1 9 9 6 – 1 9 9 7

V. I. P.
ADDRESS
BOOK

Edited by James M. Wiggins, Ph.D.

ASSOCIATED MEDIA COMPANIES, LTD.

1996 – 1997
V.I.P.
ADDRESS
BOOK

Library of Congress Catalog Card Number   89-656029
(ISSN 1043-0261)
The V.I.P. address book/edited by James M. Wiggins, Ph.D.
Bibliography: p.
Includes index.
1. Celebrities—Directories. 2. Celebrities—United States—Directories. 3. Social registers. 4. United States—Social registers.
I. Wiggins, James M., 1933-   .   II. Title: VIP address book.
CT120.VI5 1990í   920'.0025'73 - dcí   89-656029 (ISSN 1043-0261)
International Standard Book Number 0-938731-12-2
Manufactured in the United States of America

TABLE OF CONTENTS

INTRODUCTION

Purpose of the Book

The purpose of the the V.I.P. ADDRESS BOOK is to provide readers a means of reaching Very Important People — Celebrities, Government Officials, Business Leaders, Entertainers, Sports Stars, Scientists and Artists.

It is genuinely hoped that people will use this volume to write for information about an entrant's work or to express encouragement. Compliments and praise for one's efforts are always appreciated. Being at the top of one's chosen profession is no exception. And for those who are no longer active in a field, it is especially flattering to be contacted about one's past accomplishments.

Methodology

The determination of candidates for inclusion in this reference work has been a five-year process.

Committees of prominent and knowledgeable people were brought together for discussions about who should be included. The nine major areas covered are Public Service, Adventure, Business, Religion, Education, Life and Leisure, Communications, Fine Arts, Sciences, Entertainment, Athletics.

Public Service includes World Leaders, Government Officials (both U.S. and International), Law Enforcement Officials and Members of the Legal and Judicial Fields.

Adventure includes Military Leaders (both U.S. and International), Astronauts and Cosmonauts, Heroes and Explorers.

Business, Religion and Education includes Financial and Labor Leaders as well as Businesspeople and Nobel Prize Winners in Economics and Peace.

Life and Leisure includes Fashion Design, Modeling, Beauty and Health Care and Social and Political Activists.

Communications encompasses Columnists, Commentators, Editors and Publishers, along with Editorial and Comic Book Cartoonists.

Fine Arts includes Architects, Artists, Opera, Ballet and Dance Performers, Conductors, Concert Artists, Composers (both classical and popular), Writers, Photographers and Nobel Literature Laureates.

Science covers Nobel Prize winners in Chemistry, Medicine and Physics, Engineers, Inventors, Earth and Space Scientists, Psychologists and Psychiatrists, Medical and Research Scientists.

Entertainment includes stars of Radio, Stage and Screen, Musicians, Cinematographers, Producers and Directors.

Sports includes all major spectator and participatory sports.

The challenge for the committees was to define the parameters of the people included and to prepare a list of candidates. This work was exhaustive with candidates running into many thousands. Once these lists were presented, the research staff began its detailed check and update procedures.

Locating the Addresses

In the last year, the candidates - or their designated representatives - were contacted in an effort to obtain the best mailing address. Some prefer home addresses, others prefer places of business and some prefer contact through agents. The actual task of finding appropriate addresses fell to a worldwide staff of experienced researchers and veteran investigative reporters. This work is ongoing to maintain the integrity of the information.

In the final months before printing, we have attempted to verify each address and feel reasonably certain that the book is offering its readers the best way to reach listees.

People, however, do move, change jobs and change agents. The U.S. post office customarily forwards mail for up to six months. If the change is abrupt, mail may not be forwarded. We encourage users of this work to inform us if they find incorrect addresses. The V.I.P. ADDRESS BOOK UPDATES, an accompanying publication for this master volume, publishes updated and additional addresses on a regular basis.

Occupations and Titles

The category listed after a person's name is selected to best describe his/her most noteworthy accomplishment. No distinction is made whether a person still holds that position. It is felt a person who made a name for herself/himself still retains that identity even if it was done several years ago.

Additional VIPs

While this volume contains addresses for more than 20,000 VIPs, it by no means exhausts the ranks of internationally prominent people. Often we were unable to confirm an address despite continuous efforts to do so. Because of this, some people have been omitted from this basic reference work.

The book's editors will consider nominations for inclusion in later editions. Address corrections are welcome as well. We invite readers to participate in the nomination process and forms for this purpose are included in the back of the book.

HOW ADDRESSES ARE OBTAINED

The editors of the V.I.P. ADDRESS BOOK have made every effort possible to insure that the addresses listed are accurate and current.Once it is determined a person is eligible for inclusion in the book, we contact that person to determine which address he or she prefers. If a person prefers a home address, it is included. If a person prefers a business address or one in care of an agent or representative, that address is included. If a person specifically asks that their name not be included, their name is omitted. Once an address is listed, we continue efforts to verify that the address has not changed. These efforts include random sampling of the entire database, follow-up on all returned mailings received which includes those received from users of the book.

Users of the book should realize that people's addresses are in a state of constant change. The U.S. Bureau of Statistics says that almost 20 percent of people move each year. Not only do people change places of residence, they may also change business affiliations. Businesses move their headquarters as well as downsizing, merging or selling portions of their companies. Athletes get traded or retire. Entertainers change agents or personal managers and television shows get canceled. Politicians leave office or run for new positions. In addition, there are deaths almost daily which affect the address listings.

THE NATIONAL CHANGE OF ADDRESS PROGRAM

Our staff notes changes on a daily basis by watching television news shows and reading newspapers around the world. But we also take an extra step which no other directory or address book attempts. We match addresses of all U.S. listees with the U.S. Postal Service's National Change of Address program.The National Change of Address match is a process that compares mailing lists with more than 100 million address change cards filed by postal customers over the past three years. Address change information is provided for mailing list records that match with information from address change cards.

If a person/family/business moves, there are several factors which determine whether the National Change of Address is effective. These include whether the mover filed an address change with the

Postal Service, when the change was filed, whether the mover lived in an area covered by the automated address change systems (which includes more than 90 percent of the United States) and whether the name and address information in our files matches the information provided by the mover.

BAD ADDRESSES

There are some things to bear in mind about bad addresses. Our files list more than 50,000 people and we have up to 15 addresses for some of the people in the book.

We welcome information from users of the book about bad addresses. But we need to know which address is invalid. Therefore we request that the front of the envelope with any markings placed by the postal service be sent. This tells us which address is bad and the reason given by the carrier on a particular route. Be aware, though, that many celebrities have their own stamps which they will sometime put on envelopes they wish to decline. These markings look official but often are not. By seeing the front of those envelopes, this can usually be detected. Don't take literally the markings on the front, even those from the postal service. Carriers will often use the stamp nearest at hand rather than the one which would correctly list the status of the address. They do not always forward letters, nor do they always provide the latest forwarding address.

ENVELOPE MARKINGS

On your outgoing letters, you should always write "Address Correction Requested" beneath your return address in a clear and noticeable manner. If you do this, postal workers are supposed to send along the forwarding address for a nominal fee. This is often not done because it takes extra effort. But if you have not requested an address correction, you can be reasonably sure it will not be provided.

UPDATES

Realizing the ever changing aspect of addresses, we also publish V.I.P. ADDRESS BOOK UPDATES which are available mid-year for an additional fee. In a year's time, the UPDATES list several thousand address changes and new addresses as well as informing subscribers of the names of celebrities who pass away.

If you have a request for a specific address, please carefully follow the detailed procedures outlined in the back of this book. We have an affiliate service which checks our files for alternate addresses as time permits. That service requires the front of the returned envelope with all postal service markings and a self-addressed, stamped envelope. There is also a small service charge for use of the service.

RECOMMENTATIONS FOR INCLUSION IN THE BOOK

If you are interested in people who are not listed in the book, send us a letter with their name, address and biographical information. If these people are deemed worthy for inclusion, they will be listed in a future edition of the V.I.P. ADDRESS BOOK.

Until people stop moving or changing jobs (which will never happen), there are going to be address changes. We want to provide the best service possible and we think we have the highest percentage of accuracy of any directory or address book.

If you have suggestions for improving accuracy beyond random follow-ups, following daily news events, checking on all bad address notifications and using the Postal Service's National Change of Address service, let us know your ideas.

FORMS OF ADDRESS

An important part of writing to people — regardless of their positions — is to properly address envelopes and the salutations of the enclosed letters. Although the titles and positions of people listed
Continued on page xii

1 9 9 6 – 1 9 9 7

V.I.P. ADDRESS BOOK

Publisher and Editor
James M. Wiggins, Ph.D.

President and Managing Editor
Adele M. Cooke

Vice President of Technical Affairs
Michael K. Maloy

Design Director
Lee Ann Nelson

Publisher
ASSOCIATED MEDIA COMPANIES LTD.
1212 Porta Ballena
Alameda, CA 94501-3611
United States of America

TABLE OF ABBREVIATIONS

A

AB	Alberta
AFB	Air Force Base
AK	Alaska
AL	Alabama
Aly	Alley
APO	Army Post Office
AR	Arkansas
Arc	Arcade
AS	American Samoa
Assn	Association
Assoc	Associates
Ave	Avenue
AZ	Arizona

B

BC	British Columbia
Bd	Board
Beds	Bedfordshire
Berks	Berkshire
Bldg	Building
Blvd	Boulevard
Br	Branch
Bros	Brothers
Bucks	Buckinghamshire
BWI	British West Indies
Byp	Bypass

C

CA	California
Cambs	Cambridgeshire
Cir	Circle
CM	Mariana Islands
CMH	Medal of Honor Winner
CO	Colorado
Co	Company
Corp	Corporation
Cres	Crescent
Cswy	Causeway
CT	Connecticut
Ct	Court
Ctr	Center
Cts	Courts
CZ	Canal Zone

D

DC	District of Columbia
DE	Delaware
Dept	Department
Dis	District
Dr	Drive
Drwy	Driveway

E

E	East
Edin	Edinburgh
Expy	Expressway
Ext	Extended, Extension

F

Fedn	Federation
FL	Florida
FPO	Fleet Post Office
Ft	Fort
Fwy	Freeway

G

GA	Georgia
Gdns	Gardens
Glos	Gloucestershire
Grp	Group
Grv	Grove
Gt	Great
GU	Guam

H

Hants	Hampshire
Herts	Hertfordshire
HI	Hawaii
Hts	Heights
Hwy	Highway

I

IA	Iowa
ID	Idaho
IL	Illinois
IN	Indiana
Inc	Incorporated
Inst	Institute

J

Jr	Junior

K

KS	Kansas
KY	Kentucky

L

LA	Louisiana
Lancs	Lancashire
Lincs	Lincolnshire
Ln	Lane
Ltd	Limited

M

MA	Massachusetts
MB	Manitoba
MD	Maryland
ME	Maine
MI	Michigan
MN	Minnesota
MO	Missouri
Mon	Monmouthshire
MS	Mississippi
MT	Montana
Mt	Mount

N

N	North
NB	New Brunswick
NC	North Carolina
ND	North Dakota
NE	Northeast, Nebraska
NF	Newfoundland
NH	New Hampshire
NJ	New Jersey
NM	New Mexico
Northants	Northamptonshire
Notts	Nottinghamshire
NS	Nova Scotia
NSW	New South Wales
NT	Northwest Territories
NV	Nevada
NW	Northwest
NY	New York

O

OH	Ohio
OK	Oklahoma
ON	Ontario
OR	Oregon
Oxon	Oxfordshire

P

PA	Pennsylvania
PE	Prince Edward Island
Pkwy	Parkway
Pl	Place
Plz	Plaza
PO	Post Office
PQ	Province of Quebec
PR	Puerto Rico
Pt	Point

Q

Qld	Queensland

R

RD	Rural Delivery
Rd	Road
RI	Rhode Island
RR	Rural Route

S

S	South
SC	South Carolina
SD	South Dakota
SE	Southeast
SK	Saskatchewan
Spdwy	Speedway
Sq	Square
St	Saint, Street
SW	Southwest

T

Ter	Territory
Terr	Terrace
TN	Tennessee
Trl	Trail
Tpke	Turnpike
TX	Texas

U

Univ	University
US	United States
USSR	Russia
UT	Utah

V

VA	Virginia
VC	Victoria Cross Winner
VIC	Victoria
VI	Virgin Islands
VT	Vermont

W

W	West
WA	Washington
WI	Wisconsin
Worcs	Worcestershire
WV	West Virginia
WY	Wyoming

X-Y-Z

Yorks	Yorkshire
YK	Yukon Territory

in this directory are too numerous to cover, there are a number of people whose forms of address are worth noting.The Table below is a guide to enhance the likelihood your letter being received in a favorable light.

POSITION	ENVELOPE/ADDRESS	SALUTATION
Presidents of Countries	The President	Dear Mr./Madam President - - -
Vice Presidents of Countries	The Vice President	Dear Mr./Madam Vice President - - -
Cabinet Officers	The Honorable John/Jane Doe Secretary of - - -	Dear Mr./Madam Secretary - - -
Judges	The Honorable John/Jane/Jane Doe, Judge, U.S. - - - Court	Dear Judge - - -
U.S. Ambassadors	The Honorable John/Jane Doe U.S. Ambassador to (Country)	Dear Mr./Ms. Ambassador - - -
Foreign Ambassadors	His/Her Excellency John/Jane Doe	Dear Mr./Ms. Ambassador - - -
Kings/Queens	His/Her Royal Highness - - - , King/Queen of - - -	Your Royal Highness - - -
Military Leaders (Attention should be given to the actual rank.)	General/Admiral John/Jane Doe	Dear General/ Admiral - - -
Governors	The Honorable John/Jane Doe,	Dear Governor - - - Governor of - - -
Mayors	The Honorable John/Jane Doe,	Dear Mayor - - - Mayor of - - -
The Clergy		
Catholic		
The Pope	His Eminence the Pope - - -	Your Holiness - - -
Cardinals	His Eminence, John Cardinal Doe	Dear Your Eminence Cardinal
Episcopalian	The Rt. Rev. John Doe	Dear Bishop - - -
Protestant	The Rev. John Doe	Dear Mr./Ms. - - -
Eastern Orthodox Patriarch	His Holiness, the Patriarch - - -	Your Holiness - - -
Jewish	Rabbi John Doe	Dear Rabbi - - -

Forms of addresses can vary to almost impossible proportions. For instance, if the head of a Protestant church holds a degree, you are supposed to add the degree after the name on the envelope. But who knows which degrees someone holds? If you are a real stickler for proper protocol, you will need to obtain one of the many excellent reference books on etiquette or consult your local reference librarians for assistance.Times are less formal so if you are polite and spell names correctly, your letter should be favorably received

THE
DIRECTORY
OF
ADDRESS
LISTINGS

Although we have made every effort to provide
current correct addresses, we assume no responsibility
for addresses which become outdated.
Neither do we guarantee that people listed in the
book will personally answer their mail or
that they will respond to correspondence.

Aames, Willie	*Actor*
901 Bringhan Ave, Los Angeles, CA 90049, USA	
Aamodt, Kjetil Andre	*Skier*
Min Ditleffrvei 7-A, 862 Oslo 8, Norway	
Aaron, Henry L (Hank)	*Baseball Player, Executive*
1611 Adams Dr SW, Atlanta, GA 30311, USA	
Aaron, Tommy	*Golfer*
%Stouffer Pine Isle Resort, PO Drawer 545, Buford, GA 30518, USA	
Aas, Roald	*Speed Skater*
Enebakkvn 252, 1187 Oslo 11, Norway	
Aase, Donald W (Don)	*Baseball Player*
5055 Via Ricardo, Yorba Linda, CA 92686, USA	
Abacha, Sani	*President, Nigeria; Army General*
%President's Office, Lagos, Nigeria	
Abakanowicz, Magdalena	*Artist*
Ul Bzowa 1, 02-708 Warsaw, Poland	
Abbado, Claudio	*Conductor*
Piazzetta Bossi 1, 20121 Milan, Italy	
Abbe, Elfriede M	*Artist*
Applewood, Manchester Center, VT 05255, USA	
Abbott, D Thomas	*Businessman*
%Savin Corp, 333 Ludlow St, Stamford, CT 06902, USA	
Abbott, Diahnne	*Actress*
460 W Ave 46, Los Angeles, CA 90065, USA	
Abbott, James A (Jim)	*Baseball Player*
3110 Pencombe Pl, #12-A, Flint, MI 48503, USA	
Abbott, John	*Actor*
6424 Ivarene Ave, Los Angeles, CA 90068, USA	
Abbott, Philip	*Actor*
%Nelson Co, 5400 Shirley Ave, Tarzana, CA 91356, USA	
Abbott, Preston S	*Psychologist*
1305 Namassin Rd, Alexandria, VA 22308, USA	
Abboud, A Robert	*Businessman*
%A Robert Abboud Co, 212 Stone Hill Center, Fox River Grove, IL 60021, USA	
Abboud, Joseph M	*Fashion Designer*
650 5th Ave, #2700, New York, NY 10019, USA	
Abdnor, James	*Senator, SD*
PO Box 217, Kennebec, SD 57544, USA	
Abdoo, Richard A	*Businessman*
%Wisconsin Energy Corp, 231 W Michigan St, Milwaukee, WI 53202, USA	
Abdrashitov, Vadim Y	*Movie Director*
3d Frunzenskaya 8, #211, 119270 Moscow, Russia	
Abdul Ahad Mohmand	*Cosmonaut, Afghanistan*
%Potchta Kosmonavtov, 141 160 Svyosdny Gorodok, Moskovskoi Oblasti, Russia	
Abdul, Paula	*Singer, Dancer*
14046 Aubrey Rd, Beverly Hills, CA 90210, USA	
Abdul-Jabbar, Kareem	*Basketball Player*
1436 Summitridge Dr, Beverly Hills, CA 90210, USA	
Abdullah	*Prince, Jordan*
%Royal Palace, Ammam, Jordan	
Abdullah Ibn Abdul Aziz	*Crown Prince, Saudi Arabia*
%Council of Ministers, Jeddah, Saudi Arabia	
Abe, Yazuru	*Businessman*
%Nisshin Steel, 3-4-1 Marunouchi, Chiyodaku, Tokyo 100, Japan	
Abegg, Martin G	*Educator*
PO Box 429, Fish Creek, WI 54212, USA	
Abel, Robert, Jr	*Ophthalmologist*
1300 Harrison St, Wilmington, DE 19806, USA	
Abell, Murray R	*Pathologist*
%American Pathology Board, 5401 W Kennedy Blvd, Tampa, FL 33609, USA	
Abelson, Alan	*Editor, Columnist*
%Barron's Magazine, Editorial Dept, 200 Liberty St, New York, NY 10281, USA	
Abelson, Philip H	*Physicist*
4244 50th St NW, Washington, DC 20016, USA	
Abelson, Robert P	*Psychiatrist*
827 Whitney Ave, New Haven, CT 06511, USA	
Aberastain, Jose M	*Ballet Instructor*
%Southern Methodist University, Dance Division, Dallas, TX 75275, USA	

A

Aames - Aberastain

Aberconway of Bodnant, Charles M M — *Businessman*
25 Edgerton Terrace, London SW3, England

Abernethy, Robert — *Commentator*
%NBC-TV, News Dept, 4001 Nebraska Ave NW, Washington, DC 20016, USA

Abert, Donald B — *Publisher*
%Milwaukee Journal, 333 W State St, Milwaukee, WI 53203, USA

Ablon, R Richard — *Businessman*
%Ogden Corp, 2 Pennsylvania Plaza, New York, NY 10121, USA

Ablon, Ralph E — *Businessman*
%Ogden Corp, 2 Pennsylvania Plaza, New York, NY 10121, USA

Aborn, Foster L — *Businessman*
%John Hancock Mutual Life Insurance, PO Box 111, Boston, MA 02117, USA

Abraham, Edward P — *Biochemist*
%Sir William Dunn School of Pathology, South Parks Rd, Oxford, England

Abraham, F Murray — *Actor*
40 5th Ave, #2-C, New York, NY 10011, USA

Abraham, Seth — *Television Executive*
%Time Warner Sports, HBO, 1100 Ave of Americas, New York, NY 10036, USA

Abrahams, J H — *Businessman*
%Security Benefit Life Insurance, 700 SW Harrison St, Topeka, KS 66603, USA

Abrahamsen, Samuel — *Educator*
%Brooklyn College, Judiac Studies Dept, Brooklyn, NY 11210, USA

Abram, Morris B — *Educator, Diplomat*
PO Box 402, Green Farms, CT 06436, USA

Abramovitz, Max — *Architect*
176 Honey Hollow Rd, Pound Ridge, NY 10576, USA

Abramovitz, Moses — *Economist*
762 Dolores St, Stanford, CA 94305, USA

Abramowitz, Morton I — *Diplomat*
800 25th St NW, Washington, DC 20037, USA

Abrams, Elliott — *Government Official*
%Hudson Institute, 1015 18th St NW, #200, Washington, DC 20036, USA

Abrams, Herbert L — *Radiologist*
714 Alvarado Row, Stanford, CA 94305, USA

Abrams, John N — *Army General*
Commanding General, V Corps, US Army Europe & 7th Army, APO, AE 09014, USA

Abramson, Leslie — *Attorney*
4929 Wilshire Blvd, Los Angeles, CA 90010, USA

Abrew, Frederick H — *Businessman*
%Equitable Resources, 420 Blvd of Allies, Pittsburgh, PA 15219, USA

Abroms, Edward M — *Television Director, Executive*
%EMA Enterprises, 1866 Marlowe St, Thousand Oaks, CA 91360, USA

Abruzzo, Ray — *Actor*
20334 Pacific Coast Hwy, Malibu, CA 90265, USA

Abshire, David M — *Diplomat*
%Ctr for Strategic/International Studies, 1800 "K" St NW, Washington, DC 20006, USA

Abzug, Bella S — *Representative, NY*
2 5th Ave, New York, NY 10011, USA

Accola, Paul — *Skier*
Bolgenstr 17, 7270 Davos Platz, Switzerland

Acconci, Vito — *Conceptual Artist*
39 Pearl St, Brooklyn, NY 11201, USA

Achebe, Chinua — *Writer*
%Bard College, Language & Literature Department, Annandale, NY 12504, USA

Achidi Achu, Simon — *Prime Minister, Cameroon Republic*
%Prime Minister's Office, Boite Postale 1057, Yaounde, Cameroon Republic

Acker, Joseph E — *Cardiologist*
1307 Old Weisgarber Rd, Knoxville, TN 37909, USA

Acker, Sharon — *Actress*
332 N Palm Dr, #401, Beverly Hills, CA 90210, USA

Ackeren, Robert V — *Movie Director*
%Kurfurstendamm 132-A, 10711 Berlin, Germany

Ackerman, Bettye — *Actress*
302 N Alpine Dr, Beverly Hills, CA 90210, USA

Ackerman, E Duane — *Businessman*
%BellSouth Corp, 1155 Peachtree St NE, Atlanta, GA 30309, USA

Ackerman, Helen P — *Librarian*
310 20th St, Santa Monica, CA 90402, USA

Ackerman, Roger G — *Businessman*
%Corning Inc, Houghton Park, Corning, NY 14831, USA

Ackermann, Rosemarie — *Track Athlete*
Str der Jugend 72, 03050 Cottbus, Germany

Ackland, Joss — *Actor*
%International Creative Mgmt, 76 Oxford St, London W1N 0AX, England

Ackley, Gardner — *Government Official, Educator*
907 Berkshire Rd, Ann Arbor, MI 48104, USA

Ackroyd, David — *Actor*
%Gold Marshak Assoc, 3500 W Olive Ave, #1400, Burbank, CA 91505, USA

Ackroyd, Peter — *Writer*
%Anthony Sheil Assoc, 43 Doughty St, London WL1N 2LF, England

Acton, Loren W — *Astronaut*
108 W Arnold St, Bozeman, MT 59715, USA

Aczel, Janos D — *Mathematician*
97 McCarron Crescent, Waterloo ON N2L 5M9, Canada

Ada, James — *Governor, GU*
%Governor's Office, Government Offices, Agana, GU 96910, USA

Adair, Deborah — *Actress*
1605 Lindamere Pl, Los Angeles, CA 90077, USA

Adair, Paul N (Red) — *Oil Well Fire Fighter*
%Red Adair Oil Well Fires & Blowouts Control, 8101 Pinemont, Houston, TX 77040, USA

Adam, Robert — *Architect*
Crooked Pightie, Crawley, Winchester, Hants SO21 2PN, England

Adam, Theo — *Opera Singer*
Schillerstr 14, 01326 Dresden, Germany

Adamany, David W — *Educator*
%Wayne State University, President's Office, Detroit, MI 48202, USA

Adamek, Donna — *Bowler*
%Ladies Professional Bowlers Tour, 7171 Cherryvale Blvd, Rockford, IL 61112, USA

Adamle, Mike — *Sportscaster*
%ABC-TV, Sports Dept, 77 W 66th St, New York, NY 10023, USA

Adams, Brock — *Secretary, Transportation; Senator, WA*
1415 42nd Ave E, Seattle, WA 98112, USA

Adams, Brooke — *Actress*
43 W 61st St, New York, NY 10023, USA

Adams, Bryan — *Singer, Composer*
%Bruce Allen Talent, 406-68 Water St, Vancouver BC V6B 1A4, Canada

Adams, Charles J — *Religious Leader*
%Progressive National Baptist Convention, 601 50th St NE, Washington, DC 20019, USA

Adams, Cindy — *Movie Critic*
1050 5th Ave, New York, NY 10028, USA

Adams, Don — *Actor*
%Ted Witzer Agency, 6310 San Vicente Blvd, #407, Los Angeles, CA 90048, USA

Adams, Douglas — *Writer*
%Ed Victor Ltd, 162 Wardour St, London W1V 3AT, England

Adams, Edie — *Actress*
8040 Okean Terrace, Los Angeles, CA 90046, USA

Adams, Gerard (Gerry) — *Political Leader, Northern Ireland*
%Sinn Fein/IRA, 51/55 Falls Rd, Belfast BT 12, Northern Ireland

Adams, Greg — *Hockey Player*
%Dallas Stars, 901 Main St, #2301, Dallas, TX 75202, USA

Adams, James L — *Theologian*
3 Pooks Hill Rd, #715, Bethesda, MD 20814, USA

Adams, Joey — *Comedian, Writer*
1050 5th Ave, New York, NY 10028, USA

Adams, John C — *Businessman*
%Russell Corp, PO Box 272, Alexander City, AL 35011, USA

Adams, John H — *Religious Leader*
%African Methodist Church, Box 19039, Germantown Station, Philadelphia, PA 19138, USA

Adams, John L — *Financier*
%Texas Commerce Bank, 712 Main St, Houston, TX 77002, USA

Adams, John W — *Financier*
%Adams Harkness Hill Inc, 60 State St, Boston, MA 02109, USA

Adams, Julie — *Actress*
2446 N Commonwealth Ave, Los Angeles, CA 90027, USA

Adams, Kenneth S (Bud) — *Football Executive*
%Houston Oilers, 6910 Fannin St, Houston, TX 77030, USA

A

Adams, Kim *Actress*
%LA Talent, 8335 Sunset Blvd, Los Angeles, CA 90069, USA

Adams, Lucian *WW II Army Hero (CMH)*
4323 Valleyfield Dr, San Antonio, TX 78222, USA

Adams, Lyle B *Financier*
%America First Credit Union, PO Box 9199, Ogden, UT 84409, USA

Adams, Mark *Artist*
3816 22nd St, San Francisco, CA 94114, USA

Adams, Mason *Actor*
49 Owenoke Park, Westport, CT 06880, USA

Adams, Maud *Actress*
2791 Ellison Dr, Beverly Hills, CA 90210, USA

Adams, Michael *Basketball Player*
%Charlotte Hornets, 1 Hive Dr, Charlotte, NC 28217, USA

Adams, Noah *Commentator*
%National Public Radio, 2025 "M" St NW, Washington, DC 20036, USA

Adams, Pat *Artist*
370 Elm St, Bennington, VT 05201, USA

Adams, Richard *Writer*
Benwell's, 26 Church St, Whitechurch, Hants RG28 7AR, England

Adams, Richard N *Anthropologist*
%University of Texas, Anthropology Dept, Austin, TX 78712, USA

Adams, Robert *Sculptor*
Rangers Hall, Great Maplestead, Halstead, Essex, England

Adams, Robert M, Jr *Anthropologist*
PO Box ZZ, Basalt, CO 81621, USA

Adams, Sam *Football Player*
%Seattle Seahawks, 11220 NE 53rd St, Kirkland, WA 98033, USA

Adams, Samuel H *Conductor, Composer*
%University of Rochester, Eastman School of Music, Rochester, NY 14604, USA

Adams, Scott *Cartoonist (Dilbert)*
%United Feature Syndicate, 200 Park Ave, New York, NY 10166, USA

Adams, Stanley T *Korean War Army Hero (CMH)*
20454 Whistle Point Rd, Bend, OR 97702, USA

Adams, William R *Historian*
%Historic Property Assoc, PO Box 1002, St Augustine, FL 32085, USA

Adamson, James B *Businessman*
%Flagstar Companies, 203 E Main St, Spartanburg, SC 29319, USA

Adamson, James C *Astronaut*
%Lockheed Engineering & Science Co, 2625 Bay Area Blvd, Houston, TX 77058, USA

Adamson, John W *Hematologist*
%New York Blood Center, 310 E 67th St, New York, NY 10021, USA

Adcock, Joseph W (Joe) *Baseball Player*
PO Box 385, Coushatta, LA 71019, USA

Adderley, Terence E *Businessman*
%Kelly Services, 999 W Big Beaver Rd, Troy, MI 48084, USA

Adderly, Herb *Football Player*
%Adderly Industries, PO Box 513, Thorofare, NJ 08086, USA

Adderly, Nat *Jazz Trumpter*
%Producers Inc, 11806 N 56th St, Tampa, FL 33617, USA

Addis, Don *Cartoonist (Bent Offerings)*
%Creators Syndicate, 5777 W Century Blvd, #700, Los Angeles, CA 90045, USA

Ade, King Sunny *Singer*
%Island Records, 400 Lafayette St, #500, New York, NY 10003, USA

Adel, Arthur *Physicist*
PO Box 942, Flagstaff, AZ 86002, USA

Adelman, Irma G *Economist*
10 Rosemont Ave, Berkeley, CA 94708, USA

Adelman, Kenneth L *Government Official*
%Int'l Contemporary Studies Institute, 4018 27th St N, Arlington, VA 22207, USA

Adelman, Rick *Basketball Coach*
%Golden State Warriors, Oakland Coliseum Arena, Oakland, CA 94621, USA

Adelson, Mervyn L *Television Executive*
600 Sarbonne Rd, Los Angeles, CA 90077, USA

Adey, Christopher *Conductor*
137 Anson Rd, Willesden Green NW2 4AH, England

Adhikary, Man Mohan *Prime Minister, Nepal*
%Prime Minister's Office, Singhadurbar, Katmandu, Nepal

Adams - Adhikary

Adik, Stephen P *Businessman*
%Northern Indiana Public Service Co, 5265 Hohman Ave, Hammond, IN 46320, USA

Adjani, Isabelle *Actress*
%Association Des Amis, BP 166, 75523 Paris Cedex 11, France

Adjodhia, Jules *Prime Minister, Suriname*
%Prime Minister's Office, Kleine Combeweg 1, Paramaribo, Suriname

Adkisson, Perry L *Educator*
%Texas A&M University, Chancellor's Office, College Station, TX 77843, USA

Adleman, Leonard *Computer Theorist*
%University of Southern California, Computer Math Dept, Los Angeles, CA 90089, USA

Adler, Freda S *Criminologist*
30 Waterside Plaza, #37-J, New York, NY 10010, USA

Adler, Frederick R *Financier*
222 Lakeview Ave, #160, West Palm Beach, FL 33401, USA

Adler, Julius *Biologist, Biochemist*
%University of Wisconsin, Biochemistry Dept, Madison, WI 53706, USA

Adler, Larry *Concert Mouth Organist*
%MBA Literary Agents, 45 Fitzroy St, London W1, England

Adler, Lee *Artist*
Lime Kiln Farm, Climax, NY 12042, USA

Adler, Lou *Actor, Movie Director, Producer*
%Ode Sounds & Visuals, 3969 Villa Costera, Malibu, CA 90265, USA

Adler, Mortimer J *Writer, Philosopher*
1320 N State Pkwy, Chicago, IL 60610, USA

Adler, Renata *Writer*
PO Box 9, Danbury, CT 06813, USA

Adler, Richard *Composer, Lyricist*
8 E 83rd St, New York, NY 10028, USA

Adler, Steven *Drummer (Guns N' Roses)*
%Artists & Audience Entertainment, 83 Riverside Dr, New York, NY 10024, USA

Adni, Daniel *Concert Pianist*
64-A Menelik Rd, London NW2 3RH, England

Adolfo (Sardina) *Fashion Designer*
%Adolfo Inc, 36 E 57th St, New York, NY 10022, USA

Adoor, Gopalakrishnan *Movie Director*
Darsanam, Trivandrum, 695 017 Kerala, India

Adorjan, J Joseph *Businessman*
%Emerson Electric Co, 8000 W Florissant Ave, St Louis, MO 63136, USA

Adrian, Barbara *Artist*
420 E 64th St, New York, NY 10021, USA

Adriani, John *Physician*
67 N Park Pl, New Orleans, LA 70124, USA

Adyebo, George Kosmas *Prime Minister, Uganda*
%Prime Minister's Office, Kampala, Uganda

Afanasyev, Viktor M *Cosmonaut*
%Potchta Kosmonavtov, 141 160 Svyosdny Gorodok, Moskovskoi Oblasti, Russia

Africk, Jack *Businessman*
%Duty Free International Inc, 2300 Glades Rd, #220-W, Boca Raton, FL 33431, USA

Aga Khan IV, Prince Karim *Spiritual Leader*
Aiglemont, 60270 Gouvieux, France

Agajanian, Ben *Football Player*
3940 E Broadway, Long Beach, CA 90803, USA

Agam, Yaacov *Artist*
26 Rue Boulard, 75014 Paris, France

Agar, John *Actor*
639 N Hollywood Way, Burbank, CA 91505, USA

Agase, Alex *Football Player, Coach*
2105 Glencoe Hills Dr, #5, Ann Arbor, MI 48108, USA

Agassi, Andre *Tennis Player*
8921 Andre Dr, Las Vegas, NV 89113, USA

Aghayan, Ray *Costume Designer*
431 S Fairfax Ave, #3, Los Angeles, CA 90036, USA

Agnelli, Giovanni *Businessman*
%Fiat SpA, Corso G Marconi 10/20, 10125 Turin, Italy

Agnelli, Umberto *Businessman*
%Fiat SpA, Corso G Marconi 10/20, 10125 Turin, Italy

Agnew, Harold M *Physicist*
322 Punta Baja Dr, Solana Beach, CA 92075, USA

A

Agnew, James K — *Businessman*
%McCann Erikson Inc, 495 Lexington Ave, New York, NY 10017, USA

Agnew, M H Julian — *Art Dealer*
Egmere Farm House, Egmere Near Walsingham, Norfolk, England

Agnew, Rudolph I J — *Businessman*
%Hanson PLC, 1 Grosvenor Pl, London SW1, England

Agnew, Spiro T — *Vice President*
10000 Coastal Hwy, #1108, Ocean City, MD 21842, USA

Agnew, Valerie — *Drummer (7 Year Bitch)*
%Talent House, 1407 E Madison, #41, Seattle, WA 98122, USA

Agoglia, John — *Television Executive*
%NBC Productions, NBC-TV, 30 Rockfeller Plaza, New York, NY 10020, USA

Agresti, Jack J — *Businessman*
%Guy F Atkinson Co, 1001 Bayhill Dr, San Bruno, CA 94066, USA

Agria, John J — *Educator*
%University of Dubuque, President's Office, Dubuque, IA 52001, USA

Agronsky, Martin — *Commentator*
%WUSA-TV, 4100 Wisconsin Ave NW, Washington, DC 20016, USA

Agt, Andries A M Van — *Prime Minister, Netherlands*
Europa House, 9-15 Sanbancho, Chiyodaku, Tokyo 102, Japan

Agutter, Jenny — *Actress*
6884 Camrose Dr, Los Angeles, CA 90068, USA

Ahlfors, Lars V — *Mathematician*
160 Commonwealth Ave, Boston, MA 02116, USA

Ahlmann, Kaj — *Businessman*
%Employers Reinsurance Corp, 5200 Metcalf, Overland Park, KS 66202, USA

Ahmed, Khandakar M — *President, Bangladesh*
%Democratic League, 68 Jigatold, Dhaka 9, Bangladesh

Aho, Esko — *Prime Minister, Finland*
%Prime Minister's Office, Aleksanterinkatu 3-D, Helsinki, Finland

Ahrends, Peter — *Architect*
%Ahrends Burton Koralek, 7 Chalcot Rd, London NW1 8LH, England

Ahrens, Joseph — *Composer*
Huningerstr 26, 14195 Berlin, Germany

Ahronovitch, Yuri — *Conductor*
%Stockholm Philharmonic, Hotorget 8, Stockholm, Sweden

Ahtisaari, Martti — *President, Finland*
%Presidential Palace, Pohjoisesplandi 1, 00170 Helsinki 17, Finland

Aida, Takefumi — *Architect*
1-3-2 Okubo, Shinjukuku, Tokyo 169, Japan

Aiello, Danny — *Actor*
195 Surrey Ct, Ramsey, NJ 07446, USA

Aiken, Joan D — *Writer*
Hermitage, Petworth, West Sussex GU28 OAB, England

Aiken, Linda H — *Sociologist*
%University of Pennsylvania, Nursing School, Philadelphia, PA 19104, USA

Aiken, Michael T — *Educator*
%University of Illinois, Chancellor's Office, Champaign,IL 61801, USA

Aikman, Troy — *Football Player*
%Dallas Cowboys, 1 Cowboys Pkwy, Irving, TX 75063, USA

Ailes, Roger E — *Publisher*
%Ailes Communications, 440 Park Ave S, New York, NY 10016, USA

Ailes, Stephen — *Government Official*
4521 Wetherill Rd, Bethesda, MD 20816, USA

Aimee, Anouk — *Actress*
%Artmedia, 10 Ave George V, 75008 Paris, France

Ainge, Danny — *Basketball Player*
%Phoenix Suns, 201 E Jefferson St, Phoenix, AZ 85004, USA

Aini, Mohsen Ahmed al- — *Prime Minister, Yemen*
%Yemen Arab Republic Embassy, 600 New Hampshire NW, Washington, DC 20037, USA

Ainsworth-Land, George T — *Philosopher*
230 North St, Buffalo, NY 14201, USA

Aishwarya Rajya Laxmi Devi Rana — *Queen, Nepal*
%Narayanhiti Royal Palace, Durbag Marg, Kathmandu, Nepal

Aitay, Victor — *Concert Violinist*
212 Oak Knoll Terrace, Highland Park, IL 60035, USA

Akalaitis, JoAnne — *Theater Director*
%Mabou Mines, 150 1st Ave, New York, NY 10009, USA

Akama, Yoshihiro
%Mitsubishi Trust & Banking, 4-5-1 Marunouchi, Tokyo 100, Japan — *Financier*

Akashi, Toshio
%Sanwa Bank, 4-10 Fushimi, Higashiku, Osaka 541, Japan — *Financier*

Akashi, Yasushi
%Foreign Affairs Ministry, 2-2 Kasumigaseki, Chiyodaku, Tokyo, Japan — *Diplomat, Japan*

Akayev, Askar
%President's Office, Government House, Bishkek 720003, Kyrgystan — *President, Kyrgyzstan*

Akbar, Taufik
Jalan Simp, Pahlawan III/24, Bandung 40124, Indonesia — *Astronaut, Indonesia*

Akebono (Chad Rowan)
%Azumazeki Stable, 4-6-4 Higashi Komagata, Rypgpku, Tokyo, Japan — *Sumo Wrestler*

Akers, Fred
%Purdue University, Athletic Dept, West Lafayette, IN 47907, USA — *Football Coach*

Akers, John F
1 Sturges Hwy, Westport, CT 06880, USA — *Businessman*

Akers, Thomas D
%NASA, Johnson Space Center, 2101 NASA Rd, Houston, TX 77058, USA — *Astronaut*

Akhmadulina, Bella
Chernyachovskogo Str 4, #37, 125319 Moscow, Russia — *Poet*

Akhmedov, Khan A
%Council of Ministers, Vaiaku, Ashkabad, Turkmenistan — *Prime Minister, Turkmenistan*

Akihito
%Imperial Palace, 1-1 Chiyoda, Chiyodaku, Tokyo 100, Japan — *Emperor, Japan*

Akins, James E
2904 Garfield Terrace, Washington, DC 20008, USA — *Diplomat*

Akira, Yeiri
%Bridgestone Corp, 10-1-1 Kyobashi, Chuoku, Tokyo 104, Japan — *Businessman*

Akita, Masaya
%Daido Steel, 11-18 Nishiki, Nakaku, Nagoya 460, Japan — *Businessman*

Akiyama, Kazuyoshi
%Syracuse Symphony, 411 Montgomery St, Syracuse, NY 13202, USA — *Conductor*

Akiyama, Toyohiro
%Tokyo Broadcasting Systems, 3-6-5 Akasaka, Minatoku, Tokyo 107, Japan — *Astronaut, Journalist*

Akiyoshi, Toshiko
38 W 94th St, New York, NY 10025, USA — *Jazz Pianist, Composer*

Aksenov, Vladimir V
Astrakhansky Per 5, Kv 100, 129010 Moscow, Russia — *Cosmonaut*

Aksyonov, Vassily P
%George Mason University, English Dept, Fairfax, VA 22030, USA — *Writer*

Aladjem, Silvio
%Bronson Hospital, 252 E Lovell St, Kalamazoo, MI 49007, USA — *Obstetrician, Gynecologist*

Alaia, Azzeddine
18 Rue de la Verrerie, 75008 Paris, France — *Fashion Designer*

Alain, Marie-Claire
1 Ave Jean-Jaures, 78580 Maule, France — *Concert Organist*

Alan, Buddy
600 E Gilbert Dr, Tempe, AZ 85281, USA — *Singer*

Albanese, Licia
Nathan Hale Dr, Wilson Point, South Norwalk, CT 06854, USA — *Opera Singer*

Albeck, Stan
%Bradley University, Athletic Dept, Peoria, IL 61625, USA — *Basketball Coach*

Albee, Arden L
2040 Midlothian Dr, Altadena, CA 91001, USA — *Geologist*

Albee, Edward
14 Harrison St, New York, NY 10013, USA — *Writer*

Alberghetti, Anna Maria
10333 Chrysanthemum Ln, Los Angeles, CA 90077, USA — *Singer, Actress*

Albers, Hans
%BASF AG, Carl-Bosch-Str 38, 78351 Ludwigshafen, Germany — *Businessman*

Albert
%Palais de Monaco, Boite Postal 518, 98015 Monte Carlo, Monaco — *Prince, Monaco*

Albert II
%Koninklijk Palais, Rue de Brederode, 1000 Brussels, Belgium — *King, Belgium*

Albert, Calvin
2359 SE 14th St, Pompano Beach, FL 33062, USA — *Sculptor*

Albert, Carl B
1831 Word Rd, McAlester, OK 74501, USA — *Representative, OK; Speaker*

A

Albert - Aleksiy (A M Ridiger)

Albert, Eddie   *Actor*
719 Amalfi Dr, Pacific Palisades, CA 90272, USA

Albert, Edward   *Actor*
Hawks Ranch, 27320 Winding Way, Malibu, CA 90265, USA

Albert, Frankie   *Football Player*
1 Stanford Dr, Rancho Mirage, CA 92270, USA

Albert, Ken   *Sportscaster*
%Fox TV, Sports Dept, 205 E 67th St, New York, NY 10021, USA

Albert, Marv   *Sportscaster*
%NBC-TV, Sports Dept, 30 Rockefeller Plaza, New York, NY 10112, USA

Alberts, Trev   *Football Player*
2709 Edgewood Dr, Cedar Falls, ID 50613, USA

Alberty, Robert A   *Chemist*
7 Old Dee Rd, Cambridge, MA 02138, USA

Albicocco, Gabriel J   *Movie Director*
%L'Alpicella, 171 Ave Frederic Mistral, 06250 Mougains, France

Albino, Judith E N   *Educator*
%University of Colorado, President's Office, Boulder, CO 80309, USA

Albrecht, Gerd   *Conductor*
%Mariedi Anders Mgmt, 535 El Camino Del Mar, San Francisco, CA 94121, USA

Albrecht, Ronald F   *Anestheologist*
1020 Chestnut Ave, Wilmette, IL 60091, USA

Albright (Zsissly), Malvin Marr   *Artist*
1500 N Lake Shore Dr, Chicago, IL 60610, USA

Albright, Jack L   *Animal Scientist*
188 Blueberry Ln, West Lafayette, IN 47906, USA

Albright, Lola   *Actress*
PO Box 250070, Glendale, CA 91225, USA

Albright, Madeleine K   *Diplomat*
%US Mission, 799 United Nations Plaza, New York, NY 10017, USA

Albright, Tenley   *Figure Skater*
Carlton House, 2 Commonwealth Ave, Boston, MA 02116, USA

Albuquerque, Lita   *Artist*
305 Boyd St, Los Angeles, CA 90013, USA

Alcott, Amy S   *Golfer*
%Little Women Enterprises, PO Box 956, Pacific Palisades, CA 90272, USA

Alda, Alan   *Actor*
641 Lexington Ave, #1400, New York, NY 10022, USA

Alden, Ginger   *Model, Actress*
4152 Royal Crest Pl, Memphis, TN 38115, USA

Alden, Norman   *Actor*
106 N Croft Ave, Los Angeles, CA 90048, USA

Alder, Berni J   *Theoretical Physicist*
%Lawrence Radiation Laboratory, PO Box 808, Livermore, CA 94551, USA

Alderman, Darrell   *Drag Racing Driver*
%D A Construction Co, 8145 Flemingsburg Rd, Morehead, KY 40351, USA

Aldinger, William F   *Financier*
%Household International, 2700 Sanders Rd, Prospect Heights, IL 60070, USA

Aldiss, Brian W   *Writer*
Woodlands, Foxcombe Rd, Boars Hill, Oxford OX1 5DL, England

Aldred, Sophie   *Actress*
%McKenna & Grantham, 1-B Montagu Mews North, London W1H 1AJ, England

Aldredge, Theoni V   *Costume Designer*
425 Lafayette St, New York, NY 10003, USA

Aldridge, Donald O   *Air Force General*
%Aldridge Assoc, 159 Orange Blossom Cir, Folsom, CA 95630, USA

Aldridge, Edward C (Pete), Jr   *Government Official*
%Aerospace Corp, 2350 E El Segundo, El Segundo, CA 90245, USA

Aldrin, Edwin E (Buzz), Jr   *Astronaut*
%Starcraft Enterprises, 233 Emerald Bay, Laguna Beach, CA 92651, USA

Alechinsky, Pierre   *Artist*
2 Bis Rue Henri Barbusse, 78380 Bougival, France

Alegre, Norberto Costa   *Prime Minister, Sao Tome & Principe*
%Prime Minister's Office, CP 38, Sao Tome, Sao Tome & Principe

Alekseev, Dimitri   *Concert Pianist*
IMG Artist, Media House, 3 Burlington Ln, Chiswick, London W4 2TH, England

Aleksiy (A M Ridiger)   *Religious Leader*
%Moscow Patriarchy, Chisty Per 5, Moscow, Russia

Alesana, Tofilau Eti — *Prime Minister, Western Samoa*
%Prime Minister's Office, PO Box 193, Apia, Western Samoa

Aletter, Frank — *Actor*
1508 Calle De Sur, Santa Fe, NM 87505, USA

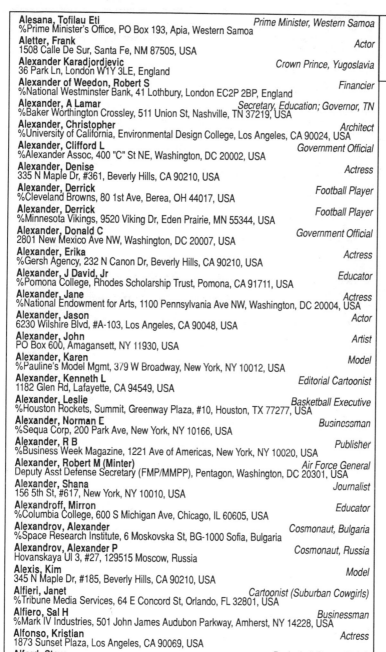

A

Alexander Karadjordjevic — *Crown Prince, Yugoslavia*
36 Park Ln, London W1Y 3LE, England

Alexander of Weedon, Robert S — *Financier*
%National Westminster Bank, 41 Lothbury, London EC2P 2BP, England

Alexander, A Lamar — *Secretary, Education; Governor, TN*
%Baker Worthington Crossley, 511 Union St, Nashville, TN 37219, USA

Alexander, Christopher — *Architect*
%University of California, Environmental Design College, Los Angeles, CA 90024, USA

Alexander, Clifford L — *Government Official*
%Alexander Assoc, 400 "C" St NE, Washington, DC 20002, USA

Alexander, Denise — *Actress*
335 N Maple Dr, #361, Beverly Hills, CA 90210, USA

Alexander, Derrick — *Football Player*
%Cleveland Browns, 80 1st Ave, Berea, OH 44017, USA

Alexander, Derrick — *Football Player*
%Minnesota Vikings, 9520 Viking Dr, Eden Prairie, MN 55344, USA

Alexander, Donald C — *Government Official*
2801 New Mexico Ave NW, Washington, DC 20007, USA

Alexander, Erika — *Actress*
%Gersh Agency, 232 N Canon Dr, Beverly Hills, CA 90210, USA

Alexander, J David, Jr — *Educator*
%Pomona College, Rhodes Scholarship Trust, Pomona, CA 91711, USA

Alexander, Jane — *Actress*
%National Endowment for Arts, 1100 Pennsylvania Ave NW, Washington, DC 20004, USA

Alexander, Jason — *Actor*
6230 Wilshire Blvd, #A-103, Los Angeles, CA 90048, USA

Alexander, John — *Artist*
PO Box 600, Amagansett, NY 11930, USA

Alexander, Karen — *Model*
%Pauline's Model Mgmt, 379 W Broadway, New York, NY 10012, USA

Alexander, Kenneth L — *Editorial Cartoonist*
1182 Glen Rd, Lafayette, CA 94549, USA

Alexander, Leslie — *Basketball Executive*
%Houston Rockets, Summit, Greenway Plaza, #10, Houston, TX 77277, USA

Alexander, Norman E — *Businessman*
%Sequa Corp, 200 Park Ave, New York, NY 10166, USA

Alexander, R B — *Publisher*
%Business Week Magazine, 1221 Ave of Americas, New York, NY 10020, USA

Alexander, Robert M (Minter) — *Air Force General*
Deputy Asst Defense Secretary (FMP/MMPP), Pentagon, Washington, DC 20301, USA

Alexander, Shana — *Journalist*
156 5th St, #617, New York, NY 10010, USA

Alexandroff, Mirron — *Educator*
%Columbia College, 600 S Michigan Ave, Chicago, IL 60605, USA

Alexandrov, Alexander — *Cosmonaut, Bulgaria*
%Space Research Institute, 6 Moskovska St, BG-1000 Sofia, Bulgaria

Alexandrov, Alexander P — *Cosmonaut, Russia*
Hovanskaya Ul 3, #27, 129515 Moscow, Russia

Alexis, Kim — *Model*
345 N Maple Dr, #185, Beverly Hills, CA 90210, USA

Alfieri, Janet — *Cartoonist (Suburban Cowgirls)*
%Tribune Media Services, 64 E Concord St, Orlando, FL 32801, USA

Alfiero, Sal H — *Businessman*
%Mark IV Industries, 501 John James Audubon Parkway, Amherst, NY 14228, USA

Alfonso, Kristian — *Actress*
1873 Sunset Plaza, Los Angeles, CA 90069, USA

Alford, Steve — *Basketball Player, Coach*
%Southwestern Missouri State University, Athletic Dept, Springfield, MO 65804, USA

Alford, William — *Writer*
31 Athens St, Cambridge, MA 02138, USA

Ali Haider Khan Bangash — *WW II Pakistan Army Hero (VC)*
PO Hangu, Tehsil Hangu, Distt Kohat Mohallah, Khan Bari, Pakistan

Ali, Kamal Hassan — *Prime Minister, Egypt; General*
110 Amar Ibn Yassar, Misr El Gadida, Egypt

A

Ali, Muhammad *Boxer*
Ali Farm, PO Box 187, Berrien Springs, MI 49103, USA

Aliev, Geidar Ali Rza Ogly *President, Azerbaijan; Army General*
%President's Office, 37066 Baku, Azerbaijan

Alimo, Mark *Actor*
%Craig Agency, 8485 Melrose Pl, #E, Los Angeles, CA 90069, USA

Alioto, Joseph L *Attorney, Mayor*
650 California St, #2500, San Francisco, CA 94108, USA

Aliyev, Geidar A *President, Azerbaijan*
%President's Office, Parliament, Baku, Azerbaijan

Allain, William A *Governor, MS*
401 Capitol St, Jackson, MS 39201, USA

Allaire, Paul A *Businessman*
%Xerox Corp, 800 Long Ridge Rd, Stamford, CT 06902, USA

Allais, Maurice *Nobel Economics Laureate*
15 Rue des Gate-Ceps, 92210 Saint Cloud, France

Allam, Mark W *Veterinarian*
%Strath Haven, #809, Swathmore, PA 19081, USA

Allan, Jed *Actor*
PO Box 5302, Blue Jay, CA 92317, USA

Allan, William *Artist*
327 Melrose, Mill Valley, CA 94941, USA

Allard, Linda M *Fashion Designer*
%Ellen Tracy Corp, 575 7th Ave, New York, NY 10018, USA

Allbritton, Joe L *Financier*
%Perpetual Corp, 800 17th St NW, Washington, DC 20006, USA

Allen, Andrew M *Astronaut*
%NASA, Johnson Space Center, 2101 NASA Rd, Houston, TX 77058, USA

Allen, Betty *Classical, Opera Singer*
%Harlem School of Arts, 645 St Nicholas Ave, New York, NY 10030, USA

Allen, Chad *Actor*
6489 Cavalleri Rd, #204, Malibu, CA 90265, USA

Allen, Corey *Actor, Director*
8642 Hollywood Blvd, Los Angeles, CA 90069, USA

Allen, Darryl F *Businessman*
%Trinova Corp, 3000 Strayer, Maumee, OH 43537, USA

Allen, Debbie *Singer, Songwriter, Actress*
607 Marguerita Ave, Santa Monica, CA 90402, USA

Allen, Duane D *Singer (Oak Ridge Boys)*
329 Rockland Rd, Hendersonville, TN 37075, USA

Allen, Eric A *Football Player*
%New Orleans Saints, 1500 Poydras, New Orleans, LA 70112, USA

Allen, George F *Governor, VA*
%Governor's Offfice, State Capitol Bldg, Richmond, VA 23219, USA

Allen, Herbert A *Financier*
%Allen & Co, 711 5th Ave, New York, NY 10022, USA

Allen, J Presson *Screenwriter, Producer*
%Lewis Allen Productions, 1501 Broadway, #1614, New York, NY 10036, USA

Allen, Joan *Actress*
%International Creative Mgmt, 8942 Wilshire Blvd, Beverly Hills, CA 90211, USA

Allen, Joseph P, IV *Astronaut*
%Space Industries International, 800 Connecticut Ave NW, Washington, DC 20006, USA

Allen, Karen *Actress*
PO Box 237, Monterey, MA 01245, USA

Allen, Lew, Jr *Air Force General*
%Draper Laboratory, 555 Technology Sq, Cambridge, MA 02139, USA

Allen, Marcus *Football Player*
433 Ward Parkway, #29, Kansas City, MO 64112, USA

Allen, Marty *Comedian*
1991 Pago Ct, Las Vegas, NV 89117, USA

Allen, Maryon P *Senator, AL*
3215 Cliff Rd, Birmingham, AL 35205, USA

Allen, Mel *Sportscaster*
21 Weavers Hill, #C, Greenwich, CT 06831, USA

Allen, Nancy *Actress*
%Agency For Performing Arts, 9000 Sunset Blvd, #1200, Los Angeles, CA 90069, USA

Allen, Paul G *Co-Developer (PC Language)*
%Asymetrix Corp, 110 110th NE, Bellvue, WA 98004, USA

Ali - Allen

Allen, Phillip Richard — *Actor*
%Gersh Agency, 232 N Canon Dr, Beverly Hills, CA 90210, USA

Allen, Raymond B — *Educator*
14136 Wadsworth Ct, Annandale, VA 22003, USA

Allen, Rex — *Actor*
Lone Star Ranch, Box 1111, Sonoita, AZ 85637, USA

Allen, Rex, Jr — *Singer*
128 Pine Oak Dr, Hendersonville, TN 37075, USA

Allen, Richard (Rick) — *Drummer (Def Leppard)*
%Q Prime Mgmt, 729 7th Ave, #1400, New York, NY 10019, USA

Allen, Richard A (Richie) — *Baseball Player*
11140 Camarillo St, #4, North Hollywood, CA 91602, USA

Allen, Richard R — *Businessman*
%LADD Furniture, 1 Plaza Center, High Point, NC 27261, USA

Allen, Richard V — *Government Official*
905 16th St NW, Washington, DC 20006, USA

Allen, Robert E — *Businessman*
%American Telephone & Telegraph, 32 Ave of Americas, New York, NY 10013, USA

Allen, Ronald W — *Businessman*
%Delta Air Lines, Hartsfield International Airport, Atlanta, GA 30320, USA

Allen, Sian Barbara — *Actress*
1622 Sierra Bonita Ave, Los Angeles, CA 90046, USA

Allen, Steve — *Comedian, Writer*
15201 Burbank Blvd, #B, Van Nuys, CA 91411, USA

Allen, Thomas — *Opera Singer*
%Lies Askonas Ltd, 186 Drury Ln, London WC2B 5RY, England

Allen, Tim — *Actor*
%Messina Baker Miller, 7920 Sunset Blvd, #400, Los Angeles, CA 90046, USA

Allen, W Wayne — *Businessman*
%Phillips Petroleum, Phillips Bldg, 4th & Keeler Sts, Bartlesville, OK 74004, USA

Allen, Willard M — *Physician*
211 Key Hwy, Baltimore, MD 21230, USA

Allen, William H — *Editor*
%National Geographic Magazine, 17th & "M" NW, Washington, DC 20036, USA

Allen, Woody — *Actor, Comedian, Director*
930 5th Ave, New York, NY 10021, USA

Allende, Fernando — *Actor*
%William Morris Agency, 151 S El Camino Dr, Beverly Hills, CA 90212, USA

Allende, Isabel — *Writer*
15 Nightingale Ln, San Rafael, CA 94901, USA

Aller, Lawrence H — *Astronomer*
18118 W Kingsport Dr, Malibu, CA 90265, USA

Alley, Kirstie — *Actress*
%Wolf/Kasteler, 1033 Gayley Ave, #208, Los Angeles, CA 90024, USA

Alley, L Eugene (Gene) — *Baseball Player*
10236 Steuben Dr, Glen Allen, VA 23060, USA

Alley, William J — *Businessman*
%American Brands Inc, 1700 E Putnam Ave, Old Greenwich, CT 06870, USA

Allfrey, Vincent G — *Biochemist*
24 Winthrop Ct, Tenafly, NJ 07670, USA

Allimadi, E Otema — *Prime Minister, Uganda*
PO Box Gulu, Gulu District, Uganda

Alling, Abigail — *Biospherian*
%Biosphere II, Hwy 77, Mile Marker 96.5, Oracle, AZ 85623, USA

Allison, Bobby — *Auto Racing Driver*
140 Church St, Hueytown, AL 35023, USA

Allison, Glenn — *Bowler*
%Professional Bowlers Assn, 1720 Merriman Rd, Akron, OH 44313, USA

Allison, John A, IV — *Financier*
%Southern National Corp, 500 N Chestnut St, Lumberton, NC 28358, USA

Allison, Mose — *Jazz Pianist, Composer*
34 Dogwood Dr, Smithtown, NY 11787, USA

Allison, Robert J, Jr — *Businessman*
%Anadarko Petroleum Corp, 17001 Northchase Dr, Houston, TX 77060, USA

Allison, Stacy — *Mountaineer*
7003 SE Reed College Pl, Portland, OR 97202, USA

Allison, Wick — *Publisher*
31 Beach Ave, Larchmont, NY 10538, USA

A

Allen - Allison

Alliss, Peter *Sportscaster*
%International Management Group, 1 Erieview Plaza, #1300, Cleveland, OH 44114, USA

Allman, Greg *Singer, Songwriter*
%Hemming Morse, 650 California St, San Francisco, CA 94108, USA

Allott, Gordon L *Senator, CO*
1764 Mesa Ridge Ln, Castle Rock, CO 80104, USA

Allouache, Merzak *Movie Director*
Cite des Asphodeles, Bt D-15, 183 Ben Aknoun, Algiers, Algeria

Allport, Christopher *Actor*
%Susan Smith Assoc, 121 N San Vicente Blvd, Beverly Hills, CA 90211, USA

Allred, Gloria R *Attorney*
6300 Wilshire Blvd, #15, Los Angeles, CA 90048, USA

Allyson, June *Actress*
1651 Foothill Rd, Ojai, CA 93023, USA

Almen, Lowell G *Religious Leader*
%Evangelical Lutheran Church, 8765 W Higgins Rd, Chicago, IL 60631, USA

Almodovar, Pedro *Movie Director*
El Deseo SA, Ruiz Perello 25, 28028 Madrid, Spain

Almond, Lincoln C *Governor, RI*
%Governor's Office, 222 State House, Providence, RI 02903, USA

Alomar, Roberto V *Baseball Player*
Urb Monserrate B-56, Box 367, Salinas, PR 00751, USA

Alomar, Santo C (Sandy), Jr *Baseball Player*
%Cleveland Indians, Cleveland Stadium, Cleveland, OH 44114, USA

Alonso, Alicia *Ballerina*
%Cuban National Ballet, Havana, Cuba

Alonso, Maria Conchita *Actress*
PO Box 537, Beverly Hills, CA 90213, USA

Alonzo, John *Cinematographer*
310 Avondale Ave, Los Angeles, CA 90049, USA

Alou, Felipe R *Baseball Player, Manager*
PO Box 1287, Santo Domingo, Dominican Republic

Alpernin, Barry J *Businessman*
%Hasbro Inc, 1027 Newport Ave, Pawtucket, RI 02861, USA

Alpert, Herb *Musician*
31930 Pacific Coast Hwy, Malibu, CA 90265, USA

Alport of Colchester, Cuthbert J M *Government Official, England*
Cross House, Layer de la Haye, Colchester, Essex, England

Alt, Carol *Model*
%Elite Model Mgmt, 111 E 22nd St, #200, New York, NY 10010, USA

Alt, John *Football Player*
%Kansas City Chiefs, 1 Arrowhead Dr, Kansas City, KS 64129, USA

Altenberg, Wolfgang *Army General, Germany*
Birkenhof 44, 28759 Brenen-St Magnus, Germany

Alter, Dennis *Financier*
%Advanta Inc, Horsham Business Center, 300 Welsh Rd, Horsham, PA 19044, USA

Alter, Hobie *Surfboard, Boat Designer*
PO Box 1008, Oceanside, CA 92051, USA

Altman, Jeff *Actor*
5065 Calvin Ave, Tarzana, CA 91356, USA

Altman, Robert B *Movie Director, Producer*
%Sandcastle 5 Productions, 502 Park Ave, #15-G, New York, NY 10022, USA

Altman, Scott D *Astronaut*
15911 Manor Square Dr, Houston, TX 77062, USA

Altman, Sidney *Nobel Chemistry Laureate*
%Yale University, Chemistry Dept, New Haven, CT 06520, USA

Altman, Steven *Educator*
1540 Wabasso Way, Glendale, CA 91208, USA

Altman, Stuart H *Educator*
11 Bakers Hill Rd, Weston, MA 02193, USA

Altmeyer, Jeannine *Opera Singer*
%Metropolitan Opera Assn, Lincoln Center Plaza, New York, NY 10023, USA

Altobello, Daniel J *Businessman*
%Cateair International, 6550 Rock Spring Dr, Bethesda, MD 20817, USA

Alvarado, Natividad (Naty) *Handball Player*
%Equitable of Iowa, 2700 N Main, Santa Ana, CA 92705, USA

Alvarado, Trini *Actress*
233 Park Ave S, #1000, New York, NY 10003, USA

Alvary, Lorenzo *Opera Singer*
205 W 57th St, New York, NY 10019, USA

Alvord, Joel B *Businessman*
%Shawmut National Corp, 1 Federal St, Boston, MA 02110, USA

Alworth, Lance *Football Player*
%Del Mar Corporate Center, 990 Highland Dr, #300, Solana Beach, CA 92075, USA

Amacher, Ryan C *Educator*
%University of Texas at Arlington, President's Office, Arlington, TX 76019, USA

Amador, Jorge *Writer*
Rua Alagoinhas 33, Rio Vermelho-Salvador, Bahia, Brazil

Amanpour, Christiane *News Correspondent*
%Cable News Int'l, News Dept, 25 Rue de Ponthieu, 75008 Paris, France

Amara, Lucine *Opera Singer*
260 West End Ave, #7-A, New York, NY 10023, USA

Amaral, Donald J *Businessman*
%OrNda HealthCorp, 3401 West End Ave, Nashville, TN 37203, USA

Amateau, Rodney *Movie Director*
133 1/2 S Linden Dr, Beverly Hills, CA 90212, USA

Amato, Giuliano *Prime Minister, Italy*
%Carmera dei Deputati, Piazza di Montecitorio, 00186 Rome, Italy

Amaya, Armando *Sculptor*
Lopex 137, Depto 1, Mexico City 06070 CP, Mexico

Ambartsumyan, Victor A *Astrophysicist*
%Armenian Academy of Sciences, 24 Marshal Bagramian Ave, Erevan, Armenia

Ambasz, Emilio *Architect*
%Emilio Ambasz Design Group, 636 Broadway, #1100, New York, NY 10012, USA

Ambler, Eric *Writer*
Bourg Dessous 28, 1814 La Tour de Peilz, Switzerland

Amdahl, Gene M *Businessman, Computer Engineer*
%Andor International, 10131 Bubb Rd, Cupertino, CA 95014, USA

Ameling, Elly *Opera Singer*
%Sheldon Soffer Mgmt, 130 W 56th St, New York, NY 10019, USA

Amelio, Gilbert F *Businessman*
%National Semiconductor Corp, 2900 Semiconductor Dr, Santa Clara, CA 95051, USA

Ament, Jeff *Guitarist (Pearl Jam)*
%Curtis Mgmt, 207 1/2 1st Ave S, #300, Seattle, WA 98104, USA

Amerman, John W *Businessman*
%Mattel Inc, 333 Continental Blvd, El Segundo, CA 90245, USA

Amery of Lustleigh, H Julian *Government Official, England*
112 Eaton Sq, London SW1W 9AF, England

Ames, Bruce N *Biochemist*
1324 Spruce St, Berkeley, CA 94709, USA

Ames, Ed *Actor, Singer*
1457 Claridge Dr, Beverly Hills, CA 90210, USA

Ames, Frank Anthony *Concert Percussionist*
1235 Potamac St NW, Washington, DC 20007, USA

Ames, Louise Bates *Child Psychologist*
283 Edwards St, New Haven, CT 06511, USA

Ames, Rachel *Actress*
%Atkins Assoc, 303 S Crescent Heights Blvd, Los Angeles, CA 90048, USA

Amick, Madchen *Actress*
%International Creative Mgmt, 8942 Wilshire Blvd, Beverly Hills, CA 90211, USA

Amies, Hardy *Fashion Designer*
%Hardy Amies Ltd, 14 Savile Row, London SW1, England

Amin Dada, Idi *President, Uganda; Army Field Marshal*
PO Box 8948, Jidda 214942, Saudi Arabia

Amis, Kingsley *Writer*
%Jonathan Clowes, Iron Bridge House, London NW1 8BD, England

Amis, Martin *Writer*
%Peters Fraser Dunlop, Chelsea Harbour, Lots Rd, London SW10 0XF, England

Amis, Suzy *Actress, Model*
%International Creative Mgmt, 8942 Wilshire Blvd, Beverly Hills, CA 90211, USA

Amling, Warren E *Football Player*
541 Eaton St, London, OH 43140, USA

Ammaccapane, Danielle *Golfer*
%Ladies Professional Golf Assn, 2570 Volusia Ave, Daytona Beach, FL 32114, USA

Ammons, A R *Poet*
423 Cayuga Heights Rd, Ithaca, NY 14850, USA

A

Amory, Cleveland *Writer*
%Fund for the Animals, 200 W 57th St, New York, NY 10019, USA

Amos, Daniel P *Financier*
%AFLAC Inc, 1932 Wynnton Rd, Columbus, GA 31999, USA

Amos, John *Actor*
PO Box 587, Califon, NJ 07830, USA

Amos, John B *Businessman*
%American Family Corp, 1932 Wynnton Rd, Columbus, GA 31999, USA

Amos, Paul S *Financier*
%AFLAC Inc, 1932 Wynnton Rd, Columbus, GA 31999, USA

Amos, Tori *Singer, Songwriter*
PO Box 8456, Clearwater, FL 34618, USA

Amos, Wally (Famous) *Businessman*
215 Lanipo Dr, Kailua, HI 96734, USA

Amram, David *Composer, Conductor*
Peekskill Hollow Farm, Peekskill Hollow Rd, Putnam Valley, NY 10579, USA

Amsterdam, Morey *Comedian*
1012 N Hillcrest Rd, Beverly Hills, CA 90210, USA

Amte, Baba *Religious Leader*
Anandwan 442914, Via Warora, Dist Chandrapur, Maharashtra, India

Ana-Alicia *Actress*
%Century Artists, 9744 Wilshire Blvd, #308, Beverly Hills, CA 90212, USA

Anagnostopoulos, Constantine E *Heart Surgeon*
29 Portland Dr, St Louis, MO 63131, USA

Anand Panyarachun *Prime Minister, Thailand*
Government House, Thanon Nakhon Pathom Rd, Bangkok 10300, Thailand

Ananiashvili, Nina *Ballerina*
119270 Frunzenskaya Nab 46, #79, Moscow, Russia

Anathan, Mone, III *Businessman*
%Filene's Basement Corp, 40 Walnut St, Wellesley, MA 02181, USA

Anaya, Toney *Governor, NM*
%MALDEF, 634 S Spring, Los Angeles, CA 90014, USA

Anders, William A *Astronaut, Air Force General*
%Apogee Group, PO Box 1630, Eastsound, WA 98245, USA

Andersen Watts, Teresa *Sychronized Swimmer*
2582 Marsha Way, San Jose, CA 95125, USA

Andersen, Anthony L *Businessman*
%H B Fuller Co, 2400 Energy Park Dr, St Paul, MN 55108, USA

Andersen, Elmer L *Governor, MN; Businessman*
1483 Bussard Ct, Arden Hills, MN 55112, USA

Andersen, Hjalmar *Speed Skater*
%Velferden for Handelsflaten, Trondheimsvn 2, 0560 Oslo 5, Norway

Andersen, John *Publisher*
%Chicago Sun-Times, 401 N Wabash, Chicago, IL 60611, USA

Andersen, Ladell *Basketball Coach*
%Brigham Young University, Athletic Dept, Provo, UT 84602, USA

Andersen, Mogens *Artist*
Strandagervej 28, 2900 Hellerup, Copenhagen, Denmark

Andersen, Morton *Football Player*
%Atlanta Falcons, 2745 Burnett Rd, Suwanee, GA 30174, USA

Andersen, Reidar *Ski Jumper*
%National Ski Hall of Fame, PO Box 191, Ishpeming, MI 49849, USA

Anderson, Barbara *Actress*
PO Box 10118, Santa Fe, NM 87504, USA

Anderson, Beaufort T *WW II Army Hero (CMH)*
22105 Ranchito Dr, Salinas, CA 93908, USA

Anderson, Beiron *Model*
%Nina Blanchard Enterprises, 957 N Cole Ave, Los Angeles, CA 90038, USA

Anderson, Bill *Singer, Guitarist, Songwriter*
%Anderson/Chad, 6147 Landon Ave, Hesperia, CA 92345, USA

Anderson, Brad *Drag Racing Driver*
%National Hot Rod Assn, 2023 Financial Way, Glendora, CA 91741, USA

Anderson, Bradbury H *Businessman*
%Best Buy Co, PO Box 9312, Minneapolis, MN 55440, USA

Anderson, Bradley J (Brad) *Cartoonist (Marmaduke)*
13022 Wood Harbour Dr, Montgomery, TX 77356, USA

Anderson, Brett *Singer (Suede)*
PO Box 3431, London N1 7LW, England

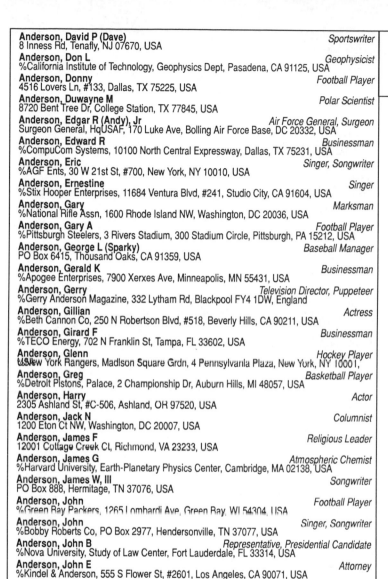

Anderson, David P (Dave) *Sportswriter*
8 Inness Rd, Tenafly, NJ 07670, USA

Anderson, Don L *Geophysicist*
%California Institute of Technology, Geophysics Dept, Pasadena, CA 91125, USA

Anderson, Donny *Football Player*
4516 Lovers Ln, #133, Dallas, TX 75225, USA

Anderson, Duwayne M *Polar Scientist*
8720 Bent Tree Dr, College Station, TX 77845, USA

Anderson, Edgar R (Andy), Jr *Air Force General, Surgeon*
Surgeon General, HqUSAF, 170 Luke Ave, Bolling Air Force Base, DC 20332, USA

Anderson, Edward R *Businessman*
%CompuCom Systems, 10100 North Central Expressway, Dallas, TX 75231, USA

Anderson, Eric *Singer, Songwriter*
%AGF Ents, 30 W 21st St, #700, New York, NY 10010, USA

Anderson, Ernestine *Singer*
%Stix Hooper Enterprises, 11684 Ventura Blvd, #241, Studio City, CA 91604, USA

Anderson, Gary *Marksman*
%National Rifle Assn, 1600 Rhode Island NW, Washington, DC 20036, USA

Anderson, Gary A *Football Player*
%Pittsburgh Steelers, 3 Rivers Stadium, 300 Stadium Circle, Pittsburgh, PA 15212, USA

Anderson, George L (Sparky) *Baseball Manager*
PO Box 6415, Thousand Oaks, CA 91359, USA

Anderson, Gerald K *Businessman*
%Apogee Enterprises, 7900 Xerxes Ave, Minneapolis, MN 55431, USA

Anderson, Gerry *Television Director, Puppeteer*
%Gerry Anderson Magazine, 332 Lytham Rd, Blackpool FY4 1DW, England

Anderson, Gillian *Actress*
%Beth Cannon Co, 250 N Robertson Blvd, #518, Beverly Hills, CA 90211, USA

Anderson, Girard F *Businessman*
%TECO Energy, 702 N Franklin St, Tampa, FL 33602, USA

Anderson, Glenn *Hockey Player*
%New York Rangers, Madison Square Grdn, 4 Pennsylvania Plaza, New York, NY 10001,

Anderson, Greg *Basketball Player*
%Detroit Pistons, Palace, 2 Championship Dr, Auburn Hills, MI 48057, USA

Anderson, Harry *Actor*
2305 Ashland St, #C-506, Ashland, OR 97520, USA

Anderson, Jack N *Columnist*
1200 Eton Ct NW, Washington, DC 20007, USA

Anderson, James F *Religious Leader*
12001 Cottage Creek Ct, Richmond, VA 23233, USA

Anderson, James G *Atmospheric Chemist*
%Harvard University, Earth-Planetary Physics Center, Cambridge, MA 02138, USA

Anderson, James W, III *Songwriter*
PO Box 888, Hermitage, TN 37076, USA

Anderson, John *Football Player*
%Green Bay Packers, 1265 Lombardi Ave, Green Bay, WI 54304, USA

Anderson, John *Singer, Songwriter*
%Bobby Roberts Co, PO Box 2977, Hendersonville, TN 37077, USA

Anderson, John B *Representative, Presidential Candidate*
%Nova University, Study of Law Center, Fort Lauderdale, FL 33314, USA

Anderson, John E *Attorney*
%Kindel & Anderson, 555 S Flower St, #2601, Los Angeles, CA 90071, USA

Anderson, John, Jr *Governor, KS*
16609 W 133rd, Olathe, KS 66062, USA

Anderson, Jon *Singer (Yes)*
%Sun Artists, 9 Hillgate St, London W8 7SP, England

Anderson, June *Opera Singer*
%Columbia Artists Mgmt Inc, 165 W 57th St, New York, NY 10019, USA

Anderson, Kenny *Football Player, Coach*
%Cincinnati Bengals, 200 Riverfront Stadium, Cincinnati, OH 45202, USA

Anderson, Kenny *Basketball Player*
%New Jersey Nets, Byrne Meadowlands Arena, East Rutherford, NJ 07073, USA

Anderson, Laurie *Performance Artist*
%Original Artists, 45 E 9th St, New York, NY 10003, USA

Anderson, Loni *Actress*
3355 Clarendon Rd, Beverly Hills, CA 90210, USA

Anderson, Lynn *Singer*
4925 Tyne Valley Blvd, Nashville, TN 37220, USA

Anderson - Anderson

Anderson, Lynn L *Financier*
%Frank Russell Trust, PO Box 1454, Tacoma, WA 98401, USA

Anderson, Marcus A (Mark) *Air Force General*
Inspector General's Office, 1140 Air Force Pentagon, Washington, DC 20330, USA

Anderson, Melissa Sue *Actress*
20722 Pacific Coast Hwy, Malibu, CA 90265, USA

Anderson, Melody *Actress*
301 E 64th St, #18-B, New York, NY 10021, USA

Anderson, Michael J *Movie Director*
%Paul Burford, 52 Yorkminster Rd, North York ON M2P 1M3, Canada

Anderson, N Christian, III *Editor, Publisher*
%Gazette Telegraph, 30 S Prospect St, Colorado Springs, CO 80903, USA

Anderson, Nick *Basketball Player*
%Orlando Magic, Orlando Arena, 1 Magic Pl, Orlando, FL 32801, USA

Anderson, Pamela *Actress*
%Manzella Entertainment, 345 N Maple Dr, #185, Beverly Hills, CA 90210, USA

Anderson, Paul M *Businessman*
%Panhandle Eastern Corp, 5400 Westheimer Ct, Houston, TX 77056, USA

Anderson, Peter J *Financier*
%IDS Advisory Group, 80 S 8th St, Minneapolis, MN 55402, USA

Anderson, Philip W *Nobel Physics Laureate*
%Princeton University, Physics Dept, Princeton, NJ 08544, USA

Anderson, Poul W *Writer*
3 Las Palomas, Orinda, CA 94563, USA

Anderson, Randy *Drag Racing Driver*
%National Hot Rod Assn, 2023 Financial Way, Glendora, CA 91741, USA

Anderson, Reid B *Ballet Dancer, Artistic Director*
%National Ballet of Canada, 157 King St E, Toronto ON M5C 1G9, Canada

Anderson, Richard *Actor*
10120 Cielo Dr, Beverly Hills, CA 90210, USA

Anderson, Richard C *Businessman*
%Lands' End Inc, 1 Lands' End Ln, Dodgeville, WI 53595, USA

Anderson, Richard Dean *Actor*
%Wolf/Kasteler, 1033 Gayley Ave, #208, Los Angeles, CA 90024, USA

Anderson, Robert G W *Museum Director*
%British Museum, London WC1B 3DG, England

Anderson, Robert W *Writer*
14 Sutton Pl S, New York, NY 10022, USA

Anderson, Ron *Basketball Player*
%Philadelphia 76ers, Veterans Stadium, Box 25040, Philadelphia, PA 19147, USA

Anderson, Ronald R *Businessman*
%Southern Farm Bureau Casualty Insurance, PO Box 1800, Richmond, VA 23214, USA

Anderson, Ross *Journalist*
%Seattle Times, Editorial Dept, 1120 John St, Seattle, WA 98109, USA

Anderson, Shelly *Drag Racing Driver*
%National Hot Rod Assn, 2023 Financial Way, Glendora, CA 91741, USA

Anderson, Terry *Hostage, Journalist*
69 Rockledge Rd, Bronxville, NY 10708, USA

Anderson, Thomas L *Businessman*
%FoxMeyer Health Corp, 1220 Senlac Dr, Carrollton, TX 75006, USA

Anderson, W French *Biochemist, Geneticist*
%University of Southern California Med School, 144 E Lake, Los Angeles, CA

Anderson, Warren M *Businessman*
270 Park Ave, New York, NY 10017, USA

Anderson, Webster *Vietnam War Army Hero (CMH)*
Rt 2, Box 17-H, Winnsboro, SC 29180, USA

Anderson, Wendell R *Governor/Senator, MN*
%Larkin & Hoffman, 1700 First Bank Pl W, Minneapolis, MN 55402, USA

Anderson, Weston *Physicist*
%Varian Assoc, 611 Hansen Way, Palo Alto, CA 94304, USA

Anderson, William R *Representative, TN; Navy Officer*
10906 Lake Wildermere Dr, Great Falls, VA 22066, USA

Anderson, Willie *Basketball Player*
%Toronto Raptors, 20 Bay St, #1702, Toronto ON M5J 2N8, Canada

Andersson, Bibi *Actress*
Tykovagen 28, Lidingo 18161, Sweden

Andersson, Harriet *Actress*
Roslagsgatan 15, 11355 Stockholm, Sweden

Anderson - Andersson

Andes, G Thomas *Financier*
%Magna Group, 1401 S Brentwood Blvd, St Louis, MO 63144, USA

Andes, Karen *Body Builder*
%G P Putnam's Sons, 200 Madison Ave, New York, NY 10016, USA

Andre, Carl *Sculptor*
PO Box 1001, Cooper Station, New York, NY 10249, USA

Andreas, Dwayne O *Businessman*
%Archer Daniels Midland Co, 4666 Faries Pkwy, Decatur, IL 62526, USA

Andreas, Michael D *Businessman*
%Archer Daniels Midland Co, 4666 Faries Pkwy, Decatur, IL 62526, USA

Andreessen, Marc *Computer Software Designer (Mosiac)*
%Netscape Communications Corp, 501 E Middlefield Rd, Mountain View, CA 94043, USA

Andreotti, Giulio *Prime Minister, Italy*
326 Corso Vittorio Emanuele, Rome, Italy

Andress, Tuck *Jazz Guitarist (Tuck & Patti)*
%Q Entertainment, 584 N Larchmont Blvd, Los Angeles, CA 90004, USA

Andress, Ursula *Actress*
Lamonstr 9, 81679 Munich, Germany

Andretti, John *Auto Racing Driver*
PO Box 34156, Indianapolis, IN 46234, USA

Andretti, Mario *Auto Racing Driver*
53 Victory Ln, Nazareth, PA 18064, USA

Andretti, Michael M *Auto Racing Driver*
3310 Airport Rd, Allentown, PA 18103, USA

Andrew *Prince, England*
%Buckingham Palace, London SW1, England

Andrews, Andy *Comedian*
PO Box 17321, Nashville, TN 37217, USA

Andrews, Anthony *Actor*
%Peters Fraser Dunlop, Chelsea Harbour, Lots Rd, London SW10 0XF, England

Andrews, Bernard W *Businessman*
%Montgomery Ward Co, 619 W Chicago Ave, Chicago, IL 60610, USA

Andrews, George E *Football Player*
9972 Sunderland St, Santa Ana, CA 92705, USA

Andrews, James E *Religious Leader*
%Presbyterian Church (USA), 100 Witherspoon St, Louisville, KY 40202, USA

Andrews, John H *Architect*
%John Andrews Int'l, 1017 Barrenjoey Rd, Palm Beach NSW 2108, Australia

Andrews, Julie *Actress*
PO Box 666, Beverly Hills, CA 90213, USA

Andrews, Mark *Senator, ND*
RR 1, PO Box 146, Mapleton, ND 58059, USA

Andrews, Maxene *Singer (Andrews Sisters)*
14200 Carriage Oaks Ln, Auburn, CA 95603, USA

Andrews, Patti *Singer (Andrews Sisters)*
9823 Aldea Ave, Northridge, CA 91325, USA

Andrews, Robert F *Religious Leader*
5536 N Roff Ave, Oklahoma City, OK 73112, USA

Andrews, Steven *Businessman*
%AM International Inc, 1800 W Central Rd, Mt Prospect, IL 60056, USA

Andrews, Theresa *Swimmer*
2004 Homewood Rd, Annapolis, MD 21402, USA

Andrews, Tige *Actor*
4914 Encino Terrace, Encino, CA 91316, USA

Andrews, William L *Football Player*
811 Tahoe Rdg, #I-55, Roswell, GA 30076, USA

Andreychuck, Dave *Hockey Player*
%Toronto Maple Leafs, 60 Carlton St, Toronto ON M5B 1L1, Canada

Andrie, George *Football Player*
%George Andrie Assoc, Rt 2, Box 748, Whitney, TX 76692, USA

Androutsopoulos, Adamantios *Prime Minister, Greece*
63 Academias St, Athens, Greece

Andrus, Cecil D *Secretary, Interior; Governor, ID*
1280 Candleridge Rd, Boise, ID 83712, USA

Andujar, Joaquin *Baseball Player*
400 Randal Ave, #106, Spring, TX 77388, USA

Ane, Charles T (Charlie), Jr *Football Player*
741 16th Ave, Honolulu, HI 96816, USA

A

Angel, Daniel D *Educator*
%Stephen F Austin State University, President's Office, Nacogdoches, TX 75962, USA

Angel, Heather H *Photographer*
Highways, 6 Vicarage Hill, Farnham, Surrey GU9 8HJ, England

Angel, J Roger P *Astronomer*
%Steward Observatory, University of Arizona, Tucson, AZ 85721, USA

Angelopoulos, Theo *Movie Director*
Solmou 18, 106 82 Athens, Greece

Angelou, Maya *Writer*
3240 Valley Rd, Winston-Salem, NC 27106, USA

Anger, Kenneth *Movie Director*
354 E 91st St, #9, New York, NY 10128, USA

Angerer, Peter *Biathlete*
Wagenau 2, 17326 Hammer, Germany

Angew, Patrick J *Financier*
%St Paul Bancorp, 6700 W North Ave, Chicago, IL 60635, USA

Angier, Natalie M *Journalist*
%New York Times, Editorial Dept, 229 W 43rd St, New York, NY 10036, USA

Anglin, Jennifer *Actress*
651 N Kilkea Dr, Los Angeles, CA 90048, USA

Anguiano, Raul *Artist*
Anaxagoras 1326, Colonia Narvate, Mexico 13 DF, Mexico

Angus, Michael *Businessman*
%Unilever PLC, PO Box 68, Unilever House, London EC4P 4BQ, England

Anhalt, Edward *Movie Director*
500 Amalfi Dr, Pacific Palisades, CA 90272, USA

Aniston, Jennifer *Actress*
%Innovative Artists, 1999 Ave of Stars, #2850, Los Angeles, CA 90067, USA

Anka, Paul *Singer, Songwriter*
12078 Summit Cir, Beverly Hills, CA 90210, USA

Anker, Robert A *Businessman*
%Lincoln National Corp, 200 E Berry St, Fort wayne, IN 46802, USA

Anlyan, William *Surgeon*
First Union Plaza, 2200 W Main St, #1066, Durham, NC 27705, USA

Ann-Margret (Smith) *Actress, Singer, Dancer*
2707 Benedict Canyon Rd, Beverly Hills, CA 90210, USA

Annabella *Actress*
1 Rue Pierret, 92200 Neuilly, France

Annakin, Ken *Movie Director*
1643 Lindacrest Dr, Beverly Hills, CA 90210, USA

Annand, Richard Wallace *WW II British Army Hero (VC)*
Springwell House, Whitesmocks, Durham City DH1 4ZL, England

Annaud, Jean-Jacques *Movie Director*
55 Rue de Varenne, 75007 Paris, France

Anne *Princess, England*
%Gatecombe Park, Gloucestershire, England

Anne of Bourbon-Palma *Queen, Romania*
%Villa Serena, 77 Chemin Louis-Degallier, 1290 Versoix-Geneva, Switzerland

Annenberg, Wallis *Publisher*
10273 Century Woods Dr, Los Angeles, CA 90067, USA

Annenberg, Walter H *Publisher, Diplomat*
71231 Tamarisk Ln, Rancho Mirage, CA 92270, USA

Annis, Francesca *Actress*
2 Vicarage Ct, London W8, England

Ansara, Michael *Actor*
4624 Park Mirasol, Calabasas, CA 91302, USA

Anspach, Susan *Actress*
2369 Beach Ave, Venice, CA 90291, USA

Anspaugh, David *Movie Director*
%International Creative Mgmt, 8942 Wilshire Blvd, Beverly Hills, CA 90211, USA

Ant (Stuart Goddard), Adam *Singer*
2452 Meadow Valley Terrace, Los Angeles, CA 90039, USA

Ant, Adam *Singer*
2452 Meadow Valley Terrace, Los Angeles, CA 90039, USA

Antes, Horst *Artist*
Hohenbergstr 11, 19322 Karlsruhe, Germany

Anthony, Barbara Cox *Businesswoman*
%Cox Enterprises, 1400 Lake Hearn Dr NE, Atlanta, GA 30319, USA

Anthony, Earl R *Bowler*
6750 Regional St, Dublin, CA 94568, USA

Anthony, Greg *Basketball Player*
%Vancouver Grizzlies, 788 Beatty St, #300, Vancouver BC V6B 2M1, Canada

Anthony, Lysette *Actress*
125 W 76th St, #6-B, New York, NY 10023, USA

Anthony, Ray *Orchestra Leader, Trumpeter*
9288 Kinglet Dr, Los Angeles, CA 90069, USA

Antoci, Mario J *Financier*
%American Savings Bank, 17877 Von Karman Ave, Irvine, CA 92714, USA

Anton, Susan *Actress*
16830 Ventura Blvd, #1616, Encino, CA 91436, USA

Antonakakis, Suzana M *Architect*
Atelier 66, Em Benaki 118, Athens 114-73 Athens, Greece

Antonakos, Stephen *Artist*
435 W Broadway, New York, NY 10012, USA

Antonelli, Ferdinando Cardinal *Religious Leader*
Piazza S Calisto 16, 00153 Rome, Italy

Antonelli, John A (Johnny) *Baseball Player*
PO Box 580, Pittsford, NY 14534, USA

Antonio *Spanish Dancer*
Coslada 7, Madrid, Spain

Antonio, Jim *Actor*
%Henderson/Hogan Agency, 247 S Beverly Dr, #102, Beverly Hills, CA 90212, USA

Antonio, Lou *Actor*
530 Gaylord Dr, Burbank, CA 91505, USA

Antonioni, Michelangelo *Movie Director*
Via Vincenzo Tiberio 18, 00191 Rome, Italy

Antoun (Khouri), Bishop *Religious Leader*
%Antiochian Orthodox Christian Archdiocese, 358 Mountain Rd, Englewood, NJ 07631, USA

Antuofermo, Vito *Boxer*
160-19 81st St, Howard Beach, NY 11414, USA

Anuszkiewicz, Richard J *Artist*
76 Chestnut St, Englewood, NJ 07631, USA

Anwar, Gabrielle *Actress*
%AIM, 5 Denmark St, London WC2H 8LP, England

Aoi, Joichi *Businessman*
%Toshiba Corp, 72 Horikawacho, Saiwaiku, Kawasaki 210, Japan

Aoki, Chieko N *Businesswoman*
%Westin Hotels Co, Westin Building, 2001 6th Ave, Seattle, WA 98121, USA

Aoki, Ikuro *Businessman*
%Kanebo Ltd, 1-2-2 Umeda, Kitaku, Osaka 530, Japan

Aoki, Rocky *Boat Racing Driver, Businessman*
%Benihana of Tokyo, 8685 NW 53rd Terrace, Miami, FL 33166, USA

Aouita, Said *Track Athlete*
%Abdejil Bencheikh, 9 Rue Soivissi, Loubira, Rabat, Morocco

Aparicio, Luis E *Baseball Player*
Calle 67, #26-82, Maracaibo, Venezuela

Apfalter, Heribert *Businessman*
%Voest-Alpine, Muldenstr 5, 4010 Linz, Austria

Apodaca, Jerry *Governor, NM*
1328 Camino Corrales, Santa Fe, NM 87505, USA

Apollonia (Patty Kotero) *Model, Actress, Singer*
%Charter Mgmt, 8200 Wilshire Blvd, #218, Beverly Hills, CA 90211, USA

Appel, Karel *Artist*
%Galerie Statler, 51 Rue de Seine, Paris, France

Apple, Raymond W, Jr *Journalist*
%New York Times, Editorial Dept, 1627 "I" St NW, Washington, DC 20006, USA

Applebaum, Eugene *Businessman*
%Arbor Drugs, 3331 W Big Beaver Rd, Troy, MI 48084, USA

Appleberry, James B *Educator*
5610 Wisconsin Ave, #704, Bethesda, MD 20815, USA

Applegate, Christina *Actress*
20411 Chapter Dr, Woodland Hills, CA 91364, USA

Appleton, James R *Educator*
%University of Redlands, President's Office, Redlands, CA 92373, USA

Appleton, Myra *Editor*
%Cosmopolitan Magazine, Editorial Dept, 224 W 57th St, New York, NY 10019, USA

A

Anthony - Appleton

A

Appleton, Steven R *Businessman*
%Micron Technology, 2805 E Columbia Rd, Boise, ID 83706, USA

Apps, Syl *Hockey Player*
241 Alwington Pl, Northboro, MA 01532, USA

Apt, Jerome (Jay) *Astronaut*
806 Shorewood Dr, Seabrook, TX 77586, USA

Apted, Michael D *Movie Director*
19 Latimer Rd, Santa Monica, CA 90402, USA

Aquilino, Thomas J, Jr *Judge*
%US Court of International Trade, 1 Federal Plaza, New York, NY 10278, USA

Aquino, Corazon C *President, Philippines*
Pius XVI Center, UN Center, Manila, Philippines

Arafat, Yasser *Palestine; Nobel Peace Laureate*
%PLO Chairman's Office, Gaza City, Gaza Strip, Palestine, Israel

Aragall, Giacomo *Opera Singer*
%Robert Lombardo Assoc, 61 W 62nd St, New York, NY 10023, USA

Aragones, Sergio *Cartoonist (Mad Comics)*
%Mad Magazine, 485 Madison Ave, New York, NY 10022, USA

Arai, Kazuo *Businessman*
%Kao Corp, 14-10 Nihonbashi, Kayabacho, Chuoku, Tokyo 103, Japan

Araiza, Francisco *Opera Singer*
%Kunstler Mgmt Kursidem, Kurfurstenstr 8, 80799 Munich, Germany

Arakawa, Ichiro *Businessman*
%Kanto Auto Works, Taura-Minatomachi, Yokosuka City 237, Japan

Arakawa, Masashi *Businessman*
%Hino Motors, 3-1-1 Hinodal, Hino City, Tokyo 191, Japan

Arakawa, Toyozo *Pottery Maker*
4-101, O-Hatacho, Tokyo, Japan

Aramburu, Juan Carlos Cardinal *Religious Leader*
Arzobispado, Suipacha 1034, Buenos Aires 1008, Argentina

Arana Osorio, Carlos M *President, Guatemala; Army General*
%President's Office, Palacio Nacional, Guatemala City, Guatemala

Aranauskas, Leonas S *Architect*
Glavmozarchitectura, Mayakovsky Square 1, 103001 Moscow, Russia

Araskog, Rand V *Businessman*
%ITT Corp, 1330 Ave of Americas, New York, NY 10019, USA

Arau, Alfonso *Movie Director*
Productions AA, Privada Rafael Oliva 8, Coyoacan 04120 Mexico City, Mexico

Arbanas, Fred V *Football Player*
3350 SW Hook Rd, Lee's Summit, MO 64082, USA

Arbeid, Murray *Fashion Designer*
202 Ebury St, London SW1W 8UN, England

Arber, Werner *Nobel Medicine Laureate*
70 Klingelbergstr, 4056 Basel, Switzerland

Arbour, Al *Hockey Coach, Executive*
%New York Islanders, Veterans Memorial Coliseum, Uniondale, NY 11553, USA

Arbulu Galliani, Guillermo *Prime Minister, Peru; Army General*
%Foreign Affairs Ministry, Lima, Peru

Arbus, Allan *Actor*
2208 N Beverly Glen, Los Angeles, CA 90077, USA

Arcaro, G Edward (Eddie) *Thoroughbred Racing Jockey, Sportscaster*
11111 Biscayne Blvd, Miami, FL 33181, USA

Archer, Anne *Actress*
13201 Old Oak Ln, Los Angeles, CA 90049, USA

Archer, Beverly *Actress*
%Judy Schoen Assoc, 606 N Larchmont Blvd, #309, Los Angeles, CA 90004, USA

Archer, George *Golfer*
%Bullet Golf Ball, 2803 S Yale St, Santa Ana, CA 92704, USA

Archer, Jeffrey H *Government Official, England; Writer*
93 Albert Embankment, London SE1, England

Archer, John *Writer*
10901 176th Cir NE, #3601, Redmond, WA 98052, USA

Archerd, Army *Journalist*
%Variety Magazine, Editorial Dept, 5700 Wilshire Blvd, Los Angeles, CA 90036, USA

Archibald, Nathaniel (Tiny) *Basketball Player*
%Harlem Armory Homeless Shelter, 40 W 143rd St, New York, NY 10037, USA

Arciniega, Tomas A *Educator*
%California State College, President's Office, Bakersfield, CA 93311, USA

Arciniegas, German *Writer, Diplomat*
%Academia Colombiana de Histora, Calle 92, 10-21 Bogota, Colombia

Ard, William D (Bill) *Football Player*
41 Vail Ln, Watchung, NJ 07060, USA

Ardalan, Nader *Architect*
177 Milk St, Boston, MA 02109, USA

Ardant, Fanny *Actress*
%Artmedia, 10 Ave George V, 75008 Paris, France

Arden, John *Playwright*
%Casorotto Ramsay Ltd, 60-66 Wardour St, London W1V 3HP, England

Arden, Toni *Singer*
34-34 75th St, Jackson Heights, NY 11372, USA

Ardia, Stephen V *Businessman*
3 W Lake St, Skancateles, NY 13152, USA

Aregood, Richard L *Journalist*
%Philadelphia Daily News, Editoral Dept, 400 N Broad St, Philadelphia, PA 19130, USA

Arens, Moshe *Government Official, Israel*
49 Hagderot, Savyon, Israel

Aretsky, Ken *Restauranteur*
%21 Club, 21 W 52nd St, New York, NY 10019, USA

Argento, Dominick *Composer*
%University of Minnesota, Music Dept, Ferguson Hall, Minneapolis, MN 55455, USA

Argerich, Martha *Concert Pianist*
%Goette Konzert Direktion, Colonnaden 70, 20354 Hamburg, Germany

Argyros, George L *Baseball Executive*
%Seattle Mariners, Kingdome, PO Box 4100, Seattle, WA 98104, USA

Arian, David *Labor Leader*
%International Longshoremen's Union, 1188 Franklin St, San Francisco, CA 94109, USA

Arias Sanchez, Oscar *President, Costa Rica; Nobel Laureate*
%Arias Foundation for Peace, Apdo 8-6410-1000, San Jose, Costa Rica

Arias, Ricardo M *President, Panama*
Apdo 4549, Panama City, Panama

Arinze, Francis Cardinal *Religious Leader*
%Pontifical Council for Non-Christians, 00120 Vatican City, Italy

Arison, M Micky *Businessman*
%Carnival Corp, 3655 NW 87th Ave, Miami, FL 33178, USA

Aristide, Jean-Bertrand *President, Haiti*
%Palace du Gouvernement, Port-Au-Prince, Haiti

Aristides, George *Businessman*
%Graco Inc, 4050 Olson Memorial Pkwy, Minneapolis, MN 55422, USA

Ariyaratne, Ahangamage *Agricutural Economist*
%Sarvodaya Shramadana, Sri Lanka

Ariyoshi, George R *Governor, HI*
745 Fort St, #500, Honolulu, HI 96813, USA

Ariyoshi, Shingo *Businessman*
%Mitsui Mining, 1-1-1 Nihonbashi Muromachi, Chuoku, Tokyo 103, Japan

Arizin, Paul J *Basketball Player*
227 Lewis Rd, Springfield, PA 19064, USA

Arkhipova, Irina K *Opera Singer*
%Union of Musicians, Nezhdanovoy Str 2/14, #27, 103009 Moscow, Russia

Arkin, Adam *Actor*
%Innovative Artists, 1999 Ave of Stars, #2850, Los Angeles, CA 90067, USA

Arkin, Alan *Actor*
%International Creative Mgmt, 40 W 57th St, New York, NY 10019, USA

Arkoff, Samuel Z *Movie Producer*
3205 Oakdell Ln, Studio City, CA 91604, USA

Arledge, David A *Businessman*
%Coastal Corp, 9 Greenway Plaza, Houston, TX 77046, USA

Arledge, Roone *Television Executive*
535 Park Ave, #13-A, New York, NY 10021, USA

Arlen, Michael J *Writer*
%New Yorker Magazine, Editorial Dept, 25 W 43rd St, New York, NY 10036, USA

Arliss, Dimitra *Actress*
%Aspen Music Assn, PO Box AA, Aspen, CO 81612, USA

Armacost, Michael H *Diplomat*
%US Embassy, 10-5-1 Akasaka, Minatoku, Tokyo, Japan

Arman, (Armand P) *Sculptor*
%Arman Studios, 430 Washington St, New York, NY 10013, USA

A

Arciniegas - Arman

A

Armani, Giorgio — *Fashion Designer*
Palazzo Durini 24, 20122 Milan, Italy

Armas, Antonio R (Tony) — *Baseball Player*
Los Mercedes, #37, P Piruto-Edo, Anzoatequi, Venezuela

Armatrading, Joan — *Singer, Songwriter*
%Running Dog Mgmt, Lower Hampton Rd, Sunbury, Middx TW16 5PR, England

Armedariz, Pedro, Jr — *Actor*
%Diamond Artists, 215 N Barrington Ave, Los Angeles, CA 90049, USA

Armfield, William J, IV — *Businessman*
%Unifi Inc, 7201 W Friendly Rd, Greensboro, NC 27410, USA

Armitage, Karole — *Choreographer, Dancer*
350 W 21st St, New York, NY 10011, USA

Armitage, Kenneth — *Artist*
22-A Avonmore Rd, London W14 8RR, England

Armitage, Richard L — *Government Official*
%Secretary's Office, Department of Army, Pentagon, Washington, DC 20310, USA

Arms, Russell — *Actor, Singer*
2918 Davis Way, Palm Springs, CA 92262, USA

Armstrong, A James — *Religious Leader*
%Broadway Methodist Church, 1100 W 42nd St, Indianapolis, IN 46208, USA

Armstrong, Anne L — *Diplomat, Educator*
Armstrong Ranch, Armstrong, TX 78338, USA

Armstrong, B J — *Basketball Player*
%Toronto Raptors, 20 Bay St, #1702, Toronto ON M5J 2N8, Canada

Armstrong, Bess — *Actress*
%William Morris Agency, 151 S El Camino Dr, Beverly Hills, CA 90212, USA

Armstrong, Bruce C — *Football Player*
%New England Patriots, Foxboro Stadium, Rt 1, Foxboro, MA 02035, USA

Armstrong, Garner Ted — *Evangelist*
PO Box 2525, Tyler, TX 75710, USA

Armstrong, Gillian — *Movie Director*
%William Morris Agency, 151 S El Camino Dr, Beverly Hills, CA 90212, USA

Armstrong, Lance — *Cyclist*
%US Cycling Federation, 1750 E Boulder St, Colorado Springs, CO 80909, USA

Armstrong, Malcolm B (Mac) — *Air Force General*
Commander, 21st Air Force, 1907 E Arnold, McGuire Air Force Base, NJ 08641, USA

Armstrong, Neil A — *Astronaut*
%AIL Systems, 5200 Springfield Pike, Dayton, OH 45431, USA

Armstrong, R G — *Actor*
3856 Reklaw Dr, Studio City, CA 91604, USA

Armstrong, Robb — *Cartoonist (Jump Start)*
%United Feature Syndicate, 200 Park Ave, New York, NY 10166, USA

Armstrong, Thomas H W — *Concert Organist*
1 East St, Olney, Bucks MK46 4AP, England

Armstrong, Thomas R — *Financier*
%Advent International, 101 Federal St, Boston, MA 02110, USA

Armstrong, Tom — *Cartoonist (Marvin)*
%North America Syndicate, 235 E 45th St, New York, NY 10017, USA

Armstrong, Valorie — *Actress*
%Contemporary Artists, 1427 3rd St Promenade, #205, Santa Monica, CA 90401, USA

Armstrong, Warren B — *Educator*
3038 Coves, Afton, OK 74331, USA

Arn, Edward — *Governor, KS*
9434 E Bent Tree Cir, Wichita, KS 67226, USA

Arnason, Hjorvardur H — *Art Historian*
4 E 89th St, New York, NY 10128, USA

Arnaud, Jean-Loup — *Government Official, France*
15 Quai Louis Bleriot, 75016 Paris, France

Arnaz, Desi, Jr — *Actor*
%Success Without Stress, 12626 Ojai Rd, Santa Paula, CA 93060, USA

Arnaz, Lucie — *Actress*
RR 3, Flintlock Ridge Rd, Katonah, NY 10536, USA

Arnell, Richard A S — *Composer*
Benhall Lodge, Benhall, Suffolk IP17 1DJ, England

Arnesen, Liv — *Distance Polar Skier*
Trostevn 6, 1340 Bekkestua, Norway

Arness, James — *Actor*
PO Box 49004, Los Angeles, CA 90049, USA

Armani - Arness

Arnett, Jon — Football Player
PO Box 4077, Palos Verdes Estates, CA 90274, USA

Arnett, Peter — Commentator
%Cable News Network, News Dept, 820 1st St NE, Washington, DC 20002, USA

Arnette, Jeanetta — Actress
9024 Dorrington Ave, Los Angeles, CA 90048, USA

Arnhold, Henry H — Financier
%Arnhold & S Bleichroeder, 45 Broadway, New York, NY 10006, USA

Arno, Ed — Cartoonist
PO Box 4203, New York, NY 10017, USA

Arnold, Anna Bing — Philanthropist
%Anna Bing Arnold Foundation, 9700 W Pico Blvd, Los Angeles, CA 90035, USA

Arnold, Debbie — Actress
%M Arnold Mgmt, 12 Cambridge Park, East Twickenham, Middx TW1 2PF, England

Arnold, Eddy — Singer
PO Box 97, Franklin Rd, Brentwood, TN 37024, USA

Arnold, Gary H — Movie Critic
5133 N 1st St, Arlington, VA 22203, USA

Arnold, Harry L, Jr — Dermatologist, Writer
250 Laurel St, #301, San Francisco, CA 94118, USA

Arnold, Jackson D — Navy Admiral
%Cubic Corp, 9333 Balboa Ave, San Diego, CA 92123, USA

Arnold, James R — Chemist
%University of California, Space Institute, La Jolla, CA 92307, USA

Arnold, John B — Businessman
%Network Equipment Technologies, 800 Saginaw Dr, Redwood City, CA 94063, USA

Arnold, Malcolm — Composer
%Faber Music Co, 3 Queen Sq, London WC1N 3AU, England

Arnold, Murray — Basketball Coach
%Western Kentucky University, Athletic Dept, Bowling Green, KY 42101, USA

Arnold, Steven L — Army General
%Commanding General, 3rd US Army, Fort McPherson, GA 30330, USA

Arnold, Stuart — Publisher
%Fortune Magazine, Rockefeller Center, New York, NY 10020, USA

Arnold, Tom — Comedian
PO Box 15458, Beverly Hills, CA 90209, USA

Arnoldi, Charles A — Artist
721 Hampton Dr, Venice, CA 90291, USA

Arns, Paulo E Cardinal — Religious Leader
Avenida Higienopolos 890, 01238 Sao Paulo, SP, Brazil

Aronson, Arthur H — Businessman
%Allegheny Ludlum Corp, 1000 6 PPG Pl, Pittsburgh, PA 15222, USA

Arp, Halton C — Astronomer
%Max Planck Physics/Radiology Institute, 84518 Garching Munich, Germany

Arpel, Adrien — Beauty Consultant
666 5th Ave, New York, NY 10103, USA

Arpino, Gerald P — Choreographer
%City Center Joffrey Ballet, 130 W 56th St, New York, NY 10019, USA

Arquette, Patricia — Actress
%United Talent Agency, 9560 Wilshire Blvd, #500, Beverly Hills, CA 90212, USA

Arquette, Rosanna — Actress
13596 Contour Dr, Sherman Oaks, CA 91423, USA

Arrindell, Clement A — Governor General, St Kitts & Nevis
Government House, Basseterre, St Kitts, St Kitts & Nevis

Arriola, Gus — Cartoonist (Gordo)
PO Box 3275, Carmel, CA 93921, USA

Arrison, Clement R — Businessman
%Mark IV Industries, 501 John James Audubon Parkway, Amherst. NJ 14228, USA

Arrow, Kenneth J — Nobel Economics Laureate
580 Constanzo St, Stanford, CA 94305, USA

Arroyo, Luis E — Baseball Player
Box 354, Penuelas, PR 00624, USA

Arroyo, Martina — Opera Singer
%Thea Dispeker, 59 E 54th St, New York, NY 10022, USA

Arthur, Beatrice — Actress
2000 Old Ranch Rd, Los Angeles, CA 90049, USA

Arthur, Maureen — Actress
PO Box 280009, Northridge, CA 91328, USA

Arnett - Arthur

A

Arthur, Rebeca *Actress*
%Paul Kohner Inc, 9300 Wilshire Blvd, #555, Beverly Hills, CA 90212, USA

Arthur, Stanley R *Navy Admiral*
Vice Chief of Naval Operations, Navy Dept, Washington, DC 20350, USA

Artschwager, Richard E *Artist*
116 S Portland Ave, Brooklyn, NY 11217, USA

Artsebarsky, Anatoly *Cosmonaut*
%Potchta Kosmonavtov, 141 160 Svyosdny Gorodok, Moskovskoi Oblasti, Russia

Artyukhin, Yuri P *Cosmonaut*
%Potchta Kosmonavtov, 141 160 Svyosdny Gorodok, Moskovskoi Oblasti, Russia

Artzt, Alice J *Concert Guitarist*
180 Claremont Ave, #31, New York, NY 10027, USA

Artzt, Edwin L *Businessman*
%Procter & Gamble Co, 1 Procter & Gamble Plaza, Cincinnati, OH 45202, USA

Arum, Robert *Boxing Promoter*
%Top Rank, 3900 Paradise Rd, Las Vegas, NV 89109, USA

Arvesen, Nina *Actress*
950 Lake St, #2, Venice, CA 90291, USA

Asahina, Takashi *Conductor*
%Osaka Philharmonic, 1-1-44 Kishinosato-Nishinariku, Osaka 557, Japan

Asby, Joseph W *Air Force General*
Commander, Air Training Command, Randolph Air Force Base, TX 78150, USA

Aschenbrenner, Frank *Football Player*
16372 E Jacklin Dr, Fountain Hills, AZ 85268, USA

Ash, Mary Kay W *Businesswoman*
%Mary Kay Cosmetics, 8787 N Stemmons Fwy, Dallas, TX 75247, USA

Ash, Roy L *Businessman, Government Official*
655 Funchal Rd, Los Angeles, CA 90077, USA

Ashbery, John L *Writer*
%Bard College, Language & Literature Dept, Annandale-On-Hudson, NY 12504, USA

Ashbrook, Dana *Actor*
7019 Melrose Ave, #332, Los Angeles, CA 90038, USA

Ashbrook, Daphne *Actress*
%Innovative Artists, 1999 Ave of Stars, #2850, Los Angeles, CA 90067, USA

Ashburn, Richie *Baseball Player*
11440 Harbor Way, Largo, FL 34644, USA

Ashbury, Beverly A *Religious Leader*
%Vanderbilt University, Religious Affairs Office, Nashville, TN 37204, USA

Ashby, Jeffrey S *Astronaut*
%NASA, Johnson Space Center, 2101 NASA Rd, Houston, TX 77058, USA

Ashdown, J J D (Paddy) *Government Official, England*
Vane Cottage, Norton Sub Hamdon, Somerset TA14 6SG, England

Ashenfelter, Horace, III *Track Athlete*
100 Hawthorne Ave, Glen Ridge, NJ 07028, USA

Asher, Barry *Bowler*
%Professional Bowlers Assn, 1720 Merriman Rd, Akron, OH 44313, USA

Asher, Jane *Actress*
24 Cale St, London SW3 3QU, England

Asher, Peter *Record Producer, Singer (Peter & Gordon)*
%Peter Asher Mgmt, 644 N Doheny Dr, Los Angeles, CA 90069, USA

Asherson, Renee *Actress*
28 Elsworthy Rd, London NW3, England

Ashford, Evelyn *Track Athlete*
818 Plantation Ln, Walnut, CA 91789, USA

Ashford, Matthew *Actor*
7948 Blackburn, #5, Los Angeles, CA 90048, USA

Ashford, Nick *Singer (Ashford & Simpson)*
%Hopsack & Silk Productions, 254 W 72nd St, #1-A, New York, NY 10023, USA

Ashihara, Yoshinobu *Architect*
%Ashihara Architects, 31-15 Sakuragaokacho, Shibuyaku, Tokyo 150, Japan

Ashkenasi, Shmuel *Concert Pianist*
3800 N Lake Shore Dr, Chicago, IL 60613, USA

Ashkenazy, Vladimir D *Concert Pianist, Conductor*
Kappelistr 15, 6045 Meggen, Switzerland

Ashley *Model*
%Ford Model Agency, 344 E 59th St, New York, NY 10022, USA

Ashley, Elizabeth *Actress*
1223 N Ogden Dr, Los Angeles, CA 90046, USA

Ashley, Merrill — *Ballerina*
%New York City Ballet, Lincoln Center Plaza, New York, NY 10023, USA

Ashmore, Edward B — *Navy Fleet Admiral, England*
%Naval Secretary, Ministry of Defense, London SW1, England

Ashmore, Harry S — *Editor, Foundation Executive*
1373 E Valley Rd, Santa Barbara, CA 93108, USA

Ashrawi, Hanan — *Political Leader, Palestine*
%Bir Zeit University, PO Box 14, West Bank, Bir Zeit, Israel

Ashton, Alan C — *Businessman*
%WordPerfect Corp, 1555 N Technology Way, Orem, UT 84057, USA

Ashton, Harris J — *Businessman*
%General Host Corp, Metro Center, 1 Station Pl, Stamford, CT 06902, USA

Ashton, John — *Actor*
700 Hinsdale Dr, Fort Collins, CO 80526, USA

Asiel, E Nelson — *Financier*
%Asiel Co, 20 Broad St, New York, NY 10005, USA

Askew, Reubin O — *Governor, FL*
%Akerman Senterfitt Edson, 255 S Orange Ave, Orlando, FL 32801, USA

Askin, Leon — *Actor*
PO Box 847, Beverly Hills, CA 90213, USA

Asmis, Herbert — *Businessman*
%Schering, Mullerstr 170-178, 12487 Berlin, Germany

Asner, Edward — *Actor*
PO Box 7407, Studio City, CA 91614, USA

Asplin, Edward W — *Businessman*
730 2nd Ave S, # 825, Minneapolis, MN 55402, USA

Assad, Hafez al- — *President, Syria*
%President's Palace, Muharreen, Abu Rumanch, Al-Rashid St, Damascus, Syria

Assante, Armand — *Actor*
Rt 1, Box 561, Campbell Hall, NY 10916, USA

Assylmuratova, Altynai — *Ballerina*
%Kirov Ballet Theatre, 1 Ploshchad Iskusstr, St Petersburg, Russia

Ast, Pat — *Actress*
4439 Worster Ave, Studio City, CA 91604, USA

Astin, Allen V — *Physicist*
5008 Battery Ln, Bethesda, MD 20814, USA

Astin, John — *Actor, Director*
1271 Stoner Ave, #408, Los Angeles, CA 90025, USA

Astin, Sean — *Actor*
%Byron Ltd, 4354 Laurel Canyon Blvd, #301, Studio City, CA 91604, USA

Astley, Thea — *Writer*
PO Box 23, Cambewarra, NSW 2540, Australia

Astor, Brooke — *Foundation Executive*
%Vincent Astor Foundation, 405 Park Ave, New York, NY 10022, USA

Asturaga, Nova — *Government Official, Nicaragua*
%Permanent Mission of Nicaragua, 820 2nd Ave, #801, New York, NY 10017, USA

Asylmuratova, Altynai — *Ballerina*
%Mariinsky Theater, Teatralnaya Pl 1, St Petersburg, Russia

Atchison, David W — *Religious Leader*
%Southern Baptist Convention, 5452 Grannywhite Pike, Brentwood, TN 37027, USA

Atchley, Bill L — *Educator*
%University of Pacific, President's Office, Stockton, CA 95211, USA

Athanassiades, Ted — *Businessman*
%Metropolitan Life Insurance, 1 Madison Ave, New York, NY 10010, USA

Atherton, Alfred L, Jr — *Diplomat*
4301 Massachusetts Ave NW, #5003, Washington, DC 20016, USA

Atherton, David — *Conductor*
%San Diego Symphony, 770 "B" St, #402, San Diego, CA 92101, USA

Atherton, Michael A — *Cricketer*
%Lancashire County Cricket Club, Old Trafford, Manchester M16 0PX, England

Atherton, William — *Actor*
5102 San Feliciano Dr, Woodland Hills, CA 91364, USA

Athow, Kirk L — *Plant Pathologist*
2104 Crestview Ct, Lafayette, IN 47905, USA

Atiyeh, Victor — *Governor, OR*
%Victor Atiyeh Co, 519 SW Park, #208, Portland, OR 97205, USA

Atkins, Chester B (Chet) — *Guitarist*
1096 Lynwood Blvd, Nashville, TN 37215, USA

A

Atkins, Christopher *Actor*
7072 Park Manor Ave, North Hollywood, CA 91605, USA

Atkins, Doug *Football Player*
PO Box 14007, Knoxville, TN 37914, USA

Atkins, Thomas E *WW II Army Hero (CMH)*
Rt 2, Box 433, Inman, SC 29349, USA

Atkins, Tom *Actor*
%Paradigm Agency, 10100 Santa Monica Blvd, #2500, Los Angeles, CA 90067, USA

Atkinson, Ray N *Businessman*
%Guy F Atkinson Co, 1001 Bayhill Dr, San Bruno, CA 94066, USA

Atkinson, Richard C *Educator*
%University of California System, 300 Lakeside Dr, Oakland, CA 94612, USA

Atkinson, Rick *Journalist*
%Kansas City Times, Editorial Dept, 1729 Grand Ave, Kansas City, MO 64108, USA

Atkisson, Curtis, Jr *Businessman*
%SPX Corp, 700 Terrace Point Dr, Muskegon, MI 49440, USA

Atkov, Oleg Y *Cosmonaut*
%Potchta Kosmonavtov, 141 160 Svyosdny Gorodok, Moskovskoi Oblasti, Russia

Atlantov, Vladimir *Opera Singer*
%Bolshoi Theatre, Teatralnaya Pl 1, 103009 Moscow, Russia

Attenborough, David *Television Broadcaster, Writer*
5 Park Rd, Richmond, Surrey TW10 GNS, England

Attenborough, Richard S *Actor, Director*
Beaver Lodge, Richmond Green, Surrey TW9 1NQ, England

Attkisson, Sharyl *Commentator*
%Cable News Network, News Dept, 1050 Techwood Dr NW, Atlanta, GA 30318, USA

Attles, Al *Basketball Player, Coach*
%Golden State Warriors, Oakland Coliseum Arena, Oakland, CA 94621, USA

Atwater, Stephen D (Steve) *Football Player*
%Denver Broncos, 13655 E Dove Valley Pkwy, Englewood, CO 80112, USA

Atwood, J Leland *Businessman*
PO Box 1587, Vista, CA 92085, USA

Atwood, Margaret E *Writer*
%McClelland/Stewart, 481 University Ave, #900, Toronto ON M5G 2E9, Canada

Atzmon, Moshe *Conductor*
Marignanostr 12, 4059 Basel, Switzerland

Auberjonois, Rene *Actor*
448 S Arden Blvd, Los Angeles, CA 90020, USA

Aubert, Pierre *President, Switzerland*
%Federal Dept of Foreign Affairs, Palais Federal, 3003 Berne, Switzerland

Aubrecht, Richard A *Businessman*
%Moog Inc, Jamison Rd, East Aurora, NY 14052, USA

Aubry, Cecile *Actress*
Le Moulin Bleu, 6 Chemin Moulin Bleu, 91410 Saint-Cyr Sous Dourdan, France

Aubry, Eugene E *Architect*
8021 Marina Isles Ln, Bradenton Beach, FL 34217, USA

Aubut, Marcel *Hockey Executive*
%Quebec Nordiques, 2205 Ave du Colisee, Quebec City PQ G1L 4W7, Canada

Auchincloss, Louis S *Writer*
1111 Park Ave, #14-D, New York, NY 10128, USA

Audran, Stephane *Actress*
95 Bis Rue de Chezy, 92200 Neuilly-sur-Seine, France

Auel, Jean M *Writer*
PO Box 430, Sherwood, OR 97140, USA

Auer, Peter L *Plasma Physicist*
220 Devon Rd, Ithaca, NY 14850, USA

Auerbach, Arnold J (Red) *Basketball Coach, Executive*
%Boston Celtics, 151 Merrimac St, #500, Boston, MA 02114, USA

Auerbach, Frank *Artist*
%Marlborough Fine Art Gallery, 6 Albermarle St, London W1X 4BY, England

Auerbach, Stanley I *Ecologist*
24 Wildwood Dr, Oak Ridge, TN 37830, USA

Auermann, Nadja *Model*
Via San Viottore 40, 20123 Milan, Italy

Auger, Claudine *Actress*
%William Morris Agency, 151 S El Camino Dr, Beverly Hills, CA 90212, USA

Auger, Pierre V *Physicist*
12 Rue Emile Faguet, 75014 Paris, France

Augmon, Stacey   *Basketball Player*
%Atlanta Hawks, 1 CNN Center, South Tower, Atlanta, GA 30303, USA
Augstein, Rudolf   *Publisher*
%Spiegel-Verloff Augstein, Brandstwiete 19, 20457 Hamburg, Germany
August, Bille   *Movie Director*
2800 Lyngby, Denmark
Augustain, Ira   *Actor*
%Diamond Artists, 215 N Barrington Ave, Los Angeles, CA 90049, USA
Augustine, Norman R   *Businessman*
%Martin Marietta Corp, 6801 Rockledge Dr, Bethesda, MD 20817, USA
Augustnyiak, Jerry   *Drummer (10,000 Maniacs)*
%New York End Ltd, 143 W 69th St, #4-A, New York, NY 10023
Auker, Eldon L   *Baseball Player*
15 Sailfish Rd, Vero Beach, FL 32960, USA
Aulby, Mike   *Bowler*
1591 Springmill Ponds Cir, Carmel, IN 46032, USA
Ault, James M   *Religious Leader*
%United Methodist Church, 168 Mt Vernon St, Newtonville, MA 02160, USA
Aumont, Jean-Pierre   *Actor*
4 Allee des Brouillards, 75018 Paris, France
Aung San Suu Kyi   *Nobel Peace Laureate*
%National League for Democracy, 54-56 University Ave, Yangon, Myanmar
Aurand, Calvin W, Jr   *Businessman*
%Banta Corp, River Place, 225 Main St, Menasha, WI 54952, USA
Auriemma, Gino   *Basketball Coach*
%University of Connecticut, Athletic Dept, 211 Hillside Rd, Storrs, CT 06269, USA
Austin, Debbie   *Golfer*
6733 Bittersweet Ln, Orlando, FL 32819, USA
Austin, Denise   *Physical Fitness Instructor*
%Getting Fit, PO Box 3771, San Clemente, CA 92674, USA
Austin, Karen   *Actress*
3356 Rowona Ave, #3, Los Angeles, CA 90027, USA
Austin, Patti   *Singer*
641 5th Ave, New York, NY 10022, USA
Austin, Philip E   *Educator*
%University of Alabama System, Chancellor's Office, Tuscaloosa, AL 35401, USA
Austin, Teri   *Actress*
4245 Laurel Grove, Studio City, CA 91604, USA
Austin, Tracy   *Tennis Player*
26406 Dunwood Rd, Rolling Hills Estates, CA 90274, USA
Austregesilo de Athayde, Belarmino M   *Journalist*
Rua Cosme Velho 599, Rio de Janeiro RJ, Brazil
Austrian, Robert   *Physician*
%Univ of Pennsylvania Med Center, 36th & Hamilton Walk, Philadelphia, PA 19130, USA
Auth, Tony   *Editorial Cartoonist*
1137 Rodman St, Philadelphia, PA 19147, USA
Authement, Ray   *Educator*
%Southwestern Louisiana University, President's Office, Lafayette, LA 70506, USA
Autry, Alan   *Actor*
%Artists Group, 10100 Santa Monica Blvd, #2490, Los Angeles, CA 90067, USA
Autry, Gene   *Actor, Singer, Baseball Executive*
4383 Colfax Ave, Studio City, CA 91604, USA
Avalon, Frankie   *Singer, Actor*
6311 DeSoto Ave, #1, Woodland Hills, CA 91367, USA
Avansio, Raymond C, Jr   *Businessman*
%Hilton Hotels Corp, 9336 Santa Monica Blvd, Beverly Hills, CA 90209, USA
Avdelsayed, Gabriel   *Religious Leader*
%Coptic Orthodox Church, 427 West Side Ave, Jersey City, NJ 07304, USA
Avedon, Richard   *Photographer*
407 E 75th St, New York, NY 10021, USA
Averback, Hy   *Movie Director*
65 Old Ranch Rd, Palm Desert, CA 92211, USA
Avery, James   *Actor*
%Abrams Artists, 9200 Sunset Blvd, #625, Los Angeles, CA 90069, USA
Avery, Margaret   *Actress*
2807 Pelham Pl, Los Angeles, CA 90068, USA
Avery, Phyllis   *Actress*
609 Sterling Pl, South Pasadena, CA 91030, USA

A

Augmon - Avery

A

Avery, R Stanton *Businessman*
%Avery International Group, 150 N Orange Grove, Pasadena, CA 91103, USA

Avery, Steven T (Steve) *Baseball Player*
22128 Haig, Taylor, MI 48180, USA

Avery, Val *Actor*
84 Grove St, #19, New York, NY 10014, USA

Avery, William H *Governor, KS*
Rt 2, Wakefield, KS 67487, USA

Avery, William J *Businessman*
%Crown Cork & Seal Co, 9300 Ashton Rd, Philadelphia, PA 19114, USA

Avila, Roberto R G (Bobby) *Baseball Player*
Navegantes FR-19, Reforma-Veracruz, Mexico

Avildsen, John G *Movie Director*
45 E 89th St, #37-A, New York, NY 10128, USA

Ax, Emmanuel *Concert Pianist*
173 Riverside Dr, #12-G, New York, NY 10024, USA

Axelrod, George *Playwright*
1840 Carla Ridge St, Beverly Hills, CA 90210, USA

Axelrod, Julius *Nobel Medicine Laureate*
10401 Grosvenor Pl, Rockville, MD 20852, USA

Axton, Hoyt W *Singer, Songwriter*
%Lady Jane Music, PO Box 976, Hendersonville, TN 37077, USA

Ay-O *Artist*
2-6-38 Matsuyama, Kiyoseshi, Tokyo, Japan

Ayckbourn, Alan *Playwright*
%M Ramsay, 14-A Goodwins Ct, St Martin's Ln, London WC2N 4LL, England

Aycock, Alice *Artist*
62 Green St, New York, NY 10012, USA

Ayer, Donald B *Attorney*
%Jones Davis Reavis Pogue, 1450 "G" St NW, Washington, DC 20005, USA

Ayer, Ramani *Businessman*
%ITT Hartford, Hartford Plaza, Hartford, CT 06115, USA

Ayers, Chuck *Cartoonist (Crankshaft)*
%Creators Syndicate, 5777 W Century Blvd, #700, Los Angeles, CA 90045, USA

Ayers, Randy *Basketball Coach*
%Ohio State University, St John Arena, Columbus, OH 43210, USA

Ayers, Richard H *Businessman*
%Stanley Works, 1000 Stanley Dr, New Britain, CT 06053, USA

Ayers, Thomas G *Businessman*
200 Wyndemere Cir, #W-134, Wheaton, IL 60187, USA

Aynes, Richard *Educator*
%University of Akron, President's Office, Akron, OH 44325, USA

Ayres, Lew *Actor*
675 Walther Way, Los Angeles, CA 90049, USA

Azcarraga Milmo, Emilio *Publisher*
%Televisa SA, Avda Chapultepec 28, 06 724 Mexico City, Mexico

Azenberg, Emanuel *Theater Producer*
165 W 46th St, New York, NY 10036, USA

Azinger, Paul *Golfer*
4520 Bent Tree Blvd, Sarasota, FL 34241, USA

Aziz, Tariq *Prime Minister, Iraq*
%Prime Minister's Office, Karadat Mariam, Baghdad, Iraq

Azlan Muhibuddin Shan *Sultan, Malaysia*
%Sultan's Palace, Kuala Lumpur, Malaysia

Aznavour, Charles *Singer, Actor*
12 Chemin du Chateau Blanc, 1231 Conches, Switzerland

Azoff, Irving *Record Company Executive*
%Warner Bros Records, 3300 Warner Blvd, Burbank, CA 91505, USA

Azuma, Norio *Artist*
276 Riverside Dr, New York, NY 10025, USA

Azuma, Takimitsu *Architect*
%Azuma Architects, 3-6-1 Minami-Aoyama Minatoku, Tokyo 107, Japan

Azzara, Candice *Actress*
%David Shapira Assoc, 15301 Ventura Blvd, #345, Sherman Oaks, CA 91403, USA

Azzato, Louis E *Businessman*
%Foster Wheeler Corp, Perryville Corporate Park, Clinton, NJ 08809, USA

Avery - Azzato

Baba, Corneliu — *Artist*
Uniunea Artistilor Plastici, Str Nicolae Iorga 42, Bucharest, Romania

Baba, Encik Abdul Ghafar Bin — *Prime Minister, Malaysia*
%Rural Development Ministry, Jalan Raja Laut, 50606 Kuala Lampur, Malaysia

Babangida, Ibrahim — *Head of State, Nigeria; Army General*
Minna, Niger State, Nigeria

Babashoff, Shirley — *Swimmer*
16260 Mercury Dr, Westminster, CA 92683, USA

Babb, Albert L — *Biomedical Engineer*
3237 Lakewood Ave S, Seattle, WA 98144, USA

Babb, Ralph W, Jr — *Financier*
%Mercantile Bancorp, Mercantile Tower, PO Box 524, St Louis, MO 63166, USA

Babb-Sprague, Kristen — *Synchronized Swimmer*
19015 N Davis Rd, Lodi, CA 95242, USA

Babbidge, Homes D, Jr — *Educator*
3 Diving St, Stonington, CT 06378, USA

Babbio, Lawrence T, Jr — *Businessman*
%Bell Atlantic Corp, 1717 Arch St, Philadelphia, PA 19103, USA

Babbitt, Bruce E — *Secretary, Interior*
%Interior Department, 1849 "C" St NW, Washington, DC 20240, USA

Babbitt, J Randolph — *Labor Leader*
%Air Line Pilots Assn, 1625 Massachusetts Ave NW, Washington, DC 20036, USA

Babbitt, Milton B — *Composer*
222 Western Way, Princeton, NJ 08540, USA

Babcock, Barbara — *Actress*
%Paradigm Agency, 10100 Santa Monica Blvd, #2500, Los Angeles, CA 90067, USA

Babcock, Horace W — *Astronomer*
%Carnegie Institution Observatories, 813 Santa Barbara St, Pasadena, CA 91101, USA

Babcock, Tim — *Governor, MT*
%Ox Bow Ranch, PO Box 877, Helena, MT 59624, USA

Babenco, Hector E — *Movie Director*
%International Creative Mgmt, 8942 Wilshire Blvd, Beverly Hills, CA 90211, USA

Babich, Bob — *Football Player*
4412 Tivoli St, San Diego, CA 92107, USA

Babilonia, Tai — *Figure Skater*
13889 Valley Vista Blvd, Sherman Oaks, CA 91423, USA

Baca, Edward D — *Army General*
Chief, National Guard Bureau, HdqsUSArmy, Pentagon, Washington, DC 20310, USA

Baca, John — *Vietnam War Army Hero (CMH)*
%Southern California College, Box 316, 55 Fair Dr, Costa Mesa, CA 92626, USA

Bacall, Lauren — *Actress*
%Dakota Hotel, 1 W 72nd St, #43, New York, NY 10023, USA

Bach, Barbara — *Actress*
2029 Century Park East, #1690, Los Angeles, CA 90067, USA

Bach, Catherine — *Actress*
14000 Davanna Terrace, Sherman Oaks, CA 91423, USA

Bach, Pamela — *Actress*
%Marion Rosenberg Office, 8428 Melrose Place, #C, Los Angeles, CA 90069, USA

Bach, Richard — *Writer*
%Dell Publishing, 1540 Broadway, New York, NY 10036, USA

Bach, Steven K — *Movie Producer*
746 S Orange Dr, Los Angeles, CA 90036, USA

Bacharach, Burt — *Composer, Musician*
10 Ocean Park Blvd, #4, Santa Monica, CA 90405, USA

Bachardy, Don — *Writer*
145 Adelaide Dr, Santa Monica, CA 90402, USA

Bacher, Robert F — *Physicist*
1300 Hot Springs Rd, Montecito, CA 93108, USA

Bachrach, Louis F, Jr — *Photographer*
%Bachrach Inc, 44 Hunt St, Watertown, MA 02172, USA

Backe, John D — *Entertainment Executive*
%Backe Group, 1646 W Chester Pike, Westtown, PA 19395, USA

Backer, William M — *Businessman*
%Backer Spielvogel Bates, 405 Lexington Ave, New York, NY 10174, USA

Backman, Jules — *Economist, Writer*
59 Crane Rd, Scarsdale, NY 10583, USA

Backman, Walter W (Wally) — *Baseball Player*
PO Box 223, Ione, OR 97843, USA

B

Baba - Backman

B

Backus, George E *Theoretical Geophysicist*
9362 La Jolla Farms Rd, La Jolla, CA 92037, USA

Backus, John *Computer Programmer, Mathematician*
91 St Germaine Ave, San Francisco, CA 94114, USA

Backus, Sharron *Softball Coach*
%University of California, Athletic Dept, Los Angeles, CA 90024, USA

Bacon, Edmund N *Architect*
2117 Locust St, Philadelphia, PA 19103, USA

Bacon, James *Columnist*
10982 Topeka Dr, Northridge, CA 91326, USA

Bacon, Kevin *Actor*
%Creative Artists Agency, 9830 Wilshire Blvd, Beverly Hills, CA 90212, USA

Bacon, Nicky D *Vietnam War Army Hero (CMH)*
PO Box 9000, Conway, AR 72033, USA

Bacot, J Carter *Financier*
48 Porter Pl, Montclair, NJ 07042, USA

Bacquier, Gabriel *Opera Singer*
141 Rue de Rome, 75017 Paris, France

Bacs, Ludovic *Conductor, Composer*
31 D Golescu, Sc III, E7 V Ap 87, Bucharest 1, Romania

Bada, Jeffrey *Chemist*
%Scripps Institute of Oceanography, Chemistry Dept, La Jolla, CA 92093, USA

Badgro, Morris H (Red) *Football Player*
1010 E Temperance St, Kent, WA 98031, USA

Badham, John M *Movie Director*
%William Morris Agency, 151 S El Camino Dr, Beverly Hills, CA 90212, USA

Badran, Mudar *Prime Minister, Jordan*
Shmaisani, Amman, Jordan

Badura-Skoda, Paul *Concert Pianist*
Zuckerkandlgass 14, 1190 Vienna, Austria

Baer, Kenneth P *Businessman*
33 Costa del Lago Lane, Hot Springs, AR 71909, USA

Baer, Max, Jr *Actor, Movie Producer, Director*
%Max Baer Productions, 10433 Wilshire Blvd, #103, Los Angeles, CA 90024, USA

Baer, Olaf *Opera Singer*
Olbersdorferstr 7, 01324 Dresden, Germany

Baer, Parley *Actor*
4967 Bilmoor Ave, Tarzana, CA 91356, USA

Baer, Robert J (Jacob) *Army General*
6213 Militia Ct, Fairfax Station, VA 22039, USA

Baez, Joan *Singer*
%Diamonds & Rust Productions, PO Box 1026, Menlo Park, CA 94026, USA

Bafile, Corrado Cardinal *Religious Leader*
Via P Pancrazio Pfeiffer 10, 00193 Rome, Italy

Bagdasarian, Ross *Actor*
1465 Lindacrest Dr, Beverly Hills, CA 90210, USA

Bagdikian, Ben H *Educator, Journalist*
25 Stonewall Rd, Berkeley, CA 94705, USA

Baggett, Lee, Jr *Navy Admiral*
1650 Copa de Oro, La Jolla, CA 92037, USA

Baggetta, Vincent *Actor*
3928 Madelia Ave, Sherman Oaks, CA 91403, USA

Baggio, Roberto *Soccer Player*
%Federazione Giuoco Calcio, Via Gregorio Allegri 14, 00198 Rome, Italy

Bagian, James P *Astronaut*
%Somanetics Corp, 1653 E Maple Rd, Troy, MI 48083, USA

Bagley, John *Basketball Player*
92 Harral Ave, Bridgeport, CT 06604, USA

Bagnall, Nigel T *Army Field Marshal, England*
%Royal Bank of England, 49 Charing Cross Rd, London SW1A 2DX, England

Bagwell, Jeffrey R (Jeff) *Baseball Player*
1422 Sugar Creek Blvd, Sugarland, TX 77478, USA

Bahcall, John N *Astrophysicist*
%Institute for Advanced Study, Natural Sciences School, Princeton, NJ 08540, USA

Bahouth, Peter *Association Executive*
%Greenpeace, 1436 "U" St NW, Washington, DC 20009, USA

Bahr, Egon *Government Official, West Germany*
%Institut fur Friedensforschung, Falkenstein 1, 22587 Hamburg, Germany

Bahr, Matt — *Football Player*
%New England Patriots, Foxboro Stadium, Rt 1, Foxboro, MA 02035, USA

Bahr, Morton — *Labor Leader*
%Communications Workers Union, 501 3rd St NW, Washington, DC 20001, USA

Bahrenburg, D Claeys — *Publisher*
%Hearst Corp, 959 8th Ave, New York, NY 10019, USA

Bailar, Benjamin F — *Government Official, Educator*
2121 Kirby Dr, #141, Houston, TX 77019, USA

Bailey, Colin — *Businessman*
%Calon Carbon Corp, 400 Calgon Carbon Dr, Pittsburgh, PA 15230, USA

Bailey, David — *Actor*
10 E 44th St, #700, New York, NY 10017, USA

Bailey, David — *Photographer*
%Camera Eye Ltd, 24-26 Brownlow Mews, London WC1N 2LA, England

Bailey, F Lee — *Attorney*
1400 Centre Park Blvd, #909, West Palm Beach, FL 33401, USA

Bailey, G W — *Actor*
4972 Calvin Ave, Tarzana, CA 91356, USA

Bailey, Irving W, II — *Businessman*
%Providian Corp, 400 W Market St, Louisville, KY 40202, USA

Bailey, Jerome H — *Financier*
%Salomon Inc, 7 World Trade Center, New York, NY 10048, USA

Bailey, Jim — *Actor, Singer*
5909 W Colgate Ave, Los Angeles, CA 90036, USA

Bailey, John — *Cinematographer*
%United Talent Agency, 9560 Wilshire Blvd, #500, Beverly Hills, CA 90212, USA

Bailey, Keith E — *Businessman*
%Williams Companies, 1 Williams Center, Tulsa, OK 74172, USA

Bailey, Leonard L — *Heart Surgeon*
%Loma Linda University, Medical School, Loma Linda, CA 92350, USA

Bailey, Michael — *Psychologist*
%Northwestern University, Psychology Dept, Evanston, IL 60208, USA

Bailey, Norman S — *Opera Singer*
84 Warham Rd, South Croydon, Surrey CR2 6LB, England

Bailey, Paul — *Writer*
79 Davisville Rd, London W12 9SH, England

Bailey, Philip — *Singer (Earth Wind & Fire)*
%International Creative Mgmt, 8942 Wilshire Blvd, Beverly Hills, CA 90211, USA

Bailey, Ralph E — *Businessman*
%E I du Pont de Nemours Co, 1807 Market St, Wilmington, DE 19802, USA

Bailey, Razzy — *Singer, Songwriter*
PO Box 943, Madison, TN 37116, USA

Bailey, Robert L — *Businessman*
%State Auto Financial Corp, 518 E Broad St, Columbus, OH 43215, USA

Bailey, Thomas H — *Financier*
%Janus Capital Corp, 100 Fillmore St, Denver, CO 80206, USA

Bailey, Thurl — *Basketball Player*
%Minnesota Timberwolves, Target Center, 600 1st Ave N, Minneapolis, MN 55403, USA

Bailey, William — *Artist*
223 E 10th St, New York, NY 10003, USA

Bailyn, Bernard — *Historian*
170 Clifton St, Belmont, MA 02178, USA

Bain, Barbara — *Actress*
1501 Skylark Lane, West Hollywood, CA 90069, USA

Bain, Conrad — *Actor*
1230 Chickory Lane, Los Angeles, CA 90049, USA

Bainbridge, Beryl — *Actress, Writer*
42 Albert St, London NW1 7NU, England

Bainbridge, Kenneth T — *Physicist*
%Brookhaven , 1010 Waltham St, #441-B, Lexington, MA 02173, USA

Baines, Harold D — *Baseball Player*
PO Box 335, Saint Michaels, MD 21663, USA

Bainum, Stewart — *Businessman*
%Manor Care Inc, 10750 Columbia Pike, Silver Spring, MD 20901, USA

Bainum, Stewart, Jr — *Businessman*
%Manor Care Inc, 10750 Columbia Pike, Silver Spring, MD 20901, USA

Baio, Jimmy — *Actor*
4333 Forman Ave, Toluca Lake, CA 91602, USA

B

Bahr - Baio

Baio, Scott — *Actor*
11662 Duque Dr, Studio City, CA 91604, USA

Baird, Charles F — *Businessman*
4423 Boxwood Rd, Bethesda, MD 20816, USA

Baird, Dugald E — *Businessman*
%Schlumberger Ltd, 277 Park Ave, New York, NY 10172, USA

Baird, Euan — *Businessman*
%Schlumberger Ltd, 277 Park Ave, New York, NY 10172, USA

Baird, James M — *Religious Leader*
%Presbyterian Church, PO Box 1428, Decatur, GA 30031, USA

Baird, William D, Jr — *Financier*
%Chemical Bank New Jersey, 2 Tower Center, East Brunswick, NJ 08816, USA

Baird, Zoe — *Attorney*
%Aetna Life & Casualty, 151 Farmington Ave, Hartford, CT 06156, USA

Baitz, Jon Robin — *Playwright*
%William Morris Agency, 1325 Ave of Americas, New York, NY 10019, USA

Baiul, Oksana — *Figure Skater*
%International Skating Center, 1375 Hopmeadow St, Simsbury, CT 06070, USA

Baker Guadagnino, Kathy — *Golfer*
%International Management Group, 1 Erieview Plaza, #1300, Cleveland, OH 44114, USA

Baker, Anita — *Singer*
%BNB Assoc, 345 N Maple Dr, Beverly Hills, CA 90210, USA

Baker, Blanche — *Actress*
70 Flower Ave, Hastings-on-Hudson, NY 10706, USA

Baker, Buddy — *Auto Racing Driver*
4860 Moonlite Bay Dr, Sherrills Frd, NC 28673, USA

Baker, Carroll — *Actress*
630 Masselin Ave, #221, Los Angeles, CA 90036, USA

Baker, D Kenneth — *Educator*
495 E 12th St, Claremont, CA 91711, USA

Baker, Dexter F — *Businessman*
%Air Products & Chemicals Inc, PO Box 25738, Lehigh Valley, PA 18002, USA

Baker, Diane — *Actress*
PO Box 480492, Los Angeles, CA 90048, USA

Baker, Dylan — *Actor*
%International Creative Mgmt, 8942 Wilshire Blvd, Beverly Hills, CA 90211, USA

Baker, Ellen Shulman — *Astronaut*
%NASA, Johnson Space Center, 2101 NASA Rd, Houston, TX 77058, USA

Baker, Ginger — *Drummer (Cream, Masters of Reality)*
%Twist Mgmt, 4230 Del Rey Ave, #621, Marina del Rey, CA 90292, USA

Baker, Graham — *Movie Director*
10 Buckingham St, London WC2, England

Baker, Howard H, Jr — *Senator, TN*
PO Box 8, Huntsville, TN 37756, USA

Baker, James A, III — *Secretary, State*
%Baker & Botts, 555 13th St NW, #500-E, Washington, DC 20004, USA

Baker, James K — *Businessman*
%Arvin Industries, Noblitt Plaza, PO Box 3000, Columbus, IN 47202, USA

Baker, Janet — *Opera, Concert Singer*
450 Edgeware Rd, London W2, England

Baker, Joe Don — *Actor*
23339 Hatteras St, Woodland Hills, CA 91367, USA

Baker, John D, II — *Businessman*
%Florida Rock Industries, 155 E 21st St, Jacksonville, FL 32206, USA

Baker, John F, Jr — *Vietnam War Army Hero (CMH)*
3832 Trogon Way, Las Vegas, NV 89103, USA

Baker, John H, Jr — *Football Player*
5 Farnham Park Dr, Houston, TX 77024, USA

Baker, John R — *Businessman*
%UtiliCorp United, 911 Main St, Kansas City, MO 64105, USA

Baker, John T — *Publisher*
%JAMA Magazine, 535 N Dearborn St, Chicago, IL 60610, USA

Baker, Johnnie B (Dusty) — *Baseball Player, Manager*
40 Livingston Terrace Dr, San Bruno, CA 94066, USA

Baker, Jordan — *Actress*
%J Michael Bloom Ltd, 9255 Sunset Blvd, #710, Los Angeles, CA 90069, USA

Baker, Kathy — *Actress*
1623 Hillcrest Ave, Glendale, CA 91202, USA

Baker, Kendall L — *Educator*
%University of North Dakota, President's Office, Grand Forks, ND 58202, USA

Baker, Lavern — *Singer*
%Alan Eichler Assoc, 1524 La Baig Ave, Los Angeles, CA 90028, USA

Baker, Leslie M, Jr — *Financier*
%Wachovia Corp, 301 N Main St, Winston-Salem, NC 27150, USA

Baker, Margaret B — *Financier*
%First Options of Chicago, 440 S LaSalle, Chicago, IL 60605, USA

Baker, Mark — *Bowler*
665 Park Dr, #20, Costa Mesa, CA 92627, USA

Baker, Michael A (Mike) — *Astronaut*
%NASA, Johnson Space Center, 2101 NASA Rd, Houston, TX 77058, USA

Baker, Nicholson — *Writer*
%Melanie Jackson Agency, 256 W 57th St, #1119, New York, NY 10019, USA

Baker, Paul T — *Anthropologist*
47-450 Lulani St, Kaneohe, HI 96744, USA

Baker, R Robinson — *Surgeon*
8717 McDonogh Rd, McDonogh, MD 21208, USA

Baker, Raymond — *Actor*
%William Morris Agency, 151 S El Camino Dr, Beverly Hills, CA 90212, USA

Baker, Roy Ward — *Actor*
Whitehall, 125 Gloucester Rd, London SW7 4TE, England

Baker, Russell W — *Journalist, Columnist*
%New York Times, Editorial Dept, 229 W 43rd St, New York, NY 10036, USA

Baker, Sherman — *Businessman*
%J Baker Inc, 555 Turnpike St, Canton, MA 02021, USA

Baker, Thane — *Track Athlete*
2812 Bonnywood, Dallas, TX 75233, USA

Baker, Thomas A — *Air Force General*
Commander, 12th Air Force, E Gafford, Davis Mountain Air Force Base, AZ 85707, USA

Baker, Vin — *Basketball Player*
%Milwaukee Bucks, Bradley Center, 1001 N 4th St, Milwaukee, WI 53203, USA

Baker, Warren J — *Educator*
%California Poly University, President's Office, San Luis Obispo, CA 93407, USA

Baker, William O — *Research Chemist*
%ATT Bell Telephone Laboratories, 600 Mountain Ave, Murray Hill, NJ 07974, USA

Baker-Finch, Ian — *Golfer*
%Professional Golfer's Assn, PO Box 109601, Palm Beach Gardens, FL 33410, USA

Bakke, Brenda — *Actress*
12754 Sarah St, Studio City, CA 91604, USA

Bakken, Jim — *Football Player*
230 Glen Hollow, Madison, WI 53705, USA

Bakker Messner, Tammy Faye — *Religious Leader*
72727 Country Club Dr, Rancho Mirage, CA 92270, USA

Bakker, James O (Jim) — *Religious Leader*
%New Covenant Church, PO Box 94, Largo, FL 34649, USA

Bakshi, Ralph — *Animator*
%Gang Tyre Ramer Brown, 6400 Sunset Blvd, Los Angeles, CA 90028, USA

Bakula, Scott — *Actor*
%United Talent Agency, 9560 Wilshire Blvd, #500, Beverly Hills, CA 90212, USA

Balaguer Ricardo, Joaquin — *President, Dominican Republic*
%Partido Reformista, Ensanche LA Fe, Santo Domingo, Dominican Republic

Balandin, Alexander N — *Cosmonaut*
%Potchta Kosmonavtov, 141 160 Svyosdny Gorodok, Moskovskoi Oblasti, Russia

Balassa, Sandor — *Composer*
14 Arnyas Str, Budapest 1121, Hungary

Balayan, Roman G — *Movie Director*
Gogolevskaya Str 37/2, #15, Kiev 252053, Ukraine

Balderstone, James S — *Businessman*
115 Mont Albert Rd, Canterbury 3126, Vic, Australia

Baldessari, John — *Conceptual Artist*
2001 1/2 Main St, Santa Monica, CA 90405, USA

Baldrige, Letitia — *Businesswoman*
%Letitia Baldrige Enterprises, PO Box 32287, Washington, DC 20007, USA

Baldschun, Jack E — *Baseball Player*
492 Bader St, Green Bay, WI 54302, USA

Baldwin, Alec — *Actor*
%Wolf/Kasteller, 1033 Gayley Ave, #208, Los Angeles, CA 90024, USA

B

Baker - Baldwin

B

Baldwin, H Furlong *Financier*
%Mercantile Bankshares Corp, 2 Hopkins Plaza, Baltimore, MD 21201, USA

Baldwin, Howard *Hockey Executive*
%Pittsburgh Penguins, Civic Arena, Centre Ave, Pittsburgh, PA 15219, USA

Baldwin, Jack *Auto Racing Driver*
4748 Balmoral Way, Marietta, GA 30068, USA

Baldwin, John A (Jack), Jr *Navy Admiral*
2032 Ferry Farms Rd, Annapolis, MD 21402, USA

Baldwin, William *Actor*
%Creative Artists Agency, 9830 Wilshire Blvd, Beverly Hills, CA 90212, USA

Bale, Christian *Actor*
%Pine Files Ltd, 6-A Wyndham Place, London W1H 1TN, England

Balemian, Robert *Businessman*
%Griffon Corp, 100 Jericho Quadrangle, Jericho, NY 11753, USA

Balfanz, John C *Ski Jumper*
7770 E Iliff Ave, #G, Denver, CO 80231, USA

Baliles, Gerald L *Governor, VA*
%Hunton & Williams, PO Box 1535, Richmond, VA 23212, USA

Balin, Marty *Singer, Songwriter*
%Joe Buchwald, 436 Belvedere St, San Francisco, CA 94117, USA

Ball, Eugene N *Financier*
%Pentagon Federal Credit Union, PO Box 1432, Alexandria, VA 22313, USA

Ball, Robert M *Government Official*
1776 Massachusetts Ave NW, Washington, DC 20036, USA

Balladur, Edouard *Prime Minister, France*
35039 Marburg 1, France

Ballantine, Duncan S *Educator*
5107 Saugapore Rd, Bethesda, MD 20816, USA

Ballard, Carroll *Movie Director*
PO Box 556, Mt Helena, CA 94574, USA

Ballard, Del, Jr *Bowler*
%Professional Bowlers Assn, 1720 Merriman Rd, Akron, OH 44313, USA

Ballard, Donald E *Vietnam War Navy Hero (CMH)*
PO Box 34593, North Kansas City, MO 64116, USA

Ballard, Hank *Singer, Songwriter*
%Bon Ton West, PO Box 8406, Santa Cruz, CA 95061, USA

Ballard, Howard *Football Player*
%Seattle Seahawks, 11220 NE 53rd St, Kirkland, WA 98033, USA

Ballard, J G *Writer*
36 Old Charlton Rd, Shepperton, Middx, England

Ballard, Kaye *Actress*
91475 Mashi Dr, Rancho Mirage, CA 92270, USA

Ballard, Larry C *Businessman*
%Sentry Insurance, 1800 N Point Dr, Stevens Point, WI 54482, USA

Ballard, Robert D *Oceanographer (Titanic Discoverer)*
%Woods Hole Oceanographic Institute, Woods Hole, MA 02543, USA

Ballengee, Jerry H *Businessman*
%Union Camp Corp, 1600 Valley Rd, Wayne, NJ 07470, USA

Ballesteros, Seveiano (Seve) *Golfer*
Ruiz Zorilla 16-20J, 39009 Santander, Spain

Ballestrero, Anastasio Cardinal *Religious Leader*
Via Arcivescovado 12, 10121 Turin, Italy

Ballhaus, Michael *Cinematographer*
PO Box 2230, Los Angeles, CA 90078, USA

Ballhaus, William F, Jr *Aeronautical Engineer*
%Martin Marietta Civil Space & Communication Co, PO Box 179, Denver, CO 80201, USA

Ballou, Clinton E *Biochemist*
%University of California, Chemistry Dept, Berkeley, CA 94720, USA

Ballou, Mark *Actor*
145 Ave of Americas, #200, New York, NY 10013, USA

Balmaseda, Liz *Journalist*
%Miami Herald, Editorial Dept, 1 Herald Plaza, Miami, FL 33132, USA

Balmuth, Marc I *Businessman*
%Caldor Corp, 20 Glover Ave, Norwalk, CT 06850, USA

Balousek, Jack B *Businessman*
1255 Battery St, San Francisco, CA 94111, USA

Balsam, Martin *Actor*
%Marshak-Wyckoff Assoc, 280 S Beverly Dr, #400, Beverly Hills, CA 90212, USA

Baldwin - Balsam

Balsam, Talia *Actress*
9220 W Sunset Blvd, #206, Los Angeles, CA 90069, USA

Balser, Glennon *Religious Leader*
%Advent Christian Church, 6315 Studley Rd, Mechanicsville, VA 23111, USA

Balsley, Philip E *Singer (Statler Brothers)*
PO Box 2703, Staunton, VA 24402, USA

Balson, John B *Businessman*
%Interpublic Group of Companies, 1271 Ave of Americas, New York, NY 10020, USA

Baltensweiler, Armin *Businessman*
%Sulzer Brothers Ltd, 8401 Winterthur, Switzerland

Balthus *Artist*
Grand Chalet Rossiniere, Canton de Vaux, Switzerland

Baltimore, David *Nobel Medicine Laureate*
28 Donnell St, Cambridge, MA 02138, USA

Baltsa, Agnes *Opera Singer*
%R Schultz Mgmt, Rutistr 52, 8044 Zurich-Gockhausen, Switzerland

Baltz, Lewis *Photographer*
11693 San Vicente Blvd, #527, Los Angeles, CA 90049, USA

Balukas, Jean *Billiards Player*
9818 4th Ave, Brooklyn, NY 11209, USA

Bama, Jim *Artist*
PO Box 148, Wapiti, WY 82450, USA

Bamberger, George I *Baseball Manager*
455 N Bath Club Blvd, North Redington Beach, FL 33708, USA

Banach, Ed *Wrestler*
2128 Country Club Blvd, Ames, IA 50014, USA

Banachowski, Andy *Volleyball Coach*
%University of California, Athletic Dept, Los Angeles, CA 90024, USA

Banana, Canaan S *President, Zimbabwe*
Burroughs House, PO Box 8136, Causeway, Zimbabwe

Banaszynski, Jacqui *Journalist*
%St Paul Pioneer Press Dispatch, Editorial Dept, 345 Cedar, St Paul, MN 55101, USA

Banazek, Cas *Football Player*
2520 Nanette, San Carlos, CA 94070, USA

Banbury, F H Frith *Theater Director*
18 Park St James, Prince Albert Rd, London NW8 7LE, England

Bancroft, Anne *Actress*
2301 La Mesa Dr, Santa Monica, CA 90402, USA

Bancroft, Ian P *Government Leader, England*
%House of Lords, Westminster, London SW1A 0PW, England

Bandaranaike, Sirimavo R D *Prime Minister, Sri Lanka*
301 T B Jayah Mawatha, Colombo 10, Sri Lanka

Banderas, Antonio *Actor*
%Creative Artists Agency, 9830 Wilshire Blvd, Beverly Hills, CA 90212, USA

Bando, Salvatore L (Sal) *Baseball Player*
104 W Juniper Lane, Mequon, WI 53092, USA

Bandy, Moe *Singer, Songwriter*
PO Box 748, Adkins, TX 78101, USA

Banfield, Edward C *Educator*
%Harvard University, Littauer Center, Cambridge, MA 02138, USA

Bangemann, Martin *Government Official, West Germany*
Sannentalstr 9, 72555 Metzingen, Germany

Bangerter, Hans E *Soccer Official*
Hubelgasse 25, 3065 Bolligen BE, Switzerland

Bangerter, Norman H *Governor, UT*
%NHB Construction Co, 2976 W 10000 S, South Jordan, UT 84095, USA

Bani-Sadr, Abolhassan *Prime Minister, Iran*
16 Ave Pont Royal, 94230 Cachan, France

Bank, Aaron *WW II Army Hero*
239 Avenida Montalvo, San Clemente, CA 92672, USA

Bankler, Alain *Financier*
%BANEXI International, 499 Park Ave, New York, NY 10022, USA

Banks, Carl *Football Player*
%Washington Redskins, 21300 Redskin Park Dr, Ashburn, VA 22011, USA

Banks, Chip *Football Player*
%Indianapolis Colts, 7001 W 56th St, Indianapolis, IN 46254, USA

Banks, David R *Businessman*
%Beverly Enterprises, 5111 Rogers Ave, Fort Smith, AR 72919, USA

Banks, Dennis *Indian Activist*
%General Delivery, Oglala, SD 57764, USA

Banks, Ernest (Ernie) *Baseball Player*
PO Box 24302, Los Angeles, CA 90024, USA

Banks, Jonathan *Actor*
909 Euclid St, #8, Santa Monica, CA 90403, USA

Banks, Russell *Businessman*
%Grow Group Inc, 200 Park Ave, New York, NY 10166, USA

Banks, Steven *Comedian*
%Agency For Performing Arts, 9000 Sunset Blvd, #1200, Los Angeles, CA 90069, USA

Banks, Ted *Track Coach*
%Riverside Community College, Athletic Dept, Riverside, CA 92506, USA

Banks, Tony *Keyboardist (Genesis)*
%Hit & Run Music, 25 Ives St, London SW3 2ND, England

Banks, Tyra *Model*
Box 36 East 18th, Los Angeles, CA 90053, USA

Banks, Willie *Track Athlete*
PO Box 4108, Salt Lake City, UT 84110, USA

Bannen, Ian *Actor*
%London Mgmt, 2-4 Noel St, London W1V 3RB, England

Banner, Bob *Movie Producer, Director*
210 S Lasky Dr, Beverly Hills, CA 90212, USA

Bannister, Floyd F *Baseball Player*
6701 Caball Dr, Paradise Valley, AZ 85253, USA

Bannister, Roger G *Track Athlete, Neurologist*
21 Bardwell Rd, Oxford OX2 6SV, England

Bannon, Jack *Actor*
5923 Wilbur Ave, Tarzana, CA 91356, USA

Banois, Vincent J *Football Player*
24256 J Tamarack Trail, Southfield, MI 48075, USA

Banowsky, William S *Educator, Businessman*
%Gaylord Broadcasting Co, PO Box 25125, Oklahoma City, OK 73125, USA

Banta, Merle H *Businessman*
180 E Pearson St, #5006, Chicago, IL 60611, USA

Bantom, Mike *Basketball Player*
%NBA Properties, Olympic Tower, 645 5th Ave, New York, NY 10022, USA

Banton, Julian W *Financier*
%SouthTrust Bank of Alabama, 420 N 20th St, Birmingham, AL 35203, USA

Baquet, Dean P *Journalist*
%New York Times, Editorial Dept, 229 W 43rd St, New York, NY 10036, USA

Bar-Josef, Ofer *Archeologist*
%Harvard University, Archeology Dept, Cambridge, MA 02138, USA

Barad, Jill Elikann *Businesswoman*
%Mattel Inc, 333 Continetal Blvd, El Segundo, CA 90245, USA

Barak, Ehud *Army General, Israel*
%Defense Ministry, Kaplan St, Hakirya, Tel-Aviv 67659, Israel

Baranski, Christine *Actress*
1325 Ave of Americas, #1500, New York, NY 10019, USA

Barany, Istvan *Swimmer*
I Attila Ut 87, 01012 Budapest, Hungary

Barba, Carlos *Entertainment Executive*
%Univision Television Group, 9405 NW 41st St, Miami, FL 33178, USA

Barbakow, Jeffrey C *Businessman*
%National Medical Enterprises, 2700 Colorado Ave, Santa Monica, CA 90404, USA

Barbara, Agatha *President, Malta*
Wied Il-Ghajn St, Zabbar, Malta

Barbeau, Adrienne *Actress*
PO Box 1839, Studio City, CA 91614, USA

Barber of Wentbridge, Anthony P L *Financier*
%Standard Chartered Bank, 10 Clements Lane, London EC4N 7AB, England

Barber, Glynis *Actress*
%Billy Marsh Agency, 19 Denmark St, London WC2H 8NA, England

Barber, Miller *Golfer*
PO Box 2202, Sherman, TX 75091, USA

Barber, William E *Korean War Marine Corps Hero (CMH)*
15231 Chalon Cir, Irvine, CA 92714, USA

Barbera, Joseph *Animator*
12003 Briarvale Lane, Studio City, CA 91604, USA

B

Barbi, Shane — *Model (Barbi Twins)*
PO Box 36066, Los Angeles, CA 90036, USA

Barbi, Sia — *Model (Barbi Twins)*
PO Box 36066, Los Angeles, CA 90036, USA

Barbieri, Fedora — *Opera Singer*
Viale Belfiore 9, Florence, Italy

Barbieri, Gato — *Jazz Saxophonist*
200 W 51st St, #1410, New York, NY 10019, USA

Barbieri, Paula — *Model*
61 E 86th St, #52, New York, NY 10028, USA

Barbot, Ivan — *Law Enforcement Official*
%Presidence Interpol, 50 Quai Achille Lignon, 69006 Lyon, France

Barbour, Haley — *Political Leader*
%Republican National Committee, 310 1st St SE, Washington, DC 20003, USA

Barbour, John — *Comedian, Writer*
2282 Trafalgar Ct, Henderson, NV 89014, USA

Barclay, George M — *Financier*
%Federal Home Loan Bank, 5605 N MacArthur Blvd, Irving, TX 75038, USA

Barco Vargas, Virgilio — *President, Colombia*
%Colombian Embassy, 3 Hans Crescent, #3-A, London SW1X 0LR, England

Bard, Allen J — *Chemist*
6202 Mountainclimb Dr, Austin, TX 78731, USA

Bardis, Panos D — *Writer*
%University of Toledo, Sociology Dept, Toledo, OH 43606, USA

Bardot, Brigitte — *Actress*
La Madrigue, 83990 St Tropez, Var, France

Bare, Bobby — *Singer, Songwriter*
2401 Music Valley Dr, Nashville, TN 37214, USA

Bare, Richard L — *Television Director*
700 Harbor Island Dr, Newport Beach, CA 92660, USA

Barenboim, Daniel — *Conductor, Concert Pianist*
%Chicago Symphony Orchestra, 220 S Michigan Ave, Chicago, IL 60604, USA

Bares, William G — *Businessman*
%Lubrizol Corp, 29400 Lakeland Blvd, Wickliffe, OH 44092, USA

Barfield, Jesse L — *Baseball Player*
4208 Canterwood Dr, Houston, TX 77068, USA

Barfod, Hakon — *Yachtsman*
Jon Ostensensv 15, 1360 Nesbru, Norway

Barfoot, Van T — *WW II Army Hero (CMH)*
Leaning Oaks, Rt 1, Box 32-A, Ford, VA 23850, USA

Barker, Clive — *Writer*
%Harper & Row Publishers, 10 E 53rd St, New York, NY 10022, USA

Barker, Gordon — *Businesman*
%Thrifty Payless, 9275 SW Peyton Lane, Wilsonville, OR 97070, USA

Barker, Horace A — *Biochemist*
561 Santa Clara Ave, Berkeley, CA 94707, USA

Barker, Richard A — *Religious Leader*
%Orthodox Presbyterian Church, 303 Horsham Rd, #G, Horsham, PA 19044, USA

Barker, Robert W (Bob) — *Entertainer*
1851 Outpost Dr, Los Angeles, CA 90068, USA

Barker, Ronnie — *Actor*
%Zahl, 57 Great Cumberland Pl, London W1H 7LJ, England

Barker, Tom — *Actor*
%Barry Burnett, Grafton House, 2-3 Golden Sq, London W1R 3AD, England

Barkin, Ellen — *Actress*
%Creative Artists Agency, 9830 Wilshire Blvd, Beverly Hills, CA 90212, USA

Barkley, Charles W — *Basketball Player*
%Phoenix Suns, 201 E Jefferson St, Phoenix, AZ 85004, USA

Barkley, Richard C — *Diplomat*
%State Department, 2201 "C" St NW, Washington, DC 20520, USA

Barkman Tyler, Janie — *Swimmer*
%Princeton University, Athletic Dept, Princeton, NJ 08544, USA

Barks, Carl — *Cartoonist (Uncle Scrooge, Ducksburg)*
%Carl Barks Studios, PO Box 524, Grants Pass, OR 97526, USA

Barletta, Joseph — *Publisher*
%TV Guide Magazine, 100 Matsonford Rd, Radnor, PA 19080, USA

Barletta, Nicolas Ardito — *President, Panama*
PO Box 7737, Panama City 9, Panama

Barbi - Barletta

B

Barlick, Albert J (Al) 2071 N 6th, Springfield, IL 62702, USA	*Baseball Umpire*
Barmore, Leon %Louisiana Tech University, Athletic Dept, Ruston, LA 71272, USA	*Basketball Coach*
Barnard, Christiaan N PO Box 6143, Welgemoed, 7538 Capetown, South Africa	*Heart Surgeon*
Barnes, Binnie 838 N Doheny Dr, #B, Los Angeles, CA 90069, USA	*Actress*
Barnes, Clive A %New York Post, 210 South St, New York, NY 10002, USA	*Dance, Theater Critic*
Barnes, Edward Larrabee 320 W 13th St, New York, NY 10014, USA	*Architect*
Barnes, Erich 255 W 85th St, New York, NY 10024, USA	*Football Player*
Barnes, Harry G, Jr Hapenny Rd, Peachum, VT 05862, USA	*Diplomat*
Barnes, James E %Mapco Inc, PO Box 645, Tulsa, OK 74101, USA	*Businessman*
Barnes, Jhane E %Jhane Barnes Inc, 575 7th Ave, New York, NY 10018, USA	*Fashion Designer*
Barnes, Joanna 2160 Century Park E, #2101-N, Los Angeles, CA 90067, USA	*Actress*
Barnes, Julian P %A D Peters, 10 Buckingham St, London WC2H 6BO, England	*Writer*
Barnes, Priscilla %Marion Rosenberg Office, 8428 Melrose Place, #C, Los Angeles, CA 90069, USA	*Actress*
Barnes, Robert H %Texas Tech University Medical School, PO Box 4349, Lubbock, TX 79409, USA	*Psychiatrist*
Barnes, Wallace %Barnes Group, 123 Main St, Bristol, CT 06010, USA	*Businessman*
Barnet, Will %National Arts Club, 15 Gramercy Park, New York, NY 10003, USA	*Artist, Educator*
Barnett of Heywood & Royton, Joel B 24 John Islip St, #92, London SW1, England	*Government Official, England*
Barnett, Gary %Northwestern University, Athletic Dept, Evanston, IL 60208, USA	*Football Coach*
Barnett, Harlon %Minnesota Vikings, 9520 Viking Dr, Eden Prairie, MN 55344, USA	*Football Player*
Barnett, Jim 7 Kittiwake Rd, Orinda, CA 94563, USA	*Basketball Player*
Barnett, Jonathan 4501 Connecticut Ave NW, Washington, DC 20008, USA	*Architect*
Barnett, Sabrina %Next Model Mgmt, 115 E 57th St, #1540, New York, NY 10022, USA	*Model*
Barnett, Tommy %Phoenix First Assembly Church, 13613 N Cave Creek Rd, Phoenix, AZ 85022, USA	*Religious Leader*
Barnette, Curtis H (Hank) %Bethlehem Steel Corp, 1170 8th Ave, Bethlehem, PA 18018, USA	*Businessman*
Barnette, Joseph D, Jr %Bank One Indianapolis, 111 Monument Circle, Indianapolis, IN 46204, USA	*Financier*
Barnevik, Barney %ASEA AB, 721 83 Vasteras, Sweden	*Businessman*
Barnevik, Percy N %Skanska AB, 182 25 Danderyd, Stockholm, Sweden	*Businessman*
Barney, Lem 23195 Laurel Valley, Southfield, MI 48034, USA	*Football Player*
Barnidge, Tom %Sporting News, Editorial Dept, 1212 N Lindbergh Blvd, St Louis, MO 63132, USA	*Editor*
Barnum, Harvey C, Jr 2101 Cabot's Point Lane, Reston, VA 22091, USA	*Vietnam War Marine Corps Hero (CMH)*
Barnum, Robert T %American Savings Bank, 17877 Von Karman Ave, Irvine, CA 92714, USA	*Financier*
Baron Crespo, Enrique %European Parliament, 97/113 Rue Velliard, 1040 Brussels, Belgium	*Government Official, Spain*
Baron, Carolyn %Dell Publishing, 666 5th Ave, New York, NY 10103, USA	*Editor*
Barr, Doug 515 S Irving Blvd, Los Angeles, CA 90020, USA	*Actor*

Barlick - Barr

Barr, Joseph W — *Secretary, Treasury*
Houyhnhnm Farm, Hume, VA 22639, USA

Barr, Julia — *Actress*
%St Laurent Assoc, Cherokee Station, PO Box 20191, New York, NY 10028, USA

Barr, Murray L — *Anatomist, Geneticist*
411-312 Oxford St W, London ON N6H 4N7, Canada

Barr, Nevada — *Writer*
%G P Putnam's Sons, 200 Madison Ave, New York, NY 10016, USA

Barr, William P — *Attorney General*
%Shaw Pittman Potts Trowbridge, 2300 "N" St NW, Washington, DC 20037, USA

Barrasso, Tom — *Hockey Player*
%Pittsburgh Penguins, Civic Arena, Centre Ave, Pittsburgh, PA 15219, USA

Barraud, Henry — *Composer*
1 Chemin de Presles, 94410 Saint-Maurice, France

Barrault, Marie-Christine — *Actress*
19 Rue de Lisbonne, 75008 Paris, France

Barre, Raymond — *Prime Minister, France*
4-6 Ave Emile-Acollas, 75007 Paris, France

Barreto, Bruno — *Movie Director*
3000 Olympic Blvd, #2325, Santa Monica, CA 90404, USA

Barrett, Charles S — *Physicist, Metallurgist*
%University of Denver, Metallurgy Materials Division, Denver, CO 80208, USA

Barrett, Craig R — *Businessman*
%Intel Corp, 2200 Mission College Blvd, Santa Clara, CA 95054, USA

Barrett, Majel — *Actress*
%Twentieth Century Artists, 15315 Magnolia Blvd, #429, Sherman Oaks, CA 91403, USA

Barrett, Martin G (Marty) — *Baseball Manager*
3140 Clamdigger, Las Vegas, NV 89117, USA

Barrett, Rona — *Columnist, Commentator*
PO Box 1410, Beverly Hills, CA 90213, USA

Barrett, Tom H — *Businessman*
2135 Stockbridge Rd, Akron, OH 44313, USA

Barrett, William — *Philosopher*
34 Harwood Ave, North Tarrytown, NY 10591, USA

Barrie, Barbara — *Actress*
15 W 72nd St, #2-A, New York, NY 10023, USA

Barris, Chuck — *Television Producer*
1990 Bundy Ave, Los Angeles, CA 90025, USA

Barron, Donald J — *Financier*
%Midland Bank, Poultry, London EC2P 2BX, England

Barron, Kenny — *Jazz Pianist*
%Joanne Klein, 130 W 28th St, New York, NY 10001, USA

Barron, William W — *Governor, WV*
Nassau House, 301 N Ocean Blvd, #603, Pompano Beach, FL 33062, USA

Barrow, Ruth Nita — *Governor-General, Barbados*
Government House, St Michael, Bridgetown, Barbados

Barrows, Sidney — *Businessman*
%Pittway Corp, 200 S Wacker Dr, Chicago, IL 60606, USA

Barrs, Jay — *Archer*
6395 Senoma Dr, Salt Lake City, UT 84121, USA

Barry, A L — *Religious Leader*
%Lutheran Church - Missouri Synod, 421 S 2nd St, Elkhart, IN 46516, USA

Barry, Brent — *Basketball Player*
%Los Angeles Clippers, Sports Arena, 3939 S Figueroa St, Los Angeles, CA 90037, USA

Barry, Dave — *Journalist*
%Miami Herald, Editorial Dept, 1 Herald Plaza, Miami, FL 33132, USA

Barry, David A — *Financier*
%Bariston Holdings, 1 International Place, Boston, MA 02110, USA

Barry, Gene — *Actor*
%Merlis Green Assoc, 10390 Santa Monica Blvd, Los Angeles, CA 90025, USA

Barry, John — *Composer*
540 Centre Island Rd, Oyster Bay, NY 11771, USA

Barry, John J — *Labor Official*
%Int'l Brotherhood of Electrical Workers, 1125 15th St NW, Washington, DC 20005, USA

Barry, Jon — *Basketball Player*
%Milwaukee Bucks, Bradley Center, 1001 N 4th St, Milwaukee, WI 53203, USA

Barry, Lynda — *Cartoonist (Ernie Pook's Comeck)*
PO Box 5286, Evanston, IL 60204, USA

B

Barr - Barry

Barry, Patricia — *Actress*
12742 Highwood St, Los Angeles, CA 90049, USA

Barry, Philip S, Jr — *Movie Producer, Writer*
PO Box 49895, Los Angeles, CA 90049, USA

Barry, Richard F D (Rick) — *Basketball Player, Sportscaster*
%Seattle Supersonics, 190 Queen Ave N, PO Box C-900911, Seattle, WA 98109, USA

Barry, Seymour (Sy) — *Cartoonist (Flash Gordon, Phantom)*
34 Saratoga Dr, Jericho, NY 11753, USA

Barrymore, Drew — *Actress*
612 N Sepulveda Blvd, #10, Los Angeles, CA 90049, USA

Barrymore, John, III — *Actor*
144 S Peck Dr, Beverly Hills, CA 90212, USA

Barschall, Henry H — *Physicist*
1110 Tumalo Trail, Madison, WI 53711, USA

Barshai, Rudolf B — *Conductor*
Homberg Str 6, 4433 Ramlinsburg, Sweden

Barsotti, Charles — *Cartoonist*
%New Yorker Magazine, Editorial Dept, 20 W 43rd St, New York, NY 10036, USA

Barstow, Josephine — *Opera Singer*
%John Coast, 31 Sinclair Rd, London W14 ONS, England

Bart, Lionel — *Composer, Lyricist*
8-10 Bulstrode St, London W1M 6AH, England

Bart, Peter B — *Editor*
2270 Betty Lane, Beverly Hills, CA 90210, USA

Bartel, Paul — *Actor*
7860 Fareholm Dr, Los Angeles, CA 90046, USA

Bartels, Joseph — *Businessman*
%Carlson Companies, Carlson Parkway, PO Box 59159, Minneapolis, MN 55459, USA

Barth, John S — *Writer*
%Johns Hopkins University, Writing Seminars, Baltimore, MD 21218, USA

Barth, Robert — *Religious Leader*
%Churches of Christ in Christian Union, Box 30, Circleville, OH 43113, USA

Bartholomay, William C — *Businessman, Baseball Executive*
%Turner Broadcasting System, 1 CNN Center, Atlanta, GA 30303, USA

Bartholomew, Reginald — *Diplomat*
%State Department, 2201 "C" St NW, Washington, DC 20520, USA

Bartholomew, Samuel W, Jr — *Attorney*
%Federal National Mortgage Assn, 1133 15th St NW, Washington, DC 20005, USA

Bartlett, Bonnie — *Actress, Singer*
12805 Hortense St, Studio City, CA 91604, USA

Bartlett, Jennifer L — *Artist*
%Paula Cooper Gallery, 155 Wooster St, New York, NY 10012, USA

Bartlett, Neil — *Chemist*
6 Oak Dr, Orinda, CA 94563, USA

Bartlett, Paul D — *Chemist*
%Brookhavem, 1010 Waltham St, Lexington, MA 02173, USA

Bartlett, Thomas A — *Educator*
%State University of New York, Chancellor's Office, Albany, NY 12246, USA

Bartley, Robert L — *Editor*
%Wall Street Journal, Editorial Dept, 200 Liberty St, New York, NY 10281, USA

Bartoe, John-David F — *Astronaut*
2121 Cabots Point Lane, Reston, VA 22091, USA

Bartoletti, Bruno — *Conductor*
%Chicago Lyric Opera, 20 N Wacker Dr, Chicago, IL 60606, USA

Bartoli, Cecilia — *Opera Singer*
%La Scala, Via Filodrammatici 2, 20100 Milan, Italy

Barton, Derek H R — *Nobel Chemistry Laureate*
%Texas A&M University, Chemistry Dept, College Station, TX 77843, USA

Barton, Glen A — *Businessman*
%Caterpillar Inc, 100 NE Adams St, Peoria, IL 61629, USA

Barton, Greg — *Kayak Athlete*
6657 58th Ave NE, Seattle, WA 98115, USA

Barton, Harris — *Football Player*
%San Francisco 49ers, 4949 Centennial Blvd, Santa Clara, CA 95054, USA

Barton, Jacqueline K — *Chemist*
%California Institute of Technology, Chemistry Dept, Pasadena, CA 91125, USA

Barton, Peter — *Actor*
2265 Westwood Blvd, #2619, Los Angeles, CA 90064, USA

Bartow, Gene   *Basketball Coach*
%University of Alabama, Athletic Dept, Birmingham, AL 35294, USA

Barty, Billy   *Actor*
4502 Farmdale Ave, North Hollywood, CA 91602, USA

Baryshnikov, Mikhail   *Ballet Dancer*
35 E 12th St, #5-D, New York, NY 10003, USA

Barzun, Jacques   *Educator*
1170 5th Ave, New York, NY 10029, USA

Baschnagel, Brian D   *Football Player*
1823 Sunset Ridge Rd, Glenview, IL 60025, USA

Baselitz, Georg   *Artist*
Schloss Derneburg, 3201 Holle Bei Hildesheim, Germany

Bashir, Omar Hassan Ahmed   *Prime Minister, Sudan; Army General*
%Prime Minister's Office, Revolutionary Command Council, Khartoum, Sudan

Bashmet, Yuri A   *Concert Viola Player*
Nezhdanovoy Str 7, #16, 103009 Moscow, Russia

Basia   *Singer*
%Creative Artists Agency, 9830 Wilshire Blvd, Beverly Hills, CA 90212, USA

Basilio, Carmen   *Boxer*
67 Boxwood Dr, Rochester, NY 14617, USA

Basinger, Kim   *Actress*
%Creative Artists Agency, 9830 Wilshire Blvd, Beverly Hills, CA 90212, USA

Baskin, Leonard   *Artist*
PO Box 413, Leeds, MA 01053, USA

Basov, Nikolai G   *Nobel Physics Laureate*
%Lebedev Physical Institute, 53 Lenin Prospect, Moscow, Russia

Basri, Gibor   *Astronomer*
%University of California, Astronomy Dept, Berkeley, CA 94720, USA

Bass, Bob   *Basketball Coach, Executive*
%San Antonio Spurs, 600 E Market St, #102, San Antonio, TX 78205, USA

Bass, Edward P   *Businessman*
%Bass Brothers Enterprises, 201 Main St, Fort Worth, TX 76102, USA

Bass, Lee   *Businessman*
%Bass Brothers Enterprises, 201 Main St, Fort Worth, TX 76102, USA

Bass, Louis N   *Agronomist, Plant Physiologist*
1117 Fairview, Fort Collins, CO 80521, USA

Bass, Perry R   *Businessman*
%Bass Brothers Enterprises, 201 Main St, Fort Worth, TX 76102, USA

Bass, Richard L (Dick)   *Football Player*
12801 Rosecrans Ave, #344, Norwalk, CA 90650, USA

Bass, Robert M   *Businessman*
%Bass Brothers Enterprises, 201 Main St, Fort Worth, TX 76102, USA

Bass, Saul   *Movie Director, Producer*
337 S Las Palmas Ave, Los Angeles, CA 90020, USA

Bass, Sid   *Businessman*
%Bass Brothers Enterprises, 201 Main St, Fort Worth, TX 76102, USA

Basset, Brian   *Editorial Cartoonist, Cartoonist (Adam)*
%Seattle Times, Editorial Dept, Fairview Ave N & John St, Seattle, WA 98111, USA

Bassett, Angela   *Actress*
6427 1/2 Troost Ave, North Hollywood, CA 91606, USA

Bassett, Edward P   *Educator, Journalist*
%University of Washington, Communications School, Seattle, WA 98195, USA

Bassett, Leslie R   *Composer*
1618 Harbal Dr, Ann Arbor, MI 48105, USA

Bassett-Seguso, Carling   *Tennis Player*
%Women's Tennis Assn, 133 1st St NE, St Petersburg, FL 33701, USA

Bassey, Shirley   *Singer*
Villa Capricorn, 55 Via Campoine, 6816 Bissone, Switzerland

Bastian, Bruce W   *Businessman*
%WordPerfect Corp, 1555 N Technology Way, Orem, UT 84057, USA

Basu, Asit Prakas   *Statistician*
1800 Valley Vista Ct, Columbia, MO 65203, USA

Batalov, Aleksey V   *Movie Director*
%VGIK, Wilgelm Piek Str 3, 129226 Moscow, Russia

Batchelor, Joy E   *Animator*
%Educational Film Center, 5-7 Kean St, London WC2B 4AT, England

Bate, Anthony   *Actor*
%Al Parker, 55 Park Lane, London W1Y 3DD, England

B

Bartow - Bate

B

Bateman, Jason — Actor
2623 2nd St, Santa Monica, CA 90405, USA

Bateman, Justine — Actress
11288 Ventura Blvd, #190, Studio City, CA 91604, USA

Bateman, Robert M — Artist
Box 115, Fulford Harbour BC V0S 1C0, Canada

Bateman, Walter R — Businessman
%Harleysville Mutual Insurance, 355 Maple Ave, Harleysville, PA 19438, USA

Bates, Alan — Actor
122 Hamilton Terrace, London NW8, England

Bates, Charles C — Oceanographer
136 W La Pintura, Green Valley, AZ 85614, USA

Bates, Kathy — Actress
%Susan Smith Assoc, 121 N San Vicente Blvd, Beverly Hills, CA 90211, USA

Bates, Robert T — Labor Leader
%Railroad Signalmen Brotherhood, 601 W Golf Rd, Mount Prospect, IL 60056, USA

Bateson, Mary Catherine — Anthropologist
10220 Bushman Dr, #211, Oakton, VA 22124, USA

Bathgate, Andy — Hockey Player
43 Brentwood Dr, Bramlee ON L6T 1R1, Canada

Batiuk, Thomas M (Tom) — Cartoonist (Crankshaft)
%Creators Syndicate, 5777 W Century Blvd, #700, Los Angeles, CA 90045, USA

Batiz Campbell, Enrique — Conductor
Periferico Sur 5141, Col Fabela, Dele Tlalan, Mexico City DF 14030, Mexico

Batliner, Gerard — Head of Government, Liechtenstein
Am Schragen, Weg 2, 9490 Vaduz, Liechtenstein

Batson, Arthur E, Jr — Labor Leader
%Marine & Shipbuilding Workers Union, 5101 River Rd, Bethesda, MD 20816, USA

Batt, Phil — Governor, ID
%Governor's Office, State Capitol, Boise, ID 83720, USA

Batten, William M — Stock Exchange Executive
7 Hadley Lane, Hilton Head Island, SC 29926, USA

Battey, Charles W — Businessman
%K N Energy, 370 Van Gordon, Lakewood, CO 80228, USA

Battista, Orlando A — Businessman, Inventor
%Knowledge Olympics, 3863 South West Loop 829, #100, Fort Worth, TX 76133, USA

Battle, Hinton — Dancer, Actor
%Borinstein Bogart Agency, 8271 Melrose Ave, #110, Los Angeles, CA 90046, USA

Battle, Kathleen D — Opera Singer
%Columbia Artists Mgmt Inc, 165 W 57th St, New York, NY 10019, USA

Battle, Lucius D — Educator, Diplomat
4856 Rockwood Parkway NW, Washington, DC 20016, USA

Battram, Richard L — Businessman
%May Department Stores, 611 Olive St, St Louis, MO 63101, USA

Batts, Warren L — Businessman
%Premark International, 1717 Deerfield Rd, Deerfield, IL 60015, USA

Baucom, Tyndall L — Businessman
%Dominion Resources, Riverfront Plaza West, 901 E Byrd St, Richmond, VA 23219, USA

Baudo, Serge — Conductor
Jas du Ferra, Chemin Charre, 13600 Ceyreste, France

Baudrillard, Jean — Philosopher
%Editions Galilee, 9 Rue Linne, 75005 Paris, France

Bauer, Belinda — Actress
%Gersh Agency, 232 N Canon Dr, Beverly Hills, CA 90210, USA

Bauer, Chris M — Financier
%Firstar Bank Milwaukee, 777 E Wisconsin Ave, Milwaukee, WI 53202, USA

Bauer, Erwin A — Photographer
PO Box 987, Livingston, MT 59047, USA

Bauer, Henry A (Hank) — Baseball Player, Manager
Quivira Falls, 12705 W 108th St, Overland Park, KS 66210, USA

Bauer, Jaime Lyn — Actress
%Tyler Kjar Agency, 10643 Riverside Dr, Toluca Lake, CA 91602, USA

Bauer, Michelle — Actress
16032 Sherman Way, #73, Van Nuys, CA 91406, USA

Bauer, Peggy — Photographer
PO Box 987, Livingston, MT 59047, USA

Bauer, Steven — Actor
5820 Wilshire Blvd, #400, Los Angeles, CA 90036, USA

Bateman - Bauer

Baugh, John F — *Businessman*
%Sysco Corp, 1390 Enclave Parkway, Houston, TX 77077, USA

Baugh, Laura — *Golfer*
%Ladies Professional Golf Assn, 2570 Volusia Ave, Daytona Beach, FL 32114, USA

Baugh, Sammy — *Football Player*
General Delivery, Rotan, TX 79546, USA

Baughan, Maxie C — *Football Player, Coach*
%Minnesota Vikings, 9520 Viking Dr, Eden Prairie, MN 55344, USA

Baughman, Gary — *Businessman*
%Tyco Toys Inc, 6000 Midlantic Dr, Mount Laurel, NJ 08054, USA

Baughn, William H — *Educator*
555 Baseline Rd, Boulder, CO 80302, USA

Baulieu, Etienne-Emile — *Biochemist, Inventor*
%Laboratoire des Hormones, Hopital de Bicetre, Le Kremlin-Bicetre, France

Baum, Herbert M — *Businessman*
%Quaker State Corp, 255 Elm St, Oil City, PA 16301, USA

Baum, Jonathan E — *Financier*
%George K Baum Co, 120 W 12th St, Kansas City, MO 64105, USA

Baum, Robert H — *Financier*
%Inland Group, 2901 Butterfield Rd, Oak Brook, IL 60521, USA

Baum, Warren C — *Economist*
%International Bank of Reconstruction, 1818 "H" St NW, Washington, DC 20433, USA

Baum, William W Cardinal — *Religious Leader*
Piazza della Citta, Lemonina 9, 00193 Rome, Italy

Bauman, G Duncan — *Publisher*
37 Conway Close Rd, St Louis, MO 63124, USA

Bauman, Jon (Bowzer) — *Singer*
3168 Oakshire Dr, Los Angeles, CA 90068, USA

Baumann, Alex — *Swimmer*
2617 Field St, Sudbury ON P3E 4X8, Canada

Baumann, Dieter — *Track Athlete*
Akazienweg 3, 79737 Herrlingen/Blaustein, Germany

Baumann, Frank M — *Baseball Player*
7712 Sunray Lane, St Louis, MO 63123, USA

Baumbauer, Frank — *Theater Director*
%Deutsches Schauspielhaus, Kirchenallee 39, 20099 Hamburg, Germany

Baumgartner, Bruce — *Wrestler*
%Edinboro University, Athletic Dept, McComb Field House, Edinboro, PA 16444, USA

Baumgartner, William — *Surgeon*
%Johns Hopkins Hospital, 600 N Wolfe St, Baltimore, MD 21205, USA

Baumhart, Raymond C — *Educator*
6525 N Sheridan Rd, Chicago, IL 60626, USA

Baumol, William J — *Economist*
PO Box 1502, Princeton, NJ 08542, USA

Bausch, Pina — *Dancer, Choreographer*
%Wuppertal Dance Theatre, Spinnstr 4, 42283 Wuppertal, Germany

Bavaro, Mark — *Football Player*
%Philadelphia Eagles, 3501 S Broad St, Philadelphia, PA 19148, USA

Bavasi, Peter J — *Baseball Executive*
%Telerate Sports Inc, 600 Plaza 2, Harborside, Jersey City, NJ 07311, USA

Baxandall, Lee — *Association Executive*
%Naturist Society, PO Box 132, Oshkosh, WI 54902, USA

Baxter, Frank E — *Financier*
%Jeffries Group, 11100 Santa Monica Blvd, Los Angeles, CA 90025, USA

Baxter, Glen — *Cartoonist*
%Aitken & Stone, 29 Fernshaw Rd, London SW10 0TG, England

Baxter, Les — *Orchestra Leader*
6430 Sunset Blvd, #1002, Los Angeles, CA 90028, USA

Baxter, Meredith — *Actress*
%William Morris Agency, 151 S El Camino Dr, Beverly Hills, CA 90212, USA

Baxter, William F — *Government Official*
%Stanford University, Law School, Stanford, CA 94305, USA

Bay, Howard — *Movie, Theater Designer*
159 W 53rd St, New York, NY 10019, USA

Bay, Willow — *Model*
%"Inside Stuff" Show, NBC-TV, 30 Rockfeller Plaza, New York, NY 10020, USA

Baye, Nathalie — *Actress*
%Artmedia, 10 Ave George V, 75008 Paris, France

B

Baugh - Baye

Bayes, G E *Religious Leader*
%Free Methodist Church, PO Box 535002, Winona Lake, IN 46590, USA

Bayh, Birch E, Jr *Senator, IN*
%Bayh Connaughton Festerheim Malone, 1350 "I" St NW, Washington, DC 20005, USA

Bayh, Evan *Governor, IN*
%Governor's Office, State House, #206, Indianapolis, IN 46204, USA

Bayi, Filbert *Track Athlete*
PO Box 60240, Dar es Salaam, Tanzania

Bayle, Jean-Michel *Motorcycle Racing Rider*
%General Delivery, Manosque, France

Baylis, Robert M *Financier*
%First Boston Corp, 55 E 52nd St, New York, NY 10055, USA

Baylor, Don E *Baseball Player, Manager*
5 Fieldstone Lane, South Natick, MA 01760, USA

Baylor, Elgin G *Basketball Player, Executive*
%Los Angeles Clippers, Sports Arena, 3939 S Figueroa St, Los Angeles, CA 90037, USA

Bazell, Robert J *Commentator*
%NBC-TV, News Dept, 4001 Nebraska Ave NW, Washington, DC 20016, USA

Bazin, Marc L *President, Haiti*
2-E Ave du Trvail, #8, Port-au-Prince, Haiti

Beach, Edward L *WW II Navy Hero, Writer*
%Henry Holt Inc, 115 W 18th St, New York, NY 10011, USA

Beach, Roger C *Businessman*
%Unocal Corp, 1201 W 5th St, Los Angeles, CA 90017, USA

Beacham, Stephanie *Actress*
PO Box 6446, Malibu, CA 90264, USA

Beagle, Ron *Football Player*
3830 San Ysidro Way, Sacramento, CA 95864, USA

Beake, John *Football Executive*
%Denver Broncos, 13655 E Dove Valley Parkway, Englewood, CO 80112, USA

Beal, Bernard B *Financier*
%M R Beal Co, 565 5th Ave, New York, NY 10017, USA

Beal, David *Financier*
%BarclaysAmerican/Mortgage Corp, 8 Parkway Plaza, Charlotte, NC 28217, USA

Beal, Jack *Artist*
HC 64, Box 83-A, Oneonta, NY 13820, USA

Beal, John *Actor*
205 W 54th St, New York, NY 10019, USA

Beale, Betty *Columnist*
2926 Garfield St NW, Washington, DC 20008, USA

Beall, Donald R *Businessman*
%Rockwell International Corp, 2201 Seal Beach Blvd, Seal Beach, CA 90740, USA

Beals, Jennifer *Actress*
335 N Maple Dr, #250, Beverly Hills, CA 90210, USA

Beals, Vaughn L, Jr *Businessman, Motorcycle Executive*
%Harley-Davidson Inc, 3700 W Juneau Ave, Milwaukee, WI 53208, USA

Beam, C Arlen *Judge*
%US Court of Appeals, Federal Building, 100 Centennial Mall N, Lincoln, NE 68508, USA

Beaman, Sally *Writer*
%Bantam Books, 1540 Broadway, New York, NY 10036, USA

Bean, Alan L *Astronaut*
26 Sugarberry Circle, Houston, TX 77024, USA

Bean, Andy *Golfer*
3216 Carleton Circle, Lakeland, FL 33803, USA

Bean, Orson *Actor, Comedian*
%Gage Group, 9255 Sunset Blvd, #515, Los Angeles, CA 90069, USA

Bean, William Bennett *Physician*
11 Rowland Ct, Iowa City, IA 52246, USA

Beard, Alfred (Butch) *Basketball Player; Coach*
%New Jersey Nets, Byrne Meadowlands Arena, East Rutherford, NJ 07073, USA

Beard, Frank *Golfer*
%PGA Seniors Tour, 112 T P C Blvd, Ponte Vedra Beach, FL 32082, USA

Beard, Frank *Drummer (ZZ Top)*
%Lone Wolf Mgmt, PO Box 163690, Austin, TX 78716, USA

Beard, Percy *Track Athlete, Coach*
832 NW 22nd St, Gainesville, FL 32603, USA

Beard, Ronald S *Attorney*
%Gibson Dunn Crutcher, 333 S Grand Ave, Los Angeles, CA 90071, USA

Bearden, H Eugene (Gene)   *Baseball Player*
PO Box 176, Helena, AR 72342, USA

Bearse, Amanda   *Actress*
4177 Klump Ave, North Hollywood, CA 91602, USA

Beart, Emmanuelle   *Actress*
9 Rue Constant-Coquelin, 75007 Paris, France

Beart, Guy   *Singer, Songwriter*
%Editions Temporel, 2 Rue Du Marquis de Mores, 92380 Garches, France

Beasley, Allyce   *Actress*
2415 Castillian Dr, Los Angeles, CA 90068, USA

Beasley, Bruce M   *Artist*
322 Lewis St, Oakland, CA 94607, USA

Beasley, David   *Governor, SC*
%Governor's Office, State Capitol, PO Box 11369, Columbia, SC 29211, USA

Beasley, Jere L   *Governor, AL*
%Beasley Wilson Allen Mendelsohn, 207 Montgomery, #1000, Montgomery, AL 36104, USA

Beasley, Terry P   *Football Player*
4449 Central Plank Rd, Wetumpka, AL 36092, USA

Beathard, Bobby   *Football Executive*
%San Diego Chargers, Jack Murphy Stadium, San Diego, CA 92160, USA

Beatrix   *Queen, Netherlands*
Huis Ten Bosch, The Hague, Netherlands

Beattie, Ann   *Writer*
%Janklow & Nesbit, 598 Madison Ave, New York, NY 10022, USA

Beattie, Bob   *Skier*
%World Wide Ski Corp, 402 Pacific Ave, #D, Aspen, CO 81611, USA

Beatty, Ned   *Actor*
2706 N Beachwood Dr, Los Angeles, CA 90068, USA

Beatty, Warren   *Actor, Director, Producer*
13671 Mulholland Dr, Beverly Hills, CA 90210, USA

Beaupre, Don   *Hockey Player*
%Ottawa Senators, 301 Moodle Dr, #200, Nepean ON K2H 9C4, Canada

Beauvais, Garcelle   *Model, Actress*
%Nina Blanchard Enterprises, 957 N Cole Ave, Los Angeles, CA 90038, USA

Beavogui, Louis Lansana   *Prime Minister, Guinea*
%Prime Minister's Office, Conakry, Guinea

Bebey, Francis   *Guitarist, Composer*
18 Rue du Camp de L'Alouette, 25013 Paris, France

Becaud, Gilbert   *Singer*
24 Rue de Longchamp, 75016 Paris, France

Becherer, Hans W   *Businessman*
%Deere Co, John Deere Rd, Moline, IL 61265, USA

Bechtel, Riley P   *Businessman*
%Bechtel Group, 50 Beale St, San Francisco, CA 94105, USA

Bechtel, Stephen D, Jr   *Businessman*
%Bechtel Group, 50 Beale St, San Francisco, CA 94105, USA

Bechtol, Hubert   *Football Player*
7917 Taranto Dr, Austin, TX 78729, USA

Beck Hilton, Kimberly   *Actress*
%Badgley Connor, 9229 Sunset Blvd, #311, Los Angeles, CA 90069, USA

Beck, Aaron T   *Psychiatrist*
3600 Market St, #700, Philadelphia, PA 19104, USA

Beck, Barry   *Hockey Player*
%New York Rangers, Madison Square Garden, 4 Penn Plaza New York, NY 10001, USA

Beck, Chip   *Golfer*
%Professional Golfer's Assn, PO Box 109601, Palm Beach Gardens, FL 33410, USA

Beck, Conrad   *Composer*
St Johann Vorstadt, Basel, Switzerland

Beck, Jeff   *Singer, Guitarist (Yardbirds)*
%Ernest Chapman Mgmt, 11 Old Square Lincoln's Inn, London WC2, England

Beck, John   *Actor*
%Camden ITG Talent Agency, 822 S Robertson Blvd, #200, Los Angeles, CA 90035, USA

Beck, Julian   *Theater Producer, Director*
800 West End Ave, New York, NY 10025, USA

Beck, Marilyn M   *Columnist*
2152 El Roble Lane, Beverly Hills, CA 90210, USA

Beck, Martin   *Actor*
%Terry Lichtman Agency, 4439 Worster Ave, Studio City, CA 91604, USA

B

Beck, Mat *Cinematographer*
%Dream Quest Images, 2635 Park Center Dr, Simi Valley, CA 93065, USA

Beck, Michael *Actor*
%Innovative Artists, 1999 Ave of Stars, #2850, Los Angeles, CA 90067, USA

Beckenbauer, Franz *Soccer Player, Coach*
Am Lutzenberg 15, 6370 Kitzbuhel, Austria

Becker, Boris *Tennis Player*
La Rocca Bella, 24 Ave Princess Grace, Monte Carlo, Monaco

Becker, Douglas *Educator*
%Sylvan Learning Corp, 2400 Presidents Dr, Montgomery, AL 36116, USA

Becker, Gary S *Nobel Economics Laureate*
1308 E 58th St, Chicago, IL 60637, USA

Becker, George *Labor Leader*
%United Steelworkers of America, 5 Gateway Center, Pittsburgh, PA 15222, USA

Becker, Gert O *Businessman*
Friedrichstr 100, 61476 Kronberg Im Taunus, Germany

Becker, Harold *Movie Director*
%Creative Artists Agency, 9830 Wilshire Blvd, Beverly Hills, CA 90212, USA

Becker, Isidore A *Businessman*
10155 Collins Ave, Miami, FL 33154, USA

Becker, John A *Financier*
%Firstar Corp, 777 W Wisconsin Ave, Milwaukee, WI 53233, USA

Becker, Quinn H *Army General, Surgeon*
154 Banner Farm Rd, Horse Shoe, NC 28742, USA

Becker, Robert J *Allergist*
1 Tower Lane, #1140, Villa Park, IL 60181, USA

Becket, MacDonald G *Architect*
%Becket Group, 2501 Colorado Blvd, Santa Monica, CA 90404, USA

Beckett, Margaret M *Government Official, England*
%House of Commons, Westminster, London SW1A 0AA, England

Beckman, Arnold O *Inventor (Acidity Testing Apparatus)*
%SmithKline Beckman Corp, 1 Franklin Plaza, Philadelphia, PA 19154, USA

Becton, C W *Religious Leader*
%United Pentacostal Free Will Baptist Church, 8855 Dunn Rd, Hazelwood, MO 63042, USA

Becton, Henry P, Jr *Businessman*
%WGBH-TV, 125 Western Ave, Allston, MA 02134, USA

Becton, Julius W, Jr *Army General, Educator*
%Prairie View A&M University, President's Office, Prairie View, TX 77446, USA

Bedard, Myriam *Biathlete*
3329 Pinecourt, Neufchatel PQ G2B 2E4, Canada

Bedelia, Bonnie *Actress*
1021 Georgina Ave, Santa Monica, CA 90402, USA

Bedford, Brian *Actor*
%Paradigm Agency, 10100 Santa Monica Blvd, #2500, Los Angeles, CA 90067, USA

Bedford, Sybille *Writer*
%Messrs Coutts, 1 Old Park Lane, London W1Y 4BS, England

Bedi, Bisban Singh *Cricketer*
Ispat Bhawan, Lodhi Rd, New Delhi 3, India

Bedi, Kabir *Actor*
%Conway Van Gelder Ltd, 18-21 Jermyn St, London SW1Y 6HP, England

Bednarik, Charles (Chuck) *Football Player*
6379 Winding Rd, Coppersburg, PA 18036, USA

Bednorz, J Georg *Nobel Physics Laureate*
%IBM Research Laboratory, Saumerstr 4, 8803 Ruschlikon, Switzerland

Bedrosian, Stephen W (Steve) *Baseball Player*
3335 Gordon Rd, Senoia, GA 30276, USA

Bedser, Alec V *Cricketer*
%Initial Cleaning Services, 33/34 Hoxton Sq, London N1 6NN, England

Bee, Molly *Actress, Singer*
PO Box 722, Esparto, CA 95627, USA

Beebe, Stephen A *Businessman*
%J R Simplot Co, 1 Capital Center, Boise, ID 83707, USA

Beebe, William T *Businessman*
%Delta Air Lines, Hartsfield International Airport, Atlanta, GA 30320, USA

Beeby, Clarence E *Architect*
%Hammond Beeby Babka, 400 N Wells St, Chicago, IL 60610, USA

Beedle, Lynn S *Civil Engineer*
102 Cedar Rd, Hellertown, PA 18055, USA

Beck - Beedle

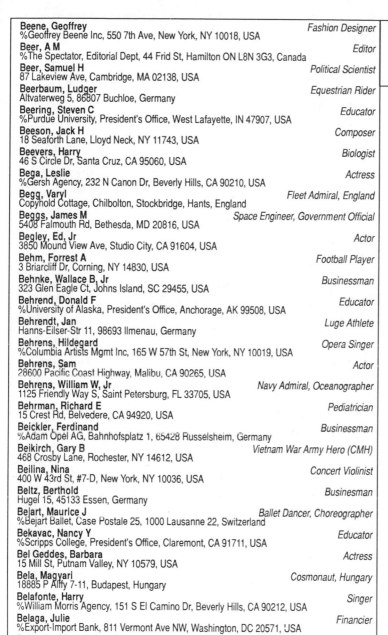

Beene, Geoffrey — *Fashion Designer*
%Geoffrey Beene Inc, 550 7th Ave, New York, NY 10018, USA

Beer, A M — *Editor*
%The Spectator, Editorial Dept, 44 Frid St, Hamilton ON L8N 3G3, Canada

Beer, Samuel H — *Political Scientist*
87 Lakeview Ave, Cambridge, MA 02138, USA

Beerbaum, Ludger — *Equestrian Rider*
Altvaterweg 5, 86807 Buchloe, Germany

Beering, Steven C — *Educator*
%Purdue University, President's Office, West Lafayette, IN 47907, USA

Beeson, Jack H — *Composer*
18 Seaforth Lane, Lloyd Neck, NY 11743, USA

Beevers, Harry — *Biologist*
46 S Circle Dr, Santa Cruz, CA 95060, USA

Bega, Leslie — *Actress*
%Gersh Agency, 232 N Canon Dr, Beverly Hills, CA 90210, USA

Begg, Varyl — *Fleet Admiral, England*
Copyhold Cottage, Chilbolton, Stockbridge, Hants, England

Beggs, James M — *Space Engineer, Government Official*
5408 Falmouth Rd, Bethesda, MD 20816, USA

Begley, Ed, Jr — *Actor*
3850 Mound View Ave, Studio City, CA 91604, USA

Behm, Forrest A — *Football Player*
3 Briarcliff Dr, Corning, NY 14830, USA

Behnke, Wallace B, Jr — *Businessman*
323 Glen Eagle Ct, Johns Island, SC 29455, USA

Behrend, Donald F — *Educator*
%University of Alaska, President's Office, Anchorage, AK 99508, USA

Behrendt, Jan — *Luge Athlete*
Hanns-Eilser-Str 11, 98693 Ilmenau, Germany

Behrens, Hildegard — *Opera Singer*
%Columbia Artists Mgmt Inc, 165 W 57th St, New York, NY 10019, USA

Behrens, Sam — *Actor*
28600 Pacific Coast Highway, Malibu, CA 90265, USA

Behrens, William W, Jr — *Navy Admiral, Oceanographer*
1125 Friendly Way S, Saint Petersburg, FL 33705, USA

Behrman, Richard E — *Pediatrician*
15 Crest Rd, Belvedere, CA 94920, USA

Beickler, Ferdinand — *Businessman*
%Adam Opel AG, Bahnhofsplatz 1, 65428 Russelsheim, Germany

Beikirch, Gary B — *Vietnam War Army Hero (CMH)*
468 Crosby Lane, Rochester, NY 14612, USA

Beilina, Nina — *Concert Violinist*
400 W 43rd St, #7-D, New York, NY 10036, USA

Beltz, Berthold — *Businessman*
Hugel 15, 45133 Essen, Germany

Bejart, Maurice J — *Ballet Dancer, Choreographer*
%Bejart Ballet, Case Postale 25, 1000 Lausanne 22, Switzerland

Bekavac, Nancy Y — *Educator*
%Scripps College, President's Office, Claremont, CA 91711, USA

Bel Geddes, Barbara — *Actress*
15 Mill St, Putnam Valley, NY 10579, USA

Bela, Magyari — *Cosmonaut, Hungary*
18885 P Alffy 7-11, Budapest, Hungary

Belafonte, Harry — *Singer*
%William Morris Agency, 151 S El Camino Dr, Beverly Hills, CA 90212, USA

Belaga, Julie — *Financier*
%Export-Import Bank, 811 Vermont Ave NW, Washington, DC 20571, USA

Belanger, Mark H — *Baseball Player*
2028 Pot Spring Rd, Timonium, MD 21093, USA

Belcher, Donald D — *Businessman*
%Banta Corp, River Place, 225 Main St, Menasha, WI 54952, USA

Beldon, Sanford T — *Publisher*
%Prevention Magazine, 33 E Minor St, Emmaus, PA 18049, USA

Belford, Christina — *Actress*
12747 Riverside Dr, #208, North Hollywood, CA 91607, USA

Belfour, Ed — *Hockey Player*
%Chicago Blackhawks, Chicago Stadium, 1800 W Madison St, Chicago, IL 60612, USA

B

Beene - Belfour

Belichik, Bill *Football Coach*
%Cleveland Browns, 80 1st Ave, Berea, OH 44017, USA

Belita *Actress*
%Rose Cottage, Crabtree Gardens, 42 Crabtree Lane, London SW6 6LW, England

Beliveau, Jean *Hockey Player*
%Montreal Canadiens, 2313 St Catherine St W, Montreal PQ H3H 1N2, Canada

Belk, John M *Businessman*
%Belk Stores Services, 2801 W Tyvola Rd, Charlotte, NC 28217, USA

Belk, Thomas M *Businessman*
%Belk Stores Services, 2801 W Tyvola Rd, Charlotte, NC 28217, USA

Bell, Archie *Singer*
%Speer Entertainment Services, PO Box 49612, Atlanta, GA 30359, USA

Bell, Bobby L, Sr *Football Player*
208 Shagbark, Lees Summit, MO 64064, USA

Bell, Clyde R (Bob) *Navy Admiral, Association Executive*
%Greater Omaha Chamber of Commerce, 1301 Harney, Omaha, NE 68102, USA

Bell, David E *Economist, Government Official*
1 Waterhouse St, Cambridge, MA 02138, USA

Bell, David G (Buddy) *Baseball Player*
9017 Decima St, Cincinnati, OH 45242, USA

Bell, Derrick A *Attorney, Educator*
%New York University, Law School, 40 Washington Sq S, New York, NY 10012, USA

Bell, Greg *Track Athlete*
831 W Maimi Ave, Logansport, IN 46947, USA

Bell, Griffin B *Attorney General*
%King & Spalding, 2500 Trust Tower, 181 Peachtree St NE, Atlanta, GA 30303, USA

Bell, Harry S *Businessman*
%Southerns Farm Bureau Life Insurance, PO Box 78, Jackson, MS 39205, USA

Bell, James D *Diplomat*
14 Kite Hill Rd, Santa Cruz, CA 95060, USA

Bell, Jay S *Baseball Player*
3835 Cold Creek Dr, Valrico, FL 33594, USA

Bell, Jerry *Baseball Executive*
%Minnesota Twins, 501 Chicago Ave S, Minneapolis, MN 55415, USA

Bell, Jorge A (George) *Baseball Player*
Bario Rest Cle T #179, San Pedro de Macoris, Dominican Republic

Bell, Larry S *Artist*
PO Box 4101, Taos, NM 87571, USA

Bell, Michael *Actor*
%Cunningham-Escott-Dipene, 10635 Santa Monica Blvd, Los Angeles, CA 90025, USA

Bell, Sam *Track Coach*
%Indiana University, Athletic Dept, Assembly Hall, Bloomington, IN 47405, USA

Bell, Terrel H *Secretary, Education*
%University of Utah, Education Dept, Salt Lake City, UT 84112, USA

Bell, Thomas D, Jr *Businessman*
%Gulfstream Aerospace Corp, PO Box 2206, Savannah, GA 31402, USA

Bell, Tom *Actor*
%Christina Shepherd, 84 Claverton St, London SW1 3AX, England

Bell, William J *Businessman*
%Cablevision Systems Corp, 1 Media Crossways, Woodbury, NY 11797, USA

Bellah, Robert N *Sociologist*
%University of California, Sociology Dept, Berkeley, CA 94720, USA

Bellamy, Carol *Association Leader*
%United Nations Children's Fund, 1 UN Plaza, New York, NY 10017, USA

Bellamy, David *Singer (Bellamy Brothers), Songwriter*
%Bellamy Brothers, 201 Restless Lane, Dade City, FL 33525, USA

Bellamy, David J *Botanist, Writer, Broadcaster*
Mill House, Bedburn, Bishop Auckland, County Durham, England

Bellamy, Howard *Singer (Bellamy Brothers), Songwriter*
%Bellamy Brothers, 201 Restless Lane, Dade City, FL 33525, USA

Belle, Albert J *Baseball Player*
10130 Westwind Dr, Shreveport, LA 71106, USA

Belle, Regina *Singer*
PO Box 4450, New York, NY 10101, USA

Bellecourt, Vernon *Social Activist, Association Executive*
%American Indian Movement, 1209 4th St SE, Minneapolis, MN 55414, USA

Beller, Kathleen *Actress*
%Paradigm Agency, 10100 Santa Monica Blvd, #2500, Los Angeles, CA 90067, USA

Belli, Melvin M — *Attorney*
30 Hotaling Pl, San Francisco, CA 94111, USA

Bellingham, Norman — *Rower*
1208 Potover Valley Rd, Rockville, MD 20850, USA

Bellini, Cal — *Actor*
%Allen Goldstein Assoc, 5015 Lemona Ave, Sherman Oaks, CA 91403, USA

Bellino, Joe — *Football Player*
45 Hayden Lane, Bedford, MA 01730, USA

Bellisario, Donald P — *Television Producer*
%Broder Kurland Webb Uffner, 9242 Beverly Blvd, #200, Beverly Hills, CA 90210, USA

Bellmon, Henry — *Governor/Senator, OK*
Rt 1, Red Rock, OK 74651, USA

Bellow, Saul C — *Nobel Literature Laureate*
745 Commonwealth Ave, Boston, MA 02215, USA

Bellows, Brian — *Hockey Player*
%Tampa Bay Lightning, Mack Center, 501 E Kennedy Blvd, Tampa, FL 33602, USA

Bellows, James G — *Journalist, Television Producer*
2337 Canyonback Rd, Los Angeles, CA 90049, USA

Bellson, Louis P (Louie) — *Drummer*
12804 Raymer St, North Hollywood, CA 91605, USA

Bellucci, Monica — *Model*
%Elite Model Mgmt, 111 E 22nd St, #200, New York, NY 10010, USA

Bellwood, Pamela — *Actress*
7444 Woodrow Wilson Dr, Los Angeles, CA 90046, USA

Bellwood, Wesley E — *Businessman*
%Wynn's International, 500 N State College Blvd, Fullerton, CA 92631, USA

Belmondo, Jean-Paul — *Actor*
9 Rue des St Peres, 75007 Paris, France

Belohlavek, Jiri — *Conductor*
%Czechoslovakia Philharmonic, Alsovo Nabr 12, 11001 Prague, Czech Republic

Belote Hamlin, Melissa — *Swimmer*
5409 Tripolis Ct, Burke, VA 22015, USA

Belousova, Ludmila — *Figure Skater*
Chalet Hubel, 3818 Grindelwald, Switzerland

Belushi, James — *Actor*
8033 Wilshire Blvd, #88, Los Angeles, CA 90046, USA

Bem, Joel E — *Labor Leader*
%Marine Engineer Beneficial Assn, 444 N Capitol St, Washington, DC 20001, USA

Ben Ami, Zine al-Abidine — *President, Tunisia; Army General*
%President's Office, Palals Presidentlel, Tunis, Tunisia

Benacerraf, Baruj — *Nobel Medicine Laureate*
111 Perkins St, Boston, MA 02130, USA

Benade, Leo Edward — *Army General*
417 Pine Ridge Rd, #A, Carthage, NC 28327, USA

Benard, Andre P J — *Businessman*
%Eurotunnel SA, Tour Franklin, Cedex 11, 92001 Paris-La-Defense 8, France

Benatar, Pat — *Singer*
8801 Eton Ave, #48, Canoga Park, CA 91304, USA

Benavidez, Roy P — *Vietnam War Army Hero (CMH)*
1700 Byrne St, El Campo, TX 77437, USA

Bench, John L (Johnny) — *Baseball Player*
105 E 4th St, #800, Cincinnati, OH 45202, USA

Benchley, Peter B — *Writer*
35 Boudinot St, Princeton, NJ 08540, USA

Bencsik, Doris D — *Businesswoman*
%Datapoint Corp, 8400 Datapoint Dr, San Antonio, TX 78229, USA

Bender, Gary N — *Sportscaster*
%Turner Sports-TNT, Sports Dept, 1050 Techwood Dr NW, Atlanta, GA 30318, USA

Bender, Myron L — *Chemist*
2514 Sheridan Rd, Evanston, IL 60201, USA

Benedict, Dirk — *Actor*
PO Box 634, Bigfork, MT 59911, USA

Benedict, Manson — *Chemical Engineer*
108 Moorings Park Dr, #206-B, Naples, FL 33942, USA

Benedict, Paul — *Actor*
84 Rockland Pl, Newton, MA 02164, USA

Benedict, William — *Actor*
1347 N Orange Grove Ave, Los Angeles, CA 90046, USA

B

Belli - Benedict

B

Benetton, Luciano	*Businessman*
%Benetton SPA, Via Chiesa Ponzano 24, 31050 Ponzano Veneto, Italy	
Benezet, Louis T	*Educator*
5101 Shelter Bay Ave, Mill Valley, CA 94941, USA	
Benglis, Lynda	*Artist*
222 Bowery St, New York, NY 10012, USA	
Bengston, Billy Al	*Artist*
805 Hampton Dr, Venice, CA 90291, USA	
Benhamou, Eric A	*Businessman*
%3Com Corp, 5400 Bayfront Plaza, Santa Clara, CA 95054, USA	
Benichou, Jacques	*Businessman*
%Snecma, 2 Blvd Victor, 75724 Paris Cedex 15, France	
Benigni, Roberto	*Actor*
Via Traversa 44, Vergaglio, Provinz di Prato, Italy	
Bening, Annette	*Actress*
13671 Mulholland Dr, Beverly Hills, CA 90210, USA	
Benirschke, Rolf J	*Football Player*
%Rolf Benirschke Enterprises, 12555 High Bluff Dr, #150, San Diego, CA 92130, USA	
Benjamin, Benoit	*Basketball Player*
%Vancouver Grizzlies, 788 Beatty St, #300, Vancouver BC V6B 2M1, Canada	
Benjamin, Curtis G	*Publisher*
Kellogg Hill Rd, Weston, CT 06880, USA	
Benjamin, Karl S	*Artist*
675 W 8th St, Claremont, CA 91711, USA	
Benjamin, Leanne	*Ballerina*
%Royal Ballet, Bow St, London WC2E 9DD, England	
Benjamin, Richard	*Actor*
%Gersh Agency, 232 N Canon Dr, Beverly Hills, CA 90210, USA	
Benn, Nigel	*Boxer*
%World Sports Corp, 212 Tower Bridge Rd, London SE1 2UP, England	
Benn, Tony	*Government Official, England*
%House of Commons, Westminster, London SW1A 0AA, England	
Bennack, Frank A, Jr	*Publisher*
%Hearst Corp, 959 8th Ave, New York, NY 10019, USA	
Bennett, Alan	*Playwright, Actor*
%A D Peters, Chambers, Chelsea Harbour, Lots Rd, London SW10 OXF, England	
Bennett, Bruce (Herman Brix)	*Actor, Track Athlete*
2702 Forester Rd, Los Angeles, CA 90064, USA	
Bennett, Cornelius	*Football Player*
%Buffalo Bills, 1 Bills Dr, Orchard Park, NY 14127, USA	
Bennett, David M	*Navy Admiral*
Inspector General, Navy Dept, Washington Naval Yard, Washington, DC 20374, USA	
Bennett, Donald D	*Businessman*
%Richfood Holdings, 2000 Richfood Rd, Richmond, VA 23261, USA	
Bennett, Emmett L	*Classical Scholar*
%University of Wisconsin, Classics Dept, Madison, WI 53706, USA	
Bennett, Hywel	*Actor*
%James Sharkey Assoc, 21 Golden Square, London W1R 3PA, England	
Bennett, Jack F	*Businessman*
141 Taconic Rd, Greenwich, CT 06831, USA	
Bennett, Jill	*Actress*
%James Sharkey Assoc, 21 Golden Square, London W1R 3PA, England	
Bennett, Mario	*Basketball Player*
%Phoenix Suns, 201 E Jefferson St, Phoenix, AZ 85004, USA	
Bennett, Nelson	*Skier*
807 S 20th Ave, Yakima, WA 98902, USA	
Bennett, Richard Rodney	*Composer*
%Lemon & Durbridge, 24 Pottery Lane, Holland Park, London W11 4LZ, England	
Bennett, Robert F	*Governor, KS*
9535 Ash St, #211, Shawnee Mission, KS 66207, USA	
Bennett, Robert J	*Financier*
%ONBANCorp, 101 S Salina St, Syracuse, NY 13202, USA	
Bennett, Robert R	*Businessman*
%Home Shopping Network, 2501 118th Ave N, St Petersburg, FL 33716, USA	
Bennett, Robert S	*Attorney*
%Skadden Arps Slate Meagher Flom, 1440 New York Ave NW, Washington, DC 20005, USA	
Bennett, Tony	*Singer*
%Tony Bennett Enterprises, 101 W 55th St; #9-J, New York, NY 10019, USA	

Benetton - Bennett

Bennett, Tony *Football Player*
%Green Bay Packers, 1265 Lombardi Ave, Green Bay, WI 54304, USA

Bennett, Tracie *Actress*
%Annette Stone, 9 Newburgh St, London W1V 1LH, England

Bennett, Ward *Interior Designer*
%Dakota Hotel, 1 W 72nd St, PH-A, New York, NY 10023, USA

Bennett, William G *Businessman*
%Circus Circus Enterprises, 2880 Las Vegas Blvd S, Las Vegas, NV 89109, USA

Bennett, William J *Secretary, Education*
%Hudson Institute, 4401 Ford Ave, Alexandria, VA 22302, USA

Bennett, William M *Financier*
%Bank One Columbus, 100 E Broad St, Columbus, OH 43215, USA

Bennis, Warren G *Educator, Writer*
%University of Southern California, Management School, Los Angeles, CA 90007, USA

Benoit Samuelson, Joan *Marathon Runner*
95 Lower Flying Point Rd, Freeport, ME 04032, USA

Benoit, David *Jazz Pianist*
%Fitzgerald-Hartley-Simmons, 50 W Main St, Ventura, CA 93001, USA

Benshoff, Janet *Attorney, Women's Activist*
%Center for Reproductive Law & Policy, 120 Wall St, New York, NY 10005, USA

Benson, Andrew A *Biochemist, Plant Physiologist*
6044 Folsom Dr, La Jolla, CA 92037, USA

Benson, David F *Financier*
%Meditrust, 197 1st Ave, Needham Heights, MA 02194, USA

Benson, David R *Businessman*
%Cabletron Systems, 35 Industrial Way, Rochester, NH 03867, USA

Benson, George *Jazz Guitarist*
%Ken Fritz Mgmt, 648 N Robertson Blvd, Los Angeles, CA 90069, USA

Benson, Robby *Actor*
PO Box 1305, Woodland Hills, CA 91365, USA

Benson, Sidney W *Chemist*
1110 N Bundy Dr, Los Angeles, CA 90049, USA

Benson, Stephen R *Editorial Cartoonist*
%Arizona Republic, Editorial Dept, PO Box 1950, Phoenix, AZ 85001, USA

Benson, Tom *Football Executive*
%New Orleans Saints, 1500 Poydras St, New Orleans, LA 70112, USA

Bentas, Lily *Businesswoman*
%Cumberland Farms, 777 Dedham St, Canton, MA 02021, USA

Benter, Steven D *Financier*
%City National Corp, 400 N Roxbury Dr, Beverly Hills, CA 90210, USA

Bentley, Eric *Writer*
194 Riverside Dr, New York, NY 10025, USA

Bentley, John *Actor*
Wedgewood House, Peterworth, Sussex, England

Bentley, Stacey *Body Builder*
PO Box 26, Santa Monica, CA 90406, USA

Benton, Barbi *Model, Actress*
40 N 4th St, Carbondale, CO 81623, USA

Benton, Fletcher *Artist*
250 Dore St, San Francisco, CA 94103, USA

Benton, Jim *Football Player*
6200 Timber Ridge Dr, Pine Bluff, AR 71603, USA

Benton, Robert *Movie Director*
%International Creative Mgmt, 40 W 57th St, New York, NY 10019, USA

Bentsen, Lloyd M, Jr *Secretary, Treasury*
123 N Post Oak Lane, #400, Houston, TX 77024, USA

Bentyne, Cheryl *Singer (Manhattan Transfer)*
%Sony/Columbia/CBS Records, 2100 Colorado Ave, Santa Monica, CA 90404, USA

Benz, Sepp *Bobsled Athlete*
Kiefernweg 37, 8057 Zurich, Switzerland

Benzali, Daniel *Actor*
%Paul Kohner Inc, 9300 Wilshire Blvd, #555, Beverly Hills, CA 90212, USA

Benzer, Seymour *Biologist*
2075 Robin Rd, San Marino, CA 91108, USA

Benzi, Roberto *Conductor*
12 Villa St Foy, 92200 Neuilly-sur-Seine, France

Beradino, John *Actor*
1719 Ambassador Dr, Beverly Hills, CA 90210, USA

B

Bennett - Beradino

B

Beran, Bruce *Coast Guard Admiral*
Commander, Pacific Area, US Coast Guard, Coast Guard Island, Alameda, CA 94501, USA

Beran, Timothy *Financier*
%Barclays Bank, 54 Lombard St, London EC3P 3AH, England

Beras Rojas, Octavio Antonio Cardinal *Religious Leader*
Arzobispade, Apartado 186, Santo Domingo, Dominican Republic

Berbick, Trevor *Boxer*
%Carl King, Don King Productions, 32 E 69th St, New York, NY 10021, USA

Bercu, Michaela *Model*
%Elite Model Mgmt, 111 E 22nd St, #200, New York, NY 10010, USA

Berdahl, Robert M *Educator*
%University of Texas, President's Office, Austin, TX 78713, USA

Bere, Richard L *Businessman*
%Kroger Co, 1014 Vine St, Cincinnati, OH 45202, USA

Berenblum, Isaac *Pathologist*
%Weizmann Institute of Science, Pathology Dept, Rehovot, Israel

Berendzen, Richard E *Educator*
1300 Crystal Dr, Arlington, VA 22202, USA

Berenger, Tom *Actor*
853 7th Ave, #9-A, New York, NY 10019, USA

Berenson, Marisa *Actress*
80 Ave Charles de Gaulle, 92200 Neuilly, France

Beresford, Bruce *Movie Director*
3 Marathon Rd, #13, Darling Point, Sydney NSW, Australia

Beresford, Meg *Social Activist*
Abbey, Iona Community, Argull PA76 6SW, Scotland

Berezovi, Anatoli N *Cosmonaut*
%Potchta Kosmonavtov, 141 160 Svyosdny Gorodok, Moskovskoi Oblasti, Russia

Berg, Bengt *Businessman*
%Strarsforetag Group, Hamngatan 6, 103 97, Stockholm, Sweden

Berg, Jeffrey S *Entertainment Executive*
%International Creative Mgmt, 8942 Wilshire Blvd, Beverly Hills, CA 90211, USA

Berg, John P *Businessman*
%Greif Bros Corp, 621 Pennsylvania Ave, Delaware, OH 43015, USA

Berg, Patty *Golfer*
PO Box 9227, Fort Myers, FL 33902, USA

Berg, Paul *Nobel Chemistry Laureate*
%Stanford University Medical School, Beckman Center, Stanford, CA 94305, USA

Berganza, Teresa *Opera Singer*
Cafeto #5, Madrid 7, Spain

Berge, Ole M *Labor Leader*
%Maintenance of Way Brotherhood, 12050 Woodward Ave, Detroit, MI 48203, USA

Berge, Pierre V G *Businessman*
%Yves Saint Laurent SA, 5 Ave Marceau, 75116 Paris, France

Bergen, Candice *Actress*
222 Central Park South, New York, NY 10019, USA

Bergen, Frances *Actress*
1485 Carla Ridge Dr, Beverly Hills, CA 90210, USA

Bergen, Polly *Actress*
11342 Dona Lisa Dr, Studio City, CA 91604, USA

Bergen, William B *Aerospace Engineer*
%Aerospatiale, 37 Rue de Montmorency, 75016 Paris, France

Berger, Frank M *Biologist*
515 E 72nd St, New York, NY 10021, USA

Berger, Gerhard *Auto Racing Driver*
%Eurotrans, Radfeld 12-A, 6250 Kundl, Austria

Berger, Helmut *Actor*
Pundterplatz 6, 80803 Munich, Germany

Berger, John *Writer, Critic*
Quincy, Mieussy, 74440 Taninges, France

Berger, Miles *Financier*
%Heitman Financial, 180 N LaSalle St, Chicago, IL 60601, USA

Berger, Peter L *Sociologist*
%Boston University, Sociology Dept, Boston, MA 02215, USA

Berger, Richard L *Entertainment Executive*
%Cinetropolis, 4540 W Valerio St, Burbank, CA 91505, USA

Berger, Senta *Actress*
Robert-Koch-Str 10, 12621 Grunewald, Germany

Berger, Thomas L *Writer*
PO Box 11, Palisades, NY 10964, USA

Bergere, Lee *Actor*
2385 Century Hill, Los Angeles, CA 90067, USA

Bergey, William E (Bill) *Football Player*
2 Hickory Lane, Chadds Ford, PA 19317, USA

Berggren, Thommy *Actor*
%Swedish Film Institute, Kungsgatan 48, Stockholm C, Sweden

Berghaus, Ruth *Theater Director*
%Deutsche Staatsoper, Unter Den Linden 7, 10117 Berlin, Germany

Bergin, Michael *Model*
%Click Model Mgmt, 881 7th Ave, New York, NY 10019, USA

Bergin, Patrick *Actor*
%Caroline Dawson Assoc, 47 Courtfield Rd, #9, London SW7 4DB, England

Bergland, Robert S *Secretary, Agriculture*
Rt 3, Roseau, MN 56751, USA

Berglund, Dennis C *Financier*
%Century Acceptance Corp, City Center Square, Kansas City, MO 64196, USA

Berglund, Paavo A E *Conductor*
Munkkiniemenranta 41, 00330 Helsinki 33, Finland

Bergman, Alan *Lyricist*
714 N Maple Dr, Beverly Hills, CA 90210, USA

Bergman, Andrew C *Playwright, Movie Director*
555 W 57th St, #1230, New York, NY 10019, USA

Bergman, Ingmar *Movie Director*
%Swedish Film Institute, PO Box 27126, 102 52 Stockholm, Sweden

Bergman, Klaus *Businessman*
%Allegheny Power System, 12 E 49th St, #4900, New York, NY 10017, USA

Bergman, Marilyn K *Lyricist*
714 N Maple Dr, Beverly Hills, CA 90210, USA

Bergman, Martin *Movie Producer*
641 Lexington Ave, New York, NY 10022, USA

Bergman, Peter *Actor*
4799 White Oak Ave, Encino, CA 91316, USA

Bergman, Sandahl *Actress*
9903 Santa Monica Blvd, #274, Beverly Hills, CA 90212, USA

Bergmann, Arnfinn *Ski Jumper*
Nils Collett Vogtsv 58, 0765 Oslo 7, Norway

Bergonzi, Carlo *Opera Singer*
%A Ziliani ALCI, Via Paolo da Cannobio 2, 120122 Milan, Italy

Bergquist, Curt *Immunologist*
%Allergon AB, Valinge 2090, 262 92 Angelholm, Sweden

Bergson, Abram *Economist*
334 Marshall St, Belmont, MA 02178, USA

Bergsten, C Fred *Economist*
4106 Sleepy Hollow Rd, Annandale, VA 22003, USA

Bergstrom, K Sune *Nobel Medicine Laureate*
%Karolinska Institute, Nobelkansli Box 60250, 104 01 Stockholm, Sweden

Berio, Luciano *Composer*
Il Colombaio, Radicondoli, 53100 Siena, Italy

Beriosova, Svetlana *Ballerina*
10 Palliser Ct, Palliser Rd, London W14, England

Berisha, Sali *President, Albania*
%President's Office, Keshilli i Ministrave, Tirana, Albania

Berkeley, Michael F *Composer*
%Rogers Coleridge White, 20 Powis Mews, London W11 1JN, England

Berkley, Elizabeth *Actress, Model*
%United Talent Agency, 9560 Wilshire Blvd, Beverly Hills, CA 90212, USA

Berkley, William R *Businessman*
%W R Berkley Corp, 165 Mason St, Greenwich, CT 06830, USA

Berkoff, David *Swimmer*
%Harvard University, Athletic Dept, Cambridge, MA 02138, USA

Berkowitz, Bob *Entertainer*
%CNBC-TV, 2200 Fletcher Ave, Fort Lee, NJ 07024, USA

Berlant, Anthony (Tony) *Artist*
%Los Angeles Louver Gallery, 55 N Venice Blvd, Venice, CA 90291, USA

Berle, Milton *Comedian*
10750 Wilshire Blvd, #1102, Los Angeles, CA 90017, USA

B

Berger - Berle

Berlin, Isaiah *Philosopher*
Headington House, Old High St, Headington, Oxford OX3 9HU, England

Berliner, Robert W *Physician*
36 Edgehill Terrace, New Haven, CT 06517, USA

Berlinger, Warren *Actor*
10642 Arnel Pl, Chatsworth, CA 91311, USA

Berlinsky, Dmitri *Concert Violinist*
35 W 64th St, #7-F, New York, NY 10023, USA

Berlitz, Charles F *Linguist, Writer, Archaeologist*
2816 NE 25th Ct, Fort Lauderdale, FL 33305, USA

Berlusconi, Silvio *Prime Minister, Italy*
Palazzo Chigi, Piazza Colonna 370, 00187 Rome, Italy

Berman, Chris *Sportscaster*
%ESPN-TV, Sports Dept, ESPN Plaza, 935 Middle St, Bristol, CT 06010, USA

Berman, Julius *Religious Leader, Attorney*
%Kaye Scholer Fierman, 425 Park Ave, New York, NY 10022, USA

Berman, Lazar *Concert Pianist*
%Jacques Leiser Artists, Dorchester Towers, 155 W 68th St, New York, NY 10023, USA

Berman, Michael A *Financier*
%Nomura Securities, 2 World Financial Center, 200 Liberty St, New York, NY 10281, USA

Berman, Pandro S *Movie Producer*
914 N Roxbury Dr, Beverly Hills, CA 90210, USA

Berman, Shelley *Comedian*
268 Bell Canyon Rd, Bell Canyon, CA 91307, USA

Bernard, Crystal *Actress, Singer, Songwriter*
%Cedar Mgmt, 10866 Wilshire Blvd, #1200, Los Angeles, CA 90024, USA

Bernard, Ed *Actor*
PO Box 7965, Northridge, CA 91327, USA

Bernard, James W *Businessman*
%Univar Corp, 6100 Carron Point, Kirkland, WA 98033, USA

Bernard, Jason *Actor*
%Paul Kohner Inc, 9300 Wilshire Blvd, #555, Beverly Hills, CA 90212, USA

Bernardin, Joseph L Cardinal *Religious Leader*
%Archdiocese of Chicago, 1555 N State Parkway, Chicago, IL 60610, USA

Bernhard *Prince, Netherlands*
%Soestdijk Palace, Baarn, Netherlands

Bernhard, Ruth *Photographer*
2982 Clay St, San Francisco, CA 94115, USA

Bernhard, Sandra *Actress*
%Levine/Schneider, 433 N Camden Dr, Beverly Hills, CA 90210, USA

Bernhardt, Glenn R *Cartoonist*
PO Box 3772, Carmel, CA 93921, USA

Bernheimer, Martin *Music Critic*
%Los Angeles Times, Editorial Dept, Times-Mirror Sq, Los Angeles, CA 90012, USA

Bernick, Carol L *Businesswoman*
%Alberto-Culver Co, 2525 Armitage Ave, Melrose Park, IL 60160, USA

Bernick, Howard B *Businessman*
%Alberto-Culver Co, 2525 Armitage Ave, Melrose Park, IL 60160, USA

Bernier, Sylvie *Diver*
%Olympic Assn, Cite du Harve, Montreal PQ H3C 3R4, Canada

Berning, Susie *Golfer*
PO Box 321, Kailena Kona, HI 96745, USA

Bernsen, Corbin *Actor*
3541 N Knoll Dr, Los Angeles, CA 90068, USA

Bernstein, Carl *Journalist*
12 Hunters Horn Ct, Owing Mills, MD 21117, USA

Bernstein, Elmer *Composer*
2715 Pearl St, Santa Monica, CA 90405, USA

Bernstein, Jay L *Movie Producer, Agent*
%Jay Bernstein Productions, PO Box 1148, Beverly Hills, CA 90213, USA

Bernstein, Kenny *Auto Racing Driver*
1105 Seminole, Richardson, TX 75080, USA

Bernstein, Richard A *Businessman*
%Western Publishing Group, 444 Madison Ave, New York, NY 10022, USA

Bernstein, Robert L *Publisher*
%John Wiley & Sons, 605 3rd Ave, New York, NY 10158, USA

Bernstein, Zalman C *Financier*
%Sanford C Bernstein Co, 767 5th Ave, New York, NY 10153, USA

Berlin - Bernstein

Bernthal, Frederick W — *Businessman*
%BASF Corp, 3000 Continental Dr N, Mt Olive, NJ 07828, USA

Berov, Lyuben — *Prime Minister, Bulgaria*
%Prime Minister's Office, 1 Dondukov Blvd, 1000 Sofia, Bulgaria

Berra, Lawrence P (Yogi) — *Baseball Player, Manager*
19 Highland Ave, Montclair, NJ 07042, USA

Berri, Claude — *Movie Director, Producer*
%Renn Productions, 10 Rue Lincoln, 75008 Paris, France

Berrigan, Daniel — *Clergyman, Social Activist*
220 W 98th St, #11-L, New York, NY 10025, USA

Berruti, Livio — *Track Athlete*
Via Avigliana 45, 10138 Torino, Italy

Berry, Bill — *Skiing Writer*
839 N Center St, Reno, NV 89501, USA

Berry, Bill — *Drummer (REM)*
%REM/Athens Ltd, 250 W Clayton St, Athens, GA 30601, USA

Berry, Bob — *Hockey Coach*
%St Louis Blues, St Louis Arena, 5700 Oakland Ave, St Louis, MO 63110, USA

Berry, Chuck — *Singer, Songwriter*
Berry Park, 691 Buckner Rd, Wentzville, MO 63385, USA

Berry, Halle — *Actress*
4173 Tattershall Dr, Decatur, GA 30034, USA

Berry, Jan — *Singer (Jan & Dean), Songwriter*
%Jan & Dean Music Co, 1720 N Ross St, Santa Ana, CA 92706, USA

Berry, Jim — *Editorial Cartoonist*
%NEA Syndicate, 200 Park Ave, New York, NY 10166, USA

Berry, John — *Singer*
%Corlew-O'Grady Mgmt, 1503 17th Ave S, Nashville, TN 37212, USA

Berry, Ken — *Actor*
4704 Cahuenga Blvd, North Hollywood, CA 91602, USA

Berry, Kevin — *Swimmer*
28 George St, Manly NSW 2295, Australia

Berry, Michael J — *Chemist*
PO Box 1421, Pebble Beach, CA 93953, USA

Berry, Stephen J — *Journalist*
241 Stevenage Dr, Longwood, FL 32779, USA

Berry, Walter — *Basketball Player*
%Houston Rockets, Summit, Greenway Plaza, #10, Houston, TX 77277, USA

Berry, Walter — *Opera Singer*
Kahlenbergerstr 82, 1190 Vienna, Austria

Berry, Wendell — *Writer, Ecologist*
River Rd, Port Royal, KY 40058, USA

Berson, Jerome A — *Chemist*
45 Bayberry Rd, Hamden, CT 06517, USA

Berst, David — *Sports Investigator*
%National Collegiate Athletic Assn, 6201 College Blvd, Overland Park, KS 66211, USA

Bersticker, Albert C — *Businessman*
%Ferro Corp, 1000 Lakeside Ave, Cleveland, OH 44114, USA

Bertelli, Angelo B — *Football Player*
22 Springdale Ct, Clifton, NJ 07013, USA

Bertil — *Prince, Sweden*
Hert Av Halland, Kungl Slottet, 111 30 Stockholm, Sweden

Bertinelli, Valerie — *Actress*
PO Box 1984, Studio City, CA 91614, USA

Bertoli, Paolo Cardinal — *Religious Leader*
Piazza della Citta Leonina 1, 00193 Rome, Italy

Bertolucci, Bernardo — *Movie Director*
Via Della Lungara 3, 00165 Rome, Italy

Berton, Pierre — *Historian*
%Pierre Berton Enterprises, 21 Sackville St, Toronto ON M5A 3E1, Canada

Bertrand, Frederic H — *Businessman*
%National Life Insurance, 1 National Life Dr, Montpelier, VT 05604, USA

Bertuccelli, Jean-Louis A — *Movie Director*
9 Rue Benard, 75014 Paris, France

Berube, Daniel T — *Businessman*
%Montana Power Co, 40 E Broadway, Butte, MT 59707, USA

Berwanger, John J (Jay) — *Football Player*
1245 Warren Ave, Downers Grove, IL 60515, USA

B

Bernthal - Berwanger

B

Besch, Bibi — *Actress*
%Gold Marshak Assoc, 3500 W Olive Ave, #1400, Burbank, CA 91505, USA

Bessell, Ted — *Actor*
1454 Stone Canyon Rd, Los Angeles, CA 90077, USA

Bessey, Edward C — *Businessman*
%Pfizer Inc, 235 W 42nd St, New York, NY 10036, USA

Bessmertnova, Natalia — *Ballerina*
%Bolshoi Theater, Teatralnya Pl 1, 103009 Moscow, Russia

Besson, Luc — *Movie Director*
%Films du Dauphin, 25 Rue Yves-Toudic, 75010 Paris, France

Best, James — *Actor*
2166 Canyon Dr, Los Angeles, CA 90068, USA

Best, Pete — *Singer, Drummer (Beatles)*
8 Hymans Green, West Derby, Liverpool 12, England

Best, Travis — *Basketball Player*
%Indiana Pacers, Market Square Arena, 300 E Market St, Indianapolis, IN 46204, USA

Beswicke, Martine — *Actress*
131 S Sycamore Ave, Los Angeles, CA 90036, USA

Bethe, Hans A — *Nobel Physics Laureate*
%Cornell University, Nuclear Studies Laboratory, Ithaca, NY 14853, USA

Bethea, Elvin L — *Football Player*
16211 Leslie Lane, Missouri City, TX 77489, USA

Bethune, Gordon M — *Businessman*
%Continental Airlines, 2929 Allen Parkway, Houston, TX 77019, USA

Bethune, Zina — *Actress*
3096 Lake Hollywood Dr, Los Angeles, CA 90068, USA

Bettenhausen, Gary — *Auto Racing Driver*
2550 Tree Farm Rd, Martinsville, IN 46151, USA

Bettenhausen, Tony — *Auto Racing Driver*
7616 Ballinshire S, Indianapolis, IN 46254, USA

Bettger, Lyle — *Actor*
PO Box 1076, Pai, HI 96779, USA

Bettis, Jerome — *Football Player*
%St Louis Rams, 100 N Broadway, #2100, St Louis, MO 63102, USA

Bettis, Valerie — *Dancer, Choreographer*
%Valerie Bettis Dance Studio, 22 W 15th St, New York, NY 10011, USA

Bettman, Gary B — *Hockey Executive*
%National Hockey League, 650 5th Ave, #3300, New York, NY 10019, USA

Bettmann, Otto L — *Photo Archivist*
3001 Deer Creek Blvd, #563, Deerfield Beach, FL 33442, USA

Bettors, Doug — *Football Player*
%Miami Dolphins, 7500 SW 30th St, Davie, FL 33329, USA

Betts, Virginia Trotter — *Labor Leader*
%American Nurses Assn, 600 Maryland Ave SW, Washington, DC 20024, USA

Betz Addie, Pauline — *Tennis Player*
%Bidwell Friends School, Washington, DC 20000, USA

Beutel, Bill — *Commentator*
%WABC-TV, News Dept, 7 Lincoln Square, New York, NY 10023, USA

Bevan, Timothy H — *Financier*
%Barclay's Bank, 54 Lombard St, London EC3P 3AH, England

Beverly, Joe E — *Financier*
%Synovus Financial Corp, 901 Front St, Columbus, GA 31901, USA

Beverly, Nick — *Hockey Executive*
%Los Angeles Kings, Forum, PO Box 17013, Inglewood, CA 90308, USA

Bevilacqua, Anthony J Cardinal — *Religious Leader*
%Office of the Archbishop, 222 N 17th St, Philadelphia, PA 19103, USA

Bevis, Leslie — *Actress*
%Epstein-Wyckoff, 280 S Beverly Dr, #400, Beverly Hills, CA 90212, USA

Bey, Richard — *Entertainer*
445 Park Ave, #1000, New York, NY 10022, USA

Beymer, Richard — *Actor*
1818 N Fuller Ave, Los Angeles, CA 90046, USA

Beyster, J Robert — *Businessman*
%Science Applications International, 10260 Campus Point Dr, San Diego, CA 92121, USA

Bezombes, Roger — *Artist*
3 Quai Saint-Michel, 75005 Paris, France

Bhagwati, Jagdish — *Economist*
%Columbia University, Economics Dept, New York, NY 10027, USA

B

Bhandari Ram, Subadar — *WW II Indian Army Hero (VC)*
Vill & Po Auhar, Teh Ghumarwin, Distt Bilaspur HP, India

Bhatarai, Krishna Prasad — *Prime Minister, Nepal*
%Congress Central Office, Baneshwar, Kathmandu, Nepal

Bhattacharya, Basu — *Movie Director*
%Gold Mist, 36 Carter Rd, Bandra, Bombay 50, India

Bhumibol Adulyadej — *King, Thailand*
%Chitralada Villa, Bangkok, Thailand

Bhutto, Benazir — *Prime Minister, Pakistan*
%Prime Minister's Office, Old State Bank Bldg, Islamabad, Pakistan

Bialik, Mayim — *Actress*
1529 N Cahuenga Blvd, #19, Los Angeles, CA 90028, USA

Bianchi, Al — *Basketball Player, Coach*
%Miami Heat, Miami Arena, Miami, FL 33136, USA

Biasucci, Dean — *Football Player*
%Pittsburgh Steelers, 3 Rivers Stadium, 300 Stadium Circle, Pittsburgh, PA 15212, USA

Bibb, John — *Sportswriter*
%Nashville Tennessean, Editorial Dept, 1100 Broadway, Nashville, TN 37203, USA

Bible, Geoffrey C — *Businessman*
%Philip Morris Companies, 120 Park Ave, New York, NY 10017, USA

Bich, Bruno — *Businessman*
%BIC Corp, 500 Bic Dr, Milford, CT 06460, USA

Bickel, Stephen D — *Businessman*
%Variable Annuity Life Insurance, 2929 Allen Parkway, Houston, TX 77019, USA

Bickerstaff, Bernard T (Bernie) — *Basketball Coach, Executive*
%Denver Nuggets, McNichols Arena, 1635 Clay St, Denver, CO 80204, USA

Bickett, Duane — *Football Player*
%Seattle Seahawks, 11220 NE 53rd St, Kirkland, WA 98033, USA

Biddle, Melvin E — *WW II Army Hero (CMH)*
918 Essex Dr, Anderson, IN 46013, USA

Bidwell, John G — *Businessman*
%Winterthur Reinsurance Corp, 225 Liberty St, New York, NY 10281, USA

Bidwell, William V — *Football Executive*
%Arizona Cardinals, 8701 S Hardy Dr, Tempe, AZ 85284, USA

Bieber, Owen F — *Labor Leader*
%United Auto Workers Union, 8000 E Jefferson Ave, Detroit, MI 48214, USA

Biederman, Charles J — *Artist*
5840 Collischan Rd, Red Wing, MN 55066, USA

Biegler, David W — *Businessman*
%Lone Star Gas Co, 301 S Harwood St, Dallas, TX 75201, USA

Biehn, Michael — *Actor*
3737 Deervale Dr, Sherman Oaks, CA 91403, USA

Bieka, Silvestre Siale — *Prime Minister, Equatorial Guinea*
%Prime Minister's Office, Malabo, Equatorial Guinea

Bielecki, J Krzysztof — *Prime Minister, Poland*
%Prime Minister's Office, Ursad Rady Ministrow, 00-583 Warsaw, Poland

Biellmann, Denise — *Figure Skater*
Im Brachli 25, 8053 Zurich, Switzerland

Bieniemy, Eric — *Football Player*
%San Diego Chargers, Jack Murphy Stadium, San Diego, CA 92160, USA

Bietila, Walter — *Skier*
%General Delivery, Iron Mountain, MI 49801, USA

Biffi, Giacomo Cardinal — *Religious Leader*
Archdiocese of Bologna, Via Altabella 6, 40126 Bologna, Italy

Bigeleisen, Jacob — *Chemist*
PO Box 217, Saint James, NY 11780, USA

Biggs, Jeremy H — *Financier*
%Fiduciary Trust Co, 2 World Trade Center, New York, NY 10048, USA

Biggs, John H — *Businessman*
%TIAA-CREF, 730 3rd Ave, New York, NY 10017, USA

Biggs, Richard — *Actor*
728 W 28th St, Los Angeles, CA 90007, USA

Biggs, Tyrell — *Boxer*
%Cross Country Concert Corp, 310 Madison Ave, New York, NY 10017, USA

Bigley, Thomas J — *Navy Admiral*
423 Dillingham Blvd, Norfolk, VA 23511, USA

Bignotti, George — *Auto Racing Mechanic*
%Bignotti Enterprises, 7802 Eagle Creek Overlook Dr, Indianapolis, IN 46254, USA

Bhandari Ram - Bignotti

B

Bijan — *Fashion Designer*
699 5th Ave, New York, NY 10022, USA

Bikel, Theodore — *Actor, Singer*
94 Honey Hill Rd, Wilton, CT 06897, USA

Bildt, Carl — *Prime Minister, Sweden*
Stratradsbereduingen, 103 33 Stockholm, Sweden

Bileck, Pam — *Gymnast*
5742 McFadden Ave, Huntington Beach, CA 92649, USA

Biletnikoff, Fred — *Football Player, Coach*
%Oakland Raiders, Oakland Coliseum, Oakland, CA 94621, USA

Bilheimer, Robert S — *Religious Leader*
15256 Knightwood Rd, Cold Spring, MN 56320, USA

Bill, Tony — *Producer, Actor*
%Market Street Productions, 73 Market St, Venice, CA 90291, USA

Biller, Morris (Moe) — *Labor Leader*
%American Postal Workers Union, 1300 "L" St NW, Washington, DC 20005, USA

Billings, Marland P — *Geologist*
Westside Rd, RFD, North Conway, NH 03860, USA

Billingslea, Beau — *Actor*
6025 Sepulveda Blvd, #201, Van Nuys, CA 91411, USA

Billingsley, Barbara — *Actress*
PO Box 1320, Santa Monica, CA 90406, USA

Billingsley, Hobie — *Diving Coach*
%Indiana University, Athletic Dept, Bloomington, IN 47405, USA

Billingsley, Ray — *Cartoonist (Curtis)*
%King Features Syndicate, 216 E 45th St, New York, NY 10017, USA

Billington, Craig — *Hockey Player*
%Boston Bruins, Boston Garden, 150 Causeway St, Boston, MA 02114, USA

Billington, James H — *Historian, Librarian*
%Library of Congress, 101 Independence Ave SE, Washington, DC 20540, USA

Bilson, Bruce — *Television Director*
%Downwind Enterprises, 12505 Sarah St, Studio City, CA 91604, USA

Bilson, Malcolm — *Concert Pianist*
132 N Sunset Dr, Ithaca, NY 14850, USA

Binder, Gordon M — *Businessman*
%Amgen Inc, 1840 DeHavilland Dr, Thousand Oaks, CA 91320, USA

Binder, John — *Religious Leader*
%North American Baptist Conference, 1 S 210 Summit, Oakbrook Terrace, IL 60181, USA

Binder, Theodore — *Physician*
Taos Canyon, Taos, NM 87571, USA

Bindley, William E — *Businessman*
%Bindley Western Industries, 4212 W 71st St, Indianapolis, IN 46268, USA

Bing, Dave — *Basketball Player*
%Bing Steel Inc, 1130 N Grand Blvd, Detroit, MI 48208, USA

Bing, Ilse — *Photographer*
210 Riverside Dr, #6-G, New York, NY 10025, USA

Bing, R H — *Mathematician*
%University of Texas, Mathematics Dept, Austin, TX 78712, USA

Bingham, Barry, Jr — *Editor, Publisher*
%Louisville Courier Journal & Times, 525 W Broadway, Louisville, KY 40202, USA

Bingham, Eula — *Educator*
%University of Cincinnati, Graduate Studies Office, Cincinnati, OH 45221, USA

Bingham, Jean — *Financier*
%BarclaysAmerican/Mortgage Corp, 8 Parkway Plaza, Charlotte, NC 28217, USA

Binnig, Gerd K — *Nobel Physics Laureate*
%IBM Research Laboratory, Saumerstr 4, 8803 Ruschlikon, Switzerland

Binns, Malcolm — *Concert Pianist*
233 Court Rd, Orpington, Kent BR6 9BY, England

Binoche, Juliette — *Actress*
%Agency Marceline Lenoir, 99 Blvd Marlesherbes, 75008 Paris, France

Bintley, David — *Choreographer*
%Royal Ballet, Bow St, London WC2E 9DD, England

Biondi, Frank J, Jr — *Businessman*
%Viacom International Inc, 1515 Broadway, New York, NY 10036, USA

Biondi, Matt — *Swimmer*
%Nicholas A Biondi, 1404 Rimer Dr, Moraga, CA 94556, USA

Biondi, Michael J — *Financier*
%Wasserstein Perella Group, 31 W 52nd St, New York, NY 10019, USA

Bijan - Biondi

Birch, L Charles *Zoologist*
5-A/73 Yarranabbe Rd, Darling Point, NSW 2027, Australia

Birchard, Bruce *Religious Leader*
%Friends General Conference, 1216 Arch St, Philadelphia, PA 19107, USA

Birchby, Kenneth L *Financier*
%Hudson City Savings Bank, W 80 Century Rd, Paramus, NJ 07652, USA

Bird, Caroline *Writer, Social Activist*
31 Sunrise Lane, Poughkeepsie, NY 12603, USA

Bird, Larry J *Basketball Player*
6278 N Federal Highway, #296, Fort Lauderdale, FL 33308, USA

Bird, Vere C, Sr *Prime Minister, Antigua & Barbuda*
%Prime Minister's Office, Factory Rd, St John's, Antigua

Birenbaum, William M *Educator*
108 Willow St, Brooklyn, NY 11201, USA

Birendra Bir Bikram Shah Dev *King, Nepal*
%Narayanhiti Royal Palace, Durbag Marg, Kathmandu, Nepal

Birk, Roger E *Businessman*
%Federal National Mortgage Assn, 3900 Wisconsin Ave NW, Washington, DC 20016, USA

Birkavs, Valdis *Prime Minister, Latvia*
%Prime Minister's Office, Brivibus Bulv 36, Riga 336170 PDP, Latvia

Birkerts, Gunnar *Architect*
%Gunnar Birkerts Assoc, 292 Harmon St, Birmingham, MI 48009, USA

Birkin, Jane *Actress*
28 Rue de la Tour, 75016 Paris, France

Birman, Len *Actor*
%Michael Mann Mgmt, 8380 Melrose Ave, #207, Los Angeles, CA 90069, USA

Birmingham, Stephen *Writer*
%Brandt & Brandt, 1501 Broadway, New York, NY 10036, USA

Birney, David *Actor*
20 Ocean Park Blvd, #118, Santa Monica, CA 90405, USA

Birney, Earle *Writer*
1201 130 Carlton St, Toronto ON M5A 4K3, Canada

Biroc, Joseph *Cinematographer*
4427 Pettit Ave, Encino, CA 91316, USA

Birren, James E *Gerontologist*
%University of California, Borun Gerontological Center, Los Angeles, CA 90024, USA

Birtwistle, Harrison *Composer*
%Allied Artists, 42 Montpelier Sq, London SW7 1JZ, England

Bisher, J Furman *Sportswriter*
431 Lester Rd, Fayetteville, GA 30215, USA

Bishop, Elvin *Singer*
5028 Geary St, San Francisco, CA 94118, USA

Bishop, J Michael *Nobel Medicine Laureate*
%University of California, G W Hooper Foundation, San Francisco, CA 94143, USA

Bishop, Joey *Comedian*
534 Via Lido Nord, Newport Beach, CA 92663, USA

Bishop, Julie *Actress*
45134 Brest St, Mendocino, CA 95460, USA

Bishop, Keith *Football Player*
%Denver Broncos, 13655 E Dove Valley Parkway, Englewood, CO 80112, USA

Bishop, Stephen *Singer, Songwriter*
2310 Apollo Dr, Los Angeles, CA 90046, USA

Bisoglio, Val *Actor*
11684 Ventura Blvd, #476, Studio City, CA 91604, USA

Bisplinghoff, Raymond L *Aeronautical Engineer*
Tyco Laboratories, Tycor Park, Exeter, NH 03833, USA

Bissell, Charles O *Editorial Cartoonist*
4221 Farrar Ave, Nashville, TN 37215, USA

Bissell, Phil *Cartoonist*
5 Shetland Rd, Rockport, MA 01966, USA

Bissell, Whit *Actor*
2953 Valencia Dr, Santa Barbara, CA 93105, USA

Bisset, Jacqueline *Actress*
1815 Benedict Canyon Dr, Beverly Hills, CA 90210, USA

Bissett, Josie *Actress*
10350 Wilshire Blvd, #502, Los Angeles, CA 90024, USA

Bista, Kirti Nidhi *Prime Minister, Nepal*
Gyaneshawor, Kathmandu, Nepal

B

Birch - Bista

B

Biswas, Abdul Rahmana *President, Bangladesh*
%President's Office, Old Sangsad Bhaban, 12 Bangabhaban, Dhaka, Bangladesh

Bittner, Armin *Skier*
Rauchbergstr 30, 83334 Izell, Germany

Bittner, Ronald L *Businessman*
%Frontier Corp, 180 S Clinton Ave, Rochester, NY 14646, USA

Bixby, Joseph R *Businessman*
%Kansas City Life Insurance, 3520 Broadway, Kansas City, MO 64111, USA

Bixby, Walter E *Businessman*
%Kansas City Life Insurance, 3520 Broadway, Kansas City, MO 64111, USA

Biya, Paul *President, Cameroon Republic*
%Palais Presidentiel, Rue de L'Exploration, Yaounde, Cameroon Republic

Bizimungu, Pasteur *President, Rwanda*
%President's Office, Church St, Boite Postale 15, Kigali, Rwanda

Bizzaro, Angelo D *Businessman*
%Caterair International, 6550 Rock Spring Dr, Bethesda, MD 20817, USA

Bjedov-Gabrilo, Djurdjica *Swimmer*
Brace Santini 33, 5800 Split, Yugoslavia

Bjork *Singer, Songwriter*
2029 Century Park East, #600, Los Angeles, CA 90067, USA

Bjork, Anita *Actress*
AB Baggensgatan 9, 1131 Stockholm, Sweden

Bjorklund, Anders *Neurologist*
%University of Lund, Neurology Dept, Lund, Sweden

Bjorn, Anna *Actress, Model*
%Paul Kohner Inc, 9300 Wilshire Blvd, #555, Beverly Hills, CA 90212, USA

Bjornstrand, Gunnar *Actor*
Svalhas Alle 8-A, 182 63 Djursholm, Sweden

Black, Cathleen P *Publisher*
%Newspaper Assn of America, 11600 Sunrise Valley Dr, Reston, VA 22091, USA

Black, Charles L, Jr *Attorney*
%Yale University, Law School, New Haven, CT 06520, USA

Black, Cilla *Singer, Actress*
%Hindworth Mgmt, Regent House, 235-241 Regent St, London W1V 3AU, England

Black, Clint *Singer*
PO Box 299386, Houston, TX 77299, USA

Black, Conrad M *Publisher*
%Hollinger Inc, 10 Toronto St, Toronto ON M5C 2B7, Canada

Black, Daniel J *Businessman*
%Carter-Wallace Inc, Burlington House, 1345 Ave of Americas, New York, NY 10105, USA

Black, James W *Nobel Medicine Laureate*
%University of Dundee, Pharmacology Dept, Dundee DD1 4HN, Scotland

Black, Joe Ed *Golf Executive*
%Professional Golfer's Assn, PO Box 109601, Palm Beach Gardens, FL 33410, USA

Black, Karen *Actress*
%Gold Marshak Assoc, 3500 W Olive Ave, #1400, Burbank, CA 91505, USA

Black, Kent M *Businessman*
%Rockwell International Corp, 2201 Seal Beach Rd, Seal Beach, CA 90740, USA

Black, Lennox K *Businessman*
%Teleflex Inc, 630 W Germantown Pike, Plymouth Meeting, PA 19462, USA

Black, Leon D *Financier*
%Apollo Advisors, 2 Manhattanville Rd, Purchase, NY 10577, USA

Black, Mary *Singer*
%Mainstage Mgmt, 22 Spindrift Way, Annapolis, MD 21403, USA

Black, Robert P *Financier, Government Official*
10 Dahlgren Rd, Richmond, VA 23233, USA

Black, Sena Ayn *Actress*
%Sportscasting Period, 8489 W 3rd St, Los Angeles, CA 90048, USA

Black, Shirley Temple *Actress, Diplomat*
115 Lakeview Dr, Woodside, CA 94062, USA

Black, Stanley *Conductor, Composer*
8 Linnell Close, London NW11, England

Black, Steven D *Financier*
%Smith Barney Inc, 1345 Ave of Americas, New York, NY 10105, USA

Black, Theodore H *Businessman*
%Ingersoll-Rand Co, 200 Chestnut Ridge Rd, Woodcliff Lake, NJ 07675, USA

Blackburn, Charles L *Businessman*
%Maxus Energy Corp, 717 N Harwood St, Dallas, TX 75201, USA

Biswas - Blackburn

Blackie, William — *Businessman*
600 Deer Valley Rd, #1-C, San Rafael, CA 94903, USA

Blackledge, Todd A — *Football Player*
1240 7th St NE, North Canton, OH 44720, USA

Blackman, Honor — *Actress*
%Michael Ladkin Mgmt, 11 Southwick Mews, London W2 1JG, England

Blackman, Robert L (Bob) — *Football Coach*
8 Full Sweep, Palmetto Dr, Hilton Head Island, SC 29928, USA

Blackmun, Harry A — *Supreme Court Justice*
%US Supreme Court, 1 1st St NE, Washington, DC 20543, USA

Blackstone, Harry B, Jr — *Illusionist*
4370 Tujunga Ave, #150, Studio City, CA 91604, USA

Blackwell, Ewell — *Baseball Player*
80 Ariel Loop, Hendersonville, NC 28792, USA

Blackwell, Harolyn — *Opera Singer*
%Ken Benson, 165 W 57th St, New York, NY 10019, USA

Blackwell, Lloyd P — *Forester*
1212 Dubach St, Ruston, LA 71270, USA

Blackwell, Mr (Richard) — *Fashion Designer*
531 S Windsor, Los Angeles, CA 90020, USA

Blackwell, Paul E — *Army General*
Deputy CofS, Operations/Plans, HdqsUS Army, Pentagon, Washington, DC 20310, USA

Blackwood, Nina — *Entertainer*
22968 Victory Blvd, #158, Woodland Hills, CA 91367, USA

Blacque, Taurean — *Actor*
4207 Don Ortega Pl, Los Angeles, CA 90008, USA

Blades, H Benedict (Bennie) — *Football Player*
%Detroit Lions, Silverdome, 1200 Featherstone Rd, Pontiac, MI 48342, USA

Blades, Ruben — *Singer, Songwriter, Actor*
521 12th St, Santa Monica, CA 90402, USA

Blaese, R Michael — *Medical Researcher*
%National Cancer Institute, 9000 Rockville Pike, Bethesda, MD 20205, USA

Blaha, John E — *Astronaut*
%NASA, Johnson Space Center, 2101 NASA Rd, Houston, TX 77058, USA

Blahnik, Manolo — *Fashion Designer*
49-51 Old Church Rd, London SW3, England

Blaine, James — *Financier*
%State Employees' Credit Union, PO Box 27665, Raleigh, NC 27611, USA

Blair, Anthony C L (Tony) — *Government Official, England*
%House of Commons, Westminster, London SW1A 0AA, England

Blair, Betsy — *Actress*
11 Chalcot Gardens, Englands Lane, London NW3 4YB, England

Blair, Bill — *Basketball Coach*
%Minnesota Timberwolves, Target Center, 600 1st Ave N, Minneapolis, MN 55403, USA

Blair, Bonnie — *Speed Skater*
306 White Pine Rd, Delafield, WI 53018, USA

Blair, Janet — *Actress*
21650 Burbank Blvd, #107, Woodland Hills, CA 91367, USA

Blair, Linda — *Actress*
4165 Kraft Ave, Studio City, CA 91604, USA

Blair, Matthew A (Matt) — *Football Player*
2155 189th St, Jordan, MN 55352, USA

Blair, William Draper, Jr — *Conservationist*
118 E Melrose St, Bethesda, MD 20815, USA

Blair, William M, Jr — *Attorney, Diplomat*
2510 Foxhall Rd NW, Washington, DC 20007, USA

Blair, William S — *Publisher*
RD 3, Brattleboro, VT 05301, USA

Blais, Madeleine — *Journalist*
%Miami Herald, Editorial Dept, 1 Herald Plaza, Miami, FL 33132, USA

Blake, George R — *Editor*
%Cincinnati Enquirer, Editorial Dept, 617 Vine St, Cincinnati, OH 45202, USA

Blake, John C — *Artist*
Oz Voorburgwal 131, 1012 ER Amsterdam, Netherlands

Blake, Julian W (Bud) — *Cartoonist (Tiger)*
PO Box 146, Damariscotta, ME 04543, USA

Blake, Norman P, Jr — *Businessman*
%USF&G, 100 Light St, Baltimore, MD 21202, USA

B

Blackie - Blake

B

Blake, Peter *Yachtsman*
Emsworth, Hants, England

Blake, Peter *Architect*
140 Elm St, Branford, CT 06405, USA

Blake, Peter T *Artist*
%Waddington Galleries, 11 Cork St, London W1X 1PD, England

Blake, Rob *Hockey Player*
%Los Angeles Kings, Forum, PO Box 17013, Inglewood, CA 90308, USA

Blake, Robert *Actor*
%Breezy Productions, 11604 Dilling St, #8, North Hollywood, CA 91604, USA

Blake, Rockwell *Opera Singer*
1 Onondaga Lane, Plattsburgh, NY 12901, USA

Blake, Whitney *Actress*
PO Box 6088, Malibu, CA 90264, USA

Blakeley, Ronee *Actress, Singer*
8033 Sunset Blvd, #693, Los Angeles, CA 90046, USA

Blakely, Ross M *Financier*
%Coast Federal Savings, 1000 Wilshire Blvd, Los Angeles, CA 90017, USA

Blakely, Susan *Actress*
416 N Oakhurst Dr, #305, Beverly Hills, CA 90210, USA

Blakemore, Colin B *Neurophysiologist, Physiologist*
%University Laboratory of Physiology, Parks Rd, Oxford OX1 3PT, England

Blakemore, Michael H *Theater Director, Actor, Writer*
18 Upper Park Rd, London NW3 2UP, England

Blakenham of Little Blakenham, Michael J *Businessman*
%S Pearson & Son, Millbank Tower, Millbank, London SW1P 4QZ, England

Blalack, Robert *Cinematographer*
12251 Huston St, North Hollywood, CA 91607, USA

Blalock, Jane *Golfer*
197 8th St, Charlestown, MA 02129, USA

Blanc, Georges *Chef*
Le Mere Blanc, 01540 Vonnas, Ain, France

Blanc, Raymond R A *Chef*
%Le Quat'Saisons, Church Rd, Great Milton, Oxford OX44 7PD, England

Blancas, Homero *Golfer*
%Homrand Inc, Randolph Golf Course, 600 S Alvernon, Tucson, AZ 85711, USA

Blanch, E J *Businessman*
%Ford-Werke, Henry-Ford-Str 1, 50735 Cologne, Germany

Blanchard, Felix (Doc) *Football Player*
30395 Olympus, Bulverde, TX 78163, USA

Blanchard, George S *Army General*
23 Dewberry Rd, Whispering Pines, NC 28327, USA

Blanchard, James H *Financier*
%Synovus Financial Corp, 901 Front Ave, Columbus, GA 31901, USA

Blanchard, Kenneth *Writer, Business Consultant*
2048 Aldergrove, #B, Escondido, CA 92029, USA

Blanchard, Nina *Model Agency Executive*
8207 Mulholland Dr, Los Angeles, CA 90046, USA

Blanchard, Susan *Actress*
900 Chapea Rd, Pasadena, CA 91107, USA

Blanchard, Terence *Jazz Trumpeter*
%Burgess Mgmt, 6916 32nd St NW, Washington, DC 20015, USA

Blanchard, Tim *Religious Leader*
%Conservative Baptist Assn, PO Box 66, Wheaton, IL 60189, USA

Blanco-Cervantes, Raul *President, Costa Rica*
Apdo 918, San Jose, Costa Rica

Bland, Bobby (Blue) *Singer*
3500 W Olive Ave, #740, Burbank, CA 91505, USA

Blanda, George F *Football Player*
1513 Stonegate Rd, LaGrange Park, IL 60525, USA

Blanding, Robert J *Financier*
%Loomis Sayles Co, 1 Financial Center, Boston, MA 02111, USA

Blank, Arthur M *Businessman*
%Home Depot Inc, 2727 Paces Ferry Rd, Atlanta, GA 30339, USA

Blankers-Koen, Fanny *Track Athlete*
Nachtegaal, Strat 67, Utrecht, Netherlands

Blankfield, Mark *Actor*
%Rossen Agency, 11712 Moorpark St, #204, Studio City, CA 91604, USA

Blake - Blankfield

Blankley, Walter E *Businessman*
%Ametek Inc, Station Square, Paoli, PA 19301, USA

Blanton, Ray *Governor, TN*
%WLAC Radio, 10 Music Cir E, Nashville, TN 37203, USA

Blashford-Snell, John N *Explorer*
%Scientific Exploration Soc, Motcome, Shaftesbury, Dorset SP7 9PB, England

Blass, Steve (Stephen R) *Baseball Player*
1756 Quigg Dr, Pittsburgh, PA 15241, USA

Blass, William R (Bill) *Fashion Designer*
%Bill Blass Ltd, 550 7th Ave, New York, NY 10018, USA

Blassie, Freddie *Wrestler*
%World Wrestling Federation, TitanSports, 1055 Summer St, Stamford, CT 06905, USA

Blasucci, Richard *Actor*
10424 Bloomfield St, North Hollywood, CA 91602, USA

Blatnick, Jeff *Wrestler*
%Cowen Co, 80 State St, Albany, NY 12207, USA

Blatty, William Peter *Writer*
3025 Vista Linda Lane, Santa Barbara, CA 93108, USA

Blau, Francine D *Economist*
%Cornell University, Industrial and Labor Relations School, Ithaca, NY 14853, USA

Blau, Harvey R *Businessman*
%Griffon Corp, 100 Jericho Quadrangle, Jericho, NY 11753, USA

Blau, Peter M *Sociologist*
12 Cobb Terrace, Chapel Hill, NC 27514, USA

Blaug, Mark *Economist*
%University of London, Economics School, London, England

Blauvelt, Howard W *Businessman*
59 Londonderry Dr, Greenwich, CT 06830, USA

Blaylock, Kenneth T *Labor Leader*
%American Government Employees Federation, 80 "F" St NW, Washington, DC 20001, USA

Blaylock, Mookie *Basketball Player*
%Atlanta Hawks, 1 CNN Center, South Tower, Atlanta, GA 30303, USA

Blazelowski, Carol *Basketball Player*
%NBA Properties, Olympic Tower, 645 5th Ave, New York, NY 10022, USA

Bleak, David B *Korean War Army Hero (CMH)*
RR 1 Box 345, Arco, ID 83213, USA

Blech, Harry *Conductor*
The Owls, 70 Leopold Rd, Wimbledon, London SW19 T5Q, England

Bleck, Max E *Businessman*
%Raytheon Co, 141 Spring St, Lexington, MA 02173, USA

Bledsoe, Drew *Football Player*
%New England Patriots, Foxboro Stadium, Rt 1, Foxboro, MA 02035, USA

Bledsoe, Tempestt *Actress*
%Innovative Artists, 1999 Ave of Stars, #2850, Los Angeles, CA 90067, USA

Bleeth, Yasmine *Actress*
247 S Beverly Dr, #102, Beverly Hills, CA 90212, USA

Blegen, Judith *Opera Singer*
91 Central Park West, #1-B, New York, NY 10023, USA

Bleiberg, Robert M *Editor*
25 Central Park West, New York, NY 10023, USA

Bleier, Rocky *Football Player*
%Rocky Bleier Enterprises, 580 Squaw Run Rd E, Pittsburgh, PA 15238, USA

Bleifeld, Stanley *Sculptor*
27 Spring Valley Rd, Weston, CT 06883, USA

Blenis, Barry G *Financier*
%ALBANK Financial Corp, 10 N Pearl St, Albany, NY 12207, USA

Blessed, Brian *Actor*
%Vernon Conway, 5 Spring St, London W2 3RA, England

Blethen, Frank A *Publisher*
%Seattle Times, Fairview Ave N & John St, Seattle, WA 98111, USA

Blethen, John A *Publisher*
%Seattle Times, Fairview Ave N & John St, Seattle, WA 98111, USA

Bley, Carla B *Composer, Jazz Pianist*
%Watt Works Inc, Grogkill Rd, Willow, NY 12495, USA

Blinder, Alan S *Financier, Government Official*
%Federal Reserve Board, 20th St & Constitution Ave NW, Washington, DC 20551, USA

Blix, Hans M *Government Official*
%International Atomic Energy Agency, Wagramserstr 5, 1400 Vienna, Austria

B

Blankley - Blix

Blobel, Gunter *Cell Biologist*
%Rockefeller University, Cell Biology Dept, 1230 York Ave, New York, NY 10021, USA

Bloch, Erich *Government Official, Scientist*
%National Science Foundation, 1800 "C" St NW, Washington, DC 20550, USA

Bloch, Henry W *Businessman*
%H & R Block Inc, 4410 Main St, Kansas City, MO 64111, USA

Bloch, Konrad E *Nobel Medicine Laureate*
%Harvard University, Chemistry Dept, 12 Oxford St, Cambridge, MA 02138, USA

Bloch, Richard A *Businessman*
%H & R Block Inc, 4410 Main St, Kansas City, MO 64111, USA

Bloch, Thomas M *Businessman*
%H & R Block Inc, 4410 Main St, Kansas City, MO 64111, USA

Blochwitz, Hans-Peter *Opera Singer*
%Shaw Concerts, Lincoln Plaza, 1900 Broadway, #200, New York, NY 10023, USA

Block, Herbert L (Herblock) *Editorial Cartoonist*
%Washington Post, Editorial Dept, 1150 15th St NW, Washington, DC 20071, USA

Block, James A *Businessman*
%Block Drug Co, 257 Cornelison Ave, Jersey City, NJ 07302, USA

Block, John R *Secretary, Agriculture*
%Nat Am Wholesale Grocers Assn, 201 Park Washington Ct, Falls Church, VA 22046, USA

Block, Lawrence *Writer*
299 W 12th St, #12-D, New York, NY 10014, USA

Block, Leonard N *Businessman*
%Block Drug Co, 257 Cornelison Ave, Jersey City, NJ 07302, USA

Block, Sherman *Law Enforcement Official*
%L A County Sheriffs Office, 4700 W Ramona Blvd, Monterey Park, CA 91754, USA

Block, Thomas R *Businessman*
%Block Drug Co, 257 Cornelison Ave, Jersey City, NJ 07302, USA

Blocker, John *Concert Pianist, Educator*
%University of California, School of Arts, Los Angeles, CA 90024, USA

Blodgett, F Caleb *Businessman*
688 Hillside Dr, Wayzata, MN 55391, USA

Bloembergen, Nicolaas *Nobel Physics Laureate*
%Harvard University, Applied Physics Dept, Pierce Hall, Cambridge, MA 02138, USA

Blomstedt, Herbert T *Conductor*
%InterArtists, Frans Van Mierisstraat 43, 1071 RK Amsterdam, Netherlands

Blood, Edward J *Skier*
RFD 2, Beech Hill, Durham, NH 03824, USA

Bloodworth-Thomason, Linda *Television Producer, Screenwriter*
9220 Sunset Blvd, #311, Los Angeles, CA 90069, USA

Bloom, Alfred H *Educator*
%Swarthmore College, President's Office, Swarthmore, PA 19081, USA

Bloom, Anne *Actress*
11288 Ventura Blvd, #B-222, Studio City, CA 91604, USA

Bloom, Brian *Actor*
11 Croydon Ct, Dix Hills, NY 11746, USA

Bloom, Claire *Actress*
%Conway Van Gelder Ltd, 18-21 Jermyn St, London SW1Y 6HP, England

Bloom, Geoffrey B *Businessman*
%Wolverine World Wide Inc, 9341 Courtland Dr, Rockford, MI 49351, USA

Bloom, Harold *Educator*
179 Linden St, New Haven, CT 06511, USA

Bloom, Lindsay *Actress*
3907 W Alameda Ave, #101, Burbank, CA 91505, USA

Bloomfield, Coleman *Businessman*
%Minnesota Mutual Life Insurance, 400 Robert St N, St Paul, MN 55101, USA

Bloomfield, Sara *Museum Director*
%Holocaust Memorial Museum, 100 Raoul Wallenberg Pl SW, Washington, DC 20024, USA

Bloomquist, Robert O *Businessman*
%Lutheran Brotherhood, 625 4th Ave S, Minneapolis, MN 55415, USA

Blossom, Roberts *Actor*
%Gersh Agency, 232 N Canon Dr, Beverly Hills, CA 90210, USA

Blount, Lisa *Actress*
%Joel Stevens Mgmt, 7473 Mulholland Dr, Los Angeles, CA 90046, USA

Blount, Mel *Football Player, Executive*
RR 1, Box 91, Claysville, PA 15323, USA

Blount, Winton M, III *Businessman*
%Blount Inc, 4520 Executive Park Dr, Montgomery, AL 36116, USA

Blount, Winton M, Jr *Postmaster General, Businessman*
%Blount Inc, 4520 Executive Park Dr, Montgomery, AL 36116, USA

Blout, Elkan R *Biochemist*
1010 Memorial Dr, Cambridge, MA 02138, USA

Blow, Kurtis *Rapper*
201 Eastern Parkway, #3-K, Brooklyn, NY 11238, USA

Blue, Forrest *Football Player*
4451 Ashton Dr, Sacramento, CA 95864, USA

Blue, Vida *Baseball Player*
PO Box 1449, Pleasanton, CA 94566, USA

Bluford, Guion S, Jr *Astronaut*
%NYMA Inc, 2001 Aerospace Parkway, Brook Park, OH 44142, USA

Blum, Arlene *Mountaineer*
%University of California, Biochemistry Dept, Berkeley, CA 94720, USA

Blum, Michael S *Financier*
%Heller Financial, 500 W Monroe St, Chicago, IL 60661, USA

Blumberg, Baruch S *Nobel Medicine Laureate*
%Fox Chase Cancer Center, 7701 Burholme Ave, Philadelphia, PA 19111, USA

Blume, Judy S *Writer*
%Harold Ober Assoc, 425 Madison Ave, New York, NY 10017, USA

Blume, Veronica *Model*
%Ford Model Agency, 344 E 59th St, New York, NY 10022, USA

Blumenthal, W Michael *Secretary, Treasury; Financier*
%Lazard Freres Co, 1 Rockefeller Plaza, New York, NY 10020, USA

Bluth, Ray *Bowler*
%Crestwood Bowl, 9822 Highway 66, Crestwood, MO 63126, USA

Bly, Robert *Poet, Psychologist*
1904 Girard Ave S, Minneapolis, MN 55403, USA

Blyleven, R Bert *Baseball Player*
18922 Canyon Dr, Villa Park, CA 92667, USA

Blyth, Ann *Actress*
35325 Beach Rd, #PH, Capistrano Beach, CA 92624, USA

Blyth, Myrna G *Editor*
%Ladies Home Journal, Editorial Dept, 100 Park Ave, New York, NY 10017, USA

Boardman of Welford, Thomas G *Financier*
%National Westminster Bank, 41 Lothbury, London EC2P 2BP, England

Boardman, Christopher M (Chris) *Cyclist*
Mozolowski & Murray, Bridgend Industrial Estate, Kinross KY13 7ER, England

Boatman, Michael *Actor*
1571 S Kiowa Crest Dr, Diamond Bar, CA 91765, USA

Bobins, Norman H *Financier*
%LaSalle National Corp, 134 S LaSalle St, Chicago, IL 60603, USA

Bobko, Karol J *Astronaut*
%Booz Allen Hamilton, 2525 Bay Area Blvd, #290, Houston, TX 77058, USA

Bocca, Julio *Ballet Dancer*
%FPS International, 150 Broadway, New York, NY 10038, USA

Boccardi, Louis D *Publisher*
%Associated Press Broadcast Svc, 12 Norwick St, London EC4A 1BP, England

Bochco, Steven *Television Producer, Writer*
%Steven Bochco Productions, PO Box 900, Beverly Hills, CA 90213, USA

Bochner, Hart *Actor*
223 Ocean Dr, Oxnard, CA 93035, USA

Bochner, Lloyd *Actor*
42 Haldeman Rd, Santa Monica, CA 90402, USA

Bochner, Salomon *Mathematician*
4100 Greenbriar Ave, #239, Houston, TX 77098, USA

Bochte, Bruce A *Baseball Player*
3688 Hastings Ct, Lafayette, CA 94549, USA

Bock, Edward J *Businessman, Football Player*
7 Huntleigh Woods, St Louis, MO 63131, USA

Bock, Jerry *Composer*
145 Wellington Ave, New Rochelle, NY 10804, USA

Bocuse, Paul *Restauranteur*
40 Rue de la Plage, 69660 Collonges-au-Mont d'Or, France

Boddicker, Michael J (Mike) *Baseball Player*
11324 W 121st Terrace, Overland Park, KS 66213, USA

Bode, Hendrick W *Research Engineer*
%Harvard University, Pierce Hall, Cambridge, MA 02138, USA

B

Bode, Ken *Commentator*
%"Washington Week in Review" Show, WETA-TV, Box 2626, Washington, DC 20013, USA

Bode, Rolf *Cinematographer*
PO Box 2230, Los Angeles, CA 90078, USA

Bodenstein, Dietrich H F A *Biologist*
536 Valley Rd, Charlottesville, VA 22903, USA

Bodine, Brett *Auto Racing Driver*
%King Racing, 103 Center Lane, Huntersville, NC 28078, USA

Bodine, Geoff *Auto Racing Driver*
%GEB Racing, 6007 Victory Lane, Harrisburg, NC 28075, USA

Bodman, Samuel W, III *Financier*
%Cabot Corp, 75 State St, Boston, MA 02109, USA

Bodmer, Walter F *Geneticist*
%Imperial Cancer Research, Lincoln's Inn Fields, London WC2A 3PX, England

Bodner, David E *Financier*
%Julius Baer Securities, 330 Madison Ave, New York, NY 10017, USA

Boe, Nils A *Judge; Governor, SD*
PO Box 5186, Sioux Falls, SD 57117, USA

Boede, Marvin J *Labor Leader*
%Plumbing & Pipe Fitting Union, 901 Massachusetts NW, Washington, DC 20001, USA

Boeheim, Jim *Basketball Coach*
%Syracuse University, Manley Field House, Syracuse, NY 13244, USA

Boehm, Gottfried K *Art Historian*
Sevogelplatz 1, 4052 Basel, Switzerland

Boehne, Edward G *Financier*
%Federal Reserve Bank, Independence Mall, 100 N 6th St, Philadelphia, PA 19106, USA

Boekelheide, Virgil C *Chemist*
2017 Elk Dr, Eugene, OR 97403, USA

Boeker, Paul H *Diplomat*
3701 Blacktorn Ct, Chevy Chase, MD 20815, USA

Boen, Earl *Actor*
1227 Shadybrook Dr, Beverly Hills, CA 90210, USA

Boerner, Jacqueline *Speed Skater*
Bernhard-Bastlein-Str 55, 10367 Berlin, Germany

Boerwinkle, Tom *Basketball Player*
%Chicago Bulls, 1901 W Madison St, Chicago, IL 60612, USA

Boesak, Allan *Religious Leader, Social Activist*
PO Box 316, Kasselsvlei 7533, South Africa

Boeschenstein, William W *Businessman*
3 Locust St, Perrysburg, OH 43551, USA

Boese, Lawrence E (Larry) *Air Force General*
Commander, 11th Air Force, 5800 "G" St, Elmendorf Air Force Base, AK 99506, USA

Boesen, Dennis L *Astronaut*
6613 Sandra Ave NE, Albuquerque, NM 87109, USA

Boettcher, Wilfried *Conductor*
%Christopher Tennant, 11 Lawrence St, London SW3 5NB, England

Boetticher, Budd *Movie Director*
23969 Green Haven Lane, Ramona, CA 92065, USA

Boeynants, Paul V D *Prime Minister, Belgium*
41 Rue de Deux Eglises, 1040 Brussels, Belgium

Boff, Leonardo G D *Theologian*
Pr M Leao 12/204, Alto Vale Encantado, 20531-350 Rio de Janeiro, Brazil

Bofill, Angela *Singer*
1385 York Ave, #6-B, New York, NY 10021, USA

Bofill, Ricardo *Architect*
%Taller de Arquitectura, 14 Ave de la Industria, 08960 Barcelona, Spain

Bofinger, Heinz *Architect*
Biebricher Allee 49, 65187 Wiesbaden, Germany

Bogarde, Dirk *Actor*
%International Creative Mgmt, 76 Oxford St, London W1N 0AX, England

Bogart, Paul *Television, Movie Director*
760 N La Cienega Blvd, Los Angeles, CA 90069, USA

Bogdanovich, Joseph J *Businessman*
%H J Heinz Co, 600 Grant St, Pittsburgh, PA 15219, USA

Bogdanovich, Peter *Movie Director*
12451 Mulholland Dr, Beverly Hills, CA 90210, USA

Boger, Lawrence L *Educator*
5015 Woodland Dr, Stillwater, OK 74074, USA

Bode - Boger

Boggs, J Caleb — *Governor/Senator, DE*
1203 Grinnell Rd, Wilmington, DE 19803, USA

Boggs, Wade A — *Baseball Player*
6006 Windham Pl, Tampa, FL 33647, USA

Bogguss, Suzy — *Singer, Songwriter*
%Gurley Co, 3322 W End Ave, #11, Nashville, TN 37203, USA

Bogle, John C — *Financier*
%Vanguard Group, 1300 Morris Dr, Valley Forge, PA 19482, USA

Bogner, Willy — *Fashion Designer*
Sank-Veit-Str 4, 81673 Munich, Germany

Bogorad, Lawrence — *Biologist, Plant Physiologist*
%Harvard University, Biological Laboratories, Cambridge, MA 02138, USA

Bogosian, Eric — *Performance Artist, Actor*
145 Hudson St, #9-SW, New York, NY 10013, USA

Bogues, Tyrone (Muggsy) — *Basketball Player*
%Charlotte Hornets, 1 Hive Dr, Charlotte, NC 28217, USA

Boguinskaia, Svetlana — *Gymnast*
%Karolyi's World Gym, 17203 Bamwood Ave, Houston, TX 77090, USA

Boh, Robert H — *Financier*
%Hibernia Corp, 313 Carondelet St, New Orleans, LA 70130, USA

Bohan, Marc — *Fashion Designer*
55 Rue Saint-Dominique, 75007 Paris, France

Bohannon, David D — *Community Planner, Developer*
60 Hillsdale Mall, San Mateo, CA 94403, USA

Bohay, Heidi — *Actress*
48 Main St, South Bound Brook, NJ 08880, USA

Bohlin, John D — *Space Scientist*
%NASA, Solar & Heliospherics Physics Division, Washington, DC 22546, USA

Bohlin, Peter Q — *Architect*
197 Parfitt Way SW, Bainbridge Island, WA 98110, USA

Bohlmann, Ralph A — *Religious Leader*
%Lutheran Church Missouri Synod, 1333 S Kirkwood Rd, St Louis, MO 63122, USA

Bohlsen, John — *Financier*
%North Fork Bancorp, 9025 Rt 2, Mattituck, NY 11952, USA

Bohn, Robert G — *Businessman*
%Oshkosh Truck Corp, 2307 Oregon St, Oshkosh, WI 54901, USA

Bohr, Aage N — *Nobel Physics Laureate*
Strangade 34, 1-Sal, 1401 Copenhagen, Denmark

Bohrer, Corinne — *Actress*
%Metropolitan Talent Agency, 4526 Wilshire Blvd, Los Angeles, CA 90010, USA

Boisset, Yves — *Movie Director*
61 Blvd Inkerman, 92200 Neuilly-sur-Seine, France

Boitano, Brian — *Figure Skater*
%Brian Boitano Enterprises, 101 1st St, #370, Los Altos, CA 94022, USA

Boiteux, Jean — *Swimmer*
51 Ave de Merignac, 33200 Bordeaux, Cauderan, France

Boivin, Leo — *Hockey Player*
PO Box 406, Prescott ON K0E 1T0, Canada

Bok, Bart J — *Astronomer, Educator*
200 Sierra Vista Dr, Tucson, AZ 85719, USA

Bok, Chip — *Editorial Cartoonist*
709 Castle Blvd, Akron, OH 44313, USA

Bok, Derek C — *Educator*
%Harvard University, Law School, Cambridge, MA 02138, USA

Bok, Joan T — *Businessman*
%New England Electric System, 25 Research Dr, Westborough, MA 01582, USA

Bok, Sissela — *Philosopher*
75 Cambridge Parkway, #E-610, Cambridge, MA 02142, USA

Bokamper, Kim — *Football Player*
301 NW 127th Ave, Plantation, FL 33325, USA

Boklund, Thomas B — *Businessman*
%Oregon Steel Mills, 1000 SW Broadway, Portland, OR 97205, USA

Bol, Manute — *Basketball Player*
%Miami Heat, Miami Arena, Miami, FL 33136, USA

Bolack, Tom — *Governor, NM*
3701 Bloomfield Highway, Framington, NM 87401, USA

Bolcom, William E — *Composer*
3080 Whitmore Lake Rd, Ann Arbor, MI 48105, USA

B

Boggs - Bolcom

Bolden, Charles F, Jr *Astronaut, Marine Corps General*
%US Naval Academy, Deputy Commandant's Office, Annapolis, MD 21402, USA

Bolen, David B *Diplomat*
26 Wesley Dr, Foxmeadow, Hockessin, DE 19707, USA

Boles, Billy J (Bill) *Air Force General*
Deputy Chief of Staff/Personnel, Hq USAF, Washington, DC 20330, USA

Bolger, James B *Prime Minister, New Zealand*
%National Party, Parliament, Wellington, New Zealand

Bolger, Thomas E *Businessman*
%Bell Atlantic Corp, 1717 Arch St, Philadelphia, PA 19103, USA

Boliek, Luther C *Financier*
%Southern National Corp, 500 N Chestnut St, Lumberton, NC 28358, USA

Bolin, Bert *Meteorologist*
%University of Stockholm, Meteorological Institute, Stockholm, Sweden

Bolkiah Mu'izuddin Waddaulah *Sultan, Brunei Darussalam*
Istana Darul Hana, Brunei Darussalam

Bolkvadze, Elisso *Concert Pianist*
%Hillyer International, Carnegie Mews, 211 W 56th St, New York, NY 10019, USA

Bolleau, Linda *Editorial Cartoonist*
%Frankfort State Journal, Editorial Dept, 321 W Main St, Frankfort, KY 40601, USA

Bollen, Roger *Cartoonist (Animal Crackers, Catfish)*
8964 Little St, Mentor, OH 44060, USA

Bollenbach, Stephen F *Businessman*
%Host Marriott Corp, 10400 Fernwood Rd, Washington, DC 20058, USA

Bolles, Richard N *Writer*
3044 Oakraider Dr, Alamo, CA 94507, USA

Bollettieri, Nick *Tennis Coach*
%Nick Bollettieri Tennis Academy, 5500 34th St W, Bradenton, FL 34210, USA

Bolling, Claude *Jazz Pianist, Composer*
20 Ave de Lorraine, 92380 Garches, France

Bolling, Tiffany *Actress*
12483 Braddock Dr, Los Angeles, CA 90066, USA

Bollom, Daniel A *Businessman*
%WPS Resources Corp, 700 N Adams St, Green Bay, WI 54301, USA

Bologna, Joseph *Actor*
16830 Ventura Blvd, #326, Encino, CA 91436, USA

Bolton, Michael *Singer, Songwriter*
%Louis Levin Mgmt, 130 W 57th St, #10-B, New York, NY 10019, USA

Bombassaro, Gerald *Labor Leader*
%Tile Marble & Granite Cutters Union, 801 N Pitt St, Alexandria, VA 22314, USA

Bombeck, Erma L *Writer, Columnist*
%Universal Press Syndicate, 4900 Main St, #900, Kansas City, KS 64112, USA

Bon Jovi, Jon *Singer, Songwriter (Bon Jovi)*
%Bon Jovi Mgmt, 250 W 57th St, #603, New York, NY 10107, USA

Bonaly, Surya *Figure Skater*
10 Impasse du Petit Chamsigny, 94500 Champigny, France

Bonanno, Louie *Actor*
PO Box 583, Laguna Beach, CA 92652, USA

Bond, Alan *Businessman, Yachtsman*
89 Watkins Rd, Dalkeith WA 6069, Australia

Bond, Edward *Playwright*
Orchard Way, Great Wilbraham, Cambridge CB1 5KA, England

Bond, Julian *Civil Rights Activist*
6002 34th Pl NW, Washington, DC 20015, USA

Bond, Richard N *Political Leader*
%Republican National Committee, 310 1st St SE, Washington, DC 20003, USA

Bondar, Roberta *Astronaut, Canada*
%McMaster University, Health Science Center, Hamilton ON L8N 3Z5, Canada

Bondarenko, Larissa *Model*
%Elite Model Mgmt, 345 N Maple Dr, Beverly Hills, CA 90210, USA

Bonde, Peder *Businessman*
1 Farragut Square South, Washington, DC 20006, USA

Bonderman, David *Businessman*
%Continental Airlines, 2929 Allen Parkway, Houston, TX 77019, USA

Bondi, Hermann *Applied Mathematician*
60 Mill Lane, Impington, Cambridgeshire CB4 4XN, England

Bondlow, William F, Jr *Publisher*
%House & Garden Magazine, 350 Madison Ave, New York, NY 10017, USA

Bondra, Peter — *Hockey Player*
%Washington Capitals, USAir Arena, Landover, MD 20785, USA

Bonds, Barry L — *Baseball Player*
%San Francisco Giants, Candlestick Park, San Francisco, CA 94124, USA

Bonds, Bobby L — *Baseball Player*
175 Lyndhurst Ave, San Carlos, CA 94070, USA

Bonds, Gary U S — *Singer*
%Brothers Mgmt, 141 Dunbar Ave, Fords, NJ 08863, USA

Bondurant, Bob — *Auto Driving Instructor*
%School of High Performance Driving, Sears Point Raceway, Sonoma, CA 95476, USA

Bonerz, Peter — *Actor, Comedian, Director*
3637 Lowry Rd, Los Angeles, CA 90027, USA

Bonet, Lisa — *Actress*
22764 Chamera Lane, Topanga, CA 90290, USA

Bonet, Pep — *Architect*
C/Pujades 62, 08005 Barcelona, Spain

Bongiorno, John J — *Financier*
%Navistar Financial Corp, 2850 W Golf Rd, Rolling Meadows, IL 60008, USA

Bongo, Albert-Bernard O — *President, Gabon*
%President's Office, Blvd de Independence, BP 546, Libreville, Gabon

Bonham-Carter, Helena — *Actress*
%Conway Van Gelder Robinson, 18/21 Jeremy St, London SW1Y 6HB, England

Bonilla, Roberto M A (Bobby) — *Baseball Player*
2418 98th St NW, Bradenton, FL 34209, USA

Bonnefous, Jean-Pierre — *Ballet Dancer, Choreographer*
%Indiana University, Ballet Dept, Music School, Bloomington, IN 47405, USA

Bonner, Frank — *Actor*
%Paradigm Agency, 10100 Santa Monica Blvd, #2500, Los Angeles, CA 90067, USA

Bonner, James — *Biologist*
1914 Edgewood Dr, South Pasadena, CA 91030, USA

Bonner, Thomas N — *Educator*
408 Hillsboro, Bloomfield Hills, MI 48301, USA

Bonney, Barbara — *Opera Singer*
Gunnarsbyn, 671 94 Edane, Sweden

Bonney, J Dennis — *Businessman*
%Chevron Corp, 225 Bush St, San Francisco, CA 94104, USA

Bono (Paul Hewson) — *Singer, Songwriter (U-2)*
%Principle Mgmt, 30-32 Sir John Rogerson's Quay, Dublin 2, Ireland

Bono, Chastity — *Actress*
11825 Kling St, North Hollywood, CA 91607, USA

Bonoff, Karla — *Singer, Songwriter*
1691 N Crescent Heights Blvd, Los Angeles, CA 90069, USA

Bonsall, Brian — *Actor*
%Natalie Rosson Agency, 11712 Moorpark St, #216, Studio City, CA 91604, USA

Bonsall, Joseph S (Joe), Jr — *Singer (Oak Ridge Boys)*
329 Rockland Rd, Hendersonville, TN 37075, USA

Bonsignore, Joseph J — *Publisher*
%Smithsonian Magazine, 900 Jefferson Dr SW, Washington, DC 20560, USA

Bonsignore, Michael R — *Businessman*
%Honeywell Inc, PO Box 524, Minneapolis, MN 55440, USA

Bonvicini, Joan — *Basketball Coach*
%University of Arizona, Athletic Dept, McKale Memorial Center, Tucson, AZ 85721, USA

Bonynge, Richard — *Conductor*
Chalet Monet, Rte de Sonloup, 1833 Les Avants, Switzerland

Booker, Henry G — *Applied Physicist*
63 Aberdeen Pl, St Louis, MO 63105, USA

Bookout, John G — *Businessman*
%Woodmen of World Life Insurance Society, 1700 Farnam St, Omaha, NE 68102, USA

Boon, David C — *Cricketer*
%Australian Cricket Board, 90 Jollimont St, Victoria 3002, Australia

Boone, Debby — *Actress, Singer*
4334 Kester Ave, Sherman Oaks, CA 91403, USA

Boone, James T — *Financier*
%Grenada Sunburst System, 2000 Gateway, Grenada, MS 38901, USA

Boone, Mary — *Artist Representative*
420 W Broadway, New York, NY 10012, USA

Boone, Pat — *Actor, Singer*
904 N Beverly Dr, Beverly Hills, CA 90210, USA

B

Bondra - Boone

Boone, Robert R (Bob) *Baseball Player, Manager*
18571 Villa Dr, Villa Park, CA 92667, USA

Boorda, J Mike *Navy Admiral*
Office of Chief of Naval Operations, Navy Department, Washington, DC 20370, USA

Boorman, John *Movie Director*
%Merlin Films, 16 Upper Pembroke St, Dublin 2, Ireland

Boorstin, Daniel J *Historian*
3541 Ordway St NW, Washington, DC 20016, USA

Boosler, Elayne *Comedienne*
11061 Wrightwood Lane, North Hollywood, CA 91604, USA

Booth, Adrian *Actor*
3922 Glenridge Dr, Sherman Oaks, CA 91423, USA

Booth, George *Cartoonist*
PO Box 1539, Stony Brook, NY 11790, USA

Booth, I MacAllister *Businessman*
%Polaroid Corp, 549 Technology Sq, Cambridge, MA 02139, USA

Booth, James *Actor*
%Hillard/Elkins, 8306 Wilshire Blvd, #438, Beverly Hills, CA 90211, USA

Booth, John C *Financier*
%Carnegie Capital Management Co, 1228 Euclid Ave, Cleveland, OH 44115, USA

Booth, Pat *Writer*
%Crown Publishers, 225 Park Ave S, New York, NY 10003, USA

Boothe, Powers *Actor*
23629 Long Valley Rd, Hidden Hills, CA 91302, USA

Boozer, Emerson *Football Player*
25 Windham Dr, Huntington Station, NY 11746, USA

Bordaberry Arocena, Juan M *President, Uruguay*
Joaquin Suarez 2868, Montevideo, Uruguay

Boreham, Roland S, Jr *Businessman*
%Baldor Electric Co, 5711 R S Boreham Jr St, Fort Smith, AR 72901, USA

Boren, David L *Governor/Senator, OK; Educator*
%University of Oklahoma, President's Office, Norman, OK 73019, USA

Borg Olivier, George *Prime Minister, Malta*
%House of Representatives, Valletta, Malta

Borg, Bjorn R *Tennis Player*
%International Management Group, 1 Erieview Plaza, #1300, Cleveland, OH 44114, USA

Borg, Kim *Opera Singer*
Osterbrogade 158, 2100 Copenhagen, Denmark

Borge, Victor *Musician, Comedian*
Field Point Park, Greenwich, CT 06830, USA

Borgelt, Burton C *Businessman*
%DENTSPLY International, 570 W College Ave, York, PA 17404, USA

Borgman, James M (Jim) *Editorial Cartoonist*
%Cincinnati Enquirer, Editorial Dept, 617 Vine St, Cincinnati, OH 45202, USA

Borgnine, Ernest *Actor*
%Selected Artists Agency, 13111 Ventura Blvd, Studio City, CA 91604, USA

Boris, James R *Financier*
%Kemper Securities, 77 W Wacker Dr, Chicago, IL 60601, USA

Boris, Ruthanna *Ballerina, Choreographer*
%Center for Dance, 555 Pierce St, #1033, Albany, CA 94706, USA

Bork, Robert H *Judge*
%American Enterprise Institute, 1150 17th St NW, Washington, DC

Borkh, Inge *Opera Singer*
Haus Weitblick, 9405 Wienacht, Switzerland

Borkowski, Francis T *Educator*
%Applalachian State University, President's Office, Boone, NC 28606, USA

Borlaug, Norman E *Nobel Peace Laureate*
15611 Ranchita Dr, Dallas, TX 75248, USA

Borman, Frank *Businessman, Astronaut*
%Patlex Corp, 250 Cotorro Ct, #A, Las Cruces, NM 88005, USA

Born, Allen *Businessman*
%Cyprus Amax Minerals Co, 9100 E Mineral Circle, Englewood, CO 80112, USA

Bornhuetter, Ronald L *Businessman*
%NAC Re Corp, 1 Greenwich Plaza, Greenwich, CT 06830, USA

Bornstein, Steven M *Television Executive*
%ESPN-TV, News Dept, ESPN Plaza, 935 Middle St, Bristol, CT 06010, USA

Borodina, Olga V *Opera Singer*
%Mariinsky Opera Theater, Teatralnaya Ploshchad 1, St Petersburg, Russia

Borofsky, Jonathan *Artist*
57 Market St, Venice, CA 90291, USA

Borowy, Henry L (Hank) *Baseball Player*
Beacon Hill, Maryland Ave, #9-C, Point Pleasant Beach, NJ 08742, USA

Borra, Ermanno *Astrophysicist*
%Laval University, Astrophysics Dept, Quebec ON, Canada

Borrego, Jesse *Actor*
250 W 57th St, #803, New York, NY 10019, USA

Borshoff, Thomas N *Financier*
%First Federal Savings & Loan Assn, 1 First Federal Plaza, Rochester, NY 14614, USA

Borten, Per *Prime Minister, Norway*
7095 Ler, Norway

Boryer, Lucy *Actress*
2116 Ewing St, Los Angeles, CA 90039, USA

Boryla, Vince *Basketball Player, Executive*
%Denver Nuggets, McNichols Arena, 1635 Clay St, Denver, CO 80204, USA

Borysewicz, Eddy *Cycling Coach*
%Cycling Velodrome, Balboa Park, San Diego, CA 92136, USA

Borzov, Valeri F *Track Athlete*
%Sport & Youth Ministry, Esplanadna St 42, 252023 Kiev 23, Ukraine

Bosco, Philip *Actor*
337 W 43rd St, #1-B, New York, NY 10036, USA

Boskin, Michael J *Government Official*
%Stanford University, Hoover Institution, Stanford, CA 94305, USA

Bosley, Tom *Actor*
%Burton Moss Agency, 8827 Beverly Blvd, #L, Los Angeles, CA 90048, USA

Bosman, Richard A (Dick) *Baseball Player*
3058 Landmark Blvd, #1202, Palm Harbor, FL 34684, USA

Bossard, Andre *Law Enforcement Official*
%Interpol, 26 Rue Armengaud, 92210 Saint-Cloud, France

Bossen, David A *Businesman*
%Measurex Corp, 1 Results Way, Cupertino, CA 95014, USA

Bossidy, Lawrence A *Businessman*
%AlliedSignal Inc, PO Box 4000, Morristown, NJ 07962, USA

Bossier, Albert L, Jr *Businessman*
%Avondale Industries, PO Box 50280, New Orleans, LA 70150, USA

Bosson, Barbara *Actress*
694 Amalfi Dr, Pacific Palisades, CA 90272, USA

Bossy, Michael (Mike) *Hockey Player*
%New York Islanders, Veterans Memorial Coliseum, Uniondale, NY 11553, USA

Dostelle, Tom *Artist*
%Aeolian Palace Gallery, PO Box 8, Pocopson, PA 19366, USA

Bostic, Jeff *Football Player*
%Washington Redskins, 21300 Redskin Park Dr, Ashburn, VA 22011, USA

Bostic, Keith *Football Player*
%Indianapolis Colts, 7001 W 56th St, Indianapolis, IN 46254, USA

Boston, John W *Businessman*
%Wisconsin Energy Corp, 231 W Michigan St, Milwaukee, WI 53202, USA

Boston, Ralph *Track Athlete*
2970 Clairmont Rd, #285, Atlanta, GA 30329, USA

Bostwick, Barry *Actor*
2770 Hutton Dr, Beverly Hills, CA 90210, USA

Boswell, David W (Dave) *Baseball Player*
309 Roxbury Ct, Joppa, MD 21085, USA

Boswell, Thomas M *Sportswriter*
%Washington Post, Sports Dept, 1150 15th St NW, Washington, DC 20071, USA

Bosworth, Brian *Football Player, Actor*
230 Park Ave, #527, New York, NY 10169, USA

Botelho, Carlos *Artist*
Ave Joao XXI-3-3d-F, 1000 Lisbon, Portugal

Botero, Fernando *Artist*
5 Blvd du Palais, 75004 Paris, France

Botha, Pieter W *Prime Minister, South Africa*
Libertas, Bryntirion, Pretoria 0001, South Africa

Botha, Roelof F *Government Official, South Africa*
%Foreign Affairs Ministry, Union Bldgs, PB X-152, Cape Town, South Africa

Botham, Ian T *Cricketer*
Epworth, South Humberside, England

Bothmer, Bernard V *Museum Curator, Egyptologist*
%Brooklyn Museum, 188 Eastern Parkway, Brooklyn, NY 11238, USA

Botstein, Leon *Educator*
%Bard College, President's Office, Annandale-on-Hudson, NY 12504, USA

Bott, Raoul *Mathematician*
1 Richdale Ave, #9, Cambridge, MA 02140, USA

Bottari, Vic *Football Player*
52 Esta Bueno, Orinda, CA 94563, USA

Bottoms, Joseph *Actor*
%Agency For Performing Arts, 9000 Sunset Blvd, #1200, Los Angeles, CA 90069, USA

Bottoms, Sam *Actor*
4719 Willowcrest Ave, North Hollywood, CA 91602, USA

Bottoms, Timothy *Actor*
532 Hot Springs Rd, Santa Barbara, CA 93108, USA

Bottorff, Dennis C *Financier*
%First American Corp, First American Center, 4th & Union St, Nashville, TN 37237, USA

Botwinick, Michael *Museum Official*
%Newport Harbor Art Museum, 850 San Clemente Dr, Newport Beach, CA 92660, USA

Boubacar, Sidi Mohamed Ould *Prime Minister, Mauritania*
%Prime Minister's Office, Nouakchott, Mauritania

Bouchard, Emile J (Butch) *Hockey Player*
213 Marie-Victorin, Vercheres PQ J0L 2R0, Canada

Bouchard, Lucien *Government Official, Canada*
%House of Commons, Ottawa ON K1A 0AZ, Canada

Boucher, Gaetan *Speed Skater*
%Center Sportif, 3850 Edgar, St Hubert PQ J4T 368, Canada

Boucher, Pierre *Photographer*
L'Ermitage, 7 Ave Massoul, Faremountiers, 77120 Coulomiers, France

Boudreau, Louis (Lou) *Baseball Player, Manager*
15600 Ellis Ave, Dolton, IL 60419, USA

Boulet, Gilles *Educator*
%University of Quebec, President's Office, Ste Foy PQ G1V 2M3, Canada

Boulez, Pierre *Composer, Conductor*
%IRCAM, 1 Place Igor Stravinsky, 75004 Paris, France

Boulting, Roy *Movie Producer, Director*
%Charter Films, Twickenham Studios, Twickenham, Mddx TW1 2AW, England

Bourdeaux, Michael *Religious Leader*
%Keston College, Heathfield Rd, Keston, Kent BR2 6BA, England

Bourgeois, Louise *Sculptor*
347 W 20th St, New York, NY 10011, USA

Bourgignon, Serge *Movie Director*
18 Rue de General-Malterre, 75016 Paris, France

Bourjaily, Vance *Writer*
Redbird Farm, Rt 3, Iowa City, IA 52240, USA

Bourke, William O *Businessman*
%Reynolds Aluminum Co, 6601 W Broad Street Rd, Richmond, VA 23261, USA

Bourland, Clifford *Track Athlete*
380 S Carmelina Ave, Brentwood, CA 90049, USA

Bourne, Henry C, Jr *Educator*
2877 Bainbridge Way NW, Atlanta, GA 30339, USA

Bournissen, Chantal *Skier*
1983 Evolene, Switzerland

Bourque, Pierre *Horticulturist*
4101 E Sherbrooke St, Montreal PQ H1X 2B2, Canada

Bourque, Ray *Hockey Player*
%Boston Bruins, Boston Garden, 150 Causeway St, Boston, MA 02114, USA

Boussena, Sadek *Government Official, Algeria*
%Ministry of Mines & Industry, 80 Rue Ahmad Ghermoul, Algiers, Algeria

Bouteflika, Abdul Aziz *Government Official, Algeria*
138 Chemin Bachir Brahimi, El Biar, Algiers, Algeria

Boutin, Bernard L *Businessman*
PO Box 1547, Laconia, NH 03247, USA

Bouton, James A (Jim) *Baseball Player, Writer*
265 Cedar Lane, Teaneck, NJ 07666, USA

Boutros-Ghali, Boutros *Government Official, Egypt*
%United Nations, Secretary-General's Office, 1 UN Plaza, New York, NY 10017, USA

Bouvet, Didier *Skier*
%Bouvet-Sports, 74360 Abondance, France

Bowa, Lawrence R (Larry) — *Baseball Player*
1029 Morris Ave, Bryn Mawr, PA 19010, USA

Bowden, Bobby — *Football Coach*
%Florida State University, Athletic Dept, Tallahassee, FL 32306, USA

Bowden, Hugh K — *Businessman*
%Canoca Ltd, Park House, 116 Park St, London W1Y 4NN, England

Bowden, Terry — *Football Coach*
%Auburn University, Athletic Complex, PO Box 351, Auburn, AL 36831, USA

Bowdler, William G — *Diplomat*
%State Department, 2201 "C" St NW, Washington, DC 20520, USA

Bowe, Riddick L — *Boxer*
%Media Plus Services, 1901 N Moore St, #900, Arlington, VA 22209, USA

Bowe, Rosemarie — *Actress*
321 St Pierre Rd, Los Angeles, CA 90077, USA

Bowen, Donald E — *Educator*
2912 Chimney Rock Dr, #22, Nacogdoches, TX 75961, USA

Bowen, Ray M — *Educator*
%Texas A&M University, President's Office, College Station, TX 77843, USA

Bowen, Richard L — *Educator*
%Idaho State University, President's Office, Pocatello, ID 83209, USA

Bowen, William G — *Foundation Executive, Educator*
%Andrew Mellon Foundation, 140 E 62nd St, New York, NY 10021, USA

Bower, Antoinette — *Actress*
1529 N Beverly Glen Blvd, Los Angeles, CA 90077, USA

Bower, Marvin D — *Businessman*
%State Farm Life Insurance, 1 State Farm Plaza, Bloomington, IL 61710, USA

Bower, Rodney A — *Labor Leader*
%Professional & Technical Engineers, 818 Roeder Rd, Silver Spring, MD 20910, USA

Bowerman, William J — *Businessman, Track Coach*
%Nike Inc, 1 Bowerman Dr, Beaverton, OR 97005, USA

Bowers, Bryan — *Singer, Guitarist*
%Klezmer Corp, PO Box 800, Mahopac, NY 10541, USA

Bowers, John W — *Religious Leader*
%Foursquare Gospel Int'l Church, 1100 Glendale Blvd, Los Angeles, CA 90026, USA

Bowersox, Kenneth D — *Astronaut*
%NASA, Johnson Space Center, 2101 NASA Rd, Houston, TX 77058, USA

Bowes, William C — *Navy Admiral*
Commander, Air Systems Command, Navy Dept, Washington, DC 10361, USA

Bowie, David — *Singer, Actor*
%Isolar Entertainment, 641 5th Ave, #22-Q, New York, NY 10022, USA

Bowie, Lester — *Jazz Trumpeter*
%ECM, 509 Madison Ave, New York, NY 10022, USA

Bowie, Robert R — *Educator, Government Official*
6918 Travelers Rest Circle, Easton, MD 21601, USA

Bowker, Albert H — *Educator*
1523 New Hampshire Ave NW, Washington, DC 20036, USA

Bowker, Judi — *Actress*
%Howes & Prior, 66 Berkeley House, Hay Hill, London W1X 7LH, England

Bowlen, Patrick D — *Football Executive*
%Denver Broncos, 13655 E Dove Valley Parkway, Englewood, CO 80112, USA

Bowles, Paul F — *Composer, Writer*
2117 Tanger Socco, Tangier, Morocco

Bowles, Samuel — *Economist*
%University of Massachusetts, Economics Dept, Amherst, MA 01003, USA

Bowlin, Michael R — *Businessman*
%Atlantic Richfield Co, 515 S Flower St, Los Angeles, CA 90071, USA

Bowlin, Patrick L — *Religious Leader*
%Open Bible Standard Churches, 2020 Bell Ave, Des Moines, IA 50315, USA

Bowman, Christopher — *Figure Skater*
5653 Kester Ave, Van Nuys, CA 91411, USA

Bowman, F L (Skip) — *Navy Admiral*
Chief of Naval Personnel, Hdqs, USN, Pentagon, Washington, DC 20370, USA

Bowman, Harry W — *Businessman*
%Outboard Marine Corp, 100 Sea-Horse Dr, Waukegan, IL 60085, USA

Bowman, Scotty — *Hockey Coach, Executive*
%Detroit Red Wings, Joe Louis Arena, 600 Civic Center Dr, Detroit, MI 48226, USA

Bowmer, John P — *Businessman*
%Adia Services, 100 Redwood Shores Parkway, Redwood City, CA 94065, USA

B

Bowa - Bowmer

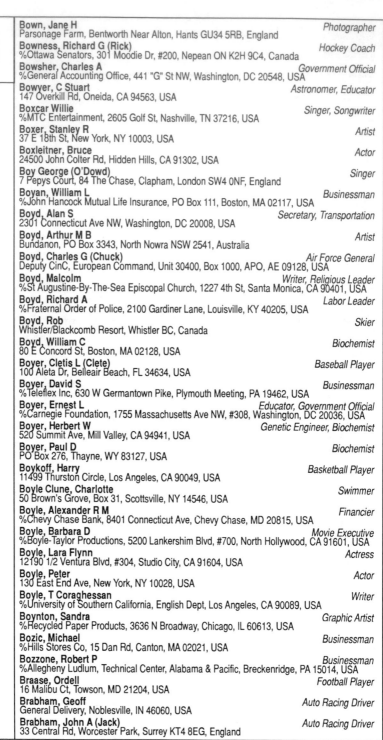

B

Bown - Brabham

Bown, Jane H — *Photographer*
Parsonage Farm, Bentworth Near Alton, Hants GU34 5RB, England

Bowness, Richard G (Rick) — *Hockey Coach*
%Ottawa Senators, 301 Moodie Dr, #200, Nepean ON K2H 9C4, Canada

Bowsher, Charles A — *Government Official*
%General Accounting Office, 441 "G" St NW, Washington, DC 20548, USA

Bowyer, C Stuart — *Astronomer, Educator*
147 Overkill Rd, Oneida, CA 94563, USA

Boxcar Willie — *Singer, Songwriter*
%MTC Entertainment, 2605 Golf St, Nashville, TN 37216, USA

Boxer, Stanley R — *Artist*
37 E 18th St, New York, NY 10003, USA

Boxleitner, Bruce — *Actor*
24500 John Colter Rd, Hidden Hills, CA 91302, USA

Boy George (O'Dowd) — *Singer*
7 Pepys Court, 84 The Chase, Clapham, London SW4 0NF, England

Boyan, William L — *Businessman*
%John Hancock Mutual Life Insurance, PO Box 111, Boston, MA 02117, USA

Boyd, Alan S — *Secretary, Transportation*
2301 Connecticut Ave NW, Washington, DC 20008, USA

Boyd, Arthur M B — *Artist*
Bundanon, PO Box 3343, North Nowra NSW 2541, Australia

Boyd, Charles G (Chuck) — *Air Force General*
Deputy CinC, European Command, Unit 30400, Box 1000, APO, AE 09128, USA

Boyd, Malcolm — *Writer, Religious Leader*
%St Augustine-By-The-Sea Episcopal Church, 1227 4th St, Santa Monica, CA 90401, USA

Boyd, Richard A — *Labor Leader*
%Fraternal Order of Police, 2100 Gardiner Lane, Louisville, KY 40205, USA

Boyd, Rob — *Skier*
Whistler/Blackcomb Resort, Whistler BC, Canada

Boyd, William C — *Biochemist*
80 E Concord St, Boston, MA 02128, USA

Boyer, Cletis L (Clete) — *Baseball Player*
100 Aleta Dr, Belleair Beach, FL 34634, USA

Boyer, David S — *Businessman*
%Teleflex Inc, 630 W Germantown Pike, Plymouth Meeting, PA 19462, USA

Boyer, Ernest L — *Educator, Government Official*
%Carnegie Foundation, 1755 Massachusetts Ave NW, #308, Washington, DC 20036, USA

Boyer, Herbert W — *Genetic Engineer, Biochemist*
520 Summit Ave, Mill Valley, CA 94941, USA

Boyer, Paul D — *Biochemist*
PO Box 276, Thayne, WY 83127, USA

Boykoff, Harry — *Basketball Player*
11499 Thurston Circle, Los Angeles, CA 90049, USA

Boyle Clune, Charlotte — *Swimmer*
50 Brown's Grove, Box 31, Scottsville, NY 14546, USA

Boyle, Alexander R M — *Financier*
%Chevy Chase Bank, 8401 Connecticut Ave, Chevy Chase, MD 20815, USA

Boyle, Barbara D — *Movie Executive*
%Boyle-Taylor Productions, 5200 Lankershim Blvd, #700, North Hollywood, CA 91601, USA

Boyle, Lara Flynn — *Actress*
12190 1/2 Ventura Blvd, #304, Studio City, CA 91604, USA

Boyle, Peter — *Actor*
130 East End Ave, New York, NY 10028, USA

Boyle, T Coraghessan — *Writer*
%University of Southern California, English Dept, Los Angeles, CA 90089, USA

Boynton, Sandra — *Graphic Artist*
%Recycled Paper Products, 3636 N Broadway, Chicago, IL 60613, USA

Bozic, Michael — *Businessman*
%Hills Stores Co, 15 Dan Rd, Canton, MA 02021, USA

Bozzone, Robert P — *Businessman*
%Allegheny Ludlum, Technical Center, Alabama & Pacific, Breckenridge, PA 15014, USA

Braase, Ordell — *Football Player*
16 Malibu Ct, Towson, MD 21204, USA

Brabham, Geoff — *Auto Racing Driver*
General Delivery, Noblesville, IN 46060, USA

Brabham, John A (Jack) — *Auto Racing Driver*
33 Central Rd, Worcester Park, Surrey KT4 8EG, England

Bracco, Lorraine — *Actress*
207-23 Melissa Ct, Bayside, NY 11360, USA

Brace, William F — *Geologist*
49 Liberty St, Concord, MA 01742, USA

Brack, Reginald K, Jr — *Publisher*
%Time Inc, Time-Life Building, Rockefeller Center, New York, NY 10020, USA

Bracken, Eddie — *Actor*
18 Fulton St, Weehauken, NJ 07087, USA

Bracken, Thomas A — *Financier*
%CoreStates New Jersey National Bank, 370 Scotch Rd, Pennington, NJ 08534, USA

Bradbury, Curt — *Financier*
%Worthen Banking Corp, 200 W Capitol Ave, Little Rock, AR 72201, USA

Bradbury, Janette Lane — *Actress*
4883 Roswell Rd NE, #M-2, Atlanta, GA 30342, USA

Bradbury, Malcolm S — *Writer*
14 Heigham Grove, Norwich NR2 3DQ, England

Bradbury, Norris E — *Physicist*
1451 47th St, Los Alamos, NM 87544, USA

Bradbury, Ray D — *Writer*
10265 Cheviot Dr, Los Angeles, CA 90064, USA

Brademas, John — *Educator; Representative, NY*
%New York University, President's Emeritus Office, New York, NY 10012, USA

Braden, Vic — *Tennis Coach*
22000 Trabuco Canyon Rd, Trabuco Canyon, CA 92678, USA

Bradford, Barbara Taylor — *Writer*
%Bradford Enterprises, 450 Park Ave, New York, NY 10022, USA

Bradford, James C — *Financier*
%J C Bradford Co, 330 Commerce St, Nashville, TN 37201, USA

Bradford, William E — *Businessman*
%Dresser Industries, PO Box 718, Dallas, TX 75221, USA

Bradlee, Benjamin C — *Editor*
3014 "N" St NW, Washington, DC 20007, USA

Bradley, Brian — *Hockey Player*
%Tampa Bay Lightning, Mack Center, 501 E Kennedy Blvd, Tampa, FL 33602, USA

Bradley, Dick — *Sports Cartoonist*
%Sporting News, Editorial Dept, 1212 N Lindbergh, St Louis, MO 63132, USA

Bradley, Edward R (Ed) — *Commentator*
%CBS-TV, News Dept, 524 W 57th St, New York, NY 10019, USA

Bradley, Patricia E (Pat) — *Golfer*
%Ladies Professional Golf Assn, 2570 Volusia Ave, Daytona Beach, FL 32114, USA

Bradley, Robert A — *Physician*
2465 S Downing, Denver, CO 80210, USA

Bradley, Shawn — *Basketball Player*
PO Box 189, Conshohocken, PA 19428, USA

Bradman, Donald G (Don) — *Cricketer*
2 Holden St, Kensington Park, SA 5068, Australia

Bradshaw, John E — *Writer, Theologian*
2412 South Blvd, Houston, TX 77098, USA

Bradshaw, Stanley J — *Financier*
%Roosevelt Bank, 900 Roosevelt Parkway, Chesterfield, MO 63017, USA

Bradshaw, Terry — *Football Player, Sportscaster*
8911 Shady Lane Dr, Shreveport, LA 71118, USA

Brady, James S — *Government Official, Journalist*
%Handgun Control, 1225 "I" St NW, #1100, Washington, DC 20005, USA

Brady, Jerome D — *Businessman*
%AM International, 1800 W Central Rd, Mt Prospect, IL 60056, USA

Brady, Kyle — *Football Player*
%New York Jets, 1000 Fulton Ave, Hempstead, NY 11550, USA

Brady, Larry D — *Businessman*
%FMC Corp, 200 E Randolph Dr, Chicago, IL 60601, USA

Brady, Nicholas F — *Secretary, Treasury; Senator, NJ*
Black River Rd, Far Hills, NJ 07931, USA

Brady, Patrick H — *Vietnam War Army Hero (CMH), General*
2809 179th Ave E, Sumner, WA 98390, USA

Brady, Ray — *Commentator*
%CBS-TV, News Dept, 524 W 57th St, New York, NY 10019, USA

Brady, Robert T — *Businessman*
%Moog Inc, Jamison Rd, Aurora, NY 14052, USA

B

Bracco - Brady

Brady, Roscoe O — *Neurogeneticist*
6026 Valerian Lane, Rockville, MD 20852, USA

Brady, Sarah — *Social Activist*
%Handgun Control, 1225 "I" St NW, #1100, Washington, DC 20005, USA

Brady, William H — *Businessman*
PO Box 571, Milwaukee, WI 53201, USA

Braeden, Eric — *Actor*
13723 Romany Dr, Pacific Palisades, CA 90272, USA

Braga, Sonia — *Actress*
295 Greenwich St, #11-B, New York, NY 10007, USA

Bragg, Billy — *Singer*
%Sincere Mgmt, 421 Harrow Rd, London W10 4RD, England

Bragg, Charles — *Artist*
%Woodland Graphics, 9713 Santa Monica Blvd, #216, Beverly Hills, CA 90210, USA

Bragg, Darrell B — *Nutritionist*
%University of British Columbia, Vancouver BC V6T 2AZ, Canada

Bragg, Don — *Track Athlete*
%D B Enterprises, PO Box 171, New Gretna, NJ 08224, USA

Bragg, Melvyn — *Writer*
12 Hampstead Hill Gardens, London NW3, England

Braidwood, Robert J — *Archaeologist, Anthropologist*
%University of Chicago, Oriental Institute, Chicago, IL 60637, USA

Brainin, Norbert — *Concert Violinist*
19 Prowse Ave, Busbey Heath, Herts, England

Braman, Norman — *Football Executive*
%Philadelphia Eagles, 3501 S Broad St, Philadelphia, PA 19148, USA

Bramble, Frank P — *Financier*
%First Maryland Bancorp, 25 S Charles St, Baltimore, MD 21201, USA

Bramlett, David A — *Army General*
Deputy Commander in Chief, US Pacific Command, Camp H M Smith, HI 96851, USA

Bramlett, Delaney — *Singer, Guitarist (Delaney & Bonnie)*
10723 Johanna Ave, Sunland, CA 91040, USA

Branagh, Kenneth — *Actor, Director*
%Marmont Mgmt, Langham House, 302-308 Regent St, London W1R 5AL, England

Branca, John G — *Attorney*
%Ziffren Brittenham Branca, 2121 Ave of Stars, #3200, Los Angeles, CA 90067, USA

Branca, Ralph T J — *Baseball Player*
%National Pension, 1025 Westchester, White Plains, NY 10604, USA

Branch, Harllee, Jr — *Businessman*
3747 Peachtree Rd NE, #1817, Atlanta, GA 30319, USA

Branch, William B — *Playwright*
53 Cortlandt Ave, New Rochelle, NY 10801, USA

Brand, Colette — *Aerials Skier*
Rigistr 24, 6340 Baar, Switzerland

Brand, Frank A — *Businessman*
249 Alexander Palm Rd, Boca Raton, FL 33432, USA

Brand, Joshua — *Television Producer*
%Creative Artists Agency, 9830 Wilshire Blvd, Beverly Hills, CA 90212, USA

Brand, Myles — *Educator*
%University of Oregon, President's Office, Eugene, OR 97403, USA

Brand, Oscar — *Singer*
%Gypsy Hill Music, 141 Baker Hill Rd, Great Neck, NY 11023, USA

Brand, Vance D — *Astronaut*
%DFRC, PO Box 273, Edwards, CA 93533, USA

Brandauer, Klaus Maria — *Actor*
Fischerndorf 76, 8992 Altausse, Austria

Brandenburg, Jim — *Basketball Coach*
%San Diego State University, Athletic Dept, San Diego, CA 92182, USA

Brandenstein, Daniel C — *Astronaut*
%Loral Space Information Systems, 2450 S Shore Blvd, Houston, TX 77258, USA

Brandis, Jonathan — *Actor*
%Gersh Agency, 232 N Canon Dr, Beverly Hills, CA 90210, USA

Brando, Marlon — *Actor*
%International Creative Mgmt, 8942 Wilshire Blvd, Beverly Hills, CA 90211, USA

Brandon, Clark — *Actor*
%Jennings Assoc, 28035 Dorothy Dr, #210-A, Agoura, CA 91301, USA

Brandon, David A — *Businessman*
%Valassis Communications, 36111 Schoolcraft Rd, Livonia, MI 48150, USA

Brandon, Edward B — Businessman
%National City Corp, 1900 E 9th St, Cleveland, OH 44114, USA

Brandon, John — Actor
%"Bold & Beautiful", Bell-Phillip Prod, 7800 Beverly Blvd, Los Angeles, CA 90036, USA

Brandon, Michael — Actor
%London Mgmt, 2-4 Noel St, London W1V 3RB, England

Brandon, Terrell — Basketball Player
%Cleveland Cavaliers, 2923 Statesboro Rd, Richfield, OH 44286, USA

Brandow, Paul — Financier
%Chase Securities, 1 Chase Manhattan Plaza, New York, NY 10081, USA

Brands, X — Actor
17171 Roscoe Blvd, #104, Northridge, CA 91325, USA

Brandt, Coleman M — Businessman
%Ark Asset Management, 1 New York Plaza, New York, NY 10004, USA

Brandt, Hank — Actor
%Contemporary Artists, 1427 3rd St Promenade, #205, Santa Monica, CA 90401, USA

Brandt, Jon — Singer, Bassist (Cheap Trick)
%Ken Adamay Assoc, 315 W Gorham St, Madison, WI 53703, USA

Brandt, Victor — Actor
859 Camino Colibri, Calabasas, CA 91302, USA

Brandy, J C — Actress
%Kazarian/Spencer Assoc, 11365 Ventura Blvd, #100, Studio City, CA 91604, USA

Branigan, Laura — Singer, Songwriter
310 E 65th St, New York, NY 10021, USA

Branitzki, Heinz — Businessman
%Porsche Dr Ing HCF, Porchenstr 42, 70435 Stuttgart, Germany

Brann, Alton J — Businessman
%Litton Industries, 21240 Burbank Blvd, Woodland Hills, CA 91367, USA

Brannan, Charles F — Secretary, Agriculture
3131 E Alameda Ave, Denver, CO 80209, USA

Brannon, Ronald — Religious Leader
%Wesleyan Church, PO Box 50434, Indianapolis, IN 46250, USA

Branscomb, B Harvie — Educator
1620 Chickering Rd, Nashville, TN 37215, USA

Branscomb, Lewis M — Physicist
%Harvard University, Kennedy School of Government, Cambridge, MA 02138, USA

Branson, Richard — Businessman, Balloonist
%Virgin Group, 120 Campden Hill Rd, London W8 7AR, England

Branstad, Terry E — Governor, IA
%Governor's Office, State Capitol Bldg, Des Moines, IA 50319, USA

Brant, Tim — Sportscaster
%ABC-TV, Sports Dept, 77 W 66th St, New York, NY 10023, USA

Brasseur, Claude — Actor
%Artmedia, 10 Ave George V, 75008 Paris, France

Brathwaite, Edward — Writer
%University of West Indies, History Dept, Mona, Kingston 7, Jamaica

Bratkowski, Zeke — Football Player, Coach
51000 Fulton Ave, Hempstead, NY 11550, USA

Bratt, Benjamin — Actor
326 Venice Way, Venice, CA 90291, USA

Bratton, Joseph K — Army General
%Ralph M Parsons Co, 100 W Walnut St, Pasadena, CA 91124, USA

Brauer, Arik — Artist
%Joram Harel Mgmt, PO Box 28, 1182 Vienna, Austria

Brauer, Jerald C — Church Historian
5620 S Blackstone Ave, Chicago, IL 60637, USA

Braugher, Andrew — Actor
%United Talent Agency, 9560 Wilshire Blvd, #500, Beverly Hills, CA 90212, USA

Braun, Lillian Jackson — Writer
%Blanche Gregory Inc, 2 Tudor Pl, New York, NY 10017, USA

Braun, Neil S — Entertainment Executive
%NBC-TV, Rockefeller Center, New York, NY 10112, USA

Braun, Pinkas — Actor, Theater Director
Unterdorf, 8261 Hemishofen/SH, Switzerland

Braver, Rita — Commentator
%CBS-TV, News Dept, 2020 "M" St NW, Washington, DC 20036, USA

Braverman, Bart — Actor
524 N Laurel Ave, Los Angeles, CA 90048, USA

Brandon - Braverman

Brawne - Brendel

Brenden, Hallgeir — *Nordic Skier*
2417 Torberget, Norway

Brendsel, Leland C — *Financier*
%Federal Home Loan Mortgage Corp, 1700 "G" St NW, Washington, DC 20552, USA

Breneman, Curtis E — *Chemist*
38 Carlyle Ave, Troy, NY 12180, USA

Brennaman, Thom — *Sportscaster*
%Fox-TV, Sports Dept, PO Box 900, Beverly Hills, CA 90213, USA

Brennan, Bernard F — *Businessman*
%Montgomery Ward Co, 619 W Chicago Ave, Chicago, IL 60610, USA

Brennan, Eileen — *Actress*
974 Mission Terrace, Camarillo, CA 93010, USA

Brennan, James F — *Hockey Executive*
%Boston Bruins, Boston Garden, 150 Causeway St, Boston, MA 02114, USA

Brennan, John J — *Financier*
%Vanguard Group, 1300 Morris Dr, Valley Forge, PA 19482, USA

Brennan, Joseph E — *Governor/Representative, ME*
104 Frances St, Portland, ME 04102, USA

Brennan, Maire — *Singer, Songwriter*
%Atlantic Records, 75 Rockefeller Plaza, New York, NY 10019, USA

Brennan, Melissa — *Actress*
6520 Platt Ave, #634, West Hills, CA 91307, USA

Brennan, Patrick E — *Businessman*
%Consolidated Papers Inc, 231 1st Ave S, Wisconsin Rapids, WI 54494, USA

Brennan, Peter J — *Secretary, Labor*
2100 Massachusetts Ave, Washington, DC 20008, USA

Brennan, Robert E — *Horse Racing Executive, Businessman*
%First Jersey Securities, 50 Broadway, #1401, New York, NY 10004, USA

Brennan, Terry — *Football Player, Coach*
1349 Chestnut St, Wilmette, IL 60091, USA

Brennan, William J, Jr — *Supreme Court Justice*
%US Supreme Court, 1 1st St NE, Washington, DC 20543, USA

Brenneman, Amy — *Actress*
9150 Wilshire Blvd, #175, Beverly Hills, CA 90212, USA

Brenner, David — *Comedian*
42 Downing St, New York, NY 10014, USA

Brenner, Donald R — *Financier*
%Trust Co of New Jersey, 35 Journal Square, Jersey City, NY 07306, USA

Brenner, Dori — *Actress*
2106 Canyon Dr, Los Angeles, CA 90068, USA

Brenner, Sydney — *Molecular Biologist*
%MRC Molecular Genetics Unit, Hills Rd, Cambridge CB2 2QH, England

Brent Ashe, Eve — *Actress*
200 N Robertson Blvd, #214, Beverly Hills, CA 90211, USA

Brescia, Richard — *Radio Executive*
%CBS Radio Network, 51 W 52nd St, New York, NY 10019, USA

Bresee, Bobbie — *Actress*
PO Box 1222, Los Angeles, CA 90078, USA

Bresky, H H — *Businessman*
%Seaboard Corp, 200 Boylston St, Chestnut Hill, MA 02167, USA

Breslawsky, Marc C — *Businessman*
%Pitney Bowes Inc, 1 Elmcroft Rd, Stamford, CT 06926, USA

Breslin, Jimmy — *Journalist*
75 Central Park West, New York, NY 10023, USA

Breslow, Lester — *Physician*
10926 Verano Rd, Los Angeles, CA 90077, USA

Breslow, Ronald C — *Chemist*
275 Broad Ave, Englewood, NJ 07631, USA

Bresson, Robert — *Movie Director*
49 Quai de Bourbon, 75004 Paris, France

Brest, Martin — *Movie Director*
831 Paseo Miramar, Pacific Palisades, CA 90272, USA

Brett, George H — *Baseball Player, Executive*
PO Box 419969, Kansas City, MO 64141, USA

Breuer, Grit — *Track Athlete*
%Neubrandenburg SC, Am Jahnstadion, 17033 Neubrandenburg, Germany

Brewer, Albert P — *Governor, AL*
%Samford University, Law School, 800 Lakeshore Dr, Birmingham, AL 35229, USA

B

Brenden - Brewer

B

Brewer, Gay *Golfer*
%Professional Golfer's Assn, PO Box 109601, Palm Beach Gardens, FL 33410, USA

Brewer, Leo *Chemist*
15 Vista del Orinda, Orinda, CA 94563, USA

Brewer, Richard G *Atomic Physicist*
%IBM Almaden Research Center, 650 Harry Rd, San Jose, CA 95120, USA

Brewer, Richard W *Businessman*
%Arbella Mutual Insurance, 1100 Crown Colony Dr, Quincy, MA 02169, USA

Brewer, Rowanne *Model*
%Elite Model Mgmt, 111 E 22nd St, #200, New York, NY 10010, USA

Brewer, Teresa *Singer*
384 Pinebrook Blvd, New Rochelle, NY 10804, USA

Breyer, Stephen G *Supreme Court Justice*
%US Supreme Court, 1 1st St NE, Washington, DC 20543, USA

Breytenbach, Breyten *Poet, Political Activist*
%Harcourt Brace Jovanovich, 111 5th Ave, New York, NY 10003, USA

Brialy, Jean-Claude *Actor*
%Theatre des Bouffes Parisiens, 4 Rue Monsigny, 75002 Paris, France

Brian, Earl W *Publisher*
%United Press International, 1400 "I" St NW, Washington, DC 20005, USA

Brice, William J *Artist*
427 Beloit St, Los Angeles, CA 90049, USA

Brickell, Beth *Movie Director*
PO Box 119, Paron, AR 72122, USA

Bricker, Neal S *Physician*
1345 S Center St, Redlands, CA 92373, USA

Brickhouse, John B (Jack) *Sportscaster*
%WGN-Continental Broadcasting Co, 2501 W Bradley Pl, Chicago, IL 60618, USA

Bricklin, Daniel S *Computer Software Designer (VisiCalc)*
%Slate Corp, 25 Needham St, Newton, MA 02161, USA

Brickman, Paul M *Movie Director*
4116 Holly Knoll Dr, Los Angeles, CA 90027, USA

Brickowski, Frank *Basketball Player*
%Seattle Supersonics, 190 Queen Ave N, PO Box C-900911, Seattle, WA 98109, USA

Bricusse, Leslie *Composer*
9903 Santa Monica Blvd, #112, Beverly Hills, CA 90212, USA

Bridges, Alan J S *Movie Director*
Wyndham House, 1 Wyndham St, Kemp Town, Brighton Sussex BN2 1AF, England

Bridges, Beau *Actor*
5525 N Jed Smith Rd, Hidden Hills, CA 91302, USA

Bridges, Jeff *Actor*
%Creative Artists Agency, 9830 Wilshire Blvd, Beverly Hills, CA 90212, USA

Bridges, Lloyd *Actor*
21540 Pacific Coast Highway, Malibu, CA 90265, USA

Bridges, Roy D, Jr *Astronaut, Air Force General*
%USAF Materials Command, Wright Patterson Air Force Base, Dayton, OH 45433, USA

Bridges, Todd *Actor*
7550 Zombar Ave, #1, Van Nuys, CA 91406, USA

Bridgewater, Bernard A, Jr *Businessman*
%Brown Group, 8300 Maryland Ave, St Louis, MO 63105, USA

Briers, Richard *Actor*
%Lorraine Hamilton, 24 Denmark St, London WC2H 8NA, England

Briggs of Lewes, Asa *Historian*
Caprons, Keere St, Lewes, Sussex, England

Briggs, Edward S *Navy Admiral*
3648 Lago Sereno, Escondido, CA 92029, USA

Briggs, Raymond R *Writer, Illustrator, Cartoonist*
Weston, Undrhill Lane, Westmeston Near Hassocks, Sussex, England

Briggs, Robert W *Biologist*
7128 Casitas Pass Rd, Carpinteria, CA 93013, USA

Bright, Harvey R (Bum) *Businessman*
4500 Lakeside Dr, Dallas, TX 75205, USA

Bright, Stanley J *Businessman*
%Iowa-Illinois Gas & Electric, 206 E 2nd St, Davenport, IA 52801, USA

Brightman, Sarah *Singer*
47 Greek St, London W1V 5LQ, England

Briles, Nelson K *Baseball Player*
1324 Clearview Dr, Greensburg, PA 15601, USA

Brewer - Briles

Brill, Charles *Actor*
3635 Wrightwood Dr, Studio City, CA 91604, USA

Brill, Francesca *Actress*
%Kate Feast, 179 Lichfield Ct, Sheen Rd, Richmond, Surrey TW9 1AZ, England

Brill, Steven *Editor, Publisher*
%American Lawyer Magazine, 600 3rd Ave, New York, NY 10016, USA

Brill, Winston J *Bacteriologist*
4134 Cherokee Dr, Madison, WI 53711, USA

Brillstein, Bernie *Television Producer, Agent*
%Brillstein Co, 9150 Wilshire Blvd, #350, Beverly Hills, CA 90212, USA

Briloff, Abraham J *Educator*
99 Grace Ave, Great Neck, NY 11021, USA

Brimley, Wilford *Actor*
%Artists Agency, 10000 Santa Monica Blvd, #305, Los Angeles, CA 90067, USA

Brimmer, Andrew F *Government Official, Economist*
%Brimmer Co, 4400 MacArthur Blvd NW, Washington, DC 20007, USA

Brimsek, Frank *Hockey Player*
1017 13th St N, Virginia, MN 55792, USA

Brinckman, Donald W *Businessman*
%Safety-Kleen Corp, 1000 N Randall Rd, Elgin, IL 60123, USA

Brinegar, Claude S *Secretary, Transportation; Businessman*
%Unocal Corp, 1201 W 5th St, Los Angeles, CA 90017, USA

Brinegar, Paul *Actor*
17322 Halsey St, Granada Hills, CA 91344, USA

Brink, Andre P *Writer*
%University of Cape Town, Rondebosch 7700, South Africa

Brink, Frank, Jr *Biophysicist*
Pine Run, #E-1, Ferry & Iron Hill Rds, Doylestown, PA 18901, USA

Brink, K Robert *Publisher*
%Town & Country Magazine, 1700 Broadway, New York, NY 10019, USA

Brink, R Alexander *Geneticist*
4237 Manitou Way, Madison, WI 53711, USA

Brinker, Norman E *Businessman*
%Brinker International, 6820 LBJ Freeway, Dallas, TX 75240, USA

Brinkhous, Kenneth M *Pathologist*
524 Dogwood Dr, Chapel Hill, NC 27516, USA

Brinkley, Christie *Model*
%Ford Model Agency, 344 E 59th St, New York, NY 10022, USA

Brinkley, David *Commentator*
%ABC-TV, News Dept, 1717 De Sales St NW, Washington, DC 20036, USA

Brinson, Gary *Financier*
%Brinson Partners, 209 S LaSalle St, Chicago, IL 60604, USA

Brinster, Ralph L *Reproductive Physiologist*
%University of Pennsylvania, Veterinary Medicine School, Philadelphia, PA 19104, USA

Briscoe, Dolph *Governor, TX*
338 Pecan St, Uvalde, TX 78801, USA

Brisebois, Danielle *Actress*
950 N Kings Rd, Los Angeles, CA 90069, USA

Briskin, Jacqueline *Writer*
%Delacorte Press, 1540 Broadway, New York, NY 10036, USA

Brisse, Leland V (Lou) *Baseball Player*
1908 White Pine Dr, North Augusta, SC 29841, USA

Bristow, Allan M *Basketball Player, Coach, Executive*
%Charlotte Hornets, 1 Hive Dr, Charlotte, NC 28217, USA

Britain, Radie *Composer*
PO Box 17, Smithville, IN 47458, USA

Britt, Mai *Actress*
PO Box 525, Zephyr Cove, NV 89448, USA

Britt, Maurice L *WW II Army Hero (CMH)*
7 Athena Ct, Little Rock, AR 72227, USA

Brittan, Leon *Government Official, England*
%European Communities Commission, 200 Rue de Loi, 1049 Brussels, Belgium

Brittany, Morgan *Model, Actress*
3434 Cornell Rd, Agoura Hills, CA 91301, USA

Britten, Roy J *Geneticist*
%Kerckhoff Marine Laboratory, 101 Dahlia Ave, Corona del Mar, CA 92625, USA

Brittenham, Harry *Attorney*
%Ziffren Brittenham Branca, 2121 Ave of Stars, #3200, Los Angeles, CA 90067, USA

B

Britton, Tony — *Actor*
%International Creative Mgmt, 76 Oxford St, London W1N 0AX, England

Britz, Jerilyn — *Golfer*
%Ladies Professional Golf Assn, 2570 Volusia Ave, Daytona Beach, FL 32114, USA

Broad, Eli — *Businessman*
%SunAmerica Inc, 1 SunAmerica Center, Los Angeles, CA 90067, USA

Broadbent, John Edward — *Government Official, Canada*
%House of Commons, Parliamentry Buildings, Ottawa ON K1A 0A6, Canada

Broadddus, J Alfred, Jr — *Financier*
%Federal Reserve Bank, 701 E Byrd St, Richmond, VA 23219, USA

Broadhead, James L — *Businessman*
%FPL Group, 700 Universe Blvd, Juno Beach, FL 33408, USA

Broccoli, Albert R (Cubby) — *Movie Producer*
809 N Hillcrest Rd, Beverly Hills, CA 90210, USA

Broches, Aron — *Attorney*
2600 Tilden Pl NW, Washington, DC 20008, USA

Brock, Louis C (Lou) — *Baseball Player*
11885 Lackland Rd, St Louis, MO 63146, USA

Brock, Stan — *Football Player*
%New Orleans Saints, 1500 Poydras St, New Orleans, LA 70112, USA

Brock, William E — *Secretary of Labor; Senator, TN*
PO Box 6646, Annapolis, MD 21401, USA

Brockert, Richard C — *Labor Leader*
%United Telegraph Workers, 701 Gude Dr, Rockville, MD 20850, USA

Brockhouse, Bertram N — *Nobel Physics Laureate*
PO Box 7338, Ancaster ON L9G 3N6, Canada

Brockington, John — *Football Player*
1205 Prospect, #550, La Jolla, CA 92037, USA

Broder, David S — *Columnist*
4024 N 27th St, Arlington, VA 22207, USA

Broder, Samuel — *Medical Administrator*
%National Cancer Institute, 9000 Rockville Pike, Bethesda, MD 20892, USA

Broderick, Beth — *Actress*
%Paul Kohner Inc, 9300 Wilshire Blvd, #555, Beverly Hills, CA 90212, USA

Broderick, John D — *Businessman*
%ITT Financial Corp, 645 Maryville Centre Dr, St Louis, MO 63141, USA

Broderick, Matthew — *Actor*
17 Charlton St, New York, NY 10014, USA

Brodie, H Keith H — *Educator, Psychiatrist*
63 Beverly Dr, Durham, NC 27707, USA

Brodie, John — *Football Player, Sportscaster*
260 Surry Pl, Los Altos, CA 94022, USA

Brodsky, Joseph A — *Nobel Literature Laureate*
%Mount Holyoke College, English Dept, South Hadley, MA 01075, USA

Brodsky, Julian A — *Businessman*
%Comcast Corp, 1500 Market St, Philadelphia, PA 19102, USA

Brody, Alexander J — *Businessman*
%Ogilvy & Mather Worldwide, 309 W 49th St, New York, NY 10019, USA

Brody, Clark L — *Concert Clarinetist*
1621 Colfax St, Evanston, IL 60201, USA

Brody, Jane E — *Journalist*
%New York Times, Editorial Dept, 229 W 43rd St, New York, NY 10036, USA

Brody, Kenneth D — *Financier*
%Export-Import Bank, 811 Vermont Ave NW, Washington, DC 20571, USA

Brody, Lane — *Singer*
%Black Stallion Country Productions, 9741 Commerce Ave, Tujunga, CA 91042, USA

Broeg, Robert W (Bob) — *Sportswriter*
%St Louis Post Dispatch, Editorial Dept, 900 N Tucker Blvd, St Louis, MO 63101, USA

Broelsch, Christopher E — *Surgeon*
%University of Chicago Medical Center, Surgery Dept, Box 259, Chicago, IL 60690, USA

Broglio, Ernest G (Ernie) — *Baseball Player*
2838 Via Carmen, San Jose, CA 95124, USA

Broidy, Steven D — *Financier*
%City National Corp, 400 N Roxbury Dr, Beverly Hills, CA 90210, USA

Brokaw, Norman R — *Entertainment Executive*
710 N Alta Dr, Beverly Hills, CA 90210, USA

Brokaw, Thomas J (Tom) — *Commentator*
941 Park Ave, #14-C, New York, NY 10028, USA

Brolin, James	*Actor*
PO Box 56927, Sherman Oaks, CA 91413, USA	
Brolin, Josh	*Actor*
PO Box 56927, Sherman Oaks, CA 91413, USA	
Bromfield, John	*Actor*
PO Box 2655, Lake Havasu City, AZ 86405, USA	
Bromley, D Allan	*Government Official, Physicist*
35 Tokeneke Dr, North Haven, CT 06473, USA	
Bromwich, John	*Tennis Player*
%International Tennis Hall of Fame, 194 Bellevue Ave, Newport, RI 02840, USA	
Bronars, Edward J	*Marine Corps General*
%Navy Mutual Aid Assn, Arlington Annex, #G-070, Washington, DC 20370, USA	
Bronfman, Charles R	*Businessman, Baseball Executive*
%Seagram Co, 1400 Peel St, Montreal PQ H3A 1S9, Canada	
Bronfman, Edgar M	*Businessman*
%Joseph E Seagram & Sons, 375 Park Ave, New York, NY 10152, USA	
Bronfman, Edgar M, Jr	*Businessman*
%Joseph E Seagram & Sons, 375 Park Ave, New York, NY 10152, USA	
Bronfman, Yefin	*Concert Pianist*
%International Creative Mgmt, 40 W 57th St, New York, NY 10019, USA	
Bronson, Charles	*Actor*
PO Box 2644, Malibu, CA 90265, USA	
Bronson, Oswald P, Sr	*Educator*
%Bethune-Cookman College, President's Office, Daytona Beach, FL 32114, USA	
Brook, Peter S P	*Movie, Theater Director*
%CICT, 9 Rue du Cirque, 75008 Paris, France	
Brooke, Edward W	*Senator, MA*
2500 Virginia Ave NW, #301-S, Washington, DC 20037, USA	
Brooke, Hilary	*Actress*
40 Via Casitas, Bonsall, CA 92003, USA	
Brooke, Peter A	*Financier*
%Advent International, 101 Federal St, Boston, MA 02110, USA	
Brooker, Gary	*Singer (Procul Harem), Songwriter*
%Strongman Mgmt, Banda House, Cambridge Grove, London W6 8LE, England	
Brookins, Gary	*Editorial Cartoonist*
%Richmond Newspapers, Editorial Dept, PO Box 85333, Richmond, VA 23293, USA	
Brookner, Anita	*Writer*
68 Elm Park Gardens, #6, London SW10 9PB, England	
Brooks, Albert	*Actor, Director*
%Scotti Bros, 2114 Pico Blvd, Santa Monica, CA 90405, USA	
Brooks, Avery	*Actor*
%Lynn Coles Productions, PO Box 93-1198, Los Angeles, CA 90093, USA	
Brooks, Derrick	*Football Player*
%Tampa Bay Buccaneers, 1 Buccaneer Place, Tampa, FL 33607, USA	
Brooks, Diana D	*Businesswoman*
%Sotheby's Holdings, 500 N Woodward Ave, Bloomfield Hills, MI 48304, USA	
Brooks, Donald M	*Fashion, Theater Designer*
158 E 70th St, New York, NY 10021, USA	
Brooks, E R	*Businessman*
%Central & South West Corp, 1616 Woodall Rogers Freeway, Dallas, TX 75202, USA	
Brooks, Elbert D	*Educator*
911 Otter Creek Rd, Nashville, TN 37220, USA	
Brooks, Foster	*Comedian*
PO Box 135, Henrietta, NY 14467, USA	
Brooks, Garth	*Singer*
%Doyle/Lewis Mgmt, 1109 17th Ave S, Nashville, TN 37212, USA	
Brooks, Gwendolyn	*Writer*
5530 S Shore Dr, #2-A, Chicago, IL 60637, USA	
Brooks, Harvey	*Physicist*
46 Brewster St, #Y, Cambridge, MA 02138, USA	
Brooks, Hubie	*Baseball Player*
15001 Olive St, Hesperia, CA 92345, USA	
Brooks, James	*Football Player*
%Cleveland Browns, 80 1st Ave, Berea, OH 44017, USA	
Brooks, James C, Jr	*Businessman*
%Life Insurance Co of Georgia, 5780 Powers Ferry Rd NW, Atlanta, GA 30327, USA	
Brooks, James L	*Movie Director, Producer, Screenwriter*
10380 Tennessee Ave, Los Angeles, CA 90064, USA	

B

Brolin - Brooks

Brooks, John E — Educator
%College of Holy Cross, President's Office, Worcester, MA 01610, USA

Brooks, Karen — Singer
5408 Clear View Lane, Waterford, WI 53185, USA

Brooks, Kix — Singer (Brooks & Dunn), Songwriter
%Bob Titley Entertainments, 706 18th Ave S, Nashville, TN 37203, USA

Brooks, Mel — Movie Director, Actor
2301 La Mesa Dr, Santa Monica, CA 90402, USA

Brooks, Michael — Football Player
%New York Giants, Giants Stadium, East Rutherford, NJ 07073, USA

Brooks, Rand — Actor
662 Juniper Pl, Franklin Lakes, NJ 07417, USA

Brooks, Randi — Actress, Model
11726 San Vicente Blvd, #900, Beverly Hills, CA 90212, USA

Brooks, Rich — Football Coach
%St Louis Rams, 100 N Broadway, #2100, St Louis, MO 63102, USA

Brooks, Roger K — Businessman
%Central Life Assurance Co, 611 5th Ave, Des Moines, IA 50309, USA

Brookshier, Tom — Sportscaster
%WIP-Radio, Sports Dept, 19th & Walnut Sts, Philadelphia, PA 19103, USA

Brophy, Kevin — Actor
15010 Hamlin St, Van Nuys, CA 91411, USA

Brophy, Theodore F — Businessman
60 Arch St, Greenwich, CT 06830, USA

Brosius, Charles C — Businessman
%Agway Inc, 333 Butternut Dr, Dewitt, NY 13214, USA

Brosnan, Pierce — Actor
28011 Paquet Pl, Malibu, CA 90265, USA

Brostek, Bern — Football Player
%St Louis Rams, 100 N Broadway, #2100, St Louis, MO 63102, USA

Brothers, Joyce D — Psychologist
1530 Palisade Ave, Fort Lee, NJ 07024, USA

Brough Clapp, Louise — Tennis Player
1808 Voluntary Rd, Vista, CA 92084, USA

Broun, Heywood Hale — Sportscaster, Columnist
184 Plochman, Woodstock, NY 12498, USA

Brouwenstyn, Gerarda — Opera Singer
3 Bachplein, Amsterdam, Netherlands

Brown Heritage, Doris — Track Athlete
%Seattle Pacific College, Athletic Dept, Seattle, WA 98119, USA

Brown, Arthur E, Jr — Army General
18 Fairway Winds Pl, Hilton Head Island, SC 29928, USA

Brown, Bill — Football Player
7524 Auto Club Cir, Bloomington, MN 55438, USA

Brown, Blair — Actress
434 W 20th St, #3, New York, NY 10011, USA

Brown, Bo — Cartoonist
218 Wyncote Rd, Jenkintown, PA 19046, USA

Brown, Bob — Football Player
1200 Lakeshore Ave, Oakland, CA 94606, USA

Brown, Bobby — Singer, Dancer, Songwriter
1324 Thomas Pl, Fort Worth, TX 76107, USA

Brown, Bruce — Photographer, Surfer
15550 Calle Real, Gaviota, CA 93117, USA

Brown, Bryan — Actor
%Creative Artists Agency, 9830 Wilshire Blvd, Beverly Hills, CA 90212, USA

Brown, Buck — Cartoonist
PO Box 122, Park Forest, IL 60466, USA

Brown, Charles — Jazz Pianist, Singer
2870 Adeline, #102, Berkeley, CA 94703, USA

Brown, Charlie — Football Player
%C Brown Real Estate Computer Service, 642 Northshore Rd, Lithonia, GA 30058, USA

Brown, Curtis L, Jr — Astronaut
%NASA, Johnson Space Center, 2101 NASA Rd, Houston, TX 77058, USA

Brown, Dale D — Basketball Coach
%Louisiana State University, Athletic Dept, Baton Rouge, LA 70803, USA

Brown, Dave — Football Player, Coach
%Seattle Seahawks, 11220 NE 53rd St, Kirkland, WA 98033, USA

Brown, David *Movie Producer*
%Zanuck/Brown Co, 200 W 57th St, New York, NY 10019, USA

Brown, Dee *Basketball Player*
%Boston Celtics, 151 Merrimac St, #500, Boston, MA 02114, USA

Brown, Denis R *Businessman*
%Pinkerton's Inc, 15910 Ventura Blvd, Encino, CA 91436, USA

Brown, Denise Scott *Architect*
%Venturi Scott Brown Assoc, 4236 Main St, Philadelphia, PA 19127, USA

Brown, Derek *Football Player*
%New York Giants, Giants Stadium, East Rutherford, NJ 07073, USA

Brown, Eddie *Football Player*
%Cincinnati Bengals, 200 Riverfront Stadium, Cincinnati, OH 45202, USA

Brown, Edmund G (Jerry), Jr *Governor, CA*
%California Democratic Party, 2424 "K" St, #100, Sacramento, CA 95816, USA

Brown, Edmund G (Pat) *Governor, CA*
2040 Ave of Stars, #C-208, Los Angeles, CA 90067, USA

Brown, Ellis L *Businessman*
%Petrolite Corp, 369 Marshall Ave, St Louis, MO 63119, USA

Brown, Faith *Actress*
%Million Dollar Music Co, 12 Praed Mews, London W2 1QY, England

Brown, Fred *Basketball Player, Coach*
%Seattle Supersonics, 190 Queen Ave N, PO Box C-900911, Seattle, WA 98109, USA

Brown, Georg Stanford *Actor*
2565 Greenvalley Rd, Los Angeles, CA 90046, USA

Brown, George C, Jr *Football Player*
1662 E Main St, #421, El Cajon, CA 92021, USA

Brown, George Mackay *Writer*
3 Mayburn Ct, Stromness, Orkey, Scotland

Brown, Harold *Secretary, Defense*
%Strategic & Int'l Studies Center, 1800 "K" St NW, #1800, Washington, DC 20006, USA

Brown, Helen Gurley *Editor, Writer*
%Cosmopolitan Magazine, Editorial Dept, 224 W 57th St, New York, NY 10019, USA

Brown, Herbert C *Nobel Chemistry Laureate*
1840 Garden St, West Lafayette, IN 47906, USA

Brown, Himan *Director*
285 Central Park W, New York, NY 10024, USA

Brown, Hubie *Basketball Coach*
120 Foxridge Rd NW, Atlanta, GA 30327, USA

Brown, J Carter *Businessman*
1201 Pennsylvania Ave NW, #621, Washington, DC 20004, USA

Brown, J Cristopher (Cris) *Baseball Player*
5015 Brighton Ave, Los Angeles, CA 90062, USA

Brown, J Gordon *Government Official, England*
%House of Commons, Westminster, London SW1A 0AA, England

Brown, J Kevin *Baseball Player*
%Baltimore Orioles, 333 W Camden Ave, Baltimore, MD 21201, USA

Brown, James *Sportscaster*
%Fox-TV, Sports Dept, 205 E 67th St, New York, NY 10021, USA

Brown, James *Singer*
%James Brown Enterprises, 1217 W Medical Park Rd, Augusta, GA 30909, USA

Brown, James N (Jim) *Football Player, Actor*
1851 Sunset Plaza Dr, Los Angeles, CA 90069, USA

Brown, James R *Air Force General*
1591 Stowe Rd, Reston, VA 22094, USA

Brown, Jesse *Secretary, Veterans Affairs*
%Veterans Affairs Department, 810 Vermont Ave NW, Washington, DC 20420, USA

Brown, Jim Ed *Singer*
%Fat City Artists, 1226 17th Ave S, #2, Nashville, TN 37212, USA

Brown, Joe *Boxer*
1615 N Broad St, New Orleans, LA 70119, USA

Brown, John O *Financier*
%Commerce Bank of Kansas City, 1000 Walnut St, Kansas City, MO 64106, USA

Brown, Joseph W, Jr *Businessman*
%Talegen Holdings, 1011 Western Ave, Seattle, WA 98104, USA

Brown, Julie *Comedienne, Actress*
11288 Ventura Blvd, #728, Studio City, CA 91604, USA

Brown, Kenneth J *Labor Leader*
%Graphic Communications Int'l Union, 1900 "L" St NW, Washington, DC 20036, USA

B

Brown, Kimberlin — *Actress*
%Pelzer, 9220 Sunset Blvd, #230, Los Angeles, CA 90069, USA

Brown, L Dean — *Diplomat*
3030 Cambridge Pl, Washington, DC 20007, USA

Brown, Larry, Jr — *Football Player*
12004 Piney Glen Lane, Potomac, MD 20854, USA

Brown, Lawrence H (Larry) — *Basketball Coach*
%Indiana Pacers, Market Square Arena, 300 E Market St, Indianapolis, IN 46204, USA

Brown, Lee P — *Government Official*
%National Drug Control Policy Office, 1600 Pennsylvania NW, Washington, DC 20500, USA

Brown, Les — *Orchestra Leader*
1417 Capri Dr, Pacific Palisades, CA 90272, USA

Brown, Lester R — *Ecologist*
%Worldwatch Institute, 1776 Massachusetts Ave NW, Washington, DC 20036, USA

Brown, Lew — *Actor*
2439 S Kihei Rd, #102-B, Kihei, Maui HI 96753, USA

Brown, Lomas, Jr — *Football Player*
%Detroit Lions, Silverdome, 1200 Featherstone Rd, Pontiac, MI 48342, USA

Brown, Mark N — *Astronaut*
%General Research Corp, Space Division, 2940 Presidential Dr, Fairborn, OH 45324, USA

Brown, Michael S — *Nobel Medicine Laureate*
5719 Redwood Lane, Dallas, TX 75209, USA

Brown, Mike — *Football Executive*
%Cincinnati Bengals, 200 Riverfront Stadium, Cincinnati, OH 45202, USA

Brown, Olivia — *Actress*
5856 College Ave, #139, Oakland, CA 94618, USA

Brown, Owsley, II — *Businessman*
%Brown-Forman Inc, 850 Dixie Highway, Louisville, KY 40210, USA

Brown, Peter — *Actor*
854 Cypress Ave, Hermosa Beach, CA 90254, USA

Brown, Peter C — *Entertainment Executive*
%AMC International, 106 W 14th St, Kansas City, MO 64105, USA

Brown, Philip — *Actor*
%Century Artists, 9744 Wilshire Blvd, #308, Beverly Hills, CA 90212, USA

Brown, Ray — *Jazz Bassist*
PO Box 845, Concord, CA 94522, USA

Brown, Reuben — *Football Player*
%Buffalo Bills, 1 Bills Dr, Orchard Park, NY 14127, USA

Brown, Richard H — *Businessman*
%Ameritech Corp, 30 S Wacker Dr, Chicago, IL 60606, USA

Brown, Rita Mae — *Writer, Social Activist*
%Wendy Weill Agency, 232 Madison Ave, New York, NY 10016, USA

Brown, Robert McAfee — *Religious Leader*
2090 Columbia Ave, Palo Alto, CA 94306, USA

Brown, Roger W — *Social Psychologist*
100 Memorial Dr, Cambridge, MA 02142, USA

Brown, Ronald H — *Publisher*
%New England Journal of Medicine, 1440 Main St, Waltham, MA 02154, USA

Brown, Ronald H — *Secretary, Commerce*
%Commerce Department, 14th St & Constitution Ave, Washington, DC 20230, USA

Brown, Roosevelt — *Football Player*
153 Van Buskirk Ave, Teaneck, NJ 07666, USA

Brown, Roscoe C, Jr — *Educator*
%City University of New York, Urban Education Policy Center, New York, NY 10031, USA

Brown, Ruth — *Singer*
600 W 165th St, #4-H, New York, NY 10032, USA

Brown, Stephen L — *Businessman*
%John Hancock Mutual Life Insurance, PO Box 111, Boston, MA 02117, USA

Brown, T Graham — *Singer*
%Starbound Mgmt, 128 Volunteer Dr, Hendersonville, TN 37075, USA

Brown, Timothy C — *Businessman*
%Thomas Industries, 4360 Brownsboro Rd, Louisville, KY 40207, USA

Brown, Timothy D (Tim) — *Football Player*
%Oakland Raiders, Oakland Coliseum, Oakland, CA 94621, USA

Brown, Tina — *Editor*
%New Yorker Magazine, Editorial Dept, 20 W 43rd St, New York, NY 10036, USA

Brown, Tom — *Football Player*
%Pemberton Houston Willoughby, Bentall Center 4, Vancouver BC, Canada

Brown - Brown

Brown, Tracy *Ballerina*
%Royal Ballet, Bow St, London WC2E 9DD, England

Brown, Trisha *Choreographer, Dancer*
%Trisha Brown Dance Co, 225 Lafayette St, #807, New York, NY 10012, USA

Brown, Vanessa *Actress*
5914 Coldwater Canyon Ave, #5, North Hollywood, CA 91607, USA

Brown, W L Lyons, Jr *Businessman*
%Brown-Forman Inc, 850 Dixie Highway, Louisville, KY 40210, USA

Brown, William D *Football Player*
7524 Auto Club Circle, Bloomington, MN 55438, USA

Brown, Willie *Football Player, Coach*
%Oakland Raiders, Oakland Coliseum, Oakland, CA 94621, USA

Browne, Jackson *Singer, Songwriter*
%Donald Miller, 12746 Kling St, Studio City, CA 91604, USA

Browne, Katherine *Actress*
%Leonard Grainger, 9903 Kip Dr, Beverly Hills, CA 90210, USA

Browne, Leslie *Ballerina, Actress*
%American Ballet Theatre, 890 Broadway, New York, NY 10003, USA

Browne, Roscoe Lee *Actor*
465 W 57th St, #1-A, New York, NY 10019, USA

Browne, Secor D *Aviation Engineer, Government Official*
2101 "L" St NW, #207, Washington, DC 20037, USA

Browne, Spencer I *Financier*
%Asset Investors Corp, 3600 S Yosemite St, Denver, CO 80237, USA

Brownell, Herbert *Attorney General*
1675 Broadway, New York, NY 10019, USA

Browner, Carol M *Government Official*
%Environmental Protection Agency, 401 "M" St SW, Washington, DC 20024, USA

Browner, Joey *Football Player*
%Minnesota Vikings, 9520 Viking Dr, Eden Prairie, MN 55344, USA

Browner, Keith *Football Player*
%San Diego Chargers, Jack Murphy Stadium, San Diego, CA 92160, USA

Browner, Ross *Football Player*
%Ross Browner Enterprises, 1135 Flamingo Dr SW, Atlanta, GA 30311, USA

Browning, Dominique *Editor*
%Mirabella Magazine, Editorial Dept, 200 Madison Ave, New York, NY 10016, USA

Browning, Edmond L *Religious Leader*
%Episcopal Church, 815 2nd Ave, New York, NY 10017, USA

Browning, John *Concert Pianist*
%Columbia Artists Mgmt Inc, 165 W 57th St, New York, NY 10019, USA

Browning, Kurt *Figure Skater*
%Royal Glenora Club, 11160 River Valley Rd, Edmonton ON T5J 2G7, Canada

Browning, Thomas L (Tom) *Baseball Player*
3094 Friars St, Covington, KY 41017, USA

Brownlow, Kevin *Movie Producer*
%Thames TV, Teddington Studios, Teddington, Middx, England

Brownmiller, Susan *Feminist Leader*
61 Jane St, New York, NY 10014, USA

Brownstein, Philip N *Government Official*
550 "N" St NW, Washington, DC 20001, USA

Broyles, Frank *Football Coach, Sportscaster*
%University of Arkansas, Broyles Athletic Complex, Fayetteville, AR 72701, USA

Brozman, Jack L *Financier*
%Century Acceptance Corp, City Center Square, Kansas City, MO 64196, USA

Brubaker, John E *Financier*
%Bay View Federal Bank, 2121 S El Camino Real, San Mateo, CA 94403, USA

Brubeck, David W (Dave) *Jazz Pianist*
221 Millstone Rd, Wilton, CT 06897, USA

Brubeck, William H *Government Official*
7 Linden St, Cambridge, MA 02138, USA

Bruce, Audray *Football Player*
%Oakland Raiders, Oakland Coliseum, Oakland, CA 94621, USA

Bruce, Carol *Actress*
1361 N Laurel Ave, #20, Los Angeles, CA 90046, USA

Bruce, Marvin E *Businessman*
%TBC Corp, 4770 Hickory Hill Rd, Memphis, TN 38141, USA

Bruce, Robert V *Historian*
28 Evans Rd, Madbury, NH 03820, USA

B

Brown - Bruce

Bruckheimer, Jerry — *Movie Producer*
%Simpson-Bruckheimer Productions, 500 S Buena Vista St, Burbank, CA 91521, USA

Brueckner, Keith A — *Physicist*
7723 Ludington Pl, La Jolla, CA 92037, USA

Bruen, John D — *Army General, Businessman*
6104 Greenlawn Ct, Springfield, VA 22152, USA

Brugger, Ernst — *President, Switzerland*
8625 Gossau ZH, Switzerland

Bruguera, Sergi — *Tennis Player*
C'Escipi'On 42, 08023 Barcelona, Spain

Brumback, Charles T — *Publisher*
%Tribune Co, 435 N Michigan Ave, Chicago, IL 60611, USA

Brumbaugh, R Dan, Jr — *Economist*
2448 Baker St, San Francisco, CA 94123, USA

Brummett, Larry W — *Businessman*
%ONEOK Inc, 100 W 5th St, Tulsa, OK 74103, USA

Brunansky, Thomas A (Tom) — *Baseball Player*
12916 Polvera Ave, San Diego, CA 92128, USA

Brundage, Howard D — *Publisher*
PO Box 766, Lyne, CT 06371, USA

Brundtland, Gro Harlem — *Prime Minister, Norway*
Det Norske Arbeiderparti, Youngstorget 2V, 0181 Oslo 1, Norway

Brunet, Andre Joly — *Figure Skater*
2805 Boyne City Rd, Boyne City, MI 49712, USA

Brunhart, Hans — *Chief of Government, Liechtenstein*
%Government Palace, Regierungsgebaude, 9490 Vaduz, Liechtenstein

Bruni, Carla — *Model*
%Wilhelmina Model Agency, 300 Park Ave, New York, NY 10022, USA

Brunner, J Terrance — *Association Executive*
%Better Government Assn, 230 N Michigan Ave, Chicago, IL 60601, USA

Brunner, Jerome S — *Psychologist, Educator*
200 Mercer St, New York, NY 10012, USA

Bruno, Frank — *Boxer*
PO Box 2266, Brentwood, Essex CM15 0AQ, England

Brunt, Jennifer — *Model*
%Elite Model Mgmt, 111 E 22nd St, New York, NY 10010, USA

Bruskin, Grisha — *Artist*
147 W 22nd St, #5-S, New York, NY 10011, USA

Brustein, Robert S — *Educator, Theater Producer, Critic*
%Harvard University, Loeb Drama Center, 64 Brattle St, Cambridge, MA 02138, USA

Bruton, John G — *Prime Minister, Ireland*
%Prime Minister's Office, Upper Merrion St, Dublin 2, Ireland

Bry, Ellen — *Actress*
8730 Sunset Blvd, #480, Los Angeles, CA 90069, USA

Bryan, David — *Keyboardist (Bon Jovi)*
%Bon Jovi Mgmt, 250 W 57th St, #603, New York, NY 10107, USA

Bryan, J Stewart, III — *Businessman*
%Media General Inc, 333 E Grace St, Richmond, VA 23293, USA

Bryan, John H, Jr — *Businessman*
%Sara Lee Corp, 3 First National Plaza, 70 W Madison St, Chicago, IL 60602, USA

Bryan, John S, III — *Publisher*
%Media General Inc, 333 E Grace St, Richmond, VA 23293, USA

Bryan, Wright — *Journalist*
3747 Peachtree Rd NE, #516, Atlanta, GA 30319, USA

Bryan, Zachary Ty — *Actor*
9105 Carmelita Ave, #101, Beverly Hills, CA 90210, USA

Bryant, Farris — *Governor, FL*
PO Box 2918, Jacksonville, FL 32203, USA

Bryant, Gay — *Editor*
34 Horatio St, New York, NY 10014, USA

Bryant, Joshua — *Actor*
%Century Artists, 9744 Wilshire Blvd, #308, Beverly Hills, CA 90212, USA

Bryant, Kelvin — *Football Player*
%Washington Redskins, 21300 Redskin Park Dr, Ashburn, VA 22011, USA

Bryden, Rod — *Hockey Executive*
%Ottawa Senators, 301 Moodie Dr, #200, Nepean ON K2H 9C4, Canada

Brymer, Jack — *Concert Clarinetist*
Underwood, Ballards Farm Rd, South Croydon, Surrey, England

Bruckheimer - Brymer

Bryson, John E — *Businessman*
%SCEcorp, 2244 Walnut Grove Ave, Rosemead, CA 91770, USA

Bryson, Peabo — *Singer, Songwriter*
%David Franklin Assoc, 999 Peachtree St, Atlanta, GA 30309, USA

Brzezinski, Zbigniew — *Government Official, Educator*
%Strategic & International Studies Center, 1800 "K" NW, Washington, DC 20006, USA

Buatta, Mario — *Interior Designer*
120 E 80th St, New York, NY 10021, USA

Bubka, Sergei N — *Track Athlete*
%Andresj Kulikowski, Vasavagen 13, 171 39 Solna, Sweden

Bucha, Paul W — *Vietnam War Army Hero (CMH)*
142 Wooster St, #4-A, New York, NY 10012, USA

Buchanan, Edna — *Journalist*
%Miami Herald, Editorial Dept, 1 Herald Plaza, Miami, FL 33132, USA

Buchanan, Ian — *Actor*
%Gold Marshak Assoc, 3500 W Olive Ave, #1400, Burbank, CA 91505, USA

Buchanan, Isobel — *Opera Singer*
%Marks Mgmt, 14 New Burlington St, London W1X 1FF, England

Buchanan, James M — *Nobel Economics Laureate*
%George Mason University, Study of Public Choice Center, Fairfax, VA 22030, USA

Buchanan, Jensen — *Actress*
200 W 57th St, #900, New York, NY 10019, USA

Buchanan, John M — *Biochemist*
56 Meriam St, Lexington, MA 02173, USA

Buchanan, Patrick J — *Columnist, Government Official*
1017 Savile Lane, McLean, VA 22101, USA

Buchen, Philip W — *Attorney, Government Official*
800 25th Ave NW, Washington, DC 20037, USA

Bucher, Lloyd — *Navy Hero*
11296 Rostrata Hill, Poway, CA 92064, USA

Buchholz, Horst — *Actor*
Kt Graubunden, 7078 Lenzerheide, Switzerland

Buchi, George H — *Chemist*
%Massachusetts Institute of Technology, Chemistry Dept, Cambridge, MA 02139, USA

Buchli, James F — *Astronaut*
%Boeing Defense/Space Group, ISSA, PO Box 58747, Houston, TX 77258, USA

Buchwald, Art — *Columnist*
2000 Pennsylvania Ave NW, Washington, DC 20006, USA

Buck, Jack — *Sportscaster*
%KMOX-TV, Sports Dept, Gateway Tower, 1 S Memorial Dr, St Louis, MO 63102, USA

Buck, Jason — *Football Player*
%Washington Redskins, 21300 Redskin Park Dr, Ashburn, VA 22011, USA

Buck, Joe — *Sportscaster*
%Fox-TV, Sports Dept, PO Box 900, Beverly Hills, CA 90213, USA

Buck, Peter — *Guitarist (REM)*
%REM/Athens Ltd, 250 W Clayton St, Athens, GA 30601, USA

Buck, Robert — *Guitarist (10,000 Maniacs)*
%New York End Ltd, 143 W 69th St, #4-A, New York, NY 10023, USA

Buck, Robert T, Jr — *Museum Director*
%Brooklyn Museum, 200 Eastern Parkway, Brooklyn, NY 11238, USA

Buckingham, Lindsey — *Musician (Fleetwood Mac)*
%Michael Brokaw Mgmt, 2934 Beverly Glen Circle, #383, Bel Air, CA 90077, USA

Bucklew, Neil S — *Educator*
%West Virginia University, President's Office, Morgantown, WV 26506, USA

Buckley, Betty — *Actress*
%William Morris Agency, 151 S El Camino Dr, Beverly Hills, CA 90212, USA

Buckley, Richard E — *Conductor*
87 Woods Rd, Branchville, NJ 07826, USA

Buckley, Terrell — *Football Player*
%Miami Dolphins, 7500 SW 30th St, Davie, FL 33329, USA

Buckley, William F, Jr — *Commentator, Editor*
%National Review Magazine, 150 E 35th St, New York, NY 10016, USA

Buckman, Frederick W — *Businessman*
%PacifiCorp, 825 NE Multnomah St, Portland, OR 97232, USA

Buckson, David P — *Governor, DE*
110 N Main St, Camden, DE 19934, USA

Buckwalter, Alan R, III — *Financier*
%Texas Commerce Bank, 712 Main St, Houston, TX 77002, USA

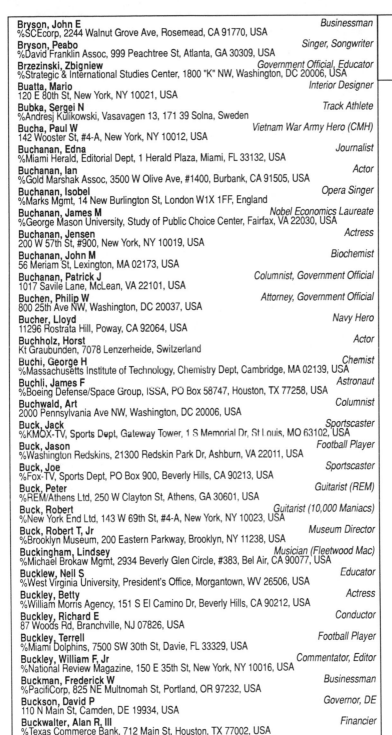

B

Bryson - Buckwalter

B

Bucyk, John — *Hockey Player*
%Boston Bruins, Boston Garden, 150 Causeway St, Boston, MA 02114, USA

Buczkowski, Bob — *Football Player*
%Oakland Raiders, Oakland Coliseum, Oakland, CA 94621, USA

Budarin, Nikolai — *Cosmonaut*
%Potchta Kosmonavtov, 141 160 Svyosdny Gorodok, Moskovskoi Oblasti, Russia

Budd Pieterse, Zola — *Track Athlete*
General Delivery, Bloemfontein, South Africa

Budd, Harold — *Composer, Poet*
%Opal/Warner Bros Records, 6834 Camrose Dr, Los Angeles, CA 90068, USA

Budd, Julie — *Actress, Singer*
%Herb Bernstein Mgmt, 180 West End Ave, New York, NY 10023, USA

Budde, Ed — *Football Player*
1176 Cherry Lane, Kansas City, MO 64106, USA

Budge, J Donald (Don) — *Tennis Player*
PO Box 789, Dingman's Ferry, PA 18328, USA

Budig, Gene A — *Baseball Executive, Educator*
%American League, 350 Park Ave, #1800, New York, NY 10022, USA

Bueche, Wendell F — *Businessman*
%IMC Global, 2100 Sanders Rd, Northbrook, IL 60062, USA

Bueno, Maria — *Tennis Player*
Rua Consolagao 3414, #10, 1001 Edificio Augustus, Sao Paulo, Brazil

Buerger, Martin J — *Mineralogist, Crystallographer*
Weston Rd, Lincoln, MA 01773, USA

Buffet, Bernard — *Artist*
%Galerie Maurice Garnier, 6 Ave Matignon, 75008 Paris, France

Buffett, Jimmy — *Singer, Songwriter*
%HK Mgmt, 80 Universal City Plaza, #401, Universal City, CA 91608, USA

Buffett, Warren E — *Businessman*
%Berkshire Hathaway Inc, 1440 Kiewit Plaza, Omaha, NE 68131, USA

Buffinton, Brian — *Actor*
%"Guidling Light" Show, CBS-TV, 51 W 52nd St, New York, NY 10019, USA

Buffkins, Archie Lee — *Performing Arts Administrator*
%Kennedy Center, Executive Suite, Washington, DC 20566, USA

Buffone, Douglas J (Doug) — *Football Player*
847 W Barry Ave, #G-A, Chicago, IL 60657, USA

Buffum, William B — *Diplomat*
%US Delegation, United Nations, New York, NY 10017, USA

Bufman, Zev — *Theater Producer*
1405 W 24th St, Miami, FL 33140, USA

Bugliosi, Vincent T — *Attorney, Writer*
8530 Wilshire Blvd, #404, Beverly Hills, CA 90211, USA

Buhari, Muhammadu — *President, Nigeria; Army General*
%GRA, Daura, Katsina State, Nigeria

Buhl, Robert R (Bob) — *Baseball Player*
26 Laurel Oak Dr, Winter Haven, FL 33880, USA

Buhrmaster, Robert C — *Businessman*
%Jostens Inc, 5501 Norman Center Dr, Minneapolis, MN 55437, USA

Bujold, Genevieve — *Actress*
27258 Pacific Coast Highway, Malibu, CA 90265, USA

Bujones, Fernando C — *Ballet Dancer*
%Boston Ballet, Community Music Center, 19 Clarendon St, Boston, MA 02116, USA

Buktenica, Raymond — *Actor*
11873 Rochester Ave, Los Angeles, CA 90025, USA

Buliach, Norman B (Norm) — *Football Player*
421 Lynn Dale Ct, Hurst, TX 76054, USA

Bulifant, Joyce — *Actress*
PO Box 6748, Snomass Village, CO 81615, USA

Bulkeley, John D — *WW II Navy Hero (CMH); Admiral*
10706 Lorain Ave, Silver Springs, MD 20901, USA

Bull, John S — *Astronaut*
1674 Alexander Court, Los Altos, CA 94024, USA

Bull, Richard — *Actor*
750 N Rush St, #3401, Chicago, IL 60611, USA

Bull, Ronald D (Ronnie) — *Football Player*
544 Michigan Ave, #2, Evanston, IL 60202, USA

Bullen, Voy M — *Religious Leader*
%Church of God, 1207 Willow Brook, Huntsville, AL 35802, USA

Bullins, Ed — *Writer*
425 Lafayette St, New York, NY 10003, USA

Bullitt, John C — *Attorney, Government Official*
%Shearman Sterling, 53 Wall St, New York, NY 10005, USA

Bullmann, Maik — *Greco-Roman Wrestler*
Leipziger Str 189, 15232 Frankfurt/Oder, Germany

Bullock, Dona — *Actress*
%Artists Agency, 10000 Santa Monica Blvd, #305, Los Angeles, CA 90067, USA

Bullock, Jm J — *Actor*
1015 N Kings Rd, #215, Los Angeles, CA 90069, USA

Bullock, Sandra — *Actress*
368 N Gardner St, Los Angeles, CA 90036, USA

Bullock, Theodore H — *Biologist*
3258 Caminito Ameca, La Jolla, CA 92037, USA

Bumbeck, David — *Artist*
Drew Lane, RD 3, Middlebury, VT 05753, USA

Bumbry, Alonzo B (Al) — *Baseball Player*
28 Tremblant Ct, Lutherville, MO 21093, USA

Bumbry, Grace — *Opera Singer*
%Herbert Breslin Inc, 119 W 57th St, New York, NY 10019, USA

Bumpus, Frederick J — *Businessman*
%Arkwright Mutual Insurance, 225 Wyman St, Waltham, MA 02154, USA

Bund, Karlheinz — *Businessman*
Huyssenallee 82-84, 45128 Essen Ruhr, Germany

Bundschuh, George A W — *Businessman*
%New York Life Insurance, 51 Madison Ave, New York, NY 10010, USA

Bundy, Brooke — *Actress*
833 N Martel Ave, Los Angeles, CA 90046, USA

Bundy, McGeorge — *Government Official, Educator*
%Carnegie Corporation, 437 Madison Ave, New York, NY 10022, USA

Bundy, William P — *Government Official, Editor*
1087 Great Rd, Princeton, NJ 08540, USA

Bunetta, Bill — *Bowler*
1176 E San Bruno, Fresno, CA 93710, USA

Bunge, Bettina — *Tennis Player*
2301 S Bayshore Dr, #14-D, Miami, FL 33133, USA

Bunker, Wallace E (Wally) — *Baseball Player*
702 E Indiana Ave, Coeur D'Alene, ID 83814, USA

Bunnell, David — *Editor, Publisher*
%PCW Communications, 555 DeHaro, San Francisco, CA 94107, USA

Bunting, James W — *Educator*
211 Lakeshore Dr, Milledgeville, GA 31061, USA

Buntrock, Dean L — *Businessman*
%WMX Technologies Inc, 3003 Butterfield Rd, Oak Brook, IL 60521, USA

Buoniconti, Nicholas A (Nick) — *Football Player, Businessman*
225 Arvida Parkway, Miami, FL 33156, USA

Burba, Edwin H, Jr — *Army General*
CinC, Forces Command, Ft McPherson, GA 30330, USA

Burbidge, E Margaret P — *Astronomer*
%University of California Astrophysics Center, 9500 Gilman, La Jolla, CA 92093, USA

Burchhardt, Helmuth — *Businessman*
%Eschweiler Bergwerks-Verein, 52134 Herzogenrath, Germany

Burchill, Thomas F (Tony) — *Radio Executive*
%RKO General, 1440 Broadway, New York, NY 10018, USA

Burchuladze, Paata — *Opera Singer*
%Metropolitan Opera Assn, Lincoln Center Plaza, New York, NY 10023, USA

Burd, Steven A — *Businessman*
%Safeway Inc, 4th & Jackson Sts, Oakland, CA 94660, USA

Burden, William A M — *Diplomat, Financier*
820 5th Ave, New York, NY 10021, USA

Burdette, S Lewis (Lew) — *Baseball Player*
2019 Beveva Rd, Sarasota, FL 34232, USA

Burdge, Jeffrey J — *Businessman*
%Harsco Corp, PO Box 8888, Camp Hill, PA 17001, USA

Burdon, Eric — *Singer (Animals); Songwriter*
%Geoffrey Blumenauer Artists, 11846 Balboa Ave, #204, Granada Hills, CA 91344, USA

Bure, Pavel — *Hockey Player*
%Vancouver Canucks, 100 N Renfrew St, Vancouver BC V5K 3N7, Canada

Burenga, Kenneth L *Businessman*
%Dow Jones Co, 200 Liberty St, New York, NY 10281, USA

Burford, Anne M *Government Official*
3853 S Hudson St, Denver, CO 80237, USA

Burford, Chris *Football Player*
377 2nd Tee Dr, Incline Village, NV 89451, USA

Burgee, John H *Architect*
Perelanda Farm, Skunks Misery Rd, Millerton, NY 12546, USA

Burgess, Greg *Track Athlete*
%US Olympic Committee, 1750 E Boulder St, Colorado Springs, CO 80909, USA

Burgess, Neil *Electrical Engineer*
8425 Kugler Mill Rd, Cincinnati, OH 45243, USA

Burgess, Robert K *Businessman*
%Pulte Corp, 33 Bloomfield Hills Parkway, Bloomfield Hills, MI 48304, USA

Burgess, Tony *Ecologist*
%US Geological Survey, 119 National Center, Reston, VA 22092, USA

Burgess, Warren D *Religious Leader*
%Reformed Church in America, 475 Riverside Dr, New York, NY 10115, USA

Burghoff, Gary *Actor*
4275 34th St S, #4, St Petersburg, FL 33711, USA

Burgin, C David *Editor*
%Oakland Tribune, Editorial Dept, 409 13th St, Oakland, CA 94612, USA

Burhoe, Ralph Wendell *Theologian*
Montgomery Place, 5550 S Shore Dr, #715, Chicago, IL 60637, USA

Burke Hederman, Lynn *Swimmer*
26 White Oak Tree Rd, Laurel Hollow, NY 11791, USA

Burke, Arleigh A *Navy Admiral*
%The Virginian, 9229 Arlington Blvd, #323, Fairfax, VA 22031, USA

Burke, Bernard F *Physicist, Astrophysicist*
10 Bloomfield St, Lexington, MA 02173, USA

Burke, Chris *Actor*
426 S Orange Grove Ave, Los Angeles, CA 90036, USA

Burke, Daniel B *Businessman*
%Capital Cities/ABC Inc, 77 W 66th St, New York, NY 10023, USA

Burke, Delta *Actress*
%Hurwitz, 427 N Canon Dr, #215, Beverly Hills, CA 90210, USA

Burke, Jack, Jr *Golfer*
%Champions Golf Club, 13722 Champions Dr, Houston, TX 77069, USA

Burke, James *Commentator*
Henley House, Terrace Barnes, London SW13 0NP, England

Burke, James D *Museum Director*
%St Louis Art Museum, Forest Park, St Louis, MO 63110, USA

Burke, James Lee *Writer*
%Hyperion Press, 114 5th Ave, New York, NY 10114, USA

Burke, John F *Surgeon, Educator*
216 Prospect St, Belmont, MA 02178, USA

Burke, Joseph *Educator*
%La Salle University, President's Office, Philadelphia, PA 19141, USA

Burke, Joseph C *Educator*
%State University of New York, Provost's Office, Albany, NY 12246, USA

Burke, Kelly Howard *Air Force General*
%Stafford Burke Hecker, 1006 Cameron St, Alexandria, VA 22314, USA

Burke, Lloyd L *Korean War Army Hero (CMH)*
700 Grand Point Dr, Hot Springs, AR 71901, USA

Burke, Michael D *Businessman*
%Tesoro Petroleum Co, 8700 Tesoro Dr, San Antonio, TX 78217, USA

Burke, Paul *Actor*
2217 Avenida Caballeros, Palm Springs, CA 92262, USA

Burke, Solomon *Singer*
%Rodgers Redding Assoc, 1048 Tatnall St, Macon, GA 31201, USA

Burket, Harriet *Editor*
700 John Ringling Blvd, Sarasota, FL 34236, USA

Burkhalter, Edward A, Jr *Navy Admiral*
%Navy Department, Pentagon, Washington, DC 20350, USA

Burkhardt, Francois *Architect*
3 Rue de Venise, 75004 Paris, France

Burkhardt, Lisa *Sportscaster*
%Madison Square Garden Network, 4 Pennsylvania Plaza, New York, NY 10001, USA

Burkholder, Barry C *Financier*
%Bank United of Texas, 3200 Southwest Freeway, Houston, TX 77027, USA

Burki, Fred A *Labor Leader*
%United Retail Workers Union, 9865 W Roosevelt Rd, Westchester, IL 60154, USA

Burkley, Dennis *Actor*
5145 Costello Ave, Sherman Oaks, CA 91423, USA

Burks, Arthur W *Applied Mathematician, Philosopher*
3445 Vintage Valley Rd, Ann Arbor, MI 48105, USA

Burleigh, William R *Businessman*
%E W Scripps Co, 312 Walnut St, Cincinnati, OH 45202, USA

Burleson, Richard P (Rick) *Baseball Player*
270 E Mira Verde Dr, La Habra Heights, CA 90631, USA

Burleson, Tom *Basketball Player*
Box 861, Newland, NC 28657, USA

Burnes, Karen *Commentator*
%CBS-TV, News Dept, 51 W 52nd St, New York, NY 10019, USA

Burnett, Carol *Actress*
%Brillstein Co, 9150 Wilshire Blvd, #350, Beverly Hills, CA 90212, USA

Burnett, Howard J *Educator*
%Washington & Jefferson College, President's Office, Washington, PA 15301, USA

Burnett, James E *Government Official*
%Transportation Safety Board, 800 Independence SW, Washington, DC 20594, USA

Burnett, Malcolm *Financier*
%Marine Midland Banks, 1 Marine Midland Center, Buffalo, NY 14203, USA

Burnett, Robert A *Publisher*
%Meredith Corp, 1716 Locust St, Des Moines, IA 50309, USA

Burnette, Rocky *Singer*
1900 Ave of Stars, #2530, Los Angeles, CA 90067, USA

Burney, Leroy E *Physician*
%Milbank Memorial Fund, 40 Wall St, New York, NY 10005, USA

Burnham, Duane L *Businessman*
%Abbott Laboratories, 100 Abbott Park Rd, Abbott Park, IL 60064, USA

Burns, Carroll D *Businessman*
%Life Insurance Co of Georgia, 5780 Powers Ferry Rd NW, Atlanta, GA 30327, USA

Burns, Eric *Television Entertainer*
%"Arts & Entertainment Revue" Show, 402 E 76th St, New York, NY 10021, USA

Burns, George *Actor, Comedian*
720 N Maple Dr, Beverly Hills, CA 90210, USA

Burns, James MacGregor *Political Scientist, Historian*
High Mowing, Bee Hill Rd, Williamstown, MA 01267, USA

Burns, Jere *Actor*
PO Box 3596, Mammoth Lakes, CA 93546, USA

Burns, John F *Journalist*
%New York Times, Editorial Dept, 229 W 43rd St, New York, NY 10036, USA

Burns, John J *Air Force General*
23 Southwind Ct, Niceville, FL 32578, USA

Burns, John J, Jr *Businessman*
%Alleghany Corp, Park Avenue Plaza, 55 E 52nd St, New York, NY 10055, USA

Burns, Kenneth L (Ken) *Documentary Director*
%Florentine Films, Maple Grove Rd, Walpole, NH 03608, USA

Burns, M Anthony *Businessman*
%Ryder System Inc, 3600 NW 82nd Ave, Miami, FL 33166, USA

Burns, Norman *Economist*
3813 N 37th Ave, Arlington, VA 22207, USA

Burns, Pat *Hockey Coach*
%Toronto Maple Leafs, 60 Carlton St, Toronto ON M5B 1L1, Canada

Burns, W L, Jr *Financier*
%CCB Financial Corp, 111 Corcoran St, Durham, NC 27701, USA

Burnside, Waldo H *Businessman*
%Carter Hawley Hale Stores, 3880 N Mission Rd, Los Angeles, CA 90031, USA

Burr, Craig L *Businessman*
%Burr Egan Deleage Co, 1 Post Office Square, Boston, MA 02109, USA

Burr, Robert *Actor*
%Fifi Oscard Assoc, 24 W 40th St, #1700, New York, NY 10018, USA

Burrell, Kenneth E (Kenny) *Jazz Guitarist, Composer*
%Tropix International, 163 W 3rd Ave, #206, New York, NY 10003, USA

Burrell, Leroy *Track Athlete*
%Santa Monica Track Club, 1801 Ocean Park Blvd, #112, Santa Monica, CA 90405, USA

B

Burkholder - Burrell

B

Burris, Robert H	*Biochemist*
1015 University Bay Dr, Madison, WI 53705, USA	
Burroughs, Jeffrey A (Jeff)	*Baseball Player*
6155 Laguna Ct, Long Beach, CA 90803, USA	
Burroughs, William S	*Writer*
PO Box 147, Lawrence, KS 66044, USA	
Burrow, Harold	*Businessman*
%Coastal Corp, 9 Greenway Plaza, Houston, TX 77046, USA	
Burrows, Darren E	*Actor*
%Twentieth Century Artists, 15315 Magnolia Blvd, #429, Sherman Oaks, CA 91403, USA	
Burrows, Eva	*Religious Leader*
%Salvation Army Int'l, 101 Queen Victoria St, London EC4 4EP, England	
Burrows, J Stuart	*Opera Singer*
%John Coast Mgmt, 31 Sinclair Rd, London W14 0NS, England	
Burrows, Stephen	*Fashion Designer*
10 W 57th St, New York, NY 10019, USA	
Bursch, Daniel W	*Astronaut*
%NASA, Johnson Space Center, 2101 NASA Rd, Houston, TX 77058, USA	
Burstein, Lawrence	*Publisher*
%Self Magazine, Conde Nast Building, 350 Madison Ave, New York, NY 10017, USA	
Burstyn, Ellen	*Actress*
Ferry House, Washington Spring Rd, Snedens Landing, Palisades, NY 10964, USA	
Burt, James M	*WW II Army Hero (CMH)*
1621 Sherwood Rd, Colony Park, Wyomissing, PA 19610, USA	
Burt, Robert N	*Businessman*
%FMC Corp, 200 E Randolph Dr, Chicago, IL 60601, USA	
Burtis, Theodore A	*Businessman*
%Sunbrook Conference Center, 601 Country Line Rd, Wayne, PA 19087, USA	
Burton, Charles	*Transglobal Explorer*
27-A Leinster Sq, London W2, England	
Burton, Gary	*Jazz Vibraphonist*
%Berklee College of Music, 1140 Boylston St, Boston, MA 02215, USA	
Burton, LeVar	*Actor*
%Peaceful Warrior Productions, 13601 Ventura Blvd, #209, Sherman Oaks, CA 91423, USA	
Burton, Nelson, Jr	*Bowler*
%Professional Bowlers Assn, 1720 Merriman Rd, Akron, OH 44313, USA	
Burton, Robert G	*Publisher*
%World Color Press, 101 Park Ave, New York, NY 10178, USA	
Burton, Ron	*Football Player*
%John Hancock Insurance, Community Affairs, 200 Clarendon St, Boston, MA 02116, USA	
Burton, Scott	*Artist*
86 Thompson St, New York, NY 10012, USA	
Burton, Steve	*Actor*
2491 Sawmill Rd, #1708, Santa Fe, NM 87505, USA	
Burton, Timothy W (Tim)	*Movie Director*
1041 N Formosa Ave, #10, Los Angeles, CA 90046, USA	
Burton, Wendell	*Actor*
6526 Costello Dr, Van Nuys, CA 91401, USA	
Burts, Stephen L, Jr	*Financier*
%Synovus Financial Corp, 901 Front Ave, Columbus, GA 31901, USA	
Burum, Stephen	*Cinematographer*
%Smith/Gosnell, 1515 Palisades Dr, #N, Pacific Palisades, CA 90272, USA	
Bury, Pol	*Sculptor*
12 Vallee de la Taupe-Perdreauville, 78200 Mantes-La-Jolie, France	
Busbee, George D	*Governor, GA*
%King & Spalding, 191 Peachtree St NW, #4900, Atlanta, GA 30303, USA	
Busby, Jack W, Jr	*Businessman*
%Hancock Fabrics, 3406 W Main St, Tupelo, MS 38801, USA	
Busby, Jheryl	*Record Company Executive*
%Motown Records, 6255 Sunset Blvd, Los Angeles, CA 90028, USA	
Busby, Steven L (Steve)	*Baseball Player*
%Texas Rangers, PO Box 901111, Arlington, TX 76004, USA	
Buscaglia, F Leonardo (Leo)	*Educator*
%LFB Inc, PO Box 599, Glenbrook, NV 89413, USA	
Busch, August A, III	*Businessman, Baseball Executive*
%Anheuser-Busch Companies, 1 Busch Place, St Louis, MO 63118, USA	
Buser, Martin	*Dog Sled Racer*
PO Box 520997, Big Lake, AK 99652, USA	

Burris - Buser

Busey, Gary	*Actor*
18424 Coastline Dr, Malibu, CA 90265, USA	
Busfield, Timothy	*Actor*
2049 Century Park East, #3700, Los Angeles, CA 90067, USA	
Bush, Barbara P	*Wife of US President*
1000 Memorial Dr, #900, Houston, TX 77007, USA	
Bush, George H W	*President, USA*
1000 Memorial Dr, #900, Houston, TX 77007, USA	
Bush, George H W, Jr	*Governor, TX*
%Governor's Office, PO Box 12404, Austin, TX 78711, USA	
Bush, Jim	*Track Coach*
5106 Bounty Lane, Culver City, CA 90230, USA	
Bush, Kate	*Singer, Songwriter*
20 Manchester Square, London W1, England	
Bush, Lesley	*Diver*
83311 Overseas Highway, Islamorada, FL 33036, USA	
Bush, Richard E	*WW II Marine Corps Hero (CMH)*
2200 Marshall Parkway, Waukegan, IL 60085, USA	
Bush, Robert E	*WW II Navy Hero (CMH)*
3148 Madrona Beach Rd NW, Olympia, WA 98502, USA	
Bush, William Green	*Actor*
%Gold Marshak Assoc, 3500 W Olive Ave, #1400, Burbank, CA 91505, USA	
Bushee, Michael F	*Financier*
%Meditrust, 197 1st Ave, Needham Heights, MA 02194, USA	
Bushinsky, Joseph M (Jay)	*Commentator*
Rehov Hatsafon 5, Savyon 56540, Israel	
Bushland, Raymond C	*Entomologist*
135 Plaza Dr, #21, Kerrville, TX 78028, USA	
Bushnell, Nolan K	*Businessman*
%Atari Inc, 1265 Borregas Ave, Sunnyvale, CA 94089, USA	
Buss, Jerry H	*Basketball Executive*
1143 Summit Dr, Beverly Hills, CA 90210, USA	
Bussard, Robert W	*Physicist*
8505 Euclid Ave, #3, Manassas Park, VA 22111, USA	
Bussell, Darcey A	*Ballerina*
155 New King's Rd, London SW6 4SJ, England	
Bussey, Dexter M	*Football Player*
2565 Bloomfield Crossing, Bloomfield Hills, MI 48304, USA	
Bustamante, Alfonso	*Government Official, Peru*
Urb Corpac, Calle 1 Oeste S/N, San Isidro, Lima 27, Peru	
Buster, John E	*Obstetrician*
%Harbor-UCLA Medical Center, PO Box 2910, Torrance, CA 90509, USA	
Butcher, Garth	*Hockey Player*
%Detroit Red Wings, Joe Louis Arena, 600 Civic Center Dr, Detroit, MI 48226, USA	
Butcher, Susan H	*Dog Sled Racer*
%Trail Breaker Kennel, 1 Eureka, Manley, AK 99756, USA	
Buthelezi, Chief Mangosuthu G	*Chief Minister, KwaZulu/Natal*
Private Bag X-01, Ulundi 3838, Kwazulu, South Africa	
Butkus, Dick	*Football Player, Actor*
%Gold Marshak Assoc, 3500 W Olive Ave, #1400, Burbank, CA 91505, USA	
Butler, Abbey J	*Businessman*
%FoxMeyer Health Corp, 1220 Senlac Dr, Carrollton, TX 75006, USA	
Butler, Bernard	*Guitarist (Suede)*
PO Box 3431, London N1 7LW, England	
Butler, Bill	*Cinematographer*
%Smith/Gosnell, 1515 Palisades Dr, #N, Pacific Palisades, CA 90272, USA	
Butler, Brett	*Comedienne*
%Gersh Agency, 232 N Canon Dr, Beverly Hills, CA 90210, USA	
Butler, Clifford E	*Businessman*
%Pilgrim's Pride Corp, 110 S Texas St, Pittsburg, TX 75686, USA	
Butler, Dan	*Actor*
%Innovative Artists, 1999 Ave of Stars, #2850, Los Angeles, CA 90067, USA	
Butler, G Lee	*Air Force General*
CinC, Strategic Air Command, 901 SAC Blvd, Offutt Air Force Base, NE 68113, USA	
Butler, Gilbert	*Financier*
%Butler Capital Corp, 767 5th Ave, New York, NY 10153, USA	
Butler, Jerry	*Football Player*
%Butler Mechanical Inc, 63 Zoar Valley Rd, Springville, NY 14141, USA	

B

Busey - Butler

Butler, Jerry (Iceman)   *Singer, Songwriter*
%Jerry Butler Productions, 164 Woodstone Dr, Buffalo Grove, IL 60089, USA

Butler, LeRoy   *Football Player*
%Green Bay Packers, 1265 Lombardi Ave, Green Bay, WI 54304, USA

Butler, Michael C   *Financier, Producer*
%Laura Lizer Assoc, 12711 Ventura Blvd, #440, Studio City, CA 91604, USA

Butler, Richard A   *Government Official, England*
Spencers, Great Yeldham, Essex CO9 4JG, England

Butler, Robert   *Television Director*
650 Club View Dr, Los Angeles, CA 90024, USA

Butler, Robert N   *Gerontologist*
%Mt Sinai Medical Center, Geriatrics Dept, 1 Levy Pl, New York, NY 10029, USA

Butler, Robert Olen   *Writer*
%McNeese State University, English Dept, Lake Charles, LA 70609, USA

Butler, Samuel C   *Attorney*
%Cravath Swain Moore, 825 8th Ave, New York, NY 10019, USA

Butler, William E   *Businessman*
%Eaton Corp, Eaton Center, 1111 Superior Ave, Cleveland, OH 44114, USA

Butsavage, Bernard   *Labor Leader*
%Molders & Allied Workers Union, 1225 E McMillan St, Cincinnati, OH 45206, USA

Butt, Charles C   *Businessman*
%HEB Grocery Co, 646 S Main Ave, San Antonio, TX 78204, USA

Butterfield, Alexander P   *Government Official*
10387 Friars Rd, #206, San Diego, CA 92120, USA

Butterfield, Jack A   *Hockey Executive*
%American Hockey League, 425 Union St, West Springfield, MA 01089, USA

Butterworth, Kenneth W   *Businessman*
%Loctite Corp, 10 Columbus Blvd, Hartford, CT 06106, USA

Buttle, Gregory E (Greg)   *Football Player*
3 Lord Joes Landing, Northport, NY 11768, USA

Buttner, Jean B   *Financier*
%Value Line Inc, 220 E 42nd St, New York, NY 10017, USA

Button, Richard T   *Figure Skater, Television Producer*
%Candid Productions, 250 W 57th St, #1818, New York, NY 10107, USA

Buttons, Red   *Actor*
778 Tortuoso Way, Los Angeles, CA 90077, USA

Butz, David R (Dave)   *Football Player*
65 Oak Grove Dr, Belleville, IL 62221, USA

Butz, Earl   *Secretary, Agriculture*
2741 N Salisbury St, West Lafayette, IN 47906, USA

Buxton, Charles I, II   *Businessman*
%Federated Mutual Insurance, 121 E Park Square, Owatonna, MN 55060, USA

Buxton, Winslow H   *Businessman*
%Pentair Inc, Waters Edge Plaza, 1500 Country Rd B-2 W, St Paul, MN 55113, USA

Buzzi, Ruth   *Comedienne*
%Artists Group, 10100 Santa Monica Blvd, #2490, Los Angeles, CA 90067, USA

Byars, Betsy C   *Writer*
126 Riverpoint Dr, Clemson, SC 29631, USA

Byars, Keith   *Football Player*
%Miami Dolphins, 7500 SW 30th St, Davie, FL 33329, USA

Byatt, Antonia Susan (A S)   *Writer*
37 Rusholme Rd, London SW15 3LF, England

Bychkov, Semyon   *Conductor*
%Buffalo Symphony Orchestra, 71 Symphony Circle, Buffalo, NY 14201, USA

Byers, Walter   *Athletic Association Executive*
PO Box 1525, Shawnee Mission, KS 66222, USA

Bykovsky, Valeri F   *Cosmonaut*
%Potchta Kosmonavtov, 141 160 Svyosdny Gorodok, Moskovskoi Oblasti, Russia

Byland, Peter   *Businessman*
%Holnam Inc, 6211 Ann Arbor Rd, Dundee, MI 48131, USA

Byner, Earnest   *Football Player*
%Cleveland Browns, 80 1st Ave, Berea, OH 44017, USA

Byner, John   *Actor*
5863 Ramirez Canyon Rd, Malibu, CA 90265, USA

Bynoe, Peter C B   *Basketball Executive*
%Denver Nuggets, McNichols Arena, 1635 Clay St, Denver, CO 80204, USA

Byrd, Benjamin F, Jr   *Physician*
2611 West End Ave, #201, Nashville, TN 37203, USA

Byrd, Charlie *Jazz Guitarist*
764 Fairview Ave, #E, Annapolis, MD 21403, USA

Byrd, Gill *Football Player*
%San Diego Chargers, Jack Murphy Stadium, San Diego, CA 92160, USA

Byrd, Harry F, Jr *Senator, VA*
%Rockingham Publishing Co, 2 N Kent St, Winchester, VA 22601, USA

Byrd, Tracy *Singer*
%Ritter/Carter Mgmt, 4345 Thomas Lane, Beaumont, TX 77706, USA

Byrne, Brendan T *Governor, NJ*
%Carella Byrne Bain Gilfillan Rhodes, Gateway 1, Newark, NJ 07102, USA

Byrne, David *Singer (Talking Heads), Songwriter*
7964 Willow Glen Rd, Los Angeles, CA 90046, USA

Byrne, Gabriel *Actor*
%International Creative Mgmt, 76 Oxford St, London W1N 0AX, England

Byrne, John *Cartoonist (Superman)*
%DC Comics, 355 Lexington Ave, New York, NY 10017, USA

Byrne, John V *Educator*
%Oregon State University, President's Office, Corvallis, OR 97330, USA

Byrne, Martha *Actress*
%International Creative Mgmt, 40 W 57th St, New York, NY 10019, USA

Byrne, Thomas J (Tommy) *Baseball Player*
442 Pineview Ave, Wake Forest, NC 27587, USA

Byrnes, Edd *Actor*
PO Box 1623, Beverly Hills, CA 90213, USA

Byrnes, William L *Financier*
%FMR Corp, 82 Devonshire St, Boston, MA 02109, USA

Byron, Jeffrey *Actor*
22918 Dolorosa St, Woodland Hills, CA 91367, USA

Byron, Kathleen *Actress*
PO Box 130, Hove, East Sussex BN3 6QU, England

Byrum, John W *Movie Director*
7435 Woodrow Wilson Dr, Los Angeles, CA 90046, USA

Bywater, William H *Labor Leader*
%International Electronic Workers, 1126 16th St NW, Washington, DC 20036, USA

B

Byrd - Bywater

Caan, James — *Actor*
1435 Stone Canyon Rd, Los Angeles, CA 90077, USA

Caballe, Montserrat — *Opera Singer*
%Carlos Caballe, Via Augusta 59, 08006 Barcelona, Spain

Cabana, Robert D — *Astronaut*
%NASA, Johnson Space Center, 2101 NASA Rd, Houston, TX 77058, USA

Cable, Thomas J — *Businessman*
%Cable & Howse Ventures, 777 108th Ave NE, Bellevue, WA 98004, USA

Cabot, John G L — *Businessman*
%Cabot Corp, 75 State St, Boston, MA 02109, USA

Cacoyannis, Michael — *Movie, Theatre Director*
15 Mouson St, Athens 401, Greece

Cadbury, Adrian — *Businessman*
%Bank of England, Threadneedle St, London EC2R 8AH, England

Caddell, Patrick H — *Statistician*
%Cambridge Research Inc, 1625 "I" St NW, Washington, DC 20006, USA

Cade, J Robert — *Medical Researcher, Inventor (Gatorade)*
%University of Florida Medical School, Physiology Dept, Gainesville, FL 32610, USA

Cadell, Ava — *Actress*
3349 W Cahuenga Blvd, #2, Los Angeles, CA 90068, USA

Cadigan, Dave — *Football Player*
83 Baldwin Ave, Point Lookout, NY 11569, USA

Cadmus, Paul — *Artist, Etcher*
PO Box 1255, Weston, CT 06883, USA

Cadorette, Mary — *Actress*
8831 Sunset Blvd, #304, Los Angeles, CA 90069, USA

Cady, Frank — *Actor*
%Greenevine Agency, 110 E 9th St, #C-1005, Los Angeles, CA 90079, USA

Caen, Herb — *Columnist, Writer*
%San Francisco Chronicle, 901 Mission St, San Francisco, CA 94103, USA

Caesar, Irving — *Lyricist*
%Irving Caesar Music Corp, 850 7th Ave, New York, NY 10019, USA

Caesar, Shirley — *Singer*
%Shirley Caesar Outreach Ministries, PO Box 3336, Durham, NC 27702, USA

Caesar, Sid — *Comedian*
1910 Loma Vista Dr, Beverly Hills, CA 90210, USA

Cafego, George — *Football Player*
405 Kittredge Ct, Knoxville, TN 37922, USA

Cafferata, Hector A, Jr — *Korean War Marine Corps Hero (CMH)*
630 Dewey Ave, Alpha, NJ 08865, USA

Caffey, Jason — *Basketball Player*
%Chicago Bulls, 1901 W Madison St, Chicago, IL 60612, USA

Caffrey, Stephen — *Actor*
12338 Cantura St, Studio City, CA 91604, USA

Cagatay, Mustafa — *Prime Minister, Cyprus Federated State*
60 Cumhuriyet Caddesi, Kyrenia, Cyprus

Cage, Michael — *Basketball Player*
%Cleveland Cavaliers, 2923 Statesboro Rd, Richfield, OH 44286, USA

Cage, Nicolas — *Actor*
%Brillstein-Grey, 9150 Wilshire Blvd, #350, Beverly Hills, CA 90212, USA

Cagigas, Donald — *Financier*
%Bank One Youngstown, 6 Federal Plaza W, Youngstown, OH 44503, USA

Caglayangil, Ihsan S — *President, Turkey*
Sehit Ersan Caddesi 30/15, Cankaya, Ankara, Turkey

Cagle, J Douglas — *Businessman*
%Cagle's Inc, 2000 Hills Ave NW, Atlanta, GA 30318, USA

Cahill, James — *Actor*
31 Chambers St, #311, New York, NY 10007, USA

Cahill, John C — *Businessman*
%Trans World Airlines, City Center, 515 N 6th St, St Louis, MO 63101, USA

Cahill, Teresa M — *Opera Singer*
65 Leyland Rd, London SE12 8DW, England

Cahill, William T — *Governor/Senator, NJ*
%Cahill Wilinski Cahill, 25 Chestnut St, Haddonfield, NJ 08033, USA

Cahouet, Frank V — *Financier*
%Mellon Bank Corp, 1 Mellon Bank Center, 500 Grant St, Pittsburgh, PA 15219, USA

Cain, Dean — *Actor*
%Centre Films, 1103 N El Centro Ave, Los Angeles, CA 90038, USA

Cain, Gordon A — *Businessman*
%Sterling Chemicals, 1200 Smith St, Houston, TX 77002, USA

Cain, Paul W — *Businessman*
%Mesa Inc, Trammell Crow Center, 2001 Ross Ave, Dallas, TX 75201, USA

Caine, Michael — *Actor*
Rectory Farm House, Northstoke, Oxfordshire, England

Cairncross, Alexander K — *Government Official, England; Economist*
14 Staverton Rd, Oxford OX2 6XJ, England

Cairns, Hugh J F — *Molecular Biologist*
Holly Grove House, Wilcote, Chipping Norton, Oxon OX7 3EA, England

Cairns, Theodore L — *Organic Chemist*
PO Box 3941, Greenville, DE 19807, USA

Calarco, Vincent A — *Businessman*
%Crompton & Knowles Corp, Metro Center, 1 Station Place, Stamford, CT 06902, USA

Calcevecchi, Mark — *Golfer*
%Professional Golfer's Assn, PO Box 109601, Palm Beach Gardens, FL 33410, USA

Calder, Iain W — *Editor*
%National Enquirer, Editorial Dept, 600 SE Coast Ave, Lantana, FL 33460, USA

Calder, Nigel — *Writer*
8 The Chase, Furnace Green, Crawley, West Sussex RH10 6HW, England

Caldera Rodriguez, Rafael — *President, Venezuela*
Ave Urdaneta 33-2, Apdo 2060, Caracas, Venezuela

Calderon Fournier, Rafael A — *President, Costa Rica*
%Casa Presidencial, Apdo 520-2010, San Jose 1000, Costa Rica

Calderon Sol, Armando — *President, El Salvador*
%President's Office, Casa Presidencial, San Salvador, El Salvador

Calderon, Alberto P — *Mathematician*
1153 E 56th St, Chicago, IL 60637, USA

Calderone, Mary S — *Physician*
%New York University, Health & Education Dept, 715 Broadway, New York, NY 10003, USA

Caldicott, Helen — *Social Activist, Pediatrician*
%Physicians for Responsibility, 639 Massachusetts Ave, Cambridge, MA 02139, USA

Caldwell, Jim — *Football Coach*
%Wake Forest University, Athletic Dept, Winston-Salem, NC 27109, USA

Caldwell, Philip — *Businessman*
%Smith Barney Shearson, 200 Vesey St, New York, NY 10281, USA

Caldwell, R Michael (Mike) — *Baseball Player*
1645 Brook Run Dr, Raleigh, NC 27614, USA

Caldwell, Sarah — *Opera Producer, Conductor*
%Boston Opera Co, 539 Washington St, Boston, MA 02111, USA

Caldwell, Wayne E — *Coast Guard Admiral*
%US Coast Guard Hdqs, 2100 2nd St SW, Washington, DC 20593, USA

Caldwell, Wiley N — *Businessman*
125 Woodstock Ave, Kenilworth, IL 60043, USA

Caldwell, William A — *Editor*
%Vineyard Gazette, Editorial Dept, S Summer St, Edgartown, MA 02539, USA

Caldwell, Zoe — *Actress*
%Whitehead-Stevens, 1501 Broadway, New York, NY 10036, USA

Cale, John — *Singer, Musician (Velvet Underground)*
PO Box 22635, Nashville, TN 37202, USA

Calegari, Maria — *Ballerina*
%New York City Ballet, Lincoln Center Plaza, New York, NY 10023, USA

Calfa, Marian — *Prime Minister, Czech Republic*
%CTL Consulting, Premyslovska 28, Prage 3, Czech Republic

Calhoon, Jesse M — *Labor Leader*
%Marine Engineers Union, 17 Battery Pl, New York, NY 10004, USA

Calhoun, Jim — *Basketball Coach*
%University of Connecticut, Athletic Dept, 2111 Hillside Rd, Storrs, CT 06269, USA

Calhoun, Rory — *Actor*
PO Box 689, Morongo Valley, CA 92256, USA

Cali, Joseph — *Actor*
25750 Vista Verde Dr, Monte Nido, CA 91302, USA

Califano, Joseph A, Jr — *Secretary, Health Education Welfare*
3551 Springfield Lane NW, Washington, DC 20008, USA

Caligiuri, Paul — *Soccer Player*
12021 Wilshire Blvd, #741, Los Angeles, CA 90025, USA

Calisher, Hortense — *Writer*
%Candida Donadio, 231 W 22nd St, New York, NY 10011, USA

Call, Brandon
Actor
5918 Van Nuys Blvd, Van Nuys, CA 91401, USA

Call, Robert V, Jr
Businessman
%Curtice Burns Foods, 90 Linden Place, Rochester, NY 14603, USA

Callaghan of Cardiff, James
Prime Minister, England
%House of Lords, Westminster, London SW1A 0PW, England

Callaghan, James T
Air Force General
Commander, Air South, Box 101, Air South, FPO, AE 09620, USA

Callahan, Daniel J
Educator
Hastings Center, 255 Elm Rd, Briarcliff Manor, NY 10510, USA

Callahan, Harry M
Photographer
145 15th St NE, #421, Atlanta, GA 30309, USA

Callahan, James
Actor
13112 Valleyheart Dr, #304, Studio City, CA 91604, USA

Callahan, John
Actor
342 N Alfred St, Los Angeles, CA 90048, USA

Callan, K
Actress
4957 Matilija Ave, Sherman Oaks, CA 91423, USA

Callan, Michael
Actor
1730 Camden Ave, #201, Los Angeles, CA 90025, USA

Callas, Charlie
Comedian
9000 Sunset Blvd, #502, Los Angeles, CA 90069, USA

Callaway, Ely R, Jr
Businessman, Inventor
%Callaway Golf Co, 2345 Camino Vida Roble, Carlsbad, CA 92009, USA

Callaway, Paul Smith
Concert Organist
%Washington Cathedral, Mount St Alban, Washington, DC 20016, USA

Callaway, Thomas
Actor
6360 Wilshire Blvd, #1707, Los Angeles, CA 90048, USA

Callejas, Rafael L
President, Honduras
%President's Office, 6-A Avda La Calle, Tegucigalpa, Honduras

Callen Jones, Gloria
Swimmer
1508 Chafton Rd, Charleston, WV 25314, USA

Calloway, D Wayne
Businessman
%PepsiCo Inc, 700 Anderson Hill Rd, Purchase, NY 10577, USA

Calne, Roy Y
Surgeon
Addenbrooke's Hospital, Surgery Dept, Hills Rd, Cambridge CB2 2QQ, England

Calugas, Jose, Sr
WW II Army Hero (CMH)
2907 Narrows Place, Tacoma, WA 98407, USA

Calvani, Terry
Government Official
1050 Connecticut Ave NW, #1200, Washington, DC 20036, USA

Calverly, Ernie
Basketball Player
36 Hillside Rd, Wakefield, RI 02879, USA

Calvert, Bruce W
Businessman
%Alliance Capital Management, 1345 Ave of Americas, New York, NY 10105, USA

Calvert, James F
Navy Admiral, Writer
900 Long Ridge Rd, Stamford, CT 06902, USA

Calvert, Phyllis
Actress
Argyll Lodge, Towersey, Thames, Oxon, England

Calvet, Corinne
Actress
%Pacific Plaza Towers, 1431 Ocean Ave, #109, Santa Monica, CA 90401, USA

Calvin, John
Actor
%Stone Manners Agency, 8091 Selma Ave, Los Angeles, CA 90046, USA

Calvin, Mack
Basketball Player, Coach
%KMPC-Radio, 5858 Sunset Blvd, Los Angeles, CA 90028, USA

Calvin, Melvin
Nobel Chemistry Laureate
2683 Buena Vista, Berkeley, CA 94708, USA

Calvin, William H
Neurobiologist
%University of Washington, Neurobiologist Dept, Seattle, WA 98195, USA

Calvo, Paul M
Governor, GU
%Governor's Office, Capitol Bldg, Agana, GU 96910, USA

Calvo-Sotelo Bustelo, Leopoldo
Prime Minister, Spain
Alcala 93, 28009 Madrid, Spain

Camacho, Hector
Boxer
Star Route, Box 113, Clewiston, FL 33440, USA

Camara, Helder P
Religious Leader
Rua Henrique Dias 208, Igreja Das Fronteiras, 50 070 Recife PE, Brazil

Camarillo, Richard J (Rich)
Football Player
%Houston Oilers, 6910 Fannin St, Houston, TX 77030, USA

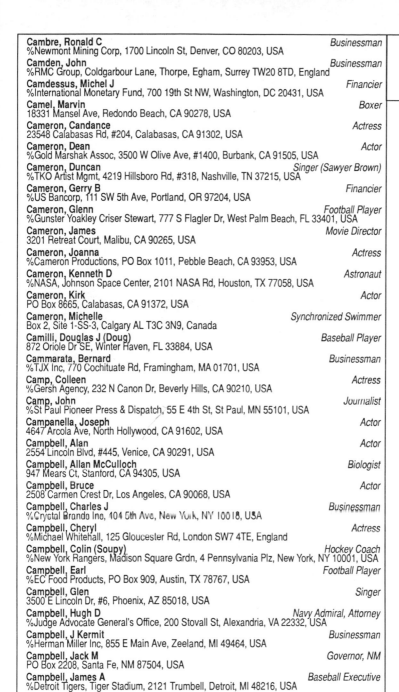

Cambre, Ronald C — *Businessman*
%Newmont Mining Corp, 1700 Lincoln St, Denver, CO 80203, USA

Camden, John — *Businessman*
%RMC Group, Coldgarbour Lane, Thorpe, Egham, Surrey TW20 8TD, England

Camdessus, Michel J — *Financier*
%International Monetary Fund, 700 19th St NW, Washington, DC 20431, USA

Camel, Marvin — *Boxer*
18331 Mansel Ave, Redondo Beach, CA 90278, USA

Cameron, Candance — *Actress*
23548 Calabasas Rd, #204, Calabasas, CA 91302, USA

Cameron, Dean — *Actor*
%Gold Marshak Assoc, 3500 W Olive Ave, #1400, Burbank, CA 91505, USA

Cameron, Duncan — *Singer (Sawyer Brown)*
%TKO Artist Mgmt, 4219 Hillsboro Rd, #318, Nashville, TN 37215, USA

Cameron, Gerry B — *Financier*
%US Bancorp, 111 SW 5th Ave, Portland, OR 97204, USA

Cameron, Glenn — *Football Player*
%Gunster Yoakley Criser Stewart, 777 S Flagler Dr, West Palm Beach, FL 33401, USA

Cameron, James — *Movie Director*
3201 Retreat Court, Malibu, CA 90265, USA

Cameron, Joanna — *Actress*
%Cameron Productions, PO Box 1011, Pebble Beach, CA 93953, USA

Cameron, Kenneth D — *Astronaut*
%NASA, Johnson Space Center, 2101 NASA Rd, Houston, TX 77058, USA

Cameron, Kirk — *Actor*
PO Box 8665, Calabasas, CA 91372, USA

Cameron, Michelle — *Synchronized Swimmer*
Box 2, Site 1-SS-3, Calgary AL T3C 3N9, Canada

Camilli, Douglas J (Doug) — *Baseball Player*
872 Oriole Dr SE, Winter Haven, FL 33884, USA

Cammarata, Bernard — *Businessman*
%TJX Inc, 770 Cochituate Rd, Framingham, MA 01701, USA

Camp, Colleen — *Actress*
%Gersh Agency, 232 N Canon Dr, Beverly Hills, CA 90210, USA

Camp, John — *Journalist*
%St Paul Pioneer Press & Dispatch, 55 E 4th St, St Paul, MN 55101, USA

Campanella, Joseph — *Actor*
4647 Arcola Ave, North Hollywood, CA 91602, USA

Campbell, Alan — *Actor*
2554 Lincoln Blvd, #445, Venice, CA 90291, USA

Campbell, Allan McCulloch — *Biologist*
947 Mears Ct, Stanford, CA 94305, USA

Campbell, Bruce — *Actor*
2508 Carmen Crest Dr, Los Angeles, CA 90068, USA

Campbell, Charles J — *Businessman*
%Crystal Brands Inc, 104 5th Ave, New York, NY 10018, USA

Campbell, Cheryl — *Actress*
%Michael Whitehall, 125 Gloucester Rd, London SW7 4TE, England

Campbell, Colin (Soupy) — *Hockey Coach*
%New York Rangers, Madison Square Grdn, 4 Pennsylvania Plz, New York, NY 10001, USA

Campbell, Earl — *Football Player*
%EC Food Products, PO Box 909, Austin, TX 78767, USA

Campbell, Glen — *Singer*
3500 E Lincoln Dr, #6, Phoenix, AZ 85018, USA

Campbell, Hugh D — *Navy Admiral, Attorney*
%Judge Advocate General's Office, 200 Stovall St, Alexandria, VA 22332, USA

Campbell, J Kermit — *Businessman*
%Herman Miller Inc, 855 E Main Ave, Zeeland, MI 49464, USA

Campbell, Jack M — *Governor, NM*
PO Box 2208, Santa Fe, NM 87504, USA

Campbell, James A — *Baseball Executive*
%Detroit Tigers, Tiger Stadium, 2121 Trumbell, Detroit, MI 48216, USA

Campbell, James R — *Financier*
%Norwest Bank Minnesota, 6th & Marquette, Minneapolis, MN 55479, USA

Campbell, John — *Harness Racing Driver*
%John D Campbell Stable, 823 Allison Dr, River Vale, NJ 07675, USA

Campbell, Julia — *Actress*
%William Morris Agency, 151 S El Camino Dr, Beverly Hills, CA 90212, USA

C

Cambre - Campbell

Campbell, Kim *Prime Minister, Canada*
PO Box 1575, Postal Station B, Ottawa ON K1P 5R5, Canada
Campbell, Louis B *Businessman*
%Textron Inc, 10 Dorrance St, Providence, RI 02903, USA
Campbell, Luther (Skywalker) *Singer (2 Live Crew)*
%Famous Artists Agency, 1700 Broadway, #500, New York, NY 10019, USA
Campbell, Marion *Publisher*
%Atlantic Monthly Co, 745 Boylston St, Boston, MA 02116, USA
Campbell, Milton *Track Athlete*
1132 St Marks Pl, Plainfield, NJ 07062, USA
Campbell, Naomi *Model, Singer*
%Ford Model Agency, 344 E 59th St, New York, NY 10022, USA
Campbell, Nicholas *Actor*
11342 Dona Lisa Dr, Studio City, CA 91604, USA
Campbell, Patrick J *Labor Leader*
%Carpenters & Joiners Union, 101 Constitution Ave NW, Washington, DC 20001, USA
Campbell, Robert H *Businessman*
%Sun Co, 10 Penn Center, 1801 Market St, Philadelphia, PA 19103, USA
Campbell, Tevin *Singer*
%Quincy Jones Productions, 3800 Barham Blvd, #503, Los Angeles, CA 90068, USA
Campbell, Tony *Basketball Player*
%Cleveland Cavaliers, 2923 Statesboro Rd, Richfield, OH 44286, USA
Campbell, Van C *Businessman*
%Corning Inc, Houghton Park, Corning, NY 14831, USA
Campbell, Vivian *Guitarist (Def Leppard)*
%Q Prime Mgmt, 729 7th Ave, #1400, New York, NY 10019, USA
Campbell, William J *Air Force General*
3267 Alex Findlay Pl, Sarasota, FL 34240, USA
Campbell, William R (Bill) *Baseball Player*
133 S Hale St, Palatine, IL 60067, USA
Campion, Jane *Movie Director*
%H Linstead Assoc, 9-13 Bronte Rd, Bondi Junction NSW 2022, Australia
Campos, Antonio C *Financier*
%Banco Central Hispano, 221 Ponce de Leon Ave, Hato Rey, PR 00917, USA
Canadeo, Tony *Football Player*
1746 Carriage Ct, Green Bay, WI 54304, USA
Canary, David *Actor*
903 S Mansfield Ave, Los Angeles, CA 90036, USA
Canby, Vincent *Movie Critic*
215 W 88th St, New York, NY 10024, USA
Candela, Felix *Engineer, Architect*
6109 Bayberry Lane, Raleigh, NC 27612, USA
Candelaria, John R *Baseball Player*
25732 Bucklestone Court, Laguna Hills, CA 92653, USA
Candeloro, Philippe *Figure Skater*
42 Rue de Lourve, 75001 Paris, France
Candilis, Georges *Architect*
17 Rue Campagne-Premiere, 75014 Paris, France
Canella, Guido *Architect*
Via Revere 7, 20123 Milan, Italy
Canepa, John C *Financier*
%Old Kent Bank & Trust Co, 1 Vandenberg Center, Grand Rapids, MI 49503, USA
Canestri, Giovanni Cardinal *Religious Leader*
Archdiocese of Genoa-Bobbio, Piazza Matteotti 4, 16123 Genoa, Italy
Canfield, William N (Bill) *Editorial Cartoonist*
143 Wayside Rd, Tinton Falls, NJ 07724, USA
Cannell, Stephen J *Television Producer*
%Stephen J Cannell Productions, 7083 Hollywood Blvd, Los Angeles, CA 90028, USA
Canning, Fred F *Businessman*
%Walgreen Co, 200 Wilmot Rd, Deerfield, IL 60015, USA
Cannon, Billy *Football Player*
656 Lobdell Ave, Baton Rouge, LA 70806, USA
Cannon, Dyan *Actress*
8033 Sunset Blvd, #254, Los Angeles, CA 90046, USA
Cannon, Freddy (Boom Boom) *Singer, Songwriter*
%Cannon Productions, 18641 Cassandra St, Tarzana, CA 91356, USA
Cannon, Howard W *Senator, NV*
6300 Evermay Dr, McLean, VA 22101, USA

Cannon, J D — *Actor*
%Gage Group, 9255 Sunset Blvd, #515, Los Angeles, CA 90069, USA

Cannon, J E — *Businessman*
%Hadson Corp, 2777 Stemmons Freeway, Dallas, TX 75207, USA

Cannon, Katherine — *Actress*
%Paradigm Agency, 10100 Santa Monica Blvd, #2500, Los Angeles, CA 90067, USA

Cannon, Robert H, Jr — *Aerospace Engineer*
%Stanford University, Aeronautics & Astronautics Dept, Stanford, CA 94305, USA

Canova, Diana — *Actress*
%Lemond, 5570 Old Highway 395 N, Carson City, NV 89707, USA

Canseco, Jose — *Baseball Player*
4525 Sheridan Ave, Miami Beach, FL 33140, USA

Cantalupo, James R — *Businessman*
%McDonald's International, 1 McDonald's Plaza, 1 Kroc Dr, Oak Brook, IL 60521, USA

Canter, Stephen E — *Financier*
%Dreyfus Corp, 200 Park Ave, New York, NY 10166, USA

Cantlay, George G — *Army General*
501 Thomas Bransby, Kingsmill on the James, Williamsburg, VA 23185, USA

Canton, Mark — *Movie Executive*
%Sony Pictures Entertainment, Columbia Plaza, Burbank, CA 91505, USA

Cantone, Vic — *Editorial Cartoonist*
%New York Daily News, Editorial Dept, 220 E 42nd St, New York, NY 10017, USA

Cantor, Charles R — *Molecular Biologist*
11 Bay St Rd, #11, Boston, MA 02215, USA

Cantor, Gerald — *Financier*
%Cantor Fitzgerald Securities, 1 World Trade Center, New York, NY 10048, USA

Cantrell, Lana — *Singer*
300 E 71st St, New York, NY 10021, USA

Cantu, Carlos H — *Businessman*
%ServiceMaster Co, 1 ServiceMaster Rd, Downers Grove, IL 60515, USA

Capa, Cornell — *Photographer*
%International Center of Photography, 1130 5th Ave, New York, NY 10128, USA

Capalbo, Carmen C — *Theater Producer, Director*
500 2nd Ave, New York, NY 10016, USA

Capecchi, Mario R — *Biologist*
%University of Utah, Biology Dept, Salt Lake City, UT 84112, USA

Capen, Richard G, Jr — *Publisher, Diplomat*
6077 San Elijo, Rancho Santa Fe, CA 92067, USA

Caperton, W Gaston, III — *Governor, WV*
%Governor's Office, State Capitol, Charleston, WV 25305, USA

Capice, Philip C — *Television Producer*
1359 Miller Dr, Los Angeles, CA 90069, USA

Capilla, Joaquin — *Diver*
Torres de Mixcoac, Lomas de Plateros, Mexico 19 DF, Mexico

Caplin, Mortimer M — *Government Official*
5610 Wisconsin Ave NW, #18-F, Bethesda, MD 20815, USA

Capobianco, Tito — *Opera Director*
%Pittsburgh Opera Co, 711 Penn Ave, #800, Pittsburgh, PA 15222, USA

Caponera, John — *Comedian*
%Messina/Baker/Miller, 7920 Sunset Blvd, #400, Los Angeles, CA 90046, USA

Cappelletti, Gino — *Football Player*
%WBZ-Radio, 1170 Soldiers Field Rd, Brighton, MA 02134, USA

Cappelletti, John R — *Football Player*
23791 Brant Lane, Laguna Niguel, CA 92677, USA

Capps, Lisa — *Actress*
%Warner Bros Records, 3300 Warner Blvd, Burbank, CA 91505, USA

Capps, Thomas E — *Businessman*
%Dominion Resources, Riverfront Plaza West, 901 E Byrd St, Richmond, VA 23219, USA

Capps, Walter H — *Humanist*
%University of California, Religion Dept, Santa Barbara, CA 93106, USA

Cappuccilli, Piero — *Opera Singer*
%S A Gorlinsky Ltd, 38 Dover St, London W1X 4NJ, England

Capra, Frank, Jr — *Movie Producer*
1695 Fernald Point Lane, Santa Barbara, CA 93108, USA

Capra, Lee W (Buzz) — *Baseball Player*
7112 Riverside Dr, Berwyn, IL 60402, USA

Capriati, Jennifer — *Tennis Player*
%International Management Group, 1 Erieview Plaza, #1300, Cleveland, OH 44114, USA

C

Cannon - Capriati

C

Caprio, Giuseppe Cardinal — *Religious Leader*
Palazzo delle Congregazione Largo del Colonnato 3, 00193 Rome, Italy

Capshaw, Kate — *Actress*
PO Box 869, Pacific Palisades, CA 90272, USA

Capucill, Terese — *Dancer*
%Martha Graham Contemporary Dance Center, 316 E 63rd St, New York, NY 10021, USA

Cara, Irene — *Singer*
8033 Sunset Blvd, #735, Los Angeles, CA 90046, USA

Carafotes, Paul — *Actor*
8033 Sunset Blvd, #3554, Los Angeles, CA 90046, USA

Caras, Roger — *Writer*
22108 Slab Bridge Rd, Freeland, MD 21053, USA

Caray, Harry C — *Sportscaster*
%WGN-TV, Sports Dept, 2501 Bradley Place, Chicago, IL 60618, USA

Caray, Skip — *Sportscaster*
%Turner Broadcasting System, 1050 Techwood Dr NW, Atlanta, GA 30318, USA

Carazo Odio, Rodrigo — *President, Costa Rica; Educator*
%UN University for Peace, Rector's Office, Ciudad Colon, Costa Rica

Carbajal, Michael — *Boxer*
914 E Filmore St, Phoenix, AZ 85006, USA

Carberry, Charles M — *Attorney*
%Jones Davis Reeve Pogue, 599 Lexington Ave, New York, NY 10022, USA

Carberry, Deirdre — *Ballerina*
%American Ballet Theater, 890 Broadway, New York, NY 10003, USA

Carberry, John Cardinal — *Religious Leader*
4445 Lindell Blvd, St Louis, MO 63108, USA

Carbine, Patricia — *Editor, Publisher*
%Ms Magazine, 370 Lexington Ave, New York, NY 10017, USA

Carbonneau, Guy — *Hockey Player*
%Dallas Stars, 211 Cowboys Parkway, Irving, TX 75063

Cardarelli, Donald P — *Businessman*
%Agway Inc, 333 Butternut Dr, Dewitt, NY 13214, USA

Carden, Joan M — *Opera Singer*
%Jennifer Eddy Mgmt, 596 St Kilda Rd, #11, Melbourne 3004, Vic, Australia

Cardiff, Jack — *Cinematographer*
%L'Epine Smith & Carney Assoc, 10 Wyndham Place, London W1H 1AS, England

Cardin, Pierre — *Fashion Designer*
59 Rue Du Faubourg-Saint-Honore, 75008 Paris, France

Cardinale, Claudia — *Actress*
Via Flaminia 118, 00188 Rome, Italy

Cardona, Manuel — *Physicist*
%Max-Planck-Institut, Heisenbergstr 1, 70569 Stuttgart, Germany

Cardoso, Fernando Henrique — *President, Brazil*
Palacio do Planalto, Praca dos Tres Poderes, 70.150 Brasilia DF, Brazil

Cardoza, Robert J — *Businessman*
%California State Automobile Assn, PO Box 422940, San Francisco, CA 94142, USA

Cardy, Robert W — *Businessman*
%Carpenter Technology Corp, 101 W Bern St, Reading, PA 19601, USA

Caretto-Brown, Patty — *Swimmer*
16079 Mesquite Cir, Santa Ana, CA 92708, USA

Carew, Rodney C (Rod) — *Baseball Player*
5144 E Crescent Dr, Anaheim, CA 92807, USA

Carey, George L — *Archbishop, Canterbury*
%Lambeth Palace, London SE1 9JU, England

Carey, Harry, Jr — *Actor*
PO Box 3256, Durango, CO 81302, USA

Carey, Hugh L — *Governor, NY*
9 Prospect Pl W, Brooklyn, NY 11217, USA

Carey, Jim — *Hockey Player*
%Washington Capitals, USAir Arena, Landover, MD 20785, USA

Carey, John J — *Businessman*
%Allendale Mutual Insurance Co, Allendale Park, Johnston, RI 02919, USA

Carey, Mariah — *Singer*
%Horizon Ent, 130 W 57th St, #12-B, New York, NY 10019, USA

Carey, Michele — *Actress*
%H David Moss Assoc, 733 N Seward St, #PH, Los Angeles, CA 90038, USA

Carey, Philip — *Actor*
427 N Canon Dr, #205, Beverly Hills, CA 90210, USA

Caprio - Carey

Carey, Raymond B, Jr — *Marine Corps General*
%Marine Corps Hdqs, Pentagon, Washington, DC 20380, USA
Carey, Richard E — *Marine Corps General*
%Marine Corps Hdqs, Pentagon, Washington, DC 20380, USA
Carey, Ron — *Actor*
419 N Larchmont Ave, Los Angeles, CA 90004, USA
Carey, Ronald R — *Labor Official*
%International Teamsters Brotherhood, 25 Louisiana Ave NW, Washington, DC 20001, USA
Carey, William D — *Publisher*
%Science Magazine, 1333 "H" St NW, 11th Floor, Washington, DC 20005, USA
Carey, William H — *Religious Leader*
%National Gay Pentecostal Alliance, PO Box 1391, Schenectady, NY 12301, USA
Cargo, David F — *Governor, NM*
6422 Concordia Rd NE, Albuquerque, NM 87111, USA
Carillo, Mary — *Sportscaster*
%CBS-TV, Sports Dept, 51 W 52nd St, New York, NY 10019, USA
Cariou, Len — *Actor*
%Paradigm Agency, 10100 Santa Monica Blvd, #2500, Los Angeles, CA 90067, USA
Carithers, William, Jr — *Physicist*
%Fermi Nat Acceleration Lab, D-Zero Collaboration, PO Box 500, Batavia, IL 60510, USA
Carl XVI Gustaf — *King, Sweden*
Kungliga Slottet, Slottsbacken, 111 30 Stockholm, Sweden
Carle, Frankie — *Pianist, Composer*
PO Box 7415, Mesa, AZ 85216, USA
Carlesimo, P J — *Basketball Coach*
%Portland Trail Blazers, 700 NE Multnomah St, #600, Portland, OR 97232, USA
Carley, John B — *Businessman*
%Albertson's Inc, 250 Parkcenter Blvd, Boise, ID 83706, USA
Carlile, Forbes — *Swimming Coach*
16 Cross St, Ryde NSW 2112, Australia
Carlin, George — *Comedian*
%Carlin Productions, 901 Bringham Ave, Los Angeles, CA 90049, USA
Carlin, John W — *Governor, KS*
3226 SW Skyline Parkway, Topeka, KS 66614, USA
Carlin, Lynn — *Actress*
%David Shapira Assoc, 15301 Ventura Blvd, #345, Sherman Oaks, CA 91403, USA
Carlin, Thomas R — *Publisher*
%St Paul Pioneer Press, 55 E 4th St, St Paul, MN 55101, USA
Carling, William D C — *Rugby Player*
%Insights Ltd, 5 Chelsea Wharf, Lots Road, London SW10 0QJ, England
Carlisle, Belinda — *Singer, Songwriter*
%Gold Mountain Ent, 3575 Cahuenga Blvd W, #450, Los Angeles, CA 90068, USA
Carlisle, Kitty — *Singer*
32 E 64th St, New York, NY 10021, USA
Carlos, Bun E — *Drummer (Cheap Trick)*
%Ken Adamay Assoc, 1818 Parmenter St, #202, Middleton, WI 53562, USA
Carlot, Maxime — *Prime Minister, Vanuatu*
%Prime Minister's Office, PO Box 10, Port Vila, Vanuatu
Carlson, Arne H — *Governor, MN*
%Governor's Office, State Capitol Bldg, #130, Minneapolis, MN 55155, USA
Carlson, Curtis — *Businessman*
%Carlson Companies, Carlson Parkway, PO Box 59159, Minneapolis, MN 55459, USA
Carlson, D H E — *Publisher*
%The Spectator, 44 Frid St, Hamilton ON L8N 3G3, Canada
Carlson, Dudley L — *Navy Admiral*
%Navy League, 2300 Wilson Blvd, Arlington, VA 22201, USA
Carlson, G Raymond — *Religious Leader*
%Assemblies of God, 1445 N Boonville Ave, Springfield, MO 65802, USA
Carlson, Jack W — *Association Executive*
%American Assn of Retired Persons, 1901 "K" St NW, Washington, DC 20006, USA
Carlson, John A — *Businessman*
%Cray Research Inc, 655-A Lone Oak Dr, Eagan, MN 55121, USA
Carlson, LeRoy T, Jr — *Businessman*
%Telephone & Data Systems, 30 N LaSalle St, Chicago, IL 60602, USA
Carlson, LeRoy T, Sr — *Businessman*
%Telephone & Data Systems, 30 N LaSalle St, Chicago, IL 60602, USA
Carlsson, Ingvar G — *Prime Minister, Sweden*
Riksdagen, 100 12 Stockholm, Sweden

C

Carey - Carlsson

C

Carlton, Paul K	*Air Force General*
2025 Shoreline Towers, 900 Gulf Shore Dr, Destin, FL 32541, USA	
Carlton, Steven N (Steve)	*Baseball Player*
PO Box 736, Durango, CO 81302, USA	
Carlucci, Frank C, III	*Businessman; Secretary, Defense*
%Carlyle Group, 1001 Pennsylvania Ave NW, Washington, DC 20004, USA	
Carlyle, Joan H	*Opera Singer*
The Griffin, Ruthin Clwyd, North Wales, England	
Carlyle, Randy	*Hockey Player, Coach*
%Winnipeg Jets, Arena, 15-1430 Maroons Rd, Winnipeg MB R3G 0L5, Canada	
Carman, Gregory W	*Judge; Representative, NY*
%US Court of International Trade, 1 Federal Plaza, New York, NY 10278, USA	
Carmen, Eric	*Singer, Songwriter*
%Carmen-Daniels Mgmt, 1015 N Doheny Dr, #1, Los Angeles, CA 90069, USA	
Carmen, Julie	*Actress*
%Innovative Artists, 1999 Ave of Stars, #2850, Los Angeles, CA 90067, USA	
Carmichael, David M	*Businessman*
%K N Energy, 370 Van Gordon, Lakewood, CO 80228, USA	
Carmichael, Harold	*Football Player*
38 Birch Lane, Glassboro, NJ 08028, USA	
Carmody, Thomas R	*Businessman*
%American Business Products, PO Box 105684, Atlanta, GA 30348, USA	
Carnahan, Mel	*Governor, MO*
PO Box 698, Rolla, MO 65402, USA	
Carne, Judy	*Comedienne*
22 Jones St, #2-F, New York, NY 10014, USA	
Carne, Marcel	*Movie Director*
16 Rue De l'Abbaye, 75006 Paris, France	
Carner, JoAnne	*Golfer*
%Ladies Professional Golf Assn, 2570 Volusia Ave, Daytona Beach, FL 32114, USA	
Carnes, Kim	*Singer*
2031 Old Natchez Trace, Franklin, TN 37064, USA	
Carnesecca, Lou	*Basketball Coach*
%St John's University, Athletic Dept, Jamaica, NY 11439, USA	
Carnevale, Bernard L (Ben)	*Basketball Coach*
113 W Kingswood Dr, Williamsburg, VA 23185, USA	
Carney, Art	*Actor*
143 Kingfisher Lane, Westbrook, CT 06498, USA	
Carney, John	*Football Player*
%San Diego Chargers, Jack Murphy Stadium, San Diego, CA 92160, USA	
Carney, Thomas P	*Army General*
Deputy Chief of Staff for Personnel, US Army, Washington, DC 20310, USA	
Carnoy, Martin	*Economist*
%Stanford University, Economic Studies Center, Stanford, CA 94305, USA	
Caro, Anthony	*Sculptor*
111 Frognal, Hampstead, London NW3, England	
Caro, Robert A	*Writer*
%Robert A Caro Assoc, 250 W 57th St, New York, NY 10107, USA	
Caroline	*Princess, Monaco*
%Palace de Monaco, 98015 Monte Carlo 518, Monaco	
Caroline, J C	*Football Player*
2501 Stanford, Champaign, IL 61820, USA	
Caron, Leslie	*Actress*
6 Rue De Bellechaisse, 75007 Paris, France	
Carothers, Robert L	*Educator*
%University of Rhode Island, President's Office, Kingston, RI 02881, USA	
Carpenter, Bob	*Hockey Player*
%Washington Capitals, USAir Arena, Landover, MD 20785, USA	
Carpenter, Bob	*Businessman*
%Dollar General Corp, 104 Woodmont Blvd, Nashville, TN 37205, USA	
Carpenter, Carleton	*Actor*
RD 2, Chardavoyne Rd, Warwick, NY 10990, USA	
Carpenter, David R	*Businessman*
%Transamerica Occidental Life Insurance, 1150 S Olive St, Los Angeles, CA 90015, USA	
Carpenter, Edmund M	*Businessman*
%General Signal Corp, 1 High Ridge Park, Stamford, CT 06905, USA	
Carpenter, John H	*Movie Director*
%International Creative Mgmt, 8942 Wilshire Blvd, Beverly Hills, CA 90211, USA	

Carlton - Carpenter

Carpenter, John M *Opera Singer*
%Maurel Enterprises, 225 W 34th St, #1012, New York, NY 10122, USA

Carpenter, John W, III *Air Force General*
177 Pine Ridge Loop, Newland, NC 28657, USA

Carpenter, Liz *Women's Activist*
116 Skyline Dr, Austin, TX 78746, USA

Carpenter, M Scott *Astronaut*
PO Box 3161, Vail, CO 81695, USA

Carpenter, Mari C *Religious Leader*
%Presbyterian Church (USA), 100 Witherspoon, Louisville, KY 40222, USA

Carpenter, Mary-Chapin *Singer, Songwriter*
%Studio One Artists, 7010 Westmoreland Ave, #100, Takoma Park, MD 20912, USA

Carpenter, Richard *Pianist, Songwriter*
9386 Raviller Dr, Downey, CA 90240, USA

Carpenter, Teresa *Journalist*
%Village Voice, Editorial Dept, 36 Cooper Sq, New York, NY 10003, USA

Carpenter, William S, Jr *Army General, Hero, Football Player*
Commanding General, CFA/DCG/EUSA, APO, AP 96258, USA

Carper, Thomas R *Governor, DE*
%Governor's Office, Tatnall Building, Dover, DE 19901, USA

Carr of Hadley, L Robert *Government Official, England*
14 North Ct, Great Peter St, London SW1, England

Carr, Alan *Movie Producer, Agent*
%Alan Carr Enterprises, PO Box 691670, Los Angeles, CA 90064, USA

Carr, Antoine *Basketball Player*
%San Antonio Spurs, 600 E Market St, #102, San Antonio, TX 78205, USA

Carr, Austin *Basketball Player*
%Cleveland Cavaliers, 2923 Statesboro Rd, Richfield, OH 44286, USA

Carr, Charles L G (Chuck), Jr *Baseball Player*
%Florida Marlins, 100 NE 3rd Ave, Fort Lauderdale, FL 33301, USA

Carr, Darleen *Actress*
1604 N Vista Ave, Los Angeles, CA 90046, USA

Carr, Gerald P (Jerry) *Astronaut*
%CAMUS Inc, PO Box 919, Huntsville, AR 72740, USA

Carr, Jane *Actress*
6200 Mt Angelus Dr, Los Angeles, CA 90042, USA

Carr, Kenneth M *Navy Admiral*
2322 Fort Scott Dr, Arlington, VA 22202, USA

Carr, Michael Leon (M L) *Basketball Player, Coach, Executive*
%Boston Celtics, 151 Merrimac St, #500, Boston, MA 02114, USA

Carr, Paul *Actor*
%H David Moss Assoc, 733 Seward St, Los Angeles, CA 90038, USA

Carr, Roger D *Football Player*
3612 Chippenham Dr, Birmingham, AL 35242, USA

Carr, Vikki *Singer*
%Vi-Carr Enterprises, PO Box 5126, Beverly Hills, CA 90209, USA

Carradine, David *Actor*
9753 La Tuna Canyon Rd, Sun Valley, CA 91352, USA

Carradine, Keith *Actor*
355 S Grand Ave, #4150, Los Angeles, CA 90071, USA

Carradine, Robert *Actor*
355 S Grand Ave, #4150, Los Angeles, CA 90071, USA

Carreker, Jim *Businessman*
%Trammell Crow Co, Trammell Crow Center, 2001 Ross Ave, Dallas, TX 75201, USA

Carreno, Jose Manuel *Ballet Dancer*
%Royal Ballet, Bow St, London WC2E 9DD, England

Carreno, Manuel *Ballet Dancer*
%American Ballet Theatre, 890 Broadway, New York, NY 10003, USA

Carrera, Barbara *Actress*
8899 Beverly Blvd, #713, Los Angeles, CA 90048, USA

Carreras, Jose *Opera Singer*
%Opera Caballe, Via Augusta 59, 08006 Barcelona, Spain

Carrere, Tia *Actress*
816 N La Cienega Blvd, #8638, Los Angeles, CA 90069, USA

Carrey, Jim *Actor*
%United Talent Agency, 9560 Wilshire Blvd, #500, Beverly Hills, CA 90212, USA

Carrier, George F *Applied Mathematician*
Rice Spring Lane, Wayland, MA 01778, USA

C

Carpenter - Carrier

Carrier, Mark A — *Football Player*
%Chicago Bears, Halas Hall, 250 N Washington Rd, Lake Forest, IL 60045, USA

Carriere, Jean P J — *Writer*
Les Broussanes, Domessargues, 30350 Ledignan, France

Carrigg, James A — *Businessman*
%New York State Electric & Gas Co, 4500 Vestal Parkway E, Binghamton, NY 13902, USA

Carrington, Laura — *Actress*
10000 Riverside Dr, #6, Toluca Lake, CA 91602, USA

Carrington, Peter A R — *Government Official, England*
Manor House, Bledlow Near Aylesbury, Bucks HP17 9PE, England

Carrion, Richard L — *Financier*
%BanPonce Corp, 209 Ponce de Leon Ave, San Juan, PR 00918, USA

Carroll, Charles A — *Businessman*
%Rubbermaid Inc, 1147 Akron Rd, Wooster, OH 44691, USA

Carroll, Charles O — *Football Player*
%Carroll Rindal Kennedy Schuck, 1200 Westlake Ave N, Seattle, WA 98109, USA

Carroll, Diahann — *Singer, Actress*
PO Box 2999, Beverly Hills, CA 90213, USA

Carroll, Earl W — *Labor Official*
%United Garment Workers of America, PO Box 239, Hermitage, TN 37076, USA

Carroll, James — *Businessman*
%Wynn's International, 500 N State College Blvd, Fullerton, CA 92631, USA

Carroll, Joe Barry — *Basketball Player*
%Denver Nuggets, McNichols Arena, 1635 Clay St, Denver, CO 80204, USA

Carroll, John — *Attorney*
%Rogers & Wells, 200 Park Ave, New York, NY 10166, USA

Carroll, John B — *Psychologist*
409 Elliott Rd N, Chapel Hill, NC 27514, USA

Carroll, John S — *Editor*
%Baltimore Sun, Editorial Dept, 501 N Calvert St, Baltimore, MD 21202, USA

Carroll, Julian M — *Governor, KY*
%Carroll Assoc, 25 Fountain Place, Frankfort, KY 40601, USA

Carroll, Kent J — *Navy Admiral*
%Country Club of North Carolina, 1600 Morganton Rd, #30-X, Pinehurst, NC 28374, USA

Carroll, L Vane, Jr — *Financier*
%Blazer Financial Services, 8900 Grand Oak Circle, Tampa, FL 33637, USA

Carroll, Leonard M — *Financier*
%Integra Financial Corp, 4 PPG Pl, Pittsburgh, PA 15222, USA

Carroll, Lester — *Cartoonist (Our Boarding House)*
21100 Beachwood Dr, Rocky River, OH 44116, USA

Carroll, Madeleine — *Actress*
6 Bis Rue Andre Chemier, 92130 Issly-Les-Moul, France

Carroll, Pat — *Actress*
6523 W Olympic Blvd, Los Angeles, CA 90048, USA

Carroll, Pete — *Football Coach*
%San Francisco 49ers, 4949 Centennial Blvd, Santa Clara, CA 95054, USA

Carruth, John Campbell — *Businessman*
%TNT Freightways Corp, 9700 Higgins Rd, Rosemont, IL 60018, USA

Carruthers, Garrey E — *Governor, NM*
PO Box 91445, Academy Station, Albuquerque, NM 87199, USA

Carruthers, James H (Red) — *Skier*
8 Malone Ave, Garnerville, NY 10923, USA

Carruthers, Kitty — *Figure Skater*
22 E 71st St, New York, NY 10021, USA

Carruthers, Peter — *Figure Skater*
22 E 71st St, New York, NY 10021, USA

Carruthers, Robert — *Electrical Engineer*
11 Badgers Copse, Radley, Abingdon, Oxon OX14 3BQ, England

Carry, Julius J, III — *Actor*
%BDP Inc, 10637 Burbank Blvd, North Hollywood, CA 91601, USA

Carsey, Marcia L P — *Television Producer*
%Carsey-Warner Productions, 4024 Radford Ave, Bldg 3, Studio City, CA 91604, USA

Carson, David E A — *Financier*
%People's Bank, 850 Main St, Bridgeport, CT 06604, USA

Carson, Edward M — *Financier*
%First Interstate Bancorp, 633 W 5th St, Los Angeles, CA 90071, USA

Carson, Harold D (Harry) — *Football Player*
732 Barrister Court, Franklin Lakes, NJ 07417, USA

Carson, Jimmy	*Hockey Player*
%Vancouver Canucks, 100 N Renfrew St, Vancouver BC V5K 3N7, Canada	
Carson, John David	*Actor*
145 S Fairfax Ave, #310, Los Angeles, CA 90036, USA	
Carson, Johnny	*Entertainer*
6862 Wildlife Rd, Malibu, CA 90265, USA	
Carson, William H (Willie)	*Thoroughbred Racing Jockey*
Minster House, Barnsley, Cirencester, Glos, England	
Carter, Arthur L	*Publisher*
%Nation Magazine, 72 5th Ave, New York, NY 10011, USA	
Carter, Benny	*Jazz Alto Saxophonist, Composer*
8321 Skyline Dr, Los Angeles, CA 90046, USA	
Carter, Betty	*Singer, Songwriter*
%Bet-Car, 117 Saint Felix St, Brooklyn, NY 11217, USA	
Carter, Carlene	*Singer, Songwriter*
%William N Carter Career Mgmt, 1114 17th Ave S, #204, Nashville, TN 37212, USA	
Carter, Clarence	*Musician*
%Rodgers Redding Assoc, 1048 Tatnall St, Macon, GA 31201, USA	
Carter, Cris	*Football Player*
%Minnesota Vikings, 9520 Viking Dr, Eden Prairie, MN 55344, USA	
Carter, Dale	*Football Player*
%Kansas City Chiefs, 1 Arrowhead Dr, Kansas City, KS 64129, USA	
Carter, Dexter	*Football Player*
%New York Jets, 1000 Fulton Ave, Hempstead, NY 11550, USA	
Carter, Dixie	*Actress*
100 Universal City Plaza, #490-A, Universal City, CA 91608, USA	
Carter, Don	*Bowler*
13600 SW 88th St, Miami, FL 33186, USA	
Carter, Donald	*Basketball Executive*
%Dallas Mavericks, Reunion Arena, 777 Sports St, Dallas, TX 75207, USA	
Carter, Donald	*Financier*
%Carter Organization, 116 John St, New York, NY 10038, USA	
Carter, E Graydon	*Editor*
%Vanity Fair Magazine, Editorial Dept, 350 Madison Ave, New York, NY 10017, USA	
Carter, Edward W	*Businessman*
%Carter Hawley Hale Stores, 3880 N Mission Rd, Los Angeles, CA 90031, USA	
Carter, Elliott C, Jr	*Composer*
31 W 12th St, New York, NY 10011, USA	
Carter, G Emmett Cardinal	*Religious Leader*
%Archdiocese of Toronto, 355 Church St, Toronto ON M5B 1Z8, Canada	
Carter, Gary E	*Baseball Player*
15 Huntly Dr, Palm Beach Gardens, FL 33418, USA	
Carter, Herbert E	*Biochemist, Educator*
2401 Cerrada de Promesa, Tucson, AZ 85718, USA	
Carter, Jack	*Comedian*
1023 Chevy Chase Dr, Beverly Hills, CA 90210, USA	
Carter, James Earl (Jimmy), Jr	*President, USA*
%Carter Presidential Center, 1 Copenhill, Atlanta, GA 30307, USA	
Carter, John Mack	*Editor*
%Good Housekeeping Magazine, Editorial Dept, 959 8th Ave, New York, NY 10019, USA	
Carter, Joseph C (Joe)	*Baseball Player*
3000 W 117th St, Leawood, KS 66211, USA	
Carter, Kevin	*Football Player*
%St Louis Rams, 100 N Broadway, #2100, St Louis, MO 63102, USA	
Carter, Ki-Jana	*Football Player*
%Cincinnati Bengals, 200 Riverfront Stadium, Cincinnati, OH 45202, USA	
Carter, Lynda	*Actress*
9200 Harrington Dr, Potomac, MD 20854, USA	
Carter, Lynne	*Actress*
%Lew Sherrell Agency, 1354 Los Robles, Palm Springs, CA 92262, USA	
Carter, Marshall N	*Financier*
%State Street Bank & Trust Co, 225 Franklin St, Boston, MA 02110, USA	
Carter, Michael	*Football Player*
3324 Flintmont Dr, San Jose, CA 95148, USA	
Carter, Nell	*Singer, Actress*
%Direct Management Group, 947 N La Cienega Blvd, #G, Los Angeles, CA 90069, USA	
Carter, Powell F, Jr	*Navy Admiral*
699 Fillmore St, Harpers Ferry, WV 25425, USA	

C

Carson - Carter

C

Carter, Ralph — *Actor*
104-60 Queens Blvd, #10, Forest Hills, NY 11375, USA

Carter, Ronald (Ron) — *Jazz Bassist*
%Bridge Agency, 8 S Oxford St, Brooklyn, NY 11217, USA

Carter, Rosalynn S — *Wife of US President*
1 Woodland Dr, Plains, GA 31780, USA

Carter, Rubin — *Football Player*
8220 SW 162nd St, Miami, FL 33157, USA

Carter, Rubin (Hurricane) — *Boxer*
1313 Brookedge Dr, Hamlin, NY 14464, USA

Carter, Russell — *Football Player*
%New York Jets, 1000 Fulton Ave, Hempstead, NY 11550, USA

Carter, Thomas — *Television Director*
10958 Strathmore Dr, Los Angeles, CA 90024, USA

Carter, W Hodding, III — *Government Official*
211 S St Asaph, Alexandria, VA 22314, USA

Carter, William G — *Army General*
Chief of Staff, Allied Forces Southern Europe, APO, AE 09620, USA

Carteri, Rosana — *Opera Singer*
%Angel Records, 810 7th Ave, New York, NY 10019, USA

Carteris, Gabrielle — *Actress*
12953 Greenleaf St, Studio City, CA 91604, USA

Cartier-Bresson, Henri — *Photographer*
%Magnum Photos, 5 Passage River, 75011 Paris, France

Cartland, Barbara — *Writer*
Camfield Place, Hatfield, Herts AL9 6JE, England

Cartledge, Raymond E — *Businessman*
%Union Camp Corp, 1600 Valley Rd, Wayne, NJ 07470, USA

Cartwright, Angela — *Actress*
4330 Bakman St, North Hollywood, CA 91602, USA

Cartwright, Bill — *Basketball Player, Executive*
%Seattle Supersonics, 190 Queen Ave N, PO Box C-900911, Seattle, WA 98109, USA

Cartwright, Carol A — *Educator*
%Kent State University, President's Office, Kent, OH 44242, USA

Cartwright, Lynn — *Actress*
3349 W Cahuenga Blvd, #2, Los Angeles, CA 90068, USA

Cartwright, Veronica — *Actress*
4342 Bakman Ave, North Hollywood, CA 91602, USA

Carty, Ricardo A J (Rico) — *Baseball Player*
5 Ens Enriquillo, San Pedro de Macoris, Dominican Republic

Caruso, Anthony — *Actor*
1706 Mandeville Lane, Los Angeles, CA 90049, USA

Caruso, David — *Actor*
%Susan Smith Assoc, 121 N San Vicente Blvd, Beverly Hills, CA 90211, USA

Carvel, Elbert N — *Governor, DE*
Clayton Ave, Laurel, DE 19956, USA

Carver, Brent — *Actor*
%Live Entertainment, 1500 Broadway, #902, New York, NY 10036, USA

Carver, Martin G — *Businessman*
%Bandag Inc, Bandag Center, 2905 N Highway 61, Muscatine, IA 52761, USA

Carver, Richard M P — *Army Field Marshal, England*
Wood End House, Wickham Near Fareham, Hants PO17 6JZ, England

Carvey, Dana — *Comedian*
%Brillstein-Grey, 9150 Wilshire Blvd, #350, Beverly Hills, CA 90212, USA

Carville, C James, Jr — *Political Consultant*
%Carville Begala, 329 Maryland Ave NE, Washington, DC 20002, USA

Cary, W Sterling — *Religious Leader*
206 Lemoyne Parkway, Oak Park, IL 60302, USA

Casablancas, John — *Model Agency Executive*
%Elite Model Mgmt, 111 E 22nd St, #200, New York, NY 10010, USA

Casadesus, Jean Claude — *Conductor*
23 Blvd de la Liberte, 59800 Lille, France

Casals, Rosemary — *Tennis Player*
%Sportswoman Inc, 85 Filbert Ave, Sausalito, CA 94965, USA

Casanova, Len — *Football Coach*
2611 Windsor Circle W, Eugene, OR 97405, USA

Casanova, Thomas R (Tommy) — *Football Player*
Rt 2, Box 307-A, Crowley, LA 70526, USA

Carter - Casanova

Casares, Maria *Actress*
8 Rue Asseline, 75014 Paris, France

Casares, Rick *Football Player*
5801 Marine St, Tampa, FL 33609, USA

Casaroli, Agostino Cardinal *Religious Leader*
%Secretary of State's Office, 00120 Vatican City, Rome, Italy

Casbarian, John *Architect*
%Taft Architects, 807 Peden St, Houston, TX 77006, USA

Case, Daniel H, III *Businessman*
%Hambrecht & Quist Inc, 1 Bush St, San Francisco, CA 94104, USA

Case, Dean W *Businessman*
%Reliance Insurance, 4 Penn Center Plaza, Philadelphia, PA 19103, USA

Case, Everett N *Educator, Foundation Official*
Van Hornesville, Hirkimer County, NY 13475, USA

Case, Scott *Football Player*
%Atlanta Falcons, 2745 Burnett Rd, Suwanee, GA 30174, USA

Casey, Albert V *Businessman, Government Official*
%Southern Methodist University, Cox Business School, Dallas, TX 75275, USA

Casey, Colleen *Actress*
%Sanders Agency, 8831 Sunset Blvd, #304, Los Angeles, CA 90069, USA

Casey, Jeremiah E *Financier*
%First Maryland Bancorp, 25 S Charles St, Baltimore, MD 21201, USA

Casey, Joe D *Law Enforcement Official*
%Police Department, 200 James Robertson Parkway, Nashville, TN 37201, USA

Casey, John D *Writer*
%University of Virginia, English Dept, Charlottesville, VA 22903, USA

Casey, John K *Businessman*
%Wendy's International, 4288 W Dublin-Granville Rd, Dublin, OH 43017, USA

Casey, John T *Businessman*
%American Medical Holdings, 14001 Dallas Parkway, Dallas, TX 75240, USA

Casey, Jon *Hockey Player*
%St Louis Blues, St Louis Arena, 5700 Oakland Ave, St Louis, MO 63110, USA

Casey, Ronald B *Journalist*
%Birmingham News, Editorial Dept, PO Box 2553, Birmingham, AL 35202, USA

Cash, Gerald C *Governor General, Bahamas*
4 Bristol St, PO Box N-476, Nassau, Bahamas

Cash, Johnny *Singer, Songwriter*
%House of Cash, 700 Johnny Cash Parkway, Hendersonville, TN 37077, USA

Cash, June Carter *Singer, Guitarist*
%House of Cash, 700 Johnny Cash Parkway, Hendersonville, TN 37077, USA

Cash, Pat *Tennis Player*
281 Clarence St, Sydney NSW 2000, Australia

Cash, R D *Businessman*
%Questar Corp, 180 E 1st S, Salt Lake City, UT 84103, USA

Cash, Rosalind *Actress*
PO Box 1605, Topanga, CA 90290, USA

Cash, Rosanne *Singer, Songwriter*
%Sony Music PR, 34 Music Sq E, Nashville, TN 37203, USA

Cash, Tommy *Singer, Songwriter*
%Capitol Mgmt, 1300 Division St, #103-A, Nashville, TN 37203, USA

Cashen, J Frank *Baseball Executive*
%New York Mets, Shea Stadium, Flushing, NY 11368, USA

Casillas, Tony *Football Player*
%New York Jets, 1000 Fulton Ave, Hempstead, NY 11550, USA

Casimir, Oye Mba *Prime Minister, Gabon*
%Prime Minister's Office, Boite Postale 546, Libreville, Gabon

Caskey, C Thomas *Geneticist, Biologist*
%Baylor College of Medicine, Molecular Genetics Dept, Houston, TX 77030, USA

Caslavska, Vera *Gymnast*
SVS Sparta Prague, Korunovacni 29, Prague 7, Czech Republic

Casoria, Giuseppe Cardinal *Religious Leader*
Via Pancrazio Pfeiffer 10, 00193 Rome, Italy

Casper, David J (Dave) *Football Player*
291 Trappers Pass, Chanhassen, MN 55317, USA

Casper, Gerhard *Educator*
%Stanford University, President's Office, Stanford, CA 94305, USA

Casper, John H *Astronaut*
%NASA, Johnson Space Center, 2101 NASA Rd, Houston, TX 77058, USA

C

Casares - Casper

Casper, William E (Billy) *Golfer*
PO Box 1088, Chula Vista, CA 91912, USA

Caspersen, Finn M W *Financier*
%Beneficial Corp, 301 N Walnut St, Wilmington, DE 19801, USA

Caspersson, Tobjorn *Biochemist, Cancer Specialist*
Emanuel Birkes Väg 2, 144 00 Ronninge, Sweden

Cassady, Howard (Hopalong) *Football Player*
539 Severn Ave, Tampa, FL 33606, USA

Cassavetes, Nick *Actor*
22223 Buena Ventura St, Woodland Hills, CA 91364, USA

Cassel, Jean-Pierre *Actor*
%International Creative Mgmt, 76 Oxford St, London W1N 0AX, England

Cassel, Seymour *Actor*
2800 Neilson Way, #1601, Santa Monica, CA 90405, USA

Cassel, Walter *Opera Singer*
%Indiana University, Music School, Bloomington, IN 47401, USA

Cassell, Ollan *Sports Executive*
%USA Track & Field, PO Box 120, Indianapolis, IN 46206, USA

Cassell, Sam *Basketball Player*
%Houston Rockets, Summit, Greenway Plaza, #10, Houston, TX 77277, USA

Cassels, A James H *Army Field Marshal, England*
Hamble End, Higham Rd, Barrow, Bury Saint Edmunds, Suffolk, England

Cassidy, David *Actor, Singer*
4155 Witzel Dr, Sherman Oaks, CA 91423, USA

Cassidy, Edward I Cardinal *Religious Leader*
%Pontifical Council for Christian Unity, Vatican City, 00120 Rome, Italy

Cassidy, Joanna *Actress*
2530 Outpost Dr, Los Angeles, CA 90068, USA

Cassidy, Patrick *Actor*
701 N Oakhurst Dr, Beverly Hills, CA 90210, USA

Cassidy, Ryan *Actor*
12546 The Vista, Los Angeles, CA 90049, USA

Cassidy, Shaun *Actor, Singer*
%International Creative Mgmt, 8942 Wilshire Blvd, Beverly Hills, CA 90211, USA

Cassilly, Richard *Opera Singer*
%Boston University, Music Dept, 855 Commonwealth Ave, Boston, MA 02215, USA

Cassini, Oleg L *Fashion Designer*
3 W 57th St, New York, NY 10019, USA

Casson, Hugh Maxwell *Architect*
6 Hereford Mansions, Hereford Rd, London W2 5BA, England

Castaneda, Carlos *Writer, Anthropologist*
%University of California Press, 2121 Berkeley Way, Berkeley, CA 94704, USA

Castaneda, Jorge A *Government Official, Mexico*
Anillo Periferico Sur 3180, #1120, Jardines del Pedregal, 01900 Mexico

Casteen, John T, III *Educator*
%University of Virginia, President's Office, Charlottesville, VA 22906, USA

Castel, Nico *Opera Singer*
%RPA Mgmt, 4 Adelaide Lane, Washingtonville, NY 10992, USA

Castelli, Leo *Art Dealer*
%Leo Castelli Gallery, 420 W Broadway, New York, NY 10012, USA

Castellini, Clateo *Businessman*
%Becton Dickinson Co, 1 Becton Dr, Franklin Lakes, NJ 07417, USA

Castille, Jeremiah *Football Player*
%Praise & Worship Ministries, 701 26th Ave, Phoenix City, AL 36869, USA

Castillo Lara, Rosalio Jose Cardinal *Religious Leader*
%Pontifical Commission for Vatican City, Vatican City, 00120 Rome, Italy

Castle of Blackburn, Barbara A *Government Official, England*
%House of Lords, Westminster, London SW1A 0PW, England

Castle, John K *Financier*
%Castle Harlan Inc, 150 E 58th St, New York, NY 10155, USA

Castleman, E Riva *Museum Curator*
%Museum of Modern Art, 11 W 53rd St, New York, NY 10019, USA

Castro Ruz, Fidel *President, Cuba*
%Palacio del Gobierno, Plaza de la Revolucion, Havana, Cuba

Castro Ruz, Raul *Prime Minister, Cuba; Army General*
%First Vice President's Office, Plaza de la Revolucion, Havana, Cuba

Castro, Emilio *Religious Leader*
%World Council of Churches, 475 Riverside Dr, New York, NY 10115, USA

Castro, Raul H — *Governor, AZ*
1433 E Thomas St, Phoenix, AZ 85014, USA

Catacosinos, William J — *Businessman*
%Long Island Lighting Co, 175 E Old Country Rd, Hicksville, NY 11801, USA

Catalano, Eduardo F — *Architect*
44 Grozier Rd, Cambridge, MA 02138, USA

Catalona, William J — *Urologist*
%Washington University School of Medicine, Urology Division, St Louis, MO 63110, USA

Catanzaro, Tony — *Dancer*
1809 Ponce De Leon Blvd, Miami, FL 33134, USA

Catell, Robert B — *Businessman*
%Brooklyn Union Gas Co, 1 Metrotech Center, Brooklyn, NY 11201, USA

Cates, Gilbert — *Movie, Television Director, Producer*
%Gilbert Cates Productions, 10920 Wilshire Blvd, #600, Los Angeles, CA 90024, USA

Cates, Phoebe — *Actress*
45 W 67th St, #27-B, New York, NY 10019, USA

Cathcart, Patti — *Singer (Tuck & Patti)*
%Q Entertainment, 584 N Larchmont Blvd, Los Angeles, CA 90004, USA

Catlett, Mary Jo — *Actress*
4357 Farmdale Ave, North Hollywood, CA 91604, USA

Catlin, Thomas (Tom) — *Football Player, Coach*
22621 NE 25th Way, Redmond, WA 98053, USA

Cato, Robert Milton — *Prime Minister, Saint Vincent*
PO Box 138, Ratho Mill, Saint Vincent & Grenadines

Caton-Jones, Michael — *Movie Director*
%Enigma Films, Pinewood Studios, Ivor Heath, Iver, Bucks SL0 0NH, England

Cattani, Richard J — *Publisher*
%Christian Science Monitor, 1 Norway St, Boston, MA 02115, USA

Catto of Cairncatto, Stephen G — *Financier*
%Morgan Grenfell Group, 23 Great Winchester St, London EC2P 2AX, England

Catto, Henry E, Jr — *Diplomat*
110 E Crockett St, San Antonio, TX 78205, USA

Cattrall, Kim — *Actress*
616 Lorna Lane, Los Angeles, CA 90049, USA

Caulfield, Lore — *Fashion Designer*
2228 Cotner, Los Angeles, CA 90064, USA

Caulfield, Maxwell — *Actor*
4770 9th St, #B, Carpinteria, CA 93013, USA

Caulo, Ralph D — *Publisher*
%Harcourt Brace Jovanovich, 6277 Sea Harbor Dr, Orlando, FL 32887, USA

Causewell, Duane — *Basketball Player*
%Sacramento Kings, 1 Sports Parkway, Sacramento, CA 95834, USA

Causley, Charles S — *Poet*
2 Cyprus Well, Launceston, Cornwall PL15 8BT, England

Cauthen, Robert S, Jr — *Businessman*
%American General Life Insurance, 2727 Allen Parkway, Houston, TX 77019, USA

Cauthen, Steve — *Thoroughbred Racing Jockey*
%Cauthen Ranch, RFD, Boone County, Walton, KY 41094, USA

Cavaco Silva, Anibal — *Prime Minister, Portugal*
%Prime Minister's Office, Rua du Imprensa a Est 8, 1300 Lisbon, Portugal

Cavaiani, Jon R — *Vietnam War Army Hero (CMH)*
10830 Yosemite Blvd, Waterford, CA 95386, USA

Cavallini, Paul — *Hockey Player*
%Dallas Stars, 211 Cowboys Parkway, Dallas, TX 75063, USA

Cavanaugh, James H — *Government Official*
%White House, 1600 Pennsylvania Ave NW, Washington, DC 20006, USA

Cavanaugh, Page — *Musician*
5442 Woodman Ave, Van Nuys, CA 91401, USA

Cavanaugh, William, III — *Businessman*
%Carolina Power & Light, 411 Fayetteville St Mall, Raleigh, NC 27601, USA

Cavaretta, Philip J (Phil) — *Baseball Player*
2206 Portside Passage, Palm Harbor, FL 34685, USA

Cavazos, Lauro F — *Secretary, Education*
173 Annursnac Hill Rd, Concord, MA 01742, USA

Cavett, Dick — *Entertainer*
2200 Fletcher Ave, Fort Lee, NJ 07024, USA

Cavezza, Carmen J — *Army General*
Commanding General, I Corps & Fort Lewis, Fort Lewis, WA 98433, USA

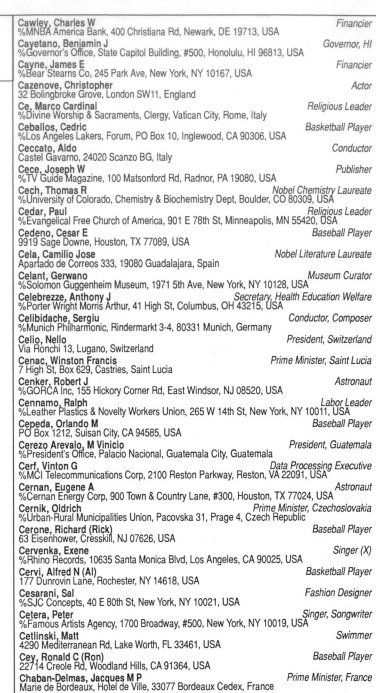

C

Cawley, Charles W — *Financier*
%MNBA America Bank, 400 Christiana Rd, Newark, DE 19713, USA

Cayetano, Benjamin J — *Governor, HI*
%Governor's Office, State Capitol Building, #500, Honolulu, HI 96813, USA

Cayne, James E — *Financier*
%Bear Stearns Co, 245 Park Ave, New York, NY 10167, USA

Cazenove, Christopher — *Actor*
32 Bolingbroke Grove, London SW11, England

Ce, Marco Cardinal — *Religious Leader*
%Divine Worship & Sacraments, Clergy, Vatican City, Rome, Italy

Ceballos, Cedric — *Basketball Player*
%Los Angeles Lakers, Forum, PO Box 10, Inglewood, CA 90306, USA

Ceccato, Aldo — *Conductor*
Castel Gavarno, 24020 Scanzo BG, Italy

Cece, Joseph W — *Publisher*
%TV Guide Magazine, 100 Matsonford Rd, Radnor, PA 19080, USA

Cech, Thomas R — *Nobel Chemistry Laureate*
%University of Colorado, Chemistry & Biochemistry Dept, Boulder, CO 80309, USA

Cedar, Paul — *Religious Leader*
%Evangelical Free Church of America, 901 E 78th St, Minneapolis, MN 55420, USA

Cedeno, Cesar E — *Baseball Player*
9919 Sage Downe, Houston, TX 77089, USA

Cela, Camilio Jose — *Nobel Literature Laureate*
Apartado de Correos 333, 19080 Guadalajara, Spain

Celant, Gerwano — *Museum Curator*
%Solomon Guggenheim Museum, 1971 5th Ave, New York, NY 10128, USA

Celebrezze, Anthony J — *Secretary, Health Education Welfare*
%Porter Wright Morris Arthur, 41 High St, Columbus, OH 43215, USA

Celibidache, Sergiu — *Conductor, Composer*
%Munich Philharmonic, Rindermarkt 3-4, 80331 Munich, Germany

Celio, Nello — *President, Switzerland*
Via Ronchi 13, Lugano, Switzerland

Cenac, Winston Francis — *Prime Minister, Saint Lucia*
7 High St, Box 629, Castries, Saint Lucia

Cenker, Robert J — *Astronaut*
%GORCA Inc, 155 Hickory Corner Rd, East Windsor, NJ 08520, USA

Cennamo, Ralph — *Labor Leader*
%Leather Plastics & Novelty Workers Union, 265 W 14th St, New York, NY 10011, USA

Cepeda, Orlando M — *Baseball Player*
PO Box 1212, Suisan City, CA 94585, USA

Cerezo Arevalo, M Vinicio — *President, Guatemala*
%President's Office, Palacio Nacional, Guatemala City, Guatemala

Cerf, Vinton G — *Data Processing Executive*
%MCI Telecommunications Corp, 2100 Reston Parkway, Reston, VA 22091, USA

Cernan, Eugene A — *Astronaut*
%Cernan Energy Corp, 900 Town & Country Lane, #300, Houston, TX 77024, USA

Cernik, Oldrich — *Prime Minister, Czechoslovakia*
%Urban-Rural Municipalities Union, Pacovska 31, Prage 4, Czech Republic

Cerone, Richard (Rick) — *Baseball Player*
63 Eisenhower, Cresskill, NJ 07626, USA

Cervenka, Exene — *Singer (X)*
%Rhino Records, 10635 Santa Monica Blvd, Los Angeles, CA 90025, USA

Cervi, Alfred N (Al) — *Basketball Player*
177 Dunrovin Lane, Rochester, NY 14618, USA

Cesarani, Sal — *Fashion Designer*
%SJC Concepts, 40 E 80th St, New York, NY 10021, USA

Cetera, Peter — *Singer, Songwriter*
%Famous Artists Agency, 1700 Broadway, #500, New York, NY 10019, USA

Cetlinski, Matt — *Swimmer*
4290 Mediterranean Rd, Lake Worth, FL 33461, USA

Cey, Ronald C (Ron) — *Baseball Player*
22714 Creole Rd, Woodland Hills, CA 91364, USA

Chaban-Delmas, Jacques M P — *Prime Minister, France*
Marie de Bordeaux, Hotel de Ville, 33077 Bordeaux Cedex, France

Chad (Stuart) — *Singer (Chad & Jeremy)*
%Agency For Performing Arts, 9000 Sunset Blvd, #1200, Los Angeles, CA 90069, USA

Chadirji, Rifat Kamil — *Architect*
28 Troy Ct, Kensington High St, London W8, England

Cawley - Chadirji

Chadli, Bendjedid — *President, Algeria*
Palace Emir Abedelkader, Algiers, Algeria

Chadnois, Lynn — *Football Player*
2048 Walden Court, Flint, MI 48532, USA

Chadwick, June — *Actress*
%Metropolitan Talent Agency, 4526 Wilshire Blvd, Los Angeles, CA 90010, USA

Chadwick, Lynn R — *Sculptor*
Lypiatt Park, Stroud, Glos GL6 7LL, England

Chadwick, Wallace L — *Construction Engineer*
475 N Taylor Dr, Claremont, CA 91711, USA

Chafetz, Sidney — *Artist*
%Ohio State University, Art Dept, Columbus, OH 43210, USA

Chailly, Riccardo — *Conductor*
Royal Concertgebrew, Jacob Obrechtstraat 51, 1071 KJ Amsterdam 41, Holland

Chakiris, George — *Actor*
7266 Clinton St, Los Angeles, CA 90036, USA

Chalfont, A G (Arthur) — *Government Official, England*
%House of Lords, Westminster, London SW1A 0PW, England

Chalsty, John S — *Financier*
%Donaldson Lufkin Jenrette Inc, 140 Broadway, New York, NY 10005, USA

Chamberlain, David M — *Businessman*
%Genesco Inc, Genesco Park, 1415 Murfreesboro Rd, Nashville, TN 37217, USA

Chamberlain, John A — *Sculptor*
%Ten Coconut Inc, 1315 10th St, Sarasota, FL 34236, USA

Chamberlain, Joseph W — *Astronomer*
%Rice University, Space Physics & Astronomy Dept, Houston, TX 77001, USA

Chamberlain, Owen — *Nobel Physics Laureate*
%University of California, Physics Dept, Berkeley, CA 94720, USA

Chamberlain, Richard — *Actor*
3711 Round Top Dr, Honolulu, HI 96822, USA

Chamberlain, Wilton N (Wilt) — *Basketball Player*
%Seymour Goldberg, 11111 Santa Monica Blvd, #1000, Los Angeles, CA 90025, USA

Chambers, Anne Cox — *Businesswoman, Diplomat*
%Cox Enterprises, 1400 Lake Hearn Dr NE, Atlanta, GA 30319, USA

Chambers, James E (Bear) — *Air Force General*
HQ US Air Force Europe/CC, Unit 3050, Box 15, APO, AE 09094, USA

Chambers, John T — *Businessman*
%Cisco Systems, 170 W Tasman Dr, San Jose, CA 95134, USA

Chambers, Tom — *Basketball Player*
%Utah Jazz, 301 W South Temple, Salt Lake City, UT 84101, USA

Chambers, Walter R — *Financier*
%Ohio Co, 155 E Broad St, Columbus, OH 43215, USA

Chambliss, C Christopher (Chris) — *Baseball Player*
1 Braves Ave, Greenville, SC 29606, USA

Chamorro, Violeta Barrios de — *President, Nicaragua*
%Casa de Gobierno, Apartado 2398, Managua, Nicaragua

Champion, Marge — *Dancer, Actress*
484 W 43rd St, New York, NY 10036, USA

Champlin, Charles D — *Movie Critic*
2169 Linda Flora Dr, Los Angeles, CA 90077, USA

Chan Sy — *Premier, Kampuchea*
%Premier's Office, Phnom-Penh, People's Republic of Kampuchea

Chan, Julius — *Prime Minister, Papua New Guinea*
PO Box 717, Rabaul, Papua New Guinea

Chance, Britton — *Biophysicist, Educator*
4014 Pine St, Philadelphia, PA 19104, USA

Chance, W Dean — *Baseball Player*
9505 W Smithville Western, Wooster, OH 44691, USA

Chancey, Malcolm B, Jr — *Financier*
%Liberty National BanCorp, 416 W Jefferson St, Louisville, KY 40202, USA

Chandler, Alice — *Educator*
%State University of New York, President's Office, New Paltz, NY 12561, USA

Chandler, Colby H — *Businessman*
%Ford Motor Co, American Rd, Dearborn, MI 48121, USA

Chandler, Don — *Football Player*
4142 S 88th E Ave, Tulsa, OK 74137, USA

Chandler, Dorothy — *Philanthropist*
455 S Lorraine Blvd, Los Angeles, CA 90020, USA

Chandler, Gene (Duke of Earl) *Singer*
%Mars Talent, 168 Orchid Dr, Pearl River, NY 10965, USA

Chandler, J Harold *Businessman*
%Provident Life & Accident Insurance, 1 Fountain Square, Chattanooga, TN 37402, USA

Chandler, J Howard *Businessman*
%Varity Corp, 672 Delaware Ave, Buffalo, NY 14209, USA

Chandler, James B *Educator*
7449 Rupert Ave, Richmond Heights, MO 63117, USA

Chandler, John W *Educator*
1818 "R" St NW, Washington, DC 20009, USA

Chandler, Kyle *Actor*
PO Box 29481, Los Angeles, CA 90029, USA

Chandler, Otis *Publisher*
%Times Mirror Co, Times Mirror Square, Los Angeles, CA 90053, USA

Chandler, Robert *Television News Executive*
21 Squaw Peak Rd, Great Barrington, MA 01230, USA

Chandola, Walter *Photographer*
%General Delivery, Annandale, NJ 08801, USA

Chandrasekhar, Bhagwat S *Cricketer*
571 31st Cross, 4th Block, Jayanagar, Bangalore 56011, India

Chaney, Don *Basketball Player, Coach*
%New York Knicks, Madison Square Grdn, 4 Pennsylvania Plz, New York, NY 10001, USA

Chaney, John *Basketball Coach*
%Temple University, Athletic Dept, Philadelphia, PA 19122, USA

Chaney, William R *Businessman*
%Tiffany Co, 727 5th Ave, New York, NY 10022, USA

Chang, Michael *Tennis Player*
PO Box 6080, Mission Viejo, CA 92690, USA

Chang, Sarah *Concert Violinist*
%International Creative Mgmt, 40 W 57th St, New York, NY 10019, USA

Chang-Diaz, Franklin R *Astronaut*
%NASA, Johnson Space Center, 2101 NASA Rd, Houston, TX 77058, USA

Channing, Carol *Actress, Singer*
9301 Flicker Way, Los Angeles, CA 90069, USA

Channing, Stockard *Actress*
%PMK Public Relations, 955 S Carillo Dr, #200, Los Angeles, CA 90048, USA

Chao, Elaine L *Association Official*
%United Way of America, 701 N Fairfax St, Alexandria, VA 22314, USA

Chao, Rosalind *Actress*
%Writers & Artists Agency, 924 Westwood Blvd, #900, Los Angeles, CA 90024, USA

Chapin, Dwight L *Publisher, Government Official*
%San Francisco Examiner, 110 5th St, San Francisco, CA 94103, USA

Chapin, Lauren *Actress*
PO Box 922, Killeen, TX 76540, USA

Chapin, Schuyler G *Opera Executive*
901 Lexington Ave, New York, NY 10021, USA

Chapin, Tom *Singer*
57 Piermont Pl, Piermont, NY 10968, USA

Chaplin, Geraldine *Actress*
Manoir de Bau, Vevey, Switzerland

Chaplin, Lita Gray *Actress*
8440 Fountain Ave, #302, Los Angeles, CA 90069, USA

Chapman, Alvah H, Jr *Publisher*
%Knight-Ridder Inc, 1 Herald Plaza, Miami, FL 33132, USA

Chapman, Bruce K *Government Official*
%Discovery Institute, 1201 3rd Ave, #4000, Seattle, WA 98101, USA

Chapman, E T *WW II British Army Hero (VC)*
%Victoria Cross Society, Old Admiralty Bldg, London SW1A 2BE, England

Chapman, James C *Businessman*
25310 W Hickory St, Antioch, IL 60002, USA

Chapman, Judith *Actress*
100 S Sunrise Way, #323, Palm Springs, CA 92262, USA

Chapman, Lonny *Actor*
3973 Goodland Ave, Studio City, CA 91604, USA

Chapman, Max C, Jr *Financier*
%Nomura Securities, 2 World Financial Center, 200 Liberty St, New York, NY 10281, USA

Chapman, Michael J *Movie Director, Cinematographer*
%Gersh Agency, 232 N Canon Dr, Beverly Hills, CA 90210, USA

Chapman, Morris M *Religious Leader*
%Southern Baptist Convention, 5452 Grannywhite Pike, Brentwood, TN 37027, USA

Chapman, Nathan A, Jr *Financier*
%Chapman Co, 401 E Pratt St, Baltimore, MD 21202, USA

Chapman, Philip K *Astronaut*
%Windowcraft Corp, 289 Gret Rd, Acton, MA 01720, USA

Chapman, Rex *Basketball Player*
%Washington Bullets, Capital Centre, 1 Truman Dr, Landover, MD 20785, USA

Chapman, Samuel B *Football Player*
11 Andrew Dr, #39, Tiburon, CA 94920, USA

Chapman, Steven Curtis *Singer, Songwriter*
%Creative Trust, 1910 Acklen Ave, Nashville, TN 37212, USA

Chapman, Tracy *Singer, Songwriter*
%Lookout Mgmt, 2644 30th St, #100, Santa Monica, CA 90405, USA

Chapman, Wes *Ballet Dancer*
%American Ballet Theater, 890 Broadway, New York, NY 10003, USA

Chappell, Fred D *Poet*
305 Kensington Rd, Greensboro, NC 27403, USA

Chappell, Robert E *Businessman*
%Penn Mutual Life Insurance, Independence Square, Philadelphia, PA 19172, USA

Chappuis, Bob *Football Player*
3115 Covington Lake Dr, Fort Wayne, IN 46804, USA

Chapuisat, Stephane *Soccer Player*
%Borussia Dortmund Soccer Club, Strobelallee, 44139 Dortmund, Germany

Charbonneau, Patricia *Actress*
%Paradigm Agency, 10100 Santa Monica Blvd, #2500, Los Angeles, CA 90067, USA

Charette, William R (Doc) *Korean War Navy Hero (CMH)*
5237 Limberlost Dr, Lake Wales, FL 33853, USA

Chargaff, Erwin *Biochemist, Educator*
350 Central Park West, #13-G, New York, NY 10025, USA

Charisse, Cyd *Actress, Dancer*
10724 Wilshire Blvd, #1406, Los Angeles, CA 90024, USA

Charles *Prince of Wales, England*
%Highgrove House, Doughton Near Tetbury, Gloucs GL8 8TN, England

Charles, Bob *Golfer*
%International Management Group, 1 Erieview Plaza, #1300, Cleveland, OH 44114, USA

Charles, Caroline *Fashion Designer*
56/57 Beauchamp Pl, London SW3, England

Charles, M Eugenia *Prime Minister, Dominica*
%Prime Minister's Office, Government House, Kennedy Ave, Roseau, Dominica

Charles, Nick *Sportscaster*
%Cable News Network, News Dept, 1050 Techwood Dr NW, Atlanta, GA 30318, USA

Charles, Ray *Singer*
%Ray Charles Enterprises, 2107 W Washington Blvd, #200, Los Angeles, CA 90018, USA

Charleson, Leslie *Actress*
2314 Live Oak Dr E, Los Angeles, CA 90068, USA

Charlesworth, James H *Theologian*
%Princeton Theological Seminary, Theology Dept, Princeton, NJ 08540, USA

Charlton, Robert (Bobby) *Soccer Player*
Garthollerton, Cleford Rd, Ollerton Near Knutsford, Cheshire, England

Charmoli, Tony *Choreographer, Director*
1271 Sunset Plaza Dr, Los Angeles, CA 90069, USA

Charnin, Martin *Theater Producer, Director, Lyricist*
%Richard Ticktin, 1345 Ave of Americas, New York, NY 10105, USA

Charo (Rasten) *Singer, Flamenco Guitarist*
%Charo's Restaurant, PO Box 1007, Hanalei, Kauai, HI 96714, USA

Charpak, Georges *Nobel Physics Laureate*
37 Rue de la Plaine, 75020 Paris, France

Charren, Peggy *Television Executive, Consumer Activist*
%Action for Children's Television, PO Box 383090, Cambridge, MA 02238, USA

Chartoff, Melanie *Actress*
%Artists Agency, 10000 Santa Monica Blvd, #305, Los Angeles, CA 90067, USA

Chartoff, Robert *Movie Producer*
PO Box 3628, Granada Hills, CA 91394, USA

Charvet, David *Actor*
%"Baywatch" Show, 5433 Beethoven St, Los Angeles, CA 90066, USA

Chase, Alison *Dance Artistic Director*
%Pilolobus Dance Theater, PO Box 388, Washington Depot, CT 06794, USA

C

Chase, Barrie	*Actress, Dancer*
3750 Beverly Ridge Dr, Sherman Oaks, CA 91423, USA	
Chase, Chevy	*Comedian*
17492 Camino de Yatasto, Pacific Palisades, CA 90272, USA	
Chase, Sylvia B	*Commentator*
%ABC-TV, News Dept, 77 W 66th St, New York, NY 10023, USA	
Chase, W Howard	*Businessman, Educator*
66 Sachem Lane, Greenwich, CT 06830, USA	
Chast, Roz	*Cartoonist*
%New Yorker Magazine, Editorial Dept, 20 W 43rd St, New York, NY 10036, USA	
Chastel, Andre	*Writer*
30 Rue De Lubeck, 75116 Paris, France	
Chatichai Choonhavan	*Prime Minister, Army General, Thailand*
%Prime Minister's Office, Luke Luang Rd, Bangkok 2, Thailand	
Chatrier, Philippe	*Tennis Executive*
7 Rue Allied Bruneau, 75016 Paris, France	
Chauvel, Bernard L	*Financier*
%Credit Agricole, 55 E Monroe St, Chicago, IL 60603, USA	
Chauvire, Yvette	*Ballerina*
21 Place di Commerce, 70015 Paris, France	
Chaves, Richard	*Actor*
%Media Artists, 8383 Wilshire Blvd, #954, Beverly Hills, CA 90211, USA	
Chavez, Ignacio	*Research Scientist*
Paseo de la Reforma 1310, Lomas, Mexico City 10 DF, Mexico	
Chavis, Boo Zoo	*Musician, Zydeco*
%King Creole Zydeco, PO Box 672661, Houston, TX 77267, USA	
Chavous, Barney L	*Football Player, Coach*
6670 S Billings Way, Englewood, CO 80111, USA	
Chawla, Kalpana	*Astronaut*
%Overset Methods Inc, 262 Warich Way, Los Altos, CA 94022, USA	
Chazov, Yevgeny I	*Cardiologist*
%Cardiology Research Center, Cherepkovskaya Ul 15-A, 121552 Moscow, Russia	
Cheaney, Calbert	*Basketball Player*
%Washington Bullets, Capital Centre, 1 Truman Dr, Landover, MD 20785, USA	
Checchi, Alfred	*Businessman*
%Northwest Airlines Corp, 5101 Northwest Dr, St Paul, MN 55111, USA	
Checker, Chubby	*Singer, Songwriter*
1646 Hilltop Rd, Birchrunville, PA 19421, USA	
Checketts, David W	*Basketball Executive*
%New York Knicks, Madison Square Grdn, 4 Pennsylvania Plz, New York, NY 10001, USA	
Cheech (Richard A Marin)	*Comedian (Cheech & Chong)*
%Joseph Mannis, 11661 San Vicente Blvd, #1010, Los Angeles, CA 90049, USA	
Cheek, James E	*Educator*
8035 16th St NW, Washington, DC 20012, USA	
Cheek, Molly	*Actress*
3690 Goodland Ave, Studio City, CA 91604, USA	
Cheeks, Maurice	*Basketball Player, Coach*
%Philadelphia 76ers, Veterans Stadium, PO Box 25040, Philadelphia, PA 19147, USA	
Cheevers, Gerry	*Hockey Player, Executive; Sportscaster*
%Boston Bruins, Boston Garden, 150 Causeway St, Boston, MA 02114, USA	
Chelberg, Bruce S	*Businessman*
%Whitman Corp, 3501 Algonwin, Rolling Meadows, IL 60008, USA	
Chelberg, Robert D	*Army General*
%George C Marshall Security Studies Center, Unit 24502, APO, AE 09053, USA	
Chelios, Christos K (Chris)	*Hockey Player*
%Chicago Blackhawks, Chicago Stadium, 1800 W Madison St, Chicago, IL 60612, USA	
Chellgren, Paul W	*Businessman*
%Ashland Oil, 1000 Ashland Dr, Russell, KY 41169, USA	
Chen Xieyang	*Conductor*
%Shanghai Symphony Orchestra, 105 Hunan Rd, Shanghai 200031, China	
Chen Zuohuang	*Conductor*
%Wichita Symphony Orchestra, Concert Hall, 225 W Douglas St, Wichita, KS 67202, USA	
Chen, Irvin S Y	*Medical Researcher*
%University of California Medical Center, Hematology Dept, Los Angeles, CA 90024, USA	
Chen, Joan	*Actress*
2601 Filbert St, San Francisco, CA 94123, USA	
Chen, Steve S	*Computer Engineer*
%Chen Systems Corp, 1414 W Hamilton Ave, Eau Claire, WI 54701, USA	

Chase - Chen

Chenault, Kenneth L — *Businessman*
%American Express Co, World Financial Center, New York, NY 10285, USA

Chenchikova, Olga — *Ballerina*
%Kirov Ballet Theatre, 1 Ploshchad Iskusstr, St Petersburg, Russia

Cheney, Lynne V — *Government Official*
%American Enterprise Institute, 1150 17th St NW, Washington, DC 20036, USA

Cheney, Richard B — *Secretary, Defense*
%Halliburton Co, Lincoln Plaza, #3600, 500 N Akard St, Dallas, TX 75201, USA

Cher (Sarkisian) — *Actress, Singer*
%Bill Sammeth Organization, PO Box 960, Beverly Hills, CA 90213, USA

Chereau, Patrice — *Movie, Opera, Theater Director*
%Nanterre-Amandiers, 7 Ave Pablo Picasso, 9200 Nanterre, France

Cherenkov, Pavel A — *Nobel Physics Laureate*
%Lebedev Physics Institute, Leninsky Prospekt 53, Moscow, Russia

Cherkassky, Shura — *Concert Pianist*
%Shaw Concerts, Lincoln Plaza, 1900 Broadway, #200, New York, NY 10023, USA

Chermayeff, Peter — *Architect*
%Cambridge Seven Assoc, 1050 Massachusetts Ave, Cambridge, MA 02138, USA

Chermayeff, Serge — *Architect, Artist*
%Design Arts, Box "NN", Wellfleet, MA 02667, USA

Chern, Shiing-Shen — *Mathematician*
8336 Kent Ct, El Cerrito, CA 94530, USA

Chernavin, Vladimir N — *Navy Admiral, Russia*
%Ministry of Defense, Kremlin, Staraya Pl 4, 103132 Moscow, Russia

Cherne, Leo — *Economist*
%Research Institute of America, 90 5th Ave, New York, NY 10011, USA

Chernin, Peter — *Movie Producer*
%Twentieth Century Fox, 10201 W Pico Blvd, Los Angeles, CA 90064, USA

Chernoff, Herman — *Statistician*
75 Crowninshield Rd, Brookline, MA 02146, USA

Chernomyrdin, Viktor S — *Prime Minister, Russia*
%Prime Minister's Office, Kremlin, Staraya Pl 4, 103132 Moscow, Russia

Chernow, Ron — *Writer*
63 Joralemon St, Brooklyn, NY 11201, USA

Cherrill, Virginia — *Actress*
160 Pomar Ave, Montecito, CA 93108, USA

Cherry, Bernard H — *Businessman*
%Oxbow Corp, 1601 Forum Pl, West Palm Beach, FL 33401, USA

Cherry, Deron — *Football Player*
%Kansas City Chiefs, 1 Arrowhead Dr, Kansas City, KS 64129, USA

Cherry, Don — *Jazz Trumpeter, Singer*
%Brad Simon Organization, 122 E 57th St, New York, NY 10022, USA

Cherry, Don S — *Hockey Coach*
%Boston Bruins, Boston Garden, 150 Causeway St, Boston, MA 02114, USA

Cherry, Neneh — *Singer*
PO Box 1622, London NW10 5TF, England

Chertok, Jack — *Movie Producer*
515 Ocean Ave, #305, Santa Monica, CA 90402, USA

Chester, Raymond T — *Football Player*
4722 Grass Valley Rd, Oakland, CA 94605, USA

Chestnutt, Jane — *Editor*
%Woman's Day Magazine, Editorial Dept, 1515 Broadway, New York, NY 10036, USA

Chestnutt, Mark — *Singer*
%BDM Co, 1106 16th Ave S, Nashville, TN 37212, USA

Chevalier, Samuel F — *Financier*
%Bank of New York Co, 1 Wall St, New York, NY 10005, USA

Chevallaz, Georges-Andre — *President, Switzerland*
1066 Epalinges, Switzerland

Cheveldae, Tim — *Hockey Player*
%Detroit Red Wings, Joe Louis Arena, 600 Civic Center Dr, Detroit, MI 48226, USA

Chevrier, Lionel — *Government Official, Canada*
500 Pl d'Armes, #1200, Montreal PQ H2Y 2W4, Canada

Chew, Geoffrey F — *Physicist*
10 Maybeck Twin Dr, Berkeley, CA 94708, USA

Chi Haotian — *General, China*
General Staff, Zhongyang Junshi Weiyuanhui, Beijing, China

Chia, Sandro — *Artist*
Castello Romitorio, Montalcino, Siena, Italy

C

Chenault - Chia

Chiang-Kai Shek (Mayling Soong), Madame *Sociologist; Government Official, China*
Locust Valley, Lattingtown, NY 11560, USA

Chiao, Leroy *Astronaut*
%NASA, Johnson Space Center, 2101 NASA Rd, Houston, TX 77058, USA

Chiara, Maria *Opera Singer*
%Columbia Artists Mgmt Inc, 165 W 57th St, New York, NY 10019, USA

Chiasson, Steve *Hockey Player*
%Calgary Flames, PO Box 1540, Station "M", Calgary AB T2P 389, Canada

Chiat, Jay *Art Director*
%Chiat/Day/Mojo Advertising, 340 Main St, Venice, CA 90291, USA

Chicago, Judy *Artist*
PO Box 5280, Santa Fe, NM 87502, USA

Chihara, Paul *Composer*
3815 W Olive Ave, #202, Burbank, CA 91505, USA

Chihuly, Dale P *Artist*
1124 Eastlake Ave, Seattle, WA 98109, USA

Chiklis, Michael *Actor*
9454 Wilshire Blvd, #405, Beverly Hills, CA 90212, USA

Child, Jane *Singer*
7095 Hollywood Blvd, #747, Los Angeles, CA 90028, USA

Child, Julia M *Food Expert, Writer*
103 Irving St, Cambridge, MA 02138, USA

Childers, Ernest *WW II Army Hero (CMH)*
13415 S 308 East Ave, Coweta, OK 74429, USA

Childress, Randolph *Basketball Player*
%Portland Trail Blazers, 700 NE Multnomah St, #600, Portland, OR 97232, USA

Childress, Raymond C (Ray), Jr *Football Player*
%Houston Oilers, 6910 Fannin St, Houston, TX 77030, USA

Childs, David M *Architect*
%Skidmore Owings Merrill, 220 E 42nd St, New York, NY 10017, USA

Childs, Toni *Singer, Songwriter*
%MFC Mgmt, 1463 Stearns Dr, Los Angeles, CA 90035, USA

Chiles, Henry G (Hank), Jr *Navy Admiral*
Deputy CinC, US Strategic Command, SAC Blvd, Offutt Air Force Base, NE 68113, USA

Chiles, Lawton M *Governor/Senator, FL*
%Governor's Office, State Capitol Bldg, Tallahassee, FL 32399, USA

Chiles, Linden *Actor*
2521 Topanga Skyline Dr, Topanga, CA 90290, USA

Chiles, Lois *Actress*
644 San Lorenzo, Santa Monica, CA 90402, USA

Chillida Juantegui, Eduardo *Sculptor*
Intz-Enea, Puerto de Faro 26, 20008 San Sebastian, Spain

Chilstrom, Herbert W *Religious Leader*
%Evangelical Lutheran Church, 8765 W Higgins Rd, Chicago, IL 60631, USA

Chilton, Alex *Singer (Box Tops)*
%Creative Entertainment Assoc, 2011 Ferry Ave, #U-19, Camden, NJ 08104, USA

Chilton, Kevin P *Astronaut*
%NASA, Johnson Space Center, 2101 NASA Rd, Houston, TX 77058, USA

Chiluba, Frederick T J *President, Zambia*
%President's Office, State House, PO Box 135, Lusaka, Zambia

Chino, Tetsuo *Businessman*
%Honda Motor Co Ltd, 1-1-2 Minami-Aoyama, Minatoku, Tokyo, Japan

Chirac, Jacques R *President, France*
%Palais de L'Elysee, 55-57 Rue de Faubourg St Honore, 75008 Paris, France

Chisholm, Shirley A S *Representative, NY*
80 Wentworth Lane, Palm Coast, FL 32164, USA

Chissano, Joaquim A *President, Mozambique*
%President's Office, Avda Julius Nyerere 2000, Maputo, Mozambique

Chitalada, Sot *Boxer*
%Home Express Co, 242/19 Moo 10, Sukhumvit Rd, Cholburi 20210, Thailand

Chittister, Joan D *Psychologist*
%St Scholastica Priory, 335 E 9th St, Erie, PA 16503, USA

Chitwood, Harold O *Businessman*
%Gold Kist Inc, 244 Perimeter Center Parkway NE, Atlanta, GA 30346, USA

Chitwood, Joey, Jr *Stunt Car Driver*
4410 W Alva St, Tampa, FL 33614, USA

Chivers, Warren *Skier*
%Vermont Academy, Saxtons River, WI 05154, USA

Cho, Margaret *Actress, Comedienne*
1815 Butler Ave, #120, Los Angeles, CA 90025, USA

Cho, Paul *Evangelist*
%Full Gospel Central Church, Yoido Plaza, Seoul, South Korea

Choate, Clyde L *WW II Army Hero (CMH)*
Rt 1, Anna, IL 62906, USA

Choate, Jerry D *Businessman*
%Allstate Insurance, Allstate Plaza, Northbrook, IL 60062, USA

Chodorow, Marvin *Physicist*
809 San Francisco Terrace, Stanford, CA 94305, USA

Chojnowska-Liskiewicz, Krystyna *Yachtswoman*
Ul Norblina 29 M 50, 80 304 Gdansk-Oliwa, Poland

Chomsky, A Noam *Linguist*
15 Suzanne Rd, Lexington, MA 02173, USA

Chomsky, Marvin J *Television Director*
4707 Ocean Front Walk, Venice, CA 90292, USA

Chong, Rae Dawn *Actress*
824 Moraga Dr, Los Angeles, CA 90049, USA

Choppin, Purnell W *Research Administrator*
%Howard Hughes Medical Institute, 4000 Jones Bridge Rd, Chevy Chase, MD 20815, USA

Choquette, Paul J, Jr *Businessman*
%Gilbane Building Co, 7 Jackson Walkway, Providence, RI 02903, USA

Chorbajian, Herbert G *Financier*
%ALBANK Financial Corp, 10 N Pearl St, Albany, NY 12207, USA

Chormann, Richard F *Financier*
%First of American Bank Corp, 211 S Rose St, Kalamazoo, MI 49007, USA

Chorzempa, Daniel W *Concert Pianist, Composer*
Grosse Budengasse 11, 50667 Cologne, Germany

Chow, Gregory C *Economist*
30 Hardy Dr, Princeton, NJ 08540, USA

Chretien, J J Jean *Prime Minister, Canada*
%Prime Minister's Office, 24 Sussex Dr, Ottawa ON K1M 0MS, Canada

Chretien, Jean-Loup *Spatinaute, France; Air Force General*
%CNES, 2 Pl Maurice Quentin, 75039 Paris Cedex 01, France

Christensen, Helena *Model*
%Marilyn Gaulthier Agence, 62 Blvd Sebastopol, 75003 Paris, France

Christensen, Kai *Architect*
100 Vester Voldgade, 1552 Copenhagen V, Denmark

Christensen, Todd *Football Player, Sportscaster*
%Management Team, 9507 Santa Monica Blvd, #304, Beverly Hills, CA 90210, USA

Christian, Claudia *Actress*
%Innovative Artists, 1999 Ave of Stars, #2850, Los Angeles, CA 90067, USA

Christian, George E *Government Official*
%George Christian Inc, 400 W 15th, #420, Austin, TX 78701, USA

Christian, Jacque *Movie Director, Screenwriter*
42 Bis Rue de Paris, 92100 Boulogne-Billancourt, France

Christiansen, Russell E *Businessman*
%Midwest Resources, 866 Grand Ave, Des Moines, IA 50309, USA

Christie, H Frederick *Businessman*
548 Paseo Del Mar, Palos Verdes Estates, CA 90274, USA

Christie, Julie *Actress, Model*
23 Linden Gardens, London W3, England

Christie, Linford *Track Athlete*
Rosedale House, Rosedale Rd, Richmond, Surrey TW9 2SZ, England

Christie, Lou *Singer*
%Dartmouth Mgmt, 228 W 71st St, #1-E, New York, NY 10023, USA

Christie, William *Concert Harpsichordist*
Les Arts Florissants, 2 Rue de Leningrad, 75008 Paris, France

Christine, Virginia *Actress*
12348 Rochedale Lane, Los Angeles, CA 90049, USA

Christman, Daniel W *Army General*
Assistant to Chairman, Joint Chiefs of Staff, Pentagon, Washington, DC 20318, USA

Christo (Javacheff) *Sculptor*
48 Howard St, New York, NY 10013, USA

Christopher, Dennis *Actor*
175 5th Ave, #2413, New York, NY 10010, USA

Christopher, Jordan *Actor*
300 Central Park West, New York, NY 10024, USA

Christopher, Robin *Actress*
%Century Artists, 9744 Wilshire Blvd, #308, Beverly Hills, CA 90212, USA

Christopher, Thom *Actor*
%Ambrosio/Mortimer, 165 W 46th St, #1109, New York, NY 10036, USA

Christopher, Warren M *Secretary, State*
%State Department, 2201 "C" St NW, Washington, DC 20520, USA

Christopher, William *Actor*
PO Box 50698, Pasadena, CA 91115, USA

Christy, James *Astronomer*
1720 W Niona Pl, Tucson, AZ 85704, USA

Christy, Robert F *Physicist*
1230 Arden Rd, Pasadena, CA 91106, USA

Chryssa *Sculptor*
565 Broadway, Soho, New York, NY 10012, USA

Chu, Paul C W *Physicist*
%University of Houston, Center for Superconductivity, Houston, TX 77204, USA

Chuan Leekpai *Prime Minister, Thailand*
%Prime Minister's Office, Government House, Luke Lang Rd, Bangkok, Thailand

Chubb, Percy, III *Businessman*
%Chubb Corp, 15 Mountain View Rd, Warren, NJ 07059, USA

Chuck D *Singer (Public Enemy)*
%Famous Artists Agency, 1700 Broadway, #500, New York, NY 10019, USA

Chung, Constance Y (Connie) *Commentator*
%CBS-TV, News Dept, 524 W 57th St, New York, NY 10019, USA

Chung, Kyung-Wha *Concert Violinist*
86 Hatton Garden, London EC1, England

Chung, Myung-Whun *Concert Pianist, Conductor*
%International Creative Mgmt, 40 W 57th St, New York, NY 10019, USA

Church, Sam *Labor Leader*
%United Mine Workers of America, 900 15th St NW, Washington, DC 20005, USA

Churches, Brady J *Businessman*
%Consolidated Stores, 1105 N Market St, Wilmington, DE 19801, USA

Churchill, Caryl *Playwright*
%Casarotto Ramsay Ltd, 60-66 Wardour St, London W1V 3HP, England

Chute, Robert M *Biologist*
RFD 1, Box 3868, Poland Spring, ME 04274, USA

Chwast, Seymour *Artist*
%Push Pin Group, 67 Irving Pl, New York, NY 10003, USA

Ciampi, Carlo A *Prime Minister, Italy*
%Palazzo Chigi, Piazza Colonna 370, 00187 Rome, Italy

Ciampi, Joe *Basketball Coach*
%Auburn University, Athletic Dept, Auburn, AL 36831, USA

Ciappi, Mario Luigi Cardinal *Religious Leader*
Via di Porto Angelica, #63, 00193 Rome, Italy

Ciccolini, Aldo *Concert Pianist*
%IMG Artists, 22 E 71st St, New York, NY 10021, USA

Ciecka, Richard J *Businessman*
%Mutual of America, 666 5th Ave, New York, NY 10103, USA

Ciller, Tansu *Prime Minister, Turkey*
T C, Basbakanlik, Ankara, Turkey

Cimino, Michael *Movie Director*
9015 Alto Cedro, Beverly Hills, CA 90210, USA

Cioffi, Charles *Actor*
Glover Ave, Norwalk, CT 06850, USA

Ciriani, Henri *Architect*
93 Rue de Montreuil, 75011 Paris, France

Cirici, Cristian *Architect*
%Cirici Arquitecte, Carrer de Pujades 63 2-N, 08005 Barcelona, Spain

Cisneros, Henry G *Secretary, Housing & Urban Development*
%Housing & Urban Development Department, 451 7th St SW, Washington, DC 20410, USA

Cisneros, Marc A *Army General*
Commanding General, 5th US Army, Fort Sam Houston, TX 78234, USA

Civalleri, Roberto *Financier*
%First Los Angeles Bank, 2049 Century Park East, Los Angeles, CA 90067, USA

Civiletti, Benjamin R *Attorney General*
%Mercantile Bank & Trust Bldg, #1800, 2 Hopkins Plaza, Baltimore, MD 21201, USA

Cizik, Robert *Businessman*
%Cooper Industries, First City Tower, 1001 Fannin St, #4000, Houston, TX 77002, USA

Claiborne Ortenberg, Elisabeth (Liz) — *Fashion Designer*
%Liz Claiborne Inc, 1441 Broadway, New York, NY 10018, USA

Claiborne, Craig — *Journalist, Food Expert*
15 Clamshell Ave, East Hampton, NY 11937, USA

Clampett, Bobby — *Golfer*
2615 Kildaire Farm Rd, Cary, NC 27511, USA

Clancy, Edward B Cardinal — *Religious Leader*
Sydney Archdiocese, Polding House, 276 Pitt St, Sydney NSW 2000, Australia

Clancy, Thomas J (Tom) — *Writer*
%William Morris Agency, 1325 Ave of Americas, New York, NY 10019, USA

Clapp, Joseph M — *Businessman*
%Roadway Services Inc, 1077 Gorge Blvd, Akron, OH 44310, USA

Clapp, Nicholas R — *Explorer (Ubar), Movie Producer*
1551 S Robertson Blvd, Los Angeles, CA 90035, USA

Clapper, James R (Jim), Jr — *Air Force General*
Director, Defense Intelligence Agency, Pentagon, Washington, DC 20340, USA

Clapton, Eric — *Singer, Guitarist*
67 Brook St, London W1, England

Clare, David R — *Businessman*
501 George St, New Brunswick, NJ 08901, USA

Clark, A James — *Businessman*
%Clark Construction Group, 7500 Old Georgetown Rd, Bethesda, MD 20814, USA

Clark, Alan — *Pianist (Dire Straits)*
%Damage Mgmt, 10 Southwick Mews, London W2, England

Clark, Bernard F — *Businessman*
%Mitchell Energy & Development Corp, 2001 Timerloch Pl, The Woodlands, TX 77380, USA

Clark, Bob — *Commentator*
%ABC-TV, News Dept, 1717 De Sales St NW, Washington, DC 20036, USA

Clark, Burton R — *Sociologist*
201 Ocean Ave, #1710-B, Santa Monica, CA 90402, USA

Clark, C Joseph (Joe) — *Prime Minister, Canada*
707 7th Ave SW, #1300, Calgary AB T2P 3H6, Canada

Clark, Candy — *Actress*
5 Briar Hill Rd, Montclair, NJ 07042, USA

Clark, Christie — *Actress*
16342 Rockaway, Placentia, CA 92670, USA

Clark, Dane — *Actor*
%Osborne, 205 W 57th St, New York, NY 10019, USA

Clark, Dick — *Entertainer, Television Producer*
%Dick Clark Productions, 3003 W Olive Ave, Burbank, CA 91505, USA

Clark, Dick C — *Senator, IA*
4424 Edmunds St NW, Washington, DC 20007, USA

Clark, Donald C — *Businessman*
%Household International, 2700 Sanders Rd, Prospect Heights, IL 60070, USA

Clark, Dwight — *Football Player, Executive*
%San Francisco 49ers, 4949 Centennial Blvd, Santa Clara, CA 95054, USA

Clark, Earl — *Diver*
1145 NE 126th St, #4, North Miami, FL 33161, USA

Clark, Eugenie — *Zoologist*
7817 Hampden Lane, Bethesda, MD 20814, USA

Clark, Gary C — *Football Player*
%Miami Dolphins, 7500 SW 30th St, Davie, FL 33329, USA

Clark, Gary M — *Businessman*
%Westinghouse Electric Corp, Gateway Center, Pittsburgh, PA 15222, USA

Clark, George W — *Physicist*
%Massachusetts Institute of Technology, Physics Dept, Cambridge, MA 02139, USA

Clark, Guy — *Singer, Songwriter*
%Vector Mgmt, PO Box 128037, Nashville, TN 37212, USA

Clark, J Desmond — *Anthropologist*
1941 Yosemite Rd, Berkeley, CA 94707, USA

Clark, Jack A — *Baseball Player*
20 Hillside Ave, Newport Beach, CA 92660, USA

Clark, James M — *Educator*
%State University of New York, President's Office, Cortland, NY 13045, USA

Clark, Joe — *Educator*
225 Kingsberry Dr, Somerset, NJ 08873, USA

Clark, Kenneth B — *Psychologist*
17 Pinecrest Dr, Hastings-on-Hudson, NY 10706, USA

C

Clark, Malcolm D *Businessman*
%Keystone International, 9600 W Gulf Bank Dr, Houston, TX 77040, USA

Clark, Marcia *Prosecutor*
%LA County District Attorney's Office, 210 W Temple St, Los Angeles, CA 90012, USA

Clark, Mary Higgins *Writer*
%Simon & Schuster Inc, 1230 Ave of Americas, New York, NY 10020, USA

Clark, Matt *Actor*
1199 Park Ave, #15-D, New York, NY 10128, USA

Clark, Perry *Football Coach*
%Tulane University, Athletic Dept, New Orleans, LA 70118, USA

Clark, Peter B *Publisher*
939 Coast Blvd, #16-E, La Jolla, CA 92037, USA

Clark, Petula *Singer*
PO Box 498, Quakertown, PA 18951, USA

Clark, Ramsey *Attorney General*
36 E 12th St, New York, NY 10003, USA

Clark, Robert A *Businessman*
Munstead Wood, Godalming, Surrey GU7 1UN, England

Clark, Robert C *Artist*
PO Box 597, Cambria, CA 93428, USA

Clark, Roy *Singer, Guitarist*
%Roy Clark Productions, 3225 S Norwood Ave, Tulsa, OK 74135, USA

Clark, Steve *Swimmer*
29 Upper Martling Rd, San Anselmo, CA 94960, USA

Clark, Susan *Actress*
7943 Woodrow Wilson Dr, Los Angeles, CA 90046, USA

Clark, Wendel *Hockey Player*
%New York Islanders, Veterans Memorial Coliseum, Uniondale, NY 11553, USA

Clark, Wesley K *Army General*
Director, Strategic Plans & Policy, Joint Staff Pentagon, Washington, DC 20318, USA

Clark, William J *Businessman*
%Massachusetts Mutual Life Insurance, 1295 State St, Springfield, MA 01111, USA

Clark, William N (Will), Jr *Baseball Player*
1000 Papworth Ave, Metairie, LA 70005, USA

Clark, William P *Secretary, Interior*
%Clark Co, 1031 Pine St, Paso Robles, CA 93446, USA

Clarke, Angela *Actress*
7557 Mulholland Dr, Los Angeles, CA 90046, USA

Clarke, Arthur C *Writer, Underwater Explorer*
Leslie's House, 25 Barnes Place, Colombo 07, Sri Lanka

Clarke, Brian Patrick *Actor*
333 N Kenwood St, #D, Burbank, CA 91505, USA

Clarke, Cyril A *Physician, Geneticist*
43 Caldy Rd, West Kirby, Wirral, Merseyside L48 2HF, England

Clarke, Don R *Businessman*
%Caldor Corp, 20 Glover Ave, Norwalk, CT 06850, USA

Clarke, Ellis E I *President, Trinidad & Tobago*
%Queens Park Cricket Club, Port of Spain, Trinidad & Tobago

Clarke, Gilmore D *Landscape Architect*
480 Park Ave, New York, NY 10022, USA

Clarke, John *Actor*
%"Days of Our Lives" Show, KNBC-TV, 3000 W Alameda Ave, Burbank, CA 91523, USA

Clarke, Kenneth H *Government Official, England*
%Chancellory of Exchequer, London, England

Clarke, Martha *Dancer, Choreographer*
%Sheldon Soffer Mgmt, 130 W 56th St, New York, NY 10019, USA

Clarke, Richard A *Businessman*
%Pacific Gas & Electric Co, PO Box 770000, San Francisco, CA 94177, USA

Clarke, Robert E (Bobby) *Hockey Player, Executive*
%Philadelphia Flyers, Spectrum, Pattison Place, Philadelphia, PA 19148, USA

Clarke, Robert F *Businessman*
%Hawaiian Electric Industries, 900 Richards St, Honolulu, HI 96813, USA

Clarke, Robert L *Government Official*
%Bracewell & Patterson, 711 Louisiana St, #2900, Houston, TX 77002, USA

Clarke, Ron *Track Athlete*
1 Bay St, Brighton VIC 3186, Australia

Clarke, Stanley *Jazz Bassist, Composer*
%Baker Winokur Ryder, 9348 Civic Center Dr, #400, Beverly Hills, CA 90210, USA

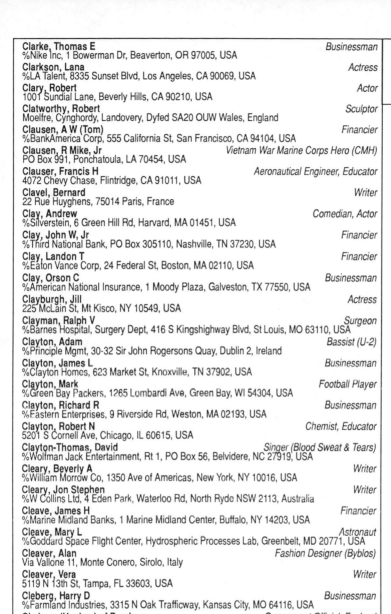

Clarke, Thomas E — *Businessman*
%Nike Inc, 1 Bowerman Dr, Beaverton, OR 97005, USA

Clarkson, Lana — *Actress*
%LA Talent, 8335 Sunset Blvd, Los Angeles, CA 90069, USA

Clary, Robert — *Actor*
1001 Sundial Lane, Beverly Hills, CA 90210, USA

Clatworthy, Robert — *Sculptor*
Moelfre, Cynghordy, Landovery, Dyfed SA20 0UW Wales, England

Clausen, A W (Tom) — *Financier*
%BankAmerica Corp, 555 California St, San Francisco, CA 94104, USA

Clausen, R Mike, Jr — *Vietnam War Marine Corps Hero (CMH)*
PO Box 991, Ponchatoula, LA 70454, USA

Clauser, Francis H — *Aeronautical Engineer, Educator*
4072 Chevy Chase, Flintridge, CA 91011, USA

Clavel, Bernard — *Writer*
22 Rue Huyghens, 75014 Paris, France

Clay, Andrew — *Comedian, Actor*
%Silverstein, 6 Green Hill Rd, Harvard, MA 01451, USA

Clay, John W, Jr — *Financier*
%Third National Bank, PO Box 305110, Nashville, TN 37230, USA

Clay, Landon T — *Financier*
%Eaton Vance Corp, 24 Federal St, Boston, MA 02110, USA

Clay, Orson C — *Businessman*
%American National Insurance, 1 Moody Plaza, Galveston, TX 77550, USA

Clayburgh, Jill — *Actress*
225 McLain St, Mt Kisco, NY 10549, USA

Clayman, Ralph V — *Surgeon*
%Barnes Hospital, Surgery Dept, 416 S Kingshighway Blvd, St Louis, MO 63110, USA

Clayton, Adam — *Bassist (U-2)*
%Principle Mgmt, 30-32 Sir John Rogersons Quay, Dublin 2, Ireland

Clayton, James L — *Businessman*
%Clayton Homes, 623 Market St, Knoxville, TN 37902, USA

Clayton, Mark — *Football Player*
%Green Bay Packers, 1265 Lombardi Ave, Green Bay, WI 54304, USA

Clayton, Richard R — *Businessman*
%Eastern Enterprises, 9 Riverside Rd, Weston, MA 02193, USA

Clayton, Robert N — *Chemist, Educator*
5201 S Cornell Ave, Chicago, IL 60615, USA

Clayton-Thomas, David — *Singer (Blood Sweat & Tears)*
%Wolfman Jack Entertainment, Rt 1, PO Box 56, Belvidere, NC 27919, USA

Cleary, Beverly A — *Writer*
%William Morrow Co, 1350 Ave of Americas, New York, NY 10016, USA

Cleary, Jon Stephen — *Writer*
%W Collins Ltd, 4 Eden Park, Waterloo Rd, North Ryde NSW 2113, Australia

Cleave, James H — *Financier*
%Marine Midland Banks, 1 Marine Midland Center, Buffalo, NY 14203, USA

Cleave, Mary L — *Astronaut*
%Goddard Space Flight Center, Hydrospheric Processes Lab, Greenbelt, MD 20771, USA

Cleaver, Alan — *Fashion Designer (Byblos)*
Via Vallone 11, Monte Conero, Sirolo, Italy

Cleaver, Vera — *Writer*
5119 N 13th St, Tampa, FL 33603, USA

Cleberg, Harry D — *Businessman*
%Farmland Industries, 3315 N Oak Trafficway, Kansas City, MO 64116, USA

Cledwyn (Hughes) of Penrhos — *Government Official, England*
Penmorfa, Trearddur, Holyhead, Gwynedd, Wales

Cleese, John — *Comedian, Writer*
%Mayday Mgmt, 68-A Delancey St, Camden Town, London NW1 7RY, England

Clegg, Johnny — *Singer*
%Alive Enterprises, 8912 Burton Way, Beverly Hills, CA 90211, USA

Cleland, J Maxwell (Max) — *Government Official*
%Secretary of State's Office, 214 State Capital Bldg, Atlanta, GA 30334, USA

Clemens, Donella — *Religious Leader*
%Mennonite Church, 722 Main St, Newton, KS 67114, USA

Clemens, W Roger — *Baseball Player*
11535 Quail Hollow, Houston, TX 77024, USA

Clement, John — *Businessman*
Tuddenham Hall, Tuddenham, Ipswich, Suffolk IP6 9DD, England

C

Clarke - Clement

C

Clement, Rene — Movie Director
5 Ave de St Roman, 98000 Monte Carlo, Monaco

Clemente, Carmine D — Anatomist
11737 Bellagio Rd, Los Angeles, CA 90049, USA

Clemente, Francesco — Artist
684 Broadway, New York, NY 10012, USA

Clements, John A — Physiologist
%University of California, Cardiovascular Research Inst, San Francisco, CA 94143, USA

Clements, Ronald F — Animator
%Walt Disney Productions, 500 S Buena Vista St, Burbank, CA 91521, USA

Clements, William P, Jr — Governor, TX
1901 N Akard, Dallas, TX 75201, USA

Cleminson, James A S — Businessman
Loddon Hall, Hales, Norfolk NR14 6TB, England

Clendenin, John L — Businessman
%BellSouth Corp, 1155 Peachtree St NE, Atlanta, GA 30309, USA

Clennon, David — Actor
%Susan Smith Assoc, 121 N San Vicente Blvd, Beverly Hills, CA 90211, USA

Cleobury, Nicholas R — Conductor
China Cottage, Church Lane, Petham, Canterbury, Kent CT4 5RD, England

Clerico, Christian — Restauranteur
%Lido-Normandie, 116 Bis Ave des Champs Elysees, 75008 Paris, France

Clerides, Glavkos J — President, Cyprus
%Presidential Palace, 5 Ioannis Clerides St, Nicosia, Cyprus

Clervoy, Jean-Francois — Spatinaut, France
%Europe Astronaut Center, Linder Hohe, Box 906096, 51127 Cologne, Germany

Cleveland, A Bruce — Financier
%Bankers Finance Investment Mgmt Corp, 1655 Fort Myer Dr, Arlington, VA 22209, USA

Cleveland, J Harlan — Diplomat, Educator
1235 Yale Pl, #802, Minneapolis, MN 55403, USA

Cleveland, Patience — Actress
21321 Providencia St, Woodland Hills, CA 91364, USA

Cliburn, Van — Concert Pianist
455 Wilder Place, Shreveport, LA 71104, USA

Cliff, Jimmy — Singer
51 Lady Musgrave Rd, Kingston, Jamaica

Clifford, Clark M — Secretary, Defense
%Clifford & Warnke, 815 Connecticut Ave NW, Washington, DC 20006, USA

Clifford, Joseph P — Financier
%TCF Financial Corp, 801 Marquette Ave, Minneapolis, MN 55402, USA

Clifford, M Richard — Astronaut
%NASA, Johnson Space Center, 2101 NASA Rd, Houston, TX 77058, USA

Clift, William B, III — Photographer
PO Box 6035, Santa Fe, NM 87502, USA

Cline, Martin J — Physician, Educator
%University of California Medical Center, Hematology Dept, Los Angeles, CA 90024, USA

Cline, Richard — Cartoonist
%New Yorker Magazine, Editorial Dept, 20 W 43rd St, New York, NY 10036, USA

Cline, Richard G — Businessman
%Nicor Inc, PO Box 3014, Naperville, IL 60566, USA

Cline, Robert S — Businessman
%Airborne Freight Corp, 3101 Western Ave, Seattle, WA 98121, USA

Clinger, Debra — Actress
4415 Auckland Ave, North Hollywood, CA 91602, USA

Clingman, J Fully — Businessman
%H E Butt Grocery Co, 646 S Main Ave, San Antonio, TX 78204, USA

Clinton, George — Singer
%Egmitt Inc, Archie Ivy, 2418 W Thoreau St, Inglewood, CA 90303, USA

Clinton, Hillary Rodham — Wife of US President
%White House, 1600 Pennsylvania Ave NW, Washington, DC 20006, USA

Clinton, William J (Bill) — President, USA
%White House, 1600 Pennsylvania Ave NW, Washington, DC 20006, USA

Clinton-Davis of Hackney, Stanley C — Government Official, England
%J Berwin Co, 236 Gray's Inn Rd, London WC1X 8HB, England

Cloherty, Patricia M — Financier
%Patricof Co Ventures, 445 Park Ave, New York, NY 10022, USA

Clohessy, Robert — Actor
%Agency For Performing Arts, 9000 Sunset Blvd, #1200, Los Angeles, CA 90069, USA

Cloninger, Tony L	Baseball Player
702 Crescent Circle, Kings Mountain, NC 28086, USA	
Clooney, George	Actor
11655 Laurelcrest Dr, Studio City, CA 91604, USA	
Clooney, Rosemary	Singer
1019 N Roxbury Dr, Beverly Hills, CA 90210, USA	
Close, Charles T (Chuck)	Artist
271 Central Park West, New York, NY 10024, USA	
Close, Glenn	Actress
%Creative Artists Agency, 9830 Wilshire Blvd, Beverly Hills, CA 90212, USA	
Clotet, Lluis	Architect
%Studio PER, Caspe 151, Barcelona 08013, Spain	
Clotworthy, Robert	Actor
%Amsel Eisenstadt Frazier, 6310 San Vicente Blvd, #401, Los Angeles, CA 90048, USA	
Cloud, Jack	Football Player
805 Janice Dr, Annapolis, MD 21403, USA	
Clough, Charles E	Businessman
%Nashua Corp, 44 Franklin St, Nashua, NH 03060, USA	
Clough, Charles M	Businessman
%Wyle Laboratories, 15370 Barranca Parkway, Irvine, CA 92718, USA	
Clough, Ray W, Jr	Structural Engineer
PO Box 4625, Sunriver, OR 97707, USA	
Clouston, Brendan R	Businessman
%Tele-Communications, 5619 DTC Parkway, Englewood, CO 80111, USA	
Clow, Lee	Businessman
%Chiat/Day/Mojo Advertising, 340 Main St, Venice, CA 90291, USA	
Clower, Jerry	Comedian, Writer
%Top Billing, PO Box 121089, Nashville, TN 37212, USA	
Clyne, Patricia	Fashion Designer
353 W 39th St, New York, NY 10018, USA	
Coachman Davis, Alice	Track Athlete
811 Gibson St, Tuskegee, AL 36083, USA	
Coan, Gaylord O	Businessman
%Gold Kist Inc, 244 Perimeter Center Parkway NE, Atlanta, GA 30346, USA	
Coase, Ronald H	Nobel Economics Laureate
%University of Chicago, Law School, 1111 E 60th St, Chicago, IL 60637, USA	
Coates, Phyllis	Actress
PO Box 1969, Boyes Hot Springs, CA 95416, USA	
Coats, Michael L	Astronaut
%LORAL Space Information Systems, 1322 Space Park Dr, Houston, TX 77058, USA	
Coats, William D	Businessman
%Coats Patons, 155 St Vincent St, Glasgow G2 5PA, England	
Cobb, Geraldyn M (Jerrie)	Astronaut
%Jerrie Cobb Foundation, PO Box 1117, Moore Haven, FL 33471, USA	
Cobb, Henry N	Architect
%Pei Cobb Freed Partners, 600 Madison Ave, #900, New York, NY 10022, USA	
Cobb, James R	Financier
%First Commercial Corp, 400 W Capitol, Little Rock, AR 72201, USA	
Cobb, Julie	Actress
10437 Sarah St, North Hollywood, CA 91602, USA	
Cobham, Billy	Jazz Drummer
%Cameron Organization, 2001 W Magnolia Blvd, Burbank, CA 91506, USA	
Coble, Hugh K	Businessman
%Fluor Corp, 3333 Michelson Dr, Irvine, CA 92730, USA	
Coblenz, Walter	Movie Director, Producer
2348 Apollo Dr, Los Angeles, CA 90046, USA	
Cobos, Jesus Lopez	Conductor
%Cincinnati Symphony, 1241 Elm St, Cincinnati, OH 45210, USA	
Coburn, James	Actor
1601 Schuyler Rd, Beverly Hills, CA 90210, USA	
Coburn, John G	Army General
Deputy CG, US Material Command, 5001 Eisenhower Ave, Alexandria, VA 22333, USA	
Coca, Imogene	Comedienne
%Joyce Agency, 370 Harrison Ave, Harrison, NY 10528, USA	
Cochereau, Pierre	Concert Organist
15 Bis Des Ursins, 75004 Paris, France	
Cochran, Barbara Ann	Skier
RFD 4, Box 2510, Montpelier, VT 05602, USA	

C

Cloninger - Cochran

Cochran, Brad *Football Player*
%Oakland Raiders, Oakland Coliseum, Oakland, CA 94621, USA

Cochran, Hank *Singer, Songwriter*
%Co-Heart Music Group, 1103 17th Ave S, Nashville, TN 37212, USA

Cochran, John *Commentator*
%ABC-TV, News Dept, 1717 De Sales St NW, Washington, DC 20036, USA

Cochran, John R *Financier*
%FirstMerit Corp, 106 S Main St, Akron, OH 44308, USA

Cochran, Johnnie L, Jr *Attorney*
4929 Wilshire Blvd, #1010, Los Angeles, CA 90010, USA

Cochran, Leslie H *Educator*
%Youngstown State University, President's Office, Youngstown, OH 44555, USA

Cockburn, Bruce *Singer, Songwriter*
%Finkelstein Mgmt, 151 John St, #301, Toronto ON M5M 2I2, Canada

Cocker, Joe *Singer*
%Creative Artists Agency, 9830 Wilshire Blvd, Beverly Hills, CA 90212, USA

Cockerell, Christopher S *Engineer, Inventor (Hovercraft)*
16 Prospect Pl, Hythe, Southampton, Hants SO4 6AU, England

Cockrell, Kenneth D *Astronaut*
%NASA, Johnson Space Center, 2101 NASA Rd, Houston, TX 77058, USA

Cockroft, Donald L (Don) *Football Player*
2377 Thornhill Dr, Colorado Springs, CO 80920, USA

Cocks of Hartcliffe, Michael F L *Government Official, England*
%House of Lords, Westminster, London SW1A 0PW, England

Code, Arthur D *Astronomer*
%WUPPE Project, University of Wisconsin, Astronomy Dept, Madison, WI 53706, USA

Codrescu, Andrei *Writer*
%Louisiana State University, English Dept, Baton Rouge, LA 70803, USA

Cody, Iron Eyes *Actor*
4470 Sunset Dr, #503, Los Angeles, CA 90027, USA

Coe, David Allan *Singer, Guitarist, Songwriter*
PO Box 1387, Goodlettsville, TN 37070, USA

Coe, George *Actor*
%Bauman Hiller Assoc, 5757 Wilshire Blvd, #PH5, Los Angeles, CA 90036, USA

Coe, Sebastian N *Track Athlete*
Starswood, High Barn Rd, Effingham, Surrey KT24 5PW, England

Coe, Sue *Artist*
%Galerie St Etienne, 24 W 57th St, New York, NY 10019, USA

Coe-Jones, Dawn *Golfer*
%Ladies Professional Golf Assn, 2570 Volusia Ave, Daytona Beach, FL 32114, USA

Coelho, Susie *Actress*
11759 Iowa Ave, Los Angeles, CA 90025, USA

Coen, Ethan *Movie Director, Screenwriter*
%United Talent Agency, 9560 Wilshire Blvd, #500, Beverly Hills, CA 90212, USA

Coen, Joel *Movie Director, Screenwriter*
%United Talent Agency, 9560 Wilshire Blvd, #500, Beverly Hills, CA 90212, USA

Coetzee, Gerrie *Boxer*
Bolesburg Township, South Africa

Coetzee, John M *Writer*
PO Box 92, Rondebosch, Cape Province 7700, South Africa

Cofer, Mike *Football Player*
%Detroit Lions, Silverdome, 1200 Featherstone Rd, Pontiac, MI 48342, USA

Coffey, John L *Judge*
%US Court of Appeals, US Courthouse, 517 E Wisconsin Ave, Milwaukee, WI 53202, USA

Coffey, Paul *Hockey Player*
%Detroit Red Wings, Joe Louis Arena, 600 Civic Center Dr, Detroit, MI 48226, USA

Coffey, Shelby, III *Editor*
%Los Angeles Times, Editorial Dept, Times Mirror Square, Los Angeles, CA 90053, USA

Coffin, Tad *Equestrian Rider*
%General Delivery, Strafford, VT 05072, USA

Coffin, Tristam *Writer*
%Washington Spectator, PO Box 70023, Washington, DC 20088, USA

Coffin, William Sloane, Jr *Social Activist, Religious Leader*
%SANE/Freeze, 55 Van Dyke Ave, Hartford, CT 06106, USA

Coffman, Stanley K, Jr *Educator*
%State University of New York, English Dept, Albany, NY 12203, USA

Coffy, Robert Cardinal *Religious Leader*
Archdiocese of Marseille, Marseille, France

Cogan, John F, Jr *Financier*
%Pioneer Group, 60 State St, Boston, MA 02109, USA

Cogan, Kevin *Auto Racing Driver*
%Championship Auto Racing Teams, 755 W Big Beaver Rd, #800, Troy, MI 48084, USA

Coggan of Canterbury, F Donald *Religious Leader*
28 Lions Hall, St Swithun St, Winchester SO23 9HW, England

Cogger, Harold W *Businessman*
%Colonial Group, 1 Financial Center, Boston, MA 02111, USA

Coghlan, Eamon *Track Athlete*
%International Management Group, 1 Erieview Plaza, #1300, Cleveland, OH 44114, USA

Cohan, Chris *Basketball Executive*
%Golden State Warriors, Oakland Coliseum Arena, Oakland, CA 94621, USA

Cohan, Edward J, Jr *Financier*
%Adler Coleman Clearing Corp, 20 Broad St, New York, NY 10005, USA

Coheleach, Guy J *Artist*
%Pandion Art, PO Box 96, Bernardsville, NJ 07924, USA

Cohen, Aaron *Space Administrator*
1310 Essex Green, College Station, TX 77845, USA

Cohen, Alexander H *Movie Producer*
25 W 54th St, #5-F, New York, NY 10019, USA

Cohen, Bennett R (Ben) *Businessman*
%Ben & Jerry's Homemade Inc, Rt 100, PO Box 240, Waterbury, VT 05676, USA

Cohen, Israel *Businessman*
%Giant Food Co, 6300 Sheriff Rd, Landover, MD 20785, USA

Cohen, Joel E *Educator*
%Rockefeller University, Populations Dept, 1230 York Ave, New York, NY 10021, USA

Cohen, Joseph *Television Executive*
%Hughes Television Network, 4 Pennsylvania Plaza, New York, NY 10001, USA

Cohen, Joseph M *Hockey Executive*
%Los Angeles Kings, Forum, PO Box 17013, Inglewood, CA 90308, USA

Cohen, Joseph M *Financier*
%Cowen Co, Financial Sq, New York, NY 10005, USA

Cohen, Leonard N *Poet, Singer, Songwriter*
%Premier Talent Agency, 3 E 54th St, #1400, New York, NY 10022, USA

Cohen, Mark A *Businessman*
%Bradlees Inc, 1 Bradlees Circle, Braintree, MA 02184, USA

Cohen, Morris *Metallurgist, Materials Scientist*
491 Puritan Rd, Swampscott, MA 01907, USA

Cohen, Robert *Concert Cellist*
%Intermusica Artists, 16 Duncan Terrace, London N1 8BZ, England

Cohen, Seymour S *Biochemist*
10 Carrot Hill Rd, Woods Hole, MA 02543, USA

Cohen, Sheldon S *Government Official*
5518 Trent St, Chevy Chase, MD 20815, USA

Cohen, Stanley *Nobel Medicine Laureate*
%Vanderbilt University Medical Center, 1161 21st Ave, Nashville, TN 37232, USA

Cohen, Stanley N *Geneticist*
%Stanford University Medical Center, Genetics Dept, Stanford, CA 94305, USA

Cohn, Marc *Singer*
%Creative Artists Agency, 9830 Wilshire Blvd, Beverly Hills, CA 90212, USA

Cohn, Mildred *Biochemist, Biophysicist*
747 Clarendon Rd, Narbeth, PA 19104, USA

Cohn, Mindy *Actress*
913 18th St, #2, Santa Monica, CA 90403, USA

Coia, Arthur A *Labor Leader*
%Laborers' International Union, 905 16th St NW, Washington, DC 20006, USA

Coker, Charles W, Jr *Businessman*
%Sonoco Products Co, N 2nd St, Hartsville, SC 29550, USA

Colalillo, Mike *WW II Army Hero (CMH)*
3677 Riley Rd, Duluth, MN 55803, USA

Colalucci, Gianluigi *Art Restorer*
%Office of Restoration, Vatican City, Rome, Italy

Colangelo, Jerry J *Basketball Executive*
%Phoenix Suns, 201 E Jefferson St, Phoenix, AZ 85004, USA

Colasuonno, Louis C *Editor*
%New York Daily News, Editorial Dept, 220 E 42nd St, New York, NY 10017, USA

Colbert, Claudette *Actress*
Bellerive, St Peter, Barbados, West Indies

C

Cogan - Colbert

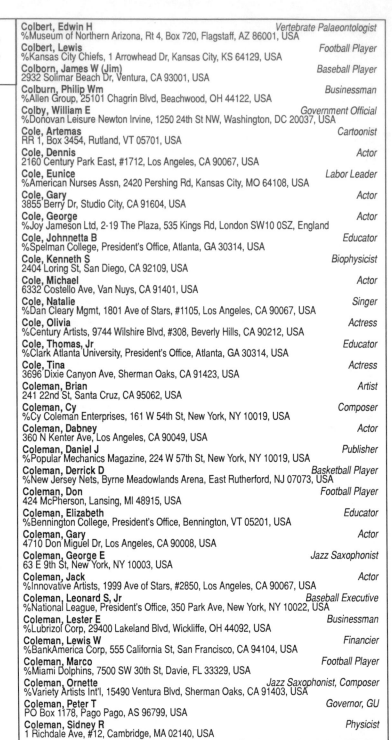

C

Colbert, Edwin H *Vertebrate Palaeontologist*
%Museum of Northern Arizona, Rt 4, Box 720, Flagstaff, AZ 86001, USA

Colbert, Lewis *Football Player*
%Kansas City Chiefs, 1 Arrowhead Dr, Kansas City, KS 64129, USA

Colborn, James W (Jim) *Baseball Player*
2932 Solimar Beach Dr, Ventura, CA 93001, USA

Colburn, Philip Wm *Businessman*
%Allen Group, 25101 Chagrin Blvd, Beachwood, OH 44122, USA

Colby, William E *Government Official*
%Donovan Leisure Newton Irvine, 1250 24th St NW, Washington, DC 20037, USA

Cole, Artemas *Cartoonist*
RR 1, Box 3454, Rutland, VT 05701, USA

Cole, Dennis *Actor*
2160 Century Park East, #1712, Los Angeles, CA 90067, USA

Cole, Eunice *Labor Leader*
%American Nurses Assn, 2420 Pershing Rd, Kansas City, MO 64108, USA

Cole, Gary *Actor*
3855 Berry Dr, Studio City, CA 91604, USA

Cole, George *Actor*
%Joy Jameson Ltd, 2-19 The Plaza, 535 Kings Rd, London SW10 0SZ, England

Cole, Johnnetta B *Educator*
%Spelman College, President's Office, Atlanta, GA 30314, USA

Cole, Kenneth S *Biophysicist*
2404 Loring St, San Diego, CA 92109, USA

Cole, Michael *Actor*
6332 Costello Ave, Van Nuys, CA 91401, USA

Cole, Natalie *Singer*
%Dan Cleary Mgmt, 1801 Ave of Stars, #1105, Los Angeles, CA 90067, USA

Cole, Olivia *Actress*
%Century Artists, 9744 Wilshire Blvd, #308, Beverly Hills, CA 90212, USA

Cole, Thomas, Jr *Educator*
%Clark Atlanta University, President's Office, Atlanta, GA 30314, USA

Cole, Tina *Actress*
3696 Dixie Canyon Ave, Sherman Oaks, CA 91423, USA

Coleman, Brian *Artist*
241 22nd St, Santa Cruz, CA 95062, USA

Coleman, Cy *Composer*
%Cy Coleman Enterprises, 161 W 54th St, New York, NY 10019, USA

Coleman, Dabney *Actor*
360 N Kenter Ave, Los Angeles, CA 90049, USA

Coleman, Daniel J *Publisher*
%Popular Mechanics Magazine, 224 W 57th St, New York, NY 10019, USA

Coleman, Derrick D *Basketball Player*
%New Jersey Nets, Byrne Meadowlands Arena, East Rutherford, NJ 07073, USA

Coleman, Don *Football Player*
424 McPherson, Lansing, MI 48915, USA

Coleman, Elizabeth *Educator*
%Bennington College, President's Office, Bennington, VT 05201, USA

Coleman, Gary *Actor*
4710 Don Miguel Dr, Los Angeles, CA 90008, USA

Coleman, George E *Jazz Saxophonist*
63 E 9th St, New York, NY 10003, USA

Coleman, Jack *Actor*
%Innovative Artists, 1999 Ave of Stars, #2850, Los Angeles, CA 90067, USA

Coleman, Leonard S, Jr *Baseball Executive*
%National League, President's Office, 350 Park Ave, New York, NY 10022, USA

Coleman, Lester E *Businessman*
%Lubrizol Corp, 29400 Lakeland Blvd, Wickliffe, OH 44092, USA

Coleman, Lewis W *Financier*
%BankAmerica Corp, 555 California St, San Francisco, CA 94104, USA

Coleman, Marco *Football Player*
%Miami Dolphins, 7500 SW 30th St, Davie, FL 33329, USA

Coleman, Ornette *Jazz Saxophonist, Composer*
%Variety Artists Int'l, 15490 Ventura Blvd, Sherman Oaks, CA 91403, USA

Coleman, Peter T *Governor, GU*
PO Box 1178, Pago Pago, AS 96799, USA

Coleman, Sidney R *Physicist*
1 Richdale Ave, #12, Cambridge, MA 02140, USA

Coleman, Vincent M (Vince) — *Baseball Player*
7785 E Vaquero Dr, Scottsdale, AZ 85258, USA

Coleman, William T, Jr — *Secretary, Transportation*
%O'Melveny & Myers, 555 13th St NW, #500, Washington, DC 20004, USA

Coles, Kim — *Actress*
325 Westbourne Dr, Los Angeles, CA 90048, USA

Coles, Robert M — *Psychiatrist*
%Harvard University Health Services, 75 Mt Auburn St, Cambridge, MA 02138, USA

Colescott, Warrington W — *Artist*
Rt 1, Hollandale, WI 53544, USA

Colgrass, Michael C — *Composer*
583 Palmerston Ave, Toronto ON M6G 2P6, Canada

Colin, Margaret — *Actress*
%Agency For Performing Arts, 9000 Sunset Blvd, #1200, Los Angeles, CA 90069, USA

Coll, Stephen W — *Journalist*
%Washington Post, Editorial Dept, 1150 15th St NW, Washington, DC 20071, USA

Collard, Jean-Philippe — *Concert Pianist*
Boite Postal 210, 75426 Paris Cedex 09, France

Collen, Desire — *Medical Researcher*
%University of Leuven, Leuven, Belgium

Collen, Phil — *Guitarist (Def Leppard)*
%Q Prime Mgmt, 729 7th Ave, #1400, New York, NY 10019, USA

Collett, Elmer — *Football Player*
10 Avenida Farralone, PO Box 522, Stinson Beach, CA 94970, USA

Collette, Buddy — *Jazz Musician*
900 S Sierra Bonita Ave, Los Angeles, CA 90036, USA

Colley, Ed — *Cartoonist (Suburban Cowgirls)*
%Tribune Media Services, 435 N Michigan Ave, #1417, Chicago, IL 60611, USA

Collie, Mark — *Singer, Songwriter*
%Don Light Talent, 2102 W Linden Ave, Nashville, TN 37212, USA

Collier, Lesley F — *Ballerina*
%Royal Ballet Co, 155 Talgarth Rd, London W14, England

Collings, Charles L — *Businessman*
%Raley's, 500 W Capitol Ave, West Sacramento, CA 95605, USA

Collins, Arthur D, Jr — *Businessman*
%Medtronic Inc, 7000 Central Ave NE, Minneapolis, MN 55432, USA

Collins, Atwood, III — *Financier*
%East New York Savings Bank, 350 Park Ave, New York, NY 10022, USA

Collins, Bud — *Sportscaster*
%NBC-TV, Sports Dept, 30 Rockefeller Plaza, New York, NY 10112, USA

Collins, David E — *Businessman*
%Schering-Plough Corp, 1 Giralda Farms, Madison, NJ 07940, USA

Collins, Doug — *Basketball Player, Coach*
%Detroit Pistons, Palace, 2 Championship Dr, Auburn Hills, MI 48057, USA

Collins, Duane E — *Businessman*
%Parker Hannifin Corp, 17325 Euclid Ave, Cleveland, OH 44112, USA

Collins, Eileen M — *Astronaut*
%NASA, Johnson Space Center, 2101 NASA Rd, Houston, TX 77058, USA

Collins, Francis S — *Geneticist*
%National Institutes of Health, 9000 Rockville Pike, Bethesda, MD 20892, USA

Collins, Gary — *Actor*
2751 Hutton Dr, Beverly Hills, CA 90210, USA

Collins, Gary — *Football Player*
PO Box 455, Palmyra, PA 17078, USA

Collins, George J — *Financier*
%T Rowe Price Assoc, 100 E Pratt St, Baltimore, MD 21202, USA

Collins, Glen L — *Football Player*
817 E River Pl, Jackson, MS 39202, USA

Collins, Jack — *Actor*
%Contemporary Artists, 1427 3rd St Promenade, #205, Santa Monica, CA 90401, USA

Collins, Jackie — *Writer*
PO Box 10581, Burbank, CA 91510, USA

Collins, James A — *Businessman*
%Sizzler International, 12655 W Jefferson Blvd, Los Angeles, CA 90066, USA

Collins, Joan — *Actress*
%Judy Bryer, 15363 Mulholland Dr, Los Angeles, CA 90077, USA

Collins, John G — *Financier*
%UJB Financial Corp, Carnegie Center, PO Box 2066, Princeton, NJ 08543, USA

C

Coleman - Collins

C

Collins, John W *Businessman*
%Clorox Co, 1221 Broadway, Oakland, CA 94612, USA

Collins, Judy *Singer, Songwriter*
39 Wagon Wheel Rd, Redding, CT 06896, USA

Collins, Larry *Writer*
La Biche Niche, 83350 Ramatuelle, France

Collins, Mark *Football Player*
%Kansas City Chiefs, 1 Arrowhead Dr, Kansas City, KS 64129, USA

Collins, Martha Layne *Governor, KY; Educator*
%St Catherine College, President's Office, St Catherine, KY 40061, USA

Collins, Marva *Educator*
%Westside Preparatory School, 4146 W Chicago Ave, Chicago, IL 60651, USA

Collins, Michael *Astronaut, Air Force General*
PO Box 600, Avon, NC 27915, USA

Collins, Pat *Hypnotist*
524 W 57th St, New York, NY 10019, USA

Collins, Patrick *Actor*
9200 Sunset Blvd, #702, Los Angeles, CA 90069, USA

Collins, Paul J *Financier*
29 Wilton Crescent, London SW1, England

Collins, Pauline *Actress*
%James Sharkey Assoc, 21 Golden Square, London W1R 3PA, England

Collins, Phil *Singer, Drummer, Songwriter*
Lockswood, Sussex, England

Collins, Samuel C *Mechanical Engineer, Cryogenist*
12322 Riverview Rd, Oxon Hill, MD 20744, USA

Collins, Stephen *Actor*
21 E 90th St, #10-A, New York, NY 10128, USA

Collinson, John T *Businessman*
%Chessie System Inc, 1126 Terminal Tower, Cleveland, OH 44113, USA

Collinsworth, Cris *Sportscaster*
%NBC-TV, Sports Dept, 30 Rockefeller Plaza, New York, NY 10112, USA

Colnbrook of Waltham (H E G Atkins) *Government Official, England*
%House of Lords, Westminster, London SW1A 0PW, England

Colodny, Edwin I *Businessman*
%USAir Group Inc, 2345 Crystal Dr, Arlington, VA 22227, USA

Colombo, Emilio *Prime Minister, Italy*
Via Aurelia 239, Rome, Italy

Colombo, Giovanni Cardinal *Religious Leader*
Palazzo Arcivescovile, Piazza Fontana 2, Milan, Italy

Colomby, Scott *Actor*
%Borinstein Oreck Bogart Agency, 8271 Melrose Ave, #110, Los Angeles, CA 90046, USA

Colson, Charles W *Religious Leader, Watergate Figure*
%Prison Fellowship, PO Box 17500, Washington, DC 20041, USA

Colson, Elizabeth F *Anthropologist*
%University of California, Anthropology Dept, Berkeley, CA 94720, USA

Colt, Marshall *Actor*
333 Elm St, Denver, CO 80220, USA

Colter, Jessie *Singer*
1117 17th Ave S, Nashville, TN 37212, USA

Coltman, Charles L, III *Financier*
%CoreStates Financial Corp, Broad & Chestnut Sts, Philadelphia, PA 19101, USA

Colton, Frank B *Inventor (Oral Contraceptive)*
3901 Lyons St, Evanston, IL 60203, USA

Colton, Sterling D *Businessman*
%Marriott International, Marriott Dr, Washington, DC 20058, USA

Coltrane, Robby *Actor*
%Caroline Dawson Assoc, 47 Courtfield Rd, #9, London SW7 4DB, England

Columbu, Franco *Body Builder*
%Franco Columbu Productions, 2947 S Sepulveda Blvd, Los Angeles, CA 90064, USA

Colussy, Dan A *Businessman*
%UNC Inc, 175 Admiral Cochrane Dr, Annapolis, MD 21401, USA

Colville, Alex *Artist*
408 Main St, Wolfville NS B0P 1XP, Canada

Colvin, Jack L *Actor*
%Century Artists, 9744 Wilshire Blvd, #308, Beverly Hills, CA 90212, USA

Colvin, Shawn *Singer, Songwriter*
%Sony/Columbia/CBS Records, 2100 Colorado Ave, Santa Monica, CA 90404, USA

Collins - Colvin

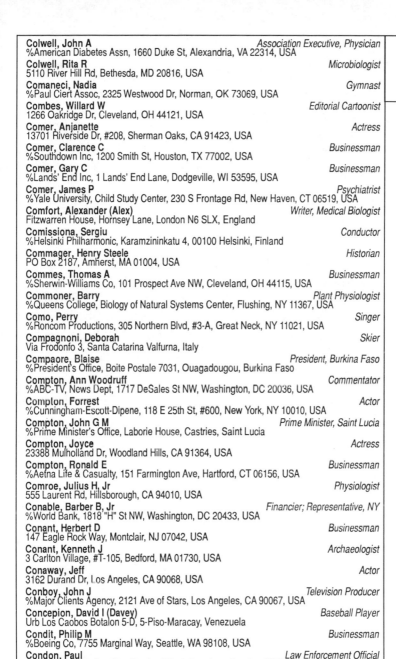

Colwell, John A *Association Executive, Physician*
%American Diabetes Assn, 1660 Duke St, Alexandria, VA 22314, USA

Colwell, Rita R *Microbiologist*
5110 River Hill Rd, Bethesda, MD 20816, USA

Comaneci, Nadia *Gymnast*
%Paul Ciert Assoc, 2325 Westwood Dr, Norman, OK 73069, USA

Combes, Willard W *Editorial Cartoonist*
1266 Oakridge Dr, Cleveland, OH 44121, USA

Comer, Anjanette *Actress*
13701 Riverside Dr, #208, Sherman Oaks, CA 91423, USA

Comer, Clarence C *Businessman*
%Southdown Inc, 1200 Smith St, Houston, TX 77002, USA

Comer, Gary C *Businessman*
%Lands' End Inc, 1 Lands' End Lane, Dodgeville, WI 53595, USA

Comer, James P *Psychiatrist*
%Yale University, Child Study Center, 230 S Frontage Rd, New Haven, CT 06519, USA

Comfort, Alexander (Alex) *Writer, Medical Biologist*
Fitzwarren House, Hornsey Lane, London N6 SLX, England

Comissiona, Sergiu *Conductor*
%Helsinki Philharmonic, Karamzininkatu 4, 00100 Helsinki, Finland

Commager, Henry Steele *Historian*
PO Box 2187, Amherst, MA 01004, USA

Commes, Thomas A *Businessman*
%Sherwin-Williams Co, 101 Prospect Ave NW, Cleveland, OH 44115, USA

Commoner, Barry *Plant Physiologist*
%Queens College, Biology of Natural Systems Center, Flushing, NY 11367, USA

Como, Perry *Singer*
%Roncom Productions, 305 Northern Blvd, #3-A, Great Neck, NY 11021, USA

Compagnoni, Deborah *Skier*
Via Frodonfo 3, Santa Catarina Valfurna, Italy

Compaore, Blaise *President, Burkina Faso*
%President's Office, Boite Postale 7031, Ouagadougou, Burkina Faso

Compton, Ann Woodruff *Commentator*
%ABC-TV, News Dept, 1717 DeSales St NW, Washington, DC 20036, USA

Compton, Forrest *Actor*
%Cunningham-Escott-Dipene, 118 E 25th St, #600, New York, NY 10010, USA

Compton, John G M *Prime Minister, Saint Lucia*
%Prime Minister's Office, Laborie House, Castries, Saint Lucia

Compton, Joyce *Actress*
23388 Mulholland Dr, Woodland Hills, CA 91364, USA

Compton, Ronald E *Businessman*
%Aetna Life & Casualty, 151 Farmington Ave, Hartford, CT 06156, USA

Comroe, Julius H, Jr *Physiologist*
555 Laurent Rd, Hillsborough, CA 94010, USA

Conable, Barber B, Jr *Financier; Representative, NY*
%World Bank, 1818 "H" St NW, Washington, DC 20433, USA

Conant, Herbert D *Businessman*
147 Eagle Rock Way, Montclair, NJ 07042, USA

Conant, Kenneth J *Archaeologist*
3 Carlton Village, #T-105, Bedford, MA 01730, USA

Conaway, Jeff *Actor*
3162 Durand Dr, Los Angeles, CA 90068, USA

Conboy, John J *Television Producer*
%Major Clients Agency, 2121 Ave of Stars, Los Angeles, CA 90067, USA

Concepion, David I (Davey) *Baseball Player*
Urb Los Caobos Botalon 5-D, 5-Piso-Maracay, Venezuela

Condit, Philip M *Businessman*
%Boeing Co, 7755 Marginal Way, Seattle, WA 98108, USA

Condon, Paul *Law Enforcement Official*
%Metropolitan Police, New Scotland Yard, Broadway, London SW1H 0BG, England

Condon, Richard T *Writer*
3436 Ashbury, Dallas, TX 75205, USA

Condron, Christopher M *Financier*
%Mellon Bank Corp, 1 Mellon Bank Center, 500 Grant St, Pittsburgh, PA 15219, USA

Cone Vanderbush, Carin *Swimmer*
116 Washington Rd, #B, West Point, NY 10996, USA

Cone, David B *Baseball Player*
17080 Harbour Point Dr, Fort Myers, FL 33908, USA

C

Colwell - Cone

Conefry, John J, Jr *Financier*
%Long Island Savings Bank, 201 Old Country Rd, Melville, NY 11747, USA

Conerly, Charles A *Football Player*
1045 Lynn Dr, Clarkesdale, MS 38614, USA

Conforti, Gino *Actor*
%Cunningham-Escott-Dipene, 10635 Santa Monica Blvd, Los Angeles, CA 90025, USA

Conger, Harry M *Businessman*
%Homestake Mining Co, 650 California St, San Francisco, CA 94108, USA

Conlan, John *Football Player*
%San Diego Chargers, Jack Murphy Stadium, San Diego, CA 92160, USA

Conlan, Shane *Football Player*
RR 1, Box 146-A, DeWittville, NY 14728, USA

Conley, Clare D *Editor*
Hemlock Farms, Hawley, PA 18428, USA

Conley, Darlene *Actress*
1840 S Beverly Glen Blvd, #501, Los Angeles, CA 90025, USA

Conley, Earl Thomas *Singer, Songwriter*
%ETC Enterprises, 48 Music Sq E, Nashville, TN 37203, USA

Conley, Joe *Actor*
PO Box 6487, Thousand Oaks, CA 91359, USA

Conlon, James J *Conductor*
%Columbia Artists Mgmt Inc, 165 W 57th St, New York, NY 10019, USA

Conn, Didi *Actress*
14820 Valley Vista Blvd, Sherman Oaks, CA 91403, USA

Connell, Elizabeth *Opera Singer*
%S A Gorlinsky, 33 Dover St, London W1X 4NJ, England

Connell, Evan S, Jr *Writer*
Fort Macy 13, 320 Artist Rd, Santa Fe, NM 87501, USA

Connell, John MacFarlane *Businessman*
%Distillers Co, 12 Torphechen St, Edinburgh EH3 8YT, Scotland

Connell, Thurman C *Financier*
%Federal Home Loan Bank, 907 Walnut St, Des Moines, IA 50309, USA

Connelly, Jennifer *Actress*
50 Bethel St, Cranston, RI 02920, USA

Connelly, Michael *Writer*
%Little Brown Co, 34 Beacon St, Boston, MA 02108, USA

Conner, Bart *Gymnast*
PO Box 1013, Norman, OK 73070, USA

Conner, Bruce *Artist*
45 Sussex St, San Francisco, CA 94131, USA

Conner, Dennis *Yachtsman*
%Dennis Conner Sports, PO Box 2911, National City, CA 91951, USA

Conner, Finis F *Businessman*
%Conner Peripherals, 3081 Zanker Rd, San Jose, CA 95134, USA

Connery, Jason *Actor*
%Joy Jameson Ltd, The Plaza, #219, 555 Kings Rd, London SW10 0SZ, England

Connery, Sean *Actor*
Casa Malibu, Fuente del Rodeo, Nueva Andalusia, Malaga, Spain

Connery, Vincent L *Labor Leader*
%National Treasury Employees Union, 1730 "K" St NW, Washington, DC 20006, USA

Connery, W Hudson, Jr *Businessman*
%Healthtrust Inc, 4525 Harding Rd, Nashville, TN 37205, USA

Connick, Harry, Jr *Pianist, Singer*
%Wilkins Mgmt, 260 Brookline St, #200, Cambridge, MA 02139, USA

Connick, Robert E *Chemist*
50 Marguerita Rd, Berkeley, CA 94707, USA

Conniff, Cal *Skier*
157 Pleasantview Ave, Longmeadow, MA 01106, USA

Conniff, Ray *Conductor, Composer*
2154 Hercules Dr, Los Angeles, CA 90046, USA

Connolly, Billy *Actor*
%John Reid Ent, Singes House, 32 Galena Rd, London W6 0LT, England

Connolly, Eugene B, Jr *Businessman*
%USG Corp, 125 S Franklin St, Chicago, IL 60606, USA

Connolly, Harold *Track Athlete*
%Santa Monica High School, 601 Pico Blvd, Santa Monica, CA 90405, USA

Connolly, Norma *Actress*
%Agency For Performing Arts, 9000 Sunset Blvd, #1200, Los Angeles, CA 90069, USA

Connolly, Olga — *Track Athlete*
11027 Ocean Dr, Culver City, CA 90230, USA

Connor, George — *Football Player*
235 E Walton Place, #5, Chicago, IL 60611, USA

Connor, John T — *Secretary, Commerce*
11854 Turtle Beach Rd, North Palm Beach, FL 33408, USA

Connor, Joseph E — *Businessman, Government Official*
%UnderSecretary-Generals Office, United Nations, UN Plaza, New York, NY 10021, USA

Connor, Ralph — *Chemist*
9866 Highwood Court, Sun City, AZ 85373, USA

Connor, Richard L — *Publisher*
%Fort Worth Star-Telegram, 400 W 7th St, Fort Worth, TX 76102, USA

Connors, Carol — *Songwriter*
1709 Ferrari Dr, Beverly Hills, CA 90210, USA

Connors, James S (Jimmy) — *Tennis Player*
200 S Refugio Rd, Santa Ynez, CA 93460, USA

Connors, Mike — *Actor*
4810 Louise Ave, Encino, CA 91316, USA

Conombo, Joseph I — *Prime Minister, Upper Volta*
Ave de la Liberte, BP 613, Dadoya, Ouagadougou, Burkina Faso

Conrad Hefner, Kimberly — *Model*
10236 Charing Cross Rd, Los Angeles, CA 90024, USA

Conrad, Charles (Pete), Jr — *Astronaut*
%McDonnell Douglas, 5301 Bolsa Ave, Huntington Beach, CA 92647, USA

Conrad, Charles A — *Businessman*
%Quaker State Corp, 255 Elm St, Oil City, PA 16301, USA

Conrad, James A — *Financier*
%Source One Mortgage Services, 27555 Farmington Rd, Farmington Hills, MI 48334, USA

Conrad, John H — *Astronaut*
%Hughes Aircraft Space Communications Group, Box 92919, Los Angeles, CA 90009, USA

Conrad, Paul F — *Editorial Cartoonist*
28649 Crestridge Rd, Palos Verdes, CA 90275, USA

Conrad, Robert — *Actor*
21006 Dumetz Rd, Woodland Hills, CA 91364, USA

Conradt, Judy — *Basketball Coach*
%University of Texas, Athletic Dept, Austin, TX 78712, USA

Conran, Jasper A T — *Fashion Designer*
49/50 Great Marlborough St, London W1V 1DB, England

Conran, Terence O — *Interior Designer*
512 Butler Wharf Building, 36 Shad Thames, London SE1 2YE, England

Conroy, D Patrick (Pat) — *Writer*
%Old New York Book Shop, 1069 Juniper St NE, Atlanta, GA 30309, USA

Conroy, Frank — *Writer*
%Houghton Mifflin Co, 215 Park Ave S, New York, NY 10003, USA

Consagra, Pietro — *Sculptor*
Via Cassia 1162, Rome, Italy

Considine, John — *Actor*
16 1/2 Red Coat Lane, Greenwich, CT 06830, USA

Considine, Tim — *Actor*
506 N Alpine Dr, Beverly Hills, CA 90210, USA

Constable, George — *Editor*
%Time-Life Books, Editorial Dept, Rockefeller Center, New York, NY 10020, USA

Constantine II — *King, Greece*
4 Linnell Dr, Hampstead Way, London NW11, England

Constantine, Kevin — *Hockey Coach*
%San Jose Sharks, 525 W Santa Clara St, San Jose, CA 95113, USA

Conte, John — *Actor*
75600 Beryl Dr, Indian Wells, CA 92210, USA

Conte, Lansana — *President, Guinea; Army General*
%President's Office, Conakry, Guinea

Conte, Lou — *Choreographer*
%Hubbard Street Dance Co, 218 S Wabash Ave, Chicago, IL 60604, USA

Conte, Richard L — *Businessman*
%Community Psychiatric Centers, 6600 W Chalreston, Las Vegas, NV 89102, USA

Conti, Bill — *Composer*
117 Fremont Pl W, Los Angeles, CA 90005, USA

Conti, Tom — *Actor*
%Chatto & Linnit, Prince of Wales, Coventry St, London W1V 7FE, England

C

Connolly - Conti

Contino, Dick	*Accordianist*
3355 Nahatan Way, Las Vegas, NV 89109, USA	
Converse, Peggy	*Actress*
2525 Briarcrest Rd, Beverly Hills, CA 90210, USA	
Conway, Gary	*Actor*
%Gary Conway Information Group, PO Box 5617, San Angelo, TX 76902	
Conway, Jill K	*Historian*
65 Commonwealth Ave, #8-B, Boston, MA 02116, USA	
Conway, Kevin	*Actor*
25 Century Park West, New York, NY 10023, USA	
Conway, Tim	*Comedian*
%Tim Conway Enterprises, PO Box 17047, Encino, CA 91416, USA	
Coobar, Abdulmegid	*Prime Minister, Libya*
Asadu El-Furat St 29, Garden City, Tripoli, Libya	
Cooder, Ry	*Singer, Guitarist, Composer*
326 Entrada Dr, Santa Monica, CA 90402, USA	
Coody, Charles	*Golfer*
%Professional Golfer's Assn, PO Box 109601, Palm Beach Gardens, FL 33410, USA	
Coogan, Keith	*Actor*
1640 S Sepulveda Blvd, #218, Los Angeles, CA 90025, USA	
Cook, Antoinette	*Government Official*
%Federal Communication Commission, 1919 "M" St NW, Washington, DC 20554, USA	
Cook, Barbara	*Actress, Singer*
%JKE Services, 205 Lexington Ave, New York, NY 10016, USA	
Cook, Beryl	*Artist*
3 Athenaeum St, The Hoe, Plymouth PL1 2RQ, England	
Cook, Bruce	*Writer*
502 N Plymouth Blvd, Los Angeles, CA 90004, USA	
Cook, Carole	*Comedienne*
8829 Ashcroft Ave, Los Angeles, CA 90048, USA	
Cook, Don	*Golfer*
%Professional Golfer's Assn, PO Box 109601, Palm Beach Gardens, FL 33410, USA	
Cook, G Bradford	*Stock Exchange Executive*
Woman Lake, Longville, MN 56655, USA	
Cook, Jeff	*Singer, Guitarist (Alabama)*
PO Box 35967, Fort Payne, AL 35967, USA	
Cook, John	*Golfer*
1111 Tahquitz E, #121, Palm Springs, CA 92262, USA	
Cook, Judy	*Bowler*
%Ladies Professional Bowlers Tour, 7171 Cherryvale Blvd, Rockford, IL 61112, USA	
Cook, Lodwrick M	*Businessman*
%Atlantic Richfield Co, 515 S Flower St, Los Angeles, CA 90071, USA	
Cook, Paul M	*Businessman*
%Raychem Corp, 300 Constitution Dr, Menlo Park, CA 94025, USA	
Cook, Peter F C	*Architect*
54 Compayne Gardens, London NW6 3RY, England	
Cook, Robert	*Opera Singer*
The Quavers, 53 Friars Ave, Fiern Barnet, London N2O OXG, England	
Cook, Robert F (Robin)	*Government Official, England*
%House of Commons, Westminster, London SW1A 0AA, England	
Cook, Robin	*Writer*
4601 Gulf Shore Blvd, #P-4, Naples, FL 33940, USA	
Cook, Scott	*Businessman*
%Intuit, 155 Linfield Dr, Menlo Park, CA 94025, USA	
Cook, Stanton R	*Publisher*
%Tribune Co, 435 N Michigan Ave, Chicago, IL 60611, USA	
Cook, V N	*Businessman*
%Science Applications International, 10260 Campus Point Dr, San Diego, CA 92121, USA	
Cooke, A Alistair	*Writer, Commentator*
1150 5th Ave, New York, NY 10128, USA	
Cooke, Howard	*Governor General, Jamaica*
King's House, Hope Rd, Kingston 10, Jamaica	
Cooke, Jack Kent	*Football Executive*
Kent Farms, Middleburg, VA 22117, USA	
Cooke, Janis	*Journalist*
%Washington Post, Editorial Dept, 1150 15th St NW, Washington, DC 20071, USA	
Cooke, Robert H	*Financier*
%Sanwa Bank California, 444 Market St, San Francisco, CA 94111, USA	

Cooks, Johnie *Football Player*
%Cleveland Browns, 80 1st Ave, Berea, OH 44017, USA

Cooksey, Dave *Religious Leader*
%Brethren Church, 524 College Ave, Ashland, OH 44805, USA

Cookson, Catherine A *Writer*
White Lodge, 23 Glastonbury Grove, Newcastle Upon Tyne NE2 2HB, England

Cooley, Denton A *Surgeon*
%Texas Heart Institution, 6621 Fannin St, Houston, TX 77030, USA

Coolidge, Charles H *WW II Army Hero (CMH)*
1054 Balmoral Dr, Signal Mountain, TN 37377, USA

Coolidge, E David, III *Financier*
%William Blair Co, 222 W Adams St, Chicago, IL 60606, USA

Coolidge, Harold J *Conservationist*
38 Standley St, Beverly, MA 01915, USA

Coolidge, Martha *Movie Director*
2129 Coldwater Canyon, Beverly Hills, CA 90210, USA

Coolidge, Rita *Singer*
%Jerry Schwartz Agency, 9595 Wilshire Blvd, #1020, Beverly Hills, CA 90212, USA

Coombe, George W *Attorney*
%Graham & James, 1 Maritime Plaza, San Francisco, CA 94111, USA

Coombs, Philip H *Economist*
River Rd, Essex, CT 06426, USA

Cooney, Joan Ganz *Educator, Television Executive*
%Children's TV Workshop, 1 Lincoln Plaza, New York, NY 10023, USA

Cooney, Thomas M *Businessman*
9200 Montgomery Rd, #23-A, Cincinnati, OH 45242, USA

Cooper, Alexander *Architect*
%Cooper Robertson & Partners, 311 W 43rd St, New York, NY 10036, USA

Cooper, Alice *Singer, Songwriter*
4135 E Keim St, Paradise Valley, AZ 85253, USA

Cooper, Amy Levin *Editor*
%Mademoiselle Magazine, Editorial Dept, 350 Madison Ave, New York, NY 10017, USA

Cooper, Arthur M *Editor*
%Gentlemen's Quarterly Magazine, 350 Madison Ave, New York, NY 10017, USA

Cooper, Cecil C *Baseball Player*
1431 Misty Bend, Katy, TX 77494, USA

Cooper, Charles A *Economist*
360 N Wilton Rd, New Canaan, CT 06840, USA

Cooper, Charles G *Marine Corps General*
3410 Barger Dr, Falls Church, VA 22044, USA

Cooper, Cortz *Religious Leader*
%Presbyterian Church in America, 1852 Century Place, Atlanta, GA 30345, USA

Cooper, Daniel L *Navy Admiral*
Assistant CNO, Undersea Warfare, OP-02, Navy Department, Washington, DC 20350, USA

Cooper, Frederick E *Businessman*
%Jones Davis Heavis, 1st Peachtree Center, 303 Peachtree St, Atlanta, GA 30308, USA

Cooper, Hal *Television Director*
2651 Hutton Dr, Beverly Hills, CA 90210, USA

Cooper, Harry *Golfer*
7 Verne Place, Hartsdale, NY 10530, USA

Cooper, Henry *Boxer*
36 Brampton Grove, London NW4, England

Cooper, Jackie *Movie Director, Actor*
9621 Royalton Dr, Beverly Hills, CA 90210, USA

Cooper, Jeanne *Actress*
8401 Edwin Dr, Los Angeles, CA 90046, USA

Cooper, Jilly *Writer*
%Desmond Elliott, 38 Bury St, London SW1Y 6AU, England

Cooper, John *Football Coach*
%Ohio State University, Athletic Dept, Columbus, OH 43210, USA

Cooper, John A D *Physician*
4118 N River Rd, Arlington, VA 22207, USA

Cooper, L Gordon, Jr *Astronaut*
7402 Hayvenhurst Ave, Van Nuys, CA 91436, USA

Cooper, Leon N *Nobel Physics Laureate*
49 Intervale Rd, Providence, RI 02906, USA

Cooper, Lester I *Television Producer*
45 S Moringside Dr, Westport, CT 06880, USA

Cooper, Marilyn	*Actress*
%Gage Group, 315 W 57th St, #4-H, New York, NY 10019, USA	
Cooper, Michael	*Basketball Player, Executive*
%Los Angeles Lakers, Forum, PO Box 10, Inglewood, CA 90306, USA	
Cooper, Paula	*Art Dealer*
%Paula Cooper Gallery, 155 Wooster St, New York, NY 10012, USA	
Cooper, Philip D	*Financier*
%ORIX Credit Alliance, 300 Lighting Way, Secaucus, NJ 07094, USA	
Cooper, Ron	*Artist*
1310 Main St, Venice, CA 90291, USA	
Cooper, Wayne	*Artist*
126 W 1025 S, Kouts, IN 46347, USA	
Cooper, William A	*Financier*
%TCF Financial Corp, 801 Marquette Ave, Minneapolis, MN 55402, USA	
Cooper, Wilma Lee	*Singer, Guitarist*
%Cooper Enterprises, PO Box 2505, Brentwood, TN 37024, USA	
Coor, Lattie F	*Educator*
%Arizona State University, President's Office, Tempe, AZ 85287, USA	
Coords, Robert H	*Financier*
%SunBank/Miami, 777 Brickell Ave, Miami, FL 33131, USA	
Coors, Jeffrey H	*Businessman*
%ACH Techs Inc, 16000 Table Mountain Parkway, Golden, CO 80403, USA	
Coors, Joseph	*Businessman*
%Adolph Coors Co, 1221 Ford St, Golden, CO 80403, USA	
Coors, William K	*Businessman*
%Adolph Coors Co, 1221 Ford St, Golden, CO 80403, USA	
Coover, Robert	*Writer*
%Georges Borchardt Inc, 136 E 57th St, New York, NY 10022, USA	
Cope, Derrike	*Auto Racing Driver*
PO Box 1542, Cornelius, NC 28031, USA	
Copeland, Al	*Powerboat Racing Driver, Businessman*
5001 Folse Dr, Metairie, LA 70006, USA	
Copeland, John W	*Businessman*
%Ruddick Corp, 2 First Union Center, Charlotte, NC 28282, USA	
Copeland, Johnny	*Singer*
%Peter Noble Ent, 7 Federal Rd, Binna Berra NSW 2481, Australia	
Copeland, Kenneth	*Evangelist*
%Kenneth Copeland Ministries, PO Box 2908, Fort Worth, TX 76113, USA	
Copeland, Lila	*Artist*
305 W 28th St, #21-E, New York, NY 10001, USA	
Copley, Helen K	*Publisher*
%Copley Press, 7776 Ivanhoe Ave, La Jolla, CA 92037, USA	
Copley, Teri	*Actress, Model*
18435 San Fernando Mission Blvd, Northridge, CA 91326, USA	
Copperfield, David	*Illusionist*
515 Post Oak Blvd, #300, Houston, TX 77027, USA	
Copping, Allen A	*Educator*
%Louisiana State University System, President's Office, Baton Rouge, LA 70808, USA	
Coppola, Alicia	*Actress*
%William Morris Agency, 151 S El Camino Dr, Beverly Hills, CA 90212, USA	
Coppola, Francis Ford	*Movie Director*
%Zoetrope Studios, 916 Kearny St, San Francisco, CA 94133, USA	
Coppola, Joseph R	*Businessman*
%Giddings & Lewis Inc, 142 Doty Rd, Fond Du Lac, WI 54935, USA	
Corbally, John E	*Educator*
1507 151st Pl SE, Mill Creek, WA 98012, USA	
Corbett, Gretchen	*Actress*
%Connor, 9229 Sunset Blvd, #311, Los Angeles, CA 90069, USA	
Corbett, Mike	*Rock Climber*
PO Box 917, Yosemite National Park, CA 95389, USA	
Corbett, Ronnie	*Comedian*
%International Artistes Ltd, 235 Regent St, London W1R 8AX, England	
Corbin, Barry	*Actor*
4519 Tyrone Ave, Sherman Oaks, CA 91423, USA	
Corbus, William	*Football Player*
1100 Union St, #1100, San Francisco, CA 94109, USA	
Corby, Ellen	*Actress*
9024 Harratt St, Los Angeles, CA 90069, USA	

Corcoran, Kevin *Actor*
8617 Balcom Ave, Northridge, CA 91325, USA
Cord, Alex *Actor*
4559 Morella Ave, North Hollywood, CA 91607, USA
Corday, Barbara *Entertainment Executive*
532 S Windsor Blvd, Los Angeles, CA 90020, USA
Corday, Mara *Actress, Model*
PO Box 800393, Valencia, CA 91380, USA
Cordero, Angel T, Jr *Thoroughbred Racing Jockey*
%New York Racing Assn, PO Box 90, Jamaica, NY 11417, USA
Cordovez Zegers, Diego *Government Official, Ecuador*
%Foreign Affairs Ministry, Avda 10 Agosta y Carrion, Quito, Ecuador
Corea, Chick *Jazz Pianist, Composer*
%Chick Corea Productions, 2635 Griffith Park Blvd, Los Angeles, CA 90039, USA
Corelli, Franco *Opera Singer*
%S A Gorlinsky Ltd, 33 Dover St, London W1X 4NJ, England
Corey, (Professor) Irwin *Comedian*
58 Nassau Dr, Great Neck, NY 11021, USA
Corey, Elias James *Nobel Chemistry Laureate*
20 Avon Hill St, Cambridge, MA 02140, USA
Corey, Jeff *Actor*
29445 Bluewater Rd, Malibu, CA 90265, USA
Corey, Ronald *Hockey Executive*
%Montreal Canadiens, 2313 St Catherine St W, Montreal PQ H3H 1N2, Canada
Corfield, Kenneth G *Businessman*
14 Elm Walk, Hampstead, London NW3 7UP, England
Cori, Carl T *Businessman*
%Sigma-Aldrich Corp, 3050 Spruce St, St Louis, MO 63103, USA
Corigliano, John P *Composer*
365 West End Ave, New York, NY 10024, USA
Corkle, Francesca *Ballerina*
%Pittsburgh Ballet Theatre, 244 Blvd of Allies, Pittsburgh, PA 15222, USA
Corley, Al *Actor*
3323 Corinth Ave, Los Angeles, CA 90066, USA
Corley, Pat *Actor*
%Agency For Performing Arts, 9000 Sunset Blvd, #1200, Los Angeles, CA 90069, USA
Cormack, Allan MacLeod *Nobel Medicine Laureate*
18 Harrison St, Winchester, MA 01890, USA
Corman, Avery *Writer*
%International Creative Mgmt, 40 W 57th St, New York, NY 10019, USA
Corman, Roger W *Movie Director, Producer*
2501 La Mesa Dr, Pacific Palisades, CA 90402, USA
Corn, Alfred *Poet*
350 W 14th St, #6-A, New York, NY 10014, USA
Corneille *Artist*
%Society of Independent Artists, Cours la Reine, 75008 Paris, France
Cornelis, Francois *Businessman*
%Petrofina SA, Rue de l'Industrie 52, 1040 Brussels, Belgium
Cornelius, Don *Television Producer*
12685 Mulholland Dr, Beverly Hills, CA 90210, USA
Cornelius, Helen *Singer, Songwriter*
PO Box 2977, Hendersonville, TN 37077, USA
Cornelius, William E *Businessman*
2 Dunlora Lane, St Louis, MO 63131, USA
Cornell, Don *Singer*
%Cornell Productions, 100 Bayview Dr, #1521, North Miami Beach, FL 33160, USA
Cornell, Harry M, Jr *Businessman*
%Leggett & Platt Inc, 1 Leggett Rd, Carthage, MO 64836, USA
Cornell, Lydia *Actress*
142 S Bedford Dr, Beverly Hills, CA 90212, USA
Cornelsen, Rufus *Religious Leader*
415 S Chester Rd, Swarthmore, PA 19081, USA
Corness, Colin R *Businessman*
%Redland, Redland House, Reigate, Surrey RH2 0SJ, England
Cornforth, John W *Nobel Chemistry Laureate*
Saxon Down, Cuilfail, Lewes, East Sussex BN7 2BE, England
Cornog, Robert A *Businessman*
%Snap-on Tools Corp, 2801 80th St, Kenosha, WI 53143, USA

C

Corns, Johnnie H — *Army General*
Commanding General, US Army Pacific, Fort Shafter, HI 96858, USA

Cornthwaite, Robert — *Actor*
19533 Renaldi St, #48, Northridge, CA 91326, USA

Cornwell, Patricia D — *Writer*
500 Libbie Ave, #1-B, Richmond, VA 23226, USA

Corr, Edwin G — *Diplomat*
544 Shawnee, Norman, OK 73071, USA

Corrado, Fred — *Businessman*
%Great Atlantic & Pacific Tea Co, 2 Paragon Dr, Montvale, NJ 07645, USA

Correa, Charles M — *Architect*
Sonmarg, Napean Sea Rd, Bombay 40006, India

Correia, Carlos — *Prime Minister, Guinea-Bissau*
%Prime Minister's Office, Bissau, Guinea-Bissau

Correll, A D — *Businessman*
%Georgia-Pacific Corp, 133 Peachtree St NE, Atlanta, GA 30303, USA

Corri, Adrienne — *Actress*
%London Mgmt, 2-4 Noel St, London W1V 3RB, England

Corrick, Ann Marjorie — *Journalist*
3050 Dover Dr, #56, Santa Cruz, CA 95065, USA

Corrigan, Douglas (Wrong Way) — *Aviator*
2828 N Flower St, Santa Ana, CA 92706, USA

Corrigan, E Gerald — *Government Official, Financier*
%Goldman Sachs Co, 85 Broad St, New York, NY 10004, USA

Corrigan, Wilfred J — *Businessman*
%LSI Logic, 1551 McCarthy Blvd, Milpitas, CA 95035, USA

Corrigan-Maguire, Mairead — *Nobel Peace Laureate*
%Peace People Community, 224 Lisburn Rd, Belfast BT9 6GE, North Ireland

Corripio Ahumada, Ernesto Cardinal — *Religious Leader*
Apartado Postal 24-433, Mexico 7 DF, Mexico

Corrock-Luby, Susie — *Skier*
PO Box 424, Edwards, CO 81632, USA

Corry, Charles A — *Businessman*
%USX Corp, 600 Grant St, Pittsburgh, PA 15219, USA

Corsaro, Frank A — *Theater, Opera Director*
33 Riverside Dr, New York, NY 10023, USA

Corso, Gregory N — *Poet*
%New Directions, 80 8th Ave, New York, NY 10011, USA

Corson, Dale R — *Physicist, Educator*
144 Northview Rd, Ithaca, NY 14850, USA

Corson, Fred P — *Religious Leader*
Cornwall Manor, Cornwall, PA 17016, USA

Corson, Keith D — *Businessman*
%Coachman Industries, 601 E Beardsley Ave, Elkhart, IN 46514, USA

Corson, Shayne — *Hockey Player*
%St Louis Blues, St Louis Arena, 5700 Oakland Ave, St Louis, MO 63110, USA

Corson, Thomas H — *Businessman*
%Coachman Industries, 601 E Beardsley Ave, Elkhart, IN 46514, USA

Cort, Bud — *Actor*
2149 Lyric Ave, Los Angeles, CA 90027, USA

Cortese, Joe — *Actor*
2065 Coldwater Canyon Dr, Beverly Hills, CA 90210, USA

Cortese, Valentina — *Actress*
Pretta S Erasmo 6, 20121 Milan, Italy

Cortright, Edgar M, Jr — *Aerospace Engineer*
9701 Calvin St, Northridge, CA 91324, USA

Corvin, Joe E — *Businessman*
%Oregon Steel Mills, 1000 SW Broadway, Portland, OR 97205, USA

Corwin, Norman — *Writer*
1840 Fairburn Ave, #302, Los Angeles, CA 90025, USA

Coryell, Larry — *Musician*
%Ted Kurland Assoc, 173 Brighton Ave, Boston, MA 02134, USA

Corzine, Jon S — *Financier*
%Goldman Sachs Co, 85 Broad St, New York, NY 10004, USA

Cosbie, Douglas D (Doug) — *Football Player*
1664 Fallen Leaf Lane, Los Altos, CA 94024, USA

Cosby, Bill — *Comedian*
PO Box 4049, Santa Monica, CA 90411, USA

Coscarelli, Kate — *Writer*
%Don Carter, PO Box 10927, Beverly Hills, CA 90213, USA

Cosenza, G Joseph — *Financier*
%Inland Group, 2901 Butterfield Rd, Oak Brook, IL 60521, USA

Cosgrave, Liam — *Prime Minister, Ireland*
Beachpark, Templeogue County, Dublin, Ireland

Cosgrove, Howard E — *Businessman*
%Delmarva Power & Light Co, 800 King St, Wilmington, DE 19801, USA

Coslet, Bruce N — *Football Coach*
1084 Hickory Ridge Lane, Loveland, OH 45140, USA

Cosmovici, Cristiano B — *Astronaut, Italy*
%Istituto Fisica Spazio Interplanetario, CP 27, 00044 Frascati, Italy

Coss, Kenneth L — *Labor Leader*
%United Rubber Cork Linoleum Plastics Workers, 570 White Pond, Akron, OH 44320, USA

Cossotto, Fiorenza — *Opera Singer*
%Columbia Artists Mgmt Inc, 165 W 57th St, New York, NY 10019, USA

Cossutta, Carlo — *Opera Singer*
%S A Gorlinsky Ltd, 33 Dover St, London W1X 4NJ, England

Costa, Gal — *Singer*
%Performers of the World, 8901 Melrose Ave, #200, Los Angeles, CA 90069, USA

Costa, Mary — *Opera Singer*
3340 Kingston Pike, #1, Knoxville, TN 37919, USA

Costa-Gavras, Konstaninos — *Movie Director*
24 Rue Saint-Jacques, 75005 Paris, France

Costanza, Margaret (Midge) — *Government Official*
4518 Agnes Ave, Studio City, CA 91607, USA

Costas, Robert Q (Bob) — *Sportscaster*
%NBC-TV, Sports Dept, 30 Rockefeller Plaza, New York, NY 10112, USA

Costello, Billy — *Boxer*
15 Laura Dr, New Paultz, NY 12561, USA

Costello, Elvis — *Singer*
%Riviera Global, 18 The Green, Richmond, Surrey TW9 1PY, England

Costello, John D — *Coast Guard Admiral*
%Coast Guard Hdqs Pacific, Coast Guard Island, Alameda, CA 94501, USA

Costello, Larry — *Basketball Player, Coach*
%Utica College, Athletic Dept, Utica, NY 13502, USA

Costello, Mariclare — *Actress*
%Borinstein Oreck Bogart Agency, 8271 Melrose Ave, #110, Los Angeles, CA 90046, USA

Costelloe, Paul — *Fashion Designer*
%Moygashel Mills, Dungannon BT71 7PB, Northern Ireland

Coster, Nicolas — *Actor*
1624 N Vista, Los Angeles, CA 90046, USA

Costie Burke, Candy — *Synchronized Swimmer*
5732 NE 190th St, Seattle, WA 98155, USA

Costle, Douglas M — *Government Official, Educator*
%Harvard University, Public Health School, Cambridge, MA 02138, USA

Costner, Kevin — *Actor, Director*
PO Box 275, Montrose, CA 91021, USA

Cotchett, Joseph W — *Attorney*
840 Malcolm Rd, Burlingame, CA 94010, USA

Cotlow, Lewis N — *Explorer*
132 Lakeshore Dr, North Palm Beach, FL 33408, USA

Cotros, Charles H — *Businessman*
%SYSCO Corp, 1390 Enclave Parkway, Houston, TX 77077, USA

Cotrubas, Ileana — *Opera Singer*
%Royal Opera House, Covent Garden, Bow St, London WC2, England

Cotsworth, Stats — *Actor*
360 E 55th St, New York, NY 10022, USA

Cottee, Kay — *Yachtswoman*
%Showcase Productions, 113 Willoughby Rd, Crows Nest NSW 2065, Australia

Cotti, Flavio — *President, Switzerland*
%Foreign Affairs Dept, Bundeshaus-West, 3003 Berne, Switzerland

Cotting, James C — *Businessman*
%Navistar International, 455 N Cityfront Plaza Dr, Chicago, IL 60611, USA

Cottingham, Robert — *Artist*
PO Box 604, Blackman Rd, Newtown, CT 06470, USA

Cotton, Francis E (Fran) — *Rugby Player*
Beechwood, Hulme Hall Road, Cheadle Hulme, Stockport, Che SK8 6JZ, England

C

Coscarelli - Cotton

Cotton, Frank A — *Chemist*
4101 Sand Creek Rd, Bryan, TX 77808, USA

Cotton, James — *Singer*
%Antone's Records & Tapes, 609 W 6th St, #B, Austin, TX 78701, USA

Cotton, Josie — *Singer*
8406 Cresthill Rd, Los Angeles, CA 90069, USA

Cotton, Marcus — *Football Player*
%Seattle Seahawks, 11220 NE 53rd St, Kirkland, WA 98033, USA

Cottrell, Donald P — *Educator*
445 Hutchinson Ave, #210, Columbus, OH 43235, USA

Cottrell, Ralph — *Religious Leader*
%Baptist Missionary Assn, PO Box 1203, Van, TX 75790, USA

Couch, John C — *Businessman*
%Alexander & Baldwin Inc, 822 Bishop St, Honolulu, HI 96813, USA

Couch, John N — *Botanist*
1109 Caroll Woods, Chapel Hills, NC 27514, USA

Coughlin, Bernard J — *Educator*
%Gonzaga University, President's Office, Spokane, WA 99258, USA

Coughlin, Timothy C — *Financier*
%Riggs National Corp, 808 17th St NW, Washington, DC 20006, USA

Coughlin, Tom — *Football Coach*
%Jacksonville Jaguars, 1 Stadium Place, Jacksonville, FL 32202, USA

Coughlin, William H — *Financier*
%George K Baum Co, 120 W 12th St, Kansas City, MO 64105, USA

Coulier, David — *Actor*
%Brillstein-Grey, 9150 Wilshire Blvd, #350, Beverly Hills, CA 90212, USA

Coulter, Arthur E — *Hockey Player*
10600 SW 128th St, Miami, FL 33176, USA

Coulter, David A — *Financier*
%Bank of America Corp, 555 California St, San Francisco, CA 94104, USA

Counsilman, James E — *Swimming Coach*
3602 William Court, Bloomington, IN 47401, USA

Countryman, Garl L — *Businessman*
%Liberty Mutual Insurance, 175 Berkeley St, Boston, MA 02116, USA

Counts, Mel — *Basketball Player*
1581 Matheny Rd, Gervais, OR 97026, USA

Couples, Fred — *Golfer*
%Players Group, 8251 Greensboro Dr, #1150, McLean, VA 22102, USA

Courant, Ernest D — *Physicist*
109 Bay Ave, Bayport, NY 11705, USA

Couric, Katherine (Katie) — *Commentator*
%NBC-TV, News Dept, 30 Rockefeller Plaza, New York, NY 10112, USA

Courier, James S (Jim), Jr — *Tennis Player*
306 E Southview Ave, Dade City, FL 33525, USA

Courlouris, George — *Actor*
Chestnut Cottage, Vale of Heath, Hampstead, London NW3, England

Cournoyer, Yvan — *Hockey Player*
%Brasserie 12, 625 32nd St, Lachine PQ H8T 3G6, Canada

Courreges, Andre — *Fashion Designer*
27 Rue Delabordere, 92 Neuilly-Sur-Seine, France

Court, Hazel — *Actress*
%Taylor, 1111 San Vicente Blvd, Santa Monica, CA 90402, USA

Courtenay, Margaret — *Actress*
%Barry Burnett, Grafton House, 2-3 Golden Sq, London W1R 3AD, England

Courtenay, Tom — *Actor*
%Michael Whitehall, 125 Gloucester Rd, London SW7 4TE, England

Courtney, Jacqueline — *Actress*
10 E 44th St, 700, New York, NY 10017, USA

Courtney, Tom — *Track Athlete*
PO Box 8186, Naples, FL 33941, USA

Cousin, Philip R — *Religious Leader*
%Episcopal Church, 11th District Hdqs, PO Box 2970, Jacksonville, FL 32203, USA

Cousins, Ralph W — *Royal Navy Admiral*
Leconfield House, Curzon St, London W1Y 8JR, England

Cousins, Robin — *Figure Skater*
9229 W Sunset Blvd, #303, Los Angeles, CA 90069, USA

Cousteau, Jacques-Yves — *Oceanographer*
%Musee Oceanografique, Ave Saint-Martin, Monaco-Ville MC, Monaco

C

Cousteau, Jean-Michel *Oceanographer*
%Cousteau Society, 870 Greenbriar Circle, #402, Chesapeake, VA 23320, USA

Cousy, Robert J (Bob) *Basketball Player*
427 Salisbury St, Worcester, MA 01609, USA

Coutinho, Antonio A R *Navy Admiral, Portugal*
Rua Carlos Malheiro Dias 18, 3 Esq, 1700 Lisbon, Portugal

Couve de Murville, J Maurice *Prime Minister, France*
44 Rue Du Bac, 75007 Paris, France

Cover, Franklin *Actor*
1422 N Sweetzer, #402, Los Angeles, CA 90069, USA

Coverly, Dave *Editorial Cartoonist*
%Bloomington Herald-Times, Editorial Dept, 1900 S Walnut, Bloomington, IN 47401, USA

Covert, James (Jimbo) *Football Player*
450 Hunter Lane, Lake Forest, IL 60045, USA

Covey, Harold D *Businessman*
%State Farm Fire & Casualty, 112 E Washington St, Bloomington, IL 61701, USA

Covey, Richard O *Astronaut*
%Unisys Space Systems, 600 Gemini Ave, Houston, TX 77058, USA

Cowan, George A *Chemist*
%Santa Fe Institute, 1660 Old Pecos Trail, #A, Santa Fe, NM 87505, USA

Cowdrey, M Colin *Cricketer*
54 Lombard St, London EC3P 3AH, England

Cowen, Donna *Actress, Dancer*
340 S Ocean Blvd, Palm Beach, FL 33480, USA

Cowens, Alfred E (Al) *Baseball Player*
1758 E 111th Place, Los Angeles, CA 90059, USA

Cowens, David W (Dave) *Basketball Player*
%Dave Cowens Basketball School, 433 Grove St, Needham, MA 02192, USA

Cowher, Bill *Football Coach*
%Pittsburgh Steelers, 3 Rivers Stadium, 300 Stadium Circle, Pittsburgh, PA 15212, USA

Cowhill, William J *Navy Admiral*
1336 Elsinore Ave, McLean, VA 22102, USA

Cowie, Lennox L *Astronomer*
%University of Hawaii, Astronomy Dept, Honolulu, HI 96822, USA

Cowley, William M *Hockey Player*
75 Sunnyside St, Ottawa ON, Canada

Cowper, Nicola *Actress*
%Brunskill Mgmt, 169 Queens Gate, #A-8, London SW7 5EH, England

Cox, Allan V *Geophysicist*
%Stanford University, Earth Sciences School, Stanford, CA 94305, USA

Cox, Archibald *Attorney, Government Official*
%Harvard University, Law School, Cambridge, MA 02138, USA

Cox, Bryan *Football Player*
%Miami Dolphins, 7500 SW 30th St, Davie, FL 33329, USA

Cox, Charles C *Government Official*
%Lexecon Inc, 002 0 Michigan Ave, Chicago, IL 60604, USA

Cox, Courteney *Actress*
606 Alta Ave, Santa Monica, CA 90402, USA

Cox, Danny B *Baseball Manager*
306 Feagin Mill Rd, Warner Robbins, GA 31088, USA

Cox, Frederick W (Fred) *Football Player*
401 E River St, Monticello, MN 55362, USA

Cox, G David *Religious Leader*
%Church of God, Box 2420, Anderson, IN 46018, USA

Cox, Glenn A, Jr *Businessman*
%WestStar Bank Building, 4th & Keeler, Bartlesville, OK 74004, USA

Cox, Harvey G, Jr *Educator, Theologian*
%Harvard University, Divinity School, Cambridge, MA 02140, USA

Cox, John W *Navy Admiral, Physician*
%Surgeon General's Office, Navy Department, Washington, DC 20372, USA

Cox, Lynne *Distance Swimmer*
%Advanced Sport Research, 4141 Ball Rd, #142, Cypress, CA 90630, USA

Cox, Mark *Tennis Player*
The Oaks, Ashtead Woods Rd, Astead, Surrey KT21 2ER, England

Cox, Paul *Movie Director*
%Illumination Films, 1 Victoria Ave, Albert Park, Vic 3208, Australia

Cox, Robert J (Bobby) *Baseball Manager, Executive*
4030 River Ridge Chase, Marietta, GA 30067, USA

Cousteau - Cox

Cox, Ronny — *Actor*
13948 Magnolia Blvd, Sherman Oaks, CA 91423, USA

Cox, Stephen J — *Artist*
154 Barnsbury Rd, Islington, London N1 0ER, England

Cox, Warren J — *Architect*
3111 "N" St NW, Washington, DC 20007, USA

Coyne, Frank J — *Businessman*
%General Accident Insurance Group, 436 Walnut St, Philadelphia, PA 19106, USA

Coyote, Peter — *Actor*
9 Rose Ave, Mill Valley, CA 94941, USA

Cozzarelli, Nicholas — *Biologist*
%University of California, Biology Dept, Berkeley, CA 94720, USA

Craddock, Billy (Crash) — *Singer, Songwriter*
%Mercer Assoc, 8447 Stults Rd, Dallas, TX 75243, USA

Craft, Christine — *Commentator*
%KRBK-TV, News Dept, 500 Media Pl, Sacramento, CA 95815, USA

Craft, Clarence B — *WW II Army Hero (CMH)*
902 W 12th St, Fayetteville, AR 72701, USA

Craft, Robert — *Conductor*
%Alfred A Knopf Inc, 201 E 50th St, New York, NY 10022, USA

Craig of Radley, David B — *Royal Air Force Marshal, England*
%House of Lords, Westminster, London SW1A 0PW, England

Craig, Andrew B, III — *Financier*
%Boatmen's BancShares, 800 Market St, St Louis, MO 63101, USA

Craig, Eugene W — *Editorial Cartoonist*
73 E Kramer St Canal, Winchester, OH 43110, USA

Craig, Helen — *Actress*
%Beal, 205 W 54th St, New York, NY 10019, USA

Craig, Jenny — *Nutritionist*
445 Marine View Dr, #300, Del Mar, CA 92014, USA

Craig, Jim — *Hockey Player*
15 Jyra Lane, North Easton, MA 02356, USA

Craig, Michael — *Actor*
%Chatto & Linnit, Prince of Wales, Coventry St, London W1V 7FE, England

Craig, Roger — *Football Player*
2453 Canora Ave, Alpine, CA 91901, USA

Craig, Roger L — *Baseball Player, Manager*
26658 San Felipe Ave, Warner Springs, GA 92086, USA

Craig, William — *Government Official, England*
23 Annadale Ave, Belfast BT7 3JJ, Northern Ireland

Craig, Yvonne — *Actress*
PO Box 827, Pacific Palisades, CA 90272, USA

Craighead, Frank C, Jr — *Ecologist*
%Craighead Environmental Research Institute, PO Box 156, Moose, WY 83012, USA

Crain, Jeanne — *Actress*
354 Hilgard Ave, Los Angeles, CA 90024, USA

Crain, Keith E — *Publisher*
%Crain Communications, 1400 Woodbridge Ave, Detroit, MI 48207, USA

Crain, Rance — *Publisher*
%Crain Communications, 740 N Rush St, Chicago, IL 60611, USA

Crais, Robert — *Writer*
12829 Landale St, Studio City, CA 91604, USA

Cram, Donald J — *Nobel Chemistry Laureate*
405 Hilgard Ave, Los Angeles, CA 90024, USA

Cram, Steve — *Track Athlete*
%General Delivery, Jarrow, England

Cramer, Floyd — *Pianist*
5109 Old Haven Lane, Tampa, FL 33617, USA

Cramer, Grant — *Actor*
9911 W Pico Blvd, #1060, Los Angeles, CA 90035, USA

Cramer, Richard Ben — *Journalist*
%Philadelphia Inquirer, Editorial Dept, 400 N Broad St, Philadelphia, PA 19130, USA

Crampton, Barbara — *Actress*
501 S Beverly Dr, #300, Beverly Hills, CA 90212, USA

Crampton, Bruce — *Golfer*
406 Tapatio Dr W, #2, Boerne, TX 78006, USA

Crandall, Delmar W (Del) — *Baseball Player*
25 Rock Cliff Place, Pomona, CA 91766, USA

Crandall, Robert L — *Businessman*
%AMR Corp, PO Box 619616, Dallas-Fort Worth Airport, TX 75261, USA

Crane, Horace R — *Physicist*
830 Avon Rd, Ann Arbor, MI 48104, USA

Crane, Irving D — *Pocket Billiards Player*
270 Yarmouth Rd, Rochester, NY 14610, USA

Cranston, Alan — *Senator, CA*
27080 W Fremont Rd, Los Altos, CA 94022, USA

Cranz, Christl — *Skier*
Steibis 61, 87534 Oberstaufen, Germany

Craven, Wes — *Movie Director*
%Wes Craven Films, 10000 W Washington Blvd, #3011, Culver City, CA 90232, USA

Crawford, Bruce E — *Businessman, Opera Official*
%Omnicom Group, 437 Madison Ave, New York, NY 10022, USA

Crawford, Bryce L, Jr — *Chemist*
1545 Branston St, St Paul, MN 55108, USA

Crawford, Cindy — *Model*
26 E 10th St, #PH, New York, NY 10003, USA

Crawford, Elbert — *Football Player*
%New England Patriots, Foxboro Stadium, Rt 1, Foxboro, MA 02035, USA

Crawford, Henry C (Shag) — *Baseball Umpire*
1530 Virginia Ave, Havertown, PA 19083, USA

Crawford, Johnny — *Actor*
2440 El Contento Dr, Los Angeles, CA 90068, USA

Crawford, Marc — *Hockey Coach*
%Quebec Nordiques, 2205 Ave du Colisee, Quebec City PQ G1L 4W7, Canada

Crawford, Michael — *Actor, Singer*
%International Creative Mgmt, 76 Oxford St, London W1N 0AX, England

Crawford, Randy — *Singer*
911 Park St SW, Grand Rapids, MI 49504, USA

Crawford, William A — *Diplomat*
4982 Sentinel Dr, #406, Bethesda, MD 20816, USA

Crawford, William J — *WW II Army Hero (CMH)*
Box 4, Palmer Lake, CO 80133, USA

Crawley, John B — *Publisher*
%Times Mirror Magazines, 2 Park Ave, New York, NY 10016, USA

Craxi, Bettino — *Prime Minister, Italy*
Hammamet, Tunisia

Cray, Robert — *Singer*
%Rosebud Agency, PO Box 170429, San Francisco, CA 94117, USA

Cray, Seymour R — *Computer Engineer*
%Cray Computer Co, 1110 Bayfield Dr, Colorado Springs, CO 80906, USA

Crean, John C — *Businessman*
%Fleetwood Enterprises, 3125 Myers St, Riverside, CA 92503, USA

Crecine, John P — *Educator*
%Georgia Institute of Technology, President's Office, Atlanta, GA 30602, USA

Creech, Wilbur L — *Air Force General*
20 Quail Run Rd, Henderson, NV 89014, USA

Creekmur, Louis (Lou) — *Football Player*
7521 SW 1st St, Plantation, FL 33317, USA

Creeley, Robert W — *Writer*
PO Box 384, Waldoboro, ME 04572, USA

Creighton, John D — *Publisher*
%Toronto Sun, 333 King St E, Toronto ON M5A 3X5, Canada

Creighton, John O — *Astronaut*
%Boeing Commercial Airplane Group, PO Box 3707, Seattle, WA 98124, USA

Creighton, John W, Jr — *Businessman*
%Weyerhaeuser Co, 33663 Weyerhaeuser Ave S, Auburn, WA 98001, USA

Creighton, Norman P — *Financier*
%Imperial Bank, PO Box 92991, Los Angeles, CA 90009, USA

Cremins, Bobby — *Basketball Coach*
%Georgia Institute of Technology, Athletic Dept, Atlanta, GA 30332, USA

Crenkovski, Branko — *Prime Minister, Macedonia*
%Prime Minister's Office, Dame Grueva 6, 9100 Skopje, Macedonia

Crenna, Richard — *Actor*
3941 Valley Meadow Rd, Encino, CA 91436, USA

Crenshaw, Ben — *Golfer*
%US Golf Assn, Liberty Corners Rd, Far Hills, NJ 07931, USA

C

Crenshaw, George — Cartoonist
%King Features Syndicate, 216 E 45th St, New York, NY 10017, USA

Crespin, Regine — Opera Singer
%Musicaglotz, 3 Ave Frochet, 75009 Paris, France

Cresson, Edith — Prime Minister, France
Ville de Chatellerault, 86106 Chatellerault Cedex, France

Creswell, Isaiah T — Educator
6315 Balky St, San Antonio, TX 78240, USA

Creutz, Edward C — Physicist
PO Box 2757, Rancho Santa Fe, CA 92067, USA

Crewdson, John M — Journalist
%Chicago Tribune, Editorial Dept, 435 N Michigan Ave, Chicago, IL 60611, USA

Crewe, Albert V — Nobel Physics Laureate
63 Old Creek Rd, Palos Park, IL 60464, USA

Crews, David — Psychobiologist
%University of Texas, Zoology Dept, Austin, TX 78712, USA

Crews, John R — WW II Army Hero (CMH)
1324 SW 54th St, Oklahoma City, OK 73119, USA

Crews, Phillip — Chemist
%University of California, Chemistry Dept, Santa Cruz, CA 99504, USA

Cribbins, Bernard — Actor
Hamm Court, Weybridge, Surrey, England

Crichton, Charles — Actor
%MacNaughton Lowe Representation, 200 Fulham Rd, London SW10 9PN, England

Crichton, Michael — Writer, Movie Director
2210 Wilshire Blvd, #433, Santa Monica, CA 90403, USA

Crick, Francis H C — Nobel Medicine Laureate
1792 Colgate Circle, La Jolla, CA 92037, USA

Crickhowell of Pont Esgob, Nicholas E — Government Leader, England
%House of Lords, Westminster, London SW1A 0PW, England

Crier, Catherine — Commentator
%ABC-TV, News Dept, 77 W 66th St, New York, NY 10023, USA

Crile, Susan — Artist
168 W 86th St, New York, NY 10024, USA

Crim, Jack C — Businessman
%Talley Industries, 2702 N 44th St, Phoenix, AZ 85008, USA

Crippen, Robert L — Astronaut
%NASA Headquarters, Mail Code CD, Kennedy Space Center, FL 32899, USA

Criqui, Don — Sportscaster
%NBC-TV, Sports Dept, 30 Rockefeller Plaza, New York, NY 10112, USA

Criser, Marshall M — Educator
6740 Epping Forest Way N, Jacksonville, FL 32217, USA

Crisman, Craig — Businessman
%Applied Magnetics Corp, 75 Robin Hill Rd, Goleta, CA 93117, USA

Crisostomo, Manny — Photographer
%Pacific Daily News, PO Box DN, Agana, GU 96910, USA

Crisp, Quentin — Actor
46 E 3rd St, New York, NY 10003, USA

Crisp, Terry A — Hockey Coach
%Tampa Bay Lightning, Mack Center, 501 E Kennedy Blvd, Tampa, FL 33602, USA

Criss, Peter — Singer, Drummer (Kiss)
PO Box 827, Hagerstown, MD 21741, USA

Crist, George B — Marine Corps General
%CBS-TV, News Dept, 51 W 52nd St, New York, NY 10019, USA

Crist, Judith — Journalist
180 Riverside Dr, New York, NY 10024, USA

Cristal, Linda — Actress
9129 Hazen Dr, Beverly Hills, CA 90210, USA

Cristofer, Michael — Playwright
%Richard Lovett, 9830 Wilshire Blvd, Beverly Hills, CA 90212, USA

Cristol, Stanley J — Chemist
2918 3rd St, Boulder, CO 80304, USA

Critchfield, Charles L — Physicist
391 El Conejo, Los Alamos, NM 87544, USA

Critchfield, Jack B — Businessman
%Florida Progress Corp, 1 Progress Plaza, St Petersburg, FL 33701, USA

Crockett, Bruce L — Businessman
%COMSAT Corp, 6560 Rock Spring Dr, Bethesda, MD 20817, USA

Croel, Mike — *Football Player*
%New York Giants, Giants Stadium, East Rutherford, NJ 07073, USA

Crofts, Dash — *Singer (Seals & Crofts)*
%Nationwide Entertainment Svcs, 770 Regents Rd, #113-905, San Diego, CA 92122, USA

Croker, Stephen B (Steve) — *Air Force General*
Commander, 8th Air Force, 245 Davis Ave E, Barksdale Air Force Base, LA 71110, USA

Cromwell, James — *Actor*
4821 Katherine Ave, Sherman Oaks, CA 91423, USA

Cromwell, Nolan — *Football Player, Coach*
%Green Bay Packers, 1265 Lombardi Ave, Green Bay, WI 54304, USA

Cronbach, Lee J — *Educator, Psychologist*
850 Webster St, #623, Palo Alto, CA 94301, USA

Cronenberg, David — *Movie Director*
%David Cronenberg Productions, 217 Avenue Rd, Toronto ON M5R 2J3, Canada

Cronenweth, Jordan — *Cinematographer*
990 Camino San Acacio, Santa Fe, NM 87501, USA

Cronin, James W — *Nobel Physics Laureate*
5825 S Dorchester St, Chicago, IL 60637, USA

Cronin, Robert J — *Businessman*
%Wallace Computer Services, 4600 W Roosevelt Rd, Hillside, IL 60162, USA

Cronkite, Eugene P — *Physician*
%Brookhaven National Laboratory, Medical Dept, Upton, NY 11973, USA

Cronkite, Walter L, Jr — *Commentator*
%CBS-TV, News Dept, 51 W 52nd St, New York, NY 10019, USA

Cronyn, Hume — *Actor*
42 W 58th St, New York, NY 10019, USA

Crook, Edward — *Boxer*
4512 Moline Ave, Columbus, GA 31907, USA

Crooke, Edward A — *Businessman*
%Baltimore Gas & Electric Co, 39 W Lexington St, Baltimore, MD 21201, USA

Croom, John H, III — *Businessman*
%Columbia Gas System, 20 Montchanin Rd, Wilmington, DE 19807, USA

Crosbie, John C — *Political Leader, Canada*
PO Box 9192, Station "B", St John's NF A1A 2X9, Canada

Crosby, Cathy Lee — *Actress*
1223 Wilshire Blvd, #404, Santa Monica, CA 90403, USA

Crosby, Denise — *Actress*
935 Embury St, Pacific Palisades, CA 90272, USA

Crosby, Gordon E, Jr — *Businessman*
%USLife Corp, 125 Maiden Lane, New York, NY 10038, USA

Crosby, John O — *Conductor*
%Santa Fe Opera, PO Box 2408, Santa Fe, NM 87504, USA

Crosby, Kathryn — *Actress*
101 Robbin Dr, Hillsborough, CA 94010, USA

Crosby, Lucinda — *Actress*
4942 Vineland Ave, #200, North Hollywood, CA 91601, USA

Crosby, Mary — *Actress*
5454 Gentry Ave, North Hollywood, CA 91607, USA

Crosby, Norm — *Comedian*
1400 Londonderry Place, Los Angeles, CA 90069, USA

Crosby, Phil — *Actor*
21801 Providencia St, Woodland Hills, CA 91364, USA

Crosetti, Frank P J — *Baseball Player*
65 W Monterey Ave, Stockton, CA 95204, USA

Cross, Ben — *Actor*
29 Burlington Gardens, London W4, England

Cross, Burton — *Governor, ME*
934 Riverside Dr, Augusta, ME 04330, USA

Cross, Christopher — *Singer, Songwriter*
PO Box 63, Marble Falls, TX 78654, USA

Cross, George L — *Educator*
812 Mockingbird Lane, Norman, OK 73071, USA

Cross, K Patricia — *Educator*
%University of California, Education School, Berkeley, CA 94720, USA

Cross, Marcia — *Actress*
8722 Burton Way, #309, Los Angeles, CA 90048, USA

Cross, Randy — *Football Player, Sportscaster*
%NBC-TV, Sports Dept, 30 Rockefeller Plaza, New York, NY 10112, USA

Crossfield, A Scott — *Test Pilot*
12100 Thoroughbred Rd, Herndon, VA 22071, USA

Crouch, Andrae — *Singer*
%William Morris Agency, 151 S El Camino Dr, Beverly Hills, CA 90212, USA

Crouch, Helen B — *Educator*
%Literacy Volunteers of America, 404 Oak St, Syracuse, NY 13203, USA

Crouch, Paul — *Evangelist*
%Trinity Broadcasting Network, PO Box "A", Santa Ana, CA 92711, USA

Crouch, Stanley — *Writer*
%Georges Borchardt Agency, 136 E 57th St, New York, NY 10022, USA

Crouch, William W — *Army General*
Commander in Chief, US Army Europe/7th Army, APO, AE 09014, USA

Crouse, Lindsay — *Actress*
%Agency For Performing Arts, 9000 Sunset Blvd, #1200, Los Angeles, CA 90069, USA

Crow, Elizabeth S — *Editor*
%Mademoiselle Magazine, Editorial Dept, 350 Madison Ave, New York, NY 10017, USA

Crow, F Trammell — *Businessman*
%Trammell Crow Co, Trammell Crow Center, 2001 Ross Ave, Dallas, TX 75201, USA

Crow, James F — *Geneticist*
24 Glenway St, Madison, WI 53705, USA

Crow, John David — *Football Player, Coach*
%Texas A&M University, Athletic Dept, College Station, TX 77843, USA

Crow, Martin D — *Cricketer*
Millbrook Golf Resort, PO Box 160, Queenstown, New Zealand

Crow, Sheryl — *Singer, Songwriter*
10345 W Olympic Blvd, #200, Los Angeles, CA 90064, USA

Crowe, Tonya — *Actress*
13030 Mindanao Way, #4, Marina del Rey, CA 90292, USA

Crowe, William J, Jr — *Navy Admiral, Diplomat*
%American Embassy, 24/31 Grosvenor Sq, London W1A 1AE, England

Crowell, Craven H, Jr — *Government Official*
%Tennessee Valley Authority, 400 W Summit Hill Dr, Knoxville, TN 37902, USA

Crowell, Donald W — *Financier*
%Crowell Weedon Co, 1 Wilshire Blvd, Los Angeles, CA 90017, USA

Crowell, Richard A — *Financier*
%PanAgora Asset Management, 260 Franklin St, Boston, MA 02110, USA

Crowell, Rodney J — *Singer, Songwriter*
PO Box 120576, Nashville, TN 37212, USA

Crowley, Joseph N — *Educator*
%University of Nevada, President's Office, Reno, NV 89557, USA

Crowley, Mart — *Playwright*
8955 Beverly Blvd, Los Angeles, CA 90048, USA

Crowley, Patricia — *Actress*
150 W 56th St, #4603, New York, NY 10019, USA

Crown, David A — *Criminologist*
3103 Jessie Court, Fairfax, VA 22030, USA

Crowson, Richard — *Editorial Cartoonist*
%Wichita Eagle-Beacon, Editorial Dept, 825 E Douglas Ave, Wichita, KS 67202, USA

Crozer, Robert P — *Businessman*
%Flowers Industries, 200 US Highway 19 S, Thomasville, GA 31792, USA

Crozier, William M, Jr — *Financier*
%BayBanks Inc, 175 Federal St, Boston, MA 02110, USA

Cruickshank, John A — *WW II Royal Air Force Hero (VC)*
34 Frogston Rd W, Edinburgh EH10 7AJ, Scotland

Cruikshank, Thomas H — *Businessman*
%Halliburton Co, Lincoln Plaza, #3600, 500 N Akard St, Dallas, TX 75201, USA

Cruise, Tom — *Actor*
%Odin Productions, 4400 Coldwater Canyon Ave, #220, Studio City, CA 91604, USA

Crum, E Denzel (Denny) — *Basketball Coach*
%University of Louisville, Crawford Gym, Louisville, KY 40292, USA

Crumb, George H — *Composer*
240 Kirk Lane, Media, PA 19063, USA

Crumley, James R, Jr — *Religious Leader*
362 Little Creek Dr, Leesville, SC 29070, USA

Crutcher, Lawrence M — *Publisher*
%Book-of-the-Month Club, Rockefeller Center, New York, NY 10020, USA

Crutchfield, Edward E, Jr — *Financier*
%First Union National Bank, 301 S Tryon St, Charlotte, NC 28288, USA

Cruyff, Johan — *Soccer Player, Coach*
%FC Barcelona, Aristides Maillol S/N, 08 028, Barcelona, Spain

Cruz, Celia — *Singer*
PO Box P-11007, Cambria Heights, NY 11411, USA

Cruz, Jose D — *Baseball Player*
B-15 Jardines Lafayette, Arroyo, PR 00615, USA

Cruz-Romo, Gilda — *Opera Singer*
1315 Lockhill-Selma Rd, San Antonio, TX 78213, USA

Cryer, Gretchen — *Playwright, Lyricist, Actress*
885 West End Ave, New York, NY 10025, USA

Cryer, Jon — *Actor*
%United Talent Agency, 9560 Wilshire Blvd, #500, Beverly Hills, CA 90212, USA

Cryner, Bobbie — *Singer*
%Erv Woolsey Co, 1000 18th Ave S, Nashville, TN 37212, USA

Crystal, Billy — *Comedian*
%Creative Artists Agency, 9830 Wilshire Blvd, Beverly Hills, CA 90212, USA

Crystal, Ronald G — *Molecular Biologist*
%National Heart Lung Blood Institute, 9000 Rockville Pike, Bethesda, MD 20892, USA

Csikszentmihalyi, Mihaly — *Psychologist*
%University of Chicago, Psychology Dept, Chicago, IL 60637, USA

Csonka, Larry — *Football Player*
37256 Hunter Camp Rd, Lisbon, OH 44432, USA

Cuckney, John G — *Financier*
%Brooke Bond Group, 45 Berkeley St, London EC4R 1DH, England

Cuellar, Miguel (Mike) — *Baseball Player*
PO Box 50016, Levittown, PA 00950, USA

Cuevas, Jose Luis — *Artist*
Galeana 109, San Angel Inn, Mexico City 20 DF, Mexico

Cuff, Ward — *Football Player*
16611 NE 26th, Bellevue, WA 98008, USA

Culbertson, Frank L, Jr — *Astronaut*
%NASA, Johnson Space Center, 2101 NASA Rd, Houston, TX 77058, USA

Culkin, Macaulay — *Actor*
%William Morris Agency, 151 S El Camino Dr, Beverly Hills, CA 90212, USA

Cullberg, Brigit R — *Choreographer*
Kommendorsgatan 8-C, 114 80 Stockholm, Sweden

Cullen, Brett — *Actor*
%Gersh Agency, 232 N Canon Dr, Beverly Hills, CA 90210, USA

Cullen, James G — *Businessman*
%Bell Atlantic Corp, 1717 Arch St, Philadelphia, PA 19103, USA

Culligan, John W — *Businessman*
%American Home Products, 5 Giralda Farms, Madison, NY 07940, USA

Cullinan, Edward H — *Architect*
The Wharf, Baldwin Terrace, London N1 7RU, England

Cullman, Edgar M, Jr — *Businessman*
%Culbro Corp, 387 Park Ave S, New York, NY 10016, USA

Cullman, Edgar M, Sr — *Businessman*
%Culbro Corp, 387 Park Ave S, New York, NY 10016, USA

Cullman, Joseph F, III — *Businessman*
%Philip Morris Companies, 100 Park Ave, New York, NY 10017, USA

Cullum, John — *Actor, Singer*
%International Creative Mgmt, 40 W 57th St, New York, NY 10019, USA

Cullum, Leo — *Cartoonist*
2900 Valmere Dr, Malibu, CA 90265, USA

Cullum, Mark E — *Editorial Cartoonist*
549 Benbow Dr, Birmingham, AL 35226, USA

Culp, Curley — *Football Player*
12311 Wycliff Lane, Austin, TX 78727, USA

Culp, Robert — *Actor*
1718 Ferrari Dr, Beverly Hills, CA 90210, USA

Culver, David M — *Businessman*
3429 Drummond St, Montreal H3G 1X6, Canada

Culver, John C — *Senator, IA*
5409 Spangler Ave, Bethesda, MD 20816, USA

Cumby, George E — *Football Player*
4418 W 43rd St, Houston, TX 77092, USA

Cumming, Ian M — *Businessman*
%Leucadia National Corp, 315 Park Ave S, New York, NY 10010, USA

C

Cruyff - Cumming

Cummings, Constance *Actress*
68 Old Church St, London SW3 6EP, England

Cummings, Herbert W *Financier*
%Citizens Financial Group, 1 Citizens Plaza, Providence, RI 02903, USA

Cummings, Quinn *Actress*
%Pietragallo Agency, 398 Collins Dr, Pittsburgh, PA 15235, USA

Cummings, Ralph W *Agriculturist*
812 Rosemont Ave, Raleigh, NC 27607, USA

Cummings, Stephen E *Financier*
%Bowles Howowell Conner Co, 227 W Trade St, Charlotte, NC 28202, USA

Cummings, Walter J *Judge*
%US Court of Appelas, 219 S Dearborn St, Chicago, IL 60604, USA

Cummins, Peggy *Actress*
Butler Farm, Hurstnonceaus, Sussex, England

Cundey, Dean *Cinematographer*
%Smith/Gosnell, 1515 Palisades Dr, #N, Pacific Palisades, CA 90272, USA

Cunniff, John *Hockey Coach*
%New Jersey Devils, Meadowlands Arena, PO Box 504, East Rutherford, NJ 07073, USA

Cunningham, Bill *Musician (Box Tops)*
%Creative Entertainment Assoc, 2011 Ferry Ave, #U-19, Camden, NJ 08104, USA

Cunningham, Jeffrey M *Publisher*
%Forbes Magazine, 60 5th Ave, New York, NY 10011, USA

Cunningham, John *Test Pilot*
Canley, Kinsbourne Green, Harpenden, Herts, England

Cunningham, John *Actor*
%Gage Group, 9255 Sunset Blvd, #515, Los Angeles, CA 90069, USA

Cunningham, John A (Jack) *Government Official, England*
%House of Commons, Westminster, London SW1A 0AA, England

Cunningham, John F *Educator*
%Providence College, President's Office, Providence, RI 02918, USA

Cunningham, John P *Businessman*
%International Aluminum Corp, 767 Monterey Pass Rd, Monterey Park, CA 91754, USA

Cunningham, Merce *Choreographer*
55 Bethune St, New York, NY 10014, USA

Cunningham, R Walter *Astronaut*
%Alcorn Ventures, 520 Post Oak Blvd, #130, Houston, TX 77027, USA

Cunningham, Randall *Football Player*
%Philadelphia Eagles, 3501 S Broad St, Philadelphia, PA 19148, USA

Cunningham, Sean S *Movie Director, Producer*
4420 Hayvenhurst Ave, Encino, CA 91436, USA

Cunningham, Stephen *Astronaut*
%Hughes Space/Communications Group, PO Box 92919, Los Angeles, CA 90009, USA

Cunningham, William J (Billy) *Basketball Player, Coach, Executive*
%Miami Heat, Miami Arena, Miami, FL 33136, USA

Cuomo, Mario M *Governor, NY*
%Wilkie Farr Gallagher, 153 E 53rd St, New York, NY 10022, USA

Cuozzo, Gary S *Football Player*
911 Middletown Lincroft Rd, Middletown, NJ 07748, USA

Curb, Mike *Record Producer*
3907 W Alameda Ave, #2, Burbank, CA 91505, USA

Curbeam, Robert L, Jr *Astronaut*
%NASA, Johnson Space Center, 2101 NASA Rd, Houston, TX 77058, USA

Curd, Howard R *Businessman*
%Jamesway Corp, 40 Hartz Way, Secaucus, NJ 07094, USA

Cureton, Thomas K *Swimming Contributor*
501 E Washington, Urbana, IL 61801, USA

Curl, Gregory L *Financier*
%Boatmen's Bancshares, 800 Market St, St Louis, MO 63101, USA

Curley, John F, Jr *Financier*
%Legg Mason Inc, 111 S Calvert St, Baltimore, MD 21202, USA

Curley, John J *Publisher*
%Gannett Co, 1100 Wilson Blvd, Arlington, VA 22234, USA

Curley, Thomas *Publisher*
%USA Today, 1000 Wilson Blvd, Arlington, VA 22209, USA

Curley, Walter J P, Jr *Diplomat, Financier*
885 3rd Ave, #1200, New York, NY 10022, USA

Curnin, Thomas F *Attorney*
%Cahill Gordon Reindel, 80 Pine St, New York, NY 10005, USA

Curran, Charles E — *Theologian*
%Southern Methodist University, Dallas Hall, Dallas, TX 75275, USA

Currey, Francis S — *WW II Army Hero (CMH)*
RR 2, Box 185, Selkirk, NY 12158, USA

Currie, Louise — *Actress*
1317 Delresto Dr, Beverly Hills, CA 90210, USA

Currie, Sondra — *Actress*
3951 Longridge Ave, Sherman Oaks, CA 91423, USA

Curry, Bill — *Football Player, Coach*
%University of Alabama, Athletic Dept, Univesity, AL 35486, USA

Curry, Eric — *Football Player*
%Tampa Bay Buccaneers, 1 Buccaneer Place, Tampa, FL 33607, USA

Curry, John — *Tennis Executive*
%All England Lawn Tennis Club, Wimbledon, England

Curry, Tim — *Singer, Actor*
26666 Aberdeen Ave, Los Angeles, CA 90027, USA

Curti, Merle E — *Historian*
110 S Henry St, Madison, WI 53703, USA

Curtin, David S — *Journalist*
%Colorado Springs Gazette Telegraph, 30 S Prospect, Colorado Springs, CO 80903, USA

Curtin, David Y — *Chemist*
3 Montclair Rd, Urbana, IL 61801, USA

Curtin, Jane — *Actress*
PO Box 1070, Sharon, CT 06069, USA

Curtin, John J, Jr — *Attorney*
%Bingham Dana Gould, 150 Federal St, #3500, Boston, MA 02110, USA

Curtin, Phyllis — *Opera Singer*
%Boston University, School for Arts, Boston, MA 02215, USA

Curtin, Valerie — *Actress*
%Creative Artists Agency, 9830 Wilshire Blvd, Beverly Hills, CA 90212, USA

Curtis Cuneo, Ann — *Swimmer*
35 Golden Hinde Blvd, San Rafael, CA 94903, USA

Curtis, Carl T — *Senator, NE*
Windsor Square, 1300 "G" St, #104-G, Lincoln, NE 68508, USA

Curtis, Daniel M — *Movie Director*
143 S Rockingham Ave, Los Angeles, CA 90049, USA

Curtis, Isaac F — *Football Player*
711 Clinton Springs, Cincinnati, OH 45229, USA

Curtis, Jamie Lee — *Actress*
%Creative Artists Agency, 9830 Wilshire Blvd, Beverly Hills, CA 90212, USA

Curtis, Joe J — *Financier*
%Commerce Bank, 8000 Forsyth Blvd, Clayton, MO 63105, USA

Curtis, Keene — *Actor*
6363 Ivarene Ave, Los Angeles, CA 90068, USA

Curtis, Kenneth M — *Governor, ME; Diplomat*
1154 Shore Rd, Cape Elizabeth, ME 04107, USA

Curtis, Robin — *Actress*
%Artists Agency, 10000 Santa Monica Blvd, #305, Los Angeles, CA 90067, USA

Curtis, Todd — *Actor*
2046 14th St, #10, Santa Monica, CA 90405, USA

Curtis, Tony — *Actor*
11831 Folkstone Lane, Los Angeles, CA 90077, USA

Cusack, Joan — *Actress*
540 N Lakeshore Dr, #722, Chicago, IL 60611, USA

Cusack, John — *Actor*
838 Sheridan, Evanston, IL 60202, USA

Cusack, Sinead — *Actress*
%Markham & Froggatt Ltd, 4 Windmill St, London W1P 1HF, England

Cusick, Thomas A — *Financier*
%TCF Financial Corp, 801 Marquette Ave, Minneapolis, MN 55402, USA

Cussler, Clive E — *Writer*
7731 W 72nd Place, Arvada, CO 80005, USA

Cuthbeth, Betty — *Track Athlete*
4/7 Karara Close, Hall's Head, Mandurah WA 6210, Australia

Cuti, Anthony J — *Businessman*
%Pathmark Stores, 301 Blair Rd, Woodbridge, NJ 07095, USA

Cutler, A Roden — *WW II Australian Army Hero (VC)*
22 Ginahgulla RD, Bellevue Hill NSW 2023, Australia

C

Curran - Cutler

C

Cutler, Alexander M *Businessman*
%Eaton Corp, Eaton Center, 1111 Superior Ave, Cleveland, OH 44114, USA

Cutler, Bruce *Attorney*
41 Madison Ave, New York, NY 10010, USA

Cutler, Laurel *Businesswoman*
%Foote Cone Belding Communications, 767 5th Ave, New York, NY 10153, USA

Cutler, Lloyd N *Government Official*
3115 "O" St NW, Washington, DC 20007, USA

Cutler, Walter L *Diplomat*
%Meridian International Center, 1630 Crescent Place NW, Washington, DC 20009, USA

Cutter, Kiki *Skier*
PO Box 1317, Carbondale, CO 81623, USA

Cutter, Lise *Actress*
464 Hudson St, #268, New York, NY 10014, USA

Cutter, Slade *Football Player*
11510 Whisper Breeze, San Antonio, TX 78230, USA

Cwiertnia, Jerome W *Businessman*
%National Education Corp, 18400 Von Karman Ave, Irvine, CA 92715, USA

Cyert, Richard M *Educator*
%Carnegie-Mellon University, GSIA Building, Pittsburgh, PA 15213, USA

Cypher, Jon *Actor*
424 Manzanita Ave, Ventura, CA 93001, USA

Cyrus, Billy Ray *Singer, Songwriter*
%McFadden Artists Corp, 818 18th Ave S, Nashville, TN 37203, USA

Czarnecki, Gerald M *Businessman*
%UNC Inc, 175 Admiral Cochrane Dr, Annapolis, MD 21401, USA

Czrongursky, Jan *Prime Minister, Slovakia*
%Prime Minister's Office, Nam Slobody 1, 81370 Bratislava, Slovakia

Czyz, Bobby *Boxer*
15 Garry Place, Wanaque, NJ 07465, USA

Cutler - Czyz

D'Abo, Maryam — *Actress*
%Paul Kohner Inc, 9300 Wilshire Blvd, #555, Beverly Hills, CA 90212, USA

D'Abo, Olivia — *Actress*
%International Creative Mgmt, 8942 Wilshire Blvd, Beverly Hills, CA 90211, USA

D'Agostino, James S, Jr — *Businessman*
%AGC Life Insurance Co, American General Center, Nashville, TN 37250, USA

D'Alemberte, Talbot (Sandy) — *Educator*
%Florida State University, President's Office, Tallahassee, FL 32306, USA

D'Amboise, Jacques J — *Dancer, Choreographer*
%National Dance Institute, 244 W 71st St, New York, NY 10023, USA

D'Ambrosio, Dominick — *Labor Leader*
%Allied Industrial Workers Union, 3520 W Oklahoma Ave, Milwaukee, WI 53215, USA

D'Angelo, Beverly — *Actress*
8033 Sunset Blvd, #247, Los Angeles, CA 90046, USA

D'Angio, Giulio J — *Radiation Therapist*
%Children's Hospital, 34th & Civic Center Blvd, Philadelphia, PA 19104, USA

D'Arbanville-Quinn, Patti — *Actress*
444 E 66th St, #6-KK, New York, NY 10021, USA

D'Arbeloff, Alexander V — *Businessman*
%Teardyne Inc, 321 Harrison St, Boston, MA 02118, USA

D'Arby, Terence Trent — *Singer*
%Creative Artists Agency, 9830 Wilshire Blvd, Beverly Hills, CA 90212, USA

D'Arcy, Margaretta — *Writer*
%M Ramsay, 14-A Goodwins Court, St Martin's Lane, London WC2N 4LL, England

D'Ascoli, Bernard — *Concert Pianist*
%Van Walsum Mgmt, 40 St Peters Rd, London W6 9RH, England

D'Eath, Tom — *Boat Racing Driver*
7773 Farnsworth, Fair Haven, MI 48001, USA

D'Harnoncourt, Anne — *Museum Director*
%Philadelphia Museum of Art, 25th & Ben Franklin Parkway, Philadelphia, PA 19101, USA

D'Oriola, Christian — *Fencer*
Valdebanne, Rt de Generac, 30 Nimes, France

D'Ornellas, Robert W — *Businessman*
%Del Monte Foods, 1 Market Plaza, San Francisco, CA 94105, USA

D'Rivera, Paquito — *Jazz Saxophonist*
%Havana-New York Music Co, PO Box 777, Union City, NJ 07087, USA

Daberko, David A — *Financier*
%National City Corp, 1900 E 9th St, Cleveland, OH 44114, USA

Dabney, Hovey S — *Financier*
%Jefferson Bankshares, 123 E Main St, Charlottesville, VA 22902, USA

Dabney, Virginius — *Writer, Editor*
Tuckahoe Apartments, 5621 Cary St Rd, #213, Richmond, VA 23226, USA

Dacosta, Claude Antoine — *Prime Minister, Congo*
%Prime Minister's Office, BP 2096, Brazzaville, Congo

Dacre of Glanton (H R Trevor-Roper) — *Historian*
The Old Rectory, Didcot, Oxon, England

Daehlie, Bjorn — *Cross Country Skier*
Cathinka Guldbergs Veg 64, 2034 Holter, Norway

Dafoe, Willem — *Actor*
33 Wooster St, #200, New York, NY 10013, USA

Daggett, Tim — *Gymnast*
%Victor Randazza, 3849 NE 169th St, #C-401, North Miami Beach, FL 33160, USA

Dagworthy Prew, Wendy A — *Fashion Designer*
18 Melrose Terrace, London W6, England

Dahanayake, Wijeyananda — *Prime Minister, Ceylon*
225 Richmond Hill Rd, Galle, Sri Lanka

Dahl, Arlene — *Actress*
%Dahlmark Productions, PO Box 116, Sparkill, NY 10976, USA

Dahl, Richard J — *Financier*
%Bancorp Hawaii, Financial Plaza, 130 Merchant Plaza, Honolulu, HI 96813, USA

Dahl, Robert A — *Political Scientist*
17 Cooper Rd, North Haven, CT 06473, USA

Dahlgren, Edward C — *WW II Army Hero (CMH)*
Box 26, Mars Hill, ME 04758, USA

Dahlsten, Gunnar — *Businessman*
%Swedish Match, PO Box 16100, 103 22 Stockholm, Sweden

Dai Ailian — *Dancer, Choreographer*
Hua Qiao Gong Yu, #2-16, Hua Yuan Cun, Hai Dian, Beijing 100044, China

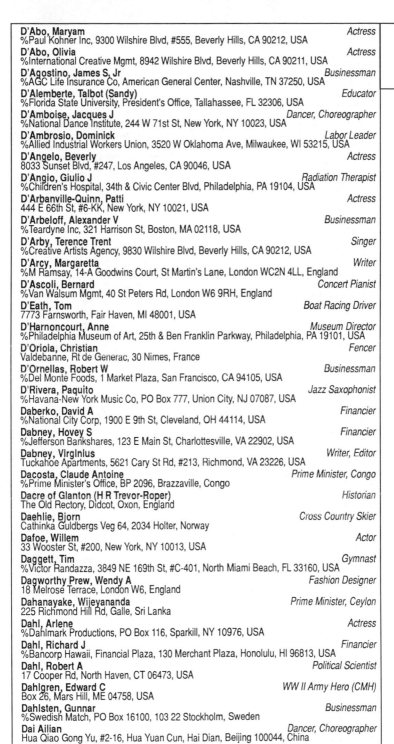

D

D'Abo - Dai Ailian

Dailey, Janet *Writer*
%Janbill Ltd, PO Box 2197, Branson, MO 65616, USA

Dailey, Peter H *Diplomat*
%State Department, 2201 "C" St NW, Washington, DC 20520, USA

Daily, Bill *Actor*
1331 Park Ave SW, #802, Albuquerque, NM 87102, USA

Daily, E G *Singer, Songwriter*
%A&M Records, 1416 N La Brea Ave, Los Angeles, CA 90028, USA

Daily, Parker *Religious Leader*
%Baptist Bible Fellowship International, PO Box 191, Springfield, MO 65801, USA

Daio, Norberto J D C A *Prime Minister, Sao Tome & Principe*
%Prime Minister's Office, CP 38, Sao Tome, Sao Tome & Principe

Dalai Lama, The *Religious Leader; Nobel Peace Laureate*
Thekchen Choeling, McLeod Ganj 176219, Dharamsal, Himachal Pradesh, India

Dale, Bruce *Photographer*
%National Geographic Magazine, 17th & "M" St NW, Washington, DC 20001, USA

Dale, Carroll *Football Player*
PO Box 1449, Wise, VA 24293, USA

Dale, Charles B *Labor Leader*
%Newspaper Guild, 8611 2nd Ave, Silver Spring, MD 20910, USA

Dale, Dick *Singer, Guitarist*
%Monarch Productions, 8803 Mayne St, Bellflower, CA 90706, USA

Dale, Jim *Actor*
26 Pembridge Villas, London W11, England

Dale, William B *Economist, Government Official*
6008 Landon Lane, Bethesda, MD 20817, USA

Daler, Jiri *Cyclist*
Jiraskova 43, 601 00 Brno, Czech Republic

Dalessandro, Peter J *WW II Army Hero (CMH)*
199 Old Niskyna Rd, Latham, NY 12110, USA

Dalhousie, Simon R *Government Official, England*
Brechin Castle, Brechin DD7 6SH, Scotland

Dalis, Irene *Opera Singer*
1731 Cherry Grove Dr, San Jose, CA 95125, USA

Dall, Bobby *Bassist (Poison)*
%Levine/Schneider, 433 N Camden Dr, Beverly Hills, CA 90210, USA

Dallenbach, Wally *Auto Racing Executive*
%Roush Racing, PO Box 1089, Liberty, NC 27298, USA

Dallesandro, Joe *Actor*
4400 Ambrose Ave, Los Angeles, CA 90027, USA

Dalrymple, Jean V K *Theater Producer*
150 W 55th St, New York, NY 10019, USA

Dalrymple, Richard W *Financier*
%Anchor Savings Bank, 1420 Broadway, Hewlett, NY 11557, USA

Dalton, Abby *Actress*
PO Box 2423, Mammoth Lakes, CA 93546, USA

Dalton, Jack *Educator*
%Columbia University, Library Service School, New York, NY 10027, USA

Dalton, James E *Air Force General*
61 Misty Acres Rd, Palos Verdes Peninsula, CA 90274, USA

Dalton, John H *Government Official*
3710 University Ave NW, Washington, DC 20016, USA

Dalton, Lacy J *Singer*
%Lacy J Dalton Enterprises, PO Box 1109, Mount Juliet, TN 37122, USA

Dalton, Robert K *Financier*
%George K Baum Co, 120 W 12th St, Kansas City, MO 64105, USA

Dalton, Timothy *Actor*
%James Sharkey Assoc, 21 Golden Square, London W1R 3PA, England

Daltry, Roger *Singer (Who)*
%Trinifold Mgmt, Harley House, 22 Marylebone Rd, London NW1 4PR, England

Daly, Cahal Brendan Cardinal *Religious Leader*
Ara Coeli Cathedral Rd, Armagh BT61 7QY, Northern Ireland

Daly, John *Movie Producer*
%Hemdale, 7960 Beverly Blvd, Los Angeles, CA 90048, USA

Daly, John *Golfer*
3710 Classic St, Memphis, TN 38125, USA

Daly, Michael J *WW II Army Hero (CMH)*
155 Redding Rd, Fairfield, CT 06430, USA

Daly, Robert A — *Entertainment Executive*
444 Loring Ave, Los Angeles, CA 90024, USA

Daly, Timothy — *Actor*
11718 Barrington Court, #252, Los Angeles, CA 90049, USA

Daly, Tyne — *Actress*
700 N Westknoll Dr, #302, Los Angeles, CA 90069, USA

Dam, Kenneth W — *Government Official*
%Universty of Chicago, Law School, 1111 E 60th St, Chicago, IL 60637, USA

Damasio, Antonio R — *Neurologist*
%University of Iowa Hospital, Neurology Dept, Iowa City, IA 52242, USA

Dame Edna (Barry Humphries) — *Comedian*
%Kate Feast, 10 Primrose Hill Studios, Fitzroy Rd, London NW1 8TR, England

Damian, Michael — *Actor*
23501 Park Sorrento, #103, Calabasas, CA 91302, USA

Damiani, Damiano — *Movie Director*
Via Delle Terme Deciane 2, 00153 Rome, Italy

Dammerman, Dennis D — *Businessman*
%Kidder Peabody Group, 10 Hanover Square, New York, NY 10005, USA

Dammeyer, Rodney F — *Businessman*
%Itel Corp, 2 N Riverside Plaza, Chicago, IL 60606, USA

Damon, Mark — *Actor*
%Kazarian/Spencer Assoc, 11365 Ventura Blvd, #100, Studio City, CA 91604, USA

Damon, Stuart — *Actor*
367 N Van Ness Ave, Los Angeles, CA 90004, USA

Damone, Vic — *Singer*
PO Box 2999, Beverly Hills, CA 90213, USA

Damson, Barrie M — *Businessman*
595 Madison Ave, New York, NY 10022, USA

Dana, Bill — *Test Pilot*
%Ames Research Center, DFRF, PO Box 273, Edwards Air Force Base, CA 93523, USA

Dana, Bill — *Comedian*
PO Box 1792, Santa Monica, CA 90406, USA

Dana, Justin — *Actor*
13111 Ventura Blvd, #102, Studio City, CA 91604, USA

Danby, Gordon T — *Inventor (Magnetic Levitation Vehicle)*
%Brookhaven National Laboratory, Upton, NY 11973, USA

Dance, Charles — *Actor*
1311 N California St, Burbank, CA 91505, USA

Dancer, Stanley — *Harness Racing Driver*
1300 S Ocean Blvd, Pompano Beach, FL 33062, USA

Dando, Evan — *Singer (Lemonheads)*
%Gold Mountain, 3575 Cahuenga Blvd W, #450, Los Angeles, CA 90068, USA

Danes, Claire — *Actress*
%Writers & Artists Agency, 924 Westwood Blvd, #900, Los Angeles, CA 90024, USA

Danforth, Douglas D — *Businessman, Baseball Executive*
%Pittsburgh Pirates, Three Rivers Stadium, Pittsburgh, PA 15212, USA

Danforth, William H — *Educator*
%Washington University, President's Office, St Louis, MO 63130, USA

Dangerfield, Rodney — *Comedian*
530 E 76th St, New York, NY 10021, USA

Daniel, Beth — *Golfer*
%Ladies Professional Golf Assn, 2570 Volusia Ave, Daytona Beach, FL 32114, USA

Daniel, Margaret Truman — *Writer*
%Scott Meredith Literary Agency, 845 3rd Ave, New York, NY 10022, USA

Daniel, Richard N — *Businessman*
%Handy & Harman, 555 Theodore Fremd Ave, #A, Rye, NY 10580, USA

Daniel-Lesur, J Y — *Composer*
101 Rue Sadi Carnot, 92800 Puteaux, France

Daniell, Averell E — *Football Player*
1150 Bower Hill Rd, #712-A, Pittsburgh, PA 15243, USA

Daniell, Martin H, Jr — *Coast Guard Admiral*
Commander, Pacific Area, Coast Guard Island, Alameda, CA 94501, USA

Daniell, Robert F — *Businessman*
%United Technologies Corp, United Technologies Building, Hartford, CT 06101, USA

Daniels, Charlie — *Singer, Songwriter*
%High Lonesome Mgmt, 17060 Central Pike, Lebanon, TN 37090, USA

Daniels, Cheryl — *Bowler*
18660 San Juan, Detroit, MI 48221, USA

Daly - Daniels

D

Daniels, Faith *Commentator*
%"Good Morning" Show, CBS-TV, 51 W 52nd St, New York, NY 10019, USA

Daniels, Jeff *Actor*
%PMK Public Relations, 1776 Broadway, #800, New York, NY 10019, USA

Daniels, John H *Businessman*
2472 Parkview Dr, Hamel, MN 55340, USA

Daniels, Mel *Basketball Player*
Circle M Ranch, RR 3, Box 420-A, Sheridan, IN 46069, USA

Daniels, William *Actor*
12805 Hortense St, Studio City, CA 91604, USA

Daniels, William B *Physicist*
100 Tanglewood Lane, Newark, DE 19711, USA

Danielsen, Egil *Track Athlete*
Roreks Gate 9, 2300 Hamar, Norway

Danielson, Donald C *Financier*
%City Securities Corp, 135 N Pennsylvania St, Indianapolis, IN 46204, USA

Danielsson, Bengt F *Anthropologist*
Box 558, Papette, Tahiti

Daniloff, Nicholas *Journalist*
PO Box 892, Chester, VT 05143, USA

Danilova, Alexandra *Ballet Dancer, Choreographer*
100 W 57th St, New York, NY 10019, USA

Danko, Rick *Singer, Bassist (The Band)*
%Skyline Music, RD 1, Jefferson, NH 03583, USA

Dankworth, John *Jazz Pianist, Composer*
Old Rectory, Wavendon, Milton Kenyes MK17 8LT, England

Danneels, Godfried Cardinal *Religious Leader*
Aartsbisdom, Wollemarkt 15, 2800 Mechelen, Belgium

Dannemiller, John C *Businessman*
%Bearings Inc, 3600 Euclid Ave, Cleveland, OH 44115, USA

Danner, Blythe *Actress*
304 21st St, Santa Monica, CA 90402, USA

Danning, Harry *Baseball Player*
212 Fox Chapel Court, Valparaiso, IN 46383, USA

Dano, Linda *Actress*
%"Another World" Show, NBC-TV, 30 Rockefeller Plaza, New York, NY 10020, USA

Danson, Ted *Actor*
%Creative Artists Agency, 9830 Wilshire Blvd, Beverly Hills, CA 90212, USA

Dante, Joe *Movie Director*
2321 Holly Dr, Los Angeles, CA 90068, USA

Dantine, Nikki *Actress*
707 N Palm Dr, Beverly Hills, CA 90210, USA

Dantley, Adrian *Basketball Player, Coach*
%Towson State University, Athletic Dept, Towson, MD 21204, USA

Danton, J Periam *Educator*
%University of California, Library Studies School, Berkeley, CA 94720, USA

Dantzig, George B *Computer Scientist*
821 Tolman Dr, Stanford, CA 94305, USA

Dantzig, Rudi Van *Choreographer*
%Het Nationale Ballet, Waterlooplein 22, 1011 PG Amsterdam, Netherlands

Danza, Tony *Actor*
25000 Malibu Rd, Malibu, CA 90265, USA

Danzig, Frederick P *Editor*
%Advertising Age, Editorial Dept, 220 E 42nd St, New York, NY 10017, USA

Danziger, Jeff *Editorial Cartoonist*
RFD, Plainfield, VT 05667, USA

Daphnis, Nassos *Artist*
362 W Broadway, New York, NY 10013, USA

Darboven, Hanne *Artist*
Am Burgberg 26, 21079 Hamburg, Germany

Darby, Kim *Actress*
%Susan Smith Assoc, 121 N San Vicente Blvd, Beverly Hills, CA 90211, USA

Darehshori, Nader F *Businessman*
%Houghton Mifflin Co, 222 Berkeley St, Boston, MA 02116, USA

Darion, Joe *Librettist, Lyricist*
PO Box 315, Pinnacle Rd, Lynne, NH 03768, USA

Dark, Alvin R *Baseball Player, Manager*
103 Cranberry Way, Easley, SC 29642, USA

Darling, Clifford — *Governor General, Bahamas*
Government House, Government Hill, PO Box N-8301, Nassau NP, Bahamas

Darling, Jennifer — *Actress*
5006 Ventura Canyon Ave, Sherman Oaks, CA 91423, USA

Darling, L Gordon — *Businessman*
%Broken Hill Proprietary Co, 140 William, Melbourne, VIC 3000, Australia

Darling, Ronald M (Ron) — *Baseball Player*
19 Woodland St, Millbury, MA 01527, USA

Darman, Richard G — *Government Official*
1137 Crest Lane, McLean, VA 22101, USA

Darnall, Robert J — *Businessman*
%Inland Steel Industries, 30 W Monroe St, Chicago, IL 60603, USA

Darnton, John — *Journalist*
%New York Times, Editorial Dept, 229 W 43rd St, New York, NY 10036, USA

Darnton, Robert C — *Historian*
6 McCosh Circle, Princeton, NJ 08540, USA

Darragh, John K — *Businessman*
%Stanfast Inc, PO Box 1167, Dayton, OH 45401, USA

Darren, James — *Singer, Actor*
PO Box 1088, Beverly Hills, CA 90213, USA

Darrieux, Danielle — *Actress*
%Nicole Cann, 1 Rue Alfred de Vigny, 75008 Paris, France

Darrow, Henry — *Actor*
%Paul Kohner Inc, 9300 Wilshire Blvd, #555, Beverly Hills, CA 90212, USA

Das Neves, Orlando — *Head of State, Sao Tome & Principe*
%Chief Executive's Office, Prago do Povo, Sao Tome, Sao Tome & Principe

Dasburg, John H — *Businessman*
%Northwest Airlines Corp, 5101 Northwest Dr, St Paul, MN 55111, USA

Dash, Leon D, Jr — *Journalist*
%Washington Post, Editorial Dept, 1150 15th Ave NW, Washington, DC 20071, USA

Dash, Samuel — *Attorney, Watergate Committee Counsel*
110 Newlands St, Chevy Chase, MD 20815, USA

Dassin, Jules — *Movie Director*
Athineon Efivon 8, Athens 11521, Greece

Dassler, Uwe — *Swimmer*
DSF 69337, 1570 Potsdam, Germany

Dater, Judy L — *Photographer*
626 Middlefield Rd, Palo Alto, CA 94301, USA

Daube, David — *Attorney, Educator*
%University of California, Law School, Berkeley, CA 94720, USA

Dauben, William G — *Chemist*
20 Eagle Hill, Kensington, CA 94707, USA

Daugherty, Bradley L (Brad) — *Basketball Player*
%Cleveland Cavaliers, 2923 Statesboro Rd, Richfield, OH 44286, USA

Daulton, Darren A — *Baseball Player*
RR 3, Box 21, Arkansas City, KS 67005, USA

Dauman, Philippe P — *Businessman*
%Viacom Inc, 1515 Broadway, New York, NY 10036, USA

Daume, Willi — *Olympic Official*
Helene-Mayer-Ring 31, 80809 Munich, Germany

Dausset, Jean B G — *Nobel Medicine Laureate*
9 Rue de Villersexel, 75007 Paris, France

Davalos, Richard — *Actor*
2311 Vista Gordo Dr, Los Angeles, CA 90026, USA

Davenport, David — *Educator*
%Pepperdine University, President's Office, Malibu, CA 90265, USA

Davenport, Nigel — *Actor*
5 Ann's Close, Kinnerton St, London SW1, England

Davi, Robert — *Actor*
6568 Beachview Dr, #209, Rancho Palos Verdes, CA 90275, USA

Daviau, Allen — *Cinematographer*
2249 Bronson Hill Dr, Los Angeles, CA 90068, USA

David, Edward E, Jr — *Underwater Sound Engineer*
%EED Inc, Box 435, Bedminster, NJ 07921, USA

David, George A L — *Businessman*
%United Technologies Corp, United Technologies Building, Hartford, CT 06101, USA

David, Hal — *Lyricist*
15 W 53rd St, New York, NY 10019, USA

Darling - David

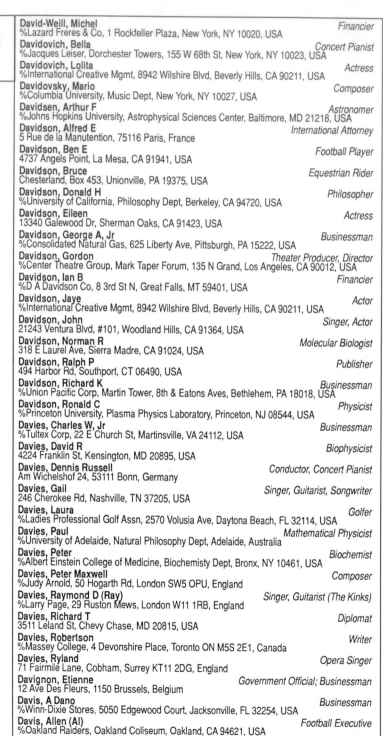

D

David-Weill, Michel — *Financier*
%Lazard Freres & Co, 1 Rockfeller Plaza, New York, NY 10020, USA

Davidovich, Bella — *Concert Pianist*
%Jacques Leiser, Dorchester Towers, 155 W 68th St, New York, NY 10023, USA

Davidovich, Lolita — *Actress*
%International Creative Mgmt, 8942 Wilshire Blvd, Beverly Hills, CA 90211, USA

Davidovsky, Mario — *Composer*
%Columbia University, Music Dept, New York, NY 10027, USA

Davidsen, Arthur F — *Astronomer*
%Johns Hopkins University, Astrophysical Sciences Center, Baltimore, MD 21218, USA

Davidson, Alfred E — *International Attorney*
5 Rue de la Manutention, 75116 Paris, France

Davidson, Ben E — *Football Player*
4737 Angels Point, La Mesa, CA 91941, USA

Davidson, Bruce — *Equestrian Rider*
Chesterland, Box 453, Unionville, PA 19375, USA

Davidson, Donald H — *Philosopher*
%University of California, Philosophy Dept, Berkeley, CA 94720, USA

Davidson, Eileen — *Actress*
13340 Galewood Dr, Sherman Oaks, CA 91423, USA

Davidson, George A, Jr — *Businessman*
%Consolidated Natural Gas, 625 Liberty Ave, Pittsburgh, PA 15222, USA

Davidson, Gordon — *Theater Producer, Director*
%Center Theatre Group, Mark Taper Forum, 135 N Grand, Los Angeles, CA 90012, USA

Davidson, Ian B — *Financier*
%D A Davidson Co, 8 3rd St N, Great Falls, MT 59401, USA

Davidson, Jaye — *Actor*
%International Creative Mgmt, 8942 Wilshire Blvd, Beverly Hills, CA 90211, USA

Davidson, John — *Singer, Actor*
21243 Ventura Blvd, #101, Woodland Hills, CA 91364, USA

Davidson, Norman R — *Molecular Biologist*
318 E Laurel Ave, Sierra Madre, CA 91024, USA

Davidson, Ralph P — *Publisher*
494 Harbor Rd, Southport, CT 06490, USA

Davidson, Richard K — *Businessman*
%Union Pacific Corp, Martin Tower, 8th & Eatons Aves, Bethlehem, PA 18018, USA

Davidson, Ronald C — *Physicist*
%Princeton University, Plasma Physics Laboratory, Princeton, NJ 08544, USA

Davies, Charles W, Jr — *Businessman*
%Tultex Corp, 22 E Church St, Martinsville, VA 24112, USA

Davies, David R — *Biophysicist*
4224 Franklin St, Kensington, MD 20895, USA

Davies, Dennis Russell — *Conductor, Concert Pianist*
Am Wichelshof 24, 53111 Bonn, Germany

Davies, Gail — *Singer, Guitarist, Songwriter*
246 Cherokee Rd, Nashville, TN 37205, USA

Davies, Laura — *Golfer*
%Ladies Professional Golf Assn, 2570 Volusia Ave, Daytona Beach, FL 32114, USA

Davies, Paul — *Mathematical Physicist*
%University of Adelaide, Natural Philosophy Dept, Adelaide, Australia

Davies, Peter — *Biochemist*
%Albert Einstein College of Medicine, Biochemisty Dept, Bronx, NY 10461, USA

Davies, Peter Maxwell — *Composer*
%Judy Arnold, 50 Hogarth Rd, London SW5 0PU, England

Davies, Raymond D (Ray) — *Singer, Guitarist (The Kinks)*
%Larry Page, 29 Ruston Mews, London W11 1RB, England

Davies, Richard T — *Diplomat*
3511 Leland St, Chevy Chase, MD 20815, USA

Davies, Robertson — *Writer*
%Massey College, 4 Devonshire Place, Toronto ON M5S 2E1, Canada

Davies, Ryland — *Opera Singer*
71 Fairmile Lane, Cobham, Surrey KT11 2DG, England

Davignon, Etienne — *Government Official; Businessman*
12 Ave Des Fleurs, 1150 Brussels, Belgium

Davis, A Dano — *Businessman*
%Winn-Dixie Stores, 5050 Edgewood Court, Jacksonville, FL 32254, USA

Davis, Allen (Al) — *Football Executive*
%Oakland Raiders, Oakland Coliseum, Oakland, CA 94621, USA

David-Weill - Davis

Davis, Allen L — *Financier*
%Provident Bank, 1 E 4th St, Cincinnati, OH 45202, USA

Davis, Andrew — *Movie Director*
%The Agency, 1800 Ave of Stars, #400, Los Angeles, CA 90067, USA

Davis, Andrew F — *Conductor*
%Harold Holt Ltd, 31 Sinclair Rd, London W14 ONS, England

Davis, Angela — *Political Activist, Educator*
%University of California, Philosophy Dept, Santa Cruz, CA 15064, USA

Davis, Ann B — *Actress*
1427 Beaver Rd, Ambridge, PA 15003, USA

Davis, Anthony — *Football Player*
9851 Oakwood Crest, Villa Park, CA 92667, USA

Davis, Anthony — *Jazz Pianist, Composer*
%American International Artists, 575 E 89th St, New York, NY 10128, USA

Davis, C Ore — *Businessman*
%MagneTek Inc, 26 Century Blvd, Nashville, TN 37214, USA

Davis, Carl — *Composer*
99 Church Rd, Barnes, London SW13 9HL, England

Davis, Clifton — *Actor*
14431 Ventura Blvd, #275, Sherman Oaks, CA 91423, USA

Davis, Clive J — *Record Producer*
%Arista Records, 6 W 57th St, New York, NY 10019, USA

Davis, Colin R — *Conductor*
%Royal Opera House, Covent Garden, Bow St, London WC2, England

Davis, Dale — *Basketball Player*
%Indiana Pacers, Market Square Arena, 300 E Market St, Indianapolis, IN 46204, USA

Davis, Danny — *Singer, Musician (Nashville Brass)*
%Danny Davis Productions, PO Box 210317, Nashville, TN 37221, USA

Davis, Darrell L — *Financier*
%Chrysler Financial Corp, 27777 Franklin Rd, Southfield, MI 48034, USA

Davis, David — *Bowler*
%DeStasio, 710 Shore Rd, Spring Lake Heights, NJ 07762, USA

Davis, Don H, Jr — *Businessman*
%Rockwell International, 2201 Seal Beach Blvd, Seal Beach, CA 90740, USA

Davis, Donald C — *Navy Admiral*
%Commander-in-Chief's Office, Pacific Fleet, Pearl Harbor, HI 96860, USA

Davis, Edgar G — *Businessman*
%Harvard University, Business-Government Center, Cambridge, MA 02138, USA

Davis, Elizabeth — *Bassist (7 Year Bitch)*
%Talent House,1407 E Madison, #41, Seattle, WA 98122

Davis, Eric K — *Baseball Player*
%Detroit Tigers, Tiger Stadium, 2121 Trumbell, Detroit, MI 48216, USA

Davis, Errol B, Jr — *Businessman*
%WPL Holdings, PO Box 2568, Madison, WI 53701, USA

Davis, Eugene I — *Businessman*
%Emerson Radio Corp, 9 Entin Rd, Parsippany, NJ 07054, USA

Davis, Geena — *Actress*
%Creative Artists Agency, 9830 Wilshire Blvd, Beverly Hills, CA 90212, USA

Davis, George K — *Nutritional Biochemist*
2903 SW 2nd Court, Gainesville, FL 32601, USA

Davis, George W — *Businessman*
%Boston Edison Co, 800 Boylston St, Boston, MA 02199, USA

Davis, Glenn E — *Baseball Player*
5002 Sedona Court, Columbus, GA 31907, USA

Davis, Glenn H — *Track Athlete*
801 Robinson Ave, Barberton, OH 44203, USA

Davis, Glenn W — *Football Player*
5241 Vantage Ave, #102, North Hollywood, CA 91607, USA

Davis, H Lowell — *Businessman*
%Potomac Electric Power Co, 1900 Pennsylvania Ave NW, Washington, DC 20068, USA

Davis, H Thomas (Tommy) — *Baseball Player*
9767 Whirlaway St, Alta Loma, CA 91737, USA

Davis, James B — *Air Force General*
Chief of Staff, SHAPE, CMR 450, APO, AE 09705, USA

Davis, James O — *Physician*
612 Maplewood Dr, Columbia, MO 65203, USA

Davis, James R (Jim) — *Cartoonist (Garfield)*
%United Feature Syndicate, 200 Park Ave, New York, NY 10166, USA

D

Davis - Davis

D

Davis, Jerry R *Businessman*
%Southern Pacific Transportation, 1 Market Plaza, San Francisco, CA 94105, USA

Davis, Jimmie *Governor, LA; Singer*
1331 Lakeridge Dr, Baton Rouge, LA 70802, USA

Davis, John K *Marine Corps General*
%Marine Corps Headquarters, Washington, DC 20380, USA

Davis, Johnny *Basketball Player, Coach*
%Los Angeles Clippers, Sports Arena, 3939 S Figueroa St, Los Angeles, CA 90037, USA

Davis, Josie *Actress*
12190 1/2 Ventura Blvd, Studio City, CA 91604, USA

Davis, Judy *Actress*
129 Bourke St, Woollomooloo, Sydney NSW 2011, Australia

Davis, Katherine W *Financier*
%Shelby Cullom Davis Co, 70 Pine St, New York, NY 10270, USA

Davis, Kenneth *Football Player*
%Buffalo Bills, 1 Bills Dr, Orchard Park, NY 14127, USA

Davis, L Edward *Religious Leader*
%Evangelical Presbyterian Church, 26049 Five Mile Rd, Detroit, MI 48239, USA

Davis, Mac *Singer, Songwriter*
759 Nimes Rd, Los Angeles, CA 90077, USA

Davis, Mark M *Microbiologist*
%Stanford University Medical Center, Microbiology Dept, Stanford, CA 94305, USA

Davis, Mark W *Baseball Player*
843 Farley, Marietta, GA 30067, USA

Davis, N Jan *Astronaut*
%NASA, Johnson Space Center, 2101 NASA Rd, Houston, TX 77058, USA

Davis, Nathaniel *Diplomat*
1783 Longwood Ave, Claremont, CA 91711, USA

Davis, Ossie *Actor*
%Emmalyn II Productions, PO Box 1318, New Rochelle, NY 10802, USA

Davis, Paul H (Butch) *Football Coach*
%University of Miami, Athletic Dept, Coral Gables, FL 33146, USA

Davis, Phyllis *Actress*
%Gage Group, 9255 Sunset Blvd, #515, Los Angeles, CA 90069, USA

Davis, Raymond G *Korean Marine Corps Hero (CMH), General*
2530 Over Lake Ave, Stockbridge, GA 30281, USA

Davis, Raymond, Jr *Chemist*
28 Bergen Lane, Blue Point, NY 11715, USA

Davis, Rennie *Political Activist*
%Birth of a New Nation, 905 S Gilpin, Denver, CO 80209, USA

Davis, Robert D *Businessman*
%Winn-Dixie Stores, 5050 Edgewood Court, Jacksonville, FL 32254, USA

Davis, Robert G *Financier*
%Bank One Columbus, 100 E Broad St, Columbus, OH 43215, USA

Davis, Robert T (Bobby), Jr *Football Player*
3721 Eaglebrook Dr, Gastonia, NC 28056, USA

Davis, Ronald (Ron) *Artist*
PO Box 276, Arroyo Hondo, NM 87513, USA

Davis, Sam H *Businessman*
%Kohler Co, 444 Highland Dr, Kohler, WI 53044, USA

Davis, Sammy L *Vietnam War Army Hero (CMH)*
RR 2, Box 80-A, Flat Rock, IL 62427, USA

Davis, Skeeter *Singer, Songwriter*
508 Seward Rd, Brentwood, TN 37027, USA

Davis, Steve *Snooker Player*
%Matchroom Snooker Ltd, 10 Western Rd, Romford, Essex RM1 3JT, England

Davis, Todd *Actor*
245 S Keystone St, Burbank, CA 91506, USA

Davis, Tom *Basketball Coach*
%University of Iowa, Athletic Dept, Iowa City, IA 52242, USA

Davis, Truman A *Labor Leader*
%Congress of Industrial Unions, 303 Ridge St, Alton, IL 62002, USA

Davis, Walt *Track Athlete*
PO Box 5608, Texarkana, TX 75505, USA

Davis, Walter *Basketball Player*
%Denver Nuggets, McNichols Arena, 1635 Clay St, Denver, CO 80204, USA

Davis, Walter S *Businessman*
%Davis & Kuelthau, 111 E Kilbourn Ave, Milwaukee, WI 53202, USA

Davis - Davis

Davis, William E — Educator
%Louisiana State University, Chancellor's Office, Baton Rouge, LA 70803, USA

Davis, William E — Businessman
%Niagara Mohawk Power, 300 Erie Blvd W, Syracuse, NY 13202, USA

Davis, William G — Government Official, Canada
%Tory Tory DesLauriers, Aetna Tower, #3000, Toronto ON M5K 1N2, Canada

Davis, William R — Financier
%Congress Financial Corp, 1133 Ave of Americas, New York, NY 10036, USA

Davis-Voss, Sammi — Actress
%Lou Coulson, 37 Berwick St, London W1V 3RF, England

Davison, Beverly C — Religious Leader
%American Baptist Churches, PO Box 851, Valley Forge, PA 19482, USA

Davison, Bruce — Actor
PO Box 57593, Sherman Oaks, CA 91413, USA

Davison, Fred C — Educator, Foundation Executive
%National Science Foundation, PO Box 15577, Augusta, GA 30919, USA

Davison, Peter — Actor
%Conway Van Gelder, 18/21 Jermyn St, London SW1V 6HP, England

Dawber, Pam — Actress
%Wings Inc, 2236 Encinitas Blvd, #A, Encinitas, CA 92024, USA

Dawes, Joseph — Cartoonist
20 Church Court, Closter, NJ 07624, USA

Dawkins, Johnny — Basketball Player
%Detroit Pistons, Palace, 2 Championship Dr, Auburn Hills, MI 48057, USA

Dawkins, Peter M (Pete) — Football Player, Businessman
178 Rumson Rd, Rumson, NJ 07760, USA

Dawsey, Lawrence — Football Player
%Tampa Bay Buccaneers, 1 Buccaneer Place, Tampa, FL 33607, USA

Dawson, Andre F — Baseball Player
6295 SW 58th Pl, Miami, FL 33143, USA

Dawson, Buck — Swimming Executive
%Swimming Hall of Fame, 1 Hall of Fame Dr, Fort Lauderdale, FL 33316, USA

Dawson, Dermontti — Football Player
%Pittsburgh Steelers, 3 Rivers Stadium, 300 Stadium Circle, Pittsburgh, PA 15212, USA

Dawson, James J — Financier
%America First Credit Union, PO Box 9199, Ogden, UT 84409, USA

Dawson, Lenny — Football Player, Sportscaster
121 W 48th St, #1906, Kansas City, MO 64112, USA

Dawson, Richard — Actor
1117 Angelo Dr, Beverly Hills, CA 90210, USA

Dawson, Thomas C, II — Economist
50 Portland Rd, Summit, NJ 07901, USA

Day, Bill — Editorial Cartoonist
%Detroit Free Press, Editorial Dept, 321 W Lafayette Blvd, Detroit, MI 48226, USA

Day, Chon — Cartoonist (Brother Sebastian)
22 Cross St, Westerly, RI 02891, USA

Day, Doris — Singer, Actress
%Doris Day Pet Foundation, PO Box 8509, Universal City, CA 91618, USA

Day, Frank R — Financier
%Trustmark National Bank, 248 E Capital St, Jackson, MS 39201, USA

Day, George E (Bud) — Vietnam War Air Force Hero (CMH)
23 Bayshore Dr, Shalimar, FL 32579, USA

Day, Guy — Businessman
%Chiat/Day/Mojo Advertising, 340 Main St, Venice, CA 90291, USA

Day, J Edward — Postmaster General
5804 Brookside Dr, Chevy Chase, MD 20815, USA

Day, Larraine — Actress
10313 Lauriston Ave, Los Angeles, CA 90025, USA

Day, Peter R — Agricultural Scientist
394 Franklin Rd, New Brunswick, NJ 08902, USA

Day, Robert — Cartoonist
Rt 1, Gravette, AR 72736, USA

Day, Robert A — Financier
%Trust Company of the West, 865 S Figoeroa St, Los Angeles, CA 90017, USA

Day, Robin — Journalist
%BBC Studios, Lime Grove, London W12, England

Day, Thomas B — Educator
%San Diego State University, President's Office, San Diego, CA 92182, USA

D

Davis - Day

Day, Todd *Basketball Player*
%Milwaukee Bucks, Bradley Center, 1001 N 4th St, Milwaukee, WI 53203, USA

Day-Lewis, Daniel *Actor*
%Alastair Reid, 65 Connaught St, London W2, England

Dayne, Taylor *Singer, Songwriter*
PO Box 476, Rockville Centre, NY 11571, USA

Days, Drews S, 3rd *Government Official*
%Justice Department, Constitution Ave & 10th St NW, Washington, DC 20530, USA

De Agostini, Doris *Skier*
6780 Airolo, Switzerland

De Almeida, Antonio *Conductor*
%S A Gorlinsky, 34 Dover St, London W1X 4NJ, England

De Bakey, Michael E *Surgeon*
%Baylor College of Medicine Med Center, 1200 Moursund Ave, Houston, TX 77030, USA

De Benning, Burr *Actor*
4235 Kingfisher Rd, Calabasas, CA 91302, USA

De Blanc, Jefferson J *WW II Marine Corps Hero (CMH)*
321 St Martin St, Saint Martinville, LA 70582, USA

De Blasis, Celeste *Writer*
Kemper Campbell Ranch, #9, Victorville, CA 92392, USA

De Boer, Ton *Financier*
%European American Bank, EAB Plaza, Uniondale, NY 11555, USA

De Bont, Jan *Cinematographer*
%Gersh Agency, 232 N Canon Dr, Beverly Hills, CA 90210, USA

De Borchgrave, Arnaud *Editor*
2141 Wyoming Ave NW, Washington, DC 20008, USA

De Branges, Louis *Mathematician*
%Purdue University, Mathematics Dept, West Lafayette, IN 47907, USA

De Burgh, Chris *Singer, Songwriter*
Bargy Castle, Tonhaggard, Wesxord, Ireland

De Camilli, Pietro *Biologist*
%Yale University, School of Medicine, Cell Biology Dept, New Haven, CT 06512, USA

De Carlo, Yvonne *Actress*
PO Box 1012, Santa Paula, CA 93061, USA

De Cordova, Frederick T *Movie, Television Producer, Director*
1875 Carla Ridge, Beverly Hills, CA 90210, USA

De Deo, Joseph E (Joe) *Businessman*
%Young & Rubicam, 285 Madison Ave, New York, NY 10017, USA

De Duve, Christian R *Nobel Medicine Laureate*
80 Central Park West, New York, NY 10023, USA

De Frank, Vincent *Conductor*
%Rhodes College of Music, 2000 N Parkway, Memphis, TN 38112, USA

De Gaspe, Philippe *Publisher*
%Canadian Living Magazine, 50 Holly St, Toronto ON M4S 3B3, Canada

De Gennes, Pierre-Gilles *Nobel Physics Laureate*
11 Place Marcelin-Berthelot, 75005 Paris, France

De Givenchy, Hubert *Fashion Designer*
3 Ave George V, 75008 Paris, France

De Grazia, Sebastian *Writer*
%Princeton University Press, PO Box 190, Princeton, NJ 08544, USA

De Hartog, Jan *Writer*
%Harper & Row Publishers, 10 E 53rd St, New York, NY 10022, USA

De Haven, Gloria *Actress*
88 Central Park West, #12-G, New York, NY 10023, USA

De Havilland, Olivia *Actress*
3 Rue Benouville, 75016 Paris, France

De Hoffmann, Frederic *Research Scientist*
1001 Genter St, #10-F, La Jolla, CA 92037, USA

De Jager, Cornelis *Astronomer*
Zonnenburg 1, 352 NL Utrecht, Netherlands

De Kieweit, Cornelis W *Historian*
22 Berkeley St, Rochester, NY 14607, USA

De Klerk, Frederik W *President, South Africa; Nobel Laureate*
%Deputy President's Office, Union Buildings, Pretoria 0001, South Africa

De Klert, Albert *Concert Organist*
Crayenesterlaan 22, Haarlem, Netherlands

De Kooning, Willem *Artist*
51 Raynor St, Freeport, NY 11520, USA

De Kruif, Robert M — *Financier*
%H F Ahmanson & Co, 4900 Rivergrade Rd, Irwindale, CA 91706, USA

De La Billiere, Peter — *Army General, England*
%Coutts Co, 440 Strand, London WC2R 0QS, England

De La Cruz, Rosie — *Model*
%Next Model Mgmt, 115 E 57th St, #1540, New York, NY 10022, USA

De la Falaise, Lucie — *Model*
%Elite Model Mgmt, 111 E 22nd St, #200, New York, NY 10010, USA

De La Hoya, Oscar — *Boxer*
445 S McDonnell Ave, Los Angeles, CA 90022, USA

De la Puente Raygada, Oscar — *Prime Minister, Peru*
%Prime Minister's Office, Urb Corpac, Calle 1 Oeste S/N, Lima, Peru

De Larrocha, Alicia — *Concert Pianist*
Farmaceutic Carbonell, 46-48 Atic, Barcelona 34, Spain

De Laurentiis, Dino — *Movie Producer*
%De Laurentiis Entertainment, 8670 Wilshire Blvd, Beverly Hills, CA 90211, USA

De Leeuw, Ton — *Composer*
Costeruslaan 4, Hilversum, Netherlands

De Leon Carpio, Ramiro — *President, Guatemala*
%President's Office, Palacio Nacional, Guatemala City, Guatemala

De Los Angeles, Victoria — *Opera Singer*
Avenida de Pedralbes 57, 08034 Barcelona, Spain

De Lucchi, Michele — *Architect*
Via Cenisio 40, 20154 Milan, Italy

De Lue, Donald — *Sculptor*
82 Highland Ave, Leonardo, NJ 07737, USA

De Maiziere, Lothar — *Prime Minister, East Germany*
Am Treptower Park 31, 12435 Berlin, Germany

De Marco, Jean — *Sculptor*
Cervaro 03044, Prov-Frosinore, Italy

De Ment, Jack — *Research Chemist*
%Oregon Health Care Center, 11325 NE Weidler St, #44, Portland, OR 97220, USA

De Merchant, Paul — *Religious Leader*
%Missionary Church, PO Box 9127, Fort Wayne, IN 46899, USA

De Mille, Katherine — *Actress*
%Morg, 10780 Santa Monica Blvd, #280, Los Angeles, CA 90025, USA

De Mita, L Ciriaco — *Prime Minister, Italy*
%Partito Democrazia Cristiana, Piazza de Gesu 46, 00186 Rome, Italy

De Montebello, Philippe L — *Museum Executive*
%Metropolitan Museum of Art, 82nd St & 5th Ave, New York, NY 10028, USA

De Mornay, Rebecca — *Actress*
%J/P/M, 760 N La Cienega Blvd, #200, Los Angeles, CA 90069, USA

De Paiva, James — *Actor*
50 Pierrepont Dr, Ridgefield, CT 06877, USA

De Palma, Brian R — *Movie Director*
270 N Canon Dr, #1195, Beverly Hills, CA 90210, USA

De Peyer, Gervase — *Concert Clarinetist, Conductor*
1250 S Washington St, Alexandria, VA 22314, USA

De Valois, Ninette — *Choreographer*
%Royal Ballet, Bow St, London WC2E 9DD, England

De Vicenzo, Roberto — *Golfer*
%Noni Lann, 5025 Veloz Ave, Tarzana, CA 91356, USA

De Villenejane, Bernard — *Businessman*
%Imetal, Tour Monparnesse, 33 Ave du Maine, 75755 Paris Cedex 1, France

De Vink, Lodewijk J R — *Businessman*
%Warner-Lambert Co, 201 Tabor Rd, Morris Plains, NJ 07950, USA

De Vries, Rimmer — *Economist*
195 Hill & Dale Rd, RFD 3, Lebanon, NJ 08833, USA

De Waart, Edo — *Conductor*
Essenlaan 68, Rotterdam 3016, Netherlands

De Weldon, Felix — *Sculptor*
219 Randolph Pl NE, Washington, DC 20002, USA

De Witt, Bryce S — *Physicist*
%University of Texas, Physics Dept, Austin, TX 78712, USA

De Witt, Joyce — *Actress*
1250 6th St, #403, Santa Monica, CA 90401, USA

De Young, Cliff — *Actor*
766 Kingman Ave, Santa Monica, CA 90402, USA

Deacon, Richard *Sculptor*
%Margarete Roeder Gallery, 545 Broadway, New York, NY 10012, USA

Deacon, Terrence *Neuroanatomist*
%Harvard University, Neuroanatomy Dept, Cambridge, MA 02138, USA

Deakin, Paul *Drummer (Mavericks)*
%AristoMedia, 1620 16th Ave S, Nashville, TN 37212, USA

Deal, Kim *Singer (Breeders)*
%Gold Mountain Ent, 3575 Cahuenga Blvd W, #450, Los Angeles, CA 90068, USA

Dean, Billy *Singer*
PO Box 870689, Stone Mountain, GA 30087, USA

Dean, Charles H, Jr *Government Official*
4021 Topside Rd, Knoxville, TN 37920, USA

Dean, Christopher *Ice Dancer*
PO Box 16, Beeston, Nottingham NG9, England

Dean, Eddie *Singer, Actor*
32161 Sailview Lane, Westlake Village, CA 91361, USA

Dean, Frederick (Fred) *Football Player, Coach*
%Howard University, Athletic Dept, PO Box 844, Washington, DC 20044, USA

Dean, Howard *Governor, VT*
%Governor's Office, Pavilion Office Building, Montpelier, VT 05609, USA

Dean, Howard M, Jr *Businessman*
%Dean Foods Co, 3600 N River Rd, Franklin Park, IL 60131, USA

Dean, Jimmy *Singer*
8000 Centerview Parkway, #400, Cordova, TN 38018, USA

Dean, John G *Diplomat*
29 Blvd Jules Sandeau, 75016 Paris, France

Dean, John W *Watergate Figure*
9496 Rembert Lane, Beverly Hills, CA 90210, USA

Dean, Laura *Choreographer, Composer*
%Dean Dance & Music Foundation, 552 Broadway, #400, New York, NY 10012, USA

Dean, Stafford R *Opera Singer*
%Harrison Parrott, 12 Penzance Place, London W11 4PA, England

Dearden, James *Movie Director*
%International Creative Mgmt, 8942 Wilshire Blvd, Beverly Hills, CA 90211, USA

Dearie, Blossom *Singer*
%Daffodil Records, PO Box 21, East Durham, NY 12423, USA

Deas, Justin *Actor*
%Paradigm Agency, 10100 Santa Monica Blvd, #2500, Los Angeles, CA 90067, USA

Deaver, E Allen *Businessman*
%Armstrong World Industries, 333 W Liberty St, Lancaster, PA 17603, USA

DeBarge, El *Singer*
%Motown Records, 6255 Sunset Blvd, Los Angeles, CA 90028, USA

DeBartolo, Edward J, Jr *Football Executive*
%Edward J DeBartolo Corp, 7620 Market St, Youngstown, OH 44512, USA

DeBartolo, Marie Denise *Businesswoman*
%Edward J DeBartolo Corp, 7620 Market St, Youngstown, OH 44512, USA

DeBerg, Steve *Football Player, Coach*
%New York Giants, Giants Stadium, East Rutherford, NJ 07073, USA

DeBold, Adolfo J *Pathologist, Physiologist*
%Ottawa Civic Hospital, 1053 Carling Ave, Ottawa ON K1Y 4E9, Canada

Debre, Michel *Prime Minister, France*
20 Rue Jacob, 75006 Paris, France

Debreu, Gerard *Nobel Economics Laureate*
267 Gravatt Dr, Berkeley, CA 94705, USA

DeBusschere, David A (Dave) *Basketball Player*
136 Hampton Rd, Garden City, NY 11530, USA

Deby, Idriss *President, Chad*
%President's Office, N'Djamena, Chad

DeCamp, Rosemary *Actress*
317 Camino de Los Colinas, Redondo Beach, CA 90277, USA

DeCastella, F Robert *Track Athlete*
%Australian Institute of Sport, PO Box 176, Belconnen ACT 2616, Australia

Decherd, Robert W *Businessman*
%A H Belo Corp, 400 S Record St, Dallas, TX 75202, USA

DeCinces, Douglas V (Doug) *Baseball Player*
2 Leesburg Court, Newport Beach, CA 92660, USA

Decio, Arthur J *Businessman*
%Skyline Corp, 2520 By-Pass Rd, Elkhart, IN 46514, USA

Decker Slaney, Mary *Track Athlete*
2923 Flintlock St, Eugene, OR 97408, USA

DeCoster, Roger *Motorcycle Racing Rider*
%MC Sports, 1919 Torrance Blvd, Torrance, CA 90501, USA

DeCrane, Alfred C, Jr *Businessman*
%Texaco Inc, 2000 Westchester Ave, White Plains, NY 10604, USA

Decter, Midge *Writer*
120 E 81st St, New York, NY 10028, USA

Dedeaux, Raoul M (Rod) *Baseball Coach*
1430 S Eastman Ave, Los Angeles, CA 90023, USA

Dedini, Eldon L *Cartoonist*
PO Box 1630, Monterey, CA 93942, USA

Dedkov, Anatoli I *Cosmonaut*
%Potchta Kosmonavtov, 141 160 Svyosdny Gorodok, Moskovskoi Oblasti, Russia

Dee, Frances *Actress*
Rt 3, Box 375, Camarillo, CA 93010, USA

Dee, Joey *Singer*
%Evans-Shulman Productions, 2 Professional Dr, #240, Gaithersburg, MD 20879, USA

Dee, Ruby *Actress*
%Emmalyn II Productions, PO Box 1318, New Rochelle, NY 10802, USA

Dee, Sandra *Actress*
%The Agency, 1800 Ave of Stars, #400, Los Angeles, CA 90067, USA

Deeb, Gary *Television Critic*
%Chicago Sun-Times, 401 N Wabash Ave, Chicago, IL 60611, USA

Deedes of Aldington, William F *Government Official, England*
New Hayters, Aldington, Kent, England

Deependra Bir Bikram Shah Dev *Crown Prince, Nepal*
%Narayanhiti Royal Palace, Durbag Marg, Kathmandu, Nepal

Deer, Ada E *Government Official*
4615 N Park Ave, #403, Chevy Chase, MD 20815, USA

Deering, Anthony W *Businessman*
%Rouse Co, 10275 Little Patuxent Parkway, Columbia, MD 21044, USA

Dees, Bowen C *Science Administrator*
140 N Camino Miramonte, Tucson, AZ 85716, USA

Dees, Rick *Entertainer*
PO Box 4352, Los Angeles, CA 90078, USA

DeFeo, Ronald M *Businessman*
%Terex Corp, 500 Post Rd E, Westport, CT 06880, USA

DeFigueiredo, Rui J P *Computer Engineer*
%University of California, Intelligent Sensors/Systems Lab, Irvine, CA 92717, USA

DeFleur, Lois B *Educator*
%State University of New York, President's Office, Binghamton, NY 13902, USA

Deford, Frank *Sportswriter*
Box 1109, Green Farms, CT 06436, USA

DeForest, Roy *Artist*
PO Box 47, Port Costa, CA 94569, USA

DeFranco, Buddy *Musician*
3724 Shoreline Circle, Panama City, FL 32405, USA

DeFrantz, Anita *Sports Executive*
%US Olympic Committee, 1750 E Boulder St, Colorado Springs, CO 80909, USA

DeGeneres, Ellen *Comedienne*
1122 S Roxbury Dr, Los Angeles, CA 90035, USA

DeHaan, Richard W *Religious Leader*
3000 Kraft Ave SE, Grand Rapids, MI 49512, USA

Dehaene, Jean-Luc *Prime Minister, Belgium*
%Prime Minister's Office, 16 Rue de la Loi, 1000 Brussels, Belgium

Dehmelt, Hans G *Nobel Physics Laureate*
1600 43rd Ave E, Seattle, WA 98112, USA

Deighton, Len *Writer*
Fairymount, Blackrock, Dundalk, County Louth, Ireland

Deihl, Richard H *Financier*
%H F Ahmanson Co, 4900 Rivergrade Rd, Irwindale, CA 91706, USA

Deisenhofer, Johann *Nobel Chemistry Laureate*
%Howard Hughes Medical Institute, 5323 Harry Hines Blvd, Dallas, TX 75235, USA

DeJohnette, Jack *Jazz Drummer, Composer*
Silver Hollow Rd, Willow, NY 11201, USA

Dekker, Desmond *Singer*
%Rhino Records, 10635 Santa Monica Blvd, Los Angeles, CA 90025, USA

D

Decker Slaney - Dekker

DeKruif, Robert M — *Financier*
%Home Savings, 4900 Rivergrade Rd, Irwindale, CA 91706, USA

Del Rio, Jack — *Football Player*
%Dallas Cowboys, 1 Cowboys Parkway, Irving, TX 75063, USA

Del Santo, Lawrence A — *Businessman*
%Vons Companies, 618 Michillinda Ave, Arcadia, CA 91007, USA

Del Tredici, David — *Composer*
463 West St, #G-121, New York, NY 10014, USA

Delacote, Jacques — *Conductor*
%IMG Artists, 3 Burlington Lane, Chiswick, London W4 2TH, England

DeLamielleure, Joe — *Football Player*
4001 Longfellow St, Lynchburg, VA 24503, USA

Delaney, Kim — *Actress*
4724 Poe St, Woodland Hills, CA 91364, USA

Delaney, Shelagh — *Playwright*
%Tess Sayle, 11 Jubilee Place, London SW3 3TE, England

Delany, Dana — *Actress*
2522 Beverly Ave, Santa Monica, CA 90405, USA

DeLap, Tony — *Artist*
225 Jasmine St, Corona del Mar, CA 92625, USA

Delchamps, Randy — *Businessman*
%Delchamps Inc, 305 Delchamps Dr, Mobile, AL 36602, USA

Deleage, Jean — *Businessman*
%Burr Egan Deleage Co, 1 Embarcadero Center, San Francisco, CA 94111, USA

DeLeo, Dean — *Guitarist (Stone Temple Pilots)*
%Atlantic Records, 9229 Sunset Blvd, #900, Los Angeles, CA 90069, USA

DeLeo, Robert — *Bassist (Stone Temple Pilots), Composer*
%Atlantic Records, 9229 Sunset Blvd, #900, Los Angeles, CA 90069, USA

Delgado, Pedro — *Cyclist*
%General Delivery, Segovia, Spain

DeLillo, Don — *Writer*
57 Rossmore Ave, Bronxville, NY 10708, USA

Dell, Donald L — *Tennis Player, Attorney*
%ProServ Inc, 888 17th St NW, #1200, Washington, DC 20006, USA

Dell, Michael S — *Businessman*
%Dell Computer Inc, 9505 Arboretum Blvd, Austin, TX 78759, USA

Della Casa-Debeljevic, Lisa — *Opera Singer*
Schloss Gottlieben, Thurgau, Switzerland

Della Femina, Jerry — *Businessman*
%Jerry & Ketchum, 527 Madison Ave, New York, NY 10022, USA

Della Malva, Joseph — *Actor*
%William Morris Agency, 151 S El Camino Dr, Beverly Hills, CA 90212, USA

DelliBovi, Alfred A — *Financier*
%Federal Home Loan Bank, 7 World Trade Center, New York, NY 10048, USA

Dellinger, Walter — *Educator, Attorney*
%Duke University, Law School, Durham, NC 27706, USA

Dello Joio, Norman — *Composer*
PO Box 154, East Hampton, NY 11937, USA

Delo, Ken — *Actor*
161 Avondale Dr, #93-8, Branson, MO 65616, USA

Delon, Alain — *Actor*
%Adel Productions, 4 Rue Chambiges, 75008 Paris, France

Deloria, Victor (Vine), Jr — *Indian Rights Activist*
%CSERA, University of Colorado, Campus Box 339, Boulder, CO 80309, USA

Delors, Jacques L J — *Government Official, France*
19 Blvd de Bercy, 75012 Paris, France

Delp, Alan F — *Businessman*
%American National Bank & Trust, 33 N LaSalle St, Chicago, IL 60602, USA

Delpy, Julie — *Actress*
%William Morris Agency, 151 S El Camino Dr, Beverly Hills, CA 90212, USA

DeLucas, Lawrence — *Astronaut*
%University of Alabama, Comprehensive Cancer Center, Birmingham, AL 35294, USA

Delugg, Milton — *Musician*
2740 Claray Dr, Los Angeles, CA 90077, USA

DeLuise, Dom — *Comedian*
1186 Corsica Dr, Pacific Palisades, CA 90272, USA

DeLuise, Peter — *Actor*
1223 Wilshire Blvd, #411, Santa Monica, CA 90403, USA

Delvecchio, Alex — *Hockey Player*
%Detroit Red Wings, Joe Louis Arena, 600 Civic Center Dr, Detroit, MI 48226, USA

Demarchelier, Patrick — *Photographer*
162 W 21st St, New York, NY 10011, USA

Demarest, Arthur A — *Archeologist*
%Vanderbilt University, Anthropology Dept, Nashville, TN 37235, USA

Demars, Bruce — *Navy Admiral*
Director, Naval Nuclear Propulsion, Navy Dept, Washington, DC 20362, USA

DeMent, Iris — *Singer, Songwriter*
%Warner Bros Records, 75 Rockefeller Plaza, New York, NY 10019, USA

Demers, Jacques — *Hockey Coach*
%Jacques Demers Restaurant, 28100 Franklin Rd, Southfield, MI 48034, USA

Demetriadis, Phokion — *Editorial Cartoonist*
3rd September St 174, Athens, Greece

DeMeuse, Donald H — *Businessman*
%Fort Howard Corp, 1919 S Broadway, Green Bay, WI 54304, USA

Demin, Lev S — *Cosmonaut*
%Potchta Kosmonavtov, 141 160 Svyosdny Gorodok, Moskovskoi Oblasti, Russia

Deming, Claiborn P — *Businessman*
%Murphy Oil Corp, 200 Peach St, El Dorado, AK 71730, USA

Demirel, Suleiman — *President, Turkey*
Adalet Partisi, Ankara, Turkey

Demme, Jonathan — *Movie Director*
%Creative Artists Agency, 9830 Wilshire Blvd, Beverly Hills, CA 90212, USA

Demos, John — *Businessman*
%Super Food Services, 3233 Newmark Dr, Miamisburg, OH 45342, USA

Dempsey, J Rickard (Rick) — *Baseball Player*
5641 Mason Ave, Woodland Hills, CA 91367, USA

Dempsey, Jerry E — *Businessman*
%PPG Industries, 5 The Trillium, Pittsburgh, PA 15238, USA

Dempsey, Patrick — *Actor*
1901 Ave of Stars, #620, Los Angeles, CA 90067, USA

Dempsey, Tom — *Football Player*
3201 St Charles Ave, New Orleans, LA 70115, USA

Demus, Jorg — *Concert Pianist*
%LYRA, Doblinger Hauptstr 77-A/10, 1190 Vienna, Austria

Demuth, Richard H — *Attorney, Financier*
5404 Bradley Blvd, Bethesda, MD 20814, USA

Den Herder, Vern — *Football Player*
%General Delivery, Sioux Center, IA 51250, USA

Den Ouden, Willy — *Swimmer*
Goudsewagenstraat 23-B, Rotterdam, Holland

Den Tagayasu — *Choreographer*
%Ondekoza, Koda Performing Arts Co, Sado Island, Japan

Denard, Michael — *Ballet Dancer*
%Paris Opera Ballet, Place de l'Opera, 75009 Paris, France

DeNault, John B — *Businessman*
%20th Century Insurance, 6301 Owensmouth Ave, Woodland Hills, CA 91367, USA

Dench, Judi — *Actress*
%Julian Belfrage, 46 Albermarle St, London W1X 4PP, England

Denenberg, Herbert S — *Educator, Government Official*
PO Box 7301, St Davids, PA 19087, USA

Denes, Agnes C — *Artist*
595 Broadway, New York, NY 10012, USA

Deneuve, Catherine — *Actress*
76 Rue Bonaparte, 75016 Paris, France

Deng Xiaoping — *Chairman, Chinese Communist Party*
%Communist Party Central Committee, Zhonganahai, Beijing, China

Denham, Maurice — *Actor*
44 Brunswick Gardens, #2, London W8, England

Denham, Robert E — *Financier*
%Salomon Inc, 7 World Trade Center, #4300, New York, NY 10048, USA

Denhardt, David T — *Biologist*
%Rutgers University, Nelson Biological Laboratories, Piscataway, NJ 08855, USA

Denig, Thomas H — *Businessman*
%TJ International, 200 E Mallard Dr, Boise, ID 83706, USA

DeNiro, Robert — *Actor*
9544 Hidden Valley Pl, Beverly Hills, CA 90210, USA

D

Delvecchio - DeNiro

D

Denison, Anthony — *Actor*
%United Talent Agency, 9560 Wilshire Blvd, #500, Beverly Hills, CA 90212, USA

Denisse, Jean-Francois — *Astronomer*
48 Rue Monsieur Le Prince, 75006 Paris, France

Denker, Henry — *Playwright*
241 Central Park West, New York, NY 10024, USA

Denlea, Leo E, Jr — *Businessman*
%Farmers Group, 4680 Wilshire Blvd, Los Angeles, CA 90010, USA

Dennehy, Brian — *Actor*
%Susan Smith Assoc, 121 N San Vicente Blvd, Beverly Hills, CA 90211, USA

Dennehy, Kathleen — *Actress*
%Susan Nathe Assoc, 8281 Melrose Ave, #200, Los Angeles, CA 90046, USA

Dennett, Daniel C — *Philosopher*
20 Ironwood Rd, Andover, MA 01845, USA

Denning of Whitechurch, Alfred T — *Judge*
The Lawn, Whitechurch, Hants, England

Dennis, Donna F — *Sculptor*
131 Duane St, New York, NY 10013, USA

Dennis, Leslie E — *Financier*
%Alaska USA Federal Credit Union, 4000 Credit Union Dr, Anchorage, AK 99503, USA

Dennison, Rachel — *Actress*
%Raymond Katz Enterprises, 345 N Maple Dr, #205, Beverly Hills, CA 90210, USA

Denny, Floyd W, Jr — *Pediatrician*
9210 Dodsons Crossroads, Chapel Hill, NC 27516, USA

Denny, James A — *Businessman*
%Sears Roebuck Co, Sears Tower, Chicago, IL 60684, USA

Denny, John A — *Baseball Player*
13430 E Camino la Cebadilla, Tucson, AZ 85749, USA

Denny, Martin — *Composer*
6770 Hawaii Kai Dr, #402, Honolulu, HI 96825, USA

Denny, Robyn — *Artist*
66 Royal Mint St, London E1 8LG, England

Densen-Gerber, Judianne — *Psychiatrist, Social Activist*
%Odyssey Resources Inc, 5 Hedley Farms Rd, Westport, CT 06880, USA

Densmore, John — *Drummer (Doors)*
49 Halderman Rd, Santa Monica, CA 90402, USA

Dent, Frederick B — *Secretary, Commerce*
221 Montgomery St, Spartenburg, SC 29302, USA

Dent, Richard L — *Football Player*
%Chicago Bears, Halas Hall, 250 N Washington Rd, Lake Forest, IL 60045, USA

Dent, Russell E (Bucky) — *Baseball Player*
2606 Verandah Lane, #816, Arlington, TX 76006, USA

Denton (Pepa), Sandi — *Singer (Salt-N-Pepa)*
%International Creative Mgmt, 8942 Wilshire Blvd, Beverly Hills, CA 90211, USA

Denton, Jeremiah A, Jr — *Senator, AL*
Rt 1, Box 305, Theodore, AL 36582, USA

Denver, Bob — *Actor*
%General Delivery, Princeton, WV 24740, USA

Denver, John — *Singer, Songwriter*
PO Box 1587, Aspen, CO 81612, USA

DeOre, Bill — *Editorial Cartoonist*
%Dallas News, Editorial Dept, Communications Center, Dallas, TX 75265, USA

Depardieu, Gerard — *Actor*
4 Place de la Chapale, 75800 Bougival, France

Depardon, Raymond — *Photographer*
18 Bis Rue Henri Barbusse, 75005 Paris, France

Depp, Johnny — *Actor*
%International Creative Mgmt, 8942 Wilshire Blvd, Beverly Hills, CA 90211, USA

DePree, Max O — *Businessman*
%Herman Miller Inc, 855 E Main St, Zeeland, MI 49464, USA

DePreist, James A — *Conductor*
%Oregon Symphony, 711 SW Alder St, #200, Portland, OR 97205, USA

Der, Lambert — *Editorial Cartoonist*
%Houston Post, Editorial Dept, 4747 Southwest Freeway, Houston, TX 77027, USA

Derbyshire, Andrew G — *Architect*
4 Sunnyfield, Hatfield, Herts AL9 5DX, England

Dercum, Max — *Skier*
PO Box 189, Dillon, CO 80435, USA

Derek, Bo *Actress*
3275 Monticello, Santa Ynez, CA 93460, USA

Derek, John *Actor*
3275 Monticello, Santa Ynez, CA 93460, USA

Dern, Bruce *Actor*
23430 Malibu Colony Rd, Malibu, CA 90265, USA

Dern, Laura *Actress*
415 N Camden Dr, #200, Beverly Hills, CA 90210, USA

Dernesch, Helga *Opera Singer*
Neutorgasse 2/22, 1013 Vienna, Austria

DeRogatis, Al *Football Player*
%Prudential Life Insurance, Prudential Plaza, Newark, NJ 07101, USA

DeRosa, Patricia *Businesswoman*
%The Gap, 900 Cherry Ave, San Bruno, CA 94066, USA

Derosier, Michael *Drummer (Heart)*
%Levine/Schneider, 433 N Camden Dr, Beverly Hills, CA 90210, USA

DeRover, Jolanda *Swimmer*
%Olympic Committee, Surinamestraat 33, 2514 La Harve, Netherlands

Derow, Peter A *Publisher*
PO Box 534, Bedford, NY 10506, USA

Derr, Kenneth T *Businessman*
%Chevron Corp, 225 Bush St, San Francisco, CA 94104, USA

Derr, Roger K *Businessman*
%Ametek Inc, Station Square, Paoli, PA 19301, USA

Derrick, John M, Jr *Businessman*
%Potomac Electric Power Co, 1900 Pennsylvania Ave NW, Washington, DC 20068, USA

Derricks, Cleavant *Actor*
192 Lexington Ave, #1204, New York, NY 10016, USA

Derrida, Jacques *Philosopher*
%Ecole des Hautes Etudes, 54 Blvd Raspail, 75006 Paris, France

Dershowitz, Alan M *Attorney, Educator*
%Harvard University, Law School, Cambridge, MA 02138, USA

DeRusha, William C *Businessman*
%Heilig-Meyers Co, 2235 Staples Mill Rd, Richmond, VA 23230, USA

Derwinski, Edward J *Secretary, Veterans Affairs*
%Derwinski Assoc, 1800 Diagonal Rd, #600, Alexandria, VA 22314, USA

DeSailly, Jean *Actor*
53 Quai des Grands Augustins, 75006 Paris, France

DesBarresm John P *Businessman*
%Transco Energy Co, 2800 Post Oak Blvd, Houston, TX 77056, USA

Desch, Carl W *Financier*
%Citibank (New York State), 99 Garnsey Rd, Pittsford, NY 14534, USA

Deschanel, Caleb *Cinematographer*
7000 Romaine St, Los Angeles, CA 90038, USA

Deschanel, Mary Jo *Actress*
844 Chautauqua Blvd, Pacific Palisades, CA 90272, USA

Deshays, Claudle *Spatinaut, France*
%Hopital Cochin, Rhumatologie Dept, 75000 Paris, France

Desiderio, Robert *Actor*
3960 Laurel Canyon Blvd, #280, Studio City, CA 91604, USA

DeSimone, Livio D *Businessman*
%Minnesota Mining & Manufacturing Co, 3-M Center, St Paul, MN 55144, USA

Desio, Ardito *Explorer, Geologist*
Viale Maino 14, 20129 Milan, Italy

Deskur, Andrzej Maria Cardial *Religious Leader*
%Council for Social Communications, Vatican City, 00120 Rome, Italy

Desny, Ivan *Actor*
Casa al Sole, 6612 Ascona-Collina, Switzerland

Despotopoulos, Johannes (Jan) *Architect*
Anapiron Polemou 7, 115 21 Athens, Greece

Detmar, Ty *Football Player*
%Green Bay Packers, 1265 Lombardi Ave, Green Bay, WI 54304, USA

Detmers, Maruschka *Actress*
%Myriam Bru, 80 Ave Charles de Gaulle, 92200 Neuilly Sur Seine, France

Detweiler, David K *Physiologist*
4636 Larchwood Ave, Philadelphia, PA 19143, USA

Detweiler, Robert C *Educator*
%California State University, President's Office, Dominguez Hills, CA 90747, USA

D

Derek - Detweiler

Deukmejian, George — *Governor, CA*
%Sidley & Austin, 555 W 5th St, Los Angeles, CA 90013, USA

Deutch, John M — *Government Official*
%Central Intelligence Agency, Director's Office, Washington, DC 20505, USA

Deutekom, Cristina — *Opera Singer*
Lancasterdreef 41, Dronten 8251 TG, Holland

Deutsch, Patti — *Actress*
1811 San Ysidro Dr, Beverly Hills, CA 90210, USA

Devan Nair, Chengara Veetil — *President, Singapore*
57 Notre Dame Rd, Bedford, MA 01730, USA

Devaney, Bob — *Football Coach*
4100 "C" St, Lincoln, NE 68510, USA

DeVarona, Donna — *Swimmer, Sportscaster*
%ABC-TV, Sports Dept, 77 W 66th St, New York, NY 10023, USA

Devening, R Randolph — *Businessman*
%Doskocil Companies, 2601 Northwest Expressway, Oklahoma City, OK 73112, USA

Devers, Gail — *Track Athlete*
20214 Leadwell, Canoga Park, CA 91306, USA

DeVille, C C — *Guitarist (Poison)*
%Levine/Schneider, 433 N Camden Dr, Beverly Hills, CA 90210, USA

Deville, Michel — *Movie Director*
36 Rue Reinhardt, 92100 Boulogne, France

Devine, Dan — *Football Coach*
%Sun Angel Foundation, 3800 N Central Ave, #D-3, Phoenix, AZ 85012, USA

DeVita, Vincent T, Jr — *Oncologist*
%Yale Comprehensive Cancer Center, 333 Cedar St, New Haven, CT 06510, USA

DeVito, Danny — *Comedian*
31020 Broad Beach Rd, Malibu, CA 90265, USA

DeVito, Mathias J — *Businessman*
%Rouse Co, 10275 Little Patuxent Parkway, Columbia, MD 21044, USA

Devitt, John — *Swimmer*
46 Beacon Ave, Beacon Hill NSW 2100, Australia

Devlin, Bruce — *Golfer*
5131 Graystone Lane, Houston, TX 77069, USA

Devlin, John — *Actor*
825 N Crescent Heights Blvd, Los Angeles, CA 90046, USA

Devlin, Robert M — *Businessman*
%American General Corp, 2929 Allen Parkway, Houston, TX 77019, USA

DeVos, Richard M — *Businessman*
%Amway Corp, 7575 E Fulton Rd E, Ada, MI 49301, USA

DeVries, William C — *Surgeon*
201 Abraham Flexner Way, #1103, Louisville, KY 40202, USA

Dewar, Donald C — *Government Official, England*
23 Cleveden Rd, Glasgow G12 OPQ, Scotland

Dewar, Jane E — *Editor*
%Legion Magazine, 359 Kent St, #504, Ottawa ON K2P 0R6, Canada

Dewar, Michael J S — *Chemist*
%University of Florida, Chemistry Dept, Gainesville, FL 32611, USA

Dewey, Duane E — *Korean War Marine Corps Hero (CMH)*
Rt 1, Box 494, Irons, MI 49644, USA

DeWilde, Edy — *Museum Director*
%Stedelijk Museum, Amsterdam, Netherlands

Dews, Peter B — *Psychiatrist*
181 Upland Rd, Newtonville, MA 02160, USA

Dexter, Peter W — *Writer*
%Sacramento Bee, Editorial Dept, 21st & "Q" Sts, Sacramento, CA 95852, USA

Dey, Susan — *Actress*
%Litke Gale Madder, 10390 Santa Monica Blvd, #300, Los Angeles, CA 90025, USA

Dezhurov, Vladimir N — *Cosmonaut*
%Potchta Kosmonavtov, 141 160 Svyosdny Gorodok, Moskovskoi Oblasti, Russia

Dezza, Paolo Cardinal — *Religious Leader*
Borgo Santo Spirito 4, 00195 Rome, Italy

Di Beligiojoso, Lodovico B — *Architect*
%Studio Architetti BBPR, 2 Via Dei Chiostri, 20121 Milan, Italy

Di Preta, Tony — *Cartoonist (Rex Morgan MD, Joe Palooka)*
%North America Syndicate, 235 E 45th St, New York, NY 10017, USA

Di Sant'Angelo, Giorgio — *Fashion Designer*
20 W 57th St, New York, NY 10019, USA

Di Stefano, Giuseppe — *Opera Singer*
Via Palatino 10, 20148 Milan, Italy

Di Suvero, Mark — *Sculptor*
PO Box 2218, Long Island, NY 11102, USA

Diamandis, Peter G — *Publisher*
%Diamandis Communications, 1515 Broadway, New York, NY 10036, USA

Diamini, Obed — *Prime Minister, Swaziland*
%Prime Minister's Office, PO Box 395, Mbabane, Swaziland

Diamond (Mike D), Michael — *Rapper (Beastie Boys)*
%Gold Mountain Ent, 3575 Cahuenga Blvd W, #450, Los Angeles, CA 90068, USA

Diamond of Gloucester, John — *Government Official, England*
Aynhoe, Doggetts Wood Lane, Chalfont Saint Giles, Bucks, England

Diamond, Abel J — *Architect*
2 Berkeley St, #600, Toronto ON M5A 2W3, Canada

Diamond, David L — *Composer*
249 Edgerton St, Rochester, NY 14607, USA

Diamond, Jared M — *Biologist*
%University of California Medical School, Physiology Dept, Los Angeles, CA 90024, USA

Diamond, Marian C — *Neuroanatomist*
2583 Virginia St, Berkeley, CA 94709, USA

Diamond, Neil — *Singer, Songwriter*
161 S Mapleton Dr, Los Angeles, CA 90024, USA

Diamond, Seymour — *Physician*
%Diamond Headache Clinic, 5252 N Western Ave, Chicago, IL 60625, USA

Diamont, Don — *Actor*
15045 Sheriew Place, Sherman Oaks, CA 91403, USA

Diana — *Princess of Wales, England*
Wilton Crescent 19, London-Belgravia, England

Diaz, Cameron — *Model, Actress*
351 N Ogden Dr, #7, Los Angeles, CA 90036, USA

DiBiaggio, John A — *Educator*
%Tufts University, President's Office, Medford, MA 02155, USA

DiBona, Richard T — *Businessman*
%M/A-Com Inc, 401 Edgewater Pl, Wakefield, MA 01880, USA

DiCaprio, Leonardo — *Actor*
%Creative Artists Agency, 9830 Wilshire Blvd, Beverly Hills, CA 90212, USA

DiCarlo, Dominick L — *Judge*
%US Court of International Trade, 1 Federal Plaza, New York, NY 10278, USA

DiCenzo, George — *Actor*
RD 1, Box 728, Stone Hollow Farm, Pipersville, PA 18947, USA

Dichter, Misha — *Concert Pianist*
%Shuman Assoc, 120 W 58th St, New York, NY 10019, USA

Dick, Douglas — *Actor*
604 Gretna Green Way, Los Angeles, CA 90049, USA

Dicke, Robert H — *Physicist*
321 Prospect Ave, Princeton, NJ 08540, USA

Dickens, Jimmy — *Singer*
5010 W Concord, Brentwood, TN 37027, USA

Dickey, James — *Writer*
Lake Katherine, 4620 Lelia's Court, Columbia, SC 29206, USA

Dickey, Lynn — *Football Player*
8842 Gallery St, Lenexa, KS 66215, USA

Dickey, William D — *Businessman*
%Cyclops Corp, 301 Grant St, Pittsburgh, PA 15219, USA

Dickinson, Angie — *Actress*
1715 Carla Ridge, Beverly Hills, CA 90210, USA

Dickinson, Bruce — *Singer (Iron Maiden)*
PO Box 391, London W4 1L2, England

Dickinson, Gary — *Bowler*
%Professional Bowlers Assn, 1720 Merriman Rd, Akron, OH 44313, USA

Dickinson, Judy — *Golfer*
%Ladies Professional Golf Assn, 2570 Volusia Ave, Daytona Beach, FL 32114, USA

Dickson, Alan T — *Businessman*
%Ruddick Corp, 2 First Union Center, Charlotte, NC 28282, USA

Dickson, Chris — *Yachtsman*
%International Management Group, 1 Erieview Plaza, #1300, Cleveland, OH 44114, USA

Dickson, Clarence — *Law Enforcement Official*
%Police Department, Metro Justice, 1351 NW 12th St, Miami, FL 33125, USA

D

Di Stefano - Dickson

D

Dickson, Jennifer — *Artist, Photographer*
20 Osborne St, Ottawa ON K1S 4Z9, Canada

Dickson, Neil — *Actor*
%International Creative Mgmt, 76 Oxford St, London W1N 0AX, England

Diddley, Bo — *Singer, Guitarist*
4426 Sorrell Lane SW, Albuquerque, NM 87105, USA

Didion, Joan — *Writer*
%Janklow & Nesbitt, 598 Madison Ave, New York, NY 10022, USA

Diebold, John — *Businessman*
%Diebold Group, PO Box 515, Bedford Hills, NY 10507, USA

Diehl, Digby R — *Journalist*
788 S Lake Ave, Pasadena, CA 91106, USA

Diemeke, Enrique A — *Conductor*
%Flint Symphony Orchestra, 1026 E Kearsley St, Flint, MI 48503, USA

Diener, Theodor O — *Plant Virologist*
4530 Powder Mill Rd, Beltsville, MD 20705, USA

Dierdof, Daniel L (Dan) — *Football Player, Sportscaster*
%ABC-TV, Sports Dept, 77 W 66th St, New York, NY 10023, USA

Dierker, Lawrence E (Larry) — *Baseball Player*
8318 N Tahoe, Houston, TX 77040, USA

Diesel, John P — *Businessman*
1203 Berthea St, Houston, TX 77006, USA

Dietrich, Dena — *Actress*
1155 N La Cienega Blvd, #302, Los Angeles, CA 90069, USA

Dietrich, William A (Bill) — *Journalist*
%Seattle Times, Editorial Dept, Fairview Ave N & John St, Seattle, WA 98111, USA

Diffie, Joe — *Singer*
%Image Management Group, 27 Music Sq E, Nashville, TN 37203, USA

DiGregorio, Ernie — *Basketball Player*
60 Chestnut Ave, Narragansett, RI 02882, USA

Dilfer, Trent — *Football Player*
%Tampa Bay Buccaneers, 1 Buccaneer Place, Tampa, FL 33607, USA

Dill, Guy — *Artist*
819 Milwood Ave, Venice, CA 90291, USA

Dill, Laddie John — *Artist*
1625 Electric Ave, Venice, CA 90291, USA

Dillard, Annie — *Writer*
%Seldes Russell Volkering, 50 W 29th St, New York, NY 10001, USA

Dillard, Harrison — *Track Athlete*
3842 E 147th St, Cleveland, OH 44128, USA

Dillard, William T, Jr — *Businessman*
%Dillard Department Stores, 1600 Cantrell Rd, Little Rock, AR 72201, USA

Dillard, William T, Sr — *Businessman*
%Dillard Department Stores, 1600 Cantrell Rd, Little Rock, AR 72201, USA

Dillehay, Thomas — *Archeologist*
%University of Kentucky, Archeology Dept, Lexington, KY 40506, USA

Diller, Barry — *Entertainment Executive*
1940 Coldwater Canyon Dr, Beverly Hills, CA 90210, USA

Diller, Phyllis — *Comedienne*
163 S Rockingham Rd, Los Angeles, CA 90049, USA

Dillman, Bradford — *Actor*
770 Hot Springs Rd, Santa Barbara, CA 93108, USA

Dillon, C Douglas — *Secretary, Treasury*
1330 Ave of Americas, #2700, New York, NY 10019, USA

Dillon, Matt — *Actor*
%Vic Ramos, 49 W 9th St, New York, NY 10011, USA

Dillon, Melinda — *Actress*
29233 Heathercliff Rd, #3, Malibu, CA 90265, USA

DiMaggio, Dominic P (Dom) — *Baseball Player*
162 Point Rd, Marion, MA 02738, USA

DiMaggio, Joseph P (Joe) — *Baseball Player*
%Morris Engelberg, 3230 Stirling Rd, Hollywood, FL 33021, USA

Dimas, Trent — *Gymnast*
%Gold Cup Gymnastics School, 6009 Carmel Ave NE, Albuquerque, NM 87113, USA

Dimbleby, David — *Journalist, Commentator*
14 King St, Richmond, Surrey TW9 1NF, England

DiMenna, Joseph — *Financier*
%Zweig Companies, 900 3rd Ave, New York, NY 10022, USA

Dickson - DiMenna

D

Dimitriou, Theodore — *Businessman*
%Wallace Computer Services, 4600 W Roosevelt Rd, Hillside, IL 60162, USA

Dimitrova, Ghena — *Opera Singer*
%KKN Enterprises, 277 West End Ave, #11-A, New York, NY 10023, USA

DiNardo, Gerry — *Football Coach*
%Louisiana State University, Athletic Dept, Baton Rouge, LA 70803, USA

Dine, James — *Artist*
%Pace Gallery, 32 E 57th St, New York, NY 10022, USA

Dineen, Kevin — *Hockey Player*
%Hartford Whalers, Coliseum, 242 Trumbell St, #800, Hartford, CT 06103, USA

Dineen, William P (Bill) — *Hockey Coach, Executive*
%Philadelphia Flyers, Spectrum, Pattison Place, Philadelphia, PA 19148, USA

Dini, Lamberto — *Prime Minister, Italy*
%Prime Minister's Office, Piazza Colonna 370, 00187 Rome, Italy

Dinitz, Simcha — *Government Official, Israel*
40 Nayot, Jerusalem, Israel

Dinitz, Simon — *Educator*
298 N Cassidy St, Columbus, OH 43209, USA

Dion (DiMucci) — *Singer*
3099 NW 63rd St, Boca Raton, FL 33496, USA

Dion, Celine — *Singer*
CP 65, Repentiguy PQ J6A 5H7, Canada

Dionne, Joseph L — *Publisher*
%McGraw-Hill Inc, 1221 Ave of Americas, New York, NY 10020, USA

Dionne, Marcel — *Hockey Player*
345 Lexington Ave, Mt Kisco, NY 10549, USA

Diop, Majhemout — *President, Senegal*
210 HCM, Guediawaye, Dakar, Senegal

Diouf, Abdou — *President, Senegal*
%President's Office, Ave Roume, Boite Postale 168, Dakar, Senegal

DiPasqua, Louis S — *Businessman*
%TBC Corp, 4770 Hickory Hill Rd, Memphis, TN 38141, USA

DiPrete, Edward D — *Governor, RI*
555 Wilbur Ave, Cranston, RI 02921, USA

Dirda, Michael — *Literary Critic*
%Washington Post, 1150 15th Ave NW, Washington, DC 20071, USA

Disch, Thomas M — *Writer*
%Karpfinger Agency, 357 W 20th St, New York, NY 10011, USA

Dischinger, Terry — *Basketball Player*
3943 SW Douglas Way, Lake Oswego, OR 97035, USA

Dishman, Cris E — *Football Player*
%Houston Oilers, 6910 Fannin St, Houston, TX 77030, USA

Dishy, Bob — *Actor*
20 E 9th St, New York, NY 10003, USA

Disney, Roy E — *Entertainment Executive*
%Shamrock Broadcasting Co, 4444 Lakeside Dr, Burbank, CA 91505, USA

Distel, Sacha — *Singer, Songwriter*
%Charley Marouani, 37 Rue Marbeuf, 75008 Paris, France

Ditka, Michael K (Mike) — *Football Player, Coach; Sportscaster*
%NBC-TV, Sports Dept, 30 Rockefeller Plaza, New York, NY 10112, USA

Dittenhafer, Brian D — *Financier*
%Collective Bancorp, 158 Philadelphia Ave, Egg Harbor, NJ 08215, USA

Ditz, Nancy — *Track Athlete*
524 Moore Rd, Woodside, CA 94062, USA

DiUlio, Albert J — *Educator*
%Marquette University, President's Office, Milwaukee, WI 53233, USA

Divac, Vlade — *Basketball Player*
%Los Angeles Lakers, Forum, PO Box 10, Inglewood, CA 90306, USA

Diwakar, R R — *Writer*
%Sri Arvind Krupa, 233 Sadashiv Nagar, Bangalore 560006, Karnataka, India

Dix, Drew D — *Vietnam War Army Hero (CMH)*
%Tundra Air, General Delivery, Manley Hot Springs, AR 99756, USA

Dixon, Alan J — *Senator, IL*
7606 Foley Dr, Belleville, IL 62223, USA

Dixon, Becky — *Sportscaster*
%ABC-TV, Sports Dept, 77 W 66th St, New York, NY 10023, USA

Dixon, D Jeremy — *Architect*
47 North Hill, Highgate, London N6, England

Dimitriou - Dixon

D

Dixon, Donna *Actress*
7708 Woodrow Wilson Ave, Los Angeles, CA 90046, USA

Dixon, Frank J *Pathologist, Immunologist*
2355 Avenida de la Playa, La Jolla, CA 92037, USA

Dixon, George F, Jr *Businessman*
1956 S Ocean Lane, Fort Lauderdale, FL 33316, USA

Dixon, Ivan *Actor*
2268 Maiden Lane, Altadena, CA 91001, USA

Dixon, James W *Businessman*
%CompuCom Systems, 10100 North Central Expressway, Dallas, TX 75231, USA

Dixon, Jeane *Psychic, Columnist*
%James L Dixon Co, 1765 "N" St NW, Washington, DC 20036, USA

Dixon, John T *Businessman*
%Penn Traffic Co, 1200 State Fair Blvd, Syracuse, NY 13209, USA

Dixon, Robert J *Air Force General*
29342 Ridgeview Terrace, Boerne, TX 78006, USA

Dixon, Rod *Track Athlete*
22 Entrican Ave, Remuera, Auckland 5, New Zealand

Dixon, Thomas F *Aerospace Engineer*
12 Beech Dr, Brunswick, ME 04011, USA

Djerassi, Carl *Inventor (Oral Contraceptive)*
%Stanford University, Chemistry Dept, Stanford, CA 94305, USA

Djerassi, Isaac *Physician*
2034 Delancey Pl, Philadelphia, PA 19103, USA

Djohar, Said Mohammed *President, Comoros*
%President's Office, Boite Postale 421, Moroni, Comoros

Djuranovic, Veselin *President, Yugoslavia*
%Federal Executive Council, Bul Lenjina 2, 11075 Novi Belgrad, Yugoslavia

Dmytryk, Edward *Movie Director*
3945 Westfall Dr, Encino, CA 91436, USA

Do Nascimento, Alexandre Cardinal *Religious Leader*
Arcebispado, CP 87, Luanda, Angola

Doan, Charles A *Physician*
4935 Oletangy Blvd, Columbus, OH 43214, USA

Doan, D T *Businessman*
%American Mutual Life Insurance, 611 5th Ave, Des Moines, IA 50309, USA

Doar, John *Attorney*
9 E 63rd St, New York, NY 10021, USA

Dobbin, Edmund J *Educator*
%Villanova University, President's Office, Villanova, PA 19085, USA

Dobbs, Glenn *Football Player*
7436 S Winston Place, Tulsa, OK 74136, USA

Dobbs, Mattiwilda *Opera Singer*
1101 S Arlington Ridge Rd, Arlington, VA 22202, USA

Dobkin, Lawrence *Movie Director, Actor*
1787 Old Ranch Rd, Los Angeles, CA 90049, USA

Dobler, Conrad F *Football Player*
8016 State Line Rd, #201, Shawnee Misson, KS 66208, USA

Dobler, David *Religious Leader*
%Presbyterian Church USA, 100 Witherspoon St, Louisville, KY 40202, USA

Dobson, James C *Religious Leader*
%Focus on the Family, 8605 Explorer Dr, Colorado Springs, CO 80920, USA

Dobson, Kevin *Actor*
PO Box 2388, Toluca Lake, CA 91610, USA

Doby, Lawrence E (Larry) *Baseball Player*
45 Nishuane Rd, Montclair, NJ 07042, USA

Dockser, William B *Financier*
%CRIIMI MAE Inc, 1200 Rockville Pike, Rockville, MD 20852, USA

Dockstader, Frederick J *Museum Director*
165 W 66th St, New York, NY 10023, USA

Doctorow, E L *Novelist*
170 Broadview Ave, New Rochelle, NY 10804, USA

Doda, Carol *Exotic Dancer*
PO Box 387, Fremont, CA 94537, USA

Dodd, Carl H *Korean War Army Hero (CMH)*
RR 4, Box 269, Corbin, KY 40701, USA

Dodd, Lamar *Artist*
%University of Georgia, Art Dept, Athens, GA 30602, USA

Dixon - Dodd

Dodd, Michael T (Mike) *Volleyball Player*
%Assn of Volleyball Pros, 15260 Ventura Blvd, #2250, Sherman Oaks, CA 91403, USA

Dodd, Patty D *Volleyball Player*
%Assn of Volleyball Pros, 15260 Ventura Blvd, #2250, Sherman Oaks, CA 91403, USA

Dodge, Brooks *Skier*
Box "C", Jackson, NH 03846, USA

Dodge, Douglas W *Financier*
%Mercantile Bankshares, 2 Hopkins Plaza, Baltimore, MD 21201, USA

Dods, Walter A, Jr *Financier*
%First Hawaiian Bank, 1132 Bishop St, Honolulu, HI 96813, USA

Doering, William V E *Chemist*
53 Francis Ave, Cambridge, MA 02138, USA

Doerr, Harriet *Writer*
%Liz Darhansoff, 1220 Park Ave, New York, NY 10128, USA

Doerr, Robert P (Bobby) *Baseball Player*
33705 Illamo-Agness Rd, Agness, OR 97406, USA

Doherty, Ken *Track Coach*
347 Michigan Ave, Swarthmore, PA 19081, USA

Doherty, Shannen *Actress*
%The Agency, 1800 Ave of Stars, #400, Los Angeles, CA 90067, USA

Dohrmann, Fred G *Businessman*
%Winnebago Industries, PO Box 152, Forest City, IA 50436, USA

Doi, Takako *Government Official, Japan*
%Daini Giinkaikan, 2-1-2 Nagatacho, Chiyodaku, Tokyo, Japan

Doi, Takao *Astronaut, Japan*
%NASDA, 2-1-1 Sengen, Tukubashi, Ibaraki 303, Japan

Dolan, Beverly Franklin (B F) *Businessman*
%Textron Inc, 10 Dorrance St, Providence, RI 02903, USA

Dolan, Charles F *Television Executive*
%Cablevision Systems Corp, 1 Media Crossways, Woodbury, NY 11797, USA

Dolan, Ellen *Actress*
%Don Buchwald Assoc, 10 E 44th St, #500, New York, NY 10017, USA

Dolan, Ronald V *Businessman*
%First Colony Corp, 700 Main St, Lynchburg, VA 24504, USA

Dolby, David C *Vietnam War Army Hero (CMH)*
Pekiomen Ave, PO Box 218, Oaks, PA 19456, USA

Dolby, Ray M *Inventor, Sound Engineer*
%Dolby Laboratories, 100 Potrero Ave, San Francisco, CA 94103, USA

Dolby, Thomas *Singer, Songwriter*
20 Manchester Square, London W1, England

Dolci, Danilo *Writer, Social Worker*
%Centro Iniziative Studi, Largo Scalia 5, Partinico/Palermo, Sicily, Italy

Dold, R Bruce *Journalist*
%Chicago Tribune, Editorial Dept, 435 N Michigan Ave, Chicago, IL 60611, USA

Dole, Elizabeth H *Secretary, Health Human Services; Labor*
%Watergate South, 2510 Virginia Ave NW, #112, Washington, DC 20037, USA

Dole, Vincent P *Medical Researcher*
%Rockefeller University, 1230 York Ave, New York, NY 10021, USA

Doleman, Christopher J (Chris) *Football Player*
%Atlanta Falcons, 2745 Burnett Rd, Suwanee, GA 30174, USA

Dolenz, Ami *Actress*
%Robert P Marcurri, 10600 Holman Ave, #1, Los Angeles, CA 90024, USA

Dolenz, Mickey *Actor, Singer, Drummer (The Monkees)*
8369 Sausalito Ave, #A, West Hills, CA 91304, USA

Dolgen, Jonathan L *Entertainment Executive*
%Viacom Entertainment, 1515 Broadway, New York, NY 10036, USA

Doll, W Richard S *Epidemiologist*
12 Rawlinson Rd, Oxford, England

Dollar, Linda *Volleyball Coach*
%Southwest Missouri State University, Athletic Dept, Springfield, MO 65804, USA

Dollfus, Audouin *Astronomer, Physicist*
%Observatoire de Paris, 5 Place Jules Janssen, 92195 Meudon, France

Domar, Evsey D *Economist*
264 Heath's Bridge Rd, Concord, MA 01742, USA

Dombasle, Arielle *Actress*
%Georges Baume, 201 Rue du Faubourg St Honore, 75008 Paris, France

Dombrowski, Jim *Football Player*
%New Orleans Saints, 1500 Poydras St, New Orleans, LA 70112, USA

D

Domingo, Placido — *Opera Singer*
150 Central Park South, New York, NY 10019, USA

Dominick, Peter H — *Senator, CO*
5050 E Quincy St, Englewood, CO 80110, USA

Domino, (Antoine) Fats — *Singer*
%New Orleans Entertainment, 3530 Rue Delphine, New Orleans, LA 70131, USA

Dominy, Charles E — *Army General*
Director of Army Staff, HdqsUSArmy, Pentagon, Washington, DC 20310, USA

Dommartin, Solveig — *Actress*
%Wim Wenders Filmproduktion, Potsdamerstr 199, 14163 Berlin, Germany

Domnanovich, Joseph (Joe) — *Football Player*
3101 Lorna Rd, #1112, Birmingham, AL 35216, USA

Donahue, Donald J — *Businessman*
%Magma Copper Co, 6400 N Oracle Rd, Tucson, AZ 85704, USA

Donahue, Elinor — *Actress*
4525 Lemp Ave, North Hollywood, CA 91602, USA

Donahue, J Christopher — *Financier*
%Federated Investors, Federal Investors Tower, Pittsburgh, PA 15222, USA

Donahue, John F — *Financier*
%Federated Investors, Federal Investors Tower, Pittsburgh, PA 15222, USA

Donahue, Kenneth — *Museum Director*
245 S Westgate Ave, Los Angeles, CA 90049, USA

Donahue, Phil — *Entertainer*
420 E 54th St, #22-F, New York, NY 10022, USA

Donahue, Richard K — *Businessman*
%Nike Inc, 1 Bowerman Dr, Beaverton, OR 97005, USA

Donahue, Terry — *Football Coach*
%University of California, Athletic Dept, Los Angeles, CA 90024, USA

Donahue, Thomas M — *Atmospheric Scientist*
1781 Arlington Blvd, Ann Arbor, MI 48104, USA

Donahue, Thomas R — *Labor Leader*
%American Federation of Labor, 815 16th St NW, Washington, DC 20006, USA

Donahue, Troy — *Actor*
1022 Euclid Ave, #1, Santa Monica, CA 90403, USA

Donald, David H — *Historian*
PO Box 158, 41 Lincoln Rd, Lincoln Center, MA 01773, USA

Donaldson of Kingsbridge, John G S — *Government Official, England*
17 Edna St, London SW11 3DP, England

Donaldson of Lymington, John F — *Judge*
%Royal Courts of Justice, Strand, London WC2, England

Donaldson, Ray — *Football Player*
%Dallas Cowboys, 1 Cowboys Parkway, Irving, TX 75063, USA

Donaldson, Robert H — *Educator*
%University of Tulsa, President's Office, Tulsa, OK 74104, USA

Donaldson, Roger — *Movie Director*
%Creative Artists Agency, 9830 Wilshire Blvd, Beverly Hills, CA 90212, USA

Donaldson, Samuel A (Sam) — *Commentator*
4452 Volta Place NW, Washington, DC 20007, USA

Donaldson, Simon K — *Mathematician*
%Mathematical Institute, 24-25 St Giles, Oxford OX1 3LB, England

Donat, Peter — *Actor*
1030 Broderick St, San Francisco, CA 94115, USA

Donath, Helen — *Opera Singer*
Bergstr 5, 30900 Wedemark, Germany

Donato, Lawrence E — *Financier*
%BHC Securities, 2005 Market St, Philadelphia, PA 19103, USA

Donegan, Dorothy — *Jazz Pianist*
%Abby Hoffer Entertainments, 223 1/2 E 48th St, New York, NY 10017, USA

Donen, Stanley — *Movie Director*
150 W 56th St, #5004, New York, NY 10019, USA

Donlan, Yolande — *Actress*
11 Mellina Place, London NW8, England

Donleavy, James Patrick (J P) — *Writer*
Levington Park, Mullingar, County Westmeath, Ireland

Donlon, Roger H C — *Vietnam War Army Hero (CMH)*
2101 Wilson Ave, Leavenworth, KS 66048, USA

Donnelley, James R — *Businessman*
%R R Donnelley & Sons, 77 W Wacker Dr, Chicago, IL 60601, USA

Donner, Clive — *Movie Director*
1466 N Kings Rd, Los Angeles, CA 90069, USA

Donner, Jorn J — *Movie Director*
Pohjoisranta 12, 00170 Helsinki 17, Finland

Donner, Richard D — *Movie Director*
%Creative Artists Agency, 9830 Wilshire Blvd, Beverly Hills, CA 90212, USA

Donohoe, Amanda — *Actress*
%Paradigm Agency, 10100 Santa Monica Blvd, #2500, Los Angeles, CA 90067, USA

Donohoe, Peter — *Concert Pianist*
82 Hampton Lane, Solihull, West Midlands B91 2RS, England

Donovan (Leitch) — *Singer, Songwriter*
8528 Walnut Dr, Los Angeles, CA 90046, USA

Donovan, Alan B — *Educator*
%State University of New York College, President's Office, Oneonta, NY 13820, USA

Donovan, Anne — *Basketball Player, Coach*
%Old Dominion University, Athletic Dept, Old Dominion, VA 23529, USA

Donovan, Arthur J (Art), Jr — *Football Player*
%Valley Country Club, 1512 Jeffers Rd, Baltimore, MD 21204, USA

Donovan, Brian — *Journalist*
%Newsday, Editorial Dept, 235 Pinelawn Rd, Melville, NY 11747, USA

Donovan, Jason — *Singer, Actor*
38 Arthur St, South Yarra, Melbourne, VIC 3141, Australia

Donovan, Richard E (Dick) — *Baseball Player*
61 Deep Run Rd, Cohasset, MA 02025, USA

Doob, Joseph L — *Mathematician*
101 W Windsor Rd, #1104, Urbana, IL 61801, USA

Doob, Leonard W — *Psychologist*
6 Clark Rd, Woodbridge, CT 06525, USA

Doody, Alison — *Actress*
%Julian Belfrage, 46 Albermarle St, London W1X 4PP, England

Doohan, James — *Actor*
22132 NE 114th St, Redmond, WA 98053, USA

Dooley, Paul — *Actor*
%Camden ITG Talent Agency, 822 S Robertson Blvd, #200, Los Angeles, CA 90035, USA

Dooley, Vincent J (Vince) — *Football Coach, Administrator*
%University of Georgia, Athletic Dept, Athens, GA 30602, USA

Doran, Ann — *Actress*
1215 Bently Ave, Los Angeles, CA 90049, USA

Dorfi, Klaus G — *Businessman*
%Atlantic Mutual Insurance, 45 Wall St, New York, NY 10005, USA

Dorfman, Ariel — *Playwright*
%Duke University, International Studies Center, 2122 Campus Dr, Durham, NC 27706, USA

Dorfman, Dan — *Columnist, Commentator*
%Money Magazine, Editorial Dept, Rockefeller Center, New York, NY 10020, USA

Dorfman, Henry S — *Businessman*
%Thorn Apple Valley Inc, 18700 W Ten Mile Rd, Southfield, MI 48075, USA

Dorfman, Joel M — *Businessman*
%Thorn Apple Valley Inc, 18700 W Ten Mile Rd, Southfield, MI 48075, USA

Dorfman, Robert — *Economist*
81 Kilburn Rd, Belmont, MA 02178, USA

Dorio, Gabriella — *Track Athlete*
%Federation of Light Athletics, Viale Tiaiano 70, 00196 Rome, Italy

Dority, Douglas H — *Labor Leader*
%United Food & Commercial Workers Union, 1775 "K" St NW, Washington, DC 20006, USA

Dorman, Gerald D — *Physician*
2365 Village Lane, Orient, NY 11957, USA

Dorn, Michael — *Actor*
3751 Multiview Dr, Los Angeles, CA 90068, USA

Dornbusch, Rudiger (Rudi) — *Economist*
%Massachusetts Institute of Technology, Economics Dept, Cambridge, MA 02139, USA

Dorney, Keith R — *Football Player*
2450 Blucher Valley Rd, Sebastopol, CA 95472, USA

Dorrance, Bennett — *Businessman*
%Campbell Soup Co, Campbell Place, Camden, NJ 08103, USA

Dorsett, Anthony D (Tony) — *Football Player*
6005 Kettering Court, Dallas, TX 75248, USA

Dorsey, Jerry E — *Businessman*
%West Co, 101 Gordon Dr, Lionville, PA 19341, USA

Donner - Dorsey

D

Dorso, Betty McLauchlen *Model*
444 N Camden Dr, Beverly Hills, CA 90210, USA

Dortort, David *Movie Producer*
133 Udine Way, Los Angeles, CA 90077, USA

Dos Santos, Alexandre J M Cardinal *Religious Leader*
Paco Arquiepiscopal, Avenida Eduardo Mondlane 1448, CP Maputo, Mozambique

Dos Santos, Jose Eduardo *President, Angola*
%President's Office, Palacio do Povo, Luanda, Angola

Doshi, Balkkrishna V *Architect*
Sangath, Thaltej Rd, Almedabad 380 054, India

Doss, Desmond T *WW II Army Medical Corps Hero (CMH)*
Rt 2, Box 307, Rising Fawn, GA 30738, USA

Doss, Reggie *Football Player*
%St Louis Rams, 100 N Broadway, #2100, St Louis, MO 63102, USA

Doti, James L *Educator*
%Chapman University, President's Office, Orange, CA 92666, USA

Dotrice, Roy *Actor*
Talbot House, 98 St Martin's Lane, London WC2, England

Dotson, Richard E *Baseball Player*
%Hicks, 3410 Heatheridge Lane, Reno, NV 89509, USA

Dotson, Santana *Football Player*
%Tampa Bay Buccaneers, 1 Buccaneer Place, Tampa, FL 33607, USA

Doty, Paul M *Biochemist*
%Harvard University, John F Kennedy Government School, Cambridge, MA 02138, USA

Douaihy, Saliba *Artist*
Vining Rd, Windham, NY 12496, USA

Doubleday, Nelson *Publisher, Baseball Executive*
%New York Mets, Shea Stadium, Flushing, NY 11368, USA

Douglas, Barry *Concert Pianist*
%Terry Harrison Mgmt, 3 Clarendon Court, Charlbury Oxon OX7 3PS, England

Douglas, Cathleen *Lawyer, Conservationist*
815 Connecticut Ave NW, Washington, DC 20006, USA

Douglas, Donna *Actress*
PO Box 49455, Los Angeles, CA 90049, USA

Douglas, Herbert R *Businessman*
%Jamesway Corp, 40 Hartz Way, Seacaucus, NJ 07094, USA

Douglas, Hugh *Football Player*
%New York Jets, 1000 Fulton Ave, Hempstead, NY 11550, USA

Douglas, James (Buster) *Boxer*
700 Ackerman Rd, #628, Columbus, OH 43202, USA

Douglas, Kenneth J *Businessman*
1101 Lake St, #401, Oak Park, IL 60301, USA

Douglas, Kirk *Actor*
805 N Rexford Dr, Beverly Hills, CA 90210, USA

Douglas, Michael *Actor, Director, Producer*
936 Hot Springs Rd, Montecito, CA 93108, USA

Douglas, Mike *Entertainer*
1876 Chartley Rd, Gates Mills, OH 44040, USA

Douglas, Sherman *Basketball Player*
%Boston Celtics, 151 Merrimac St, #500, Boston, MA 02114, USA

Douglass, Bobby *Football Player*
%Lettuce Entertain You Enterprises, 5419 N Sheridan Rd, Chicago, IL 60640, USA

Douglass, Robyn *Actress*
10 Canterbury Court, Wilmette, IL 60091, USA

Dourda, Abu Zaid Umar *Prime Minister, Libya*
%Prime Minister's Office, Bab el Aziziya Barracks, Tripoli, Libya

Dourif, Brad *Actor*
PO Box 3762, Beverly Hills, CA 90212, USA

Dove, Billie *Actress*
%Thunderbird Country Club, 70612 Highway 111, Rancho Mirage, CA 92270, USA

Dove, Rita F *Poet*
1757 Lambs Rd, Charlottesville, VA 22901, USA

Dow, Peggy *Actress*
2121 S Yorktown Ave, Tulsa, OK 74114, USA

Dow, Tony *Actor*
PO Box 1671, Topanga, CA 90290, USA

Dowdle, James C *Businessman*
%Tribune Co, 435 N Michigan Ave, Chicago, IL 60611, USA

Dorso - Dowdle

Dowdle, Walter R — Microbiologis[t]
1708 Mason Mill Rd, Atlanta, GA 30329, USA

Dowell, Anthony J — Ballet Dance[r]
%Royal Ballet, Bow St, London WC2E 9DD, England

Dowhower, Rod — Football Coac[h]
%Vanderbilt University, Athletic Dept, Nashville, TN 37212, USA

Dowiyogo, Bernard — President, Nauru
%Parliament House, Government Offices, Yaren, Nauru

Dowler, Boyd H — Football Player
%Carr Assoc, 2303 S Lila Lane, Tampa, FL 33629, USA

Dowling, Doris — Actress
9026 Elevado Ave, Los Angeles, CA 90069, USA

Dowling, John E — Biologist, Neurobiologist
%Biological Laboratories, 16 Divinity St, Cambridge, MA 02138, USA

Dowling, Vincent — Theater Director, Playwright
%Stepaside House, Box 30-A, East River Rd, Huntington, MA 01050, USA

Down, Sarah — Cartoonist (Betsey's Buddies)
%Playboy Magazine, 919 N Michigan Ave, Chicago, IL 60611, USA

Downes, Edward — Conductor
%Royal Opera House, Covent Garden, London WC2E 9DD, England

Downes, Edward O D — Music Historian
1 W 72nd St, New York, NY 10023, USA

Downes, Terry — Boxer
Milestone, Milespit, Milespit Hill, London NW7, England

Downey, James — Educator
%University of Waterloo, President's Office, Waterloo ON N2L 3G1, Canada

Downey, Morton, Jr — Entertainer
8121 Georgia Ave, Silver Spring, MD 20910, USA

Downey, Robert J — Movie Director
1350 1/2 N Harper Ave, Los Angeles, CA 90046, USA

Downey, Robert, Jr — Actor
29169 Heathercliff Rd, Malibu, CA 90265, USA

Downie, Leonard, Jr — Editor
%Washington Post, Editorial Dept, 1150 15th St NW, Washington, DC 20071, USA

Downing, Alphonso E (Al) — Baseball Player
2800 Neilson Way, #412, Santa Monica, CA 90405, USA

Downing, Brian J — Baseball Player
4861 Silver Spur Lane, Yorba Linda, CA 92686, USA

Downing, George — Surfer
%Get Wet!, 3021 Waialee Ave, Honolulu, HI 96816, USA

Downing, Walt — Football Player
516 E Mohawk Dr, Malvern, OH 44644, USA

Downing, Wayne A — General, Army
CG, US Army Special Operations Command, MacDill Air Force Base, FL 33621, USA

Downing, William E — Businessman
%Pacific Bell Group, 130 Kearny St, San Francisco, CA 94108, USA

Downs, Hugh — Journalist
%"20-20 News" Show, ABC-TV, 157 Columbus Ave, New York, NY 10023, USA

Dowson, Philip M — Architect
%Arup Assoc, 37 Fitzroy Square, London W1P 6AA, England

Doyle, David — Actor
4731 Noeline Ave, Encino, CA 91436, USA

Doyle, Francis C — Financier
%First National Bank of Commerce, 210 Barrone St, New Orleans, LA 70112, USA

Doyle, Larry — Cartoonist (Pogo)
%Los Angeles Times Syndicate, Times Mirror Square, Los Angeles, CA 90053, USA

Doyle, Mathias F — Educator
The Friary, St Bonaventure, NY 14778, USA

Doyle-Murray, Brian — Actor
555 W 57th St, #1230, New York, NY 10019, USA

Dozier, James L — Army General
%David C Brown Enterprises, 12689 New Brittany Blvd, Fort Myers, FL 33907, USA

Dozier, Lamont — Singer, Songwriter
%McMullen Co, 8500 Melrose Ave, #204, West Hollywood, CA 90069, USA

Dr Demento (Barret E Hansen) — Radio Entertainer
6102 Pimenta Ave, Lakewood, CA 90712, USA

Dr Dre (Andre Young) — Rapper
%Rush Artists Mgmt, 1600 Varick St, New York, NY 10013, USA

Dr John *Jazz Pianist, Singer*
%B&B, 532 Burgundy St, New Orleans, LA 70112, USA

Drabek, Douglas D (Doug) *Baseball Player*
15 Red Sable Point, The Woodlands, TX 77380, USA

Drabowsky, Myron W (Moe) *Baseball Player*
4741 Oak Run Dr, Sarasota, FL 34243, USA

Drager, Dieter *Businessman*
%Vista Chemical Co, 900 Threadneedle St, Houston, TX 77079, USA

Dragon, Daryl *Musician (Captain & Tennille)*
7123 Franktown Rd, Carson City, NV 89704, USA

Dragoti, Stan *Movie Director*
1800 Ave of Stars, #430, Los Angeles, CA 90067, USA

Drai, Victor *Movie Producer*
10527 Bellagio Rd, Beverly Hills, CA 90210, USA

Drake, Carl R *Businessman*
%BMC Industries, 2 Appletree Square, Minneapolis, MN 55425, USA

Drake, Frances *Actress*
1511 Summit Ridge Dr, Beverly Hills, CA 90210, USA

Drake, Frank D *Astronomer*
%Lick Observatory, University of California, Santa Cruz, CA 9064, USA

Drake, Juel D *Labor Leader*
%Iron Workers Union, 1750 New York Ave NW, Washington, DC 20006, USA

Drake, Larry *Actor*
2293 Bronson Hill Dr, Los Angeles, CA 90068, USA

Drake, Stanley A *Cartoonist (Juliet Jones, Blondie)*
46 Post Rd E, Westport, CT 06880, USA

Drake, William E. Jr *Businessman*
%Alco Standard Corp, PO Box 834, Valley Forge, PA 19482, USA

Draper, E Lynn, Jr *Businessman*
%American Electric Power Co, 1 Riverside Plaza, Columbus, OH 43215, USA

Drasner, Fred *Publisher*
%New York Daily News, 220 E 42nd St, New York, NY 10017, USA

Dravecky, David F (Dave) *Baseball Player*
19995 Chisholm Trail, Monument, CO 80132, USA

Draves, Vickie *Diver*
29591 Sea Horse Cove, Laguna Niguel, CA 92677, USA

Drazenovich, Chuck *Football Player*
4215 Woodlark Dr, Annandale, VA 22003, USA

Drechsler, Heike *Track Athlete*
Steubenstr 11, 07743 Jena, Germany

Dreesen, Tom *Comedian*
14538 Benefit St, #301, Sherman Oaks, CA 91403, USA

Dreier, R Chad *Businessman*
%Ryland Group, 1100 Broken Land Parkway, Columbia, MD 21044, USA

Drell, Sidney D *Physicist*
570 Alvarado Row, Stanford, CA 94305, USA

Drendel, Frank M *Businessman*
%M/A-Com Inc, 401 Edgewater Place, Wakefield, MA 01880, USA

Drescher, Fran *Actress*
%"The Nanny" Show, Culver Studios, 9336 W Washington Blvd, Culver City, CA 90232, USA

Dresser, Paul A, Jr *Businessman*
%Chesapeake Corp, 1021 E Cary St, Richmond, VA 23219, USA

Dressler, Alan M *Astronomer*
%Carnegie Observatories, 813 Santa Barbara St, Pasadena, CA 91101, USA

Drew, Dennis *Keyboardist (10,000 Maniacs)*
%New York End Ltd, 143 W 69th St, #4-A, New York, NY 10023, USA

Drew, Elizabeth H *Publisher*
%William Morrow Co, 1350 Ave of Americas, New York, NY 10016, USA

Drew, Jane B *Architect*
West Lodge, Cotherstone, Barnard Castle, Co Durham DH12 9PF, England

Drewitz, Henry *Financier*
%Astoria Federal Savings, Astoria Federal Plaza, Lake Success, NY 11042, USA

Drexler, Austin J *Museum Director*
%Museum of Modern Art, 11 W 53rd St, New York, NY 10019, USA

Drexler, Clyde *Basketball Player*
%Houston Rockets, Summit, Greenway Plaza, #10, Houston, TX 77277, USA

Drexler, Millard S *Businessman*
%The Gap Inc, 1 Harrison St, San Francisco, CA 94105, USA

Drexler, Richard A — *Businessman*
%Allied Products Corp, 10 S Riverside Plaza, Chicago, IL 60606, USA

Dreyfus, Lee S — *Governor, WI*
PO Box 1776, Waukeska, WI 53187, USA

Dreyfuss, Richard — *Actor*
2809 Nicholas Canyon Rd, Los Angeles, CA 90046, USA

Drickamer, Harry G — *Chemical Engineer*
304 E Pennsylvania St, Urbana, IL 61801, USA

Driedger, Florence G — *Social Agency Executive*
3833 Montaigne St, Regina SK S4S 3J6, Canada

Driesell, Charles (Lefty) — *Basketball Coach*
%James Madison University, Convocation Center, Harrisonburg, VA 22807, USA

Drinan, Robert F — *Educator, Representative, MA*
%Georgetown University, 1507 Isherwood St NE, #1, Washington, DC 20002, USA

Driscoll, John G — *Educator*
%Iona College, President's Office, New Rochelle, NY 10801, USA

Drivas, Robert — *Actor*
376 Bleecker St, New York, NY 10014, USA

Driver, William J — *Government Official*
215 W Columbia St, Falls Church, VA 22046, USA

Drnovsek, Janez — *Prime Minister, Slovenia*
%Prime Minister's Office, Presemova St 8, 61000 Ljubljana, Slovenia

Drobney, Jaroslav — *Tennis Player*
23 Kenilworth Court, Lower Richmond Rd, London SW15 1EW, England

Dropo, Walter (Walt) — *Baseball Player*
65 E India Row, Boston, MA 02110, USA

Drosdick, John G — *Businessman*
%Ultramar Corp, 2 Pickwick Plaza, Greenwich, CT 06830, USA

Drowley, Jesse R — *WW II Army Hero (CMH)*
523 E Wabash Ave, Spokane, WA 99207, USA

Dru, Joanne — *Actress*
1459 Carla Ridge Dr, Beverly Hills, CA 90210, USA

Drucker, Daniel C — *Engineer*
%University of Florida, Aerospace Engineering Building, Gainesville, FL 32611, USA

Drucker, Mort — *Cartoonist (Ort)*
%Mad Magazine, 485 Madison Ave, New York, NY 10022, USA

Drucker, Peter F — *Educator, Management Consultant, Writer*
636 Wellesley Dr, Claremont, CA 91711, USA

Druckman, Jacob — *Composer*
%Yale University, Music School, New Haven, CT 06520, USA

Druk, Mirchea — *Prime Minister, Moldova*
Str 31 August 123, #7, 277012 Kishinev, Moldova

Drummond, Roscoe — *Columnist*
6637 MacLean Dr, Olde Dominion Sq, McLean, VA 22101, USA

Drury, Allen S — *Writer*
PO Box 647, Tiburon, CA 94920, USA

Drury, James — *Actor*
12755 Mill Ridge, #622, Cypress, TX 77429, USA

Dryer, Fred — *Football Player, Actor*
4117 Radford Ave, Studio City, CA 91604, USA

Dryke, Matt — *Skeet Marksman*
4702 Davis Ave S, #2-B-102, Renton, WA 98055, USA

Drysdale, Cliff — *Tennis Player*
%Landfall, 1801 Eastwood Rd, #F, Wilmington, NC 28403, USA

Du Bain, Myron — *Businessman*
%Fireman Fund Insurance, 1 Market Plaza, #1200, San Francisco, CA 94105, USA

Du Bois, Ja'Net — *Actress*
8306 Wilshire Blvd, #189, Beverly Hills, CA 90211, USA

Du Plessis, Christian — *Opera Singer*
%Performing Arts, 1 Hinde St, London W1M 5RH, England

Du Pont, Pierre S, IV — *Governor, DE*
%Richards Layton Finger, 1 Rodney Square, PO Box 551, Wilmington, DE 19899, USA

Dubbels, Britta — *Model*
%Ford Model Agency, 344 E 59th St, New York, NY 10022, USA

Dubbie, Curtis — *Religious Leader*
%Church of Brethren, 1451 Dundee Ave, Elgin, IL 60120, USA

Dubinbaum, Gail — *Opera Singer*
%Metropolitan Opera Assn, Lincoln Center Plaza, New York, NY 10023, USA

D

Drexler - Dubinbaum

D

Dubinin, Yuri V — *Government Official, Russia*
%Ministry of Foreign Affairs, Smolenskaya-Sennaya 32/34, Moscow, Russia

DuBose, G Thomas — *Labor Leader*
%United Transportation Union, 14600 Detroit Ave, Cleveland, OH 44107, USA

Ducasse, Alain — *Chef*
%Louis XV Restaurant, Hotel de Paris, Monte Carlo, Monaco

Duchesnay, Isabelle — *Figure Skater*
Im Steinach 30, 87561 Oberstdorf, Germany

Duchesnay, Paul — *Figure Skater*
Oeschlesweg 10, 87561 Oberstdorf, Germany

Duchesne, Steve — *Hockey Player*
%Ottawa Senators, 301 Moodie Dr, #200, Nepean ON K2H 9C4, Canada

Duchin, Peter — *Jazz Pianist*
%Peter Duchin Orchestra, 305 Madison Ave, #956, New York, NY 10165, USA

Duchovny, David — *Actor*
%International Creative Mgmt, 8942 Wilshire Blvd, Beverly Hills, CA 90211, USA

Duckworth, Kevin — *Basketball Player*
%Washington Bullets, Capital Centre, 1 Truman Dr, Landover, MD 20785, USA

Duderstadt, James J — *Government Official, Educator*
%National Science Foundation, 1800 "G" St NW, Washington, DC 20550, USA

Dudikoff, Michael — *Actor*
1608 Via Zurita, Palos Verdes, CA 90274, USA

Dudinskyaya, Natalia M — *Ballerina, Ballet Director*
2 Gogol St, #13, St Petersburg 191065, Russia

Dudley, Alfred E — *Businessman*
%First Brands Corp, 83 Wooster Heights Rd, Danbury, CT 06810, USA

Dudley, Bill — *Football Player*
303 Barkley Court, Lynchburg, VA 24503, USA

Dudley, Charles B, III — *Financier*
%Boatmen's Arkansas, 200 W Capitol Ave, Little Rock, AR 72201, USA

Dudley, Chris — *Basketball Player*
%Portland Trail Blazers, 700 NE Multnomah St, #600, Portland, OR 97232, USA

Dudley, Jaquelin — *Microbiologist*
%University of Texas, Microbiology Dept, Austin, TX 78712, USA

Duenkel Fuldner, Virginia — *Swimmer*
707 Eisenhower, Monett, MO 65708, USA

Duerden, John H — *Businessman*
%Reebok International, 100 Technology Center Dr, Stoughton, MA 02072, USA

Duesenberry, James S — *Economist*
25 Fairmont St, Belmont, MA 02178, USA

Duff, Dick — *Hockey Player*
7 Elwood Ave S, Mississauga ON L5G 3JB, Canada

Duff, John B — *Educator*
%Columbia College, President's Office, New York, NY 10027, USA

Duff, John E — *Sculptor*
7 Doyers St, New York, NY 10013, USA

Duff, Thomas M — *Businessman*
%Wellman Inc, 1040 Broad St, Shrewsbury, NJ 07702, USA

Duffey, Joseph D — *Educator*
%US Information Agency, 301 4th St SW, Washington, DC 20547, USA

Duffner, Mark — *Football Coach*
%University of Maryland, Athletic Dept, College Park, MD 20740, USA

Duffy, Brian — *Astronaut*
%NASA, Johnson Space Center, 2101 NASA Rd, Houston, TX 77058, USA

Duffy, Brian — *Editorial Cartoonist*
%Des Moines Register, Editorial Dept, PO Box 957, Des Moines, IA 50304, USA

Duffy, Helen — *Actress*
%Jack Scagnetti Agency, 5330 Lankershim Blvd, North Hollywood, CA 91601, USA

Duffy, J C — *Cartoonist (Fusco Brothers)*
%Universal Press Syndicate, Time-Life Building, New York, NY 10020, USA

Duffy, John — *Composer*
%Meet the Composer, 2112 Broadway, New York, NY 10023, USA

Duffy, Julia — *Actress*
%Lacey, 5699 Kanan Rd, #285, Agoura, CA 91301, USA

Duffy, Kenneth J — *Financier*
%Commerical Union Corp, 1 Beacon St, Boston, MA 02108, USA

Duffy, Patrick — *Actor*
%Montana Power Inc, 10000 Washington Blvd, #411, Culver City, CA 90232, USA

Dubinin - Duffy

Dufour, Val	Actor
40 W 22nd St, New York, NY 10010, USA	
Dugan, Alan	Poet
PO Box 97, Truro, MA 02666, USA	
Dugan, Dennis	Actor
228 N Layton Dr, Los Angeles, CA 90049, USA	
Dugan, Michael J	Air Force General, Association Executive
%National Multiple Sclerosis Society, 733 3rd Ave, New York, NY 10017, USA	
Duggan, Ervin S	Broadcast Executive
%Public Broadcasting Service, 1320 Braddock Place, Alexandria, VA 22314, USA	
Dugger, John S	Artist
501 3rd St, San Francisco, CA 94107, USA	
Duguay, Ron	Hockey Player, Actor
150 E 58th St, #2610, New York, NY 10155, USA	
Duhe, A J	Football Player
379 Coconut Circle, Fort Lauderdale, FL 33326, USA	
Dukakis, Michael S	Governor, MA
%Florida Atlantic University, InterGovernment Studies Dept, Boca Raton, FL 33437, USA	
Dukakis, Olympia	Actress
222 Upper Mountain Rd, Montclair, NJ 07043, USA	
Duke, Bill	Movie Director
%Yagya Productions, PO Box 609, Pacific Palisades, CA 90272, USA	
Duke, Charles M, Jr	Astronaut, Air Force General
280 Lakeview, New Braunfels, TX 78130, USA	
Duke, David A	Businessman
%Corning Inc, Houghton Park, Corning, NY 14831, USA	
Duke, Patty	Actress
2950 E Nettleton Gulch Rd, Coeur D'Alene, ID 83814, USA	
Dukes, David	Actor
255 S Lorraine Blvd, Los Angeles, CA 90004, USA	
Dulbecco, Renato	Nobel Medicine Laureate
7525 Hillside Dr, La Jolla, CA 92037, USA	
Dullea, Keir	Actor
320 Fleming Lane, Fairfield, CT 06430, USA	
Dulles, Avery R	Theologian
%Fordham University, Jesuit Community, Bronx, NY 10458, USA	
Dulo, Jane	Actress
904 Hilldale Ave, #2, Los Angeles, CA 90069, USA	
Dumars, Joe, III	Basketball Player
%Detroit Pistons, Palace, 2 Championship Dr, Auburn Hills, MI 48057, USA	
Dumart, Woody	Hockey
36 Old Farm Rd, Needham, MA 02192, USA	
Dumas, Charlie	Track Athlete
10709 8th Ave, Inglewood, CA 90303, USA	
Dunaway, Faye	Actress
8721 Beverly Blvd, #200, Los Angeles, CA 90048, USA	
Dunbar, Bonnie J	Astronaut
%NASA, Johnson Space Center, 2101 NASA Rd, Houston, TX 77058, USA	
Dunbar, Vaughn	Football Player
%New Orleans Saints, 1500 Poydras St, New Orleans, LA 70112, USA	
Duncan, Angus	Actor
%Thomas Jennings Assoc, 28035 Dorothy Dr, #210-A, Agoura, CA 91301, USA	
Duncan, Charles K	Navy Admiral
813 1st St, Coronado, CA 92118, USA	
Duncan, Charles W, Jr	Secretary, Energy
9 Briarwood Court, Houston, TX 77019, USA	
Duncan, Daniel Kablan	Prime Minister, Cote d'Ivoire
%Prime Minister's Office, Boulevard Clozel, Abidjan, Cote d'Ivoire	
Duncan, David Douglas	Photojournalist
Castellaras Mouans-Sartoux 06370, France	
Duncan, Lindsay	Actor
%Ken McReddie, 91 Regent St, London W1R 7TB, England	
Duncan, Sandy	Actress
44 W 77th St, #1-B, New York, NY 10024, USA	
Duncan, William	Businessman
%Rolls-Royce Ltd, 65 Buckingham Gate, London SW1E 6AT, England	
Duncan, William M	Financier
%Chemical Bank New Jersey, 2 Tower Center, East Brunswick, NJ 08816, USA	

D

Dufour - Duncan

D

Dundee, Angelo — *Boxing Manager*
11264 Pines Blvd, Hollywood, FL 33026, USA

Dunderstadt, James — *Educator*
%University of Michigan, President's Office, Ann Arbor, MI 48109, USA

Dunham, Katherine — *Dancer, Choreographer*
%Katherine Dunham Children's Workshop, 532 N 10th St, East St Louis, IL 62201, USA

Dunham, Russell E — *WW II Army Hero (CMH)*
2144 Sunderland Rd, Jerseyville, IL 62052, USA

Duning, George W — *Composer*
PO Box 190, Borrego Springs, CA 92004, USA

Dunlap, Albert J — *Businessman*
%Scott Paper Co, 1 Scott Plaza, Philadelphia, PA 19113, USA

Dunlap, Carla — *Bodybuilder*
%Diamond, 732 Irvington Ave, Maplewood, NJ 07040, USA

Dunlap, Charles E — *Businessman*
%Crown Central Petroeum Corp, 1 N Charles, Baltimore, MD 21201, USA

Dunlap, Robert H — *WW II Marine Corps Hero (CMH)*
615 N 6th St, Monmouth, IL 61462, USA

Dunleavy, Michael J (Mike) — *Basketball Player, Coach*
%Milwaukee Bucks, Bradley Center, 1001 N 4th St, Milwaukee, WI 53203, USA

Dunlop, John T — *Secretary, Labor*
509 Pleasant St, Belmont, MA 02178, USA

Dunn, Edward K, Jr — *Financier*
%Mercantile Bankshares, 2 Hopkins Plaza, Baltimore, MD 21201, USA

Dunn, Gregory — *Publisher*
%Redbook Magazine, 224 W 57th St, New York, NY 10019, USA

Dunn, Halbert L — *Statistician*
3637 Edelmar Terrace, Rossmoor Silver Spring, MD 20906, USA

Dunn, Holly — *Singer*
PO Box 2525, Hendersonville, TN 37077, USA

Dunn, James Joseph — *Publisher*
%Forbes Magazine, 60 5th Ave, New York, NY 10011, USA

Dunn, Martin — *Editor*
%New York Daily News, Editorial Dept, 220 E 42nd St, New York, NY 10017, USA

Dunn, Mary Maples — *Educator*
%Smith College, President's Office, Northampton, MA 01063, USA

Dunn, Mignon — *Opera Singer*
%Columbia Artists Mgmt Inc, 165 W 57th St, New York, NY 10019, USA

Dunn, Ronnie — *Singer (Brooks & Dunn), Songwriter*
%Bob Titley Entertainments, 706 18th Ave S, Nashville, TN 37203, USA

Dunn, Stephen L — *Religious Leader*
%Churches of God General Conference, 7176 Glenmeadow Dr, Frederick, MD 21703, USA

Dunn, Susan — *Opera Singer*
%Herbert Breslin Inc, 119 W 57th St, New York, NY 10019, USA

Dunn, T R — *Basketball Player*
1014 19th St SW, Birmingham, AL 35211, USA

Dunn, William G — *Publisher*
%US News & World Report Magazine, 2400 "N" St NW, Washington, DC 20037, USA

Dunn, Winfield C — *Governor, TN*
40 Concord Park E, Nashville, TN 37205, USA

Dunne, Dominick — *Writer*
155 E 49th St, New York, NY 10017, USA

Dunne, Griffin — *Actor, Producer*
445 Park Ave, #701, New York, NY 10022, USA

Dunne, John Gregory — *Writer*
%Janklow & Nesbit, 598 Madison Ave, New York, NY 10022, USA

Dunne, Roisin — *Guitarist (7 Year Bitch)*
%Talent House, 1407 E Madison Ave, #41, Seattle, WA 98122, USA

Dunnigan, Frank J — *Publisher*
%Prentice-Hall Inc, Rt 9-W, Englewood Cliffs, NJ 7632, USA

Dunnigan, T Kevin — *Businessman*
%Thomas & Betts Corp, 1555 Lynnfield Ave, Memphis, TN 38119, USA

Dunphy, Jerry — *Commentator*
%KCAL-TV, 5515 Melrose Ave, Los Angeles, CA 90038, USA

Dunphy, Marv — *Volleyball Coach*
%Pepperdine University, Athletic Dept, Malibu, CA 90265, USA

Dunphy, T J Dermot — *Businessman*
%Sealed Air Corp, Park 80 Plaza E, Saddle Park, NJ 07663, USA

Dunsmore, Barrie — *Commentator*
%ABC-TV, News Dept, 1717 De Sales St NW, Washington, DC 20036, USA

Dunst, Kirsten — *Actress*
%Iris Burton Agency, PO Box 15306, Beverly Hills, CA 90209, USA

Dupard, Reggie — *Football Player*
%New England Patriots, Foxboro Stadium, Rt 1, Foxboro, MA 02035, USA

Dupont, Jacques — *Minister of State, Monaco*
%Minister of State's Office, Boite Postale 522, 98015 Monaco-Cedex, Monaco

DuPree, Billy Joe — *Football Player*
PO Box 64744, Dallas, TX 75206, USA

Duque, Pedro — *Astronaut*
%Europe Astronaut Center, Linder Hohe, Box 906096, 51127 Cologne, Germany

Duques, Henry C — *Businessman*
%First Data Corp, 401 Hackensack Ave, Hackensack, NJ 07601, USA

Duquette, Dan — *Baseball Executive*
%Montreal Expos, PO Box 500, Station "M", Montreal PQ H1V 3P2, Canada

Duran Bellen, Sixto — *President, Ecuador*
%President's Office, Gobierno Palacio, Garcia Moreno 1043, Quito, Ecuador

Duran, Roberto — *Boxer*
Nuevo Reperto El Carmen, Panama

Durang, Christopher — *Playwright*
%Helen Merrill Agency, 337 W 22nd St, New York, NY 10011, USA

Durant, Graham J — *Inventor (Antiulcer Compound)*
%Cambridge NeuroScience, 1 Kendall Square, Building 700, Cambridge, MA 02139, USA

Durante, Viviana P — *Ballerina*
20 Bristol Gardens, Little Venice, London W9, England

Duras, Marguerite — *Writer, Movie Director*
5 Rue Saint Benoit, 75006 Paris, France

Durbin, Deanna — *Actress*
BP 767, 75123 Paris Cedex 03, France

Durbin, Mike — *Bowler*
%Professional Bowlers Assn, 1720 Merriman Rd, Akron, OH 44313, USA

Durbridge, Francis — *Writer*
4 Fairacres, Roehampton Lane, London SW15 5LX, England

Durden, Allen — *Football Player*
%Detroit Lions, Silverdome, 1200 Featherstone Rd, Pontiac, MI 48342, USA

Durham, G Robert — *Businessman*
%Walter Industries, 1500 N Dale Mabry Highway, Tampa, FL 33607, USA

Durkin, John A — *Senator, NH*
%Perito Duerk Carlson Pinco, 1140 Connecticut NW, Washington, DC 20036, USA

Durning, Charles — *Actor*
10590 Wilshire Blvd, #506, Los Angeles, CA 90024, USA

Durr Browning, Francoise — *Tennis Player*
195 Rue de Lourmel, 75015 Paris, France

Durrance, Samuel T — *Astronaut, Astronomer*
118 Warwick St, Lutherville, Timonium, MD 21093, USA

Durrett, Joseph P — *Businessman*
%ADVO Inc, 1 Univac Lane, Windsor, CT 06095, USA

Durwood, Edward D — *Entertainment Executive*
%AMC Entertainment, 106 W 4th St, Kansas City, MO 64105, USA

Durwood, Stanley H — *Entertainment Executive*
%AMC Entertainment, 106 W 14th St, Kansas City, MO 64105, USA

Dury, Ian — *Singer*
%Markham & Froggatt Ltd, 4 Windmill St, London W1P 1HF, England

Dusay, Marj — *Actress*
1964 Westwood Blvd, #6-F, New York, NY 10025, USA

Dusenberry, Ann — *Actress*
11726 Laurelwood Dr, Studio City, CA 91604, USA

Dussault, Nancy — *Actress*
12211 Iredell St, North Hollywood, CA 91604, USA

Dutilleux, Henri — *Composer*
12 Rue St Louis-en-l'Isle, 75004 Paris, France

Dutoit, Charles E — *Conductor*
%Montreal Symphony, 85 St Catherine St W, Montreal PQ H2X 3P4, Canada

Dutton, Charles S — *Actor*
%"Live", Fox-TV, PO Box 900, Beverly Hills, CA 90213, USA

Duva, Lou — *Boxing Promoter*
%Main Events, 811 Totowa Rd, #100, Totowa, NJ 07512, USA

Duval, Leon-Etienne Cardinal *Religious Leader*
Notre-Dame d'Afriques, 4 Ave Gurak Ali, Bologhine-Alger, Algeria

Duvall, Jed *Commentator*
%ABC-TV, News Dept, 1717 De Sales St NW, Washington, DC 20036, USA

Duvall, Robert *Actor*
PO Box 520, The Plains, VA 22171, USA

Duvall, Sammy *Water Skier*
PO Box 871, Windermere, FL 34786, USA

Duvall, Shelley *Actress*
9595 Wilshire Blvd, #505, Beverly Hills, CA 90212, USA

Duvall-Hero, Camille *Water Skier*
PO Box 871, Windermere, FL 34786, USA

Duvignaud, Jean *Writer*
28 Rue Saint-Leonard, 1700 La Rochelle, France

Duvillard, Henri *Skier*
Le Mont d'Arbois, 74120 Megere, France

Duwez, Pol E *Applied Physicist*
1535 Oakdale St, Pasadena, CA 91106, USA

Dwight, Edward, Jr *Astronaut*
4022 Montview Blvd, Denver, CO 80207, USA

Dworkin, Andrea *Writer*
%Elaine Markson, 44 Greenwich Ave, New York, NY 10011, USA

Dworkin, David L *Businessman*
%Broadway Stores, 3880 N Mission Rd, Los Angeles, CA 90031, USA

Dworsky, Dan *Football Player, Architect*
%Daniel L Dworsky Assoc, 3530 Wilshire Blvd, #1000, Los Angeles, CA 90010, USA

Dye, Nancy Schrom *Educator*
%Oberlin College, President's Office, Oberlin, OH 44074, USA

Dye, Pat *Football Coach*
%Auburn University, Assistant to the President, Auburn, AL 36831, USA

Dyer, David F *Businessman*
%Home Shopping Network, 2501 118th Ave N, St Petersburg, FL 33716, USA

Dyke, Charles W *Army General, Association Executive*
%International Technical/Trade Assoc, 1330 Connecticut NW, Washington, DC 20036, USA

Dykes Bower, John *Concert Organist*
4-Z Artillery Mansions, Westminster, London SW1, England

Dykstra, John *Artist, Animator, Cinematographer*
%Apogee Productions, PO Box 7340, Van Nuys, CA 91409, USA

Dykstra, Lenny K (Len) *Baseball Player*
236 Chester Rd, Devon, PA 19333, USA

Dylan, Bob *Singer, Songwriter*
PO Box 870, Cooper Station, New York, NY 10276, USA

Dysart, Richard *Actor*
654 Copeland Court, Santa Monica, CA 90405, USA

Dyson, Freeman J *Physicist*
105 Battle Road Circle, Princeton, NJ 08540, USA

Dystel, Oscar *Publisher*
The Springs, Purchase Hills Dr, Purchase, NY 10577, USA

Dzau, Victor *Medical Researcher*
%Stanford University Hospital, Cardiovascular Medicine Division, Stanford, CA 94305, USA

Dzeliwe *Queen Regent, Swaziland*
%Royal Palace, Mbabane, Swaziland

Dzhanibekov, Vladimir A *Cosmonaut, Air Force General*
%Potchta Kosmonavtov, 141 160 Svyosdny Gorodok, Moskovskoi Oblasti, Russia

Dzundza, George *Actor*
%Gersh Agency, 232 N Canon Dr, Beverly Hills, CA 90210, USA

E

Eade, George J — *Air Force General*
1131 Sunnyside Dr, Healdsburg, CA 95448, USA

Eads, Ora Wilbert — *Religious Leader*
%Christian Congregation, 804 W Hemlock St, LaFollette, TN 37766, USA

Eagleburger, Lawrence S — *Secretary, State*
%Baker Worthington Assoc, 801 Pennsylvania Ave NW, #800, Washington, DC 20004, USA

Eagleson, Alan — *Labor Leader*
%NHL Players Assn, 37 Maitland St, Toronto ON M4Y 1CB, Canada

Eagleton, Thomas F — *Senator, MO*
%Thompson & Mitchell, 1 Mercantile Center, #3400, St Louis, MO 63101, USA

Eakes, Bobbie — *Actress*
5420 Sylmar Dr, #202, Van Nuys, CA 91401, USA

Eakin, Richard R — *Educator*
%East Carolina University, Chancellor's Office, Greenville, NC 27858, USA

Eanes, Antonio dos Santos R — *President, Portugal; Army General*
%Partido Renovador Democratico, Travessa do Falo 9, 1200 Lisbon, Portugal

Earl, Anthony S — *Governor, WI*
%Quarles & Brady, 1st Wisconsin Plaza, 1 S Pinckney St, Madison, WI 53703, USA

Earle, Eyvind — *Artist*
2900 Santa Lucia Ave, Carmel-by-the-Sea, CA 93923, USA

Earle, Steve — *Singer, Songwriter*
%UNI Records, MCA, 70 Universal City Plaza, Universal City, CA 91608, USA

Earle, Sylvia Alice — *Oceanographer*
12812 Skyline Blvd, Oakland, CA 94619, USA

Earley, Anthony F, Jr — *Businessman*
%Detroit Edison Co, 2000 2nd Ave, Detroit, MI 48226, USA

Earley, Michael M — *Businessman*
%Triton Group, 550 W "C" St, San Diego, CA 92101, USA

Earnhardt, R Dale — *Auto Racing Driver*
1951 Old Cuthbert Rd, Cherry Hill, NJ 08034, USA

Easterbrook, Leslie — *Actress, Singer*
5111 Louise Ave, Encino, CA 91316, USA

Easterly, David E — *Businessman*
%Cox Enterprises, 1400 Lake Hearn Dr NE, Atlanta, GA 30319, USA

Eastman, Benjamin — *Track Athlete*
1025 3100 Rd, Hotchkiss, CO 81419, USA

Eastman, Dean E — *Physicist*
806 Pines Bridge Rd, Ossining, NY 10562, USA

Eastman, John — *Attorney*
%Eastman & Eastman, 39 W 54th St, New York, NY 10019, USA

Easton, Bill — *Track Coach*
1024 Mississippi St, Lawrence, KS 66044, USA

Easton, Sheena — *Singer*
7095 Hollywood Blvd, #469, Los Angeles, CA 90028, USA

Eastwick-Field, Elizabeth — *Architect*
Low Farm, Low Rd, Denham, Eye, Suffolk IP21 5ET, England

Eastwood, Clint — *Actor, Director*
%Malpaso Productions, 4000 Warner Blvd, Bldg 154, #206, Burbank, CA 91522, USA

Easum, Donald B — *Diplomat*
801 West End Ave, #3-A, New York, NY 10025, USA

Eaton, Dan L — *Hematologist*
%Genentech Inc, 460 Point San Bruno Blvd, South San Francisco, CA 94080, USA

Eaton, John C — *Composer*
4585 N Hartstrait Rd, Bloomington, IN 47404, USA

Eaton, Robert J — *Businessman*
%Chrysler Corp, 1200 Chrysler Dr, Highland Park, MI 48288, USA

Eaton, Shirley — *Actress*
8 Harley St, London W1N 2AB, England

Eban, Abba — *Government Official, Israel*
PO Box 394, Hertzelia, Israel

Ebb, Fred — *Lyricist, Librettist*
%San Remo Apts, 146 Central Park West, #14-D, New York, NY 10023, USA

Ebbers, Bernard J — *Businessman*
%LDDS Communications, 515 E Amite St, Jackson, MS 39201, USA

Ebbesen, Samuel E — *Army General*
Dep Asst Sec of Defense (Manpower/Personnel), Pentagon, Washington, DC 20301, USA

Eber, Lorenz — *Inventor (Mechanical Cable Drum Lifter)*
927 1st Ave, Grafton, WI 53024, USA

Eade - Eber

E

Eberhard, Wolfram — *Sociologist*
22479 Golf Club Dr, Twain Harte, CA 95383, USA

Eberhart, Richard — *Poet*
80 Lyme Rd, #32, Kendal at Hanover, NH 03755, USA

Eberle, William D — *Government Official, Businessman*
13 Garland Rd, Concord, MA 01742, USA

Ebersol, Dick — *Television Executive*
%NBC-TV, Sports Dept, 30 Rockefeller Plaza, New York, NY 10112, USA

Ebersole, Christine — *Actress*
20 W 90th St, #A, New York, NY 10024, USA

Ebert, Douglas E — *Financier*
%Michigan National Corp, 27777 Inkster Rd, Farmington Hills, MI 48334, USA

Ebert, James D — *Embryologist, Biologist*
Winthrop House, 4100 N Charles St, Baltimore, MD 21218, USA

Ebert, Peter — *Opera Director*
Col di Mura, 06010 Lippiano, Italy

Ebert, Robert D — *Physician*
16 Brewster Rd, Wayland, MA 01778, USA

Ebert, Roger J — *Movie Critic*
PO Box 146366, Chicago, IL 60614, USA

Ebina, Masao — *Financier*
%Nikko Securities, 1 World Financial Center, 200 Liberty St, New York, NY 10281, USA

Ebsen, Bonnie — *Actress*
PO Box 356, Agoura, CA 91376, USA

Ebsen, Buddy — *Actor*
605 Via Horquilla, Palos Verdes Estates, CA 90274, USA

Eccles of Chute, David M — *Government Official, England*
Dean Farm, Chute Near Andover, Hants, England

Eccles, John Carew — *Nobel Medicine Laureate*
Ca'a La Gra', 6611 Contra, Ticino, Switzerland

Eccles, Spencer F — *Financier*
%First Security Corp, 79 S Main St, Salt Lake City, UT 84111, USA

Ecclestone, Bernie — *Auto Racing Executive*
%Formula One, 8 Rue de La Concorde, 70008 Paris, France

Ecevit, Bulent — *Prime Minister, Turkey*
Or-An Sehri 69/5, Ankara, Turkey

Echement, John R — *Financier*
%Integra Financial Corp, 4 PPG Place, Pittsburgh, PA 15222, USA

Echeverria Alvarez, Luis — *President, Mexico*
Magnolia 131, San Jeronimo Lidice, Magdalena Contreras, CP 10200, Mexico

Eckersley, Dennis L — *Baseball Player*
263 Morse Rd, Sudbury, MA 01776, USA

Eckhardt, William B — *Financier*
%Alaska USA Federal Credit Union, 4000 Credit Union Dr, Anchorage, AK 99503, USA

Eco, Umberto — *Writer, Educator*
Piazza Castello 13, 20121 Milan, Italy

Edberg, Stefan — *Tennis Player*
Spinnaregatan 6, 593 00 Vastervik, Sweden

Eddington, Paul — *Actor*
%International Creative Mgmt, 76 Oxford St, London W1N 0AX, England

Eddy, Duane — *Singer, Songwriter*
%Talent Consultants Int'l, 1560 Broadway, #1308, New York, NY 10036, USA

Eddy, Edward D — *Educator*
%Eddy Group, PO Box 5161, Wakefield, RI 02880, USA

Edel, J Leon — *Writer, Educator*
3817 Lurline Dr, Honolulu, HI 96816, USA

Edelin, Kenneth C — *Physician*
720 Harrison Ave, Boston, MA 02118, USA

Edell, Marc Z — *Attorney*
%Budd Larner Gross, 150 J F Kennedy Parkway, #1000, Short Hills, NJ 07078, USA

Edelman, Brad M — *Football Player*
%Edelman Productions, PO Box 512, Kenner, LA 70063, USA

Edelman, Gerald M — *Nobel Medicine Laureate*
%Scripps Research Institute, Neurobiology Dept, La Jolla, CA 92037, USA

Edelman, Herbert — *Actor*
%Green/Siegel Assoc, 8730 Sunset Blvd, #470, Los Angeles, CA 90069, USA

Edelman, Marian Wright — *Association Executive*
%Children's Defense Fund, 25 "E" St NW, Washington, DC 20001, USA

Eberhard - Edelman

Edelmann, Otto K　　　　　　　　　　　　　　　　*Opera Singer*
Breitenfurterstr 547, 1238 Wein-Kalksburg, Austria
Edelstein, Jean　　　　　　　　　　　　　　　　　　　*Artist*
354 Broome St, #5-A, New York, NY 10013, USA
Edelstein, Victor　　　　　　　　　　　　　　　*Fashion Designer*
3 Stanhope Mews West, London SW7 5RB, England
Eden of Winton, John　　　　　　　*Government Official, England*
41 Victoria Rd, London W8 5RH, England
Eden, Barbara　　　　　　　　　　　　　　　　　　*Actress*
9816 Denbigh Dr, Beverly Hills, CA 90210, USA
Eder, Richard G　　　　　　　　　　　　　　　　*Literary Critic*
%Los Angeles Times, Editorial Dept, Times Mirror Sq, Los Angeles, CA 90053, USA
Ederle Reichenback, Gertrude　　　　　　　*Channel Swimmer*
4465 SW 37th Ave, Fort Lauderdale, FL 33312, USA
Edgar, James (Jim)　　　　　　　　　　　　　　　*Governor, IL*
%Governor's Office, State House, #207, E Capitol Ave, Springfield, IL 62706, USA
Edge (Dave Evans), The　　　　　　　　　　*Guitarist (U-2)*
%Principle Mgmt, 30-32 Sir John Rogersons Quay, Dublin 2, Ireland
Edison, Harry (Sweets)　　　　　　　　　　　*Jazz Trumpeter*
%Thomas Cassidy Inc, 0366 Horseshoe Dr, Basalt, CO 81621, USA
Edler, Inge G　　　　　　　　　　　　　　　　　*Cardiologist*
%University Hospital, Cardiology Dept, Lund, Sweden
Edley, Christopher F　　　　　　　　　　*Association Director*
%United Negro College Fund, 500 E 62nd St, New York, NY 10021, USA
Edlund, Richard　　　　　　　　　　　　　　*Cinematographer*
%Boss Film Corp, 13335 Maxella Ave, Marina del Rey, CA 90292, USA
Edmiston, Mark M　　　　　　　　　　　　　　　*Publisher*
%Jordan Edmiston Group, 885 3rd Ave, New York, NY 10022, USA
Edmond, John M　　　　　　　　　　　　*Marine Geochemist*
21 Robin Hood Rd, Arlington, MA 02174, USA
Edmonds, Albert J (Al)　　　　　　　　　*Air Force General*
Director, Command Control Communications, HqUSAF, Washington, DC 20318, USA
Edmonds, Walter D　　　　　　　　　　　　　　　　*Writer*
27 River St, Concord, MA 01742, USA
Edmund-Davies, Herbert E　　　　　　　　　　　　　*Judge*
5 Gray's Inn Sq, London WC1R 5EU, England
Edsall, John T　　　　　　　　　　　　　*Biological Chemist*
985 Memorial Dr, #503, Cambridge, MA 02138, USA
Edson, Hilary　　　　　　　　　　　　　　　　　　*Actress*
%Kroll, 2211 Broadway, New York, NY 10024, USA
Eduardo dos Santos, Jose　　　　　　　　*President, Angola*
%President's Office, Palacio do Povo, Luanda, Angola
Edward　　　　　　　　　　　　　　　　　　*Prince, England*
%Buckingham Palace, London SW1A 1BA, England
Edwards, Anthony　　　　　　　　　　　　　　　　　*Actor*
15260 Ventura Blvd, #1420, Sherman Oaks, CA 91403, USA
Edwards, Barbara　　　　　　　　　　　　　*Actress, Model*
%Hansen, 7767 Hollywood Blvd, #202, Los Angeles, CA 90046, USA
Edwards, Benjamin F, III　　　　　　　　　　　　　*Financier*
%A G Edwards Inc, 1 N Jefferson Ave, St Louis, MO 63103, USA
Edwards, Blake　　　　　　　　　　*Movie Director, Producer*
11777 San Vicente Blvd, #501, Los Angeles, CA 90049, USA
Edwards, Blue　　　　　　　　　　　　　*Basketball Player*
%Vancouver Grizzlies, 788 Beatty St, #300, Vancouver BC V6B 2M1, Canada
Edwards, Charles C　　　　　　　　　　　　　　　*Physician*
Keeney Park, 10666 N Torrey Pines Rd, La Jolla, CA 92037, USA
Edwards, Charles C, Jr　　　　　　　　　　　　　*Publisher*
%Des Moines Register & Tribune, 715 Locust St, Des Moines, IA 50309, USA
Edwards, Earl　　　　　　　　　　　　　　*Football Player*
%MATOL/KM Distributor, 6612 S Forest Ave, Tempe, AZ 85283, USA
Edwards, Edwin W　　　　　　　　　　　　　　*Governor, LA*
8114 Walden Rd, Baton Rouge, LA 70808, USA
Edwards, Harry　　　　　　　　　　*Educator, Social Activist*
%University of California, Sociology Dept, Berkeley, CA 94720, USA
Edwards, James　　　　　　　　　　　　　*Basketball Player*
%Portland Trail Blazers, 700 NE Multnomah St, #600, Portland, OR 97232, USA
Edwards, James B　　　　　　　　*Secretary, Energy; Governor, SC*
100 Venning St, Mount Pleasant, SC 29464, USA

E

Edwards, Joe F, Jr	*Astronaut*
%NASA, Johnson Space Center, 2101 NASA Rd, Houston, TX 77058, USA	
Edwards, LaVell	*Football Coach*
%Brigham Young University, Athletic Dept, Provo, UT 84602, USA	
Edwards, Lena F	*Physician*
821 Woodland Dr, Lakewood, NJ 08701, USA	
Edwards, Ralph	*Entertainer*
1717 N Highland Ave, #1018, Los Angeles, CA 90028, USA	
Edwards, Robert A (Bob)	*Commentator*
%National Public Radio, News Dept, 635 Massachusetts NW, Washington, DC 20001, USA	
Edwards, Robert D	*Businessman*
%Minnesota Power, 30 W Superior St, Duluth, MN 55802, USA	
Edwards, Robert G	*Physiologist*
Duck End Farm, Dry Drayton, Cambridge CB3 8DB, England	
Edwards, Robert J	*Editor*
%Sunday Mirror, Editorial Dept, 33 Holborn, London EC1P 1DG, England	
Edwards, Stephanie	*Actress*
8075 W 3rd St, #303, Los Angeles, CA 90048, USA	
Edwards, Teresa	*Basketball Player*
Teresa Edwards Dr, Cairo, GA 31728, USA	
Edwards, Vince	*Actor*
PO Box 642, Malibu, CA 90265, USA	
Edwardson, John A	*Businessman*
%UAL Corp, 1200 E Algonquin Rd, Elk Grove Township, IL 60005, USA	
eFresco, Paolo	*Businessman*
%General Electric Co, 3135 Easton Turnpike, Fairfield, CT 06431, USA	
Egal, Mohamed Ibrahim	*Prime Minister, Somalia*
PO Box 27, Via Asha, Mogadishu, Somalia	
Egan, Peter	*Actor*
%James Sharkey Assoc, 21 Golden Square, London W1R 3PA, England	
Egan, Richard J	*Businessman*
%EMC Corp, 171 South St, Hopkinton, MA 01748, USA	
Egan, William P	*Businessman*
%Burr Egan Deleage Co, 1 Post Office Sq, Boston, MA 02109, USA	
Egdahl, Richard H	*Surgeon*
333 Commonwealth Ave, #23, Boston, MA 02115, USA	
Ege, Julie	*Actress*
Vestre Nostegate 29, 3300 Hokksund, Norway	
Egeberg, Roger O	*Physician, Government Official*
330 Independence St SW, 4039 North Bldg, Washington, DC 20201, USA	
Eggar, Samantha	*Actress*
15430 Mulholland Dr, Los Angeles, CA 90077, USA	
Egger, Roscoe L (Roger), Jr	*Government Official*
3831 S Via de La Urraca, Green Valley, AZ 85614, USA	
Eggert, Nicole	*Actress*
20591 Queens Park, Huntington Beach, CA 92646, USA	
Eggert, Robert J	*Economist*
%Eggert Economic Enterprises, PO Box 2243, Sedona, AZ 86339, USA	
Eggleston, William	*Photographer, Artist*
%Robert Miller Gallery, 41 E 57th St, New York, NY 10022, USA	
Egoyan, Atom	*Movie Director*
%Ego Film Artists, 80 Niagara St, Toronto ON M5V 1C5, Canada	
Eguchi, Tomonaru	*Businessman*
%Daihatsu Motor Co, 1-1 Daihatsucho, Ikeda City 563, Japan	
Ehlers, Beth	*Actress*
%William Morris Agency, 151 S El Camino Dr, Beverly Hills, CA 90212, USA	
Ehlers, Walter D	*WW II Army Hero (CMH)*
8382 Valley View, Buena Park, CA 90620, USA	
Ehlo, Craig	*Basketball Player*
%Atlanta Hawks, 1 CNN Center, South Tower, Atlanta, GA 30303, USA	
Ehmann, Frank A	*Businessman*
864 Bryant Ave, Winnetka, IL 60093, USA	
Ehrenreich, Barbara	*Women's Activist, Writer*
%Farrar Straus Giroux, 19 Union Square W, New York, NY 10003, USA	
Ehrlich, Paul R	*Population Biologist*
%Stanford University, Biological Sciences Dept, Stanford, CA 94305, USA	
Ehrlich, S Paul, Jr	*Physician*
6512 Lakeview Dr, Falls Church, VA 22041, USA	

Edwards - Ehrlich

190   V.I.P. Address Book

Ehrlichman, John D — *Government Official*
795 Hammond Dr NE, #2208, Atlanta, GA 30328, USA

Ehrling, Sixten — *Conductor*
%Park Ten, 10 W 66th St, New York, NY 10023, USA

Eichelberger, Charles B — *Army General*
PO Box 2569, Peachtree City, GA 30269, USA

Eichenfield, Samuel L — *Financier*
%GFC Financial, Dial Corporate Center, Phoenix, AZ 85077, USA

Eichhorn, Lisa — *Actress*
19 W 44th St, #1000, New York, NY 10036, USA

Eichner, Ira A — *Businessman*
%AAR Corp, 1111 Nicholas Blvd, Elk Grove Village, IL 60007, USA

Eickhoff, Gottfred — *Artist*
Frederiksholms Kanal 28-C, Copenhagen, Denmark

Eigen, Manfred — *Nobel Chemistry Laureate*
%Max Planck Institute, Am Fassburg, 37077 Gottingen-Nikolausberg, Germany

Eigsti, Roger H — *Businessman*
%SAFECO Corp, SAFECO Plaza, Seattle, WA 98185, USA

Eikenberry, Jill — *Actress*
2183 Mandeville Canyon Rd, Los Angeles, CA 90049, USA

Eilbacher, Lisa — *Actress*
2949 Deep Canyon Dr, Beverly Hills, CA 90210, USA

Eilber, Janet — *Actress*
%Irv Schechter Co, 9300 Wilshire Blvd, #410, Beverly Hills, CA 90212, USA

Eilenberg, Samuel — *Mathematician*
%Columbia University, Mathematics Dept, New York, NY 10027, USA

Eilts, Hermann F — *Diplomat*
67 Cleveland Rd, Wellesley, MA 02181, USA

Einhom, Edward M (Eddie) — *Baseball Executive*
%Chicago White Sox, 333 W 35th St, Chicago, IL 60616, USA

Einstein (Super Dave Osborn), Bob — *Actor*
%Super Dave Productions, 10 Universal City Plaza, #3100, Universal City, CA 91608, USA

Eisen, Herman N — *Immunologist*
9 Homestead St, Waban, MA 02168, USA

Eisenberg, Kenneth S — *Restoration Expert*
1000 Connecticut Ave NW, Washington, DC 20036, USA

Eisenberg, Lee B — *Editor*
%Edison Project, 333 Main St, Knoxville, TN 37902, USA

Eisenberg, Leon — *Psychiatrist*
9 Clement Cir, Cambridge, MA 02138, USA

Eisenhower, Milton S — *Educator*
3900 N Charles St, #1102, Baltimore, MD 21218, USA

Eisenman, Peter D — *Architect*
%Eisenman Architects, 40 W 25th St, New York, NY 10010, USA

Eisenmann, Ike — *Actor*
%Gage Group, 9255 Sunset Blvd, #515, Los Angeles, CA 90069, USA

Eisner, Michael D — *Entertainment Executive*
%Walt Disney Productions, 500 S Buena Vista St, Burbank, CA 91521, USA

Eisner, Robert — *Economist*
800 Lincoln St, Evanston, IL 60201, USA

Eisner, Thomas — *Biologist*
%Cornell University, Biological Sciences Dept, Ithaca, NY 14853, USA

Eisner, Will — *Cartoonist (The Spirit)*
%Poorhouse Press, 8333 W McNab Rd, #114, Tamarac, FL 33321, USA

Eitan, Raphael — *Army General, Israel*
%Tsomet Party, Knesset, Tel-Aviv, Israel

Eizenstat, Stuart E — *Government Official, Diplomat*
%Powell Goldstein Frazer, 1001 Pennsylvania Ave NW, Washington, DC 20004, USA

Ekandem, Dominic Cardinal — *Religious Leader*
PO Box 286, Garki, Abiya, Nigeria

Ekberg, Paul H — *Businessman*
%Birmingham Steel Corp, 1000 Urban Center Dr, Birmingham, AL 35242, USA

Ekland, Britt — *Actress*
16830 Ventura Blvd, #501, Encino, CA 91436, USA

Eklund, A Sigvard — *Nuclear Physicist*
Krapfenwaldgasse 48, 1190 Vienna, Austria

Elam, Jack — *Actor*
PO Box 5718, Santa Barbara, CA 93150, USA

E

Elbert, P O — *Businessman*
%Pitt-Des Moines Inc, 3400 Grand Ave, Pittsburgh, PA 15225, USA

Elcar, Dana — *Actor*
22920 Hatteras St, Woodland Hills, CA 91367, USA

Elder, Mark P — *Conductor*
%National Opera, London Coliseum, St Martin's Lane, London WC2N 4ES, Engla

Elder, R Lee — *Golfer*
%Lee Elder Enterprises, 4130 Palm-Sire Dr W, #302-B, Pompano Beach, FL 33069, USA

Elder, Will — *Cartoonist (Little Annie Fanny)*
143 Booth Ave, Englewood, NJ 07631, USA

Elders, M Jocelyn — *Government Official, Pediatrician*
%University of Arkansas Medical School, Pediatrics Dept, Little Rock, AR 72205, USA

Eldredge, Todd — *Figure Skater*
6000 Revere Pl, #H, Bloomfield, MI 48301, USA

Elegant, Robert S — *Writer*
Manor House, Middle Green Near Langley, Bucks SL3 6BS, England

Eleniak, Erika — *Actress*
%Deloitte/Touche, 2029 Century Park East, #300, Los Angeles, CA 90067, USA

Elewonibi, Mohammed (Moe) — *Football Player*
%Buffalo Bills, 1 Bills Dr, Orchard Park, NY 14127, USA

Elfman, Danny — *Singer, Composer*
%Oingo Bongo Secret Society, PO Box 10815, Beverly Hills, CA 90213, USA

Elfner, Albert H, III — *Financier*
%Keystone Group, 200 Berkeley St, Boston, MA 02116, USA

Elg, Taina — *Actress*
%Michael Hartig Agency, 114 E 28th St, New York, NY 10016, USA

Elgart, Larry J — *Orchestra Leader*
%Ted Schmidt Assoc, 2149 NE 63rd St, Fort Lauderdale, FL 33308, USA

Elia, Claudio — *Businessman*
%Air & Water Technologies, US Highway 22 W & Station Rd, Branchburg, NJ 08876, USA

Elias, Eddie — *Bowling Executive*
%Professional Bowlers Assn, 1720 Merriman Rd, Akron, OH 44313, USA

Elias, Eliane — *Jazz Pianist*
%Denon Records, 130 W 50th St, #1915, New York, NY 10020, USA

Elias, John W — *Businessman*
%Seagull Energy Corp, 1001 Fannin St, Houston, TX 77002, USA

Elias, Peter — *Electrical Engineer*
102 Raymond St, Cambridge, MA 02140, USA

Elias, Rosalind — *Opera Singer*
%Columbia Artists Mgmt Inc, 165 W 57th St, New York, NY 10019, USA

Elicker, Paul H — *Businessman*
5600 Wisconsin Ave, #19-D, Chevy Chase, MD 20815, USA

Elie, Mario — *Basketball Player*
%Houston Rockets, Summit, Greenway Plaza, #10, Houston, TX 77277, USA

Eliel, Ernest L — *Chemist*
725 Kenmore Rd, Chapel Hill, NC 27514, USA

Elinson, Jack — *Sociomedical Scientist*
1181 E Laurelton Parkway, Teaneck, NJ 07666, USA

Elion, Gertrude B — *Nobel Medicine Laureate*
1 Banbury Lane, Chapel Hill, NC 27514, USA

Elish, Herbert — *Businessman*
%Weirton Steel Corp, 400 Three Springs Dr, Weirton, WV 26062, USA

Elisha, Walter Y — *Businessman*
%Springs Industries, 205 N White St, Fort Hill, SC 29715, USA

Elizabeth — *Queen Mother, Great Britain*
%Clarence House, London SW1A 1BA, England

Elizabeth II — *Queen, Great Britain & Northern Ireland*
%Buckingham Palace. London SW1A 1AA, England

Elizondo, Hector — *Actor*
5040 Noble Ave, Sherman Oaks, CA 91403, USA

Elkes, Joel — *Psychiatrist*
%University of Louisville, Psychiatry/Behavioral Sci Dept, Louisville, KY 40292, USA

Elkes, Terrence A — *Businessman*
%Apollo Partners, 350 Park Ave, New York, NY 10022, USA

Elkins, Hillard — *Theater Producer*
1335 N Doheny Dr, Los Angeles, CA 90069, USA

Ellard, Henry — *Football Player*
%Washington Redskins, 21300 Redskin Park Dr, Ashburn, VA 22011, USA

Elbert - Ellard

Ellena, Jack — *Football Player*
%Mountain Meadow Ranch, PO Box 610, Susanville, CA 96130, USA

Ellenstein, Robert — *Actor*
5215 Sepulveda Blvd, #23-F, Culver City, CA 90230, USA

Ellenthal, Ira — *Publisher*
%New York Daily News, 220 E 42nd St, New York, NY 10017, USA

Eller, Carl — *Football Player, Executive*
1035 Washburn Ave N, Minneapolis, MN 55411, USA

Ellerbee, Linda — *Commentator*
%Lucky Duck Productions, 96 Morton St, #600, New York, NY 10014, USA

Elliman, Donald M, Jr — *Publisher*
%Sports Illustrated Magazine, Rockefeller Center, New York, NY 10020, USA

Elliot, Jane — *Actress*
%Judy Schoen Assoc, 606 N Larchmont Blvd, #309, Los Angeles, CA 90004, USA

Elliot, Win — *Sportscaster*
14 October Pl, Weston, CT 06883, USA

Elliott, Bill — *Auto Racing Driver*
PO Box 435, Dawsonville, GA 30534, USA

Elliott, Chalmers (Bump) — *Football Player, Coach*
%University of Iowa, Athletic Dept, Iowa City, IA 52242, USA

Elliott, David H — *Businessman*
%MBIA, 113 King St, Armonk, NY 10504, USA

Elliott, Herb — *Track Athlete*
40 Porteous Rd, Sorrento WA, Australia

Elliott, Joe — *Singer (Def Leppard)*
%Q Prime Inc, 729 7th Ave, #1400, New York, NY 10019, USA

Elliott, John, Jr — *Businessman*
%Ogilvy Group, 309 W 49th St, New York, NY 10019, USA

Elliott, Jumbo — *Football Player*
%New York Giants, Giants Stadium, East Rutherford, NJ 07073, USA

Elliott, Osborn — *Journalist*
36 E 72nd St, New York, NY 10021, USA

Elliott, Pete — *Football Player*
3003 Dunbarton Ave NW, Canton, OH 44708, USA

Elliott, Sam — *Actor*
33050 Pacific Coast Highway, Malibu, CA 90265, USA

Elliott, Sean — *Basketball Player*
%San Antonio Spurs, 600 E Market St, #102, San Antonio, TX 78205, USA

Elliott, Steven G — *Financier*
%Mellon Bank Corp, 1 Mellon Bank Center, 500 Grant St, Pittsburgh, PA 15219, USA

Ellis, Albert — *Clinical Psychologist*
%Institute for Rational-Emotional Therapy, 45 E 65th St, New York, NY 10021, USA

Ellis, Alton — *Singer*
27 McConnell House, Deeley Rd, London SW8, England

Ellis, Bret Easton — *Writer*
%International Creative Mgmt, 40 W 57th St, New York, NY 10019, USA

Ellis, Clarence — *Football Player*
PO Box 95247, Atlanta, GA 30347, USA

Ellis, Dale — *Basketball Player*
%Denver Nuggets, McNichols Arena, 1635 Clay St, Denver, CO 80204, USA

Ellis, Elmer — *Historian*
107 W Brandon Rd, Columbia, MO 65203, USA

Ellis, Herb — *Jazz Guitarist*
%Thomas Cassidy Inc, 0366 Horseshoe Dr, Basalt, CO 81621, USA

Ellis, James R — *Army General*
Commanding General, 3rd US Army, FORSCOM, Fort McPherson, GA 30330, USA

Ellis, Janet — *Actress*
%Arlington Entertainments, 1/3 Charlotte St, London W1P 1HD, England

Ellis, Kathy — *Swimmer*
3024 Woodshore, Carmel, IN 46033, USA

Ellis, LaPhonso — *Basketball Player*
%Denver Nuggets, McNichols Arena, 1635 Clay St, Denver, CO 80204, USA

Ellis, Luther — *Football Player*
%Detroit Lions, Silverdome, 1200 Featherstone Rd, Pontiac, MI 48342, USA

Ellis, Mary — *Actress*
%Chase Manhattan Bank, Woolgate House, Coleman St, London EC2, England

Ellis, Patrick (H J) — *Educator*
%Catholic University, President's Office, Washington, DC 20064, USA

E

Ellena - Ellis

E

Ellis, Ron	*Hockey Player*
BCE Place, 30 Yonge St, Toronto ON M5E 1X8, Canada	
Ellis, Samuel J (Sam)	*Baseball Player*
6111 Whiteway, Temple Terrace, FL 33617, USA	
Ellis, Scott	*Theater Director*
%Nederlander, 810 7th Ave, New York, NY 10019, USA	
Ellis, Terence S	*Financier*
%Criterion Investment Management Co, 1990 Post Oak Blvd, Houston, TX 77056, USA	
Ellis, Terry	*Singer (En Vogue)*
%William Morris Agency, 1325 Ave of Americas, New York, NY 10019, USA	
Ellison, Ernest O	*Financier*
%Trust Company of the West, 865 Figueroa St, Los Angeles, CA 90017, USA	
Ellison, Harlan J	*Writer*
3484 Coy Dr, Sherman Oaks, CA 91423, USA	
Ellison, Lawrence J	*Businessman*
%Oracle Systems Corp, 500 Oracle Parkway, Redwood City, CA 94065, USA	
Ellison, Pervis	*Basketball Player*
%Boston Celtics, 151 Merrimac St, #500, Boston, MA 02114, USA	
Ellroy, James	*Writer*
%Mysterious Press, 129 W 56th St, New York, NY 10019, USA	
Ellsberg, Daniel	*Political Activist*
90 Norwood Ave, Kensington, CA 94707, USA	
Ellsworth, Frank L	*Educator*
1530 Poppy Peak Dr, Pasadena, CA 91105, USA	
Ellsworth, Ralph E	*Librarian*
860 Willowbrook Rd, Boulder, CO 80302, USA	
Ellsworth, Richard C (Dick)	*Baseball Player*
1099 W Morris Ave, Fresno, CA 93711, USA	
Ellwood, Paul M, Jr	*Physician*
%Jackson Hole Group, PO Box 350, Teton Village, WY 83025, USA	
Elsna, Hebe	*Writer*
%Curtis Brown, 162-168 Regent St, London W1R 5TB, England	
Elton of Headington, Rodney	*Government Official, England*
%House of Lords, Westminster, London SW1A 0PW, England	
Elton, Charles S	*Zoologist*
61 Park Town, Oxford OX2 6SL, England	
Elvin, Violetta	*Ballerina*
Marina di Equa, 80066 Seiano, Bay of Naples, Italy	
Elvira (Cassandra Peterson)	*Entertainer*
%Panacea Entertainment, 2705 Glendower Ave, Los Angeles, CA 90027, USA	
Elway, John A	*Football Player*
%Denver Broncos, 13655 E Dove Valley Parkway, Englewood, CO 80112, USA	
Elwes, Cary	*Actor*
1901 Ave of Stars, #1245, Los Angeles, CA 90067, USA	
Elworthy, Charles	*Royal Air Force Marshal, England*
Gordons Valley, RD 2, Tomaru, South Canterbury, New Zealand	
Ely, Joe	*Singer, Songwriter*
%Campfire Nightmares, 7101 Highway 71 W, #A-9, Austin, TX 78735, USA	
Ely, Ron	*Actor*
4161 Mariposa Dr, Santa Barbara, CA 93110, USA	
Elytis, Odysseus	*Nobel Literature Laureate*
23 Skoufa St, Athens, Greece	
Eman, J H A (Henny)	*Prime Minister, Aruba*
Arubaanse Volkspartij, Orangestad, Aruba	
Emanuel, Elizabeth F	*Fashion Designer*
44 Grove End Rd, #7, London NW8 9NE, England	
Emanuels, Severinus D	*Prime Minister, Suriname*
98 Wassenaarse Weg, 2596 CZ The Hague, Netherlands	
Emberg, Kelly	*Actress, Model*
%Artists Agency, 10000 Santa Monica Blvd, #305, Los Angeles, CA 90067, USA	
Embry, Wayne	*Basketball Player, Executive*
%Cleveland Cavaliers, 2923 Statesboro Rd, Richfield, OH 44286, USA	
Emeneau, Murray B	*Linguist*
909 San Benito Rd, Berkeley, CA 94707, USA	
Emerson, Alice F	*Educator*
%Andrew Mellon Foundation, 140 E 62nd St, New York, NY 10021, USA	
Emerson, Daniel E	*Financier*
%First Federal Savings & Loan Assn, 1 First Federal Plaza, Rochester, NY 14614, USA	

Ellis - Emerson

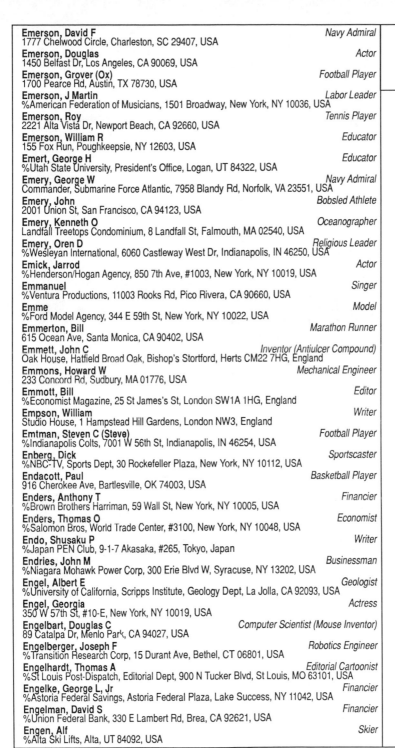

Emerson, David F — *Navy Admiral*
1777 Chelwood Circle, Charleston, SC 29407, USA

Emerson, Douglas — *Actor*
1450 Belfast Dr, Los Angeles, CA 90069, USA

Emerson, Grover (Ox) — *Football Player*
1700 Pearce Rd, Austin, TX 78730, USA

Emerson, J Martin — *Labor Leader*
%American Federation of Musicians, 1501 Broadway, New York, NY 10036, USA

Emerson, Roy — *Tennis Player*
2221 Alta Vista Dr, Newport Beach, CA 92660, USA

Emerson, William R — *Educator*
155 Fox Run, Poughkeepsie, NY 12603, USA

Emert, George H — *Educator*
%Utah State University, President's Office, Logan, UT 84322, USA

Emery, George W — *Navy Admiral*
Commander, Submarine Force Atlantic, 7958 Blandy Rd, Norfolk, VA 23551, USA

Emery, John — *Bobsled Athlete*
2001 Union St, San Francisco, CA 94123, USA

Emery, Kenneth O — *Oceanographer*
Landfall Treetops Condominium, 8 Landfall St, Falmouth, MA 02540, USA

Emery, Oren D — *Religious Leader*
%Wesleyan International, 6060 Castleway West Dr, Indianapolis, IN 46250, USA

Emick, Jarrod — *Actor*
%Henderson/Hogan Agency, 850 7th Ave, #1003, New York, NY 10019, USA

Emmanuel — *Singer*
%Ventura Productions, 11003 Rooks Rd, Pico Rivera, CA 90660, USA

Emme — *Model*
%Ford Model Agency, 344 E 59th St, New York, NY 10022, USA

Emmerton, Bill — *Marathon Runner*
615 Ocean Ave, Santa Monica, CA 90402, USA

Emmett, John C — *Inventor (Antiulcer Compound)*
Oak House, Hatfield Broad Oak, Bishop's Stortford, Herts CM22 7HG, England

Emmons, Howard W — *Mechanical Engineer*
233 Concord Rd, Sudbury, MA 01776, USA

Emmott, Bill — *Editor*
%Economist Magazine, 25 St James's St, London SW1A 1HG, England

Empson, William — *Writer*
Studio House, 1 Hampstead Hill Gardens, London NW3, England

Emtman, Steven C (Steve) — *Football Player*
%Indianapolis Colts, 7001 W 56th St, Indianapolis, IN 46254, USA

Enberg, Dick — *Sportscaster*
%NBC-TV, Sports Dept, 30 Rockefeller Plaza, New York, NY 10112, USA

Endacott, Paul — *Basketball Player*
916 Cherokee Ave, Bartlesville, OK 74003, USA

Enders, Anthony T — *Financier*
%Brown Brothers Harriman, 59 Wall St, New York, NY 10005, USA

Enders, Thomas O — *Economist*
%Salomon Bros, World Trade Center, #3100, New York, NY 10048, USA

Endo, Shusaku P — *Writer*
%Japan PEN Club, 9-1-7 Akasaka, #265, Tokyo, Japan

Endries, John M — *Businessman*
%Niagara Mohawk Power Corp, 300 Erie Blvd W, Syracuse, NY 13202, USA

Engel, Albert E — *Geologist*
%University of California, Scripps Institute, Geology Dept, La Jolla, CA 92093, USA

Engel, Georgia — *Actress*
350 W 57th St, #10-E, New York, NY 10019, USA

Engelbart, Douglas C — *Computer Scientist (Mouse Inventor)*
89 Catalpa Dr, Menlo Park, CA 94027, USA

Engelberger, Joseph F — *Robotics Engineer*
%Transition Research Corp, 15 Durant Ave, Bethel, CT 06801, USA

Engelhardt, Thomas A — *Editorial Cartoonist*
%St Louis Post-Dispatch, Editorial Dept, 900 N Tucker Blvd, St Louis, MO 63101, USA

Engelke, George L, Jr — *Financier*
%Astoria Federal Savings, Astoria Federal Plaza, Lake Success, NY 11042, USA

Engelman, David S — *Financier*
%Union Federal Bank, 330 E Lambert Rd, Brea, CA 92621, USA

Engen, Alf — *Skier*
%Alta Ski Lifts, Alta, UT 84092, USA

E

Engen, Corey — *Skier*
PO Box 774, McCall, ID 83638, USA

Engen, Donald D — *Government Official*
809 Duke St, Alexandria, VA 22314, USA

Engen, Sverre — *Skier*
9058 Green Hills Dr, Sandy, UT 84093, USA

Engholm, Bjorn — *Government Official, Germany*
Jurgen-Wallenwever-Str 9, 23566 Lubeck, Germany

England, Anthony W — *Astronaut, Geophysicist*
7949 Ridgeway Court, Dexter, MI 48130, USA

England, Richard — *Architect*
26/1 Merchants St, Valletta, Malta

Englander, Harold R — *Dental Researcher*
11502 Whisper Bluff, San Antonio, TX 78230, USA

Engle, Joe H — *Astronaut, Air Force General*
1906 Back Bay Ct, Nassau Bay, Houston, TX 77058, USA

Englehart, Robert W (Bob), Jr — *Editorial Cartoonist*
%Hartford Courant, Editorial Dept, 280 Broad St, Hartford, CT 06105, USA

Engler, John M — *Governor, MI*
%Governor's Office, State Capitol Bldg, #200, Lansing, MI 48913, USA

English, Alex — *Basketball Player*
%Dallas Mavericks, Reunion Arena, 777 Sports St, Dallas, TX 75207, USA

English, Diane — *Screenwriter*
%Shukovsky-English Ent, 4024 Radford Ave, Studio City, CA 91604, USA

English, Joseph T — *Psychiatrist*
%St Vincents Hospital, 203 W 12th St, New York, NY 10011, USA

English, Lawrence P — *Businessman*
%Connecticut General Life Insurance, 900 Cottage Grove Rd, Bloomfield, CT 06002, USA

English, Michael — *Singer*
PO Box 681598, Franklin, TN 37068, USA

Englund, Robert — *Actor*
1616 Santa Cruz St, Laguna Beach, CA 92651, USA

Engstrom, Ted W — *Association Executive*
%World Vision, 919 W Huntington Dr, Arcadia, CA 91007, USA

Enke-Kania, Karin — *Speed Skater*
%Einheit Sport Club, Dresden, Germany

Ennest, John W — *Financier*
%Citizens Banking Corp, 1 Citizens Banking Center, Flint, MI 48502, USA

Ennis, Delmar (Del) — *Baseball Player*
1332 King Rd, Huntingdon Valley, PA 19006, USA

Enright, Dennis J — *Writer, Educator*
35-A Viewfield Rd, London SW18 5JD, England

Entremont, Philippe — *Conductor, Concert Pianist*
Schwarzenbergplatz 10/7, 1040 Vienna, Austria

Entringer, James W — *Businessman*
%Selective Insurance Group, 40 Wantage Ave, Branchville, NJ 07890, USA

Entwistle, John — *Singer, Songwriter, Bassist (Who)*
1704 Queens Ct, Los Angeles, CA 90069, USA

Enzensberger, Hans M — *Poet, Writer*
%Suhrkamp Verlag, Fach 2446, 60549 Frankfurt/Main, Germany

Ephron, Nora — *Writer*
390 West End Ave, New York, NY 10024, USA

Epperson, Brenda — *Actress*
%Lee, 403 Susana Ave, Redondo Beach, CA 90277, USA

Epple-Beck, Irene — *Skier*
Aufmberg 235, 87637 Seeg, Germany

Epstein, Daniel M — *Poet, Dramatist*
843 W University Parkway, Baltimore, MD 21210, USA

Epstein, Emmanuel — *Plant Nutritionist*
%University of California, Land Air Water Resources Dept, Davis, CA 95616, USA

Epstein, Gabriel — *Architect*
3 Rue Mazet, 75006 Paris, France

Epstein, Jason — *Editor*
%Random House Inc, 201 E 50th St, New York, NY 10022, USA

Epstein, Joseph — *Writer, Educator*
522 Church St, #6-B, Evanston, IL 60201, USA

Erb, Donald — *Composer*
4073 Bluestone Rd, Cleveland, OH 44121, USA

Engen - Erb

Erb, Richard D *Government Official*
%International Monetary Fund, 700 19th St NW, Washington, DC 20431, USA

Erbe, Norman *Governor, IA*
2880 Grand Ave, #307, Des Moines, IA 50312, USA

Erben, Ralph *Businessman*
%Luby's Cafeterias, 2211 NE Loop 410, San Antonio, TX 78265, USA

Erburu, Robert F *Publisher, Businessman*
1518 Blue Jay Way, West Hollywood, CA 90069, USA

Erdman, Paul E *Writer*
1817 Lytton Springs Rd, Healdsburg, CA 95448, USA

Erdman, Richard *Actor*
5655 Greenbush Ave, Van Nuys, CA 91401, USA

Erdrich, K Louise *Writer*
%Henry Holt Inc, 115 W 18th St, New York, NY 10011, USA

Erhard, Werner *est Founder*
1945 Franklin St, San Francisco, CA 94109, USA

Erhardt, Warren R *Publisher*
455 Wakefield Dr, Metchen, NJ 08840, USA

Erhart, Charles H, Jr *Businessman*
%W R Grace Co, 1 Town Center Rd, Boca Raton, FL 33486, USA

Erickson, Arthur C *Architect*
%Arthur Erickson Architects, 1672 W 1st Ave, Vancouver BC V6J 1G1, Canada

Erickson, Dennis *Football Coach*
%Seattle Seahawks, 11220 NE 53rd St, Kirkland, WA 98033, USA

Erickson, Jeffrey H *Businessman*
%Trans World Airlines, City Center, 515 N 6th St, St Louis, MO 63101, USA

Erickson, Robert *Composer*
%University of California, Music Dept, La Jolla, CA 92093, USA

Erickson, Steve *Writer*
%Poseidon Press, 1230 Ave of Americas, New York, NY 10020, USA

Ericson, James D *Businessman*
%Northwestern Mutual Life Insurance, 720 E Wisconsin Ave, Milwaukee, WI 53202, USA

Ericson, John *Actor*
RR 3, Box 109-JK, Santa Fe, NM 87505, USA

Eriksen, Stein *Skier*
7700 Stein Way, Park City, UT 84060, USA

Erikson, Raymond L *Medical Researcher*
%Harvard University Medical School, 25 Shattuck St, Boston, MA 02115, USA

Erikson, Sheldon R *Businessman*
%Western Co of North America, 515 Post Oak Blvd, Houston, TX 77027, USA

Erixon, Jan *Hockey Player*
PO Box 90111, Arlington, TX 76004, USA

Erni, Hans *Artist*
6045 Meggen, Lucerne, Switzerland

Ernst, Markus M *Businessman*
%Arbor Drugs, 3331 W Big Beaver Rd, Troy, MI 48084, USA

Ernst, Richard R *Nobel Chemistry Laureate*
Kurlistr 24, 8404 Winterthur, Switzerland

Eros, Peter *Conductor*
7019 Bobhird Dr, San Diego, CA 92119, USA

Erroll of Hale, Frederick J *Government Official, England*
%Bowater Corp, Bowater House, Knightsbridge, London SW1X 7LR, England

Erskine, Carl D *Baseball Player*
6214 S Madison Ave, Anderson, IN 46013, USA

Erskine, Peter *Jazz Drummer*
1727 Hill St, Santa Monica, CA 90405, USA

Erskine, Ralph *Architect*
Gustav III's Vag, 170 11 Drottningholm, Sweden

Ertegun, Ahmet M *Entertainment Executive*
%Atlantic Records, 75 Rockefeller Plaza, New York, NY 10019, USA

Eruzione, Mike *Hockey Player*
274 Bowdoin St, Winthrop, MA 02152, USA

Ervine-Andrews, Harold M *WW II British Army Hero (VC)*
Trevor Cot, Gorran, St Austell, Cornwall PL26 6LW, England

Erving, Julius W (Dr J) *Basketball Player*
PO Box 8269, Cherry Hill, NJ 08002, USA

Ervins, Ricky *Football Player*
%Washington Redskins, 21300 Redskin Park Dr, Ashburn, VA 22011, USA

E

Erb - Ervins

Ervolino, Frank *Labor Leader*
%Laundry & Dry Cleaning Union, 107 Delaware Ave, Buffalo, NY 14202, USA

Erwin, Henry E *WW II Army Air Corps Hero (CMH)*
Rt 2, Box 50, Leeds, AL 35094, USA

Erwitt, Elliott R *Photographer*
88 Central Park West, New York, NY 10023, USA

Esaki, Leo *Nobel Physics Laureate*
Takezono 3-772, Tsukuba Ibaraki 305, Japan

Esau, Katherine *Botanist*
8 W Constance Ave, #8, Santa Barbara, CA 93105, USA

Escalante, Jaime A *Educator*
%Hiram Johnson High School, 6879 14th Ave, Sacramento, CA 95820, USA

Eschenbach, Christoph *Conductor, Concert Pianist*
Maspalomas, Monte Leon 760625, Gran Canaria, Spain

Esiason, Norman J (Boomer) *Football Player*
%New York Jets, 1000 Fulton Ave, Hempstead, NY 11550, USA

Esmond, Carl *Actor*
576 Tigertail Rd, Los Angeles, CA 90049, USA

Esperian, Kallen R *Opera Singer*
514 Lindseywood Cove, Memphis, TN 38117, USA

Espey, John *Writer*
PO Box 107, Topanga, CA 90290, USA

Esposito, Frank *Bowling Executive*
200 Rt 17, Paramus, NJ 07652, USA

Esposito, Philip A (Phil) *Hockey Player, Executive*
%Tampa Bay Lightning, Mack Center, 501 E Kennedy Blvd, Tampa, FL 33602, USA

Esposito, Tony *Hockey Player, Executive*
%Tampa Bay Lightning, Mack Center, 501 E Kennedy Blvd, Tampa, FL 33602, USA

Espy, A Michael (Mike) *Secretary, Agriculture*
154 Deertrail Lane, Madison, MS 39110, USA

Esquivel, Manuel *Prime Minister, Belize*
PO Box 165, Belize City, Belize

Esrey, William T *Businessman*
%Sprint Corp, 2300 Shawnee Mission Parkway, Westwood, KS 66205, USA

Esselborn, Bruce A *Businessman*
%Capsure Holdings Corp, 2 N Riverside Plaza, Chicago, IL 60606, USA

Essex, David *Singer*
%Lamplight Music, 109 Eastbourne Mews, London W2 6LQ, England

Essex, Myron E *Microbiologist*
%Harvard School of Public Health, 665 Huntington Ave, Boston, MA 02115, USA

Essian, James S (Jim) *Baseball Manager*
134 Eckford, Troy, MI 48098, USA

Essman, Alyn V *Businessman*
%CPI Corp, 1706 Washington Ave, St Louis, MO 63103, USA

Esswood, Paul L V *Concert Singer*
Jasmine Cottage, 42 Ferring Lane, Ferring, West Sussex BN12 6QT, England

Esteban, Manuel A *Educator*
%California State University, President's Office, Chico, CA 95929, USA

Estefan, Gloria *Singer, Songwriter*
%Estefan Enterprises, 6205 SW 40th St, Miami, FL 33155, USA

Estes, Clarissa Pinkola *Psychologist*
%Ballantine Books, 201 E 50th St, New York, NY 10022, USA

Estes, Howell M, III *Air Force General*
Dep CINCUNC, Korea/Commander, 7th Air Force, Unit 2047, PACAF, APO, AP 96278, USA

Estes, Howell M, Jr *Air Force General, Businessman*
7603 Shadywood Rd, Bethesda, MD 20817, USA

Estes, James *Cartoonist*
1103 Callahan, Amarillo, TX 79106, USA

Estes, Rob *Actor*
910 Idaho Ave, Santa Monica, CA 90403, USA

Estes, Simon L *Opera Singer*
%Columbia Artists Mgmt Inc, 165 W 57th St, New York, NY 10019, USA

Estes, William K *Behavioral Scientist*
95 Irving St, Cambridge, MA 02138, USA

Esteve-Coll, Elizabeth *Museum Curator*
%Victoria & Albert Museum, South Kensington, London SW7 2RL, England

Estevez, Emilio *Actor*
31725 Sea Level Dr, Malibu, CA 90265, USA

Estevez, Luis — *Fashion Designer*
122 E 7th St, Los Angeles, CA 90014, USA

Estevez, Ramon — *Actor*
837 Ocean Ave, #101, Santa Monica, CA 90403, USA

Estrada, Erik — *Actor*
3768 Eureka Dr, North Hollywood, CA 91604, USA

Estrich, Susan R — *Attorney*
%University of Southern California, Law Center, Los Angeles, CA 90089, USA

Estrin, Melvyn — *Businessman*
%FoxMeyer Health Corp, 1220 Senlac Dr, Carrollton, TX 75006, USA

Eszterhas, Joseph A — *Screenwriter*
%William Morris Agency, 151 S El Camino Dr, Beverly Hills, CA 90212, USA

Etchegaray, Roger Cardinal — *Religious Leader*
Piazza San Calisto, Vatican City, Rome, Italy

Etheridge, Melissa — *Singer, Songwriter*
PO Box 884563, San Francisco, CA 94188, USA

Ethridge, Mark F, III — *Editor*
%Business Journal of Charlotte, 128 S Tryon St, #2200, Charlotte, NC 28202, USA

Etienne, Jean-Louis — *Explorer*
%Think South, PO Box 4097, St Paul, MN 55104, USA

Etienne-Martin — *Sculptor*
7 Rue Du Pot de Fer, 75005 Paris, France

Etling, John C — *Businessman*
%General Re Corp, Financial Centre, Stamford, CT 06901, USA

Etrog, Sorel — *Artist*
PO Box 5943, Station A, Toronto ON M5W 1P3, Canada

Etsel, Ed — *Marksman*
%University of Virginia, Athletic Dept, Charlottesville, VA 22906, USA

Etter, Richard A — *Financier*
%Bank of America Nevada, 300 S 4th St, Las Vegas, NV 89101, USA

Ettore, Joseph R — *Businessman*
%Ames Department Stores, 2418 Main St, Rocky Hill, CT 06067, USA

Etzioni, Amitai W — *Sociologist*
7110 Arran Pl, Bethesda, MD 20817, USA

Etzwiler, Donnell D — *Pediatrician*
%International Diabetes Center, 5000 W 39th St, Minneapolis, MN 55416, USA

Eubanks, Bob — *Entertainer*
5900 Highridge Rd, Hidden Hills, CA 91302, USA

Eure, Wesley — *Actor*
PO Box 69405, Los Angeles, CA 90069, USA

Eustace, Joseph L — *Governor-General*
%Government House, Montrose, Saint Vincent & Grenadines

Evangelista, Linda — *Model*
%Elite Model Mgmt, 8 Bis Rue Le Cuirot, 75014 Paris, France

Evans, Andrea — *Actress*
310 W 72nd St, #7-G, New York, NY 10023, USA

Evans, Anthony H — *Educator*
%California State University, President's Office, San Bernardino, CA 92407, USA

Evans, Dale — *Actress*
15650 Seneca Rd, Victorville, CA 92392, USA

Evans, Daniel E — *Businessman*
%Bob Evans Farms, 3776 S High St, Columbus, OH 43207, USA

Evans, Daniel J — *Senator/Governor, WA*
%Daniel J Evans Assoc, 1111 3rd Ave, #3400, Seattle, WA 98101, USA

Evans, Darrell W — *Baseball Player*
RR 1, Box 141-A, Wheeling, WV 26003, USA

Evans, Dick — *Bowling Writer*
%Miami Herald, Sports Dept, Herald Plaza, Miami, FL 33101, USA

Evans, Earl A, Jr — *Biochemist*
1120 N Lake Shore Dr, Chicago, IL 60611, USA

Evans, Edward P — *Publisher*
712 5th Ave, #4900, New York, NY 10019, USA

Evans, Edwin C — *Physician*
500 Westover Dr NW, Atlanta, GA 30305, USA

Evans, Evans — *Actress*
3114 Abington Dr, Beverly Hills, CA 90210, USA

Evans, Gene — *Actor*
PO Box 93, Medon, TN 38356, USA

E

Estevez - Evans

E

Evans, Glen *Molecular Biologist*
%Salk Institute, Molecular Biology Dept, PO Box 8500, San Diego, CA 92138, USA

Evans, Greg *Cartoonist (Luann)*
660 Elm Tree Lane, San Marcos, CA 92069, USA

Evans, Harold J *Plant Physiologist*
14151 Redwood Court, Lake Oswego, OR 97034, USA

Evans, Harold M *Editor*
%Random House Inc, 201 E 50th St, New York, NY 10022, USA

Evans, J Handel *Educator*
%San Jose State University, President's Office, San Jose, CA 95192, USA

Evans, James S *Businessman*
%Media General Inc, 333 E Grace St, Richmond, VA 23293, USA

Evans, Janet *Swimmer*
424 Brower Ave, Placentia, CA 92670, USA

Evans, John *Musician (Box Tops)*
%Creative Entertainment Assoc, 2011 Ferry Ave, #U-19, Camden, NJ 08104, USA

Evans, John B *Publisher*
%Murdoch Magazines, 755 2nd Ave, New York, NY 10017, USA

Evans, John E *Businessman*
%ALLIED Group, 701 5th Ave, Des Moines, IA 50391, USA

Evans, John R *Educator, Foundation Executive*
%Rockefeller Foundation, 1133 Ave of Americas, New York, NY 10036, USA

Evans, John V *Governor, ID*
%D L Evans Bank, 397 N Overland, Burley, ID 83318, USA

Evans, Lee *Track Athlete*
%Quatar National Track Team, PO Box 7494, Dohar, Quatar

Evans, Linda *Actress*
6714 Villa Madera Dr SW, Tacoma, WA 98499, USA

Evans, Mary Beth *Actress*
PO Box 50105, Pasadena, CA 91115, USA

Evans, Michael *Actor*
12530 Collins St, North Hollywood, CA 91607, USA

Evans, Morgan J *Financier*
%First Security Corp, 79 S Main St, Salt Lake City, UT 84111, USA

Evans, Norm E *Football Player*
15731 Tiger Mountain Rd, Issaquah, WA 98027, USA

Evans, Ray R *Football Player*
5632 Pembroke Lane, Shawnee Mission, KS 66208, USA

Evans, Richard *Sports Executive*
%Madison Square Garden, 4 Pennsylvania Plaza, New York, NY 10001, USA

Evans, Richard W *Financier*
%Frost National Bank, 100 W Houston St, San Antonio, TX 78205, USA

Evans, Robert C *Mountaineer*
Ardincaple, Capel Curig, Betws-y-Coed, Northern Wales, British Isles

Evans, Robert E *Financier*
%TCF Financial Corp, 801 Marquette Ave, Minneapolis, MN 55402, USA

Evans, Robert J *Movie Producer*
%Robert Evans Productions, Paramount Pictures, 5555 Melrose, Los Angeles, 90038, USA

Evans, Robert S *Businessman*
%Crane Co, 100 1st Stamford Pl, Stamford, CT 06902, USA

Evans, Ronald M *Geneticist*
%Salk Institute, Gene Expression Laboratory, PO Box 85800, San Diego, CA 92186, USA

Evans, Rowland, Jr *Columnist*
3125 "O" St NW, Washington, DC 20007, USA

Evans, Russell W *Movie Producer*
Walnut Tree, Roehampton Gate, London SW15, England

Evans, Troy *Actor*
PO Box 834, Lakeside, MT 59922, USA

Evans, Walker *Truck, Off-Road Racing Driver*
%Walker Evans Racing, PO Box 2469, Riverside, CA 92516, USA

Evdokimova, Eva *Ballerina*
%Gregori Productions, PO Box 1586, New York, NY 10150, USA

Eve, Trevor *Actor*
%Julian Belfrage, 46 Albermarle St, London W1X 4PP, England

Everest, Frank K (Pete), Jr *Test Pilot*
General Delivery, McCall, ID 83638, USA

Everett, Chad *Actor*
5472 Island Forest Pl, Westlake Village, CA 91362, USA

Evans - Everett

Everett, Danny *Track Athlete*
%Santa Monica Track Club, 1801 Ocean Park Ave, #112, Santa Monica, CA 90405, USA

Everett, James L, III *Businessman*
323 Roberts Ave, Conshohocken, PA 19428, USA

Everett, Jim *Football Player*
%New Orleans Saints, 1500 Poydras St, New Orleans, LA 70112, USA

Everett, Malcolm E, III *Financier*
%First Union National Bank, 1 First Union Center, Charlotte, NC 28288, USA

Everett, Thomas *Football Player*
%Dallas Cowboys, 1 Cowboys Parkway, Irving, TX 75063, USA

Everhard, Nancy *Actress*
2751 Pelham Pl, Los Angeles, CA 90068, USA

Everhart, Angie *Model*
%Next Model Mgmt, 115 E 57th St, #1540, New York, NY 10022, USA

Everingham, Lyle J *Businessman*
%Kroger Co, 1014 Vine St, Cincinnati, OH 45202, USA

Everly, Don *Singer (Everly Brothers)*
PO Box 120725, Nashville, TN 37212, USA

Everly, Phil *Singer (Everly Brothers)*
10414 Camarillo St, North Hollywood, CA 91602, USA

Evers, Charles *Civil Rights Activist*
1072 Lunch St, Jackson, MS 39203, USA

Evers, Jason *Actor*
%Sekura/A Talent Agency, PO Box 931779, Los Angeles, CA 90093, USA

Evers-Williams, Myrlie *Association Executive*
%NAACP, 4805 Mt Hope Dr, Baltimore, MD 21215, USA

Eversley, Frederick J *Sculptor*
1110 W Albert Kinney Blvd, Venice, CA 90291, USA

Everson, Corinna (Cory) *Body Builder*
PO Box 5767, Beverly Hills, CA 90209, USA

Evert, Christine M (Chris) *Tennis Player*
701 NE 12th Ave, Fort Lauderdale, FL 33304, USA

Evigan, Greg *Actor, Singer*
5472 Winnetka Ave, Woodland Hills, CA 91364, USA

Evren, Kenan *President, Turkey; Army General*
Beyaz Ev Sokak 21, Armutalan, Marmaris, Turkey

Evron, Ephraim *Government Official, Israel*
%Ministry of Foreign Affairs, Tel Aviv, Israel

Ewald, Robert H *Businessman*
%Cray Research Inc, 655-A Lone Oak Dr, Eagan, MN 55121, USA .

Ewaldsen, Hans L *Businessman*
%Deutsche Babcock, Duisburgerstr 375, 46049 Oberhausen, Germany

Ewart, Gavin B *Poet*
57 Kenilworth Court, Lower Richmond Rd, London SW15 1EN, England

Ewbank, Wilbur C (Weeb) *Football Coach*
4160 Steamboat Bend E, #103, Fort Myers, FL 33919, USA

Ewell, Barney *Track Athlete*
55 Green St, Lancaster, PA 17602, USA

Ewen, David *Musician, Author*
%Century Village, Preston A-18, Boca Raton, FL 33434, USA

Ewing, Maria L *Opera Singer*
33 Bramerton St, London SW3, England

Ewing, Patrick A *Basketball Player*
%New York Knicks, Madison Square Garden, 4 Penn Plaza, New York, NY 10001, USA

Exum, Glenn *Musician, Mountaineer*
PO Box 889, Thayne, WY 83127, USA

Eyadema, E Gnassingbe *President, Togo; Army General*
%President's Office, Palais Presidentiel, Ave de la Marina, Lome, Togo

Eyes, Raymond *Publisher*
%McCall's Magazine, 110 5th Ave, New York, NY 10011, USA

Eyles, David L *Financier*
%Shawmut National Corp, 1 Federal St, Boston, MA 02110, USA

Eyre, Richard *Movie, Theater, Television Director*
%Royal National Theater, South Bank, London SE1 9PX, England

Eysenck, Hans J *Psychologist*
10 Dorchester Dr, London SE24, England

Eytchison, Ronald M *Navy Admiral*
11 Prentice Ln, Signal Mountain, TN 37377, USA

Fabares, Shelley *Actress*
PO Box 6010, Sherman Oaks, CA 91413, USA

Faber, Sandra M *Astronomer*
%Lick Observatory, Mount Hamilton, San Jose, CA 95140, USA

Fabi, Teo *Auto Racing Driver*
Via Bronzino 14, Milan, Italy

Fabian (Forte) *Singer*
%Arslanian Assoc, 6671 Sunset Blvd, #1502, Los Angeles, CA 90028, USA

Fabian, John M *Astronaut*
%ANSER, Space Systems Dept, 1215 Jefferson Davis Highway, Arlington, VA 22202, USA

Fabio (Lanzoni) *Model*
%Fabio's Helpies Bodies, PO Box 4, Inwood, NY 11696, USA

Fabiola Mora y Aragon, Dona *Queen Mother, Belgium*
%Royal Palace of Laeken, Laeken-Brussels, Belgium

Fabius, Laurent *Premier, France*
15 Place du Pantheon, 75005 Paris, France

Fabray, Nanette *Singer*
14360 Sunset Blvd, Pacific Palisades, CA 90272, USA

Fabulous Moolah *Wrestler*
%TitanSports, 1241 E Main St, Stamford, CT 06902, USA

Face, Elroy L *Baseball Player*
608 Della Dr, #5-F, North Versailles, PA 15137, USA

Fadeyechev, Aleksei *Ballet Dancer*
%Bolshoi Theater, Teatralnaya Pl 1, 103009 Moscow, Russia

Fadeyechev, Nicolai B *Ballet Dancer*
%Bolshoi Theater, Teatralnaya Pl 1, 103009 Moscow, Russia

Fadiman, Clifton *Writer*
Beach Home 13, S S Plantation, PO Box 459, Captiva, FL 33924, USA

Fagan, Garth *Choreographer*
%State University of New York, Dance Dept, Brockport, NY 14420, USA

Fagan, John J *Labor Leader*
%International Teamsters Brotherhood, 25 Louisiana Ave NW, Washington, DC 20001, USA

Fagan, Kevin *Cartoonist (Drabble)*
PO Box 2582, Mission Viejo, CA 92690, USA

Fagen, Clifford B *Basketball Executive*
1021 Royal Saint George Dr, Naperville, IL 60563, USA

Fagerbakke, Bill *Actor*
1500 Will Geer Rd, Topanga, CA 90290, USA

Faget, Maxime *Space Scientist*
%Space Industries International, 101 Courageous Dr, League City, TX 77573, USA

Fagg, George C *Judge*
%US Court of Appeals, US Courthouse, East 1st & Walnut St, Des Moines, IA 50309, USA

Faggin, Federico *Inventor (Commercial Microprocessor)*
%Synaptics Inc, 2698 Orchard Parkway, San Jose, CA 95134, USA

Faggs Starr, Mae *Track Athlete*
10152 Shady Lane, Cincinnati, OH 45215, USA

Fagin, Claire M *Educator*
1311 Remington Rd, Wynnewood, PA 19096, USA

Fagin, David K *Businessman*
%Golden Star Resources, 1990 N California Blvd, Walnut Creek, CA 94596, USA

Fahd Ibn Abdul Aziz *King, Saudi Arabia*
%Royal Palace, Royal Court, Riyadh, Saudi Arabia

Fahey, Jeff *Actor*
250 N Robertson Blvd, #518, Beverly Hills, CA 90211, USA

Fahn, Stanley *Neurologist*
%Columbia University, Neurology Dept, 710 W 168th St, New York, NY 10032, USA

Fahrenkopf, Frank J, Jr *Political Leader*
%Republican National Committee, 310 1st St SE, Washington, DC 20003, USA

Fahrney, Delmer S *Navy Admiral, Missile Expert*
10245 Vivera Dr, La Mesa, CA 91941, USA

Fain, Ferris R *Baseball Player*
PO Box 1357, Georgetown, CA 95634, USA

Fain, James A (Jim), Jr *Air Force General*
CinC, Aeronautical Systems Center, Wright Patterson Air Force Base, OH 45433, USA

Fainsilber, Adrien *Architect*
7 Rue Salvador Allende, 92000 Nanterre, France

Fairbairn, Bruce *Actor*
%Century Artists, 9744 Wilshire Blvd, #308, Beverly Hills, CA 90212, USA

Fairbanks, Douglas, Jr *Actor*
%Inverness Corp, 545 Madison Ave, New York, NY 10022, USA

Fairbanks, Jerry *Movie Director, Producer*
PO Box 50553, Santa Barbara, CA 93150, USA

Fairchild, John B *Publisher*
Chalet Bianchina, Talstr GR, 7250 Klosters, Switzerland

Fairchild, Morgan *Actress*
2424 Bowmont Dr, Beverly Hills, CA 90210, USA

Fairfield, Bill L *Businessman*
%InaCom Corp, 10810 Farnam Dr, Omaha, NE 68154, USA

Fairfield, John S *Air Force General*
Vice Commander, Pacific Air Forces, 25 "E" St, Hickam Air Force Base, HI 96853, USA

Fairly, Ronald R (Ron) *Baseball Player, Sportscaster*
342 Sunstone, Westlake Village, CA 91361, USA

Faison, Earl *Football Player*
PO Box 711355, Santee, CA 92072, USA

Faith, Adam *Singer, Actor*
Crockham Hill, Edenbridge, Kent, England

Faithfull, Marianne *Singer, Songwriter*
Yew Tree Cottage, Aldridge, Berks, England

Falcao, Jose Freire Cardinal *Religious Leader*
SHIS QL 12 Conj 12, Casa 01, 71 630-325 Brasilia, Brazil

Faldo, Nick *Golfer*
%Professional Golfer's Assn, PO Box 109601, Palm Beach Gardens, FL 33410, USA

Falk, David B *Sports Attorney*
%Falk Assoc, 5335 Wisconsin Ave NW, #850, Washington, DC 20015, USA

Falk, Isidore S *Medical Economist*
472 Whitney Ave, New Haven, CT 06511, USA

Falk, Lee H *Cartoonist (Mandrake, Phantom)*
PO Box Z, Truro, MA 02666, USA

Falk, Paul *Figure Skater*
Sybelstr 21, 40239 Dusseldorf, Germany

Falk, Peter *Actor*
1004 N Roxbury Dr, Beverly Hills, CA 90210, USA

Falk, Randall M *Religious Leader*
%Temple, 5015 Harding Rd, Nashville, TN 37205, USA

Falkenburg McCrary, Jinx *Model, Actress*
10 Shelter Rock Rd, Manhasset, NY 11030, USA

Falkenburg, Robert *Tennis Player*
259 St Pierre Rd, Los Angeles, CA 90077, USA

Falkenstein, Claire *Artist*
719 Ocean Front Walk, Venice, CA 90291, USA

Falkner, Keith *Singer*
Low Cottages, Ilketshall Saint Margaraet, Bungay, Suffolk, England

Fallaci, Oriana *Journalist*
%Rizzoli, 31 W 57th St, #400, New York, NY 10019, USA

Falldin, N O Thorbjorn *Prime Minister, Sweden*
As, 870 16 Ramvik, Sweden

Falloon, Pat *Hockey Player*
%San Jose Sharks, 525 W Santa Clara St, San Jose, CA 95113, USA

Fallows, James B *Editor*
%Atlantic Monthly Magazine, Editorial Dept, 745 Boylston St, Boston, MA 02116, USA

Faltings, Gerd *Mathematician*
%Princeton University, Mathematics Dept, Princeton, NJ 08544, USA

Faludi, Susan C *Journalist*
1032 Irving St, #204, San Francisco, CA 94122, USA

Falwell, Jerry L *Religious Leader*
%Liberty Baptist Fellowship, 3765 Candler's Mountain Rd, Lynchburg, VA 24502, USA

Fanfani, Amintore *Prime Minister, Italy*
Via XX Settembre 97, 00187 Rome, Italy

Fang Lizhi *Astrophysicist; Political Activist*
%Cambridge University, Astronomy Institute, Cambridge, England

Fann, Al *Actor*
19649 Citronia Ave, Northridge, CA 91324, USA

Fannin, Paul J *Senator, AZ*
599 Orange Blossom Lane, Phoenix, AZ 85018, USA

Fanning, Katherine W *Editor*
330 Beacon St, Boston, MA 02116, USA

F

Fano, Ugo *Physicist*
5801 S Dorchester Ave, Chicago, IL 60637, USA

Faracy, Stephanie *Actress*
8765 Lookout Mountain Rd, Los Angeles, CA 90046, USA

Farah, Roger N *Businessman*
%Woolworth Corp, Woolworth Corp, 233 Broadway, New York, NY 10279, USA

Farenthold, Frances T *Women's Activist, Educator*
2929 Buffalo Speedway, #18-B, Houston, TX 77098, USA

Farentino, Debrah *Actress*
%Innovative Artists, 1999 Ave of Stars, #2850, Los Angeles, CA 90067, USA

Farentino, James *Actor*
1340 Londonderry Place, Los Angeles, CA 90069, USA

Farer, Tom J *Educator*
%American University, International Services School, Washington, DC 20016, USA

Fares, Muhammad Ahmed Al *Cosmonaut, Syria*
PO Box 1272, Aleppo, Syria

Fargis, Joe *Equestrian Rider*
11744 Marblestone Court, West Palm Beach, FL 33414, USA

Fargo, Donna *Singer*
%Prima-Donna Entertainment, PO Box 150527, Nashville, TN 37215, USA

Farina, Battista (Pinin) *Industrial Designer*
%Pinitarina SpA, Via Lesna 78, 10095 Grugliasco, Turin, Italy

Farina, David *Religious Leader*
%Christian Church of North America, 41 Sherbrooke Rd, Trenton, NJ 08638, USA

Farina, Dennis *Actor*
1201 Greenacre Ave, Los Angeles, CA 90046, USA

Farkas, Bertalan *Cosmonaut, Hungary*
A Magyar Koztarsasag, Kutato Urhajosa, Pf 25, 1885 Budapest, Hungary

Farkas, Ferenc *Composer*
Nagyatai-Ut 12, 1026 Budapest, Hungary

Farley, Carole *Opera, Concert Singer*
270 Riverside Dr, New York, NY 10025, USA

Farley, William F *Businessman*
%Fruit of the Loom, Sears Tower, 233 S Wacker Dr, #500, Chicago, IL 60606, USA

Farling, Robert A *Businessman*
%Centerior Energy Corp, 6200 Oak Tree Blvd, Independence, OH 44131, USA

Farlow, Talmadge H (Tal) *Jazz Guitarist*
%Richard A Barz Assoc, RD 1, Box 91, Tannersville, PA 18372, USA

Farman, Richard D *Businessman*
%Pacific Enterprises, 633 W 5th St, Los Angeles, CA 90071, USA

Farmer, Art *Jazz Musician*
%Helen Keane Artists, 49 E 96th St, New York, NY 10128, USA

Farmer, James L, Jr *Civil Rights Activist*
3805 Guinea Station Rd, Fredericksburg, VA 22408, USA

Farmer, Jim G *Financier*
%Boatmen's Arkansas, 200 W Capitol Ave, Little Rock, AR 72201, USA

Farmer, Phillip W *Businessman*
%Harris Corp, 1025 W NASA Blvd, Melbourne, FL 32919, USA

Farmer, Richard G *Physician*
9126 Town Gate Lane, Bethesda, MD 20817, USA

Farnam, Walter E *Businessman*
%General Accident Insurance Group, 436 Walnut St, Philadelphia, PA 19106, USA

Farner, Donald S *Zoo Physiologist*
%University of Washington, Zoology Dept, Seattle, WA 98195, USA

Farnsworth, Richard *Actor*
PO Box 215, Lincoln, NM 88338, USA

Farquhar, John W *Physician*
%Stanford University Med School, Disease Prevention Center, Stanford, CA 94305, USA

Farquhar, Robert W *Rocket Scientist*
%Johns Hopkins University, Applied Physics Laboratory, Laurel, MD 20723, USA

Farr, Bruce *Marine Architect*
%Bruce Farr Assoc, 613 3rd St, Annapolis, MD 21403, USA

Farr, George L *Businessman*
%American Express Co, World Financial Center, New York, NY 10285, USA

Farr, Jaime *Actor*
99 Buckskin Rd, Canoga Park, CA 91307, USA

Farr, Mel, Sr *Football Player*
4525 Lakeview Court, Bloomfield Hills, MI 48301, USA

Fano - Farr

Farrakhan, Louis   *Religious Leader*
%Nation of Islam, 734 W 79th St, Chicago, IL 60620, USA

Farrar, Donald K   *Businessman*
%Imo Industries, 1009 Lenox Dr, Lawrenceville, NJ 08648, USA

Farrar, Frank L   *Governor, SD*
203 9th Ave, Britton, SD 57430, USA

Farreley, Alexander   *Governor, VI*
%Governor's Office, Government Offices, Charlotte Amalie, VI 00801, USA

Farrell, David C   *Businessman*
%May Department Stores, 611 Olive St, St Louis, MO 63101, USA

Farrell, Eileen   *Opera Singer*
72 Louis St, Staten Island, NY 10304, USA

Farrell, Jeff   *Swimmer*
2405 Capri Lane, Wichita, KS 67210, USA

Farrell, Joseph C   *Businessman*
%Pittston Co, First Stamford Pl, Stamford, CT 06912, USA

Farrell, Mike   *Actor*
PO Box 6010, Sherman Oaks, CA 91413, USA

Farrell, Sean   *Football Player*
%Denver Broncos, 13655 E Dove Valley Parkway, Englewood, CO 80112, USA

Farrell, Sharon   *Actress*
1619 Oak Dr, Topanga, CA 90290, USA

Farrell, Shea   *Actor*
125 S Bowling Green Way, Los Angeles, CA 90049, USA

Farrell, Suzanne   *Ballet Dancer*
%New York City Ballet, Lincoln Center Plaza, New York, NY 10023, USA

Farrell, Terence (Terry)   *Architect*
17 Hatton St, London NW8 8PL, England

Farrell, Terry   *Actress*
%Paul Kohner Inc, 9300 Wilshire Blvd, #555, Beverly Hills, CA 90212, USA

Farrell, Tommy   *Actor*
5225 Riverton Ave, North Hollywood, CA 91601, USA

Farrell, W James   *Businessman*
%Illinois Tool Works, 3600 W Lake Ave, Glenview, IL 60025, USA

Farrimond, Richard A   *Astronaut, England*
95 Druid Stoke Ave, Stoke Bishop, Bristol BS9 1DE, England

Farrington, Hugh G   *Businessman*
%Hannaford Bros Co, 145 Pleasant Hill Rd, Scarborough, ME 04074, USA

Farrington, Jerry S   *Businessman*
%Texas Utilities Co, 1601 Bryan St, Dallas, TX 75201, USA

Farris, G Steven   *Businessman*
%Apache Corp, 2000 Post Oak Blvd, Houston, TX 77056, USA

Farris, Joseph   *Cartoonist*
PO Box 4203, New York, NY 10017, USA

Farrow, Mia   *Actress*
124 Henry Sanford Rd, Bridgewater, CT 06752, USA

Fasanella, Ralph   *Artist*
15 Chester St, Ardskey, NY 10502, USA

Fassbaender, Brigitte   *Opera Singer*
%Jennifer Selby, Haiming 2, 83119 Obing, Germany

Fassi, Carlo   *Figure Skating Coach*
%Broadmoor World Arena Club, Colorado Springs, CO 80901, USA

Fast, Darrell   *Religious Leader*
%Mennonite Church General Conference, 722 Main St, Newton, KS 67114, USA

Fast, Howard M   *Writer*
%Houghton Mifflin Co, 2 Park Ave, Boston, MA 02116, USA

Fauci, Anthony S   *Immunologist*
%National Institue of Allergy & Infectious Diseases, Bethesda, MD 20892, USA

Faucon, Bernard   *Photographer*
6 Rue Barbanegre, 75019 Paris, France

Faulk, Marshall   *Football Player*
%Indianapolis Colts, 7001 W 56th St, Indianapolis, IN 46254, USA

Faulkner, John   *Organic Chemist*
%Scripps Institution of Oceanography, La Jolla, CA 92093, USA

Faulstich, James R   *Financier*
%Federal Home Loan Bank, 1501 4th Ave, Seattle, WA 98101, USA

Faure, Maurice H   *Government Official, France*
28 Blvd Raspail, 75007 Paris, France

F

Faurot, Donald B — *Football Coach*
%Missouri Senior Golf Assn, 108 Burnam Ave, Columbia, MO 65201, USA

Faust, Gerry — *Football Coach*
%University of Akron, Athletic Dept, Akron, OH 44325, USA

Faustino, David — *Actor*
1806 N Maple St, Burbank, CA 91505, USA

Fauvet, Jacques — *Editor*
5 Rue Louis-Boilly, 70016 Paris, France

Favier, Jean-Jacques — *Spatinaut, France*
%CEREM, CENG, 53 Ave des Martyrs, 38041 Grenoble Cedex, France

Fawcett, Don W — *Anatomist*
1224 Lincoln Rd, Missoula, MT 59802, USA

Fawcett, Farrah — *Actress, Model*
9507 Heather Rd, Beverly Hills, CA 90210, USA

Fawcett, Sherwood L — *Research Physicist*
2820 Margate Rd, Columbus, OH 43221, USA

Faxon, Brad — *Golfer*
77 Rumstick Rd, Barrington, RI 02806, USA

Fay, David B — *Golf Executive*
%U S Golf Assn, Golf House, Liberty Corner Rd, Far Hills, NJ 07931, USA

Faye, Herbie — *Actor*
1501 Kenneth Rd, Glendale, CA 91201, USA

Fazio, Tom — *Golf Course Architect*
%Fazio Golf Course Designers, 109 S Main St, Hendersonville, NC 28792, USA

Fazzini, Enrico — *Neurologist*
%New York University Medical Center, 550 1st Ave, New York, NY 10016, USA

Fears, Tom — *Football Player*
1550 Spyglass Place, Palm Springs, CA 92264, USA

Feck, Luke M — *Editor*
2494 Sheringham, Columbus, OH 43220, USA

Fedorov, Sergei — *Hockey Player*
%Detroit Red Wings, Joe Louis Arena, 600 Civic Center Dr, Detroit, MI 48226, USA

Fedoseyev, Vladimir I — *Conductor*
%Moscow House of Recording, Kachalova 24, 121069 Moscow, Russia

Feher, George — *Physicist*
%University of California, Physics Dept, 9500 Gilman Dr, La Jolla, CA 92093, USA

Fehr, Donald M — *Labor Leader*
%Major League Baseball Players Assn, 805 3rd Ave, New York, NY 10022, USA

Fehr, Steve — *Bowler*
%Fehr-Calhoun Bowlers Corral, 3363 Westbourne Dr, Cincinnati, OH 45248, USA

Feifel, Herman — *Psychologist*
360 S Burnside Ave, Los Angeles, CA 90036, USA

Feiffer, Jules — *Cartoonist*
RR 1, Box 440, Vineyard Haven, MA 02568, USA

Feigenbaum, Armand V — *Businessman, Systems Engineer*
%General Systems Co, Berkshire Common, South St, Pittsfield, MA 01201, USA

Feigenbaum, Edward A — *Computer Scientist*
1017 Cathcart Way, Stanford, CA 94305, USA

Feigenbaum, Mitchell J — *Physicist*
%Cornell University, Physics Dept, Ithaca, NY 14853, USA

Feilden, Bernard M — *Architect*
Stiffkey Old Hall, Wells-Next-to-the-Sea, Norfolk NR23 1QJ, England

Fein, Bernard — *Businessman*
%United Industrial Corp, 18 E 48th St, New York, NY 10017, USA

Fein, Rashi — *Economist*
205 Commonwealth Ave, Boston, MA 02116, USA

Feininger, Andreas B L — *Photographer*
5 E 22nd St, #15-P, New York, NY 10010, USA

Feinstein, A Richard — *Physician*
164 Linden St, New Haven, CT 06511, USA

Feinstein, Alan — *Actor*
9229 Sunset Blvd, #311, Los Angeles, CA 90069, USA

Feinstein, Michael — *Singer*
%Agency For Performing Arts, 9000 Sunset Blvd, #1200, Los Angeles, CA 90069, USA

Felch, William C — *Physician*
26337 Carmelo St, Carmel, CA 93923, USA

Feld, Eliot — *Dancer, Choreographer*
%Feld Ballet, 890 Broadway, New York, NY 10003, USA

Faurot - Feld

Feld, Kenneth — *Entertainment Executive*
%Ringling Bros-Barnum & Bailey Circus, 8607 Westwood Circle, Vienna, VA 22182, USA

Feldberg, Sumner L — *Businessman*
%TJX Companies, 770 Cochituate Rd, Framingham, MA 01701, USA

Feldenkrais, Moshe — *Psychologist*
University of Tel-Aviv, Psychology Dept, Tel-Aviv, Israel

Felder, Raoul Lionel — *Attorney*
437 Madison Ave, New York, NY 10022, USA

Feldman, Bella — *Artist*
12 Summit Lane, Berkeley, CA 94708, USA

Feldman, Corey — *Actor*
%Thomas, 3209 Tareco Dr, Los Angeles, CA 90068, USA

Feldman, Jerome M — *Physician*
%Duke University Medical Center, Box 2963, Durham, NC 27715, USA

Feldman, Myer — *Government Official*
%Ginsberg Feldman Bress, 1250 Connecticut Ave NW, Washington, DC 20036, USA

Feldon, Barbara — *Actress, Model*
14 E 74th St, New York, NY 10021, USA

Feldshuh, Tovah — *Actress*
322 Central Park West, #11-B, New York, NY 10025, USA

Feldstein, Martin S — *Government Official, Economist*
147 Clifton St, Belmont, MA 02178, USA

Felici, Pericle Cardinal — *Religious Leader*
Via Pfeiffer 10, 10093 Rome, Italy

Feliciano, Jose — *Singer*
10 Bay St, #123, Westport, CT 06880, USA

Felipe — *Crown Prince, Spain*
%Palacio de la Zarzuela, Madrid, Spain

Felisiak, Robert — *Fencer*
Kreuzberg 13, 97953 Konigheim, Germany

Felke, Petra — *Track Athlete*
%SC Motor Jena, Wollnitzevstr 42, 07749 Jena, Germany

Felker, Clay — *Editor*
322 E 57th St, New York, NY 10022, USA

Fell, Norman — *Actor*
4335 Marina City Dr, Marina del Rey, CA 90292, USA

Feller, Robert W A (Bob) — *Baseball Player*
PO Box 157, Gates Mill, OH 44040, USA

Fellner, William J — *Economist*
131 Edgehill Rd, New Haven, CT 06511, USA

Fellows, Edith — *Actress*
2016 1/2 N Vista del Mar, Los Angeles, CA 90068, USA

Felton, Norman F — *Movie, Television Producer*
%Arena Productions, 22146 Pacific Coast Highway, Malibu, CA 90265, USA

Felts, William R, Jr — *Physician*
1492 Hampton Hill Circle, McLean, VA 22101, USA

Fena, James A — *Financier*
%Alaska USA Federal Credit Union, 4000 Credit Union Dr, Anchorage, AK 99503, USA

Fencik, Gary — *Football Player*
%Chicago Bears, Halas Hall, 250 N Washington Rd, Lake Forest, IL 60045, USA

Fender, Freddy — *Singer, Songwriter*
%Refugee Mgmt, 1025 16th Ave S, #300, Nashville, TN 37212, USA

Fenech, Jeff — *Boxer*
Private Mail Bag 3, Annandale NSW 2038, Australia

Fenech-Adami, Edward — *Prime Minister, Malta*
%Education Ministry, Floriana, Auberge de Castille, Valleta, Malta

Fenical, William — *Organic Chemist*
%Scripps Institution of Oceanography, Organic Chemistry Dept, La Jolla, CA 92093, USA

Fenimore, Bob — *Football Player*
1214 Fairway Dr, Stillwater, OK 74074, USA

Fenley, Molissa — *Dancer, Choreographer*
%Molissa Fenley Dancers, PO Box 450, Prince Street Station, New York, NY 10012, USA

Fenn, Sherilyn — *Actress*
3758 Regal Vista Dr, Sherman Oaks, CA 91403, USA

Fenneman, George — *Entertainer*
11500 San Vicente Blvd, #304, Los Angeles, CA 90049, USA

Fenoglio, William R — *Businessman*
%Augat Inc, 89 Forbes Blvd, Mansfield, MA 02048, USA

F

Feld - Fenoglio

Fenswick, J Henry *Editor*
%Modern Maturity Magazine, Editorial Dept, 3200 E Carson St, Lakewood, CA 90712, USA

Feoktistov, Konstantin P *Cosmonaut*
%Potchta Kosmonavtov, 141 160 Svyosdny Gorodok, Moskovskoi Oblasti, Russia

Ferber, Norman A *Businessman*
%Ross Stores, 8333 Central Ave, Newark, CA 94560, USA

Fergason, James L (Jim) *Inventor (Therman Imaging Device)*
%Optical Shields Inc, 1390 Willow Rd, Menlo Park, CA 94025, USA

Ferguson Cullum, Cathy *Swimmer*
9212 Wilhelm Circle, Huntington Beach, CA 92646, USA

Ferguson, Charles A *Editor*
1448 Joseph St, New Orleans, LA 70115, USA

Ferguson, Clarence C, Jr *Diplomat, Lawyer*
%Harvard University, Law School, Cambridge, MA 02138, USA

Ferguson, Daniel C *Businessman*
%Newell Co, Newell Center, 29 E Stephenson St, Freeport, IL 61032, USA

Ferguson, Frederick E *Vietnam War Army Hero (CMH)*
106 E Stellar Parkway, Chandler, AZ 85226, USA

Ferguson, Jay *Actor*
PO Box 57078, Sherman Oaks, CA 91413, USA

Ferguson, Maynard *Jazz Trumpeter*
PO Box 716, Ojai, CA 93024, USA

Ferguson, Ronald E *Businessman*
%General Re Corp, 695 E Main St, Stanford, CT 06901, USA

Ferguson, Thomas A, Jr *Businessman*
%Newell Co, Newell Center, 29 E Stephenson St, Freeport, IL 61032, USA

Ferguson, Tom *Rodeo Rider*
%General Delivery, Miami, OK 74355, USA

Ferguson, William C *Businessman*
%Nynex Corp, 1095 Ave of Americas, New York, NY 10036, USA

Fergusson, Frances D *Educator*
%Vassar College, President's Office, Poughkeepsie, NY 12603, USA

Ferland, E James *Businessman*
%Public Service Enterprise Group, 80 Park Plaza, Newark, NJ 07102, USA

Ferlinghetti, Lawrence *Writer*
%City Lights Booksellers, 261 Columbus Ave, San Francisco, CA 94133, USA

Fernandez, C Sidney (Sid) *Baseball Player*
748 Kalanipuu St, Honolulu, HI 96825, USA

Fernandez, Juan R *Educator*
%University of Puerto Rico, President's Office, Rio Piedras, PR 00931, USA

Fernandez, Mario F *Artist*
1415 5th St S, #A, Hopkins, MN 55343, USA

Fernandez, Mary Joe *Tennis Player*
%Women's Tennis Assn, 133 1st St NE, St Petersburg, FL 33701, USA

Fernandez, O Antonio C (Tony) *Biologist*
Calle N-3, Restauracion, San Pedro de Macoris, Dominican Republic

Ferragamo, Vince *Football Player*
6715 Horseshoe Rd, Orange, CA 92669, USA

Ferrante, Art *Pianist (Ferrante & Teicher)*
%Avant-Garde Records Corp, 12224 Avila Dr, Kansas City, MO 64145, USA

Ferrante, Jack *Football Player*
3712 Pembroke Lane, Ocean City, NJ 08226, USA

Ferrara, Arthur V *Businessman*
%Guardian Life Insurance Co, 201 Park Ave S, New York, NY 10003, USA

Ferrare, Cristina *Model, Entertainer*
1280 Stone Canyon Rd, Los Angeles, CA 90077, USA

Ferrari, Michael R, Jr *Educator*
%Drake University, President's Office, Des Moines, IA 50311, USA

Ferrari, Tina *Dancer, Wrestler*
2901 S Las Vegas Blvd, Las Vegas, NV 89109, USA

Ferraro, Geraldine A *Representative, NY*
%Keck Mahin Cate Koehler, 220 E 42nd St, New York, NY 10017, USA

Ferraro, John *Football Player*
641 N Wilcox Ave, Los Angeles, CA 90004, USA

Ferrazzi, Ferruccio *Artist*
Piazza delle Muse, Via G G Porro 27, 00197 Rome, Italy

Ferrazzi, Pierpaolo *Kayak Athlete*
%EuroGrafica, Via del Progresso, 36035 Marano Vicenza, Italy

Ferre, Gianfranco — *Fashion Designer*
Villa Della Spiga 19/A, 20121 Milan, Italy

Ferrell, Conchata — *Actress*
1335 Seward St, Los Angeles, CA 90028, USA

Ferrell, Rachelle — *Singer*
%Dan Cleary Mgmt, 1801 Ave of Stars, #1105, Los Angeles, CA 90067, USA

Ferrer, Lupita — *Actress*
904 N Bedford Dr, Beverly Hills, CA 90210, USA

Ferrer, Mel — *Actor*
6590 Camino Caretta, Carpinteria, CA 93013, USA

Ferrer, Miguel — *Actor*
%William Morris Agency, 151 S El Camino Dr, Beverly Hills, CA 90212, USA

Ferrero, Louis P — *Businessman*
%Anacomp Inc, 11550 N Meridian St, Indianapolis, IN 46240, USA

Ferrigno, Lou — *Actor, Bodybuilder*
PO Box 1671, Santa Monica, CA 90406, USA

Ferriss, David M (Boo) — *Baseball Player*
510 Robinson Dr, Cleveland, MS 38732, USA

Territor, Daniel E — *Educator*
%University of Arkansas, Chancellor's Office, Fayetteville, AR 72701, USA

Ferron — *Singer, Songwriter*
%Cherrywood Station Records, PO Box 871, Vashon Island, WA 98070, USA

Ferry, Bryan — *Singer, Songwriter*
%Stardust Ents, 2650 Glendower Ave, Los Angeles, CA 90027, USA

Ferry, Danny — *Basketball Player*
%Cleveland Cavaliers, 2923 Statesboro Rd, Richfield, OH 44286, USA

Ferry, David — *Poet*
%Wellesley College, English Dept, Wellesley, MA 02181, USA

Ferry, John D — *Chemist*
137 N Prospect Ave, Madison, WI 53705, USA

Fery, John B — *Businessman*
609 Wyndemere Dr, Boise, ID 83702, USA

Feshbach, Herman — *Physicist*
5 Sedgwick Rd, Cambridge, MA 02138, USA

Festinger, Leon — *Psychologist*
37 W 12th St, New York, NY 10011, USA

Fetterhoff, Robert — *Religious Leader*
%Fellowship of Grace Brethren, PO Box 386, Winona Lake, IN 46590, USA

Fettman, Martin J — *Veterinarian, Astronaut*
%Colorado State University, Pathology Dept, Fort Collins, CO 80523, USA

Feuer, Cy — *Theatrical, Movie Producer*
%Feuer & Martin, 630 Park Ave, New York, NY 10021, USA

Feuillere, Edwige — *Actress*
141 Rue de Longchamp, 92200 Neuilly-Sur-Seine, France

Feulner, Edwin J, Jr — *Foundation Executive*
%Heritage Foundation, 214 Massachusetts Ave NE, Washington, DC 20002, USA

Fey, Michael — *Cartoonist (Committed)*
%United Feature Syndicate, 200 Park Ave, New York, NY 10166, USA

Fibiger, John A — *Businessman*
%Transam Life Cos, 1159 S Olive St, Los Angeles, CA 90015, USA

Fichandler, Zelda — *Theater Producer, Director*
%Arena Stages, 6th & Maine Ave SW, Washington, DC 20024, USA

Fichtel, Anja — *Fencer*
Dittigheimer Weg 20, 97941 Tauberbischofsheim, Germany

Fidrych, Mark S — *Baseball Player*
260 West St, Northboro, MA 01532, USA

Fiechter, Jonathan L — *Financier*
%Office of Thrift Supervision, 1700 "G" St NW, Washington, DC 20552, USA

Fiedler, Jens — *Cyclist*
Fritz-Lesch-Str, Herberge, 13053 Berlin, Germany

Fiedler, John — *Actor*
225 Adams St, #10-B, Brooklyn, NY 11201, USA

Fiedler, Leslie A — *Writer, Critic*
154 Morris Ave, Buffalo, NY 14214, USA

Field, Chelsea — *Actress*
%Troxell, 2335 Overland Ave, Los Angeles, CA 90064, USA

Field, Frederick (Ted) — *Entertainment Executive*
%Interscope Communications, 10900 Wilshire Blvd, Los Angeles, CA 90024, USA

F

Ferre - Field

F

Field, George B *Theoretical Astrophysicist*
%Harvard University Observatory, 60 Garden St, Cambridge, MA 02138, USA

Field, Helen *Opera Singer*
%Lies Askonas Ltd, 186 Drury Lane, London WC2B 5RY, England

Field, John W, Jr *Financier*
%J P Morgan Delaware, 902 Market St, Wilmingtonm, DE 19801, USA

Field, Marshall *Publisher*
%Field Corp, 333 W Wacker Dr, Chicago, IL 60606, USA

Field, Sally *Actress*
%Fogwood Films, PO Box 492417, Los Angeles, CA 90049, USA

Field, Shirley Ann *Actress*
%International Creative Mgmt, 76 Oxford St, London W1N 0AX, England

Fielder, Cecil G *Baseball Player*
109 Kenwood Rd, Grosse Pointe Farms, MI 48236, USA

Fields, Debbi *Businesswoman*
%Mrs Fields Cookies, 333 Main St, Park City, UT 84060, USA

Fields, Harold T, Jr *Army General*
126 Deer Run Strut, Enterprise, AL 36330, USA

Fields, Holly *Actress*
%Borinstein Oreck Bogart Agency, 8271 Melrose Ave, #110, Los Angeles, CA 90046, USA

Fields, Kim *Actress*
825 3/4 N Sweetzer Ave, Los Angeles, CA 90069, USA

Fields, Mark *Football Player*
%New Orleans Saints, 1500 Poydras St, New Orleans, LA 70112, USA

Fiennes, Ralph *Actor*
%Larry Dalzell Assoc, 17 Broad Court, #12, London WC2B 5QN, England

Fiennes, Ranulph T-W *Transglobal Explorer*
Greenlands, Exford, Minehead, West Sussex, England

Fierstein, Harvey F *Playwright, Actor*
15 Hawthorne Rd, Ridgefield, CT 06877, USA

Fife, Bernard *Businessman*
%Standard Motor Products Inc, 37-18 Northern Blvd, Long Island City, NY 11101, USA

Figini, Luigi *Architect*
Via Perone di S Martino 8, Milan, Italy

Figini, Michela *Skier*
6799 Prato-Leventina, Switzerland

Figueiredo, Joao Baptista de *President, Brazil; Army General*
Av Prefeito Mendes de Moraes 1400/802, S Conrado, Rio de Janeiro, Brazil

Figueres Olsen, Jose M *President, Costa Rica*
%President's Office, Apdo 520-2010, San Jose 1000, Costa Rica

Fikrig, Erol *Immunologist*
%Yale University Medical Center, Infectious Disease Dept, New Haven, CT 06510, USA

Filatova, Ludmila P *Opera Singer*
Ryleyevastr 6, #13, St Petersburg, Russia

Filchock, Frank *Football Player*
1725 SW Fernwood Dr, Lake Oswego, OR 97034, USA

Filipacchi, Daniel *Publisher*
%Hachette Filipacchi, 2-6 Rue Ancelle, 92525 Neuilly-Sur-Seine, France

Filipchenko, Anatoly N *Cosmonaut; Air Force General*
%Potchta Kosmonavtov, 141 160 Svyosdny Gorodok, Moskovskoi Oblasti, Russia

Fill, Dennis C *Businessman*
%Westmark International Inc, 701 5th Ave, Seattle, WA 98104, USA

Filmus, Tully *Artist*
4 Fern Hill, Great Barrington, MA 01230, USA

Finch, Jon *Actor*
%Conway Van Gelder Robinson, 18-21 Jermyn St, London SW1Y 6HB, England

Finch, Larry *Basketball Player, Coach*
%Memphis State University, Athletic Dept, Memphis, TN 38152, USA

Finch, Robert H *Secretary, Health Education & Welfare*
1106 Las Reindas, Pasadena, CA 91107, USA

Finchem, Timothy W *Golf Executive*
%Professional Golfer's Assn, Sawgrass, Ponte Vedra Beach, FL 32082, USA

Fine, Travis *Actor*
%Vaughn D Hart, 200 N Robertson Blvd, #219, Beverly Hills, CA 90211, USA

Fingers, Roland G (Rollie) *Baseball Player*
4944 Smith Canyon Court, San Diego, CA 92130, USA

Fini, Leonor *Artist*
8 Rue de la Vrilliere, 75001 Paris, France

Field - Fini

Fink, Donald E *Editor*
%Aviation Week Magazine, 1221 Ave of Americas, New York, NY 10020, USA
Fink, Gerald R *Geneticist*
40 Alston Rd, Chestnut Hill, MA 02167, USA
Finkel, Fyvush *Actor*
%Silver/Kass/Massetti, 8730 Sunset Blvd, #480, Los Angeles, CA 90069, USA
Finlay, Frank *Actor*
%Al Parker Ltd, 55 Park Lane, London W1Y 3DD, England
Finley, Charles E (Chuck) *Baseball Player*
59 Sea Pine Lane, Newport Beach, CA 92660, USA
Finley, Charles O *Baseball Executive*
601 9th Ave, Ottawa, IL 61350, USA
Finley, Karen *Conceptual Artist*
%Kitchen Center for Video-Music-Dance, 512 W 9th, New York, NY 10018, USA
Finley, Michael *Basketball Player*
%Phoenix Suns, 201 E Jefferson St, Phoenix, AZ 85004, USA
Finn, Chester E, Jr *Educator*
%Educational Excellence Network, PO Box 26919, Indianapolis, IN 46226, USA
Finn, John W *WW II Navy Hero (CMH)*
Star Route, Box 17, Pine Valley, CA 91962, USA
Finn, Richard H *Financier*
%Transamerica Finance Group, 1150 S Olive St, Los Angeles, CA 90015, USA
Finn, Tim *Singer (Split Enz, Crowded House)*
1801 Century Park E, #2400, Los Angeles, CA 90067, USA
Finnane, Daniel F *Basketball Executive*
%Golden State Warriors, Oakland Coliseum Arena, Oakland, CA 94621, USA
Finnbogagottir, Vigdis *President, Iceland*
%President's Office, Sto'rnarradshusini v/Laekjartog, Reykjavik, Iceland
Finnegan, John R, Sr *Editor*
%St Paul Pioneer Press Dispatch, 345 Cedar St, St Paul, MN 55101, USA
Finnegan, Neal F *Financier*
%UST Corp, 40 Court St, Boston, MA 02108, USA
Finneran Rittenhouse, Sharon *Swimmer*
212 Harbor Dr, Santa Cruz, CA 95062, USA
Finneran, John G *Navy Admiral*
5600 Beam Court, Bethesda, MD 20817, USA
Finney, Albert *Actor*
39 Seymour Walk, London SW10, England
Finney, Allison *Golfer*
72-750 Cactus Court, #A, Palm Desert, CA 92260, USA
Finney, Jack *Writer*
223 Ricardo Rd, Mill Valley, CA 94941, USA
Finney, Ross Lee *Composer*
2015 Geddes, Ann Arbor, MI 48104, USA
Finnie, Linda A *Concert Singer*
16 Golf Course, Girvan, Ayrshire KA26 9HW, England
Finster, Howard *Artist*
Rt 2, Box 106-A, Summerville, GA 30747, USA
Finsterwald, Dow *Golfer*
%Broadmoor Golf Club, 1 Lake Circle, Colorado Springs, CO 80906, USA
Fiona *Singer, Songwriter*
%William Morris Agency, 151 S El Camino Dr, Beverly Hills, CA 90212, USA
Fiondella, Robert W *Businessman*
%Phoenix Home Mutual Life Insurance, 150 Bright Meadow Blvd, Enfield, CT 06082, USA
Fiore, Bill *Actor*
10 E 44th St, #700, New York, NY 10017, USA
Fiorentino, Linda *Actress*
%United Talent Agency, 9560 Wilshire Blvd, #500, Beverly Hills, CA 90212, USA
Fiorillo, Elisa *Singer*
%A&M Records, 1416 N La Brea Ave, Los Angeles, CA 90028, USA
Fippin, Cornelius J *Financier*
%Golden 1 Credit Union, 6507 4th St, Sacramento, CA 95817, USA
Fireman, Paul B *Businessman*
%Reebok International, 100 Technology Center Dr, Stroughton, MA 02072, USA
Firestone, Roy *Sportscaster*
%Seizen/Wallach Productions, 257 Rodeo Dr, Beverly Hills, CA 90212, USA
Firth, Peter *Actor*
%Markham & Froggatt, 4 Windmill St, London W1P 1HF, England

F

Fink - Firth

Fischbach, Ephraim *Physicist*
120 Pathway Lane, Lafayette, IN 47906, USA

Fischer, Bill (Moose) *Football Player*
1909 Prairie, Ishpeming, MI 49849, USA

Fischer, Edmond H *Nobel Medicine Laureate*
5540 N Windermere Rd, Seattle, WA 98105, USA

Fischer, Ernst Otto *Nobel Chemistry Laureate*
Sohnckestr 16, 81479 Munich, Germany

Fischer, Gottfried B *Publisher*
PO Box 237, Old Greenwich, CT 06870, USA

Fischer, Ivan *Conductor*
Nepkoztarsasag Ut 27, 1061 Budapest, Hungary

Fischer, Michael L *Association Executive*
%California Coastal Conservancy, 1330 Broadway, #1100, Oakland, CA 94612, USA

Fischer, Robert J (Bobby) *Chess Player*
%US Chess Federation, 186 Rt 9-W, New Windsor, NY 12550, USA

Fischer, Stanley *Economist*
4804 Foxhall Crescent NW, Washington, DC 20007, USA

Fischer-Dieskau, Dietrich *Opera, Concert Singer*
Lindenallee 22, 12587 Berlin, Germany

Fischl, Eric *Artist*
%Mary Boone Gallery, 417 W Broadway, New York, NY 10012, USA

Fiscus, Robert L *Businessman*
%United Illuminating Co, 157 Church St, New Haven, CT 06510, USA

Fish, Howard M *Air Force General*
%Loral Corp, 1725 Jefferson Davis Highway, Arlington, VA 22202, USA

Fish, Lawrence K *Financier*
%Citizens Financial Group, 1 Citizens Plaza, Providence, RI 02903, USA

Fishburne, Laurence *Actor*
%Helen Sugland, 5200 Lankershim Blvd, #260, North Hollywood, CA 91601, USA

Fishel, Richard *Microbiologist*
%University of Vermont Medical Center, Microbiology Dept, Burlington, VT 05405, USA

Fisher, Anna L *Astronaut*
%NASA, Johnson Space Center, 2101 NASA Rd, Houston, TX 77058, USA

Fisher, Bernard *Surgeon*
5636 Aylesboro Ave, Pittsburgh, PA 15217, USA

Fisher, Bernard F *Vietnam War Air Force Hero (CMH)*
4200 King Rd, Rt 1, Kuna, ID 83634, USA

Fisher, Carrie *Actress, Writer*
7985 Santa Monica Blvd, #109-336, Los Angeles, CA 90046, USA

Fisher, Charles T, III *Financier*
100 Renaissance Center, #2412, Detroit, MI 48243, USA

Fisher, Donald G *Businessman*
%Gap Stores Inc, 1 Harrison St, San Francisco, CA 94105, USA

Fisher, Eddie *Singer*
1000 North Point St, #1802, San Francisco, CA 94109, USA

Fisher, Eddie G *Baseball Player*
408 Cardinal Circle S, Altus, OK 73521, USA

Fisher, Elder A (Bud) *Bowling Executive*
521 Cedar Lake Court, Carmel, IN 46032, USA

Fisher, Frances *Actress*
2337 Roscomare Rd, #2-174, Los Angeles, CA 90077, USA

Fisher, Franklin M *Economist*
130 Mt Auburn St, Cambridge, MA 02138, USA

Fisher, George A, Jr *Army General*
Chief of Staff, Forces Command, Fort McPherson, GA 30330, USA

Fisher, George M C *Businessman*
%Eastman Kodak Co, 343 State St, Rochester, NY 14650, USA

Fisher, Jeff *Football Coach*
%Houston Oilers, 6910 Fannin St, Houston, TX 77030, USA

Fisher, Joel *Sculptor*
99 Commercial St, Brooklyn, NY 11222, USA

Fisher, Jules E *Lighting Designer*
%Jules Fisher Enterprises, 126 5th Ave, New York, NY 10011, USA

Fisher, Max M *Businessman*
2700 Fisher St, Detroit, MI 48217, USA

Fisher, Richard B *Financier*
%Morgan Stanley Group, 1251 Ave of Americas, New York, NY 10020, USA

F

Fisher, Rick *Lighting Designer*
%Royale Theater, 242 W 45th St, New York, NY 10036, USA

Fisher, Roger *Guitarist (Heart)*
%Levine/Schneider, 433 N Camden Dr, Beverly Hills, CA 90210, USA

Fisher, Steve *Basketball Coach*
%University of Michigan, Crisler Arena, 1000 S State St, Ann Arbor, MI 48109, USA

Fisher, Thomas L *Businessman*
%Nicor Inc, PO Box 3014, Naperville, IL 60566, USA

Fisher, William F *Astronaut*
%Humana Hospital Clear Lake, 500 Medical Center Blvd, Webster, TX 77598, USA

Fisherman, William S *Businessman*
%ARA Services, 1101 Market St, Philadelphia, PA 19107, USA

Fishman, Jack *Businessman*
%IVAX Corp, 8800 NW 36th St, Miami, FL 33178, USA

Fishman, Jerald G *Businessman*
%Analog Devices, 1 Technology Way, Norwood, MA 02062, USA

Fishman, Michael *Actor*
%Gold Marshak Assoc, 3500 W Olive Ave, #1400, Burbank, CA 91505, USA

Fisk, Carlton E *Baseball Player*
16612 Catawba Rd, Lockport, IL 60441, USA

Fisk, James B *Physicist*
Lees Hill Rd, Basking Ridge, NJ 60441, USA

Fiske, Robert B, Jr *Attorney*
19 Juniper Rd, Darien, CT 06820, USA

Fitch, Val L *Nobel Physics Laureate*
292 Hartley Ave, Princeton, NJ 08540, USA

Fitch, William C (Bill) *Basketball Coach*
%Los Angeles Clippers, Sports Arena, 3939 S Figueroa St, Los Angeles, CA 90037, USA

Fitch, William H *Marine Corps General*
%Marine Corps Headquarters, Washington, DC 20380, USA

Fitoo, Donald V *Businessman*
%Caterpillar Inc, 100 NE Adams St, Peoria, IL 61629, USA

Fitt of Bell's Hill, Gerard *Government Official, England*
%Irish Club, 82 Eaton Square, London SW1, England

Fittipaldi, Emerson *Auto Racing Driver*
1524 Camino Sierra Vista, Santa Fe, NM 87501, USA

Fitz, Raymond L *Educator*
%University of Dayton, President's Office, Dayton, OH 45469, USA

Fitzgerald, A Ernest *Government Efficiency Advocate*
%Air Force Management Systems, Pentagon, Washington, DC 20330, USA

Fitzgerald, Ella *Singer*
%Franklyn Agency, 1010 Hammond St, #312, Los Angeles, CA 90069, USA

FitzGerald, Frances *Writer*
%Simon & Schuster Inc, 1230 Ave of Americas, New York, NY 10020, USA

FitzGerald, Garret *Prime Minister, Ireland*
%Dail Eireann, Leinster House, Kildare St, Dublin 2, Ireland

Fitzgerald, Geraldine *Actress*
50 E 79th St, New York, NY 10021, USA

Fitzgerald, Jack *Actor*
%Tisherman Agency, 6767 Forest Lawn Dr, #115, Los Angeles, CA 90068, USA

Fitzgerald, James F *Basketball Executive*
%Golden State Warriors, Oakland Coliseum Arena, Oakland, CA 94621, USA

FitzGerald, Tara *Actress*
%Caroline Dawson Assoc, 47 Courtfield Rd, #9, London SW7 4DB, England

Fitzgerald, William A *Financier*
%Commercial Federal Bank, 2120 S 72nd St, Omaha, NE 68124, USA

Fitzgibbons, James M *Businessman*
%Fieldcrest Cannon Inc, 326 E Stadium Dr, Eden, NC 27288, USA

Fitzmaurice, David J *Labor Leader*
%Electrical Radio & Machinists Union, 11256 156th St NW, Washington, DC 20005, USA

Fitzmaurice, Michael J *Vietnam War Army Hero (CMH)*
PO Box 183, Hartford, SD 57033, USA

Fitzpatrick, Barry J *Financier*
%First Virginia Banks, 6400 Arlington Blvd, Falls Church, VA 22042, USA

Fitzsimmons, Lowell (Cotton) *Basketball Coach*
%Phoenix Suns, 201 E Jefferson St, Phoenix, AZ 85004, USA

Fitzsimmons, Tom *Actor*
%Henderson/Hogan Agency, 247 S Beverly Dr, #102, Beverly Hills, CA 90212, USA

Fisher - Fitzsimmons

F

Fitzsimonds, Roger L *Financier*
%Firstar Corp, 777 E Wisconsin Ave, Milwaukee, WI 53202, USA

Fitzwater, Marlin *Government Official*
2001 Swan Terrace, Alexandria, VA 22307, USA

Fixman, Marshall *Chemist*
%Colorado State University, Chemistry Dept, Fort Collins, CO 80523, USA

Fjeldstad, Oivin *Conductor*
Damfaret 59, Bryn-Oslo 6, Norway

Flach, Ken *Tennis Player*
%Advantage International, 1025 Thomas Jefferson St NW, #450, Washington 20007, USA

Flack, Roberta *Singer, Songwriter*
PO Box 277, Tarrytown, NY 10591, USA

Flade, H Klaus-Dietrich *Cosmonaut, Germany*
Hennebuhlstr 2, 85051 Ingolstadt, Germany

Flagg, Fannie *Comedienne*
1520 Willina Lane, Montecito, CA 93108, USA

Flaherty, John F (Red) *Baseball Umpire*
9 Fowler Lane, Falmouth, MA 02540, USA

Flaherty, Peter L, Jr *Businessman*
%Mid Atlantic Medical Services, 4 Taft Ct, Rockville, MD 20850, USA

Flaherty, Thomas J *Businessman*
%Fairchild Corp, 300 W Service Rd, Chantilly, VA 22021, USA

Flanagan, Barry *Sculptor*
5-E Fawe St, London E14 6PD, England

Flanagan, David T *Businessman*
%Central Maine Power Co, Edison Dr, Augusta, ME 04336, USA

Flanagan, Ed *Football Player*
7436 Reche Canyon Rd, Colton, CA 92324, USA

Flanagan, Fionnula *Actress*
13438 Java Dr, Beverly Hills, CA 90210, USA

Flanagan, James L *Research Engineer*
%Rutgers University, Computer Aids for Industry Center, Piscataway, NJ 08855, USA

Flanagan, Michael K (Mike) *Baseball Player*
410 Stablers Church Rd, Parkton, MD 21120, USA

Flanagan, Tommy *Jazz Pianist*
%Bobbi Marcus Public Relations, 1514 17th St, #206, Santa Monica, CA 90404, USA

Flanagan, William J, Jr *Navy Admiral*
Commander, 2nd Fleet, FPO, AE 09501, USA

Flanery, Sean Patrick *Actor*
185 San Felipe Ave, San Francisco, CA 94127, USA

Flannery, Susan *Actress*
789 Riven Rock Rd, Santa Barbara, CA 93108, USA

Flannery, Thomas *Editorial Cartoonist*
911 Dartmouth Glen Way, Baltimore, MD 21212, USA

Flaten, Alfred N, Jr *Businessman*
%Nash Finch Co, 7600 France Ave S, Minneapolis, MN 55435, USA

Flathman, Richard E *Political Scientist*
819 W University Parkway, Baltimore, MD 21210, USA

Flatley, Patrick *Hockey Player*
%New York Islanders, Veterans Memorial Coliseum, Uniondale, NY 11553, USA

Flatt, Lester *Banjo Player*
PO Box 647, Hendersonville, TN 37077, USA

Flaugh, David C *Businessman*
%National Health Laboratories, 4225 Executive Square, La Jolla, CA 92037, USA

Flavell, Richard A *Immunologist*
%Yale University Medical Center, Immunology Dept, New Haven, CT 06510, USA

Flavin, Dan *Artist*
PO Box 1210, Wainscott, NY 11975, USA

Flavin, Jennifer *Model*
1144 Ocean Dr, Manhattan Beach, CA 90266, USA

Fleck, Jack *Golfer*
Rt 1, Box 140, Magazine, AR 72943, USA

Fleetwood, Ken *Fashion Designer*
14 Savile Row, London SW1, England

Fleetwood, Mick *Musician (Fleetwood Mac)*
%Courage Mgmt, 2899 Agoura Rd, #582, Westlake, CA 91361, USA

Fleischer, Arthur, Jr *Attorney*
%Fried Frank Harris Shriver Jacobson, 1 New York Plaza, New York, NY 10004, USA

Fleischer, Daniel — *Religious Leader*
%Church of Lutheran Confession, 460 75th Ave NE, Minneapolis, MN 55432, USA

Fleischer, Richard O — *Movie Director*
%Gersh Agency, 232 N Canon Dr, Beverly Hills, CA 90210, USA

Fleischmann, Martin — *Electrochemist*
Bury Lodge, Duck St, Tisbury, Wilts SP3 6LJ, England

Fleisher, Leon — *Concert Pianist, Conductor*
20 Merrymount Rd, Baltimore, MD 21210, USA

Fleishman, Joel L — *Educator, Lawyer*
205 Wood Circle, Chapel Hill, NC 27514, USA

Fleming Jenkins, Peggy — *Figure Skater*
16387 Aztec Ridge Dr, Los Gatos, CA 95032, USA

Fleming, Betty B — *Judge*
%US Court of Appeals, 1010 5th Ave, Seattle, WA 98104, USA

Fleming, James P — *Vietnam War Air Force Hero (CMH)*
5109 River Ridge Rd, Arlington, TX 76017, USA

Fleming, John M — *Businessman*
%Vauxhall Motors, Kimpton Rd, Luton, Beds LU2 0SY, England

Fleming, John V — *Educator*
183 Hartley Ave, Princeton, NJ 08540, USA

Fleming, Mac A — *Labor Leader*
%Maintenance of Ways Brotherhood, 26555 Evergreen Rd, Southfield, MI 48076, USA

Fleming, Peter E, Jr — *Attorney*
%Curtis Mallet-Prevost Colt Mosle, 101 Park Ave, New York, NY 10178, USA

Fleming, Rhonda — *Actress*
10281 Century Woods Dr, Los Angeles, CA 90067, USA

Fleming, Richard C D — *City Planner*
%Greater Denver Chamber of Commerce, 1445 Market St, Denver, CO 80202, USA

Fleming, Robben W — *Educator*
2108 Vinewood Ave, Ann Arbor, MI 48104, USA

Fleming, Scott — *Government Official*
2750 Shasta Rd, Berkeley, CA 94708, USA

Flemming, Arthur S — *Secretary, Health Education & Welfare*
%Commission on Civil Rights, 1121 Vermont Ave NW, Washington, DC 20005, USA

Flemming, William N (Bill) — *Sportscaster*
%ABC-TV, Sports Dept, 77 W 66th St, New York, NY 10023, USA

Fletcher, Andy — *Synthesizer Musician (Depeche Mode)*
PO Box 326, London SW6 6RL, England

Fletcher, Arthur A — *Government Official*
%Commission on Civil Rights, 1121 Vermont Ave NW, Washington, DC 20005, USA

Fletcher, Charles M — *Physician, Research Scientist*
2 Coastguard Cottages, Newtown PO30 4PA, England

Fletcher, Colin — *Backpacker, Writer*
%Brandt & Brandt, 1501 Broadway, New York, NY 10036, USA

Fletcher, Guy — *Keyboardist (Dire Straits)*
%Damage Mgmt, 10 Southwick Mews, London W2, England

Fletcher, Louise — *Actress*
1520 Camden Ave, #105, Los Angeles, CA 90025, USA

Fletcher, Martin — *Commentator*
%NBC-TV, News Dept, 4001 Nebraska Ave NW, Washington, DC 20016, USA

Fletcher, Philip B — *Businessman*
%ConAgra Inc, 1 ConAgra Dr, Omaha, NE 68102, USA

Flexner, James T — *Writer*
530 E 86th St, New York, NY 10028, USA

Flindt, Flemming O — *Ballet Dancer, Choreographer*
%Dallas Ballet Assn, 1925 Elm St, #300, Dallas, TX 75201, USA

Flinn, Patrick L — *Financier*
%Bank South Corp, 55 Marietta St NW, Atlanta, GA 30303, USA

Flittie, John H — *Businessman*
%NWNL Companies, 20 Washington Ave, Minneapolis, MN 55401, USA

Flom, Joseph H — *Attorney*
%Skadden Arps Slate Meagher Flom, 919 3rd Ave, New York, NY 10022, USA

Flood, Ann — *Actress*
15 E 91st St, New York, NY 10128, USA

Flood, Curtis C (Curt) — *Baseball Player*
4139 Cloverdale Ave, Los Angeles, CA 90008, USA

Flood, Howard L — *Financier*
%FirstMerit Corp, 106 S Main St, Akron, OH 44308, USA

F

Fleischer - Flood

F

Flor, Claus Peter — *Conductor*
%Mariedl Anders Artists, 535 El Camino Del Mar, San Francisco, CA 94121, USA

Florek, Dann — *Actor*
%J Michael Bloom Ltd, 9255 Sunset Blvd, #710, Los Angeles, CA 90069, USA

Floren, Myron — *Accordionist*
26 Georgeff Rd, Rolling Hills, CA 90274, USA

Flores, Patrick F — *Religious Leader*
%Archbishop's Residence, 2600 Woodlawn Ave, San Antonio, TX 78228, USA

Florio, James J (Jim) — *Governor; Representative, NJ*
%Mudge Rose Guthrie, Corporate Center 2, 1 Upper Pond Rd, Parsippany, NJ 07054, USA

Florio, Steven T — *Publisher*
%Conde Nast Publications, 350 Madison Ave, New York, NY 10017, USA

Florio, Thomas A — *Publisher*
%New Yorker Magazine, 20 W 43rd St, New York, NY 10036, USA

Flory, Med — *Actor*
6044 Ensign Ave, North Hollywood, CA 91606, USA

Flournoy, Craig — *Journalist*
%Dallas News, Editorial Dept, Communications Center, Dallas, TX 75265, USA

Flower, Joseph R — *Religious Leader*
%Assemblies of God, 1445 N Boonville Ave, Springfield, MO 65802, USA

Flowers of Queen's Gate, Brian H — *Physicist*
53 Athenaeum Rd, London N2O 9AL, England

Floyd, Carlisle — *Composer*
4491 Yoakum Blvd, Houston, TX 77006, USA

Floyd, Eddie — *Singer, Songwriter*
%TCI/Talent Consultants International, 1560 Broadway, #1308, New York, NY 10036, USA

Floyd, Eric (Sleepy) — *Basketball Player*
%New Jersey Nets, Byrne Meadowlands Arena, East Rutherford, NJ 07073, USA

Floyd, Raymond (Ray) — *Golfer*
%International Management Group, 1 Erieview Plaza, #1300, Cleveland, OH 44114, USA

Fluckey, Eugene B — *WW II Navy Hero (CMH); Admiral*
1016 Sandpiper Lane, Annapolis, MD 21403, USA

Fluegel, Darlanne — *Actress*
PO Box 78, Beckwourth, CA 96129, USA

Fluno, Jere D — *Businessman*
%W W Grainger Inc, 5500 W Howard St, Skokie, IL 60077, USA

Flutie, Doug — *Football Player*
22 Robin Hood Rd, Natick, MA 01760, USA

Flynn, Barbara — *Actress*
%Markham & Froggatt, Julian House, 4 Windmill St, London W1P 1HF, England

Flynn, William J — *Businessman*
%Mutual of America, 666 5th Ave, New York, NY 10103, USA

Flynn, William S — *Army General*
14 Annandale Rd, Newport, RI 02840, USA

Flynt, Larry — *Publisher*
%Hustler Magazine, 9171 Wilshire Blvd, #300, Beverly Hills, CA 90210, USA

Fo, Dario — *Writer*
%Pietro Sciotto, Via Alessandria 4, 20144 Milan, Italy

Foa, Joseph V — *Aeronautical Engineer*
11319 Commonwealth Dr, #101, North Bethesda, MD 20852, USA

Foale, C Michael — *Astronaut*
%NASA, Johnson Space Center, 2101 NASA Rd, Houston, TX 77058, USA

Foale, Marion A — *Fashion Designer*
Church Farm, Orton-on-the-Hill Near Atherstone, Warwicks, England

Fobes, John E — *Diplomat*
25 Beaverbrook Rd, Asheville, NC 28804, USA

Foch, Nina — *Actress*
PO Box 1884, Beverly Hills, CA 90213, USA

Focht, Michael H, Sr — *Businessman*
%National Medical Enterprises, 2700 Colorado Ave, Santa Monica, CA 90404, USA

Fock, Jeno — *Prime Minister, Hungary*
%Tech/Scien Societies Fed, Kossuth Lajos Ter 6/8, 1055 Budapest, Hungary

Fodor, Eugene N — *Concert Violinist*
22314 N Turkey Creek Rd, Morrison, CO 80465, USA

Foeger, Luggi — *Skier*
%Christopher Foeger, 230 S Balsamina Way, Portola Valley, CA 94028, USA

Fogarty, Edward T — *Businessman*
%Tambrands Inc, 777 Westchester Ave, White Plains, NY 10604, USA

Fogarty, William M — *Navy Admiral*
Commander, Joint Task Force Middle East, FPO, New York, NY 09501, USA

Fogel, Robert W — *Nobel Economics Laureate*
%University of Chicago, Population Economics Center, Chicago, IL 60637, USA

Fogelberg, Dan — *Singer, Songwriter*
PO Box 2399, Pagosa Springs, CO 81147, USA

Fogerty, John — *Singer, Songwriter*
14023 Aubrey Rd, Beverly Hills, CA 90210, USA

Foggs, Edward L — *Religious Leader*
%Church of God, PO Box 2420, Anderson, IN 46018, USA

Fogleman, Ronald R — *Air Force General*
CinC, Transportation Command, 508 Scott Dr, Scott Air Force Base, IL 62225, USA

Fogler, Eddie — *Basketball Coach*
%University of South Carolina, Athletic Dept, Columbia, SC 53233, USA

Foley, Dave — *Actor*
%"NewsRadio" Show, NBC-TV, 3000 W Alameda Ave, Burbank, CA 91523, USA

Foley, Maurice — *Government Official, England*
Gillingham House, Gillingham St, London SW1, England

Foley, Robert F — *Vietnam War Army Hero, General*
%US Military Academy, Superintendent's Office, West Point, NY 10996, USA

Foley, Sylvester R, Jr — *Navy Admiral*
%Navy Department, Pentagon, Washington, DC 20350, USA

Foley, Thomas S — *Representative, WA; Speaker*
601 W 1st Ave, #2-W, Spokane, WA 99204, USA

Foley, William P, II — *Businessman*
%CKE Restaurants, 1200 N Habor Blvd, Anaheim, CA 92801, USA

Folick, Jeffrey M — *Businessman*
%PacifiCare Health Systems, 5995 Plaza Dr, Cypress, CA 90630, USA

Foligno, Mike — *Hockey Player*
%Toronto Maple Leafs, 60 Carlton St, Toronto ON M5B 1L1, Canada

Folkenberg, Robert S — *Religious Leader*
%Seventh-Day Adventists, 12501 Old Columbia Pike, Silver Spring, MD 20904, USA

Folkers, Karl A — *Chemist*
6406 Mesa Dr, Austin, TX 78731, USA

Folkin, Vitold — *Prime Minister, Ukraine*
%Prime Minister's Office, Government Building, Kiev, Ukraine

Follett, Ken — *Writer*
PO Box 708, London SW10 0DH, England

Folon, Jean-Michel — *Artist*
Burcy, 77890 Beaumont-du-Gatinais, France

Folsom, Allan R — *Writer*
%Little Brown Co, 34 Beacon St, Boston, MA 02108, USA

Folsom, James E (Jim), Jr — *Governor, AL*
702 5th Ave E, Cullman, AL 35055, USA

Folsome, Claire — *Microbiologist*
%University of Hawaii, Microbiology Dept, Honolulu, HI 96822, USA

Fonda, Bridget — *Actress*
%United Talent Agency, 9560 Wilshire Blvd, #500, Beverly Hills, CA 90212, USA

Fonda, Jane — *Actress*
1 CNN Center NW, #St-1080, Atlanta, GA 30303, USA

Fonda, Peter — *Actor*
%Pando Co, Rt 38, Box 2024, Livingston, MT 59047, USA

Fondren, Debra Jo — *Model*
300 W Lake Ave, Madison, WI 53715, USA

Fong, Hiram L — *Senator, HI*
1102 Alewa Dr, Honolulu, HI 96817, USA

Fong, Kam — *Actor*
1088 Bishop St, #406, Honolulu, HI 96813, USA

Fontaine, Frank — *Singer*
%Suffolk Marketing, 475 5th Ave, New York, NY 10017, USA

Fontaine, Joan — *Actress*
PO Box 222600, Carmel, CA 93922, USA

Fontana, Wayne — *Singer*
%Brian Cannon Mgmt, PO Box 81, Ruyton, Oldham, Manchester OL2 5DG, England

Fontes, Wayne — *Football Coach*
626 Shellbourne Dr, Rochester Hills, MI 48309, USA

Fonville, Charles — *Track Athlete*
2040 Walden Court, Flint, MI 48532, USA

F

Fogarty - Fonville

Foot, Michael M — Government Official, England
66 Pilgrims Rd, London NW3, England

Foote, Dan — Editorial Cartoonist
%Dallas Times Herald, Editorial Dept, Herald Sq, Dallas, TX 75202, USA

Foote, Edward T, II — Educator
%University of Miami, President's Office, Coral Gables, FL 33124, USA

Foote, Horton — Playwright
95 Horatio St, #322, New York, NY 10014, USA

Foote, Shelby — Writer
542 East Parkway S, Memphis, TN 38104, USA

Foote, William C — Businessman
%USG Corp, 125 S Franklin St, Chicago, IL 60606, USA

Foray, June — Actress
22745 Erwin St, Woodland Hills, CA 91367, USA

Forbert, Steve — Singer, Guitarist
%Al Bunetta Mgmt, 33 Music Sq W, 102-A, Nashville, TN 37203, USA

Forbes, Bryan — Movie Director, Screenwriter
Bookshop, Virginia Water, Surrey, England

Forbes, Malcolm S (Steve), Jr — Editor
%Forbes Magazine, Editorial Dept, 60 5th Ave, New York, NY 10011, USA

Forbes, Walter A — Businessman
%CUC International, 707 Summer St, Stamford, CT 06901, USA

Force, John — Auto Racing Driver
%John Force Racing, 23253 E La Palma Ave, Yorba Linda, CA 92687, USA

Ford, Alan — Swimmer
1821 Ivy Lane, Midland, MI 48642, USA

Ford, Doug — Golfer
4701 Oak Terrace, Lake Worth, FL 33463, USA

Ford, Edsel B, Jr — Financier
%Ford Motor Credit Co, American Rd, Dearborn, MI 48121, USA

Ford, Edward C (Whitey) — Baseball Player
38 Schoolhouse Lane, Lake Success, NY 11020, USA

Ford, Eileen O — Model Agency Executive
%Ford Model Agency, 344 E 59th St, New York, NY 10022, USA

Ford, Elizabeth B (Betty) — Wife of US President
40365 Sand Dune Rd, Rancho Mirage, CA 92270, USA

Ford, Faith — Actress
7920 Sunset Blvd, #350, Los Angeles, CA 90046, USA

Ford, Frankie — Singer, Songwriter
PO Box 1830, New Orleans, LA 70054, USA

Ford, Gerald J — Financier
%First Nationwide Bank, 135 Main St, San Francisco, CA 94105, USA

Ford, Gerald R, Jr — President, USA
40365 Sand Dune Rd, Rancho Mirage, CA 92270, USA

Ford, Gerard W — Model Agency Executive
%Ford Model Agency, 344 E 59th St, New York, NY 10022, USA

Ford, Glenn — Actor
911 Oxford Way, Beverly Hills, CA 90210, USA

Ford, Harrison — Actor
10279 Century Woods Dr, Los Angeles, CA 90067, USA

Ford, Jesse Hill — Writer
PO Box 43, Bellevue, TN 37202, USA

Ford, Joe T — Businessman
%ALLTEL Corp, 1 Allied Dr, Little Rock, AR 72202, USA

Ford, Larry C — Gynecologic Oncologist
%University of California Medical School, OB-Gyn Dept, Los Angeles, CA 90024, USA

Ford, Lita — Singer
128 Sinclair Ave, #3, Gardena, CA 91206, USA

Ford, Richard — Writer
%International Creative Mgmt, 40 W 57th St, New York, NY 10019, USA

Ford, Ruth — Actress
%Dakota Hotel, 1 W 72nd St, New York, NY 10023, USA

Ford, William C — Businessman, Football Executive
%Ford Motor Co, American Rd, Dearborn, MI 48121, USA

Fordham, Christopher C, III — Educator
%University of North Carolina, Medical School, Chapel Hill, NC 27514, USA

Fordice, D Kirkwood (Kirk), Jr — Governor, MS
%Governor's Office, State Capitol, PO Box 139, Jackson, MS 39205, USA

Foreman, Carol L T — *Government Official*
5408 Trent St, Chevy Chase, MD 20815, USA

Foreman, Charles (Chuck) — *Football Player*
7370 Stewart Dr, Eden Prairie, MN 55346, USA

Foreman, George — *Boxer*
7639 Pine Oak Dr, Humble, TX 77396, USA

Forester, Bernard I — *Businessman*
%Anthony Industries, 4900 S Eastern Ave, Los Angeles, CA 90040, USA

Foret, Mickey P — *Businessman*
1903 Mount Curve Ave, Minneapolis, MN 55403, USA

Forget, Guy — *Tennis Player*
Rue des Pacs 2, 2000 Neuchatel, Switzerland

Forlani, Arnaldo — *Prime Minister, Italy*
Piazzale Schumann 15, Rome, Italy

Forman, Milos — *Movie Director*
Hampshire House, 150 Central Park South, New York, NY 10019, USA

Forman, Tom — *Cartoonist (Motley's Crew)*
28947 Thousand Oaks Blvd, #120, Agoura Hills, CA 91301, USA

Formia, Osvaldo — *Harness Racing Trainer*
6501 Winfield Blvd, #A-10, Margate, FL 33063, USA

Fornos, Werner H — *Association Executive*
%Population Institute, 107 2nd St NE, Washington, DC 20002, USA

Forrest, Frederic — *Actor*
4121 Wilshire Blvd, Los Angeles, CA 90010, USA

Forrest, Helen — *Singer*
1870 Camino Del Cielo, Glendale, CA 91208, USA

Forrest, Sally — *Actress*
1125 Angelo Dr, Beverly Hills, CA 90210, USA

Forrest, Steve — *Actor*
1065 Michael Lane, Pacific Palisades, CA 90272, USA

Forrestal, Robert P — *Financier, Government Official*
%Federal Reserve Bank, 104 Marietta St NW, Atlanta, GA 30303, USA

Forrester, James — *Medical Researcher*
%Cedars-Sinai Medical Center, 8700 Beverly Blvd, Los Angeles, CA 90048, USA

Forrester, Jay W — *Inventor (Digital Storage Device)*
%Massachusetts Institute of Technology, Management School, Cambridge, MA 02139, USA

Forrester, Maureen — *Concert Singer*
26 Edmond Ave, Toronto ON M4V 1H3, Canada

Forsberg, Peter — *Hockey Player*
%Colorado Avalanche, McNichols Arena, 1635 Clay St, Denver, CO 80204, USA

Forsch, Kenneth R (Ken) — *Baseball Player*
794 S Ridgeview Rd, Anaheim, CA 92807, USA

Forsch, Robert H (Bob) — *Baseball Player*
1532 Highland Valley Circle, Chesterfield, MO 63005, USA

Forster, Frederic J — *Financier*
%Home Savings, 4900 Rivergrade Rd, Irwindale, CA 91706, USA

Forster, K Dieter — *Religious Leader*
%Scientist Church of Christ, 175 Huntington Ave, Boston, MA 02115, USA

Forster, Peter H — *Businessman*
%DPL Inc, Courthouse Plaza SW, Dayton, OH 45402, USA

Forster, Robert — *Actor*
8550 Holloway Dr, #402, Los Angeles, CA 90069, USA

Forstmann, Theodore J — *Financier*
%Forstmann Little Co, 767 5th Ave, New York, NY 10153, USA

Forsyth, Bill — *Movie Director*
%Peters Fraser Dunlop, Chelsea Harbour, Lots Rd, London SW10 0XF, England

Forsyth, Bruce — *Comedian*
Kent House, Upper Ground, London SE1, England

Forsyth, Frederick — *Writer*
%Hutchinson Publishing Group, 3 Fitzroy Square, London W1P 6JD, England

Forsyth, Rosemary — *Actress*
1591 Benedict Canyon, Beverly Hills, CA 90210, USA

Forsythe, Henderson — *Actor*
204 Elm St, Tenafly, NJ 07670, USA

Forsythe, John — *Actor*
3849 Roblar Ave, Santa Ynez, CA 93460, USA

Fort, Edward B — *Educator*
%North Carolina A&T University, Chancellor's Office, Greensboro, NC 27411, USA

Foreman - Fort

F

Fort, John F, III — *Businessman*
%Tyco International, 1 Tyco Park, Exeter, NH 03833, USA

Fort-Brescia, Bernardo — *Architect*
%Arquitectonica International, 2151 Le Jeuen Rd, #300, Coral Gables, FL 33134, USA

Forte, Chet — *Television Director, Basketball Player*
PO Box 8030, Rancho Santa Fe, CA 92067, USA

Fortess, Karl E — *Artist*
311 Plochmann Lane, Woodstock, NY 12498, USA

Fortier, Claude — *Physiologist*
1014 De Grenoble, Ste-Foy, Quebec PQ G1V 2Z9, Canada

Fortune, Jimmy — *Singer (Statler Brothers)*
PO Box 2703, Staunton, VA 24402, USA

Fosbury, Dick — *Track Athlete*
680 2nd Ave N, Kethcum, ID 83340, USA

Foss, Joseph — *WW II Marine Hero (CMH); Governor, SD*
PO Box 566, Scottsdale, AZ 85252, USA

Foss, Lukas — *Composer, Conductor*
1140 5th Ave #4-B, New York, NY 10128, USA

Fossel, Jon S — *Financier*
%Oppenheimer Management Corp, 2 World Trade Center, New York, NY 10048, USA

Fossen, Steve — *Bassist (Heart)*
%Levine/Schneider, 433 N Camden Dr, Beverly Hills, CA 90210, USA

Fossey, Brigitte — *Actress*
18 Rue Troyon, 75017 Paris, France

Foster, Bill — *Basketball Coach*
%Virginia Polytechnic Institute, Athletic Dept, Blacksburg, VA 24061, USA

Foster, Bob — *Boxer*
%Bernalillo County Sheriff Dept, 401 Marquette Ave, Albuquerque, NM 87102, USA

Foster, Brendan — *Track Athlete*
Whitegates, 31 Meadowfield Rd, Stocksfield, Northumberland, England

Foster, David — *Songwriter, Musician*
PO Box 6228, Malibu, CA 90264, USA

Foster, George A — *Baseball Player*
%George Foster Pro Concepts, 15 E Putnam Ave, #320, Greenwich, CT 06830, USA

Foster, Greg — *Track Athlete*
PO Box 18204, Long Beach, CA 90807, USA

Foster, Harold E (Bud) — *Basketball Player*
24 Heritage Circle, #3, Madison, WI 53711, USA

Foster, Jodie — *Actress*
%International Creative Mgmt, 8942 Wilshire Blvd, Beverly Hills, CA 90211, USA

Foster, John S, Jr — *Physicist*
%TRW Inc, 1 Space Parkway, Redondo Beach, CA 90278, USA

Foster, Kent B — *Businessman*
%GTE Corp, 1 Stamford Forum, Stamford, CT 06901, USA

Foster, Lawrence — *Conductor*
%Harrison Parrott Ltd, 12 Penzance Place, London W11, England

Foster, Lisa-Raines — *Actress*
%Diamond Artists, 215 N Barrington Ave, Los Angeles, CA 90049, USA

Foster, Meg — *Actress*
10866 Wilshire Blvd, #1100, Los Angeles, CA 90024, USA

Foster, Norman R — *Architect*
%Foster Assoc, Riverside 3, 22 Hester Rd, London SW11 4AN, England

Foster, Todd — *Boxer*
2222 Westerland Dr, #100, Houston, TX 77063, USA

Foster, William C — *Government Official*
3304 "R" St NW, Washington, DC 20007, USA

Foster, William E — *Businessman*
%Stratus Computer, 55 Fairbanks Blvd, Marlboro, MA 01752, USA

Foster, William E (Bill) — *Basketball Coach*
%South Western Conference, 1300 W Mockingbird Lane, Dallas, TX 75247, USA

Foti, Samuel J — *Businessman*
%Mutual Life Insurance, 1740 Broadway, New York, NY 10019, USA

Foulkes, Llyn — *Artist*
6010 Eucalyptus Lane, Los Angeles, CA 90042, USA

Fountain, Peter D (Pete), Jr — *Jazz Clarinetist*
%As Was, 2 Poydras St, New Orleans, LA 70140, USA

Fouts, Daniel F (Dan) — *Football Player, Sportscaster*
%KPIX-TV, Sports Dept, 855 Battery St, San Francisco, CA 94111, USA

Fort - Fouts

Fowden, Leslie — *Plant Chemist*
31 Southdown Rd, Harpenden, Herts AL5 1PF, England

Fowler, Henry H — *Secretary, Treasury*
%Goldman Sachs Co, 85 Broad St, New York, NY 10004, USA

Fowler, Mark S — *Government Official*
%Latham & Watkins, 1001 Pennsylvania Ave NW, Washington, DC 20004, USA

Fowler, Michael — *Architect*
%Calder Fowler Styles Turner, PO Box 2692, Wellington, New Zealand

Fowler, Robert E, Jr — *Businessman*
%Vigoro Corp, 225 N Michigan Ave, Chicago, IL 60601, USA

Fowles, John — *Writer*
%Anthony Sheil Assoc, 45 Doughty St, London WC1N 2LF, England

Fowley, Douglas — *Actor*
38510 Glen Abbey Lane, Murietta, CA 92562, USA

Fox, Allen — *Tennis Player, Coach*
%Pepperdine University, Athletic Dept, Malibu, CA 90265, USA

Fox, Bernard — *Actor*
145 S Fairfax Ave, #310, Los Angeles, CA 90036, USA

Fox, Bernard M — *Businessman*
%Northeast Utilities, PO Box 270, Hartford, CT 06141, USA

Fox, Bertrand — *Economist*
12 Hayes Ave, Lexington, MA 02173, USA

Fox, Charles I — *Composer, Conductor*
4601 Vanalden Ave, Tarzana, CA 91356, USA

Fox, Edward — *Actor*
25 Maida Ave, London W2, England

Fox, J Carter — *Businessman*
%Chesapeake Corp, 1021 E Cary St, Richmond, VA 23219, USA

Fox, James — *Actor*
3 Spencer Park Rd, London SW18, England

Fox, Marye Anne — *Organic Chemist*
%University of Texas, Chemistry Dept, Austin, TX 78712, USA

Fox, Matthew — *Religious Leader*
%Grace Episcopal Cathedral, 1 Nob Hill Circle, San Francisco, CA 94100, USA

Fox, Maurice S — *Molecular Biologist*
983 Memorial Dr, #401, Cambridge, MA 02138, USA

Fox, Michael J — *Actor*
Lottery Hill Farm, South Woodstock, VT 05071, USA

Fox, Paula — *Writer*
%Robert Lescher, 67 Irving Place, New York, NY 10003, USA

Fox, Renee C — *Sociologist*
The Wellington, 135 S 19th St, Philadelphia, PA 19103, USA

Fox, Samantha — *Singer*
11 Mount Pleasant Villas, London 4HH, England

Fox, Sheldon — *Architect*
%Kohn Pedersen Fox Assoc, 111 W 57th St, New York, NY 10019, USA

Fox, Tim — *Football Player*
18 Shoreline Dr, Foxboro, MA 02035, USA

Fox, Wesley L — *Vietnam War Marine Corps Hero (CMH)*
OCS MCCOC, Development & Education Command, Quantico, VA 22134, USA

Fox, William F, Jr — *Attorney*
%Catholic University, Law School, Washington, DC 20064, USA

Foxworth, Robert — *Actor*
%Krisbo Productions, 9720 Wilshire Blvd, #300, Beverly Hills, CA 90212, USA

Foxworthy, Jeff — *Comedian*
%Longstreet Press, 2140 Newmarket Parkway, #118, Atlanta, GA 30067, USA

Foy, Eddie, III — *Actor*
13332 McCormick St, Van Nuys, CA 91401, USA

Foyt, Anthony Joseph (A J), Jr — *Auto Racing Driver*
6415 Toledo St, Houston, TX 77008, USA

Fradon, Dana — *Cartoonist*
RFD 2, Brushy Hill Rd, Newtown, CT 06470, USA

Fraenkel-Conrat, Heinz — *Molecular Biologist*
870 Grizzly Peak Blvd, Berkeley, CA 94708, USA

Frahm, Donald R — *Businessman*
%ITT Hartford, Hartford Plaza, Hartford, CT 06115, USA

Fraker, William A — *Cinematographer*
%Gersh Agency, 232 N Canon Dr, Beverly Hills, CA 90210, USA

F

Fowden - Fraker

Frakes, Jonathan *Actor*
9033 Briarcrest Dr, Beverly Hills, CA 90210, USA

Frame, Janet *Writer*
276 Glenfield Rd, Auckland 10, New Zealand

Frampton, Peter *Singer, Guitarist*
234 S Tower Dr, #1, Beverly Hills, CA 90211, USA

Franca, Celia *Ballerina, Choreographer*
250 Clenow Ave, Ottawa ON K1S 2B6, Canada

France, Bill, Jr *Auto Racing Executive*
%National Assn of Stock Car Racing, 1801 Speedway Blvd, Daytona Beach, FL 32015, USA

Francesconi, Joseph J *Businessman*
%Network Equipment Technologies, 800 Saginaw Dr, Redwood City, CA 94063, USA

Franchione, Dennis *Football Coach*
%University of New Mexico, Athletic Dept, Albuquerque, NM 87131, USA

Franciosa, Tony *Actor*
567 Tigertail Rd, Los Angeles, CA 90049, USA

Francis, Anne *Actress*
PO Box 5417, Santa Barbara, CA 93150, USA

Francis, Arlene *Actress*
%Ritz Towers, 59th & Park Ave, New York, NY 10016, USA

Francis, Clarence (Bevo) *Basketball Player*
18340 Steubenville Pike Rd, Salineville, OH 43945, USA

Francis, Connie *Singer*
50 Sullivan Dr, West Orange, NJ 07052, USA

Francis, Don *Medical Researcher*
%Genentech Inc, 460 Point San Bruno Blvd, South San Francisco, CA 94080, USA

Francis, Fred *Commentator*
%NBC-TV, News Dept, 4001 Nebraska Ave NW, Washington, DC 20016, USA

Francis, Freddie *Cinematographer*
12 The Chestnuts, Jersey Rd, Osterley, Middx TW7 5QA, England

Francis, Genie *Actress*
9033 Briarcrest Dr, Beverly Hills, CA 90210, USA

Francis, Harrison (Sam) *Football Player*
2850 S Chambery Ave, Springfield, MO 65804, USA

Francis, James *Football Player*
%Cincinnati Bengals, 200 Riverfront Stadium, Cincinnati, OH 45202, USA

Francis, Richard S (Dick) *Writer*
5100 N Ocean Blvd, #609, Sea Ranch Lakes, FL 33308, USA

Francis, Ron *Hockey Player*
%Pittsburgh Penguins, Civic Arena, Centre Ave, Pittsburgh, PA 15219, USA

Francisco, George J *Labor Leader*
%Fireman & Oilers Union, 1100 Circle 75 Parkway, Atlanta, GA 30339, USA

Franck, George H *Football Player*
2714 29th Ave, Rock Island, IL 61201, USA

Franck, John M *Businessman*
%Tultex Corp, 22 E Church St, Martinsville, VA 24112, USA

Franco, John A *Baseball Player*
111 Clifford Ave, Staten Island, NY 10305, USA

Franco, Julio C *Baseball Player*
2403 Copper Ridge Rd, Arlington, TX 76006, USA

Frank, Anthony M *Government Official, Financier*
%Independent Bancorp, 3800 N Central, Phoenix, AZ 85012, USA

Frank, Charles *Actor*
%Century Artists, 9744 Wilshire Blvd, #308, Beverly Hills, CA 90212, USA

Frank, F Charles *Physicist*
Orchard Cottage, Grove Rd, Coombe Dingle, Bristol BS9 2RL, England

Frank, Gerold *Writer*
930 5th Ave, New York, NY 10021, USA

Frank, Harold R *Businessman*
%Applied Magnetics Corp, 75 Robin Hill Rd, Goleta, CA 93117, USA

Frank, Jerome D *Psychiatrist, Educator*
603 W University Parkway, Baltimore, MD 21210, USA

Frank, Joe *Radio Personality*
%KCRW-FM, 1900 Pico Blvd, Santa Monica, CA 90405, USA

Frank, Neil L *Meteorologist*
%National Hurricane Center, 1320 S Dixie Highway, Miami, FL 33146, USA

Frank, Reuven *Television Producer*
%NBC-TV, 30 Rockefeller Plaza, New York, NY 10112, USA

Frank, Richard H — *Financier*
%World Bank Group, 1818 "H" St NW, Washington, DC 20433, USA

Frank, Richard H — *Entertainment Executive*
%Comcast Content/Communications, 1500 Market St, Philadelphia, PA 19102, USA

Frank, Sam H — *Educator*
36-24 Corporal Kennedy St, Flushing, NY 11361, USA

Frank, Sarah — *Television Executive*
%BBC/Lionheart TV, Woodlands, 80 Wood Lane, London W12 0TT, England

Franke, William A — *Businessman*
%American West Airlines, 51 W 3rd St, Tempe, AZ 85281, USA

Frankel, Max — *Editor*
%New York Times, Editorial Dept, 229 W 43rd St, New York, NY 10036, USA

Frankenheimer, John M — *Movie Director*
3114 Abington Dr, Beverly Hills, CA 90210, USA

Frankenthaler, Helen — *Artist*
173 E 94th St, New York, NY 10128, USA

Frankl, Peter — *Concert Pianist*
5 Gresham Gardens, London NW11 8NX, England

Frankl, Viktor E — *Psychiatrist, Writer*
Mariannengasse 1, Vienna 1090, Austria

Franklin, Aretha — *Singer*
8450 Linwood St, Detroit, MI 48206, USA

Franklin, Barbara Hackman — *Secretary, Commerce*
1875 Perkins St, Bristol, CT 06010, USA

Franklin, Bonnie — *Actress*
448 W 44th St, New York, NY 10036, USA

Franklin, Charles E (Ed) — *Air Force General*
Commander, Electronic Systems, 9 Elgin St, Hanscom Air Force Base, MA 01731, USA

Franklin, Diane — *Actress*
2115 Topanga Skyline Dr, Topanga, CA 90290, USA

Franklin, John Hope — *Historian*
208 Pineview Rd, Durham, NC 27707, USA

Franklin, Jon D — *Journalist*
%University of Oregon, Journalism School, Eugene, OR 97403, USA

Franklin, Pamela — *Actress*
1280 Sunset Plaza Dr, Los Angeles, CA 90069, USA

Franklin, Richard C — *Businessman*
%Insurance Co of North America, 1601 Chestnut St, Philadelphia, PA 19192, USA

Franklin, Samuel O, III — *Financier*
%Third National Bank, PO Box 305110, Nashville, TN 37230, USA

Franklin, Tony — *Football Player*
%New England Patriots, Foxboro Stadium, Rt 1, Foxboro, MA 02035, USA

Franklyn, Sabina — *Actress*
%CCA Mgmt, 4 Court Lodge, 48 Sloane Sq, London SW1W 8AT, England

Franks, Frederick M, Jr — *Army General*
Commanding General, US Army Training/Doctrine Command, Fort Monroe, VA 23651, USA

Franks, Michael — *Singer, Songwriter, Guitarist*
%Les Schwartz, 9220 Sunset Blvd, #320, Los Angeles, CA 90069, USA

Frankston, Robert M — *Computer Software Designer (VisiCalc)*
%Slate Corp, 15035 N 73rd St, Scottsdale, AZ 85260, USA

Frann, Mary — *Actress*
11365 Santa Monica Blvd, #130, Los Angeles, CA 90025, USA

Fransioli, Thomas A — *Artist*
55 Dodges Row, Wenham, MA 01984, USA

Frantz, Chris — *Drummer (Talking Heads)*
%Overland Productions, 1775 Broadway, #700, New York, NY 10019, USA

Franz, Dennis — *Actor*
11805 Bellagio Rd, Los Angeles, CA 90049, USA

Franz, Frederick W — *Religious Leader*
%Jehovah's Witnesses, 25 Columbia Heights, Brooklyn, NY 11201, USA

Franz, Rodney (Rod) — *Football Player*
1448 Engberg Court, Carmichael, CA 95608, USA

Franzen, Jonathan — *Writer*
%Farrar Straus Giroux, 19 Union Square W, New York, NY 10003, USA

Franzen, Ulrich J — *Architect*
%Ulrich Franzen Assoc, 168 E 74th St, New York, NY 10021, USA

Frasca, Robert J — *Architect*
%Zimmer Gunsul Frasca, 320 SW Oak St, #500, Portland, OR 97204, USA

F

Frank - Frasca

Fasconi - Freedman

Frasconi, Antonio *Artist*
26 Dock Rd, South Norwalk, CT 06854, USA

Fraser Ware, Dawn *Swimmer*
87 Birchgrove Rd, Balmain NSW, Australia

Fraser, Antonia *Writer*
%Curtis Brown, 162-168 Regent St, London W1R 5TB, England

Fraser, Brendan *Actor*
2118 Wilshire Blvd, #513, Santa Monica, CA 90403, USA

Fraser, Douglas *Labor Leader*
%United Auto Workers, 8000 E Jefferson Ave, Detroit, MI 48214, USA

Fraser, Hugh *Actor*
1 Northumberland Place, London W2 5BS, England

Fraser, Ian E *WW II British Royal Navy Hero (VC)*
Innisfallen, 47 Warren Dr, Wallasey, Merseyside, England

Fraser, Malcolm *Prime Minister, Australia*
ANZ Tower, #4400, 55 Collins St, Melbourne Vic 3000, Australia

Fraser, Neale *Tennis Player*
%Tennis Australia, Private Bag 6060, Richmond South, 3121 Vic, Australia

Fratello, Michael R (Mike) *Basketball Coach*
%Cleveland Cavaliers, 2923 Statesboro Rd, Richfield, OH 44286, USA

Fratianne, Linda *Figure Skater*
1177 N Vista Vespero, Palm Springs, CA 92262, USA

Fraumeni, Joseph F, Jr *Cancer Researcher*
%National Cancer Institute, Cancer Etiology Division, Bethesda, MD 20892, USA

Frayn, Michael *Writer*
%Elaine Green Ltd, 31 Newington Glen, London N16 9PU, England

Frazer, Liz *Actress*
42/43 Grafton House, 2/3 Golden Square, London W1, England

Frazetta, Frank *Artist*
%Frazetta Art Museum, 82 S Courtland St, East Stroudsburg, PA 18301, USA

Frazier, Dallas *Singer, Songwriter*
Rt 5, Box 133, Longhollow Pike, Gallatin, TN 37066, USA

Frazier, Ian *Writer*
%Farrar Straus Giroux, 19 Union Square W, New York, NY 10003, USA

Frazier, Joe *Boxer*
2917 N Broad St, Philadelphia, PA 19132, USA

Frazier, Owsley B *Businessman*
%Brown-Forman Inc, 850 Dixie Highway, Louisville, KY 40210, USA

Frazier, Walt (Clyde) *Basketball Player*
675 Flamingo Dr SW, Atlanta, GA 30311, USA

Frears, Stephen A *Movie Director*
93 Talbot Rd, London W2, England

Freberg, Stanley V (Stan) *Comedian*
10450 Wilshire Blvd, #1-A, Los Angeles, CA 90024, USA

Freccia, Massimo *Conductor*
25 Eaton Square, London SW1, England

Frederick, Sherman R *Editor*
%Las Vegas Review-Journal, 1111 W Bonanza Rd, Las Vegas, NV 89106, USA

Fredericks, Fred *Cartoonist (Mandrake the Magician)*
Bridge Rd, Box 475, Eastham, MA 02642, USA

Frederik Andre Henrik Christian *Prince, Denmark*
%Amalienborg Palace, 1257 Copenhagen K, Denmark

Fredrickson, Donald S *Physician*
6615 Bradley Blvd, Bethesda, MD 20817, USA

Fredriksson, Gert *Canoeist*
Bruunsgat 13, 611 22 Nykoping, Sweden

Freed, Curt R *Neurobiologist*
%University of Colorado Health Sciences Center, 4200 E 9th Ave, Denver, CO 80220, USA

Freed, James Ingo *Architect*
%Pei Cobb Freed Partners, 600 Madison Ave, New York, NY 10022, USA

Freedberg, Sydney J *Museum Curator*
3328 Reservoir Rd, Washington, DC 20007, USA

Freedman, Allen R *Financier*
%Fortis Inc, 1 World Trade Center, New York, NY 10048, USA

Freedman, Eric *Journalist*
%Detroit News, Editorial Dept, 615 Lafayette Blvd, Detroit, MI 48231, USA

Freedman, Gerald A *Theater, Opera Director*
%Theatre Julliard School, Lincoln Center Plaza, New York, NY 10023, USA

Freedman, James O — *Educator*
%Dartmouth College, President's Office, Hanover, NH 03755, USA

Freedman, Michael H — *Mathematician*
%University of California, Mathematics Dept, La Jolla, CA 92093, USA

Freedman, Ronald — *Sociologist*
4380 Exeter Dr, #H-203, Longboat Key, FL 34228, USA

Freeh, Louis J — *Law Enforcement Official*
%Federal Bureau of Investigation, 9th & Pennsylvania NW, Washington, DC 20535, USA

Freehan, William A (Bill) — *Baseball Player*
%University of Michigan, 1000 S State St, Ann Arbor, MI 48109, USA

Freelon, Nnenna — *Singer*
%John Levy Enterprises, 5455 Wilshire Blvd, #2208, Los Angeles, CA 90036, USA

Freeman, Al, Jr — *Actor*
%Weingard, 1 Executive Ave, Suffern, NY 10901, USA

Freeman, Bobby — *Singer*
%Majestic Tours International, 29701 Kinderamack Rd, Oredell, NJ 07649, USA

Freeman, Charles W, Jr — *Diplomat*
2805 31st St NW, Washington, DC 20008, USA

Freeman, David — *Businessman*
%Loctite Corp, 10 Columbus Blvd, Hartford, CT 06106, USA

Freeman, J E — *Actor*
%Judy Schoen Assoc, 606 N Larchmont Blvd, #309, Los Angeles, CA 90004, USA

Freeman, Kathleen — *Actress*
6247 Orion Ave, Van Nuys, CA 91411, USA

Freeman, Kenneth W — *Businessman*
%Corning Inc, Houghton Park, Corning, NY 14831, USA

Freeman, Mona — *Actress*
608 N Alpine Dr, Beverly Hills, CA 90210, USA

Freeman, Morgan — *Actor*
2472 Broadway, #227, New York, NY 10025, USA

Freeman, Orville L — *Secretary, Agriculture*
1101 S Arlington Ridge Rd, Arlington, VA 22202, USA

Freeman, Robert M — *Financier*
%Signet Banking Corp, 7 N 8th St, Richmond, VA 23219, USA

Freeman, Ron — *Track Athlete*
61-63 Myrtle Ave, North Plainfield, NJ 07060, USA

Freeman, Russ — *Jazz Guitarist*
%Agency For Performing Arts, 9000 Sunset Blvd, #1200, Los Angeles, CA 90069, USA

Freeman, Sandi — *Commentator*
%Cable News Network, News Dept, 820 1st St NE, Washington, DC 20002, USA

Freeman, William A — *Businessman*
%Zurn Industries, 1 Zurn Place, Erie, PA 16505, USA

Fregosi, James L (Jim) — *Baseball Player, Manager*
1092 Copeland Ct, Tarpon Springs, FL 34689, USA

Frehley, Ace — *Singer, Guitarist (Kiss)*
%Kayos Productions, 16th W 19th St, #500, New York, NY 10011, USA

Frei Fruiz Tagle, Eduardo — *President, Chile*
%President's Office, Palacio de la Monedo, Santiago, Chile

Frei, Emil, III — *Physician*
%Dana-Farber Cancer Institute, 44 Binney St, Boston, MA 02115, USA

Freilicher, Jane — *Artist*
%Fishbach Gallery, 24 W 57th St, New York, NY 10019, USA

Freire, Paolo — *Educator*
%World Council of Churches, Geneva, Switzerland

Freireich, Emil J — *Physician*
%M D Anderson Medical Center, 1515 Holcombe Blvd, Houston, TX 77030, USA

Freis, Edward D — *Physician*
4515 Willard Ave, Chevy Chase, MD 20815, USA

Fremaux, Louis J F — *Conductor*
25 Edencroft, Wheeleys Rd, Birmingham B15 2LW, England

French, Charles S — *Plant Biologist*
11970 Rhus Ridge Rd, Los Altos Hills, CA 94022, USA

French, Leigh — *Actress*
1850 N Vista St, Los Angeles, CA 90046, USA

French, Marilyn — *Writer*
%Charlotte Sheedy Agency, 41 King St, New York, NY 10014, USA

Freni, Mirella — *Opera Singer*
%Columbia Artists Mgmt Inc, 165 W 57th St, New York, NY 10019, USA

F

Freedman · Freni

F

Frenzer, Peter F *Businessman*
%Nationwide Life Insurance, 1 Nationwide Plaza, Columbus, OH 43215, USA

Fresno Lorrain, Juan Cardinal *Religious Leader*
Erasmo Escala 1822, Santiago 30-D, Chile

Fretwell, Elbert K, Jr *Educator*
%University of Massachusetts, President's Office, Boston, MA 02116, USA

Freud, Lucian *Artist*
%James Kirkman, 46 Brompton Square, London SW3 2AF, England

Freund-Rosenthal, Miriam Kottler *Religious Leader*
50 W 58th St, New York, NY 10019, USA

Frewer, Matt *Actor*
6670 Wildlife Rd, Malibu, CA 90265, USA

Frey, Glenn *Singer (Eagles), Songwriter, Actor*
29623 Louis Ave, Santa Clarita, CA 91351, USA

Frey, James G (Jim) *Baseball Manager*
119 Versailles Circle, #A, Towson, MD 21204, USA

Freyndlikh, Alisa B *Actress*
Rubinstein Str 11, #7, 191002 St Petersburg, Russia

Freytag, Arny *Photographer*
22735 MacFarlane Dr, Woodland Hills, CA 91364, USA

Fribourg, Michel *Businessman*
%Continental Grain Co, 277 Park Ave, New York, NY 10172, USA

Fribourg, Paul J *Businessman*
%Continental Grain Co, 277 Park Ave, New York, NY 10172, USA

Frick, Gottlob *Opera Singer*
Eichelberg-Haus Waldfrieden, 75248 Olbronn-Durrn, Germany

Fricke, Howard R *Businessman*
%Security Benefit Insurance, 700 SW Harrison St, Topeka, KS 66603, USA

Fricke, Janie *Singer*
%Janie Fricke Concerts, PO Box 798, Lancaster, TX 75146, USA

Fricker, Brenda *Actress*
%Mayer Mgmt, Grafton House, #4, 2-3 Golden Square, London W1R 3AD, England

Friday, Elbert W, Jr *Government Official*
%US National Weather Service, 1125 East West Highway, Silver Spring, MD 20910, USA

Friday, Nancy *Writer*
%Simon & Schuster Inc, 1230 Ave of Americas, New York, NY 10020, USA

Friday, William C *Educator*
%William R Kenan Jr Fund, PO Box 3808, Chapel Hill, NC 27515, USA

Fridell, Squire *Actor*
7080 Hollywood Blvd, #704, Los Angeles, CA 90028, USA

Friderichs, Hans *Businessman*
%AEG-Telefunken, Theodor-Stern-Kai 1, 60596 Frankfurt/Main, Germany

Fridovich, Irwin *Biochemist*
3517 Courtland Dr, Durham, NC 27707, USA

Fried, Charles *Government Official, Educator*
%Harvard University, Law School, Cambridge, MA 02138, USA

Fried, Josef *Organic Chemist*
5717 S Kenwood Ave, Chicago, IL 60637, USA

Friedan, Betty *Writer, Social Activist*
1 Lincoln Plaza, #40-K, New York, NY 10023, USA

Frieder, Bill *Basketball Coach*
%Arizona State University, Athletic Dept, Tempe, AZ 85287, USA

Friedkin, William *Movie Director*
1363 Angelo Dr, Beverly Hills, CA 90210, USA

Friedlander, Lee *Artist, Photographer*
44 S Mountain Rd, New City, NY 10956, USA

Friedman, Bruce Jay *Writer*
Holly Lane, Water Mill, NY 11976, USA

Friedman, Emanuel A *Medical Educator, Obstetrician*
%Beth-Israel Hospital, 330 Brookline Ave, Boston, MA 02215, USA

Friedman, Herbert *Physicist*
2643 N Upshur St, Arlington, VA 22207, USA

Friedman, Irving S *Economist*
6620 Fernwood Court, Bethesda, MD 20817, USA

Friedman, Jerome I *Nobel Physics Laureate*
75 Greenough Circle, Brookline, MA 02146, USA

Friedman, Meyer *Cardiologist*
160 San Carlos Ave, Sausalito, CA 94965, USA

Frenzer - Friedman

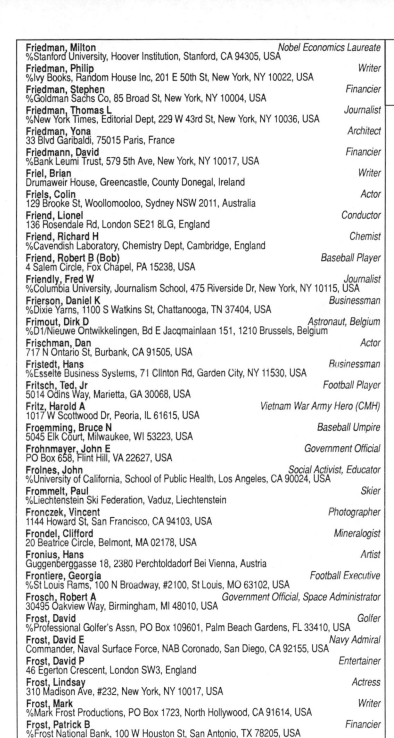

Friedman, Milton   *Nobel Economics Laureate*
%Stanford University, Hoover Institution, Stanford, CA 94305, USA

Friedman, Philip   *Writer*
%Ivy Books, Random House Inc, 201 E 50th St, New York, NY 10022, USA

Friedman, Stephen   *Financier*
%Goldman Sachs Co, 85 Broad St, New York, NY 10004, USA

Friedman, Thomas L   *Journalist*
%New York Times, Editorial Dept, 229 W 43rd St, New York, NY 10036, USA

Friedman, Yona   *Architect*
33 Blvd Garibaldi, 75015 Paris, France

Friedmann, David   *Financier*
%Bank Leumi Trust, 579 5th Ave, New York, NY 10017, USA

Friel, Brian   *Writer*
Drumaweir House, Greencastle, County Donegal, Ireland

Friels, Colin   *Actor*
129 Brooke St, Woollomooloo, Sydney NSW 2011, Australia

Friend, Lionel   *Conductor*
136 Rosendale Rd, London SE21 8LG, England

Friend, Richard H   *Chemist*
%Cavendish Laboratory, Chemistry Dept, Cambridge, England

Friend, Robert B (Bob)   *Baseball Player*
4 Salem Circle, Fox Chapel, PA 15238, USA

Friendly, Fred W   *Journalist*
%Columbia University, Journalism School, 475 Riverside Dr, New York, NY 10115, USA

Frierson, Daniel K   *Businessman*
%Dixie Yarns, 1100 S Watkins St, Chattanooga, TN 37404, USA

Frimout, Dirk D   *Astronaut, Belgium*
%D1/Nieuwe Ontwikkelingen, Bd E Jacqmainlaan 151, 1210 Brussels, Belgium

Frischman, Dan   *Actor*
717 N Ontario St, Burbank, CA 91505, USA

Fristedt, Hans   *Businessman*
%Esselte Business Systems, 71 Clinton Rd, Garden City, NY 11530, USA

Fritsch, Ted, Jr   *Football Player*
5014 Odins Way, Marietta, GA 30068, USA

Fritz, Harold A   *Vietnam War Army Hero (CMH)*
1017 W Scottwood Dr, Peoria, IL 61615, USA

Froemming, Bruce N   *Baseball Umpire*
5045 Elk Court, Milwaukee, WI 53223, USA

Frohnmayer, John E   *Government Official*
PO Box 658, Flint Hill, VA 22627, USA

Frolnes, John   *Social Activist, Educator*
%University of California, School of Public Health, Los Angeles, CA 90024, USA

Frommelt, Paul   *Skier*
%Liechtenstein Ski Federation, Vaduz, Liechtenstein

Fronczek, Vincent   *Photographer*
1144 Howard St, San Francisco, CA 94103, USA

Frondel, Clifford   *Mineralogist*
20 Beatrice Circle, Belmont, MA 02178, USA

Fronius, Hans   *Artist*
Guggenberggasse 18, 2380 Perchtoldadorf Bei Vienna, Austria

Frontiere, Georgia   *Football Executive*
%St Louis Rams, 100 N Broadway, #2100, St Louis, MO 63102, USA

Frosch, Robert A   *Government Official, Space Administrator*
30495 Oakview Way, Birmingham, MI 48010, USA

Frost, David   *Golfer*
%Professional Golfer's Assn, PO Box 109601, Palm Beach Gardens, FL 33410, USA

Frost, David E   *Navy Admiral*
Commander, Naval Surface Force, NAB Coronado, San Diego, CA 92155, USA

Frost, David P   *Entertainer*
46 Egerton Crescent, London SW3, England

Frost, Lindsay   *Actress*
310 Madison Ave, #232, New York, NY 10017, USA

Frost, Mark   *Writer*
%Mark Frost Productions, PO Box 1723, North Hollywood, CA 91614, USA

Frost, Patrick B   *Financier*
%Frost National Bank, 100 W Houston St, San Antonio, TX 78205, USA

Frost, Phillip   *Businessman*
%IVAX Corp, 8800 NW 36th St, Miami, FL 33178, USA

F

Friedman - Frost

F

Frost, Sadie	*Actress*
%Burdett-Coutts, Riverside Studios, Crisp Rd, London W6 9RL, England	
Frost, T C	*Financier*
%Cullen/Frost Bankers Inc, 100 W Houston St, San Antonio, TX 78205, USA	
Fruchtenbaum, Edward	*Businessman*
%American Greetings Corp, 1 American Rd, Cleveland, OH 44144, USA	
Fruedek, Jacques	*Physicist*
2 Rue Jean-Francois Gerbillion, 70006 Paris, France	
Fruh, Eugen	*Artist*
Romergasse 9, 8001 Zurich, Switzerland	
Fruhbeck de Burgos, Rafael	*Conductor*
Reyes Magos 20, 28007 Madrid, Spain	
Frumkin, Allan	*Art Dealer*
%Frumklin/Adams Gallery, 1185 Park Ave, New York, NY 10128, USA	
Frutig, Ed	*Football Player*
811 Mohawk St, Dearborn, MI 48124, USA	
Fruton, Joseph S	*Biochemist*
123 York St, New Haven, CT 06511, USA	
Fry Irvin, Shirley	*Tennis Player*
1970 Asylum Ave, West Hartford, CT 06117, USA	
Fry, Arthur L	*Inventor (Post-its)*
%Minnesota Mining & Manufacturing Co, 3-M Center, Bldg 230-2S, St Paul, MN 55144, USA	
Fry, Christopher	*Writer*
Toft, East Dean Near Chichester, Sussex, England	
Fry, E Maxwell	*Architect*
West Lodge, Cotherstone, Barnard Castle, County Durham DL1Z 9PF, England	
Fry, Hayden	*Football Coach*
%University of Iowa, Athletic Dept, Iowa City, IA 52242, USA	
Fry, Michael	*Cartoonist (Committed)*
%United Feature Syndicate, 200 Park Ave, New York, NY 10166, USA	
Fry, Stephen	*Comedian*
%Lorraine Hamilton, 19 Denmark St, London WC2H 8NA, England	
Fry, Thornton C	*Mathematician*
500 Mohawk Dr, Boulder, CO 80303, USA	
Fryar, Irving	*Football Player*
%Miami Dolphins, 7500 SW 30th St, Davie, FL 33329, USA	
Frye, Northrop	*Educator*
127 Clifton Rd, Toronto ON M4T 2G5, Canada	
Frye, Richard N	*Historian, Orientalist*
%Harvard University, Oriental & African Studies School, Cambridge, MA 02138, USA	
Frye, Soliel Moon	*Actress*
2713 N Keystone St, Burbank, CA 91504, USA	
Fryling, Victor J	*Businessman*
%CMS Energy Corp, Fairlane Plaza South, 330 Town Center Dr, Dearborn, MI 48126, USA	
Fthenakis, Emanuel	*Businessman*
%CEF Corp, PO Box 59708, Rockville, MD 20859, USA	
Ftorek, Robbie	*Hockey Coach*
%New Jersey Devils, Meadowlands Arena, PO Box 504, East Rutherford, NJ 07073, USA	
Fuchs, Ann Sutherland	*Publisher*
%Vogue Magazine, 350 Madison Ave, New York, NY 10017, USA	
Fuchs, Joseph L	*Publisher*
%Mademoiselle Magazine, 350 Madison Ave, New York, NY 10017, USA	
Fuchs, Michael J	*Television Executive*
%Home Box Office, 1100 Ave of Americas, New York, NY 10036, USA	
Fuchs, Victor R	*Economist*
796 Cedro Way, Stanford, CA 94305, USA	
Fuchs, Vivian E	*Explorer, Geologist*
106 Barton Rd, Cambridge, Cambs CB3 9LH, England	
Fudge, Alan	*Actor*
355 S Rexford Dr, Beverly Hills, CA 90212, USA	
Fuente, David I	*Businessman*
%Office Club Inc, 2200 Old Germantown Rd, Delray Beach, FL 33445, USA	
Fuente, Luis	*Ballet Dancer*
98 Rue Lepic, 75018 Paris, France	
Fuentealba, Victor W	*Labor Leader*
4501 Arabia Ave, Baltimore, MD 21214, USA	
Fuentes, Carlos	*Writer*
%Harvard University, Latin American Studies Dept, Cambridge, MA 02138, USA	

Fuentes, Daisy *Entertainer, Model*
%"Street Party" Show, MTV-TV, 1775 Broadway, New York, NY 10019, USA

Fugard, Athol H *Writer*
PO Box 5090, Walmer, Port Elizabeth, South Africa

Fugate, Judith *Ballerina*
%New York City Ballet, Lincoln Center Plaza, New York, NY 10023, USA

Fuglesang, Christer *Astronaut*
%Europe Astronaut Center, Linder Hohe, Box 906096, 51127 Cologne, Germany

Fuhr, Grant *Hockey Player*
%St Louis Blues, St Louis Arena, 5700 Oakland Ave, St Louis, MO 63110, USA

Fujii, Keishi *Financier*
%Bank of Tokyo Ltd, 3-2-1 Nihombasi Hongpkucho, Chuoku, Tokyo 103, Japa

Fujimori, Alberto K *President, Peru*
%President's Office, Palacio de Gobierno S/N, Plaza de Armas, Lima 1, Peru

Fujimori, Masamichi *Businessman*
%Sumitomo Metal Mining Co, 5-11-3 Shimbashi, Minatoku, Tokyo 105, Japan

Fujimori, Tetsuo *Financier*
%Dai-Ichi Kangyo Bank, 1-5-1 Uchisaiwaicho, Chiyodaku, Tokyo 100, Japan

Fujimoto, Shun *Businessman*
%Toyota Automobile Body Co, 100 Kanayama, Kariya City 448, Japan

Fujinuma, Mototoshi *Businessman*
%Sekisui Chemical Co, 2-4-4 Nishi-Tenma, Kitaku, Osaka 530, Japan

Fujisaki, Akira *Businessman*
%Sumitomo Metal Mining Co, 5-11-3 Shimbashi, Minatoku, Tokyo 105, Japan

Fujisawa, Tomokichiro *Businessman*
%Fujisawa Pharmaceutical Co, 4-3 Doshomachi, Higashiku, Osaka 541, Japan

Fujita, Hiroyuki *Microbiotics Engineer*
1-9-14 Senkawa, Toshimaku, Tokyo 171, Japan

Fujiyoshi, Tsuguhide *Businessman*
%Toray Industries, 2-2 Nihonbashi-Muromachi, Chuoku, Tokyo 103, Japan

Fukui, Kenichi *Nobel Chemistry Laureate*
%Fundamental Chemistry Inst, 34-4 Takano-Nishihiraki-cho, Kyoto 606, Japan

Fuld, Richard S, Jr *Financier*
%Lehman Brothers, 3 World Financiel Center, New York, NY 10285, USA

Fulghum, Robert *Religious Leader, Writer*
1015 Violeta Dr, Alhambra, CA 91801, USA

Fuller, Bob B *Writer*
37 Langton Way, London 5E3, England

Fuller, Charles *Playwright*
%William Morris Agency, 1325 Ave of Americas, New York, NY 10019, USA

Fuller, E Keith *Journalist*
%Associated Press, 50 Rockefeller Plaza, New York, NY 10020, USA

Fuller, H Laurance *Businessman*
%Amoco Corp, 200 E Randolph Dr, Chicago, IL 60601, USA

Fuller, Jack W *Editor, Publisher*
%Chicago Tribune, Editorial Dept, 435 N Michigan, Chicago, IL 60611, USA

Fuller, Kathryn S *Association Official*
%World Wildlife Fund, 1250 24th St NW, Washington, DC 20037, USA

Fuller, Lawrence R *Publisher*
%Argus Leader, PO Box 5034, Sioux Falls, SD 57117, USA

Fuller, Penny *Actress*
12428 Hesby St, North Hollywood, CA 91607, USA

Fuller, Robert *Actor*
6767 Forest Lawn Dr, #115, Los Angeles, CA 90068, USA

Fuller, Samuel *Movie Director*
7628 Woodrow Wilson Dr, Los Angeles, CA 90046, USA

Fuller, William H, Jr *Football Player*
%Philadelphia Eagles, 3501 S Broad St, Philadelphia, PA 19148, USA

Fullerton, C Gordon *Astronaut*
%Ames/Dryden Research Facility, PO Box 273, Edwards Air Force Base, CA 93523, USA

Fullerton, Fiona *Actress*
%London Mgmt, 2-4 Noel St, London W1V 3RB, England

Fullerton, Gail J *Educator*
1643 Tompkins Hill Rd, Fortuna, CA 95540, USA

Fullmer, Gene *Boxer*
1875 W 7800 S, West Jordan, UT 84088, USA

Fullwood, Brent *Football Player*
%Green Bay Packers, 1265 Lombardi Ave, Green Bay, WI 54304, USA

F

Fuentes - Fullwood

Fulton, Eileen *Actress, Singer*
%"As the World Turns" Show, CBS-TV, 524 W 57nd St, New York, NY 10019, USA

Fulton, Robert D *Governor, IA*
141 Hillcrest Rd, Waterloo, IA 50701, USA

Funicello, Annette *Actress*
16202 Sandy Lane, Encino, CA 91316, USA

Funk, Paul E *Army General*
Commanding General, III Corps, Fort Hood, TX 76544, USA

Funkhouser, Paul W *Businessman*
%Howell Corp, 1111 Fannin St, Houston, TX 77002, USA

Funt, Allen A *Comedian, Television Producer*
2359 Nichols Canyon, Los Angeles, CA 90046, USA

Fuoss, Raymond M *Chemist*
68 N Lake Dr, Hamden, CT 06517, USA

Furakawa, Susumu *Financier*
%Daiwa Bank, 2-21 Bingomachi, Higashiku, Osaka 541, Japan

Furlanetto, Ferruccio *Opera Singer*
%Metropolitan Opera Assn, Lincoln Center Plaza, New York, NY 10023, USA

Furlaud, Richard M *Businessman*
%American Express Co, 200 Vecsey St, New York, NY 10285, USA

Furlong, Edward *Actor*
10573 W Pico Blvd, #853, Los Angeles, CA 90064, USA

Furniss, Bruce *Swimmer*
655 Westwood St, Anaheim Hills, CA 92807, USA

Furst, Stephen *Actor*
3900 Huntercrest Court, Moorpark, CA 93021, USA

Furst, Stephen J *Businessman*
%Gottschalks Inc, 7 River Park Place E, Fresno, CA 93720, USA

Furth, George *Actor, Playwright*
8484 Wilshire Blvd, #500, Beverly Hills, CA 90211, USA

Furth, Harold P *Physicist*
36 Lake Lane, Princeton, NJ 08540, USA

Furth, Warren Wolfgang *International Official*
13 Rt de Presinge, 1241 Puplinge, Geneva, Switzerland

Furuhashi, Hironshin *Swimmer*
3-9-11 Nozawa, Setagayaku, Tokyo, Japan

Furukawa, Masaru *Swimmer*
5-5-12 Shinohara Honmachi, Nadaku, Kobe, Japan

Furuseth, Ole Kristian *Skier*
John Colletts Alle 74, 0854 Oslo, Norway

Fusina, Chuck *Football Player*
1548 King James, Pittsburgh, PA 15237, USA

Fussell, Paul *Writer, Educator*
1016 Spruce St, #2-F, Philadelphia, PA 19107, USA

Futrell, J Richard, Jr *Financier*
%Centura Banks, 124 N Church St, Rocky Mount, NC 27804, USA

Futrell, Mary H *Labor Leader*
%George Washington University, Education School, Washington, DC 20052, USA

Futter, Ellen V *Educator*
%American Museum of Natural History, Park W & 79th St, New York, NY 10024, USA

Futterknecht, James O, Jr *Businessman*
%Excel Industries, 1120 N Main St, Elkhart, IN 46514, USA

Futterman, Jack *Businessman*
%Pathmark Stores, 301 Blair Rd, Woodbridge, NJ 07095, USA

Fylstra, Daniel *Computer Software Designer*
%Visicorp, 2895 Zanken Rd, San Jose, CA 95134, USA

Fulton - Fylstra

Gaarder, Jostein — *Philosopher*
Gullkroken 22-A, 0377 Oslo, Norway

Gabelli, Mario J — *Financier*
%Gabelli Funds, 1 Corporate Center, Rye, NY 10580, USA

Gabet, Sharon — *Actress*
222 E 44th St, New York, NY 10017, USA

Gable, Christopher — *Actor*
%Ken McReddie, 91 Regent St, London W1R 7TB, England

Gable, Dan — *Wrestler, Coach*
%University of Iowa, Athletic Dept, Carver-Hawkeye Arena, Iowa City, IA 52242, USA

Gabor, Zsa Zsa — *Actress*
1001 Bel Air Rd, Los Angeles, CA 90077, USA

Gabreski, Francis S (Gabby) — *WW II Army Air Corps Hero*
106 Ryder Ave, Dix Hills, NY 11746, USA

Gabriel, Charles A — *Air Force General*
%Flight International, International Airport, Newport News, VA 23602, USA

Gabriel, John — *Actor*
130 W 42nd St, #1804, New York, NY 10036, USA

Gabriel, Juan — *Singer, Songwriter*
%Ventura Productions, 11003 Rooks Rd, Pico Rivera, CA 90660, USA

Gabriel, Peter — *Singer, Songwriter*
%Gailforce Mgmt, 81-83 Walton St, London SW3 2HP, England

Gabriel, Roman — *Football Player*
%Roman Gabriel Sports Connection, 16817 McKee Rd, Charlotte, NC 28278, USA

Gabrielle, Monique — *Model, Actress*
1560-1 Newbury Rd, #420, Newbury Park, CA 91320, USA

Gaddafi, Mu'ammar Mohammad al- — *President, Libya*
%President's Office, Bab el Aziziya Barracks, Tripoli, Libya

Gaddis, William — *Writer*
%Donadio & Ashworth, 231 W 22nd St, New York, NY 10011, USA

Gadzhiev, Raul S O — *Composer*
%Azerbaijan State Popular Orchestra, Baku, Azerbaijan

Gaetti, Gary J — *Baseball Player*
1937 Torrey Pines Place, Raleigh, NC 27615, USA

Gaffney, F Andrew — *Astronaut*
6613 Chatsworth Place, Nashville, TN 37205, USA

Gage, Nicholas — *Columnist*
37 Nelson St, North Grafton, MA 01536, USA

Gagne, Greg C — *Baseball Player*
746 Whetstone Hill Rd, Somerset, MA 02726, USA

Gagnier, Holly — *Actress*
145 S Fairfax Ave, #310, Los Angeles, CA 90036, USA

Gagnon, Edouard Cardinal — *Religious Leader*
%Pontifical Family Council, Palazzo S Calisto, 00120 Vatican City, Italy

Gago, Jenny — *Actress*
%Paul Kohner Inc, 9300 Wilshire Blvd, #555, Beverly Hills, CA 90212, USA

Gagosian, Larry — *Art Dealer*
%Gagosian Gallery, 980 Madison Ave, #PH, New York, NY 10021, USA

Gahan, David — *Singer (Depeche Mode)*
%DMB&B Entertainment, 6500 Wilshire Blvd, #1000, Los Angeles, CA 90048, USA

Gaidukov, Sergei N — *Cosmonaut*
%Potchta Kosmonavtov, 141 160 Svyosdny Gorodok, Moskovskoi Oblasti, Russia

Gaief, Andrew G — *Businessman*
%MagneTek Inc, 26 Century Blvd, Nashville, TN 37214, USA

Gail, Max — *Actor*
29451 Bluewater Rd, Malibu, CA 90265, USA

Gaillard, Bob — *Basketball Coach*
50 Bonnie Brae Dr, Novato, CA 94949, USA

Gain, Bob — *Football Player*
11 Nokomis Dr, Timberlake Village, OH 44095, USA

Gaines, Boyd — *Actor*
%Duva/Flack Assoc, 200 W St, #1407, New York, NY 10013, USA

Gaines, Ernest J — *Writer*
128 Buena Vista, Lafayette, LA 70503, USA

Gaines, Howard C — *Financier*
%First National Bank of Commerce, 210 Baronne St, New Orleans, LA 70112, USA

Gaines, James R — *Editor, Publisher*
%Time Warner Inc, Time Magazine, Rockefeller Center, New York, NY 10020, USA

G

Gaarder - Gaines

G

Gaines, John R *Thoroughbred Racing Breeder*
%Gainesway Farm, 3750 Paris Pike, Lexington, KY 40511, USA

Gaines, Rowdy *Swimmer*
6800 Hawaii Kai Dr, Honolulu, HI 96825, USA

Gaines, William C *Journalist*
%Chicago Tribune, Editorial Dept, 435 N Michigan Ave, Chicago, IL 60611, USA

Gainey, Robert M (Bob) *Hockey Player, Coach, Executive*
%Dallas Stars, 211 Cowboys Parkway, Dallas, TX 75063, USA

Gaiswinkler, Robert S *Financier*
%First Financial Corp, 1305 Main St, Stevens Point, WI 54481, USA

Gaither, Bill *Gospel Songwriter*
%Gaither Music Co, PO Box 737, Alexandria, IN 46001, USA

Gajdusek, D Carleton *Nobel Medicine Laureate*
4316 Deer Spring Rd, Middletown, MD 21769, USA

Gaje Ghale *WW II India Army Hero (VC)*
Alexendre Lines, Almora 26301 UP, India

Galambos, Robert *Neuroscientist*
8826 La Jolla Scenic Dr, La Jolla, CA 92037, USA

Galanos, James *Fashion Designer*
2254 S Sepulveda Blvd, Los Angeles, CA 90064, USA

Galarraga, Andres J P *Baseball Player*
Barrio Nuevo Chapellin, Clejon Soledad #5, Caracas, Venezuela

Galati, Frank J *Stage, Opera Director*
1144 Michigan Ave, Evanston, IL 60202, USA

Galbraith, Evan G *Diplomat, Financier*
133 E 64th St, New York, NY 10021, USA

Galbraith, J Kenneth *Government Official, Economist*
30 Francis Ave, Cambridge, MA 02138, USA

Galdikas, Birute *Anthropologist*
%Orangutan Foundation International, 822 S Wellesley Ave, Los Angeles, CA 90049, USA

Gale, Lauren (Laddie) *Basketball Player*
Hound Dog Rd, Gold Beach, OR 97444, USA

Gale, Robert P *Medical Researcher*
2501 Roscomare Rd, Los Angeles, CA 90077, USA

Galef, Andrew G *Businessman*
%Magnetek Inc, 11150 Santa Monica Blvd, #1400, Los Angeles, CA 90025, USA

Galella, Ronald E (Ron) *Photographer*
%Ron Galella Ltd, 12 Nelson Lane, Montville, NJ 07045, USA

Galer, Robert E *WW II Marine Corps Hero (CMH), General*
5588 Southern Hills Dr, Frisco, TX 75034, USA

Galiardo, John W *Businessman*
%Becton Dickinson Co, 1 Becton Dr, Franklin Lakes, NJ 07417, USA

Gall, Hugues *Opera Executive*
%Theater National de l'Opera, Place de l'Opera, 75009 Paris, France

Gall, Joseph G *Biologist*
107 Bellemore Rd, Baltimore, MD 21210, USA

Gallagher *Illusionist*
%American Mgmt, 17530 Ventura Blvd, #108, Encino, CA 91316, USA

Gallagher, Helen *Singer, Actress*
260 West End Ave, New York, NY 10023, USA

Gallagher, John *Religious Leader*
%Advent Christian Church, PO Box 551, Presque Isle, ME 04769, USA

Gallagher, Megan *Actress*
440 Landfair Ave, Los Angeles, CA 90024, USA

Gallagher, Peter *Actor*
171 W 71st St, #3-A, New York, NY 10023, USA

Gallagher, Thomas C *Businessman*
%Genuine Parts Co, 2999 Circle 75 Parkway, Atlanta, GA 30339, USA

Galland, Adolf *Army General, Germany*
Gotenstr 157 Am Hockreg, 53175 Bonn-Bad Godesberg, Germany

Gallant, Mavis *Writer*
14 Rue Jean Ferrandi, 75006 Paris, France

Gallardo, Camilio *Actor*
%Innovative Artists, 1999 Ave of Stars, #2850, Los Angeles, CA 90067, USA

Gallardo, Silvana *Actress*
201 Ruth Ave, Venice, CA 90291, USA

Gallarneau, Hugh *Football Player*
2216 Maple Dr, Northbrook, IL 60062, USA

Gallatin, Harry J — *Basketball Player*
2010 Madison Ave, Edwardsville, IL 62025, USA

Galles, John — *Association Executive*
%National Small Business United, 1155 15th St NW, #710, Washington, DC 20005, USA

Galley, Garry — *Hockey Player*
%Buffalo Sabres, Memorial Stadium, 140 Main St, Buffalo, NY 14202, USA

Galli, Robert G — *Financier*
%Oppenheimer Management Corp, 2 World Trade Center, New York, NY 10048, USA

Gallison, Joe — *Actor*
3760 Green Vista Dr, Encino, CA 91436, USA

Gallo, Ernest — *Businessman*
%E&J Gallo Winery, 600 Yosemite Blvd, Modesto, CA 95354, USA

Gallo, Frank — *Sculptor*
%University of Illinois, Art Dept, Urbana, IL 61801, USA

Gallo, Lew — *Movie Director*
915 N Beverly Dr, Beverly Hills, CA 90210, USA

Gallo, Robert C — *Research Scientist*
%Institute for Study of Viruses, University of Maryland, Baltimore, MD 21228, USA

Gallo, William V (Bill) — *Sports Cartoonist*
1 Mayflower Dr, Yonkers, NY 10710, USA

Gallogly, Jerry T — *Businessman*
%American States Insurance, 500 N Meridian St, Indianapolis, IN 46204, USA

Galloway, Don — *Actor*
1800 Century Park East, #300, Los Angeles, CA 90067, USA

Galloway, Joey — *Football Player*
%Seattle Seahawks, 11220 NE 53rd St, Kirkland, WA 98033, USA

Gallup, George H, II — *Statistician, Pollster*
53 Bank St, Princeton, NJ 08542, USA

Galotti, Donna — *Publisher*
%Ladies Home Journal, 100 Park Ave, New York, NY 10017, USA

Galotti, Ronald A — *Publisher*
%Hearst Magazines, 959 8th Ave, New York, NY 10019, USA

Galt, Barry J — *Businessman*
%Seagull Energy Corp, 1001 Fannin St, Houston, TX 77002, USA

Galtieri, Leopold F — *President, Argentina; Army General*
Chivilkoy, Buenos Aires, Argentina

Galvin, Christopher B — *Businessman*
%Motorola Inc, 1303 E Algonquin Rd, Schaumburg, IL 60196, USA

Galvin, James — *Poet*
%University of Iowa, Writers' Workshop, Iowa City, IA 52242, USA

Galvin, John R — *Army General*
791 Bluffview Dr, Columbus, OH 43235, USA

Galway, James — *Concert Flutist*
%IMG Artists, 3 Burlington Lane, London W4 2TH, England

Gam, Rita — *Actress*
180 W 58th St, #8-B, New York, NY 10019, USA

Gamba, Piero — *Conductor*
%Winnipeg Symphony Orchestra, 555 Main St, Winnipeg MB R3B 1C3, Canada

Gamble, Ed — *Editorial Cartoonist*
%Florida Times-Union, Editorial Dept, 1 Riverside Ave, Jacksonville, FL 32202, USA

Gamble, Kevin — *Basketball Player*
%Boston Celtics, 151 Merrimac St, #500, Boston, MA 02114, USA

Gambon, Michael — *Actor*
%Larry Dalzell Assoc, 17 Broad Court, #12, London WC2B 5QN, England

Gambrell, David H — *Senator, GA*
3820 Castlegate Dr NW, Atlanta, GA 30327, USA

Gambril, Don — *Swimming Coach*
%University of Alabama, Athletic Dept, University, AL 35486, USA

Gammie, Anthony P — *Businessman*
%Bowater Inc, 55 E Campendown Way, Greenville, SC 29601, USA

Gammill, Lee M, Jr — *Businessman*
%New York Life & Annuity Co, 51 Madison Ave, New York, NY 10010, USA

Gammon, James — *Actor*
%Cunningham-Escott-Dipene, 10635 Santa Monica Blvd, Los Angeles, CA 90025, USA

Gamper, Albert R, Jr — *Financier*
%CIT Group Holdings, 650 CIT Dr, Livingston, NJ 07039, USA

Ganci, Paul E — *Businessman*
%Central Hudson Gas & Electric, 284 South Ave, Poughkeepsie, NY 12601, USA

G

Gallatin - Ganci

G

Gandrud, Robert P — *Businessman*
%Lutheran Brotherhood, 625 4th Ave S, Minneapolis, MN 55415, USA

Ganellin, C Robin — *Inventor (Antiulcer Compound)*
University College, Chemistry Dept, 20 Gordon St, London WC1H OAJ, England

Gangel, Jamie — *Commentator*
%NBC-TV, News Dept, 30 Rockefeller Plaza, New York, NY 10112, USA

Gangl, Kenneth R — *Financier*
%Case Finance Co, 700 State St, Racine, WI 53404, USA

Ganju Lama — *WW II India Army Hero (VC)*
Shangderpa House, 34 Singtam Ravangla Rd, PO Ravangla, South Sikkim, India

Gannon, Robert P — *Businessman*
%Montana Power Co, 40 E Broadway, Butte, MT 59707, USA

Gant, Harry — *Auto Racing Driver*
PO Box 1258, Mooresville, NC 28115, USA

Gantin, Bernardin Cardinal — *Religious Leader*
Piazzi S Calisto 16, 00153 Rome, Italy

Garabedian, Paul R — *Mathematician*
110 Bleecker St, New York, NY 10012, USA

Garagiola, Joe — *Sportscaster, Baseball Player*
6221 E Huntress Dr, Paradise Valley, AZ 85253, USA

Garas, Kaz — *Actor*
PO Box 6736, Malibu, CA 90264, USA

Garba, Joseph N — *Army General, Diplomat, Nigeria*
%Foreign Affairs Ministry, 23 Marina, PMB 12600, Lagos, Nigeria

Garbarek, Jan — *Musician*
Niels Juels Gate 42, 0257 Oslo, Norway

Garber, H Eugene (Gene) — *Baseball Player*
771 Stonemill Dr, Elizabethtown, PA 17022, USA

Garber, Terri — *Actress*
911 15th St, Santa Monica, CA 90403, USA

Garci, Jose Luis — *Movie Director*
%Direccion General del Libro, Paseo de la Castellana 109, Madrid 16, Spain

Garcia Marquez, Gabriel — *Nobel Literature Laureate*
Fuego 144, Pedregal de San Angel, Mexico City DF, Mexico

Garcia Perez, Alan — *President, Peru*
%President's Office, Palcio del Gobierno S/N, Plaza de Armas, Lima, Peru

Garcia, Andy — *Actor*
4323 Forman Ave, Toluca Lake, CA 91602, USA

Gardelli, Lamberto — *Conductor*
%Allied Artists, 42 Montpelier Sq, London SW7 1J2, England

Gardiner of Kittisford, Gerald — *Barrister*
%Mote End, Nan Clark's Lane, Mill Hill, London NW7 4HH, England

Gardiner, John Eliot — *Conductor*
Gore Farm, Ashmore, Salisbury, Wilts, England

Gardiner, Robert K A — *United Nations Official, Ghana*
PO Box 9274, The Airport, Accra, Ghana

Gardner, Dale A — *Astronaut*
1013 Sun Dr, Colorado Springs, CO 80906, USA

Gardner, David P — *Educator, Foundation Executive*
%Hewlett Foundation, 525 Middlefield Rd, #200, Menlo Park, CA 94025, USA

Gardner, Guy S — *Astronaut*
%NASA Headquarters, Mail Code M-3, Washington, DC 20546, USA

Gardner, Howard E — *Psychologist, Neurobiologist*
%Harvard University, Graduate Education School, Cambridge, MA 02138, USA

Gardner, Jack (James H) — *Basketball Coach*
2486 Michigan Ave, Salt Lake City, UT 84108, USA

Gardner, John — *Ballet Dancer*
%American Ballet Theatre, 890 Broadway, New York, NY 10003, USA

Gardner, John W — *Secretary, Health Education Welfare*
%Stanford University, Graduate Business School, Stanford, CA 94305, USA

Gardner, M Dozier — *Financier*
%Eaton Vance Corp, 24 Federal St, Boston, MA 02110, USA

Gardner, Moe — *Football Player*
%Atlanta Falcons, 2745 Burnett Rd, Suwanee, GA 30174, USA

Gardner, Philip J — *WW II British Army Hero (VC)*
Wakehurst, 19 Princes Crescent, Hove, Sussex BN3 4GS, England

Gardner, Randy — *Figure Skater*
4640 Glencoe Ave, #6, Marina del Rey, CA 90292, USA

Gardner, Richard N — *Diplomat*
1150 5th Ave, New York, NY 10128, USA

Gardner, Wilford R — *Physicist*
%University of California, Natural Resources College, Berkeley, CA 94720, USA

Gardner, William F (Bill) — *Baseball Manager*
35 Dayton Rd, Waterford, CT 06385, USA

Gare, Danny — *Hockey Player*
%Edmonton Oilers, Northlands Coliseum, Edmonton AB T5B 4M9, Canada

Garfield, Brian W — *Writer*
345 N Maple Dr, #395, Beverly Hills, CA 90210, USA

Garfield, David C — *Businessman*
731 Manatee Cove, Vero Beach, FL 32963, USA

Garfunkel, Art — *Singer*
9 E 79th St, New York, NY 10021, USA

Garland, Beverly — *Actress*
8014 Briar Summit Dr, Los Angeles, CA 90046, USA

Garland, George D — *Geophysicist*
%Academy of Science, 207 Queen St, Ottawa ON K1G OAO, Canada

Garlits, Dan (Big Daddy) — *Drag Racing Driver*
%Garlits Racing Museum, 13700 SW 16th Ave, Ocala, FL 34473, USA

Garn, E Jacob (Jake) — *Senator, UT; Astronaut*
%Huntsman Chemical Corp, 2000 Eagle Gate Tower, Salt Lake City, UT 84111, USA

Garn, Stanley M — *Physical Anthropologist*
2410 Londonderry Rd, Ann Arbor, MI 48104, USA

Garneau, Marc — *Astronaut, Canada*
14818 Heather Valley Way, Houston, TX 77062, USA

Garner, James — *Actor*
33 Oakmont Dr, Los Angeles, CA 90049, USA

Garner, Jay M — *Army General*
Com Gen, US Army Space Command, 1941 Jeff Davis Highway, Arlington, VA 22215, USA

Garner, Philip M (Phil) — *Baseball Player, Manager*
2451 Lake Village Dr, Kingwood, TX 77339, USA

Garner, Wendell R — *Psychologist*
48 Yowago Ave, Branford, CT 06405, USA

Garner, William S — *Editorial Cartoonist*
%Memphis Commercial Appeal, Editorial Dept, 495 Union Ave, Memphis, TN 38103, USA

Garnett, Kevin — *Basketball Player*
%Minnesota Timberwolves, Target Center, 600 1st Ave N, Minneapolis, MN 55403, USA

Garofalo, Janeane — *Actress*
%United Talent Agency, 9560 Wilshire Blvd, #500, Beverly Hills, CA 90212, USA

Garouste, Gerard — *Artist*
La Mesangere, 27810 Marcilly-sur-Eure, France

Garr, Ralph A — *Baseball Player*
7819 Chaseway Dr, Missouri City, TX 77489, USA

Garr, Teri — *Actress*
8686 Lookout Mountain Dr, Los Angeles, CA 90046, USA

Garrahy, J Joseph — *Governor, RI*
474 Ocean Rd, Narragansett, RI 02882, USA

Garrels, Robert M — *Geologist*
%South Florida University, Marine Science Dept, St Petersburg, FL 33701, USA

Garrett, Betty — *Actress*
3231 Oakdell Rd, Studio City, CA 91604, USA

Garrett, George P, Jr — *Writer*
1845 Wayside Pl, Charlottesville, VA 22903, USA

Garrett, H Lawrence, III — *Government Official*
3202 Cinch Ring Court, Oakton, VA 22124, USA

Garrett, Leif — *Actor, Singer*
11524 Amanda Dr, Studio City, CA 91604, USA

Garrett, Lila — *Movie Producer*
1245 Laurel Way, Beverly Hills, CA 90210, USA

Garrett, Mike — *Football Player, Sports Administrator*
%University of Southern California, Heritage Hall, Los Angeles, CA 90089, USA

Garrett, Pat — *Singer, Songwriter*
%Dutch Kitchen, RD 1, Bethel, PA 19507, USA

Garrett, Wilbur E — *Editor*
%National Geographic Magazine, 17th & "M" Sts, Washington, DC 20036, USA

Garrett, William E — *Photographer*
209 Seneca Rd, Great Falls, VA 22066, USA

G

Gardner - Garrett

G

Garriott, Owen K — *Astronaut*
111 Lost Tree Dr SW, Huntsville, AL 35824, USA

Garrison, U Edwin — *Businessman*
%Thiokel Corp, 2475 Washington Blvd, Ogden, UT 84401, USA

Garrison, William R — *Businessman*
%CDI Corp, 1717 Arch St, Philadelphia, PA 19103, USA

Garrison-Jackson, Zina — *Tennis Player*
PO Box 272305, Houston, TX 77277, USA

Garrott, Thomas M — *Financier*
%National Commerce Bancorp, 1 Commerce St, Memphis, TN 38150, USA

Garrow, David J — *Political Scientist, Historian*
200 Cabrini Blvd, #PH-9, New York, NY 10033, USA

Garrum, Larry — *Hockey Player*
987 Pleasant St, Framingham, MA 01701, USA

Garson, Greer — *Actress*
3525 Turtle Creek Rd, Dallas, TX 75219, USA

Garth, Jennie — *Actress*
PO Box 5792, Sherman Oaks, CA 91413, USA

Gartner, Michael G — *Television Executive*
%Ames Daily Tribune, PO Box 380, Ames, IA 50010, USA

Gartner, Mike — *Hockey Player*
%Toronto Maple Leafs, 60 Carlton St, Toronto ON M5B 1L1, Canada

Garver, Kathy — *Actress*
%Atkins Assoc, 303 S Crescent Heights Blvd, Los Angeles, CA 90048, USA

Garvey, Fenwick H — *Financier*
%Ryan Beck Co, 80 Main St, West Orange, NJ 07052, USA

Garvey, Ned F — *Baseball Player*
PO Box 114, Ney, OH 43549, USA

Garvey, Steven P (Steve) — *Baseball Player*
11822 Kearsarge St, Los Angeles, CA 90049, USA

Garvin, Clifton C, Jr — *Businessman*
33 Baldwin Farms, Greenwich, CT 06831, USA

Garwin, Richard L — *Physicist*
%IBM Corp, Watson Research Center, PO Box 218, Yorktown Heights, NY 10598, USA

Gary, Cleveland — *Football Player*
%Miami Dolphins, 7500 SW 30th St, Davie, FL 33329, USA

Gary, John — *Singer*
7 Briarwood Cir, Richardson, TX 75080, USA

Gary, Lorraine — *Actress*
1158 Tower Dr, Beverly Hills, CA 90210, USA

Gascoigne, Paul J — *Soccer Player*
%Arran Gardner, Holborn Hall, London WC1X 8BY, England

Gaspari, Rich — *Body Builder*
PO Box 29, Milltown, NJ 08850, USA

Gasparro, Frank — *Sculptor*
216 Westwood Park Dr, Havertown, PA 19083, USA

Gass, William — *Philosopher*
6304 Westminster Pl, St Louis, MO 63130, USA

Gasser, Michael J — *Businessman*
%Greif Bros Corp, 621 Pennsylvania Ave, Delaware, OH 43015, USA

Gassman, Vittorio — *Actor*
Piazza S Alessio 32, 00191 Rome, Italy

Gastineau, Mark — *Football Player*
1000 Fulton Ave, Hempstead, NY 11550, USA

Gaston, Clarence E (Cito) — *Baseball Player, Manager*
505 Edgewater Dr, Dunedin, FL 34698, USA

Gaston, Gerald N — *Businessman*
%American Bankers Insurance Group, 11222 Quail Roost Dr, Miami, FL 33157, USA

Gately, George G — *Cartoonist (Heathcliff)*
%Tribune Media Services, 435 N Michigan Ave, #1417, Chicago, IL 60611, USA

Gates, Charles C — *Businessman*
%Gates Corp, 900 S Broadway St, Denver, CO 80209, USA

Gates, Daryl F — *Law Enforcement Official*
PO Box 30158, Los Angeles, CA 90030, USA

Gates, Henry L, Jr — *Educator*
%Harvard University, Afro-American Studies Dept, Cambridge, MA 02138, USA

Gates, Marshall De M, Jr — *Chemist*
41 West Brook Rd, Pittsburgh, PA 14534, USA

Garriott - Gates

Gates, William H, III — *Businessman*
%Microsoft Corp, 1 Microsoft Way, Redmond, WA 98052, USA

Gathercole, Terry — *Swimmer*
PO Box 36, Forestville NSW 2087, Australia

Gatlin, Larry W — *Singer*
%Gatlin Enterprises, 7003 Chadwick Dr, #360, Brentwood, TN 37027, USA

Gatski, Frank — *Football Player*
PO Box 677, Grafton, WV 26354, USA

Gattis, Jerry — *Businessman*
%Cagle's Inc, 2000 Hills Ave NW, Atlanta, GA 30318, USA

Gaudiani, Claire L — *Educator*
%Connecticut College, President's Office, New London, CT 06320, USA

Gaul, Gilbert M — *Journalist*
%Philadelphia Inquirer, Editorial Dept, 400 N Broad St, Philadelphia, PA 19130, USA

Gaulin, Jean — *Businessman*
%Ultramar Inc, 2 Pickwick Plaza, Greenwich, CT 06830, USA

Gault, Stanley C — *Businessman*
%Goodyear Tire & Rubber Co, 1144 E Market St, Akron, OH 44316, USA

Gault, William Campbell — *Writer*
482 Vaquero Lane, Santa Barbara, CA 93111, USA

Gault, Willie — *Football Player*
%Travis Clark Mgmt, 5700 Wilshire Blvd, #575, Los Angeles, CA 90036, USA

Gaultier, Jean-Paul — *Fashion Designer*
%Gaultier Boutique, 2 Rue Vivien, 75006 Paris, France

Gautier, Dick — *Actor*
11333 Moorpark St, #59, North Hollywood, CA 91602, USA

Gavaskar, Sunil — *Cricketer*
40 Sir Bhalchandra Rd, #A, Dadar, Bombay 400014, India

Gavazzeni, Gianandrea — *Conductor*
Via Porta Dipinta 5, Bergamo, Italy

Gavin, James J, Jr — *Businessman*
161 Thorntree Lane, Winnetka, IL 60093, USA

Gavin, John — *Actor, Diplomat*
10263 Century Woods Dr, Los Angeles, CA 90067, USA

Gaviria Trujillo, Cesar — *President, Colombia*
%Organization of American States, 1889 "F" St NW, Washington, DC 20006, USA

Gavitt, Dave — *Basketball Executive*
%Boston Celtics, 151 Merrimac St, #500, Boston, MA 02114, USA

Gavrilov, Andrei V — *Concert Pianist*
%Harold Holt Ltd, 31 Sinclair Rd, London W14 ON5, England

Gay, Peter J — *Historian*
105 Blue Trail, Hamden, CT 06518, USA

Gayle, Crystal — *Singer*
%Gayle Entertainment, 51 Music Square E, Nashville, TN 37203, USA

Gayle, Jackie — *Comedian*
2155 San Ysidro Dr, Beverly Hills, CA 90210, USA

Gaylor, Noel — *Navy Admiral*
%East-West Accords Committee, 227 Massachusetts NW, Washington, DC 20001, USA

Gaylord, Edward L — *Broadcast Executive, Publisher*
%Oakland Publishing Co, 500 N Broadway, Oklahoma City, OK 73125, USA

Gaylord, Mitch — *Gymnast*
1232 Smithwood Dr, Los Angeles, CA 90035, USA

Gaynes, George — *Actor*
3344 Campanil Dr, Santa Barbara, CA 93109, USA

Gaynor, Gloria — *Singer*
%Malcolm Field Agency, Longford Ave, Southall, Middx UB1 3QT, England

Gaynor, Mitzi — *Actress, Dancer*
610 N Arden Dr, Beverly Hills, CA 90210, USA

Gayoom, Maumoon Abdul — *President, Maldives*
%President's Office, Marine Dr N, Male, Maldives

Gazzara, Ben — *Actor*
1080 Madison Ave, New York, NY 10028, USA

Geary, Anthony — *Actor*
7010 Pacific View Dr, Los Angeles, CA 90068, USA

Geary, Cynthia — *Actress*
%William Morris Agency, 151 S El Camino Dr, Beverly Hills, CA 90212, USA

Gebel-Williams, Gunther — *Circus Animal Trainer*
%Ringling Bros Barnum & Bailey Circus, 8607 Westwood Circle, Vienna, VA 22182, USA

G

Gedda, Nicolai *Opera Singer*
%Shaw Concerts, Lincoln Plaza, 1900 Broadway, #200, New York, NY 10023, USA

Geddes, Jane *Golfer*
1865 Palm Cove Blvd, #9205, Delray Beach, FL 33445, USA

Gedrick, Jason *Actor*
%IFA Talent Agency, 9730 Sunset Blvd, #490, Los Angeles, CA 90069, USA

Gee, E Gordon *Educator*
%Ohio State University, President's Office, Columbus, OH 43210, USA

Gee, James D *Religious Leader*
%Pentecostal Church of God, 4901 Pennsylvania, Joplin, MO 64804, USA

Geer, Dennis *Financier*
%Federal Deposit Insurance Corp, 550 17th St NW, Washington, DC 20429, USA

Geer, Ellen *Actress*
21418 W Entrada Rd, Topanga, CA 90290, USA

Geertz, Clifford J *Anthropologist*
%Institute for Advanced Study, Social Science Dept, Princeton, NJ 08540, USA

Geeson, Judy *Actress*
%MLR Ltd, 200 Fulham Rd, London SW10 9PN, England

Geffen, David *Movie, Music Producer*
%DreamWorks SKG, 100 Universal City Plaza, Universal City, CA 91608, USA

Gehry, Frank O *Architect*
%Frank Gehry Assoc, 1520-B Cloverfield Blvd, Santa Monica, CA 90404, USA

Geiberger, Al *Golfer*
700 Mesa Dr, Solvang, CA 93463, USA

Geiduschek, E Peter *Biologist*
%University of California, Biology Dept, 9500 Gilman Dr, La Jolla, CA 92093, USA

Geier, James A D *Businessman*
%Cincinnati Milacron Inc, 4701 Marburg Ave, Cincinnati, OH 45209, USA

Geier, Philip H, Jr *Businessman*
%Interpublic Group of Companies, 1271 Ave of Americas, New York, NY 10020, USA

Geiger, Keith *Labor Leader*
%National Education Assn, 1201 16th St NW, Washington, DC 20036, USA

Geiger, Ken *Photographer*
%Dallas Morning News, Communications Center, Dallas, TX 75265, USA

Geiger, Roy S *Marine Corps General*
%Marine Corps Headquarters, Washington, DC 20380, USA

Geis, Bernard *Publisher*
500 5th Ave, #3600, New York, NY 10110, USA

Geithner, Paul H, Jr *Financier*
%First Virginia Banks, 6400 Arlington Blvd, Falls Church, VA 22042, USA

Gelb, Bruce S *Businessman, Diplomat*
%US Embassy, Belgium, APO, AE 09724, USA

Gelb, Ignace Jay *Linguist*
%University of Chicago, Oriental Institute, Chicago, IL 60637, USA

Gelb, Richard L *Businessman*
%Bristol-Meyers Squibb Co, 345 Park Ave, New York, NY 10154, USA

Gelbart, Larry *Movie, Television Producer; Writer*
807 N Alpine Dr, Beverly Hills, CA 90210, USA

Gelber, Jack *Writer*
230 E 18th St, #1-C, New York, NY 10003, USA

Geldof, Bob *Singer*
Davington Priory, Faversham, Kent, England

Gelin, Daniel *Actor*
72 Ave de Chartres, 28570 Abondant, France

Gell-Mann, Murray *Nobel Physics Laureate*
%California Institute of Technology, Physics Laboratory, Pasadena, CA 91125, USA

Gelles, Richard J *Sociologist*
%University of Rhode Island, Sociology Dept, Kingston, RI 02881, USA

Gellhorn, Martha *Writer*
%Douglas Rae Mgmt, 28 Charing Cross Rd, London WC2H 0DB, England

Gelman, Larry *Actor*
5121 Greenbush Ave, Sherman Oaks, CA 91423, USA

Gemar, Charles D *Astronaut*
%NASA, Johnson Space Center, 2101 NASA Rd, Houston, TX 77058, USA

Gendron, George *Editor*
%Inc Magazine, Editorial Dept, 38 Commercial Wharf, Boston, MA 02110, USA

Geneen, Harold S *Businessman*
320 Park Ave, New York, NY 10022, USA

Gedda - Geneen

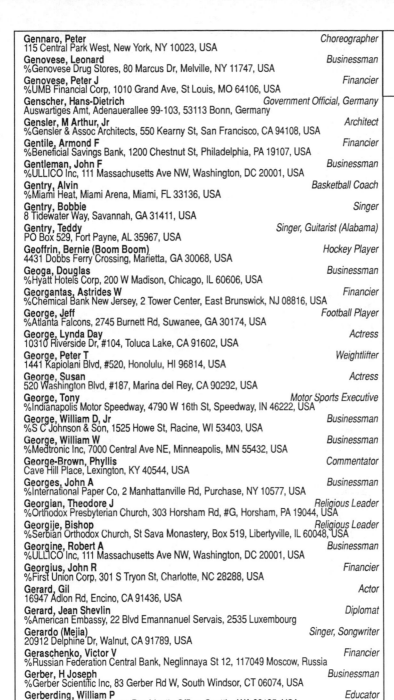

Gennaro, Peter — *Choreographer*
115 Central Park West, New York, NY 10023, USA

Genovese, Leonard — *Businessman*
%Genovese Drug Stores, 80 Marcus Dr, Melville, NY 11747, USA

Genovese, Peter J — *Financier*
%UMB Financial Corp, 1010 Grand Ave, St Louis, MO 64106, USA

Genscher, Hans-Dietrich — *Government Official, Germany*
Auswartiges Amt, Adenauerallee 99-103, 53113 Bonn, Germany

Gensler, M Arthur, Jr — *Architect*
%Gensler & Assoc Architects, 550 Kearny St, San Francisco, CA 94108, USA

Gentile, Armond F — *Financier*
%Beneficial Savings Bank, 1200 Chestnut St, Philadelphia, PA 19107, USA

Gentleman, John F — *Businessman*
%ULLICO Inc, 111 Massachusetts Ave NW, Washington, DC 20001, USA

Gentry, Alvin — *Basketball Coach*
%Miami Heat, Miami Arena, Miami, FL 33136, USA

Gentry, Bobbie — *Singer*
8 Tidewater Way, Savannah, GA 31411, USA

Gentry, Teddy — *Singer, Guitarist (Alabama)*
PO Box 529, Fort Payne, AL 35967, USA

Geoffrin, Bernie (Boom Boom) — *Hockey Player*
4431 Dobbs Ferry Crossing, Marietta, GA 30068, USA

Geoga, Douglas — *Businessman*
%Hyatt Hotels Corp, 200 W Madison, Chicago, IL 60606, USA

Georgantas, Astrides W — *Financier*
%Chemical Bank New Jersey, 2 Tower Center, East Brunswick, NJ 08816, USA

George, Jeff — *Football Player*
%Atlanta Falcons, 2745 Burnett Rd, Suwanee, GA 30174, USA

George, Lynda Day — *Actress*
10310 Riverside Dr, #104, Toluca Lake, CA 91602, USA

George, Peter T — *Weightlifter*
1441 Kapiolani Blvd, #520, Honolulu, HI 96814, USA

George, Susan — *Actress*
520 Washington Blvd, #187, Marina del Rey, CA 90292, USA

George, Tony — *Motor Sports Executive*
%Indianapolis Motor Speedway, 4790 W 16th St, Speedway, IN 46222, USA

George, William D, Jr — *Businessman*
%S C Johnson & Son, 1525 Howe St, Racine, WI 53403, USA

George, William W — *Businessman*
%Medtronic Inc, 7000 Central Ave NE, Minneapolis, MN 55432, USA

George-Brown, Phyllis — *Commentator*
Cave Hill Place, Lexington, KY 40544, USA

Georges, John A — *Businessman*
%International Paper Co, 2 Manhattanville Rd, Purchase, NY 10577, USA

Georgian, Theodore J — *Religious Leader*
%Orthodox Presbyterian Church, 303 Horsham Rd, #G, Horsham, PA 19044, USA

Georgije, Bishop — *Religious Leader*
%Serbian Orthodox Church, St Sava Monastery, Box 519, Libertyville, IL 60048, USA

Georgine, Robert A — *Businessman*
%ULLICO Inc, 111 Massachusetts Ave NW, Washington, DC 20001, USA

Georgius, John R — *Financier*
%First Union Corp, 301 S Tryon St, Charlotte, NC 28288, USA

Gerard, Gil — *Actor*
16947 Adlon Rd, Encino, CA 91436, USA

Gerard, Jean Shevlin — *Diplomat*
%American Embassy, 22 Blvd Emannanuel Servais, 2535 Luxembourg

Gerardo (Mejia) — *Singer, Songwriter*
20912 Delphine Dr, Walnut, CA 91789, USA

Geraschenko, Victor V — *Financier*
%Russian Federation Central Bank, Neglinnaya St 12, 117049 Moscow, Russia

Gerber, H Joseph — *Businessman*
%Gerber Scientific Inc, 83 Gerber Rd W, South Windsor, CT 06074, USA

Gerberding, William P — *Educator*
%University of Washington, President's Office, Seattle, WA 98195, USA

Gerbner, George — *Social Scientist*
234 Golfview Rd, Ardmore, PA 19003, USA

Gere, Richard — *Actor*
26 E 10th St, #PH, New York, NY 10003, USA

G

Gennaro - Gere

G

Gerety, Tom, Jr *Educator*
%Amherst College, President's Office, Amherst, MA 01002, USA
Gerg-Leitner, Michaela *Skier*
Jachenauer Str 26, 83661 Lenggries, Germany
Gergiev, Valery A *Conductor*
%Kirov Opera, Mariinsky Theater, Teatralnaya Pl 1, St Petersburg, Russia
Geri, Joe *Football Player*
140 Chalfont Dr, Athens, GA 30606, USA
Gerlach, Gary *Publisher*
%Des Moines Register & Tribune, 715 Locust St, Des Moines, IA 50309, USA
Gerlach, John B *Businessman*
%Lancaster Colony Corp, 37 W Broad St, Columbus, OH 43215, USA
Gerlach, John B, Jr *Businessman*
%Lancaster Colony Corp, 37 W Broad St, Columbus, OH 43215, USA
German, William *Editor*
%San Francisco Chronicle, Editorial Dept, 901 Mission, San Francisco, CA 94103, USA
Germane, Geoffrey J *Mechanical Engineer*
%Brigham Young University, Mechanical Engineering Dept, Provo, UT 84602, USA
Germani, Fernando *Concert Organist*
Via Delle Terme Deciane 11, Rome, Italy
Gerner, Robert *Behavioral Psychiatrist*
%University of California, Neuropsychiatric Institute, Los Angeles, CA 90024, USA
Geronimo, Cesar F *Baseball Player*
127 W 97th St, #9-E, New York, NY 10025, USA
Gerring, Cathy *Golfer*
%Ladies Professional Golf Assn, 2570 Volusia Ave, Daytona Beach, FL 32114, USA
Gerson, Mark *Photographer*
3 Regal Lane, Regent's Park, London NW1 7TH, England
Gerson, Samuel J *Businessman*
%Filene's Basement Corp, 40 Walnut St, Wellesley, MA 02181, USA
Gerstell, A Frederick *Businessman*
%CalMat Co, 3200 San Fernando Rd, Los Angeles, CA 90065, USA
Gerstner, Louis V, Jr *Businessman*
%International Business Machines Inc, Old Orchard Rd, Armonk, NY 10504, USA
Gerth, Donald R *Educator*
%California State University, President's Office, Sacramento, CA 95819, USA
Gertz, Jami *Actress*
%International Creative Mgmt, 8942 Wilshire Blvd, Beverly Hills, CA 90211, USA
Gervin, George *Basketball Player, Coach*
%San Antonio Spurs, 600 E Market St, #102, San Antonio, TX 78205, USA
Gerwick, Ben C, Jr *Construction Engineer*
5727 Country Club Dr, Oakland, CA 94618, USA
Getaneh, Anna *Model*
%Ford Model Agency, 344 E 59th St, New York, NY 10022, USA
Gettier, Glenn H, Jr *Businessman*
%Southwestern Life Corp, Lincoln Plaza, 500 N Akard, Dallas, TX 75201, USA
Getty, Estelle *Actress*
1240 N Wetherly Dr, Los Angeles, CA 90069, USA
Getz, John *Actor*
440 Linnie Canal, Venice, CA 90291, USA
Geyer, George *Artist*
%Karl Bornstein Gallery, 1662 12th St, Santa Monica, CA 90404, USA
Geyer, Georgie Anne *Columnist*
%Plaza, 800 25th St NW, Washington, DC 20037, USA
Gheorghiu, Ion A *Artist*
%Romanian Fine Arts Union, 21 Nicolae Iorga St, Bucharest 1, Romania
Ghiardi, John F L *Economist, Government Official*
12 Park Overlook Court, Bethesda, MD 20817, USA
Ghiglia, Oscar A *Concert Guitarist*
Helfembergstr 14, 4059 Basel, Switzerland
Ghiuselev, Nicola *Opera Singer*
Villa Elpida, Sofia 1616, Bulgaria
Ghosh, Gautam *Movie Director*
28/1A Gariahat Rd, Block 5, #50, Calcutta 700029, India
Ghostley, Alice *Actress*
3800 Reklaw Dr, Studio City, CA 91604, USA
Giacco, Alexander F *Businessman*
%Axess Corp, Phillips Point, 777 S Flagler Dr, #1112, West Palm Beach, FL 33401, USA

Gerety - Giacco

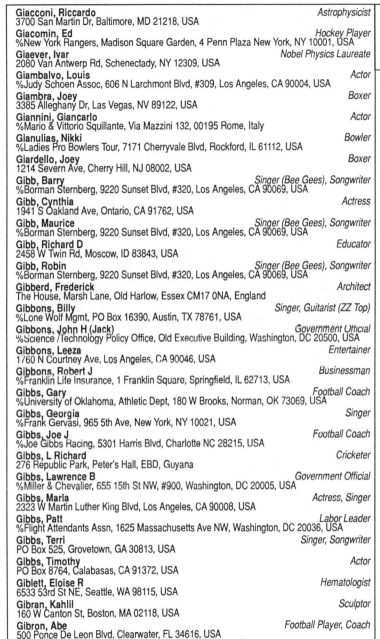

Giacconi, Riccardo *Astrophysicist*
3700 San Martin Dr, Baltimore, MD 21218, USA

Giacomin, Ed *Hockey Player*
%New York Rangers, Madison Square Garden, 4 Penn Plaza New York, NY 10001, USA

Giaever, Ivar *Nobel Physics Laureate*
2080 Van Antwerp Rd, Schenectady, NY 12309, USA

Giambalvo, Louis *Actor*
%Judy Schoen Assoc, 606 N Larchmont Blvd, #309, Los Angeles, CA 90004, USA

Giambra, Joey *Boxer*
3385 Alleghany Dr, Las Vegas, NV 89122, USA

Giannini, Giancarlo *Actor*
%Mario & Vittorio Squillante, Via Mazzini 132, 00195 Rome, Italy

Gianulias, Nikki *Bowler*
%Ladies Pro Bowlers Tour, 7171 Cherryvale Blvd, Rockford, IL 61112, USA

Giardello, Joey *Boxer*
1214 Severn Ave, Cherry Hill, NJ 08002, USA

Gibb, Barry *Singer (Bee Gees), Songwriter*
%Borman Sternberg, 9220 Sunset Blvd, #320, Los Angeles, CA 90069, USA

Gibb, Cynthia *Actress*
1941 S Oakland Ave, Ontario, CA 91762, USA

Gibb, Maurice *Singer (Bee Gees), Songwriter*
%Borman Sternberg, 9220 Sunset Blvd, #320, Los Angeles, CA 90069, USA

Gibb, Richard D *Educator*
2458 W Twin Rd, Moscow, ID 83843, USA

Gibb, Robin *Singer (Bee Gees), Songwriter*
%Borman Sternberg, 9220 Sunset Blvd, #320, Los Angeles, CA 90069, USA

Gibberd, Frederick *Architect*
The House, Marsh Lane, Old Harlow, Essex CM17 0NA, England

Gibbons, Billy *Singer, Guitarist (ZZ Top)*
%Lone Wolf Mgmt, PO Box 16390, Austin, TX 78761, USA

Gibbons, John H (Jack) *Government Official*
%Science /Technology Policy Office, Old Executive Building, Washington, DC 20500, USA

Gibbons, Leeza *Entertainer*
1760 N Courtney Ave, Los Angeles, CA 90046, USA

Gibbons, Robert J *Businessman*
%Franklin Life Insurance, 1 Franklin Square, Springfield, IL 62713, USA

Gibbs, Gary *Football Coach*
%University of Oklahoma, Athletic Dept, 180 W Brooks, Norman, OK 73069, USA

Gibbs, Georgia *Singer*
%Frank Gervasi, 965 5th Ave, New York, NY 10021, USA

Gibbs, Joe J *Football Coach*
%Joe Gibbs Racing, 5301 Harris Blvd, Charlotte NC 28215, USA

Gibbs, L Richard *Cricketer*
276 Republic Park, Peter's Hall, EBD, Guyana

Gibbs, Lawrence B *Government Official*
%Miller & Chevalier, 655 15th St NW, #900, Washington, DC 20005, USA

Gibbs, Marla *Actress, Singer*
2323 W Martin Luther King Blvd, Los Angeles, CA 90008, USA

Gibbs, Patt *Labor Leader*
%Flight Attendants Assn, 1625 Massachusetts Ave NW, Washington, DC 20036, USA

Gibbs, Terri *Singer, Songwriter*
PO Box 525, Grovetown, GA 30813, USA

Gibbs, Timothy *Actor*
PO Box 8764, Calabasas, CA 91372, USA

Giblett, Eloise R *Hematologist*
6533 53rd St NE, Seattle, WA 98115, USA

Gibran, Kahlil *Sculptor*
160 W Canton St, Boston, MA 02118, USA

Gibron, Abe *Football Player, Coach*
500 Ponce De Leon Blvd, Clearwater, FL 34616, USA

Gibson, Althea *Tennis Player*
275 Prospect St, #768, East Orange, NJ 07017, USA

Gibson, Charles D *Commentator*
%ABC-TV, News Dept, 77 W 66th St, New York, NY 10023, USA

Gibson, Christopher T *Financier*
%Capstead Mortgage Corp, 2001 Bryan Tower, Dallas, TX 75201, USA

Gibson, Debbie *Singer*
300 Main St, #201, Huntington, NY 11743, USA

G

Giacconi - Gibson

G

Gibson, Don — *Singer, Guitarist*
PO Box 50474, Nashville, TN 37205, USA

Gibson, Edward G — *Astronaut*
%Gibson International Corp, 7153 Tern Place, Carlsbad, CA 92009, USA

Gibson, Eleanor J — *Psychologist*
RD 1, Box 265-A, Middlebury, VT 05753, USA

Gibson, Everett K, Jr — *Space Scientist*
1015 Trowbridge Dr, Houston, TX 77062, USA

Gibson, Henry — *Actor*
26740 Latigo Shore Dr, Malibu, CA 90265, USA

Gibson, Kirk H — *Baseball Player*
%Detroit Tigers, Tiger Stadium, 2121 Trumbell, Detroit, MI 48216, USA

Gibson, Mel — *Actor*
%International Creative Mgmt, 8942 Wilshire Blvd, Beverly Hills, CA 90211, USA

Gibson, Quentin H — *Biochemist*
98 Dodge Rd, Ithaca, NY 14850, USA

Gibson, Ralph H — *Photographer*
331 W Broadway, New York, NY 10013, USA

Gibson, Robert (Bob) — *Baseball Player*
215 Belleview Rd S, Belleview, NE 68005, USA

Gibson, Robert L (Hoot) — *Astronaut*
%NASA, Johnson Space Center, 2101 NASA Rd, Houston, TX 77058, USA

Gibson, Verna K — *Businessman*
%Petrie Retail Inc, 70 Enterprise Ave, Secaucus, NJ 07094, USA

Gibson, William — *Writer*
%General Delivery, Stockbridge, MA 01262, USA

Gibson, William F — *Association Executive*
%NAACP, 4805 Mt Hope Dr, Baltimore, MD 21215, USA

Gideon, Miriam — *Composer*
410 Central Park West, New York, NY 10025, USA

Gideon, Raynold — *Actor, Writer*
3524 Multiview Dr, Los Angeles, CA 90068, USA

Gidwitz, Gerald S — *Businessman*
%Helene Curtis Industries, 325 N Wells St, Chicago, IL 60610, USA

Gidwitz, Joseph L — *Businessman*
%Helene Curtis Industries, 325 N Wells St, Chicago, IL 60610, USA

Giel, Paul — *Football Player, Administrator*
13400 McGintz Rd, Minneapolis, MN 55305, USA

Gielen, Michael A — *Conductor, Composer*
%Cincinnati Symphony, 1241 Elm St, Cincinnati, OH 45210, USA

Gielgud, John — *Actor*
South Pavilion, Wotton Underwood, Aylesbury Bucks HP18 0SB, England

Giella, Joe — *Cartoonist (Mary Worth)*
%King Features Syndicate, 216 E 45th St, New York, NY 10017, USA

Gierek, Edward — *Premier, Poland*
Ustronie, Silesia, Poland

Gierer, Vincent A, Jr — *Businessman*
%UST Inc, 100 W Putnam Ave, Greenwich, CT 06830, USA

Gierster, Hans — *Conductor*
Hallerwiese 4, 90419 Nurenberg, Germany

Gifford, Frank N — *Football Player, Sportscaster*
355 Taconic Rd, Greenwich, CT 06831, USA

Gifford, Kathie Lee — *Entertainer*
%"Live With Regis & Kathie Lee", WABC-TV, 7 Lincoln Square, New York, NY 10023, USA

Gift, Roland — *Singer (Fine Young Cannibals)*
%Jonathan Altaras Assoc, 2 Goodwins Court, London WC2N 4LL, England

Gil, Gilberto — *Singer, Songwriter*
%Tempest Entertainment, 200 Varick St, #500, New York, NY 10014, USA

Gilbane, William J — *Businessman*
%Gilbane Building Co, 7 Jackson Walkway, Providence, RI 02903, USA

Gilbert, Brad — *Tennis Player*
%ProServe, 1100 Woodrow Wilson Blvd, #1800, Arlington, VA 22209, USA

Gilbert, Carl A — *Businessman*
%Dravo Corp, 1 Oliver Plaza, Pittsburgh, PA 15222, USA

Gilbert, David — *Financier*
%California Federal Bank, 5700 Wilshire Blvd, Los Angeles, CA 90036, USA

Gilbert, Felix — *Historian*
266 Mercer Rd, Princeton, NJ 08540, USA

Gilbert, J Freeman *Geophysicist*
780 Kalamath Dr, Del Mar, CA 92014, USA

Gilbert, Kenneth A *Concert Harpsichordist*
23 Cloitre Notre-Dame, 28000 Chartres, France

Gilbert, Lewis *Movie Director*
17 Sheldrake Place, Dutchess of Bedford Walk, London W8, England

Gilbert, Martin J *Historian*
7 Landsdowne Crescent, London W11, England

Gilbert, Melissa *Actress*
PO Box 57593, Sherman Oaks, CA 91413, USA

Gilbert, Richard W *Publisher*
%Des Moines Register & Tribune, 715 Locust St, Des Moines, IA 50309, USA

Gilbert, Ronnie *Singer*
%Donna Korones Mgmt, PO Box 7765, Berkeley, CA 94707, USA

Gilbert, S J, Sr *Religious Leader*
%Baptist Convention of America, 6717 Centennial Blvd, Nashville, TN 37209, USA

Gilbert, Sara *Actress*
16254 High Valley Dr, Encino, CA 91346, USA

Gilbert, Sean *Football Player*
%St Louis Rams, 100 N Broadway, #2100, St Louis, MO 63102, USA

Gilbert, Simon *Drummer (Suede)*
PO Box 3431, London N1 7LW, England

Gilbert, Walter *Nobel Chemistry Laureate*
15 Gray Gardens W, Cambridge, MA 02138, USA

Gilberto, Astrud *Singer*
%International Music Network, 112 Washington St, Marblehead, MA 01945, USA

Gilbertson, Keith *Football Coach*
%University of California, Athletic Dept, Berkeley, CA 94720, USA

Gilchrist, Paul R *Religious Leader*
%Presbyterian Church in America, 1862 Century Place, Atlanta, GA 30345, USA

Gilday, Scott R *Financier*
%UAL Employees' Credit Union, 125 E Algonquin Rd, Arlington Heights, IL 60005, USA

Gilder, George F *Writer, Economist*
%General Delivery, Tyringham, MA 01264, USA

Giles, Nancy *Actress*
PO Box 16153, Beverly Hills, CA 90209, USA

Giles, William E *Editor*
667 College Hill Dr, Baton Rouge, LA 70808, USA

Giletti, Alain *Figure Skater*
103 Pl de L'Eglise, 74400 Chamonix, France

Gilgorov, Kiro *President, Macedonia*
%President's Office, Skopje, Macedonia

Gill, Brendan *Writer*
%New Yorker Magazine, 20 W 43rd St, New York, NY 10036, USA

Gill, Daniel E *Businessman*
%Bausch & Lomb Inc, 1 Chase Sq, Rochester, NY 14604, USA

Gill, George N *Publisher*
%Louisville Courier-Journal & Times, 525 W Broadway, Louisville, KY 40202, USA

Gill, Howard R, Jr *Publisher*
%Golf Digest/Tennis Magazine, 495 Westport Ave, Norwalk, CT 06851, USA

Gill, Johnny *Singer, Songwriter*
17539 Corinthian Dr, Encino, CA 91316, USA

Gill, Kendall *Basketball Player*
%Charlotte Hornets, 1 Hive Dr, Charlotte, NC 28217, USA

Gill, Vince *Singer, Songwriter*
%Fitzgerald-Hartley-Simmons, 50 W Main St, Ventura, CA 93001, USA

Gill, William A, Jr *Labor Leader, Government Official*
15975 Cove Lane, Dumfries, VA 22026, USA

Gilles, Daniel *Writer*
161 Ave Churchill, 1180 Brussels, Belgium

Gilles, Genevieve *Actress*
%Dakota Hotel, 1 W 72nd St, New York, NY 10023, USA

Gillespie, Charles A, Jr *Diplomat*
%State Department, 2201 "C" St NW, Washington, DC 20520, USA

Gillespie, Rhondda *Concert Pianist*
2 Princess Rd, St Leonards-on-Sea, East Sussex TN37 6EL, England

Gillespie, Robert W *Financier*
%KeyCorp, 127 Public Square, Cleveland, OH 44114, USA

G

Gilbert - Gillespie

Gillett, George *Publisher*
%Gillett Group, 4400 Harding Rd, Nashville, TN 37205, USA

Gillette, Anita *Actress*
501 S Beverly Dr, #3, Beverly Hills, CA 90212, USA

Gilley, Mickey *Singer, Songwriter*
%Gilley's Enterprises, PO Box 1242, Pasadena, TX 77501, USA

Gillfillan, Michael J *Financier*
%Wells Fargo Co, 420 Montgomery St, San Francisco, CA 94104, USA

Gilliam, Armon *Basketball Player*
%New Jersey Nets, Byrne Meadowlands Arena, East Rutherford, NJ 07073, USA

Gilliam, Terry V *Actor, Animator, Writer (Monty Python)*
%Poo Poo Pictures, 68-A Delancey St, Camden Town, London NW1 7RY, England

Gilligan, John G *Governor, OH*
%University of Notre Dame, Law School, Notre Dame, IN 46556, USA

Gillilan, William J, III *Businessman*
%Centex Corp, 3333 Lee Parkway, Dallas, TX 75219, USA

Gilliland, Richard *Actor*
%David Shapira Assoc, 15301 Ventura Blvd, #345, Sherman Oaks, CA 91403, USA

Gillingham, Gale *Football Player*
RR 1, Box 328, Little Falls, MN 56345, USA

Gillis, Malcolm *Educator*
%Rice University, President's Office, Houston, TX 77251, USA

Gillman, Sid *Football Coach*
2968 Playa Rd, Carlsbad, CA 92009, USA

Gilman, Alfred G *Nobel Medicine Laureate*
%Southwestern Medical Center, 5323 Harry Hines Blvd, Dallas, TX 75235, USA

Gilman, Dorothy *Writer*
50 Whitney Glen, Westport, CT 06880, USA

Gilman, Henry *Chemist*
3221 Oakland St, Ames, IA 50014, USA

Gilman, Kenneth B *Businessman*
%Limited Inc, 3 Limited Parkway, Columbus, OH 43230, USA

Gilman, Richard C *Educator*
131 Annandale Rd, Pasadena, CA 91105, USA

Gilmartin, John A *Businessman*
%Millipore Corp, 80 Ashby Rd, Bedford, MA 01730, USA

Gilmartin, Raymond V *Businessman*
%Merck Co, 1 Merck Dr, Whitehouse Station, NJ 08889, USA

Gilmer, Gary D *Businessman*
%Hamilton Life Insurance, 33045 Hamilton Court, Farmington Hills, MI 48334, USA

Gilmore, Clarence P *Editor*
19725 Creekround Ave, Baton Rouge, LA 70817, USA

Gilmore, Jimmie Dale *Singer, Songwriter*
%Mike Crowley Artists, 122 Longwood Ave, Austin, TX 78734, USA

Gilmore, Kenneth O *Editor*
Charles Rd, Mt Kisco, NY 10549, USA

Gilmour of Craigmillar, Ian *Government Official, England*
Ferry House, Old Isleworth, Middx, England

Gilmour, David *Singer, Guitarist (Pink Floyd)*
43 Portland Rd, London W11 4LJ, England

Gilmour, Doug *Hockey Player*
%Toronto Maple Leafs, 60 Carlton St, Toronto ON M5B 1L1, Canada

Gilpatric, Roswell L *Government Official*
435 E 52nd St, New York, NY 10022, USA

Gilroy, Frank D *Writer*
6 Magnin Rd, Monroe, NY 10950, USA

Gilroy, J A *Businessman*
%Varity Corp, 672 Delaware Ave, Buffalo, NY 14209, USA

Gilruth, Robert R *Aerospace Engineer*
2600 Barracks Rd, #C-38, Charlottesville, VA 22901, USA

Giltner, F Phillips *Financier*
%First National of Nebraska, 1 First National Center, Omaha, NE 68102, USA

Gimbel, Norman *Songwriter*
PO Box 50013, Santa Barbara, CA 93150, USA

Gimeno, Andres *Tennis Player*
Paseo de la Bonanova 38, Barcelona 6, Spain

Gingerich, John C *Businessman*
%Measurex Corp, 1 Results Way, Cupertino, CA 95014, USA

Ginibre, Jean-Louis	*Editor*
%Hachette Filipacchi, 1633 Broadway, New York, NY 10019, USA	
Ginsberg, Allen	*Writer, Poet*
PO Box 582, Stuyvesant Station, New York, NY 10009, USA	
Ginsburg, Ruth Bader	*Supreme Court Justice*
%US Supreme Court, 1 1st St NE, Washington, DC 20543, USA	
Gintel, Robert M	*Businessman*
%XTRA Corp, 60 State St, Boston, MA 02109, USA	
Ginty, Robert	*Actor*
16133 Ventura Blvd, #800, Encino, CA 91436, USA	
Ginzberg, Eli	*Economist*
845 West End Ave, New York, NY 10025, USA	
Ginzton, Edward L	*Electrical Engineer, Businessman*
%Varian Assoc, 3100 Hansen Way, Palo Alto, CA 94304, USA	
Giordano, Michele Cardinal	*Religious Leader*
Largo Donnaregina 22, 80138 Naples, Italy	
Giovanni, Nikki E	*Poet*
%Virginia Polytechnic Institute, English Dept, Blacksburg, VA 24061, USA	
Giraldi, Robert N (Bob)	*Movie Director*
%Giraldi Suarez, 581 6th Ave, New York, NY 10011, USA	
Girardelli, Marc	*Skier*
%Alpenhotel Bodele, 6850 Dornbirn/Bodele, Austria	
Girardot, Annie	*Actress*
%Editions Robert Laffont, 6 Pl Saint-Sulpice, 75006 Paris, France	
Giri, Tulsi	*Prime Minister, Nepal*
Jawakpurdham, District Dhanuka, Nepal	
Giri, Varahagiri Venkata	*President, India*
Girija, 1 Third Block, Jayanagar, Bangalore 56011, India	
Girod, Bernard A	*Businessman*
%Harman International Industries, 1101 Pennsylvania Ave NW, Washington, DC 20004, USA	
Giroux, Robert	*Publisher*
%Farrar Straus Giroux, 19 Union Square W, New York, NY 10003, USA	
Giscard d'Estaing, Valery	*President, France*
11 Rue Benouville, 75116 Paris, France	
Gish, Annabeth	*Actress*
%International Creative Mgmt, 8942 Wilshire Blvd, Beverly Hills, CA 90211, USA	
Giulini, Carlo Maria	*Conductor*
%General Delivery, Bolzano, Italy	
Giuranna, Bruno	*Concert Violist*
Via Bembo 96, 31011 Asolo TV, Italy	
Givens, Jack	*Basketball Player, Executive*
%Orlando Magic, Orlando Arena, 1 Magic Place, Orlando, FL 32801, USA	
Givens, Robin	*Actress*
885 3rd Ave, #2900, New York, NY 10022, USA	
Gladstone, David J	*Financier*
%Allied Capital Advisers, 1666 "K" St NW, Washington, DC 20006, USA	
Glamack, George	*Basketball Player*
50 Pleasant Way, Rochester, NY 14622, USA	
Glanville, Jerry	*Football Coach, Sportscaster*
%Fox TV, Sports Dept, 205 E 67th St, New York, NY 10021, USA	
Glaser, Daniel	*Sociologist*
901 S Ogden Dr, Los Angeles, CA 90036, USA	
Glaser, Donald A	*Nobel Physics Laureate*
%University of California, Molecular Biology Laboratory, Berkeley, CA 94720, USA	
Glaser, Milton	*Graphic Artist*
%Milton Glaser Assoc, 207 E 32nd St, New York, NY 10016, USA	
Glaser, Paul Michael	*Actor, Director*
317 Georgina Ave, Santa Monica, CA 90402, USA	
Glaser, Robert	*Psychologist*
%University of Pittsburgh, Psychology Dept, Pittsburgh, PA 15260, USA	
Glaser, Robert L	*Television Executive*
%American Film Techs Inc, 117 E 57th St, New York, NY 10022, USA	
Glasgow, William J	*Financier*
%PacifiCorp Financial Services, 824 NE Multnomah Ave, Portland, OR 97232, USA	
Glashow, Sheldon Lee	*Nobel Physics Laureate*
30 Prescott St, Brookline, MA 02146, USA	
Glaspie, April	*Diplomat*
%State Department, 2201 "C" St NW, Washington, DC 20520, USA	

G

Ginibre - Glaspie

G

Glass, David D — *Businessman*
%Wal-Mart Stores, 702 SW 8th St, Bentonville, AK 72712, USA

Glass, H Bentley — *Biologist*
PO Box 65, East Setauket, NY 11733, USA

Glass, Philip — *Composer*
231 2nd Ave, New York, NY 10003, USA

Glass, Ron — *Actor*
2485 Wild Oak Dr, Los Angeles, CA 90068, USA

Glass, William S (Bill) — *Football Player*
4299 Shiloh, Midlothian, TX 76065, USA

Glasser, Ira S — *Attorney, Legal Activist*
%American Civil Liberties Union, 132 W 43rd St, New York, NY 10036, USA

Glasser, James J — *Businessman*
%GATX Corp, 500 W Monroe St, Chicago, IL 60661, USA

Glasser, William — *Psychiatrist*
11633 San Vicente Blvd, Los Angeles, CA 90049, USA

Glavin, Denis Joseph — *Labor Leader*
%Electrical Radio & Machine Workers Union, 11 E 1st St, New York, NY 10003, USA

Glavin, William F — *Businessman, Educator*
56 Whiting Rd, Wellesley, MA 02181, USA

Glavine, Thomas M (Tom) — *Baseball Player*
89 Treble Cove Rd, Billerica, MA 01862, USA

Glazer, Nathan — *Sociologist*
12 Scott St, Cambridge, MA 02138, USA

Glazkov, Yuri N — *Cosmonaut; Air Force General*
%Potchta Kosmonavtov, 141 160 Svyosdny Gorodok, Moskovskoi Oblasti, Russia

Glazunov, Ilya S — *Artist*
Kalashny Per 2/10, #22-A, 103009 Moscow, Russia

Gleason, Alfred M — *Businessman*
%PacifiCorp, 700 NE Multnomah St, Portland, OR 97232, USA

Gleason, Andrew M — *Mathematician*
110 Larchwood Dr, Cambridge, MA 02138, USA

Gleason, Paul — *Actor*
%Paradigm Agency, 10100 Santa Monica Blvd, #2500, Los Angeles, CA 90067, USA

Gleason, Thomas D — *Businessman*
%Wolverine World Wide Inc, 9341 Courtland Dr, Rockford, IL 49351, USA

Glemp, Jozef Cardinal — *Religious Leader*
Sekretariat Prymasa, Kolski, Ul Miodowa 17, 00-246 Warsaw, Poland

Glenamara (Edward W Short) — *Government Official, England*
21 Priory Gardens, Corbridge, Northumberland, England

Glendening, Parris N — *Governor, MD*
%Governor's Office, State House, Annapolis, MD 21401, USA

Glenn, Arthur L — *Businessman*
%Air & Water Technologies, US Highway 22 & Station Rd, Branchburg, NJ 08876, USA

Glenn, David W — *Financier*
%Federal Home Loan Mortgage Corp, 8200 Jones Branch Dr, McLean, VA 22102, USA

Glenn, Scott — *Actor*
126 E De Vargas St, #1902, Santa Fe, NM 87501, USA

Glenn, Wayne E — *Labor Leader*
%United Paperworkers Int'l Union, 3340 Perimeter Hill Dr, Nashville, TN 37211, USA

Glennan, Robert E, Jr — *Educator*
%Emporia State University, President's Office, Emporia, KS 66801, USA

Glenville, Peter — *Theater Director, Actor*
%Elliott Lefkowitz, 641 Lexington Ave, New York, NY 10022, USA

Gless, Sharon — *Actress*
%William Morris Agency, 151 S El Camino Dr, Beverly Hills, CA 90212, USA

Glickenhaus, Seth M — *Financier*
%Glickenhaus Co, 6 E 43rd St, New York, NY 10017, USA

Glickman, Daniel R — *Secretary, Agriculture*
%Agriculture Department, 14th & Independence Ave SW, Washington, DC 20250, USA

Glidden, Bob — *Auto Racing Driver*
PO Box 236, Whiteland, IN 46184, USA

Glidden, Robert — *Educator*
%Ohio University, President's Office, Athens, OH 45701, USA

Glidewell, Iain — *Judge*
%Royal Courts of Justice, Strand, London WC2A 2LL, England

Glimcher, Arnold O (Arne) — *Art Dealer*
%Pace Gallery, 32 E 57th St, New York, NY 10022, USA

Glass - Glimcher

Glimm, James G — *Mathematician*
%State University of New York, Applied Math Dept, Stony Brook, NY 11794, USA

Glitman, Maynard W — *Diplomat*
%General Delivery, Jeffersonville, VT 05464, USA

Globus, Yoram — *Movie Producer*
%Pathe International, 8670 Wilshire Blvd, Beverly Hills, CA 90211, USA

Glosson, Buster C — *Air Force General*
Deputy Chief of Staff, Plans & Operations, HdqsUSAF, Washington, DC 20330, USA

Glossop, Peter — *Opera Singer*
End Cottage, 7 Gate Close, Hawkchurch Near Axminster, Devon, England

Glover, Brian — *Actor*
%DeWolfe, Manfield House, 376/378 The Strand, London WC2R OLR, England

Glover, Danny — *Actor*
PO Box 170069, San Francisco, CA 94117, USA

Glover, Jane A — *Conductor*
%Lies Askonas Ltd, 186 Drury Lane, London WC2B 5RY, England

Glover, John — *Actor*
2417 Micheltorena St, Los Angeles, CA 90039, USA

Glover, Richard — *Football Player*
5097 Eppling Lane, San Jose, CA 95111, USA

Gluck, Henry — *Businessman*
%Caesars World Inc, 1801 Century Park East, #2600, Los Angeles, CA 90067, USA

Gluck, Louis — *Physician*
%University of California, Medical School, La Jolla, CA 92093, USA

Gluck, Louise E — *Poet*
Creamery Rd, Plainfield, VA 05667, USA

Glynn, Carlin — *Actress*
1165 5th Ave, New York, NY 10029, USA

Gminski, Mike — *Basketball Player, Sportscaster*
%Charlotte Hornets, 1 Hive Dr, Charlotte, NC 28217, USA

Goalby, Bob — *Golfer*
5950 Town Hall Rd, Belleville, IL 62223, USA

Godard, Jean-Luc — *Movie Director*
15 Rue du Nord, 1180 Roulle, Switzerland

Godbold, Francis S — *Financier*
%Raymond James Financial, 880 Carillon Parkway, St Petersburg, FL 33716, USA

Goddard, David R — *Biologist*
738-A I Walcott Dr, Philadelphia, PA 19118, USA

Goddard, John — *Explorer*
4224 Beulah Dr, La Canada, CA 91011, USA

Goddard, Samuel P, Jr — *Governor, AZ*
4724 E Camelback Canyon Dr, Phoenix, AZ 85018, USA

Godden, Rumer — *Writer*
Ardnacloich, Moniaive, Thornhill, Dumfriesshire D63 4HZ, Scotland

Godfrey, Paul V — *Publisher*
%Toronto Sun, 333 King St E, Toronto ON M5A 3X5, Canada

Godley, Georgina — *Fashion Designer*
%Georgina Godley London Ltd, 19-A All Saints Rd, London W11 1HE, England

Godmanis, Ivars — *Government Official, Latvia*
Bul Brivibas 26, 226170 Riga, Latvia

Godwin, A Timothy — *Businessman*
%Tech Data Corp, 5350 Tech Data Dr, Clearwater, FL 34620, USA

Godwin, Fay S — *Photographer*
%Fay Godwin Network, 3-4 Kirby St, London E4N 8TS, England

Godwin, Gail K — *Writer*
PO Box 946, Woodstock, NY 12498, USA

Godwin, Linda M — *Astronaut*
%NASA, Johnson Space Center, 2101 NASA Rd, Houston, TX 77058, USA

Godwin, Mills E, Jr — *Governor, VA*
2180 Partridge Place, Suffolk, VA 23433, USA

Goehr, Alexander — *Composer*
%University of Cambridge, Music Faculty, 11 West Rd, Cambridge, England

Goergen, Robert G — *Businessman*
%XTRA Corp, 60 State St, Boston, MA 02109, USA

Goetz, Eric — *Yacht Builder*
%Eric Goetz Marine & Technology, 15 Broad Common Rd, Bristol, RI 02809, USA

Goffin, Gerry — *Songwriter*
9171 Hazen Dr, Beverly Hills, CA 90210, USA

G

Goh Chok Tong — *Prime Minister, Singapore*
%Prime Minister's Office, Istana Annexe, Singapore 0923, Singapore

Goheen, Robert F — *Educator, Diplomat*
1 Orchard Circle, Princeton, NJ 08540, USA

Going, Joanna — *Actress*
PO Box 154, Bronx, NY 10471, USA

Goitschel, Marielle — *Skier*
%Chalet Helrob, 73-Val D'Isere, France

Goizueta, Roberto C — *Businessman*
%Coca-Cola Co, 1 Coca-Cola Plaza, 310 North Ave NW, Atlanta, GA 30313, USA

Gola, Thomas J (Tom) — *Basketball Player*
15 Kings Oak Lane, Philadelphia, PA 19115, USA

Golan, Menahem — *Movie Producer*
%Cannon Film Group, 10000 Washington Blvd, Culver City, CA 90232, USA

Gold, Ernest — *Composer*
269 N Bellino Dr, Pacific Palisades, CA 90272, USA

Gold, Herbert — *Writer*
1051 Broadway, #A, San Francisco, CA 94133, USA

Gold, Jack — *Movie Director*
24 Wood Vale, London N1O 3DP, England

Gold, Joe — *Bodybuilder*
%World Gym, 2210 Main St, Santa Monica, CA 90405, USA

Gold, Missy — *Actress*
%Gold Marshak Assoc, 3500 W Olive Ave, #1400, Burbank, CA 91505, USA

Gold, Thomas — *Astronomer, Physicist*
7 Pleasant Grove Lane, Ithaca, NY 14850, USA

Gold, Tracey — *Actress*
12621 Addison St, North Hollywood, CA 91607, USA

Goldberg, Arthur M — *Businessman*
%Bally Entertainment Corp, 8700 W Bryn Mawr Ave, Chicago, IL 60631, USA

Goldberg, Bernard R — *Commentator*
%CBS-TV, News Dept, 51 W 52nd St, New York, NY 10019, USA

Goldberg, Carol R — *Businesswoman*
%Avcar Group, 225 Franklin St., #2700, Boston, MA 02110, USA

Goldberg, Danny — *Entertainment Executive*
%Warner Bros Records, 3300 Warner Blvd, Burbank, CA 91505, USA

Goldberg, Edward D — *Geochemist*
750 Val Sereno Dr, Encinitas, CA 92024, USA

Goldberg, Leonard — *Movie, Television Producer*
%Spectradyne Inc, 1501 N Plano Rd, Richardson, TX 75081, USA

Goldberg, Luella G — *Educator*
%Wellesley College, President's Office, Wellesley, MA 02181, USA

Goldberg, Marshall — *Football Player*
180 E Pearson, #4202, Chicago, IL 60611, USA

Goldberg, Michael — *Artist*
222 Bowery Place, New York, NY 10012, USA

Goldberg, Michael A — *Businessman*
%National Indemnity Co, 3024 Harney St, Omaha, NE 68131, USA

Goldberg, Stan — *Cartoonist (Archie)*
%Archie Comics, 325 Fayette Ave, Mamaroneck, NY 10543, USA

Goldberg, Whoopi — *Comedienne, Actress*
%Whoop Inc, 5555 Melrose Ave, #114, Los Angeles, CA 90038, USA

Goldberger, Marvin L — *Educator*
621 Mira Monte, La Jolla, CA 92037, USA

Goldberger, Paul J — *Journalist, Architecture Critic*
%New York Times, Editorial Dept, 229 W 43rd St, New York, NY 10036, USA

Goldblatt, Stephen — *Cinematographer*
%Smith/Gosnell, 1515 Palisades Dr, #N, Pacific Palisades, CA 90272, USA

Goldblum, Jeff — *Actor*
%International Creative Mgmt, 8942 Wilshire Blvd, Beverly Hills, CA 90211, USA

Golden, Diana — *Skier*
%Sharf Marketing Group, 822 Boylston St, #203, Chestnut Hill, MA 02167, USA

Golden, Harry — *Bowling Executive*
%Professional Bowlers Assn, 1720 Merriman Rd, Akron, OH 44313, USA

Golden, Raymond L — *Financier*
%James D Wolfensohn Inc, 599 Lexington Ave, New York, NY 10022, USA

Golden, William Lee — *Singer (Oak Ridge Boys); Songwriter*
329 Rockland Rd, Hendersonville, TN 37075, USA

Goldenson, Leonard H — *Television Executive*
%American Broadcasting Companies, 1330 Ave of Americas, New York, NY 10019, USA

Goldfus, Donald W — *Businessman*
%Apogee Enterprises, 7900 Xerxes Ave S, Minneapolis, MN 55431, USA

Goldhaber, Gertrude S — *Physicist*
91 S Gillette Ave, Bayport, NY 11705, USA

Goldhaber, Maurice — *Physicist*
91 S Gillette Ave, Bayport, NY 11705, USA

Goldhirsh, Bernard A — *Publisher*
%Inc Magazine, 38 Commercial Wharf, Boston, MA 02110, USA

Goldin, Claudia D — *Economist*
%Harvard University, Economics Dept, Cambridge, MA 02138, USA

Goldin, Daniel S — *Government Official, Space Administrator*
%NASA Hdqs, Code A, 300 "E" St SW, Washington, DC 20546, USA

Goldin, Ricky Paull — *Actor*
365 W 52nd St, #L-E, New York, NY 10019, USA

Goldman, Bo — *Screenwriter*
%Creative Artists Agency, 9830 Wilshire Blvd, Beverly Hills, CA 90212, USA

Goldman, James — *Writer*
%Barbara Deren Assoc, 965 5th Ave, New York, NY 10021, USA

Goldman, Robert I — *Financier*
%Congress Financial Corp, 1133 Ave of Americas, New York, NY 10036, USA

Goldman, William — *Writer*
50 E 77th St, #30, New York, NY 10021, USA

Goldman-Rakic, Patricia — *Neuroscientist*
%Yale University Medical School, Neurology Dept, New Haven, CT

Goldmark, Peter C, Jr — *Foundation Executive*
%Rockefeller Foundation, 420 5th Ave, New York, NY 10018, USA

Goldovsky, Boris — *Concert Pianist, Opera Educator*
183 Clinton Rd, Brookline, MA 02146, USA

Goldreich, Peter — *Astronomer*
471 S Catalina Ave, Pasadena, CA 91106, USA

Goldsboro, Bobby — *Singer, Songwriter*
%Jim Stephany Mgmt, 1021 Preston Dr, Nashville, TN 37206, USA

Goldschmidt, Berthold — *Composer*
13 Belsize Crescent, London NW3 5QY, England

Goldsmith, Bram — *Financier*
%City National Corp, 400 N Roxbury Dr, Beverly Hills, CA 90210, USA

Goldsmith, Jerry — *Composer*
6525 Sunset Blvd, #402, Los Angeles, CA 90028, USA

Goldsmith, Judy — *Social Activist*
%National Organization for Women, 425 13th St NW, Washington, DC 20002, USA

Goldstein, Abraham S — *Attorney*
%Yale University, Law School, 127 Wall St, New Haven, CT 06511, USA

Goldstein, Allan L — *Biochemist, Immunologist*
0407 Bradley Blvd, Bethesda, MD 20817, USA

Goldstein, Avram — *Pharmacologist*
735 Dolores St, Stanford, CA 94305, USA

Goldstein, Jack — *Businessman*
%OMI Corp, 90 Park Ave, New York, NY 10016, USA

Goldstein, Joseph L — *Nobel Medicine Laureate*
%University of Texas Medical Center, 5324 Harry Hines Blvd, Dallas, TX 75235, USA

Goldstein, Michael — *Businessman*
%Toys "R" Us Inc, 461 From Rd, Paramus, NJ 07652, USA

Goldstein, Murray — *Physician, Association Executive*
%United Cerebral Palsey Foundation, 1522 "K" St NW, #1112, Washington, DC 20005, USA

Goldstein, Stanley P — *Businessman*
%Melville Corp, 1 Theall Rd, Rye, NY 10580, USA

Goldstine, Herman H — *Mathematician*
1900 Rittenhouse Sq, #13-B, Philadelphia, PA 19103, USA

Goldstone, Jeffrey — *Physicist*
18 Orchard Rd, Brookline, MA 02146, USA

Goldstone, Richard J — *Judge*
PO Box 258, Bloemfontein 9300, South Africa

Goldthwait, Bob (Bobcat) — *Comedian*
3950 Fredonia Dr, Los Angeles, CA 90068, USA

Goldwater, Barry M — *Senator, AZ*
6250 N Hogan Dr, Scottsdale, AZ 85253, USA

G

Goldenson - Goldwater

G

Goldwater, John L *Cartoonist (Archie)*
8 White Birch Lane, Scarsdale, NY 10583, USA

Goldwyn, Samuel J, Jr *Movie Producer*
%Samuel Goldwyn Co, 10203 Santa Monica Blvd, #500, Los Angeles, CA 90067, USA

Golic, Bob *Football Player, Sportscaster*
%NBC-TV, Sports Dept, 30 Rockefeller Plaza, New York, NY 10112, USA

Golino, Valeria *Actress*
8033 W Sunset Blvd, #419, Los Angeles, CA 90046, USA

Golonka, Arlene *Actress*
17849 Duncan St, Reseda, CA 91335, USA

Golub, Harvey *Businessman*
%American Express Co, American Express Tower, New York, NY 10285, USA

Golub, Leon A *Artist*
530 LaGuardia Place, New York, NY 10012, USA

Gombrich, Ernst *Art Historian*
19 Briardale Gardens, London NW3 7PN, England

Gomer, Robert *Chemist*
4824 S Kimbark Ave, Chicago, IL 60615, USA

Gomes, Francisco da Costa *President, Portugal; Army Marshal*
Ave Dos Eua 121-9-C, Lisbon, Portugal

Gomez, Jill *Opera Singer*
16 Milton Park, London N6 5QA, England

Gomez, Ruben *Baseball Player*
T2-8 Iquaza Park Gardens, Rio Piedra, PR 00928, USA

Gomory, Ralph E *Mathematician, Foundation Executive*
%Alfred P Sloan Foundation, 630 5th Ave, New York, NY 10111, USA

Goncalves, Vascos dos Santos *Prime Minister, Portugal; Army General*
Ave Estados Unidos da America 86, 5 Esq, 1700 Lison, Portugal

Goncz, Arpad *President, Hungary*
%President's Office, Kossuth Lajos Ter 1, 1055 Budapest, Hungary

Gonda, Leslie L *Financier*
%International Lease Finance Corp, 1999 Ave of Stars, Los Angeles, CA 90067, USA

Gong Li *Actress*
%Xi'an Film Studio, Xi'an City, Shaanxi Province, China

Gonick, Larry *Cartoonist*
247 Missouri St, San Francisco, CA 94107, USA

Gonshaw, Francesca *Actress*
%Greg Mellard, 12 D'Arblay St, #200, London W1V 3FP, England

Gonzales, Dalmacio *Opera Singer*
%Metropolitan Opera Assn, Lincoln Center Plaza, New York, NY 10023, USA

Gonzalez Marquez, Felipe *Prime Minister, Spain*
%Prime Minister's Office, Complejo de las Moncloa, 28071 Madrid, Spain

Gonzalez Martin, Marcelo Cardinal *Religious Leader*
Arco de Palacio 1, Toledo, Spain

Gonzalez, Hector *Religious Leader*
%Baptist Churches USA, PO Box 851, Valley Forge, PA 19482, USA

Gonzalez, Juan A *Baseball Player*
Ext Catoni A-9, Vega Baja, PR 00693, USA

Gonzalez, Peter W *Financier*
%Adler Coleman Clearing Corp, 20 Broad St, New York, NY 10005, USA

Gooch, Gerald *Artist*
%Hansen Fuller Gallery, 228 Grant Ave, San Francisco, CA 94108, USA

Gooch, Graham A *Cricketer*
%Essex County Club, New Writtle St, Chelmsford, Essex CM2 0PG, England

Good, Hugh W *Religious Leader*
%Primitive Advent Christian Church, 395 Frame Rd, Elkview, WV 25071, USA

Good, Robert A *Physician*
%All Children's Hospital, 801 6th St S, St Petersburg, FL 33701, USA

Goodacre Connick, Jill *Model*
%Elite Model Mgmt, 111 E 22nd St, #200, New York, NY 10010, USA

Goodall, Caroline *Actress*
%Jonathan Altaras Assoc, 2 Goodwins Court, London WC2N 4LL, England

Goodall, Jack W *Businessman*
%Foodmaker Inc, 9330 Balboa Ave, San Diego, CA 92123, USA

Goodall, Jane *Ethologist, Primatologist*
%Jane Goodall Institute, 310 Main St, Ridgefield, CT 06877, USA

Goode, David R *Businessman*
%Norfolk Southern Corp, 3 Commercial Place, Norfolk, VA 23510, USA

Goldwater - Goode

Goode, Joe — *Artist*
1645 Electric Ave, Venice, CA 90291, USA

Goode, Richard S — *Concert Pianist*
%Frank Salomon Assoc, 201 W 54th St, New York, NY 10019, USA

Gooden, Dwight E — *Baseball Player*
6755 30th St S, St Petersburg, FL 33712, USA

Goodenough, Ward H — *Antropologist*
204 Fox Lane, Wallingford, PA 19086, USA

Goodes, Melvin R — *Businessman*
%Warner-Lambert Co, 201 Tabor Rd, Morris Plains, NJ 07950, USA

Goodeve, Charles P — *Physical Chemist*
38 Middleway, London NW11, England

Goodeve, Grant — *Actor*
21416 NE 68th Court, Redmond, WA 98053, USA

Goodfellow, Peter N — *Geneticist*
%Cancer Research Fund, Lincoln Inn Fields, London WC2A 3PX, England

Goodfriend, Lynda — *Actress*
%Cohen & Luckienbache, 740 N La Brea Ave, Los Angeles, CA 90038, USA

Gooding, Cuba, Jr — *Actor*
4789 Vineland Ave, #100, North Hollywood, CA 91602, USA

Goodlad, John I — *Educator*
%University of Washington, Education College, Seattle, WA 98185, USA

Goodman, Alfred — *Composer*
Bodenstedtstr 31, 81241 Munich, Germany

Goodman, Corey S — *Neurobiologist*
Howard Hughes Medical Institute, Molecular-Cell Biology Dept, Berkeley, CA 94720, USA

Goodman, Dody — *Comedienne*
%Ruth Webb Enterprises, 7500 Devista Dr, Los Angeles, CA 90046, USA

Goodman, Ellen H — *Columnist*
%Boston Globe, 135 Morrissey Blvd, Boston, MA 02128, USA

Goodman, John — *Actor*
5180 Louise Ave, Encino, CA 91316, USA

Goodman, Julian — *Broadcast Executive*
%National Broadcasting Co, 30 Rockefeller Plaza, New York, NY 10112, USA

Goodman, Linda — *Writer*
%Mannu United, 137 Hayden St, Cripple Creek, CO 80813, USA

Goodman, Nelson — *Philosopher*
%Harvard University, Philosophy Dept, Cambridge, MA 02138, USA

Goodman, Oscar — *Attorney*
520 S 4th St, Las Vegas, NV 89101, USA

Goodpaster, Andrew J — *Army General*
%Atlantic Council, 1616 "H" St NW, Washington, DC 20006, USA

Goodreault, Gene — *Football Player*
95 Colby St, Bradford, MA 01835, USA

Goodrum, Richard W — *Businessman*
%Tredegar Industries, 1100 Boulders Parkway, Richmond, VA 23225, USA

Goodson, R Eugene — *Businessman*
%Oshkosh Truck Corp, 2307 Oregon St, Oshkosh, WI 54901, USA

Goodspeed, Richard F — *Businessman*
%Vons Companies, 618 Michillinda Ave, Arcadia, CA 91007, USA

Goodwin, C W — *Businessman*
%Woodman of the World Life Insurance Society, 1700 Farnam St, Omaha, NE 68102, USA

Goodwin, Dan — *Climber (Sears Tower)*
%Goodwin Enterprises, PO Box 3209, Benician Meadows, San Rafael, CA 94912, USA

Goodwin, Daniel L — *Financier*
%Inland Group, 2901 Butterfield Rd, Oak Brook, IL 60521, USA

Goodwin, Michael — *Labor Leader*
%Office & Professional Employees Union, 265 W 14th St, New York, NY 10011, USA

Goodwin, Michael — *Actor*
%Susan Smith Assoc, 121 N San Vicente Blvd, Beverly Hills, CA 90211, USA

Goodwin, Ron — *Composer, Conductor*
Black Nest Cottage, Hockford Lane, Br Com, Reading RG7 4RP, England

Goodwin, V John — *Businessman*
%National Steel Corp, 4100 Edison Lakes Parkway, Mishawaka, IN 46545, USA

Goody, Joan E — *Architect*
%Goody Clancy Assoc, 334 Boylston St, Boston, MA 02116, USA

Goodyear, Scott — *Auto Racing Driver*
%Shierson Racing, 4650 W US 223, Adrian, MI 49221, USA

G

Goode - Goodyear

Goolagong Cawley, Evonne — *Tennis Player*
80 Dutroon Ave, Roseville NSW, Australia

Gorbachev, Mikhail S — *Gen Sec, USSR; Nobel Peace Laureate*
Leningradsky Prospekt 49, 125468 Moscow, Russia

Gorbatko, Viktor V — *Cosmonaut; Air Force General*
%Potchta Kosmonavtov, 141 160 Svyosdny Gorodok, Moskovskoi Oblasti, Russia

Gorbunovs, Anatolijs V — *Chairman, Latvia*
%Supreme Council, 11 Jeraba St, PDP 226811 Riga, Latvia

Gordeeva, Ekaterina — *Figure Skater*
%International Skating Center, 1375 Hopmeadow St, Simsbury, CT 06070, USA

Gordeyev, Vyacheslav M — *Ballet Dancer, Choreographer*
Tverskaya Str 9, #78, 103009 Moscow, Russia

Gordimer, Nadine — *Nobel Literature Laureate*
7 Frere Rd, Parktown, Johannesburg 2193, South Africa

Gordin, Sidney — *Artist*
903 Camilia St, Berkeley, CA 94710, USA

Gordon, Barry — *Actor*
18140 Superior St, Northridge, CA 91325, USA

Gordon, Bridgette — *Basketball Player*
421 E Chelsea St, Deland, FL 32724, USA

Gordon, Cyrus H — *Educator*
130 Dean Rd, Brookline, MA 02146, USA

Gordon, David — *Choreographer*
%David Gordon/Pick Up Co, 131 Varick St, #901, New York, NY 10013, USA

Gordon, Don — *Actor*
2095 Linda Flora Dr, Los Angeles, CA 90077, USA

Gordon, Gerald — *Actor*
%Lichtman Co, 12456 Ventura Blvd, #1, Studio City, CA 91604, USA

Gordon, Hannah — *Actress*
%Hutton Mgmt, 200 Fulham Rd, London SW10 9PN, England

Gordon, Irving — *Composer*
20444 W Pacific Coast Highway, Malibu, CA 90265, USA

Gordon, Jeff — *Auto Racing Driver*
%Hendrick Motor Sports, 5325 Stowe Lane, PO Box 9, Harrisburg, NC 28075, USA

Gordon, Lawrence — *Entertainment Executive*
%Largo Entertainment, 20th Century Fox, 10201 W Pico Blvd, Los Angeles, CA 90064, USA

Gordon, Leo — *Actor*
9977 Wornom Ave, Sunland, CA 91040, USA

Gordon, Lincoln — *Economist, Diplomat*
3069 University Terrace NW, Washington, DC 20016, USA

Gordon, Mark — *Actor*
10 E 44th St, #700, New York, NY 10017, USA

Gordon, Mary C — *Writer*
%Viking Penguin, 375 Hudson St, New York, NY 10014, USA

Gordon, Milton A — *Educator*
%California State University, President's Office, Fullerton, CA 99264, USA

Gordon, Mita — *Governor General, Belize*
Belize House, Belnopan, Belize

Gordon, Nathan G — *WW II Navy Hero (CMH)*
%Gordon & Gordon, PO Box 558, Morrilton, AR 72110, USA

Gordon, Richard F, Jr — *Astronaut*
%Space Age America, 9800 S Sepulveda Blvd, #818, Los Angeles, CA 90045, USA

Gordon, Robby — *Auto, Truck Racing Driver*
1463 Kennymead Ave, Orange, CA 92669, USA

Gordon, Roger L — *Financier*
%SFFED Corp, 88 Kearny St, San Francisco, CA 94108, USA

Gordon, William E — *Radio Physicist*
%Rice University, Space Physics Dept, PO Box 1892, Houston, TX 77251, USA

Gordone, Charles — *Playwright*
%Texas A&M University, Speech Communication College, College Station, TX 77843, USA

Gordy, Berry — *Record Company Executive*
878 Stradella Rd, Los Angeles, CA 90077, USA

Gordy, John — *Football Player*
30100 Town Center Dr, #O-223, Laguna Niguel, CA 92677, USA

Gordy, Walter — *Physicist*
2521 Perkins Rd, Durham, NC 27706, USA

Gore, Albert A — *Senator, TN*
%Gore Farms, Rt 2, Elmwood Rd, Carthage, TN 37030, USA

Gore, Albert A, Jr *Vice President*
%Vice President's Office, Old Executive Office Bldg, Washington, DC 20501, USA

Gore, Lesley *Singer*
170 E 77th St, #2-A, New York, NY 10021, USA

Gore, Martin *Synthesizer Musician (Depeche Mode)*
%DMB&B Entertainment, 6500 Wilshire Blvd, #1000, Los Angeles, CA 90048, USA

Gorecki, Henryk M *Composer*
Ul Feliksa Kona 4 M 1, 40-133 Katowice, Poland

Goren, Shlomo *Religious Leader, Army General*
Chief Rabbinate, Hechal Shlomo, Jerusalem, Israel

Gorie, Dominic L *Astronaut*
%NASA, Johnson Space Center, 2101 NASA Rd, Houston, TX 77058, USA

Goring, Marius *Actor*
Film Rights, 483 Southbank House, Black Prince Rd, London SE1 7SJ, England

Gorman, Cliff *Actor*
%Paradigm Agency, 200 W 57th St, #900, New York, NY 10019, USA

Gorman, Joseph T *Businessman*
%TRW Inc, 1900 Richmond Rd, Cleveland, OH 44124, USA

Gorman, Kenneth J *Businessman*
%Atlantic Mutual Insurance, 45 Wall St, New York, NY 10005, USA

Gorman, Patrick *Actor*
%Dade/Schultz Agency, 11846 Ventura Blvd, #100, Studio City, CA 91604, USA

Gorman, R C *Artist*
PO Box 1258, El Prado, NM 87529, USA

Gorman, Tom *Tennis Player*
%US Tennis Assn, 1212 Ave of Americas, New York, NY 10036, USA

Gorme, Eydie *Singer*
820 Greenway Dr, Beverly Hills, CA 90210, USA

Gormley, Dennis J *Businessman*
%Federal-Mogul Corp, 26555 Northwestern Parkway, Southfield, MI 48034, USA

Gorney, Karen Lynn *Actress*
%Kroll, 390 West End Ave, New York, NY 10024, USA

Gorrell, Bob *Editorial Cartoonist*
%Richmond Newspapers, Editorial Dept, PO Box 85333, Richmond, VA 23293, USA

Gorrell, Fred *Balloonist*
501 E Port Au Prince Lane, Phoenix, AZ 85022, USA

Gorshin, Frank *Comedian*
72 Cross Way, Westport, CT 06880, USA

Gorski, Mark *Cyclist*
4503 N Pennsylvania St, Indianapolis, IN 46205, USA

Gorter, Cornelis J *Physicist*
Klobenlersburgwal 29, Amsterdam, Netherlands

Gortner, Marjoe *Actor*
PO Box 46266, Los Angeles, CA 90046, USA

Gorton, John G *Prime Minister, Australia*
8 Hamelin Croooont, Narrabundah ACT 2604, Australia

Gosdin, Vern *Singer, Songwriter*
2509 W Marquette Ave, Tampa, FL 33614, USA

Gosman, Abraham D *Financier*
%Meditrust, 197 1st Ave, Needham Heights, MA 02194, USA

Goss, Robert F *Labor Leader*
%Oil Chemical & Atomic International, 1636 Champa St, Denver, CO 80202, USA

Gossage, Richard M (Goose) *Baseball Player*
35 Marland Dr, Colorado Springs, CO 80906, USA

Gossage, Thomas L *Businessman*
%Hercules Inc, Hercules Plaza, Wilmington, DE 19894, USA

Gossard, Stone *Guitarist (Pearl Jam)*
%Curtis Mgmt, 207 1/2 1st Ave S, #300, Seattle, WA 98104, USA

Gosselaar, Mark-Paul *Actor*
27512 Wesley Way, Valencia, CA 91354, USA

Gosselin, Mario *Hockey Player*
%Quebec Nordiques, 2205 Ave du Colisee, Quebec City PQ G1L 4W7, Canada

Gossett, D Bruce *Football Player*
6151 Oak Forest Way, San Jose, CA 95120, USA

Gossett, Louis, Jr *Actor*
5916 Bonsall Dr, Malibu, CA 90265, USA

Gossick Crockatt, Sue *Diver*
13768 Christian Barrett Dr, Moorpark, CA 93021, USA

G

Gore - Gossick Crockatt

G

Gottesman, David S — *Financier*
%First Manhattan Co, 437 Madison Ave, New York, NY 10022, USA

Gottfried, Brian — *Tennis Player*
4030 Inverrary Dr, Lauderhill, FL 33319, USA

Gottlieb, Michael — *Movie Director*
2436 Washington Ave, Santa Monica, CA 90403, USA

Gottlieb, Richard D — *Businessman*
%Lee Enterprises, 214 N Main St, Davenport, IA 52801, USA

Gottlieb, Robert A — *Editor, Publisher*
237 E 48th St, New York, NY 10017, USA

Gottschalk, Carl W — *Physician*
1300 Mason Farm Rd, Chapel Hill, NC 27514, USA

Gottwald, Bruce C — *Businessman*
%Ethyl Corp, 330 S 4th St, Richmond, VA 23219, USA

Gottwald, Bruce C, Jr — *Businessman*
%First Colony Corp, 700 Main St, Lynchburg, VA 24504, USA

Gottwald, Floyd D, Jr — *Businessman*
%Ethyl Corp, 330 S 4th St, Richmond, VA 23219, USA

Gottwald, John D — *Businessman*
%Tredegar Industries, 1100 Boudlers Parkway, Richmond, VA 23225, USA

Gough, Michael — *Actor*
Torleigh Green Lane, Ashmore, Salisbury, Wilts SP5 5AQ, England

Gould Innes, Shane — *Swimmer*
General Delivery, Post Office, Margaret River 6285, Australia

Gould, Edward P — *Financier*
%Trust Company Bank, 25 Park Place NE, Atlanta, GA 30303, USA

Gould, Elliott — *Actor*
21250 Califa, #201, Woodland Hills, CA 91367, USA

Gould, Harold — *Actor*
603 Ocean Ave, #4-East, Santa Monica, CA 90402, USA

Gould, Laurence M — *Geologist*
201 E Rudasill Rd, Tucson, AZ 85704, USA

Gould, Morton — *Composer, Conductor*
231 Shoreward Dr, Great Neck, NY 11021, USA

Gould, Samuel B — *Educator*
4822 Ocean Blvd, Sarasota, FL 34242, USA

Gould, Stephen Jay — *Paleontologist*
%Museum of Comparative Zoology, Harvard University, Cambridge, MA 02138, USA

Gould, Thomas W — *WW II British Royal Navy Hero (VC)*
6 Howlands, Orton Gold Hay, Peterborough, Cambridgeshire, England

Gould, William B, IV — *Government Official*
%National Labor Relations Board, 1009 14th St NW, Washington, DC 20005, USA

Gouled Aptidon, Hassan — *President, Djibouti Republic*
%President's Office, 8-18 Ahmed Nessin St, Djibouti

Goulet, Michel — *Hockey Player*
%Chicago Blackhawks, Chicago Stadium, 1800 W Madison St, Chicago, IL 60612, USA

Goulet, Robert — *Singer*
3110 Monte Rosa Ave, Las Vegas, NV 89120, USA

Goulian, Mehran — *Physician, Biochemist*
8433 Prestwick Dr, La Jolla, CA 92037, USA

Gourad Hamadou, Barkad — *Prime Minister, Djibouti Republic*
%Prime Minister's Office, PO Box 2086, Djibouti, Djibouti Republic

Gouyon, Paul Cardinal — *Religious Leader*
Ma Maison, 181 Rue Judaique, 33000 Bordeaux Cedex, France

Gowan, James — *Architect*
2 Linden Gardens, London W2 4ES, England

Gowdy, Curt — *Sportscaster*
300 Boylston St, #506, Boston, MA 02116, USA

Gowdy, Robert C — *Financier*
%Commercial Union Corp, 1 Beacon St, Boston, MA 02108, USA

Gower, Bob G — *Businessman*
%Lyondell Petrochemical Co, 1221 McKinney St, Houston, TX 77010, USA

Gower, David I — *Cricketer*
%David Gower Promotions, 6 George St, Nottingham NG1 3BE, England

Gowrie (A P G Hore-Ruthven), Earl of — *Government Official, England*
%Arts Council, 14 Great Peter St, London SW1P 3NQ, England

Goycoechea, Sergio — *Soccer Player*
%Argentine Football Assn, Via Monte 1366-76, 1053 Buenos Aires, Argentina

Gqozo, Oupa — *Head of State, Ciskei; Army General*
%Military Council, Zwelitsha, Ciskei

Grabe, Ronald J — *Astronaut*
%Orbital Science Corp, Launch Systems Group, 217000 Atlantic, Dulles, VA 20166, USA

Graber, Bill — *Track Athlete*
1136 N Columbia Ave, Ontario, CA 91764, USA

Graber, Pierre — *President, Switzerland*
1073 Savugny, Switzerland

Grabois, Neil R — *Educator*
%Colgate University, President's Office, Hamilton, NY 13346, USA

Grabowski, James S (Jim) — *Football Player*
1523 W Withorn Lane, Palatine, IL 60067, USA

Grace, Barnett — *Financier*
%First Commercial Corp, 400 W Capitol, Little Rock, AR 72201, USA

Grace, Bud — *Cartoonist (Ernie)*
PO Box 66, Oakton, VA 22124, USA

Gracey, James S — *Coast Guard Admiral, Businessman*
1141 21st St S, Arlington, VA 22202, USA

Grachev, Pavel S — *Army Marshal, Russia*
%Defense Ministry, Novy Arbat 19, K-160 Moscow, Russia

Gracq, Julien — *Writer*
3 Rue du Grenier a Del, 49410 St Florent Le Vieil, France

Grad, Harold — *Mathematician*
248 Overlook Rd, New Rochelle, NY 10804, USA

Graddy, Sam — *Track Athlete, Football Player*
%Oakland Raiders, Oakland Coliseum, Oakland, CA 94621, USA

Grade of Elstree, Lew — *Television Executive*
Embassy House, Mayfair, 8 Queen St, London W1X 7PH, England

Grade, Jeffery T — *Businessman*
%Harnischfeger Corp, 13400 Bishops Lane, Brookfield, WI 53005, USA

Gradishar, Randy — *Football Player*
2255 Cherryville Circle, Littleton, CO 80121, USA

Grady, Don — *Actor, Songwriter*
4444 Lankershim Blvd, #207, North Hollywood, CA 91602, USA

Grady, James T — *Labor Leader*
%International Teamsters Brotherhood, 25 Louisiana Ave NW, Washington, DC 20001, USA

Grady, Wayne — *Golfer*
8619 French Oak Dr, Orlando, FL 32835, USA

Graf, Steffi — *Tennis Player*
Normannenstra 14, 68782 Bruhl, Germany

Graff, Randy — *Actress*
%Marion Rosenberg Office, 8428 Melrose Place, #C, Los Angeles, CA 90069, USA

Graffin, Guillaume — *Ballet Dancer*
%American Ballet Theatre, 890 Broadway, New York, NY 10003, USA

Graffman, Gary — *Concert Pianist*
PO Box 30, Tenafly, NJ 07670, USA

Grafton, Sue — *Writer*
PO Box 41447, Santa Barbara, CA 93140, USA

Graham, Alex — *Cartoonist (Fred Basset)*
%Tribune Media Services, 435 N Michigan Ave, #1417, Chicago, IL 60611, USA

Graham, Bruce J — *Architect*
%Graham & Graham, PO Box 8589, Hobe Sound, FL 33475, USA

Graham, Charles J — *Educator*
1675 Ridgewood Lane S, St Paul, MN 55113, USA

Graham, Charles P — *Army General*
330 Martins Trail, Roswell, GA 30076, USA

Graham, David — *Golfer*
5619 Preston Fairways Dr, Dallas, TX 75252, USA

Graham, Dirk — *Hockey Player*
%Chicago Blackhawks, Chicago Stadium, 1800 W Madison St, Chicago, IL 60612, USA

Graham, Donald E — *Publisher*
%Washington Post Co, 1150 15th St NW, Washington, DC 20071, USA

Graham, Heather — *Actress*
28721 Timberlane St, Agoura Hills, CA 91301, USA

Graham, John R — *Astronomer*
%Univesity of California, Astronomy Dept, Berkeley, CA 94720, USA

Graham, Jorie — *Poet*
%University of Iowa, Writers' Workshop, Iowa City, IA 55242, USA

G

Graham, Katharine M *Businesswoman*
%Washington Post Co, 1150 15th St NW, Washington, DC 20071, USA

Graham, Larry *Guitarist (Sly & Family Stone), Singer*
%Mister 1 Mouse Ltd, 920 Dickson St, Marina del Rey, CA 90292, USA

Graham, Lou *Golfer*
%Professional Golfer's Assn, PO Box 109601, Palm Beach Gardens, FL 33410, USA

Graham, Otto E, Jr *Football Player, Coach*
2216 Riviera Dr, Sarasota, FL 34232, USA

Graham, Patricia A *Educator*
%Spencer Foundation, 900 N Michigan Ave, #2800, Chicago, IL 60611, USA

Graham, Robert *Sculptor*
35 Market St, Venice, CA 90291, USA

Graham, Virginia *Commentator*
211 E 70th St, New York, NY 10021, USA

Graham, William B *Businessman*
%Baxter International, 1 Baxter Parkway, Deerfield, IL 60015, USA

Graham, William E, Jr *Businessman*
409 Hillandale Dr, Raleigh, NC 27609, USA

Graham, William F (Billy) *Evangelist*
1300 Harmon Place, Minneapolis, MN 55403, USA

Graham, William R *Government Official*
%Xsirius Inc, 1110 N Glebe Rd, #620, Arlington, VA 22201, USA

Grahn, Nancy Lee *Actress*
4910 Agnes Ave, North Hollywood, CA 91607, USA

Grainger, David W *Businessman*
%W W Grainger Inc, 5500 W Howard St, Skokie, IL 60077, USA

Gralish, Tom *Photographer*
%Philadelphia Inquirer, Editorial Dept, 400 N Broad St, Philadelphia, PA 19130, USA

Gralla, Lawrence *Publisher*
%Gralla Publications, 1515 Broadway, New York, NY 10036, USA

Gralla, Milton *Publisher*
%Gralla Publications, 1515 Broadway, New York, NY 10036, USA

Gramlich, Edward M *Economist*
%University of Michigan, Public Policy Studies Institute, Ann Arbor, MI 48109, USA

Gramm, Lou *Singer (Foreigner)*
%Car-Sharpe Entertainment, 9320 Wilshire Blvd, #200, Beverly Hills, CA 90212, USA

Gramm, Wendy L *Government Official*
%Commodity Futures Trading Commission, 2033 "K" St NW, Washington, DC 20006, USA

Grammer, Kathy *Actress*
%Artists Agency, 10000 Santa Monica Blvd, #305, Los Angeles, CA 90067, USA

Grammer, Kelsey *Actor*
3266 Cornell Rd, Agoura Hills, CA 91301, USA

Granatelli, Andy *Auto Racing Builder*
%TuneUp Masters, 21031 Ventura Blvd, Woodland Hills, CA 91364, USA

Grandin, Temple *Animal Scientist*
2918 Silver Plume Dr, #C-3, Fort Collins, CO 80526, USA

Grandy, Fred *Actor, Representative, IA*
2506 W Solway St, Sioux City, IA 51104, USA

Grandy, John *Royal Air Force Marshal, England*
%White's, St James's St, London SW1, England

Granger, Farley *Actor*
18 W 72nd St, #25-D, New York, NY 10023, USA

Granlund, Paul T *Sculptor*
%Adolphus College, Art Dept, St Peter, MN 56082, USA

Granrud, Jerome H *Army General*
Commanding General, US Army Japan/IX Corps, APO, AP 96343, USA

Grant, Amy *Singer, Songwriter*
Riverston Farm, Moran Rd, Franklin, TN 37064, USA

Grant, B Donald *Television Executive*
%CBS Entertainment, 51 W 52nd St, New York, NY 10019, USA

Grant, Boyd *Basketball Coach*
%Colorado State University, Athletic Dept, Fort Collins, CO 80523, USA

Grant, Deborah *Actress*
%Larry Dalzall, 17 Broad Ct, #12, London WC2B 5QN, England

Grant, Gogi *Singer*
10323 Alamo Ave, #202, Los Angeles, CA 90064, USA

Grant, Harvey *Basketball Player*
%Portland Trail Blazers, 700 NE Multnomah St, #600, Portland, OR 97232, USA

Grant, Horace	*Basketball Player*
%Orlando Magic, Orlando Arena, 1 Magic Place, Orlando, FL 32801, USA	
Grant, Hugh	*Actor*
PO Box 8394, London SW7 2ZB, England	
Grant, James T (Mudcat)	*Baseball Player*
1020 S Dunsmuir, Los Angeles, CA 90019, USA	
Grant, Lee	*Actress, Director*
610 West End Ave, #7-B, New York, NY 10024, USA	
Grant, Rodney A	*Actor*
%Omar, 526 N Larchmont Blvd, Los Angeles, CA 90004, USA	
Grant, Toni	*Radio Psychologist*
610 S Ardmore Ave, Los Angeles, CA 90005, USA	
Grant, Verne E	*Biologist*
2811 Fresco Dr, Austin, TX 78731, USA	
Grant, William R	*Businessman*
%SmithKline Beckman Corp, 1 Franklin Plaza, Philadelphia, PA 19154, USA	
Grantham, Jeremy	*Financier*
%Grantham Mayo Van Otterloo Co, 40 Rowes Wharf, Boston, MA 02110, USA	
Granzow, Paul H	*Businessman*
%Standard Register Co, 626 Albany St, Dayton, OH 45408, USA	
Grappelli, Stephane	*Jazz Violinist*
87 Rue de Dunkerque, 75009 Paris, France	
Grass, Alexander	*Businessman*
%Rite Aid Corp, 30 Hunter Lane, Camp Hill, PA 17011, USA	
Grass, Gunter	*Writer*
Niedstr 13, 12159 Berlin, Germany	
Grass, Martin L	*Businessman*
%Rite Aid Corp, 30 Hunter Lane, Camp Hill, PA 17011, USA	
Grassle, Karen	*Actress*
3717 Edmond Lane, Louisville, KY 40207, USA	
Grau, Shirley Ann	*Writer*
210 Baronne St, #1120, New Orleans, LA 70112, USA	
Graubard, Seymour	*Businessman*
2784 S Ocean Blvd, Palm Beach, FL 33480, USA	
Graubard, Stephen R	*Educator, Historian, Editor*
8 Maple Ave, Cambridge, MA 02139, USA	
Graveline, Duane E	*Astronaut*
PO Box 92, Underhill Center, VT 05490, USA	
Gravelle, Peter W	*Businessman*
%Kysor Industrial Corp, 1 Madison Ave, Cadillac, MI 49601, USA	
Graves, Adam	*Hockey Player*
%New York Rangers, Madison Square Garden, 4 Penn Plaza New York, NY 10001, USA	
Graves, Bill	*Governor, KS*
%Governor's Office, State Capitol, Topeka, KS 66612, USA	
Graves, Denyce	*Opera Singer*
%Metropolitan Opera Assn, Lincoln Center Plaza, New York, NY 10023, USA	
Graves, Earl G	*Publisher*
%Black-Enterprise Magazine, 130 5th Ave, New York, NY 10011, USA	
Graves, Harold N, Jr	*Journalist, Government Official*
4816 Grantham Ave, Chevy Chase, MD 20815, USA	
Graves, Howard D	*Army General, Educator*
%US Military Academy, Superintendent's Office, West Point, NY 10996, USA	
Graves, Michael	*Architect*
341 Nassau St, Princeton, NJ 08540, USA	
Graves, Morris	*Artist*
%Willard Gallery, 29 E 72nd St, New York, NY 10021, USA	
Graves, Nancy S	*Artist*
69 Wooster St, New York, NY 10012, USA	
Graves, Peter	*Actor*
660 E Channel Rd, Santa Monica, CA 90402, USA	
Graves, Ray	*Football Coach*
%University of Florida, Athletic Assn, PO Box 14485, Gainesville, FL 32604, USA	
Gray, Alasdair J	*Writer*
%McAlpine, 2 Marchmont Terrace, Glasgow G12 9LT, Scotland	
Gray, Alfred M, Jr	*Marine Corps General*
%Commandant's Office, US Marine Corps, Washington, DC 20380, USA	
Gray, Barry S	*Commentator*
425 E 58th St, New York, NY 10022, USA	

G

Grant - Gray

G

Gray, Charles *Actor*
%London Mgmt, 2-4 Noel St, London W1V 3RB, England

Gray, Coleen *Actress*
1432 N Kenwood St, Burbank, CA 91505, USA

Gray, D'Wayne *Marine Corps General*
3423 Barger Dr, Falls Church, VA 22044, USA

Gray, Dulcie *Actress*
Shardeloes, Amersham, Bucks, England

Gray, Erin *Model, Actress*
10921 Alta View Dr, Studio City, CA 91604, USA

Gray, Harry B *Chemist*
1415 E California Blvd, Pasadena, CA 91106, USA

Gray, Jerry *Football Player*
%Tampa Bay Buccaneers, 1 Buccaneer Place, Tampa, FL 33607, USA

Gray, Ken *Football Player*
%Right Guard International, Rt 7, Box 212, Llano, TX 78643, USA

Gray, L Patrick, III *Director, FBI*
PO Box 1591, New London, CT 06320, USA

Gray, Linda *Actress*
PO Box 1370, Santa Clarita, CA 91386, USA

Gray, Mel *Football Player*
%Houston Oilers, 6910 Fannin St, Houston, TX 77030, USA

Gray, Peter (Pete) *Baseball Player*
203 Phillips St, Nanticoke, PA 18634, USA

Gray, Robert E *Army General*
Deputy CinC, US Army & 7th Army, APO, AE 09014, USA

Gray, Robert K *Government Official*
4953 Rock Spring Rd, Arlington, VA 22207, USA

Gray, Simon J H *Writer*
%Judy Daish Assoc, 83 Eastbourne Mews, London W2 6LQ, England

Gray, William H, III *Association Leader; Representative, PA*
%United Negro College Fund, 500 E 62nd St, New York, NY 10021, USA

Graydon, Michael J *Royal Air Chief Marshal, England*
%Lloyds Bank, Cox & King's Branch, 7 Pall Mall, London SW1Y 5NA, England

Graysmith, Robert *Editorial Cartoonist*
%San Francisco Chronicle, 901 Mission St, San Francisco, CA 94103, USA

Grayson, C Jackson, Jr *Government Official, Educator*
123 N Post Oak Lane, Houston, TX 77024, USA

Grazzola, Kenneth E *Publisher*
%Aviation Week Magazine, 1221 Ave of Americas, New York, NY 10020, USA

Greatbatch, Wilson *Inventor (Cardiac Pacemaker)*
%Wilson Greatbatch Prosthetics, 10871 Main St, Clarence, NY 14031, USA

Grebenshchikov, Boris *Singer, Guitarist (Akvarium)*
2 Marata St, #3, 191025 St Petersburg, Russia

Grebstein, Sheldon N *Educator*
%State University of New York, President's Office, Purchase, NY 10577, USA

Grechko, Georgi M *Cosmonaut*
%Potchta Kosmonavtov, 141 160 Svyosdny Gorodok, Moskovskoi Oblasti, Russia

Greco, Buddy *Singer, Pianist*
%Cornell Productions, 100 Bayview Dr, #1521, North Miami Beach, FL 33160, USA

Greco, Emilio *Sculptor*
Viale Cortina d'Ampezzo 132, 00135 Rome, Italy

Greco, Jose *Dancer, Choreographer*
224 W 49th St, New York, NY 10019, USA

Greco, Juliette *Singer*
%Maurice Maraouani, 37 Rue Marbeuf, 75008 Paris, France

Greco, Rosemarie B *Financier*
%CoreStates Bank, Centre Square Building, Philadelphia, PA 19101, USA

Greeley, Andrew M *Writer, Sociologist*
6030 S Ellis Ave, Chicago, IL 60637, USA

Greeley, William E *Businessman*
%Valero Energy Corp, 530 McCullough Ave, San Antonio, TX 78215, USA

Green, A C *Basketball Player*
%Phoenix Suns, 201 E Jefferson St, Phoenix, AZ 85004, USA

Green, Adolph *Lyricist*
211 Central Park West, #19-E, New York, NY 10024, USA

Green, Al *Singer, Clergyman*
%A&M Records, 1416 N La Brea Ave, Los Angeles, CA 90028, USA

Green, Benny *Jazz Pianist*
%DL Media, 155 E 23rd St, #607, New York, NY 10010, USA

Green, Brian Austin *Actor*
11333 Moorpark St, #27, Studio City, CA 91602, USA

Green, Cyril K *Businessman*
%Fred Meyer Inc, 3800 SE 22nd Ave, Portland, OR 97202, USA

Green, Darrell *Football Player*
%Washington Redskins, 21300 Redskin Park Dr, Ashburn, VA 22011, USA

Green, David *Movie Director*
%International Creative Mgmt, 76 Oxford St, London W1N 0AX, England

Green, David E *Chemist*
5339 Brody Dr, Madison, WI 53705, USA

Green, Dennis *Football Coach*
%Minnesota Vikings, 9520 Viking Dr, Eden Prairie, MN 55344, USA

Green, Eric *Football Player*
%Pittsburgh Steelers, 3 Rivers Stadium, 300 Stadium Circle, Pittsburgh, PA 15212, USA

Green, G Dallas *Baseball Manager, Executive*
RR 1, Box 227-A, West Grove, PA 19390, USA

Green, Gary *Football Player*
12206 Melon, San Antonio, TX 78247, USA

Green, Gerald *Writer*
88 Arrowhead Trail, New Canaan, CT 06840, USA

Green, Hamilton *Prime Minister, Guyana*
Plot "D" Lodge, Georgetown, Guyana

Green, Holcombe T, Jr *Businessman*
%WestPoint Stevens, 400 W 10th St, West Point, GA 31833, USA

Green, Howard *Cellular Physiologist*
%Harvard Medical School, Physiology & Biophysics Dept, Boston, MA 02115, USA

Green, Hubert *Golfer*
PO Box 28030, Panama City, FL 32411, USA

Green, Hugh *Football Player*
%Miami Dolphins, 7500 SW 30th St, Davie, FL 33329, USA

Green, Jacob *Football Player*
%Seattle Seahawks, 11220 NE 53rd St, Kirkland, WA 98033, USA

Green, John L, Jr *Educator*
12018 Connell, Overland Park, KS 66213, USA

Green, Julian *Writer*
%Editions Fayard, 75 Rue des Saints-Peres, 75006 Paris, France

Green, Kate *Writer*
%Delacorte Press, 1540 Broadway, New York, NY 10036, USA

Green, Lucinda *Equestrian Rider*
Appleshaw House, Andover, Hants, England

Green, Mark J *Activist, Attorney, Writer*
%Democracy Project, 67 Irving Pl, #4, New York, NY 10003, USA

Green, Marshall *Diplomat*
5063 Millwood Lane NW, Washington, DC 20016, USA

Green, Maurice Spurgeon *Editor*
Hermitage, Twyford House, Hants, England

Green, Mike *Football Player*
8842 Polanco St, San Diego, CA 92129, USA

Green, Norman *Hockey Executive*
%Dallas Stars, 211 Cowboys Parkway, Dallas, TX 75063, USA

Green, Peter J F *Businessman*
85 Burton Court, London SW3 4SX, England

Green, Richard C, Jr *Businessman*
%UtiliCorp United, 911 Main St, Kansas City, MO 64105, USA

Green, Rick *Hockey Player*
%Detroit Red Wings, Joe Louis Arena, 600 Civic Center Dr, Detroit, MI 48226, USA

Green, Tammie *Golfer*
%Ladies Professional Golf Assn, 2570 Volusia Ave, Daytona Beach, FL 32114, USA

Green, Tim *Sportscaster*
%Fox-TV, Sports Dept, PO Box 900, Beverly Hills, CA 90213, USA

Greenaway, Peter *Movie Director*
%Allarts Ltd, 387-B King St, London W6 9NH, England

Greenberg, Alan C *Financier*
%Bear Stearns Co, 245 Park Ave, New York, NY 10167, USA

Greenberg, Bernard *Biological Scientist, Entomologist*
1463 E 55th Pl, Chicago, IL 60637, USA

G

Green - Greenberg

Greenberg, Carl	*Journalist*
6001 Canterbury Dr, Culver City, CA 90230, USA	
Greenberg, Frank S	*Businessman*
%Burlington Industries, PO Box 21207, Greensboro, NC 27420, USA	
Greenberg, Jack M	*Businessman*
%McDonald's Corp, McDonald's Plaza, 1 Kroc Dr, Oak Brook, IL 60521, USA	
Greenberg, Jeffrey W	*Businessman*
%American Home Assurance Co, 70 Pine St, New York, NY 10270, USA	
Greenberg, Joseph H	*Anthropologist*
860 Mayfield St, Stanford, CA 94305, USA	
Greenburg, Dan	*Writer*
323 E 50th St, New York, NY 10022, USA	
Greenburg, Paul	*Journalist*
5900 Scenic Dr, Little Rock, AR 72207, USA	
Greenbush, Rachel Lindsay	*Actress*
%Gold Marshak Assoc, 3500 W Olive Ave, #1400, Burbank, CA 91505, USA	
Greenbush, Sidney Robin	*Actress*
%Gold Marshak Assoc, 3500 W Olive Ave, #1400, Burbank, CA 91505, USA	
Greene of Harrow Weald, Sidney F	*Labor Leader*
26 Kynaston Wood, Boxtree Rd, Harrow Weald, Middx HA3 6UA, England	
Greene Raine, Nancy	*Skier*
%Nancy Greene Hotel, PO Box 418, Whistler/Blackcomb BC V0N 1B0, Canada	
Greene, Allen S	*Financier*
%Ryan Beck Co, 80 Main St, West Orange, NJ 07052, USA	
Greene, Charlie	*Track Athlete*
%International Special Olympics, 1350 New York Ave NW, Washington, DC 20005, USA	
Greene, Ellen	*Actress, Singer*
%William Morris Agency, 151 S El Camino Dr, Beverly Hills, CA 90212, USA	
Greene, Graham	*Actor*
%Susan Smith Assoc, 121 N San Vicente Blvd, Beverly Hills, CA 90211, USA	
Greene, Jack P	*Historian*
1606 Hishfield House, 4000 N Charles St, Baltimore, MD 21218, USA	
Greene, Joseph (Mean Joe)	*Football Player, Coach*
%Miami Dolphins, Robbie Stadium, 2269 NW 199th St, Miami, FL 33056, USA	
Greene, Kevin	*Football Player*
%Pittsburgh Steelers, 3 Rivers Stadium, 300 Stadium Circle, Pittsburgh, PA 15212, USA	
Greene, Kim Morgan	*Actress*
%Paul Kohner Inc, 9300 Wilshire Blvd, #555, Beverly Hills, CA 90212, USA	
Greene, Leonard M	*Inventor (Airplane Stall Warning Device)*
6 Hickory Rd, Scarsdale, NY 10583, USA	
Greene, Michele	*Actress*
PO Box 1543, Los Angeles, CA 90078, USA	
Greene, Robert B (Bob), Jr	*Columnist*
%Chicago Tribune, Editorial Dept, 435 N Michigan Ave, Chicago, IL 60611, USA	
Greene, Shecky	*Comedian*
612 S Lorraine Blvd, Los Angeles, CA 90005, USA	
Greenfield, James L	*Journalist*
850 Park Ave, New York, NY 10021, USA	
Greenfield, Jerry	*Businessman*
%Ben & Jerry's Homemade Inc, Duxtown Common Plaza, Waterbury, CT 05676, USA	
Greenfield, Meg	*Journalist*
3318 "R" St NW, Washington, DC 20007, USA	
Greenhill, Robert F	*Financier*
%Smith Barney Shearson Inc, 1345 Ave of Americas, New York, NY 10105, USA	
Greeniaus, H John	*Businessman*
%RJR Nabisco Holdings, 1301 Ave of Americas, New York, NY 10019, USA	
Greenlaw, Douglas J	*Businessman*
%Multimedia Inc, 305 S Main St, Greenville, SC 29601, USA	
Greenspan, Alan	*Financier, Government Official*
%Federal Reserve Board, 20th St & Constitution Ave NW, Washington, DC 20551, USA	
Greenspan, Bud	*Producer, Director*
%Cappy Productions, 33 E 68th St, New York, NY 10021, USA	
Greenstein, Jesse L	*Astronomer*
1763 Royal Oaks Dr, #5-B, Duarte, CA 91010, USA	
Greenwald, Gerald	*Businessman*
%UAL Corp, 1200 Algonquin Rd, Elk Grove Township, IL 60005, USA	
Greenwald, Joseph A	*Economist, Diplomat*
Town House, 8-5-25 Asaka, Minatoku, Tokyo 107, Japan	

Greenwald, Milton — *Paleontologist*
%University of California, Museum of Paleontology, Berkeley, CA 94720, USA

Greenwalt, Clifford — *Businessman*
%CIPSCO Inc, 607 E Adams St, Springfield, IL 62739, USA

Greenwalt, T Jack — *Medical Administrator*
328 Compton Hills Dr, Cincinnati, OH 45215, USA

Greenwell, Michael L (Mike) — *Baseball Player*
151 Brookline St, Needham, MA 02192, USA

Greenwood, Bruce — *Actor*
%Agency For Performing Arts, 9000 Sunset Blvd, #1200, Los Angeles, CA 90069, USA

Greenwood, David — *Basketball Player*
%San Antonio Spurs, 600 E Market St, #102, San Antonio, TX 78205, USA

Greenwood, Joan — *Actress*
27 Slaidburn St, Chelsea, London SW10, England

Greenwood, Lee — *Singer, Songwriter*
%Lee Greewood Inc, 1311 Elm Hill Pike, Nashville, TN 37210, USA

Greenwood, Richard M — *Businessman*
%Fidelity Federal Bank, 600 N Brand Blvd, Glendale, CA 91203, USA

Greer, C Scott — *Businessman*
%Echlin Inc, 100 Double Beach Rd, Branford, CT 06405, USA

Greer, Dabbs — *Actor*
284 S Madison Ave, Pasadena, CA 91101, USA

Greer, David S — *Internist*
%Brown University, Medicine Program, Box G-B221, Providence, RI 02901, USA

Greer, Germaine — *Writer, Feminist*
%University of Tulsa, English Dept, 600 S College Ave, Tulsa, OK 74104, USA

Greer, Gordon G — *Editor*
%Better Homes & Gardens Magazine, 1716 Locust St, Des Moines, IA 50309, USA

Greer, Harold E (Hal) — *Basketball Player*
1213 Rennie Ave, Richmond, VA 23227, USA

Greer, Howard E — *Navy Admiral*
1121 Waieli St, Honolulu, HI 96821, USA

Greer, Jane — *Actress*
966 Moraga Dr, Los Angeles, CA 90049, USA

Greer, Janet L — *Nutritionist*
%University of Wisconsin, Nutritional Sciences Dept, Madison, WI 53706, USA

Greevy, Bernadette — *Concert Singer*
Melrose, 672 Howth Rd, Dublin 5, Ireland

Gregg, A Forrest — *Football Player, Coach, Administrator*
4244 Potomac, Dallas, TX 75205, USA

Gregg, Hugh — *Governor, NH*
RFD 5, 17 Gregg Rd, Nashua, NH 03062, USA

Gregg, Julie — *Actress*
12304 Santa Monica Blvd, #104, Los Angeles, CA 90024, USA

Gregg, Ricky Lynn — *Singer*
%Wemus Entertainment, 4301 Arroyo, #2, Dallas, TX 75354, USA

Gregg, Stephen R — *WW II Army Hero (CMH)*
130 Lexington Ave, Bayonne, NJ 07002, USA

Gregoire, Paul Cardinal — *Religious Leader*
%Archbishopric, 2000 Rue Sherbrooke Quest, Montreal PQ H3H 1G4, Canada

Gregorian, Vartan — *Educator*
%Brown University, President's Office, Providence, RI 02912, USA

Gregorio, Rose — *Actress*
%Paul Kohner Inc, 9300 Wilshire Blvd, #555, Beverly Hills, CA 90212, USA

Gregorios, Metropolitan Paulos M — *Religious Leader*
%Orthodox Seminary, PO Box 98, Kottayam, Kerala 686001, India

Gregory, Bettina L — *Commentator*
%ABC-TV, News Dept, 1717 DeSales St NW, Washington, DC 20036, USA

Gregory, Cynthia — *Ballet Dancer*
%American Ballet Theatre, 890 Broadway, New York, NY 10003, USA

Gregory, Dick — *Comedian, Social Activist*
PO Box 3270, Plymouth, MA 02361, USA

Gregory, Frederick D — *Astronaut*
%NASA Headquarters, Safety & Mission Quality, Code Q, Washington, DC 20546, USA

Gregory, Jack, Jr — *Football Player*
%Jack Gregory Enterprises, 108 Robertson St, Okolona, MS 38860, USA

Gregory, James — *Actor*
55 Cathedral Rock Dr, #33, Sedona, AZ 86351, USA

G

Gregory, James M — *Hockey Executive*
%National Hockey League, 75 International Blvd, Rexdale ON M9W 6L9, Canada

Gregory, Mary — *Actress*
1350 N Highland Ave, #24, Los Angeles, CA 90028, USA

Gregory, Paul — *Movie Producer*
PO Box 38, Palm Springs, CA 92263, USA

Gregory, Richard — *Religious Leader*
%Independent Fundamental Churches, 2684 Meadow Ridge, Byron Center, MI 49315, USA

Gregory, Robert E, Jr — *Businessman*
%Gitano Group, 1411 Broadway, New York, NY 10018, USA

Gregory, Stephen — *Actor*
%Carey, 64 Thornton Ave, London W4 1QQ, England

Gregory, William G — *Astronaut*
%NASA, Johnson Space Center, 2101 NASA Rd, Houston, TX 77058, USA

Gregory, William H — *Editor*
%Aviation Week Magazine, 1221 Ave of Americas, New York, NY 10020, USA

Grehl, Michael — *Editor*
%Memphis Commercial Appeal, Editorial Dept, 495 Union Ave, Memphis, TN 38103, USA

Greif, Michael — *Theater Director*
%La Jolla Playhouse, PO Box 12039, La Jolla, CA 92039, USA

Greiner, William R — *Educator*
%State University of New York, President's Office, Buffalo, NY 14260, USA

Greist, Kim — *Actress*
%Innovative Artists, 1999 Ave of Stars, #2850, Los Angeles, CA 90067, USA

Grentz, Theresa Shank — *Basketball Coach*
%University of Illinois, Athletic Dept, Champaign, IL 61820, USA

Gressette, L M, Jr — *Businessman*
%SCANA Corp, 1426 Main St, Columbia, SC 29201, USA

Gretzky, Wayne — *Hockey Player*
14135 Beresford Dr, Beverly Hills, CA 90210, USA

Grewal, Alexi — *Cyclist*
11400 N Brownstone Dr, Parker, CO 80134, USA

Grewcock, William L — *Businessman*
%Peter Kiewit Sons, 1000 Kiewit Plaza, Omaha, NE 68131, USA

Grey, Beryl E — *Ballerina*
Fernhill, Priory Rd, Forest Row, East Sussex RH18 5JE, England

Grey, Jennifer — *Actress*
%Creative Artists Agency, 9830 Wilshire Blvd, Beverly Hills, CA 90212, USA

Grey, Joel — *Actor*
9119 Thrasher Ave, Los Angeles, CA 90069, USA

Grey, Linda — *Publisher*
%Linda Grey Books, 201 E 50th St, New York, NY 10022, USA

Grey, Richard E — *Businessman*
%Tyco Toys, 6000 Midlantic Dr, Mount Laurel, NJ 08054, USA

Grey, Virginia — *Actress*
15101 Magnolia Blvd, #54, Sherman Oaks, CA 91403, USA

Grich, Robert A (Bobby) — *Baseball Player*
206 Prospect Ave, Long Beach, CA 90803, USA

Grieco, Richard — *Actor*
2934 1/2 N Beverly Glen Circle, #252, Los Angeles, CA 90077, USA

Griem, Helmut — *Actor*
Holbeinstr 4, 81677 Munich, Germany

Grier, Pam — *Actress*
PO Box 370958, Denver, CO 80237, USA

Grier, Roosevelt (Rosey) — *Football Player, Actor*
11656 Montana Ave, #301, Los Angeles, CA 90049, USA

Griese, Robert A (Bob) — *Football Player, Sportscaster*
1030 Andora Ave, Miami, FL 33146, USA

Griesemer, John N — *Government Official*
RR 2, Box 204-B, Springfield, MO 65802, USA

Grieve, Pierson M — *Businessman*
%Ecolab Inc, Ecolab Center, 370 Wabasha St N, St Paul, MN 55102, USA

Griffey, G Kenneth (Ken) — *Baseball Player*
3942 Mack Rd, #9, Fairfield, OH 45014, USA

Griffey, G Kenneth (Ken), Jr — *Baseball Player*
1420 NW Gilman Blvd, #2717, Issawuah, WA 98027, USA

Griffin, Archie — *Football Player*
7750 Slate Ridge Blvd, Reynoldsville, OH 44131, USA

Griffin, Donald R — *Biologist*
Brookhaven, #A-212, 1010 Waltham St, Lexington, MA 02173, USA

Griffin, G Lee — *Financier*
%Premier Bancorp, 451 Florida St, Baton Rouge, LA 70801, USA

Griffin, James Bennett — *Anthropologist*
5023 Wyandot Court, Bethesda, MD 20816, USA

Griffin, Merv E — *Entertainer*
%Merv Griffin Enterprises, 9860 Wilshire Blvd, Beverly Hills, CA 90210, USA

Griffin, Robert P — *Senator, MI*
%Michigan Supreme Court, PO Box 30052, Lansing, MI 48909, USA

Griffin, Thomas N, Jr — *Army General*
9749 S Park Circle, Fairfax Station, VA 22039, USA

Griffith Joyner, Florence D — *Track Athlete*
%Flo-Jo Int'l, 27758 Santa Margarita Parkway, #385, Mission Viejo, CA 92691, USA

Griffith, Alan R — *Financier*
%Bank of New York Co, 48 Wall St, New York, NY 10005, USA

Griffith, Andy — *Actor*
PO Box 1968, Manteo, NC 27954, USA

Griffith, Bill — *Cartoonist (Zippy the Pinhead)*
%Innovative Artists, 1999 Ave of Stars, #2850, Los Angeles, CA 90067, USA

Griffith, Ed — *Actor*
8721 Santa Monica Blvd, #21, West Hollywood, CA 90069, USA

Griffith, Ernest S — *Political Scientist*
1941 Parkside Dr NW, Washington, DC 20012, USA

Griffith, Melanie — *Actress*
231 N Orchard Dr, Burbank, CA 91506, USA

Griffith, Nanci — *Singer, Songwriter*
%Vector Mgmt, 1500 17th Ave S, Nashville, TN 37212, USA

Griffith, Ronald H — *Army General*
%Vice Chief of Staff, Hdqs USArmy, Pentagon, Washington, DC 20310, USA

Griffith, Steve C, Jr — *Businessman*
%Duke Power Co, 422 S Church St, Charlotte, NC 28242, USA

Griffith, Thomas — *Editor*
25 East End Ave, New York, NY 10028, USA

Griffith, Tom W — *Labor Leader*
%Rural Letter Carriers Assn, 1448 Duke St, #100, Alexandria, VA 22314, USA

Griffiths, Arthur R — *Hockey Executive*
%Vancouver Canucks, 100 N Renfrew St, Vancouver BC V5K 3N7, Canada

Griffiths, Phillip A — *Mathematician*
%Advanced Study Institute, Director's Office, Olden Lane, Princeton, NJ 08540, USA

Grigg, Charles W — *Businessman*
%SPS Technologies, 101 Greenwood Ave, Jenkintown, PA 19046, USA

Grigg, William H — *Businessman*
%Duke Power Co, 422 S Church St, Charlotte, NC 28242, USA

Griggs, Robyn — *Actress*
%"Another World" Show, NBC-TV, 79 Madison Ave, #500, New York, NY 10016, USA

Grigsbym Bernard C, II — *Financier*
%Barclays de Zoete Wedd Secuities, 222 Broadway, New York, NY 10038, USA

Grigson, Geoffrey — *Poet*
Broad Town Farm, Broad Town Near Swindon, Wilts, England

Griliches, Zvi — *Economist*
62 Shephard St, Cambridge, MA 02155, USA

Grim, Robert A (Bob) — *Baseball Player*
13723 W 58th Terrace, #3, Shawnee, KS 66216, USA

Grimaud, Helene — *Concert Pianist*
%Columbia Artists Mgmt Inc, 165 W 57th St, New York, NY 10019, USA

Grimes, Martha — *Writer*
%Montgomery College, English Dept, Takoma Park, MD 20012, USA

Grimes, Tammy — *Actress, Singer*
%Don Buchwald Assoc, 10 E 44th St, #500, New York, NY 10017, USA

Grimm, Russ — *Football Player, Coach*
%Washington Redskins, 21300 Redskin Park Dr, Ashburn, VA 22011, USA

Grimshaw, Nicolas T — *Architect*
1 Conway St, Fitzroy Square, London W1P 5HA, England

Grimsley, Ross A — *Baseball Player*
39 Judges Lane, Towson, MD 21204, USA

Grinham Rawley, Judy — *Swimmer*
103 Green Lane, Northwood, Middx HA6 1AP, England

G

Griffin - Grinham Rawley

Grinkov, Sergei *Figure Skater*
%International Skating Center, 1375 Hopmeadow St, Simsbury, CT 06070, USA

Grinnell, Alan D *Physiologist*
%University of California Medical School, Lewis Center, Los Angeles, CA 90024, USA

Grinstead, Eugene A *Navy Admiral*
%Director's Office, Defense Logistics Agency, Alexandria, VA 22314, USA

Grinstein, Gerald *Businessman*
%Burlington Northern, Continental Plaza, 777 Main St, Fort Worth, TX 76102, USA

Grinville, Patrick *Writer*
Academie Goncourt, 38 Rue du Faubourg Saint Jacques, 75014 Paris, France

Grisanti, Eugene P *Businessman*
%International Flavors & Fragrances, 521 W 57th St, New York, NY 10019, USA

Grisez, Germain *Theologian*
%Mount Saint Mary's College, Christian Ethics Dept, Emmitsburg, MD 21727, USA

Grisham, John *Writer*
PO Box 1780, Oxford, MS 38655, USA

Grishin, Evgenii *Speed Skater*
%Committee of Physical Culture, Skatertny P 4, Moscow, Russia

Grissom, Marquis D *Baseball Player*
%Montreal Expos, PO Box 500, Station "M", Montreal PQ H1V 3P2, Canada

Grist, Reri *Opera Singer*
%Columbia Artists Mgmt Inc, 165 W 57th St, New York, NY 10019, USA

Grizzard, George *Actor*
400 E 54th St, New York, NY 10022, USA

Groat, Richard M (Dick) *Baseball, Basketball Player*
%Champion Lakes, PO Box 288, Bolivar, PA 15923, USA

Groebli, Werner (Mr Frick) *Ice Skater*
PO Box 7886, Incline Village, NV 89452, USA

Groener, Harry *Actor*
%Susan Smith Assoc, 121 N San Vicente Blvd, Beverly Hills, CA 90211, USA

Groening, Matthew (Matt) *Cartoonist (Life in Hell, Simpsons)*
241 Howland Canal, Venice, CA 90291, USA

Groer, Hans Hermann Cardinal *Religious Leader*
Erzbischofliches, Wollzeile 2, 1010 Vienna, Austria

Grogan, Steve *Football Player*
%New England Patriots, Foxboro Stadium, Rt 1, Foxboro, MA 02035, USA

Groh, David *Actor*
301 N Canon Dr, #305, Beverly Hills, CA 90210, USA

Grondal, Benedikt *Prime Minister, Iceland*
Hjallaland 26, 108 Reykjavik, Iceland

Gronk (Glugio Gronk Nicandro) *Artist*
%Saxon-Lee Gallery, 7525 Beverly Blvd, Los Angeles, CA 90036, USA

Gronouski, John A *Postmaster General*
1108 S Monroe Ave, Green Bay, WI 54301, USA

Grooms, Red *Artist*
85 Walker St, New York, NY 10013, USA

Gropp, Louis Oliver *Editor*
140 Riverside Dr, #6-G, New York, NY 10024, USA

Grosbard, Ulu *Movie Director*
29 W 10th St, New York, NY 10011, USA

Gross, Ludwik *Physician*
%Veterans Administration Hospital, 130 W Kingsbridge Rd, Bronx, NY 10468, USA

Gross, Michael *Swimmer*
Paul-Ehrlich-Str 6, 60596 Frankfurt/Main, Germany

Gross, Michael *Actor*
PO Box 522, La Canada, CA 91012, USA

Gross, Robert A *Physicist*
14 Sunnyside Way, New Rochelle, NY 10804, USA

Gross, Terry R *Commentator*
%WHYY-Radio, News Dept, Independence Mall W, Philadelphia, PA 19104, USA

Grossfeld, Stanley *Photographer*
%Boston Globe, 135 Morrissey Blvd, Boston, MA 02128, USA

Grossi, Richard J *Businessman*
%United Illuminating Co, 157 Church St, New Haven, CT 06510, USA

Grossman, Judith *Writer*
%Warren Wilson College, English Dept, Swammanoa, NC 28778, USA

Grossman, Robert *Illustrator*
19 Crosby St, New York, NY 10013, USA

Grosvenor, Gilbert M — *Foundation Executive, Publisher*
%National Geographic Society, 17th & "M" NW, Washington, DC 20036, USA

Grotowski, Jerzy — *Theater Director*
%Centro Per la Sperimentazione, Via Manzoni 22, 56025 Pontedera, Italy

Grout, James — *Actor*
%Crouch Assoc, 59 Firth St, London W1V 5TA, England

Grove, Andrew S — *Businessman*
%Intel Corp, 2200 Mission College Blvd, Santa Clara, CA 95054, USA

Grove, Jon A — *Financier*
%ASR Investments, 335 N Wilmot, Tucson, AZ 85711, USA

Groza, Louis R (Lou) — *Football Player*
287 Parkway Dr, Berea, OH 44017, USA

Grubbs, Gary — *Actor*
%Fields Talent Agency, 3325 Wilshire Blvd, #749, Los Angeles, CA 90010, USA

Grubbs, Gerald R — *Businessman*
%LADD Furniture, 1 Plaza Center, High Point, NC 27261, USA

Gruber, Kelly W — *Baseball Player*
2934 Oestrick Lane, Austin, TX 78733, USA

Grubman, Allen J — *Attorney*
%Grubman Indursky Schindler Goldstein, 152 W 57th St, New York, NY 10019, USA

Grum, Clifford J — *Businessman*
%Temple-Inland Inc, 303 S Temple Dr, Diboll, TX 75941, USA

Grumbach, Melvin M — *Physician*
%University of California Med School, Pediatrics Dept, San Francisco, CA 94143, USA

Grummer, Elisabeth — *Opera Singer*
Am Schlachtensee 104, 14163 Berlin, Germany

Grundfest, Joseph A — *Government Official*
%Stanford University, Law School, Stanford, CA 94305, USA

Grundhofer, Jerry A — *Financier*
%Star Banc Corp, 425 Walnut St, Cincinnati, OH 45202, USA

Grundhofer, John F — *Financier*
%First Bank System, First Bank Pl, Minneapolis, MN 55480, USA

Grune, George V — *Publisher, Foundation Executive*
36 Hyde Lane, Westport, CT 06880, USA

Grunewald, Herbert — *Businessman*
%Bayer, 17192 Leverkusen, Germany

Grunfeld, Ernie — *Basketball Player, Executive*
%New York Knicks, Madison Square Garden, 4 Penn Plaza, New York, NY 10001, USA

Grunsfeld, John M — *Astronaut*
%NASA, Johnson Space Center, 2101 NASA Rd, Houston, TX 77058, USA

Grunwald, Ernest M — *Chemist*
%Brandeis University, Chemistry Dept, Waltham, MA 02154, USA

Grunwald, Henry A — *Editor, Diplomat*
50 E 72nd St, New York, NY 10021, USA

Grushin, Pyotr D — *Aviation Engineer*
%Academy of Sciences, 14 Lenisky Prospekt, Moscow, Russia

Grusin, Dave — *Composer*
%GRP Records, 555 W 57th St, New York, NY 10019, USA

Grutman, N Roy — *Attorney*
%Grutman Miller Greenspoon Hendler, 505 Park Ave, New York, NY 10022, USA

Grzelecki, Frank E — *Businessman*
%Handy & Harman, 555 Theodore Fremd Ave, #A, Rye, NY 10580, USA

Guadagnino, Kathy — *Golfer*
%Ladies Professional Golf Assn, 2570 Volusia Ave, Daytona Beach, FL 32114, USA

Guardino, Harry — *Actor*
2949 Via Vaquero, Palms Springs, CA 92262, USA

Guare, John — *Playwright*
%R Andrew Boose, 1 Dag Hammarskjold Plaza, New York, NY 10017, USA

Guarrera, Frank — *Concert, Opera Singer*
4514 Latona Ave NE, Seattle, WA 98105, USA

Gubarev, Alexei A — *Cosmonaut; Air Force General*
%Potchta Kosmonavtov, 141 160 Svyosdny Gorodok, Moskovskoi Oblasti, Russia

Guber, Peter — *Movie Producer*
%Columbia Pictures, 10202 W Washington Blvd, #1070, Culver City, CA 90232, USA

Gubicza, Mark S — *Baseball Player*
593 Monastery Ave, Philadelphia, PA 19128, USA

Guccione, Robert (Bob) — *Publisher*
%Penthouse Magazine, 1965 Broadway, New York, NY 10023, USA

G

Grosvenor - Guccione

G

Guckel, Henry *Microbiotics Engineer*
%University of Wisconsin, Engineering Dept, Madison, WI 53706, USA

Gudelski, Leonard S *Financier*
%Hudson City Savings Bank, W 80 Century Rd, Paramus, NJ 07652, USA

Guenther, Johnny *Bowler*
%Professional Bowlers Assn, 1720 Merriman Rd, Akron, OH 44313, USA

Guenther, Otto J *Army General*
Director, Information Systems, HdqsUSA, Pentagon, Washington, DC 20310, USA

Guerard, Michel E *Chef*
Les Pres d'Eugenie, 40320 Eugenie les Bains, France

Guerin, Richie *Basketball Player*
%Bear Stearns Co, 55 Water St, New York, NY 10041, USA

Guerrero, Pedro *Baseball Player*
435 S Lafayette Park Pl, #308, Los Angeles, CA 90057, USA

Guerrero, Roberto *Auto Racing Driver*
%Championship Auto Racing Teams, 2655 Woodward Ave, Bloomfield Hills, MI 48304, USA

Guest, Douglas *Concert Organist*
Gables, Minchinhampton, Glos GL6 9JE, England

Guffey, John W, Jr *Businessman*
%Coltec Industries, 430 Park Ave, New York, NY 10022, USA

Guglielmi, Ralph *Football Player*
8501 White Pass Court, Potomac, MD 20854, USA

Gugliotta, Tom *Basketball Player*
%Minnesota Timberwolves, Target Center, 600 1st Ave N, Minneapolis, MN 55403, USA

Guida, Lou *Harness Racing Breeder*
%General Delivery, Yardley, PA

Guidoni, Umberto *Astronaut*
15010 Cobre Valley Dr, Houston, TX 77062, USA

Guidry, Ronald A (Ron) *Baseball Player*
PO Box 278, Scott, LA 70583, USA

Guilbert, Ann *Actress*
%Bauman Hiller Assoc, 5757 Wilshire Blvd, #PH5, Los Angeles, CA 90036, USA

Guilford, Joy Paul *Psychologist*
PO Box 1288, Beverly Hills, CA 90213, USA

Guillaime, R K *Financier*
%Liberty National Bank & Trust, 416 W Jefferson St, Louisville, KY 40202, USA

Guillaume, Robert *Actor*
11963 Crest Place, Beverly Hills, CA 90210, USA

Guillem, Sylvie *Ballerina*
%Royal Ballet, Bow St, London WC2E 9DD, England

Guillemin, Roger C L *Nobel Medicine Laureate*
%Whittier Diabetes/Endocrinology Institute, 9894 Genesse Ave, La Jolla, CA 92037, USA

Guillen, Oswaldo J (Ozzie) *Baseball Player*
%Cle San Jose 52, El Rodeo Del Tuy, Mirando, Venezuela

Guillerman, John *Movie Director*
309 S Rockingham Ave, Los Angeles, CA 90049, USA

Guindon, Richard G *Cartoonist (Guindon)*
321 W Lafayette Blvd, Detroit, MI 48226, USA

Guinier, Lani *Attorney, Educator*
%University of Pennsylvania, Law School, 3400 Chestnut, Philadelphia, PA 19104, USA

Guinn, Kenny C *Financier*
%Southwest Gas Corp, 5241 Spring Mountain Rd, Las Vegas, NV 89150, USA

Guinness, A F B *Businessman*
%Arthur Guinness & Sons, Park Royal Brewery, London NW10 7RR, England

Guinness, Alec *Actor*
Kettlebrook Meadows, Steep Marsh, Petersfield, Hants, England

Guisewite, Cathy L *Cartoonist (Cathy)*
4039 Camilla Ave, Studio City, CA 91604, USA

Guizar, Tito *Guitarist, Actor*
Sierra Madre, 640 Lomas de Chapultepec, Mexico City DF 10-09999, Mexico

Gulbinowicx, Henryk Roman Cardinal *Religious Leader*
%Metropolita Wroclawski, Ul Katedraina 11, 50-328 Wroclaw, Poland

Gullett, Donald E (Don) *Baseball Player*
130 Meadow Ave, Raceland, KY 41169, USA

Gullickson, William L (Bill) *Baseball Player*
300 Brentvale Lane, Brentwood, TN 37027, USA

Gulliver, Harold *Editor*
%Atlanta Constitution, Editorial Dept, 72 Marieta St NW, Atlanta, GA 30303, USA

Gulyas, Denes *Opera Singer*
%Hungarian State Opera, Andrassy Ut 22, Budapest 1062, Hungary

Guman, Michael D (Mike) *Football Player*
3913 Pleasant Ave, Allentown, PA 18103, USA

Gumbel, Bryant C *Broadcaster*
%NBC-TV, News Dept, 30 Rockefeller Plaza, New York, NY 10112, USA

Gumbel, Greg *Sportscaster*
%NBC-TV, Sports Dept, 30 Rockefeller Plaza, New York, NY 10112, USA

Gumbiner, Burke F *Businessman*
%FHP International Corp, 9900 Talbert Ave, Fountain Valley, CA 92708, USA

Gumbiner, Robert *Businessman*
%FHP International Corp, 9900 Talbert Ave, Fountain Valley, CA 92708, USA

Gumede, Josiah Z *President, Zimbabwe*
29 Barbour Fields, PO Mzilikazi, Bulawayo, Zimbabwe

Gund, Agnes *Museum Executive*
%Musuem of Modern Art, 11 W 53rd St, New York, NY 10019, USA

Gund, George, III *Hockey Executive*
%San Jose Sharks, 525 W Santa Clara St, San Jose, CA 95113, USA

Gundeck, Robert W *Businessman*
%American Business Products, PO Box 105684, Atlanta, GA 30348, USA

Gunderson, Richard L *Businessman*
%Aid Assn for Lutherans, 4321 N Ballard Rd, Appleton, WI 54915, USA

Gundling, Beulah *Synchronized Swimmer*
%Coral Ridge South, 3333 NE 34th St, #1517, Fort Lauderdale, FL 33308, USA

Gunn, James P *Astronomer*
%Princeton University, Astrophysics Dept, Princeton, NJ 08544, USA

Gunn, Thomson W (Thom) *Poet*
1216 Cole St, San Francisco, CA 94117, USA

Gunnell, Sally *Track Athlete*
7 Old Patcham Mews, Old London Rd, Brighton, Eoor Susscx, England

Gunnoe, Larry R *Businessman*
%Idaho Power Co, 1221 W Idaho St, Boise, ID 83702, USA

Gunsalus, Irwin C *Biochemist, Writer*
716 W Iowa, Urbana, IL 61801, USA

Gunst, Robert A *Businessman*
%Good Guys Inc, 7000 Marina Blvd, Brisbane, CA 94005, USA

Guokas, Matt *Basketball Coach, Executive*
%Orlando Magic, Orlando Arena, 1 Magic Place, Orlando, FL 32801, USA

Gupta, Sudhir *Immunologist*
%University of California, Medicine Dept, Irvine, CA 92717, USA

Gur, Mordechai *Army General, Israel*
25 Mishmeret St, Afeka, Tel-Aviv 69694, Israel

Gura, Larry C *Baseball Player*
PO Box 94, Litchfield Park, AZ 85340, USA

Gurash, John T *Businessman*
%Horace Mann Educators Corp, 1 Horace Mann Plaza, Springfield, IL 62701, USA

Gurchenko, Ludmilla M *Actress*
%Union of Cinematographists, Vasilyevskaya 13, 103056 Moscow, Russia

Gurney, A R, Jr *Writer*
Wellers Bridge Rd, Roxbury, CT 06783, USA

Gurney, Daniel S (Dan) *Auto Racing Driver, Builder*
%All-American Racers Inc, 2334 S Broadway, Santa Ana, CA 92707, USA

Gurney, Edward J *Senator, FL*
617 N Interlachen Ave, Winter Park, FL 32789, USA

Gurraggchaa, Jugderdemidijn *Cosmonaut, Mongolia; Air Force General*
Lyotchik Kosmonavt, MNR, Central Post Office Box 378, Ulan Bator, Mongolia

Gusella, James *Medical Researcher*
%Harvard Medical School, 25 Shattuck St, Boston, MA 02115, USA

Gushiken, Koji *Gymnast*
%Nippon Physical Education College, Judo School, Tokyo, Japan

Gustafson, Cliff *Baseball Coach*
%University of Texas, Athletic Dept, PO Box 7399, Austin, TX 78713, USA

Gustafson, Steven *Bassist (10,000 Maniacs)*
%New York End Ltd, 143 W 69th St, #4-A, New York, NY 10023, USA

Gustafsson, Bengt *Hockey Player*
%Washington Capitals, USAir Arena, Landover, MD 20785, USA

Gut, Rainer E *Financier*
%CS First Boston, Park Ave Plaza, 55 E 52nd St, New York, NY 10055, USA

G

Gulyas - Gut

Gutensohn-Knopf, Katrin — *Skier*
Oberfeldweg 12, 83080 Oberaudorf, Germany

Guth, Alan H — *Physicist*
%Massachusetts Institute of Technology, Physics Dept, Cambridge, MA 02139, USA

Guth, John E, Jr — *Businessman*
%National-Standard Co, 1618 Terminal Rd, Niles, MI 49120, USA

Guth, Wilfried — *Financier*
%Deutsche Bank, Taunusanlage 12, 60262 Frankfurt/Main, Germany

Guthart, Leo A — *Businessman*
%Pittway Corp, 200 S Wacker Dr, Chicago, IL 60606, USA

Guthman, Edwin O — *Editor*
%Philadelphia Inquirer, Editorial Dept, 400 N Broad St, Philadelphia, PA 19130, USA

Guthrie, Arlo — *Singer*
The Farm, Washington, MA 01223, USA

Gutierrez, Gerald A — *Theater Director*
%William Morris Agency, 1325 Ave of Americas, New York, NY 10019, USA

Gutierrez, Gustavo — *Theologian*
Belisario Flores, 647 Lince, Ap 3090, Lima 100, Peru

Gutierrez, Horacio — *Concert Pianist*
%Shaw Concerts, Lincoln Plaza, 1900 Broadway, #200, New York, NY 10023, USA

Gutierrez, Sidney M — *Astronaut*
%Sandia National Laboratories, Strategic PO Box 5800, Albuquerque, NM 87185, USA

Gutman, Natalia G — *Concert Cellist*
%Harold Holt Ltd, 31 Sinclair Rd, London W14 ONS, England

Gutman, Roy W — *Journalist*
13132 Curved Iron Rd, Herndon, VA 22071, USA

Gutman, Steve — *Football Executive*
%New York Jets, 1000 Fulton Ave, Hempstead, NY 11550, USA

Gutowsky, Herbert S — *Physical Chemist*
202 W Delaware Ave, Urbana, IL 61801, USA

Guttenberg, Steve — *Actor*
15237 Sunset Blvd, #48, Pacific Palisades, CA 90272, USA

Guttman, Zoltan (Lou) — *Financier*
%New York Mercantile Exchange, 4 World Trade Center, New York, NY 10048, USA

Gutton, Andre H G — *Architect*
3 Ave Vavin, 75006 Paris, France

Guy, Buddy — *Singer, Guitarist*
%Cameron Organization, 2001 W Magnolia Blvd, Burbank, CA 91506, USA

Guy, Jasmine — *Actress*
%Pantich, 21243 Ventura Blvd, #101, Woodland Hills, CA 91364, USA

Guy, William L — *Governor, ND*
3330 Prairiewood Dr W, Fargo, ND 58103, USA

Guyon, John C — *Educator*
%Southern Illinois University, President's Office, Carbondale, IL 62901, USA

Guze, Samuel B — *Psychiatrist*
%Washington University, Medical School, Psychiatry Dept, St Louis, MO 63110, USA

Guzy, Carol — *Photographer*
%Washington Post, Editorial Dept, 1150 15th St NW, Washington, DC 20071, USA

Guzzle, Timothy L — *Businessman*
%TECO Energy, 702 N Franklin St, Tampa, FL 33602, USA

Gwathmey, Charles — *Architect*
%Gwathmey Siegel Architects, 475 10th Ave, New York, NY 10018, USA

Gwinn, Mary Ann — *Journalist*
%Seattle Times, Editorial Dept, Fairview Ave N & John St, Seattle, WA 98111, USA

Gwynn, Anthony K (Tony) — *Baseball Player*
15643 Boulder Ridge Lane, Poway, CA 92064, USA

Gwynne, A Patrick — *Architect*
Homewood, Esher, Surrey KT10 9JL, England

Gyenge Garay, Valerie — *Swimmer*
5 Highland Ave, Toronto ON M4W 2A2, Canada

Gyll, J Soren — *Businessman*
%Volvo AB, 405 08 Goteborg, Sweden

Gyllenhammar, Pehr G — *Businessman*
%Volvo AB, 405 08 Goteborg, Sweden

Haab, Larry D — *Businessman*
%Illinova Corp, 500 S 27th St, Decatur, IL 62521, USA

Haacke, Hans C C — *Artist*
%Cooper Union for Advancement of Science, Cooper Square, New York, NY 10003, USA

Haag, Rudolf — *Physicist*
Oeltingsalle 20, 25421 Pinneberg, Germany

Haakon — *Crown Prince, Norway*
Det Kongeligel Slottet, Drammensveien 1, 0010 Oslo, Norway

Haas, Andrew T — *Labor Leader*
%Auto Aero & Agricultural Union, 1300 Connecticut NW, Washington, DC 20036, USA

Haas, Ernst — *Photographer*
853 7th Ave, New York, NY 10019, USA

Haas, Jay — *Golfer*
%Professional Golfer's Assn, PO Box 109601, Palm Beach Gardens, FL 33410, USA

Haas, Lukas — *Actor*
%Wolf/Kasteler, 1033 Gayley Ave, #208, Los Angeles, CA 90024, USA

Haas, Marvin I — *Businessman*
%Chock Full O'Nuts Corp, 425 Lexington Ave, New York, NY 10017, USA

Haas, Paul R — *Businessman*
4500 Ocean Blvd, #9-A, Corpus Christi, TX 78412, USA

Haas, Peter E — *Businessman*
%Levi Strauss Assoc, 1155 Battery St, San Francisco, CA 94111, USA

Haas, Richard J — *Artist*
361 W 36th St, New York, NY 10018, USA

Haas, Robert D — *Businessman*
%Levi Strauss Asscc, 1155 Battery St, San Francisco, CA 94111, USA

Haavelmo, Trygve — *Nobel Economics Laureate*
%University of Oslo, PO Box 1072, Blindern, 0316 Oslo 3, Norway

Habash, George — *Palestinian Leader*
Palais Essaada La Marsa, Tunis, Tunisia

Habel, Karl — *Medical Researcher*
%Reading Institute of Rehabilitation, Rt 1, Box 252, Reading, PA 19607, USA

Haber, Bill — *Entertainment Executive*
%Creative Artists Agency, 9830 Wilshire Blvd, Beverly Hills, CA 90212, USA

Haber, Norman — *Inventor (Electromolecular Propulsion)*
%Haber Inc, 470 Main Rd, Towaco, NJ 07082, USA

Habib, Munir — *Cosmonaut, Syria*
%Potchta Kosmonavtov, 141 160 Svyosdny Gorodok, Moskovskoi Oblasti, Russia

Habig, Douglas A — *Businessman*
%Kimball International, 1600 Royal St, Jasper, IN 47549, USA

Habig, Thomas L — *Businessman*
%Kimball International, 1600 Royal St, Jasper, IN 47549, USA

Habiger, Eugene E (Gene) — *Air Force General*
Vice Commander, Air Education Training Cmd, Randolph Air Force Base, TX 78150, USA

Hachette, Jean-Louis — *Publisher*
79 Blvd Saint-Germain, 75006 Paris, France

Hack, Shelley — *Model, Actress*
209 12th St, Santa Monica, CA 90402, USA

Hacken, Mark B — *Businessman*
%FHP International Corp, 9900 Talbert Ave, Fountain Valley, CA 92708, USA

Hackett, Buddy — *Comedian*
800 N Whittier Dr, Beverly Hills, CA 90210, USA

Hackford, Taylor — *Movie Director*
2003 La Brea Terrace, Los Angeles, CA 90016, USA

Hackl, Georg — *Luge Athlete*
Caftehaus Soamatl, Ramsauerstr 100, 83471 Berchtesgaden-Engedey, Germany

Hackman, Gene — *Actor*
118 S Beverly Dr, #201, Beverly Hills, CA 90212, USA

Hackney, F Sheldon — *Educator*
%Nat'l Endowment for Humanities, 1100 Pennsylvania NW, Washington, DC 20004, USA

Hackney, Roderick P — *Architect*
St Peter's House, Windmill St, Macclesfield, Cheshire SK11 7HS, England

Hackworth, David H — *Korean, Vietnam Army Hero*
706 2nd St E, Whitefish, MT 59937, USA

Hackworth, Michael — *Businessman*
%Cirrus Logic, 3100 W Warren Ave, Fremont, CA 94538, USA

Haddock, Ron W — *Businessman*
%FINA Inc, FINA Plaza, 8350 N Central Expressway, Dallas, TX 75206, USA

H

Haab - Haddock

H

Haddon, Dayle	*Model, Actress*
38 E 64th St, #4, New York, NY 10021, USA	
Haddon, Larry	*Actor*
%Atkins Assoc, 303 S Crescent Heights Blvd, Los Angeles, CA 90048, USA	
Haden, Charlie	*Jazz Bassist, Composer*
%Quartet West, Merlin Co, 17609 Ventura Blvd, #212, Encino, CA 91316, USA	
Haden, Pat	*Football Player, Sportscaster*
%Riodan & McKinzie, 300 S Grand Ave, Los Angeles, CA 90071, USA	
Hadlee, Richard J	*Cricketer*
PO Box 29186, Christchurch, New Zealand	
Hadley, Brett	*Actor*
5070 Woodley Ave, Encino, CA 91436, USA	
Hadley, Jerry	*Opera Singer*
%Lyric Arts Group, 204 W 10th St, New York, NY 10014, USA	
Hadley, Leonard A	*Businessman*
%Maytag Corp, 403 W 4th St N, Newton, IA 50208, USA	
Haebler, Ingrid	*Concert Pianist*
%Ibbs & Tillett Ltd, 420-452 Edgware Rd, London W2 1EG, England	
Haeckel, John C	*Businessman*
%Broadway Stores, 3880 N Mission Rd, Los Angeles, CA 90031, USA	
Haegg, Gunder	*Track Athlete*
%Swedish Olympic Committee, Idrottens Hus, 123 87 Farsta, Sweden	
Haendel, Ida	*Concert Violinist*
%Harold Holt Ltd, 31 Sinclair Rd, London W14 0N8, England	
Haenicke, Diether H	*Educator*
%Western Michigan University, President's Office, Kalamazoo, MI 49008, USA	
Haensel, Vladimir	*Catalytic Chemist*
83 Larkspur Dr, Amherst, MA 01002, USA	
Haeusgen, Helmut	*Financier*
%Dresdner Bank, Jurgen-Ponto-Platz 1, 60329 Frankfurt/Main, Germany	
Haffner, Charles C, III	*Businessman*
1524 N Astor St, Chicago, IL 60610, USA	
Hafner, Dudley H	*Foundation Executive*
%American Heart Assn, 7320 Greenville Ave, Dallas, TX 75231, USA	
Hafstein, Johann	*Prime Minister, Iceland*
Sjalfstaedisflokkurinn, Laufasvegi 46, Reykjavik, Iceland	
Haft, Herbert H	*Businessman*
%Dart Group Corp, 3300 75th Ave, Landover, MD 20785, USA	
Haft, Ronald	*Businessman*
%Dart Group Corp, 3300 75th Ave, Landover, MD 20785, USA	
Hagale, John E	*Businessman*
%Burlington Resources Inc, PO Box 4239, Houston, TX 77210, USA	
Hagan, Clifford O (Cliff)	*Basketball Player*
3637 Castlegate West Wynd, Lexington, KY 40502, USA	
Hagan, Molly	*Actress*
%Ellis Artists Agency, 3441 Harrison St, Evanston, IL 60201, USA	
Hagan, Ward S	*Businessman*
%Warner-Lambert Co, 201 Tabor Rd, Morris Plains, NJ 07950, USA	
Hagar, Sammy	*Singer*
PO Box 5395, Novato, CA 94948, USA	
Hagegard, Hakan	*Opera Singer*
Gunnarsbyn, 670 30 Edane, Sweden	
Hagemeister, Charles C	*Vietnam War Army Hero (CMH)*
811 N 16th Terrace Court, Leavenworth, KS 66048, USA	
Hagen, Donald F	*Navy Admiral, Physician*
Chief, Bureau of Medicine & Surgery, Navy Dept, Washington, DC 20372, USA	
Hagen, James A	*Businessman*
%Conrail Corp, 2001 Market St, Philadelphia, PA 19103, USA	
Hagen, Kevin	*Actor*
941 N Mansfield Ave, #C, Los Angeles, CA 90038, USA	
Hagen, Nina	*Singer*
%BMG Ariola Munich, Postfach 800149, 50670 Cologne, Germany	
Hagen, Uta	*Actress*
%Kroll, 390 West End Ave, New York, NY 10024, USA	
Hager, Robert	*Commentator*
%NBC-TV, News Dept, 4001 Nebraska Ave NW, Washington, DC 20016, USA	
Hagerty, Julie	*Actress*
%Don Buchwald Assoc, 10 E 44th St, #500, New York, NY 10017, USA	

Haddon - Hagerty

Haggard, Merle *Singer, Songwriter*
%HAG Inc, Box 536, Palo Cedro, CA 96073, USA

Hagge, Marlene *Golfer*
%Ladies Professional Golf Assn, 2570 Volusia Ave, Daytona Beach, FL 32114, USA

Haggerty, Charles A *Businessman*
%Western Digital Corp, 8105 Irvine Center Dr, Irvine, CA 92718, USA

Haggerty, Dan *Actor*
11684 Ventura Blvd, #211, Studio City, CA 91604, USA

Haggerty, H B *Actor*
%First Artists Agency, 10000 Riverside Dr, #10, Toluca Lake, CA 91602, USA

Haggerty, Tim *Cartoonist (Ground Zero)*
%United Feature Syndicate, 200 Park Ave, New York, NY 10166, USA

Hagiwara, Kokichi *Businessman*
%National Steel Corp, 4100 Edison Lakes Parkway, Mishawaka, IN 46545, USA

Hagler, Marvin *Boxer*
%Peter Devener, 112 Island St, Stoughton, MA 02072, USA

Hagman, Larry *Actor*
23730 Malibu Colony Rd, Malibu, CA 90265, USA

Hahn, Carl H *Businessman*
%Volkswagenwerk AG, 78730 Wolfsburg, Germany

Hahn, Erwin L *Physicist*
69 Stevenson Ave, Berkeley, CA 94708, USA

Hahn, Jessica *Model*
6345 Balboa Blvd, #375, Encino, CA 91316, USA

Hahn, Michael J *Financier*
%Churchill Capital, 333 S 7th St, Minneapolis, MN 55402, USA

Hahn, T Marshall, Jr *Businessman*
%Georgia-Pacific Corp, 133 Peachtree St NE, Atlanta, GA 30303, USA

Haid, Alan P *Businessman*
%MicroAge Inc, 2308 S 55th St, Tempe, AZ 85280, USA

Haid, Charles *Actor*
4376 Forman Ave, North Hollywood, CA 91602, USA

Haig, Alexander M, Jr *Secretary, State; Army General*
1155 15th St NW, #800, Washington, DC 20005, USA

Haignere, Jean-Pierre *Spatinaut, France*
CNES, 2 Place Maurice Quentin, 75039 Paris Cedeux, France

Hailey, Arthur *Writer*
Lyford Cay, PO Box N-7776, Nassau, Bahamas

Hailsham of St Marylebone (Q M Hogg) *Government Official, England*
Corner House, Heathview Gardens, London SW15 OPW, England

Haim, Corey *Actor*
3209 Taresco Dr, Los Angeles, CA 90068, USA

Haimovitz, Matt *Concert Cellist*
%International Creative Mgmt, 40 W 57th St, New York, NY 10019, USA

Haines, Connie *Singer*
13816 Bora Bora Way, Marina del Rey, CA 90292, USA

Haines, George *Swimming Coach*
1218 Cordelia Ave, San Jose, CA 95129, USA

Haines, James S, Jr *Businessman*
%Western Resources Co, 818 Kansas Ave, Topeka, KS 66612, USA

Haines, Randa *Movie Director*
1429 Avon Park Terrace, Los Angeles, CA 90026, USA

Haines, Terry L *Businessman*
%A Schulman Inc, 3550 W Market St, Akron, OH 44333, USA

Hair, Jay D *Foundation Executive, Environmentalist*
%National Wildlife Federation, 1412 16th St NW, Washington, DC 20036, USA

Haire, John E *Publisher*
%Time Magazine, Rockefeller Center, New York, NY 10020, USA

Hairston, Carl B *Football Player, Coach*
4713 Chalfont Dr, Virginia Beach, VA 23464, USA

Hairston, Harold (Happy) *Basketball Player*
%Happy Hairston Youth Foundation, 1801 Ave of Stars, Los Angeles, CA 90067, USA

Hairston, Jester J *Composer*
5047 Valley Ridge Ave, Los Angeles, CA 90043, USA

Haise, Fred W, Jr *Astronaut*
3730 Chiara Dr, Titusville, FL 32796, USA

Haitink, Bernard *Conductor*
%Harold Holt Ltd, 31 Sinclair Rd, London W14 ONS, England

H

Haje, Khrystyne — *Actress*
PO Box 8750, Universal City, CA 91618, USA

Hajt, Bill — *Hockey Player*
%Buffalo Sabres, Memorial Stadium, 140 Main St, Buffalo, NY 14202, USA

Hakamada, Kunio — *Businessman*
%Daido Steel Co, 11-18 Nishiki, Nakaku, Nagoya 460, Japan

Hakansson, Nils — *Economist*
252 Clyde Dr, Walnut Creek, CA 94598, USA

Hakashima, Tamotsu — *Businessman*
%Nihon Cement Co, 1-6-1 Otemachi, Chiyodaku, Tokyo 100, Japan

Hakulinen, Veikko — *Nordic Skier*
%General Delivery, Valkeakoski, Finland

Halaby, Najeeb E — *Businessman, Government Official*
175 Chain Bridge Rd, McLean, VA 22101, USA

Halas, John — *Animator*
%Educational Film Center, 5-7 Kean St, London WC2B 4AT, England

Halberstam, David — *Writer*
%William Morrow Co, 1350 Ave of Americas, New York, NY 10016, USA

Halbreich, Kathy — *Museum Director*
%Walker Art Center, 725 Vineland Pl, Minneapolis, MN 55403, USA

Hale, Barbara — *Actress*
PO Box 1980, North Hollywood, CA 91614, USA

Hale, Edwin F, Sr — *Financier*
%Baltimore Bancorp, 120 E Baltimore St, Baltimore, MD 21202, USA

Hale, Georgina — *Actress*
74-A St John's Wood, High St, London NW8, England

Hale, James H — *Publisher*
%Kansas City Star-Tribune, 1729 Grand Ave, Kansas City, MO 64108, USA

Hale, John H — *Businessman*
71 Eaton Terrace, London SW1W 8TN, England

Hale, Roger E — *Businessman*
%LG&E Energy Corp, 220 W Main St, Louisville, KY 40202, USA

Haley, Charles L — *Football Player*
%Dallas Cowboys, 1 Cowboys Parkway, Irving, TX 75063, USA

Haley, Jack, Jr — *Movie Director, Producer*
1443 Devlin Dr, Los Angeles, CA 90069, USA

Haley, Maria — *Financier*
%Export-Import Bank, 811 Vermont Ave NW, Washington, DC 20571, USA

Half, Robert — *Businessman*
%Robert Half International, 565 5th Ave, #12, New York, NY 10017, USA

Halford, Rob — *Singer (Judas Priest)*
%Sony/Columbia/CBS Records, 2100 Colorado Ave, Santa Monica, CA 90404, USA

Hall Greff, Kaye — *Swimmer*
906 3rd St, Mukilteo, WA 98275, USA

Hall, A Stewart, Jr — *Businessman*
%Hughes Supply Inc, 30 N Orange Ave, Orlando, FL 32801, USA

Hall, Arnold A — *Businessman*
%Hawker Siddeley Group, 18 St James's Sq, London SW1Y 4LJ, England

Hall, Arsenio — *Entertainer*
10989 Bluffside Dr, #3418, Studio City, CA 91604, USA

Hall, Charles — *Inventor (Waterbed)*
%Basic Designs, 5815 Bennett Valley Rd, Santa Rosa, CA 95404, USA

Hall, Conrad L — *Cinematographer*
%G G Gundry Agency, 23715 Malibu Rd, #383, Malibu, CA 90265, USA

Hall, Daryl — *Singer (Hall & Oates), Songwriter*
%Horizon Entertainment, 130 W 57th St, #12-B, New York, NY 10019, USA

Hall, Deidre — *Actress*
215 Strada Corta Rd, Los Angeles, CA 90077, USA

Hall, Delores — *Singer, Actress*
%Agency For Performing Arts, 888 7th Ave, New York, NY 10106, USA

Hall, Donald — *Writer*
Eagle Pond Farm, Danbury, NH 03230, USA

Hall, Donald J — *Businessman*
%Hallmark Cards, 2501 McGee St, Kansas City, MO 64108, USA

Hall, Doug — *Cartoonist (Simple Beasts)*
%Tribune Media Services, 435 N Michigan Ave, #1417, Chicago, IL 60611, USA

Hall, Edward T — *Anthropologist, Writer*
707 E Palace Ave, #13, Santa Fe, NM 87501, USA

Hall, Erv — *Track Athlete*
%Citicorp Mortgage, 670 Mason Ridge Center Dr, St Louis, MO 63141, USA

Hall, Fawn — *Government Secretary*
1319 Bishop Lane, Alexandria, VA 22302, USA

Hall, Floyd D — *Businessman*
%Kmart Corp, 3100 W Big Beaver Rd, Troy, MI 48084, USA

Hall, Galen — *Football Coach*
%University of Florida, Athletic Dept, Gainesville, FL 32611, USA

Hall, Gary — *Swimmer*
3123 E Vermont Ave, Phoenix, AZ 85016, USA

Hall, Gary C — *Test Pilot, Engineer*
PO Box 715, Rosamond, CA 93560, USA

Hall, Glenn — *Hockey Player*
Stony Plain AB T7Z 1X9, Canada

Hall, Gus — *Political Party Official*
%Communist Party of America, 215 W 23rd St, #700, New York, NY 10011, USA

Hall, Huntz — *Actor*
12512 Chandler Blvd, #307, North Hollywood, CA 91607, USA

Hall, James E — *Auto Race Car Builder, Driver*
Rt 7, Box 640, Midland, TX 79706, USA

Hall, Jerry — *Model, Actress*
2 Munroe Terrace, London SW10 0DL, England

Hall, Jerry — *Geneticist*
%George Washington University Med Center, 2300 "I" St NW, Washington, DC 20037, USA

Hall, Jim — *Jazz Guitarist*
%Jazz Tree, 211 Thompson St, #1-D, New York, NY 10012, USA

Hall, Joe B — *Basketball Coach*
%Central Bank & Trust Co, 300 W Vine St, Lexington, KY 40507, USA

Hall, John R — *Businessman*
%Ashland Oil Inc, 1000 Ashland Dr, Russell, KY 41169, USA

Hall, Karen — *Screenwriter*
9242 Beverly Dr, #200, Beverly Hills, CA 90210, USA

Hall, Kevan — *Fashion Designer*
%Kevan Hall Studio, 756 S Spring St, #11-F, Los Angeles, CA 90014, USA

Hall, Lani — *Singer*
31930 Pacific Coast Highway, Malibu, CA 90265, USA

Hall, Lanny — *Educator*
%Hardin-Simmons University, President's Office, Abilene, TX 79698, USA

Hall, Larry D — *Businessman*
%K N Energy, 370 Van Gordon, Lakewood, CO 80228, USA

Hall, Lawrence — *Physicist*
%University of California, Physics Dept, Berkeley, CA 94720, USA

Hall, Llody M, Jr — *Religious Leader*
%Congregation Christian Churches National Assn, Box 1620, Oak Creek, MI 53154, USA

Hall, Monty — *Entertainer*
519 N Arden Dr, Beverly Hills, CA 90210, USA

Hall, Nigel J — *Artist*
11 Kensington Park Gardens, London, W11 3HD, England

Hall, Parker — *Football Player*
4712 Cole Rd, Memphis, TN 38117, USA

Hall, Peter R F — *Theater, Opera, Movie Director*
%Peter Hall Co, 18 Exeter St, London WC2E 7DU, England

Hall, Sonny — *Labor Leader*
%Transport Workers Union, 80 West End Ave, New York, NY 10023, USA

Hall, Tom T — *Singer, Songwriter*
PO Box 1246, Franklin, TN 37065, USA

Hall, William E — *WW II Navy Hero (CMH)*
4131 Mercier St, Kansas City, MO 64111, USA

Hall, William K — *Businessman*
%Eagle Industries, 2 N Riverside Plaza, #1160, Chicago, IL 60606, USA

Hallahan, Charles — *Actor*
1975 W Silverlake Dr, Los Angeles, CA 90039, USA

Halligan, James E — *Educator*
%New Mexico State University, President's Office, Las Cruces, NM 88003, USA

Hallinan, Joseph T — *Journalist*
%Newhouse News Service, 2000 Pennsylvania Ave NW, Washington, DC 20006, USA

Hallstrom, Lasse — *Movie Director*
%International Creative Mgmt, 8942 Wilshire Blvd, Beverly Hills, CA 90211, USA

H

Hall - Hallstrom

Hallyday, Estelle — *Model*
%Elite Model Mgmt, 111 E 22nd St, New York, NY 10010, USA

Halperin, Bertrand I — *Physicist*
%Harvard University, Physics Dept, Cambridge, MA 02138, USA

Halperin, Robert M — *Businessman*
80 Reservoir Rd, Atherton, CA 94027, USA

Halpern, Daniel — *Writer*
60 Pheasant Hill Rd, Princeton, NJ 08540, USA

Halpern, Jack — *Chemist*
5630 S Dorchester Ave, Chicago, IL 60637, USA

Halpern, Merril M — *Financier*
%Charterhouse Group International, 535 Madison Ave, New York, NY 10022, USA

Halpern, Ralph M — *Businessman*
%Burton Group, 214 Oxford St, London W1N 9DF, England

Halprin, Lawrence — *Landscape Architect, Planner*
444 Brannan St, San Francisco, CA 94107, USA

Halsell, James D, Jr — *Astronaut*
%NASA, Johnson Space Center, 2101 NASA Rd, Houston, TX 77058, USA

Halver, John E — *Biochemist, Nutritionist*
16502 41st NE, Seattle, WA 98155, USA

Ham, Jack R — *Football Player*
%Ham Enterprises, 509 Hegner Way, Sewickley, PA 15143, USA

Ham, James M — *Educator*
135 Glencairn Ave, Toronto ON M4R 1N1, Canada

Hamada, Hiroshi — *Businessman*
%Ricoh Co, 1-5-5 Minami-Aoyama, Minatoku, Tokyo 107, Japan

Hamann, H J — *Businessman*
%Schering, Mullerstr 170-178, 12487 Berlin, Germany

Hamari, Julia — *Opera Singer*
Max Brod-Weg 14, 70437 Stuttgart, Germany

Hambling, Maggi — *Artist*
%Bernard Jacobson Gallery, 14-A Clifford St, London W1X 1RF, England

Hambrecht, William R — *Businessman*
%Hambrecht & Quist Inc, 1 Bush St, San Francisco, CA 94104, USA

Hambro, Leonid — *Concert Pianist*
%California Institute of Arts, Music Dept, Valencia, CA 91355, USA

Hamburger, Michael P L — *Poet*
%John Johnson Ltd, 45/47 Clerkenwell Green, London EC1R 0HT, England

Hamed, Nihad — *Religious Leader*
%Islamic Assn in US/Canada, 25351 5 Mile Rd, Redford Township, MI 48239, USA

Hamel, Veronica — *Actress*
129 N Woodburn Dr, Los Angeles, CA 90049, USA

Hamer, Jean Jerome Cardinal — *Religious Leader*
Piazza di S Uffizio 11, 00193 Rome, Italy

Hamerow, Theodore S — *Educator*
466 S Segoe Rd, Madison, WI 53711, USA

Hamill, Dorothy S — *Figure Skater*
79490 Fairway Dr, Indian Wells, CA 92210, USA

Hamill, Mark — *Actor*
PO Box 55, Malibu, CA 90265, USA

Hamill, W Pete — *Writer*
%Esquire Magazine, 250 W 55th St, New York, NY 10019, USA

Hamilton, Ashley — *Actor*
10230 Wilshire Blvd, #1705, Los Angeles, CA 90024, USA

Hamilton, Carrie — *Actress*
415 N Camden Dr, #121, Beverly Hills, CA 90210, USA

Hamilton, Chico — *Jazz Drummer*
%Chico Hamilton Productions, 321 E 45th St, #PH-A, New York, NY 10017, USA

Hamilton, David — *Photographer*
41 Blvd du Montparnasse, 75006 Paris, France

Hamilton, George — *Actor*
9255 Doheny Rd, #2302, Los Angeles, CA 90069, USA

Hamilton, George, IV — *Singer, Guitarist, Songwriter*
PO Box 1558, Gainesville, FL 32602, USA

Hamilton, Guy — *Movie Director*
22 Mont Port, Puerto Andraitz, Mallorca, Baleares, Spain

Hamilton, Linda — *Actress*
19900 Pacific Coast Highway, Malibu, CA 90265, USA

Hamilton, Richard *Artist*	**H**
Northend Farm, Northend, Oxon RG9 6LQ, England	

Hamilton, Richard *Artist*
Northend Farm, Northend, Oxon RG9 6LQ, England

Hamilton, Robert A (Bones) *Football Player*
PO Box Y, Rancho Mirage, CA 92270, USA

Hamilton, Scott S *Figure Skater*
%Michael Sterling Assoc, 4242 Van Nuys Blvd, Sherman Oaks, CA 91403, USA

Hamilton, Suzanna *Actress*
%Julian Belfrage, 46 Albermarle St, London W1X 4PP, England

Hamilton, Thomas H *Financier*
%Collective Bancorp, 158 Philadelphia Ave, Egg Harbor City, NJ 08215, USA

Hamilton, Tom *Bassist (Aerosmith)*
%Collins Mgmt, 5 Bigelow St, Cambridge, MA 02139, USA

Hamilton, William *Cartoonist, Writer*
152 S Almont Dr, Los Angeles, CA 90048, USA

Hamlin, Harry *Actor*
612 N Sepulveda Blvd, #10, Los Angeles, CA 90049, USA

Hamlisch, Marvin *Composer*
970 Park Ave, #501, New York, NY 10028, USA

Hamm, Charles J *Financier*
%Independence Savings Bank, 195 Montague St, Brooklyn, NY 11201, USA

Hamm, Richard L *Religious Leader*
130 E Washington St, Indianapolis, IN 46204, USA

Hammel, Eugene A *Anthropologist*
%University of California, Anthroplogy Dept, Berkeley, CA 94720, USA

Hammer (Stanley K Burrell) *Rapper*
44896 Vista Del Sol, Fremont, CA 94539, USA

Hammerly, Harry A *Businessman*
%Minnesota Mining & Manufacturing, 3-M Center, St Paul, MN 55144, USA

Hammerman, Stephen L *Financier*
%Merrill Lynch Co, World Financial Center, 2 Vesey St, New York, NY 10007, USA

Hammerstein, Mike *Football Player*
%Cincinnati Bengals, 200 Riverfront Stadium, Cincinnati, OH 45202, USA

Hammett, Louis P *Chemist*
288 Medford Leas, Medford, NJ 08055, USA

Hammond Innes, Ralph *Writer*
Ayres End, Kersey by Ipswich, Suffolk 1P7 6EB, England

Hammond, Caleb D, Jr *Publisher, Cartographer*
61 Woodland Rd, Maplewood, NJ 07040, USA

Hammond, George S *Chemist*
27 Timber Lane, Painted Post, NY 14870, USA

Hammond, James T *Religious Leader*
%Pentecostal Free Will Baptist Church, PO Box 1568, Dunn, NC 28335, USA

Hammond, Jay S *Governor, AK*
Lake Charles Lodge, Port Alsworth, AK 99652, USA

Hammond, Joan H *Opera Singer*
46 Lansell Rd, Toorak Vic 3142, Australia

Hammond, L Blaine, Jr *Astronaut*
2255 Broadlawn Dr, Houston, TX 77058, USA

Hammond, Tom *Sportscaster*
%NBC-TV, Sports Dept, 30 Rockefeller Plaza, New York, NY 10112, USA

Hammons, David *Sculptor*
%Exit Art, 578 Broadway, #800, New York, NY 10012, USA

Hammons, Roger *Religious Leader*
%Primitive Advent Christian Church, 395 Frame Rd, Elkview, WV 25071, USA

Hamnett, Katharine *Fashion Designer*
%Katharine Hamnett Ltd, 202 New North Rd, London N1, England

Hampel, Ronald C *Businessman*
%Imperial Chemical Industries, 9 Millbank, London SW1P 3JF, England

Hampshire, Susan *Actress*
%Chatto & Linnit, Prince of Wales, Coventry St, London W1V 7FE, England

Hampson, Thomas *Opera Singer*
Starkfriedgasse 53, 1180 Vienna, Austria

Hampton, Christopher J *Playwright*
2 Kensington Park Gardens, London W11, England

Hampton, Dan *Football Player*
%Chicago Bears, Halas Hall, 250 N Washington Rd, Lake Forest, IL 60045, USA

Hampton, Henry E, Jr *Movie, Television Producer*
%Backside Inc, 486 Shawmut Ave, Boston, MA 02118, USA

Hamilton - Hampton

Hampton, James — Actor
15741 Haynes St, Van Nuys, CA 91406, USA

Hampton, Lionel — Jazz Vibraharpist, Conductor
20 W 64th St, #28-K, New York, NY 10023, USA

Hampton, Ralph C, Jr — Religious Leader
%Free Will Baptist Bible College, 3606 West End Ave, Nashville, TN 37205, USA

Han Suyin — Writer
37 Montoie, Lausanne, Switzerland

Han, Maggie — Actress
%J Michael Bloom Ltd, 9255 Sunset Blvd, #710, Los Angeles, CA 90069, USA

Hanafusa, Hidesaburo — Microbiologist
%Rockefeller University, 1230 York Ave, New York, NY 10021, USA

Hanaka, Martin — Businessman
%Staples Inc, 100 Pennsylvania Ave, Framingham, MA 01701, USA

Hanauer, Chip — Speed Boat Racer
%Hanauer Enterprises, 2702 NE 88th St, Seattle, WA 98115, USA

Hanburger, Chris, Jr — Football Player
10701 Mattaponi Rd, Upper Marlboro, MA 20772, USA

Hanbury-Tenison, Robin — Explorer
%Maidenwell, Cardinham, Bodmin, Cornwall PL3O 4DW, England

Hance, James H, Jr — Financier
%NationsBank Corp, NationsBank Plaza, Charlotte, NC 28255, USA

Hancock, Herbert J (Herbie) — Jazz Pianist, Composer
%Hancock Music, 1250 N Doheny Dr, Los Angeles, CA 90069, USA

Hancock, John D — Movie Director
7355 N Fail Rd, La Porte, IN 46350, USA

Hancock, Walker K — Artist
Lanesville, PO Box 7133, Gloucester, MA 01930, USA

Hand, Elbert O — Businessman
%Hartmarx Inc, 101 N Wacker Dr, Chicago, IL 60606, USA

Handelsman, J B — Cartoonist
%New Yorker Magazine, Editorial Dept, 20 W 43rd St, New York, NY 10036, USA

Handelsman, Walt — Editorial Cartoonist
%New Orleans Times-Picayune, 3800 Howard Ave, New Orleans, LA 70140, USA

Handke, Peter — Writer
%Farrar Straus Giroux, 19 Union Square W, New York, NY 10003, USA

Handleman, David — Businessman
%Handleman Co, 500 Kirts Blvd, Troy, MI 48084, USA

Handley, Vernon G — Conductor
Hen Gerrig, Pen-y-Fan Near Monmouth, Gwent NP5 4RA, Wales

Handlin, Oscar — Historian, Educator
18 Agassiz St, Cambridge, MA 02140, USA

Hands, William A (Bill) — Baseball Player
Willow Terrace, Orient, NY 11957, USA

Haney, Lee — Body Builder
%Lee Haney Enterprises, PO Box 491269, Atlanta, GA 30349, USA

Hanfmann, George M A — Archaeologist
%Harvard University, Fogg Art Museum, 32 Quincy St, Cambridge, MA 02138, USA

Hanft, Ruth S — Medical Researcher
600 21st St NW, Washington, DC 20006, USA

Hanifan, Jim — Football Coach
%Washington Redskins, 21300 Redskin Park Dr, Ashburn, VA 22011, USA

Hanin, Roger — Actor
9 Rue du Boccador, 75008 Paris, France

Hanks, Tom — Actor
PO Box 1650, Pacific Palisades, CA 90272, USA

Hanley, Edward T — Labor Leader
%Hotel-Restaurant Employees Union, 1219 28th St NW, Washington, DC 20007, USA

Hanley, Frank — Labor Leader
%Int'l Union of Operating Engineers, 1125 17th St NW, Washington, DC 20036, USA

Hanna, Bill — Businessman
%Koch Industries, PO Box 2256, Wichita, KS 67201, USA

Hanna, David S — Financier
%Bank of America Arizona, PO Box 16290, Phoenix, AZ 85011, USA

Hanna, Robert C — Businessman
%Imperial Holly Inc, 8016 Highway 90-A, Sugar Land, TX 77478, USA

Hanna, William D — Animator (Flintstones, Yogi Bear)
%Hanna-Barbera Productions, 3400 W Cahuenga Blvd, Los Angeles, CA 90068, USA

Hampton - Hanna

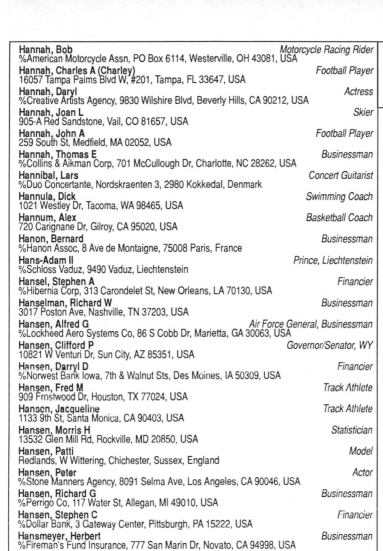

Hannah, Bob — *Motorcycle Racing Rider*
%American Motorcycle Assn, PO Box 6114, Westerville, OH 43081, USA

Hannah, Charles A (Charley) — *Football Player*
16057 Tampa Palms Blvd W, #201, Tampa, FL 33647, USA

Hannah, Daryl — *Actress*
%Creative Artists Agency, 9830 Wilshire Blvd, Beverly Hills, CA 90212, USA

Hannah, Joan L — *Skier*
905-A Red Sandstone, Vail, CO 81657, USA

Hannah, John A — *Football Player*
259 South St, Medfield, MA 02052, USA

Hannah, Thomas E — *Businessman*
%Collins & Aikman Corp, 701 McCullough Dr, Charlotte, NC 28262, USA

Hannibal, Lars — *Concert Guitarist*
%Duo Concertante, Nordskraenten 3, 2980 Kokkedal, Denmark

Hannula, Dick — *Swimming Coach*
1021 Westley Dr, Tacoma, WA 98465, USA

Hannum, Alex — *Basketball Coach*
720 Carignane Dr, Gilroy, CA 95020, USA

Hanon, Bernard — *Businessman*
%Hanon Assoc, 8 Ave de Montaigne, 75008 Paris, France

Hans-Adam II — *Prince, Liechtenstein*
%Schloss Vaduz, 9490 Vaduz, Liechtenstein

Hansel, Stephen A — *Financier*
%Hibernia Corp, 313 Carondelet St, New Orleans, LA 70130, USA

Hanselman, Richard W — *Businessman*
3017 Poston Ave, Nashville, TN 37203, USA

Hansen, Alfred G — *Air Force General, Businessman*
%Lockheed Aero Systems Co, 86 S Cobb Dr, Marietta, GA 30063, USA

Hansen, Clifford P — *Governor/Senator, WY*
10821 W Venturi Dr, Sun City, AZ 85351, USA

Hansen, Darryl D — *Financier*
%Norwest Bank Iowa, 7th & Walnut Sts, Des Moines, IA 50309, USA

Hansen, Fred M — *Track Athlete*
909 Frostwood Dr, Houston, TX 77024, USA

Hansen, Jacqueline — *Track Athlete*
1133 9th St, Santa Monica, CA 90403, USA

Hansen, Morris H — *Statistician*
13532 Glen Mill Rd, Rockville, MD 20850, USA

Hansen, Patti — *Model*
Redlands, W Wittering, Chichester, Sussex, England

Hansen, Peter — *Actor*
%Stone Manners Agency, 8091 Selma Ave, Los Angeles, CA 90046, USA

Hansen, Richard G — *Businessman*
%Perrigo Co, 117 Water St, Allegan, MI 49010, USA

Hansen, Stephen C — *Financier*
%Dollar Bank, 3 Gateway Center, Pittsburgh, PA 15222, USA

Hansmeyer, Herbert — *Businessman*
%Fireman's Fund Insurance, 777 San Marin Dr, Novato, CA 94998, USA

Hanson of Edgerton, James E — *Businessman*
1 Grosvenor Place, London SW1X 7JH, England

Hanson, Curtis — *Movie Director*
%United Talent Agency, 9560 Wilshire Blvd, #500, Beverly Hills, CA 90212, USA

Hanson, Duane E — *Sculptor*
6109 SW 55th Ct, Davie, FL 33314, USA

Hanson, John K — *Businessman*
%Winnebago Industries, PO Box 152, Forest City, IA 50436, USA

Hanson, Robert A — *Businessman*
2200 29th Ave Court, Moline, IL 61265, USA

Hanson, William R — *Artist*
78 W Notre Dame, Glens Falls, NY 12801, USA

Harad, George J — *Businessman*
%Boise Cascade Corp, 1111 Jefferson Square, Boise, ID 83702, USA

Harald V — *King, Norway*
Det Kongelige Slott, Drammensveien 1, 0010 Oslo, Norway

Haran, Mary Cleere — *Singer*
%Agency For Performing Arts, 9000 Sunset Blvd, #1200, Los Angeles, CA 90069, USA

Harbaugh, Gregory J — *Astronaut*
%NASA, Johnson Space Center, 2101 NASA Rd, Houston, TX 77058, USA

Hannah - Harbaugh

H

Harbaugh, Robert E *Neurosurgeon*
%Dartmouth-Hitchcock Medical Center, Surgery Dept, Hanover, NH 03756, USA

Harbison, John H *Composer*
479 Franklin St, Cambridge, MA 02139, USA

Hard, Darlene *Tennis Player*
22924 Erwin St, Woodland Hills, CA 91367, USA

Hardaway, Anfernee (Penny) *Basketball Player*
%Orlando Magic, Orlando Arena, 1 Magic Place, Orlando, FL 32801, USA

Hardaway, Timothy D (Tim) *Basketball Player*
%Golden State Warriors, Oakland Coliseum Arena, Oakland, CA 94621, USA

Harder, Melvin L (Mel) *Baseball Player*
130 Center St, #6-A, Chardon, OH 44024, USA

Hardgrove, Richard L *Financier*
%First National Bank of Ohio, 106 S Main St, Akron, OH 44308, USA

Hardin, Clifford M *Secretary, Agriculture*
10 Roan Lane, St Louis, MO 63124, USA

Hardin, Melora *Actress*
%William Morris Agency, 151 S El Camino Dr, Beverly Hills, CA 90212, USA

Hardin, Paul, III *Educator*
%University of North Carolina, Chancellor's Office, Chapel Hill, NC 27599, USA

Harding of Petherton, John *Army Field Marshal*
Lower Farm, Nether Compton, Sherborne, Dorset, England

Harding, John H *Businessman*
%National Life Insurance, 1 National Life Dr, Montpelier, VT 05604, USA

Harding, John Wesley *Singer*
%William Morris Agency, 1325 Ave of Americas, New York, NY 10019, USA

Harding, Peter R *Royal Air Force Marshal, England*
%Ministry of Defence, Whitehall, London SW1, England

Harding, Tonya *Figure Skater*
13610 Tarleton Court SW, Tigard, OR 97224, USA

Hardis, Stephen R *Businessman*
%Eaton Corp, Eaton Center, 1111 Superior Ave, Cleveland, OH 44114, USA

Hardison, Kadeem *Actor*
19743 Valleyview Dr, Topanga, CA 90290, USA

Hardt, Eloise *Actress*
%Dale Garrick International, 8831 Sunset Blvd, #402, Los Angeles, CA 90069, USA

Hardwick, Billy *Bowler*
1576 S White Station, Memphis, TN 38117, USA

Hardwick, Elizabeth *Writer*
15 W 67th St, New York, NY 10023, USA

Hardy, Francoise *Singer, Songwriter*
13 Rue Halle, 75014 Paris, France

Hardy, Hugh *Architect*
%Hardy Holzman Pfeiffer, 902 Broadway, New York, NY 10010, USA

Hardy, Robert *Actor*
Upper Bolney House, Upper Bolney, Henley-on-Thames, Oxon RG9 4AQ, England

Hardymon, James F *Businessman*
%Textron Inc, 10 Dorrance St, Providence, RI 02903, USA

Hare, David *Playwright*
95 Linden Gardens, London WC2, England

Harewood, Dorian *Actor*
1289 S Oak Knoll Ave, Pasadena, CA 91106, USA

Hargis, Billy James *Clergyman*
Rose of Sharon Farm, Neosho, MO 64850, USA

Hargitay, Mariska *Actress*
9274 Warbler Way, Los Angeles, CA 90069, USA

Hargrove, D Michael (Mike) *Baseball Player, Manager*
%Cleveland Indians, Cleveland Stadium, Cleveland, OH 44114, USA

Hargrove, Roy *Jazz Trumpeter*
%Verve Records, Worldwide Plaza, 825 8th Ave, New York, NY 10019, USA

Haring, Robert W *Editor*
%Tulsa World, Editorial Dept, 315 S Boulder Ave, Tulsa, OK 74103, USA

Hariri, Rafiq Al- *Prime Minister, Lebanon*
%Prime Minister's Office, Serail, Place de L'Etoile, Beirut, Lebanon

Harker, David *Biophysicist*
56 Lexington Ave, Buffalo, NY 14222, USA

Harkin, Ruth R *Financier*
%Overseas Private Investment Corp, 1100 New York Ave NW, Washington, DC 20527, USA

Harkness, Rebekah — *Philanthropist, Ballet Director*
4 E 75th St, New York, NY 10021, USA

Harlan, Jack R — *Plant Geneticist*
1016 N Hagan St, New Orleans, LA 70119, USA

Harlan, Kevin — *Sportscaster*
%Fox TV, Sports Dept, PO Box 900, Beverly Hills, CA 90213, USA

Harlan, Leonard M — *Financier*
%Castle Harlan Inc, 150 E 58th St, New York, NY 10155, USA

Harlan, Neil E — *Businessman*
1170 Sacramento St, #13-D, San Francisco, CA 94108, USA

Harlin, Renny — *Movie Director*
%Midnight Sun Pictures, 8800 Sunset Blvd, #400, Los Angeles, CA 90069, USA

Harling, C Gene — *Financier*
%First Federal Michigan Corp, 1001 Woodward Ave, Detroit, MI 48226, USA

Harman, Gilbert H — *Philosopher*
106 Broadmead St, Princeton, NJ 08540, USA

Harman, Sidney — *Businessman*
%Harman International Industries, 1155 Connecticut Ave NW, Washington, DC 20036, USA

Harmon, James A — *Financier*
%Wertheim Schroder Co, Equitable Center, 787 7th Ave, New York, NY 10019, USA

Harmon, Kelly — *Actress*
13224 Old Oak Lane, Los Angeles, CA 90049, USA

Harmon, Mark — *Actor*
%Wings Inc, 2236 Encinitas Blvd, #A, Encinitas, CA 92024, USA

Harmon, Merle — *Sportscaster*
424 Lamar Blvd E, #210, Arlington, TX 76011, USA

Harness, William E — *Opera Singer*
2132 W 235th Place, Torrance, CA 90501, USA

Harnett, Gordon D — *Businessman*
%Brush Wellman Inc, 17876 St Clair Ave, Cleveland, OH 44110, USA

Harney, Paul — *Golfer*
72 Club Valley Dr, East Falmouth, MA 02536, USA

Harnick, Sheldon M — *Lyricist*
%Kraft Haiken Bell, 551 5th Ave, #900, New York, NY 10176, USA

Harnoncourt, Nikolaus — *Conductor*
38 Piarlstangasse, 1080 Vienna, Austria

Harnoy, Ofra — *Concert Cellist*
122 Alfred Ave, Willowdale ON M2N 3H9, Canada

Haroian, Gary E — *Businessman*
%Stratus Computer, 55 Fairbanks Blvd, Marlboro, MA 01752, USA

Harout, Magda — *Actress*
13452 Vose St, Van Nuys, CA 91405, USA

Harper, Alvin — *Football Player*
%Tampa Bay Buccaneers, 1 Buccaneer Place, Tampa, FL 33607, USA

Harper, Chandler — *Golfer*
4412 Gannon Rd, Portsmouth, VA 23703, USA

Harper, Charles M — *Businessman*
%RJR Nabisco Holdings, 1301 Ave of Americas, New York, NY 10019, USA

Harper, Craig — *Basketball Player*
%Chicago Bulls, 1901 W Madison St, Chicago, IL 60612, USA

Harper, Derek — *Basketball Player*
%New York Knicks, Madison Square Garden, 4 Penn Plaza, New York, NY 10001, USA

Harper, Heather M — *Opera Singer*
20 Milverton Rd, London NW6 7AS, England

Harper, Jessica — *Actress*
3454 Glorietta Place, Sherman Oaks, CA 91423, USA

Harper, Judson M — *Chemical Engineer*
1818 Westview Rd, Fort Collins, CO 80524, USA

Harper, Ron — *Basketball Player*
%Chicago Bulls, 1901 W Madison St, Chicago, IL 60612, USA

Harper, Tess — *Actress*
2271 Betty Lane, Beverly Hills, CA 90210, USA

Harper, Valerie — *Actress*
616 N Maple Dr, Beverly Hills, CA 90210, USA

Harrah, Colbert D (Toby) — *Baseball Player*
6120 Ten Mile Bridge Rd, Fort Worth, TX 76135, USA

Harrar, J George — *Nutritionist*
125 Puritan Dr, Scarsdale, NY 10583, USA

H

Harkness - Harrar

Harrell, Henry H *Businessman*
%Universal Corp, 1501 N Hamilton St, Richmond, VA 23230, USA

Harrell, James A *Geologist*
%University of Toledo, Geology Dept, Toledo, OH 43606, USA

Harrell, Lynn M *Concert Cellist*
%International Management Group, 22 E 71st St, New York, NY 10021, USA

Harrelson, Derrell M (Bud) *Baseball Player, Manager*
25 Falcon Dr, Hauppauge, NY 11788, USA

Harrelson, Kenneth S (Ken) *Baseball Player*
150 Crossways Park W, Woodbury, NY 11797, USA

Harrelson, Woody *Actor*
10780 Santa Monica Blvd, #280, Los Angeles, CA 90025, USA

Harrick, Jim *Basketball Coach*
%University of California, Athletic Dept, Pauley Pavilion, Los Angeles, CA 90024, USA

Harriman, Pamela D C *Diplomat*
%US Embassy, PSC 166, APO, AE 09777, USA

Harrington, Donald J *Educator*
%St John's University, President's Office, Jamaica, NY 11439, USA

Harrington, Pat *Actor*
730 Marzella Ave, Los Angeles, CA 90049, USA

Harris, Arthur T *Royal Air Force Marshal, England*
Ferry House, Goring-on-Thames RG8 9DX, England

Harris, Barbara *Actress*
823 W Montrose Ave, #100, Chicago, IL 60613, USA

Harris, Barbara C *Religious Leader*
%Episcopal Diocese of Massachusetts, 138 Tremont St, Boston, MA 02111, USA

Harris, Bernard A, Jr *Astronaut*
%NASA, Johnson Space Center, 2101 NASA Rd, Houston, TX 77058, USA

Harris, Bill *Movie Critic*
12747 Riverside Dr, #208, Valley Village, CA 91607, USA

Harris, Chauncy D *Geographer*
5649 S Blackstone Ave, Chicago, IL 60637, USA

Harris, Cliff *Football Player*
%Penta Exploration Co, 6820 LBJ Freeway, #140, Dallas, TX 75240, USA

Harris, D George *Businessman*
399 Park Ave, #3200, New York, NY 10022, USA

Harris, Ed *Actor*
%Creative Artists Agency, 9830 Wilshire Blvd, Beverly Hills, CA 90212, USA

Harris, Eddie *Jazz Saxophonist*
%Vonlo Inc, PO Box 45614, Los Angeles, CA 90045, USA

Harris, Emmylou *Singer*
PO Box 158568, Nashville, TN 37215, USA

Harris, Franco *Football Player*
995 Greentree Rd, Pittsburgh, PA 15220, USA

Harris, Irving B *Businessman*
%Pittway Corp, 200 S Wacker Dr, Chicago, IL 60606, USA

Harris, Joe Frank *Governor, GA*
712 West Ave, Cartersville, GA 30120, USA

Harris, John R *Architect*
24 Devonshire Place, London W1N 2BX, England

Harris, Jonathan *Actor*
16830 Marmaduke Pl, Encino, CA 91436, USA

Harris, Julie *Actress*
132 Barn Hill Rd, West Chatham, MA 02669, USA

Harris, King W *Businessman*
%Pittway Corp, 200 S Wacker Dr, Chicago, IL 60606, USA

Harris, Lew *Editor*
%Los Angeles Magazine, 1888 Century Park East, Los Angeles, CA 90067, USA

Harris, Louis *Statistician*
%Louis Harris Research, 152 E 38th St, New York, NY 10016, USA

Harris, Mel *Actress*
%Gersh Agency, 232 N Canon Dr, Beverly Hills, CA 90210, USA

Harris, Neil Patrick *Actor*
13351 Riverside Dr, #D-450, Sherman Oaks, CA 91423, USA

Harris, Neison *Businessman*
%Pittway Corp, 200 S Wacker Dr, Chicago, IL 60606, USA

Harris, Nelson G *Businessman*
%American Water Works Co, 1025 Laurel Oak Rd, Voorhees, NJ 08043, USA

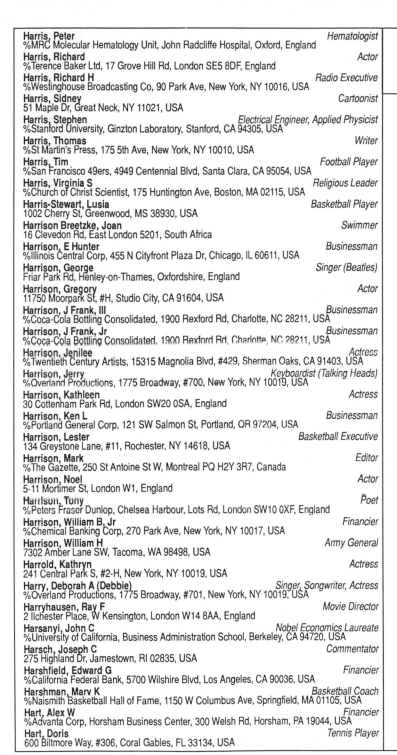

Harris, Peter *Hematologist*
%MRC Molecular Hematology Unit, John Radcliffe Hospital, Oxford, England

Harris, Richard *Actor*
%Terence Baker Ltd, 17 Grove Hill Rd, London SE5 8DF, England

Harris, Richard H *Radio Executive*
%Westinghouse Broadcasting Co, 90 Park Ave, New York, NY 10016, USA

Harris, Sidney *Cartoonist*
51 Maple Dr, Great Neck, NY 11021, USA

Harris, Stephen *Electrical Engineer, Applied Physicist*
%Stanford University, Ginzton Laboratory, Stanford, CA 94305, USA

Harris, Thomas *Writer*
%St Martin's Press, 175 5th Ave, New York, NY 10010, USA

Harris, Tim *Football Player*
%San Francisco 49ers, 4949 Centennial Blvd, Santa Clara, CA 95054, USA

Harris, Virginia S *Religious Leader*
%Church of Christ Scientist, 175 Huntington Ave, Boston, MA 02115, USA

Harris-Stewart, Lusia *Basketball Player*
1002 Cherry St, Greenwood, MS 38930, USA

Harrison Breetzke, Joan *Swimmer*
16 Clevedon Rd, East London 5201, South Africa

Harrison, E Hunter *Businessman*
%Illinois Central Corp, 455 N Cityfront Plaza Dr, Chicago, IL 60611, USA

Harrison, George *Singer (Beatles)*
Friar Park Rd, Henley-on-Thames, Oxfordshire, England

Harrison, Gregory *Actor*
11750 Moorpark St, #H, Studio City, CA 91604, USA

Harrison, J Frank, III *Businessman*
%Coca-Cola Bottling Consolidated, 1900 Rexford Rd, Charlotte, NC 28211, USA

Harrison, J Frank, Jr *Businessman*
%Coca-Cola Bottling Consolidated, 1900 Rexford Rd, Charlotte, NC 28211, USA

Harrison, Jenilee *Actress*
%Twentieth Century Artists, 15315 Magnolia Blvd, #429, Sherman Oaks, CA 91403, USA

Harrison, Jerry *Keyboardist (Talking Heads)*
%Overland Productions, 1775 Broadway, #700, New York, NY 10019, USA

Harrison, Kathleen *Actress*
30 Cottenham Park Rd, London SW20 0SA, England

Harrison, Ken L *Businessman*
%Portland General Corp, 121 SW Salmon St, Portland, OR 97204, USA

Harrison, Lester *Basketball Executive*
134 Greystone Lane, #11, Rochester, NY 14618, USA

Harrison, Mark *Editor*
%The Gazette, 250 St Antoine St W, Montreal PQ H2Y 3R7, Canada

Harrison, Noel *Actor*
5-11 Mortimer St, London W1, England

Harrison, Tony *Poet*
%Peters Fraser Dunlop, Chelsea Harbour, Lots Rd, London SW10 0XF, England

Harrison, William B, Jr *Financier*
%Chemical Banking Corp, 270 Park Ave, New York, NY 10017, USA

Harrison, William H *Army General*
7302 Amber Lane SW, Tacoma, WA 98498, USA

Harrold, Kathryn *Actress*
241 Central Park S, #2-H, New York, NY 10019, USA

Harry, Deborah A (Debbie) *Singer, Songwriter, Actress*
%Overland Productions, 1775 Broadway, #701, New York, NY 10019, USA

Harryhausen, Ray F *Movie Director*
2 Ilchester Place, W Kensington, London W14 8AA, England

Harsanyi, John C *Nobel Economics Laureate*
%University of California, Business Administration School, Berkeley, CA 94720, USA

Harsch, Joseph C *Commentator*
275 Highland Dr, Jamestown, RI 02835, USA

Harshfield, Edward G *Financier*
%California Federal Bank, 5700 Wilshire Blvd, Los Angeles, CA 90036, USA

Harshman, Marv K *Basketball Coach*
%Naismith Basketball Hall of Fame, 1150 W Columbus Ave, Springfield, MA 01105, USA

Hart, Alex W *Financier*
%Advanta Corp, Horsham Business Center, 300 Welsh Rd, Horsham, PA 19044, USA

Hart, Doris *Tennis Player*
600 Biltmore Way, #306, Coral Gables, FL 33134, USA

H

Harris - Hart

Hart, Freddie — *Singer, Guitarist, Songwriter*
%Richard Davis Mgmt, 1030 N Woodland Dr, Kansas City, MO 64118, USA

Hart, Gary W — *Senator, CO*
9785 S Maroon Circle, #210, Englewood, CO 80112, USA

Hart, H L A — *Solicitor*
11 Manor Place, Oxford, England

Hart, James W (Jim) — *Football Player, Sports Administrator*
Rt 6, Box 21, Brush Hill, Carbondale, IL 62901, USA

Hart, John — *Actor*
35109 Highway 79, #134, Warner Springs, CA 92086, USA

Hart, John L (Johnny) — *Cartoonist (BC, Wizard of Id)*
%Creators Syndicate, 5777 W Century Blvd, #700, Los Angeles, CA 90045, USA

Hart, John R — *Commentator*
%International Creative Mgmt, 40 W 57th St, New York, NY 10019, USA

Hart, Larry M — *Businessman*
%International Technology Corp, 23456 Hawthorne Blvd, Torrance, CA 90505, USA

Hart, Leon J — *Football Player*
3904 Cotton Tail Lane, Birmingham, MI 48301, USA

Hart, Mary — *Entertainer*
150 S El Camino Dr, #303, Beverly Hills, CA 90212, USA

Hart, Mickey — *Drummer (Grateful Dead)*
PO Box 1073, San Rafael, CA 94915, USA

Hart, Parker T — *Diplomat*
4705 Berkeley Terrace NW, Washington, DC 20007, USA

Hart, Roxanne — *Actress*
%International Creative Mgmt, 8942 Wilshire Blvd, Beverly Hills, CA 90211, USA

Hart, Stanley R — *Geologist*
53 Quonset Rd, Falmouth, MA 02540, USA

Hart, Terry J — *Astronaut*
47 Parker Dr, Morris Plaines, NJ 07950, USA

Harte, Houston H — *Publisher*
%Harte-Hanks Communications, 200 Concord Plaza Dr, San Antonio, TX 78216, USA

Harter, Carol C — *Educator*
%State University of New York, President's Office, Genesco, NY 14454, USA

Hartford, John C — *Singer, Songwriter*
PO Box 443, Madison, TN 37116, USA

Harth, Sidney — *Concert Violinist*
135 Westland Dr, Pittsburgh, PA 15217, USA

Hartigan, Grace — *Artist*
1701 1/2 Eastern Ave, Baltimore, MD 21231, USA

Hartke, Vance — *Senator, IN*
%Hartke & Hartke, 7637 Leesburg Pike, Falls Church, VA 22043, USA

Hartley, Harry J — *Educator*
%University of Connecticut, President's Office, Storrs, CT 06269, USA

Hartley, John T, Jr — *Businessman*
%Harris Corp, 1025 W NASA Blvd, Melbourne, FL 32919, USA

Hartley, Mariette — *Actress*
10110 Empryian Way, #304, Los Angeles, CA 90067, USA

Hartley-Leonard, Darryl — *Businessman*
%Hyatt Hotels & Resorts, 200 W Madison Ave, Chicago, IL 60606, USA

Hartling, Poul — *Prime Minister, Denmark*
Emilievej 6E, 2920 Charlottenlund, Denmark

Hartman Black, Lisa — *Actress*
8606 Allenwood Rd, Los Angeles, CA 90046, USA

Hartman, Arthur A — *Diplomat*
2738 McKinley St NW, Washington, DC 20015, USA

Hartman, David — *Actor, Commentator*
%Trascott Alyson Craig, 222 Cedar Lane, Teaneck, NJ 07666, USA

Hartman, George E — *Architect*
3525 Hamlet Place, Bethesda, MD 20815, USA

Hartman, Phil — *Comedian*
%"NewsRadio" Show, NBC-TV, 3000 W Alameda Ave, Burbank, CA 91523, USA

Hartman, William C (Bill), Jr — *Football Player*
%National Life of Vermont, 1160 S Milledge Ave, #220, Athens, GA 30605, USA

Hartmann, Frederick W — *Editor*
%Florida Times-Union, Editorial Dept, 1 Riverside Ave, Jacksonville, FL 32202, USA

Hartmann, Robert T — *Government Official*
5001 Baltimore Ave, Bethesda, MD 20816, USA

Hart - Hartmann

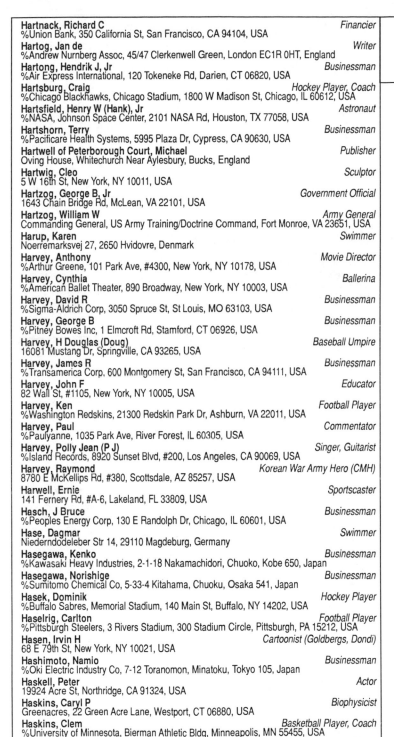

Hartnack, Richard C — *Financier*
%Union Bank, 350 California St, San Francisco, CA 94104, USA

Hartog, Jan de — *Writer*
%Andrew Nurnberg Assoc, 45/47 Clerkenwell Green, London EC1R 0HT, England

Hartong, Hendrik J, Jr — *Businessman*
%Air Express International, 120 Tokeneke Rd, Darien, CT 06820, USA

Hartsburg, Craig — *Hockey Player, Coach*
%Chicago Blackhawks, Chicago Stadium, 1800 W Madison St, Chicago, IL 60612, USA

Hartsfield, Henry W (Hank), Jr — *Astronaut*
%NASA, Johnson Space Center, 2101 NASA Rd, Houston, TX 77058, USA

Hartshorn, Terry — *Businessman*
%Pacificare Health Systems, 5995 Plaza Dr, Cypress, CA 90630, USA

Hartwell of Peterborough Court, Michael — *Publisher*
Oving House, Whitechurch Near Aylesbury, Bucks, England

Hartwig, Cleo — *Sculptor*
5 W 16th St, New York, NY 10011, USA

Hartzog, George B, Jr — *Government Official*
1643 Chain Bridge Rd, McLean, VA 22101, USA

Hartzog, William W — *Army General*
Commanding General, US Army Training/Doctrine Command, Fort Monroe, VA 23651, USA

Harup, Karen — *Swimmer*
Noerremarksvej 27, 2650 Hvidovre, Denmark

Harvey, Anthony — *Movie Director*
%Arthur Greene, 101 Park Ave, #4300, New York, NY 10178, USA

Harvey, Cynthia — *Ballerina*
%American Ballet Theater, 890 Broadway, New York, NY 10003, USA

Harvey, David R — *Businessman*
%Sigma-Aldrich Corp, 3050 Spruce St, St Louis, MO 63103, USA

Harvey, George B — *Businessman*
%Pitney Bowes Inc, 1 Elmcroft Rd, Stamford, CT 06926, USA

Harvey, H Douglas (Doug) — *Baseball Umpire*
16081 Mustang Dr, Springville, CA 93265, USA

Harvey, James R — *Businessman*
%Transamerica Corp, 600 Montgomery St, San Francisco, CA 94111, USA

Harvey, John F — *Educator*
82 Wall St, #1105, New York, NY 10005, USA

Harvey, Ken — *Football Player*
%Washington Redskins, 21300 Redskin Park Dr, Ashburn, VA 22011, USA

Harvey, Paul — *Commentator*
%Paulyanne, 1035 Park Ave, River Forest, IL 60305, USA

Harvey, Polly Jean (P J) — *Singer, Guitarist*
%Island Records, 8920 Sunset Blvd, #200, Los Angeles, CA 90069, USA

Harvey, Raymond — *Korean War Army Hero (CMH)*
8780 E McKellips Rd, #380, Scottsdale, AZ 85257, USA

Harwell, Ernie — *Sportscaster*
141 Fernery Rd, #A-6, Lakeland, FL 33809, USA

Hasch, J Bruce — *Businessman*
%Peoples Energy Corp, 130 E Randolph Dr, Chicago, IL 60601, USA

Hase, Dagmar — *Swimmer*
Niederndodeleber Str 14, 29110 Magdeburg, Germany

Hasegawa, Kenko — *Businessman*
%Kawasaki Heavy Industries, 2-1-18 Nakamachidori, Chuoko, Kobe 650, Japan

Hasegawa, Norishige — *Businessman*
%Sumitomo Chemical Co, 5-33-4 Kitahama, Chuoku, Osaka 541, Japan

Hasek, Dominik — *Hockey Player*
%Buffalo Sabres, Memorial Stadium, 140 Main St, Buffalo, NY 14202, USA

Haselrig, Carlton — *Football Player*
%Pittsburgh Steelers, 3 Rivers Stadium, 300 Stadium Circle, Pittsburgh, PA 15212, USA

Hasen, Irvin H — *Cartoonist (Goldbergs, Dondi)*
68 E 79th St, New York, NY 10021, USA

Hashimoto, Namio — *Businessman*
%Oki Electric Industry Co, 7-12 Toranomon, Minatoku, Tokyo 105, Japan

Haskell, Peter — *Actor*
19924 Acre St, Northridge, CA 91324, USA

Haskins, Caryl P — *Biophysicist*
Greenacres, 22 Green Acre Lane, Westport, CT 06880, USA

Haskins, Clem — *Basketball Player, Coach*
%University of Minnesota, Bierman Athletic Bldg, Minneapolis, MN 55455, USA

H

Hartnack - Haskins

H

Haskins, Don — *Basketball Coach*
%University of Texas, Athletic Dept, El Paso, TX 79968, USA

Haskins, Sam — *Photographer*
PO Box 59, Wimbledon, London SW19, England

Haslam of Bolton, Robert — *Businessman*
%British Steel Corp, 9 Albert Embankment, London SE1 7SN, England

Hasler, Arthur D — *Zoologist*
1233 Sweet Briar Bd, Madison, WI 53705, USA

Hasluck, Paul M C — *Government Official, Australia*
2 Adams Rd, Dalkeith WA 6009, Australia

Hass, Robert — *Poet*
%University of California, English Dept, Berkeley, CA 94720, USA

Hassan Ibn Talal — *Crown Prince, Jordan*
%Crown Prince's Office, Royal Palace, Amman, Jordan

Hassan II — *King, Morocco*
%Royal Palais, Rabat, Morocco

Hassanali, Noor Mohamed — *President, Trinidad & Tobago*
%President's House, St Ann's, Port of Spain, Trinidad & Tobago

Hassel, Odd — *Nobel Chemistry Laureate*
Holsteinveien 10, Oslo 8, Norway

Hasselhoff, David — *Actor*
11342 Dona Lisa Dr, Studio City, CA 91604, USA

Hasselmo, Nils — *Educator*
%University of Minnesota, President's Office, Minneapolis, MN 55455, USA

Hassenfeld, Alan G — *Businessman*
%Hasbro Inc, 1027 Newport Ave, Pawtucket, RI 02861, USA

Hassett, Marilyn — *Actress*
%Contemporary Artists, 1427 3rd St Promenade, #205, Santa Monica, CA 90401, USA

Hasso, Signe — *Actress*
582 S Orange Grove Ave, Los Angeles, CA 90036, USA

Hasson, Maurice — *Concert Violinist*
18 West Heath Court, North End Rd, London NW11, England

Hast, Adele — *Editor*
%Newberry Library, 60 W Walton St, Chicago, IL 60610, USA

Hastings, A Baird — *Chemist*
233 Prospect Ave, La Jolla, CA 92037, USA

Hastings, Barry G — *Financier*
%Northern Trust Corp, 50 S LaSalle St, Chicago, IL 60603, USA

Hastings, Don — *Actor*
%Schneiderman Assoc, 400 Park Ave, New York, NY 10022, USA

Hatakeyama, Seiji — *Businessman*
%EBARA Corp, 11-1 Hanedacho, Otaku, Tokyo 144, Japan

Hatch, Harold A — *Marine Corps General*
8655 White Beach Way, Vienna, VA 22182, USA

Hatch, Henry J — *Army General*
%Law Cos International Group, 1000 Abernathy Rd NE, Atlanta, GA 30328, USA

Hatch, Monroe W, Jr — *Air Force General*
%Air Force Assn, 1501 Lee Highway, Arlington, VA 22209, USA

Hatch, Richard — *Actor*
12304 Santa Monica Blvd, #140, Los Angeles, CA 90025, USA

Hatch, Robert W — *Businessman*
%Mohasco Corp, 4401 Fair Lakes Court, Fairfax, VA 22033, USA

Hatchell, Sylvia — *Basketball Coach*
%University of North Carolina, Athletic Dept, Chapel Hill, NC 27515, USA

Hatcher, Kevin — *Hockey Player*
%Dallas Stars, 211 Cowboys Parkway, Irving, TX, USA

Hatcher, Teri — *Actress*
PO Box 1101, Sunland, CA 91041, USA

Hatfield, Bobby — *Singer (Righteous Brothers)*
1824 Port Wheeler Dr, Newport Beach, CA 92660, USA

Hatfield, Hurd — *Actor*
Ballinterry House, Rathcormac, County Cork, Ireland

Hatfield, James E — *Labor Leader*
%Glass Pottery & Plastics Union, 608 E Baltimore Pike, Media, PA 19063, USA

Hatfield, Juliana — *Singer*
%Geronimo Mgmt, 1 Camp St, #2, Cambridge, MA 02140, USA

Hathaway, Charles G — *Businessman*
%Southern Farm Bureau Life Insurance, PO Box 78, Jackson, MS 39205, USA

Hathaway, Derek C *Businessman*
%Harsco Corp, PO Box 8888, Camp Hill, PA 17001, USA

Hathaway, Stanley K *Secretary, Interior; Governor, WY*
2424 Pioneer Ave, Cheyenne, WY 82001, USA

Hathaway, William D *Senator, ME*
80 Orchard St, Auburn, ME 04210, USA

Hatsopoulos, George N *Businessman*
%Thermo Electron Corp, 81 Wyman St, Waltham, MA 02154, USA

Hatten, Tom *Actor*
1759 Sunset Plaza Dr, Los Angeles, CA 90069, USA

Hattersley, Roy S G *Government Official, England*
%House of Commons, Westminster, London SW1A 0AA, England

Hattestad, Stine Lise *Moguls Skier*
Sundlia 1-B, 1315 Nesoya, Norway

Hattori, Kunio *Businessman*
%Bridgestone Tire Co, 1-10-1 Kyobashi, Chuoku, Tokyo 104, Japan

Hauck, Frederick H (Rick) *Astronaut*
1437 Foxhall Rd NW, Washington, DC 20007, USA

Hauer, Rutger *Actor*
%William Morris Agency, 151 S El Camino Dr, Beverly Hills, CA 90212, USA

Haugen, Richard M *Businessman*
%Allergan Inc, 2525 DuPont Dr, Irvine, CA 92715, USA

Haughey, Charles J *Prime Minister, Ireland*
Abbeville, Kinsakey, Malahide County Dublin, Ireland

Haugland, Aage *Opera Singer*
Skovbrinken 7, 3450 Allerod, Denmark

Hauptfuhrer, Robert P *Businessman*
602 Old Eagle Rd, Wayne, PA 19087, USA

Hauptman, Herbert A *Nobel Chemistry Laureate*
%Medical Foundation of Buffalo, 73 High St, Buffalo, NY 14203, USA

Hauptman, Michael *Radio Executive*
13 Carriage Rd, Cos Cob, CT 06807, USA

Haurwitz, Bernhard *Meteorologist*
%Colorado State University, Atmospheric Science Dept, Fort Collins, CO 80523, USA

Hauser, Erich *Sculptor*
78628 Rottweil-Wurtt, Germany

Hauser, Tim *Singer (Manhattan Transfer)*
3855 Lankershim Blvd, #214, North Hollywood, CA 91604, USA

Hauser, Wings *Actor*
14126 Marquesas Way, Marina del Rey, CA 90292, USA

Hausman, Jerry A *Economist*
%Massachusetts Institute of Technology, Economics Dept, Cambridge, MA 02139, USA

Hauspurg, Arthur *Businessman*
%Consolidated Edison of New York, 4 Irving Place, New York, NY 10003, USA

Havel, Richard J *Physician*
PO Box 1791, Ross, CA 94957, USA

Havel, Vaclav *President, Czech Republic; Playwright*
%Kancelar Prezidenta Republiky, Hradecek, 119 08 Prague 1, Czech Republic

Havelange, Jean M F G (Joao) *Soccer Executive*
Rua Prudente de Maroes 1700, #1001, 20420-042 Rio de Janiero, Brazil

Havens, Richie *Singer*
%Wolfson, 123 W 44th St, New York, NY 10036, USA

Haver, June *Actress*
485 Halvern Dr, Los Angeles, CA 90049, USA

Havers, Nigel *Actor*
%Michael Whitehall, 125 Gloucester Rd, London SW7 4TE, England

Haverty, Harold V *Businessman*
%Deluxe Corp, 1080 W Country Rd "F", St Paul, MN 55126, USA

Havighurst, Clark C *Attorney, Educator*
3610 Dover Rd, Durham, NC 27707, USA

Havlicek, John *Basketball Player*
24 Beech Rd, Weston, MA 02193, USA

Havoc, June *Actress*
405 Old Long Ridge Rd, Stamford, CT 06903, USA

Hawerchuk, Dale *Hockey Player*
%St Louis Blues, St Louis Arena, 5700 Oakland Ave, St Louis, MO 63110, USA

Hawk, John D *WW II Army Hero (CMH)*
3243 Solie Ave, Bremerton, WA 98310, USA

Hawke, Ethan — *Actor*
%Creative Artists Agency, 9830 Wilshire Blvd, Beverly Hills, CA 90212, USA

Hawke, Robert J L — *Prime Minister, Australia*
Westfield Towers, #1300, 100 William St, Sydney NSW 2000, Australia

Hawkes, Christopher — *Archaeologist*
19 Walton St, Oxford OX1 2HQ, England

Hawkes, Jacquetta — *Archaeologist*
Littlecote, Leysbourne, Chipping Campden, Glos GL55 6HL, England

Hawkes, John — *Writer*
18 Everett Ave, Providence, RI 02906, USA

Hawking, Stephen W — *Theoretical Physicist*
%University of Cambridge, Applied Math Dept, Cambridge CB3 9EW, England

Hawkins, Connie — *Basketball Player*
%Phoenix Suns, 201 E Jefferson St, Phoenix, AZ 85004, USA

Hawkins, Edwin — *Vocal Group Leader*
%PAZ Entertainment, 2041 Locust St, Philadelphia, PA 19103, USA

Hawkins, Hersey — *Basketball Player*
%Seattle Supersonics, 190 Queen Ave N, PO Box C-900911, Seattle, WA 98109, USA

Hawkins, M Andrew (Andy) — *Baseball Player*
PO Box 8812, Waco, TX 76714, USA

Hawkins, Paula — *Senator, FL*
1214 Park Ave N, Winter Park, FL 32789, USA

Hawkins, Ronnie — *Singer*
%Backstage Productions, 1-3015 Kennedy Rd, Scarborough ON M1V 1E7, Canada

Hawkins, Sophie B — *Singer*
550 Madison Ave, #2500, New York, NY 10022, USA

Hawkins, Tommy — *Basketball Player*
2445 Banyon Dr, Los Angeles, CA 90049, USA

Hawley, Frank J, Jr — *Businessman*
%Morgan Products, 75 Tri-State International Building, Lincolnshire, IL 60069, USA

Hawley, Michael C — *Businessman*
%Gillette Co, Prudential Tower Building, Boston, MA 02199, USA

Hawley, Richard E (Dick) — *Air Force General*
SAF/Air Force Acquisitions, 1060 Air Force Pentagon, Washington, DC 20330, USA

Hawley, Samuel W — *Financier*
%People's Bank, 850 Main St, Bridgeport, CT 06604, USA

Hawley, Steven A — *Astronaut*
3929 Walnut Pond Dr, Houston, TX 77059, USA

Hawn, Goldie — *Actress*
%Hawn-Sylbert Co, 500 S Buena Vista St, #10-D-06, Burbank, CA 91521, USA

Haworth, Jill — *Actress*
300 E 51st St, New York, NY 10022, USA

Haworth, Lionel — *Aeronautical Engineer*
10 Hazelwood Rd, Sneryd Park, Bristol BS9 1PX, England

Hawpe, David V — *Editor*
%Louisville Courier-Journal, 525 W Broadway, Louisville, KY 40202, USA

Hawthorne, Nigel — *Actor*
Radwell Grange Near Radwell, Baldock, Herts SG7 5EU, England

Hawthorne, William — *Thermodynamics Engineer*
%Churchill College, Engineering School, Cambridge CB3 0DS, England

Hay, Alexandra — *Actress*
20910 Bandera St, Woodland Hills, CA 91364, USA

Hay, Andrew O — *Businessman*
2 Glen Rd, Toorak, VIC 3142, Australia

Hay, Raymond A — *Businessman*
%LTV Corp, 25 W Prospect Ave, Cleveland, OH 44115, USA

Hayden, J Michael (Mike) — *Governor, KS*
%E C Mellick Agency, 406 State St, Atwood, KS 67730, USA

Hayden, Jim — *Publisher*
%Philadelphia Inquirer, 400 N Broad St, Philadelphia, PA 19130, USA

Hayden, Neil Steven — *Publisher*
749 Rivenwood Rd, Franklin Lakes, NJ 07417, USA

Hayden, Tom — *Political Activist (Chicago 7)*
152 Wadsworth, Santa Monica, CA 90405, USA

Hayden, William G — *Governor General, Australia*
16 East St, Ipswich, QLD 4305, Australia

Hayden, William J — *Businessman*
%Jaguar Cars Ltd, Browns Lane, Coventry, West Midlands CV5 9DR, England

Hawke - Hayden

Haydon Jones, Ann *Tennis Player*
85 Westerfield Rd, Edgloaston, Birmingham 15, England

Hayes, Bill *Actor*
4528 Beck Ave, North Hollywood, CA 91602, USA

Hayes, Bob *Football Player, Track Athlete*
%Staubach Co, 6750 LBJ Freeway, #1100, Dallas, TX 75240, USA

Hayes, Charles A *Businessman*
%Guilford Mills Inc, 4925 W Market St, Greensboro, NC 27407, USA

Hayes, Denis A *Environmentalist*
%Green Seal, PO Box 18237, Washington, DC 20036, USA

Hayes, Dennis C *Engineer, Co-Inventor (Modem)*
%Hayes Microcomputer Products, PO Box 105203, Atlanta, GA 30348, USA

Hayes, Elvin *Basketball Player*
%Great Cleveland Ford-Mercury, PO Box 148, Cleveland, TX 77328, USA

Hayes, Isaac *Composer*
PO Box 674891, Marietta, GA 30067, USA

Hayes, John B *Coast Guard Admiral*
%Coast Guard Headquarters, 2100 2nd St SW, Washington, DC 20593, USA

Hayes, John E, Jr *Businessman*
%Western Resources, 818 Kansas Ave, Topeka, KS 66601, USA

Hayes, John P *Economist*
51 Enfield Rd, Brentford, Middx TW8 9PA, England

Hayes, Peter Lind *Actor*
3538 Pueblo Way, Las Vegas, NV 89109, USA

Hayes, Robert M *Social Activist*
%National Coalition for the Homeless, 105 E 22nd St, New York, NY 10010, USA

Hayes, Samuel B, III *Financier*
%Boatmen's National Bank (St Louis), 800 Market St, St Louis, MO 63101, USA

Haylett, Ward *Track Coach*
%College Hills Skilled Nursing Center, 2423 Kimball Ave, Manhattan, KS 66502, USA

Haymon, Monte R *Businessman*
%Ply Gem Inc, 777 3rd Ave, New York, NY 10017, USA

Haynes, Al *Airline Pilot Hero*
4410 S 182nd St, Seattle, WA 98188, USA

Haynes, Marques *Basketball Player*
PO Box 9246, Tulsa, OK 74157, USA

Haynes, Richard *Attorney*
2701 Fannin St, Houston, TX 77002, USA

Haynie, Hugh *Editorial Cartoonist*
%Louisville Courier-Journal, 525 W Broadway, Louisville, KY 40202, USA

Haynie, Sandra *Golfer*
%Ladies Professional Golf Assn, 2570 Volusia Ave, Daytona Beach, FL 32114, USA

Hays, Robert *Actor*
%Creative Artists Agency, 9830 Wilshire Blvd, Beverly Hills, CA 90212, USA

Hays, Ronald J *Navy Admiral*
711 Kapiolani Blvd, #200, Honolulu, HI 96813, USA

Hays, Thomas A *Businessman*
%May Department Stores, 611 Olive St, St Louis, MO 63101, USA

Hays, Thomas C *Businessman*
%American Brands Inc, 1700 E Putnam Ave, Old Greenwich, CT 06870, USA

Hayward, Charles E *Publisher*
%Little Brown Co, Time-Life Building, Rockefeller Center, New York, NY 10020, USA

Hayward, Justin *Singer, Songwriter (Moody Blues)*
%Wolfman Jack Entertainment, Rt 1, PO Box 56, Belvidere, NC 27919, USA

Hayward, Thomas B *Navy Admiral*
1556 Aulena Place, Honolulu, HI 96821, USA

Hayward-Surry, Jeremy *Businessman*
%Pall Corp, 2200 Northern Blvd, East Hills, NY 11548, USA

Haza, Ofra *Singer*
%Warner Bros Records, 75 Rockefeller Plaza, New York, NY 10019, USA

Hazen, Paul M *Financier*
%Wells Fargo Co, 420 Montgomery St, San Francisco, CA 94104, USA

Hazzard, Shirley *Writer*
200 E 66th St, New York, NY 10021, USA

He Kang *Government Official, China*
%Agriculture Ministry, Nun Zen Nan Li, Beijing, China

He Xiaohua *Writer*
%China Federation of Literature & Art, Beijing, China

Heacock, Raymond L _Space Engineer_
%Jet Propulsion Laboratory, 4800 Oak Grove Dr, Pasadena, CA 91109, USA

Head, G O _Financier_
%First Investors Management Co, 95 Wall St, New York, NY 10005, USA

Head, James W _Space Scientist_
%Brown University, Geological Sciences Dept, Providence, RI 02912, USA

Head, Kathryn S _Financier_
%First Investors Management Co, 95 Wall St, New York, NY 10005, USA

Headly, Glenne _Actress_
7929 Hollywood Blvd, Los Angeles, CA 90046, USA

Heagy, Thomas C _Financier_
%LaSalle National Corp, 135 S LaSalle St, Chicago, IL 60603, USA

Healey, Denis W _Government Official, England_
%House of Lords, Westminster, London SW1A 0PW, England

Healey, Derek E _Composer_
29 Stafford Rd, Ruislip Gardens, Middx H4A 6PB, England

Healey, John G _Association Executive_
%Amnesty International USA, 322 8th Ave, New York, NY 10001, USA

Healy, Bernadine P _Medical Administrator_
%Cleveland Clinic Foundation, 9500 Euclid Ave, Cleveland, OH 44106, USA

Healy, Cornelius T _Labor Leader_
%Plate Die Engravers Union, 228 S Swarthmore Ave, Ridley Park, PA 19078, USA

Healy, Jane E _Journalist_
%Orlando Sentinel, Editorial Dept, 633 N Orange Ave, Orlando, FL 32801, USA

Healy, Jeremiah _Writer_
%Pocket Books, 1230 Ave of Americas, New York, NY 10020, USA

Healy, Mary _Actress_
3538 Pueblo Way, Las Vegas, NV 89109, USA

Heaney, Robert A _Financier_
%Chase Manhattan Bank (USA), 1 Chase Manhattan Plaza, Wilmington, DE 19801, USA

Heaney, Seamus J _Nobel Literature Laureate_
%Faber & Faber, 3 Queen Square, London WC1N 3RU, England

Heaps, Alvin E _Labor Leader_
%Retail Wholesale Department Store Union, 30 E 29th St, New York, NY 10016, USA

Heard, G Alexander _Educator_
2100 Golf Club Lane, Nashville, TN 37215, USA

Heard, John _Actor_
347 W 84th St, #5, New York, NY 10024, USA

Hearn, Chick _Sportscaster_
%Los Angeles Lakers, Forum, PO Box 10, Inglewood, CA 90306, USA

Hearn, George _Actor_
200 W 57th St, #900, New York, NY 10019, USA

Hearn, J Woodrow _Religious Leader_
%United Methodist Church, PO Box 320, Nashville, TN 37202, USA

Hearn, James T (Jim) _Baseball Player_
1678 Beverly Wood Court, Chamblee, GA 30341, USA

Hearn, Thomas K, Jr _Educator_
%Wake Forest University, President's Office, Winston-Salem, NC 27109, USA

Hearnes, Warren E _Governor, MO_
PO Box 349, Rt 3, Charleston, MO 63834, USA

Hearns, Thomas _Boxer_
19785 W 12 Mile Rd, Southfield, MI 48076, USA

Hearst, George R, Jr _Publisher_
318 N Rockingham Ave, Los Angeles, CA 90049, USA

Hearst, Randolph A _Publisher_
%Hearst Corp, 959 8th Ave, New York, NY 10019, USA

Hearth, Donald P _Aeronautical Engineer_
%Langley Research Center, NASA, Hampton, VA 23665, USA

Heath, Edward R G _Prime Minister, England_
%House of Commons, Westminster, London SW1A 0AA, England

Heath, Jimmy _Jazz Saxophonist, Composer_
%Ted Kurland Assoc, 173 Brighton Ave, Boston, MA 02134, USA

Heath, Percy _Jazz Bassist (Modern Jazz Quartet)_
%Ellen Levine Mgmt, 8033 Sunset Blvd, #1037, Los Angeles, CA 90046, USA

Heath-Stubbs, John F A _Poet_
22 Artesian Rd, London W2 5AR, England

Heathcote, Jud _Basketball Coach_
%Michigan State University, Jenison Gym, East Lansing, MI 48824, USA

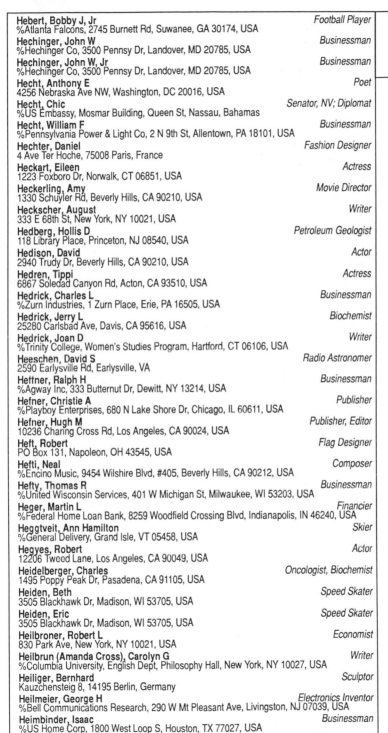

Hebert, Bobby J, Jr	*Football Player*
%Atlanta Falcons, 2745 Burnett Rd, Suwanee, GA 30174, USA	
Hechinger, John W	*Businessman*
%Hechinger Co, 3500 Pennsy Dr, Landover, MD 20785, USA	
Hechinger, John W, Jr	*Businessman*
%Hechinger Co, 3500 Pennsy Dr, Landover, MD 20785, USA	
Hecht, Anthony E	*Poet*
4256 Nebraska Ave NW, Washington, DC 20016, USA	
Hecht, Chic	*Senator, NV; Diplomat*
%US Embassy, Mosmar Building, Queen St, Nassau, Bahamas	
Hecht, William F	*Businessman*
%Pennsylvania Power & Light Co, 2 N 9th St, Allentown, PA 18101, USA	
Hechter, Daniel	*Fashion Designer*
4 Ave Ter Hoche, 75008 Paris, France	
Heckart, Eileen	*Actress*
1223 Foxboro Dr, Norwalk, CT 06851, USA	
Heckerling, Amy	*Movie Director*
1330 Schuyler Rd, Beverly Hills, CA 90210, USA	
Heckscher, August	*Writer*
333 E 68th St, New York, NY 10021, USA	
Hedberg, Hollis D	*Petroleum Geologist*
118 Library Place, Princeton, NJ 08540, USA	
Hedison, David	*Actor*
2940 Trudy Dr, Beverly Hills, CA 90210, USA	
Hedren, Tippi	*Actress*
6867 Soledad Canyon Rd, Acton, CA 93510, USA	
Hedrick, Charles L	*Businessman*
%Zurn Industries, 1 Zurn Place, Erie, PA 16505, USA	
Hedrick, Jerry L	*Biochemist*
25280 Carlsbad Ave, Davis, CA 95616, USA	
Hedrick, Joan D	*Writer*
%Trinity College, Women's Studies Program, Hartford, CT 06106, USA	
Heeschen, David S	*Radio Astronomer*
2590 Earlysville Rd, Earlysville, VA	
Heffner, Ralph H	*Businessman*
%Agway Inc, 333 Butternut Dr, Dewitt, NY 13214, USA	
Hefner, Christie A	*Publisher*
%Playboy Enterprises, 680 N Lake Shore Dr, Chicago, IL 60611, USA	
Hefner, Hugh M	*Publisher, Editor*
10236 Charing Cross Rd, Los Angeles, CA 90024, USA	
Heft, Robert	*Flag Designer*
PO Box 131, Napoleon, OH 43545, USA	
Hefti, Neal	*Composer*
%Encino Music, 9454 Wilshire Blvd, #405, Beverly Hills, CA 90212, USA	
Hefty, Thomas R	*Businessman*
%United Wisconsin Services, 401 W Michigan St, Milwaukee, WI 53203, USA	
Heger, Martin L	*Financier*
%Federal Home Loan Bank, 8259 Woodfield Crossing Blvd, Indianapolis, IN 46240, USA	
Heggtveit, Ann Hamilton	*Skier*
%General Delivery, Grand Isle, VT 05458, USA	
Hegyes, Robert	*Actor*
12206 Tweed Lane, Los Angeles, CA 90049, USA	
Heidelberger, Charles	*Oncologist, Biochemist*
1495 Poppy Peak Dr, Pasadena, CA 91105, USA	
Heiden, Beth	*Speed Skater*
3505 Blackhawk Dr, Madison, WI 53705, USA	
Heiden, Eric	*Speed Skater*
3505 Blackhawk Dr, Madison, WI 53705, USA	
Heilbroner, Robert L	*Economist*
830 Park Ave, New York, NY 10021, USA	
Heilbrun (Amanda Cross), Carolyn G	*Writer*
%Columbia University, English Dept, Philosophy Hall, New York, NY 10027, USA	
Heiliger, Bernhard	*Sculptor*
Kauzchensteig 8, 14195 Berlin, Germany	
Heilmeier, George H	*Electronics Inventor*
%Bell Communications Research, 290 W Mt Pleasant Ave, Livingston, NJ 07039, USA	
Heimbinder, Isaac	*Businessman*
%US Home Corp, 1800 West Loop S, Houston, TX 77027, USA	

H

Hebert - Heimbinder

H

Heimbold, Charles A, Jr *Businessman*
%Bristol-Myers Squibb Co, 345 Park Ave, New York, NY 10154, USA

Heimbuch, Babette *Financier*
%FirstFed Financial Corp, 401 Wilshire Blvd, Santa Monica, CA 90401, USA

Heimlich, Henry J *Physician*
%Heimlich Institute, 2368 Victory Parkway, #410, Cincinnati, OH 45206, USA

Heine, Jutta *Track Athlete*
Blaue Muhle, 57614 Burglahr, Germany

Heineken, Alfred H *Businessman*
%Heineken Holding, 2-E Weteringplantsoen 5, 1017-ZD Amsterdam, Netherlands

Heinemann, Stephen *Neurobologist*
%Salk Biological Studies Institute, 10010 N Torrey Pines Rd, La Jolla, CA 92037, USA

Heinsohn, Thomas W (Tom) *Basketball Player, Coach*
31 Columbia Ave, Newton, MA 02164, USA

Heinze, Bernard T *Conductor*
101 Victoria Rd, Bellevue Hill, Sydney NSW, Australia

Heinzer, Franz *Skier*
Lauenen, 6432 Rickenbach/Schwyz, Switzerland

Heiskell, Andrew *Publisher*
870 United Nations Plaza, New York, NY 10017, USA

Heisley, Michael E *Businessman*
%Robertson-Ceco Corp, 222 Berkeley St, Boston, MA 02116, USA

Heiss Jenkins, Carol *Figure Skater*
809 Lafayette Dr, Akron, OH 44303, USA

Heist, L C *Businessman*
%Champion International Corp, 1 Champion Plaza, Stamford, CT 06921, USA

Heitmann, Scott K *Financier*
%LaSalle Talman Bank, 135 S LaSalle St, Chicago, IL 60603, USA

Heitz, Mark *Businessman*
%AmVestors Financial Corp, 415 SW 8th Ave, Topeka, KS 66603, USA

Hejduk, John Q *Architect*
5721 Huxley Ave, Riverdale, NY 10471, USA

Hekman, Peter M, Jr *Navy Admiral*
Commander, Naval Sea Systems Command, Navy Dept, Washington, DC 20362, USA

Hekmatyar, Gulbuddin *Prime Minister, Afghanistan*
%Prime Minister's Office, Shar Rahi Sedarat, Kabul, Afghanistan

Held, Al *Artist*
%Andre Emmerich Gallery, 41 E 57th St, New York, NY 10022, USA

Held, Charles W *Financier*
%Bank One Dayton, Kettering Tower, Dayton, OH 45401, USA

Held, Franklin (Bud) *Track Athlete*
13367 Caminito Mar Villa, Del Mar, CA 92014, USA

Held, Richard M *Psychologist*
%Massachusetts Institute of Technology, Psychology Dept, Cambridge, MA 02139, USA

Heldman, Gladys *Tennis Magazine Editor*
1002 Old Pecos Trail, Santa Fe, NM 87501, USA

Helfer, Ricki Tigert *Financier*
%Federal Deposit Insurance Corp, 550 17th St NW, Washington, DC 20429, USA

Helgenberger, Marg *Actress*
1275 N Harper Ave, Los Angeles, CA 90046, USA

Heliker, John *Artist*
865 West End Ave, #3-C, New York, NY 10025, USA

Helinski, Donald R *Biologist*
%University of California, Molecular Genetics Center, La Jolla, CA 92093, USA

Heller, Daniel M *Attorney*
Israel Discount Bank Building, 14 NE 1st Ave, Miami, FL 33132, USA

Heller, John H *Research Scientist*
74 Horseshoe Rd, Wilton, CT 06897, USA

Heller, Joseph *Writer*
%NHP Inc, 1225 1st St NW, Washington, DC 20001, USA

Hellerman, Fred *Singer (Weavers), Songwriter*
83 Goodhill Rd, Weston, CT 06883, USA

Helligbrodt, L William *Businessman*
%Service Corp International, 1929 Allen Parkway, Houston, TX 77019, USA

Helliwell, Robert A *Radio Scientist*
2240 Page Mill Rd, Palo Alto, CA 94304, USA

Hellman, Monte *Movie Director*
8588 Appian Way, Los Angeles, CA 90046, USA

Hellman, Peter S	*Businessman*
%TRW Inc, 1900 Richmond Rd, Cleveland, OH 44124, USA	
Hellmann, Martina	*Track Athlete*
Neue Leipziger Str 14, 04205 Leipzig, Germany	
Hellmuth, George F	*Architect*
5 Conway Lane, St Louis, MO 63124, USA	
Hellyer, Paul T	*Government Official, Canada*
65 Harbour Square, #506, Toronto ON M5J 2L4, Canada	
Helm, Brigitte	*Actress*
Via Collinetta Rocca Vispa, 6120 Ascona, Switzerland	
Helm, Levon	*Singer, Drummer (The Band); Actor*
%Susan Smith Assoc, 121 N San Vicente Blvd, Beverly Hills, CA 90211, USA	
Helmerich, Otto	*Businessman*
%Helmerich & Payne Inc, Utica & 21st St, Tulsa, OK 74114, USA	
Helmerich, Walter H, III	*Businessman*
%Helmerich & Payne Inc, Utice & 21st St, Tulsa, OK 74114, USA	
Helmond, Katherine	*Actress*
2035 Davies Way, Los Angeles, CA 90046, USA	
Helmreich, Ernst J M	*Physiological Chemist*
%University of Wurzburg Biozentrum, Am Hubland, 97074 Wurzburg, Germany	
Helms, Richard M	*Government Official*
%Safeer Co, 1627 "K" St, #402, Washington, DC 20006, USA	
Helms, Susan J	*Astronaut*
%NASA, Johnson Space Center, 2101 NASA Rd, Houston, TX 77058, USA	
Helmsley, Leona M	*Businesswoman*
%Helmsley Hotels, 455 Madison Ave, New York, NY 10022, USA	
Heloise (Cruse Evans)	*Journalist*
PO Box 795000, San Antonio, TX 78279, USA	
Helou, Charles	*President, Lebanon*
Kaslik, Jounieh, Lebanon	
Helpern, David M	*Businessman*
%Joan & David Halpern Inc, 4 W 58th St, New York, NY 10019, USA	
Helpern, Joan G	*Fashion Designer*
%Joan & David Helpern Inc, 4 W 58th St, New York, NY 10019, USA	
Heltau, Michael	*Actor*
Sulzweg 11, 1190 Vienna, Austria	
Helton, Bill D	*Businessman*
%Southwestern Public Service, Tyler & 6th, Amarillo, TX 79170, USA	
Helvin, Marie	*Model*
%IMG, 23 Eyot Gardens, London W6 9TN, England	
Hemingway, Margaux	*Model, Actress*
2824 La Costa Ave, Rancho La Costa, CA 92009, USA	
Hemingway, Mariel	*Model, Actress*
PO Box 2249, Ketchum, ID 83340, USA	
Hemminghaus, Roger R	*Businessman*
%Diamond Shamrock R&M, 9830 Colonnade Blvd, San Antonio, TX 78230, USA	
Hemmings, David	*Actor*
PO Box 5836, Sun Valley, ID 83340, USA	
Hempel, Amy	*Writer*
%Alfred A Knopf Inc, 201 E 50th St, New York, NY 10022, USA	
Hempel, Kathleen J	*Businesswoman*
%Fort Howard Corp, 1919 S Broadway, Green Bay, WI 54304, USA	
Hemphill, Shirley	*Actress*
PO Box 897, West Covina, CA 91793, USA	
Hempstone, Smith, Jr	*Columnist, Diplomat*
7611 Fairfax Rd, Bethesda, MD 20814, USA	
Hemsley, Sherman	*Actor*
%Kenny Johnston, 15043 Valley Heart Dr, Sherman Oaks, CA 91403, USA	
Hencken, John	*Swimmer*
1441 Yellowstone Ave, Milpitas, CA 95035, USA	
Henderson, Alan	*Basketball Player*
%Atlanta Hawks, 1 CNN Center, South Tower, Atlanta, GA 30303, USA	
Henderson, David L (Dave)	*Baseball Player*
6004 142nd Court SE, Bellvue, WA 98006, USA	
Henderson, Donald A	*Epidemiologist*
3802 Greenway, Baltimore, MD 21218, USA	
Henderson, Florence	*Actress, Singer*
%FHB Productions, PO Box 11295, Marina del Rey, CA 90295, USA	

H

Hellman - Henderson

H

Henderson, George W, III	*Businessman*
%Burlington Industries, PO Box 21207, Greensboro, NC 27420, USA	
Henderson, Gordon	*Fashion Designer*
%World Hong Kong, 80 W 40th St, New York, NY 10018, USA	
Henderson, Greer F	*Businessman*
%USLIFE Corp, 125 Maiden Lane, New York, NY 10038, USA	
Henderson, Horace E	*Government Official*
1100 Gough St, #15-F, San Francisco, CA 94109, USA	
Henderson, J Nicholas	*Government Official, England*
6 Fairholt St, London SW7 1EG, England	
Henderson, James A	*Businessman*
%Cummins Engine Co, PO Box 3005, Columbus, IN 47202, USA	
Henderson, Joe	*Jazz Saxophonist*
%Verve Records, Worldwide Plaza, 825 8th Ave, New York, NY 10019, USA	
Henderson, Julia	*International Official*
1735 Forest Rd, Venice, FL 34293, USA	
Henderson, Loy W	*Diplomat*
2727 29th St NW, Washington, DC 20008, USA	
Henderson, Lyle R C (Skitch)	*Pianist, Conductor, Composer*
Hunt Hill Farm, 44 Upland Rd, RFD 3, New Milford, CT 06776, USA	
Henderson, Michael C	*Financier*
%PacifiCorp Financial Services, 825 NE Multnomah Ave, Portland, OR 97232, USA	
Henderson, Paul	*Journalist*
%Seattle Times, Editorial Dept, Fairview Ave N & John St, Seattle, WA 98111, USA	
Henderson, Rickey H	*Baseball Player*
10561 Englewood Dr, Oakland, CA 94605, USA	
Henderson, Roy A	*Financier*
%Bank of California, 400 California St, San Francisco, CA 94104, USA	
Henderson, William D	*Businessman*
%Smith Corona Corp, 65 Locust Ave, New Canaan, CT 06840, USA	
Hendrick, George A	*Baseball Player*
1027 Park Circle Dr, Torrance, CA 90502, USA	
Hendricks, Barbara	*Opera Singer*
%Miguel Esteban, 26 Rue Lamartine, 1203 Geneva, Switzerland	
Hendricks, John	*Television Executive*
%Discovery Communications, 7700 Wisconsin Ave, Bethesda, MD 20814, USA	
Hendricks, Jon	*Singer*
%Hendricks Music, Gateway Plaza, 375 South End Ave, #33-U, New York, NY 10280, USA	
Hendricks, Theodore P (Ted)	*Football Player*
165 Sunset Way, Miami Springs, FL 33166, USA	
Hendrix, Dennis R	*Businessman*
%Panhandle Eastern Corp, 5400 Westheimer Court, Houston, TX 77056, USA	
Hendrix, James R	*WW II Army Hero (CMH)*
PO Box 164, Davenport, FL 33837, USA	
Henkel, Heike	*Track Athlete*
Tannenbergstr 57, 51373 Leverkusen, Germany	
Henkel, Konrad	*Businessman*
%Degussa, Weissfrauenstr 9, 60311 Frankfurt/Main, Germany	
Henkin, Louis	*Attorney, Educator*
460 Riverside Dr, New York, NY 10027, USA	
Henle, Gertrude	*Virologist*
533 Ott Rd, Bala-Cynwyd, PA 19004, USA	
Henley, Don	*Singer, Drummer (Eagles), Songwriter*
%Front Line Mgmt, 8900 Wilshire Blvd, #300, Beverly Hills, CA 90211, USA	
Henley, Edward T	*Labor Leader*
%Hotel & Restaurant Employees Union, 1219 28th St NW, Washington, DC 20007, USA	
Henley, Elizabeth B (Beth)	*Playwright*
%William Morris Agency, 1325 Ave of Americas, New York, NY 10019, USA	
Henley, Ernest M	*Physicist*
4408 5th Ave NE, Seattle, WA 98105, USA	
Henley, Larry	*Composer*
%Creative Directions, 713 18th Ave S, Nashville, TN 37203, USA	
Henley, William B	*Educator*
Creston Circle Ranch, Paso Robles, CA 93446, USA	
Henn, Mark	*Animator (Little Mermaid)*
%Walt Disney Animation, PO Box 10200, Lake Buena Vista, FL 32830, USA	
Henn, Walter	*Architect*
Ramsachleite 13, 82418 Murnau, Germany	

Henderson - Henn

Henner, Marilu *Actress*
%William Morris Agency, 151 S El Camino Dr, Beverly Hills, CA 90212, USA

Hennessy, Jill *Actress*
%William Morris Agency, 151 S El Camino Dr, Beverly Hills, CA 90212, USA

Hennessy, John B *Archaeologist*
%University of Sydney, Archaeology Dept, Sydney NSW 2006, Australia

Hennig, Frederick E *Businessman*
%Woolworth Corp, Woolworth Building, 233 Broadway, New York, NY 10279, USA

Hennigan, Charlie *Football Player*
7800 Youree, #2700-G, Shreveport, LA 71105, USA

Henning, Dan *Football Coach*
%Boston College, Athletic Dept, Boston, MA 02167, USA

Henning, Doug *Illusionist*
6747 Odessa Ave, #105, Van Nuys, CA 91406, USA

Henning, John F, Jr *Publisher*
%Sunset Magazine, 80 Willow Rd, Menlo Park, CA 94025, USA

Henning, Linda Kaye *Actress*
4250 Navajo St, North Hollywood, CA 91602, USA

Henning, Lorne E *Hockey Coach*
%Chicago Blackhawks, Chicago Stadium, 1800 W Madison St, Chicago, IL 60612, USA

Henning-Walker, Anne *Speed Skater*
9959 E Peakview Ave, Englewood, CO 80111, USA

Hennings, Chad *Football Player*
%Dallas Cowboys, 1 Cowboys Parkway, Irving, TX 75063, USA

Henrich, Thomas D (Tommy) *Baseball Player*
1985 Shadow Valley Dr, Prescott, AZ 86301, USA

Henricks, Jon N *Swimmer*
254 N Laurel Ave, Des Plaines, IL 60016, USA

Henricks, Terence T (Tom) *Astronaut*
%NASA, Johnson Space Center, 2101 NASA Rd, Houston, TX 77058, USA

Henrik *Prince, Denmark*
%Amalienborg Palace, 1257 Copenhagen K, Denmark

Henriksen, Lance *Actor*
%Agency For Performing Arts, 9000 Sunset Blvd, #1200, Los Angeles, CA 90069, USA

Henriquez, Ron *Actor*
PO Box 38027, Los Angeles, CA 90038, USA

Henry, Buck *Actor, Screenwriter*
117 E 57th St, New York, NY 10022, USA

Henry, Carl F H *Theologian*
1141 Hus Dr, #206, Watertown, WI 53098, USA

Henry, Gloria *Actress*
%Dade/Schultz Agency, 11846 Ventura Blvd, #100, Studio City, CA 91604, USA

Henry, Joseph L *Dentist*
%Harvard University Dental School, 188 Longwood Ave, Boston, MA 02115, USA

Henry, Justin *Actor*
3 Clark Lane, Rye, NY 10580, USA

Henry, Lenny *Comedian*
%Luff, 294 Earls Court Rd, London SW5 9BB, England

Henry, Pierre *Composer*
32 Rue Toul, 75012 Paris, France

Henry, Taylor H *Businessman*
%Shoney's Inc, 1727 Elm Hill Pike, Nashville, TN 37210, USA

Henry, William H, Jr *Publisher*
%Time-Life Books, Rockefeller Center, New York, NY 10020, USA

Henschel, Milton *Religious Leader*
%Jehovah's Witnesses, 25 Columbia Heights, Brooklyn, NY 11201, USA

Hensel, Witold *Archaeologist*
Ul Marszalkowska 84/92 M, 109 00-514 Warsaw, Poland

Hensley, Kirby J *Religious Leader*
%Universal Life Church, 601 3rd St, Modesto, CA 95351, USA

Hensley, Pamela *Actress*
9526 Dalegrove Dr, Beverly Hills, CA 90210, USA

Henson, Lisa *Entertainment Executive*
%Columbia Pictures, 10202 W Washington Blvd, Culver City, CA 90232, USA

Henson, Lou *Basketball Coach*
%University of Illinois, Athletic Dept, Assembly Hall, Champaign, IL 61820, USA

Henson, Paul H *Businessman*
%Kansas City Southern Industries, 114 W 11th St, Kansas City, MO 64105, USA

H

Hentoff, Nathan I (Nat)

Hentoff, Nathan I (Nat) — *Jazz Critic*
%Village Voice, Editorial Dept, 36 Cooper Sq, New York, NY 10003, USA

Hentrich, Helmut — *Architect*
Dusseldorfer Str 67, 40545 Dusseldorf-Oberkassel, Germany

Henze, Hans Werner — *Composer, Conductor*
Weihergarten 1-5, 55116 Mainz, Germany

Hepburn, Katharine — *Actress*
244 E 49th St, New York, NY 10017, USA

Heppel, Leon A — *Biochemist*
%Cornell University, Biochemistry Dept, Ithaca, NY 14850, USA

Herb, Raymond G — *Physicist*
RR 1, Box 223-A, Middleton, WI 53704, USA

Herbert (Mr Wizard), Don — *Educator*
%"Mr Wizard's World" Show, PO Box 83, Canoga Park, CA 91305, USA

Herbert of Hemingford, Nicholas — *Publisher*
The Old Rectory, Hemingford Abbots, Huntington Cambs PE18 9AN, England

Herbert, Gavin S, Jr — *Businessman*
%Allergan Pharmaceuticals, 2525 Dupont Dr, Irvine, CA 92715, USA

Herbert, Michael K — *Editor*
990 Grove St, Evanston, IL 60201, USA

Herbert, Raymond E (Ray) — *Baseball Player*
9360 Taylors Turn, Stanwood, AL 35901, USA

Herbert, Walter W (Wally) — *Explorer*
Old Vicarage, Vicarage Rd, Stoke Gabriel, Devon TQ9 6QP, England

Herbig, George H — *Astronomer*
%University of Hawaii, Astronomy Institute, 2680 Woodlawn Dr, Honolulu, HI 96822, USA

Herbig, Gunther — *Conductor*
%Toronto Symphony, 60 Simcoe St, #C-116, Toronto ON MJ5 2H5, Canada

Herbold, Robert J — *Businessman*
%Microsoft Corp, 1 Microsoft Way, Redmond, WA 98052, USA

Herbst, Edward I — *Financier*
%Cowen Co, Financial Square, New York, NY 10005, USA

Herd, Richard — *Actor*
%Innovative Artists, 1999 Ave of Stars, #2850, Los Angeles, CA 90067, USA

Herda, Frank A — *Vietnam War Army Hero (CMH)*
PO Box 34239, Cleveland, OH 44134, USA

Herincx, Raimund — *Opera Singer*
Monks' Vineyard, Larkbarrow, Shepton Mallet, Somerset BA4 4NR, England

Herman (Paul Reubens), Pee Wee — *Actor*
PO Box 29373, Los Angeles, CA 90029, USA

Herman, George E — *Commentator*
4500 "Q" Lane NW, Washington, DC 20007, USA

Herman, Jerry — *Composer, Lyricist*
10847 Bellagio Rd, Los Angeles, CA 90077, USA

Hermann, Allen M — *Physicist*
2704 Lookout View Dr, Golden, CO 80401, USA

Hermaszewski, Miroslav — *Cosmonaut, Poland; Air Force General*
Ul Czeczota 25, 02-650 Warsaw, Poland

Hermon, John C — *Law Enforcement Official*
Warren Road, Donaghadee, County Down, Northern Ireland

Hern, Dick — *Thoroughbred Racing Trainer*
%West Ilsley Stables, West Ilsley, Newbury Berks RG16 0AE, England

Hernandez Colon, Rafael — *Govenor, PR*
La Fortaleza, PO Box 82, Trujillo Alto, PR 00977, USA

Hernandez, Amalia — *Dancer, Choreographer*
%Ballet Folklorico de Mexico, Palace of Fine Arts, Mexico City DF, Mexico

Hernandez, Guillermo (Willie) — *Baseball Player*
Bo Espina, Calle C Buzon 125, Aguada, PR 00602, USA

Hernandez, Keith — *Baseball Player*
255 E 49th St, #28-D, New York, NY 10017, USA

Hernandez, Rodolfo P — *Korean War Army Hero (CMH)*
5328 Bluewater Place, College Lakes, Fayetteville, NC 28311, USA

Heron, Patrick — *Artist*
Eagles Nest, Zennor Near St Ives, Cornwall, England

Herr, John C — *Immunologist*
%University of Virginia Med Center, Immunology Dept, Charlottesville, VA 22903, USA

Herr, Thomas M (Tommy) — *Baseball Player*
1077 Olde Forge Crossing, Lancaster, PA 17601, USA

Hentoff - Herr

294   V.I.P. Address Book

Herrera, Carolina — *Fashion Designer*
%Carolina Herrera Ltd, 501 7th Ave, #1700, New York, NY 10018, USA

Herrera, Pamela — *Ballerina*
%American Ballet Theatre, 890 Broadway, New York, NY 10003, USA

Herrera, Silvestre S — *WW II Army Hero (CMH)*
7222 W Windsor Blvd, Glendale, AZ 85303, USA

Herres, Robert T — *Air Force General, Businessman*
%United Services Automobile Assn, USAA Building, San Antonio, TX 78288, USA

Herrick, Kenneth G — *Businessman*
%Tecumseh Products Co, 100 E Patterson St, Tecumseh, MI 49286, USA

Herrick, Todd W — *Businessman*
%Tecumseh Products Co, 100 E Patterson St, Tecumseh, MI 49286, USA

Herries, Michael R Y — *Financier*
%Royal Bank of Scotland, 42 St Andrew Square, Edinburg EH2 2YE, Scotland

Herring, Leonard G — *Businessman*
%Loew's Companies, State Highway 268 E, North Wilkesboro, NC 28659, USA

Herring, Rufus G — *WW II Navy Hero (CMH)*
PO Box 128, Roseboro, NC 28382, USA

Herring, W Conyers — *Physicist*
3945 Nelson Dr, Palo Alto, CA 94306, USA

Herringer, Frank C — *Businessman*
%Transamerica Corp, 600 Montgomery St, San Francisco, CA 94111, USA

Herrington, John S — *Secretary, Education; Businessman*
%Harcourt Brace Jovanovich Inc, 6277 Sea Harbor Dr, Orlando, FL 32887, USA

Herrmann, Edward — *Actor*
%William Morris Agency, 151 S El Camino Dr, Beverly Hills, CA 90212, USA

Herron, Cindy — *Singer (En Vogue)*
%William Morris Agency, 1325 Ave of Americas, New York, NY 10019, USA

Hersant, Robert J E — *Publisher*
%Le Figaro, 12 Rue De Presbourg, 75116 Paris, France

Herschbach, Dudley R — *Nobel Chemistry Laureate*
64 Linnaean St, Cambridge, MA 02138, USA

Herschler, David — *Artist*
PO Box 5859, Santa Barbara, CA 93150, USA

Hersh, Kristin — *Singer, Songwriter*
%Throwing Mgmt, 520 Southview Dr, Athens, GA 30605, USA

Hersh, Seymour M — *Writer*
1211 Connecticut Ave NW, Washington, DC 20036, USA

Hershberger, Larry D — *Financier*
%TIAA-CREF, 730 3rd Ave, New York, NY 10017, USA

Hershey, Alfred D — *Nobel Medicine Laureate*
RD Box 1640, Moores Hill Rd, Syosset, NY 11791, USA

Hershey, Barbara — *Actress*
1007 Montana Ave, Santa Monica, CA 90403, USA

Hershiser, Orel L Q — *Baseball Player*
1585 Orlando Rd, Pasadena, CA 91106, USA

Hertog, Roger — *Financier*
%Sanford C Bernstein Co, 767 5th Ave, New York, NY 10153, USA

Hertz, C Hellmuth — *Physicist*
%Lund Institute of Technology, Physics School, Lund, Sweden

Hertz, Roy — *Obstetrician, Pharmacologist*
RR 3, Box 582, Hollywood, MD 20636, USA

Hertzberg, Arthur — *Religious Leader*
83 Glenwood Rd, Englewood, NJ 07631, USA

Hertzberg, Daniel — *Journalist*
%Wall Street Journal, Editorial Dept, 200 Liberty St, New York, NY 10281, USA

Hertzberger, Herman — *Architect*
%Architectourstudio, Box 74665, 1070 BR Amsterdam, Netherlands

Herzberg, Gerhard — *Nobel Chemistry Laureate*
190 Lakeway Dr, Rockcliffe Park, Ottawa ON K1L 5B3, Canada

Herzigova, Eva — *Model*
%Metropolitan Model Mgmt, 20 W 20th St, #600, New York, NY 10011, USA

Herzog, Arthur, III — *Writer*
4 E 81st St, New York, NY 10028, USA

Herzog, Chaim — *President, Israel*
Beit Amot Hamisphat, 8 Shaul Hamelech Blvd, 64733 Tel-Aviv, Israel

Herzog, Dorrel N E (Whitey) — *Baseball Manager, Executive*
9426 Sappington Estates Dr, St Louis, MO 63127, USA

H

Herrera - Herzog

H

Herzog, George — *Anthropologist*
%Holt Rinehart & Winston, 383 Madison Ave, New York, NY 10017, USA

Herzog, Maurice — *Mountaineer*
84 Chemin De La Tournette, 74400 Chamoinix-Mont-Blanc, France

Herzog, Roman — *President, Germany*
%President's Office, Kaiser-Friederich-Str 16, 53113 Bonn, Germany

Herzog, Werner — *Movie Director*
%Herzog Film Productions, Turkenstr 91, 80799 Munich, Germany

Hesburgh, Theodore M — *Educator*
%University of Notre Dame, Hesburgh Library, Notre Dame IN 46556, USA

Heseltine, Michael R D — *Government Official, England*
Thenford House, Near Banbury, Oxon OX17 2BX, England

Hess, Erika — *Skier*
Aeschi, 6388 Gratenort, Switzerland

Hess, Leon — *Businessman, Football Executive*
%Amerada Hess Corp, 1185 Ave of Americas, New York, NY 10036, USA

Hesse, James D — *Businessman*
%Wheeling-Pittsburgh Steel Corp, 1134 Market St, Wheeling, WV 26003, USA

Hesseman, Howard — *Actor*
7146 La Pesa Dr, Los Angeles, CA 90068, USA

Hessler, Curtis A — *Publisher*
%Times-Mirror Co, Times-Mirror Square, Los Angeles, CA 90053, USA

Hester, Jessie — *Football Player*
%Indianapolis Colts, 7001 W 56th St, Indianapolis, IN 46254, USA

Heston, Charlton — *Actor*
2859 Coldwater Canyon, Beverly Hills, CA 90210, USA

Hetfield, James — *Singer, Guitarist (Metallica)*
%Q Prime Inc, 729 7th Ave, #1400, New York, NY 10019, USA

Hettich, Arthur M — *Editor*
606 Shore Acres Dr, Mamaroneck, NY 10543, USA

Hetzel, C Charles — *Businessman*
%Ark Asset Management, 1 New York Plaza, New York, NY 10004, USA

Heuga, Jimmie — *Skier*
%Jimmie Heuga Health Center, PO Box 5480, Avon, CO 81620, USA

Hewett, Christopher — *Actor*
1422 N Sweetzer Ave, #110, Los Angeles, CA 90069, USA

Hewish, Anthony — *Nobel Physics Laureate*
Pryor's Cottage, Kingston, Cambridge CB3 7NQ, England

Hewitt, Bob — *Tennis Player*
%Pender Sports Corp, 29 Tower Rd, Newton, MA 02164, USA

Hewitt, Don S — *Television Producer*
%"Sixty Minutes" Show, CBS-TV, 555 W 57th St, New York, NY 10019, USA

Hewlett, William R — *Inventor (Oscillarion Generator)*
%Hewlett-Packard Co, 3000 Hanover St, Palo Alto, CA 94304, USA

Hewson, Jeffrey — *Businessman*
%United Stationers, 2200 E Golf Rd, Des Plaines, IL 60016, USA

Hewson, John — *Government Official, Australia*
%Parliament House, Canberra ACT 2600, Australia

Hextall, Ron — *Hockey Player*
%Philadelphia Flyers, Spectrum, Pattison Place, Philadelphia, PA 19148, USA

Hey, J Stanley — *Astronomer*
4 Shortlands Close, Eastbourne, East Sussex BN22 0JE, England

Heyerdahl, Thor — *Explorer, Anthropologist*
Guimar, Tenerife, Canary Islands, Spain

Heyman, I Michael — *Association Executive, Educator*
%Smithsonian Institution, 1000 Jefferson Dr SW, Washington, DC 20560, USA

Heyman, Richard — *Geneticist*
%Ligand Pharmaceuticals, 9393 Town Center Dr, #100, San Diego, CA 92121, USA

Heyman, Samuel J — *Businessman*
%GAF Corp, 1361 Alps Rd, Wayne, NJ 07470, USA

Heyssel, Robert M — *Physician*
230 Stoney Run Lane, Baltimore, MD 21210, USA

Heywood, Anne — *Actress*
9966 Liebe Dr, Beverly Hills, CA 90210, USA

Hiatt, Andrew — *Molecular Biologist*
%Scripps Clinic-Research Foundation, 10666 N Torrey Pines Rd, La Jolla, CA 92037, USA

Hibbard, Dwight H — *Businessman*
%Cincinnati Bell Inc, 201 E 4th St, Cincinnati, OH 45202, USA

Herzog - Hibbard

Hick, Anna *Financier*
%Alaska USA Federal Credit Union, 4000 Credit Union Dr, Anchorage, AK 99503, USA

Hick, Graeme A *Cricketer*
%Worcestershire County Cricket Club, New Road, Worcester, England

Hickel, Walter J *Secretary, Interior; Governor, AK*
935 W 5th Ave, Anchorage, AK 99501, USA

Hickey, James A Cardinal *Religious Leader*
%Archdiocesan Pastoral Center, 5002 Eastern Ave, Washington, DC 20017, USA

Hickey, Maurice *Publisher*
%Denver Post, 650 15th St, Denver, CO 80202, USA

Hickman, Dwayne *Actor*
812 16th St, #1, Santa Monica, CA 90403, USA

Hickman, Fred *Sportscaster*
%Cable News Network, News Dept, 1050 Techwood Dr NW, Atlanta, GA 30318, USA

Hickox, Richard S *Conductor*
35 Ellington St, London N7 8PN, England

Hicks, Catherine *Actress*
15422 Brownwood Place, Los Angeles, CA 90077, USA

Hicks, Dan *Sportscaster*
%NBC-TV, Sports Dept, 30 Rockefeller Plaza, New York, NY 10112, USA

Hicks, John *Football Player*
3287 Green Cook Rd, Johnstown, OH 43031, USA

Hicks, Marshall M *Labor Leader*
%Utility Workers Union of America, 815 16th St NW, Washington, DC 20006, USA

Hicks, Scottie B *Labor Leader*
%National Rural Letter Carriers Assn, 1630 Duke St, Alexandria, VA 22314, USA

Hickson, Joan *Actress*
%Plunket & Greene, 21 Golden Square, London W1R 3PA, England

Hidalgo, John *Government Official*
%Mays Valentine Davenport Moore, 1899 "L" St NW, Washington, DC 20036, USA

Hieb, Richard J *Astronaut*
%Allied Signal Technical Services, 7515 Mission Dr, Lanham, MD 20706, USA

Hiebert, Erwin N *Historian*
40 Payson Rd, Belmont, MA 02178, USA

Hier, Marvin *Religious Leader, Social Activist*
%Simon Wiesenthal Holocaust Center, 9766 W Pico Blvd, Los Angeles, CA 90035, USA

Hieronymus, Clara W *Journalist*
%Tennessean, Editorial Dept, 1100 Broad St, Nashville, TN 37203, USA

Higdon, Bruce *Cartoonist*
2631 Birdsong Ave, Murfreesboro, TN 37129, USA

Higdon, Ernest D *Labor Leader*
%Coopers International Union, 400 Sherburn Lane, #207, Louisville, KY 40207, USA

Higginbotham, Richard A *Financier*
%Fleet Bank-RI, 111 Westminster St, Providence, RI 02903, USA

Higgins, George G *Religious Leader*
%Catholic University of America, Curley Hall, Washington, DC 20064, USA

Higgins, George V *Writer*
15 Brush Hill Lane, Milton, MA 02186, USA

Higgins, Jack *Editorial Cartoonist*
9545 S Bell Ave, Chicago, IL 60643, USA

Higgins, Jack *Writer*
September Tide, Mont de la Roque, Jersey, Channel Islands, England

Higgins, Joel *Actor*
24 Old Hill Rd, Westport, CT 06880, USA

Higgins, John *Swimmer, Swimming Coach*
40 Williams Dr, Annapolis, MD 21401, USA

Higgins, Robert J *Financier*
%Fleet Financial Group, 50 Kennedy Plaza, Providence, RI 02903, USA

Higgins, Stephen E *Law Enforcement Official*
%Alcohol Tobacco Firearms Bureau, 650 Massachusetts NW, Washington, DC 20001, USA

Higginson, John *Pathologist*
9650 Rockville Pike, Bethesda, MD 20814, USA

Higham, John *Historian*
309 Tuscany Rd, Baltimore, MD 21210, USA

Hightower, John B *Museum Director*
1600 Chesapeake Ave, Hampton, VA 23661, USA

Higuera, Teodoro V *Baseball Player*
%Milwaukee Brewers, County Stadium, 201 S 46th St, Milwaukee, WI 53214, USA

Hijikata, Takeshi *Businessman*
%Sumitomo Chemical Co, 5-33-4 Kitahama, Chuoku, Osaka 541, Japan

Hijuelos, Oscar *Writer*
%Hofstra University, English Dept, 10000 Fulton Ave, Hempstead, NY 11550, USA

Hilbe, Alfred J *Head of Government, Liechtenstein*
9494 Schaan, Garsill 11, Liechtenstein

Hilbert, Stephen C *Businessman*
%Conseco, 11825 N Pennsylvania St, Carmel, IN 46032, USA

Hildegarde *Singer*
230 E 48th St, New York, NY 10017, USA

Hildreth, Eugene A *Physician*
%Reading Hospital & Medical Center, PO Box 16052, Reading, PA 19612, USA

Hilfiger, Tommy *Fashion Designer*
%Tommy Hilfiger USA, 25 W 39th St, #1300, New York, NY 10018, USA

Hilgard, Ernest R *Psychologist*
850 Webster, #518, Palo Alto, CA 94301, USA

Hilger, Wolfgang *Businessman*
%Hoechst AG, Postfach 800320, 65903 Frankfurt, Germany

Hill of Luton, Baron *Government Official, Journalist*
5 Bamville Wood, East Common, Harpenden, Herts, England

Hill Smith, Marilyn *Opera Singer*
%Music International, 13 Ardilaun Rd, Highbury, London N5 2QR, England

Hill, A Alan *Government Official*
102 Coleman Dr, San Rafael, CA 94901, USA

Hill, A Derek *Artist*
%National Art Collections Fund, 20 John Islip St, London SW1, England

Hill, Anita *Educator*
%Oklahoma University, Law School, Norman, OK 73069, USA

Hill, Arthur *Actor*
1515 Club View Dr, Los Angeles, CA 90024, USA

Hill, Bob *Basketball Coach*
%San Antonio Spurs, 600 E Market St, #102, San Antonio, TX 78205, USA

Hill, Brian *Basketball Coach*
%Orlando Magic, Orlando Arena, 1 Magic Place, Orlando, FL 32801, USA

Hill, Brian *Businessman*
%California State Automobile Assn, PO Box 422940, San Francisco, CA 94142, USA

Hill, Calvin *Football Player, Baseball Executive*
%Baltimore Orioles, 333 W Camden Ave, Baltimore, MD 21201, USA

Hill, Dan *Football Player*
171 Montrose Dr, Dunbarton, Durham, NC 27707, USA

Hill, Dave *Golfer*
%Eddie Elias Enterprises, 1720 Merriman Rd, #5118, Akron, OH 44313, USA

Hill, Draper *Editorial Cartoonist*
368 Washington Rd, Grosse Pointe, MI 48230, USA

Hill, Drew *Football Player*
%Houston Oilers, 6910 Fannin St, Houston, TX 77030, USA

Hill, Dusty *Singer, Bassist (ZZ Top)*
%Lone Wolf Mgmt, PO Box 163690, Austin, TX 78716, USA

Hill, Eddie *Drag Racing Driver*
2130 McGrath Lane, Wichita Falls, TX 76309, USA

Hill, Faith *Singer*
2502 Belmont Blvd, #B, Nashville, TN 37212, USA

Hill, Gary *Artist*
%Cornish College of the Arts Galleries, 710 E Roy St, Seattle, WA 98102, USA

Hill, George Roy *Movie Director*
%Pan Arts Productions, 59 E 54th St, #73, New York, NY 10022, USA

Hill, Grant *Basketball Player*
%Detroit Pistons, Palace, 2 Championship Dr, Auburn Hills, MI 48057, USA

Hill, Jim *Sportscaster*
%ABC-TV, Sports Dept, 77 W 66th St, New York, NY 10023, USA

Hill, Kent A *Football Player*
630 Hawthorne Place, Fayetteville, GA 30214, USA

Hill, Phil *Auto Racing Driver*
266 20th St, Santa Monica, CA 90402, USA

Hill, Robert L *Biochemist*
%Duke University Medical Center, Biochemistry Dept, Durham, NC 27710, USA

Hill, Ron *Track Athlete*
PO Box 11, Hyde, Cheshire SK14 1RD, England

Hill, S Richardson, Jr	*Educator*
3337 E Briarcliff Rd, Birmingham, AL 35223, USA	
Hill, Steven	*Actor*
18 Jill Lane, Monsey, NY 10952, USA	
Hill, Susan E	*Writer*
Longmoor Farmhouse, Ebrington, Chipping Campden, Glos GL55 6NW, England	
Hill, Terence	*Actor*
PO Box 818, Stockbridge, MA 01262, USA	
Hill, Terrell L	*Biophysicist, Chemist*
433 Logan St, Santa Cruz, CA 95062, USA	
Hill, Virgil	*Boxer*
%Top Rank Inc, 3900 Paradise Rd, #227, Las Vegas, NV 89109, USA	
Hill, Walter	*Movie Director*
31368 Broad Beach Rd, Malibu, CA 90265, USA	
Hill-Norton, Peter J	*Navy Fleet Admiral, England*
Cass Cottage, Hyde, Fordingbridge, Hampshire, England	
Hillaby, John	*Writer*
%Constable Co, Lanchesters, 102 Fulham Palace Rd, London W6 9ER, England	
Hillaire, Marcel	*Actor*
637 1/2 S Burnside Ave, Los Angeles, CA 90036, USA	
Hillary, Edmund P	*Mountaineer, Explorer*
278-A Remuera Rd, Auckland SE2, New Zealand	
Hille, Einar	*Mathematician*
8862 La Jolla Scenic Dr N, La Jolla, CA 92037, USA	
Hillebrecht, Rudolf F H	*Architect*
Gneiststr 7, 30169 Hanover, Germany	
Hillel, Shlomo	*Government Official, Israel*
%Knesset, Jerusalem, Israel	
Hilleman, Maurice R	*Virologist*
%Merck Institute for Therapeutic Research, West Point, PA 19486, USA	
Hillenbrand, Daniel A	*Businessman*
%Hillenbrand Industries, 700 State Rt 46 E, Batesville, IN 47006, USA	
Hillenbrand, Martin J	*Diplomat*
%University of Georgia, Global Policy Studies Center, Athens, GA 30602, USA	
Hillenbrand, W August	*Businessman*
%Hillenbrand Industries, 700 State Rt 46 E, Batesville, IN 47006, USA	
Hiller, Arthur	*Movie Director*
1218 Benedict Canyon, Beverly Hills, CA 90210, USA	
Hiller, Susan	*Artist*
%Gimpel Fils, 30 Davies St, London W1, England	
Hiller, Wendy	*Actress*
Spindles, Stratton Rd, Beaconsfield, Bucks, England	
Hillerman, John	*Actor*
7102 La Presa Dr, Los Angeles, CA 90068, USA	
Hillerman, Tony	*Writer*
1632 Francisca Rd NW, Albuquerque, NM 87107, USA	
Hillery, Patrick J	*President, Ireland*
Grasmere, Greenfield Rd, Sutton, Dublin 13, Ireland	
Hillier, James	*Inventor (Electron Lens Corrector)*
22 Arreton Rd, Princeton, NJ 08540, USA	
Hillis, W Daniel (Danny)	*Computer Scientist*
%Thinking Machines Corp, 245 1st St, Cambridge, MA 02142, USA	
Hillman, Chris	*Singer, Bassist (Byrds), Songwriter*
PO Box 729, Ojai, CA 93024, USA	
Hills, Carla A	*Secretary, Housing & Urban Development*
%Hills Co, 1200 19th St NW, Washington, DC 20036, USA	
Hills, Lee	*Publisher, Editor*
%Knight-Ridder Newspapers, 1 Herald Plaza, Miami, FL 33132, USA	
Hills, Roderick M	*Government Official*
%Mudge Rose Guthrie Alexander Ferdon, 1200 19th St NW, Washington, DC 20036, USA	
Hilly, Francis Billy	*Prime Minister, Solomon Islands*
%Prime Minister's Office, Legakiki Ridge, Honiara, Solomon Islands	
Hilmers, David C	*Astronaut*
18502 Point Lookout Dr, Houston, TX 77058, USA	
Hilsman, Roger	*Diplomat*
251 Hamburg Cove, Lyme, CT 06371, USA	
Hilton, Barron	*Businessman*
%Hilton Hotels Corp, 9336 Civic Center Dr, Beverly Hills, CA 90210, USA	

H

Hill - Hilton

H

Hilton, Eric M — *Businessman*
%Hilton Hotels Corp, 9336 Civic Center Dr, Beverly Hills, CA 90210, USA

Hilton, Janet — *Concert Clarinetist*
Holly House, East Downs Rd, Bowdon, Altrincham, Cheshire WA14 2LH, England

Himmelfarb, Gertrude — *Historian*
%City University of New York, Graduate School, New York, NY 10036, USA

Hinault, Bernard — *Cyclist*
Ouest Levure, 7 Rue de la Sauvaie, 21 Sud-Est, 35000 Rennes, France

Hinckley, Gordon B — *Religious Leader*
%Church of Latter Day Saints, 50 E North Temple, Salt Lake City, UT 84150, USA

Hindman, Earl — *Actor*
%"Home Improvment", Disney TV, 500 S Buena Vista St, Burbank, CA 91521, USA

Hinds, Bruce J — *Test Pilot*
5915 Alleppo Lane, Palmdale, CA 93551, USA

Hinds, Samuel A A — *Prime Minister, Guyana*
%Prime Minister's Office, Public Buildings, Georgetown, Guyana

Hinds, William E — *Cartoonist (Tank McNamara)*
1301 Spring Oaks Circle, Houston, TX 77055, USA

Hine, Maynard K — *Dentist*
1121 W Michigan St, Indianapolis, IN 46202, USA

Hine, Patrick — *Royal Air Force Marshal, England*
%Lloyd's Bank, Cox's & Kings, 7 Pall Mall, London SW1 5NA, England

Hiner, Glen H — *Businessman*
%Owens-Corning Fiberglas Corp, Fiberglas Tower, Toledo, OH 43659, USA

Hines, Gregory — *Dancer, Actor*
377 W 11th St, #PH, New York, NY 10014, USA

Hines, Jerome — *Opera Singer*
%Shaw Concerts, Lincoln Plaza, 1900 Broadway, #200, New York, NY 10023, USA

Hines, Patrick — *Actor*
46 W 95th St, New York, NY 10025, USA

Hingle, Pat — *Actor*
PO Box 2228, Carolina Beach, NC 28428, USA

Hingsen, Jurgen — *Track Athlete*
655 Circle Dr, Santa Barbara, CA 93108, USA

Hino, Kazuyoshi — *Fashion Designer*
%Hino & Malee Inc, 3701 N Ravenswood Ave, Chicago, IL 60613, USA

Hinshaw, Horton C — *Physician*
400 Deer Valley Rd, #41, San Rafael, CA 94903, USA

Hinson, David — *Government Official*
%Federal Aviation Administration, 800 Independence SW, Washington, DC 20591, USA

Hinson, Roy — *Basketball Player*
%Atlanta Hawks, 1 CNN Center, South Tower, Atlanta, GA 30303, USA

Hinson, Walter F, III — *Financier*
%Coral Gables Federal Savings, 2511 Ponce de Leon Blvd, Coral Gables, FL 33134, USA

Hinton of Bankside, Christopher — *Government Official, England; Engineer*
Tiverton Lodge, Dulwich Common, London SG2 7EW, England

Hinton, Christopher J (Chris) — *Football Player*
%Minnesota Vikings, 9520 Viking Dr, Eden Prairie, MN 55344, USA

Hinton, John D — *WW II Army Hero (VC)*
30 Waitaki St, Bexley, Christchurch 7, New Zealand

Hinton, Leslie F — *Television Executive*
%Fox Television Stations, 5746 Sunset Blvd, Los Angeles, CA 90028, USA

Hinton, Milt (Judge) — *Jazz Bassist*
%Thomas Cassidy Inc, 0366 Horseshoe Dr, Basalt, CO 81621, USA

Hinton, S E — *Writer*
%Delacorte Press, 1540 Broadway, New York, NY 10036, USA

Hinton, Sam — *Singer, Songwriter*
9420 La Jolla Shores Dr, La Jolla, CA 92037, USA

Hiort, Esbjorn — *Architect*
%Bel Colles Farm, Parkvej 6, 2960 Rungsted Kyst, Denmark

Hipp, W Hayne — *Businessman*
%Liberty Life Insurance, PO Box 789, Greenville, SC 29602, USA

Hirata, Kusuo — *Businessman*
%Fuji Photo Film Co, 26-30 Nishiazabu, Minatoku, Tokyo 106, Japan

Hird, Thora — *Actress*
Old Loft, 21 Leinster Mews, Lancaster Gate, London W2 3EX, England

Hiro, Keitaro — *Businessman*
%Kubota Ltd, 2-47 Shikitsuhigashi, Naniwaku, Osaka 556, Japan

Hilton - Hiro

Hirsch, Elroy (Crazy Legs) — *Football Player*
50 Oak Creek Trail, Madison, WI 53717, USA

Hirsch, Gary D — *Businessman*
%Penn Traffic Co, 1200 State Fair Blvd, Syracuse, NY 13209, USA

Hirsch, Judd — *Actor*
%Morton L Leavy, 11 E 44th St, New York, NY 10017, USA

Hirsch, Laurence E — *Businessman*
%Centex Corp, 3333 Lee Parkway, Dallas, TX 75219, USA

Hirsch, Leon C — *Businessman*
%US Surgical Corp, 150 Glover Ave, Norwalk, CT 06850, USA

Hirsch, Robert P — *Actor*
1 Place du Palais Bourbon, 75007 Paris, France

Hirschfeld, Albert (Al) — *Artist, Illustrator*
122 E 95th St, New York, NY 10128, USA

Hirschfield, Gerald J — *Cinematographer*
361 Scenic Dr, Ashland, OR 97520, USA

Hirschman, Albert O — *Economist*
16 Newlin Rd, Princeton, NJ 08540, USA

Hirschmann, Ralph F — *Chemist*
740 Palmer Place, Blue Bell, PA 19422, USA

Hirsig, Alan R — *Businessman*
%ARCO Chemical Co, 3801 Westchester Pike, Newton Square, PA 19073, USA

Hirt, Al — *Jazz Trumpeter*
1920 Frankel Ave, Metairie, LA 70003, USA

Hirt, F William — *Businessman*
%Erie Insurance Group, 100 Erie Insurance Place, Erie, PA 16530, USA

Hisle, Larry E — *Baseball Player*
%Ferguson, PO Box 84, Portsmouth, OH 45662, USA

Hiss, Alger — *Attorney*
%Rosenman & Colin, 575 Madison Ave, New York, NY 10022, USA

Hitchcock, Russell — *Singer (Air Supply)*
PO Box 25909, Los Angeles, CA 90025, USA

Hitchings, George H — *Nobel Medicine Laureate*
%Burroughs Wellcome Co, 3030 Cornwallis Rd, Research Triangle, NC 27709, USA

Hite, Ronald V — *Army General*
Military Deputy/Director Acquisition Corps, Pentagon, Washington, DC 20310, USA

Hite, Shere D — *Writer*
PO Box 1037, New York, NY 10028, USA

Hitt, John C — *Educator*
%University of Central Florida, President's Office, Orlando, FL 32816, USA

Hix, Charles — *Fashion Expert, Writer*
%Simon & Schuster Inc, 1230 Ave of Americas, New York, NY 10020, USA

Hlass, I Jerry — *Aeronautical Engineer*
%National Space Technology Laboratories, NSTL Station, MS 39529, USA

Hlinka, Nichol — *Ballerina*
%New York City Ballet, Lincoln Center Plaza, New York, NY 10023, USA

Hnatyshyn, Ramon J — *Governor General, Canada*
Government House, Rideau Hall, 1 Sussex Dr, Ottawa ON K1A 0A1, Canada

Ho, Donald T (Don) — *Singer*
277 Lewers St, Honolulu, HI 96815, USA

Ho, Tao — *Architect*
Upper Deck, North Point West, Passenger Ferry Pier, North Point, Hong Kong

Ho, Ya-Ming — *Biochemist*
%Massachusetts Institute of Technology, Biology Dept, Cambridge, MA 02139, USA

Hoag, David H — *Businessman*
%LTV Corp, 25 W Prospect Ave, Cleveland, OH 44115, USA

Hoag, Peter C — *Test Pilot*
%McDonnell Douglas Ltd, M/C 1064850, PO Box 516, St Louis, MO 63166, USA

Hoage, Terry — *Football Player*
%Washington Redskins, 21300 Redskin Park Dr, Ashburn, VA 22011, USA

Hoagland, Edward — *Writer*
RR 1, Box 2977, Bennington, VT 05201, USA

Hoagland, Jimmie L (Jim) — *Journalist*
%Washington Post, Editorial Dept, 1150 15th St NW, Washington, DC 20071, USA

Hoagland, Mahlon B — *Biochemist*
Academy Rd, Thetford, VT 05074, USA

Hoaglin, Fred — *Football Player, Coach*
80 Fisher Rd, #30, Cumberland, RI 02864, USA

Hirsch - Hoaglin

Hoar, Joseph P *Marine Corps General*
%Commander, US Central Command, MacDill Air Force Base, FL 33621, USA

Hoban, Russell C *Writer*
%David Higham, Golden Square, 5-8 Lower John St, London W1R 4HA, England

Hobart, Nick *Cartoonist*
133 Indiana Ave, New Port Richey, FL 33552, USA

Hobson, Allan *Neuroscientist*
%Harvard University, Sleep Laboratory, Cambridge, MA 02138, USA

Hobson, Clell L (Butch) *Baseball Player, Manager*
6415 Nelson Rd, Fairhope, AL 36532, USA

Hobson, Valerie *Writer*
Old Barn Cottage, Upton Grey, Hampshire RG25 2RM, England

Hoch, Orion L *Businessman*
%Litton Industries, 21240 Burbank Blvd, Woodland Hills, CA 91367, USA

Hoch, Scott *Golfer*
%Professional Golfer's Assn, PO Box 109601, Palm Beach Gardens, FL 33410, USA

Hochhuth, Rolf *Playwright*
PO Box 661, 4002 Basel, Switzerland

Hochstrasser, Robin M *Chemist*
%University of Pennsylvania, Chemistry Dept, Philadelphia, PA 19104, USA

Hockaday, Irvine O, Jr *Businessman*
%Hallmark Cards Inc, 2501 McGee St, Kansas City, MO 64108, USA

Hockenberry, John *Commentator*
%"Day One" Show, 147 Columbus Ave, New York, NY 10023, USA

Hockenbrocht, David W *Businessman*
%Sparton Corp, 2400 E Ganson St, Jackson, MI 49202, USA

Hockett, Charles F *Anthropologist*
145 N Sunset Dr, Ithaca, NY 14850, USA

Hockney, David *Artist*
2907 Montcalm Ave, Los Angeles, CA 90046, USA

Hodder, Kenneth *Religious Leader*
%Salvation Army, 615 Slaters Lane, Alexandria, VA 22314, USA

Hodder, William A *Businessman*
%Donaldson Co, 1400 W 94th St, Minneapolis, MN 55431, USA

Hoddinott, Alun *Composer*
86 Mill Rd, Lisvane, Cardiff CF4 5UG, Wales

Hodge, Charlie *Hockey Player*
4088 198th St, Langley BC V3A 1E2, Canada

Hodge, Ken *Hockey Player*
%New York Rangers, Madison Square Garden, 4 Penn Plaza New York, NY 10001, USA

Hodge, Patricia *Actress*
%International Creative Mgmt, 76 Oxford St, London W1N 0AX, England

Hodges, Bill *Basketball Coach*
%Georgia College, Athletic Dept, Milledgeville, GA 31061, USA

Hodges, Carl N *Environmental Scientist*
%University of Arizona, Environmental Research Laboratory, Tucson, AZ 85721, USA

Hodgkin, Alan Lloyd *Nobel Medicine Laureate*
%Cambridge University, Physiology Lab, Downing St, Cambridge, England

Hodgkin, Howard *Artist*
32 Coptic St, London WC1, England

Hodgson, James D *Secretary, Labor*
10132 Hillgrove Dr, Beverly Hills, CA 90210, USA

Hodgson, Maurice *Businessman*
Kent House, #75/76, 87 Regent St, London W1, England

Hodgson, Thomas R *Businessman*
%Abbott Laboratories, 100 Abbott Park Rd, Abbott Park, IL 60064, USA

Hodler, Marc *Ski Executive*
%Int'l Ski Federation, Worbstr 210, 3073 Gumligen B Bern, Switzerland

Hodowal, John R *Businessman*
%IPALCO Enterprises, 25 Monument Cir, Indianapolis, IN 46204, USA

Hoeft, William F (Billy) *Baseball Player*
2243 S Huron Parkway, Ann Arbor, MI 48104, USA

Hoegh, Leo A *Governor, IA*
1472 W Desert Hills Dr, Green Valley, AZ 85614, USA

Hoelscher, Ludwig *Concert Cellist*
Graf Viereggstr 2, 82327 Tutzing Bei Muchen, Germany

Hoenig, Thomas M *Financier*
%Federal Reserve Bank, 925 Grand Ave, Kansas City, MO 64198, USA

Hoepner, Theodore J — *Financier*
%SunBank, 200 S Orange Ave, Orlando, FL 32801, USA

Hoerni, Jean A — *Electronics Consultant*
302 Lakeside Ave S, Seattle, WA 98144, USA

Hoest, Bunny — *Cartoonist (Lockhorns)*
%William Hoest Enterprises, 27 Watch Way, Lloyd Neck, Huntington, NY 11743, USA

Hoff, James E — *Educator*
%Xavier University, President's Office, Cincinnati, OH 45207, USA

Hoff, Marcian E (Ted), Jr — *Inventor (Commercial Microprocessor)*
12226 Colina Dr, Los Altos, CA 94024, USA

Hoff, Philip H — *Governor, VT*
%Hoff Wilson Powell Lang, 192 College St, Burlington, VT 05401, USA

Hoff, Sydney (Syd) — *Writer, Cartoonist*
PO Box 2463, Miami Beach, FL 33140, USA

Hoffman, Alan J — *Mathematician*
%IBM Research Center, Box 218, Yorktown Heights, NY 10598, USA

Hoffman, Alice — *Writer*
3 Hurlbut St, Cambridge, MA 02138, USA

Hoffman, Basil — *Actor*
4456 Cromwell Ave, Los Angeles, CA 90027, USA

Hoffman, Dustin — *Actor*
315 E 65th St, New York, NY 10021, USA

Hoffman, Grace — *Singer*
Bergstr 19, 72666 Neckartailfingen, Germany

Hoffman, Jeffrey A — *Astronaut*
%NASA, Johnson Space Center, 2101 NASA Rd, Houston, TX 77058, USA

Hoffman, Michael L — *Economist, Journalist*
RFD, Vineyard Haven, MA 02568, USA

Hoffman, Robert B — *Businessman*
%Monsanto Co, 800 N Lindbergh Blvd, St Louis, MO 63167, USA

Hoffman, Ted, Jr — *Bowling Executive*
1568 Partarian Way, San Jose, CA 95129, USA

Hoffman, William M — *Playwright, Lyricist*
190 Prince St, New York, NY 10012, USA

Hoffmann, Frank (Nordy) — *Football Player*
400 N Capitol St NW, #327, Washington, DC 20001, USA

Hoffmann, Jorg — *Swimmer*
M Curie 14, 16303 Schwedt, Germany

Hoffmann, Roald — *Nobel Chemistry Laureate*
4 Sugarbush Lane, Ithaca, NY 14850, USA

Hoffs, Susanna — *Singer*
%Stiefel-Phillips Ent, 9720 Wilshire Blvd, #400, Beverly Hills, CA 90212, USA

Hoflehner, Rudolf — *Artist*
Ottensteinstr 62, 2344 Maria Enzersdorf, Austria

Hofman, Leonard J — *Religious Leader*
%Christian Reformed Church, 2850 Kalamazoo Ave SE, Grand Rapids, MI 49560, USA

Hofmann, Douglas — *Artist*
8602 Saxon Circle, Baltimore, MD 21236, USA

Hofmann, Isabella — *Actress*
%Susan Smith Assoc, 121 N San Vicente Blvd, Beverly Hills, CA 90211, USA

Hofmann, Klaus — *Biochemist*
1467 Mohican Dr, Pittsburgh, PA 15228, USA

Hofmann, Peter — *Opera Singer*
%Fritz Hofmann, Schlosse Schonreith, 834191 Schonreuth, Germany

Hofstatter, Peter R — *Psychologist*
Lehmkuhleweg 16, 21614 Buxtehude, Germany

Hogan, A Paul — *Editor*
%Tampa Tribune, Editorial Dept, 202 S Parker St, Tampa, FL 33606, USA

Hogan, Ben W — *Golfer*
%Ben Hogan Co, 6000 Western Pl, #111, Fort Worth, TX 76107, USA

Hogan, Craig — *Astronomer*
%University of Washington, Astronomy Dept, Seattle, WA 98195, USA

Hogan, Gerald F — *Businessman*
%Home Shopping Network, 2501 118th Ave N, St Petersburg, FL 33716, USA

Hogan, Hulk — *Wrestler*
4505 Morella Ave, Valley Village, CA 91607, USA

Hogan, Jack — *Actor*
%Alex Brewis Agency, 12429 Laurel Terrace Dr, Studio City, CA 91604, USA

H

Hogan, Paul *Actor*
%JP Productions, 7 Parr Ave, North Curl, NSW 2099, Australia

Hogan, Robert *Actor*
%Borinstein-Oreck-Bogart, 8271 Melrose, #110, Los Angeles, CA 90046, USA

Hogarth, A Paul *Artist*
%Tessa Sayle, 11 Jubilee Place, London SW3 3TE, England

Hogarth, Burne *Cartoonist (Tarzan)*
6026 W Lindenhurst Ave, Los Angeles, CA 90036, USA

Hogestyn, Drake *Actor*
%Gage Group, 9255 Sunset Blvd, #515, Los Angeles, CA 90069, USA

Hogg, Sonya *Basketball Coach*
%Baylor University, Athletic Dept, Waco, TX 76798, USA

Hogwood, Christopher J H *Concert Harpsichordist, Conductor*
10 Brookside, Cambridge CB2 1JE, England

Hohenberg, John *Journalist, Educator*
7118 Sheffield Dr, Knoxville, TN 37909, USA

Hohmann, John *Anthropologist*
%Louis Berger Assoc, 1110 E Missouri Ave, #200, Phoenix, AZ 85014, USA

Hohn, Harry G *Businessman*
%New York Life Insurance Co, 51 Madison Ave, New York, NY 10010, USA

Hoiby, Lee *Composer, Concert Pianist*
800 Rock Valley Rd, Long Eddy, NY 12760, USA

Hokinson, Helen E *Cartoonist*
%New Yorker Magazine, Editorial Dept, 20 W 43rd St, New York, NY 10036, USA

Holbrook, Anthony B *Businessman*
%Advanced Micro Devices, 1 AMD Place, PO Box 3453, Sunnyvale, CA 94088, USA

Holbrook, Bill *Cartoonist (On the Fastrack)*
1321 Weatherstone Way, Atlanta, GA 30324, USA

Holbrook, Hal *Actor*
639 N Larchmont Blvd, #201, Los Angeles, CA 90004, USA

Holcombe, James C *Businessman*
%Nevada Power Co, 6226 W Sahara Ave, Las Vegas, NV 89151, USA

Holden, Rebecca *Singer*
%Box Office, 1010 16th Ave S, Nashville, TN 37212, USA

Holden-Brown, Derrick *Businessman*
Copse House, Milford-on-Sea, Lymington, Hants, England

Holder, Geoffrey *Actor, Dancer*
%Don Buchwald Assoc, 10 E 44th St, #500, New York, NY 10017, USA

Holder, Leonard D, Jr *Army General*
Commanding General, USArmy Combined Arms Center, Fort Leavenworth, KS 66027, USA

Holder, Richard G *Businessman*
%Reynolds Metals Co, 6603 W Broad St, Richmond, VA 23230, USA

Holderness of Bishop Wilton (R F Wood) *Government Official, England*
65 Les Collines De Guerrevieille, 83120 Ste Maxime, France

Holdorf, Willi *Track Athlete*
%Adidas KG, 91074 Herzogenaurach, Germany

Holdren, John P *Educator*
%University of California, Energy & Resources Group, Berkeley, CA 94720, USA

Holdsworth, G Trevor *Businessman*
%British Satellite Broadcasting, Queenstown Rd, London SW8 4NQ, England

Holiday, Harry, Jr *Businessman*
1616 Schirm Dr, Middletown, OH 45042, USA

Holl, Steven M *Architect*
%Steven Holl Architects, 435 Hudson St, #500, New York, NY 10014, USA

Holladay, Wilhelmina *Museum Official*
%National Museum of Women in Arts, 1250 New York NW, Washington, DC 20005, USA

Holland, Heinrich D *Geologist*
%Harvard University, Hoffman Laboratory, Cambridge, MA 02138, USA

Holland, Jeffrey R *Educator*
%LDS Church, 47 E South Temple, Salt Lake City, UT 84150, USA

Holland, John B *Businessman*
%Fruit of the Loom Inc, Sears Tower, 233 S Wacker Dr, Chicago, IL 60606, USA

Holland, John R *Religious Leader*
%Foursquare Gospel Int'l Church, 1910 W Sunset Blvd, Los Angeles, CA 90026, USA

Holland, Terry *Basketball Coach, Administrator*
%Davidson College, Athletic Dept, Davidson, NC 28036, USA

Holland, Tom *Artist*
%San Francisco Art Institute, 800 Chestnut St, San Francisco, CA 94133, USA

Holland, Willard R, Jr — *Businessman*
%Ohio Edison, 76 S Main St, Akron, OH 44308, USA

Hollander, John — *Poet*
%Yale University, English Dept, New Haven, CT 06520, USA

Hollander, Lorin — *Concert Pianist*
210 W 101st St, #PH, New York, NY 10025, USA

Hollander, Nicole — *Cartoonist (Sylvia)*
%Sylvia Syndicate, 1440 N Dayton St, Chicago, IL 60622, USA

Holldobler, Berthold K — *Writer, Biologist, Zoologist*
%Harvard University, Biology Dept, Cambridge, MA 02138, USA

Hollein, Hans — *Architect*
Eiskellerstr 1, 40213 Dusseldorf, Germany

Hollen, Stanley C — *Financier*
%Golden 1 Credit Union, 6507 4th Ave, Sacramento, CA 95817, USA

Hollerer, Walter F — *Writer, Critic*
Heerstr 99, 14055 Berlin, Germany

Holliday, Fred — *Actor*
4610 Forman Ave, North Hollywood, CA 91602, USA

Holliday, Jennifer — *Singer, Actress*
%Bowen Agency, 504 W 168th St, New York, NY 10032, USA

Holliday, Polly — *Singer, Actress*
201 E 17th St, #23-H, New York, NY 10003, USA

Holliger, Heinz — *Concert Oboist, Composer*
%Ingpen & Williams, 14 Kensington Court, London W8, England

Holliman, Earl — *Actor*
PO Box 1969, Studio City, CA 91614, USA

Hollings, Michael R — *Religious Leader*
St Mary of Angels, Moorhouse Rd, Bayswater, London W2 5DJ, England

Hollins, Lionel — *Basketball Player*
%Phoenix Suns, 201 E Jefferson St, Phoenix, AZ 85004, USA

Holloway, James L, III — *Navy Admiral*
1694 Epping Farms Lane, Annapolis, MD 21401, USA

Holloway, Randy — *Football Player*
%New England Patriots, Foxboro Stadium, Rt 1, Foxboro, MA 02035, USA

Holly, Lauren — *Actress*
13601 Ventura Blvd, #99, Sherman Oaks, CA 91423, USA

Holm Whalen, Eleanor — *Swimmer*
1800 NE 114th St, #1503, North Miami, FL 33181, USA

Holm, Celeste — *Actress*
88 Central Park West, New York, NY 10023, USA

Holm, Ian — *Actor*
%Julian Belfrage, 46 Albermarle St, London W1X 4PP, England

Holm, Jeanne M — *Air Force General*
2707 Thyme Dr, Edgewater, MD 21037, USA

Holm, Joan — *Bowler*
%Women's International Dowling Congress, 5301 S 76th St, Greendale, WI 53129, USA

Holm, Richard H — *Chemist*
40 Temple St, Belmont, MA 02178, USA

Holman, C Ray — *Businessman*
%Mallinckrodt Group, 7733 Forsyth Blvd, St Louis, MO 63105, USA

Holman, Marshall — *Bowler*
%Professional Bowlers Assn, 1720 Merriman Rd, Akron, OH 44313, USA

Holman, Ralph T — *Biochemist*
1403 2nd Ave SW, Austin, MN 55912, USA

Holman, William G — *Financier*
%Baring Securities, 667 Madison Ave, New York, NY 10021, USA

Holmboe, Vagn — *Composer*
Holmboevej 4-6, Ramlose, 3200 Helsinge, Denmark

Holmes, D Brainerd — *Space Engineer, Businessman*
%Bay Colony Corp Center, 950 Winter St, #4350, Waltham, MA 02154, USA

Holmes, David R — *Businessman*
%Reynolds & Reynolds Inc, 115 S Ludlow St, Dayton, OH 45402, USA

Holmes, E Paul — *Navy Admiral*
5700 Williamsburg Landing Dr, #107, Williamsburg, VA 23185, USA

Holmes, Jay T — *Businessman*
%Bausch & Lomb Inc, 1 Chase Square, Rochester, NY 14604, USA

Holmes, Jennifer — *Actress*
PO Box 6303, Carmel, CA 93921, USA

Holland - Holmes

H

Holmes, Larry — *Boxer*
%Holmes Enterprises, 43 Northampton St, Easton, PA 18042, USA

Holmes, Ron — *Football Player*
%Tampa Bay Buccaneers, 1 Buccaneer Place, Tampa, FL 33607, USA

Holmes, Thomas F (Tommy) — *Baseball Player*
1 Pine Dr, Woodbury, NY 11797, USA

Holmgren, Mike — *Football Coach*
%Green Bay Packers, 1265 Lombardi Ave, Green Bay, WI 54304, USA

Holmgren, Paul — *Hockey Player, Coach*
%Hartford Whalers, Coliseum, 242 Trumbell St, #800, Hartford, CT 06103, USA

Holmquest, Donald L — *Astronaut*
%Holmquest Assoc, 3721 Tangley Rd, Houston, TX 77005, USA

Holmstrom, Carl — *Skier*
1703 E 3rd St, #101, Duluth, MN 55812, USA

Holomisa, Bantu — *President, Transkei; General*
%President's Office, Military Council, Umtata, Transkei

Holovak, Mike — *Football Player, Coach, Executive*
%Houston Oilers, 6910 Fannin St, Houston, TX 77030, USA

Holroyd, Michael — *Writer*
85 St Marks Rd, London W10 6JS England

Holst, Per — *Movie Producer*
%Per Holst Film A/S, Rentemestervej 69-A, 2400 Copenhagen NV, Denmark

Holt, David Lee — *Guitarist (Mavericks)*
%AristoMedia, 1620 16th Ave S, Nashville, TN 37212, USA

Holt, Glenn L — *Labor Leader*
%Metal Workers Union, 5578 Montgomery Rd, Cincinnati, OH 45212, USA

Holt, Leon C, Jr — *Businessman*
Pocono Lake, Preserve, PA 18348, USA

Holtermann, E Louis, Jr — *Publisher*
%Glamour Magazine, 350 Madison Ave, New York, NY 10017, USA

Holton, A Linwood, Jr — *Governor, VA*
6010 Claiborne Dr, McLean, VA 22101, USA

Holton, Earl — *Businessman*
%Meijer Inc, 2929 Walker NW, Grand Rapids, MI 49544, USA

Holton, Gerald — *Physicist*
64 Francis Ave, Cambridge, MA 02138, USA

Holton, Richard H — *Educator*
87 Southampton Ave, Berkeley, CA 94707, USA

Holton, Robert J — *Labor Leader*
%Plasters/Cement Masons International Assn, 1125 17th NW, Washington, DC 20036, USA

Holtz, Louis L (Lou) — *Football Coach*
%University of Notre Dame, Athletic Dept, PO Box 518, Notre Dame, IN 46556, USA

Holtzman, Jerome — *Sportswriter*
1225 Forest Ave, Evanston, IL 60202, USA

Holtzman, Kenneth D (Ken) — *Baseball Player*
933 Providence, Buffalo Grove, IL 60089, USA

Holtzman, Wayne H — *Psychologist*
3300 Foothill Dr, Austin, TX 78731, USA

Holub, E J — *Football Player*
Mullendore Cross Bell Ranch, RR 1, Copan, OK 74022, USA

Holum, Dianne — *Speed Skater*
280 Weldwood Dr, Elgin, IL 60120, USA

Holyfield, Evander — *Boxer*
794 Highway 279, Fairburn, GA 30213, USA

Holz, Ernest W — *Religious Leader*
%Salvation Army, Commander's Office, 120 W 14th St, New York, NY 10011, USA

Holzer, Jenny — *Artist*
245 Eldridge St, New York, NY 10002, USA

Holzman, Malcolm — *Architect*
%Hardy Holzman Pfeiffer, 902 Broadway, New York, NY 10010, USA

Holzman, William (Red) — *Basketball Coach*
%New York Knicks, Madison Square Garden, 4 Penn Plaza, New York, NY 10001, USA

Homeier, Skip — *Actor*
247 N Castellana, Palm Desert, CA 92260, USA

Homfeld, Conrad — *Equestrian Rider*
%Sandron, 11744 Marblestone Court, West Palm Beach, FL 33414, USA

Honderich, Beland H — *Publisher*
%Toronto Star, 1 Yonge St, Toronto ON M5E 1E6, Canada

Holmes - Honderich

Honderich, John H	*Editor*
%Toronto Star, Editorial Dept, 1 Yonge St, Toronto ON M5E 1E6, Canada	
Honea, T Milton	*Businessman*
%NorAm Energy Corp, 1600 Smith St, Houston, TX 77002, USA	
Honegger, Fritz	*President, Switzerland*
Schloss-Str 29, 8803 Ruschlikon, Switzerland	
Honeycutt, Frederick W (Rick)	*Baseball Player*
207 Forrest Rd, Fort Oglethorpe, GA 30742, USA	
Honeycutt, Van B	*Businessman*
%Computer Sciences Corp, 2100 E Grand Ave, El Segundo, CA 90245, USA	
Honeyghan, Lloyd	*Boxer*
50 Barnfield Wood Rd, Park Langley, Beckenham, Kent, England	
Honeyman, Janice	*Actress*
8-A Seymour St, Westdene, Johannesburg 2092, South Africa	
Hong, James	*Actor*
11684 Ventura Blvd, #948, Studio City, CA 91604, USA	
Honig, Edwin	*Writer*
%Brown University, English Dept, Providence, RI 02912, USA	
Hood, Edward E, Jr	*Businessman*
917 Lake House Dr, Lost Tree Village, FL 33408, USA	
Hood, Leroy E	*Biologist*
5534 55th Ave NE, Seattle, WA 98105, USA	
Hood, Robert	*Editor*
%Boys Life Magazine, Editorial Dept, 1325 Walnut Hill Lane, Irving, TX 75038, USA	
Hood, Robin	*Golfer*
%Ladies Professional Golf Assn, 2570 Volusia Ave, Daytona Beach, FL 32114, USA	
Hooglandt, Jan D	*Businessman*
%Hoogovens Group, 1970 CA Nijmegen, Netherlands	
Hook, Harold S	*Businessman*
%American General Corp, 2929 Allen Parkway, Houston, TX 77019, USA	
Hooker, Charles R	*Artist*
28 Whippingham Rd, Brighton, Sussex BN2 3PG, England	
Hooker, John Lee	*Singer, Guitarist*
%Rosebud Agency, PO Box 170429, San Francisco, CA 94117, USA	
Hooker, Michael K	*Educator*
%University of Massachusetts, President's Office, Boston, MA 02108, USA	
Hooks, Benjamin L	*Civil Rights Activist*
200 Wagner Pl, #407-8, Memphis, TN 38103, USA	
Hooks, Jan	*Actress*
%William Morris Agency, 151 S El Camino Dr, Beverly Hills, CA 90212, USA	
Hooks, Robert	*Actor*
145 N Valley St, Burbank, CA 91505, USA	
Hookstratten, Edward G	*Attorney*
9012 Beverly Blvd, Los Angeles, CA 90048, USA	
Hoops, Alan R	*Businessman*
%PacifiCare Health Systems, 5995 Plaza Dr, Cypress, CA 90630, USA	
Hooten, Burt C	*Baseball Player*
3619 Granby Court, San Antonio, TX 78217, USA	
Hoover, William R	*Businessman*
%Computer Sciences Corp, 2100 E Grand Ave, El Segundo, CA 90245, USA	
Hope, Alec	*Poet*
66 Arthur Circle, Forrest ACT, Australia	
Hope, Bob	*Comedian*
10346 Moorpark St, North Hollywood, CA 91602, USA	
Hope, Maurice	*Boxer*
%Boxing Control Board, Ramilles Building, Hills Place, London W1, England	
Hopfield, John J	*Biophysicist*
931 Canon Dr, Pasadena, CA 91106, USA	
Hopkins, Anthony	*Actor*
%Conway Van Gelder Robinson, 18-21 Jermyn St, London SW1Y 6HB, England	
Hopkins, Bo	*Actor*
6628 Ethel Ave, North Hollywood, CA 91606, USA	
Hopkins, Godfrey T	*Photographer*
Wilmington Cottage, Wilmington Rd, Seaford, East Sussex BN25 2EH, England	
Hopkins, Linda	*Singer*
2055 N Ivar St, #PH-21, Los Angeles, CA 90068, USA	
Hopkins, Michael J	*Architect*
27 Broadley Terrace, London NW1 6LG, England	

H

Honderich - Hopkins

H

Hopkins, Telma *Actress, Singer*
%Innovative Artists, 1999 Ave of Stars, #2850, Los Angeles, CA 90067, USA

Hopkins, Wes *Football Player*
%Kansas City Chiefs, 1 Arrowhead Dr, Kansas City, KS 64129, USA

Hopp, John L (Johnny) *Baseball Player*
1914 Ave "M", Scottsbluff, NE 69361, USA

Hoppe, Wolfgang *Bobsled Athlete*
Dieterstedter Str 11, 99510 Apolda, Germany

Hopper, Dennis *Actor, Director*
330 Indiana Ave, Venice, CA 90291, USA

Hopson, Dennis *Basketball Player*
%Chicago Bulls, 1901 W Madison St, Chicago, IL 60612, USA

Horak, H Lynn *Financier*
%Norwest Bank, 7th & Walnut Sts, Des Moines, IA 50309, USA

Horan, Mike *Football Player*
%New York Giants, Giants Stadium, East Rutherford, NJ 07073, USA

Horecker, Bernard L *Biochemist*
1621 Sand Castle Rd, Sanibel Island, FL 33957, USA

Horgan, Patrick *Actor*
201 E 89th St, New York, NY 10128, USA

Horlen, Joel E *Baseball Player*
3718 Chartwell Dr, San Antonio, TX 78230, USA

Horlock, John H *Mechanical Engineer, Educator*
2 The Avenue, Ampthill, Bedford MK45 2NR, England

Horn, Carol *Fashion Designer*
575 7th Ave, New York, NY 10018, USA

Horn, Charles G *Businessman*
%Fieldcrest Cannon Inc, 326 E Stadium Dr, Eden, NC 27288, USA

Horn, Francis H *Educator*
42 Upper College Rd, Kingston, RI 02881, USA

Horn, Gyula *Prime Minister, Hungary*
%Parliament, Kossuth Lajos Ter 1/3, 1055 Budapest, Hungary

Horn, Karen N *Financier*
%Banc One Corp Cleveland, 600 Superior Ave, Cleveland, OH 44114, USA

Horn, Paul J *Jazz Flutist*
4601 Leyns Rd, Victoria BC V8N 3A1, Canada

Horn, Ralph *Financier*
%First Tennessee National Corp, 165 Madison Ave, Memphis, TN 38103, USA

Horn, Shirley *Singer*
%Bennett Morgan Assoc, 1282 Rt 376, Wappingers Falls, NY 12590, USA

Hornacek, Jeff *Basketball Player*
%Utah Jazz, 301 W South Temple, Salt Lake City, UT 84101, USA

Horne, Donald R *Writer*
53 Grosvenor St, Woollahra, Sydney NSW, Australia

Horne, John R *Businessman*
%Navistar International, 455 N Cityfront Plaza Dr, Chicago, IL 60611, USA

Horne, Lena *Singer*
%Volney Apts, 23 E 74th St, New York, NY 10021, USA

Horne, Marilyn *Opera Singer*
%Columbia Artists Mgmt Inc, 165 W 57th St, New York, NY 10019, USA

Horner, Charles A *Air Force General*
2824 Jack Nicklaus Way, Shalimar, FL 32579, USA

Horner, Freeman V *WW II Army Hero (CMH)*
PO Box 6144, Columbus, GA 31907, USA

Horner, J Robert (Bob) *Baseball Player*
209 Steeplechase Dr, Irving, TX 75062, USA

Horner, James *Composer*
728 Brooktree Rd, Pacific Palisades, CA 90272, USA

Horner, John R (Jack) *Palentologist*
%Museum of the Rockies, Montana State University, Bozeman, MT 59717, USA

Horner, Martina S *Educator, Businesswoman*
%TIAA-CREF, 730 3rd Ave, New York, NY 10017, USA

Hornig, Donald F *Chemist*
16 Longfellow Park, Cambridge, MA 02138, USA

Hornsby, Bruce *Singer, Pianist*
PO Box 3545, Williamsburg, VA 23187, USA

Hornung, Paul *Football Player*
5800 Creighton Hill Rd, Louisville, KY 40207, USA

Hopkins - Hornung

Horovitz (Ad-Rock), Adam *Rapper (Beastie Boys)*
%Gold Mountain Ent, 3575 Cahuenga Blvd W, #450, Los Angeles, CA 90068, USA
Horovitz, Israel A *Playwright*
146 W 11th St, New York, NY 10011, USA
Horovitz, Joseph *Composer*
%Royal College of Music, Prince Consort Rd, London SW7 2BS, England
Horowitz, David C *Commentator*
4267 Marina City Dr, #810, Marina Del Rey, CA 90292, USA
Horowitz, David H *Businessman*
141 E 72nd St, New York, NY 10021, USA
Horowitz, Jerome P *Medical Researcher*
%Michigan Cancer Foundation, 110 E Warren Ave, Detroit, MI 48201, USA
Horowitz, Norman H *Biologist*
2495 Brighton Rd, Pasadena, CA 91104, USA
Horowitz, Paul *Physician*
111 Chilton St, Cambridge, MA 02138, USA
Horrigan, Edward A, Jr *Businessman*
228 Locha Dr, Jupiter, FL 33458, USA
Horry, Robert *Basketball Player*
%Houston Rockets, Summit, Greenway Plaza, #10, Houston, TX 77277, USA
Horsford, Anna Maria *Actress*
PO Box 48082, Los Angeles, CA 90048, USA
Horsley, Lee *Actor*
PO Box 456, Gypsum, CO 81637, USA
Horsley, Richard D *Financier*
%Regions Financial Corp, 417 N 20th St, Birmingham, AL 35203, USA
Horton, Frank E *Educator*
%University of Toledo, President's Office, Toledo, OH 43606, USA
Horton, Peter *Actor*
409 Santa Monica Blvd, #PH, Santa Monica, CA 90401, USA
Horton, Robert *Actor*
5317 Andasol Ave, Encino, CA 91316, USA
Horton, William W (Willie) *Baseball Player*
%Reid, 15124 Warwick, Detroit, MI 48223, USA
Horvath, Les *Football Player*
2667 Bogue Dr, Glendale, CA 91208, USA
Hoskins, Bob *Actor*
30 Steele Rd, London NW3 4RE, England
Hosmer, Bradley C (Brad) *Air Force General*
%Superintendent's Office, 2304 Cadet Dr, USAF Air Force Academy, CO 80840, USA
Hossein, Robert *Actor, Theater Director*
%Ghislaine De Wing, 10 Rue Du Docteur Roux, 75015 Paris, France
Hostetler, Jeff W *Foobtall Player*
%Oakland Raiders, Oakland Coliseum, Oakland, CA 94621, USA
Hostetter, G Richard *Religious Leader*
%Presbyterian Church in America, 1852 Century Place, Atlanta, GA 30345, USA
Hotani, Hirokazu *Microbiotics Engineer*
%Teikyo University, Biosciences Dept, Toyosatodai, Utsunomiya 320, Japan
Hotard, Edgar G *Businessman*
%Praxair Inc, 39 Old Ridgebury Rd, Danbury, CT 06810, USA
Hotchkiss, Harley *Hockey Executive*
%Calgary Flames, PO Box 1540, Station "M", Calgary AB T2P 389, Canada
Hotchkiss, Rollin D *Bacterial Physiologist*
%State University of New York, Biology Dept, Albany, NY 12222, USA
Hotson, Leslie *Educator*
White Hollow Rd, Northford, CT 06472, USA
Hottel, Hoyt C *Chemical Engineer*
27 Cambridge St, Winchester, MA 01890, USA
Hottelet, Richard C *Commentator*
120 Chestnut Hill Rd, Wilton, CT 06897, USA
Hotter, Hans *Opera Singer*
%Bayerische Staatsoper, Portiastr 8, 81545 Munich, Germany
Hou Runyu *Conductor*
1710-3-602 Huai-Hai-Zhong Rd, Shanghai, China
Hou, Ya-Ming *Biologist*
%Massachusetts Institute of Technology, Biology Dept, Cambridge, MA 02139, USA
Houbregs, Bob *Basketball Player*
3403 207th Ave SE, Issaquah, WA 98029, USA

H

Horovitz (Ad-Rock) - Houbregs

Hough, Charles O (Charlie) — Baseball Player
2266 Shade Tree Circle, Brea, CA 92621, USA

Hough, John — Movie Director
8 Queen St, Mayfair, London W1, England

Hough, Lawrence A — Businessman
%Student Loan Marketing Assn, 1050 Thomas Jefferson NW, Washington, DC 20007, USA

Hough, Richard — Writer
31 Meadowbank, London NW3 1AY, England

Hough, Stephen A G — Concert Pianist
%Harrison Parrott Ltd, 12 Penzance Place, London W11 4PA, England

Houghton of Sowerby, Douglas — Government Official, England
110 Marsham Court, London SW1, England

Houghton, James R — Businessman
%Corning Inc, Houghton Park, Corning, NY 14831, USA

Houghton, John — Physicist
%Rutherford Appleton Laboratory, Chilton, Didcot Oxon OX11 0QX, England

Houghton, Katherine — Actress
134 Steele Rd, West Hartford, CT 06119, USA

Houk, Ralph G — Baseball Manager
3000 Plantation Rd, Winter Haven, FL 33884, USA

Houle, Cyril O — Educator
700 John Ringling Blvd, #1705, Sarasota, FL 34236, USA

Hounsfield, Godfrey N — Nobel Medicine Laureate
15 Crane Park Rd, Whitton, Twickenham, Middx, England

House, Karen E — Journalist
%Wall Street Journal, Editorial Dept, 22 Cortlandt St, New York, NY 10007, USA

Housley, Phil — Hockey Player
%Calgary Flames, PO Box 1540, Station "M", Calgary AB T2P 389, Canada

Houssels, J K — Businessman
%Showboat Inc, 2800 E Fremont St, Las Vegas, NV 89104, USA

Houssels, J Kell, III — Businessman
%Showboat Inc, 2800 E Fremont St, Las Vegas, NV 89104, USA

Houston, Allan — Basketball Player
%Detroit Pistons, Palace, 2 Championship Dr, Auburn Hills, MI 48057, USA

Houston, Cissy — Singer
2160 N Central Rd, Fort Lee, NJ 07024, USA

Houston, James A — Writer
24 Main St, Stonington, CT 06378, USA

Houston, Jim — Football Player
3625 Hughestown Dr, Akron, OH 44333, USA

Houston, Ken — Football Player
3603 Forest Village Dr, Kingwood, TX 77339, USA

Houston, Thelma — Singer
4296 Mt Vernon Dr, Los Angeles, CA 90008, USA

Houston, Wade — Basketball Coach
%University of Tennessee, Athletic Dept, Knoxville, TN 37901, USA

Houston, Whitney — Singer
%Nippy Inc, 2160 N Central Rd, Fort Lee, NJ 07024, USA

Houthakker, Hendrik S — Economist
348 Payson Rd, Belmont, MA 02178, USA

Houtte, Jean Van — Prime Minister, Belgium
54 Blvd St Michel, Brussels, Belgium

Hove, Andrew C, Jr — Financier
%Federal Deposit Insurance Corp, 550 17th St NW, Washington, DC 20429, USA

Hovhaness, Alan — Composer
%C F Peters Corp, 373 Park Ave S, New York, NY 10016, USA

Hovind, David J — Businessman
%Paccar Inc, 777 106th Ave NE, Bellevue, WA 98004, USA

Hoving, Thomas — Museum Director, Editor
%Hoving Assoc, 150 E 73rd St, New York NY 10021, USA

Hovnanian, Ara K — Businessman
%Hovnanian Enterprises, 10 Highway 35, Red Bank, NJ 07701, USA

Hovnanian, Kevork S — Businessman
%Hovnanian Enterprises, 10 Highway 35, Red Bank, NJ 07701, USA

Hovsepian, Vatche — Religious Leader
%Armenian Church of America (West), 1201 N Vine St, Los Angeles, C 90038, USA

Howard, Alan — Actor
%Julian Belfrage, 46 Albermarle St, London W1X 4PP, England

Howard, Ann *Opera Singer*
%Stafford Law Assoc, 26 Mayfield Rd, Weybridge, Surrey KT13 8XB, England

Howard, Desmond *Football Player*
%Jacksonville Jaguars, 1 Stadium Place, Jacksonville, FL 32202, USA

Howard, Frank O *Baseball Player*
15626 Bernardo Center Dr, #2802, San Diego, CA 92127, USA

Howard, Greg *Cartoonist (Sally Forth)*
3403 W 28th St, Minneapolis, MN 55416, USA

Howard, Harry N *Historian*
6508 Greentree Rd, Bradley Hills Grove, Bethesda, MD 20817, USA

Howard, Jack R *Publisher*
%Scripps-Howard Newspapers, 200 Park Ave, New York, NY 10166, USA

Howard, James J, III *Businessman*
%Northern States Power Co, 414 Nicollett Mall, Minneapolis, MN 55401, USA

Howard, James Newton *Composer*
%Gorfaine/Schwarz/Roberts, 3301 Barham Blvd, #201, Los Angeles, CA 90068, USA

Howard, Jan *Singer*
%Tessier-Marsh Talent, 505 Canton Pass, Madison, TN 37115, USA

Howard, Juwan *Basketball Player*
%Washington Bullets, Capital Centre, 1 Truman Dr, Landover, MD 20785, USA

Howard, Ken *Actor*
%Ken Howard Productions, 59 E 54th St, #22, New York, NY 10022, USA

Howard, Michael *Government Official, England*
%House of Commons, Westminster, London SW1A 0AA, England

Howard, Rance *Actor*
4286 Clybourn Ave, Burbank, CA 91505, USA

Howard, Richard *Writer*
23 Waverly Place, #5-X, New York, NY 10003, USA

Howard, Robert L *Vietnam War Army Hero (CMH)*
8450 Cambridge St, #1203, Houston, TX 77054, USA

Howard, Ron *Actor, Director*
%Imagine Entertainment, 1925 Century Park East, #2300, Los Angeles, CA 90067, USA

Howard, Sherri *Track Athlete*
14059 Bridle Ridge Rd, Sylmar, CA 91342, USA

Howard, Susan *Actress*
PO Box 1456, Boerne, TX 78006, USA

Howarth, Thomas *Architect*
%University of Toronto, 230 College St, Toronto ON M5S 1R1, Canada

Howatch, Susan *Writer*
%Aitken & Stone, 29 Fernshaw Rd, London SW10 0TG, England

Howe of Aberavon, R E Geoffrey *Government Official, England*
%Barclays Bank, Cavendish Square Branch, 4 Vere St, London W1, England

Howe, Arthur *Journalist*
%Philadelphia Inquirer, Editorial Dept, 400 N Broad St, Philadelphia, PA 19130, USA

Howe, Arthur H (Art) *Baseball Player, Manager*
711 Kahlddon Court, Houston, TX 77079, USA

Howe, G Woodson *Editor*
%Omaha World-Herald, Editorial Dept, World-Herald Square, Omaha, NE 68102, USA

Howe, Gordon (Gordie) *Hockey Player*
6645 Peninsula Dr, Traverse City, MI 49686, USA

Howe, Harold, II *Educator*
55 Alcott Rd, Concord, MA 01742, USA

Howe, Jonathan T *Navy Admiral*
3946 Saint Johns Ave, #123, Jacksonville, FL 32205, USA

Howe, Mark *Hockey Player, Executive*
%Detroit Red Wings, Joe Louis Arena, 600 Civic Center Dr, Detroit, MI 48226, USA

Howe, Oscar *Artist*
128 Walker St, Vermillion, SD 57069, USA

Howe, Robert W *Businessman*
%MAPCO Inc, PO Box 645, Tulsa, OK 74101, USA

Howe, Stanley M *Businessman*
%HON Industries, 414 E 3rd St, Muscatine, IA 52761, USA

Howe, Steven R (Steve) *Baseball Player*
PO Box 1355, Warsaw, IN 46581, USA

Howe, Tina *Playwright*
333 West End Ave, New York, NY 10023, USA

Howell, C Thomas *Actor*
1491 Stone Canyon Blvd, Los Angeles, CA 90077, USA

H

Howard - Howell

Howell, Francis C — *Anthropologist*
1994 San Antonio Ave, Berkeley, CA 94707, USA

Howell, Harry — *Hockey Player*
General Delivery, Carslyle ON L0R 1H0, Canada

Howell, John R — *Financier*
%UJB Financial Corp, Carnegie Center, PO Box 2066, Princeton, NJ 08543, USA

Howell, Margaret — *Fashion Designer*
5 Garden House, 8 Battersea Park Rd, London SW8, England

Howell, Paul N — *Businessman*
%Howell Corp, 1111 Fannin St, Houston, TX 77002, USA

Howell, W Nathaniel, III — *Diplomat*
%State Department, 2201 "C" St NW, Washington, DC 20520, USA

Howell, William R — *Businessman*
%J C Penney Co, PO Box 10001, Dallas, TX 75301, USA

Howells, Anne E — *Opera Singer*
Milestone, Broom Close, Esher, Surrey, England

Howells, William W — *Anthropologist*
11 Lawrence Lane, Kittery Point, ME 03905, USA

Howes, Sally Ann — *Actress*
%Saraband Assoc, 265 Liverpool Rd, London N1 1LX, England

Howland, Beth — *Actress*
255 Amalfi Dr, Santa Monica, CA 90402, USA

Howley, Charles L (Chuck) — *Football Player*
%Howley Uniform Rental Inc, 5422 Redfield St, Dallas, TX 75235, USA

Howse, Elwood D, Jr — *Businessman*
%Cable & Howse Ventures, 777 108th Ave NE, Bellevue, WA 98004, USA

Howson, Robert E — *Businessman*
%McDermott International Inc, 1450 Poydras St, New Orleans, LA 70112, USA

Hoyle, Fred — *Astronomer, Mathematician*
%Royal Society, 6 Carlton House Terrace, London SW1Y 5AG, England

Hoyt, Henry H, Jr — *Businessman*
%Carter-Wallace Inc, Burlington House, 1345 Ave of Americas, New York, NY 10105, USA

Hoyte, Hugh Desmond — *President, Guyana*
14 North Rd, Bourda, Georgetown, Guyana

Hrabosky, Alan T (Al) — *Baseball Player, Sportscaster*
16216 Pepper View Court, Chesterfield, MO 63005, USA

Hrawi, Elias — *President, Lebanon*
%President's Office, Palais de Baebda, Beirut, Lebanon

Hrudey, Kelly — *Hockey Player*
%Los Angeles Kings, Forum, PO Box 17013, Inglewood, CA 90308, USA

Hruska, Roman L — *Senator, NE*
2139 S 38th St, Omaha, NE 68105, USA

Hu Qili — *Government Official, China*
%Chinese Communist Party, Beijing, China

Huarte, John — *Football Player*
1448 E Northshore Dr, Tempe, AZ 85283, USA

Hubbard, Elizabeth — *Actress*
165 W 46th St, #1214, New York, NY 10036, USA

Hubbard, Frederick D (Freddie) — *Jazz Trumpeter*
%Merlin Co, 17609 Ventura Blvd, #212, Encino, CA 91316, USA

Hubbard, Gregg — *Singer (Sawyer Brown)*
%TKO Artist Mgmt, 4213 Hillsboro Rd, #318, Nashville, TN 37215, USA

Hubbard, John — *Artist*
Chilcombe House, Chilcombe Near Bridport, Dorset, England

Hubbard, Phil — *Basketball Player*
%New York Knicks, Madison Square Garden, 4 Penn Plaza, New York, NY 10001, USA

Hubbell, Frederick S — *Businessman*
%Equitable of Iowa Companies, 604 Locust St, Des Moines, IA 50309, USA

Hubble, Don W — *Businessman*
%National Service Industries, 1420 Peachtree St NE, Atlanta, GA 30309, USA

Hubel, David H — *Nobel Medicine Laureate*
98 Collins Rd, Newton, MA 02168, USA

Hubenthal, Karl — *Editorial Cartoonist*
5536 Via La Mesa, #A, Laguna Hills, CA 92653, USA

Huber, Anke — *Tennis Player*
Dieselstr 10, 76689 Karlsdorf-Neuthard, Germany

Huber, Richard L — *Businessman*
%Aetna Life & Casualty Co, 151 Farmington Ave, Hartford, CT 06156, USA

Huber, Robert *Nobel Chemistry Laureate*
Max Planck Biochemie Institut, Am Klopferspitz, 82152 Martinsried, Germany

Hubers, David R *Financier*
%American Express Financial Corp, IDS Tower 10, Minneapolis, MN 55440, USA

Hubley, Faith E *Animator*
%Hubley Studio, 2575 Palisade Ave, #12-L, Riverdale, NY 10463, USA

Hubley, Season *Actress*
46 Wavecrest Ave, Venice, CA 90291, USA

Huckstep, Ronald L *Orthopedic Surgeon*
108 Sugarloaf Crescent, Castlecrag, Syndey NSW 2068, Australia

Huddleston, David *Actor*
%Abrams-Rubaloff Lawrence, 8075 W 3rd St, #303, Los Angeles, CA 90048, USA

Huddleston, Trevor *Religious Leader*
House of Resurrection, Mirfield, W Yorks WF14 OBN, England

Huddleston, Walter D *Senator, KY*
Seminole Rd, Elizabethtown, KY 42701, USA

Hudecek, Vaclav *Concert Violinist*
Londynska 25, 120 00 Prague 2, Czech Republic

Hudner, Thomas J, Jr *Korean War Navy Hero (CMH)*
31 Allen Farm Lane, Concord, MA 01742, USA

Hudson, Bannus B *Businessman*
%US Shoe Corp, 1 Eastwood Dr, Cincinnati, OH 45227, USA

Hudson, C B, Jr *Businessman*
%Liberty National Life Insurance, PO Box 2612, Birmingham, AL 35202, USA

Hudson, Clifford G *Financier*
%Securities Investor Protection Corp, 805 15th St NW, Washington, DC 20005, USA

Hudson, Garth *Organist (The Band)*
%Storm Mgmt, 256 Centre Rd, Bentleigh, Vic 3204, Australia

Hudson, Hugh *Movie Director*
%Hudson Films Ltd, 11 Queensgate Place Mews, London SW7 5BG, England

Hudson, James *Psychiatrist*
%Harvard Medical School, 25 Shattuck St, Boston, MA 02115, USA

Hudson, James T *Businessman*
%Hudson Foods Inc, 1225 Hudson Rd, Rogers, AR 72756, USA

Hudson, Michael T *Businessman*
%Hudson Foods Inc, 1225 Hudson Rd, Rogers, AR 72756, USA

Hudson, Sally *Skier*
PO Box 2343, Olympic Valley, CA 96146, USA

Hudson, William J *Businessman*
%AMP Inc, 470 Friendship Rd, Harrisburg, PA 17111, USA

Huebner, Robert J *Medical Research Scientist*
12100 Whippoorwil Lane, Rockville, MD 20852, USA

Huet, Philippe E J *Businessman*
%Charbonnages de France, BP 396 08, 73560 Paris Cedex, France

Huey, Ward L, Jr *Businessman*
%A H Belo Corp, 400 S Record St, Dallas, TX 75202, USA

Huff, Kenneth W (Ken) *Football Player*
105 Blackford Court, Durham, NC 27712, USA

Huff, Sam *Football Player*
824 Emerald Dr, Wellington, VA 22308, USA

Huffington, Arianna *Writer*
1250 "H" St NW, #550, Washington, DC 20005, USA

Hufstedler, Shirley M *Secretary, Education*
%Hufstedler Kaus Ettinger, 355 S Grand Ave, Los Angeles, CA 90071, USA

Huggard, E Douglas *Businessman*
%Atlantic Energy, 6801 Black Horse Pike, Pleasantville, NJ 08234, USA

Huggins, Bob *Basketball Coach*
%University of Cincinnati, Athletic Dept, Cincinnati, OH 45221, USA

Huggins, Charles B *Nobel Medicine Laureate*
%University of Chicago, Ben May Institute, 5841 S Maryland, Chicago, IL 60637, USA

Hugh-Kelly, Daniel *Actor*
%Gersh Agency, 232 N Canon Dr, Beverly Hills, CA 90210, USA

Hughes, Barnard *Actor*
1244 11th St, #A, Santa Monica, CA 90401, USA

Hughes, David H *Businessman*
%Hughes Supply Inc, 20 N Orange Ave, Orlando, FL 32801, USA

Hughes, Finola *Actress*
4234 S Bel Air Dr, La Canada, CA 91011, USA

Huber - Hughes

H

Hughes, H Richard — *Architect*
47 Chiswick Quay, London W4 3UR, England

Hughes, Harold E — *Governor, IA*
%Harold Hughes Centers, 600 E 14th St, Des Moines, IA 50316, USA

Hughes, Harold E — *Senator, NJ*
%Democratic National Committee, 1625 Massachusetts NW, Washington, DC 20036, USA

Hughes, Harry R — *Governor, MD*
%Patton Boggs Blow, 250 W Pratt St, #1100, Baltimore, MD 21201, USA

Hughes, John W — *Movie Director, Screenwriter*
%Hughes Entertainment, 1 E Westminster Rd, Lake Forest, IL 60045, USA

Hughes, Keith W — *Financier*
%Associated Corp of North America, 250 Carpenter Freeway, Dallas, TX 75266, USA

Hughes, Ken — *Movie Director*
2218 N Beachwood Dr, #301, Los Angeles, CA 90068, USA

Hughes, Merv — *Cricketer*
%Australian Cricket Board, 90 Jollimant St, Melbourne VIC 3002, Australia

Hughes, Richard H (Dick) — *Baseball Player*
PO Box 598, Stephens, AR 71764, USA

Hughes, Robert S F — *Art Critic*
%Time Magazine, Editorial Dept, Rockefeller Center, New York, NY 10020, USA

Hughes, Ted — *Poet*
%Faber & Faber Ltd, 3 Queen Square, London WC1N 3AN, England

Hughes, Thomas J, Jr — *Navy Admiral*
%Navy Federal Credit Union, 820 Folin Lane SE, Vienna, VA 22180, USA

Hughes, Tyrone — *Football Player*
%New Orleans Saints, 1500 Poydras St, New Orleans, LA 70112, USA

Hughes, Wendy — *Actress*
345 N Maple Dr, #183, Beverly Hills, CA 90210, USA

Hughes-Fulford, Millie — *Astronaut*
%Veterans Affairs Dept, Medical Center, 4150 Clement St, San Francisco, CA 94121, USA

Hugstedt, Petter — *Ski Jumper*
3600 Kongsberg, Norway

Huguenin, G Richard — *Inventor (Portable Gun Detector Camera)*
%Millitech Corp, South Deerfield, MA

Huizenga, H Wayne — *Businessman*
%Blockbuster Entertainment Corp, PO Box 29002, Fort Lauderdale, FL 33302, USA

Huizenga, John R — *Nuclear Chemist*
43 McMichael Dr, Pinehurst, NC 28374, USA

Hulce, Tom — *Actor*
2305 Stanley Hills Dr, Los Angeles, CA 90046, USA

Hull, Brett A — *Hockey Player*
%St Louis Blues, St Louis Arena, 5700 Oakland Ave, St Louis, MO 63110, USA

Hull, Kent — *Football Player*
RR 1 Box 574-B, Greenwood, MS 38930, USA

Hull, Robert M (Bobby) — *Hockey Player*
115 E Maple St, Hinsdale, IL 60521, USA

Hull, Roger H — *Educator*
%Union College, Chancellor's Office, Schenectady, NY 12308, USA

Hullar, Theodore L — *Educator*
PO Box 1606, Davis, CA 95617, USA

Hulme, Denis — *Auto Racing Driver*
CI-6, RDTE Puke, Bay of Plenny, New Zealand

Hulse, Russell A — *Nobel Physics Laureate*
%Princeton University, Plasma Physics Laboratory, Princeton, NJ 08544, USA

Humann, L Phillip — *Financier*
%SunTrust Banks, 22 Park Place NE, Atlanta, GA 30303, USA

Humbard, Rex — *Evangelist*
Cathedral of Tomorrow, 2700 State Rd, Cuyahoga Falls, OH 44223, USA

Humbert, John O — *Religious Leader*
%Christian Church Disciples of Christ, 222 S Downey, Indianapolis, IN 46219, USA

Humble, Weldon — *Football Player*
12219 Broken Bough Dr, Houston, TX 77024, USA

Hume, A Britton (Brit) — *Commentator*
%ABC-TV, News Dept, 1717 De Sales St NW, Washington, DC 20036, USA

Hume, G Basil Cardinal — *Religious Leader*
%Archbishop's House, Westminister, London SW1, England

Hume, John — *Political Leader, Northern Ireland*
6 West End Park, Derry BT48 9JF, Northern Ireland

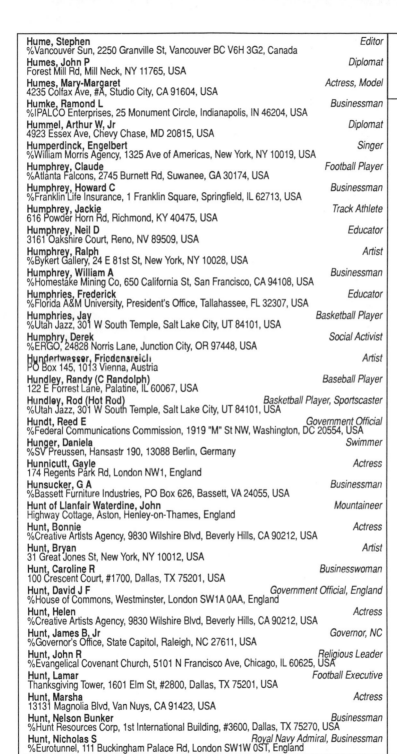

Hume, Stephen	*Editor*
%Vancouver Sun, 2250 Granville St, Vancouver BC V6H 3G2, Canada	
Humes, John P	*Diplomat*
Forest Mill Rd, Mill Neck, NY 11765, USA	
Humes, Mary-Margaret	*Actress, Model*
4235 Colfax Ave, #A, Studio City, CA 91604, USA	
Humke, Ramond L	*Businessman*
%IPALCO Enterprises, 25 Monument Circle, Indianapolis, IN 46204, USA	
Hummel, Arthur W, Jr	*Diplomat*
4923 Essex Ave, Chevy Chase, MD 20815, USA	
Humperdinck, Engelbert	*Singer*
%William Morris Agency, 1325 Ave of Americas, New York, NY 10019, USA	
Humphrey, Claude	*Football Player*
%Atlanta Falcons, 2745 Burnett Rd, Suwanee, GA 30174, USA	
Humphrey, Howard C	*Businessman*
%Franklin Life Insurance, 1 Franklin Square, Springfield, IL 62713, USA	
Humphrey, Jackie	*Track Athlete*
616 Powder Horn Rd, Richmond, KY 40475, USA	
Humphrey, Neil D	*Educator*
3161 Oakshire Court, Reno, NV 89509, USA	
Humphrey, Ralph	*Artist*
%Bykert Gallery, 24 E 81st St, New York, NY 10028, USA	
Humphrey, William A	*Businessman*
%Homestake Mining Co, 650 California St, San Francisco, CA 94108, USA	
Humphries, Frederick	*Educator*
%Florida A&M University, President's Office, Tallahassee, FL 32307, USA	
Humphries, Jay	*Basketball Player*
%Utah Jazz, 301 W South Temple, Salt Lake City, UT 84101, USA	
Humphry, Derek	*Social Activist*
%ERGO, 24828 Norris Lane, Junction City, OR 97448, USA	
Hundertwasser, Friedensreich	*Artist*
PO Box 145, 1013 Vienna, Austria	
Hundley, Randy (C Randolph)	*Baseball Player*
122 E Forrest Lane, Palatine, IL 60067, USA	
Hundley, Rod (Hot Rod)	*Basketball Player, Sportscaster*
%Utah Jazz, 301 W South Temple, Salt Lake City, UT 84101, USA	
Hundt, Reed E	*Government Official*
%Federal Communications Commission, 1919 "M" St NW, Washington, DC 20554, USA	
Hunger, Daniela	*Swimmer*
%SV Preussen, Hansastr 190, 13088 Berlin, Germany	
Hunnicutt, Gayle	*Actress*
174 Regents Park Rd, London NW1, England	
Hunsucker, G A	*Businessman*
%Bassett Furniture Industries, PO Box 626, Bassett, VA 24055, USA	
Hunt of Llanfair Waterdine, John	*Mountaineer*
Highway Cottage, Aston, Henley-on-Thames, England	
Hunt, Bonnie	*Actress*
%Creative Artists Agency, 9830 Wilshire Blvd, Beverly Hills, CA 90212, USA	
Hunt, Bryan	*Artist*
31 Great Jones St, New York, NY 10012, USA	
Hunt, Caroline R	*Businesswoman*
100 Crescent Court, #1700, Dallas, TX 75201, USA	
Hunt, David J F	*Government Official, England*
%House of Commons, Westminster, London SW1A 0AA, England	
Hunt, Helen	*Actress*
%Creative Artists Agency, 9830 Wilshire Blvd, Beverly Hills, CA 90212, USA	
Hunt, James B, Jr	*Governor, NC*
%Governor's Office, State Capitol, Raleigh, NC 27611, USA	
Hunt, John R	*Religious Leader*
%Evangelical Covenant Church, 5101 N Francisco Ave, Chicago, IL 60625, USA	
Hunt, Lamar	*Football Executive*
Thanksgiving Tower, 1601 Elm St, #2800, Dallas, TX 75201, USA	
Hunt, Marsha	*Actress*
13131 Magnolia Blvd, Van Nuys, CA 91423, USA	
Hunt, Nelson Bunker	*Businessman*
%Hunt Resources Corp, 1st International Building, #3600, Dallas, TX 75270, USA	
Hunt, Nicholas S	*Royal Navy Admiral, Businessman*
%Eurotunnel, 111 Buckingham Palace Rd, London SW1W 0ST, England	

H

Hume - Hunt

H

Hunt, Richard	*Sculptor*
1017 W Lill Ave, Chicago, IL 60614, USA	
Hunt, Robert L, II	*Financier*
%Coast Savings Financial, 1000 Wilshire Blvd, Los Angeles, CA 90017, USA	
Hunt, Robert M	*Publisher*
%New York Daily News, 220 E 42nd St, New York, NY 10017, USA	
Hunt, Ronald K (Ron)	*Baseball Player*
2806 Jackson Rd, Wentzville, MO 63385, USA	
Hunten, Donald M	*Astronomer*
10 Calle Corta, Tucson, AZ 85716, USA	
Hunter (Ed McBain), Evan	*Writer*
324 Main Ave, #339, Norwalk, CT 06851, USA	
Hunter, Charles D	*Businessman*
%Walgreen Co, 200 Wilmot Rd, Deerfield, IL 60015, USA	
Hunter, Holly	*Actress*
1223 Wilshire Blvd, #668, Santa Monica, CA 90403, USA	
Hunter, James A (Jim Catfish)	*Baseball Player*
RR1, Box 895, Hertford, NC 27944, USA	
Hunter, Jim	*Skier*
%Jungle Jim Hunter Mgmt, 864 Woodpark Way SW, Calgary AB T2W 2V8, Canada	
Hunter, John	*Businessman*
%Coca-Cola Co, 1 Coca-Cola Plaza, 310 North Ave NW, Atlanta, GA 30313, USA	
Hunter, Kaki	*Actress*
%Gersh Agency, 232 N Canon Dr, Beverly Hills, CA 90210, USA	
Hunter, Kim	*Actress*
42 Commerce St, New York, NY 10014, USA	
Hunter, Lindsey	*Basketball Player*
%Detroit Pistons, Palace, 2 Championship Dr, Auburn Hills, MI 48057, USA	
Hunter, R Alan	*Businessman*
%Stanley Works, 1000 Stanley Dr, New Britain, CT 06053, USA	
Hunter, Rachel	*Model*
%Ford Model Agency, 344 E 59th St, New York, NY 10022, USA	
Hunter, Rita	*Opera Singer*
Cornways, 70 Embercourt Rd, Thams Ditton, Surrey KT7 0LW, England	
Hunter, Robert C	*Financier*
%Texas Commerce Bank, 712 Main St, Houston, TX 77002, USA	
Hunter, Robert D	*Financier*
%Chase Manhattan Bank (USA), 1 Chase Manhattan Plaza, Wilmington, DE 19801, USA	
Hunter, Ross	*Movie Producer*
370 Trousdale Place, Beverly Hills, CA 90210, USA	
Hunter, Tab	*Actor*
223 N Guadalupe St, #292, Santa Fe, NM 87501, USA	
Hunter-Gault, Charlayne	*Commentator*
%McNeill/Lehrer News Hour, 356 W 58th St, New York, NY 10019, USA	
Hunthausen, Raymond G	*Religious Leader*
%Catholic Archdiocese of Seattle, 910 Marion, Seattle, WA 98104, USA	
Huntington, Ellery C	*Football Player*
219 Wolfe St, Alexandria, VA 22314, USA	
Huntington, Lawrence S	*Financier*
%Fiduciary Trust Co, 2 World Trade Center, New York, NY 10048, USA	
Huntsman, Stanley H	*Track Coach*
5532 Timbercrest Trail, Knoxville, TN 37909, USA	
Hunyadfi, Steven	*Swimming Coach*
838 Ridgewood Dr, #12, Fort Wayne, IN 46805, USA	
Hunyady, Emese	*Speed Skater*
%Haus des Sports, Prinz-Eugen-Str 12, 1040 Vienna, Austria	
Huo Yaobang	*General Secretary, China*
%Communist Party Central Committee, Zhongguo Gongchan Dang, Beijing, China	
Hupp, Robert P	*Religious Leader, Social Worker*
%Father Flanagan's Boys Home, Boys Town, NE 68010, USA	
Huppert, Isabelle	*Actress*
18 Rue Rousselet, 75007 Paris, France	
Hurd, Douglas R	*Government Official, England*
5 Mitford Cottages, Westwell, Burford, Oxon, England	
Hurd, G David	*Businessman*
%Principal Financial Group, 711 High St, Des Moines, IA 50392, USA	
Hurd, Gale Anne	*Movie Producer*
%Pacific Western Productions, 270 N Canon Dr, #1195, Beverly Hills, CA 90210, USA	

Hurford, Peter J *Concert Organist*
Broom House, St Bernard's Rd, St Albans, Herts AL3 5RA, England

Hurlburt, Wendell F *Businessman*
%Esterline Technologies, 10800 NE 8th St, Bellevue, WA 98004, USA

Hurley, Alfred F *Historian*
%University of North Texas, President's Office, Denton, TX 76203, USA

Hurley, Bobby *Basketball Player*
%Sacramento Kings, 1 Sports Parkway, Sacramento, CA 95834, USA

Hurley, Denis E *Religious Leader*
%Emanuel Catholic Cathedral, Cathedral Rd, Durban 4001, South Africa

Hurley, Elizabeth *Model, Actress*
3 Cromwell Place, London DW 2JE, England

Hurn, David *Photographer*
Prospect Cottage, Tintern, Gwent, Wales

Hurnik, Ilja *Concert Pianist*
Narodni Trida 35, 11000 Prague 1, Czech Republic

Hurt, Frank *Labor Leader*
%Bakery Confectionery Tobacco Union, 10401 Connecticut, Kensington, MD 20895, USA

Hurt, John *Actor*
%Julian Belfrage, 46 Albermarle St, London W1X 4PP, England

Hurt, Mary Beth *Actress*
1619 Broadway, #900, New York, NY 10019, USA

Hurt, William *Actor*
370 Lexington Ave, #808, New York, NY 10017, USA

Hurtt, Caleb B *Businessman*
%Martin Marietta Corp, 6801 Rockledge Dr, Bethesda, MD 20817, USA

Hurvich, Leo M *Psychologist*
%University of Pennsylvania, Psychology Dept, Philadelphia, PA 19104, USA

Hurwitz, Charles E *Businessman*
%Maxxam Inc, PO Box 572887, Houston, TX 77257, USA

Hurwitz, Emanuel *Concert Violinist*
25 Dollis Ave, London N3 1DA, England

Hurwitz, Jerard *Molecular Biologist*
%Einstein College of Medicine, Yeshiva University, Bronx, NY 10461, USA

Husa, Karel J *Composer, Conductor*
1032 Hanshaw Rd, Ithaca, NY 14850, USA

Husband, Rick D *Astronaut*
%NASA, Johnson Space Center, 2101 NASA Rd, Houston, TX 77058, USA

Husen, Torsten *Educator*
%Int'l Educational Institute, Armfeltsgatan 10, 115 34 Stockholm, Sweden

Huseynov, Surat *Prime Minister, Azerbaijan*
%Prime Minister's Office, Baku, Azerbaijan

Husky, Ferlin *Singer, Songwriter*
%Ace Productions, 4825 Shasta Dr, Old Hickory, TN 37138, USA

Hussein At-Takriti, Saddam *President, Iraq*
%Revolutionary Command Council, Al-Sijoud Majalis, Baghdad, Iraq

Hussein Ibn Talal *King, Jordan*
%Royal Palace, Amman, Jordan

Hussey, Olivia *Actress*
21334 Colina Dr, Topanga, CA 90290, USA

Hussey, Ruth *Actress*
3361 Don Pablo Dr, Carlsbad, CA 92008, USA

Huston, Anjelica *Actress*
74 Market St, Venice, CA 90291, USA

Hutcherson, Bobby *Jazz Vibraphonist*
%DeLeon Artists, 4031 Panama Court, Piedmont, CA 94611, USA

Hutchins, Will *Actor*
3461 Waverly Dr, #108, Los Angeles, CA 90027, USA

Hutchinson, Barbara *Labor Leader*
%American Federation of Labor, 815 15th St NW, Washington, DC 20005, USA

Hutchinson, Frederick E *Educator*
%University of Maine, President's Office, Orono, ME 04469, USA

Hutchinson, J Maxwell *Architect*
10 St Augustine's Rd, London NW1 9RN, England

Hutchinson, Josephine *Actress*
360 E 55th St, New York, NY 10022, USA

Hutchinson, Pemberton *Businessman*
%Westmoreland Coal Co, Bellvue, 200 S Broad St, #700, Philadelphia, PA 19102, USA

Hutchinson, W R — *Financier*
%Amoco Credit Corp, 200 E Randolph Dr, Chicago, IL 60601, USA

Hutchison, Clyde A, Jr — *Chemist*
%University of Chicago, Searle Laboratory, Chemistry Dept, Chicago, IL 60637, USA

Hutchison, Theodore M — *Businessman*
%Principal Financial Group, 711 High St, Des Moines, IA 50392, USA

Huth, Edward J — *Editor, Physician*
1124 Morris Ave, Bryn Mawr, PA 19010, USA

Hutson, Don — *Football Player*
%Thunderbird Country Club, PO Box Y, Rancho Mirage, CA 92270, USA

Hutson, Don — *Businessman*
%TIG Insurance, 5205 N O'Connor Blvd, Irving, TX 75039, USA

Hutt, Peter B — *Attorney*
%Covington & Burling, 1201 Pennsylvania Ave NW, Washington, DC 20004, USA

Hutton, Betty — *Actress*
1350 N Highland, Newport, RI 02840, USA

Hutton, Edward L — *Businessman*
%Chemed Corp, Chemed Center, 255 E 5th St, Cincinnati, OH 45202, USA

Hutton, Lauren — *Model, Actress*
382 Lafayette St, #6, New York, NY 10003, USA

Hutton, Leonard — *Cricketer*
Ebor House, 1 Coombe, Surrey KT2 7HW, England

Hutton, Ralph — *Swimmer*
%Vancouver Police Department, 312 Main St, Vancouver BC, Canada

Hutton, Timothy — *Actor*
RR 2, Box 331-B, Cushman Rd, Patterson, NY 12563, USA

Huxley, Andrew F — *Nobel Medicine Laureate*
Master's Lodge, Trinity College, Cambridge CB2 1TQ, England

Huxley, Elspetha J — *Writer*
Green End, Oaksey Near Malmesbury, Wilts SN16 9TL, England

Huxley, Laura — *Therapist, Writer*
6233 Mulholland Dr, Los Angeles, CA 90068, USA

Huxtable, Ada Louise — *Architectural Critic*
969 Park Ave, New York, NY 10028, USA

Huyck, Willard — *Movie Director*
39 Oakmont Dr, Los Angeles, CA 90049, USA

Hwang, David Henry — *Playwright*
70 W 36th St, #501, New York, NY 10018, USA

Hyams, Joseph I (Joe), Jr — *Writer*
10375 Wilshire Blvd, #4-D, Los Angeles, CA 90024, USA

Hyams, Peter — *Movie Director*
932 Hilts Ave, Los Angeles, CA 90024, USA

Hyatt, Joel Z — *Attorney, Businessman*
%Hyatt Legal Services, 1215 Superior Ave E, Cleveland, OH 44114, USA

Hybl, William J — *Sports Official*
%US Olympic Committee, 1750 E Boulder St, Colorado Springs, CO 80909, USA

Hyer, Martha — *Actress*
1216 La Rambla, Santa Fe, NM 87501, USA

Hyland, Brian — *Singer*
%Stone Buffalo, PO Box 101, Silver Lakes, CA 92342, USA

Hyland, William G — *Government Official*
%Council on Foreign Relations, 58 E 68th St, New York, NY 10021, USA

Hylton, Thomas J — *Journalist*
%Pottstown Mercury, Editorial Dept, Hanover & King Sts, Pottstown, PA 19464, USA

Hyman, Dick — *Jazz Pianist*
4146 Lankershim Blvd, #300, North Hollywood, CA 91602, USA

Hyman, Earle — *Actor*
%Manhattan Towers, 484 W 43rd St, #33-E, New York, NY 10036, USA

Hyman, Morton P — *Businessman*
%Overseas Shipholding Group, 1114 Ave of Americas, New York, NY 10036, USA

Hynde, Chrissie — *Singer, Guitarist, Songwriter*
%Pretenders, Cheval Music Ltd, 73 Market St, Venice, CA 90291, USA

Hynes, Samuel — *Writer*
130 Moore St, Princeton, NJ 08540, USA

Hynter, Nicholas R — *Theater Director*
%National Theatre, South Bank, London SE1 9PX, England

Hyser, Joyce — *Actress*
%Paradigm Agency, 10100 Santa Monica Blvd, #2500, Los Angeles, CA 90067, USA

Iacobellis, Sam F *Businessman, Aeronautical Engineer*
%Rockwell International, 2201 Seal Beach Blvd, Seal Beach, CA 90740, USA

Iacocca, Lido A (Lee) *Businessman*
30 Scenic Oaks Dr N, Bloomfield Hills, MI 48304, USA

Iafrate, Al A *Hockey Player*
%Boston Bruins, Boston Garden, 150 Causeway St, Boston, MA 02114, USA

Iakovos, Primate Archbishop *Religious Leader*
%Greek Orthodox Archdiocese, 8-10 E 79th St, New York, NY 10021, USA

Ian, Janis *Singer, Songwriter*
1875 Century Park East, #200, Los Angeles, CA 90067, USA

Ibbetson, Arthur *Cinematographer*
%Tanglewood, Chalfont Lane, Chorlry Wood, Herts, England

Ibers, James A *Chemist*
2657 Orrington Ave, Evanston, IL 60201, USA

Ibiam, Francis A *Religious Leader*
Ganymede, Unwana, PO Box 240, Afikpo, Imo State, Nigeria

Ibuka, Masaru *Inventor, Businessman*
%Sony Corp, 6-7-35 Kitashinagawa, Shinagawaku, Tokyo 141, Japan

Ibuka, Yaeko *Social Worker*
%Fukusei Byoin, Leprosarium, Mount Fuji, Japan

Icahn, Carl C *Businessman*
%Icahn Co, 100 S Bedford Rd, Mount Kisco, NY 10549, USA

Ice Cube (O'Shea Jackson) *Rapper*
6709 Victoria Ave, Los Angeles, CA 90043, USA

Ice T (Tracy Marrow) *Rapper*
2287 Sunset Plaza Dr, Los Angeles, CA 90069, USA

Ickx, Jacky *Auto Racing Driver*
171 Chaussee de la Hulpe, 1170 Brussels, Belgium

Idei, Nobuyuki *Businessman*
%Sony Corp, 6-7-35 Kitashinagawa, Shingawaku, Tokyo 141, Japan

Idle, Eric *Comedian (Monty Python)*
%Mayday Mgmt, 68-A Delancey St, Camden Town, London NW1 7RY, England

Idol, Billy *Singer, Songwriter*
%Fast End Mgmt, 8209 Melrose Ave, #200, Los Angeles, CA 90046, USA

Iduarte Foucher, Andres *Writer*
Calle Edimburgo 3, Colonia del Valle, Mexico City 12 DF, Mexico

Iger, Robert A *Broadcast Executive*
%Capital Cities/ABC Inc, 77 W 66th St, New York, NY 10023, USA

Iglesias, Julio *Singer*
1177 Kane Concourse, Miami, FL 33154, USA

Ignatius Zakka I Iwas, Patriarch *Religious Leader*
%Syrian Orthodox Patriarchate, Bab Toma, PB 22260, Damascus, Syria

Ignatius, Paul R *Government Official*
3650 Fordham Rd, Washington, DC 20016, USA

Ignatow, David *Poet*
PO Box 1458, East Hampton, NY 11937, USA

Ihara, Michio *Sculptor*
63 Wood St, Concord, MA 01742, USA

Ihnatowicz, Zbigniew *Architect*
Ul Mokotowska 31 M 15, 00-560 Warsaw, Poland

Iida, Yotaro *Businessman*
%Mitsubishi Heavy Industries, 2-5-1 Marunouchi, Chiyodaku, Tokyo, Japan

Ikagawa, Tadaichi *Financier*
%Sumitomo Bank of California, 320 California St, San Francisco, CA 94104, USA

Ike, Reverend *Evangelist*
4140 Broadway, New York, NY 10033, USA

Ikeda, Daisaku *Religious Leader*
%Soka Gakkai, 32 Shinanomachi, Shinjuku, Tokyo 160, Japan

Ikenberry, Stanley O *Educator*
%University of Illinois, Admin Office, 506 S Wright St, Urbana, IL 61801, USA

Ikle, Fred C *Social Scientist*
7010 Glenbrook Rd, Washington, DC 20014, USA

Ilchman, Alice Stone *Educator*
%Sarah Lawrence College, President's Office, Bronxville, NY 10708, USA

Iley, Barbara *Actress*
%Paradigm Agency, 10100 Santa Monica Blvd, #2500, Los Angeles, CA 90067, USA

Ilg, Raymond P *Navy Admiral*
5504 Teak Court, Alexandria, VA 22309, USA

I

Iliescu, Ion *President, Romania*
%President's Office, Calle Victoriei 49-53, Bucharest, Romania

Ilitch, Marian *Hockey Executive, Baseball Executive*
%Detroit Red Wings, Joe Louis Arena, 600 Civic Center Dr, Detroit, MI 48226, USA

Ilitch, Michael *Hockey Executive, Baseball Executive*
%Detroit Red Wings, Joe Louis Arena, 600 Civic Center Dr, Detroit, MI 48226, USA

Illich, Ivan *Educator, Writer, Theologian*
Apdo Postal 1-479, 62001 Cuernavaca, Morelos, Mexico

Illmann, Margaret *Ballerina*
%National Ballet of Canada, 157 E King St, Toronto ON M5C 1G9, Canada

Illsley, John *Bassist (Dire Straits)*
%Damage Mgmt, 10 Southwick Mews, London W2, England

Imai, Kenji *Architect*
4-12-28 Kitazawa, Setagayaku, Tokyo, Japan

Imai, Nobuko *Concert Viola Player*
%Harrison Mgmt, Clarendon Court, Park St, Charlbury Oxon OX7 3PS, England

Imamura, Shohei *Movie Director*
%Toei Co, 3-2-17 Ginza, Chuoku, Tokyo 104, Japan

Iman (Abudulmajid) *Model*
639 N Larchmont Blvd, #207, Los Angeles, CA 90004, USA

Imbert, Bertrand S M *Explorer, Engineer*
50 Rue de Turenne, 75003 Paris, France

Imbert, Peter M *Law Enforcement Official*
%New Scotland Yard, Broadway, London SW1H 0BG, England

Imbrie, Andrew W *Composer*
2625 Rose St, Berkeley, CA 94708, USA

Imhoff, Gary *Actor*
%Gold Marshak Assoc, 3500 W Olive Ave, #1400, Burbank, CA 91505, USA

Imie, John F, Jr *Businessman*
%Unocal Corp, 1201 W 5th St, Los Angeles, CA 90017, USA

Imshenetsky, Aleksandr A *Microbiologist*
%Russian Academy of Sciences, Profsoyuznaya Ul 7, Moscow, Russia

Inaba, Kosaku *Businessman*
%Ishikawajima-Harima Heavy Industries, 2-1 Ohtemachi, Tokyo 100, Japan

Inai, Yoshihiro *Businessman*
%Mitsubishi Metal Corp, 1-5-2 Otemachi, Chiyodaku, Tokyo 100, Japan

Inatome, Rick *Businessman*
%InaCom Corp, 10810 Farnam Dr, Omaha, NE 68154, USA

Inbal, Eliahu *Conductor*
%Hessischer Rundfunk, Bertramstr 8, 60320 Frankfurt/Main, Germany

Incaviglia, Peter J (Pete) *Baseball Player*
PO Box 526, Pebble Beach, CA 93953, USA

Inderbitzin, Paul H *Businessman*
%American Re Corp, 555 College Rd E, Princeton, NJ 08540, USA

Indiana, Robert *Artist*
Star of Hope, Vinalhaven, ME 04863, USA

Indurain, Miguel *Cyclist*
%Banesto, Avenida Bajona 37, 31011 Pamplona, Spain

Iness, Sim *Track Athlete*
455 W Oak Ave, Porterville, CA 93257, USA

Infill, O Urcille, Jr *Religious Leader*
%African Methodist Church, Box 19039, Germantown Station, Philadelphia, PA 19138, USA

Ingalls, Daniel H H *Educator*
The Yard, Hot Springs, VA 24445, USA

Inge, Peter A *Army General, England*
%Barclays Bank, Market Place, Leyburn, North Yorkshire DL8 5BQ, England

Ingels, Marty *Actor, Comedian*
%Ingels Entertainment, 8127 Melrose Ave, West Hollywood, CA 90046, USA

Ingersoll, Mary *Actress*
%Whitaker Agency, 12725 Ventura Blvd, #F, Studio City, CA 91604, USA

Ingersoll, Ralph, II *Publisher*
%Ingersoll Publications, PO Box 1869, Lakeville, CT 06039, USA

Inghram, Mark G *Physicist*
3077 Lakeshore Ave, Holland, MI 49424, USA

Ingle, Robert D *Editor*
%San Jose Mercury News, Editorial Dept, 750 Ridder Park Dr, San Jose, CA 95190, USA

Ingman, Einar H, Jr *Korean War Army Hero (CMH)*
W-4053 N Silver Lake Rd, Irma, WI 54442, USA

Ingraham, Hubert A — *Prime Minister, Bahamas*
%Prime Minister's Office, Whitfield Center, Box CB-10980, Nassau, Bahamas

Ingram, James — *Singer, Songwriter*
867 Muirfield Rd, Los Angeles, CA 90005, USA

Ingram, Lonnie — *Microbiologist*
%University of Florida, Microbiology-Cell Science Dept, Gainesville, FL 32611, USA

Ingram, Vernon M — *Biochemist*
%Massachusetts Institute of Technology, Biochemistry Dept, Cambridge, MA 02139, USA

Ingrao, Pietro — *Government Official, Italy*
%Centro Studie Iniziative Per La Reforma, Via Della Vite 13, Rome, Italy

Ingrassia, Paul J — *Journalist*
111 Division Ave, New Providence, NJ 07974, USA

Ingstad, Helge M — *Explorer*
Vettalivei 24, 0389 Oslo 3, Norway

Inkeles, Alex — *Sociologist*
1001 Hamilton Ave, Palo Alto, CA 94301, USA

Inkster, Juli — *Golfer*
%Ladies Professional Golf Assn, 2570 Volusia Ave, Daytona Beach, FL 32114, USA

Inman, Bobby Ray — *Navy Admiral, Government Official*
3300 Bee Cave Rd, #650-221, Austin, TX 78746, USA

Inman, John — *Actor*
%Nick Thomas Artistes, 11-13 Broad Court, London WC2B 5QN, England

Innauer, Toni — *Ski Jumper, Coach*
%Olympic Committee, Prinz-Eugen-Str 12, 1040 Vienna, Austria

Innaurato, Albert F — *Playwright*
325 W 22nd St, New York, NY 10011, USA

Innis, Roy E A — *Civil Rights Activist*
%Congress of Racial Equality, 310 Cooper Square, New York, NY 10003, USA

Innocenti, Antonio Cardinal — *Religious Leader*
%Pontifical Commission, Vatican City, 00120 Rome, Italy

Inoue, Shinya — *Biologist, Photographer*
%Marine Biological Laboratory, 167 Water St, Woods Hole, MA 02543, USA

Inoue, Yulchl — *Artist*
Ohkamiyashiki, 2475-2 Kurami, Samakawamachi 253-01, Kozagun, Kam, Japan

Inskeep, J Jerry, Jr — *Financier*
%Columbia Management, 1300 SW 6th St, Portland, OR 97201, USA

Insko, Del — *Harness Racing Driver*
Rt 1, Box 65, South Beloit, IL 61080, USA

Insley, Will — *Artist*
231 Bowery, New York, NY 10002, USA

Insolia, Anthony — *Editor*
%Newsday, Editorial Dept, 235 Pinelawn, Melville, NY 11747, USA

Ioannisiani, Bagrat K — *Astronomer*
%State Institute of Optics, St Petersburg, Russia

Iordanou, Constantine D — *Financier*
%Zurich-American Group, 1400 American Lane, Schaumburg, IL 60196, USA

Iott, Richard B — *Businessman*
%Seaway Food Town, 1020 Ford St, Maumee, OH 43537, USA

Iott, Wallace D — *Businessman*
%Seaway Food Town, 1020 Ford St, Maumee, OH 43537, USA

Ipcar, Dahlov — *Illustrator, Artist*
HCR-33, PO Box 432, Bath, ME 04530, USA

Ippolito, Angelo — *Artist*
Powderhouse Rd, Box 45, Vestal, NY 13851, USA

Irani, Ray R — *Businessman*
%Occidental Petroleum, 10889 Wilshire Blvd, Los Angeles, CA 90024, USA

Irbe, Arturs — *Hockey Plyaer*
%San Jose Sharks, 525 W Santa Clara St, San Jose, CA 95113, USA

Iredale, Randle W — *Architect*
1151 W 8th Ave, Vancouver BC V6H 1C5, Canada

Ireland, Kathy — *Model*
%Sterling/Winters, 1900 Ave of Stars, #739, Los Angeles, CA 90067, USA

Ireland, Patricia — *Association Executive*
%National Organization for Women, 1000 16th St NW, Washington, DC 20036, USA

Irizarry, Vincent — *Actor*
%Agency For Performing Arts, 9000 Sunset Blvd, #1200, Los Angeles, CA 90069, USA

Irons, Jeremy — *Actor*
194 Old Brompton Rd, London SW5, England

Ingraham - Irons

I

Irrera, Dom — *Comedian*
%Metropolitan Talent Agency, 4526 Wilshire Blvd, Los Angeles, CA 90010, USA

Irsay, Robert — *Football Executive*
%Indianapolis Colts, 7001 W 56th St, Indianapolis, IN 46254, USA

Irvan, Ernie — *Auto Racing Driver*
80 Louve Ave, Conford, NC 28027, USA

Irvin, John — *Movie Director*
6 Lower Common St, London SW10, England

Irvin, Michael J — *Football Player*
%Dallas Cowboys, 1 Cowboys Parkway, Irving, TX 75063, USA

Irvin, Monford M (Monte) — *Baseball Player*
11 Douglas Court S, Homosassa, FL 34446, USA

Irvin, Tinsley H — *Businessman*
3027 Bakers Meadow Lane NW, Atlanta, GA 30339, USA

Irving, Amy — *Actress*
11693 San Vicente Blvd, #335, Los Angeles, CA 90049, USA

Irwin, Bill — *Entertainer, Clown*
56 7th Ave, #4-E, New York, NY 10011, USA

Irwin, Hale S — *Golfer*
745 Old Frontenac Square, #260, St Louis, MO 63131, USA

Irwin, John C — *Coast Guard Admiral*
%Vice Commandant's Office, US Coast Guard, Washington, DC 20593, USA

Irwin, John Nichol, II — *Government Official*
848 Weed St, New Canaan, CT 06840, USA

Irwin, Malcolm R — *Biologist*
4720 Regent St, Madison, WI 53705, USA

Irwin, Paul G — *Association Executive*
%Humane Society of the United States, 2100 "L" St NW, Washington, DC 20037, USA

Irwin, Robert W — *Artist*
%Pace Gallery, 32 E 57th St, New York, NY 10022, USA

Isaacs, Donald L — *Financier*
%BayBanks, 175 Federal St, Boston, MA 02110, USA

Isaacs, Jeremy I — *Opera Director*
%Royal Opera House, Covent Garden, Bow St, London WC2 7Q4, England

Isaacs, John — *Basketball Player*
1412 Crotona Ave, Bronx, NY 10456, USA

Isaacs, Susan — *Writer*
%Harper Collins Publishers, 10 E 53rd St, New York, NY 10022, USA

Isaacson, Julius — *Labor Leader*
%Novelty & Production Workers Union, 1815 Franklin Ave, Valley Stream, NY 11581, USA

Isaak, Chris — *Singer, Songwriter*
PO Box 547, Larkspur, CA 94977, USA

Isaak, Russell — *Businessman*
%CPI Corp, 1706 Washington Ave, St Louis, MO 63103, USA

Isacksen, Peter — *Actor*
4635 Placidia Ave, North Hollywood, CA 91602, USA

Isard, Walter — *Regional Economist*
3218 Garrett Rd, Drexel Hill, PA 19026, USA

Isenberg, Eugene M — *Businessman*
%Nabors Industries, 515 W Greens Rd, Houston, TX 77067, USA

Isenburger, Eric — *Artist*
140 E 56th St, New York, NY 10022, USA

Ishibashi, Kanichiro — *Businessman*
%Bridgestone Tire Co, 1-10-1 Kyobashi, Chuoku, Tokyo 104, Japan

Ishida, Jim — *Actor*
871 N Vail Ave, Montebello, CA 90640, USA

Ishiguro, Kazuo — *Writer*
%Faber & Faber Ltd, 3 Queens Square, London WC1N 3AO, England

Ishihara, Shintaro — *Government Official, Japan*
%Liberal Democratic Party, Diet, Tokyo, Japan

Ishihara, Takashi — *Businessman*
%Nissan Motor Co, 6-17-1 Ginza, Chuoku, Tokyo 104, Japan

Ishii, Kazuhiro — *Architect*
4-14-27 Akasaka, Minatoku, Tokyo 107, Japan

Ishimaru, Akira — *Electrical Engineer*
%University of Washington, Electrical Engineering Dept, Seattle, WA 98195, USA

Ishizaka, Kimishige — *Allergist*
%Allergy/Immunology Institute, 11149 N Torrey Pines Rd, La Jolla, CA 92037, USA

Ishizaka, Teruko *Allergist*
%Good Samaritan Hospital, 5601 Loch Raven Blvd, Baltimore, MD 21239, USA

Isley, Ron *Singer*
1211 Sunset Plaza Dr, #401, Los Angeles, CA 90069, USA

Ismail, Ahmed Sultan *Mechanical Engineer*
43 Ahmed Abdel Aziz St, Dokki, Cairo, Egypt

Ismail, Raghib (Rocket) *Football Player*
%Oakland Raiders, Oakland Coliseum, Oakland, CA 94621, USA

Isola, Thomas M *Businessman*
%Petroleum Heat & Power, 2187 Atlantic St, Stamford, CT 06902, USA

Isom, Gerald A *Businessman*
%Insurance Co of North America, 1601 Chestnut St, Philadelphia, PA 19192, USA

Ison, Christopher J *Journalist*
%Minneapolis-St Paul Star Tribune, 425 Portland Ave, Minneapolis, MN 55488, USA

Isozaki, Arata *Architect*
%Arata Assoc, 6-17-9 Akasaka, Minatoku, Tokyo 107, Japan

Israel, Franklin D *Architect*
6204 Banner St, #2, Los Angeles, CA 90038, USA

Issel, Daniel P (Dan) *Basketball Player, Coach, Executive*
%Denver Nuggets, McNichols Arena, 1635 Clay St, Denver, CO 80204, USA

Isselbacher, Kurt J *Physician*
%Massachusetts General Hospital, Cancer Center, Charleston, MA 02129, USA

Issley, John *Bassist (Dire Straits)*
%Damage Mgmt, 10 Southwick Mews, London W2, England

Istel, Yves-Andre *Financier*
%Rothschild Inc, 1251 Ave of Americas, New York, NY 10020, USA

Istock, Verne G *Financier*
%NBD Bancorp, 611 Woodward Ave, Detroit, MI 48226, USA

Istomin, Eugene G *Concert Pianist*
225 W 71st St, New York, NY 10023, USA

Itami, Juzo *Movie Director*
%Itami Productions, Sekaeya Bldg, 4-8-6 Akasaka, Minatoku, Tokyo, Japan

Ito, Masatoshi *Businessman*
%Southland Corp, 2711 N Haskell Ave, Dallas, TX 75204, USA

Ito, Masayoshi *Government Official, Japan*
1-28-3 Chitose-Dai, Setagayaku, Tokyo 157, Japan

Ito, Midori *Figure Skater*
%Skating Federation, Kryshi Taaikukan 1-1-1, Shibuyaku, Tokyo 10, Japan

Ito, Robert *Actor*
%Diamond Artists, 215 N Barrington Ave, Los Angeles, CA 90049, USA

Ito, Shinsui *Artist*
Kita-Kamakura, Kanagawa Prefecture, Japan

Itoh, Junji *Businessman*
%Kanebo Ltd, 5-90-1 Tomobuchicho, Miyakojimaku, Osaka 534, Japan

Iue, Satoshi *Businessman*
%Sanyo Electric Co, 2-18 Keihan-Hondori, Moriguchi City 570, Japan

Ivan, Thomas N *Hockey Player*
557 N King Muir Rd, Lake Forest, IL 60045, USA

Ivanchenkov, Alexander S *Cosmonaut*
%Potchta Kosmonavtov, 141 160 Svyosdny Gorodok, Moskovskoi Oblasti, Russia

Ivanisevic, Goran *Tennis Player*
Alijnoviceva 28, 58000 Split, Yugoslavia

Iverson, F Kenneth *Businessman*
%Nucor Corp, 2100 Rexford Rd, Charlotte, NC 28211, USA

Ives, J Atwood *Businessman*
%Eastern Enterprises, 9 Riverside Rd, Weston, MA 02193, USA

Ivester, M Douglas *Businessman*
%Coca-Cola Co, 1 Coca-Cola Plaza, 310 North Ave NW, Atlanta, GA 30313, USA

Ivey, Dana *Actress*
%Paradigm Agency, 10100 Santa Monica Blvd, #2500, Los Angeles, CA 90067, USA

Ivey, James B *Editorial Cartoonist*
561 Obispo Ave, Orlando, FL 32807, USA

Ivey, Judith *Actress*
4470 W Sunset Blvd, #131, Los Angeles, CA 90027, USA

Ivins, Marsha S *Astronaut*
%NASA, Johnson Space Center, 2101 NASA Rd, Houston, TX 77058, USA

Ivory, James F *Movie Director, Producer*
%Merchant-Ivory Productions, 46 Lexington St, London W1P 3LH, England

Iwago, Mitsuaki *Photographer*
Edelhof Daichi Bldg, #2-F, 8 Honsio-cho, Shinjuka-ku, Tokyo 160, Japan

Iwata, Kazuo *Businessman*
%Toshiba Corp, 72 Horikawacho, Sawwaiku, Kawasaki 210, Japan

Iwerks, Donald W *Entertainment Executive*
%Iwerks Entertainment, 4540 Valerio St, Burbank, CA 91505, USA

Izetbegovic, Alija *President, Bosnia-Herzegovina*
%President's Office, Marsala Titz 7-A, 71000 Sarajevo, Bosnia-Herzegovina

Jablonski, Henryk *President of Council, Poland*
Ul Filtrowa 61 M 4, 02-056 Warsaw, Poland

Jacke, Chris *Football Player*
%Green Bay Packers, 1265 Lombardi Ave, Green Bay, WI 54304, USA

Jackee (Harry) *Actress*
8649 Metz Place, Los Angeles, CA 90069, USA

Jacklin, Tony *Golfer*
Golfscape, Quothquhan Lodge Near Biggar, Lanarkshire ML12 6NB, Scotland

Jackson, Alan *Singer, Songwriter*
%Ten Ten Mgmt, 66 Music Square W, Nashville, TN 37203, USA

Jackson, Anne *Actress*
90 Riverside Dr, New York, NY 10024, USA

Jackson, Arthur J *WW II Marine Corps Hero (CMH)*
1290 E Spring Court, Boise, ID 83712, USA

Jackson, Betty *Fashion Designer*
33 Tottenham St, London W1, England

Jackson, Danny L *Baseball Player*
%Philadelphia Phillies, Veterans Stadium, PO Box 7575, Philadelphia, PA 19101, USA

Jackson, Daryl S *Architect*
161 Hoham St, East Melbourne, VIC 3002, Australia

Jackson, Donald *Figure Skater*
504 Gordon Baker Rd, Willowdale ON M2H 3B4, Canada

Jackson, Frederick W, III *Publisher*
%Town & Country Magazine, 959 8th Ave, New York, NY 10019, USA

Jackson, Glenda *Actress*
51 Harvey Rd, Blackheath, London SE3, England

Jackson, Harold *Journalist*
%Birmingham News, Editorial Dept, 2200 N 4th Ave N, Birmingham, AL 35203, USA

Jackson, Harry A *Artist*
PO Box 2836, Cody, WY 82414, USA

Jackson, Janet *Singer, Dancer*
%HK Mgmt, 8900 Wilshire Blvd, #300, Beverly Hills, CA 90211, USA

Jackson, Jermaine *Singer, Songwriter*
4641 Hayvenhurst Dr, Encino, CA 91436, USA

Jackson, Jesse L *Evangelist, Civil Rights Activist*
%Operation Push, 930 E 50th St, Chicago, IL 60615, USA

Jackson, Jim *Basketball Player*
%Dallas Mavericks, Reunion Arena, 777 Sports St, Dallas, TX 75207, USA

Jackson, Joe *Singer, Songwriter*
%Basement Music, Trinity House, 6 Pembridge Rd, London W11, England

Jackson, Joe M *Vietnam War Air Force Hero (CMH)*
25320 38th Ave S, Kent, WA 98032, USA

Jackson, John *Football Player*
%Pittsburgh Steelers, 3 Rivers Stadium, 300 Stadium Circle, Pittsburgh, PA 15212, USA

Jackson, John E, Jr *Air Force General*
Vice Commander, Air Mobility Cmd, 402 Scott Dr, Scott Air Force Base, IL 62225, USA

Jackson, Kate *Actress*
1628 Marlay Dr, Los Angeles, CA 90069, USA

Jackson, Keith M *Sportscaster*
%ABC-TV, Sports Dept, 77 W 66th St, New York, NY 10023, USA

Jackson, Larry R *Labor Leader*
%American Grain Millers Fed, 4949 Olson Memorial Parkway, Minneapolis, MN 55422, USA

Jackson, LaToya *Singer*
%Waldorf Astoria Hotel, 301 Park Ave, #1970, New York, NY 10022, USA

Jackson, Mark *Basketball Player*
%Indiana Pacers, Market Square Arena, 300 E Market St, Indianapolis, IN 46204, USA

Jackson, Mary *Actress*
2055 Grace Ave, Los Angeles, CA 90068, USA

Jackson, Michael *Commentator*
%KABC-Radio, News Dept, 3321 S LaCienega Blvd, Los Angeles, CA 90016, USA

Jackson, Michael — *Singer, Songwriter*
Sycamore Valley Ranch, Zacca Landeras, Santa Ynez, CA 93460, USA

Jackson, Millie — *Singer, Songwriter*
%Headline Talent Inc, 1650 Broadway, #508, New York, NY 10019, USA

Jackson, Milton (Bags) — *Jazz Pianist*
%Ted Kurland Assoc, 173 Brighton Ave, Boston, MA 02134, USA

Jackson, Philip — *Actor*
%Markham & Froggatt, Julian House, 4 Windmill St, London W1P 1HF, England

Jackson, Philip D (Phil) — *Basketball Player, Coach*
%Chicago Bulls, 1901 W Madison St, Chicago, IL 60612, USA

Jackson, R Graham — *Architect*
%Calhoun Tungate Jackson Dill Architects, 6200 Savoy Dr, Houston, TX 77036, USA

Jackson, Rebbie — *Singer, Songwriter*
4641 Hayvenhurst Dr, Encino, CA 91436, USA

Jackson, Reginald M (Reggie) — *Baseball Player*
325 Elder Ave, Sunnyside, CA 93955, USA

Jackson, Richard A — *Religious Leader*
%North Phoenix Baptist Church, 5757 N Central Ave, Phoenix, AZ 85012, USA

Jackson, Richard S (Richie) — *Football Player*
%All Pro Inc, 6000 Kingston Court, New Orleans, LA 70131, USA

Jackson, Rickey — *Football Player*
%San Francisco 49ers, 4949 Centennial Blvd, Santa Clara, CA 95054, USA

Jackson, Robert W — *Businessman*
%CIPSCO Inc, 607 E Adams St, Springfield, IL 62739, USA

Jackson, Roy I — *International Civil Servant*
%Food/Agriculture Organization, Via delle Terme di Caracalla, Rome, Italy

Jackson, Samuel L — *Actor*
%Creative Artists Agency, 9830 Wilshire Blvd, Beverly Hills, CA 90212, USA

Jackson, Sherry — *Actress*
4933 Encino Ave, Encino, CA 91316, USA

Jackson, Stonewall — *Singer, Songwriter*
6007 Cloverland Dr, Brentwood, TN 37027, USA

Jackson, Stoney — *Actor*
%The Agency, 1800 Ave of Stars, #400, Los Angeles, CA 90067, USA

Jackson, Tito — *Singer (Jacksons)*
4425 Costa De Oro, Oxnard, CA 93035, USA

Jackson, Tom — *Football Player*
%Denver Broncos, 13655 E Dove Valley Parkway, Englewood, CO 80112, USA

Jackson, Victoria — *Actress*
%William Morris Agency, 1325 Ave of Americas, New York, NY 10019, USA

Jackson, Vincent E (Bo) — *Football, Baseball Player*
PO Box 453, Mobile, AL 36601, USA

Jackson, Wanda — *Singer*
%Wanda Jackson Entertainments, 725 N Broadway Ave, Oklahoma City, OK 73102, USA

Jacob, Francois — *Nobel Medicine Laureate*
%Institut Pasteur, 25 Rue du Dr Roux, 75015 Paris, France

Jacob, John E — *Civil Rights Activist*
%National Urban League, 500 E 62nd St, New York, NY 10021, USA

Jacob, Stanley W — *Surgeon*
1055 SW Westwood Court, Portland, OR 97201, USA

Jacobi, Derek — *Actor*
%International Creative Mgmt, 76 Oxford St, London W1N 0AX, England

Jacobi, Lou — *Actor*
240 Central Park South, New York, NY 10019, USA

Jacobs, Bernard B — *Theater Producer*
%Shubert Organization, 225 W 44th St, New York, NY 10036, USA

Jacobs, Helen Hull — *Tennis Player*
36 James Lane, #B, East Hampton, NY 11937, USA

Jacobs, Irwin L — *Businessman*
%Genmar Industries, 100 S 5th St, Minneapolis, MN 55402, USA

Jacobs, Jack H — *Vietnam War Army Hero (CMH)*
%Bankers Trust Co, 1 Appold St, London EC2A 2HE, England

Jacobs, Jane — *Writer*
%Random House Inc, 201 E 50th St, New York, NY 10022, USA

Jacobs, Jerrold L — *Businessman*
%Atlantic Energy, 6801 Black Horse Pike, Pleasantville, NJ 08234, USA

Jacobs, Jim — *Playwright*
%International Creative Mgmt, 40 W 57th St, New York, NY 10019, USA

J

Jacobs, Joseph J — *Businessman*
%Jacobs Engineering Group, 251 S Lake Ave, Pasadena, CA 91101, USA

Jacobs, Julien I — *Judge*
%US Tax Court, 400 2nd St NW, Washington, DC 20217, USA

Jacobs, Lawrence-Hilton — *Actor*
3804 Evans St, #2, Los Angeles, CA 90027, USA

Jacobs, Marc — *Fashion Designer*
%Marc Jacobs Co, 113 Spring St, #300, New York, NY 10012, USA

Jacobs, Norman J — *Publisher*
%Century Publishing Co, 990 Grove St, Evanston, IL 60201, USA

Jacobs, Robert — *Pharmacologist*
%University of California, Pharmacology Dept, Santa Barbara, CA 93106, USA

Jacobs, Rodney L — *Financier*
%Wells Fargo Co, 420 Montgomery St, San Francisco, CA 94104, USA

Jacobs, Wilfred E — *Governor General, Antigua & Barbuda*
Government House, St John's, Antigua

Jacobsen, James C — *Businessman*
%Kellwood Co, 600 Kellwood Parkway, St Louis, MO 63017, USA

Jacobsen, Peter — *Golfer*
%Fred Meyer Challenge, 8700 SW Nimbus Ave, #B, Beaverton, OR 97008, USA

Jacobsen, Steven C — *Microbiotics Engineer*
%University of Utah, Engineering Design Center, Salt Lake City, UT 84112, USA

Jacobsen, Thomas H — *Financier*
%Mercantile Bancorp, Mercantile Tower, PO Box 524, St Louis, MO 63166, USA

Jacobson, A Thurl — *Petroleum Geologist*
1734 N Oak Crest Dr, Orem, UT 84057, USA

Jacobson, Allen F — *Businessman*
%Minnesota Mining & Manufacturing Co, 3-M Center, St Paul, MN 55144, USA

Jacobson, Herbert L — *Diplomat, Journalist*
Apartado 160, Escazu, Costa Rica

Jacobson, Nathan — *Mathematician*
2 Prospect Court, Hamden, CT 06517, USA

Jacoby, Scott — *Actor*
PO Box 461100, Los Angeles, CA 90046, USA

Jacot, Michele — *Skier*
Residence du Brevent, 74 Chamonix, France

Jacquet, Illinois — *Jazz Saxophonist*
%Bowen Agency, 504 W 168th St, New York, NY 10032, USA

Jacquot, Pierre E — *Army General, France*
15 Ave de Villars, 75007 Paris, France

Jacuzzi, Roy — *Businessman*
%Jacuzzi Whirlpool Bath Inc, 2121 N California Blvd, Walnut Creek, CA 94596, USA

Jadot, Jean L O — *Religious Leader*
Ave de l'Atlantique 71-B-12, Brussels 1150, Belgium

Jaeckel, Richard — *Actor*
23388 Mulholland Dr, Woodland Hills, CA 91364, USA

Jaeckin, Just — *Movie Director*
8 Villa Mequillet, 92200 Neuilly/Seine, France

Jaeger, Andrea — *Tennis Player*
%Kids Stuff Foundation, Silver Lining Ranch, PO Box 10970, Aspen, CO 81612, USA

Jaffe, Arthur M — *Mathematical Physicist*
27 Lancaster St, Cambridge, MA 02140, USA

Jaffe, Bruce M — *Businessman*
%Bell Industries, 11812 San Vicente Blvd, Los Angeles, CA 90049, USA

Jaffe, Harold W — *Epidemiologist*
%Centers for Disease Control, 1600 Clifton Rd, Atlanta, GA 30333, USA

Jaffe, Leo — *Movie Executive*
425 E 58th St, New York, NY 10022, USA

Jaffe, Leonard W — *Businessman*
%National Education Corp, 18400 Von Karman Ave, Irvine, CA 92715, USA

Jaffe, Rona — *Writer*
%Janklow & Nesbit Assoc, 598 Madison Ave, New York, NY 10022, USA

Jaffe, Stanley R — *Entertainment Executive*
152 W 57th St, #5200-F, New York, NY 10019, USA

Jaffe, Susan — *Ballerina*
%American Ballet Theatre, 890 Broadway, New York, NY 10003, USA

Jagan, Cheddi — *President, Guyana*
%President's Office, New Garden & South, Georgetown, Guyana

Jagendorf, Andre T — *Plant Physiologist*
309 Brookfield Rd, Ithaca, NY 14850, USA

Jagge, Finn Christian — *Skier*
Michelets Vei 108, 1320 Stabekk, Norway

Jagger, Bianca — *Actress, Model*
530 Park Ave, #18-D, New York, NY 10021, USA

Jagger, Mick — *Singer, Harmonicist (Rolling Stones)*
Cheyne Walk, Chelsea, London SW3, England

Jaglom, Henry — *Movie Director*
9165 W Sunset Blvd, #300, Los Angeles, CA 90069, USA

Jagr, Jaromir — *Hockey Player*
%Pittsburgh Penguins, Civic Arena, Centre Ave, Pittsburgh, PA 15219, USA

Jahn, Helmut — *Architect*
224 S Michigan Ave, Chicago, IL 60604, USA

Jahn, Sigmund — *Cosmonaut, East Germany; General*
Fontanestr 35, 15344 Strausberg, Germany

Jaidah, Ali Mohammed — *Government Official, Qatar*
%Qatar Petroleum Corp, PO Box 3212, Doha, Qatar

Jakes, John — *Writer*
%Rembar & Curtis, 19 W 44th St, New York, NY 10036, USA

Jaki, Stanley L — *Physicist, Theologian*
PO Box 167, Princeton, NJ 08542, USA

Jakobovits, Immanuel — *Religious Leader*
%Rabbi's Residence, Adler House, Tavistock Square, London WC1, England

Jakobson, Maggie — *Actress*
%Writers & Artists Agency, 924 Westwood Blvd, #900, Los Angeles, CA 90024, USA

Jakobson, Max — *Journalist; Government Official, Finland*
Rahapajankatu 3B 17, 00160 Helsinki 16, Finland

Jakosits, Michael — *Marksman*
Karlsbergstr 140, 66424 Homburg/Saar, Germany

Jalloud, Abdul Salam — *Prime Minister, Libya*
%General Secretariat, General People's Congress, Tripoli, Libya

Jamail, Joseph D, Jr — *Attorney*
%Jamail & Kolius, 500 Dallas St, #3434, Houston, TX 77002, USA

Jamal, Ahmad — *Jazz Pianist*
%Shubra Productions, PO Box 295, Ashley Falls, MA 01222, USA

Jambor, Agi — *Concert Pianist*
%Beethoven Apartments, 1518 Park Ave, #104-N, Baltimore, MD 21217, USA

Jamerson, James L (Jim) — *Air Force General*
Commander, 12th Air Force, Davis Mountain Air Force Base, AZ 85707, USA

James of Holland Park, Phyllis D — *Writer*
%Elaine Green Ltd, 37-A Goldhawk Rd, London W12 SQQ, England

James, Anthony — *Actor*
%CNA, 1801 Ave of Stars, #1250, Los Angeles, CA 90067, USA

James, Bob — *Jazz Pianist*
%Record Music Inc, 84-19 63rd Ave, Middle Village, NY 11379, USA

James, Charmayne — *Rodeo Rider*
%General Delivery, Clayton, NM 88415, USA

James, Cheryl (Salt) — *Singer*
%International Creative Mgmt, 8942 Wilshire Blvd, Beverly Hills, CA 90211, USA

James, Clifton — *Actor*
95 Buttonwood Dr, Dix Hills, NY 11746, USA

James, Clive V L — *Broadcaster, Journalist*
%A D Peters Co, Chambers, #500, Chelsea Harbour, London SW10 0XF, England

James, D Clayton — *Historian*
902 Providence Pl, Lexington, VA 24450, USA

James, Dennis — *Entertainer*
3681 Caribeth Dr, Encino, CA 91436, USA

James, Etta — *Singer*
PO Box 5025, Gardena, CA 90249, USA

James, Forrest H (Fob), Jr — *Governor, AL*
%Governor's Office, State Capitol, 11 Union St, Montgomery, AL 36130, USA

James, Gene A — *Businessman*
%CF Industries, 1 Salem Lake Dr, Long Grove, IL 60047, USA

James, Geraldine — *Actress*
%Julian Belfrage, 46 Albermarle St, London W1X 4PP, England

James, Harold L — *Geologist*
%US Geological Survey, 1617 Washington St, Port Townsend, WA 98368, USA

James, John *Actor*
PO Box 3248, Hilton Head Island, SC 29928, USA

James, Joni *Singer*
%Alan Eichler Assoc, 1524 LaBaig Ave, Los Angeles, CA 90028, USA

James, Kate *Model*
%Men/Women Agency, 107 Greene St, #200, New York, NY 10012, USA

James, Larry *Track Athlete*
%Stockton State College, Athletic Dept, Pomona, NJ 08240, USA

James, Lionel *Football Player*
%San Diego Chargers, Jack Murphy Stadium, San Diego, CA 92160, USA

James, P D *Writer*
%Elaine Greene Ltd, 37-A Goldhawk Rd, London W12 8QQ, England

James, S A *Governor General, St Lucia*
Government House, The Morne, Castries, St Lucia

James, Sheryl *Journalist*
%St Petersburg Times, Editorial Dept, 490 1st Ave, St Petersburg, FL 33731, USA

James, Sonny *Singer, Guitarist, Songwriter*
PO Box 158433, Nashville, TN 37215, USA

James, Stanislaus *Governor General, St Lucia*
Government House, The Morue, Castries, St Lucia

James, Steve W *Actor*
%Artists Agency, 10000 Santa Monica Blvd, #305, Los Angeles, CA 90067, USA

James, Thomas A *Financier*
%Raymond James Financial, 880 Carillon Parkway, St Petersburg, FL 33716, USA

Jameson, Arlen D (Dirk) *Air Force General*
Commander, 20th Air Force, 7100 Saber Rd, Warren Air Force Base, WY 82005, USA

Jamieson, David A *WW II British Army Hero (VC)*
Drove House, Thornham, Hunstandton, Norfolk, England

Jamieson, John K *Businessman*
601 Jefferson St, #975, Houston, TX 77002, USA

Jamison, Judith *Dancer, Dance Director, Choreographer*
%Alvin Ailey American Dance Theater, 1515 Broadway, New York, NY 10036, USA

Jandernoa, Michael J *Businessman*
%Perrigo Co, 117 Water St, Allegan, MI 49010, USA

Janecyk, Bob *Hockey Player*
%Los Angeles Kings, Forum, PO Box 17013, Inglewood, CA 90308, USA

Janeway, Elizabeth H *Writer*
350 E 79th St, New York, NY 10021, USA

Janeway, Michael C *Editor*
%Northwestern University, Fisk Hall, Evanston, IL 60201, USA

Janeway, Richard *Physician*
PO Box 188, Blowing Rock, NC 28605, USA

Janis, Conrad *Actor, Jazz Trombonist*
1434 N Genesee Ave, Los Angeles, CA 90046, USA

Janklow, Morton L *Literary Agent, Attorney*
%Morton L Janklow Assoc, 598 Madison Ave, New York, NY 10022, USA

Jankowski, Gene F *Television Executive*
%American Film Institute, 901 15th St NW, #700, Washington, DC 20005, USA

Janofsky, Leonard S *Law Enforcement Official*
661 Thayer Ave, Los Angeles, CA 90024, USA

Janowicz, Victor F (Vic) *Football Player*
1966 Jervis Rd, Columbus, OH 43221, USA

Janowitz, Gundula *Opera Singer*
Rehetobelstr 81, 9000 St Gallen, Switzerland

Janowitz, Tama *Writer*
%Pocket Books, 1230 Ave of Americas, New York, NY 10020, USA

Jansen, Daniel E (Dan) *Speed Skater*
4428 S 85th St, Greenfield, WI 53228, USA

Jansen, Lawrence J (Larry) *Baseball Player*
3207 NW Highway 47, Forest Grove, OR 97116, USA

Jansen, Raymond A *Publisher*
%Newsday Inc, 235 Pinelawn Rd, Melville, NY 11747, USA

Jansons, Maris *Conductor*
%Oslo Philharmonic, PO Box 1607, 0119 Oslo, Norway

Janss, William C *Businessman*
PO Box 107, Sun Valley, ID 83353, USA

January, Don *Golfer*
%Professional Golfer's Assn, PO Box 109601, Palm Beach Gardens, FL 33410, USA

January, Lois *Actress*
225 N Crescent Dr, #103, Beverly Hills, CA 90210, USA

Jany, Alex *Swimmer*
104 Blvd Livon, 13007 Marseille, France

Janzen, Daniel H *Biologist*
%University of Pennsylvania, Biology Dept, Philadelphia, PA 19104, USA

Janzen, Edmund *Religious Leader*
%General Conference of Mennonite Brethren, 8000 W 21st St, Wichita, KS 67205, USA

Janzen, Lee *Golfer*
%Professional Golfer's Assn, PO Box 109601, Palm Beach Gardens, FL 33410, USA

Jaquish, John E *Air Force General*
Assisstant to Secretary Air Force for Acquisition, HqUSAF, Washington, DC 20330, USA

Jardine, Al *Singer (Beach Boys)*
PO Box 36, Big Sur, CA 93920, USA

Jarman, Claude, Jr *Actor*
11 Dos Encinas, Orinda, CA 94563, USA

Jarre, Maurice A *Composer*
27011 Sea Vista Dr, Malibu, CA 90265, USA

Jarreau, Al *Singer*
%Patrick Rains Assoc, 1543 7th St, #3, Santa Monica, CA 90401, USA

Jarrett, Dale *Auto Racing Driver*
PO Box 564, Conover, NC 28613, USA

Jarrett, Keith *Jazz Pianist, Composer*
%Vincent Ryan, 135 W 16th St, New York, NY 10011, USA

Jarrett, Will *Editor*
%Dallas Times Herald, Editorial Dept, Herald Square, Dallas, TX 75202, USA

Jarriel, Thomas E (Tom) *Commentator*
%ABC-TV, News Dept, 77 W 66th St, New York, NY 10023, USA

Jarring, Gunnar *Government Official, Sweden*
Pontus Ols Vaeg 7, 260 40 Viken, Sweden

Jarrott, Charles *Movie Director*
4314 Marina City Dr, #418, Marina del Rey, CA 90292, USA

Jarryd, Anders *Tennis Player*
Maaneskoldsgatan 37, 531 00 Lidkoping, Sweden

Jaruzelski, Wojciech *Head of State, Poland*
Ul Ikara 5, Warsaw, Poland

Jarvi, Neeme *Conductor*
PO Box 305, Sea Bright, NJ 07760, USA

Jarvik, Robert K *Heart Surgeon*
%University of Utah Medical College, Surgery Dept, Salt Lake City, UT 84102, USA

Jarvis, Doug *Hockey Player*
%Hartford Whalers, Coliseum, 242 Trumbell St, #800, Hartford, CT 06103, USA

Jarvis, Graham *Actor*
15351 Via De Las Olas, #531, Pacific Palisades, CA 90272, USA

Jarvis, Morris O *Businessman*
%Hancock Fabrics, 3406 W Main St, Tupelo, MS 38801, USA

Jason, Sybil *Actress*
PO Box 40024, Studio City, CA 91614, USA

Jasrai, Puntsagiin *Prime Minister, Mongolia*
%Prime Minister's Office, Ulan Bator, Mongolia

Jastremski, Chet *Swimmer*
2611 Olcott Blvd, Bloomington, IN 47401, USA

Jastrow, Robert *Physicist, Writer*
%Wilson Observatory, 740 Holladay Rd, Pasadena, CA 91106, USA

Jastrow, Terry L *Movie Director*
13201 Old Oak Lane, Los Angeles, CA 90049, USA

Jatoi, Ghulan Mustafa *Prime Minister, Pakistan*
%Jatoi House, 18 Khayaban-E-Shamsheer Housing, #V, Karachi, Pakistan

Jaudes, Robert C *Businessman*
%Laclede Gas Co, 720 Olive St, St Louis, MO 63101, USA

Javan, Ali *Physicist*
12 Hawthorne St, Cambridge, MA 02138, USA

Javierre Ortas, Antonio M Cardinal *Religious Leader*
%Biblioteca Apostolica Vatican, Vatican City, Rome, Italy

Jawara, Dawda K *President, Gambia*
%President's Office, State House, Banjul, Gambia

Jaworski, Ronald V (Ron) *Football Player*
8 Silver Hill Lane, West Berlin, NJ 08043, USA

Jay of Batteresea, Douglas P T — *Government Official, England*
Causeway Cottage, Minster Lovell, Oxford OX8 5RN, England

Jay, John — *Ski Photographer*
PO Box 3131, Rancho Santa Fe, CA 92067, USA

Jay, Joseph R (Joey) — *Baseball Player*
7209 Battenwood Court, Tampa, FL 33615, USA

Jay, Peter — *Government Official, England*
39 Castlebar Rd, London W5 2DJ, England

Jay, Ricky — *Illusionist*
%W&V Dailey Booksellers, 8216 Melrose Ave, Los Angeles, CA 90046, USA

Jayawardene, Junius Richard — *President, Sri Lanka*
66 Ward Place, Colombo 7, Sri Lanka

Jayston, Michael — *Actor*
%Michael Whitehall Ltd, 125 Gloucester Rd, London SW7 4TE, England

Jazy, Michel — *Track Athlete*
Clos Saint-Marc, 18 Rue la Fontaine, 77330 Ozoire-la-Ferriere, France

Jean — *Grand Duke, Luxembourg*
%Palais Grand-Ducal, Marche-Aux-Herbes, 1728 Luxembourg-Ville, Luxembourg

Jean, Gloria — *Actress*
6625 Variel Ave, Canoga Park, CA 91303, USA

Jeanmaire, Zizi — *Ballet Dancer, Actress*
22 Rue de la Paix, 75002 Paris, France

Jeannette, Harry (Buddy) — *Basketball Player*
2 New Castle Dr, #3, Nashua, NH 03060, USA

Jeantot, Philippe — *Sailor, Explorer*
%General Delivery, Quimper, France

Jeffcoat, Jim — *Football Player*
%Buffalo Bills, 1 Bills Dr, Orchard Park, NY 14127, USA

Jefferson, John — *Football Player*
%Cleveland Browns, 80 1st Ave, Berea, OH 44017, USA

Jefferson, Margo — *Journalist*
%New York Times, Editorial Dept, 229 W 43rd St, New York, NY 10036, USA

Jeffrey, Richard C — *Philosopher*
55 Patton Ave, Princeton, NJ 08540, USA

Jeffreys, Anne — *Actress*
%Sterling, 121 S Bentley Ave, Los Angeles, CA 90049, USA

Jeffreys, Harold — *Astronomer*
160 Huntingdon Rd, Cambridge CB3 0LB, England

Jeffreys, Richard C — *Philosopher*
%Princeton University, Philosophy Dept, Princeton, NJ 08544, USA

Jeffries, Carson D — *Physicist*
%University of California, Physics Dept, Berkeley, CA 94720, USA

Jeffries, Francis E — *Financier*
%Duff & Phelps Corp, 55 E Monroe St, Chicago, IL 60603, USA

Jeffries, Herb — *Singer*
849 S Broadway, #750, Los Angeles, CA 90014, USA

Jeffries, John T — *Astronomer*
1652 E Camino Cielo, Tucson, AZ 85718, USA

Jeffries, Lionel — *Actor*
%International Creative Mgmt, 76 Oxford St, London W1N 0AX, England

Jeffs, Thomas H, II — *Financier*
%NBD Corp, 611 Woodward Ave, Detroit, MI 48226, USA

Jellicoe, Geoffrey — *Architect*
14 Highpoint, North Hill, Highgate, London N6 4BA, England

Jellicoe, George P J R — *Government Official, England*
97 Onslow Square, London SW7, England

Jemison, Mae C — *Astronaut*
2726 Lighthouse Dr, Houston, TX 77058, USA

Jemison, Theodore J — *Religious Leader*
%National Baptist Convention USA, 1620 White's Creek Pike, Nashville, TN 37207, USA

Jencks, William P — *Biochemist*
11 Revere St, Lexington, MA 02173, USA

Jenes, Theodore G, Jr — *Army General*
809 169th Place SW, Lynwood, WA 98037, USA

Jenifer, Franklyn G — *Educator*
%University of Texas, President's Office, Richardson, TX 75083, USA

Jenkin of Roding, Patrick F — *Government Official, England*
703 Howard House, Dolphin Sq, London SW1V 3PQ, England

Jenkins of Hillhead, Roy H — *Government Official, England*
2 Kensington Park Gdns, London W11 3BH, England

Jenkins, Alfred — *Football Player*
%Anhaeuser Busch, 33354 Overland Lane, Solon, OH 44139, USA

Jenkins, Alfred le Sesne — *Diplomat*
Stalsama High Knob, PO Box 586, Front Royal, VA 22630, USA

Jenkins, Charles — *Track Athlete, Coach*
%Villanova University, Athletic Dept, Villanova, PA 19085, USA

Jenkins, Daniel — *Actor*
%J Michael Bloom Ltd, 9255 Sunset Blvd, #710, Los Angeles, CA 90069, USA

Jenkins, Don J — *Vietnam War Army Hero (CMH)*
3783 Bowling Green Rd, Morgantown, KY 42261, USA

Jenkins, Ferguson A (Fergie), Jr — *Baseball Player*
PO Box 1202, Guthrie, OK 73044, USA

Jenkins, George — *Stage Designer, Movie Art Director*
740 Kingman Ave, Santa Monica, CA 90402, USA

Jenkins, Greg G — *Businessman*
%Hadson Corp, 2777 Stemmons Freeway, Dallas, TX 75207, USA

Jenkins, Hayes Alan — *Figure Skater*
809 Lafayette Dr, Akron, OH 44303, USA

Jenkins, Jackie (Butch) — *Actor*
Rt 6, Box 541-G, Fairview, NC 28730, USA

Jenkins, Loren — *Journalist*
%Washington Post, Editorial Dept, 1150 15th St NW, Washington, DC 20071, USA

Jenkins, Paul — *Artist*
%Imago Terrae, PO Box 6833, Yorkville Station, New York, NY 10128, USA

Jenkins, Robert W — *Financier*
%WestCorp, 23 Pasteur Rd, Irvine, CA 92718, USA

Jenkins, William — *Businessman*
%CalMat Co, 3200 San Fernando Rd, Los Angeles, CA 90065, USA

Jenner, Bruce — *Track Athlete, Actor*
3133 Abington Dr, Beverly Hills, CA 90210, USA

Jennings, Christopher R — *Financier*
%Dauphin Deposit Corp, 213 Market St, Harrisburg, PA 17101, USA

Jennings, Delbert O — *Vietnam War Army Hero (CMH)*
640 9th Ave, #A, Honolulu, HI 96816, USA

Jennings, Drue — *Businessman*
%Kansas City Power & Light, 1201 Walnut St, Kansas City, MO 64106, USA

Jennings, Elizabeth — *Writer*
%David Higham Assoc, 5-8 Lower John St, London W1R 4HA, England

Jennings, Jesse D — *Anthropologist*
21801 Siletz Highway, Siletz, OR 97380, USA

Jennings, Joseph L, Jr — *Businessman*
%WestPoint Stevens, 400 W 10th St, West Point, GA 31833, USA

Jennings, Lynn — *Track Athlete*
17 Cushing Rd, Newmarket, NH 03857, USA

Jennings, Peter C — *Commentator*
%ABC-TV, News Dept, 77 W 66th St, New York, NY 10023, USA

Jennings, Waylon — *Singer, Songwriter*
%WGJ Productions, 1117 17th Ave S, Nashville, TN 37212, USA

Jenrette, Richard H — *Businessman*
%Equitable Companies, 787 7th Ave, New York, NY 10019, USA

Jens, Salome — *Actress*
9400 Readcrest Dr, Beverly Hills, CA 90210, USA

Jens, Walter — *Writer*
Sonnenstr 5, 72076 Tubingen, Germany

Jensen, Arthur R — *Educational Psychologist*
30 Canyon View Dr, Orinda, CA 94563, USA

Jensen, Elwood V — *Biochemist*
%Hormone/Fertility Research Inst, Grandweg 64, 22529 Hamburg, Germany

Jensen, James — *Geologist*
%Brigham Young University, Geology Dept, Provo, UT 84602, USA

Jensen, Karen — *Actress*
111 S Kings Rd, Los Angeles, CA 90048, USA

Jensen, Robert P — *Businessman*
%Jostens Inc, 5501 Norman Center Dr, Minneapolis, MN 55437, USA

Jepsen, Roger W — *Senator, IA*
608 W Mulberry Lane, Long Grove, IA 52756, USA

Jenkins of Hillhead - Jepsen

Jeremiah, David E *Navy Admiral*
Vice Chairman, Joint Chiefs of Staff, Pentagon, Washington, DC 20318, USA

Jeremy (Clyde) *Singer (Chad & Jeremy)*
%Agency For Performing Arts, 9000 Sunset Blvd, #1200, Los Angeles, CA 90069, USA

Jergens, Adele *Actress*
32108 Village, #32, Camarillo, CA 93012, USA

Jermoluk, Thomas A *Businessman*
%Silicon Graphics Inc, 2011 N Shoreline Blvd, Mountain View, CA 94043, USA

Jernberg, Sixten *Skier*
Fritidsby 780, 64 Lima, Sweden

Jernigan, Tamara E (Tammy) *Astronaut*
%NASA, Johnson Space Center, 2101 NASA Rd, Houston, TX 77058, USA

Jerome, Jerrold V *Businessman*
%Unitrin Inc, 1 E Wacker Dr, Chicago, IL 60601, USA

Jerusalem, Siegfried *Opera Singer*
Sudring 9, 90542 Eckental, Germany

Jessee, Michael A *Financier*
%Federal Home Loan Bank, 1 Financial Center, Boston, MA 02111, USA

Jeter, Bob *Football Player*
7147 S Paxton Ave, Chicago, IL 60649, USA

Jeter, Gary *Football Player*
32725 Shadowbrook Dr, Solon, OH 44139, USA

Jeter, Michael *Actor*
4571 N Figueroa St, #20, Los Angeles, CA 90065, USA

Jethroe, Samuel (Sam) *Baseball Player*
340 E 14th St, Erie, PA 16503, USA

Jett, Joan *Singer*
%QBQ Entertainment, 341 Madison Ave, #1400, New York, NY 10017, USA

Jewett, George F, Jr *Businessman*
%Potlatch Corp, 1 Maritime Plaza, San Francisco, CA 94111, USA

Jewison, Norman F *Movie Director, Producer*
3000 Olympic Blvd, #1314, Santa Monica, CA 90404, USA

Jhabvala, Ruth Prawer *Writer*
400 E 52nd St, New York, NY 10022, USA

Jiang Zemin *President, China*
%General Secretary's Office, Zhonganahai, Beijing, China

Jillian, Ann *Actress*
4241 Woodcliffe Rd, Sherman Oaks, CA 91403, USA

Jillson, Joyce *Actress, Astrologist*
PO Box 5931, Sherman Oaks, CA 91413, USA

Jiscke, Martin C *Educator*
%Iowa State University, President's Office, Ames, IA 50011, USA

Jobe, Edward B *Businessman*
%American Re Corp, 555 College Rd E, Princeton, NJ 08540, USA

Jobe, Frank W *Orthopedic Surgeon*
501 E Hardy St, #200, Inglewood, CA 90301, USA

Jobert, Michel *Government Official, France*
21 Quai Alphonse-Le Gallo, 92100 Boulogne-Billancourt, France

Jobs, Steven P *Businessman*
%NeXT Inc, 900 Chesapeake Dr, Redwood City, CA 94063, USA

Jochum, George T *Businessman*
%Mid Atlantic Medical Services, 4 Taft Court, Rockville, MD 20850, USA

Joel, Billy *Singer, Songwriter*
%Maritime Music, 200 W 57th St, #308, New York, NY 10019, USA

Joffe, Roland I V *Movie Director, Producer*
2934 1/2 N Beverly Glen Circle, #270, Los Angeles, CA 90077, USA

Johanos, Donald *Conductor*
%Honolulu Symphony, 1441 Kapiolani Blvd, #1515, Honolulu, HI 96814, USA

Johanson, Donald C *Anthropologist*
1288 9th St, Berkeley, CA 94710, USA

Johansson, Ingemar *Boxer*
Rakegaton 9, 413 20 Goteborg, Sweden

John Paul II, Pope *Religious Leader*
Palazzo Apostolico, Vatican City, Italy

John, Caspar *Fleet Admiral, England*
Trethewey, Mousehole, Penzance, Cornwall, England

John, David D *Museum Official, Explorer*
7 Cyncoed Ave, Cardiff CF2 6ST, Wales

John, Elton — *Singer*
%John Reid Ent, Singes House, 32 Galena Rd, London W6 0LT, England

John, Thomas E (Tommy) — *Baseball Player*
3133 N 16th St, Terre Haute, IN 47804, USA

John-Roger (Hinkins) — *Religious Leader*
%John Roger Foundation, 2101 Wilshire Blvd, Santa Monica, CA 90403, USA

Johncock, Gordon — *Auto Racing Driver*
1042 Becker Rd, Hastings, MI 49058, USA

Johns, Charley E — *Governor, FL*
%Community State Bank, 131 S Walnut St, Starke, FL 32091, USA

Johns, Glynis — *Actress*
11645 Gorham Ave, #309, Los Angeles, CA 90049, USA

Johns, Jasper — *Artist*
225 E Houston St, New York, NY 10002, USA

Johns, John E — *Educator*
1209 Roe Ford Rd, Greenville, SC 29609, USA

Johns, Lori — *Drag Racing Driver*
4418 Congressional Dr, Corpus Christi, TX 78413, USA

Johns, Mervyn — *Actor*
%Richards, 42 Hazlebury Rd, London SW6, England

Johnson, A Clark, Jr — *Businessman*
%Union Texas Inc, 1330 Post Oak Blvd, Houston, TX 77056, USA

Johnson, Alexander (Alex) — *Baseball Player*
7650 Grand River Ave, Detroit, MI 48204, USA

Johnson, Anne-Marie — *Actress*
2606 Ivan Hill Terrace, Los Angeles, CA 90039, USA

Johnson, Arte — *Comedian*
2725 Bottlebrush Dr, Los Angeles, CA 90077, USA

Johnson, Avery — *Basketball Player*
%San Antonio Spurs, 600 E Market St, #102, San Antonio, TX 78205, USA

Johnson, Axel A — *Businessman*
%A Johnson & Co HAB, 103 75 Stockholm, Sweden

Johnson, Ben — *Track Athlete*
40 Oak Ave, Richmond Hill ON L4C 6R7, Canada

Johnson, Ben — *Actor*
%Mesa Entertainment, 2466 Leisure World, Mesa, AZ 85206, USA

Johnson, Betsey L — *Fashion Designer*
%Betsey Johnson Co, 209 W 38th St, New York, NY 10018, USA

Johnson, Beverly — *Model, Actress*
%Robert Kosden Agency, 7135 Hollywood Blvd, #PH-2, Los Angeles, CA 90046, USA

Johnson, Bill — *Skier*
472-750 Richmond Rd, Susanville, CA 96130, USA

Johnson, Brad — *Model, Actor*
%Creative Artists Agency, 9830 Wilshire Blvd, Beverly Hills, CA 90212, USA

Johnson, Brooks — *Track Coach*
%Stanford University, Athletic Dept, Stanford, CA 94305, USA

Johnson, Butch — *Football Player*
%Denver Broncos, 13655 E Dove Valley Parkway, Englewood, CO 80112, USA

Johnson, Charles — *Writer*
%University of Washington, English Dept, Seattle, WA 98105, USA

Johnson, Charles — *Football Player*
%Pittsburgh Steelers, 3 Rivers Stadium, 300 Stadium Circle, Pittsburgh, PA 15212, USA

Johnson, Charles B — *Financier*
%Franklin Resources, 777 Mariners Island Blvd, San Mateo, CA 94404, USA

Johnson, Charles M — *Financier*
%Wells Fargo Co, 420 Montgomery St, San Francisco, CA 94104, USA

Johnson, Claudia (Lady Bird) — *Wife of US President*
LBJ Ranch, Stonewall, TX 78671, USA

Johnson, Cletus — *Artist*
%Leo Castelli Gallery, 420 W Broadway, New York, NY 10012, USA

Johnson, Dale A — *Businessman*
%SPX Inc, 700 Terrace Point Dr, Muskegon, MI 49440, USA

Johnson, Darrell D — *Baseball Manager*
2305 "M" St, Ord, NE 68862, USA

Johnson, Dave — *Track Athlete*
%Bill Goldstein, 545 Madison Ave, New York, NY 10022, USA

Johnson, Dave — *Labor Leader*
%United Garment Workers, 4207 Lebanon Rd, Hermitage, TN 37076, USA

J

John - Johnson

Johnson, David A (Davey) — *Baseball Manager*
1064 Howell Branch Rd, Winter Park, FL 32789, USA

Johnson, David G — *Economist*
5617 S Kenwood Ave, Chicago, IL 60637, USA

Johnson, David W — *Businessman*
%Campbell Soup Co, Campbell Place, Camden, NJ 08103, USA

Johnson, Dennis — *Basketball Player*
%Boston Celtics, 151 Merrimac St, #500, Boston, MA 02114, USA

Johnson, Don — *Actor*
231 N Orchard Dr, Burbank, CA 91506, USA

Johnson, Don J — *Bowler*
%Professional Bowlers Assn, 1720 Merriman Rd, Akron, OH 44313, USA

Johnson, Earvin (Magic) — *Basketball Player, Coach*
Beverly Estates, 13100 Mulholland Dr, Beverly Hills, CA 90210, USA

Johnson, Eddie — *Basketball Player*
%Indiana Pacers, Market Square Arena, 300 E Market St, Indianapolis, IN 46204, USA

Johnson, Edward C, III — *Financier*
%FMR Corp, 82 Devonshire St, Boston, MA 02109, USA

Johnson, Ellis — *Football Player*
%Indianapolis Colts, 7001 W 56th St, Indianapolis, IN 46254, USA

Johnson, Eric — *Singer*
%Joe Priesnitz Artist Mgmt, PO Box 5249, Austin, TX 78763, USA

Johnson, Erik E — *Businessman*
%International Shipbuilding Corp, 650 Poydras St, New Orleans, LA 70130, USA

Johnson, F Ross — *Businessman*
%RJM Associates, 200 Galleria Parkway, #970, Atlanta, GA 30339, USA

Johnson, G Griffith, Jr — *Government Official*
300 Locust Ave, Annapolis, MD 21401, USA

Johnson, Gary — *Governor, NM*
%Governor's Office, State Capitol, Santa Fe, NM 87503, USA

Johnson, Georgann — *Actress*
%Gage Group, 9255 Sunset Blvd, #515, Los Angeles, CA 90069, USA

Johnson, George W — *Educator*
%George Mason University, President's Office, Fairfax, VA 22030, USA

Johnson, Glendon E — *Businessman*
%John Alden Financial Corp, 7300 Corporate Center Dr, Miami, FL 33102, USA

Johnson, H Richard — *Businessman*
%Watkins-Johnson Co, 3333 Hillview Ave, Palo Alto, CA 94304, USA

Johnson, Hansford T — *Air Force General*
%USAA Capital Corp, 9800 Fredericksburg Rd, San Antonio, TX 78284, USA

Johnson, Harold — *Boxer*
139 W Tulpehocken St, #H-2, Philadelphia, PA 19144, USA

Johnson, Haynes B — *Journalist*
%George Washington University, Communications Studies Ctr, Washington, DC 20052, USA

Johnson, Hazel W — *Army General*
%Army Nurse Corps, Army Dept, Pentagon, Washington, DC 20310, USA

Johnson, Howard B — *Businessman*
%Howard Johnson Co, 1 Howard Johnson Plaza, Boston, MA 02125, USA

Johnson, Howard M — *Baseball Player*
%Colorado Rockies, 2001 Blake St, Denver, CO 80205, USA

Johnson, Howard W — *Educator*
1558 Sand Castle Rd, Sanibel, FL 33957, USA

Johnson, J J — *Jazz Trombonist, Composer*
4001 Murietta Ave, Sherman Oaks, CA 91423, USA

Johnson, James A — *Financier*
%Federal National Mortgage Assn, 3900 Wisconsin Ave NW, Washington, DC 20016, USA

Johnson, James C — *Financier*
%Loyola Federal Savings Bank, 1300 N Charles St, Baltimore, MD 21201, USA

Johnson, James E (Johnnie) — *WW II Royal Air Force Hero, England*
Stables, Hargate Hall, Buxton, Derbyshire SK17 8TA, England

Johnson, Jannette — *Skier*
PO Box 901, Sun Valley, ID 83353, USA

Johnson, Jenna — *Swimmer, Coach*
%University of Tennessee, Athletic Dept, PO Box 15016, Knoxville, TN 37901, USA

Johnson, Jimmy — *Football Player*
656 Amaranth Blvd, Mill Valley, CA 94941, USA

Johnson, Jimmy — *Football Coach, Sportscaster*
%Fox-TV, Sports Dept, 205 E 67th St, New York, NY 10021, USA

Johnson, Joe — *Educator*
%University of Tennessee, President's Office, Knoxville, TN 37901, USA

Johnson, Joel W — *Businessman*
%Hormel Foods Corp, 1 Hormel Place, Austin, MN 55912, USA

Johnson, John G, Jr — *Businessman*
%Safety-Kleen Corp, 1000 N Randall Rd, Elgin, IL 60123, USA

Johnson, John H — *Publisher*
%Johnson Publishing Co, 820 S Michigan Ave, Chicago, IL 60605, USA

Johnson, John Henry — *Football Player*
1543 East Blvd, #3, Cleveland, OH 44106, USA

Johnson, Johnnie — *Singer, Songwriter*
%Creative Music Consultants, 119 W 57th St, #911, New York, NY 10019, USA

Johnson, Joseph E, III — *Physician*
%The Philadelphian, 2401 Pennsylvania Ave, #15-C-44, Philadelphia, PA 19130, USA

Johnson, Junior — *Auto Racing Driver, Builder*
%Johnson Assoc, Rt 2, PO Box 162, Ronda, NC 28670, USA

Johnson, Keith — *Labor Leader*
%Woodworkers of America Union, 1622 N Lombard St, Portland, OR 97217, USA

Johnson, Kevin — *Basketball Player*
%Phoenix Suns, 201 E Jefferson St, Phoenix, AZ 85004, USA

Johnson, Lamont — *Movie Director*
900 Alameda Ave, Monterey, CA 93940, USA

Johnson, Larry D — *Basketball Player*
%Charlotte Hornets, 1 Hive Dr, Charlotte, NC 28217, USA

Johnson, Laura — *Actress*
1917 Weepah Way, Los Angeles, CA 90046, USA

Johnson, Lawrence M — *Financier*
%Bancorp Hawaii, Financial Plaza, 130 Merchant Plaza, Honolulu, HI 96813, USA

Johnson, Leon W — *WW II Air Force Hero (CMH), General*
2550 N Bonanza Ave, Tucson, AZ 85749, USA

Johnson, Lester D — *Businessman*
%Consolidated Natural Gas Co, 625 Liberty Ave, Pittsburgh, PA 15222, USA

Johnson, Lynn-Holly — *Actress*
6605 Hollywood Blvd, #220, Los Angeles, CA 90028, USA

Johnson, Manuel H, Jr — *Economist, Government Official*
%George Mason University, Global Market Studies Center, Fairfax, VA 22030, USA

Johnson, Michelle — *Actress, Model*
%Gores/Fields Agency, 10100 Santa Monica Blvd, #2500, Los Angeles, CA 90067, USA

Johnson, Nicholas — *Attorney, Writer*
PO Box 1876, Iowa City, IA 52244, USA

Johnson, Niels W — *Businessman*
%International Shipbuilding Corp, 650 Poydras St, New Orleans, LA 70130, USA

Johnson, Norm — *Football Player*
%Pittsburgh Steelers, 3 Rivers Stadium, 300 Stadium Circle, Pittsburgh, PA 15212, USA

Johnson, Ora J — *Religious Leader*
%General Assn of General Baptists, 100 Stinson Dr, Popular Bluff, MO 63901, USA

Johnson, Oscar G — *WW II Army Hero (CMH)*
121 Garfield St, Iron Mountain, MI 49801, USA

Johnson, Paul B — *Historian, Journalist*
Coach House, Over Stowey Near Bridgewater, Somerset TA5 1HA, England

Johnson, Pepper — *Football Player*
%New York Giants, Giants Stadium, East Rutherford, NJ 07073, USA

Johnson, Philip C — *Architect*
%John Burgee Architects, 885 3rd Ave, New York, NY 10022, USA

Johnson, R E — *Labor Leader*
%Train Dispatchers Assn, 1401 S Harlem Ave, Berwyn, IL 60402, USA

Johnson, Rafer — *Track Athlete*
%Special Olympics California, 501 Colorado Ave, #200, Santa Monica, CA 90401, USA

Johnson, Ralph E — *Architect*
%Perkins & Will, 123 N Wacker Dr, Chicago, IL 60606, USA

Johnson, Randall D (Randy) — *Baseball Player*
16110 SE Cougar Mountain Way, Bellevue, WA 98006, USA

Johnson, Raymond A — *Businessman*
%Nordstrom Inc, 1501 5th Ave, Seattle, WA 98101, USA

Johnson, Richard — *Actor*
%United British Artists, 2 Stokenchurch St, London SW6 3TR, England

Johnson, Richard C — *Businessman*
%H B Fuller Co, 200 Energy Park Dr, St Paul, MN 55108, USA

Johnson, Richard J V *Publisher*
%Houston Chronicle, 801 Texas St, Houston, TX 77002, USA

Johnson, Rick *Motorcycle Racing Rider, Auto Driver*
%American Honda Racing, 100 W Alondra Blvd, Gardena, CA 90248, USA

Johnson, Robert L *Entertainment Executive*
%Black Entertainment Television, 1232 31st St NW, Washington, DC 20007, USA

Johnson, Roger W *Government Official, Businessman*
%General Services Administration, 18th & "F" Sts NW, Washington, DC 20405, USA

Johnson, Ron *Football Player*
226 Summit Ave, Summit, NJ 07901, USA

Johnson, Roy *Labor Leader*
%Roofers & Waterproofers Union, 1125 17th St NW, Washington, DC 20036, USA

Johnson, Russell *Actor*
PO Box 3135, La Jolla, CA 92038, USA

Johnson, Samuel C *Businessman*
%S C Johnson & Son, 1525 Howe St, Racine, WI 53403, USA

Johnson, Sonia *Women's, Religious Activist*
3318 2nd St S, Arlington, VA 22204, USA

Johnson, Steve *Basketball Player*
%Seattle Supersonics, 190 Queen Ave N, PO Box C-900911, Seattle, WA 98109, USA

Johnson, Thomas S *Financier*
%GreenPoint Bank, 41-60 Main St, Flushing, NY 11355, USA

Johnson, Tim *Football Player*
%Washington Redskins, 21300 Redskin Park Dr, Ashburn, VA 22011, USA

Johnson, Tish *Bowler*
%Ladies Professional Bowlers Tour, 7171 Cherryvale Blvd, Rockford, IL 61112, USA

Johnson, Tom *Hockey Player*
%Boston Bruins, Boston Garden, 150 Causeway St, Boston, MA 02114, USA

Johnson, U Alexis *Diplomat*
3133 Connecticut Ave NW, Washington, DC 20008, USA

Johnson, Van *Actor*
405 E 54th St, New York, NY 10022, USA

Johnson, Vaughan *Football Player*
%New Orleans Saints, 1500 Poydras St, New Orleans, LA 70112, USA

Johnson, Virginia *Ballerina*
%Dance Theatre of Harlem, 215 E 94th St, New York, NY 10128, USA

Johnson, Virginia E *Sex Therapist*
%Johnson & Masters Institute, Campbell Plaza, 59th & Arsenal, St Louis, MO 63118, USA

Johnson, W Thomas (Tom), Jr *Television Executive*
%CNN 1 CNN Center, Atlanta, GA 30303, USA

Johnson, Warren *Drag Racing Driver*
PO Box 1294, Duluth, GA 30136, USA

Johnson, Warren C *Chemist*
946 Bellclair Rd SE, Grand Rapids, MI 49506, USA

Johnston McKay, Mary H *Astronaut*
%University of Tennessee, Space Institute, Tullahoma, TN 37388, USA

Johnston, Alastair *Sports Agent*
%International Mgmt Group, 75490 Fairway Dr, Indian Wells, CA 92210, USA

Johnston, Allen H *Religious Leader*
%Bishop's House, 3 Wymer Terrace, PO Box 21, Hamilton, New Zealand

Johnston, Cathy *Golfer*
%Ladies Professional Golf Assn, 2570 Volusia Ave, Daytona Beach, FL 32114, USA

Johnston, Darryl *Football Player*
%Dallas Cowboys, 1 Cowboys Parkway, Irving, TX 75063, USA

Johnston, David L *Educator*
%McGill University, Chancellor's Office, Montreal PQ H3A 2T5, Canada

Johnston, Douglas *Publisher*
%Vanity Fair Magazine, 350 Madison Ave, New York, NY 10017, USA

Johnston, Edward J *Hockey Executive*
%Pittsburgh Penguins, Civic Arena, Centre Ave, Pittsburgh, PA 15219, USA

Johnston, Freedy *Singer, Songwriter*
%Do Easy Booking, 2135 W Augusta Blvd, #2, Chicago, IL 60622, USA

Johnston, Harold S *Chemist*
285 Franklin St, Harrisonburg, VA 22801, USA

Johnston, James W *Businessman*
%RJR Nabisco Holdings, 1301 Ave of Americas, New York, NY 10019, USA

Johnston, John Dennis *Actor*
%Century Artists, 9744 Wilshire Blvd, #308, Beverly Hills, CA 90212, USA

Johnston, Lynn *Cartoonist (For Better or For Worse)*
%Universal Press Syndicate, 4900 Main St, #900, Kansas City, KS 64112, USA

Johnston, Lynn H *Businessman*
%Life Insurance Co of Georgia, 5780 Powers Ferry RD NW, Atlanta, GA 30327, USA

Johnstone, George W *Businessman*
%American Water Works Co, 1025 Laurel Oak Rd, Voorhees, NJ 08043, USA

Johnstone, John W, Jr *Businessman*
%Olin Corp, 120 Long Ridge Rd, Stamford, CT 06902, USA

Johore *Sultan, Malaysia*
%Istana Bukit Serene, Johore Bahru, Johore, Malaysia

Joiner, Charlie *Football Player, Coach*
%Buffalo Bills, 1 Bills Dr, Orchard Park, NY 14127, USA

Joklik, W Karl *Microbiologist*
%Duke University Medical Center, Microbiology/Immunology Dept, Durham, NC 27710, USA

Jolly, Allison *Yachtswoman*
3440 Knoxville Ave, Long Beach, CA 90808, USA

Jonckheer, Efrain *Prime Minister, Netherlands Antilles*
%Royal Netherlands Embassy, Calle 21, Avda 10, San Jose, Costa Rica

Jones (Amiri Baraka), LeRoi *Poet*
%State University of New York, Afro-American Studies Dept, Stony Brook, NY 11794, USA

Jones, Alex S *Journalist*
225 W 86th St, #309, New York, NY 10024, USA

Jones, Allen *Artist*
%41 Charterhouse Square, London EC1M 6EA, England

Jones, Arthur *Inventor (Nautilus Exercise Machine)*
%MedX, 1155 NE 77th St, Ocala, FL 34479, USA

Jones, Ben J *Prime Minister, Grenada*
Archibald Ave, St George's, Grenada

Jones, Bert *Football Player*
%Mid-States Wood Preservers, PO Box 298, Simsboro, LA 71275, USA

Jones, Bill T *Choreographer*
%Bull T Jones/Arnie Zane Dance Co, 853 Broadway, #1706, New York, NY 10003, USA

Jones, Bobby *Basketball Player*
5109 Panview Dr, Mathews, NC 28105, USA

Jones, Brent *Football Player*
%San Francisco 49ers, 4949 Centennial Blvd, Santa Clara, CA 95054, USA

Jones, Brereton C *Governor, KY*
%Governor's Office, State Capitol Bldg, #100, Frankfort, KY 40601, USA

Jones, Charles M (Chuck) *Animator (Road Runner, Pepe le Pew)*
PO Box 2319, Costa Mesa, CA 92628, USA

Jones, Charles W *Labor Leader*
%Brotherhood of Boilermakers, 753 8th Ave, Kansas City, KS 66105, USA

Jones, Charlie *Sportscaster*
8080 El Paseo Grande, La Jolla, CA 92037, USA

Jones, Courtney J L *Figure Skating Executive*
%National Skating Assn, 15-27 Gee St, London EC1V 3RE, England

Jones, Cranston E *Editor*
8 E 96th St, New York, NY 10128, USA

Jones, D Michael *Financier*
%West One Bancorp, 101 S Capitol Blvd, Boise, ID 83702, USA

Jones, D Paul, Jr *Financier*
%Compass BancShares, 15 S 20th St, Birmingham, AL 35233, USA

Jones, Dale P *Businessman*
%Halliburton Co, Lincoln Plaza, 500 N Akard St, Dallas, TX 75201, USA

Jones, Darryl *Bassist (Rolling Stones)*
1776 Broadway, #507, New York, NY 10019, USA

Jones, David (Deacon) *Football Player, Executive*
%Calgary Stampeders, 1817 Crowchild Trail NW, Calgary AB T2M 4R6, Canada

Jones, David A *Businessman*
%Humana Inc, 500 W Main St, Louisville, KY 40202, USA

Jones, David C *Businessman*
%National Education Corp, 18400 Von Karman Ave, Irvine, CA 92715, USA

Jones, David R *Businessman*
%Atlanta Gas Light Co, 303 Peachtree St NE, Atlanta, GA 30308, USA

Jones, Davy *Singer, Guitarist (Monkees)*
%Dome Press, PO Box 400, Beavertown, PA 17813, USA

Jones, Dean *Actor*
5055 Casa Dr, Tarzana, CA 91356, USA

J

Johnston - Jones

Jones, Dean M — *Cricketer*
%Durham Club, Mercantile Rd, Houghton-Le-Sring, Durham DH4 5PH, England

Jones, E Bradley — *Businessman*
3881-2 Lander Rd, Chagrin Falls, OH 44022, USA

Jones, E Edward — *Religious Leader*
%Baptist Convention of America, 777 S R L Thornton Freeway, Dallas, TX 75203, USA

Jones, E Fay — *Architect*
1330 N Hillcrest St, Fayetteville, AR 72703, USA

Jones, Earl — *Track Athlete*
15114 Petroskey Ave, Detroit, MI 48238, USA

Jones, Eddie J — *Football Executive*
%Miami Dolphins, 7500 SW 30th St, Davie, FL 33329, USA

Jones, Elvin — *Jazz Drummer*
%Keiko Jones Mgmt, 415 Central Park West, New York, NY 10025, USA

Jones, George — *Singer, Songwriter*
RR 3, Box 150, Murphy, NC 28906, USA

Jones, Geraint I — *Conductor*
Long House, Arkley Lane, Barnet Rd, Arkley, Herts, England

Jones, Grace — *Model, Actress*
PO Box 82, Great Neck, NY 11022, USA

Jones, Grandpa — *Comedian*
172 Happy Valley Rd, Goodlettsvlle, TN 37072, USA

Jones, Greg — *Skier*
PO Box 500, Tahoe City, CA 96145, USA

Jones, Gwyneth — *Opera Singer*
PO Box 556, 8037 Zurich, Switzerland

Jones, Hayes — *Track Athlete*
11799 Corbett, Detroit, MI 48213, USA

Jones, Henry — *Football Player*
%Buffalo Bills, 1 Bills Dr, Orchard Park, NY 14127, USA

Jones, Henry — *Actor*
502 9th St, Santa Monica, CA 90402, USA

Jones, Jack — *Singer*
78-825 Osage Trail, Indian Wells, CA 92210, USA

Jones, James Earl — *Actor*
390 West End Ave, New York, NY 10024, USA

Jones, James L (Jack) — *Labor Leader*
74 Ruskin Park House, Champion Hill, London SE5, England

Jones, Janet — *Actress*
14135 Beresford Dr, Beverly Hills, CA 90210, USA

Jones, Jeff — *Basketball Coach*
%University of Virginia, Athletic Dept, Charlottesville, VA 22903, USA

Jones, Jeffrey — *Actor*
%J Michael Bloom Ltd, 9255 Sunset Blvd, #710, Los Angeles, CA 90069, USA

Jones, Jennifer — *Actress*
264 N Glenroy Ave, Los Angeles, CA 90049, USA

Jones, Jenny — *Entertainer, Comedienne*
%Jenny Jones Show, NBC-Tower, 454 N Columbus Dr, #400, Chicago, IL 60611, USA

Jones, Jerrauld C (Jerry) — *Football Executive*
%Dallas Cowboys, 1 Cowboys Parkway, Irving, TX 75063, USA

Jones, John E — *Businessman*
%CBI Industries, 800 Jorie Blvd, Oak Brook, IL 60521, USA

Jones, John Paul — *Sculptor*
22370 3rd Ave, South Laguna, CA 92677, USA

Jones, June — *Football Coach*
%Atlanta Falcons, 2745 Burnett Rd, Suwanee, GA 30174, USA

Jones, K C — *Basketball Player, Coach*
%Detroit Pistons, Palace, 2 Championship Dr, Auburn Hills, MI 48057, USA

Jones, L Q — *Actor*
2144 1/2 N Cahuenga Blvd, Los Angeles, CA 90068, USA

Jones, Landon Y — *Editor*
%People Magazine, Editorial Dept, Rockefeller Center, New York, NY 10020, USA

Jones, Leilani — *Actress*
%Writers & Artists Agency, 924 Westwood Blvd, #900, Los Angeles, CA 90024, USA

Jones, Lyle V — *Psychologist*
RR 7, Pittsboro, NC 27312, USA

Jones, Marcia Mae — *Actress*
4541 Hazeltine, #4, Sherman Oaks, CA 91423, USA

Jones, Marvin — *Football Player*
%New York Jets, 1000 Fulton Ave, Hempstead, NY 11550, USA

Jones, Mary Ellen — *Biochemist*
%University of North Carolina, Biochemistry Dept, Chapel Hill, NC 27599, USA

Jones, Maxine — *Singer (En Vogue)*
%William Morris Agency, 1325 Ave of Americas, New York, NY 10019, USA

Jones, Nathaniel R — *Judge*
%US Court of Appeals, US Courthouse, 5th & Walnut Sts, Cincinnati, OH 45202, USA

Jones, Norman T — *Businessman*
%CF Industries, 1 Salem Lake Dr, Long Grove, IL 60047, USA

Jones, Parnelli — *Auto Racing Driver, Builder*
20550 Earl St, Torrance, CA 90503, USA

Jones, Philip M — *Concert Trumpeter*
14 Hamilton Terrace, London NW8 9UG, England

Jones, Pirkle — *Photographer*
663 Lovell Ave, Mill Valley, CA 94941, USA

Jones, Quincy — *Composer, Conductor*
PO Box 11509, Burbank, CA 91510, USA

Jones, Randall L (Randy) — *Baseball Player*
14934 La Manda Dr, Poway, CA 92064, USA

Jones, Randy — *Publisher*
%Esquire Magazine, 250 W 55th St, New York, NY 10019, USA

Jones, Reginald V — *Physicist*
8 Queen's Terrace, Aberdeen AB1 1XL, Scotland

Jones, Renee — *Actress*
%Innovative Artists, 1999 Ave of Stars, #2850, Los Angeles, CA 90067, USA

Jones, Richard M — *Businessman*
%Savings & Profit Sharing Fund, Sears Tower, Chicago, IL 60684, USA

Jones, Rickie Lee — *Singer, Songwriter*
%Gold Mountain Entertainment, 3575 Barham Blvd, #450, Los Angeles, CA 90068, USA

Jones, Robert T — *Aerospace Scientist*
25005 La Loma Dr, Los Altos, CA 94022, USA

Jones, Robert Trent — *Golf Course Architect*
705 Forest Ave, Palo Alto, CA 94301, USA

Jones, Roy, Jr — *Boxer*
%Stanley Levin, 226 S Palafox Place, Pensacola, FL 32501, USA

Jones, Rulon — *Football Player*
%Denver Broncos, 13655 E Dove Valley Parkway, Englewood, CO 80112, USA

Jones, Russel C — *Educator, Civil Engineer*
12 Boysenberry Dr, Hockessin, DE 19707, USA

Jones, Samuel (Sam) — *Basketball Player*
15417 Tierra Dr, Wheaton, MD 20906, USA

Jones, Shirley — *Actress, Singer*
701 N Oakhurst Dr, Beverly Hills, CA 90210, USA

Jones, Stan — *Football Player, Coach*
1202 Clear Pond Dr, Walpole, MA 02081, USA

Jones, Stephen — *Attorney*
%Jones & Wyatt, PO Box 472, Enid, OK 73702, USA

Jones, Steve — *Golfer*
%Professional Golfer's Assn, PO Box 109601, Palm Beach Gardens, FL 33410, USA

Jones, Steven — *Physicist*
%Brigham Young University, Physics Dept, Provo, UT 84602, USA

Jones, Terry — *Animator, Director (Monty Python)*
%Python Productions, 68-A Delancey St, London NW1 7RY, England

Jones, Thomas D — *Astronaut*
%NASA, Johnson Space Center, 2101 NASA Rd, Houston, TX 77058, USA

Jones, Thomas V — *Businessman*
1050 Moraga Dr, Los Angeles, CA 90049, USA

Jones, Thomas W — *Businessman*
%TIAA-CREF, 730 3rd Ave, New York, NY 10017, USA

Jones, Tom — *Singer*
363 Copa de Oro Rd, Los Angeles, CA 90077, USA

Jones, Tommy Lee — *Actor*
PO Box 966, San Saba, TX 76877, USA

Jones, William (Dub) — *Football Player*
326 Glendale, Ruston, LA 71270, USA

Jones, William K — *Marine Corps General*
1211 Huntly Place, Alexandria, VA 22307, USA

J

Jones - Jones

Jong, Erica M *Writer*
%K D Burrows, 425 Park Ave, New York, NY 10022, USA

Jonsen, Albert R *Physician*
%University of Washington Medical School, Medical Ethics Dept, Seattle, WA 98195, USA

Joo Hyong Kyong *Businessman*
%Samsung Co, 250 Ka Taepyungro, Chungku, Seoul, South Korea

Joon Silk Koh *Businessman*
%Pohang Iron & Steel, 5 Dongchondon, Pohang City, Kyungbok, South Korea

Joost, Edwin D (Eddie) *Baseball Player*
303 Belhaven Circle, Santa Rosa, CA 95409, USA

Jopling, T Michael *Government Official, England*
Clyder Howe Cottage, Windermere, Cumbria, England

Jordan, Bryce *Educator*
3403 Ledgestone Dr, Austin, TX 78731, USA

Jordan, Charles M *Automobile Designer*
PO Box 8330, Rancho Santa Fe, CA 92067, USA

Jordan, Don D *Businessman*
%Houston Industries, 4400 Post Oak Park, Houston, TX 77027, USA

Jordan, Glenn *Movie Director*
9401 Wilshire Blvd, #700, Beverly Hills, CA 90212, USA

Jordan, I King *Educator*
%Gallaudet University, President's Office, 800 Florida NW, Washington, DC 20001, USA

Jordan, Jerry L *Financier*
%Federal Reserve Bank, 1455 E 6th St, Cleveland, OH 44114, USA

Jordan, Kathy *Tennis Player*
1604 Union St, San Francisco, CA 94123, USA

Jordan, Lee Roy *Football Player*
%Redwood Lumber Co, 2425 Burbank St, Dallas, TX 75235, USA

Jordan, Michael H *Businessman*
%Westinghouse Electric Corp, Gateway Center, Pittsburgh, PA 15222, USA

Jordan, Michael J *Basketball Player*
%Chicago Bulls, 1901 W Madison St, Chicago, IL 60612, USA

Jordan, Neil P *Movie Director*
6 Sorrento Terrace, Dalkey, County Dublin, Ireland

Jordan, Payton *Track Coach*
439 Knoll Dr, Los Altos, CA 94024, USA

Jordan, Stanley *Jazz Guitarist*
%David Rubinson, 100 Broderick St, #601, San Francisco, CA 94117, USA

Jordan, Steven R (Steve) *Football Player*
%Minnesota Vikings, 9520 Viking Dr, Eden Prairie, MN 55344, USA

Jordan, Vernon E, Jr *Civil Rights Activist*
%Akin Gump Strauss Hauer, 1333 New Hampshire Ave NW, Washington, DC 20036, USA

Jordan, W Hamilton M *Government Official, Publisher*
%Whittle Communications, 333 W Main Ave, Knoxville, TN 37902, USA

Jordan, William *Actor*
10806 Lindbrook Ave, #4, Los Angeles, CA 90024, USA

Jorgensen, Anker *Prime Minister, Denmark*
Borgbjergvej 1, 2450 SV Copenhagen, Denmark

Jorgensen, Paul E *Educator*
%Virginia Polytechnic Institute, President's Office, Blacksburg, VA 24061, USA

Jorgenson, Dale W *Economist*
1010 Memorial Dr, #14-C, Cambridge, MA 02138, USA

Jorginho *Soccer Player*
Rua Levi Carreiro 420, Barra de Tijuca, Brazil

Jorndt, L Daniel *Businessman*
%Walgreen Co, 200 Wilmot Rd, Deerfield, IL 60015, USA

Jose, Jose *Singer*
%Ventura Productions, 11003 Rooks Rd, Pico Rivera, CA 90660, USA

Josefowicz, Leila *Concert Violinist*
%Jascha Brodsky, Curtis Institute of Music, 1726 Locust, Philadelphia, PA 19103, USA

Joseph, Curtis *Hockey Player*
%Edmonton Oilers, Northlands Coliseum, Edmonton AB T5B 4M9, Canada

Joseph, Marcel P *Businessman*
%Augat Inc, 89 Forbes Blvd, Mansfield, MA 02048, USA

Joseph, Stephen *Physician*
%New York City Department of Health, 125 Worth St, New York, NY 10013, USA

Josephine Charlotte *Princess, Luxembourg*
Grand Ducal Palace, Luxembourg, Luxembourg

Josephs, Wilfred *Composer*
4 Grand Union Walk, Kentish Town Rd, Camden Town, London NW1 9LP, England

Josephson, Brian D *Nobel Physics Laureate*
%Cavendish Laboratory, Madingley Rd, Cambridge CB3 0HE, England

Josephson, Erland *Actor*
%Royal Dramatic Theater, Nybroplan, Box 5037, 102 41 Stockholm, Sweden

Josephson, Karen *Synchronized Swimmer*
1923 Junction Dr, Concord, CA 94518, USA

Josephson, Marvin *Entertainment Executive*
%International Creative Mgmt, 40 W 57th St, New York, NY 10019, USA

Josephson, Sarah *Synchronized Swimmer*
1923 Junction Dr, Concord, CA 94518, USA

Joslin, Roger S *Businessman*
%State Farm Fire & Casualty, 112 E Washington St, Bloomington, IL 61701, USA

Joubert, Beverly *Photographer*
%National Geographic Magazine, 17th & "M" Sts NW, Washington, DC 20036, USA

Joubert, Dereck *Photographer*
%National Geographic Magazine, 17th & "M" Sts NW, Washington, DC 20036, USA

Joulwan, George A *Army General*
Supreme Allied Command, Supreme Hdqs, Allied Powers Europe, APO, AP 09705, USA

Jourdan, Louis *Actor*
1139 Maybrook Dr, Beverly Hills, CA 90210, USA

Jovanovich, Peter W *Publisher*
%MacMillan Inc, 866 3rd Ave, New York, NY 10022, USA

Joyce, Andrea *Sportscaster*
%Home Box Office, Sports Dept, 1100 Ave of Americas, New York, NY 10036, USA

Joyce, Burton M *Businessman*
%Terra Industries, 600 4th St, Sioux City, IA 51101, USA

Joyce, Edward M *Television Executive*
%Columbia Broadcasting System, 51 W 52nd St, New York, NY 10019, USA

Joyce, Elaine *Actress*
%Twentieth Century Artists, 15315 Magnolia Blvd, #429, Sherman Oaks, CA 91403, USA

Joyce, Joan *Softball Player, Golfer*
22856 Marbella Circle, Boca Raton, FL 33433, USA

Joyce, John T *Labor Leader*
%Bricklayers & Allied Craftsmen, 815 15th St NW, Washington, DC 20005, USA

Joyce, Kevern R *Businessman*
%TNP Enterprises, PO Box 2943, Fort Worth, TX 76113, USA

Joyce, William *Artist, Writer*
3302 Centenary Blvd, Shreveport, LA 71104, USA

Joyce, William H *Businessman*
%Union Carbide Corp, 39 Old Ridgebury Rd, Danbury, CT 06817, USA

Joyner, Al *Track Athlete*
21214 Leadwell St, Canoga Park, CA 91304, USA

Joyner, Seth *Football Player*
%Arizona Cardinals, 8701 S Hardy Dr, Tempe, AZ 85284, USA

Joyner, Wallace K (Wally) *Baseball Player*
11923 Alley Jackson Rd, Lees Summit, MO 64086, USA

Joyner-Kersee, Jacqueline (Jackie) *Track Athlete*
21214 Leadwell St, Canoga Park, CA 91304, USA

Jozwiak, Brian J *Football Player, Coach*
51 Rohor Ave, Buckhannon, WV 26201, USA

Juan Carlos I *King, Spain*
%Palacio de la Zarzuela, 28671 Madrid, Spain

Juantorena, Alberto *Track Athlete*
%National Institute for Sports, Sports City, Havana, Cuba

Jubany Arnau, Narciso Cardinal *Religious Leader*
%Arquebisbe de Barcelone, Bisbe Irurita 5, 08002 Barcelona, Spain

Juckes, Gordon W *Hockey Executive*
General Delivery, Zurich ON N0M 2T0, Canada

Judd, Ashley *Actress*
PO Box 2504, Malibu, CA 90265, USA

Judd, Howard L *Obstetrician*
%University of California Medical Center, OB-Gyn Dept, Los Angeles, CA 90024, USA

Judd, Naomi *Singer (The Judds), Songwriter*
1321 Murfreesboro Rd, #100, Nashville, TN 37217, USA

Judd, Wynonna *Singer (The Judds)*
PO Box 682068, Franklin, TN 37068, USA

J

Judge, George — *Economist*
%University of California, Economics Dept, Berkeley, CA 94720, USA

Judge, Mike — *Animator (Beavis & Butt-Head)*
%"Beavis & Butt-Head" Show, MTV-TV, 1515 Broadway, New York, NY 10036, USA

Judge, Thomas L — *Governor, MT*
579 Diehl Dr, Helena, MT 59601, USA

Jugnauth, Anerood — *Prime Minister, Mauritius*
%Government House, New Government Center, Port Louis, Mauritius

Juhl, Finn — *Furniture Designer*
%Kratvaenget 15, 2920 Chartottenlund, Denmark

Julian, Alexander, II — *Fashion Designer*
%Alexander Julian Inc, 63 Copps Hill Rd, Ridgefield, CT 06877, USA

Julian, Janet — *Actress*
%Borinstein Oreck Bogart Agency, 8271 Melrose Ave, #110, Los Angeles, CA 90046, USA

Juliana — *Queen, Netherlands*
%Palace of Soestdijk, Amsterdamsestraatweg 1, 2513 AA Baarn, Netherlands

Julien, Max — *Actor*
6051 Fulton Ave, Van Nuys, CA 91401, USA

Jumblatt, Walid — *Government Official, Lebanon*
%Druze Headquarters, Mokhtara, Lebanon

Jump, Gordon — *Actor*
1631 Hillcrest Ave, Glendale, CA 91202, USA

Jumper, John P — *Air Force General*
Commander, 9th Air Force, 524 Shaw Dr, Shaw Air Force Base, SC 29152, USA

Junck, Mary — *Publisher*
%Baltimore Sun Co, 501 N Calvert St, Baltimore, MD 21202, USA

Juneau, Joe — *Hockey Player*
%Washington Capitals, USAir Arena, Landover, MD 20785, USA

Juneau, Pierre — *Government Official, Canada*
%Canadian Broadcast Co, 1500 Bronson Ave, Ottawa ON N1G 3J5, Canada

Jung, Ernst — *Writer*
88515 Lagenensligen/Wiltlingen, Germany

Jung, Richard — *Neurologist*
Waldhofstr 42, 71691 Freiburg, Germany

Junker, Edward P, III — *Financier*
%PNC Bank Corp, 5th Ave & Wood St, Pittsburgh, PA 15222, USA

Junkins, Jerry R — *Businessman*
%Texas Instruments, 13500 North Central Expressway, Dallas, TX 75243, USA

Junz, Helen B — *Economist*
%Int'l Monetary Fund, 58 Rue de Moillebeau, 1209 Geneva, Switzerland

Juppe, Alain M — *Prime Minister, France*
%Prime Minister's Office, 57 Rue de Varenne, 75700 Paris, France

Juran, Joseph M — *Engineer, Management Consultant*
%Juran Institute, 11 River Rd, Wilton, CT 06897, USA

Jurasik, Peter — *Actor*
969 1/2 Manzanita St, Los Angeles, CA 90029, USA

Jurgensen, Christian A (Sonny), III — *Football Player*
PO Box 53, Mount Vernon, VA 22121, USA

Jurick, Geoffrey — *Businessman*
%Emerson Radio Corp, 9 Entin Rd, Parsippany, NJ 07054, USA

Jurinac, Sena — *Opera Singer*
%State Opera House, Opernring 2, 10100 Vienna, Austria

Just, Walter — *Publisher*
%Milwaukee Journal, 333 W State St, Milwaukee, WI 53203, USA

Just, Ward S — *Writer*
36 Ave Junot, Paris, France

Justice, Charlie (Choo Choo) — *Football Player*
PO Box 819, Cherryville, NC 28021, USA

Justice, David C — *Baseball Player*
4173 Tattershall Dr, Decatur, GA 30034, USA

Justice, Donald R — *Poet, Educator*
338 Rocky Shore Dr, Iowa City, IA 52246, USA

Judge - Justice

Kaassorla, Irene *Psychologist*
10231 Charing Cross Rd, Los Angeles, CA 90024, USA

Kabat, Elvin A *Immunochemist*
70 Haven Ave, New York, NY 10032, USA

Kabua, Amata *President, Marshall Islands*
%President's Office, Cabinet Building, PO Box 2, Majuro, Marshall Islands

Kaczmarek, Jane *Actress*
304 E 65th St, #5-A, New York, NY 10021, USA

Kadanoff, Leo P *Physicist*
5421 Cornell Ave, Chicago, IL 60615, USA

Kadare, Ismael *Writer*
%Editions Fayard, 75 Rue De St Peres, 75006 Paris, France

Kadish, Mike *Football Player*
5485 Red Bank Rd, Galena, OH 43021, USA

Kael, Pauline *Writer*
2 Berkshire Heights Rd, Great Barrington, MA 01230, USA

Kaelin, Brian (Kato) *Celebrity*
8383 Wilshire Blvd, #954, Beverly Hills, CA 90211, USA

Kaestle, Carl F *Historian*
1345 E Madison Park, #1, Chicago, IL 60615, USA

Kafi, Ali *President, Algeria*
%President's Office, Council of State, Al-Mouradia, Algiers, Algeria

Kagame, Paul *Army General, Rwanda*
%Vice Chairman's Office, Church St, Kigali, Rwanda

Kagan, Jeremy Paul *Movie Director*
2024 N Curson Ave, Los Angeles, CA 90046, USA

Kagge, Erling *Polar Skier*
Munkedamsveien 86, 0270 Oslo, Norway

Kagoshima, Juzo *Dollmaker*
1-14 Toyotamakami, Nerimaku, Tokyo, Japan

Kahana, Aron *Financier*
%Israel Discount Bank of New York, 511 5th Ave, New York, NY 10017, USA

Kahane, Jeffrey *Concert Pianist*
%IMG Artists, 22 E 71st St, New York, NY 10021, USA

Kahn, Alfred E *Government Official, Economist*
1679 Taughannock Blvd, Trumansburg, NY 14886, USA

Kahn, Jenette S *Publisher*
%DC Comics, 1325 Ave of Americas, New York, NY 10019, USA

Kahn, Madeline *Actress*
975 Park Ave, #9-A, New York, NY 10028, USA

Kahn, Philippe *Businessman*
%Borland International, 100 Borland Way, Scotts Valley, CA 95066, USA

Kaifu, Toshiki *Prime Minister, Japan*
%House of Representatives, Tokyo, Japan

Kailbourne, Erland E *Financier*
%Fleet Bank, Kiernan Plaza, Albany, NY 12207, USA

Kain, Karin A *Ballet Dancer*
%National Ballet of Canada, 157 E King St, Toronto ON M5C 1G9, Canada

Kairamo, Kari *Businessman*
%Nokia Group, Mikonkatu 15 A, 00101 Helsinki 10, Finland

Kaiser, A Dale *Biochemist*
832 Santa Fe Ave, Stanford, CA 94305, USA

Kaiser, George B *Financier*
%Bank of Oklahoma, Bank of Oklahoma Tower, PO Box 2300, Tulsa, OK 74102, USA

Kaiser, Philip M *Diplomat*
%SRI International, 1611 N Kent St, Arlington, VA 22209, USA

Kaiserman, William *Fashion Designer*
29 W 56th St, New York, NY 10019, USA

Kaizaki, Yoichiro *Businessman*
%Bridgestone Corp, 10-1-1 Kyobashi, Chuoku, Tokyo 104, Japan

Kaji, Gautam S *Financier*
%World Bank Group, 1818 "H" St NW, Washington, DC 20433, USA

Kaku, Ryuzaburo *Businessman*
%Canon Inc, 2-7-1 Nishi-shinku, Shinjuku, Tokyo 169, Japan

Kalainov, Samuel C *Businessman*
%American Mutual Life Insurance, 611 5th Ave, Des Moines, IA 50309, USA

Kalangis, Ike *Financier*
%Boatmen's Sunwest, 303 Roma Ave NW, Albuquerque, NM 87102, USA

K

Kalb, Marvin *Commentator, Educator*
%Harvard University, Barone Center, 79 J F Kennedy St, Cambridge, MA 02138, USA

Kalber, Floyd *Commentator*
%NBC-TV, News Dept, 30 Rockefeller Plaza, New York, NY 10112, USA

Kalember, Patricia *Actress*
324 W 83rd St, #3-B, New York, NY 10024, USA

Kaleri, Alexander Y *Cosmonaut*
141 160 Svyosdny Gorodok, Moskovskoi Oblasti, Potchta Kosmonavtor, Russia

Kalikow, Peter S *Publisher*
%H J Kalikow Co, 101 Park Ave, New York, NY 10178, USA

Kalikowski, Frederick R *Financier*
%City Bank (New York State), 99 Garnsey Rd, Pittsford, NY 14534, USA

Kalina, Mike *Chef*
%"Travelin' Gourmet" Show, PBS-TV, 1320 Braddock Place, Alexandria, VA 22314, USA

Kalina, Richard *Artist*
44 King St, New York, NY 10014, USA

Kaline, Albert W (Al) *Baseball Player*
945 Timberlake Dr, Bloomfield Hills, MI 48302, USA

Kalish, Martin *Labor Leader*
%School Administrators Federation, 853 Broadway, New York, NY 10003, USA

Kalish, Robert P *Financier*
%Government National Mortgage Assn, 451 7th St SW, Washington, DC 20410, USA

Kalitta, Connie *Drag Racing Driver*
%National Hot Rod Assn, 2023 Financial Way, Glendora, CA 91741, USA

Kall (Kevin Kallaugher) *Editorial Cartoonist*
%Baltimore Sun, Editorial Dept, 501 N Calvert St, Baltimore, MD 21202, USA

Kallai, Gyula *Prime Minister, Hungary*
%Patriotic People's Front Council, Belgrad Rakpart 24, Budapest 5, Hungary

Kalleres, Michael P *Navy Admiral*
Commander, Military Sealift Command, 901 "M" St SE, Washington, DC 20398, USA

Kallman, Donald H *Businessman*
%Manhattan Industries, 1114 Ave of Americas, New York, NY 10036, USA

Kaltinick, Paul R *Financier*
%Frank Russell Trust, PO Box 1454, Tacoma, WA 98401, USA

Kalule, Ayub *Boxer*
%Palle, Skjulet, Bagsvaert 12, Copenhagen 2850, Denmark

Kalvaria, Leon *Businessman*
%Triarc Companies, 900 3rd Ave, New York, NY 10022, USA

Kamali, Norma *Fashion Designer*
%OMO Norma Kamali, 11 W 56th St, New York, NY 10019, USA

Kaman, Charles H *Businessman*
%Kaman Corp, 1332 Blue Hills Ave, Bloomfield, CT 06002, USA

Kamarck, Martin A *Financier*
%Export-Import Bank, 811 Vermont Ave NW, Washington, DC 20571, USA

Kamb, Alexander *Geneticist*
1103 E 600 South, Salt Lake City, UT 84102, USA

Kamberg, Kenneth E *Financier*
%Coral Gable Federal Savings, 2511 Ponce de Leon Blvd, Coral Gables, FL 33134, USA

Kamei, Masao *Businessman*
34-11-1 Kyodo, Setagayaku, Tokyo 156, Japan

Kamen, Harry P *Businessman*
%Metropolitan Life Insurance, 1 Madison Ave, New York, NY 10010, USA

Kamen, Martin D *Chemist*
Casa Burinda, #B-58, 300 Hot Springs Rd, Montecito, CA 93108, USA

Kamen, Michael *Composer*
%Gorfaine/Schwarz/Roberts, 3301 Barham Blvd, #201, Los Angeles, CA 90068, USA

Kamerschen, Robert J *Businessman*
%ADVO Inc, 1 Univac Lane, Windsor, CT 06095, USA

Kaminsky, Arthur C *Sports Attorney*
%Athletes & Artists, 421 7th Ave, #1400, New York, NY 10001, USA

Kamm, Henry *Journalist*
%New York Times, Editorial Dept, 229 W 43rd St, New York, NY 10036, USA

Kampelman, Max M *Government Official, Diplomat*
3154 Highland Place NW, Washington, DC 20008, USA

Kampouris, Emmanuel A *Businessman*
%American Standard Inc, 1 Centennial Place, Piscataway, NJ 08854, USA

Kamu, Okko *Conductor*
%Svensk Konsertdirektion Ab, Box 5076, 402 22 Goteborg, Sweden

Kalb - Kamu

K

Kan, Yuet Wai *Geneticist*
20 Yerba Buena Ave, San Francisco, CA 94127, USA
Kanaly, Steve *Actor*
838 Foothill Lane, Ojai, CA 93023, USA
Kanamori, Masao *Businessman*
%Mitsubishi Heavy Industries, 5-2-1 Marunouchi, Chiyodaku, Tokyo, Japan
Kananin, Roman G *Architect*
%Joint-Stock Co Mosprojekt, 13/14 1 Brestkaya Str, 125190 Moscow, Russia
Kanao, Minoru *Businessman*
%Nippon Kokan, 1-1-2 Marunouchi, Chiyodaku, Tokyo 100, Japan
Kanas, John A *Financier*
%North Fork Bancorp, 9025 Rt 25, Mattituck, NY 11952, USA
Kanazawa, Shuzo *Businessman*
%Mitsubishi Paper Co, 2-3-19 Kyobashi, Chuoku, Tokyo 104, Japan
Kandel, Eric R *Neurobiologist*
9 Sigma Place, Riverdale, NY 10471, USA
Kander, John H *Composer*
12203 Octagon St, Los Angeles, CA 90049, USA
Kane Elson, Marion *Synchronized Swimmer*
4669 Badger Rd, Santa Rosa, CA 95409, USA
Kane, Big Daddy *Rapper, Lyricist*
%Famous Artists Agency, 1700 Broadway, #500, New York, NY 10019, USA
Kane, Bob *Cartoonist (Batman)*
8455 Fountain Ave, #725, Los Angeles, CA 90069, USA
Kane, Carol *Actress*
1416 N Havenhurst Dr, #1-C, Los Angeles, CA 90046, USA
Kane, Douglas C *Businessman*
%MDU Resources Group, 400 N 4th St, Bismarck, ND 58501, USA
Kane, James *Labor Leader*
%United Electrical Workers Union, 11 E 51st St, New York, NY 10022, USA
Kane, John C *Businessman*
%Cardinal Health Inc, 655 Metro Place S, Dublin, OH 43017, USA
Kane, John R *WW II Army Air Corps Hero (CMH)*
1420 Lawndale Rd, Havertown, PA 19083, USA
Kane, Joseph N *Historian*
%H W Wilson Co, 950 University Ave, Bronx, NY 10452, USA
Kaneda, Masaichi *Baseball Player*
%Nippon Television, 14 Nibancho, Chiyodaku, Tokyo 102, Japan
Kaneko, Hisashi *Businessman*
%NEC Corp, 5-33-1 Shiba, Minatoku, Tokyo 108, Japan
Kanew, Jeffrey R *Movie Director*
%Gersh Agency, 232 N Canon Dr, Beverly Hills, CA 90210, USA
Kang Song San *Prime Minister, North Korea*
%Prime Minister's Office, Pyongyang, North Korea
Kanin, Fay *Writer*
653 Ocean Front Walk, Santa Monica, CA 90402, USA
Kanin, Garson *Writer*
200 W 57th St, #1203, New York, NY 10019, USA
Kann Valar, Paula *Skier*
PO Box 906, Franconia, NH 03580, USA
Kann, Peter R *Businessman, Publisher*
%Dow Jones Co, 200 Liberty St, New York, NY 10281, USA
Kannenberg, Bernd *Track Athlete*
Sportschule, 87527 Sonthofen/Allgau, Germany
Kano, Eisuke *Financier*
%IBJ Schroder Bank & Trust, 1 State St, New York, NY 10004, USA
Kanovitz, Howard *Artist*
463 Broome St, New York, NY 10013, USA
Kanter, Hal *Movie, TV Producer; Screenwriter*
%Hecox Horn Wheeler, 4730 Woodman Ave, Sherman Oaks, CA 91423, USA
Kanter, Rosabeth M *Economist*
%Harvard University, Business School, Boston, MA 02163, USA
Kantner, Paul *Musician (Jefferson Airplane, Starship)*
%Little Dragon Publishers, 3145 Geary Blvd, #416, San Francisco, CA 94118, USA
Kantor, Michael (Mickey) *Government Official*
%Office of US Trade Representative, 600 17th St NW, Washington, DC 20006, USA
Kantrowitz, Adrian *Heart Surgeon*
70 Gallogly Rd, Pontiac, MI 48326, USA

Kan - Kantrowitz

Kantrowitz - Karlen

Kantrowitz, Arthur R *Physicist*
4 Downing Rd, Hanover, NH 03755, USA

Kapioitas, John *Businessman*
%ITT Sheraton Corp, 60 State St, Boston, MA 02109, USA

Kaplan, Gabe *Actor, Comedian*
9551 Hidden Valley Rd, Beverly Hills, CA 90210, USA

Kaplan, Jonathan S *Movie Director*
8275 Kirkwood Dr, Los Angeles, CA 90046, USA

Kaplan, Justin *Writer*
16 Francis Ave, Cambridge, MA 02138, USA

Kaplan, Marvin *Actor*
7600 Claybeck Ave, Burbank, CA 91505, USA

Kaplan, Morton A *Political Scientist*
5446 S Ridgewood Circle, Chicago, IL 60615, USA

Kaplan, Nathan O *Biochemist*
8587 La Jolla Scenic Dr, La Jolla, CA 92037, USA

Kaplan, Richard *Editor*
%Star Magazine, Editoral Dept, 660 White Plains Rd, Tarrytown, NY 10591, USA

Kaplansky, Irving *Mathematician*
%Mathematical Sciences Research Institute, 100 Centennial Dr, Berkeley, CA 94720, USA

Kaplow, Herbert E *Commentator*
211 N Van Buren St, Falls Church, VA 22046, USA

Kapoor, Anish *Sculptor*
33 Coleherne Rd, London SW10, England

Kapoor, Shashi *Actor*
%Film Valas, Janki Kutir, Juhu Church Rd, Bombay 400049, India

Kapor, Mitchell D *Computer Programer*
%Electronic Frontier Foundation, 238 Main St, Cambridge, MA 02142, USA

Kapp, Joe *Football Player, Coach*
233 Edelen Ave, Los Gatos, CA 95030, USA

Kappner, Augusta Sousa *Educator*
%Education Dept, Vocational/Adult Education, 330 "C" St SW, Washington, DC 20201, USA

Kappock, Thomas J *Financier*
%Bancorp Hawaii, Financial Plaza, 130 Merchant Plaza, Honolulu, HI 96813, USA

Kaprisky, Valerie *Actress*
%Artmedia, 10 Ave George V, 75008 Paris, France

Kapture, Mitzi *Actress*
11866 Tiara St, North Hollywood, CA 91607, USA

Karageorghis, Vassos *Archaeologist*
%Foundation Anastasios Leventis, 28 Sofoulis St, Nicosia, Cyprus

Karan, Donna *Fashion Designer*
%Donna Karan Co, 550 7th Ave, New York, NY 10018, USA

Karanik, John A *Businessman*
%Maryland Insurance Group, 3910 Keswick Rd, Baltimore, MD 21211, USA

Karathanasis, Sotirios K *Medical Researcher*
%Harvard Medical School, 25 Shattuck St, Boston, MA 02115, USA

Karcher, Carl *Businessman*
%Carl Karcher Enterprises, 1200 N Harbor Blvd, Anaheim, CA 92801, USA

Kardos, Paul J *Businessman*
%Horace Mann Educators Corp, 1 Horace Mann Plaza, Springfield, IL 62715, USA

Karelskaya, Rimma K *Ballerina*
%Bolshoi Theater, Teatralnaya Pl 1, 103009 Moscow, Russia

Karg, Uschi *Model*
%Ford Model Agency, 344 E 59th St, New York, NY 10022, USA

Karim-Lamrani, Mohammed *Prime Minister, Morocco*
Rue Du Mont Saint Michel, Anfa Superieur, Casablanca 21300, Morocco

Karimov, Islam M *President, Uzbekistan*
%President's Office, Tashkent, Uzbekistan

Karina, Anna *Actress*
%JFPM, 11 Rue Chanez, 75781 Paris, France

Karkow, Richard E *Businessman*
%Minstar Inc, 100 S 5th St, Minneapolis, MN 55402, USA

Karl, George *Basketball Coach*
%Seattle Supersonics, 190 Queen Ave N, PO Box C-900911, Seattle, WA 98109, USA

Karle, Jerome *Nobel Chemistry Laureate*
US Navy Structure of Matter Research Laboratory, Code 6030, Washington, DC 20375, USA

Karlen, John *Actor*
911 2nd St, #16, Santa Monica, CA 90403, USA

Karlin, Samuel *Mathematician*
%Stanford University, Mathematics Dept, Stanford, CA 94305, USA

Karling, John S *Mycologist*
1219 Tuckahoe Lane, West Lafayette, IN 47906, USA

Karlstad, Geir *Speed Skater*
Hamarveien 5-A, 1472 Fjellhamar, Norway

Karlya, Paul *Hockey Player*
%Mighty Ducks of Anaheim, 1313 S Harbor Blvd, Anaheim, CA 92803, USA

Karlzen, Mary *Singer, Songwriter*
%Atlantic Records, 9229 Sunset Blvd, #900, Los Angeles, CA 90069, USA

Karmanos, Peter, Jr *Hockey Executive*
%Hartford Whalers, Coliseum, 242 Trumbell St, #800, Hartford, CT 06103, USA

Karmi, Ram *Architect*
%Karmi Architects, 5 Ben-Zion Blvd, Tel-Aviv, Israel

Karmi-Melamede, Ada *Architect*
%Karmi Architects, 5 Ben-Zion Blvd, Tel Aviv, Israel

Karn, Richard *Actor*
%Contemporary Artists, 1427 3rd St Promenade, #205, Santa Monica, CA 90401, USA

Karnes, David K *Senator, NE*
%Kutak Rock, Omaha Building, 1650 Farnam St, Omaha, NE 68102, USA

Karnow, Stanley *Journalist*
10850 Spring Knolls Dr, Potomac, MD 20854, USA

Karolyi, Bela *Gymnastics Coach*
%Karolyi's World Gym, 17203 Bamwood Dr, Houston, TX 77090, USA

Karoui, Hamed *Prime Minister, Tunisia*
%Prime Minister's Office, Place du Gouvernement, Tunis, Tunisia

Karp, David *Writer*
300 E 56th St, #3-C, New York, NY 10022, USA

Karpati, Gyorgy *Water Polo Player*
Il Liva U 1, 1025 Budapest, Hungary

Karpatkin, Rhoda H *Publisher*
%Consumer Reports Magazine, 101 Truman Ave, Yonkers, NY 10703, USA

Karplus, Martin *Chemist*
%Harvard University, Chemistry Dept, Cambridge, MA 02138, USA

Karpov, Anatoly *Chess Player*
%Russian Chess Federation, Luzhnetskaya 8, 119270 Moscow, Russia

Karppinen, Pentti *Rowing Athlete*
General Delivery, Turku, Finland

Karr, Mary *Poet*
%Syracuse University, English Dept, Syracuse, NY 13244, USA

Karras, Alex G *Football Player, Actor*
7943 Woodrow Wilson Dr, Los Angeles, CA 90046, USA

Karrass, Chester L *Writer*
1633 Stanford St, Santa Monica, CA 90404, USA

Karsh, Yousuf *Photographer*
%Chateau Laurier Hotel, #660, 1 Rideau St, Ottawa ON K1N 8S7, Canada

Karusseit, Ursula *Actress*
%Volksbuhne, Rasa Luxemburg Platz, 10178 Berlin, Germany

Kasaks, Sally Frame *Businesswoman*
%AnnTaylor Stores Corp, 142 W 57th St, New York, NY 10019, USA

Kasatkina, Natalya K *Ballerina, Choreographer*
St Karietny Riad, H 5/10, B 37, Moscow, Russia

Kasatonov, Alexei *Hockey Player*
%St Louis Blues, St Louis Arena, 5700 Oakland Ave, St Louis, MO 63110, USA

Kasdan, Lawrence E *Movie Director*
%United Talent Agency, 9560 Wilshire Blvd, #500, Beverly Hills, CA 90212, USA

Kasem, Casey *Entertainer*
138 N Mapleton Dr, Los Angeles, CA 90077, USA

Kasem, Jean *Actress*
138 N Mapleton Dr, Los Angeles, CA 90077, USA

Kaser, Helmut A *Soccer Executive*
Hitzigweg 11, 8032 Zurich, Switzerland

Kasha, Al *Composer*
8665 Burton Way, #313, Los Angeles, CA 90048, USA

Kashiwagi, Yusuke *Financier*
%Bank of Tokyo, 1-6-3 Nihombashi, Hongokucho, Chuoku, Tokyo 106, Japan

Kaske, Karlheinz *Businessman*
%Siemens AG, Wittelsbacherplatz 2, 80333 Munich, Germany

K

Karlin - Kaske

K

Kasle, Donald H *Financier*
%Bank One Dayton, Kettering Tower, Dayton, OH 45401, USA

Kasparov, Garri K *Chess Player*
%Russian Chess Federation, Luzhnetskaya 8, 119270 Moscow, Russia

Kasper, Steve *Hockey Player*
%Boston Bruins, Boston Garden, 150 Causeway St, Boston, MA 02114, USA

Kasrashvili, Makvala *Opera Singer*
%Bolshoi Theater, Teatralnaya Ol 1, 103009 Moscow, Russia

Kassar, Mario F *Movie Producer*
%Carolco Pictures, 1901 Ave of Stars, #1100, Los Angeles, CA 90067, USA

Kassell, Carl *Commentator*
%National Public Radio, 635 Massachusetts Ave, Washington, DC 20001, USA

Kassirer, Jerome P *Physician, Editor*
%New England Journal of Medicine, 1440 Main St, Waltham, MA 02154, USA

Kassorla, Irene C *Psychologist*
PO Box 11001, Beverly Hills, CA 90213, USA

Kassulke, Karl *Football Player*
%Bethel College, Athletic Dept, St Paul, MN 55112, USA

Kasten, G Frederick, Jr *Businessman*
%Robert W Baird Co, 777 E Wisconsin Ave, Milwaukee, WI 53202, USA

Kasten, Robert W, Jr *Senator, WI*
%Strategic/International Studies Center, 1800 "K" St NW, Washington, DC 20006, USA

Kasten, Stan *Baseball, Basketball Executive*
%Atlanta Braves, Atlanta-Fulton County Stadium, PO Box 4064, Atlanta, GA 30302, USA

Kastner, Elliott *Movie Producer*
%Winkast Films, Pinewood Studios, Iver Heath, Iver SLO ONH, England

Katayama, Nihachiro *Businessman*
%Mitsubishi Electric Corp, 2-2-3 Marunouchi, Chiyodaku, Tokyo 100, Japan

Kates, Robert W *Geographer*
PO Box 8075, Ellsworth, ME 04605, USA

Katims, Milton *Conductor, Concert Violinist*
Fairway Estates, 8001 Sand Point Way NE, Seattle, WA 98115, USA

Katin, Peter *Concert Pianist*
%Maureen Lunn, Top Farm, Parish Lane, Hedgerley, Bucks SL2 3JH, England

Katleman, Harris L *Entertainment Executive*
%Mark Goodson Productions, 5750 Wilshire Blvd, #475, Los Angeles, CA 90036, USA

Katritzky, Alan R *Chemist*
1221 SW 21st Ave, Gainesville, FL 32601, USA

Katt, William *Actor*
26608 Sunflower Court, Calabasas, CA 91302, USA

Katz, Abraham *Diplomat*
%US Council for International Business, 1212 Ave of Americas, New York, NY 10036, USA

Katz, Alex *Artist*
435 W Broadway, New York, NY 10012, USA

Katz, Bernard *Nobel Medicine Laureate*
%University College, Biophysics Dept, Gower St, London WC1, England

Katz, Douglas J *Navy Admiral*
Commander, IDEastFor, US Naval Forces, Central Command, FPO, AE 09501, USA

Katz, Harold *Basketball Executive*
%Philadelphia 76ers, Veterans Stadium, PO Box 25040, Philadelphia, PA 19147, USA

Katz, Hilda *Artist*
915 West End Ave, #5-D, New York, NY 10025, USA

Katz, Jerome L *Financier*
%Charterhouse Group International, 535 Madison Ave, New York, NY 10022, USA

Katz, Lillian Hochberg *Businesswoman*
%Lillian Vernon Corp, 543 Main St, New Rochelle, NY 10801, USA

Katz, Michael *Pediatrician*
%March of Dimes Foundation, 1275 Mamaroneck Ave, White Plains, NY 10605, USA

Katz, Omri *Actor*
%J H Productions, 23679 Calabasas Rd, #333, Calabasas, CA 91302, USA

Katz, Samuel L *Pediatrician*
1917 Wildcat Creek Rd, Chapel Hill, NC 27516, USA

Katz, Sydney L *Businessman*
%Grossman's Inc, 200 Union St, Braintree, MA 02184, USA

Katz, Tonnie L *Editor*
%Orange County Register, Editorial Dept, 625 N Grand Ave, Santa Ana, CA 92701, USA

Katzenbach, Nicholas deB *Attorney General*
906 The Great Rd, Princeton, NJ 08540, USA

Kasle - Katzenbach

Katzenberg, Jeffrey _Entertainment Executive_
%DreamWorks SKG, 100 Universal City Plaza, Universal City, CA 91608, USA
Katzir, Ephraim _President, Israel_
%Weizmann Institute of Science, PO Box 26, Rehovot, Israel
Katzman, Jerry _Entertainment Executive_
%William Morris Agency, 151 S El Camino Dr, Beverly Hills, CA 90212, USA
Kaufman, Henry _Financier_
%Henry Kaufman Co, 65 E 55th St, New York, NY 10022, USA
Kaufman, Napoleon _Football Player_
%Oakland Raiders, Oakland Coliseum, Oakland, CA 94621, USA
Kaufman, Philip _Movie Director_
%Creative Artists Agency, 9830 Wilshire Blvd, Beverly Hills, CA 90212, USA
Kaufman, Stephen P _Businessman_
%Arrow Electronics Inc, 25 Hub Dr, Melville, NY 11747, USA
Kaufman, Victor A _Entertainment Executive_
%Savoy Pictures, 152 W 57th St, New York, NY 10019, USA
Kaufmann, Bob _Basketball Player_
1677 Rivermist Dr, Lilburn, GA 30247, USA
Kauzmann, Walter J _Chemist_
301 N Harrison St, #152, Princeton, NJ 08540, USA
Kavanaugh, Ken _Football Player_
4907 Palm Aire Dr, Sarasota, FL 34243, USA
Kavandi, Janet L _Astronaut_
%NASA, Johnson Space Center, 2101 NASA Rd, Houston, TX 77058, USA
Kavner, Julie _Actress_
25154 Malibu Rd, #2, Malibu, CA 90265, USA
Kawai, Ryoichi _Businessman_
%Komatsu Ltd, 2-3-6 Akasaka, Minatoku, Tokyo 107, Japan
Kawakami, Genichi _Businessman_
%Yamata Motor Co, 2500 Shingai, Iwata City 438, Japan
Kawakami, Tetsuro _Businessman_
%Sumitomo Electric Industries, 5-15 Kltahama, Higashiku, Osaka 541, Japan
Kawakubo, Rei _Fashion Designer_
%Comme des Garcons, 5-11-5 Minamiaoyama, Minatoku, Tokyo, Japan
Kawawa, Rashidi M _Prime Minister, Tanzania_
%Ministry of Defense, Dar es Salaam, Tanzania
Kay, Dianne _Actress_
1559 Palisades Dr, Pacific Palisades, CA 90272, USA
Kay, John _Singer, Guitarist (Steppenwolf)_
%Ron Rainey Mgmt, 315 S Beverly Dr, #206, Beverly Hills, CA 90212, USA
Kay, W Gordon _Businessman_
%Inland Steel Industries, 30 W Monroe St, Chicago, IL 60603, USA
Kaye, Harvey J _Social Scientist_
523 Larscheid St, Green Bay, WI 54302, USA
Kaye, Judy _Actress, Singer_
870 N Vine St, #G, Los Angeles, CA 90038, USA
Kaye, Tony _Keyboardist (Yes)_
%Sun Artists, 9 Hillgate St, London W8 7SP, England
Kaysen, Carl _Economist_
41 Holden St, Cambridge, MA 02138, USA
Kayser, Elmer L _Historian_
2921 34th St NW, Washington, DC 20008, USA
Kayser, Uwe _Financier_
%Deutsche Credit Corp, 2333 Waukegan Rd, Deerfield, IL 60015, USA
Kazan, Elia _Movie Director_
174 E 95th St, New York, NY 10128, USA
Kazan, Lainie _Singer_
9903 Santa Monica Blvd, #283, Beverly Hills, CA 90212, USA
Kazankina, Tatyana _Track Athlete_
Hoshimina St, 111211 St Petersburg, Russia
Kazarnovskaya, Lubov Y _Opera Singer_
Hohenbergstr 50, 1120 Vienna, Austria
Kazin, Alfred _Writer_
%City University of New York, English Dept, 33 W 42nd St, New York, NY 10036, USA
Kazmaier, Richard W (Dick), Jr _Football Player_
%Kazmaier Assoc, 676 Elm St, Concord, MA 01742, USA
Keach, Stacy _Actor_
27425 Winding Way, Malibu, CA 90265, USA

Katzenberg - Keach

K

Keach, Stacy, Sr — *Movie Producer, Director*
3969 Longridge Ave, Sherman Oaks, CA 91423, USA

Keady, Gene — *Basketball Coach*
%Purdue University, Mackey Arena, West Lafayette, IN 47907, USA

Kean, Jane — *Actress*
28128 W Pacific Coast Highway, Malibu, CA 90265, USA

Kean, Thomas H — *Governor, NJ, Educator*
%Drew University, President's Office, 36 Madison Ave, Madison, NJ 07940, USA

Keanan, Staci — *Actress*
%Talent Group Inc, 9250 Wilshire Blvd, #208, Beverly Hills, CA 90212, USA

Keane, Bil — *Cartoonist (Family Circus)*
5815 E Joshua Tree Lane, Paradise Valley, AZ 85253, USA

Keane, Glen — *Animator (Little Mermaid)*
%Walt Disney Studios, 500 S Buena Vista St, Burbank, CA 91521, USA

Keane, Kerrie — *Actress*
1801 Ave of Stars, #902, Los Angeles, CA 90067, USA

Kear, David — *Geologist*
14 Christiana Grover, Lower Hutt, Ohope, Wellington, New Zealand

Kearns Goodwin, Doris — *Writer*
%General Delivery, Concord, MA 01742, USA

Kearns, David T — *Businessman, Government Official*
%Education Department, 400 Maryland Ave SW, Washington, DC 20202, USA

Keathley, George — *Movie Director*
%Missouri Repertory Theater, 4949 Cherry St, Kansas City, MO 64110, USA

Keating, Charles — *Actor*
%Don Buchwald Assoc, 10 E 44th St, #500, New York, NY 10017, USA

Keating, Frank — *Governor, OK*
%Governor's Office, State Capitol Building, Oklahoma City, OK 73105, USA

Keating, H R F — *Writer*
35 Northumberland Place, London W2 5AS, England

Keating, Paul J — *Prime Minister, Australia*
%Prime Minister's Office, Parliament House, Canberra ACT 2600, Australia

Keating, Stephen F — *Businessman*
340 Peavey Rd, Wayzata, MN 55391, USA

Keaton, Diane — *Actress*
%William Morris Agency, 1325 Ave of Americas, New York, NY 10019, USA

Keaton, Michael — *Actor*
11901 Santa Monica Blvd, #547, Los Angeles, CA 90025, USA

Kebich, Vyacheslau F — *Prime Minister, Belarus*
%Council of Ministers, Government House, Dom Urada, 220010 Minsk, Belarus

Keck, Donald B — *Inventor (Silica Optical Waveguide)*
2877 Chequers Circle, Big Flats, NY 14814, USA

Keck, Herman, Jr — *Religious Leader*
%Calvary Grace Christian Church of Faith, US Box 4266, Norton AFB, CA 92409, USA

Keck, Howard B — *Philanthropist*
%Keck Foundation, 555 S Flower St, #3640, Los Angeles, CA 90071, USA

Keck, William — *Architect*
5551 University Ave, #300, Chicago, IL 60637, USA

Kedah — *Sultan, Kedah*
Alor Setar, Kedah, Malaysia

Kedrova, Lila — *Actress*
50 Forest Manor Rd, #3, Willowdale ON M2J 1M1, Canada

Keefe, Adam — *Basketball Player*
%Atlanta Hawks, 1 CNN Center, South Tower, Atlanta, GA 30303, USA

Keefe, Mike — *Editorial Cartoonist*
%Denver Post, Editorial Dept, PO Box 1709, Denver, CO 80201, USA

Keefer, Don — *Actor*
4146 Allott Ave, Sherman Oaks, CA 91423, USA

Keegan, Gerald C — *Financier*
%Greater New York Savings Bank, 1 Pennsylvania Plaza, New York, NY 10119, USA

Keegan, John — *Historian*
%Jonathan Cape Ltd, 32 Bedford Square, London WC1B 3EL, England

Keel, Alton G, Jr — *Buisnessman, Diplomat*
%Carlyle International, 1001 Pennsylvania Ave NW, Washington, DC 20004, USA

Keel, Howard — *Singer, Actor*
%Lake Country Club, 394 Red River Rd, Palm Desert, CA 92211, USA

Keeler, James L — *Businessman*
%WLR Foods, PO Box 7000, Broadway, VA 22815, USA

Keach - Keeler

Keeler, William H Cardinal *Religious Leader*
%National Conference of Catholic Bishops, 3211 4th St, Washington, DC 20017, USA

Keeley, Robert V *Diplomat*
3814 Livingston St NW, Washington, DC 20015, USA

Keen, Robert Earl *Singer, Songwriter*
PO Box 1734, Bandera, TX 78003, USA

Kennan, John F *Judge*
%US District Court, US Courthouse, Foley Square, New York, NY 10007, USA

Keenan, Joseph D *Labor Leader*
2727 29th St NW, Washington, DC 20008, USA

Keenan, Mike *Hockey Coach, Executive*
%St Louis Blues, St Louis Arena, 5700 Oakland Ave, St Louis, MO 63110, USA

Keeshan, Bob *Actor (Captain Kangaroo)*
PO Box 1243, Norwich, VT 05055, USA

Keezer, Geoff *Jazz Pianist*
%Jazz Tree, 211 Thompson St, #1-D, New York, NY 10012, USA

Kegel, Oliver *Canoist*
Am Bogen 23, 13589 Berlin, Germany

Kehaya, Ery W *Businessman*
%Standard Commercial Corp, 2201 Miller Rd, Wilson, NC 27893, USA

Kehoe, Rick *Hockey Player*
%Pittsburgh Penguins, Civic Arena, Centre Ave, Pittsburgh, PA 15219, USA

Keightley, David N *Historian*
%University of California, History Dept, Berkeley, CA 94720, USA

Keillor, Garrison E *Writer, Broadcaster*
%A Prairie Home Companion, 45 7th St E, St Paul, MN 55101, USA

Keiser, John H *Educator*
%Boise State University, President's Office, Boise, ID 83725, USA

Keiser, Robert L *Businessman*
%Oryx Energy Corp, 13155 Noel Rd, Dallas, TX 75240, USA

Keltel, Harvey *Actor*
110 Hudson St, #9-A, New York, NY 10013, USA

Keith, Brian *Actor*
23449 Malibu Canyon Rd, Malibu, CA 90265, USA

Keith, David *Actor*
304 Stone Rd, Knoxville, TN 37920, USA

Keith, Garnett L, Jr *Businessman*
%Prudential Insurance, Prudential Plaza, 751 Broad St, Newark, NJ 07102, USA

Keith, Leroy, Jr *Educator*
%Morehouse College, President's Office, Atlanta, GA 30314, USA

Keith, Louis *Physician*
333 E Superior St, #476, Chicago, IL 60611, USA

Keith, Penelope *Actress*
66 Berkeley House, Hay Hill, London SW3, England

Keleti, Agnes *Gynmast*
%Wingate Institute for Physical Education & Sport, Matanya 42902, Israel

Kelker-Kelly, Robert *Actor*
%Judy Schoen Assoc, 606 N Larchmont Blvd, #309, Los Angeles, CA 90004, USA

Kell, George C *Baseball Player*
700 E 9th St, #13-M, Little Rock, AR 72202, USA

Kellaway, Roger *Composer*
%Pat Phillips Mgmt, 520 E 81st St, #PH-C, New York, NY 10028, USA

Kelleher, Herbert D *Businessman*
%Southwest Airlines Co, PO Box 36611, 2702 Love Field Dr, Dallas, TX 75235, USA

Kellen, Stephen M *Financier*
%Arnhold & S Bleichroeder, 45 Broadway, New York, NY 10006, USA

Keller, Bill *Journalist*
%New York Times, Editorial Dept, 229 W 43rd St, New York, NY 10036, USA

Keller, Erhard *Speed Skater*
Sudliche Munchneustr 6-A, 82031 Grunwald, Germany

Keller, Joseph B *Mathematician*
820 Sonoma Terrace, Stanford, CA 94305, USA

Keller, Leonard B *Vietnam War Army Hero (CMH)*
310 Majzun Rd, Milton, FL 32570, USA

Keller, Marthe *Actress*
%Lemonstr 9, 81679 Munich, Germany

Keller, Mary Page *Actress*
%William Morris Agency, 151 S El Camino Dr, Beverly Hills, CA 90212, USA

K

Keeler - Keller

Keller, Richard F — *Army General*
Chief of Staff, US European Command, APO, AE 09128, USA

Kellerman, Jonathan S — *Writer*
%Karpfinger Agency, 357 W 20th St, New York, NY 10011, USA

Kellerman, Sally — *Actress*
7944 Woodrow Wilson Dr, Los Angeles, CA 90046, USA

Kellermann, Susan — *Actress*
%Judy Schoen Assoc, 606 N Larchmont Blvd, #309, Los Angeles, CA 90004, USA

Kelley, Clarence M — *Director, FBI*
Alameda Towers, 400 W 49th Terrace, Kansas City, MO 64112, USA

Kelley, David E — *Television Producer, Screenwriter*
2210 Wilshire Blvd, #998, Santa Monica, CA 90403, USA

Kelley, DeForest — *Actor*
%Lincoln Enterprises, 14710 Arminta St, Van Nuys, CA 91403, USA

Kelley, Edward F — *Physicist*
%National Standards & Technology Institute, Rt I-270, Gaithersburg, MD 20878, USA

Kelley, Edward W, Jr — *Financier, Government Official*
%Federal Reserve Board, 20th & Constitution NE, Washington, DC 20551, USA

Kelley, Gaynor N — *Businessman*
%Perkin-Elmer Corp, 761 Main Ave, Norwalk, CT 06859, USA

Kelley, Harold H — *Psychologist*
21634 Rambla Vista St, Malibu, CA 90265, USA

Kelley, Jay W — *Air Force General*
Commander, Air University, 55 LeMay Plaza S, Maxwell Air Force Base, AL 36112, USA

Kelley, John A (Marathon) — *Marathon Runner*
136 Cedar Hill Rd, East Dennis, MA 02641, USA

Kelley, Kitty — *Writer*
1228 Eton Court NW, Washington, DC 20007, USA

Kelley, Larry — *Football Player*
5917 Strickland Place, Pensacola, FL 32506, USA

Kelley, Mike — *Sculptor*
2472 Eastman Ave, #35-36, Ventura, CA 93003, USA

Kelley, Paul X — *Marine Corps General*
1600 N Oak St, #1619, Arlington, VA 22209, USA

Kelley, Robert — *Businessman*
%Noble Affiliates, 110 W Broadway, Ardmore, OK 73401, USA

Kelley, Sheila — *Actress*
2910 N Beachwood Dr, Los Angeles, CA 90068, USA

Kelley, Steve — *Editorial Cartoonist*
%San Diego Union, 350 Camino de la Reina, PO Box 191, San Diego, CA 92112, USA

Kelley, Terry — *Financier*
%Bank One Texas, 1717 Main St, Dallas, TX 75201, USA

Kelley, Thomas G — *Vietnam War Navy Hero (CMH)*
4400 Rena Rd, #T-2, Suitland, MD 20746, USA

Kelley, Wendell J — *Businessman*
65 Dellwood Dr, Decatur, IL 62521, USA

Kelley, William G — *Businessman*
%Consolidated Stores, 1105 N Market St, Wilmington, DE 19801, USA

Kellner, Alexander R (Alex) — *Baseball Player*
3716 N Jackson Ave, Tucson, AZ 85719, USA

Kellogg, Clark — *Basketball Player, Sportscaster*
%CBS-TV, Sports Dept, 51 W 52nd St, New York, NY 10019, USA

Kelly, Donald P — *Businessman*
%Envirodyne Industries, 701 Harger Rd, Hinsdale, IL 60521, USA

Kelly, Eamon M — *Educator*
%Tulane University, President's Office, New Orleans, LA 70118, USA

Kelly, Edmund F — *Businessman*
%Liberty Mutual Insurance, 175 Berkeley St, Boston, MA 02116, USA

Kelly, Ellsworth — *Artist*
RD, PO Box 170-B, Chatham, NY 12037, USA

Kelly, Gail P — *Educator*
%State University of New York, Educational Studies Faculty, Amherst, NY 14260, USA

Kelly, Gene — *Dancer, Actor*
725 N Rodeo Dr, Beverly Hills, CA 90210, USA

Kelly, Hugh J — *Financier*
%Hibernia Corp, 313 Carondelet St, New Orleans, LA 70130, USA

Kelly, J Thomas (Tom) — *Baseball Manager*
%Minnesota Twins, 501 Chicago Ave S, Minneapolis, MN 55415, USA

Keller - Kelly

Kelly, James — *Businessman*
%United Parcel Service, 55 Glenlake Parkway NE, Atlanta, GA 30328, USA

Kelly, James E (Jim) — *Football Player*
%Buffalo Bills, 1 Bills Dr, Orchard Park, NY 14127, USA

Kelly, John F — *Businessman*
%Alaska Air Group, 19300 Pacific Highway S, Seattle, WA 98168, USA

Kelly, John H — *Diplomat*
%State Department, 2201 "C" St NW, Washington, DC 20520, USA

Kelly, Leroy — *Football Player*
74 Club House Dr, Willingboro, NJ 08046, USA

Kelly, Moira — *Actress*
501 N Spaulding Ave, #5, Los Angeles, CA 90036, USA

Kelly, Patsy — *Comedienne*
%Gloria Safier, 667 Madison Ave, New York, NY 10021, USA

Kelly, Paula — *Actress, Dancer*
7020 La Presa Dr, Los Angeles, CA 90068, USA

Kelly, Robert (R) — *Rapper, Songwriter*
%Famous Artists Agency, 1700 Broadway, #500, New York, NY 10019, USA

Kelly, Robert J (Barney) — *Navy Admiral*
Commander, US Pacific Fleet, Pearl Harbor, HI 96860, USA

Kelly, Thomas J, III — *Photographer*
PO Box 2208, Sanatoga Branch, Pottstown, PA 19464, USA

Kelly, Thomas W — *Army General*
%George Washington University, Engineering School, Washington, DC 20052, USA

Kelly, William R — *Businessman*
%Kelly Services Inc, 999 W Big Beaver Rd, Troy, MI 48084, USA

Kelman, Arthur — *Plant Pathologist*
615 Yarmouth Rd, Raleigh, NC 27607, USA

Kelman, Charles D — *Ophthalmologist*
Empire State Building, 350 5th Ave, #2100, New York, NY 10118, USA

Kelser, Gregory — *Basketball Player*
%Detroit Pistons, Palace, 2 Championship Dr, Auburn Hills, MI 48057, USA

Kelsey, Frances O — *Pharmacologist*
%Federal Drug Administration, 5600 Fishers Lane, Rockville, MD 20852, USA

Kelsey, Linda — *Actress*
1116 S Alvera St, Los Angeles, CA 90035, USA

Kemal, Yashar — *Writer*
PK 14 Basinkoy, Istanbul, Turkey

Kemble, Edwin C — *Physicist*
8 Ash Street Place, Cambridge, MA 02138, USA

Kemme, Thomas — *Labor Leader*
%Stove Furnance & Appliance Union, 2929 S Jefferson Ave, St Louis, MO 63118, USA

Kemp, Jack F — *Secretary, Housing & Urban Development*
%Empower America, 1776 "I" St NW, #800, Washington, DC 20006, USA

Kemp, Jeremy — *Actor*
%Marina Martin, 6-A Danbury St, London N1 8JU, England

Kemp, Shawn T — *Basketball Player*
%Seattle Supersonics, 190 Queen Ave N, PO Box C-900911, Seattle, WA 98109, USA

Kemp, Steve F — *Baseball Player*
171 Linden Court, Pittsburgh, PA 15237, USA

Kemper, David W, II — *Financier*
%Commerce Bancshares Inc, 1000 Walnut St, Kansas City, MO 64106, USA

Kemper, Jonathan — *Financier*
%Commerce Bancshares, 1000 Walnut St, Kansas City, MO 64106, USA

Kemper, R Crosby — *Financier*
%UMB Financial Corp, 1010 Grand Ave, Kansas City, MO 64106, USA

Kemper, Randolph E (Randy) — *Fashion Designer*
%Randy Kemper Corp, 530 7th Ave, #1400, New York, NY 10018, USA

Kemper, Victor W — *Cinematographer*
10313 W Pico Blvd, Los Angeles, CA 90064, USA

Kempner, I H, III — *Businessman*
%Imperial Holly Corp, 8016 Highway 90-A, Sugar Land, TX 77478, USA

Kempner, James C — *Businessman*
%Imperial Holly Corp, 8016 Highway 90-A, Sugar Land, TX 77478, USA

Kempner, Walter — *Nutritionist*
1505 Virginia Ave, Durham, NC 27705, USA

Kempton, George R — *Businessman*
%Kysor Industrial Corp, 1 Madison Ave, Cadillac, MI 49601, USA

K

Kelly - Kempton

K

Kempton, Murray — *Journalist*
%Newsday, Editorial Dept, 235 Pinelawn Rd, Melville, NY 11747, USA

Kendal, Felicity — *Actress*
%Chatto & Linnit, Prince of Wales, Coventry St, London W1V 7FE, England

Kendall, Barbara — *Yachtswoman*
%Kendall Distributing, 82-B Great South Rd, Otahuhu, Auckland, New Zealand

Kendall, Bruce — *Boardsailor*
6 Pedersen Place, Bucklands Beach, Auckland, New Zealand

Kendall, Donald M — *Businessman*
%PepsiCo Inc, Anderson Hill Rd, Purchase, NY 10577, USA

Kendall, Henry W — *Nobel Physics Laureate*
%Massachusetts Institute of Technology, Physics Dept, Cambridge, MA 02139, USA

Kendall, Suzy — *Actress*
Dentham House, #44, The Mount, Hampstead NW3, England

Kendall, Tom — *Auto Racing Driver*
708 Ivy St, Glendale, CA 91204, USA

Kendler, Bob — *Handball, Raquetball Player*
%US Handball Assn, 4101 Dempster St, Skokie, IL 60076, USA

Kendrew, John C — *Nobel Chemistry Laureate*
The Old Guildhall, 4 Church Lane, Linton, Cambridge CB1 6JX, England

Keneally, Thomas M — *Writer*
24 The Serpentine, Bilgola Beach NSW 2107, Australia

Kengo Wa Dondo — *Prime Minister, Zaire*
%Prime Minister's Office, Mont Ngakuena, Kinshasa, Zaire

Kenilorea, Peter — *Prime Minister, Solomon Islands*
%Foreign Affairs Ministry, Honiara, Guadalcanal, Solomon Islands

Kenn, Mike — *Football Player*
%Atlanta Falcons, 2745 Burnett Rd, Suwanee, GA 30174, USA

Kenna, E Douglas — *Businessman, Football Player*
%Carlisle Companies, 250 S Clinton, Syracuse, NY 13202, USA

Kenna, Edward — *WW II Australian Army Hero (VC)*
121 Coleraine Rd, Hamilton, Vic 3300, Australia

Kennan, Elizabeth Topham — *Educator*
%Mount Holyoke College, Presidents' Office, South Hadley, MA 01075, USA

Kennan, George F — *Diplomat*
%Institute for Advanced Study, Princeton, NJ 08540, USA

Kenneally, John P — *WW II Irish Army Hero (VC)*
7 Station Lane, Lapworth, Warwks, England

Kennedy, Anthony M — *Supreme Court Justice*
%US Supreme Court, 1 lst St NE, Washington, DC 20543, USA

Kennedy, Bernard J — *Businessman*
%National Fuel Gas Co, 10 Lafayette Square, Buffalo, NY 14203, USA

Kennedy, Burt R — *Movie Director*
%Brigade Productions, 13138 Magnolia Blvd, Sherman Oaks, CA 91423, USA

Kennedy, Cortez — *Football Player*
%Seattle Seahawks, 11220 NE 53rd St, Kirkland, WA 98033, USA

Kennedy, D James — *Religious Leader*
%Coral Ridge Presbyterian Church, 5554 N Federal Highway, Fort Lauderdale, 33308, USA

Kennedy, David M — *Secretary, Treasury*
3793 Parkview Dr, Salt Lake City, UT 84124, USA

Kennedy, Donald — *Educator*
%Stanford University, International Studies Institute, Stanford, CA 94305, USA

Kennedy, Eugene P — *Biological Chemist*
221 Mt Auburn St, Cambridge, MA 02138, USA

Kennedy, George — *Actor*
%Paradigm Agency, 10100 Santa Monica Blvd, #2500, Los Angeles, CA 90067, USA

Kennedy, James C — *Businessman*
%Cox Communications Inc, 1400 Lake Hearn Dr NE, Atlanta, GA 30319, USA

Kennedy, Jayne — *Actress*
230 Sunridge St, Playa del Rey, CA 90293, USA

Kennedy, Joey D (Joe), Jr — *Journalist*
%Birmingham News, Editorial Dept, 2200 4th Ave N, Birmingham, AL 35203, USA

Kennedy, John Milton — *Actor*
7100 Balboa Blvd, #606, Van Nuys, CA 91406, USA

Kennedy, John R, Jr — *Businessman*
%Federal Paper Board Co, 75 Chestnut Ridge Rd, Montvale, NJ 07645, USA

Kennedy, Kevin C — *Baseball Manager*
5040 Cascade, Tarzana, CA 91356, USA

Kennedy, Leon Isaac *Actor*
9427 Via Monique, Burbank, CA 91504, USA

Kennedy, Lincoln *Football Player*
%Atlanta Falcons, 2745 Burnett Rd, Suwanee, GA 30174, USA

Kennedy, Mimi *Actress*
%Agency For Performing Arts, 9000 Sunset Blvd, #1200, Los Angeles, CA 90069, USA

Kennedy, Nigel *Concert Violinist*
%Pamela Esterson, 81 Landor Rd, London SW9 9RT, England

Kennedy, Robert D *Businessman*
%Union Carbide Corp, 39 Old Ridgbury Rd, Danbury, CT 06817, USA

Kennedy, Ted *Hockey Player*
290 Russell Hill Rd, Toronto ON M4V 2T6, Canada

Kennedy, Terrence E (Terry) *Baseball Player*
6822 22nd Ave N, #428, St Petersburg, FL 33710, USA

Kennedy, Tom *Television Host*
%William Morris Agency, 151 S El Camino Dr, Beverly Hills, CA 90212, USA

Kennedy, W Keith, Jr *Businessman*
%Watkins-Johnson Co, 3333 Hillview Ave, Palo Alto, CA 94304, USA

Kennedy, William J *Writer*
%State University of New York, English Dept, Albany, NY 12468, USA

Kennedy, X J *Writer*
4 Fern Way, Bedford, MA 01730, USA

Kennet of Dene, Wayland Y *Government Official, England*
%House of Lords, Westminster, London SW1A 0PW, England

Kenney, Stephen F (Steve) *Football Player*
1105 Silver Oaks Court, Raleigh, NC 27614, USA

Kenny G *Saxophonist*
%Boulevard Mgmt, 16130 Ventura Blvd, #550, Encino, CA 91436, USA

Kenny, Douglas T *Educator*
4180 Crown Crescent, Vancouver BC V6R 2A9, Canada

Kenny, Michael *Sculptor*
71 Stepney Green, London E1 3LE, England

Kenny, Shirley Strum *Educator*
%State University of New York, President's Office, Stony Brook, NY 11794, USA

Kenrich, John L *Businessman*
116 Wickersham Dr, Savannah, GA 31411, USA

Kensit, Patsy *Actress*
14 Lambton Place, Nottinghill, London W11 2SH, England

Kent, Allegra *Ballerina*
%New York City Ballet, Lincoln Center Plaza, New York, NY 10023, USA

Kent, Arthur *Commentator*
%A K's O K, Box 695, New Hartford, CT 06057, USA

Kent, Bruce *Social Activist*
%Nuclear Disarmament Campaign, 22-24 Underwood St, London N1 7JG, England

Kent, Geoffrey C *Businessman*
Hill House, Gonalston, Nottingham NG14 7JA, England

Kent, Jean *Actress*
%London Mgmt, 2-4 Noel St, London W1V 3RB, England

Kent, Jonathan *Theater Director*
%International Creative Mgmt, 76 Oxford St, London W1N 0AX, England

Kent, Julie *Ballerina*
%American Ballet Theatre, 890 Broadway, New York, NY 10003, USA

Kent, Peter *Geologist*
43 Trinity Court, Gray's Inn Rd, London WC1, England

Kentner, Louis P *Concert Pianist*
1 Mallord St, London SW3, England

Kenyon, Alfred K *Businessman*
%Kemper Corp, 1 Kemper Dr, Long Grove, IL 60047, USA

Kenyon, Mel *Auto Racing Driver*
2645 S 25 West, Lebanon, IN 46052, USA

Kenzo (Takada) *Fashion Designer*
3 Place des Victories, 75001 Paris, France

Keogh, James *Government Official*
Byram Dr, Belle Haven, Greenwich, CT 06830, USA

Keohane, Nannerl O *Educator*
%Duke University, President's Office, Durham, NC 27706, USA

Keon, Dave *Hockey Player*
%Toronto Maple Leafs, 60 Carlton St, Toronto ON M5B 1L1, Canada

K

Kennedy - Keon

K

Keough, Donald R *Financier*
%Allen & Co, 711 5th Ave, New York, NY 10022, USA

Kepes, Gyorgy *Artist*
PO Box 1423, Wellfleet, MA 02667, USA

Kerber, James R *Businessman*
%Southwestern Life Insurance, Lincoln Plaza, 500 N Akard, Dallas, TX 75201, USA

Kercheval, Ken *Actor*
PO Box 325, Goshen, KY 40026, USA

Keresztes, K Sandor *Architect*
Fo Utca 44/50, 1011 Budapest, Hungary

Kerkorian, Kirk *Businessman*
%MGM/UA Communications, 9454 Wilshire Blvd, Beverly Hills, CA 90212, USA

Kern, Geof *Photographer*
1355 Conant St, Dallas, TX 75207, USA

Kern, Rex W *Football Player*
4648 Stonehaven Dr, Columbus, OH 43220, USA

Kerns, David V, Jr *Microbiotics Engineer*
%Vanderbilt University, Electrical Engineering Dept, Nashville, TN 37235, USA

Kerns, Joanna *Actress*
PO Box 49216, Los Angeles, CA 90049, USA

Kerr, Clark *Educator*
8300 Buckingham Dr, El Cerrito, CA 94530, USA

Kerr, Deborah *Actress*
Los Monteros, 29600 Marbella, Malaga

Kerr, Donald M, Jr *Physicist*
%Science Applications International, 1241 Cave St, La Jolla, CA 92037, USA

Kerr, Jean *Writer*
1 Beach Ave, Larchmont Manor, NY 10538, USA

Kerr, John *Basketball Player, Sportscaster*
%WMAQ-AM, Sports Dept, Merchandise Mart, Chicago, IL 60654, USA

Kerr, Judy *Actress*
6827 Pacific View Dr, Los Angeles, CA 90068, USA

Kerr, Pat *Fashion Designer*
%Pat Kerr Inc, 200 Wagner Pl, Memphis, TN 38103, USA

Kerr, Tim *Hockey Player, Coach*
%Springfield Indians, PO Box 4896, Springfield, MA 01101, USA

Kerr, Walter F *Drama Critic*
1 Beach Ave, Larchmont Manor, NY 10538, USA

Kerr, William T *Businessman*
%Meredith Corp, 1716 Locust St, Des Moines, IA 50309, USA

Kerrigan, Nancy *Figure Skater*
7 Cedar Ave, Stoneham, MA 02180, USA

Kershaw, Doug *Fiddler*
13063 Ventura Blvd, #203, Studio City, CA 91604, USA

Kershaw, Sammy *Singer*
PO Box 121739, Nashville, TN 37212, USA

Kershner, Irvin *Movie Director*
424 Sycamore Rd, Santa Monica, CA 90402, USA

Kerwin, Brian *Actor*
10402 1/2 Wheatland Ave, Sunland, CA 91040, USA

Kerwin, Joseph P *Astronaut*
1802 Royal Fern Court, Houston, TX 77062, USA

Kerwin, Lance *Actor*
PO Box 237, Lake Elsinore, CA 92531, USA

Kerwin, Larkin *Physicist*
Canadian Space Agency, 500 Blvd Rene-Levesque, Montreal PQ H2Z 1Z7, Canada

Kesey, Ken *Writer*
Rt 8, Box 477, Pleasant Hill, OR 97455, USA

Kessel, Barney *Jazz Guitarist, Composer*
1136 Madison Ave, San Diego, CA 92116, USA

Kessler, David A *Physician, Government Official*
%US Food & Drug Administration, 5600 Fishers Lane, Rockville, MD 20852, USA

Kestelman, Sara *Actress*
%Shephendswell Productions, 34 S Molton St, London W1, England

Kesten, Hermann *Writer*
Im Tiefen Boden 25, 4059 Basel, Switzerland

Kestner, Boyd *Actor*
%Metropolitan Talent Agency, 4526 Wilshire Blvd, Los Angeles, CA 90010, USA

Keough - Kestner

Ketchum, Hal *Singer, Songwriter*
%Fitzgerald Hartley Simmons, 50 W Main St, Ventura, CA 93001, USA

Ketchum, Howard *Color Engineer*
3800 Washington Rd, West Palm Beach, FL 33405, USA

Ketelsen, James L *Businessman*
%Monroe Auto Equipment Co, 1 International Dr, Monroe, MI 48161, USA

Ketner, Ralph W *Businessman*
936 Confederate Ave, Salisbury, NC 28144, USA

Kett, Herbert J *Businessman*
%Geonvese Drug Stores, 80 Marcus Dr, Melville, NY 11747, USA

Kettell, Russell W *Financier*
%Golden West Financial Corp, 1901 Harrison St, Oakland, CA 94612, USA

Kety, Seymour S *Physiologist, Pscholobiolgist*
%National Institutes of Health, 9000 Rockville Pike, Bethesda, MD 20892, USA

Kevorkian, Jack *Medical Activist*
4870 Lockhart St, West Bloomfield, MI 48323, USA

Key, James E (Jimmy) *Baseball Player*
%New York Yankees, Yankee Stadium, 161st St & River Ave, Bronx, NY 10451, USA

Key, Ted *Cartoonist (Hazel)*
1694 Glenhardie Rd, Wayne, PA 19087, USA

Keyes, Evelyn *Actress*
999 N Doheny Dr, #509, Los Angeles, CA 90069, USA

Keyes, James H *Businessman*
%Johnson Controls Inc, 5757 N Green Bay Ave, Milwaukee, WI 53209, USA

Keyes, Leroy *Football Player*
8527 Cratin Pl, Philadelphia, PA 19153, USA

Keyes, Robert W *Physicist, Engineer*
%IBM Research Division, PO Box 218, Yorktown Heights, NY 10598, USA

Keyfitz, Nathan *Statistician*
61 Mill Rd, North Hampton, NH 03862, USA

Keys, Donald *Educator*
%Planetary Citizens, 777 United Nations Plaza, New York, NY 10017, USA

Keyser, F Ray, Jr *Governor, VT*
64 Warner Ave, Proctor, VT 05765, USA

Keyser, Richard L *Businessman*
%W W Grainger Inc, 5500 W Howard St, Skokie, IL 60077, USA

Keyworth, George A, II *Government Official*
%Keyworth Meyer International, PO Box 25566, Washington, DC 20007, USA

Khajag Barsamian *Religious Leader*
%Armenian Church of America, Eastern Diocese, 630 2nd Ave, New York, NY 10016, USA

Khaled (Hadj Brahlm) *Singer*
%Mango/Polygram Records, Worldwide Plaza, 825 8th Ave, New York, N 10019, USA

Khalifa al-Thani, Hamad Bin *Prime Minister, Qatar; Prince*
%Royal Palace, PO Box 923, Doha, Qatar

Khalifa, Sheikh Hamed bin Isa al- *Crown Prince, Bahrain*
%Crown Prince's Office, Rifa's Palace, Manama, Bahrain

Khalifa, Sheikh Isa bin Sulman al- *Emir, Bahrain*
%Rifa's Palace, Manama, Bahrain

Khalifa, Sheikh Khalifa bin Sulman al- *Prime Minister, Bahrain*
%Prime Minister's Office, Government House, Government Rd, Manama, Bahrain

Khalil, Mustafa *Prime Minister, Egypt*
9-A El Maahad El Swisry St, Zamalek, Cairo, Egypt

Khamenei, Hojatolislam Sayyed Ali *President, Iran*
%Religious Leader's Office, Teheran, Iran

Khamtay Siphandone *Prime Minister, Laos; Army General*
%Prime Minister's Office, Council of Ministers, Vientiane, Laos

Khan, Chaka *Singer, Actress*
PO Box 16680, Beverly Hills, CA 90209, USA

Khan, Gulam Ishaq *President, Pakistan*
3-B University Town, Jamrud Road, Peshawar, Pakistan

Khan, Inamullah *Religious Leader*
%Muslim Congress, D-26, Block 8, Gulshan-E-Iqbal, Karachi 75300, Pakistan

Khan, Niazi Imran *Cricketer*
%Shankat Khanum Memorial Trust, 29 Shah Jamal, Lahore 546000, Pakistan

Khanh, Emmanuelle *Fashion Designer*
%Emanuelle Khan International, 45 Ave Victor Hugo, 75116 Paris, France

Khanzadian, Vahan *Opera Singer*
3604 Broadway, #2-N, New York, NY 10031, USA

K

Ketchum - Khanzadian

Khashoggi, Adnan M *Businessman*
La Baraka, Marbella, Spain

Khatib, Ahmed al- *President, Syria*
%Syrian Ba'ath Party, Damascus, Syria

Khavin, Vladimir Y *Architect*
%Glavmosarchitectura, Mayakovsky Square 1, 103001 Moscow, Russia

Khayat, Edward (Eddie) *Football Player, Coach*
3455 Harrowgate Rd, York, PA 17402, USA

Kheel, Theodore W *Labor Mediator*
280 Park Ave, New York, NY 10017, USA

Khokhlov, Boris *Ballet Dancer*
Myaskovsky St 11-13, #102, 121019 Moscow, Russia

Khoraiche, Antoine Pierre Cardinal *Religious Leader*
Patriarcat Maronite, Dimane, Lebanon

Khorana, Har Gobind *Nobel Medicine Laureate*
%Massachusetts Institute of Technology, Biology Dept, Cambridge, MA 02139, USA

Khrennikov, Tikhon N *Composer*
Plotnikov Per 10/28, #19, 121200 Moscow, Russia

Khrunov, Yevgeni V *Cosmonaut*
%Potchta Kosmonavtov, 141 160 Svyosdny Gorodok, Moskovskoi Oblasti, Russia

Khvorostovsky, Dimitri A *Opera Singer*
%Elen Victorova, Mosfilmovskaya 26, #5, Moscow, Russia

Kiam, Victor E, II *Football Executive, Businessman*
119 Wire Mill Rd, Stamford, CT 06903, USA

Kibrick, Anne *Medical Educator*
381 Clinton Rd, Brookline, MA 02146, USA

Kidd, Billy *Skier*
PO Box 1178, Steamboat Springs, CO 80477, USA

Kidd, Jason *Basketball Player*
%Dallas Mavericks, Reunion Arena, 777 Sports St, Dallas, TX 75207, USA

Kidd, Michael *Choreographer*
%William Morris Agency, 1325 Ave of Americas, New York, NY 10019, USA

Kidder Lee, Barbara *Skier*
1308 W Highland, Phoenix, AZ 85013, USA

Kidder, C Robert *Businessman*
%Borden Inc, 180 E Broad St, Columbus, OH 43215, USA

Kidder, Margot *Actress*
PO Box 829, Los Angeles, CA 90078, USA

Kidder, Tracy *Writer*
%George Borchardt, 136 E 57th St, New York, NY 10022, USA

Kidman, Nicole *Actress*
%Odin Productions, 4400 Coldwater Canyon Ave, #220, Studio City, CA 91604, USA

Kiechel, Walter, III *Editor*
%Fortune Magazine, Editorial Dept, 1291 Ave of Americas, New York, NY 10020, USA

Kiedis, Anthony *Singer (Red Hot Chili Peppers)*
3120 Hollyridge Dr, Los Angeles, CA 90068, USA

Kiefer, Adolph *Swimmer*
42125 N Hunt Club Rd, Wadsworth, IL 60083, USA

Kiehl, Marina *Skier*
Engadinerstr 2, 81475 Munich, Germany

Kiel, Richard *Actor*
40356 Oak Park Way, #T, Oakhurst, CA 93644, USA

Kiernan, Charles E *Businessman*
%Duracell International, Berkshire Corporate Park, Bethel, CT 06801, USA

Kiesler, Charles A *Educator*
%University of Missouri, Chancellor's Office, Columbia, MO 65211, USA

Kight Wingard, Lenore *Swimmer*
6281 Cary Ave, Cincinnati, OH 45224, USA

Kihune, Robert K U *Navy Admiral*
Chief, Naval Education & Training, 250 Dallas St, Pensacola, FL 32508, USA

Kiick, James F (Jim) *Football Player*
8190 SW 28th St, Davie, FL 33328, USA

Kikuchi, Rioko *Astronaut, Photographer*
%Tokyo Broadcasting System, 5-3-6 Akasaka, Minatoku, Tokyo 107-06, Japan

Kikutake, Kiyonori *Architect*
1-11-15 Otsuka, Bunkyoku, Tokyo, Japan

Kilbourne, Wendy *Actress*
9300 Wilshire Blvd, #410, Beverly Hills, CA 90212, USA

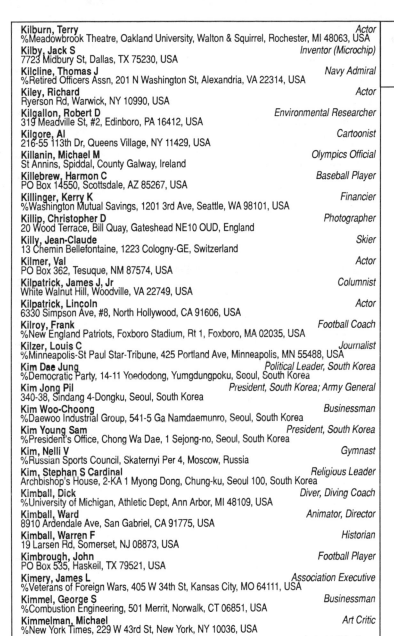

Kilburn, Terry *Actor*
%Meadowbrook Theatre, Oakland University, Walton & Squirrel, Rochester, MI 48063, USA

Kilby, Jack S *Inventor (Microchip)*
7723 Midbury St, Dallas, TX 75230, USA

Kilcline, Thomas J *Navy Admiral*
%Retired Officers Assn, 201 N Washington St, Alexandria, VA 22314, USA

Kiley, Richard *Actor*
Ryerson Rd, Warwick, NY 10990, USA

Kilgallon, Robert D *Environmental Researcher*
319 Meadville St, #2, Edinboro, PA 16412, USA

Kilgore, Al *Cartoonist*
216-55 113th Dr, Queens Village, NY 11429, USA

Killanin, Michael M *Olympics Official*
St Annins, Spiddal, County Galway, Ireland

Killebrew, Harmon C *Baseball Player*
PO Box 14550, Scottsdale, AZ 85267, USA

Killinger, Kerry K *Financier*
%Washington Mutual Savings, 1201 3rd Ave, Seattle, WA 98101, USA

Killip, Christopher D *Photographer*
20 Wood Terrace, Bill Quay, Gateshead NE10 OUD, England

Killy, Jean-Claude *Skier*
13 Chemin Bellefontaine, 1223 Cologny-GE, Switzerland

Kilmer, Val *Actor*
PO Box 362, Tesuque, NM 87574, USA

Kilpatrick, James J, Jr *Columnist*
White Walnut Hill, Woodville, VA 22749, USA

Kilpatrick, Lincoln *Actor*
6330 Simpson Ave, #8, North Hollywood, CA 91606, USA

Kilroy, Frank *Football Coach*
%New England Patriots, Foxboro Stadium, Rt 1, Foxboro, MA 02035, USA

Kilzer, Louis C *Journalist*
%Minneapolis-St Paul Star-Tribune, 425 Portland Ave, Minneapolis, MN 55488, USA

Kim Dae Jung *Political Leader, South Korea*
%Democratic Party, 14-11 Yoedodong, Yumgdungpoku, Seoul, South Korea

Kim Jong Pil *President, South Korea; Army General*
340-38, Sindang 4-Dongku, Seoul, South Korea

Kim Woo-Choong *Businessman*
%Daewoo Industrial Group, 541-5 Ga Namdaemunro, Seoul, South Korea

Kim Young Sam *President, South Korea*
%President's Office, Chong Wa Dae, 1 Sejong-no, Seoul, South Korea

Kim, Nelli V *Gymnast*
%Russian Sports Council, Skaternyi Per 4, Moscow, Russia

Kim, Stephan S Cardinal *Religious Leader*
Archbishop's House, 2-KA 1 Myong Dong, Chung-ku, Seoul 100, South Korea

Kimball, Dick *Diver, Diving Coach*
%University of Michigan, Athletic Dept, Ann Arbor, MI 48109, USA

Kimball, Ward *Animator, Director*
8910 Ardendale Ave, San Gabriel, CA 91775, USA

Kimball, Warren F *Historian*
19 Larsen Rd, Somerset, NJ 08873, USA

Kimbrough, John *Football Player*
PO Box 535, Haskell, TX 79521, USA

Kimery, James L *Association Executive*
%Veterans of Foreign Wars, 405 W 34th St, Kansas City, MO 64111, USA

Kimmel, George S *Businessman*
%Combustion Engineering, 501 Merrit, Norwalk, CT 06851, USA

Kimmelman, Michael *Art Critic*
%New York Times, 229 W 43rd St, New York, NY 10036, USA

Kimura, Kazuo *Industrial Designer*
%Japan Design Foundation, 2-2 Cenba Chuo, Higashiku, Osaka 541, Japan

Kimura, Motoo *Geneticist, Biologist*
%Institute of Genetics, Yata 1, 111, Mishima, Shizuoka-ken 411, Japan

Kincaid, Aron *Actor*
12307 Ventura Blvd, #C, North Hollywood, CA 91604, USA

Kincaid, Jamaica *Writer*
%New Yorker Magazine, 25 W 43rd St, New York, NY 10036, USA

Kincses, Veronika *Opera Singer*
%Hungarian State Opera, Andrassy Ut 22, 1061 Budapest, Hungary

K

Kilburn - Kincses

K

Kind, Peter A — *Army General*
Director, Information Systems, OSA, Washington, DC 20310, USA

Kind, Roslyn — *Actress, Singer*
8871 Burton Way, #303, Los Angeles, CA 90048, USA

Kinder, Melvyn — *Psychologist*
521 N LaCienega Blvd, #209, Los Angeles, CA 90048, USA

Kinder, Richard D — *Businessman*
%Enron Corp, PO Box 1188, Houston, TX 77251, USA

Kindleberger, Charles P — *Economist*
Brookhaven, #A-406, 1010 Waltham St, Lexington, KY 02173, USA

Kindred, David A — *Sportswriter*
%Atlanta Constitution, 72 Marietta St, Atlanta, GA 30303, USA

Kiner, Ralph M — *Baseball Player, Sportscaster*
271 Silver Spur Trail, Palm Desert, CA 92260, USA

Kines, Joe — *Football Coach*
%University of Arkansas, Broyles Athletic Complex, Fayetteville, AR 72701, USA

King Hogue, Micki — *Diver*
3509 Colt Neck Lane, Lexington, KY 40502, USA

King of Wartnaby, John Leonard — *Businessman*
Ensearch House, 8 St James's Square, London SW1Y 4JU, England

King, Alan — *Comedian*
%William Morris Agency, 151 S El Camino Dr, Beverly Hills, CA 90212, USA

King, Albert — *Basketball Player*
%San Antonio Spurs, 600 E Market St, #102, San Antonio, TX 78205, USA

King, Allen B — *Businessman*
%Universal Corp, 1501 N Hamilton St, Richmond, VA 23230, USA

King, Angus — *Governor, ME*
%Governor's Office, Blaine House, Augusta, ME 04333, USA

King, B B — *Singer, Guitarist*
PO Box 4396, Las Vegas, NV 89127, USA

King, Ben E — *Singer*
%Smiling Clown Music, PO Box 1097, Teaneck, NJ 07666, USA

King, Betsy — *Golfer*
%General Delivery, Limekiln, PA 19535, USA

King, Billie Jean — *Tennis Player*
%World Team Tennis, 445 N Wells St, #404, Chicago, IL 60610, USA

King, Bruce — *Governor, NM*
PO Box 83, Stanley, NM 87056, USA

King, Carole — *Composer, Singer*
Robinson Bar Ranch, Stanley, ID 83278, USA

King, Coretta S — *Civil Rights Leader*
671 Beckwith St SW, Atlanta, GA 30314, USA

King, Dana — *Commentator*
%CBS-TV, News Dept, 524 W 57th St, New York, NY 10019, USA

King, Dennis — *Artist*
3857 26th St, San Francisco, CA 94131, USA

King, Dexter Scott — *Association Executive*
%M L King Nonviolent Social Change Center, 449 Auburn Ave NE, Atlanta, GA 30312, USA

King, Don — *Boxing Promoter*
%Don King Productions, 968 Pinehurst Dr, Las Vegas, NV 89109, USA

King, Edward J — *Governor, MA*
%A J Lane Co, 1500 Worcester Rd, Framingham, MA 01701, USA

King, Evelyn (Champagne) — *Singer*
%Famous Artists Agency, 1700 Broadway, #500, New York, NY 10019, USA

King, Francis H — *Writer*
19 Gordon Place, London W8 4JE, England

King, Gordon D — *Football Player*
2641 Highwood Dr, Roseville, CA 95661, USA

King, Harold D — *Financier*
%Colonial BancGroup, 1 Commerce St, Montgomery, AL 36104, USA

King, Ivan R — *Astronomer*
%University of California, Astronomy Dept, Berkeley, CA 94720, USA

King, James A — *Opera Singer*
%Denis Laggelier Artists, 40 Alexander St, Toronto ON M4Y 1B5, Canada

King, James B — *Editor*
%Seattle Times, Editorial Dept, Fairview Ave N & John St, Seattle, WA 98111, USA

King, John W — *Governor, NH*
Kennedy Hill Rd, RD 1, Goffstown, NH 03045, USA

Kind - King

King, Larry *Commentator*
4218 10th St NE, Washington, DC 20010, USA

King, Mary-Claire *Geneticist*
%University of California, Molecular-Cell Biology Dept, Berkeley, CA 94720, USA

King, Michael *Television Executive*
%King World Productions, 1700 Broadway, New York, NY 10019, USA

King, Miles B *Businessman*
%Alexander & Baldwin Inc, 822 Bishop St, Honolulu, HI 96813, USA

King, Morgana *Singer*
%Bowen Agency, 504 W 168th St, New York, NY 10032, USA

King, Olin B *Businessman*
%SCI Systems Inc, 2101 W Clinton Ave, Huntsville, AL 35805, USA

King, Pee Wee *Singer, Songwriter*
%Ressier, 505 Canton Pass, Madison, TN 37115, USA

King, Perry *Actor*
3647 Wrightwood Dr, Studio City, CA 91604, USA

King, Phillip *Sculptor*
%New Rowan Gallery, 25 Dover St, London W1X 3PA, England

King, Roger *Television Executive*
%King World Productions, 1700 Broadway, New York, NY 10019, USA

King, Stacey *Basketball Player*
%Minnesota Timberwolves, Target Center, 600 1st Ave N, Minneapolis, MN 55403, USA

King, Stephen E *Writer*
%Juliann Eugley, 49 Florida Ave, Bangor, ME 04401, USA

King, Thomas J (Tom) *Government Official, England*
%House of Commons, Westminster, London SW1A 0AA, England

King, Thomas L *Businessman*
%Standex International Corp, 6 Manor Parkway, Salem, NH 03079, USA

King, Tony *Actor*
1333 N Sweetzer, #2-G, Los Angeles, CA 90069, USA

King, W David *Hockey Coach*
%Calgary Flames, PO Box 1540, Station "M", Calgary AB T2P 389, Canada

King, Woodie, Jr *Theater Producer*
417 Convent Ave, New York, NY 10031, USA

King, Zalman *Movie Director*
308 Alta Ave, Santa Monica, CA 90402, USA

Kingdom, Roger *Track Athlete*
322 Mall Blvd, #303, Monroeville, PA 15146, USA

Kingman, David A (Dave) *Baseball Player*
PO Box 11771, Zephyr Cove, NV 89448, USA

Kingman, Dong *Artist*
21 W 58th St, New York, NY 10019, USA

Kings Norton (Harold R Cox) *Engineer, Scientist*
Westcote House, Chipping Campden, Glos, England

Kingsbury Smith, Joseph *Journalist*
1701 Pennsylvania Ave NW, Washington, DC 20006, USA

Kingsley, Ben *Actor*
New Penworth House, Stratford Upon Avon, Warwickshire 0V3 7QX, England

Kingsolver, Barbara E *Writer*
PO Box 5275, Tucson, AZ 85703, USA

Kingston, Maxine Hong *Writer*
%University of California, English Dept, Berkeley, CA 94720, USA

Kinkel, Klaus *Government Official, Germany*
%Auswartigen Amt, Adenauerallee 101, 53113 Bonn, Germany

Kinmont Boothe, Jill *Skier*
Rt 1, Box 11, 310 Sunland Dr, Bishop, CA 93515, USA

Kinmont, Kathleen *Actress*
641 S Mariposa Dr, Burbank, CA 91506, USA

Kinnear, George E R, II *Navy Admiral*
%New England Digital Corp, 7 New England Executive Park, Burlington, MA 01803, USA

Kinnear, James W, III *Businessman*
%Ten Standard Forum, PO Box 120, Stamford, CT 06904, USA

Kinnell, Galway *Writer*
RFD, Sheffield, VT 05866, USA

Kinnock, Neil G *Government Official, England*
%House of Commons, Westminster, London SW1A 0AA, England

Kinoshita, Keisuke *Movie Director*
1366 Tsujido, Fujisawa, Kanagawa Prefecture, Japan

K

King - Kinoshita

K

Kinsella, John — *Swimmer*
Canterberry Court, Hinsdale, IL 60521, USA

Kinsella, Thomas — *Poet*
Killalane, Laragh, County Wicklow, Ireland

Kinsella, W P — *Writer*
PO Box 2162, Blaine, WA 98231, USA

Kinser, Steve — *Auto Racing Driver*
%King Racing, 103 Center Lane, Huntsville, NC 28078, USA

Kinsey, Stan — *Entertainment Executive*
%Iwerks Entertainment, 4540 Valerio St, Burbank, CA 91505, USA

Kinshofer-Guthlein, Crista — *Skier*
Munchnerstr 44, 83026 Rosenheim, Germany

Kinskey, Leonid — *Actor*
15009 N Tamarack Lane, Fountain Hill, AZ 85268, USA

Kinski, Nastassja — *Actress*
%William Morris Agency, 151 S El Camino Dr, Beverly Hills, CA 90212, USA

Kinsler, Richard — *Publisher*
%Playboy Magazine, 680 N Lake Shore Dr, Chicago, IL 60611, USA

Kinsley, Michael E — *Editor*
%New Republic Magazine, Editorial Dept, 1220 19th St NW, Washington, DC 20036, USA

Kinsman, T Jim — *Vietnam War Army Hero (CMH)*
111 Howe Rd E, Winlock, WA 98596, USA

Kintner, William R — *Political Scientist*
%Foreign Policy Research Institute, 3508 Market St, Philadelphia, PA 19104, USA

Kinugasa, Sachio — *Baseball Player*
%Hiroshima Toyo Carp, 5-25 Moto-Machi, Nakaku, Hiroshima 730, Japan

Kiplinger, Austin H — *Publisher*
1729 "H" St NW, Washington, DC 20006, USA

Kipnis, Igor — *Concert Harpsichordist*
20 Drummer Lane, West Redding, CT 06896, USA

Kipniss, Robert — *Artist*
26 E 33rd St, New York, NY 10016, USA

Kiraly, Charles F (Karch) — *Volleyball Player, Coach*
%Pepperdine University, Athletic Dept, Malibu, CA 90265, USA

Kirby, Bruce — *Actor*
629 N Orlando Ave, #3, Los Angeles, CA 90048, USA

Kirby, Bruno — *Actor*
%Metropolitan Talent Agency, 4526 Wilshire Blvd, Los Angeles, CA 90010, USA

Kirby, Durwood — *Actor*
Rt 7, Box 374, Sherman, CT 06784, USA

Kirby, F M — *Businessman*
%Alleghany Corp, Park Avenue Plaza, 55 E 52nd St, New York, NY 10055, USA

Kirby, Jerry L — *Financier*
%Citizens Federal Bank, 1 Citizens Federal Centre, Dayton, OH 45402, USA

Kirby, Ronald H — *Architect*
PO Box 337, Melville, 2109 Johannesburg, South Africa

Kirchner, Leon — *Composer*
%Harvard University, Music Dept, Cambridge, MA 02138, USA

Kirchner, Mark — *Biathlete*
Hauptstr 66-B, 98749 Scheib-Alsbach, Germany

Kirchschlager, Rudolf — *President, Austria*
Anderg 9, 1170 Vienna, Austria

Kirgo, George — *Actor, Screenwriter*
178 N Carmelina Ave, Los Angeles, CA 90049, USA

Kirk, Claude R, Jr — *Governor, FL*
%Kirk Co, 926 Village Rd, North Palm Beach, FL 33408, USA

Kirk, Grayson L — *Educator*
28 Sunnybrook Rd, Bronxville, NY 10708, USA

Kirk, James L — *Businessman*
%OHM Corp, 16406 US Rt 224 E, Findlay, OH 45839, USA

Kirk, Larry G — *Businessman*
%Hancock Fabrics, 3406 W Main St, Tupelo, MS 38801, USA

Kirk, Phyllis — *Actress*
321 S Beverly Dr, #M, Beverly Hills, CA 90212, USA

Kirkby, Emma — *Concert Singer*
%Consort of Music, 54-A Leamington Road Villas, London W11 1HT, England

Kirkeby, Per — *Artist*
%Margarete Roeder Gallery, 545 Broadway, New York, NY 10012, USA

Kinsella - Kirkeby

Kirkland, Gelsey *Ballerina*
191 Silver Moss Dr, Vero Beach, FL 32963, USA

Kirkland, Sally *Actress*
17 E 89th St, New York, NY 10128, USA

Kirkman, Rick *Cartoonist (Baby Blues)*
%Creators Syndicate, 5777 W Century Blvd, #700, Los Angeles, CA 90045, USA

Kirkpatrick, Clayton *Editor*
471 Stagecoach Run, Glen Ellyn, IL 60137, USA

Kirkpatrick, Jeane J *Government Official*
6812 Granby St, Bethesda, MD 20817, USA

Kirkpatrick, Ralph *Concert Harpsichordist*
Old Quarry, Guilford, CT 06437, USA

Kirkup, James *Writer*
%British Monomarks, BM-Box 2780, London WC1V 6XX, England

Kirpal, Prem Nath *Educator*
%UNESCO Executive Board, Place de Fintenoy, 75700 Paris, France

Kirschner, David *Entertainment Executive*
%Hanna-Barbera Productions, 3400 W Cahuenga Blvd, Los Angeles, CA 90068, USA

Kirschstein, Ruth L *Physician*
%National Institutes of Health, 9000 Rockville Pike, Bethesda, MD 20205, USA

Kirshbaum, Laurence J *Publisher*
%Warner Books, Time-Life Building, Rockefeller Center, New York, NY 10020, USA

Kirst, Michael *Educator*
%Stanford University, Education School, Stanford, CA 94305, USA

Kirstein, Lincoln *Ballet Promoter*
%American Ballet Theatre, 890 Broadway, New York, NY 10003, USA

Kirszenstein Szewinska, Irena *Track Athlete*
Ul Bagno 5 m 80, 00-112 Warsaw, Poland

Kirwan, William E, II *Educator*
%University of Maryland, President's Office, College Park, MD 20742, USA

Kishlansky, Mark A *Historian*
%Harvard University, History Dept, Cambridge, MA 02138, USA

Kisio, Kelly *Hockey Player*
%San Jose Sharks, 525 W Santa Clara St, San Jose, CA 95113, USA

Kison, Bruce E *Baseball Player*
1403 Riverside Cir, Bradenton, FL 33529, USA

Kissin, Evgeni I *Concert Pianist*
%Harold Holt Ltd, 31 Sinclair Rd, London W14 0NS, England

Kissinger, Henry A *Secretary, State; Nobel Peace Laureate*
River House, 435 E 52nd St, New York, NY 10022, USA

Kissling, Conny *Freestyle Skier*
Hubel, 3254 Messen, Switzerland

Kissling, Walter *Businessman*
%H B Fuller Co, 2400 Energy Park Dr, St Paul, MN 55108, USA

Kistler, Darci *Ballerina*
%New York City Ballet, Lincoln Center Plaza, New York, NY 10023, USA

Kitaen, Tawny *Actress*
PO Box 16693, Beverly Hills, CA 90209, USA

Kitaj, R B *Artist*
%Marlborough Fine Art Ltd, 6 Albemarle St, London W1, England

Kitamura, Kusuo *Swimmer*
%Nippon Suiei Renmei, 25 Kannami, Shibuyaku, Tokyo, Japan

Kitaro *Musician, Composer*
%Geffen Records, 9100 Sunset Blvd, Los Angeles, CA 90069, USA

Kitayenko, Dmitri G *Conductor*
%Moscow Philharmonic, Moscow Conservatory, Moscow, Russia

Kitbunchu, M Michai Cardinal *Religious Leader*
%Assumption Cathedral, 51 Oriental Ave, Bangkok 10500, Thailand

Kitchen, Lawrence O *Businessman*
%Lockheed Corp, 4500 Park Grenada Blvd, Calabasas, CA 91302, USA

Kite, Greg *Basketball Player*
%Greg Kite Assoc, 5202 Greenway Dr, Orlando, FL 32819, USA

Kite, Thomas O (Tom), Jr *Golfer*
%Pros Inc, PO Box 673, Richmond, VA 23206, USA

Kitora, Fumio *Financier*
%Daiwa Bank Trust, 75 Rockefeller Plaza, New York, NY 10019, USA

Kitt, A J *Skier*
15 Hidden Valley Rd, Rochester, NY 14624, USA

K

Kirkland - Kitt

K

Kitt, Eartha *Singer, Actress*
125 Boulder Ridge Rd, Scarsdale, NY 10583, USA

Kittel, Charles *Physicist*
%University of California, Physics Dept, Berkeley, CA 94720, USA

Kittinger, Joe *Parachutist, Balloonist*
300 N Main St, Las Vegas, NV 89101, USA

Kittle, Ronald D (Ron) *Baseball Player*
742 N Old Suman Rd, Valparaiso, IN 46383, USA

Kitzhaber, John *Governor, OR*
%Governor's Office, State Capitol, #224, Salem, OR 97310, USA

Kiyokawa Seiji, Masaji *Swimmer*
%Kanematsu-Gosho Ltd, CPO Box 141, Tokyo, Japan

Kizer, Carolyn A *Poet*
%University of Arizona, English Dept, Tucson, AZ 85721, USA

Kizim, Leonid D *Cosmonaut; Air Force General*
%Mojaysky Military School, Russian Space Forces, St Petersburg, Russia

Kjus, Lasse *Skier*
Rugdeveien 2-C, 1404 Siggerud, Norway

Klabunde, Charles S *Artist*
68 W 3rd St, New York, NY 10012, USA

Klammer, Franz *Skier*
Mooswald 22, 9712 Friesach/Ktn, Austria

Klatsky, Bruce J *Businessman*
%Phillips-Van Heusen Corp, 1290 Ave of Americas, New York, NY 10104, USA

Klatte, Gunther *Businessman*
%Rheinische Braunkohlenwerke, Stuttgenweg 2, 50935 Cologne, Germany

Klaus, Josef *Chancellor, Austria*
Osterreichische Volkspartei, 1 Karntnerstr 51, Vienna, Austria

Klaus, Vaclav *Prime Minister, Czech Republic*
%Prime Minister's Office, Nabr E Benese 4, 118 01 Prague, Czech Republic

Klaw, Spencer *Editor*
280 Cream Hill Rd, West Cornwall, CT 06796, USA

Klebanoff, Michael *Businessman*
%OMI Corp, 90 Park Ave, New York, NY 10016, USA

Klebe, Giselher *Composer*
Bruchstr 16, 32756 Detmold, Germany

Kleiber, Carlos *Conductor*
Max-Joseph-Platz 2, 80539 Munich, Germany

Kleihues, Josef P *Architect*
Schlickweg 4, 14129 Berlin, Germany

Klein, Calvin R *Fashion Designer*
%Calvin Klein Industries, 205 W 39th St, New York, NY 10018, USA

Klein, George *Tumor Biologist*
Kottlavagen 10, 181 61 Lidingo, Sweden

Klein, Heinrich J *Businessman*
%Carl-Zeiss-Stiftung, Postfach 1369, 73447 Oberkochen, Germany

Klein, Herbert G *Publisher, Government Official*
%Copley Press, 350 Camino de Reina, San Diego, CA 92108, USA

Klein, Lawrence R *Nobel Economics Laureate*
1317 Medford Rd, Wynnewood, PA 19096, USA

Klein, Lester A *Urologist*
%Scripps Clinic, Urology Dept, 10666 N Torrey Pines Rd, La Jolla, CA 92037, USA

Klein, Robert *Entertainer*
%Conversation Co, 697 Middle Neck Rd, Great Neck, NY 11023, USA

Klein, Robert O (Bob) *Football Player*
15933 Alcima Ave, Pacific Palisades, CA 90272, USA

Klein, Yves *Artist*
%Marisa del Re Gallery, 41 E 57th St, New York, NY 10022, USA

Kleindienst, Richard G *Attorney General*
%Favour Moore Wilhelmsen, 1580 Plaza W, Prescott, AZ 86302, USA

Kleine, Joe *Basketball Player*
%Phoenix Suns, 201 E Jefferson St, Phoenix, AZ 85004, USA

Kleinert, Harold E *Microsurgeon*
225 Abraham Flexner Way, Louisville, KY 40202, USA

Kleinman, Arthur M *Anthropologist*
%Harvard University, Anthropology Dept, Cambridge, MA 02138, USA

Kleinrock, Leonard *Computer Scientist*
318 N Rockingham Ave, Los Angeles, CA 90049, USA

Klemmer, John *Saxophonist*
%Boardman, 10548 Clearwood Court, Los Angeles, CA 90077, USA

Klemperer, Werner *Actor*
44 W 62nd St, #1000, New York, NY 10023, USA

Klemperer, William *Chemist*
53 Shattuck Rd, Watertown, MA 02172, USA

Klemt, Becky *Attorney*
%Pence & MacMillan, PO Box 1285, Laramie, WY 82070, USA

Klensch, Else *Fashion Commentator*
%Cable News Network, News Dept, 1050 Techwood Dr NW, Atlanta, GA 30318, USA

Kleppe, Thomas S *Secretary, Interior*
7100 Darby Rd, Bethesda, MD 20817, USA

Klestil, Thomas *President, Austria*
Prasidentschaftskanzlei, Hofburg, 1014 Vienna, Austria

Kliesmet, Robert B *Labor Leader*
%Union of Police Assns, 815 16th St NW, #307, Washington, DC 20006, USA

Kliks, Rudolf R *Architect*
%Russian Chamber of Commerce, Ul Kuibysheva 6, Moscow, Russia

Klimke, Reiner *Equestrian Rider*
Krumme Str 3, 48143 Munster, Germany

Klimuk, Pyotr I *Cosmonaut, Air Force General*
%Potchta Kosmonavtov, 141 160 Svyosdny Gorodok, Moskovskoi Oblasti, Russia

Kline, Kevin *Actor*
45 W 67th St, #27-B, New York, NY 10023, USA

Kling, Richard W *Businessman*
%IDS Life Insurance of New York, PO Box 5144, Albany, NY 12205, USA

Klingensmith, Michael J *Publisher*
%Entertainment Weekly Magazine, Rockefeller Center, New York, NY 10020, USA

Klinger, Georgette *Beauty Consultant*
312 N Rodeo Dr, Beverly Hills, CA 90210, USA

Klinsmann, Jurgen *Soccer Player*
%Tottenham Hotspurs, 748 High St, Tottenham, London W1V 3RB, England

Kljusev, Nikola *Prime Minister, Macedonia*
%Prime Minister's Office, Dame Grueva 6, 91000 Skopje, Macedonia

Kloska, Ronald F *Businessman*
%Skyline Corp, 2520 By-Pass Rd, Elkhart, IN 46514, USA

Klotz, Irving M *Chemist, Biochemist*
2515 Pioneer Rd, Evanston, IL 60201, USA

Klous, Patricia *Actress*
18096 Karen Dr, Encino, CA 91316, USA

Klug, Aaron *Nobel Physics Laureate*
%Medical Research Council Centre, Hills Rd, Cambridge CB2 2QH, England

Kluge, John W *Businessman*
%Metromedia Co, 1 Meadowlands Plaza, #300, East Rutherford, NJ 07073, USA

Klugman, Jack *Actor*
22548 W Pacific Coast Highway, #110, Malibu, CA 90265, USA

Klutznick, Philip M *Secretary, Commerce*
875 N Michigan Ave, #4044, Chicago, IL 60611, USA

Klyszewski, Waclaw *Architect*
Ul Gornoslaska 16, M 15-A, 00-432 Warsaw, Poland

Knabusch, Charles T *Businessman*
%La-Z-Boy Chair Co, 1284 N Telegraph Rd, Monroe, MI 48162, USA

Knape Lindberg, Ulrike *Diver*
Drostvagen 7, 691 33 Karlskoga, Sweden

Knapp, Charles B *Educator*
%University of Georgia, President's Office, Athens, GA 30602, USA

Knapp, Cleon T *Publisher*
%Talewood Corp, 10100 Santa Monica Blvd, #2000, Los Angeles, CA 90067, USA

Knapp, John W *Educator, Army General*
%Virginia Military Institute, Superintendent's Office, Lexington, VA 24450, USA

Knapp, Stefan *Artist*
The Studio, Sandhills, Godalming, Surrey, England

Knappenberger, Alton W *WW II Army Hero (CMH)*
PO Box 364, Main St, Schwenksville, PA 19473, USA

Kneale, R Bryan C *Sculptor*
10-A Muswell Rd, London N10 2BG, England

Knebel, John A *Secretary, Agriculture*
1418 Laburnum St, McLean, VA 22101, USA

K

Klemmer - Knebel

K

Knef, Hildegard *Actress, Singer*
%Agentur Lentz, Holbeinstr 4, 81679 Munich, Germany

Knepper, Robert W (Bob) *Baseball Player*
2045 Oakhill Rd, Roseburg, OR 97470, USA

Kness, Richard M *Opera Singer*
240 Central Park South, #3-N, New York, NY 10019, USA

Kneuer, Cameo *Physical Fitness Expert*
%Starshape by Cameo, 2554 Lincoln Blvd, #640, Marina del Rey, CA 90291, USA

Knievel, Evel *Motorcycle Stunt Rider*
160 E Flamingo Rd, Las Vegas, NV 89109, USA

Knight Pulliam, Keshia *Actress*
PO Box 866, Teaneck, NJ 07666, USA

Knight, Andrew S B *Editor*
%News International, PO Box 495, Virginia St, London W1 9XY, England

Knight, Charles F *Businessman*
%Emerson Electric Co, 8000 W Florissant Ave, St Louis, MO 63136, USA

Knight, Christopher *Actor*
7738 Chandelee Place, Los Angeles, CA 90046, USA

Knight, Curt *Football Player*
5300 Holmes Run Parkway, #301, Alexandria, VA 22304, USA

Knight, Douglas M *Educator*
68 Upper Creek Rd, Stockton, NJ 08559, USA

Knight, Gladys *Singer*
%Shakeki Mgmt, 3221 La Mirada Ave, Las Vegas, NV 89120, USA

Knight, Michael E *Actor*
%Paradigm Agency, 10100 Santa Monica Blvd, #2500, Los Angeles, CA 90067, USA

Knight, Philip H *Businessman*
%Nike Inc, 1 Bowerman Dr, Beaverton, OR 97005, USA

Knight, Ray (C Ray) *Baseball Player*
2308 Tara Dr, Albany, GA 31707, USA

Knight, Robert M (Bobby) *Basketball Coach*
%Indiana University, Athletic Dept, Assembly Hall, Bloomington, IN 47405, USA

Knight, Shirley *Actress*
2130 N Beachwood Dr, #8, Los Angeles, CA 90068, USA

Knight, William J (Pete) *Test Pilot*
220 Eagle Lane, Palmdale, CA 93551, USA

Knipling, Edward F *Entomologist*
2623 Military Rd, Arlington, VA 22207, USA

Knodel, William C *Businessman*
%Vista Chemical Co, 900 Threadneedle St, Houston, TX 77079, USA

Knol, Monique *Cyclist*
Draarlier 6, 3766 Et Soest, Holland

Knoll, Jozsef *Pharmacologist*
%Semmelweis Medical University, Pharmacology Dept, 1089 Budapest, Hungary

Knopfler, Mark *Singer, Guitarist (Dire Straits)*
%Damage Mgmt, 16 Lamberton Place, London W11 2SH, England

Knopoff, Leon *Geophysicist*
%University of California, Geophysics Institute, Los Angeles, CA 90024, USA

Knotts, Don *Comedian*
1854 S Beverly Glen Blvd, #402, Los Angeles, CA 90025, USA

Knowles, John *Writer*
PO Box 939, Southampton, NY 11969, USA

Knowles, Michael R *Medical Researcher*
%University of North Carolina, Medical School, Chapel Hill, NC 27599, USA

Knowles, Patric *Actor*
6243 Randi Ave, Woodland Hills, CA 91367, USA

Knowles, Tony *Governor, AK*
%Governor's Office, State Capitol Building, Little Rock, AK 72201, USA

Knowlton, Richard L *Businessman*
%Hormel Foods Corp, 1 Hormel Place, Austin, MN 55912, USA

Knowlton, Steve R *Skier*
%Palmer Yeager Assoc, 6600 E Hampden Ave, #210, Denver, CO 80224, USA

Knox, Buddy *Singer, Songwriter*
RR 3, C-10 Evans, Armstrong BC VOE 1BO, Canada

Knox, Elyse *Actress*
320 N Gunston Ave, Los Angeles, CA 90049, USA

Knox, Northrup R *Financier*
%Marine Midland Banks Inc, 1 Marine Midland Center, Buffalo, NY 14203, USA

Knef - Knox

Knox, Terence *Actor*
%International Creative Mgmt, 8942 Wilshire Blvd, Beverly Hills, CA 90211, USA
Knox-Johnston, Robin *Sailor*
26 Sefton St, Putney, London SW15, England
Knudsen, Arthur G *Skier*
311 Blaine Ave, Racine, WI 53405, USA
Knudsen, Conrad C *Businessman*
%MacMillan Bloedel Ltd, 925 W Georgia St, Vancouver BC V6E 3R9, Canada
Knudson, Alfred G, Jr *Geneticist*
%Institute for Cancer Research, 7701 Burlhome Ave, Philadelphia, PA 19111, USA
Knudson, Darrell G *Financier*
%Fourth Financial Corp, 100 N Broadway, Wichita, KS 67202, USA
Knudson, Thomas J *Journalist*
%Sacramento Bee, Editorial Dept, 21st & "Q" Sts, Sacramento, CA 95852, USA
Knussen, S Oliver *Conductor, Composer*
167 West End Lane, #3, London NW6 2LG, England
Knuth, Donald E *Computer Scientist*
%Stanford University, Computer Sciences Dept, Stanford, CA 94305, USA
Knutson, John A *Financier*
%Jackson National Life Insurance, 5901 Executive Dr, Lansing, MI 48911, USA
Knutson, Ronald *Religious Leader*
%Free Lutheran Congregations Assn, 402 W 11th St, Canton, SD 57013, USA
Kobayashi, Hisao *Financier*
%CUT Group Holdings, 650 CIT Dr, Livingston, NJ 07039, USA
Kobayashi, Kaoru *Businessman*
%Matsushita Electric Works, 1048 Kadomashi, Osaka 571, Japan
Kobayashi, Koji *Businessman*
%NEC Corp, 7-1-5 Shiba, Minatoku, Tokyo 108, Japan
Kobayashi, Taiyu *Businessman*
%Fujitsu Ltd, 2-6-1 Marunouchi, Chiyodaku, Tokyo 100, Japan
Kober, Jeff *Actor*
907 Parkman Ave, #2, Los Angeles, CA 90026, USA
Kober, Roger W *Businessman*
%Rochester Gas & Electric, 89 East Ave, Rochester, NY 14604, USA
Koch, Bill *Cross Country Skier*
13 Circle Dr, Underwood, WA 98651, USA
Koch, Charles G *Businessman*
%Koch Industries, PO Box 2256, Wichita, KS 67201, USA
Koch, Charles John *Financier*
%Charter One Financial, 1215 Superior Ave, Cleveland, OH 44114, USA
Koch, David A *Businessman*
%Graco Inc, 4050 Olson Memorial Parkway, Minneapolis, MN 55422, USA
Koch, Howard W *Movie Producer, Director*
704 N Crescent Dr, Beverly Hills, CA 90210, USA
Koch, William I *Yachtsman, Businessman*
%Oxbow Corp, 1601 Forum Place, West Palm Beach, FL 33401, USA
Kocherga, Anatoli I *Opera Singer*
Gogolevskaya 37/2/47, 254053 Kiev, Russia
Kochi, Jay K *Chemist*
4372 Faculty Lane, Houston, TX 77004, USA
Kocsis, Zoltan *Concert Pianist, Composer*
Narcisa Ut 29, 1126 Budapest, Hungary
Kodes, Jan *Tennis Player*
Na Berance 18, 160 00 Prague 6/Dejvioe, Czech Republic
Koehn, George W *Financier*
%SunBank of Tampa Bay, 315 E Madison St, Tampa, FL 33602, USA
Koelle, George B *Pharmacologist*
205 College Ave, Swarthmore, PA 19081, USA
Koen, Karleen *Writer*
%Random House Inc, 201 E 50th St, New York, NY 10022, USA
Koencamp, Fred *Cinematographer*
9756 Shoshine Ave, Northridge, CA 91325, USA
Koenig, Pierre *Architect*
12221 Dorothy St, Los Angeles, CA 90049, USA
Koenig, Walter *Actor*
PO Box 4395, North Hollywood, CA 91617, USA
Koenigswald, G H Ralph von *Paleoanthropologist*
%Senckenberg Museum, Senckenberganlage 25, 60325 Frankfurt/Maim, Germany

K

Knox - Koenigswald

K

Koffigoh, Joseph K — *Prime Minister, Togo*
%Prime Minister's Office, PO Box 1161, Lome, Togo

Koffman, Morley — *Businessman*
%TNT Freightways, 9700 Higgins Rd, Rosemont, IL 60018, USA

Kogan, Richard J — *Businessman*
%Schering-Plough Corp, 1 Giraldo Farms, Madison, NJ 07940, USA

Kohde-Kilsch, Claudia — *Tennis Player*
Elsa-Brandstrom-Str 22, 66119 Saarbrucken, Germany

Kohjima, Sachio — *Financier*
%Bank of Tokyo Trust, 1251 Ave of Americas, New York, NY 10116, USA

Kohl, Helmut — *Chancellor, Germany*
Marbacherstr 11, 78351 Ludwigshafen/Rhein-Obbersheim, Germany

Kohlberg, Jerome, Jr — *Financier*
%Kohlberg Co, 111 Radio Circle, Mt Kisco, NY 10549, USA

Kohler, Herbert V, Jr — *Businessman*
%Kohler Co, 444 Highland Dr, Kohler, WI 53044, USA

Kohlsaat, Peter — *Cartoonist (Single Slices)*
5282 Greenwood Rd, Duluth, MN 55804, USA

Kohn, A Eugene — *Architect*
%Kohn Pedersen Fox Assoc, 111 W 57th St, New York, NY 10019, USA

Kohn, Walter — *Physicist*
%University of California, Physics Dept, Santa Barbara, CA 93106, USA

Kohner, Susan — *Actress*
710 Park Ave, #14-E, New York, NY 10021, USA

Kohoutek, Lubos — *Astronomer*
Corthumstr 5, 21029 Hamburg, Germany

Koike, Hisao — *Businessman*
%Yamaha Motor Co, 2500 Shingai, Iwata City 438, Japan

Kojac, George — *Swimmer*
13015 Point Pleasant Dr, Fairfax, VA 22033, USA

Kok Oudegeest, Mary — *Swimmer*
Escuela Nacional de Natacion, Izarra, Alava, Spain

Kokonin, Vladimir — *Opera, Ballet Administrator*
%Bolshoi Theater, Teatralnaya Pl 1, 103009 Moscow, Russia

Kolar, Jiri — *Poet, Artist*
61 Rue Olivier-Metra, 75020 Paris, France

Kolb Thomas, Claudia — *Swimmer, Coach*
%Stanford University, Athletic Dept, Stanford, CA 94305, USA

Kolb, David L — *Businessman*
%Mohawk Industries, 1755 The Exchange, Atlanta, GA 30339, USA

Kolbert, Kathryn — *Attorney*
%Center for Reproductive Law & Policy, 120 Wall St, New York, NY 10005, USA

Kolehmainen, Mikko — *Kayak Athlete*
Poppelitie 18, 50130 Mikkeli, Finland

Kolff, Willem J — *Inventor (Soft-Shelled Mushroom Heart)*
2894 Crestview Dr, Salt Lake City, UT 84108, USA

Kolingba, Andre — *President, Central African Republic*
%Palais de la Renaissance, Bangui, Central African Republic

Koller, William — *Medical Researcher*
%University of Kansas, School of Medicine, Lawrence, KS 66045, USA

Kollias, Konstantinos V — *Prime Minister, Greece*
124 Vassil Sophias St, Ampelokipi, Athens, Greece

Kollo, Rene — *Opera Singer*
%Marguerite Kollo Mgmt, Lietzenseeufer 8, 14057 Berlin, Germany

Kolm, Henry V — *Electrical Engineer (Magnetic Train)*
Weir Meadow Rd, Wayland, MA 01778, USA

Kolodner, Richard D — *Biochemist, Cancer Researcher*
%Dana-Farber Cancer Institute, 44 Binney St, Boston, MA 02115, USA

Kolpakova, Irina A — *Ballerina*
%American Ballet Theatre, 890 Broadway, New York, NY 10003, USA

Kolsti, Paul — *Editorial Cartoonist*
%Dallas News, Editorial Dept, Communications Center, Dallas, TX 75265, USA

Kolvenbach, Peter-Hans — *Religious Leader*
Borgo Santo Spirito 5, CP 6139, 00195 Rome, Italy

Komack, James — *Television Producer, Director*
617 N Beverly Dr, Beverly Hills, CA 90210, USA

Komansky, David H — *Financier*
%Merrill Lynch Co, World Financial Center, New York, NY 10281, USA

Koffigoh - Komansky

Komar, Vitaly *Artist*
%Ronald Freeman Fine Arts, 31 Mercer St, New York, NY 10013, USA

Komarkova, Vera *Mountaineer*
%University of Colorado, INSTAAR, Boulder, CO 80302, USA

Komatsu, Koh *Financier*
%Sumitomo Bank, 3-2-1 Marunouchi, Chiyodaku, Tokyo 100, Japan

Komer, Robert W *Diplomat*
1211 Villsmsy Blvd, Alexandria, VA 22307, USA

Kominsky, Cheryl *Bowler*
%Ladies Professional Bowlers Tour, 7171 Cherryvale Blvd, Rockford, IL 61112, USA

Komleva, Gabriela T *Ballerina*
Fontanka River 116, #34, 198005 St Petersburg, Russia

Komlos, Peter *Concert Violinist*
Torokvesz Ut 94, 1025 Budapest, Hungary

Komunyakaa, Yusef *Poet*
%Indiana University, English Dept, Bloomington, IN 47405, USA

Konan Bedie, Henri *President, Cote D'Ivoire*
Blvd Clozel, Boite Postale 1354, Abidjan, Cote D'Ivoire

Konare, Alpha Oumar *President, Mali*
%President's Office, Boite Postale 1463, Bamako, Mali

Koncak, Jon *Basketball Player*
%Orlando Magic, Orlando Arena, 1 Magic Place, Orlando, FL 32801, USA

Konchalovsky, Andrei *Movie Director*
%Creative Artists Agency, 9830 Wilshire Blvd, Beverly Hills, CA 90212, USA

Kondakova, Yelena V *Cosmonaut*
Scientific Industrial Assn, Ulica Lenina 4-A, 141 070 Kaliningrad, Russia

Kondratiyeva, Maria V *Ballerina*
%Bolshoi Theater, Teatralnaya Pl 1, 103009 Moscow, Russia

Konig, Franz Cardinal *Religious Leader*
Erzbischofliches Sekretariat, Rotenturmstr 2, 1010 Vienna, Austria

Konrad, John H *Astronaut*
%Hughes Space-Communications Group, PO Box 92919, Los Angeles, CA 90009, USA

Konstantinidis, Aris *Architect*
4 Vasilissis Sofias Blvd, 106 74 Athens, Greece

Kontos, Constantine W *Government Official*
3606 Warren St NW, Washington, DC 20008, USA

Koons, Fred B *Financier*
%Chase Home Mortgage Corp, 4915 Independence Parkway, Tampa, FL 33634, USA

Koons, Jeff *Artist*
600 Broadway, New York, NY 10012, USA

Koontz, Dean R *Writer*
PO Box 9529, Newport Beach, CA 92658, USA

Koontz, Richard H *Businessman*
%Bowne Co, 345 Hudson St, New York, NY 10014, USA

Koop, C Everett *Physician, Pediatrician*
6707 Democracy Blvd, #107, Bethesda, MD 20817, USA

Koopmans-Kint, Cor *Swimmer*
Pacific Sands C'Van Park, Nambucca Heads NSW 2448, Australia

Koosman, Jerry M *Baseball Player*
4101 Pelicans Nest Dr, Bonita Springs, FL 33923, USA

Kopell, Bernie *Actor*
19413 Olivos Dr, Tarzana, CA 91356, USA

Kopins, Karen *Actress*
%Sutton Barth Vennari, 145 S Fairfax Ave, #310, Los Angeles, CA 90036, USA

Kopit, Arthur *Writer*
5 Glen Hill Rd, Wilton, CT 06897, USA

Koplovitz, Kay *Entertainment Executive*
%USA Network, 1230 Ave of Americas, #1800, New York, NY 10020, USA

Kopp, Wendy *Association Executive*
%Teach for America Foundation, PO Box 5114, New York, NY 10185, USA

Koppel, Ted *Commentator*
%ABC-TV, News Dept, 1717 DeSales St NW, Washington, DC 20036, USA

Koppelman, Chaim *Artist*
498 Broome St, New York, NY 10013, USA

Kopper, Hilmar *Financier*
%Deutsche Bank AG, Taunusanlage 12, 60325 Frankfurt/Main, Germany

Koprowski, Hilary *Microbiologist*
334 Fairhill Rd, Wynnewood, PA 19096, USA

K

Komar - Koprowski

K

Korbut, Olga *Gymnast*
4705 Masters Court, Duluth, GA 30136, USA

Kord, Kazimierz *Conductor*
%International Creative Mgmt, 40 W 57th St, New York, NY 10019, USA

Korda, Michael V *Writer*
%Simon & Schuster Inc, 1230 Ave of Americas, New York, NY 10020, USA

Korell, Mark L *Financier*
%GMAC Mortgage, 8360 Old York Rd, Elkins Park, PA 19027, USA

Koren, Edward B *Cartoonist*
%New Yorker Magazine, Editorial Dept, 20 W 43rd St, New York, NY 10036, USA

Korjus, Tapio *Track Athlete*
%General Delivery, Lapua, Finland

Korman, Harvey *Comedian*
1136 Stradella Rd, Los Angeles, CA 90077, USA

Korman, Lewis J *Entertainment Executive*
%Savoy Entertainment, 152 W 57th St, New York, NY 10019, USA

Korman, Maxime Carlot *Prime Minister, Vanuatu*
%Prime Minister's Office, PO Box 110, Port Vila, Vanuatu

Korn, Lester B *Businessman*
237 Park Ave, New York, NY 10017, USA

Kornberg, Arthur *Nobel Medicine Laureate*
365 Golden Oak Dr, Portola Valley, CA 94028, USA

Kornberg, Hans L *Biochemist*
Master's Lodge, Christ College, Cambridge CB2 3BU, England

Koroma, Sorie Ibrahim *Prime Minister, Sierra Leone*
%First Vice President's Office, Tower Hill, Freetown, Sierra Leone

Korot, Alla *Actress*
%Gores/Fields Agency, 10100 Santa Monica Blvd, #2500, Los Angeles, CA 90067, USA

Korowi, Wiwa *Governor General, Papua New Guinea*
Government House, Konedobu, Box 79, Port Moresby, Boroko, Papua New Guinea

Korpan, Richard *Businessman*
%Florida Progress Corp, 1 Progress Plaza, St Petersburg, FL 33701, USA

Korry, Edward M *Diplomat*
RR 2, Stonington, CT 06378, USA

Kors, Michael *Fashion Designer*
119 W 24th St, #900, New York, NY 10011, USA

Korth, Fred *Government Official*
1700 "K" St NW, #501, Washington, DC 20006, USA

Korvald, Lars *Prime Minister, Norway*
Vinkelgaten 6, 3050 Mjondalen, Norway

Kosar, Bernie, Jr *Football Player*
%Miami Dolphins, 7500 SW 30th St, Davie, FL 33329, USA

Koshalek, Richard *Museum Director*
%Museum of Contemporary Art, 250 S Grand Ave, Los Angeles, CA 90012, USA

Koshiro, Matsumoto, IV *Kabuki Actor*
%Kabukiza Theatre, 12-15-4 Ginza, Chuoku, Tokyo 104, Japan

Koshland, Daniel E, Jr *Biochemist*
3991 Happy Valley Rd, Lafayette, CA 94549, USA

Kosler, Zdenek *Conductor*
Nad Sarkou 35, 16000 Prague 6, Czech Republic

Koslow, Lauren *Actress*
14724 Ventura Blvd, #401, Sherman Oaks, CA 91403, USA

Kosmi, John C *Financier*
%Bethpage Federal Credit Union, 899 S Oyster Bay Rd, Bethpage, NY 11714, USA

Kosner, Edward A *Editor*
%Esquire Magazine, Editorial Dept, 250 W 55th St, New York, NY 10019, USA

Koss, Johann Olav *Speed Skater*
Dagaliveien 21, 0387 Oslo, Norway

Koss, John C *Television Inventor*
%Koss Corp, 4129 N Port Washington Ave, Milwaukee, WI 53212, USA

Kosterlitz, Hans W *Pharmacist*
16 Glendor Terrace, Cults, Aberdeen AB1 9HX, Scotland

Kosuth, Joseph *Artist*
591 Broadway, New York, NY 10012, USA

Kotcheff, W Theodore (Ted) *Movie Director*
%Ted Kotcheff Productions, 13451 Firth Dr, Beverly Hills, CA 90210, USA

Koterba, Jeff *Sports Cartoonist*
%Kansas City Star, 1729 Grand Ave, Kansas City, MO 64108, USA

Korbut - Koterba

Kotite, Rich *Football Coach*
%New York Jets, 1000 Fulton Ave, Hempstead, NY 11550, USA

Kotlarek, Gene *Ski Jumper*
4611 W 89th Way, Westminster, CO 80030, USA

Kotlarek, George *Skier*
330 N Arlington Ave, #512, Duluth, MN 55811, USA

Kotler, Steven *Financier*
%Wertheim Schroder Co, Equitable Center, 787 7th Ave, New York, NY 10019, USA

Kotsonis, Ieronymous *Religious Leader*
%Archdiocese of Athens, Hatzichristou 8, Athens 402, Greece 53212, USA

Kott, Jan K *Writer, Educator*
29 Quaker Path, Stony Brook, NY 11790, USA

Kottke, Leo *Singer, Songwriter*
PO Box 7308, Carmel, CA 93921, USA

Kotto, Yaphet *Actor*
%Metropolitan Talent Agency, 4526 Wilshire Blvd, Los Angeles, CA 90010, USA

Kotulak, Ronald *Editor*
%Chicago Tribune, Editorial Dept, 435 N Michigan Ave, Chicago, IL 60611, USA

Kotzky, Alex S *Cartoonist (Apartment 3-G)*
203-17 56th Ave, Bayside, NY 11364, USA

Kouchner, Bernard *Physician*
%Action D'Humanitaire Foundation, 99 Blvd Malesherbes, 75008 Paris, France

Koufax, Sanford (Sandy) *Baseball Player*
PO Box 88, Carpinteria, CA 93014, USA

Koumakoye, Kassire D *Prime Minister, Chad*
%Prime Minister's Office, N'Djamena, Chad

Kourkoumelis, Dan *Businessman*
%Quality Food Centers, 10116 NE 8th St, Bellevue, WA 98004, USA

Kourpias, George J *Labor Leader*
%International Machinists Assn, 9000 Machinist Place, Upper Marlboro, MD 20772, USA

Koushouris, John L *Television Executive*
%Hughes Television Network, 4 Pennsylvania Plaza, New York, NY 10001, USA

Kovac, Vladimir *President, Slovakia*
%President's Office, Nam Slobody 1, 813 70 Bratislava, Slovakia

Kovacevich, Richard M *Financier*
%Norwest Corp, 1200 Peavey Building, 6th & Marquette, Minneapolis, MN 55403, USA

Kovacevich, Stephen *Concert Pianist*
%Van Walsum Mgmt, 26 Wadham Rd, London SW15 2LR, England

Kovach, William *Editor*
%Harvard University, Nieman Fellows Program, Cambridge, MA 02138, USA

Kovacic, Ernst *Concert Violinist*
%Tennant Artists' Mgmt, 39 Tadema Rd, #2, London SW10 0PY, England

Kovacic-Ciro, Zdravko *Water Polo Player*
JP Kamova 57, 51000 Rijeka, Yugoslavia

Kovacs, Andras *Movie Director*
Magyar Jakobinusok Tere 2/3, 1122 Budapest, Hungary

Kovacs, Denes *Concert Violinist*
Iranyi Ut 12, Budapest V, Hungary

Kovacs, Laszlo *Cinematographer*
%American Society of Cinematographers, 1782 N Orange Dr, Los Angeles, CA 90028, USA

Kovalenok, Vladimir S *Cosmonaut, Air Force General*
3 Ap 22, Hovanskaya St, 129 515 Moscow, Russia

Kove, Martin *Actor*
19155 Rosita St, Tarzana, CA 91356, USA

Kowal, Charles T *Astronomer*
%Space Telescope Science Institute, Homewood Campus, Baltimore, MD 21218, USA

Koy, Ernest M (Ernie) *Football Player*
7 E Hacienda, Bellville, TX 77418, USA

Kozak, Harley Jane *Actress*
2329 Stanley Hills Dr, Los Angeles, CA 90046, USA

Kozlova, Valentina *Ballerina*
%New York City Ballet, Lincoln Center Plaza, New York, NY 10023, USA

Kozlowski, L Dennis *Businessman*
%Tyco International, 3 Tyco Park, Exeter, NH 03833, USA

Kozlowski, Linda *Actress*
%Gersh Agency, 232 N Canon Dr, Beverly Hills, CA 90210, USA

Kozol, Jonathan *Writer*
PO Box 145, Byfield, MA 01922, USA

K

Kozyrev, Andrei V — *Government Official, Russia*
%Foreign Affairs Ministry, Smolenskaya-Sennaya 32/34, Moscow, Russia

Krabbe, Jeroen — *Actor*
Van Eeghaustraat 107, 1071 EZ Amsterdam, Netherlands

Krabbe, Katrin — *Track Athlete*
Am Jahnstadion, 17033 Neubrandenburg, Germany

Krackow, Jurgen — *Businessman*
Schumannstr 100, 40237 Dusseldorf, Germany

Kraft, Christopher C, Jr — *Space Administrator*
%Rockwell International Systems Division, 555 Gemini Ave, Houston, TX 77058, USA

Kraft, Leo A — *Composer*
9 Dunster Rd, Great Neck, NY 11021, USA

Kraft, Robert — *Composer*
4722 Noeline Ave, Encino, CA 91436, USA

Kraft, Robert P — *Astrophysicist*
%University of California, Lick Observatory, Santa Cruz, CA 95064, USA

Krainik, Ardis — *Opera Executive*
%Chicago Lyric Opera, 20 N Wacker St, Chicago, IL 60606, USA

Kramek, Robert E — *Coast Guard Admiral*
Commandant, US Coast Guard, 2100 2nd St SW, Washington, DC 20593, USA

Kramer, Billy J — *Singer*
%Global Entertainment Network, 332 Southdown Rd, Lloyd Harbor, NY 11743, USA

Kramer, Erik — *Football Player*
%Chicago Bears, Halas Hall, 250 N Washington Rd, Lake Forest, IL 60045, USA

Kramer, Gerald (Jerry) — *Football Player*
Rt 1, Highway 95, PO Box 370, Parma, ID 83660, USA

Kramer, Jack — *Tennis Player, Promoter*
231 N Glenroy Place, Los Angeles, CA 90049, USA

Kramer, Joel R — *Editor*
%Minneapolis Star Tribune, 425 Portland Ave, Minneapolis, MN 55488, USA

Kramer, Joey — *Drummer (Aerosmith)*
%Collins Mgmt, 5 Bigelow St, Cambridge, MA 02139, USA

Kramer, John H (Jack) — *Baseball Player*
2126 Pauline St, New Orleans, LA 70117, USA

Kramer, Larry — *Social Activist, Playwright*
%Gay Men's Health Crisis, 129 W 20th St, New York, NY 10011, USA

Kramer, Ron — *Football Player*
10153 Walnut Shores Dr, Fenton, MI 48430, USA

Kramer, Stanley E — *Movie Director*
5230 Shira Dr, Valley Village, CA 91607, USA

Kramer, Stepfanie — *Actress*
8455 Beverly Blvd, #505, Los Angeles, CA 90048, USA

Kramer, Tommy — *Football Player*
%Minnesota Vikings, 9520 Viking Dr, Eden Prairie, MN 55344, USA

Krantz, Judith T — *Writer*
%Thorndike Press, PO Box 159, Thorndike, ME 04986, USA

Krasnoff, Eric — *Businessman*
%Pall Corp, 2200 Northern Blvd, East Hills, NY 11548, USA

Krasnow, Robert A — *Businessman*
%Nonesuch Records, 75 Rockefeller Plaza, New York, NY 10019, USA

Krasny, Yuri — *Artist*
%Sloane Gallery, Oxford Office Building, 1612 17th St, Denver, CO 80202, USA

Krauch, Carl-Heinrich — *Businessman*
%Chemische Werke Huels, Postfach 1320, 45743 Marl, Germany

Kraus, Alfredo — *Opera Singer*
61 W 62nd St, #6-F, New York, NY 10023, USA

Kraus, Eileen S — *Financier*
%Shawmut National Corp, 1 Federal St, Boston, MA 02110, USA

Kraus, Otakar — *Opera Singer*
223 Hamlet Gardens, London W6, England

Krause, Chester L — *Publisher*
Krause Publications, 700 E State St, Iola, WI 54990, USA

Krause, Jerome R (Jerry) — *Basketball Executive*
%Chicago Bulls, 1901 W Madison St, Chicago, IL 60612, USA

Krause, Paul J — *Football Player*
18099 Judicial Way N, Lakeville, MN 55044, USA

Krause, Richard M — *Immunologist*
4000 Cathedral Ave NW, #413-B, Washington, DC 20016, USA

Kozyrev - Krause

Kraushaar, William L *Physicist*
462 Togstad Glen, Madison, WI 53711, USA
Krauskopf, Konrad B *Geologist*
806 La Mesa Dr, Menlo Park, CA 94028, USA
Krauss, Alison *Singer, Fiddler*
%Keith Case Mgmt, 59 Music Square W, Nashville, TN 37203, USA
Krausse, Stefan *Luge Athlete*
Heinrich-Hertz-Str 39, 98693 Ilmenau, Germany
Krauthammer, Charles *Columnist*
%Washington Post Writers Group, 1150 15th St NW, Washington, DC 20071, USA
Kravchuk, Leonid M *President, Ukraine*
%President's Office, Bankivska Ul 11, 252009 Kiev, Ukraine
Kravis, Henry *Financier*
%Kohlberg Kravis Roberts Co, 9 W 57th St, New York, NY 10019, USA
Kravitz, Lenny *Singer, Songwriter*
14681 Harrison St, Miami, FL 33176, USA
Krayer, Otto H *Pharmacologist*
4140 E Cooper St, Tucson, AZ 85711, USA
Krebs, Edwin G *Nobel Medicine Laureate*
%University of Washington, Hughes Medical Institute, Seattle, WA 98195, USA
Krebs, Robert D *Businessman*
%Santa Fe Southern Pacific Corp, 1700 E Golf Rd, #700, Schaumburg, IL 60173, USA
Krebs, Susan *Actress*
3782 Redwood Ave, Los Angeles, CA 90066, USA
Krehbiel, Frederick A, II *Businessman*
%Molex Corp, 222 Wellington Court, Lisle, IL 60532, USA
Krehbiel, John H, Jr *Businessman*
%Molex Inc, 2222 Wellington Court, Lisle, IL 60532, USA
Kreile, Reinhold *Businessman*
%Friedrich Flick Group, Monchenwerther Str 15, 40545 Dusseldorf, Germany
Krementz, Jill *Photographer*
%Dial Books Young, 375 Hudson St, New York, NY 10014, USA
Kremer, Gidon *Concert Violinist*
%International Creative Mgmt, 40 W 57th St, New York, NY 10019, USA
Krens, Thomas *Museum Administrator*
%Solomon R Guggenheim Museum, 1071 5th Ave, New York, NY 10128, USA
Krentz (Amanda Quick), Jayne Ann *Writer*
%Axelrod Agency, 66 Church St, Lenox, MA 01240, USA
Krenz, Donald A *Businessman*
19 Beachside Common, Westport, CT 06880, USA
Krenz, Egon *Chairman, East Germany*
Majakowskiweg 9, 13156 Berlin, Germany
Krenz, Jan *Composer, Conductor*
Al 1 Armii Wojska Polskiego 16/38, 00-582 Warsaw, Poland
Kreps, David M *Economist*
%Stanford University, Graduate Business School, Stanford, CA 94305, USA
Kreps, Juanita M *Secretary, Commerce*
1407 W Pettigrew St, Durham, NC 27705, USA
Kresa, Kent *Businessman*
%Northrop Corp, 1840 Century Park East, Los Angeles, CA 90067, USA
Kreskin *Illusionist*
PO Box 1383, West Caldwell, NJ 07007, USA
Kretchmer, Arthur *Editor*
%Playboy Magazine, Editorial Dept, 680 N Lake Shore Dr, Chicago, IL 60611, USA
Kretz, Eric *Drummer (Stone Temple Pilots)*
%Atlantic Records, 9229 Sunset Blvd, #900, Los Angeles, CA 90069, USA
Kretzer, William T *Businessman*
%Unifi Inc, 7201 W Friendly Ave, Greensboro, NC 27410, USA
Kreutzmann, Bill *Drummer (Grateful Dead)*
PO Box 1073, San Rafael, CA 94915, USA
Kriangsak Chomanan *Prime Minister, Thailand; Army General*
%National Assembly, Bangkok, Thailand
Krick, Irving P *Meteorologist*
1200 S Orange Grove Blvd, #13, Pasadena, CA 91105, USA
Krieg, Arthur M *Immunologist*
%University of Iowa, College of Medicine, Immunology Dept, Iowa City, IA 52242, USA
Krieg, Dave *Football Player*
%Arizona Cardinals, 8701 S Hardy Dr, Tempe, AZ 85284, USA

K

Kraushaar - Krieg

K

Kriegel, David I _Businessman_
%Drug Emporium, 155 Hidden Ravines Dr, Powell, OH 43065, USA

Krieger, Robbie _Guitarist (Doors), Songwriter_
8033 Sunset Blvd, #76, Los Angeles, CA 90046, USA

Krier, Leon _Architect_
16 Belsize Park, London NW3, England

Krige, Alice _Actress_
10816 Lindbrook Dr, Los Angeles, CA 90024, USA

Krikalev, Sergei K _Cosmonaut_
%Potchta Kosmonavtov, 141 160 Svyosdny Gorodok, Moskovskoi Oblasti, Russia

Krim, Mathilde _Philanthropist_
%Amer Foundation for AIDS Research, 5900 Wilshire Blvd, Los Angeles, CA 90036, USA

Krimsky, John, Jr _Sports Executive_
%US Olympic Committee, 1750 E Boulder St, Colorado Springs, CO 80909, USA

Krinsky, Paul L _Coast Guard Admiral_
%US Merchant Marine Academy, Superintendent's Office, Kings Point, NY 11024, USA

Kripke, Saul A _Philosopher_
%Princeton University, Philosophy Dept, Princeton, NJ 08544, USA

Kriss, Gerard A _Astronomer_
%Johns Hopkins University, Astronomy Dept, Baltimore, MD 21218, USA

Kristel, Sylvia _Actress_
%Edrick/Rich Mgmt, 2400 Whitman Place, Los Angeles, CA 90068, USA

Kristiansen, Ingrid _Track Athlete_
Nils Collett Vogts Vei 51-B, 0765 Oslo, Norway

Kristof, Kathy M _Columnist_
%Los Angeles Times, Times Mirror Square, Los Angeles, CA 90053, USA

Kristof, Nicholas D _Journalist_
%New York Times, Editorial Dept, 229 W 43rd St, New York, NY 10036, USA

Kristofferson, Kris _Singer, Songwriter_
PO Box 2147, Malibu, CA 90265, USA

Kristol, Irving _Educator_
%Public Interest Magazine, 1112 16th St NW, Washington, DC 20036, USA

Kriwet, Heinz _Businessman_
%Thyssen AG, Kaiser-Wilhelm-Str 100, 47166 Duisburg, Germany

Kroc, Joan B _Businesswoman_
%Joan B Kroc Foundation, 8989 Villa La Jolla Dr, La Jolla, CA 92037, USA

Kroeger, Gary _Actor_
%Barbara Lawrence, 317 S Carmelia Ave, Los Angeles, CA 90049, USA

Krofft, Marty _Puppeteer_
700 Greentree Rd, Pacific Palisades, CA 90272, USA

Krofft, Sid _Puppeteer_
7710 Woodrow Wilson Dr, Los Angeles, CA 90046, USA

Kroft, Steve _Commentator_
%CBS-TV, News Dept, 51 W 52nd St, New York, NY 10019, USA

Krogman, Wilton _Physical Anthropologist_
1127 Spring Grove Ave, Lancaster, PA 17603, USA

Krol, John A _Businessman_
%E I Du Pont de Nemours Co, 1007 N Market St, Wilmington, DE 19898, USA

Krol, John Cardinal _Religious Leader_
%Philadelphia Archdiocese, 222 N 17th St, Philadelphia, PA 19103, USA

Kroll, Lucien _Architect_
Ave Louis Berlaimont 20, Boite 9, 1160 Brussels, Belgium

Kromm, Bob _Hockey Coach_
%Detroit Red Wings, Joe Louis Arena, 600 Civic Center Dr, Detroit, MI 48226, USA

Kronberger, Petra _Skier_
Ellmautal 37, 5452 Pfarrwerfen, Austria

Krone, Julie _Thoroughbred Racing Jockey_
%Monmouth Park Race Track, Oceanport Ave, Oceanport, NJ 07757, USA

Krongard, A B _Financier_
%Alex Brown & Sons, 135 E Baltimore St, Baltimore, MD 21202, USA

Kroon, Ciro D _Prime Minister, Netherlands Antilles_
%Banco Mercantil Venezolano, PO Box 565, Willenstad, Netherlands Antilles

Kropfeld, Jim _Boat Racing Driver_
%Hydroplanes Inc, 9117 Zoellner Dr, Cincinnati, OH 45251, USA

Kross, Kris _Singer_
%Entertainment Resources Int'l, 9380 SW 72nd St, #B-220, Miami, FL 33173, USA

Kross, Walter (Walt) _Air Force General_
Commander, 15th Air Force, 575 Waldron St, Travis Air Force Base, CA 94535, USA

Kriegel - Kross

Krowe, Allen J — *Businessman*
%Texaco Inc, 2000 Westchester Ave, White Plains, NY 10604, USA
Kruegar, Charlie — *Football Player*
44 Regency Dr, Clayton, CA 94517, USA
Krueger, Robert C — *Senator, TX; Diplomat*
%US Embassy-Burundi, State Department, 2201 "C" St NW, Washington, DC 20521, USA
Kruger, Hardy — *Actor*
Albert-Beit-Weg, 20149 Hamburg, Germany
Kruger, Pit — *Actor*
Geleitstr 10, 60599 Frankfurt/Main, Germany
Krugman, Paul R — *Economist*
506 Governors Ave, Stanford, CA 94305, USA
Krugman, Saul — *Physician*
300 E 33rd St, New York, NY 10016, USA
Krugman, Wilton — *Physical Anthropologist*
1127 Spring Grove Ave, Lancaster, PA 17603, USA
Krulak, Charles C — *Marine Corps General*
%Commandant's Office, HdqsUS Marine Corps, Navy Annex, Washington, DC 20380, USA
Krulwich, Robert — *Commentator*
%CBS-TV, News Dept, 524 W 57th St, New York, NY 10019, USA
Krumrie, Tim — *Football Player*
%Cincinnati Bengals, 200 Riverfront Stadium, Cincinnati, OH 45202, USA
Kruschen, Jack — *Actor*
8733 Farralone Ave, Canoga Park, CA 91304, USA
Kruse, Earl J — *Labor Leader*
%Roofers/Waterproofers/Allied Workers, 1125 17th St NW, Washington, DC 20036, USA
Kruse, Martin — *Religious Leader*
Neue Grunstr 19-20, 10179 Berlin, Germany
Kryuchkov, Vasiliy D — *Government Official, Ukraine*
4 Vinogradniy St, #74, Kiev, Ukraine
Krzyzewski, Mike — *Basketball Coach*
%Duke University, Cameron Indoor Stadium, Durham, NC 27706, USA
Kubasov, Valery N — *Cosmonaut*
%Potchta Kosmonavtov, 141 160 Svyosdny Gorodok, Moskovskoi Oblasti, Russia
Kubek, Anthony C (Tony) — *Baseball Player, Sportscaster*
8323 North Shore Rd, Menasha, WI 54952, USA
Kubiak, Gary — *Football Player, Coach*
%Denver Broncos, 13655 E Dove Valley Parkway, Englewood, CO 80112, USA
Kubler-Ross, Elisabeth — *Physician, Writer*
%Celestial Arts Publishing, PO Box 7327, Berkeley, CA 94707, USA
Kubrick, Stanley — *Movie Director*
PO Box 123, Borehamwood, Herts, England
Kucan, Milan — *President, Slovenia*
%President's Office, Erjavcera 17, 61000 Ljubljana, Slovenia
Kucharski, John M — *Businessman*
%EG&G Inc, 45 William St, Wellesley, MA 02181, USA
Kuchma, Leonid D — *President, Ukraine*
%President's Office, Bankivska Ul 11, 252009 Kiev, Ukraine
Kudelka, James — *Choreographer*
%National Ballet of Canada, 157 E King St, Toronto ON M5C 1G9, Canada
Kudelski, Bob — *Hockey Player*
%Ottawa Senators, 301 Moodie Dr, #200, Nepean ON K2H 9C4, Canada
Kudlow, Lawrence A — *Government Official, Economist*
%Bear Stearns Co, 245 Park Ave, New York, NY 10167, USA
Kudrna, Julius — *Canoeist*
Sekaninova 36, 120 00 Prague 2, Czech Republic
Kudrow, Lisa — *Actress*
%Creative Artists Agency, 9830 Wilshire Blvd, Beverly Hills, CA 90212, USA
Kuester, Dennis J — *Financier*
%M&I Marshall & Ilsley Bank, 770 N Water St, Milwaukee, WI 53202, USA
Kufeldt, James — *Businessman*
%Winn-Dixie Stores, 5050 Edgewood Ct, Jacksonville, FL 32254, USA
Kuharic, Franjo Cardinal — *Religious Leader*
%Archdiocese of Zagreb, 41101 Zagreb, Yugoslavia
Kuhaulua, Jesse — *Sumo Wrestler*
%Azumazeki Stable, 4-6-4 Higashi Komagata, Ryogoku, Tokyo, Japan
Kuhlmann, Kathleen M — *Opera Singer*
37 Sydenham Park Rd, London SE26, England

K

Kuhn, Bowie K — *Baseball Executive*
%Kent Group, PO Box 65, Quogue, NY 11959, USA

Kuhn, Steve — *Jazz Pianist*
%Berkeley Agency, 2608 9th St, Berkeley, CA 94710, USA

Kuhn, Thomas S — *Philosopher*
%Massachusetts Institute of Technology, Philosophy Dept, Cambridge, MA 02139, USA

Kuhnen, Harald — *Businessman*
%Thyssen, Kaiser-Wilhelm-Str 100, 31089 Duisburg, Germany

Kukoc, Toni — *Basketball Player*
%Chicago Bulls, 1901 W Madison St, Chicago, IL 60612, USA

Kulick, Bruce — *Musician (Kiss)*
%Levine/Schneider, 433 N Camden Dr, Beverly Hills, CA 90210, USA

Kulikov, Viktor G — *Army Marshal, USSR*
%Defense Ministry, Krasnopresnenskaya Nat 2, 103116 Moscow, Russia

Kulkarni, Shrinivas R — *Astronomer*
%California Institute of Technology, Astronomy Dept, Pasadena, CA 91125, USA

Kull, Lorenz A — *Businessman*
%Science Applications International, 10260 Campus Point Dr, San Diego, CA 92121, USA

Kumagai, Yoshifumi — *Businessman*
5-33-4 Kitahama, Chuoku, Osaka 541, Japan

Kumagai, Yoshiro — *Businessman*
%Sumitomo Metal Industries, 1-1-3 Otemachi, Chiyodaku, Tokyo 100, Japan

Kumar, Sanjay — *Businessman*
%Computer Associates Int'l, 1 Computer Associated Plaza, Islandia, NY 11788, USA

Kumaratunga, Chandrika B — *Prime Minister, Sri Lanka*
%Prime Minister's Office, 58 Mawatha, Sri Jayewardenepura Kotte, Sri Lanka

Kume, Tadashi — *Businessman*
%Honda Motor Co, 27-8-6 Jingumae, Shibuyaku, Tokyo 150, Japan

Kume, Yutaka — *Businessman*
%Nissan Motor Co Ltd, 6-17-1 Ginza, Chuoku, Tokyo 104, Japan

Kumin, Maxine W — *Writer*
Joppa Rd, Warner, NH 03278, USA

Kumler, Kipton C — *Businessman*
%Commercial Intertech Corp, 1775 Logan Ave, Youngstown, OH 44505, USA

Kummer, Glenn F — *Businessman*
%Fleetwood Enterprises, 3125 Myers St, Riverside, CA 92503, USA

Kump, Ernest J — *Architect*
17 Rue Chanoinesse, 75004 Paris, France

Kundera, Milan — *Writer*
%University of Rennes, 6 Ave Gaston Berger, 35043 Rennes, France

Kung, Hans — *Theologian*
Waldhauserstr 23, 72076 Tubingen, Germany

Kung, Patrick C — *Pharmacologist*
%T Cell Sciences, 38 Sidney St, Cambridge, MA 02139, USA

Kunin, Madeline M — *Governor, VT*
%National Arts-Humanities Foundation, 1100 Pennsylvania, Washington, DC 20004, USA

Kunisch, Robert D — *Businessman*
%PHH Corp, 11333 McCormick Rd, Hunt Valley, MD 21031, USA

Kunitz, Stanley J — *Writer*
37 W 12th St, New York, NY 10011, USA

Kunkel, Louis M — *Pediatrician*
%Children's Hospital, 300 Longwood Ave, Boston, MA 02115, USA

Kunkle, John F — *Religious Leader*
%Evangelical Methodist Church, 3000 W Kellogg Dr, Wichita, KS 67213, USA

Kunz, George J — *Football Player*
8215 S Bermuda, Las Vegas, NV 89123, USA

Kunzel, Erich, Jr — *Conductor*
%Cincinnati Symphony, Music Hall, 1241 Elm St, Cincinnati, OH 45210, USA

Kupchak, Mitch — *Basketball Player*
1123 Manning Ave, Los Angeles, CA 90024, USA

Kupcinet, Irv — *Columnist*
%Chicago Sun-Times, Editorial Dept, 401 N Wabash Ave, Chicago, IL 60611, USA

Kupcinet, Kari — *Actress*
1730 N Clark St, #3311, Chicago, IL 60614, USA

Kupfer, Carl — *Ophthalmologist*
%National Eye Institute, 9000 Rockville Pike, Bethesda, MD 20205, USA

Kupfer, Harry — *Opera Director*
%Komische Oper, Behrenstr 55-57, 10117 Berlin, Germany

Kuhn - Kupfer

Kupferberg, Sabine _Ballerina_
%Dans Theater 3, Scheldoldoekshaven 60, 2511 EN Gravenhage, Netherlands

Kurabayashi, Ikushiro _Businessman_
%Takeda Chemical Industries, 2-27 Doshomachi, Higashiku, Osaka 541, Japan

Kuralt, Charles B _Commentator_
119 W 57th St, #PH-1601, New York, NY 10019, USA

Kuranari, Tadashi _Government Official, Japan_
2-18-12 Daita, Setangayaku, Tokyo 155, Japan

Kureishi, Hanif _Writer_
81 Comeragh Rd, London W14 9HS, England

Kurland, Robert A (Bob) _Basketball Player_
1200 Brookside, Bartlesville, OK 74006, USA

Kurland, Stanford L _Financier_
%Countrywide Credit Industries, 155 N Lake Ave, Pasadena, CA 91101, USA

Kurokawa, Kisho _Architect_
Aoyama Bldg, #11-F, 1-2-3 Kita Aoyama, Minatoku, Tokyo, Japan

Kurosawa, Akira _Movie Director_
%Kurosawa Production, 3-2-1 Kirigaoka Midori-ku, Yokohama, Japan

Kurri, Jari _Hockey Player_
%Los Angeles Kings, Forum, PO Box 17013, Inglewood, CA 90308, USA

Kurtz, Swoosie _Actress_
320 Central Park West, New York, NY 10025, USA

Kurtzig, Sandra L _Businesswoman_
%ASK Group Inc, 2880 Scott Blvd, Santa Clara, CA 95050, USA

Kurz, Herbert _Businessman_
%Presidential Life Insurance, 69 Lydecker St, Nyack, NY 10960, USA

Kurzweil, Raymond _Inventor_
%Kurzweil Applied Intelligence, 411 Waverly Oaks Rd, Waltham, MA 02154, USA

Kuschak, Metropolitan Andrei _Religious Leader_
%Ukranian Orthodox Church in America, 90-34 139th St, Jamaica, NY 11435, USA

Kuse, James R _Businessman_
%Georgia Gulf Corp, 400 Perimeter Center Terrace, Atlanta, GA 30346, USA

Kushner, Robert E _Artist_
%Reinhold-Brown Gallery, 26 E 78th St, New York, NY 10021, USA

Kushner, Tony _Playwright_
%Joyce Ketay Agency, 334 W 89th St, New York, NY 10024, USA

Kuter, Kay E _Actor_
6207 Satsuma Ave, North Hollywood, CA 91606, USA

Kuti, Fela A _Musician_
The Shrine, Kalakuta, Lagos, Nigeria

Kutner, Mal _Football Player_
3 River Hollow Lane, Houston, TX 77027, USA

Kuttner, Stephan G _Historian_
2270 Le Conte Ave, #601, Berkeley, CA 94709, USA

Kuykendall, John W _Educator_
%Davidson College, President's Office, Davidson, NC 28036, USA

Kuznetsov, Vacheslav _Government Official, Belarus_
%Chairman's Office, Dom Pravitelstva, Minsk 220010, Belarus

Kuzyk, Mimi _Actress_
%J Michael Bloom Ltd, 9255 Sunset Blvd, #710, Los Angeles, CA 90069, USA

Kwalick, Ted _Football Player_
14375 New Jersey Ave, San Jose, CA 95124, USA

Kwan, Nancy _Actress_
%Contemporary Artists, 1427 3rd St Promenade, #205, Santa Monica, CA 90401, USA

Kwasniewski, Aleksander _Government Leader, Poland_
Ul Wiktorii Wiedenskiej 1/7, 02-954 Warsaw, Poland

Kwoh, Yik San _Electrical Engineer_
%Memorial Medical Center, PO Box 1428, Long Beach, CA 90801, USA

Ky, Machiko _Actress_
%Uni Japan Films, 9-13-5 Ginza, Chuoku, Tokyo, Japan

Ky, Nguyen Cao _Prime Minister, South Vietnam; General_
15701 Sunburst Lane, Huntington Beach, CA 92647, USA

Kylian, Jiri _Ballet Dancer_
%Dance Theatre, Scheldeldoekshaven 60, 2511 EN Gravenhage, Netherlands

Kyo, Machiko _Actress_
Olimpia Copu, 6-35 Jingumae, Shibuyaku, Tokyo, Japan

Kyprianou, Spyros _President, Cyprus_
Antistaseos 1, Engomi, Nicosia, Cyprus

K

Kupferberg - Kyprianou

L'Engle, Madeleine — *Writer*
%Crosswicks, Goshen, CT 06756, USA

La Belle, Patti — *Singer*
1212 Grennox Rd, Wynnewood, PA 19096, USA

La Fosse, Robert — *Choreographer*
%New York City Ballet, Lincoln Center Plaza, New York, NY 10023, USA

La Planche, Rosemary — *Actress*
13914 Hartsook St, Sherman Oaks, CA 91423, USA

La Rosa, Julius — *Singer*
67 Sycamore Lane, Irvington, NY 10533, USA

La Rue, Lash — *Actor*
RR 1, Box 634-A, Broadway, NC 27505, USA

La Sala, Francis J — *Financier*
%BHF Securities Corp, 70 Pine St, New York, NY 10270, USA

La Sala, James — *Labor Leader*
%Amalgamated Transit Workers, 5025 Wisconsin Ave NW, Washington, DC 20016, USA

La Salle, Eriq — *Actor*
%Gersh Agency, 232 N Canon Dr, Beverly Hills, CA 90210, USA

La Tourette, John E — *Educator*
3734 N Pine Grove, #304, Chicago, IL 60613, USA

Laage, Gerhart — *Architect*
Weidenallee 26-A, 20357 Hamburg, Germany

Laar, Mart — *Prime Minister, Estonia*
%Prime Minister's Office, Lossi Plats 1-A, Tallinn 0100, Estonia

Laatasi, Kamuta — *Prime Minister, Tuvalu*
%Prime Minister's Office, Vaiaku, Funafuti, Tuvalu

Labaff, Ernie — *Labor Leader*
%Aluminum Brick Glass Workers Union, 3362 Hollenberg, Bridgeton, MO 63044, USA

Labis, Attilo — *Ballet Dancer, Choreographer*
36 Rue du Chemin-de-fer, 78380 Bougival, France

LaBoa, Guy A J — *Army General*
Commanding General, 2nd US Army, Fort Gillem, GA 30050, USA

Labonte, Terry — *Auto Racing Driver*
PO Box 4617, Archdale, NC 27263, USA

Laborde, Alden J — *Businessman*
63 Oriole St, New Orleans, LA 70124, USA

Labrecque, Thomas G — *Financier*
%Chase Manhattan Corp, 270 Park Ave, New York, NY 10017, USA

Lacalle Herrera, Luis A — *President, Uruguay*
%President's Office, Ave Luis Alberto de Herrera 3350, Montevideo, Uruguay

Lace, Jerry E — *Figure Skating Executive*
15750 Spur Ranch Rd, Peyton, CO 80831, USA

Lacey, Deborah — *Actress*
1801 Ave of Stars, #1250, Los Angeles, CA 90067, USA

Lach, Elmer J — *Hockey Player*
4557 Rosedale Ave, Montreal PQ H4B 2H1, Canada

Lachemann, Rene G — *Baseball Player, Manager*
%Florida Marlins, 100 NE 3rd Ave, Fort Lauderdale, FL 33301, USA

Lachey, James M (Jim) — *Football Player*
%Washington Redskins, 21300 Redskin Park Dr, Ashburn, VA 22011, USA

Lachiman Gurung — *WW II Nepal Army Hero (VC)*
Village Dahakhani, Village Development, Conmelle, Ward 4, Chitwan, Nepal

Lackey, Brad — *Motorcycle Racing Rider*
%Badco, 35 Monument Plaza, Pleasant Hill, CA 94523, USA

Laclavere, Georges — *Geophysicist*
53 Ave de Breteuil, 70075 Paris, France

Laclotte, Michel R — *Museum Director*
%Musee du Louvre, 4 Quai des Tuileries, 75041 Paris Cedex 1, France

Lacombe, Henri — *Oceanographer*
20 Bis Ave de Lattre de Tassigny, 92340 Bourg-La-Reine, France

Lacoste, Catherine — *Golfer*
Calle B-6, #4, El Soto de la Moraleja Alcobendas, Madrid, Spain

Lacoste, Rene — *Tennis Player*
Lacostenia, Chantaco, 64500 St Jean-de-Luz, France

LaCroix, Anthony A — *Financier*
%Advest Group, Commercial Plaza, 280 Trumbull St, Hartford, CT 06103, USA

Lacroix, Christian M M — *Fashion Designer*
73 Rue du Faubourg St Honore, 75008 Paris, France

Lacy, Linwood A, Jr *Businessman*
%Ingram Industries, 4400 Harding Rd, Nashville, TN 37205, USA

Lacy, William H *Financier*
%MGIC Investment Corp, 250 E Kilbourn Ave, Milwaukee, WI 53202, USA

Ladd, Alan W, Jr *Movie Producer*
706 N Elm Dr, Beverly Hills, CA 90210, USA

Ladd, Cheryl *Actress*
PO Box 1329, Santa Ynez, CA 93460, USA

Ladd, Diane *Actress*
PO Box 17111, Beverly Hills, CA 90209, USA

Ladd, Edward H *Financier*
%Standish Ayer & Wood, 1 Financial Center, Boston, MA 02111, USA

Ladd, Margaret *Actress*
444 21st St, Santa Monica, CA 90402, USA

Ladehoff, Leo W *Businessman*
%Amcast Industrial Corp, 7887 Washington Village Dr, Dayton, OH 45459, USA

Laderman, Ezra *Composer*
%Yale University, Music School, New Haven, CT 06520, USA

Laettner, Christian *Basketball Player*
%Minnesota Timberwolves, Target Center, 600 1st Ave N, Minneapolis, MN 55403, USA

Laffer, Arthur *Economist*
24255 Pacific Coast Highway, Malibu, CA 90263, USA

Lafleur, Guy *Hockey Player*
3400 Chemin Ste-Foy, Ste Foy PQ G1X 1X6, Canada

Lafontaine, Oskar *Political Leader, West Germany*
Staatskanzle, Am Ludwigsplatz 14, 66117 Saarbrucken, Germany

LaFontaine, Pat *Hockey Player*
%Buffalo Sabres, Memorial Stadium, 140 Main St, Buffalo, NY 14202, USA

Lagerfeld, Karl *Fashion Designer*
14 Blvd de la Madeleine, 75008 Paris, France

Laghi, Pio Cardinal *Religious Leader*
%Catholic Education Congregation, Piazza Pio XII 3, 00193 Rome, Italy

Lahav, Gideon *Financier*
%Israel Discount Bank of New York, 511 5th Ave, New York, NY 10017, USA

Lahourcade, John B *Businessman*
%Luby's Cafeterias, 2211 NE Loop 410, San Antonio, TX 78265, USA

Lahti, Christine *Actress*
%Creative Artists Agency, 9830 Wilshire Blvd, Beverly Hills, CA 90212, USA

Lai, Francis *Composer*
23 Rue Franklin, 75016 Paris, France

Laine, Cleo *Singer*
%International Artists, 235 Regent St, London W1R 8AX, England

Laine, Frankie *Singer*
352 San Gorgonio St, San Diego, CA 92106, USA

Laingon, L Druce *Diplomat*
5627 Old Chester Rd, Bethesda, MD 20814, USA

Laird, Melvin R *Secretary, Defense; Businessman*
%COMSAT Corp, 6560 Rock Spring Dr, Bethesda, MD 20817, USA

Laird, Peter *Cartoonist (Ninja Turtles)*
%TMNT, PO Box 417, Haydenville, MA 01039, USA

Laird, Ron *Track Athlete*
4706 Diane Dr, Astabula, OH 44004, USA

Laithwaite, Eric R *Electrical Engineer*
%Imperial College, Electrical Engineering Dept, London SW7 2BT, England

Laitman, Jeffrey *Anatomist*
%Mt Sinai Medical Center, Anatomy Dept, 1 Gustave Levy Place, New York, NY 10029, USA

Lake, James A *Molecular Biologist*
%University of California, Molecular Biology Institute, Los Angeles, CA 90024, USA

Lake, N Anthony *Government Official*
%National Security Council, Old Executive Office Building, Washington, DC 20506, USA

Lake, Ricki *Actress*
%Ricki Lake Show, 401 5th Ave, New York, NY 10016, USA

Laker, Frederick A *Businessman*
Princess Tower, West Sunrise, Box F-207, Freeport, Grand Bahamas, Bahamas

Laker, Jim *Cricketer*
Oak End, 9 Portinscale Rd, Putney, London SW15, England

Lakes, Gary *Opera Singer*
%Herbert Barrett Mgmt, 1776 Broadway, New York, NY 10019, USA

L

Lacy - Lakes

L

Lakoue, Enoch Devant *Prime Minister, Central African Republic*
%Prime Minister's Office, Bangui, Central African Republic

LaLanne, Jack *Physical Fitness Expert*
%BeFit Enterprises, PO Box 1023, San Luis Obispo, CA 93406, USA

Laliberte-Bourque, Andree *Museum Director*
%Musee du Quebec, 1 Ave Wolfe-Montcalm, Quebec PQ G1R 5H3, Canada

Lalli, Frank *Editor*
%Money Magazine, Editorial Dept, Rockefeller Center, New York, NY 10020, USA

LaMacchia, John T *Businessman*
%Cincinnati Bell Inc, 201 E 4th St, Cincinnati, OH 45202, USA

LaMaina, Lawrence J, Jr *Financier*
%Dauphin Deposit Corp, 213 Market St, Harrisburg, PA 17101, USA

Lamarr, Hedy *Actress*
568 Orange Dr, #47, Altamonte Springs, FL 32701, USA

Lamas, Lorenzo *Actor*
PO Box 500907, San Diego, CA 92150, USA

Lamb, Brian *Entertainment Executive*
%C-SPAN, 400 N Capitol St NW, Washington, DC 20001, USA

Lamb, Dennis *Diplomat*
19 Rue de Franqueville, 75016 Paris, France

Lamb, Gil *Comedian*
6476 San Marcos Circle, Los Angeles, CA 90069, USA

Lamb, Ronald M *Businessman*
%Casey's General Stores, 1 Convenience Blvd, Ankeny, IA 50021, USA

Lamb, Willis E, Jr *Nobel Physics Laureate*
%University of Arizona, Optical Sciences Center, Tucson, AZ 85721, USA

Lambert, Christopher *Actor*
9 Ave Trempley, C/Lui, 1209 Geneva, Switzerland

Lambert, Jack *Football Player*
%Pro Football Hall of Fame, 2121 George Halas Dr NW, Canton, OH 44708, USA

Lambert, Phyllis *Architect*
%Centre d'Architecture, 1920 Rue Baile, Montreal PQ H3H 2S6, Canada

Lamberti, Donald E *Businessman*
%Casey's General Stores, 1 Convenience Blvd, Ankeny, IA 50021, USA

Lambro, Phillip *Composer, Pianist*
%Trigram Music, 1888 Century Park East, #10, Los Angeles, CA 90067, USA

Lambsdorff, Otto *Government Official, West Germany*
Fritz-Erler-Str 23, 53113 Bonn, Germany

Lamm, Donald S *Publisher*
%W W Norton Co, 500 5th Ave, New York, NY 10110, USA

Lamm, Norman *Educator*
101 Central Park West, New York, NY 10023, USA

Lamm, Richard D *Governor, CO*
400 E 8th Ave, Denver, CO 80203, USA

Lamm, Robert *Singer, Keyboardist (Chicago)*
%Front Line Mgmt, 8900 Wilshire Blvd, #300, Beverly Hills, CA 90211, USA

Lamonica, Darryl *Football Player*
8796 N 6th St, Fresno, CA 93720, USA

Lamonica, Roberto de *Artist*
Rua Anibal de Mendanca 180, AP 202, Rio de Janeiro ZC-37 RJ, Brazil

Lamont, Gene W *Baseball Manager*
4966 Fallcrest Circle, Sarasota, FL 34233, USA

Lamont, Norman S H *Government Official, England*
%House of Commons, Westminster, London SW1A 0AA, England

Lamoriello, Lou *Hockey Executive*
%New Jersey Devils, Meadowlands Arena, PO Box 504, East Rutherford, NJ 07073, USA

LaMothe, William E *Businessman*
%Kellogg Co, 1 Kellogg Square, 235 Porter St, Battle Creek, MI 49017, USA

LaMotta, Jake *Boxer*
400 E 57th St, New York, NY 10022, USA

LaMotta, Vikki *Model*
235 Beacon Dr, Phoenixville, PA 19460, USA

Lamour, Dorothy *Actress*
5309 Goodland Ave, North Hollywood, CA 91607, USA

Lamparski, Richard *Writer*
1220 Mesa Rd, Santa Barbara, CA 93108, USA

Lampert, Zohra *Actress*
666 West End Ave, New York, NY 10025, USA

Lamphers, Gilbert H · *Businessman*
%Illinois Central Corp, 455 N Cityfront Plaza Dr, Chicago, IL 60611, USA

Lampley, Jim · *Sportscaster*
3347 Tareco Dr, Los Angeles, CA 90068, USA

Lampton, Michael · *Astronaut*
%University of California, Space Science Laboratory, Berkeley, CA 94720, USA

Lance, T Bert · *Government Official*
409 E Line St, PO Box 637, Calhoun, GA 30703, USA

Lanchbery, John A · *Conductor*
17 Harwicke Rd, London W4 5EA, England

Landau, Irvin · *Editor*
%Consumer Reports Magazine, 101 Truman Ave, Yonkers, NY 10703, USA

Landau, Jacob · *Artist*
2 Pine Dr, Roosevelt, NJ 08555, USA

Landau, Martin · *Actor*
1501 Skylark Lane, Los Angeles, CA 90069, USA

Landau, Saul · *Writer*
%Institute for Policy Studies, 1601 Connecticut Ave NW, Washington, DC 20009, USA

Landazuri Ricketts, Juan Cardinal · *Religious Leader*
Arzobispado, Plazo de Armas, Apartado Postal 1512, Lima 100, Peru

Landeck, Armin · *Artist*
RD 1, Litchfield, CT 06759, USA

Lander, David L · *Actor*
4138 Pulido Court, Calabasas, CA 91302, USA

Landers (Eppie Lederer), Ann · *Columnist*
%Chicago Tribune, 435 N Michigan Ave, Chicago, IL 60611, USA

Landers, Audrey · *Actress, Singer*
%Queen Bee Productions, 3112 Nicada Dr, Bel Air, CA 90077, USA

Landers, Judy · *Actress*
1913 N Beverly Dr, Beverly Hills, CA 90210, USA

Landes, David S · *Historian*
24 Highland St, Cambridge, MA 02138, USA

Landesberg, Steve · *Actor*
%Rick Bernstein Enterprises, 355 N Genesee Ave, Los Angeles, CA 90036, USA

Landeta, Sean · *Football Player*
%St Louis Rams, 100 N Broadway, #2100, St Louis, MO 63102, USA

Landguth, Daniel P · *Businessman*
%Black Hills Corp, 625 9th St, Rapid City, SD 57701, USA

Landini, Richard G · *Educator*
%Indiana State University, English Dept, Root Hall, Terre Haute, IN 47809, USA

Landis, John D · *Movie Director*
9402 Beverly Crest Dr, Beverly Hills, CA 90210, USA

Lando, Joe · *Actor*
%William Morris Agency, 151 S El Camino Dr, Beverly Hills, CA 90212, USA

Landon, Howard · *Writer*
Chateau de Foncoussieres, 81800 Rabastens, Tarn, France

Landon, R Kirk · *Businessman*
%American Bankers Insurance Group, 11222 Quail Roost Dr, Miami, FL 33157, USA

Landrieu, Moon · *Secretary, Housing & Urban Development*
4301 S Prieur St, New Orleans, LA 70125, USA

Landry, Greg · *Football Player, Coach*
%Detroit Lions, Silverdome, 1200 Featherstone Rd, Pontiac, MI 48342, USA

Landry, Thomas W (Tom) · *Football Executive*
%Landry Investment Co, 8411 Preston Rd, #720, Dallas, TX 75225, USA

Landsburg, Valerie · *Actress*
22745 Chamera Lane, Topanga Canyon, CA 90290, USA

Lane of St Ippollitts, Geoffrey D · *Judge*
%Royal Courts of Justice, Strand, London WC2A 2LL, England

Lane, Abbe · *Singer, Actress*
444 N Faring Rd, Los Angeles, CA 90077, USA

Lane, Charles · *Actor*
321 Gretna Green Way, Los Angeles, CA 90049, USA

Lane, Cristy · *Singer*
1225 Apache Lane, Madison, TN 37115, USA

Lane, Diane · *Actress*
111 W 40th St, #2000, New York, NY 10018, USA

Lane, Donald D · *Businessman*
%CKE Restaurants, 1200 N Harbor Blvd, Anaheim, CA 92801, USA

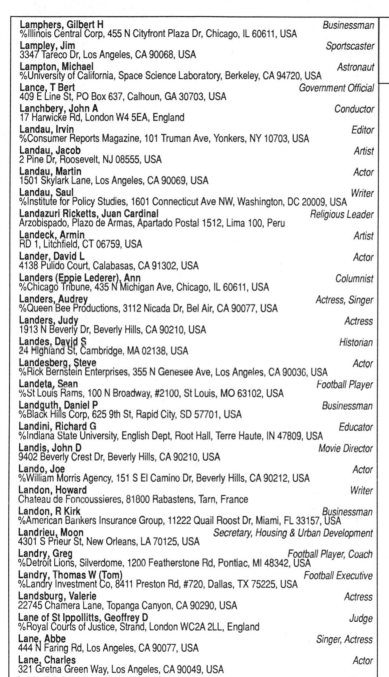

L

Lamphers - Lane

Lane, Jeffrey B *Financier*
%Smith Barney Inc, 1345 Ave of Americas, New York, NY 10105, USA

Lane, John R (Jack) *Museum Curator*
%San Francisco Museum of Modern Art, 151 3rd St, San Francisco, CA 94103, USA

Lane, Kenneth Jay *Fashion Designer*
%Kenneth Jay Lane Inc, 20 W 37th St, New York, NY 10018, USA

Lane, Lawrence W, Jr *Publisher, Diplomat*
3000 Sandhill Rd, #215, Menlo Park, CA 94025, USA

Lane, Melvin B *Publisher*
99 Tallwood Court, Menlo Park, CA 94027, USA

Lane, Mike *Editorial Cartoonist*
%Baltimore Evening Sun, Editorial Dept, 501 N Calvert St, Baltimore, MD 21202, USA

Lane, Richard (Night Train) *Football Player*
1510 North Loop, #431, Austin, TX 78756, USA

Lane, William W *Businessman*
%William Lane Assoc, 30 E 60th St, #901, New York, NY 10022, USA

Laney, James T *Educator, Diplomat*
2080 Renault Lane NE, Atlanta, GA 30345, USA

Laney, Sandra E *Businesswoman*
%Chemed Corp, Chemed Center, 255 E 5th St, Cincinnati, OH 45202, USA

Lang, Anton *Plant Physiologist*
1538 Cahill Dr, East Lansing, MI 48823, USA

Lang, Belinda *Actress*
%Ken McReddie, 91 Regent St, London W1R 7TB, England

Lang, Ed *Photographer*
%Elysium Growth Press, 814 Robinson Rd, Topanga, CA 90290, USA

Lang, Eugene M *Businessman*
912 5th Ave, New York, NY 10021, USA

Lang, George C *Vietnam War Army Hero (CMH)*
3786 Clark St, Seaford, NY 11783, USA

Lang, Jack *Government Official, France*
17 Place des Vosges, 75004 Paris, France

Lang, Jack *Sportswriter*
%Baseball Writers' Assn, 36 Brookfield Rd, Fort Salonga, NY 11768, USA

Lang, June *Actress*
12756 Kahlenberg Lane, North Hollywood, CA 91607, USA

Lang, K D *Singer*
%Bumstead Productions, 1616 W 3rd Ave, #200, Vancouver BC V6J 1K2, Canada

Lang, Katherine Kelly *Actress*
317 S Carmelina Ave, Los Angeles, CA 90049, USA

Lang, Pearl *Dancer, Choreographer*
382 Central Park West, New York, NY 10025, USA

Langbo, Arnold G *Businessman*
%Kellogg Co, 1 Kellogg Square, 235 Porter St, Battle Creek, MI 49017, USA

Langdon, Harry *Photographer*
PO Box 16816, Beverly Hills, CA 90209, USA

Langdon, Michael *Opera Singer*
34 Warnham Ct, Grand Ave, Hove, Sussex, England

Langdon, Sue Ane *Actress*
24115 Long Valley Rd, Calabasas, CA 91302, USA

Lange, David R *Prime Minister, New Zealand*
14 Ambury Rd, Mangere Bridge, Auckland, New Zealand

Lange, Hope *Actress*
803 Bramble Way, Los Angeles, CA 90049, USA

Lange, Jessica *Actress*
%Creative Artists Agency, 9830 Wilshire Blvd, Beverly Hills, CA 90212, USA

Lange, Ted *Actor*
5321 Coldwater Canyon Ave, #C, Sherman Oaks, CA 91401, USA

Lange, Thomas *Rowing Athlete*
Burgermeister-Kock-Str 5, 23909 Bak, Germany

Langella, Frank *Actor*
%Innovative Artists, 1999 Ave of Stars, #2850, Los Angeles, CA 90067, USA

Langenberg, Frederick C *Businessman*
%Interlake Corp, 550 Warrenville Rd, Lisle, IL 60532, USA

Langenkamp, Heather *Actress*
4238 Ocean View Dr, Malibu, CA 90265, USA

Langer, Bernhard *Golfer*
1120 SW 21st Lane, Boca Raton, FL 33486, USA

Langer, James J (Jim)   *Football Player*
4111 McKay Rd N, Brainerd, MN 56401, USA
Langford, Frances   *Singer*
PO Box 96, Jensen Beach, FL 34958, USA
Langford, John   *Aeronautical Engineer*
%Aurora Flight Sciences, 10601 Observation Rd, Manassas, VA 22111, USA
Langham, Antonio   *Football Player*
%Cleveland Browns, 80 1st Ave, Berea, OH 44017, USA
Langham, Michael   *Theater Director*
%Julliard School, Drama Division, 144 W 66th St, New York, NY 10023, USA
Langhammer, Fred H   *Businessman*
%Estee Lauder Companies, 767 5th Ave, New York, NY 10153, USA
Langley, H Desmond A   *Governor General, Bermuda; Army General*
%Governor's Office, 11 Langton Hill, Pembroke, Hamilton HM 13, Bermuda
Langley, Roger   *Skier*
Broad St, Barre, MA 01005, USA
Langlois, Lisa   *Actress*
9105 Carmelita Ave, #1, Beverly Hills, CA 90210, USA
Langsam, Walter C   *Educator*
%University of Cincinnati, President Emeritus' Office, Cincinnati, OH 45221, USA
Langston, J William   *Neurologist*
%Parkinson's Foundation, 2444 Moorpark Ave, San Jose, CA 95128, USA
Langston, Mark E   *Baseball Player*
4801 Copa de Oro, Anaheim, CA 92807, USA
Langway, Rod   *Hockey Player*
%Winnipeg Jets, Arena, 15-1430 Maroons Rd, Winnipeg MB R3G 0L5, Canada
Laniak, David K   *Businessman*
%Rochester Gas & Electric, 89 East Ave, Rochester, NY 14604, USA
Lanier, Hal (Harold C)   *Baseball Manager*
19380 SW 90th Lane Rd, Dunnellon, FL 34432, USA
Lanier, J Hicks   *Businessman*
%Oxford Industries, 222 Piedmont Ave NE, Atlanta, GA 30308, USA
Lanier, Max (H Max)   *Baseball Player*
11250 SW Rio Vista Dr, Dunnellon, FL 31630, USA
Lanier, Robert J (Bob)   *Basketball Player, Coach*
%Golden State Warriors, Oakland Coliseum Arena, Oakland, CA 94621, USA
Lanier, Willie E   *Football Player*
2911 W Brigstock Rd, Midlothian, VA 23113, USA
Lanigan, Robert J   *Businessman*
13145 Valewood Dr, Naples, FL 33999, USA
Lanin, Lester   *Musician*
%Blue Ox Talent Agency, 4130 N Goldwater Blvd, #121, Scottsdale, AZ 85251, USA
Lanker, Brian   *Photographer*
1993 Kimberly Dr, Eugene, OR 97405, USA
Lankford, Ronald B   *Financier*
%Old National Bancorp, 420 Main St, Evansville, IN 47708, USA
LaNoue, Alcide M   *Army General*
Surgeon General's Office, USA/PEO, 5109 Leesburg Pike, Falls Church, VA 22041, USA
Lansbury, Angela   *Actress*
635 N Bonhill Rd, Los Angeles, CA 90049, USA
Lansdowne, J Fenwick   *Artist*
941 Victoria Ave, Victoria BC V8S 4N6, Canada
Lansford, Carney R   *Baseball Player*
RR, 1 Box 66, Baker City, OR 97814, USA
Lansing, Sherry L   *Movie Producer*
1363 Angelo Dr, Beverly Hills, CA 90210, USA
Lanvin, Bernard   *Fashion Designer*
22 Rue du Faubourg St Honore, 70008 Paris, France
Lanz, David   *Pianist*
Siddons Assoc, 584 N Larchmont Blvd, Los Angeles, CA 90004, USA
Lanza, Frank C   *Businessman*
%Loral Corp, 600 3rd Ave, New York, NY 10016, USA
Laperriere, Jacques   *Hockey Player*
1983 Nice, Chomedey Est, Laval PQ H7S 1G5, Canada
Lapham, Lewis H   *Editor*
%Harper's Magazine, Editorial Dept, 666 Broadway, New York, NY 10012, USA
Laphen, James A   *Financier*
%Commercial Federal Corp, 2120 S 72nd St, Omaha, NE 68124, USA

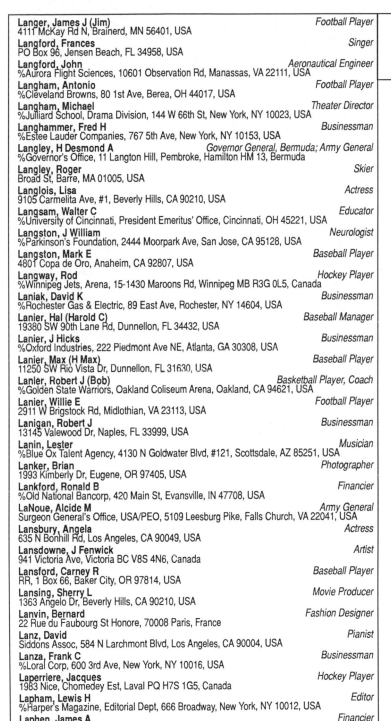

L

Langer - Laphen

Lapidus, Alan *Architect*
%Lapidus Assoc, 43 W 61st St, New York, NY 10023, USA

Lapidus, Edmond (Ted) *Fashion Designer*
35 Rue Francois 1er, 75008 Paris, France

Lapierre, Dominique *Writer, Historian*
Les Bignoles, 8350 Ramatuelle, France

Lapine, James E *Playwright, Theater Director*
85 Mill River Rd, South Salem, NY 10590, USA

LaPlaca, Alison *Actress*
8380 Melrose Ave, #207, Los Angeles, CA 90069, USA

LaPlante, Laura *Actress*
23388 Mulholland Dr, Woodland Hills, CA 91364, USA

Lapointe, Guy *Hockey Player*
%Montreal Canadiens, 2313 St Catherine St W, Montreal PQ H3H 1N2, Canada

LaPorte, Danny *Motorcycle Racing Rider*
949 Via Del Monte, Palos Verdes Estates, CA 90274, USA

Laporte, William F *Businessman*
%American Home Products Corp, 685 3rd Ave, New York, NY 10017, USA

Laposata, Joseph S *Army General*
%Battle Monuments Commission, 20 Massachusetts, Washington, DC 20314, USA

Lapotaire, Jane *Actress*
92 Oxford Gardens, #C, London W10, England

Lappin, Richard C *Businessman*
%Fruit of the Loom Inc, Sears Tower, 233 S Wacker Dr, Chicago, IL 60606, USA

Laprade, Edgar *Hockey Player*
12 Shunick St, Thunder Bay ON P7A 2Y8, Canada

Laquer, Walter *Historian*
%Georgetown University, Strategic Studies, 1800 "K" St NW, Washington, DC 20006, USA

Laragh, John H *Physician, Educator*
435 E 70th St, New York, NY 10021, USA

Larch, John *Actor*
4506 Varna Ave, Sherman Oaks, CA 91423, USA

Lardner, George, Jr *Journalist*
%Washington Post, Editorial Dept, 1150 15th St NW, Washington, DC 20071, USA

Lardner, Ring, Jr *Writer*
55 Central Park West, New York, NY 10023, USA

Lardy, Henry A *Biochemist*
1829 Thorstrand Rd, Madison, WI 53705, USA

Laredo, Ruth *Classical Pianist*
%Sony/Columbia/CBS Records, 51 W 52nd St, New York, NY 10019, USA

Large, David C *Historian*
1359 7th Ave, San Francisco, CA 94122, USA

Large, James M, Jr *Financier*
%Anchor BanCorp, 1420 Broadway, Hewlett, NY 11557, USA

Larkin, Barry L *Baseball Player*
5022 Rollman Estates Dr, Cincinnati, OH 45236, USA

Larkin, Thomas E, Jr *Financier*
%Trust Company of the West, 865 S Figueroa St, Los Angeles, CA 90017, USA

Larkins, Gary L *Businessman*
%House of Fabrics, 13400 Riverside Dr, Sherman Oaks, CA 91423, USA

Larmer, Steve *Hockey Player*
%New York Rangers, Madison Square Garden, 4 Penn Plaza New York, NY 10001, USA

LaRoche, Philippe *Aerial Skier*
%Club de Ski Acrobatique, Lac Beauport PQ G0A 20Q, Canada

LaRocque, Gene R *Government Official, Navy Admiral*
3140 Davenport St NW, Washington, DC 20008, USA

LaRouche, Lyndon H, Jr *Political Activist*
%Executive Intelligence Review, PO Box 17390, Washington, DC 20041, USA

Larrabee, Martin G *Biophysicist*
4227 Long Green Rd, Glen Arm, MD 21057, USA

Larroquette, John *Actor*
5874 Deerfield Rd, Malibu, CA 90265, USA

Larrouilh, Michel *Financier*
%Bank of the West, 1450 Treat Blvd, Walnut Creek, CA 94596, USA

Larsen, Art *Tennis Player*
203 Lorraine Blvd, San Leandro, CA 94577, USA

Larsen, Bruce *Editor*
%Vancouver Sun, 2250 Granville St, Vancouver BC V6H 3G2, Canada

Larsen, Don J — *Baseball Player*
PO Box 2863, Hayden Lake, ID 83835, USA

Larsen, Gary L — *Football Player*
4612 141st Court SE, Bellevue, WA 98006, USA

Larsen, Libby — *Composer*
2205 Kenwood Parkway, Minneapolis, MN 55405, USA

Larsen, Paul E — *Religious Leader*
%Evangelical Convenant Church, 5101 N Francisco Ave, Chicago, IL 60625, USA

Larsen, Ralph S — *Businessman*
%Johnson & Johnson, 1 Johnson & Johnson Plaza, New Brunswick, NJ 08904, USA

Larsen, Terrence A — *Financier*
%CoreStates Financial Corp, Broad & Chestnut Sts, Philadelphia, PA 19101, USA

Larson, April U — *Religious Leader*
%Evangelical Lutheran Church, PO Box 4900, Rochester, MN 55903, USA

Larson, Charles R (Chuck) — *Navy Admiral*
Commander, US Pacific Command, Box 64028, Camp H M Smith, HI 96861, USA

Larson, Eric — *Publisher*
%TV Guide Magazine, 100 Matsonford Rd, Radnor, PA 19080, USA

Larson, Gary — *Cartoonist (Far Side)*
%Universal Press Syndicate, 4900 Main St, #900, Kansas City, KS 64112, USA

Larson, Glen — *Television Producer*
351 Delfern Dr, Los Angeles, CA 90077, USA

Larson, Jack — *Actor*
449 Skyewiay Rd N, Los Angeles, CA 90049, USA

Larson, Jill — *Actress*
%St Laurent Assoc, PO Box 20191, Cherokee Station, New York, NY 10023, USA

Larson, Lance — *Swimmer*
1872 N Tustin Ave, Orange, CA 92665, USA

Larson, Nicolette — *Singer, Songwriter*
%Rick Alter Mgmt, 1114 17th Ave S, Nashville, TN 37212, USA

Larsson, Gunnar — *Swimmer*
Synalsvagen 9, 724 76 Vasteras, Sweden

LaRue, Florence — *Actress, Singer (The Fifth Dimension)*
%Sterling/Winters Co, 1900 Ave of Stars, #739, Los Angeles, CA 90067, USA

LaRussa, Anthony (Tony), Jr — *Baseball Manager*
%Oakland Athletics, Oakland Coliseum, Oakland, CA 94621, USA

Lary, Yale — *Football Player*
9366 Lansdale Rd, Fort Worth, TX 76116, USA

LaSalle, Denise — *Singer*
%Ordena Ents, 210 E Main St, #B, Jackson, TN 38301, USA

Lasdun, Denys L — *Architect*
146 Grosvenor Rd, London SW1V 3JY, England

Lash, Bill — *Skier*
PO Box 509, Sun Valley, ID 83353, USA

Lasorda, Thomas C (Tommy) — *Baseball Manager*
1473 W Maxzim Ave, Fullerton, CA 92633, USA

Lassally, Walter — *Cinematographer*
The Abbey, Eye, Suffolk, England

Lassaw, Ibram — *Sculptor*
PO Box 487, East Hampton, NY 11937, USA

Lasser, Lawrence J — *Financier*
%Putnam Investments, 1 Post Office Square, Boston, MA 02109, USA

Lasser, Louise — *Actress, Comedienne*
200 E 71st St, #20-C, New York, NY 10021, USA

Lassiter, Phillip B — *Businessman*
%Ambac, 1 State Street Plaza, New York, NY 10004, USA

Lasswell, Fred — *Cartoonist (Barney Google)*
1111 N Westshore Blvd, #604, Tampa, FL 33607, USA

Laster, Danny B — *Animal Research Scientist*
%Hruska Meat Animal Research Center, PO Box 166, Clay Center, NE 68933, USA

Laster, Ralph W, Jr — *Businessman*
%AmVestors Financial Corp, 415 SW 8th Ave, Topeka, KS 66603, USA

Lastinger, Allen L, Jr — *Financier*
%Barnett Banks, 50 N Laura St, Jacksonville, FL 32202, USA

Laszlo, Andrew — *Cinematographer*
%Smith/Gosnell, 1515 Palisades Dr, #N, Pacific Palisades, CA 90272, USA

Latham, Louise — *Actress*
%Badgley Connor, 9229 Sunset Blvd, #311, Los Angeles, CA 90069, USA

Lathiere, Bernard — *Businessman*
%Airbus-Industrie, 5 Ave de Villiers, 75017 Paris, France

Lathon, Lamar — *Football Player*
%Houston Oilers, 6910 Fannin St, Houston, TX 77030, USA

Lathrop, Philip — *Cinematographer*
PO Box 1166, Pacific Palisades, CA 90272, USA

Latiolais, Rene L — *Businessman*
%Freeport-McMoRan Inc, 1615 Poydras St, New Orleans, LA 70112, USA

LaTorre, L Donald — *Businessman*
%Engelhard Corp, 101 Wood Ave, Iselin, NJ 08830, USA

Lattner, Johnny — *Football Player*
933 Wenonah Ave S, Oak Park, IL 60304, USA

Latzer, Richard N — *Financier*
%Transamerica Investment Services, 1150 S Olive St, Los Angeles, CA 90015, USA

Laub, Larry — *Bowler*
%Professional Bowlers Assn, 1720 Merriman Rd, Akron, OH 44313, USA

Lauda, Andreas-Nikolaus (Niki) — *Auto Racing Driver*
5322 Hof/Salzburg, Austria

Lauder, Estee — *Businesswoman*
%Estee Lauder Inc, 767 5th Ave, New York, NY 10153, USA

Lauder, Leonard A — *Businessman*
%Estee Lauder Inc, 767 5th Ave, New York, NY 10153, USA

Lauder, Ronald S — *Diplomat*
767 5th Ave, #4200, New York, NY 10153, USA

Lauer, Andrew — *Actor*
%Gersh Agency, 232 N Canon Dr, Beverly Hills, CA 90210, USA

Lauer, Martin — *Track Athlete*
Hardstr 41, 77886 Lauf, Germany

Lauer, Matt — *Commentator*
%"Today" Show, NBC-TV, 30 Rockefeller Plaza, New York, NY 10112, USA

Lauer, Tod R — *Astronomer*
6471 N Tierra de Las Catalina, Tucson, AZ 85718, USA

Laufgraben, Allan — *Businessman*
%Petrie Retail Inc, 70 Enterprise Ave, Secaucus, NJ 07094, USA

Laughlin, James — *Publisher*
Meadow House, Mountain Rd, Norfolk, CT 06058, USA

Laughlin, John — *Actor*
%Laughlin Enterprises, 13116 Albers, Van Nuys, CA 91401, USA

Laughlin, Tom — *Actor*
PO Box 25355, Los Angeles, CA 90025, USA

Lauper, Cyndi — *Singer, Songwriter*
%Gold Mountain Ent, 3575 Cahuenga Blvd W, #450, Los Angeles, CA 90068, USA

Laurance, Matthew — *Actor*
1951 Hillcrest Rd, Los Angeles, CA 90068, USA

Laurel, Salvador H — *Prime Minister, Philippines*
Partido Nacionalista Ng Philipinas, Manila, Philippines

Lauren, Ralph — *Fashion Designer*
1107 5th Ave, New York, NY 10128, USA

Lauren, Tammy — *Actress*
%William Morris Agency, 151 S El Camino Dr, Beverly Hills, CA 90212, USA

Laurens, Andre — *Editor*
%Le Monde, Editorial Dept, 15 Rue Falguiere, 75015 Paris, France

Laurents, Arthur — *Playwright*
PO Box 582, Quoque, NY 11959, USA

Lauria, Dan — *Actor*
601 N Cherokee Ave, Los Angeles, CA 90004, USA

Lauricella, Francis (Hank) — *Football Player*
%Lauricella Land Co, 900 Commerce Rd E, #100, Harahan, LA 70123, USA

Laurie, Hugh — *Comedian*
%Lorraine Hamilton Mgmt, 19 Denmark St, London WC2H 8NA, England

Laurie, Piper — *Actress*
2210 Wilshire Blvd, #931, Santa Monica, CA 90403, USA

Lauristin, Marju — *Prime Minister, Estonia*
Toompuiestee 12, Tallinn, Estonia

Lauritzen, Bruce R — *Financier*
%First National of Nebraska, 1 First National Plaza, Omaha, NE 68102, USA

Lauritzen, John R — *Financier*
%First National of Nebraska, 1 First National Plaza, Omaha, NE 68102, USA

Lauter, Ed — *Actor*
270 N Canon Dr, #PH, Beverly Hills, CA 90210, USA

Lauterbur, Paul C — *Chemist*
%University of Illinois, Chemistry Dept, Urbana, IL 61801, USA

Lautner, Georges C — *Movie Director*
1 Blvd Richard-Wallace, 92200 Neuilly-Sur-Seine, France

Lave, Lester B — *Economist*
1008 Devonshire Rd, Pittsburgh, PA 15213, USA

Laveikin, Aleksandr I — *Cosmonaut*
%Potchta Kosmonavtov, 141 160 Svyosdny Gorodok, Moskovskoi Oblasti, Russia

Lavelli, Dante — *Football Player*
12555 Lake Ave, Lakewood, OH 44107, USA

Lavelli, Tony — *Basketball Player*
37 Spring St, Somerville, MA 02143, USA

Laventhol, David A — *Publisher*
%Los Angeles Times, Times Mirror Square, Los Angeles, CA 90053, USA

Laventhol, Henry L (Hank) — *Artist*
805 Hanover St, Yorktown Heights, NY 10598, USA

Laver, Rodney G (Rod) — *Tennis Player*
PO Box 4798, Hilton Head, SC 29938, USA

Lavery, Sean — *Ballet Dancer*
%New York City Ballet, Lincoln Center Plaza, New York, NY 10023, USA

Lavi, Daliah — *Actress*
2000 S Bayshore Dr, #26, Miami, FL 33133, USA

Lavin, Bernice E — *Businesswoman*
%Alberto-Culver Co, 2525 Armitage Ave, Melrose Park, IL 60160, USA

Lavin, Leonard H — *Businessman*
%Alberto-Culver Co, 2525 Armitage Ave, Melrose Park, IL 60160, USA

Lavin, Linda — *Actress*
20781 Big Rock Rd, Malibu, CA 90265, USA

Lavin, Mary — *Writer*
5 Gilford Pines, Gilford Rd, Sandymount, Dublin 4, Ireland

Law, Bernard F Cardinal — *Religious Leader*
%Archdiocese of Boston, 2121 Commonwealth Ave, Brighton, MA 02135, USA

Law, John Phillip — *Actor*
1339 Miller Dr, Los Angeles, CA 90069, USA

Law, Vernon S — *Baseball Player*
1718 N 1050 West, Provo, UT 84604, USA

Lawless, Robert W — *Educator*
%Texas Tech University, President's Office, Lubbock, TX 79409, USA

Lawley, William R, Jr — *WW II Army Air Corps Hero (CMH)*
3547 Dalraida Court, Montgomery, AL 36109, USA

Lawn, John C — *Law Enforcement Official*
%New York Yankees, Yankee Stadium, 161st St & River Ave, Bronx, NY 10451, USA

Lawrence, Andrea Meade — *Skier*
PO Box 43, Mammoth Lakes, CA 93546, USA

Lawrence, Carol — *Actress, Singer*
12337 Ridge Circle, Los Angeles, CA 90049, USA

Lawrence, David, Jr — *Publisher*
%Miami Herald, 1 Herald Plaza, Miami, FL 33132, USA

Lawrence, Francis L — *Educator*
%Rutgers University, President's Office, New Brunswick, NJ 08903, USA

Lawrence, Henry — *Football Player*
6330 Green Valley Circle, #307, Culver City, CA 90230, USA

Lawrence, Henry S — *Physician, Immunologist*
343 E 30th St, New York, NY 10016, USA

Lawrence, Jacob — *Artist*
4316 37th Ave NE, Seattle, WA 98105, USA

Lawrence, Jerome — *Playwright*
21506 Las Flores Mesa Dr, Malibu, CA 90265, USA

Lawrence, Joey — *Actor*
846 N Cahuenga Blvd, Los Angeles, CA 90038, USA

Lawrence, Marc — *Actor*
2200 N Vista Grande Ave, Palm Springs, CA 92262, USA

Lawrence, Martin — *Comedian*
%United Talent Agency, 9560 Wilshire Blvd, #500, Beverly Hills, CA 90212, USA

Lawrence, Robert S — *Physician*
15 W 72nd St, #37-G, New York, NY 10023, USA

L

Lauter - Lawrence

Lawrence, Sharon — *Actress*
2144 Beech Knoll Dr, West Hollywood, CA 90046, USA

Lawrence, Steve — *Singer*
820 Greenway Dr, Beverly Hills, CA 90210, USA

Lawrence, Tracy — *Singer, Songwriter*
%Music Matters Mgmt, 1100 17th Ave S, Nashville, TN 37212, USA

Lawrence, Vicki — *Actress, Singer*
6000 Lido Ave, Long Beach, CA 90803, USA

Lawrence, Wendy B — *Astronaut*
%NASA, Johnson Space Center, 2101 NASA Rd, Houston, TX 77058, USA

Lawson of Blaby, Nigel — *Government Official, England*
32 Sutherland Walk, London SE17, England

Lawson, A Lowell — *Businessman*
%E-Systems Inc, 6250 LBJ Freeway, Dallas, TX 75266, USA

Lawson, Richard — *Actor*
4279 Clybourn Ave, Toluca Lake, CA 91602, USA

Lawson, Richard L — *Air Force General*
6910 Clifton Rd, Clifton, VA 22024, USA

Lawwill, Theodore — *Ophthalmologist*
PO Box 8741, Prairie Village, KS 66208, USA

Lax, Melvin — *Physicist*
12 High St, Summit, NJ 07901, USA

Lax, Peter D — *Mathematician*
%New York University, Courant Mathematics Institute, New York, NY 10012, USA

Laxalt, Paul — *Governor/Senator, NV*
%Laxalt Washington Willard, 1455 Pennsylvania NW, #975, Washington, DC 20004, USA

Lay, Kenneth L — *Businessman*
%Enron Corp, PO Box 1188, Houston, TX 77251, USA

Layden, Francis P (Frank) — *Basketball Coach, Executive*
%Utah Jazz, 301 W South Temple, Salt Lake City, UT 84101, USA

Laye, Evelyn — *Actress*
60 Dorset House, Gloucester Place, London NW1, England

Layman, Harold E — *Businessman*
%Blount Inc, 4520 Executive Park Dr, Montgomery, AL 36116, USA

Laynie, Tamrat — *Prime Minister, Ethiopia*
%Prime Minister's Office, PO Box 1013, Addis Ababa, Ethiopia

Lazar, Laurence — *Religious Leader*
%Romanian Orthodox Episcopate, 2522 Grey Tower Rd, Jackson, MI 49201, USA

Lazarev, Alexander N — *Conductor*
%Christopher Tennant Artists, 39 Tadema Rd, #2, London SW10 0PY, England

Lazarus, Charles — *Businessman*
%Toys "R" Us Inc, 461 From Rd, Paramus, NJ 07652, USA

Lazarus, Mell — *Cartoonist (Miss Peach, Momma)*
%North America Syndicate, 235 E 45th St, New York, NY 10017, USA

Lazenby, George — *Actor*
1127 21st St, Santa Monica, CA 90403, USA

Le Beauf, Sabrina — *Actress*
917 Nowita Place, Venice, CA 90291, USA

Le Bon, Simon — *Singer, Songwriter (Duran Duran)*
25 Tewkesbury Ave, Pinner, Middx, England

Le Bon, Yasmin — *Model*
25 Tewkesbury Ave, Pinner, Middx, England

Le Brun, Christopher M — *Artist*
%Nigel Greenwood, 4 New Burlington St, London W1X 1FE, England

Le Carre (David J M Cornwell), John — *Writer*
Tregiffian, Saint Buryan, Penzance, Cornwall, England

Le Duc Anh — *President, Vietnam; Army General*
%President's Office, Hoang Hoa Tham, Hanoi, Vietnam

Le Mat, Paul — *Actor*
1100 N Alta Loma Rd, #805, West Hollywood, CA 90069, USA

Le Mesurier, John — *Actor*
56 Barron's Keep, London W14, England

Le Pelley, Guernsey — *Editorial Cartoonist*
841 Whitecap Circle, Venice, FL 34285, USA

Le Shana, David C — *Educator*
5737 Charles Circle, Lake Oswego, OR 97035, USA

Le Vier, Anthony W (Tony) — *Test Pilot*
%SAFE, 5108 Solliden Lane, La Canada, CA 91011, USA

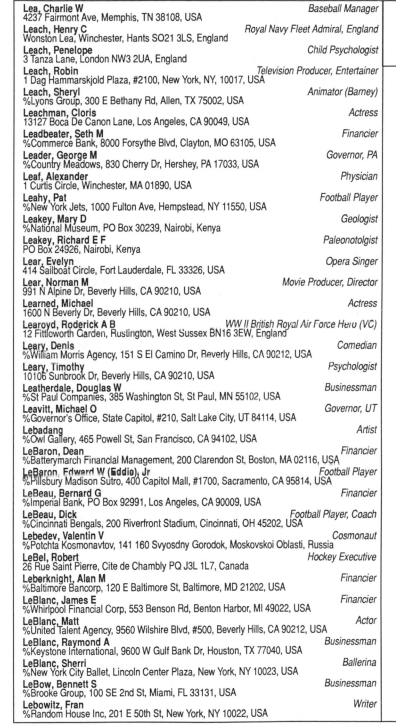

Lea, Charlie W   *Baseball Manager*
4237 Fairmont Ave, Memphis, TN 38108, USA

Leach, Henry C   *Royal Navy Fleet Admiral, England*
Wonston Lea, Winchester, Hants SO21 3LS, England

Leach, Penelope   *Child Psychologist*
3 Tanza Lane, London NW3 2UA, England

Leach, Robin   *Television Producer, Entertainer*
1 Dag Hammarskjold Plaza, #2100, New York, NY, 10017, USA

Leach, Sheryl   *Animator (Barney)*
%Lyons Group, 300 E Bethany Rd, Allen, TX 75002, USA

Leachman, Cloris   *Actress*
13127 Boca De Canon Lane, Los Angeles, CA 90049, USA

Leadbeater, Seth M   *Financier*
%Commerce Bank, 8000 Forsythe Blvd, Clayton, MO 63105, USA

Leader, George M   *Governor, PA*
%Country Meadows, 830 Cherry Dr, Hershey, PA 17033, USA

Leaf, Alexander   *Physician*
1 Curtis Circle, Winchester, MA 01890, USA

Leahy, Pat   *Football Player*
%New York Jets, 1000 Fulton Ave, Hempstead, NY 11550, USA

Leakey, Mary D   *Geologist*
%National Museum, PO Box 30239, Nairobi, Kenya

Leakey, Richard E F   *Paleonotolgist*
PO Box 24926, Nairobi, Kenya

Lear, Evelyn   *Opera Singer*
414 Sailboat Circle, Fort Lauderdale, FL 33326, USA

Lear, Norman M   *Movie Producer, Director*
991 N Alpine Dr, Beverly Hills, CA 90210, USA

Learned, Michael   *Actress*
1600 N Beverly Dr, Beverly Hills, CA 90210, USA

Learoyd, Roderick A B   *WW II British Royal Air Force Hero (VC)*
12 Fittleworth Garden, Rustington, West Sussex BN16 3EW, England

Leary, Denis   *Comedian*
%William Morris Agency, 151 S El Camino Dr, Beverly Hills, CA 90212, USA

Leary, Timothy   *Psychologist*
10106 Sunbrook Dr, Beverly Hills, CA 90210, USA

Leatherdale, Douglas W   *Businessman*
%St Paul Companies, 385 Washington St, St Paul, MN 55102, USA

Leavitt, Michael O   *Governor, UT*
%Governor's Office, State Capitol, #210, Salt Lake City, UT 84114, USA

Lebadang   *Artist*
%Owl Gallery, 465 Powell St, San Francisco, CA 94102, USA

LeBaron, Dean   *Financier*
%Batterymarch Financial Management, 200 Clarendon St, Boston, MA 02116, USA

LeBaron, Edward W (Eddie), Jr   *Football Player*
%Pillsbury Madison Sutro, 400 Capitol Mall, #1700, Sacramento, CA 95814, USA

LeBeau, Bernard G   *Financier*
%Imperial Bank, PO Box 92991, Los Angeles, CA 90009, USA

LeBeau, Dick   *Football Player, Coach*
%Cincinnati Bengals, 200 Riverfront Stadium, Cincinnati, OH 45202, USA

Lebedev, Valentin V   *Cosmonaut*
%Potchta Kosmonavtov, 141 160 Svyosdny Gorodok, Moskovskoi Oblasti, Russia

LeBel, Robert   *Hockey Executive*
26 Rue Saint Pierre, Cite de Chambly PQ J3L 1L7, Canada

Leberknight, Alan M   *Financier*
%Baltimore Bancorp, 120 E Baltimore St, Baltimore, MD 21202, USA

LeBlanc, James E   *Financier*
%Whirlpool Financial Corp, 553 Benson Rd, Benton Harbor, MI 49022, USA

LeBlanc, Matt   *Actor*
%United Talent Agency, 9560 Wilshire Blvd, #500, Beverly Hills, CA 90212, USA

LeBlanc, Raymond A   *Businessman*
%Keystone International, 9600 W Gulf Bank Dr, Houston, TX 77040, USA

LeBlanc, Sherri   *Ballerina*
%New York City Ballet, Lincoln Center Plaza, New York, NY 10023, USA

LeBow, Bennett S   *Businessman*
%Brooke Group, 100 SE 2nd St, Miami, FL 33131, USA

Lebowitz, Fran   *Writer*
%Random House Inc, 201 E 50th St, New York, NY 10022, USA

L

Lebowitz, Joel L *Mathematician*
%Rutgers University, Mathematics Dept, New Brunswick, NJ 08903, USA

Leboyer, Frederick *Physician*
%Georges Borchardt, 136 E 57th St, New York, NY 10022, USA

LeBrock, Kelly *Actress*
PO Box 727, Los Olivos, CA 93441, USA

Leburton, Edmond *Prime Minister, Belgium*
%Ministre D'Etat, 36 Clos de Hesbaye, 4300 Waremme, Belgium

LeClair, J M *Businessman*
%Grand Trunk Western Railroad, 1333 Brewery Park Blvd, Detroit, MI 48207, USA

Leconte, Henri *Tennis Player*
58 Chemin Hauts-Crets, 1223 Cologny, Switzerland

Ledbetter, Donald N *Labor Leader*
%Postal Supervisors Assn, 490 L'Enfant Plaza SW, Washington, DC 20005, USA

Leder, Philip *Geneticist*
%Harvard University Medical School, 25 Shattuck St, Boston, MA 02115, USA

Lederberg, Joshua *Nobel Medicine Laureate*
%Rockefeller University, President's Office, 1230 York Ave, New York, NY 10021, USA

Lederer, Francis *Actor*
23134 Sherman Way, Canoga Park, CA 91307, USA

Lederer, Jerome *Aerospace Engineer*
468 Calle Cadiz, #D, Laguna Beach, CA 92653, USA

Lederman, Leon M *Nobel Physics Laureate*
34 Overbrook Rd, Dobbs Ferry, NY 10522, USA

Ledford, Frank F, Jr *Army General*
%Southwest Foundation for Biomedical Research, Box 28147, San Antonio, TX 78228, USA

Ledley, Robert S *Inventor (Diagnostic X-Ray Systems)*
%Georgetown University, National Biomed Research Center, Washington, DC 20007, USA

LeDoux, Chris *Singer*
4205 Hillsboro Rd, #208, Nashville, TN 37215, USA

Ledsinger, Charles A, Jr *Businessman*
%Promus Companies, 1023 Cherry Rd, Memphis, TN 38117, USA

Lee Kuan Yew *Prime Minister, Singapore*
Senior Minister's Office, Istana Annexe, Istana, Singapore 0923, Singapore

Lee Teng-Hui *President, Taiwan*
%President's Office, Chung-King South Rd, Section 1, Taipei 100, Taiwan

Lee, Anna *Actress*
4031 Hollyline Ave, Sherman Oaks, CA 91423, USA

Lee, Bertram M *Basketball Executive*
%Denver Nuggets, McNichols Arena, 1635 Clay St, Denver, CO 80204, USA

Lee, Beverly *Singer (Shirelles)*
%Bevi Corp, PO Box 100, Clifton, NJ 07011, USA

Lee, Brenda *Singer*
%Brenda Lee Mgmt, 2174 Carson St, Nashville, TN 37211, USA

Lee, Carl *Football Player*
%New Orleans Saints, 1500 Poydras St, New Orleans, LA 70112, USA

Lee, Charles R *Businessman*
%GTE Corp, 1 Stamford Forum, Stamford, CT 06901, USA

Lee, Chester M *Space Engineer*
8540 Westown Way, Vienna, VA 22182, USA

Lee, Christopher *Actor*
5 Sandown House, Wheat Field Terrace, London W4, England

Lee, Daniel R *Businessman*
%Mirage Resorts International, 3400 Las Vegas Blvd S, Las Vegas, NV 89109, USA

Lee, David H *Astronomer, Writer*
%Plenum Publishing Group, 233 Spring St, New York, NY 10013, USA

Lee, Dorothy *Actress*
2664 Narcissus Dr, San Diego, CA 92106, USA

Lee, Geddy *Singer, Bassist (Rush)*
%SRO Mgmt, 189 Carlton St, Toronto ON M5A 2K7, Canada

Lee, Gordon (Porky) *Actor*
905 W 103rd Place, #202-D, Denver, CO 80221, USA

Lee, H Douglas *Educator*
%Stetson University, President's Office, Deland, FL 32720, USA

Lee, Howard V *Vietnam War Marine Corps Hero (CMH)*
529 King Arthur Dr, Virginia Beach, VA 23464, USA

Lee, J Bracken *Governor, UT*
PO Box 58371, Salt Lake Cty, UT 84158, USA

Lee, Jared B *Cartoonist*
%Jared B Lee Studio, 2942 Hamilton Rd, Lebanon, OH 45036, USA

Lee, Jason Scott *Actor*
%United Talent Agency, 9560 Wilshire Blvd, #500, Beverly Hills, CA 90212, USA

Lee, Joe R *Businessman*
%General Mills Inc, PO Box 1113, Minneapolis, MN 55440, USA

Lee, John J *Businessman*
%Hexcel Corp, 5794 W Las Positas Blvd, Pleasanton, CA 94588, USA

Lee, Johnny *Singer, Songwriter*
8748 Holloway Dr, Los Angeles, CA 90069, USA

Lee, Jonna *Actress*
%Dremann, 13219 Albers Place, Van Nuys, CA 91401, USA

Lee, Keith *Basketball Player*
%Orlando Magic, Orlando Arena, 1 Magic Place, Orlando, FL 32801, USA

Lee, Laurie *Poet*
9/40 Elm Park Gardens, London SW10 9NZ, England

Lee, Lawrence H *Businessman*
%Delta Air Lines, 6060 Avion Dr, Los Angeles, CA 90045, USA

Lee, Mark C *Astronaut*
%NASA, Johnson Space Center, 2101 NASA Rd, Houston, TX 77058, USA

Lee, Michelle *Actress*
830 Birchwood Dr, Los Angeles, CA 90024, USA

Lee, Peggy *Singer, Actress*
11404 Bellagio Rd, Los Angeles, CA 90049, USA

Lee, R William, Jr *Businessman*
%Oxford Industries, 222 Piedmont Ave NE, Atlanta, GA 30308, USA

Lee, Raphael C *Surgeon*
%Massachusetts Institute Technology, Engineering Dept, Cambridge, MA 02139, USA

Lee, Rex E *Educator, Government Official*
2840 Iroquois Dr, Provo, UT 84604, USA

Lee, Ruta *Actress*
2623 Laurel Canyon Rd, Los Angeles, CA 90046, USA

Lee, Sammy *Diver, Coach*
16537 Harbour Lane, Huntington Beach, CA 92649, USA

Lee, Shelton M (Spike) *Movie Director*
%Forty Acres & A Mule Filmworks, 124 DeKalb Ave, #2, Brooklyn, NY 11217, USA

Lee, Stan *Publisher, Cartoonist*
%Marvel Entertainment, 1440 S Sepulveda Blvd, #114, Los Angeles, CA 90025, USA

Lee, Thomas H *Businessman*
%Hills Stories Co, 15 Dan Rd, Canton, MA 02021, USA

Lee, Thornton S *Baseball Player*
9054 Calle Norlo E, Tucson, AZ 85710, USA

Lee, Tommy *Drummer (Motley Crue)*
31341 Mulholland Highway, Malibu, CA 90265, USA

Lee, Tsung-Dao *Nobel Physics Laureate*
25 Claremont Ave, New York, NY 10027, USA

Lee, Vernon R *Religious Leader*
%Wyatt Baptist Church, 4621 W Hillsboro St, El Dorado, AR 71730, USA

Lee, William F (Bill) *Baseball Player*
RR 1, Box 145, Craftsburg, VT 05826, USA

Lee, Yuan T *Nobel Chemistry Laureate*
%University of California, Chemistry Dept, Berkeley, CA 94720, USA

Leeds, Laurence C, Jr *Businessman*
%Manhattan Industries, 1114 Ave of Americas, New York, NY 10036, USA

Leeds, Phil *Actor*
7135 Hollywood Blvd, #102, Los Angeles, CA 90046, USA

Leek, Sybil *Self-Acclaimed Witch*
%Prentice-Hall Inc, Rt 9-W, Englewood Cliffs, NJ 7632, USA

Leese, Howard *Guitarist (Heart)*
219 1st Ave N, #333, Seattle, WA 98109, USA

Leestma, David C *Astronaut*
%NASA, Johnson Space Center, 2101 NASA Rd, Houston, TX 77058, USA

Leetch, Brian *Hockey Player*
%New York Rangers, Madison Square Garden, 4 Penn Plaza New York, NY 10001, USA

Leeves, Jane *Actress*
21724 Ventura Blvd, #212, Woodland Hills, CA 91364, USA

LeFebure, Estelle *Model*
%Elite Model Mgmt, 111 E 22nd St, #200, New York, NY 10010, USA

L

Lee - LeFebure

L

Lefebvre, James K (Jim) *Baseball Manager*
9120 N 106th Place, Scottsdale, AZ 85258, USA

LeFevre, David E *Hockey, Baseball Executive*
%Reid & Priest, 40 W 57th St, New York, NY 10019, USA

LeFrak, Richard S *Businessman*
%LeFrak Organization, 97-77 Queens Blvd, Forest Hills, NY 11374, USA

LeFrak, Samuel J *Businessman*
%LeFrak Organization, 97-77 Queens Blvd, Forest Hills, NY 11374, USA

Leggett, Reid G *Financier*
%Bowles Hollowell Conner Co, 227 W Trade St, Charlotte, NC 28202, USA

Leghari, Farooq A *President, Pakistan*
%President's Office, Awan-e-sadr, Mall Rd, Islamabad, Pakistan

Legorreta Vilchis, Ricardo *Architect*
%Palacio de Versalles, #285-A, C Lomas Reforma, Mexico City 10 DF, Mexico

Legrand, Michel *Composer*
Le Grand Moulin, 28 Rouves, France

LeGuin, Ursula K *Writer*
%Virginia Kidd, Box 278, Milford, PA 18337, USA

Lehman, Ronald F, II *Government Official*
693 Encina Grande Dr, Palo Alto, CA 94306, USA

Lehmann, Edie *Actress*
PO Box 7217, Northridge, CA 91327, USA

Lehmann, Eric L *Statistician*
2550 Dana St, Berkeley, CA 94704, USA

Lehmann, Jens *Cyclist*
Breite Str 4, 04317 Leipzig, Germany

Lehmann, Richard J *Financier*
%Banc One Corp, 100 E Broad St, Columbus, OH 43215, USA

Lehmberg, Stanford E *Historian*
2300 S Willow Lane, Minneapolis, MN 55416, USA

Lehn, Jean-Marie P *Nobel Chemistry Laureate*
21 Rue d'Oslo, 67000 Strasbourg, France

Lehninger, Albert L *Biochemist*
15020 Tanyard Rd, Sparks, MD 21152, USA

Lehrer, James C (Jim) *Commentator*
1775 Broadway, #608, New York, NY 10019, USA

Lehrer, Robert I *Molecular Biologist*
%UCLA Medical Center, Hematology & Oncology Div, Los Angeles, CA 90024, USA

Lehrer, Thomas A (Tom) *Entertainer*
%Cowell College, University of California, Santa Cruz, CA 95064, USA

Lehtinen, Dexter *Attorney, Government Official*
%US Attorney's Office, Justice Dept, 155 S Miami Ave, Miami, FL 33130, USA

Leibman, Ron *Actor*
10530 Strathmore Dr, Los Angeles, CA 90024, USA

Leibovitz, Annie *Photographer*
%Annie Leibovitz Studio, 55 Vandam St, New York, NY 10013, USA

Leibovitz, Mitchell G *Businessman*
%Pep Boys-Manny Moe & Jack, 3111 W Allegheny Ave, Philadelphia, PA 19132, USA

Leibowitz, Martin *Businessman*
%TIAA-CREF, 730 3rd Ave, New York, NY 10017, USA

Leifer, Carol *Comedienne*
1123 N Flores St, #17, Los Angeles, CA 90069, USA

Leiferkus, Sergei P *Opera Singer*
5 The Paddocks, Abberbury Rd, Iffley, Oxford OX4 4ET, England

Leigh, Janet *Actress*
1625 Summitridge Dr, Beverly Hills, CA 90210, USA

Leigh, Jennifer Jason *Actress*
%Edrick/Rich Mgmt, 2400 Whitman Place, Los Angeles, CA 90068, USA

Leigh, Mike *Movie, Theater Director*
8 Earlham Grove, London N22, England

Leigh, Mitch *Composer*
29 W 57th St, #1000, New York, NY 10019, USA

Leighton, Laura *Actress*
10350 Wilshire Blvd, #502, Los Angeles, CA 90024, USA

Leighton, Robert B *Physicist*
%California Institute of Technology, Physics Dept, Pasadena, CA 91125, USA

Leimkuehler, Paul *Amputee Skier, Businessman*
351 Darbys Run, Bay Village, OH 44140, USA

Lefebvre - Leimkuehler

Leisenring, E B, Jr *Businessman*
%Westmoreland Coal Co, Bellevue, 200 S Broad St, Philadelphia, PA 19102, USA

Leisure, David *Actor*
14071 Roblar Rd, Sherman Oaks, CA 91423, USA

Lejeune, Michael L *Government Official*
80 Conejo Rd, Santa Barbara, CA 93103, USA

Lekang, Anton *Ski Jumper*
47 Pratt St, Winsted, CT 06098, USA

Lelouch, Claude *Movie Director*
15 Ave Hoche, 75008 Paris, France

Lelyveld, Joseph *Editor*
%New York Times, Editorial Dept, 229 W 43rd St, New York, NY 10036, USA

Lem, Stanislaw *Writer*
%Franz Rottensteiner, Marchettigasse 9/17, 1060 Vienna, Austria

Lemaire, Jacques *Hockey Player, Coach*
%New Jersey Devils, Meadowlands Arena, PO Box 504, East Rutherford, NJ 07073, USA

Lembeck, Michael *Actor*
9171 Wilshire Blvd, #436, Beverly Hills, CA 90210, USA

Lemelson, Jerome H *Inventor*
48 Parkside Dr, Princeton, NJ 08540, USA

Lemieux, Claude *Hockey Player*
%Colorado Avalanche, McNichols Arena, 1635 Clay St, Denver, CO, USA

Lemieux, Joseph H *Businessman*
%Owens-Illinois Inc, 1 Sea Gate, Toledo, OH 43604, USA

Lemieux, Mario *Hockey Player*
%Pittsburgh Penguins, Civic Arena, Centre Ave, Pittsburgh, PA 15219, USA

Lemmon, Chris *Actor*
80 Murray St, South Gastonbury, CT 06073, USA

Lemmon, Jack *Actor*
%Jalem Productions, 141 S El Camino Dr, #201, Beverly Hills, CA 90212, USA

Lemon, Chet (Chester E) *Baseball Player*
4805 Highlands Place Dr, Lakeland, FL 33813, USA

Lemon, Meadowlark *Basketball Player*
%Blue Ox Talent Agency, 4130 N Goldwater Blvd, #121, Scottsdale, AZ 85251, USA

Lemon, Peter C *Vietnam War Army Hero (CMH)*
595 Saddlemountain Rd, Colorado Springs, CO 80919, USA

Lemon, Robert G (Bob) *Baseball Player, Manager*
1141 Clairborne Dr, Long Beach, CA 90807, USA

LeMond, Greg *Cyclist*
%Greg LeMond Pro Centers, 241 Ridge St, #205, Reno, NV 89501, USA

Lemons, A E (Abe) *Basketball Coach*
%Oklahoma City University, Athletic Dept, Oklahoma City, OK 73106, USA

Lemper, Ute *Singer, Dancer*
%Les Visiteurs du Soir, 21 Rue du Grand Prieure, 75011 Paris, France

Lenahan, Edward P *Publisher*
%Fortune Magazine, Rockefeller Center, New York, NY 10020, USA

Lendl, Ivan *Tennis Player*
800 North St, Greenwich, CT 06831, USA

Lenfant, Claude J M *Physician*
%National Heart Institute, 9000 Rockville Pike, Bethesda, MD 20205, USA

Lenihan, Brian J *Government Official, Ireland*
24 Park View, Castleknock, County Dublin, Ireland

Lenk, Maria *Swimmer*
Rua Cupertino Durao 16, Leblon, Rio de Janeiro 22441, Brazil

Lenk, Thomas *Sculptor*
Gemeinde Braunsbach, 7176 Schloss Tierberg, Germany

Lenkin, Melvin *Financier*
%Columbia First Bank, 1560 Wilson Blvd, Arlington, VA 22209, USA

Lennon, Julian *Singer, Songwriter*
12721 Mulholland Dr, Beverly Hills, CA 90210, USA

Lennon, Max *Educator*
%Clemson University, President's Office, Clemson, SC 29634, USA

Lennon, Sean *Singer*
%Dakota Hotel, 1 W 72nd St, New York, NY 10023, USA

Lennox, Annie *Singer (Eurythmics)*
28 Alexander St, London W2, England

Leno, Jay *Comedian*
1151 Tower Dr, Beverly Hills, CA 90210, USA

L

L

Lenoir, William B *Astronaut*
%Booz-Allen Hamilton Inc, 4330 E West Highway, Bethesda, MD 20814, USA

Lenska, Rula *Model*
306-16 Euston Rd, London NW13, England

Lenz, Kay *Actress*
%Gage Group, 9255 Sunset Blvd, #515, Los Angeles, CA 90069, USA

Lenzie, Charles A *Businessman*
%Nevada Power Co, 6226 W Sahara Ave, Las Vegas, NV 89151, USA

Lenzmeier, Allen U *Businessman*
%Best Buy Co, PO Box 9312, Minneapolis, MN 55440, USA

Leonard, Bobby *Basketball Player, Coach*
%Indiana Pacers, Market Square Arena, 300 E Market St, Indianapolis, IN 46204, USA

Leonard, Dennis P *Baseball Player*
4102 Evergreen Lane, Blue Springs, MO 64015, USA

Leonard, Elmore *Writer*
2192 Yarmouth Rd, Bloomfield Village, MI 48301, USA

Leonard, Hugh *Playwright*
Theros, Coliemore Rd, Dalkey, County Dublin, Ireland

Leonard, J Wayne *Businessman*
%CINergy Corp, 139 E 4th St, Cincinnati, OH 45202, USA

Leonard, Joanne *Photographer*
%University of Michigan, Art Dept, Ann Arbor, MI 48109, USA

Leonard, Nelson J *Chemist*
389 California Terrace, Pasadena, CA 91105, USA

Leonard, Ray C (Sugar Ray) *Boxer*
9110 Stapleford Hill Rd, Potomac, MD 20854, USA

Leonard, Richard H *Editor*
330 E Beaumont Ave, Milwaukee, WI 53217, USA

Leonard, Sheldon *Actor, Producer*
1141 Loma Vista Dr, Beverly Hills, CA 90210, USA

Leonard, Walter F (Buck) *Baseball Player*
605 Atlantic Ave, Rocky Mount, NC 27801, USA

Leone, Giovanni *Prime Minister, Italy*
%Senato, Piazzi Madama 1, 00186 Rome, Italy

Leonetti, Matthew *Cinematographer*
%Innovative Artists, 1999 Ave of Stars, #2850, Los Angeles, CA 90067, USA

Leonhart, William *Diplomat*
2618 30th St NW, Washington, DC 20008, USA

Leoni, Tea *Actress*
2054 Clifton Dr, Chicago, IL 60614, USA

Leonis, John M *Businessman*
%Litton Industries, 21240 Burbank Blvd, Woodland Hills, CA 91367, USA

Leonov, Aleksei A *Cosmonaut, Air Force General*
%Chetek Corp, Varvarka Str 15, 103 012 Moscow, Russia

Leontief, Wassily *Nobel Economics Laureate*
%New York University, Economic Analysis Institute, New York, NY 10003, USA

Leopold, Luna B *Hydraulic Engineer*
400 Vermont Ave, Berkeley, CA 94707, USA

Leppard, Raymond J *Conductor*
%Indianapolis Symphony, 45 Monument Circle, Indianapolis, IN 46204, USA

Lepping, George *Governor General, Solomon Islands*
Government House, Hoinara, Guadalcanal, Solomon Islands

Lerner, Alfred *Financier*
%MBNA Corp, 400 Christine Rd, Newark, DE 19713, USA

Lerner, Michael *Actor*
%Dale Olson Assoc, 6310 San Vicente Blvd, #340, Los Angeles, CA 90048, USA

LeRoy, Gloria *Actress*
%Gold Marshak Assoc, 3500 W Olive Ave, #1400, Burbank, CA 91505, USA

Leroy, Pierre E *Businessman*
%Deere & Co, John Deere Rd, Moline, IL 61265, USA

Leschly, Jan *Businessman*
%SmithKline Beecham Corp, 1 Franklin Plaza, Philadelphia, PA 19154, USA

Leser, Bernard H *Publisher*
%Conde Nast Publications, Conde Nast Bldg, 350 Madison Ave, New York, NY 10017, USA

Leser, Lawrence A *Businessman*
%E W Scripps Co, 312 Walnut St, Cincinnati, OH 45202, USA

Lesh, Phil *Bassist (Grateful Dead)*
PO Box 1073, San Rafael, CA 94915, USA

Lenoir - Lesh

Leslie, Bethel *Actress*
393 West End Ave, #11-C, New York, NY 10024, USA

Leslie, Joan *Actress*
2228 N Catalina St, Los Angeles, CA 90027, USA

Less, Anthony A (Tony) *Navy Admiral*
Commander, Naval Air Force Atlantic, 1729 Franklin St, Norfolk, VA 23511, USA

Lesser, Len *Actor*
934 N Evergreen St, Burbank, CA 91505, USA

Lesser, Richard L *Businessman*
%TJX Companies, 770 Cochituate Rd, Framingham, MA 01701, USA

Lessin, Robert H *Financier*
%Smith Barney Inc, 1345 Ave of Americas, New York, NY 10105, USA

Lessing, Doris M *Writer*
11 Kingscroft Rd, #3, London NW2 3QE, England

Lester, Darrell *Football Player*
3103 Meadow Oaks Dr, Temple, TX 76502, USA

Lester, Ketty *Actress, Singer*
5931 Comey Ave, Los Angeles, CA 90034, USA

Lester, Mark L *Movie Director*
17268 Camino Yatasto, Pacific Palisades, CA 90272, USA

Lester, Richard *Movie Director*
River Lane, Petersham, Surrey, England

Lester, Ronnie *Basketball Player, Executive*
%Los Angeles Lakers, Forum, PO Box 10, Inglewood, CA 90306, USA

Letlow, W R (Russ) *Football Player*
1876 Thelma Dr, San Luis Obispo, CA 93405, USA

Leto, Jared *Actor*
%Innovative Artists, 1999 Ave of Stars, #2850, Los Angeles, CA 90067, USA

Letsie III *King, Lesotho*
%Royal Palace, PO Box 524, Maseru, Lesotho

Letterman, David *Entertainer, Comedian*
%CBS-TV, Ed Sullivan Theatre, 1697 Broadway, New York, NY 10019, USA

Leutze, James R *Educator*
%University of North Carolina, Public Radio Center, Chapel Hill, NC 28403, USA

Leva, James R *Businessman*
%General Public Utilities, 100 Interspace Parkway, Parsippany, NJ 07054, USA

LeVan, David M *Businessman*
%Conrail Inc, 2001 Market St, Philadelphia, PA 19103, USA

Levato, Joseph A *Businessman*
%Triarc Companies, 900 3rd Ave, New York, NY 10022, USA

LeVay, Simon *Neuroscientist*
970 Palm Ave, West Hollywood, CA 90069, USA

Level, Leon J *Businessman*
%Computer Sciences Corp, 2100 E Grand Ave, El Segundo, CA 90245, USA

Levenson, Harvey S *Businessman*
%Kamen Corp, 1332 Blue Hills Ave, Bloomfield, CT 06002, USA

Leventhal, Bernard A *Businessman*
%Burlington Industries, PO Box 21207, Greensboro, NC 27420, USA

Leventhal, Kathy Neisloss *Publisher*
%Vanity Fair Magazine, Conde Nast Building, 350 Madison Ave, New York, NY 10017, USA

Levertow, Denise *Poet*
%New Directions Publishers, 80 8th Ave, New York, NY 10011, USA

Levi, Edward H *Attorney General*
4950 Chicago Beach Dr, Chicago, IL 60615, USA

Levi-Montalcini, Rita *Nobel Medicine Laureate*
%Cell Biology Institute, Piazzale Aldo Moro 7, 00185 Rome, Italy

Levi-Strauss, Claude *Anthropologist*
2 Rue Des Marronniers, 75016 Paris, France

Levin, Gerald M *Publisher*
%Time Warner Inc, 75 Rockefeller Plaza, New York, NY 10019, USA

Levin, Ira *Writer*
%Harry Ober Agency, 425 Madison Ave, New York, NY 10017, USA

Levin, Richard E *Educator*
%Yale University, President's Office, New Haven, CT 06520, USA

Levin, Robert J *Businessman*
65 Grove St, #343, Wellesley, MA 02181, USA

Levin, Wilbur A *Financier*
%Independence Savings Bank, 195 Montague St, Brooklyn, NY 11201, USA

L

Leslie - Levin

Levine, David — Artist
161 Henry St, Brooklyn, NY 11201, USA

Levine, Ellen R — Editor
%Good Housekeeping Magazine, 959 8th Ave, New York, NY 10019, USA

Levine, Irving R — Commentator
%NBC-TV, News Dept, 4001 Nebraska Ave NW, Washington, DC 20016, USA

Levine, Jack — Artist
68 Morton St, New York, NY 10014, USA

Levine, James — Conductor
%Metropolitan Opera Assn, Lincoln Center Plaza, New York, NY 10023, USA

Levine, Leon — Businessman
%Family Dollar Stores, 10401 Old Monroe Rd, Charlotte, NC 28201, USA

Levine, Philip — Poet
4549 N Van Ness Blvd, Fresno, CA 93704, USA

Levine, Rachmiel — Endocrinologist
2024 Canyon Rd, Arcadia, CA 91006, USA

Levine, S Robert — Businessman
%Cabletron Systems, 35 Industrial Way, Rochester, NH 03867, USA

Levine, Seymour — Psychobiologist
927 Valdez Place, Stanford, CA 94305, USA

Levine, Sol — Sociologist
30 Powell St, Brookline, MA 02146, USA

Levine, Ted — Actor
%Innovative Artists, 1999 Ave of Stars, #2850, Los Angeles, CA 90067, USA

Levingston, Cliff — Basketball Player
%Denver Nuggets, McNichols Arena, 1635 Clay St, Denver, CO 80204, USA

Levingstone, Ken — Government Official, England
%House of Commons, Westminster, London SW1A 0AA, England

Levinson, Barry — Movie Director
%Creative Artists Agency, 9830 Wilshire Blvd, Beverly Hills, CA 90212, USA

Levinthal, Cyrus — Biologist
%Columbia University, Biological Sciences Dept, New York, NY 10027, USA

Levitin, Lloyd A — Businessman
%Pacific Enterprises, 633 W 5th St, Los Angeles, CA 90071, USA

Levitow, John L — Vietnam War Air Force Hero (CMH)
148 Old Farm Rd, South Windsor, CT 06074, USA

Levy, Bernard-Henri — Philosopher
%Editions Bernans Grasset, 61 Rue des Saints-Penes, 75006 Paris, France

Levy, David — Government Official, Israel
%New Way Party, Knesset, Jerusalem, Israel

Levy, David — Astronomer
%Mt Palomar Observatory, Palomar Mounain, Mt Palomar, CA 92060, USA

Levy, Irvin L — Businessman
%NCH Corp, 2727 Chemsearch Blvd, Irving, TX 75062, USA

Levy, Joseph W — Businessman
%Gottschalks Inc, 7 River Park Place E, Fresno, CA 93720, USA

Levy, Leon — Financier
%Odyssey Partners, 31 W 52nd St, New York, NY 10019, USA

Levy, Leonard W — Historian
1025 Timberline Terrace, Ashland, OR 97520, USA

Levy, Lester A — Businessman
%NCH Corp, 2727 Chemsearch Blvd, Irving, TX 75062, USA

Levy, Marvin D (Marv) — Football Coach
%Buffalo Bills, 1 Bills Dr, Orchard Park, NY 14127, USA

Levy, Michael R — Publisher
%Texas Monthly Magazine, PO Box 1569, Austin, TX 78767, USA

Levy, Paul — Editor
2014 7th Court S, Lake Worth, FL 33461, USA

Levy, Robert I — Physician
%Wyeth-Ayest Laboratories, PO Box 8299, Philadelphia, PA 19101, USA

Lewent, Judy C — Businesswoman
%Merck & Co, 1 Merck Dr, Whitehouse Station, NJ 08889, USA

Lewin of Greenwich, Terence T — Royal Navy Fleet Admiral, England
%House of Lords, Westminster, London SW1A 0PW, England

LeWinter, Nancy Nadler — Publisher
%Esquire Magazine, 250 W 55th St, New York, NY 10019, USA

Lewis (Christianni Brand), Mary — Writer
88 Maida Vale, London W9, England

L

Levine - Lewis (Christianni Brand)

Lewis, Al *Actor*
PO Box 277, New York, NY 10044, USA

Lewis, Albert *Football Player*
%Oakland Raiders, Oakland Coliseum, Oakland, CA 94621, USA

Lewis, Alex *Financier*
%State Employees' Credit Union, PO Box 27665, Raleigh, NC 27611, USA

Lewis, Allen *Government Official, Saint Lucia*
Beaver Lodge, The Morn, PO Box 1076, Castries, Saint Lucia, West Indies

Lewis, Andrew L (Drew), Jr *Secretary, Transportation; Businessman*
%Union Pacific Corp, Martin Tower, 8th & Eaton Aves, Bethlehem, PA 18018, USA

Lewis, Anthony *Columnist*
%New York Times, Editorial Dept, 2 Faneuil Hall, Boston, MA 02109, USA

Lewis, Bernard *Historian*
%Princeton University, Near Eastern Studies Dept, Princeton, NJ 08544, USA

Lewis, Bill *Football Coach*
%Georgia Institute of Technology, Athletic Dept, Atlanta, GA 30332, USA

Lewis, Carl *Track Athlete*
PO Box 571990, Houston, TX 77257, USA

Lewis, Charles E *Physician*
221 Burlingame Ave, Los Angeles, CA 90049, USA

Lewis, Charlotte *Actress*
%Metropolitan Talent Agency, 4526 Wilshire Blvd, Los Angeles, CA 90010, USA

Lewis, Clea *Actress*
%Bresler Kelly Kipperman, 15760 Ventura Blvd, #1730, Encino, CA 91436, USA

Lewis, D D *Football Player*
%PCS Sales, 2619 Forest Grove Dr, Richardson, TX 75080, USA

Lewis, David K *Philosopher*
%Princeton University, Philosophy Dept, Princeton, NJ 08544, USA

Lewis, David Levering *Writer*
%Rutgers University, History Dept, East Rutherford, NJ 08903, USA

Lewis, Dawnn *Actress*
9229 Sunset Blvd, #311, Los Angeles, CA 90069, USA

Lewis, Edward B *Nobel Medicine Laureate*
%California Institute of Technology, Biology Dept, Pasadena, CA 91125, USA

Lewis, Emmanuel *Actor*
1900 Ave of Stars, #2800, Los Angeles, CA 90067, USA

Lewis, Flora *Writer, Journalist*
%New York Times, Editorial Dept, 229 W 43rd St, New York, NY 10036, USA

Lewis, G Wade *Businessman*
%Duracell International, Berkshire Corporate Park, Bethel, CT 06801, USA

Lewis, Gary *Singer (Gary Lewis & Playboys)*
701 Balin Court, Nashville, TN 37221, USA

Lewis, Geoffrey *Actor*
6120 Shirley Ave, Tarzana, CA 91356, USA

Lewis, Henry *Conductor*
%Herbert H Breslin Inc, 119 W 57th St, New York, NY 10019, USA

Lewis, Huey *Singer*
%Hulex Corp, PO Box 819, Mill Valley, CA 94942, USA

Lewis, Jerome A *Businessman*
%Princeps Partners, 1775 Sherman St, Denver, CO 80203, USA

Lewis, Jerry *Comedian*
1701 Waldman Ave, Las Vegas, NV 89102, USA

Lewis, Jerry Lee *Singer*
Lewis Farms, Nesbit, MS 38651, USA

Lewis, John *Jazz Pianist, Composer*
%Ted Kurland Assoc, 173 Brighton Ave, Boston, MA 02134, USA

Lewis, John C, Jr *Businessman*
%Amdahl Corp, 1250 E Arques Ave, Sunnyvale, CA 94086, USA

Lewis, John D *Financier*
%Comerica Inc, 500 Woodward Ave, Detroit, MI 48226, USA

Lewis, Juliette *Actress*
4128 Whitsett Ave, #202, Studio City, CA 91604, USA

Lewis, Kenneth D *Financier*
%NationsBank Corp, NationsBank Plaza, Charlotte, NC 28255, USA

Lewis, Lennox *Boxer*
%Champion Enterprises, 84 Greens Lanes, London N16 9EJ, England

Lewis, Marilyn W *Businessman*
%American Water Works Co, 1025 Laurel Oak Rd, Voorhees, NJ 08043, USA

L

Lewis - Lewis

L

Lewis, Monica — *Singer*
%Lang, 606 Mountain Rd, Beverly Hills, CA 90210, USA

Lewis, Peter B — *Businessman*
%Progressive Corp, 6300 Wilson Mills Rd, Mayfield Village, OH 44143, USA

Lewis, Ramsey — *Jazz Pianist, Composer*
%Joyce Agency, 370 Harrison Ave, Harrison, NY 10528, USA

Lewis, Richard — *Comedian*
8001 Hemet Place, Los Angeles, CA 90046, USA

Lewis, Robert — *Writer*
%Stein & Day, 122 E 42nd St, New York, NY 10168, USA

Lewis, Russell T — *Publisher*
%New York Times, 229 W 43rd St, New York, NY 10036, USA

Lewis, Samuel W — *Diplomat*
%US Institute for Peace, 4701 Willard Ave, #1216, Bethesda, MD 20815, USA

Lewis, Shari — *Ventriloquist, Puppeteer*
603 N Alta Dr, Beverly Hills, CA 90210, USA

Lewis, Thyme — *Actor*
%"Days of Our Lives" Show, NBC-TV, 3000 W Alameda Ave, Burbank, CA 91523, USA

Lewit-Nirenberg, Julie — *Publisher*
%Mademoiselle Magazine, 350 Madison Ave, New York, NY 10017, USA

Lewitt, Sol — *Artist*
20 Pratt St, Chester, CT 06412, USA

Lewitzky, Bella — *Dancer, Choreographer*
%Lewitzky Dance Co, 1055 Wilshire Blvd, #1140, Los Angeles, CA 90017, USA

Ley, Rick — *Hockey Coach*
%Vancouver Canucks, 100 N Renfrew St, Vancouver BC V5K 3N7, Canada

Leygue, Louis Georges — *Sculptor*
6 Rue de Docteur Blanche, 75016 Paris, France

Leyland, James R (Jim) — *Baseball Manager*
30 Midway Rd, Pittsburgh, PA 15216, USA

Leyton, John — *Actor*
53 Keyes House, Dolphin Square, London SW1V 3NA, England

Leyva, Nicholas T (Nick) — *Baseball Manager*
1098 Tilghman Rd, Wayne, PA 19087, USA

Li Ka-Shing — *Businessman*
%Hutchison Whampoa Ltd, Hutchison House, 10 Harvard Rd, Hong Kong

Li Peng — *Premier, China*
%Communist Central Committee, Zhonganahai, Beijing, China

Li, Choh H — *Biochemist*
901 Arlington Ave, Berkeley, CA 94707, USA

Liacouras, Peter J — *Educator*
%Temple University, President's Office, Philadelphia, PA 19122, USA

Liaklev, Reidar — *Speed Skater*
2770 Jaren, Norway

Liberati, Anthony W — *Businessman*
%Edward J DeBartolo Corp, 7620 Market St, Youngstown, OH 44512, USA

Liberman, Alexander — *Editor, Artist*
%Conde Nast Publications, 350 Madison Ave, New York, NY 10017, USA

Libertini, Richard — *Actor*
2313 McKinley Ave, Venice, CA 90291, USA

Lichfield, Earl of (T Patrick J A) — *Photographer*
133 Oxford Gardens, London 10 6NE, England

Lichtenberg, Byron K — *Astronaut*
%Omega Aerospace Inc, 728 Wolfsnare Crescent, Virginia Beach, VA 23454, USA

Lichtenberger, H William — *Businessman*
%Praxair Inc, 39 Old Ridgebury Rd, Danbury, CT 06817, USA

Lichtenstein, Harvey — *Musical Director*
%Brooklyn Academy of Music, 30 Lafayette Ave, Brooklyn, NY 11217, USA

Lichtenstein, Roy — *Artist*
PO Box 1369, Southampton, NY 11969, USA

Lichti, Todd — *Basketball Player*
%Orlando Magic, Orlando Arena, 1 Magic Place, Orlando, FL 32801, USA

Liddy, G Gordon — *Watergate Figure*
9909 E Joshua Tree Lane, #E, Scottsdale, AZ 85253, USA

Liddy, Richard A — *Businessman*
%General American Life Insurance Co, 700 Market St, St Louis, MO 63101, USA

Lidov, Arthur — *Artist*
Pleasant Ridge Rd, Poughquag, NY 12570, USA

Lewis - Lidov

Lidow, Eric — *Businessman*
%International Rectifier Corp, 233 Kansas St, El Segundo, CA 90245, USA

Lieber, Larry — *Cartoonist (Amazing Spider-Man)*
%Marvel Comics Group, 387 Park Ave S, New York, NY 10016, USA

Lieberman, Myron — *Educator*
4600 Connecticut Ave NW, #823, Washington, DC 20008, USA

Lieberman, Seymour — *Biochemist*
%St Luke's-Roosevelt Health Science Institute, 432 W 58th St, New York, NY 10019, USA

Lieberman, William S — *Museum Curator*
%Metropolitan Museum of Art, 5th Ave & 82nd St, New York, NY 10028, USA

Liebeskind, John — *Brain Surgeon, Psychologist*
%University of California Medical Center, Surgery Dept, Los Angeles, CA 90024, USA

Liebowitz, Leo — *Businessman*
%Getty Petroleum Corp, 125 Jericho Turnpike, Jericho, NY 11753, USA

Liefeld, Rob — *Cartoonist (Youngblood)*
%Image Comics, PO Box 25468, Anaheim, CA 92825, USA

Lien Chan — *Prime Minister, Taiwan*
%Prime Minister's Office, 1 Chunghsiano East Rd, Section 1, Taipei, Taiwan

Liepa, Adris — *Ballet Dancer*
%Kirov Ballet Theatre, 1 Ploshchad Iskusstr, St Petersburg, Russia

Lietzke, Bruce — *Golfer*
%Professional Golfer's Assn, PO Box 109601, Palm Beach Gardens, FL 33410, USA

Lifeson, Alex — *Guitarist (Rush)*
%SRO Mgmt, 189 Carlton St, Toronto ON M5A 2K7, Canada

Lifford, Tina — *Actress*
301 N Canon Dr, #305, Beverly Hills, CA 90210, USA

Lifvendahl, Harold R — *Publisher*
%Orlando Sentinel, 633 N Orange Ave, Orlando, FL 32801, USA

Ligeti, Gyorgy — *Composer*
Himmelhofgasse 34, 1130 Vienna, Austria

Light, Judith — *Actress*
2930 Beverly Glen Circle, #30, Los Angeles, CA 90077, USA

Light, Murray B — *Editor*
%Buffalo News, Editorial Dept, 1 News Plaza, Buffalo, NY 14203, USA

Lightfoot, Gordon — *Singer, Songwriter*
1365 Yonge St, #207, Toronto ON M4T 2P7, Canada

Lightner, Candy — *Social Activist*
%Berman Co, 607 14th St NW, Washington, DC 20005, USA

Lightstone, Steve — *Businessman*
%Payless Cashways Inc, 2301 Main, Kansas City, MO 64108, USA

Liguori, Frank N — *Businessman*
%Olsten Corp, 175 Broad Hollow Rd, Melville, NY 11747, USA

Likens, Gene E — *Ecologist*
%Ecosystem Studies Institute, New Botanical Gardens, Box AB, Millbrook, NY 12545, USA

Likins, Peter W — *Educator*
%Lehigh University, President's Office, Bethlehem, PA 18015, USA

Lilic, Zoran — *President, Yugoslavia*
%President's Office, Bul Lenjina 2, 11 070 Novi Belgrade, Yugoslavia

Lilienfeld, Abraham M — *Epidemiologist*
3203 Old Post Dr, Pikesville, MD 21208, USA

Lill, John R — *Concert Pianist*
%Harold Holt Ltd, 31 Sinclair Rd, London W14 0NS, England

Lillee, Dennis K — *Cricketer*
%WACA Ground, Nelson Crescent, East Perth 6000 WA, Australia

Lillehei, C Walton — *Surgeon*
73 Otis Lane, St Paul, MN 55104, USA

Lilley, James R — *Diplomat*
7301 Maple Ave, Bethesda, MD 20815, USA

Lillie, John M — *Businessman*
%American President Companies, 1111 Broadway, Oakland, CA 94607, USA

Lilly, Frank — *Geneticist*
%Albert Einstein Medical College, Yeshiva University, Bronx, NY 10461, USA

Lilly, John C — *Dolphin Researcher*
%Human/Dolphin Foundation, 11930 Oceanaire Lane, Malibu, CA 90265, USA

Lilly, Robert L (Bob) — *Football Player*
120 Fawn Trail, Graham, TX 76450, USA

Lima, Luis — *Opera Singer*
1950 Redondela Dr, Rancho Palos Verdes, CA 90275, USA

L

Lidow - Lima

L

Liman, Arthur L — *Attorney*
%Paul Weiss Rifkin Wharton Garrison, 1285 Ave of Americas, New York, NY 10019, USA

Limbaugh, Rush — *Entertainer*
124 W 60th St, #47-H, New York, NY 10023, USA

Lime, Yvonne — *Actress*
16071 Royal Oak Rd, Encino, CA 91436, USA

Lin Ching-Hsia — *Actress*
%Taiwan Cinema-Drama Assn, 196 Chunghua Rd, 10/F, Sec 1 Taipei, Taiwan

Lin, Bridget — *Actress*
8 Fei Ngo Shan Rd, Kowloon, Hong Kong

Lin, Chia-Chiao — *Applied Mathematician*
%Massachusetts Institute of Technology, Mathematics Dept, Cambridge, MA 02139, USA

Lin, Cho-Liang — *Concert Violinist*
1 Sherman Square, #28-K, New York, NY 10023, USA

Lin, Maya Ying — *Sculpturess, Achitect*
%Sidney Janis Gallery, 110 W 57th St, New York, NY 10019, USA

Lin, Tsung-Yi — *Psychiatrist*
6287 MacDonald St, Vancouver BC V6N 1E7, Canada

Lin, Tung Yen — *Civil Engineer*
8701 Don Carol Dr, El Cerrito, CA 94530, USA

Linander, Nils — *Businessman*
%Saab-Scania, 581 88 Linkoping, Sweden

Lincoln, Abbey — *Singer*
645 West End Ave, New York, NY 10025, USA

Lincoln, Keith P — *Football Player*
SE 770 Ridgeview Court, Pullman, WA 99163, USA

Lind, Don L — *Astronaut*
%Utah State University, Physics Dept, Logan, UT 84322, USA

Lind, Geoffrey E — *Financier*
%UMB Financial Corp, 1010 Grand Ave, St Louis, MO 64106, USA

Lind, Joan — *Rowing Athlete*
240 Euclid Ave, Long Beach, CA 90803, USA

Lind, Marshall L — *Educator*
%University of Alaska, Chancellor's Office, Juneau, AK 99801, USA

Lindbeck, Assar — *Economist*
50 Ostermalmsgatan, 11426 Stockholm, Swedem

Lindbergh, Anne Morrow — *Writer*
PO Box 98, St Johnsbury, VT 05819, USA

Linden, Hal — *Actor*
416 N Bristol Ave, Los Angeles, CA 90049, USA

Lindenauer, Arthur — *Businessman*
%Schlumberger Ltd, 277 Park Ave, New York, NY 10172, USA

Linder, Kate — *Actress*
9111 Wonderland Ave, Los Angeles, CA 90046, USA

Lindes, Hal — *Guitarist (Dire Straits)*
%Damage Mgmt, 10 Southwick Mews, London W2, England

Lindfors, Viveca — *Actress*
172 E 95th St, New York, NY 10128, USA

Lindgren, Astrid — *Writer*
Dalagatan 46, 113 24 Stockholm, Sweden

Lindig, Bill M — *Businessman*
%SYSCO Corp, 1390 Enclave Parkway, Houston, TX 77077, USA

Lindley, Audra — *Actress*
200 N Swall Dr, #PH-58, Beverly Hills, CA 90211, USA

Lindner, Carl H — *Businessman*
%Chiquita Brands International, 250 E 5th St, Cincinnati, OH 45202, USA

Lindner, Keith E — *Businessman*
%Chiquita Brands International, 250 E 5th St, Cincinnati, OH 45202, USA

Lindner, Philip G — *Businessman*
%Midwest Resources, 666 Grand Ave, Des Moines, IA 50309, USA

Lindner, Robert D — *Financier*
%American Financial Corp, 1 E 4th St, Cincinnati, OH 45202, USA

Lindner, William G — *Labor Leader*
%Transport Workers Union, 80 West End Ave, New York, NY 10023, USA

Lindros, Eric — *Hockey Player*
%Philadelphia Flyers, Spectrum, Pattison Place, Philadelphia, PA 19148, USA

Lindsay, Jack — *Writer*
56 Maids Causeway, Cambridge, England

Liman - Lindsay

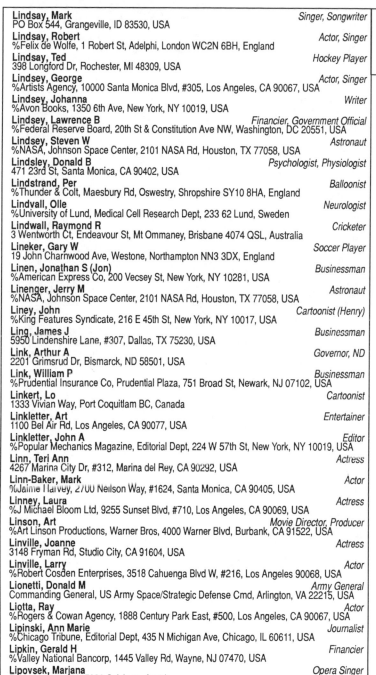

Lindsay, Mark *Singer, Songwriter*
PO Box 544, Grangeville, ID 83530, USA

Lindsay, Robert *Actor, Singer*
%Felix de Wolfe, 1 Robert St, Adelphi, London WC2N 6BH, England

Lindsay, Ted *Hockey Player*
398 Longford Dr, Rochester, MI 48309, USA

Lindsey, George *Actor, Singer*
%Artists Agency, 10000 Santa Monica Blvd, #305, Los Angeles, CA 90067, USA

Lindsey, Johanna *Writer*
%Avon Books, 1350 6th Ave, New York, NY 10019, USA

Lindsey, Lawrence B *Financier, Government Official*
%Federal Reserve Board, 20th St & Constitution Ave NW, Washington, DC 20551, USA

Lindsey, Steven W *Astronaut*
%NASA, Johnson Space Center, 2101 NASA Rd, Houston, TX 77058, USA

Lindsley, Donald B *Psychologist, Physiologist*
471 23rd St, Santa Monica, CA 90402, USA

Lindstrand, Per *Balloonist*
%Thunder & Colt, Maesbury Rd, Oswestry, Shropshire SY10 8HA, England

Lindvall, Olle *Neurologist*
%University of Lund, Medical Cell Research Dept, 233 62 Lund, Sweden

Lindwall, Raymond R *Cricketer*
3 Wentworth Ct, Endeavour St, Mt Ommaney, Brisbane 4074 QSL, Australia

Lineker, Gary W *Soccer Player*
19 John Charnwood Ave, Westone, Northampton NN3 3DX, England

Linen, Jonathan S (Jon) *Businessman*
%American Express Co, 200 Vecsey St, New York, NY 10281, USA

Linenger, Jerry M *Astronaut*
%NASA, Johnson Space Center, 2101 NASA Rd, Houston, TX 77058, USA

Liney, John *Cartoonist (Henry)*
%King Features Syndicate, 216 E 45th St, New York, NY 10017, USA

Ling, James J *Businessman*
5950 Lindenshire Lane, #307, Dallas, TX 75230, USA

Link, Arthur A *Governor, ND*
2201 Grimsrud Dr, Bismarck, ND 58501, USA

Link, William P *Businessman*
%Prudential Insurance Co, Prudential Plaza, 751 Broad St, Newark, NJ 07102, USA

Linkert, Lo *Cartoonist*
1333 Vivian Way, Port Coquitlam BC, Canada

Linkletter, Art *Entertainer*
1100 Bel Air Rd, Los Angeles, CA 90077, USA

Linkletter, John A *Editor*
%Popular Mechanics Magazine, Editorial Dept, 224 W 57th St, New York, NY 10019, USA

Linn, Teri Ann *Actress*
4267 Marina City Dr, #312, Marina del Rey, CA 90292, USA

Linn-Baker, Mark *Actor*
%Jaime Harvey, 2700 Neilson Way, #1624, Santa Monica, CA 90405, USA

Linney, Laura *Actress*
%J Michael Bloom Ltd, 9255 Sunset Blvd, #710, Los Angeles, CA 90069, USA

Linson, Art *Movie Director, Producer*
%Art Linson Productions, Warner Bros, 4000 Warner Blvd, Burbank, CA 91522, USA

Linville, Joanne *Actress*
3148 Fryman Rd, Studio City, CA 91604, USA

Linville, Larry *Actor*
%Robert Cosden Enterprises, 3518 Cahuenga Blvd W, #216, Los Angeles 90068, USA

Lionetti, Donald M *Army General*
Commanding General, US Army Space/Strategic Defense Cmd, Arlington, VA 22215, USA

Liotta, Ray *Actor*
%Rogers & Cowan Agency, 1888 Century Park East, #500, Los Angeles, CA 90067, USA

Lipinski, Ann Marie *Journalist*
%Chicago Tribune, Editorial Dept, 435 N Michigan Ave, Chicago, IL 60611, USA

Lipkin, Gerald H *Financier*
%Valley National Bancorp, 1445 Valley Rd, Wayne, NJ 07470, USA

Lipovsek, Marjana *Opera Singer*
Rottmaygrasse 16, 5020 Salzburg, Austria

Lipp, Robert I *Financier*
%Travelers Inc, 65 E 55th St, New York, NY 10022, USA

Lipper, Kenneth *Financier*
%Lipper Co, 101 Park Ave, New York, NY 10178, USA

L

Lindsay - Lipper

L

Lippold, Richard *Artist*
PO Box 248, Locust Valley, NY 11560, USA

Lipps, Louis *Football Player*
%Pittsburgh Steelers, 3 Rivers Stadium, 300 Stadium Circle, Pittsburgh, PA 15212, USA

Lipschitz, Louis *Businessman*
%Toys "R" Us Inc, 461 From Rd, Paramus, NJ 07652, USA

Lipscomb, William N, Jr *Chemist*
44 Langdon St, Cambridge, MA 02138, USA

Lipset, Seymour M *Sociologist*
900 N Stafford St, #2131, Arlington, VA 22203, USA

Lipsett, Mortimer B *Physician*
%National Institutes of Health, 9000 Rockville Pike, Bethesda, MD 20205, USA

Lipsey, Stanford *Publisher*
%Buffalo News, 1 News Plaza, Buffalo, NY 14203, USA

Lipshutz, Bruce H *Organic Chemist*
%University of California, Chemistry Dept, Santa Barbara, CA 93106, USA

Lipson, D Herbert *Publisher*
%Philadelphia Magazine, 1500 Walnut St, Philadelphia, PA 19102, USA

Lipton, Martin *Attorney*
%Wachtell Lipton Rosen Katz, 51 W 52nd St, New York, NY 10019, USA

Lipton, Peggy *Actress*
2576 Benedict Canyon Dr, Beverly Hills, CA 90210, USA

Liquori, Marty *Track Athlete, Sportscaster*
2915 NW 58th Blvd, Gainesville, FL 32606, USA

Lisi, Virna *Actress*
Via di Filomarino 4, Rome, Italy

Lissouba, Pascal *President, Congo*
%President's Office, Palace du Peuple, Brazzaville, Congo

List, Robert F *Governor, NV*
50 W Liberty St, #210, Reno, NV 89501, USA

Lister, Alton *Basketball Player*
%Golden State Warriors, Oakland Coliseum Arena, Oakland, CA 94621, USA

Listowel (William F Hare), Earl of *Government Official, England*
10 Downshire Hill, London NW3, England

Lithgow, John *Actor*
1319 Warnall Ave, Los Angeles, CA 90024, USA

Little Anthony (Gordine) *Singer*
%Evans-Schulam Productions, 11 Delmar Ct, Brigantine, NJ 08203, USA

Little Richard (Penniman) *Singer*
%Hyatt Sunset Hotel, 8401 W Sunset Blvd, Los Angeles, CA 90069, USA

Little Steven *Singer*
%Premier Talent Agency, 3 E 54th St, #1400, New York, NY 10022, USA

Little, Carole *Fashion Designer*
%Carole Little Inc, 102 E Martin Luther King Blvd, Los Angeles, CA 90011, USA

Little, Floyd D *Football Player*
31315 22nd Ave SW, Federal Way, WA 98023, USA

Little, Larry *Football Player, Coach*
5310 Lacy Rd, Durham, NC 27713, USA

Little, Rich *Comedian*
%Rich Little Enterprises, 21550 Oxnard St, #630, Woodland Hills, CA 91367, USA

Little, Robert A *Chef*
49 Firth St, London W1V 5TE, England

Little, Sally *Golfer*
%Endicott Assoc, 42-081 Beacon Hill, #A, Palm Desert, CA 92211, USA

Little, Tawny *Entertainer*
17941 Sky Park Circle, #F, Irvine, CA 92714, USA

Little, William G *Businessman*
%West Co, 101 Gordon Dr, Lionville, PA 19341, USA

Littler, Gene *Golfer*
PO Box 1919, Rancho Santa Fe, CA 92067, USA

Littles, Gene *Basketball Coach*
%Denver Nuggets, McNichols Arena, 1635 Clay St, Denver, CO 80204, USA

Littleton, Harvey *Glass Sculptor*
Rt 1, Box 843, Spruce Pine, NC 28777, USA

Litton, Andrew *Conductor*
%IMG Artists, Media House, 3 Burlington Lane, London W4 2TH, England

Littrell, Gary L *Vietnam War Army Hero (CMH)*
4302 Belle Vista Dr, St Petersburg, FL 33706, USA

Lippold - Littrell

Litwack, Harry   *Basketball Coach*
1818 Oakwynne Rd, Huntingdon Valley, PA 19006, USA

Liu, Lee   *Businessman*
%IES Industries, 200 1st St SE, Cedar Rapids, IA 52401, USA

Liut, Mike   *Hockey Player*
%Washington Capitals, USAir Arena, Landover, MD 20785, USA

Liuzzi, Robert C   *Businessman*
%CF Industries, 1 Salem Lake Dr, Long Grove, IL 60047, USA

Lively, Penelope M   *Writer*
Duck End, Great Rollright, Chipping, Northern Oxfordshire OX7 5SB, England

Livingston, Barry   *Actor*
11310 Blix St, North Hollywood, CA 91602, USA

Livingston, James E   *Vietnam Marine Corps Hero (CMH), General*
Naval Support Activity, 102 Constitution St, New Orleans, LA 70114, USA

Livingston, Stanley   *Actor*
PO Box 1782, Studio City, CA 91614, USA

Lizer, Kari   *Actress*
4249 Costello Ave, Sherman Oaks, CA 91423, USA

LL Cool J (James T Smith)   *Rapper*
%Rush Artists Mgmt, 1600 Varick St, New York, NY 10013, USA

Llewellyn, John A   *Astronaut*
4202 E Fowler Ave, Tampa, FL 33620, USA

Lloyd Webber, Andrew   *Composer*
%Really Useful Group PLC, 20 Greek St, London W1V 5LF, England

Lloyd, Christopher   *Actor*
%Managemint, PO Box 491246, Los Angeles, CA 90049, USA

Lloyd, Clive   *Cricketer*
%Harefield, Harefield Dr, Wilmslow, Cheshire SK9 1NJ, England

Lloyd, Emily   *Actress*
%Malcolm Sheddon Mgmt, 1 Charlotte Square, London W1P 1DH, England

Lloyd, George W S   *Conductor, Composer*
109 Clarence Gate Gardens, Glentworth St, London NW1 6AU, England

Lloyd, Greg   *Football Player*
%Pittsburgh Steelers, 3 Rivers Stadium, 300 Stadium Circle, Pittsburgh, PA 15212, USA

Lloyd, Kathleen   *Actress*
%Paradigm Agency, 10100 Santa Monica Blvd, #2500, Los Angeles, CA 90067, USA

Lloyd, Norman   *Actor*
1813 Old Ranch Rd, Los Angeles, CA 90049, USA

Lloyd, Robert A   *Opera Singer*
67-B Fortis Green, London SE1 9HL, England

Lloyd, Seton   *Archaeologist*
Woolstone Lodge, Faringdon, Oxon SN7 7QL, England

Lloyd-Jones, David M   *Conductor*
94 Whitelands House, Cheltenham Terrace, London SW3 4RA, England

Lo Bianco, Tony   *Actor*
327 Central Park W, #16-B, New York, NY 10025, USA

Loach, Kenneth   *Movie Director*
%Judy Daish Assoc, 83 Eastbourne Mews, London W2 6LQ, England

Lobbia, John E   *Businessman*
%Detroit Edison Co, 2000 2nd Ave, Detroit, MI 48226, USA

Lobkowicz, Nicholas   *Philosopher*
%Katholische Universitat, 85071 Eichstalt, Germany

Lobo, Rebecca   *Basketball Player*
%University of Connecticut, Athletic Dept, 211 Hillside Rd, Storrs, CT 06269, USA

Local, Ivars Godmanis   *Prime Minister, Latvia*
Brivibus Bluv 36, PDP Riga 226170, Latvia

Locane, Amy   *Actress*
%Don Buchwald Assoc, 10 E 44th St, #500, New York, NY 10017, USA

Locatelli, Paul L   *Educator*
%Santa Clara University, President's Office, Santa Clara, CA 95053, USA

Locher, Dick   *Editorial Cartoonist*
%Chicago Tribune, Editorial Dept, 435 N Michigan Ave, Chicago, IL 60611, USA

Lochhead, Kenneth C   *Artist*
35 Wilton Crescent, Ottawa ON K1S 2T4, Canada

Lochner, Philip R, Jr   *Government Official, Businessman*
%Time Warner Inc, 75 Rockefeller Plaza, New York, NY 10019, USA

Lochrie, Robert B, Jr   *Financier*
%SunBank/South Florida, 501 E Las Olas Blvd, Fort Lauderdale, FL 33301, USA

L

Litwack - Lochrie

Lockard, John A *Financier*
%Navy Federal Credit Union, PO Box 3000, Merrifield, VA 22119, USA

Locke, Sondra *Actress*
PO Box 69865, Los Angeles, CA 90069, USA

Lockhart, Anne *Actress*
191 Upper Lake Rd, Thousand Oaks, CA 91361, USA

Lockhart, Eugene *Football Player*
%New England Patriots, Foxboro Stadium, Rt 1, Foxboro, MA 02035, USA

Lockhart, James *Conductor*
105 Woodcock Hill, Harrow, Middx HA3 0JJ, England

Lockhart, June *Actress*
PO Box 260207, Encino, CA 91426, USA

Lockhart, Keith *Conductor*
%Boston Pops Orchestra, Symphony Hall, 301 Massachusetts Ave, Boston, MA 02115, USA

Lockhart, Michael D *Businessman*
%General Signal Corp, 1 High Ridge Park, Stamford, CT 06905, USA

Locklear, Heather *Actress*
4970 Summit View Dr, Westlake Village, CA 91362, USA

Lockridge, Richard K *Businessman*
%Dynatech Corp, 3 New England Executive Park, Burlington, MA 01803, USA

Lockwood, Gary *Actor*
3083 1/2 Rambla Pacifica, Malibu, CA 90265, USA

Lockwood, Julia *Actress*
112 Castlenan, London SW13, England

Loderbaum, Jeffrey S *Businessman*
%Mohawk Industries, 1755 The Exchange, Atlanta, GA 30339, USA

Loe, Harald A *Dentist*
%National Dental Research Institute, 9000 Rockville Pike, Bethesda, MD 20205, USA

Loeb, David S *Financier*
%Countrywide Credit Industries, 155 N Lake Ave, Pasadena, CA 91101, USA

Loeb, Jerome T *Businessman*
%May Department Stores, 611 Olive St, St Louis, MO 63101, USA

Loeb, John L, Jr *Financier, Diplomat*
%Loeb Partners, 375 Park Ave, #801, New York, NY 10152, USA

Loeb, Marshall R *Editor*
31 Montrose Rd, Scarsdale, NY 10583, USA

Lofgren, Nils *Singer, Guitarist, Songwriter*
%Anson Smith Mgmt, 3 Bethesda Metro Center, #505, Bethesda, MD 20814, USA

Lofton, Fred C *Religious Leader*
%Progressive National Baptist Convention, 601 50th St NE, Washington, DC 20019, USA

Lofton, James *Football Player*
931 W Pleasant Run Rd, De Soto, TX 75115, USA

Loftus, Stephen F *Navy Admiral*
Deputy CNO, Logistics, Navy Dept, Washington, DC 20350, USA

Logan, David *Football Player*
%Tampa Bay Buccaneers, 1 Buccaneer Place, Tampa, FL 33607, USA

Logan, Don *Businessman*
%Time Inc, Time-Life Building, Rockefeller Center, New York, NY 10020, USA

Logan, James M *WW II Army Hero (CMH)*
801 Emmons, Kilgore, TX 75662, USA

Logan, Johnny (John) *Baseball Player*
6115 W Cleveland Ave, Milwaukee, WI 53219, USA

Logan, Robert *Actor*
%BDP Assoc, 10637 Burbank Blvd, North Hollywood, CA 91601, USA

Logan, Steve *Football Coach*
%East Carolina University, Athletic Dept, Greenville, NC 27858, USA

Loggia, Robert *Actor*
12659 Promontory Rd, Los Angeles, CA 90049, USA

Loggins, Kenny *Singer, Songwriter*
3281 Padaro Ln, Carpinteria, CA 93013, USA

Loh, John M *Air Force General*
CinChief, Air Combat Command, 205 Dodd Blvd, Langley Air Force Base, VA 23665, USA

Lohman, Gordon R *Businessman*
%Amsted Industries, 205 N Michigan Ave, Chicago, IL 60601, USA

Lohman, James J *Businessman*
%Excel Industries, 1120 N Main St, Elkhart, IN 46514, USA

Lohrum, Fred C *Financier*
%R I Hospital Trust National Bank, Hospital Trust Plaza, Providence, RI 02903, USA

Lokoloko, Tore *Governor General, Papua New Guinea*
%Indosuez Niugine Bank, Burns House, Port Moresby, Papua New Guinea

Lolich, Michael S (Mickey) *Baseball Player*
6252 Robin Hill, Washington, MI 48094, USA

Lollobrigida, Gina *Actress*
Via Appia Antica 223, 00178 Rome, Italy

Lom, Herbert *Actor*
%International Creative Mgmt, 76 Oxford St, London W1N 0AX, England

Lomas, Eric J *Businessman*
%Willcox & Gibbs Inc, 150 Alhambra Circle, Coral Gables, FL 33134, USA

Lomax, Alan *Folk Song Collector, Producer*
450 W 41st St, #600, New York, NY 10036, USA

Lomax, Neil V *Football Player*
11510 SW Military Court, Portland, OR 97219, USA

Lombard, Karina *Model, Actress*
%William Morris Agency, 151 El Camino, Beverly Hills, CA 90212, USA

Lombard, Louise *Actress*
%Annette Stone Assoc, 9 Newburgh St, London W1V 1LH, England

Lombardi, John V *Educator*
%University of Florida, President's Office, Gainesville, FL 32611, USA

Lombardo, John M *Businessman*
%Munich American Reinsurance Co, 560 Lexington Ave, New York, NY 10022, USA

Lombreglio, Ralph *Writer*
%Doubleday Co, 1540 Broadway, New York, NY 10036, USA

Lonborg, James R (Jim) *Baseball Player*
498 First Parish Rd, Scituate, MA 02066, USA

London, Irving M *Physician*
%Harvard-MIT Health Sciences, 77 Massachusetts Ave, Cambridge, MA 02139, USA

London, Julie *Actress, Singer*
16074 Royal Oak Rd, Encino, CA 91436, USA

London, Lisa *Actress, Model*
1680 N Vine St, #203, Los Angeles, CA 90028, USA

Lone, John *Actor*
%Levine Thall Plotkin, 1740 Broadway, New York, NY 10019, USA

Long, Chuck *Football Player*
%Detroit Lions, Silverdome, 1200 Featherstone Rd, Pontiac, MI 48342, USA

Long, Dale W *Publisher*
%Working Woman Magazine, 342 Madison Ave, New York, NY 10173, USA

Long, David L *Publisher*
%Sports Illustrated Magazine, Rockefeller Center, New York, NY 10020, USA

Long, Elizabeth Valk *Publisher*
%Time Magazine, Rockefeller Center, New York, NY 10020, USA

Long, Francis A *Businessman*
%Pennsylvania Power & Light, 2 N 9th St, Allentown, PA 18101, USA

Long, Franklin A *Chemist*
050 Harrison Ave, #446, Claremont, CA 91711, USA

Long, Howie *Football Player, Sportscaster*
PO Box 210, Ivy, VA 22945, USA

Long, Joan D *Movie Producer*
La Burrage Place, Lindfield 2070 NSW, Australia

Long, R M *Businessman*
%Longs Drug Stores, 141 N Civic Dr, Walnut Creek, CA 94596, USA

Long, Richard *Artist*
Old School, Lower Failand, Bristol BS8 3SL, England

Long, Robert *Paleontologist*
%University of California, Paleontology Museum, Berkeley, CA 94720, USA

Long, Robert L J *Navy Admiral*
247 Heamans Way, Annapolis, MD 21401, USA

Long, Robert R *Financier*
%Trust Company Bank, 25 Park Place NE, Atlanta, GA 30303, USA

Long, Russell B *Senator, LA*
1455 Pennsylvania Ave NW, Washington, DC 20004, USA

Long, Sharon R *Molecular Geneticist*
%Stanford University, Biological Sciences Dept, Stanford, CA 94305, USA

Long, Shelley *Actress*
%Creative Artists Agency, 9830 Wilshire Blvd, Beverly Hills, CA 90212, USA

Longden, Johnny *Thoroughbred Racing Jockey, Trainer*
5401 Palmer Dr, Banning, CA 92220, USA

Longfield, William H *Businessman*
%C R Bard Inc, 730 Central Ave, Murray Hill, NJ 07974, USA

Longford (Francis A Pakenham), Earl of *Government Official, England*
Bernhurst, Hurst Green, East Sussex TN19 7QN, England

Longmire, William P, Jr *Physician*
10102 Empyrean Way, #8-203, Los Angeles, CA 90067, USA

Longo, Jeannie Ciprelli- *Cyclist*
9 Rue Massena, 38000 Grenoble, France

Longo, Robert *Artist*
%Longo Studio, 224 Center St, New York, NY 10013, USA

Longstreet, Stephen *Writer*
1133 Miradero Rd, Beverly Hills, CA 90210, USA

Longuet-Higgins, H Christopher *Chemist*
%Experimental Psych Lab, Sussex Univ, Falmer, Brighton BN1 9Q4, England

Lonsbrough Porter, Anita *Swimmer*
6 Rivendell Gardens, Tettendall, Wolverhampton WV6 8SY, England

Loob, Hakan *Hockey Player*
%Calgary Flames, PO Box 1540, Station "M", Calgary AB T2P 389, Canada

Loomis, Henry *Government Official*
4661 Ortega Island Dr, Jacksonville, FL 32210, USA

Looney, Donald L *Football Player*
1447 Wakefield Dr, Houston, TX 77018, USA

Looney, Ralph E *Editor*
6101 Casa De Vida Dr NE, Albuquerque, NM 87111, USA

Lopes, David E (Davey) *Baseball Player*
%Baltimore Orioles, 333 W Camden Ave, Baltimore, MD 21201, USA

Lopes-Graca, Fernando *Composer*
El Mi Paraiso, 2 Avenida da Republica, 2775 Parede, Portugal

Lopez Arellano, Oswaldo *President, Honduras; Air Force General*
Servico Aereo de Honduras, Apdo 129, Tegucigalpa DC, Honduras

Lopez Michelsen, Alfonso *President, Colombia*
%Partido Liberal, Avda Jimenez 8-56, Bogota, Colombia

Lopez Rodriguez, Nicolas de Jesus *Religious Leader*
Archdiocese of Santo Domingo, Santo Domingo, AP 186, Dominican Republic

Lopez Trujillo, Alfonso Cardinal *Religious Leader*
Arzobispado, Calle 57, N 48-28 , Medellin, Colombia

Lopez, Albert A (Al) *Baseball Player*
3601 Beach Dr, Tampa, FL 33629, USA

Lopez, Dan *Cartoonist*
77 N Ellsworth Ave, San Mateo, CA 94401, USA

Lopez, George *Comedian*
%Harvey Elkin Mgmt, 6515 Sunset Blvd, #305, Los Angeles, CA 90028, USA

Lopez, Jose M *WW II Army Hero (CMH)*
3223 Hatton Dr, San Antonio, TX 78237, USA

Lopez, Lourdes *Ballerina*
%New York City Ballet, Lincoln Center Plaza, New York, NY 10023, USA

Lopez, Nancy *Golfer*
2308 Tara Dr, Albany, GA 31707, USA

Lopez, Priscilla *Actress*
%Don Buchwald Assoc, 10 E 44th St, #500, New York, NY 10017, USA

Lopez, Robert S *Historian*
41 Richmond Ave, New Haven, CT 06515, USA

Lopez, T Joseph *Navy Admiral*
DCNO Warfare Requirements/Assessments, Navy Dept, Washington, DC 20350, USA

Lopez, Trini *Singer, Actor*
1139 Abrigo Rd, Palm Springs, CA 92262, USA

Lopez-Cobos, Jesus *Conductor*
%Terry Harrison Mgmt, 1 Clarendon Court, Charlbury, Oxon OX7 3PS, England

Lopez-Garcia, Antonio *Artist*
%Marlborough Fine Art Ltd, 6 Albermarle St, London W1, England

Loprete, Joseph F *Businessman*
%York International, 631 S Richland Ave, York, PA 17403, USA

Lorant, Stefan *Writer*
PO Box 803, Lenox, MA 01240, USA

Lord, Jack *Actor*
4999 Kahala Ave, Honolulu, HI 96816, USA

Lord, M G *Editorial Cartoonist*
%Newsday, Editorial Dept, 235 Pinelawn Rd, Melville, NY 11747, USA

Lord, Marjorie — *Actress*
1110 Maytor Place, Beverly Hills, CA 90210, USA

Lord, Michael — *Artist*
14227 71st Ave, Surrey BC V3W 2K9, Canada

Lord, Walter — *Writer*
116 E 68th St, New York, NY 10021, USA

Lord, Winston — *Diplomat*
740 Park Ave, New York, NY 10021, USA

Loren, Sophia — *Actress*
La Concordia Ranch, 1151 Hidden Valley Rd, Thousand Oaks, CA 91361, USA

Lorengar, Pilar — *Opera Singer*
19 Frankenallee 12, 14052 Berlin, Germany

Lorenz, Lee — *Cartoonist*
PO Box 131, Easton, CT 06612, USA

Lorenzoni, Andrea — *Astronaut, Italy*
Via B Vergine del Carmelo 168, 00144 Rome, Italy

Loring, Gloria — *Singer, Actress*
4125 Parva Ave, Los Angeles, CA 90027, USA

Loring, John R — *Artist*
860 5th Ave, New York, NY 10021, USA

Loring, Lynn — *Actress*
506 N Camden Dr, Beverly Hills, CA 90210, USA

Loriod, Yvonne — *Concert Pianist*
%Bureau de Concerts, 7 Rue de Richepanse, 75008 Paris, France

Lorring, Joan — *Actress*
345 E 68th St, New York, NY 10021, USA

Lorsch, George A — *Businessman*
%Armstrong World Industries, 313 W Liberty St, Lancaster, PA 17603, USA

Lorscheider, Aloisio Cardinal — *Religious Leader*
%Arquidiocese de Fortaleza, CP D-6, 60.000 Fortaleza, Ceara, Brazil

Lortel, Lucille — *Theater Producer*
%Lucille Lortel Theatre, 121 Christopher St, New York, NY 10014, USA

Lortie, Louis — *Concert Pianist*
%G Guibord, 4666 De Bullion, Montreal PQ H2T 1Y6, Canada

Losee, Thomas P, Jr — *Publisher*
PO Box 471, Cold Spring Harbor, NY 11724, USA

Losh, J Michael — *Businessman*
%General Motors Corp, 3044 W Grand Blvd, Detroit, MI 48202, USA

Lott, Felicity A — *Opera Singer*
%Lies Askonas Ltd, 186 Drury Lane, London WC2B 5RY, England

Lott, Ronnie — *Football Player*
%Kansas City Chiefs, 1 Arrowhead Dr, Kansas City, KS 64129, USA

Loucks, Vernon R, Jr — *Businessman*
%Baxter International, 1 Baxter Parkway, Deerfield, IL 60015, USA

Loudon, Dorothy — *Actress*
101 Central Park West, New York, NY 10023, USA

Loudon, Rodney — *Theoretical Physicist*
3 Gaston St, East Bergholt, Colchester, Essex CO7 6SD, England

Louganis, Greg — *Diver*
PO Box 4130, Malibu, CA 90264, USA

Loughery, Kevin — *Basketball Player, Coach, Executive*
%Miami Heat, Miami Arena, Miami, FL 33136, USA

Loughlin, Lori — *Actress, Singer*
%William Morris Agency, 151 S El Camino Dr, Beverly Hills, CA 90212, USA

Loughlin, Mary Anne — *Commentator*
%WTBS, 1050 Techwood Dr NW, Atlanta, GA 30318, USA

Loughran, James — *Conductor*
Rookery, Bollington Cross, Macclesfield, Cheshire SK10 5EL, England

Louis, John J, Jr — *Diplomat, Publisher*
%Combined Communications Corp, 1 Northfield Plaza, #510, Northfield, IL 60093, USA

Louis, Murray — *Dancer, Choreographer*
%Nikolais/Louis Foundation, 375 W Broadway, New York, NY 10012, USA

Louis-Dreyfus, Julia — *Actress*
131 S Rodeo Dr, #300, Beverly Hills, CA 90212, USA

Louis-Dreyfus, Robert L M — *Businessman*
%Saatchi & Saatchi Co, 83/89 Whitfield St, London W1A 4XA, England

Louisa, Maria — *Model*
%Next Model Mgmt, 115 E 57th St, #1540, New York, NY 10022, USA

L

Lord - Louisa

Louise, Tina *Actress*
310 E 46th St, #18-T, New York, NY 10017, USA

Louisy, Allan *Prime Minister, Saint Lucia*
Laborie, Castries, Saint Lucia, West Indies

Lounge, John M (Mike) *Astronaut*
%Spacehab Inc, 1215 Jefferson Davis Highway, #150, Arlington, VA 22202, USA

Lourdusamy, Simon Cardinal *Religious Leader*
Palazzo dei Convertendi, 34 Via della Conciliazione, 00193 Rome, Italy

Lousma, Jack R *Astronaut*
2722 Roseland St, Ann Arbor, MI 48103, USA

Loutfy, Ali *Prime Minister, Egypt*
29 Ahmed Hesmat St, Zamalek, Cairo, Egypt

Louvier, Alain *Composer*
Conservatoire Nat Musique Superieur, 14 Rue de Madrid, 75008 Paris, France

Louvin, Charlie *Singer, Guitarist, Songwriter*
%Joe Taylor Artist Agency, 2802 Columbine Pl, Nashville, TN 37204, USA

Lovano, Joe *Jazz Saxophonist*
206 W 23rd St, #2, New York, NY 10011, USA

Love, Ben H *Association Executive*
%Boy Scouts of America, 4407 Eaton Circle, Colleyville, TX 76034, USA

Love, Bob *Basketball Player*
%Chicago Bulls, 1901 W Madison St, Chicago, IL 60612, USA

Love, Courtney *Singer (Hole), Songwriter*
332 Southdown Rd, Lloyd Harbor, NY 11743, USA

Love, Darlene *Singer*
%Shore Fire Media, 193 Joralemon St, Brooklyn, NY 11201, USA

Love, Davis, III *Golfer*
%Professional Golfer's Assn, PO Box 109601, Palm Beach Gardens, FL 33410, USA

Love, Gael *Editor*
%Connoisseur Magazine, Editorial Dept, 1790 Broadway, New York, NY 10019, USA

Love, Howard M *Businessman*
1440 Bennington Ave, Pittsburgh, PA 15217, USA

Love, John A *Governor, CO; Businessman*
%Ideal Basic Industries, 950 17th St, Denver, CO 80202, USA

Love, Mike *Singer (Beach Boys)*
101 Mesa Lane, Santa Barbara, CA 93109, USA

Love, Nancy *Editor*
%Mademoiselle Magazine, Editorial Dept, 350 Madison Ave, New York, NY 10017, USA

Love, Susan *Surgeon, Oncologist*
%University of California Medical Plaza, Breast Center, Los Angeles, CA 90024, USA

Lovejoy, David R *Financier*
%Mellon Bank Corp, 1 Meeon Bank Center, 500 Grant St, Pittsburgh, PA 15219, USA

Lovelace, Jon B, Jr *Financier*
%Capital Research & Management Co, 333 S Hope St, Los Angeles, CA 90071, USA

Loveless, Patty *Singer, Songwriter*
%Fitzgerald Hartley Co, 1212 16th Ave S, Nashville, TN 37212, USA

Lovell, A C Bernard *Astronomer*
Quinta, Swettenham Near Congleton, Cheshire, England

Lovell, James A, Jr *Astronaut*
%Lovell Communications, PO Box 49, Lake Forest, IL 60045, USA

Lovelock, James E *Chemist, Inventor*
Coombe Mill, St Giles-on-the-Heath, Launceston, Cornwall PL15 9RY, England

Lover, Seth *Inventor, Engineer (Humbucking Pickup)*
12752 Adrian Circle, Garden Grove, CA 92640, USA

Lovering, Thomas S *Geologist, Geochemist*
2663 Tallant Rd, Santa Barbara, CA 93105, USA

Lovett, Lyle *Singer, Songwriter*
%Vector Mgmt, PO Box 128037, Nashville, TN 37212, USA

Lovitz, Jon *Actor*
%Creative Artists Agency, 9830 Wilshire Blvd, Beverly Hills, CA 90212, USA

Low, Francis E *Physicist*
28 Adams St, Belmont, MA 02178, USA

Low, G David *Astronaut*
%NASA, Johnson Space Center, 2101 NASA Rd, Houston, TX 77058, USA

Low, George M *Space Scientist, Educator*
2005 Tibbits Ave, Troy, NY 12180, USA

Low, Stephen *Diplomat*
2855 Tilden St NW, Washington, DC 20008, USA

Lowder, Robert E *Financier*
%Colonial BancGroup, 1 Commerce St, Montgomery, AL 36104, USA

Lowe, Chad *Actor*
%Wisnicki & Robbins, 1642 Westwood Blvd, #300, Los Angeles, CA 90024, USA

Lowe, Kevin *Hockey Player*
%New York Rangers, Madison Square Garden, 4 Penn Plaza New York, NY 10001, USA

Lowe, Nick *Singer*
%International Creative Mgmt, 40 W 57th St, New York, NY 10019, USA

Lowe, Rob *Actor*
270 N Canon Dr, #1072, Beverly Hills, CA 90210, USA

Lowe, Woodrow *Football Player, Coach*
%Kansas City Chiefs, 1 Arrowhead Dr, Kansas City, KS 64129, USA

Lowell, Carey *Actress*
%International Creative Mgmt, 8942 Wilshire Blvd, Beverly Hills, CA 90211, USA

Lowenstein, Louis *Attorney, Educator*
1 Fountain Square, Larchmont, NY 10538, USA

Lowery, Dominic G (Nick) *Football Player*
%New York Jets, 1000 Fulton Ave, Hempstead, NY 11550, USA

Lowery, Joseph E *Civil Rights Activist*
%Southern Christian Leadership, 334 Auburn Ave NE, Atlanta, GA 30303, USA

Lowman, Frank A *Financier*
%Federal Home Loan Bank, 2 Townsite Plaza, Topeka, KS 66601, USA

Lown, Bernard *Cardiologist*
%Harvard University Medical School, 25 Shattuck St, Boston, MA 02115, USA

Lowrey, Tyler A *Businessman*
%Micron Technology, 2805 E Columbia Rd, Boise, ID 83706, USA

Lowry of Crossgar, Robert L E *Judge*
White Hill, Crossgar, County Down, Northern Ireland

Lowry, Bates *Art Historian*
255 Massachusetts Ave, Boston, MA 02115, USA

Lowry, Mike *Governor/Senator, WA*
PO Box 4246, Seattle, WA 98104, USA

Lowry, Oliver H *Pharmacologist*
%Washington University Medical School, Pharmacology Dept, St Louis, MO 63110, USA

Loy, Frank E *Environmentalist*
%Marshall German Fund, 11 Dupont Circle NW, Washington, DC 20036, USA

Loynd, Richard B *Businessman*
%Interco Inc, 101 S Hanley Rd, St Louis, MO 63105, USA

Lozano, Ignacio E, Jr *Editor*
%La Opinion, 411 W 5th St, Los Angeles, CA 90013, USA

Lozano, Silvia *Choreographer*
%Ballet Folklorico, 31 Esq Con Riva Palacio, Mexico City DF, Mexico

Lu Qihui *Sculptor*
351 Flats Shuang-Feng Rd, #10-5, Shanghai, China

Lu, Edward T *Astronaut*
%NASA, Johnson Space Center, 2101 NASA Rd, Houston, TX 77058, USA

Luan Jujie *Fencer*
146 Shuang Le Yuan, #301, Qin-Huai Region, Nanjing, China

Luan Jujie *Fencer*
146 Shuang-Le Yuan, #301, Qin-Huai Region, Nanjing, China

Lubachivsky, Myroslav Cardinal *Religious Leader*
%Piazza Madonna dei Monti 3, 00184 Rome, Italy

Lubbers, Ruud F M *Prime Minister, Netherlands*
%Prime Minister's Office, Binnenhof 20, 2500 EA The Hague, Netherlands

Lubich Silvia, Chiara *Evangelist*
%Focolare Movement, 306 Via di Frascati, 00040 Rocca di Papa RM, Italy

Lubin, Steven *Concert Pianist*
%J B Keller, 600 W 111th St, #129, New York, NY 10025, USA

Lubotsky, Mark *Concert Violinist*
Overtoom 329 III, 1054 JM Amsterdam, Netherlands

Lubovitch, Lar *Dancer, Choreographer*
%Lar Lubovitch Dance Co, 15-17 W 18th St, New York, NY 10011, USA

Lubs, Herbert A *Geneticist*
%University of Miami Medical School, Pediatrics Dept, Box 16820, Miami, FL 33101, USA

Lubys, Bronislovas *Prime Minister, Lithuania*
%Prime Minister's Office, Tuo-Vaizganto 2, Vilnius, Lithuania

Lucas, Aubrey K *Educator*
%University of Southern Mississippi, President's Office, Hattiesburg, MS 39406, USA

L

Lucas, Craig *Lyricist*
%William Morris Agency, 1325 Ave of Americas, New York, NY 10019, USA

Lucas, George *Movie Director*
%LucasFilm Ltd, PO Box 2009, San Rafael, CA 94912, USA

Lucas, Jack H *WW II Marine Corps Hero (CMH)*
75 Elks Lake Rd, Hattiesburg, MS 39401, USA

Lucas, John H, Jr *Basketball Player, Coach*
%Philadelphia 76ers, Veterans Stadium, PO Box 25040, Philadelphia, PA 19147, USA

Lucas, Maurice *Basketball Player, Coach*
%Portland Trail Blazers, 700 NE Multnomah St, #600, Portland, OR 97232, USA

Lucas, Richard J (Richie) *Football Player*
%Pennsylvania State University, Athletic Dept, University Park, PA 16802, USA

Lucas, Robert E, Jr *Nobel Economics Laureate*
5441 S Hyde Park Blvd, Chicago, IL 60615, USA

Lucas, William *Government Official*
%Justice Department, Constitution & 10th NW, Washington, DC 20530, USA

Lucassen, Sigurd *Labor Leader*
%Brotherhood of Carpenters/Joiners, 101 Constitution NW, Washington, DC 20001, USA

Lucchesini, Andrea *Concert Pianist*
%Columbia Artists Mgmt Inc, 165 W 57th St, New York, NY 10019, USA

Lucci, Susan *Actress*
16 Carteret Place, Garden City, NY 11530, USA

Luce, Charles F *Businessman*
1 Stoneleigh, #1-L, Bronxville, NY 10708, USA

Luce, Henry, III *Publisher*
Mill Hill Rd, Mill Neck, NY 11765, USA

Luce, R Duncan *Psychologist*
20 Whitman Ct, Irvine, CA 92715, USA

Luce, Richard N *Government Official, England*
%House of Commons, Westminster, London SW1A 0AA, England

Lucebert (L J Swaanswijk) *Artist*
Boendermakerhof 10, 1861 TB Bergen N-H, Netherlands

Lucey, Patrick J *Governor, WI*
6200 Highway 57, Rt 3, Sturgeon Bay, WI 54235, USA

Luchko, Klara *Actress*
Kotelmicheskaya Nab 1/15 Korp B, #308, 109240 Moscow, Russia

Luciano, Robert P *Businessman*
%Schering-Plough Corp, 1 Giralda Farms, Madison, NJ 07940, USA

Lucid, Shannon W *Astronaut*
1622 Gunwale Rd, Houston, TX 77062, USA

Luck, Gary E *Army General*
CinC, UN Command/US Forces Korea, Unit 15237, APO, AP 96205, USA

Luckinbill, Lawrence *Actor*
RR 3, Flintlock Ridge Rd, Katonah, NY 10536, USA

Luckman, Charles *Architect*
%Luckman Management Co, 9220 Sunset Blvd, Los Angeles, CA 90069, USA

Luckman, Sid *Football Player*
5303 St Charles Rd, Bellwood, IL 60104, USA

Luckovich, Mike *Editorial Cartoonist*
%Atlanta Constitution, Editorial Dept, 72 Marietta St, Atlanta, GA 30303, USA

Lucky Dube *Rapper*
%Fast Lane Productions, 5125 MacArthur Blvd NW, #14, Washington, DC 20016, USA

Lucky, Robert W *Electrical Engineer*
48 Gillespie Ave, Fair Haven, NJ 07704, USA

Luder, Owen H *Architect*
%Communication in Construction, 2 Smith Square, London SW1P 3H5, England

Ludes, John T *Businessman*
%American Brands Inc, 1700 E Putnam Ave, Old Greenwich, CT 06870, USA

Luding-Rothenburger, Christa *Speed Skater*
Hutbergstr 80, 01326 Dresden, Germany

Ludlum, Robert *Writer*
%Henry Morrison Inc, PO Box 235, Bedford Hills, NY 10507, USA

Ludwig, Christa *Opera Singer*
Rigistr 14, 6045 Meggen, Switzerland

Ludwig, Ken *Playwright*
%Steptoe & Johnson, 1330 Connecticut Ave NW, Washington, DC 20036, USA

Luening, Otto *Composer*
460 Riverside Dr, New York, NY 10027, USA

Lucas - Luening

Luers, William H
%Metropolitan Museum of Art, 1000 5th Ave, New York, NY 10028, USA
Diplomat, Museum Executive

Luft, Lorna
5757 Wilshire Blvd, #240, Los Angeles, CA 90036, USA
Actress

Lugbill, Jon
%American Canoe Assn, PO Box 1190, Newington, VA 22122, USA
Kayak Athlete

Luikart, John F
%Sutro Co, 201 California St, San Francisco, CA 94111, USA
Financier

Luisetti, Angelo (Hank)
2659 Summit Dr, Burlingame, CA 94010, USA
Basketball Player

Luisi, James
14315 Riverside Dr, #111, Sherman Oaks, CA 91423, USA
Actor

Luiso, Anthony
%International Multifoods, 33 S 6th St, Minneapolis, MN 55402, USA
Businessman

Lujack, Johnny
3700 Harrison St, Davenport, IA 52806, USA
Football Player

Lujan, Manuel, Jr
%Manuel Lujan Agencies, PO Box 3727, Albuquerque, NM 87190, USA
Secretary, Interior

Lukas, D Wayne
%Santa Anita Race Track, Barn 66, 285 W Huntington Dr, Arcadia, CA 91007, USA
Thoroughbred Racing Trainer

Lukas, J Anthony
890 West End Ave, #10-B, New York, NY 10025, USA
Journalist, Writer

Lukashenko, Aleksandr
%President's Office, Government House, Dom Urada, 210010 Minsk, Belarus
President, Belarus

Luke, John A, Jr
%Westvaco Corp, 299 Park Ave, New York, NY 10171, USA
Businessman

Lukin, Matt
%Reprise Records, 3300 Warner Blvd, Burbank, CA 91505, USA
Bassist (Mudhoney)

Lukkarinen, Marjut
%Lohja Ski Team, Lohja, Finland
Cross Country Skier

Lulu
%Susan Angel Assoc, 12 D'Arblay St, #100, London W1V 3FP, England
Singer, Actress

Lumbly, Carl
5875 Carolos Dr, Los Angeles, CA 90068, USA
Actor

Lumet, Sidney
1 W 81st St, #4-DB, New York, NY 10024, USA
Movie Director

Lumley, Harry
680 4th Ave E, Owen Sound ON N4K 2N4, Canada
Hockey Player

Lumley, Joanna
%Caroline Renton, 23 Crescent Lane, London SW4 9PT, England
Actress

Lumsden, David J
Melton House, Soham, Cambridgeshire, England
Conductor, Concert Organist

Luna, Barbara
18026 Rodarte Way, Encino, CA 91316, USA
Actress

Lund, Deanna
545 Howard Dr, Salem, VA 24153, USA
Actress

Lund, Francis (Pug)
9999 Wayzata Blvd, Minnetonka, MN 55305, USA
Football Player

Lund, Victor L
%American Stores Co, 709 E South Temple, Salt Lake City, UT 84102, USA
Businessman

Lundberg, Fred Borre
Skogbrynet 11, 9250 Bardu, Norway
Nordic Combined Athlete

Lundberg, George D, II
%JAMA Magazine, Editorial Dept, 515 N State St, Chicago, IL 60610, USA
Editor, Physician

Lunden, Joan
%"Good Morning America" Show, ABC-TV, 77 W 66th St, New York, NY 10023, USA
Commentator

Lundgren, Dolph
29055 Cliffside Dr, Malibu, CA 90265, USA
Actor

Lundgren, Lauren
%Washington Federal Savings, 425 Pike St, Seattle, WA 98101, USA
Financier

Lundquist, Steve
3448 Southbay Dr, Jonesboro, GA 30236, USA
Swimmer

Lundquist, Verne
%CBS-TV, Sports Dept, 51 W 52nd St, New York, NY 10019, USA
Sportscaster

Lundy, Victor A
%Victor A Lundy Assoc, 701 Mulberry Lane, Bellaire, TX 77401, USA
Architect

Luns, Joseph M A H
117 Ave Franklin Roosevelt, 1050 Brussels, Belgium
Government Official, Netherlands

L

Luers - Luns

Lupberger, Edwin A — *Businessman*
%Entergy Corp, 639 Loyola Ave, New Orleans, LA 70113, USA

LuPone, Patti — *Singer, Actress*
%Lantz Office, 888 7th Ave, #2500, New York, NY 10106, USA

Lupu, Radu — *Concert Pianist*
%Terry Harrison Mgmt, 3 Clarendon Court, Charlbury, Oxon OX7 3PS, England

Lupus, Peter — *Actor*
11375 Dona Lisa Dr, Studio City, CA 91604, USA

Lurie, Alison — *Writer*
%Cornell University, English Dept, Ithaca, NY 14850, USA

Lurie, Jeff — *Football Executive*
%Philadelphia Eagles, 3501 S Broad St, Philadelphia, PA 19148, USA

Lurie, Ranan R — *Editorial Cartoonist*
%Cartoonnews International, 9 Mountain Laurel Dr, Greenwich, CT 06831, USA

Lustgarten, Marc A — *Businessman*
%Cablevision Systems Corp, 1 Media Crossways, Woodbury, NY 11797, USA

Lustiger, Jean-Marie Cardinal — *Religious Leader*
Archeveche de Paris, 32 Rue Barbet de Jouy, 75007 Paris, France

Lutali, A P — *Governor, AS*
%Governor's Office, Government Offices, Pago Pago, Tutuila, AS 90799, USA

Luter, Joseph W, III — *Businessman*
%Smithfield Foods Inc, 501 N Church St, Smithfield, VA 23430, USA

Lutnick, Howard W — *Financier*
%Cantor Fitzgerald Securities, 1 World Trade Center, New York, NY 10048, USA

Luttwak, Edward N — *Political Scientist*
4510 Drummond Ave, Chevy Chase, MD 20815, USA

Lutz, Bob — *Tennis Player*
%US Tennis Assn, 1212 Ave of Americas, New York, NY 10036, USA

Lutz, Robert A — *Businessman*
%Chrysler Corp, 12000 Chrysler Dr, Highland Park, MI 48288, USA

Lux, Philip G — *Businessman*
%Coachmen Industries, 601 E Beardsley Ave, Elkhart, IN 46514, USA

Luxon, Benjamin — *Opera Singer*
Lower Cox Street Farm, Detling, Maidstone, Kent ME14 3HE, England

Luyendyk, Arie — *Auto Racing Driver*
%Indy Regency Racing, 7051 Corporate Circle, Indianapolis, IN 46278, USA

Luzinski, Gregory M (Greg) — *Baseball Player*
320 Jackson Rd, Medford, NJ 08055, USA

Lyakhov, Vladimir A — *Cosmonaut*
%Potchta Kosmonavtov, 141 160 Svyosdny Gorodok, Moskovskoi Oblasti, Russia

Lyburger, Stanley A — *Financier*
%Bank of Oklahoma, Bank of Oklahoma Tower, PO Box 2300, Tulsa, OK 74102, USA

Lydon, Jimmy — *Actor*
1317 Los Arboles Ave NW, Albuquerque, NM 87107, USA

Lydon, Thomas J — *Judge*
%US Circuit Court, 717 Madison Place NW, Washington, DC 20005, USA

Lyght, Todd — *Football Player*
%St Louis Rams, 100 N Broadway, #2100, St Louis, MO 63102, USA

Lyle, Sandy — *Golfer*
%Professional Golfer's Assn, PO Box 109601, Palm Beach Gardens, FL 33410, USA

Lyman, Richard W — *Foundation Executive, Educator*
%Stanford University, Education School, Stanford, CA 94305, USA

Lympany, Moura — *Concert Pianist*
%Helen Jennings, 2 Hereford House, Links Rd, London W3 OHX, England

Lynam, Jim — *Basketball Coach, Executive*
%Washington Bullets, Capital Centre, 1 Truman Dr, Landover, MD 20785, USA

Lynch, Allen J — *Vietnam War Army Hero (CMH)*
438 Belle Plaine Ave, Gurnee, IL 60031, USA

Lynch, David K — *Movie Director*
PO Box 93624, Los Angeles, CA 90093, USA

Lynch, Gary — *Government Official, Attorney*
%Davis Polk Wardwell, 1 Chase Manhatten Plaza, New York, NY 10005, USA

Lynch, James E (Jim) — *Football Player*
1009 W 67th St, Kansas City, MO 64113, USA

Lynch, John M — *Prime Minister, Ireland*
21 Garville Ave, Rathgar, Dublin 6, Ireland

Lynch, Kelly — *Model, Actress*
1970 Mandeville Canyon Rd, Los Angeles, CA 90049, USA

Lynch, Peter S	*Financier*
27 State St, Boston, MA 02109, USA	
Lynch, Richard	*Actor*
%Sindell, 8271 Melrose Ave, #202, Los Angeles, CA 90046, USA	
Lynch, Richard (Dick)	*Football Player*
203 Manor Rd, Douglaston, NY 11363, USA	
Lynch, Robert P	*Financier*
%Lord Abbett Co, 767 5th Ave, New York, NY 10153, USA	
Lynch, Thomas C	*Navy Admiral*
%Rules/Mission Studies Grp, Navy Department, Pentagon, Washington, DC 20350, USA	
Lynden-Bell, Donald	*Astronomer*
%Institute of Astronomy, Madingley Rd, Cambridge CB3 0HA, England	
Lynds, Roger	*Astronomer*
%Kitt Peak National Observatory, Tucson, AZ 85726, USA	
Lyne, Adrian	*Movie Director*
2825 Seattle Dr, Los Angeles, CA 90046, USA	
Lynley, Carol	*Actress*
PO Box 2190, Malibu, CA 90265, USA	
Lynn Salomon, Janet	*Figure Skater*
1716 Grandview , Rochester Hills, MI 48306, USA	
Lynn, Frederic M (Fred)	*Baseball Player*
7336 El Fuerte St, Carlsbad, CA 92009, USA	
Lynn, James T	*Secretary, Housing & Urban Development*
151 Farmington Ave, Hartford, CT 06115, USA	
Lynn, Loretta	*Singer, Songwriter*
%Loretta Lynn Ent, PO Box 120369, Nashville, TN 37212, USA	
Lynn, Meredith Scott	*Actress*
%Gores/Fields Agency, 10100 Santa Monica Blvd, #2500, Los Angeles, CA 90067, USA	
Lynne, Gillian	*Dance Director, Choreographer*
%Lean-2 Productions, 18 Rutland St, Knightsbridge, London SW7 1EF, England	
Lynne, Jeff	*Singer, Songwriter*
PO Box 5850, Santa Barbara, CA 93150, USA	
Lynne, Shelby	*Singer*
%Debbie Doebler Business Mgmt, 48 Music Square E, Nashville, TN 37203, USA	
Lyon, Lisa	*Body Builder*
%Jungle Gym, PO Box 585, Santa Monica, CA 90406, USA	
Lyon, Sue	*Actress*
1244 N Havenhurst Dr, Los Angeles, CA 90046, USA	
Lyon, Wayne B	*Businessman*
%Masco Corp, 21001 Van Born Rd, Taylor, MI 48180, USA	
Lyon, William	*Businessman, Air Force General*
%William Lyon Co, 4490 Von Karman Ave, Newport Beach, CA 92660, USA	
Lyons, Robert F	*Actor*
1801 Ave of Stars, #1250, Los Angeles, CA 90067, USA	
Lyons, Warren R	*Financier*
%Avco Financial Services, 3349 Michelson Dr, Irvine, CA 92715, USA	
Lysinger, Rex J	*Businessman*
%Energen Corp, 2101 6th Ave N, Birmingham, AL 35203, USA	
Lyst, John H	*Editor*
%Indianapolis Star, Editorial Dept, 307 N Pennsylvania, Indianapolis, IN 46204, USA	
Lytle, L Ben	*Businessman*
%Associated Insurance, 120 Monument Circle, Indianapolis, IN 46204, USA	
Lytle, Ronn K	*Financier*
%Capstead Mortgage Corp, 2001 Bryan Tower, Dallas, TX 75201, USA	
Lyubimov, Yuri P	*Theater Director*
%Royal Opera, Covent Garden, 48 Floral St, London WC2E 7QA, England	

L

Lynch - Lyubimov

M

M C Lyte *Rapper*
%First Priority Music, 824 St Johns Place, Brooklyn, NY 11216, USA

M'Bow, Amadou-Mahtar *Government Official, Senegal*
BP 5276, Dakar-Fann, Senegal

Ma, Yo-Yo *Concert Cellist*
%International Creative Mgmt, 40 W 57th St, New York, NY 10019, USA

Maag, Peter *Conductor*
Casa Maag, 7504 Pontresina, Switzerland

Maas, Bill *Football Player*
%Green Bay Packers, 1265 Lombardi Ave, Green Bay, WI 54304, USA

Maas, Peter *Writer*
%International Creative Mgmt, 40 W 57th St, New York, NY 10019, USA

Maathai, Wangari *Environmentalist*
%Green Belt Movement, PO Box 67545, Nariobi, Kenya

Maatman, Gerald L *Businessman*
%Kemper National Insurance Companies, 1 Kemper Dr, Long Grove, IL 60047, USA

Maazel, Lorin *Conductor, Concert Violinist*
%Pittsburgh Symphony, 600 Pennsylvania Ave, Pittsburgh, PA 15146, USA

Mabe, Manabu *Artist*
Rua das Canjeranas 321, Jabaquara, Sao Paulo SP, Brazil

Mabee, John *Thoroughbred Racing Executive*
4346 54th St, San Diego, CA 92115, USA

Mabus, Raymond E, Jr *Governor, MS*
PO Box 200, Jackson, MS 39205, USA

MacAfee, Ken *Football Player*
26 W Elm Terrace, Brockton, MA 02401, USA

MacArthur, Douglas, II *Diplomat*
2101 Connecticut Ave NW, Washington, DC 20008, USA

MacArthur, James *Actor*
74092 Covered Wagon Trail, Palm Desert, CA 92260, USA

MacArthur, John R (Rick) *Publisher*
%Harper's Magazine, 666 Broadway, New York, NY 10012, USA

MacArthur, Robert B *Financier*
%UAL Employees' Credit Union, 125 E Algonquin Rd, Arlington Heights, IL 60005, USA

Macaskill, Bridget A *Financier*
%Oppenheimer Management Corp, 2 World Trade Center, New York, NY 10048, USA

Macauley, Edward C *Basketball Player*
1455 Reauville Dr, St Louis, MO 63122, USA

MacCarthy, John Peters *Financier*
%Boatmen's Bancshares, 800 Market St, St Louis, MO 63101, USA

Macchio, Ralph *Actor*
451 Deerpark Ave, Dix Hills, NY 11746, USA

MacColl, Kristy *Singer, Songwriter*
%XL Talent, 27-A Penbridge Villas, Studio 7, London W11 3EP, England

MacCorkindale, Simon *Actor*
520 Washington Blvd, #187, Marina del Rey, CA 90292, USA

MacCormac, Richard C *Architect*
9 Heneage St, London E1 5LJ, England

MacCready, Paul B *Aeronautical Engineer*
%AeroVironment Inc, 222 E Huntington Dr, Monrovia, CA 91016, USA

MacDermot, Galt *Composer*
%MacDermot Assoc, 12 Silver Lake Rd, Staten Island, NY 10301, USA

MacDonald, Gordon J F *Geophysicist*
%Mitre Corp, 1820 Dolly Madison Blvd, McLean, VA 22102, USA

Macdonald, J Ross *Physicist*
308 Laurel Hill Rd, Chapel Hill, NC 27514, USA

MacDowell, Andie *Model, Actress*
%International Creative Mgmt, 8942 Wilshire Blvd, Beverly Hills, CA 90211, USA

MacEachen, Allan J *Government Official, Canada*
RR 1, Whycocomagh, NS BOE 3MO, Canada

MacGillivary, Charles A *WW II Army Hero (CMH)*
38 Fallon Circle, Braintree, MA 02184, USA

MacGraw, Ali *Actress*
27040 Malibu Cove Colony Dr, Malibu, CA 90265, USA

MacGregor, Ian K *Government Official, England*
Castleton House, Lochgilphead, Argyll, Scotland

MacGregor, John R R *Government Official, England*
%House of Commons, Westminster, London SW1A 0AA, England

Macharski, Franciszak Cardinal   *Religious Leader*
%Metropolita Krakowski, Ul Franciszkanska 3, 31-004 Krakow, Poland

Machiz, Leon   *Businessman*
%Avnet Inc, 80 Cutter Mill Rd, Great Neck, NY 11021, USA

Machlis, Gail   *Cartoonist (Quality Time)*
%Chronicle Features, 901 Mission St, San Francisco, CA 94103, USA

Machover, Tod   *Composer*
%Massachusetts Institute of Technology, Media Laboratory, Cambridge, MA 02139, USA

Machungo, Mario de Graca   *Prime Minister, Mozambique*
%Prime Minister's Office, Avenida Julius Nyerere 1780, Maputo, Mozambique

MacInnis, Al   *Hockey Player*
%St Louis Blues, St Louis Arena, 5700 Oakland Ave, St Louis, MO 63110, USA

MacInnis, Frank T   *Businessman*
%EMCOR Group, 101 Merritt Seven, Norwalk, CT 06851, USA

MacIntosh, Craig   *Cartoonist (Sally Forth)*
%King Features Syndicate, 216 E 45th St, New York, NY 10017, USA

MacIver, Loren   *Artist*
61 Perry St, New York, NY 10014, USA

Mack, John E   *Psychiatrist*
%Harvard University Medical School, 25 Shattuck St, Boston, MA 02115, USA

Mack, John E, III   *Businessman*
%Central Hudson Gas & Electric, 284 South Ave, Poughkeepsie, NY 12601, USA

Mack, John J   *Financier*
%Morgan Stanley Group, 1251 Ave of Americas, New York, NY 10020, USA

Mack, Kevin   *Football Player*
%Cleveland Browns, 80 1st Ave, Berea, OH 44017, USA

Mackay, Harvey   *Writer*
%Mackay Envelope Corp, 2100 Elm St SE, Minneapolis, MN 55414, USA

Macke, Kenneth A   *Businessman*
%Dayton Hudson Corp, 777 Nicollet Mall, Minneapolis, MN 55402, USA

Macke, Richard C   *Navy Admiral*
Director, Joint Staff, Pentagon, Washington, DC 20318, USA

MacKenzie, Gisele   *Singer*
11014 Blix Ave, North Hollywood, CA 91602, USA

MacKenzie, Kelvin   *Editor*
%The Sun, Editorial Dept, PO Box 481, Virginia St, London EC1 9BD, England

MacKenzie, Warren   *Ceramist*
8695 68th St N, Stillwater, MN 55082, USA

Mackerras, Charles   *Conductor*
10 Hamilton Terrace, London NW8 9UG, England

Mackey, George W   *Mathematician*
25 Coolidge Hill Rd, Cambridge, MA 02138, USA

Mackey, John   *Football Player*
5324 Marina Pacifica Dr S, Long Beach, CA 90803, USA

Mackie, Hobert G (Bob)   *Fashion Designer*
%Bob Mackie Originals, 225 W 39th St, New York, NY 10018, USA

MacKinnon, Catherine   *Attorney, Social Activist*
%University of Michigan, Law School, Ann Arbor, MI 48109, USA

Mackintosh, Cameron A   *Theater Producer*
%Cameron Mackintosh Ltd, 1 Bedford Square, London WC1B 3RA, England

Macklin, David   *Actor*
5410 Wilshire Blvd, #227, Los Angeles, CA 90036, USA

Macklin, J Stanley   *Financier*
%Regions Financial Corp, 417 N 20th St, Birmingham, AL 35203, USA

Mackovic, John   *Football Coach*
%University of Texas, Athletic Dept, PO Box 7399, Austin, TX 78713, USA

MacLachlan, Janet   *Actress*
1919 N Taft Ave, Los Angeles, CA 90068, USA

MacLachlan, Kyle   *Actor*
828 Venezia Ave, Venice, CA 90291, USA

MacLaine, Shirley   *Actress*
25200 Old Malibu Rd, Malibu, CA 90265, USA

MacLane, Saunders   *Mathematician*
5712 S Dorchester Ave, Chicago, IL 60637, USA

MacLaury, Bruce K   *Educator*
%Brookings Institute, 1775 Massachusetts Ave NW, Washington, DC 20036, USA

MacLean, Don   *Basketball Player*
%Washington Bullets, Capital Centre, 1 Truman Dr, Landover, MD 20785, USA

M

Macharski - MacLean

MacLean - Madigan

M

MacLean, Doug *Hockey Coach*
%Florida Panthers, 100 NE 3rd Ave, #1000, Fort Lauderdale, FL 33301, USA

MacLean, Steven G *Astronaut, Canada*
%Astronaut Program, 6767 Rte de l'Aeroport, Sainte-Hubert PQ J3Y 8Y9, Canada

Maclellan, Hugh O, Jr *Businessman*
%Provident Life & Accident Insurance, 1 Fountain Square, Chattanooga, TN 37402, USA

Maclennan, Robert A R *Government Official, England*
74 Abingdon Villas, London W8 6XB, England

MacLeod, Gavin *Actor*
11641 Curry Ave, Granada Hills, CA 91344, USA

MacLeod, John *Basketball Coach*
%University of Notre Dame, Athletic Dept, Notre Dame, IN 46556, USA

MacLeod, Robert *Football Player*
110 Malibu Colony Dr, Malibu, CA 90265, USA

MacMahon, Brian *Epidemiologist*
89 Warren St, Needham, MA 02192, USA

MacMillan, Whitney *Businessman*
%Cargill Inc, PO Box 9300, Minneapolis, MN 55440, USA

MacNabb, B Gordon *Missile Engineer*
5604 Blue Bluff, Cheyenne, WY 82009, USA

Macnee, Patrick *Actor*
PO Box 1685, Palm Springs, CA 92263, USA

MacNeil, Cornell H *Opera Singer*
%Columbia Artists Mgmt Inc, 165 W 57th St, New York, NY 10019, USA

MacNeil, Robert *Commentator*
%"MacNeil/Lehrer Newshour" Show, WNET-TV, 356 W 58th St, New York, NY 10019, USA

MacNeish, Richard S *Archaeologist*
%Andover Archeological Research Foundation, PO Box 83, Andover, MA 01810, USA

MacNelly, Jeff *Editorial Cartoonist (Pluggers)*
333 E Grace St, Richmond, VA 23293, USA

Macomber, George B H *Skier*
Russia Wharf, 530 Atlantic Ave, Boston, MA 02210, USA

Macomber, William B, Jr *Diplomat, Museum Official*
27 Monomoy Rd, Nantucket, MA 02554, USA

MacPhail, Leland S, Jr *Baseball Executive*
%American League, 350 Park Ave, New York, NY 10022, USA

MacPhee, Donald A *Educator*
%State University College of New York, President's Office, Fredonia, NY 14063, USA

MacPherson, Duncan I *Editorial Cartoonist*
%Toronto Daily Star, 1 Yonge St, Toronto ON M5E 1E6, Canada

Macpherson, Elle *Model*
%Women Inc, 107 Greene St, #200, New York, NY 10012, USA

MacQuitty, Jonathan *Medical Inventor*
%GenPharm International, 2375 Garcia Ave, Mountain View, CA 94043, USA

MacRae, Meredith *Actress*
518 Pacific Ave, Manhattan Beach, CA 90266, USA

MacRae, Sheila *Actress, Singer*
301 N Canon Dr, #305, Beverly Hills, CA 90210, USA

Macy, Bill *Actor*
10130 Angelo Circle, Beverly Hills, CA 90210, USA

Madden, D S *Religious Leader*
%American Baptist Assn, 4605 N State Line, Texarkana, TX 75503, USA

Madden, David *Writer*
%Louisiana State University, US Civil War Center, Baton Rouge, LA 70803, USA

Madden, J Kevin *Publisher*
%Conde Nast Publications, 360 Madison Ave, #1200, New York, NY 10017, USA

Maddox, Lester *Governor, GA*
3155 Johnson Ferry Rd NE, Marietta, GA 30062, USA

Maddox, Rose *Singer*
749 E Nevada St, Ashland, OR 97520, USA

Maddrey, E Erwin, II *Businessman*
%Delta Woodside Industries, Hammond Square, 233 N Main St, Greenville, SC 29601, USA

Maddux, Gregory A (Greg) *Baseball Player*
8124 Desert Jewel Circle, Las Vegas, NV 89128, USA

Madigan, Amy *Actress*
22031 Carbon Mesa Rd, Malibu, CA 90265, USA

Madigan, John W *Publisher*
%Tribune Co, 435 N Michigan Ave, Chicago, IL 60611, USA

Madigan, Martha   *Photographer*
%Tyler School of Art, Beech & Penrose Aves, Philadelphia, PA 19126, USA

Madison, Guy   *Actor*
PO Box 1281, Morongo Valley, CA 92256, USA

Madlock, Bill   *Baseball Player*
453 E Decatur St, Decatur, IL 62521, USA

Madonna (Ciccone)   *Singer, Actress*
3143 Durand Dr, Los Angeles, CA 90068, USA

Madrazo, Ignacio N   *Surgeon*
%Instituto Mexicano del Seguro Social, Mexico City, Mexico

Madsen, Loren   *Sculptor*
426 Broome St, New York, NY 10013, USA

Madsen, Virginia   *Actress*
9354 Claircrest Dr, Beverly Hills, CA 90210, USA

Maegle, Richard (Dick)   *Football Player*
4047 Aberdeen Way, Houston, TX 77025, USA

Maehata Hyodo, Hideko   *Swimmer*
1294 Nagamorikuramae, Gifu City, Japan

Maffie, Michael O   *Businessman*
%Southwestern Gas Corp, 5241 Spring Mountain Rd, Las Vegas, NV 89150, USA

Magaw, John W   *Law Enforcement Official*
%Alcohol Tobacco Firearms Bureau, 650 Massachusetts NW, Washington, DC 20001, USA

Magaziner, Henry J   *Architect*
1901 Walnut St, #15-B, Philadelphia, PA 19103, USA

Magdol, Michael O   *Financier*
%Fiduciary Trust Co, 2 World Trade Center, New York, NY 10048, USA

Maggio, Kirk   *Football Player*
%Green Bay Packers, 1265 Lombardi Ave, Green Bay, WI 54304, USA

Magilton, Gerard E (Jerry)   *Astronaut*
%Martin Marietta Astro Space, PO Box 800, Princeton, NJ 08543, USA

Magness, Bob   *Businessman*
%Tele-Communications, 5619 DTC Parkway, Englewood, CO 80111, USA

Magnus, Edie   *Commentator*
%CBS-TV, News Dept, 2020 "M" St NW, Washington, DC 20036, USA

Magnuson, Ann   *Actress*
1317 Maltman Ave, Los Angeles, CA 90026, USA

Magoon, Bob   *Powerboat Racing Driver*
1688 Meridian Ave, Miami Beach, FL 33139, USA

Magowan, Peter A   *Businessman, Football Executive*
%Safeway Inc, 4th & Jackson Sts, Oakland, CA 94660, USA

Magri, Charles G (Charlie)   *Boxer*
345 Bethnal Green Rd, Bethnal Green, London E2 6LG, England

Maguire, Deirdre   *Model*
%Elite Model Mgmt, 111 E 22nd St, #200, New York, NY 10010, USA

Maguire, John D   *Educator*
%Claremont Graduate School, President's Office, Claremont, CA 91711, USA

Maguire, Michael   *Actor*
%Agency For Performing Arts, 9000 Sunset Blvd, #1200, Los Angeles, CA 90069, USA

Maguire, Paul   *Sportscaster*
%NBC-TV, Sports Dept, 30 Rockefeller Plaza, New York, NY 10112, USA

Magyar, Gabriel   *Concert Cellist*
101 W Windsor Rd, #3103, Urbana, IL 61801, USA

Mahaffey, John   *Golfer*
3100 Richmond Ave, #500, Houston, TX 77098, USA

Mahaffey, Valerie   *Actress*
%Susan Smith Assoc, 121 N San Vicente Blvd, Beverly Hills, CA 90211, USA

Mahal, Taj   *Musician, Composer*
%Folklore Productions, 1671 Appian Way, Santa Monica, CA 90401, USA

Mahan, Larry   *Rodeo Rider*
PO Box 41, Camp Verde, TX 78010, USA

Mahanes, Walter J   *Businessman*
%Minstar Inc, 100 S 5th St, Minneapolis, MN 55402, USA

Maharidge, Dale D   *Writer*
%Stanford University, Communications Dept, Stanford, CA 94305, USA

Maharis, George   *Actor*
13150 Mulholland Dr, Beverly Hills, CA 90210, USA

Maharishi Mahesh Yogi   *Religious Leader*
%Institute of World Leadership, Maharishi University, Fairfield, IA 52556, USA

M

Mahathir Bin Mohamed, Datuk Seri   *Prime Minister, Malaysia*
%Prime Minister's Office, Jalan Dato Onn, 50502 Kuala Lumpur, Malaysia

Maher, Bill   *Commentator, Comedian*
%Brillstein Co, 9150 Wilshire Blvd, #350, Beverly Hills, CA 90212, USA

Maher, James R   *Businessman*
%Laboratory Corp of America Holdings, 358 S Main St, Burlington, NC 27215, USA

Maher, John F   *Financier*
%Great Western Financial Corp, 8484 Wilshire Blvd, Beverly Hills, CA 90211, USA

Mahfouz, Naguib   *Nobel Literature Laureate*
%American University Press, 113 Sharia Kasr El Aini, Cairo, Egypt

Mahoney, David J   *Businessman*
277 Park Ave, New York, NY 10172, USA

Mahoney, John   *Actor*
%International Creative Mgmt, 8942 Wilshire Blvd, Beverly Hills, CA 90211, USA

Mahoney, Joseph A   *Financier*
%Adler Coleman Clearing Corp, 20 Broad St, New York, NY 10005, USA

Mahoney, Richard J   *Businessman*
%Monsanto Co, 800 N Lindbergh Blvd, St Louis, MO 63167, USA

Mahoney, Robert W   *Businessman*
%Diebold Inc, 818 Mulberry Rd SE, Canton, OH 44707, USA

Mahoney, William E   *Businessman*
%Witco Corp, 1 American Lane, Greenwich, CT 06831, USA

Mahony, Roger Cardinal   *Religious Leader*
%Archdiocese of Los Angeles, PO Box 15052, Los Angeles, CA 90015, USA

Mahorn, Rick   *Basketball Player*
%New Jersey Nets, Byrne Meadowlands Arena, East Rutherford, NJ 07073, USA

Mahovlich, Frank   *Hockey Player*
27 Glenridge Dr, RR1, Unionville ON L6C 1A2, Canada

Mahre, Phil   *Skier*
White Pass Dr, Naches, WA 98937, USA

Mahre, Steve   *Skier*
2408 N 52nd Ave, Yakima, WA 98903, USA

Mai, Vincent   *Financier*
%AEA Investors, 65 E 55th St, New York, NY 10022, USA

Maida, Adam J Cardinal   *Religious Leader*
%Archdiocese of Detroit, 1234 Washington Blvd, Detroit, MI 48226, USA

Maiden-Naccarato, Jeanne   *Bowler*
1 Stadium Way N, #4, Tacoma, WA 98403, USA

Maier, Sepp   *Soccer Player*
Parkstr 62, 84405 Anzing, Germany

Mailer, Norman K   *Writer*
142 Columbia Heights Place, Brooklyn, NY 11201, USA

Maisel, Jay   *Photographer*
190 The Bowery, New York, NY 10012, USA

Maisel, Sherman J   *Economist*
2164 Hyde St, San Francisco, CA 94109, USA

Maitland, Beth   *Actress*
%Craig Agency, 8485 Melrose Place, #E, Los Angeles, CA 90069, USA

Majdarzavyn Ganzorig   *Cosmonaut, Mongolia*
%Academy of Sciences, Peace Ave 54-B, Ulan Bator 51, Mongolia

Majerle, Daniel L (Dan)   *Basketball Player*
%Cleveland Cavaliers, 2923 Statesboro Rd, Richfield, OH 44286, USA

Majerus, Rick   *Basketball Coach*
%University of Utah, Athletic Dept, Huntsman Center, Salt Lake City, UT 84112, USA

Majewski, Janusz   *Movie Director*
Ul Forteczna 1-A, 01-540 Warsaw, Poland

Majkowski, Don   *Football Player*
%Detroit Lions, Silverdome, 1200 Featherstone Rd, Pontiac, MI 48342, USA

Major, Clarence L   *Writer*
%University of California, English Dept, Sproul Hall, Davis, CA 95616, USA

Major, John   *Prime Minister, England*
%Prime Minister's Office, 10 Downing St, London SW1A 2AA, England

Majors, John T (Johnny)   *Football Player, Coach*
%University of Pittsburgh, Athletic Dept, PO Box 7436, Pittsburgh, PA 15213, USA

Majors, Lee   *Actor*
625 San Marco Dr, Fort Lauderdale, FL 33301, USA

Makarov, Askold A   *Ballet Dancer*
%Askold Makarov's State Ballet, 15 Mayakovsky St, St Petersburg, Russia

Mahathir Bin Mohamed - Makarov

Makarov, Oleg G — *Cosmonaut*
%Potchta Kosmonavtov, 141 160 Svyosdny Gorodok, Moskovskoi Oblasti, Russia

Makarova, Inna — *Actress*
Ukrainian Blvd 11, 121059 Moscow, Russia

Makarova, Natalia R — *Ballerina*
%Herbert Breslin Inc, 119 W 57th St, New York, NY 10019, USA

Makeba, Miriam — *Singer*
%Performers of the World, 8901 Melrose Ave, #201, Los Angeles, CA 90069, USA

Makhalina, Yulia — *Ballerina*
%State Kirov Ballet, 1 Ploschad Iskusstr, St Petersburg, Russia

Maki, Fumihiko — *Architect*
5-16-22 Higashi-Gotanda, Shinagawaku, Tokyo, Japan

Makk, Karoly — *Movie Director*
Hankoczy Jeno Ut 15, 1022 Budapest, Hungary

Mako — *Actor*
%Amsel Eisenstadt Frazier, 6310 San Vicente Blvd, #401, Los Angeles, CA 90048, USA

Mako, C Gene — *Tennis Player*
430 S Burnside Ave, #M-C, Los Angeles, CA 90036, USA

Maksimova, Yekaterina S — *Ballerina*
%Bolshoi Theater, Teatralnaya Pl 1, 103009 Moscow, Russia

Maksymiuk, Jerzy — *Conductor*
%BBC Scottish Symphony, Queen Margaret Dr, Glasgow G12 8BC, Scotland

Maktoum, Sheikh Rashid bin Said al- — *Prime Minister, United Arab Emirates*
%Royal Palace, PO Box 899, Abu Dhubai, United Arab Emirates

Malandro, Kristina — *Actress*
2518 Cardigan Court, Los Angeles, CA 90077, USA

Malara, Anthony C — *Television Executive*
%CBS-TV Network, 51 W 52nd St, New York, NY 10019, USA

Malarchuk, Clint — *Hockey Player*
%Quebec Nordiques, 2205 Ave du Colisee, Quebec City PQ G1L 4W7, Canada

Malcolm, George J — *Concert Harpsichordist*
99 Wimbledon Hill Rd, London SW19 4BE, England

Malden, Karl — *Actor*
1845 Mandeville Canyon, Los Angeles, CA 90049, USA

Malecela, John — *Prime Minister, Tanzania*
%Prime Minister's Office, PO Box 980, Dodoma, Dar es Salaam, Tanzania

Malee, Chompoo — *Fashion Designer*
%Hino & Malee Inc, 3701 N Ravenswood Ave, Chicago, IL 60613, USA

Maleeva, Katerina — *Tennis Player*
Mladostr 1, #45, NH 14, Sofia 1174, Bulgaria

Maleeva-Fragniere, Manuela — *Tennis Player*
%Women's Tennis Assn, 133 1st St NE, St Petersburg, FL 33701, USA

Malenick, Donal H — *Businessman*
%Worthington Industries, 1205 Dearborn Dr, Columbus, OH 43085, USA

Malerba, Franco F — *Astronaut*
Via Cantore 10, 16149 Genova, Italy

Malfitano, Catherine — *Opera Singer*
%Metropolitan Opera Assn, Lincoln Center Plaza, New York, NY 10023, USA

Malick, Wendie — *Actress*
%Camden ITG Talent Agency, 822 S Robertson Blvd, #200, Los Angeles, CA 90035, USA

Malicky, Neal — *Educator*
%Baldwin-Wallace College, President's Office, Berea, OH 44017, USA

Malietoa Tanumafili II — *King, Western Samoa*
%Government House, Vailima, Apia, Western Samoa

Maliponte, Adrianna — *Opera Singer*
%Gorlinsky Promotions, 35 Darer, London W1, England

Malkan, Matthew A — *Astronomer*
%University of Arizona, Steward Observatory, Tucson, AZ 85721, USA

Malkhov, Vladimir — *Ballet Dancer*
%American Ballet Theatre, 890 Broadway, New York, NY 10003, USA

Malkovich, John — *Actor*
1322 S Genesee Ave, Los Angeles, CA 90019, USA

Mallary, Robert — *Sculptor*
PO Box 97, Conway, MA 01341, USA

Malle, Louis — *Movie Director*
Le Couel, 46260 Limogne en Quercy, France

Mallea, Eduardo — *Writer*
Posadas 1120, Buenos Aires, Argentina

M

Mallender, William H *Businessman*
%Talley Industries, 2702 N 44th St, Phoenix, AZ 85008, USA

Mallette, Alfred J *Army General*
4578 Bedford Court, Evans, GA 30809, USA

Malley, Kenneth C *Navy Admiral*
Commander, Naval Sea Systems Command, Navy Dept, Washington, DC 20362, USA

Mallick, Don *Test Pilot*
42045 N Tilton Dr, Quartz Hill, CA 93536, USA

Mallon, Meg *Golfer*
%Ladies Professional Golf Assn, 2570 Volusia Ave, Daytona Beach, FL 32114, USA

Mallory, Carole *Actress*
2300 5th Ave, New York, NY 10037, USA

Malloy, Edward A *Educator*
%University of Notre Dame, President's Office, Notre Dame, IN 46556, USA

Malloy, Larkin *Actor*
1501 Broadway, #703, New York, NY 10036, USA

Malloy, Patrick E, III *Financier*
%New York Bancorp, 241-02 Northern Blvd, Douglaston, NY 11362, USA

Malo, Raul *Singer (Mavericks), Songwriter*
%AristoMedia, 1620 16th Ave S, Nashville, TN 37212, USA

Maloff, Sam *Furniture Designer*
PO Box 51, Alta Loma, CA 91701, USA

Malone, Dorothy *Actress*
PO Box 7287, Dallas, TX 75209, USA

Malone, James R *Businessman*
%Anchor Glass Container Corp, 4343 Anchor Plaza Parkway, Tampa, FL 33634, USA

Malone, James W *Religious Leader*
%National Catholic Bishops Conference, 1312 Massachusetts, Washington, DC 20005, USA

Malone, Jeff *Basketball Player*
%Philadelphia 76ers, Veterans Stadium, PO Box 25040, Philadelphia, PA 19147, USA

Malone, John C *Television Executive*
%Tele-Communications, 5619 DTC Parkway, Englewood, CO 80111, USA

Malone, Karl *Basketball Player*
%Utah Jazz, Delta Center, 301 W South Temple, Salt Lake City, UT 84101, USA

Malone, Michael P *Educator*
%Montana State University, President's Office, Bozeman, MT 59717, USA

Malone, Moses *Basketball Player*
%San Antonio Spurs, 600 E Market St, #102, San Antonio, TX 78205, USA

Malone, Nancy *Actress*
11624 Sunshine Terrace, Studio City, CA 91604, USA

Malone, Robert B *Financier*
%SunBank/South Florida, 501 E Las Olas Blvd, Fort Lauderdale, FL 33301, USA

Malone, Thomas F *Geophysicist*
300 Woodcroft Parkway, Durham, NC 27713, USA

Malone, Wallace D, Jr *Financier*
%SouthTrust Corp, 420 N 20th St, Birmingham, AL 35203, USA

Maloney, Dan *Hockey Coach*
%Winnipeg Jets, Arena, 15-1430 Maroons Rd, Winnipeg MB R3G 0L5, Canada

Maloney, Don *Hockey Player*
22 Park Dr S, Rye, NY 10580, USA

Maloney, James W (Jim) *Baseball Player*
7027 N Teilman Ave, #102, Fresno, CA 93711, USA

Maloney, William R *Marine Corps General*
%Navy Mutual Aid Assn, Board of Directors, Arlington Annex, Washington, DC 20370, USA

Malott, Deane W *Educator*
322 Wait Ave, Ithaca, NY 14850, USA

Maloy, Robert *Educator, Librarian*
PO Box 524, Washington, DC 20044, USA

Malozemoff, Plato *Businessman*
230 Park Ave, #1154, New York, NY 10169, USA

Maltby, John N *Businessman*
Broadford House, Stratfield Turgis, Basingstoke, Hants RG27 0AS, England

Maltby, Richard E, Jr *Lyricist*
1111 Park Ave, #4-D, New York, NY 10128, USA

Maltin, Leonard *Television Critic*
10424 Whipple St, Toluca Lake, CA 91602, USA

Malyshev, Yuri V *Cosmonaut*
%Potchta Kosmonavtov, 141 160 Svyosdny Gorodok, Moskovskoi Oblasti, Russia

Mallender - Malyshev

Mamet, David A — *Playwright*
%General Delivery, Cabot, VT 05647, USA

Mammel, Russell N — *Businessman*
%Nash Finch Co, 7600 France Ave S, Minneapolis, MN 55435, USA

Mamo, Anthony J — *President, Malta*
49 Stella Maris St, Sliema, Malta

Mamula, Mike — *Football Player*
%Arizona Cardinals, 8701 S Hardy Dr, Tempe, AZ 85284, USA

Manakov, Gennadi M — *Cosmonaut*
%Potchta Kosmonavtov, 141 160 Svyosdny Gorodok, Moskovskoi Oblasti, Russia

Manarov, Musa C — *Cosmonaut*
Khovanskeya 3, 129 515 Moscow, Russia

Manasseh, Leonard S — *Architect*
6 Bacon's Lane, Highgate, London N6 6BL, England

Manatt, Charles T — *Political Leader*
4814 Woodway Lane NW, Washington, DC 20016, USA

Mancha, Vaughn — *Football Player*
1308 High Rd, Tallahassee, FL 32304, USA

Mancham, James R M — *President, Seychelles*
%Lloyd's Bank, 81 Edgware Rd, London W2 2HY, England

Mancheski, Frederick J — *Businessman*
%Echlin Inc, 100 Double Beach Rd, Branford, CT 06405, USA

Manchester, Melissa — *Singer, Songwriter*
15822 High Knoll Rd, Encino, CA 91436, USA

Manchester, William — *Writer*
PO Box 329, Wesleyan Station, Middletown, CT 06457, USA

Mancini, Ray (Boom Boom) — *Boxer*
2611 25th St, Santa Monica, CA 90405, USA

Mancuso, Frank G — *Movie Executive*
%MGM/United Artists, 1350 Ave of Americas, New York, NY 10010, USA

Mancuso, Nick — *Actor*
7160 Grasswood Ave, Malibu, CA 90265, USA

Mandan, Robert — *Actor*
4160 Dixie Canyon Rd, Sherman Oaks, CA 91423, USA

Mandel, Howie — *Actor*
24710 Robert Guy Rd, Hidden Hills, CA 91302, USA

Mandel, Johnny — *Composer*
28946 Cliffside Dr, Malibu, CA 90265, USA

Mandel, Marvin — *Governor, MD*
%Frank A Defilippo, Cross Keys Rd, Baltimore, MD 21210, USA

Mandela, N Winnie — *Social Activist*
Orlando West, Soweto, Johannesburg, South Africa

Mandela, Nelson R — *President, South Africa; Nobel Laureate*
%President's Office, Union Buildings, PB X-1000, Pretoria 0001, South Afri

Mandelbrot, Benoit B — *Mathematician*
%IBM, PO Box 218, Yorktown Heights, NY 10598, USA

Mandell, Samuel W W — *Businessman*
%Bradlees Inc, 1 Bradlees Circle, Braintree, MA 02184, USA

Mandich, Jim — *Football Player*
16101 Aberdeen Way, Miami Lakes, FL 33014, USA

Mandle, E Roger — *Museum Director*
%Rhode Island School of Design, President's Office, Providence, RI 02903, USA

Mandles, Martinn H — *Businessman*
%ABM Industries, 50 Fremont St, San Francisco, CA 94105, USA

Mandlikova, Hanna — *Tennis Player*
Vymolova 8, 150 00 Prague 5, Czech Republic

Mandrell, Barbara — *Singer*
%Mandrell Mgmt, PO Box 800, Hendersonville, TN 37077, USA

Mandrell, Erline — *Singer*
%Mandrell Mgmt, PO Box 800, Hendersonville, TN 37077, USA

Mandrell, Louise — *Singer*
%Mandrell Mgmt, PO Box 800, Hendersonville, TN 37077, USA

Mandylor, Costas — *Actor*
%William Morris Agency, 151 S El Camino Dr, Beverly Hills, CA 90212, USA

Manekshaw, Sam H F J — *Army Field Marshal, India*
Stavka Springfield, Coonor, Nilgiris, South India, India

Manetti, Larry — *Actor*
4615 Winnetka Ave, Woodland Hills, CA 91364, USA

M

Mamet - Manetti

M

Mangelsdorf, David *Geneticist*
%Salk Institute, Gene Expression Laboratory, PO Box 85800, San Diego, CA 92186, USA

Mangelsdorf, Paul C *Geneticist*
510 Caswell Rd, Chapel Hill, NC 27514, USA

Mangieri, John *Educator*
%Arkansas State University, President's Office, State University, AK 72467, USA

Mangione, Chuck *Jazz Trumpeter, Composer*
%Gates Music, 1845 Winton Rd S, #2000, Rochester, NY 14618, USA

Mangold, Sylvia *Artist*
1 Bull Rd, Washingtonville, NY 10992, USA

Maniatis, Thomas P *Genetics Engineer, Molecular Biolgist*
%Harvard University, Biochemistry Dept, Cambridge, MA 02138, USA

Manilow, Barry *Singer, Songwriter*
%Stiletto Entertainment, 5443 Beethoven St, Los Angeles, CA 90066, USA

Mankiller, Wilma P *Social Activist*
%Cherokee Nation, PO Box 948, Tahlequah, OK 74465, USA

Mankowitz, Wolf *Writer*
Bridge House, Ahakista, County Cork, Ireland

Manley, Elizabeth *Figure Skater*
%M A Rosenberg, 73271 Riata Trail, Palm Desert, CA 92260, USA

Manley, Michael N *Prime Minister, Jamaica*
%People's National Party, 89 Old Hope Rd, Kingston 6, Jamaica

Mann, Abby *Writer*
602 N Whittier Dr, Beverly Hills, CA 90210, USA

Mann, Carol *Golfer*
6 Cape Chestnut, The Woodlands, TX 77381, USA

Mann, Charles *Football Player*
%Washington Redskins, 21300 Redskin Park Dr, Ashburn, VA 22011, USA

Mann, David W *Religious Leader*
10025 Crown Point Dr, Fort Wayne, IN 46804, USA

Mann, Delbert *Movie Director, Producer*
%Caroline Productions, 401 S Burnside Ave, #11-D, Los Angeles, CA 90036, USA

Mann, Herbie *Jazz Flutist*
%Kokopelli Music, PO Box 8200, Santa Fe, NM 87504, USA

Mann, Johnny *Composer, Conductor*
78516 Gorman Lane, Indio, CA 92203, USA

Mann, Larry D *Actor*
%Allen Goldstein Assoc, 5015 Lemona Ave, Sherman Oaks, CA 91403, USA

Mann, Marvin L *Businessman*
%Lexmark International, 55 Railroad Ave, Greenwich, CT 06830, USA

Mann, Michael K *Television Producer, Director*
13746 Sunset Blvd, Pacific Palisades, CA 90272, USA

Mann, Robert *Football Player*
David Stott Building, #3500, 1150 Griswold St, Detroit, MI 48226, USA

Mann, Robert W *Biomedical Engineer*
5 Pelham Rd, Lexington, MA 02173, USA

Mann, Shelley *Swimmer*
315 S Ivy St, Arlington, VA 22204, USA

Mann, Thomas C *Government Official*
8105 Middle Court, Austin, TX 78759, USA

Manners, David *Actor*
3011 Foothill Rd, Santa Barbara, CA 93105, USA

Manning, Archie *Football Player, Sportscaster*
1420 1st St, New Orleans, LA 70130, USA

Manning, Daniel R (Danny) *Basketball Player*
%Phoenix Suns, 201 E Jefferson St, Phoenix, AZ 85004, USA

Manning, Irene *Actress*
3165 La Mesa Dr, San Carlos, CA 94070, USA

Manning, Jane *Opera Singer*
2 Wilton Square, London N1, England

Manning, Kenneth P *Businessman*
%Universal Foods Corp, 443 E Michigan St, Milwaukee, WI 53202, USA

Manning, Patrick A M *Prime Minister, Trinidad & Tobago*
%Prime Minister's Office, Central Bank Building, Port of Spain, Trinidad

Manning, Richard E (Rick) *Baseball Player*
12151 Newq Market, Chagrin Falls, OH 44026, USA

Manning, Robert J *Editor*
191 Commonwealth Ave, Boston, MA 02116, USA

Mannino, Franco — *Conductor*
%Studio Mannino, Via Citta di Castello 14, 00191 Rome, Italy

Manoff, Dinah — *Actress*
21244 Ventura Blvd, #126, Sherman Oaks, CA 91423, USA

Manoogian, Richard A — *Businessman*
%Masco Corp, 21001 Van Born Rd, Taylor, MI 48180, USA

Manos, Pete L — *Businessman*
%Giant Food Inc, 6300 Sheriff Rd, Landover, MD 20785, USA

Mansbach, Peter J — *Financier*
%Republic National Bank of New York, 452 5th Ave, New York, NY 10018, USA

Mansell, Nigel — *Auto Racing Driver*
Portland House, Station Rd, Box 1, Ballasalla, Isle of Man, United Kingdom

Manser, Michael J — *Architect*
%Manser Assoc, 8 Hammersmith Broadway, London W6 7AL, England

Mansfield, Michael J (Mike) — *Senator, MT; Diplomat*
1101 Pennsylvania Ave NW, #900, Washington, DC 20004, USA

Mansholt, Sicco L — *Government Official, Netherlands*
Oosteinde 18, 8351 HB Wapserveen, Netherlands

Manske, Edgar — *Football Player*
1031 Lanza Court, San Marcos, CA 92069, USA

Manson, Dave — *Hockey Player*
%Edmonton Oilers, Northlands Coliseum, Edmonton AB T5B 4M9, Canada

Mansouri, Lotfi — *Opera Director*
%San Francisco Opera House, 301 Van Ness Ave, San Francisco, CA 94102, USA

Mantee, Paul — *Actor*
3709 Las Flores Canyon Rd, #4, Malibu, CA 90265, USA

Mantegna, Joe — *Actor*
10415 Sarah St, Toluca Lake, CA 91602, USA

Mantooth, Randolph — *Actor*
PO Box 280, Agoura, CA 91376, USA

Manuel, Robert — *Actor*
La Maison du Buisson, 22-26 Rue Jules Regnier, 78370 Plaisir, France

Manuelidis, Laura — *Neuropathologist*
%Yale University Medical School, Neuropathology Dept, New Haven, CT 06520, USA

Manz, Wolfgang — *Concert Pianist*
Pasteuralle 55, 30655 Hanover, Germany

Manzarek, Ray — *Keyboardist (Doors)*
232 S Rodeo Dr, Beverly Hills, CA 90212, USA

Manzi, Jim P — *Businessman*
%Lotus Development Corp, 55 Cambridge Parkway, Cambridge, MA 02142, USA

Manzoni, Giacomo — *Composer*
Viale Papiniano 31, 20123 Milan, Italy

Mara, Adele — *Actress*
1928 Mandeville Canyon Rd, Los Angeles, CA 90049, USA

Mara, Kamisese K T — *Prime Minister, Fiji*
6 Berkeley Crescent, Suva, Fiji

Mara, Wellington T — *Football Executive*
%New York Giants, Giants Stadium, East Rutherford, NJ 07073, USA

Marafino, Vincent N — *Businessman*
%Lockheed Corp, 4500 Park Granada Blvd, Calabasas, CA 91302, USA

Marais, Jean — *Actor*
%Cineart, 34 Ave de Champs-Elysees, 75008 Paris, France

Maraniss, David — *Journalist*
%Washington Post, Editorial Dept, 1150 15th St NW, Washington, DC 20071, USA

Marbut, Robert G — *Publisher*
%Argyle Communications, 100 NE Loop, #1400, San Antonio, TX 78216, USA

Marc, Alessandra — *Opera Singer*
%Columbia Artists Mgmt Inc, 165 W 57th St, New York, NY 10019, USA

Marca-Relli, Conrad — *Artist*
%Jaffe Baker Blau Gallery, 608 Banjan Trail, Boca Raton, FL 33431, USA

Marceau, Marcel — *Mime*
%Compagne de Mime, 32 Rue de Londres, 75009 Paris, France

March, Barbara — *Actress*
%Judy Schoen Assoc, 606 N Larchmont Blvd, #309, Los Angeles, CA 90004, USA

March, Jane — *Actress*
%Storm Model Mgmt, 5 Jubilee Place, #100, London SW3 3TD, England

Marchais, Georges — *Government Official, France*
%Parti Communiste Francais, 2 Place du Colonel Fabien, 75019 Paris, France

M

Mannino - Marchais

M

Marchand, Nancy — *Actress*
205 W 89th St, #6-S, New York, NY 10024, USA

Marchetti, Gino — *Football Player*
324 Devon Way, West Chester, PA 19380, USA

Marchetti, Leo V — *Labor Leader*
%Fraternal Order of Police, 5613 Belair Rd, Baltimore, MD 21206, USA

Marchibroda, Theodore J (Ted) — *Football Player, Coach*
%Indianapolis Colts, 7001 W 56th St, Indianapolis, IN 46254, USA

Marchuk, Guri I — *Applied Mathematician*
%Computing Math Institute, Leninsky Prosp 32-A, 117334 Moscow, Russia

Marchuk, Yevhen — *Prime Minister, Ukraine*
%Prime Minister's Office, Kiev, Ukraine

Marcinkevicius, Iustinas M — *Poet*
Mildos Str 33, #6, 232055 Vilnius, Lithuania

Marcinkus, Paul C — *Religious Leader*
%Institute for Religious Work, Vatican City, Rome, Italy

Marciulionis, Sarunas — *Basketball Player*
%Sacramento Kings, 1 Sports Parkway, Sacramento, CA 95834, USA

Marcovicci, Andrea — *Actress*
8273 W Norton Ave, Los Angeles, CA 90046, USA

Marcum, Joseph L — *Financier*
%Ohio Casualty Corp, 136 N 3rd St, Hamilton, OH 45025, USA

Marcus, Bernard — *Businessman*
%Home Depot Inc, 2727 Paces Ferry Rd, Atlanta, GA 30339, USA

Marcus, Ken — *Photographer*
6916 Melrose Ave, Los Angeles, CA 90038, USA

Marcus, Rudolph A — *Nobel Chemistry Laureate*
331 S Hill Ave, Pasadena, CA 91106, USA

Marcus, Ruth B — *Philosopher*
311 St Roman St, New Haven, CT 06511, USA

Marcus, Stanley — *Businessman*
NCNB Center, 4800 Tower II, Dallas, TX 75201, USA

Mardall, Cyril L — *Architect*
5 Boyne Terrace Mews, London W11 3LR, England

Marden, Brice — *Artist*
54 Bond St, New York, NY 10012, USA

Marden, Robert A — *Financier*
%People Heritage Financial Group, 1 Portland Square, Portland, ME 04101, USA

Maree, Sydney — *Track Athlete*
%Olympic Job Opportunity Program, 1750 E Boulder, Colorado Springs, CO 80909, USA

Margal, Albert M — *Prime Minister, Sierra Leone*
8 Hornsey Rise Gardens, London N19, England

Margaret Rose — *Princess, England*
Kensington Palace, London W8 4PU, England

Margeot, Jean Cardinal — *Religious Leader*
Bonne Terre, Vacoas, Mautitius

Margerison, Richard W — *Businessman*
%Tyler Corp, San Jacinto Tower, 2121 San Jacinto St, Dallas, TX 75201, USA

Margoliash, Emmanuel — *Biochemist*
%University of Chicago, Biological Sciences Dept, Box 4348, Chicago, IL 60680, USA

Margolin, Stuart — *Actor*
2809 2nd St, #1, Santa Monica, CA 90405, USA

Margolis, Karl — *Businessman*
%McCrory Corp, 667 Madison Ave, New York, NY 10021, USA

Margrave, John L — *Chemist*
5012 Tangle Lane, Houston, TX 77056, USA

Margrethe II — *Queen, Denmark*
%Amalienborg Palace, 1257 Copenhagen K, Denmark

Margulies, James H (Jimmy) — *Editorial Cartoonist*
%Hackensack Record, Editorial Dept, 150 River St, Hackensack, NJ 07601, USA

Margulies, Julianna — *Actress*
%Gersh Agency, 232 N Canon Dr, Beverly Hills, CA 90210, USA

Margulis, Lynn — *Biologist, Botanist*
2 Cummington St, Boston, MA 02215, USA

Mariategui, Sandro — *Prime Minister, Peru*
Congreso Del Peru, #301, Plaza Bolivar, Lima, Peru

Marichal, Juan A S — *Baseball Player*
3178 NW 19th St, Miami, FL 33125, USA

Marchand - Marichal

M

Marie — *Princess, Lichtenstein*
%Schloss Vaduz, 9490 Vaduz, Liechtenstein

Marie, Aurelius J B L — *President, Dominica*
Zicack, Portsmouth, Danica

Marie, Lisa — *Model*
%Click Model Mgmt, 881 7th Ave, New York, NY 10019, USA

Marie, Teena — *Singer*
1000 Laguna Rd, Pasadena, CA 91105, USA

Marimow, William K — *Journalist*
1025 Winding Way, Baltimore, MD 21210, USA

Marinaro, Edward F (Ed) — *Actor, Football Player*
1466 N Doheny Dr, Los Angeles, CA 90069, USA

Marineau, Philip A — *Businessman*
%Quaker Oats Co, 321 N Clark St, Chicago, IL 60610, USA

Marinella, Sabino — *Businessman*
%Keyport Life Insurance, 125 High St, Boston, MA 02110, USA

Marini, Marino — *Sculptor*
Piazza Mirabella 2, 20121 Milan, Italy

Marino, Daniel C (Dan), Jr — *Football Player*
%Miami Dolphins, 7500 SW 30th St, Davie, FL 33329, USA

Marino, John — *Cyclist*
%Race Across America, 64 Bennington, Irvine, CA 92720, USA

Mario, Ernest — *Pharmacist, Businessman*
%Alza Corp, 950 Page Mill Rd, Palo Alto, CA 94304, USA

Mariotti, Ray — *Editor*
%Austin American-Statesman, Editorial Dept, 166 E Riverside, Austin, TX 78704, USA

Marisol (Escobar) — *Sculptor*
%Marlborough Gallery, 40 W 57th St, New York, NY 10019, USA

Mark, Hans M — *Government Official, Physicist, Educator*
1715 Scenic Dr, Austin, TX 78703, USA

Mark, Mary Ellen — *Photographer*
%International Center of Photography, 1130 15th Ave, New York, NY 10128, USA

Mark, Reuben — *Businessman*
%Colgate-Palmolive Co, 300 Park Ave, New York, NY 10022, USA

Mark, Robert — *Law Enforcement Official*
Esher, Surrey KT10 8LU, England

Markaryants, Vladimir S — *Government Official, Armenia*
%Council of Ministers, Yerevan, Armenia

Marken, William R — *Editor*
%Sunset Magazine, Editorial Dept, 80 Willow Rd, Menlo Park, CA 94025, USA

Markert, Clement L — *Biologist*
4005 Wakefield Dr, Colorado Springs, CO 80906, USA

Markey, Lucille P — *Thoroughbred Racing Breeder*
18 La Gorce Circle Lane, La Gorce Island, Miami Beach, FL 33141, USA

Markham, Monte — *Actor*
PO Box 607, Malibu, CA 90265, USA

Markkula, A C (Mike), Jr — *Businessman*
%Apple Computer Inc, 1 Infinite Loop, Cupertino, CA 95014, USA

Markle, C Wilson — *Film Engineer*
%Colorization Inc, 26 Soho St, Toronto ON M5T 1Z7, Canada

Markle, Peter — *Movie Director*
7510 W Sunset Blvd, #509, Los Angeles, CA 90046, USA

Markov, Victor — *Football Player*
5512 NE Windemere Rd, Seattle, WA 98105, USA

Markova, Alicia — *Ballerina*
%Barclays Bank Ltd, 137 Brompton Rd, London SW3 1QB, England

Markowitz, Harry M — *Nobel Economics Laureate*
1010 Turquoise St, #245, San Diego, CA 92109, USA

Markowitz, Michael — *Artist*
%23rd Street Gallery, 3747 23rd St, San Francisco, CA 94114, USA

Markowitz, Robert — *Movie Director, Producer*
11521 Amanda Dr, Studio City, CA 91604, USA

Marks, Albert J — *Pageant Director*
%Miss American Pageant, 1325 Broadway, Atlantic City, NJ 08401, USA

Marks, Bruce — *Ballet Dancer, Artistic Director*
%Boston Ballet Co, 19 Clarendon St, Boston, MA 02116, USA

Marks, Leonard H — *Government Official*
2833 McGill Terrace NW, Washington, DC 20008, USA

Marie - Marks

M

Marks, Paul A *Oncologist, Cell Biologist*
PO Box 1485, Washington Depot, CT 06793, USA

Marks, William L *Financier*
%Whitney National Bank, 228 St Charles Ave, New Orleans, LA 70130, USA

Marlen, John S *Businessman*
%Ameron Inc, 245 S Los Robles Ave, Pasadena, CA 91101, USA

Marler, Peter R *Biologist*
Reservoir Rd, Staatsburg, NY 12580, USA

Marlette, Douglas N (Doug) *Editorial Cartoonist*
PO Box 32188, Charlotte, NC 28232, USA

Marley, James E *Businessman*
%AMP Inc, 470 Friendship Rd, Harrisburg, PA 17111, USA

Marley, Ziggy *Singer*
Jack's Hill, Kingston, Jamaica

Marlin, Sterling *Auto Racing Driver*
%Stavola Brothers Racing, PO Box 139, Harrisburg, NC 28075, USA

Marm, Walter J, Jr *Vietnam War Army Hero (CMH)*
220 Oak Hill Dr, Hatboro, PA 19040, USA

Marohn, William D *Businessman*
%Whirlpool Corp, 2000 N State St, Rt 63, Benton Harbor, MI 49022, USA

Maroney, Daniel V, Jr *Labor Leader*
%Amalgamated Transit Union, 5025 Wisconsin Ave NW, Washington, DC 20016, USA

Marotte, Gilles *Hockey Player*
%Agence Prestige, 4777 Blvd Bourque, Rock Forest PQ J1N 1A6, Canada

Marr, Dave *Golfer*
%Riviere-Marr, 2100 W Loop St, #800, Houston, TX 77027, USA

Marriner, Neville *Conductor*
67 Cornwell Gardens, London SW7 4BA, England

Marriott, Alice S *Businesswoman*
%Marriott Corp, 10400 Fernwood Rd, Bethesda, MD 20817, USA

Marriott, J Willard, Jr *Businessman*
%Marriott International, Marriott Dr, Washington, DC 20058, USA

Marriott, Richard E *Businessman*
%Host Marriott Corp, 10400 Fernwood Rd, Washington, DC 20058, USA

Marro, Anthony J *Editor*
%Newsday, Editorial Dept, 235 Pinelawn Rd, Melville, NY 11747, USA

Marron, Donald B *Financier*
%PaineWebber Group, 1285 Ave of Americas, New York, NY 10019, USA

Mars, Forrest, Jr *Businessman*
%Mars Inc, 6885 Elm St, McLean, VA 22101, USA

Mars, Kenneth *Actor*
10820 Shoshone Ave, Granada Hills, CA 91344, USA

Marsalis, Branford *Musician, Composer*
9520 Cedarbrook Rd, Beverly Hills, CA 90210, USA

Marsalis, Wynton *Trumpeter, Composer*
3 Lincoln Center, #2911, New York, NY 10023, USA

Marsden, Roy *Actor*
%London Mgmt, 2-4 Noel St, London W1V 3RB, England

Marsh of Mannington, Richard W *Government Official, England*
Laurentian House, Barnwood, Gloucs GL4 7RZ, England

Marsh, Brad *Hockey Player*
%Ottawa Senators, 301 Moodie Dr, #200, Nepean ON K2H 9C4, Canada

Marsh, Caryl G *Army General*
Commanding General, I Corps, Fort Lewis, WA 98433, USA

Marsh, Henry *Track Athlete*
%General Delivery, Bountiful, UT 84010, USA

Marsh, Jean *Actress*
%International Creative Mgmt, 76 Oxford St, London W1N 0AX, England

Marsh, Linda *Actress*
170 West End Ave, 22-P, New York, NY 10023, USA

Marsh, Marian *Actress*
PO Box 1, Palm Desert, CA 92261, USA

Marsh, Michael (Mike) *Track Athlete*
2425 Holly Hall St, #152, Houston, TX 77054, USA

Marsh, Miles L *Businessman*
%James River Corp of Virginia, 120 Tredegar St, Richmond, VA 23219, USA

Marsh, Robert T *Air Force General, Businessman*
%Thiokel Corp, 6327 Manchester Way, Alexandria, VA 22304, USA

Marks - Marsh

Marshall, Barry J *Medical Researcher*
%University of Virginia Med Center, Immunolgy Dept, Charlottesville, VA 22908, USA

Marshall, Burke *Attorney*
Castle Meadow Rd, Newton, CT 06470, USA

Marshall, Carolyn M *Religious Leader*
%United Methodist Church, 204 N Newlin St, Veedersburg, IN 47987, USA

Marshall, Dale Rogers *Educator*
%Wheaton College, President's Office, Norton, MA 02766, USA

Marshall, David L *Businessman*
%Pittston Co, 100 First Stamford Place, Stamford, CT 06902, USA

Marshall, Donyell *Basketball Player*
%Golden State Warriors, Oakland Coliseum Arena, Oakland, CA 94621, USA

Marshall, E G *Actor*
Bryan Lake Rd, RFD 2, Mt Kisco, NY 10549, USA

Marshall, Esme *Model*
%Fame Models Ltd, 133 E 58th St, New York, NY 10022, USA

Marshall, F Ray *Secretary, Labor*
%University of Texas, LBJ Public Affairs School, Austin, TX 78712, USA

Marshall, Frank W *Movie Producer*
%Amblin Entertainment, 100 Universal City Plaza, #477, Universal City, CA 91608, USA

Marshall, Garry K *Movie Director*
10459 Sarah St, Toluca Lake, CA 91602, USA

Marshall, Gordon S *Businessman*
%Marshall Industries, 9320 Telstar Ave, El Monte, CA 91731, USA

Marshall, Harold D *Financier*
%Associates Corp of America, 250 Carpenter Freeway, Dallas, TX 75266, USA

Marshall, James *Actor*
30710 Monte Lado Dr, Malibu, CA 90265, USA

Marshall, John *Prime Minister, New Zealand*
%Buddle Findlay Barristers, PO Box 2694, Wellington, New Zealand

Marshall, Joseph W *Businessman*
%Idaho Power Co, 1221 W Idaho St, Boise, ID 83702, USA

Marshall, Ken *Actor*
%Paradigm Agency, 10100 Santa Monica Blvd, #2500, Los Angeles, CA 90067, USA

Marshall, Leonard *Football Player*
%New York Jets, 1000 Fulton Ave, Hempstead, NY 11550, USA

Marshall, Margaret A *Opera Singer*
Woodside, Main St, Gargunnock, Stirling FKS 3BP, Scotland

Marshall, Michael A (Mike) *Baseball Player*
13063 Ventura Blvd, Studio City, CA 91604, USA

Marshall, Michael G (Mike) *Baseball Player*
%West Texas A&M, Athletic Dept, Canyon, TX 79016, USA

Marshall, Penny *Actress, Director*
7150 La Presa Dr, Los Angeles, CA 90068, USA

Marshall, Peter *Television Host*
16714 Oak View Dr, Encino, CA 91436, USA

Marshall, Robert C *Businessman*
%Tandem Computers Inc, 19333 Vallco Parkway, Cupertino, CA 95014, USA

Marshall, Wilber *Football Player*
%New York Jets, 1000 Fulton Ave, Hempstead, NY 11550, USA

Marshall, Willard W *Baseball Player*
1090 Arcadian Way, Fort Lee, NJ 07024, USA

Marshall, William *Actor*
11351 Dronfield Ave, Pacoima, CA 91331, USA

Marston, Robert Q *Educator*
Rt 1, Box 20-A, Alachua, FL 32615, USA

Martell, Dominic A *Labor Leader*
%Plasters Cement Masons Int'l Assn, 1125 17th St NW, Washington, DC 20036, USA

Martens, Wilfried *Prime Minister, Belgium*
%Europese Volkspartij, 16 Rue de la Victoire, 1060 Brussels, Belgium

Martika (Marrero) *Singer*
%Lobeline Communications, 8995 Elevado Ave, Los Angeles, CA 90069, USA

Martin (Miss Manners), Judith *Journalist*
1651 Harvard St NW, Washington, DC 20009, USA

Martin, Agnes *Artist*
414 Placitas Rd, Taos, NM 87571, USA

Martin, Alastair B *Tennis Contributor*
%Bessemer Trust Co, 630 5th Ave, New York, NY 10111, USA

M

Martin, Albert C — *Architect*
%Albert C Martin Assoc, 811 W 7th St, #800, Los Angeles, CA 90017, USA

Martin, Andrea — *Actress*
%William Morris Agency, 1325 Ave of Americas, New York, NY 10019, USA

Martin, Ann — *Commentator*
%KCBS-TV, News Dept, 6121 Sunset Blvd, Los Angeles, CA 90028, USA

Martin, Anne-Marie — *Actress*
%Belson & Klass Assoc, 144 S Beverly Blvd, #405, Beverly Hills, CA 90212, USA

Martin, Archer J P — *Nobel Chemistry Laureate*
47 Roseford Rd, Cambridge CB4 2HA, England

Martin, Betsy — *Publisher*
%Money Magazine, Rockefeller Center, New York, NY 10020, USA

Martin, Charles N, Jr — *Businessman*
%OrNda HealthCorp, 3401 West End Ave, Nashville, TN 37203, USA

Martin, David — *Commentator*
%CBS-TV, News Dept, 2020 "M" St NW, Washington, DC 20036, USA

Martin, Dean — *Singer, Actor*
511 N Maple Dr, Beverly Hills, CA 90210, USA

Martin, Dewey — *Actor*
1430 Stonewood Court, San Pedro, CA 90732, USA

Martin, Dick — *Comedian*
11030 Chalon Rd, Los Angeles, CA 90077, USA

Martin, Eric — *Football Player*
%New Orleans Saints, 1500 Poydras St, New Orleans, LA 70112, USA

Martin, George C — *Aeronautical Engineer*
900 University St, #5-P, Seattle, WA 98101, USA

Martin, Harvey — *Football Player*
%Dallas Cowboys, 1 Cowboys Parkway, Irving, TX 75063, USA

Martin, Henry R — *Cartoonist (Good News Bad News)*
100 Dodds Lane, Princeton, NJ 08540, USA

Martin, J Landis — *Businessman*
%NL Industries, 2 Greenspoint Dr, 16825 Northchase Dr, Houston, TX 77060, USA

Martin, J Leslie — *Architect*
Church Street Barns, Great Shelford, Cambridge, England

Martin, James E — *Businessman*
205 N Michigan Ave, #3900, Chicago, IL 60601, USA

Martin, James G — *Governor, NC*
PO Box 32861, Charlotte, NC 28232, USA

Martin, Jared — *Actor*
%Paul Kohner Inc, 9300 Wilshire Blvd, #555, Beverly Hills, CA 90212, USA

Martin, Joe — *Cartoonist (Mister Boffo)*
%Tribune Media Services, 435 N Michigan Ave, #1417, Chicago, IL 60611, USA

Martin, John H — *Educator*
%JHM Corp, 3930 RCA Blvd, #3240, Palm Beach Gardens, FL 33410, USA

Martin, Kellie — *Actress*
5918 Van Nuys Blvd, Van Nuys, CA 91401, USA

Martin, LeRoy — *Law Enforcement Official*
%Chicago Police Dept, Superintendent's Office, Chicago, IL 60602, USA

Martin, Marilyn — *Singer*
%Atlantic Records, 9229 Sunset Blvd, #900, Los Angeles, CA 90069, USA

Martin, Mark — *Auto Racing Driver*
%Roush Racing, PO Box 1089, Liberty, NC 27298, USA

Martin, Marsha P — *Financier*
%Farm Credit Administration, 1501 Farm Credit Dr, McLean, VA 22102, USA

Martin, Millicent — *Actress, Singer*
%London Mgmt, 2-4 Noel St, London W1V 3RB, England

Martin, Nan — *Actress*
33604 Pacific Coast Highway, Malibu, CA 90265, USA

Martin, Pamela Sue — *Actress*
4108 Farmdale Ave, North Hollywood, CA 91604, USA

Martin, Paul — *Government Official, Canada*
%House of Commons, Confederation Building, Ottawa ON K1A 0A6, Canada

Martin, Paul E — *Religious Leader*
%American Rescue Workers, 2827 Frankford Ave, Philadelphia, PA 19134, USA

Martin, Peter M — *Financier*
%Provident Bankshares Corp, 114 E Lexington St, Baltimore, MD 21202, USA

Martin, Preston — *Government Official, Financier*
1130 N Lake Shore Dr, #4-E, Chicago, IL 60611, USA

Martin - Martin

Martin, R Bruce   *Chemist*
%University of Virginia, Chemistry Dept, Charlottesville, VA 22903, USA

Martin, Ray   *Billiards Player*
11-05 Cadmus Place, Fairlawn, NJ 07410, USA

Martin, Ray   *Financier*
%Coast Savings Financial, 1000 Wilshire Blvd, Los Angeles, CA 90017, USA

Martin, Robert M   *Financier*
%Deutsche Credit Corp, 2333 Waukegan Rd, Deerfield, IL 60015, USA

Martin, Ronald D   *Editor*
%Atlanta Journal-Constitution, Editorial Dept, 72 Marietta, Atlanta, GA 30303, USA

Martin, Slater N   *Basketball Player*
2615 Ella Blvd, Houston, TX 77008, USA

Martin, Steve   *Comedian*
PO Box 929, Beverly Hills, CA 90213, USA

Martin, Todd   *Tennis Player*
%Advantage International, 1025 Thomas Jefferson St NW, #450, Washington 20007, USA

Martin, Tony   *Singer, Actor*
10724 Wilshire Blvd, #1406, Los Angeles, CA 90024, USA

Martin, William McChesney, Jr   *Government Official, Tennis Contributor*
2861 Woodland Dr NW, Washington, DC 20008, USA

Martindale, Wink   *Entertainer*
5744 Newcastle Lane, Calabasas, CA 91302, USA

Martinez, A   *Actor*
6835 Wild Life Rd, Malibu, CA 90265, USA

Martinez, Arthur C   *Businessman*
%Sears Roebuck Co, Sears Tower, Chicago, IL 60684, USA

Martinez, Conchita   *Tennis Player*
%International Management Group, 1 Erieview Plaza, #1300, Cleveland, OH 44114, USA

Martinez, Daniel J   *Artist*
%University of California, Studio Art Dept, Irvine, CA 92717, USA

Martinez, Edgar   *Baseball Player*
%Seattle Mariners, Kingdome, PO Box 4100, Seattle, WA 98104, USA

Martinez, J Dennis   *Baseball Player*
9400 SW 63rd Court, Miami, FL 33156, USA

Martinez, Ramon J   *Baseball Player*
Bo San Miguel #9, Managuayaba, Santo Domingo, Dominican Republic

Martini, Carlo Maria Cardinal   *Religious Leader*
Palazzo Arcivescovile, Piazza Fontana 2, 20122 Milan, Italy

Martino, Al   *Musician*
927 N Rexford Dr, Beverly Hills, CA 90210, USA

Martino, Frank D   *Labor Leader*
%Chemical Workers Union, 1655 W Market St, Akron, OH 44313, USA

Martins, Peter   *Ballet Dancer, Artistic Director*
%New York City Ballet, Lincoln Center Plaza, New York, NY 10023, USA

Martinson, Ida M   *Educator*
%University of California, Family Care Nursing Dept, San Francisco, CA 94143, USA

Marton, Eva   *Opera Singer*
%Organization of International Opera, 19 Rue Vignon, 75008 Paris, France

Marty, Martin E   *Theologian*
239 Scottswood Rd, Riverside, IL 60546, USA

Martzke, Rudy   *Sportswriter*
%USA Today, Editorial Dept, 1000 Wilson Blvd, Arlington, VA 22209, USA

Marx, Gilda   *Fashion Designer*
%Gilda Marx Industries, 11755 Exposition Blvd, Los Angeles, CA 90064, USA

Marx, Gyorgy   *Physicist*
%Eotvos University, Atomic Physics Dept, Pushkin 5, 1088 Budapest, Hungary

Marx, Jeffrey A   *Journalist*
%Lexington Herald-Leader, Editorial Dept, Main & Midland, Lexington, KY 40507, USA

Marx, Richard   *Singer, Songwriter*
15250 Ventura Blvd, #900, Sherman Oaks, CA 91403, USA

Maryland, Russell   *Football Player*
%Dallas Cowboys, 1 Cowboys Parkway, Irving, TX 75063, USA

Marzich, Andy   *Bowler*
2709 W 235th St, #D, Torrance, CA 90505, USA

Marzio, Peter C   *Museum Director*
%Houston Museum of Fine Arts, 1001 Bissonnet, PO Box 6826, Houston, TX 77265, USA

Masak, Ron   *Actor*
5440 Shirley Ave, Tarzana, CA 91356, USA

M

Martin - Masak

M

Masakayan, Linda *Volleyball Player*
%Women's Pro Volleyball Assn, 1730 Oak St, Santa Monica, CA 90405, USA

Masco, Judit *Model*
%Next Model Mgmt, 115 E 57th St, #1540, New York, NY 10022, USA

Mascotte, John P *Businessman*
%Continental Corp, 180 Maiden Lane, New York, NY 10038, USA

Masekela, Hugh *Jazz Trumpeter*
%Sam Nole, 230 Park Ave, #1221, New York, NY 10169, USA

Mashburn, Jamal *Basketball Player*
%Dallas Mavericks, Reunion Arena, 777 Sports St, Dallas, TX 75207, USA

Masin, Michael T *Businessman*
%GTE Corp, 1 Stamford Forum, Stamford, CT 06901, USA

Masire, Quett K J *President, Botswana*
%President's Office, State House, Private Bag 001, Gaborone, Botswana

Maske, Henry *Boxer*
%Rudi Sahr, Kommunardenwerg 9, 15232 Frankfurt/Oder, Germany

Maslak, Samuel H *Businessman*
%Acuson Corp, 1220 Charleston Rd, Mountain View, CA 94043, USA

Maslansky, Paul *Movie Producer, Director*
%Henry Barnberger, 10866 Wilshire Blvd, #1000, Los Angeles, CA 90024, USA

Mason of Barnsley, Roy *Government Official, England*
12 Victoria Ave, Barnsley, S Yorks, England

Mason, Anthony *Basketball Player*
%New York Knicks, Madison Square Garden, 4 Penn Plaza, New York, NY 10001, USA

Mason, B John *Meteorologist*
64 Christchurch Rd, East Sheen, London SW14, England

Mason, Birny, Jr *Chemical Engineer*
6 Island Dr, Rye, NY 10580, USA

Mason, Bobbie Ann *Writer*
PO Box 518, Lawrenceburg, KY 40342, USA

Mason, Bruce *Businessman*
%Foote Cone Belding Communications, 101 E Erie St, Chicago, IL 60611, USA

Mason, Herman D *Businessman*
%WLR Foods, PO Box 7000, Broadway, VA 22815, USA

Mason, Jackie *Comedian*
30 Park Ave, New York, NY 10016, USA

Mason, Marlyn *Actress, Singer*
27 Glen Oak Court, Medford, OR 97504, USA

Mason, Marsha *Actress*
RR 2, Box 269, Santa Fe, NM 87505, USA

Mason, Monica *Ballerina*
%Royal Opera House, Convent Garden, Bow St, London WC2, England

Mason, Nick *Drummer (Pink Floyd)*
%Ten Tenths Mgmt, 106 Gifford St, London M1 ODF, England

Mason, Pamela *Actress*
1018 Pamela Dr, Beverly Hills, CA 90210, USA

Mason, Raymond A *Financier*
%Legg Mason Inc, 111 S Calvert St, Baltimore, MD 21202, USA

Mason, Steven C *Businessman*
%Mead Corp, Courthouse Plaza NE, Dayton, OH 45463, USA

Mason, Thomas R *Businessman*
%California Energy Co, 10853 Old Mill Rd, Omaha, NE 68154, USA

Mason, Tom *Actor*
406 S Roxbury Dr, Beverly Hills, CA 90212, USA

Mason, Tommy *Football Player*
%Inland Beverage, 1455 Riverview Dr, San Bernardino, CA 92408, USA

Masri, Tahir Nashat *Prime Minister, Jordan*
PO Box 5550, Amman, Jordan

Massagli, Mark Tully *Labor Leader*
%American Federation of Musicians, 1501 Broadway, #600, New York, NY 10036, USA

Massengale, Martin A *Educator*
1610 Kingston Rd, Lincoln, NE 68506, USA

Massevitch, Alla G *Astronomer*
%Astronomical Council, 48 Pjatnitskaja St, 109017 Moscow, Russia

Massey, Anna *Actress*
%Markham & Froggett, 4 Windmill St, London W1P 1HF, England

Massey, Daniel *Actor*
35 Tynehan Rd, London SW11, England

Masakayan - Massey

V.I.P. Address Book

Massey, Marilyn Chapin — *Educator*
%Pitzer College, President's Office, Claremont, CA 91711, USA

Massey, T Benjamin — *Educator*
%University of Maryland, President's Office, College Park, MD 20742, USA

Masterhoff, Joe — *Playwright*
2 Horatio St, New York, NY 10014, USA

Masters, Geoff — *Tennis Player*
De Lorain St, Wavell Heights, QLD 4012, Australia

Masters, John — *Writer*
%McGraw-Hill, 1221 Ave of Americas, New York, NY 10020, USA

Masters, William H — *Sex Therapist*
%Masters & Johnson Institute, Campbell Plaza, 59th & Arsenal, St Louis, MO 63139, USA

Masterson, Mary Stuart — *Actress*
PO Box 1249, White River Junction, VT 05001, USA

Masterson, Peter — *Writer, Director, Producer*
%Writer's Guild, 555 W 57th St, New York, NY 10019, USA

Masterson, Valerie — *Opera Singer*
%Music International, 13 Ardilaun Rd, London N5 2QR, England

Mastroianni, Marcello — *Actor*
Via Maria Adelaide 8, 00196 Rome, Italy

Masur, Kurt — *Conductor*
%New York Philharmonic, Avery Fisher Hall, Lincoln Center, New York, NY 10023, USA

Masur, Richard — *Actor*
2847 Mandeville Canyon Rd, Los Angeles, CA 90049, USA

Masurok, Yuri — *Opera Singer*
%Bolshoi Theater, Teatralnaya Pl 1, 103009 Moscow, Russia

Mata'aho — *Queen, Tonga*
%Royal Palace, PO Box 6, Nuku'alofa, Tonga

Matalin, Mary — *Political Consultant*
1601 Shenandoah Shores St, Fort Royal, VA 22630, USA

Matalon, David — *Entertainment Executive*
%Tri-Star Pictures, 711 5th Ave, New York, NY 10022, USA

Matano, Tsutomo (Tom) — *Automotive Designer*
%Mazda Motor, Research/Development Dept, 7755 Irvine Center Dr, Irvine, CA 92718, USA

Mateo, Manuel M — *Financier*
%Golden 1 Credit Union, 6507 4th Ave, Sacramento, CA 95817, USA

Mateyo, George R — *Financier*
%Carnegie Capital Management Co, 1228 Euclid Ave, Cleveland, OH 44115, USA

Mather, John C — *Astrophysicist*
%Goddard Space Flight Center, Code G-85, Greenbelt, MD 20771, USA

Mathers, Jerry — *Actor*
%Artists Group, 10100 Santa Monica Blvd, #2490, Los Angeles, CA 90067, USA

Matheson, Tim — *Actor*
830 Riven Rock Rd, Santa Barbara, CA 93108, USA

Mathews, Edwin L (Eddie) — *Baseball Player*
13744 Recuordo Dr, Del Mar, CA 92014, USA

Mathews, F David — *Secretary, Health Education Welfare*
%Charles F Kettering Foundation, 200 Commons Rd, Dayton, OH 45459, USA

Mathias, Bob — *Track Athlete; Representative, CA*
7469 E Pine Ave, Fresno, CA 93727, USA

Mathias, Charles McC, Jr — *Senator, MD*
3808 Leland St, Chevy Chase, MD 20815, USA

Mathias, William — *Composer*
Y Graigwen Cadnant Rd, Menai Bridge, Anglesey, Gwynedd LL59 5NG, Wales

Mathis, Daniel W — *Financier*
%First Union National Bank, 1 First Union Center, Charlotte, NC 28288, USA

Mathis, Edith — *Opera Singer*
%Ingpen & Williams, 14 Kensington Court, London W8 5DN, England

Mathis, Johnny — *Singer*
PO Box 69278, Los Angeles, CA 90069, USA

Mathis, Samantha — *Actress*
%William Morris Agency, 151 S El Camino Dr, Beverly Hills, CA 90212, USA

Mathis, Terance — *Football Player*
%Atlanta Falcons, 2745 Burnett Rd, Suwanee, GA 30174, USA

Mathis-Eddy, Darlene — *Poet*
1409 W Cardinal St, Muncie, IN 47303, USA

Mathwich, Dale F — *Businessman*
%American Family Insurance Group, 6000 American Parkway, Madison, WI 53783, USA

M

Matlin, Marlee *Actress*
12304 Santa Monica Blvd, #119, Los Angeles, CA 90025, USA

Matlock, Jack F, Jr *Diplomat*
2913 "P" St NW, Washington, DC 20007, USA

Matola, Sharon *Zoo Director, Conservationist*
%Belize Zoo & Tropical Education Center, PO Box 1787, Belize City, Belize

Matson, Ollie *Football Player*
1319 S Hudson Ave, Los Angeles, CA 90019, USA

Matson, Randy *Track Athlete*
%Texas A&M University, Assn of Former Students, College Station, TX 77840, USA

Matsui, Kosei *Pottery Maker*
Ibaraki-ken, Kasama-shi, Kasama 350, Japan

Matsumoto, Shigeharu *Writer, Association Executive*
%International House of Japan, 11-16 Roppongi, Minatuku, Tokyo, Japan

Matsushita, Masaharu *Businessman*
%Matsushita Electrical Industrial, 1006 Kadoma City, Osaka 571, Japan

Matta del Meskin *Religious Leader*
Deir el Makarios Monastery, Cairo, Egypt

Matta, Roberto *Artist*
Boissy Sans Avoir, Seine-et-Oise, France

Matte, Thomas R (Tom) *Football Player*
8 Ferrous Court, Hunt Valley, MD 21030, USA

Mattea, Kathy *Singer*
%Bob Titley Ent, 706 18th Ave S, Nashville, TN 37203, USA

Mattesich, Rudi *Skier*
%General Delivery, Troy, VT 05868, USA

Matteson, Thomas T *Coast Guard Admiral*
%US Coast Guard Academy, Superintendent's Office, New London, CT 06320, USA

Matthaeus, Lothar *Soccer Player*
%Bayern Munich, Sabena Str 51, 81547 Munich, Germany

Matthau, Walter *Actor*
278 Toyopa Dr, Pacific Palisades, CA 90272, USA

Matthes, Roland *Swimmer*
Storkower Str 118, 10407 Berlin, Germany

Matthews, Bruce *Football Player*
%Houston Oilers, 6910 Fannin St, Houston, TX 77030, USA

Matthews, Clark J, II *Businessman*
%Southland Corp, 2711 N Haskell Ave, Dallas, TX 75204, USA

Matthews, Clay *Football Player*
%Atlanta Falcons, 2745 Burnett Rd, Suwanee, GA 30174, USA

Matthews, DeLane *Actress*
%Don Buchwald Assoc, 9229 Sunset Blvd, #710, Los Angeles, 90069, USA

Matthews, Edward E *Businessman*
%American International Group, 70 Pine St, New York, NY 10270, USA

Matthews, Raymond (Rags) *Football Player*
2501 Oak Hill Circle, #2416, Fort Worth, TX 76109, USA

Matthews, Robert L *Financier*
%Banc One Arizona, 241 N Central Ave, Phoenix, AZ 85004, USA

Matthews, William D *Businessman*
%Oneida Ltd, Kenwood Ave, Oneida, NY 13421, USA

Matthies, Nina *Volleyball Player, Coach*
%Pepperdine University, Athletic Dept, Malibu, CA 90265, USA

Matthiessen, Peter *Writer*
Bridge Lane, Sagaponack, NY 11962, USA

Mattila, Karita M *Opera Singer*
45-B Croxley Rd, London W9 3HJ, England

Mattingly, Donald A (Don) *Baseball Player*
12641 Browning Rd, Evansville, IN 47711, USA

Mattingly, Mack F *Senator, GA*
4315 10th St, East Beach, St Simons Island, GA 31522, USA

Mattingly, Thomas K, II *Astronaut, Navy Admiral*
%Martin Marietta, PO Box 85990, MZ-K1-7142, San Diego, CA 92186, USA

Mattson, Robin *Actress*
917 Manning Ave, Los Angeles, CA 90024, USA

Mattson, Walter E *Publisher*
%New York Times Co, 229 W 43rd St, New York, NY 10036, USA

Mature, Victor *Actor*
PO Box 706, Rancho Santa Fe, CA 92067, USA

Matlin - Mature

Matzdorf, Pat — *Track Athlete*
1252 Bainbridge, Naperville, IL 60563, USA

Mauch, Bill — *Actor*
538 W Northwest Highway, #C, Palatine, IL 60067, USA

Mauch, Eugene W (Gene) — *Baseball Manager*
71 Princeton, Rancho Mirage, CA 92270, USA

Maucher, Helmut — *Businessman*
%Nestle SA, Ave Nestle, 1800 Vevey, Switzerland

Maugham, R H — *Religious Leader*
%Christian & Missionary Alliance, PO Box 35000, Colorado Springs, CO 80935, USA

Mauldin, Jerry L — *Businessman*
%Entergy Corp, 639 Loyola Ave, New Orleans, LA 70113, USA

Mauldin, Robert R — *Financier*
%Centura Banks, 134 N Church St, Rocky Mount, NC 27804, USA

Mauldin, William H (Bill) — *Editorial Cartoonist*
3145 Killarney Lane, Costa Mesa, CA 92626, USA

Maulnier, Thierry — *Writer*
3 Rue Yves-Carriou, 92430 Marnes-la-Coquette, France

Maumenee, Alfred E — *Ophthalmologist*
1700 Hillside Rd, Stevenson, MD 21153, USA

Maupin, Robert W — *Businessman*
%Shelter Mutual Insurance, 1817 W Broadway, Columbia, MO 65218, USA

Maura, Carmen — *Actress*
Juan de Austria 13, 28010 Madrid, Spain

Maurer, Gilbert C — *Publisher*
%Hearst Corp, 959 8th Ave, New York, NY 10019, USA

Maurer, Ion Gheorghe — *Premier, Romania*
Bul Aviatorilor 104, Bucharest, Romania

Maurer, Jeffrey S — *Financier*
%United States Trust Co of New York, 114 W 47th St, New York, NY 10036, USA

Maurer, Robert D — *Inventor (Silica Optical Waveguide)*
6 Roche Dr, Painted Post, NY 14870, USA

Mauriac, Claude — *Writer*
24 Quai de Bethune, 75004 Paris, France

Maurin, Laurence — *Skier, Conservationist*
200 Schmidt Rd, West Bend, WI 53095, USA

Mauroy, Pierre — *Prime Minister, France*
17-19 Rue Voltaire, 59800 Lille, France

Mautner, Hans C — *Financier*
%Corporate Property Investors, 3 Dag Hammarskjold Plaza, New York, NY 10017, USA

Mawby, Russell G — *Foundation Executive*
%W K Kellogg Foundation, 1 Michigan Ave E, Battle Creek, MI 49017, USA

Max, Peter — *Artist*
118 Riverside Dr, New York, NY 10024, USA

Maxim, Joey — *Boxer*
2491 Natalie Ave, Las Vegas, NV 89121, USA

Maximova, Ekaterina — *Ballerina*
%Bolshoi Theater, Teatralnaya Pl 1, 103009 Moscow, Russia

Maxson, Robert — *Educator*
%California State State University, President's Office, Long Beach, CA 90840, USA

Maxwell, Arthur E — *Oceanographer*
8115 Two Coves Dr, Austin, TX 78730, USA

Maxwell, Charles R (Charlie) — *Baseball Player*
730 Mapleview Ave, Paw Paw, MI 49079, USA

Maxwell, Frank — *Labor Leader*
%Federation of TV-Radio Artists, 260 Madison Ave, New York, NY 10016, USA

Maxwell, Hamish — *Businessman*
%Philip Morris Companies, 120 Park Ave, New York, NY 10017, USA

Maxwell, Ian — *Publisher*
Eaton Terrace, London SW1, England

Maxwell, Kevin F H — *Publisher*
Hill Burn, Hailey Near Wallingford, Oxford OX10 6AD, England

Maxwell, Robert D — *WW II Army Hero (CMH)*
General Delivery, Parker, AZ 85344, USA

Maxwell, Vernon — *Basketball Player*
%Philadelphia 76ers, Veterans Stadium, PO Box 25040, Philadelphia, PA 19147, USA

Maxwell, William — *Writer*
%Alfred A Knopf Inc, 201 E 50th St, New York, NY 10022, USA

M

Matzdorf - Maxwell

M

May, Arthur *Architect*
%Kohn Pedersen Fox Assoc, 111 W 57th St, New York, NY 10019, USA

May, Brian *Musician, Songwriter*
%Artists & Audience Entertainment, 83 Riverside Dr, New York, NY 10024, USA

May, Elaine *Movie Director, Comedienne*
2017 California Ave, Santa Monica, CA 90403, USA

May, Gerald W *Educator*
1058 Red Oaks Loop, Albuquerque, NM 87122, USA

May, Lee A *Baseball Player*
5593 Hill & Dale Dr, Cincinnati, OH 45213, USA

May, Peter W *Businessman*
%Triarc Companies, 900 3rd Ave, New York, NY 10022, USA

May, Scott *Basketball Player*
2001 E Hillside Dr, Bloomington, IN 47401, USA

May, Thomas I *Businessman*
%Boston Edison Co, 800 Boylston St, Boston, MA 02199, USA

May, Torsten *Boxer*
%Sauerland Promotion, Hans-Bockler-Str 163, 50354 Hurth, Germany

Mayall, John *Musician, Composer*
PO Box 170429, San Francisco, CA 94117, USA

Mayall, Nicholas U *Astronomer*
7206 E Camino Vecino, Tucson, AZ 85715, USA

Mayberry, John C *Baseball Player*
11115 W 121st Terrace, Overland Park, KS 66213, USA

Mayer, John L, III *Financier*
%Robert W Baird Co, 777 E Wisconsin Ave, Milwaukee, WI 53202, USA

Mayer, Joseph E *Chemical Physicist*
2345 Via Siena, La Jolla, CA 92037, USA

Mayer, P Augustin Cardinal *Religious Leader*
Ecclesia Dei, Vatican City, Rome, Italy

Mayer, Thomas *Conductor*
%Norman McCann, Grand Buildings, #620, Trafalgar Square, London WC2, Engla

Mayfield, Curtis *Singer, Musician, Songwriter*
%Curtom Records, PO Box 724677, Atlanta, GA 31139, USA

Mayhew, Patrick B B *Government Official, England*
%House of Commons, Westminster, London SW1A 0AA, England

Maynard, Andrew *Boxer*
%Mike Trainer, 3922 Fairmont Ave, Bethesda, MD 20814, USA

Maynard, Don *Football Player*
6545 Butterfield Dr, El Paso, TX 79932, USA

Maynard, Mimi *Actress*
%Badgley Connor, 9229 Sunset Blvd, #311, Los Angeles, CA 90069, USA

Mayne, D Roger *Photographer*
Colway Manor, Colway Lane, Lyme Regis, Dorset DT7 3HD, Canada

Mayne, Ferdinand *Actor*
%Lou Coulson, 37 Berwick St, London W1V 3RF, England

Mayne, William *Writer*
%Harold Ober Assoc, 425 Madison Ave, New York, NY 10017, USA

Maynes, Charles W *Editor*
%Foreign Policy Magazine, Editorial Dept, 2400 "N" St NW, Washington, DC 20037, USA

Mayo, Richard *Financier*
%Grantham Mayo Van Otterloo Co, 40 Rowes Wharf, Boston, MA 02110, USA

Mayo, Virginia *Actress*
109 E Avenida de las Aboles, Thousand Oaks, CA 91360, USA

Mayo, Whitman *Actor*
265 Dix Leeon Dr, Fairburn, GA 30213, USA

Mayor Zaragoza, Federico *Government Official, Spain*
%UNESCO, Place de Fonteroy, 75352 Paris, France

Mayr, Ernst *Biologist, Zoologist*
11 Chauncy St, Cambridge, MA 02138, USA

Mayron, Melanie *Actress*
7510 W Sunset Blvd, Los Angeles, CA 90046, USA

Mays, Willie H *Baseball Player*
PO Box 2410, Menlo Park, CA 94026, USA

Mazanec, George L *Businessman*
%Panhandle Eastern Corp, 5400 Westheimer Court, Houston, TX 77056, USA

Mazar, Debi *Actress*
%Flick East-West Talents, 9057 Nemo St, #A, West Hollywood, CA 90069, USA

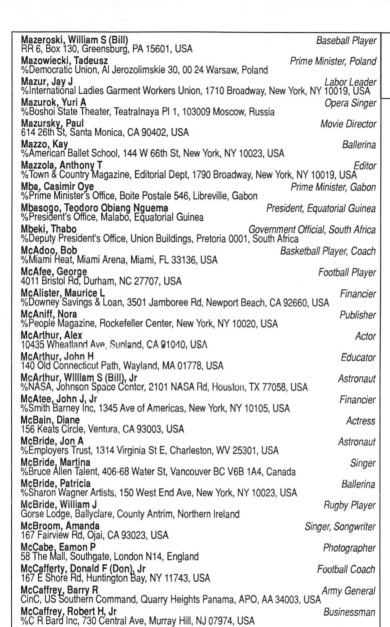

Mazeroski, William S (Bill) — *Baseball Player*
RR 6, Box 130, Greensburg, PA 15601, USA

Mazowiecki, Tadeusz — *Prime Minister, Poland*
%Democratic Union, Al Jerozolimskie 30, 00 24 Warsaw, Poland

Mazur, Jay J — *Labor Leader*
%International Ladies Garment Workers Union, 1710 Broadway, New York, NY 10019, USA

Mazurok, Yuri A — *Opera Singer*
%Boshoi State Theater, Teatralnaya Pl 1, 103009 Moscow, Russia

Mazursky, Paul — *Movie Director*
614 26th St, Santa Monica, CA 90402, USA

Mazzo, Kay — *Ballerina*
%American Ballet School, 144 W 66th St, New York, NY 10023, USA

Mazzola, Anthony T — *Editor*
%Town & Country Magazine, Editorial Dept, 1790 Broadway, New York, NY 10019, USA

Mba, Casimir Oye — *Prime Minister, Gabon*
%Prime Minister's Office, Boite Postale 546, Libreville, Gabon

Mbasogo, Teodoro Obiang Nguema — *President, Equatorial Guinea*
%President's Office, Malabo, Equatorial Guinea

Mbeki, Thabo — *Government Official, South Africa*
%Deputy President's Office, Union Buildings, Pretoria 0001, South Africa

McAdoo, Bob — *Basketball Player, Coach*
%Miami Heat, Miami Arena, Miami, FL 33136, USA

McAfee, George — *Football Player*
4011 Bristol Rd, Durham, NC 27707, USA

McAlister, Maurice L — *Financier*
%Downey Savings & Loan, 3501 Jamboree Rd, Newport Beach, CA 92660, USA

McAniff, Nora — *Publisher*
%People Magazine, Rockefeller Center, New York, NY 10020, USA

McArthur, Alex — *Actor*
10435 Wheatland Ave, Sunland, CA 91040, USA

McArthur, John H — *Educator*
140 Old Connecticut Path, Wayland, MA 01778, USA

McArthur, William S (Bill), Jr — *Astronaut*
%NASA, Johnson Space Center, 2101 NASA Rd, Houston, TX 77058, USA

McAtee, John J, Jr — *Financier*
%Smith Barney Inc, 1345 Ave of Americas, New York, NY 10105, USA

McBain, Diane — *Actress*
156 Keats Circle, Ventura, CA 93003, USA

McBride, Jon A — *Astronaut*
%Employers Trust, 1314 Virginia St E, Charleston, WV 25301, USA

McBride, Martina — *Singer*
%Bruce Allen Talent, 406-68 Water St, Vancouver BC V6B 1A4, Canada

McBride, Patricia — *Ballerina*
%Sharon Wagner Artists, 150 West End Ave, New York, NY 10023, USA

McBride, William J — *Rugby Player*
Gorse Lodge, Ballyclare, County Antrim, Northern Ireland

McBroom, Amanda — *Singer, Songwriter*
167 Fairview Rd, Ojai, CA 93023, USA

McCabe, Eamon P — *Photographer*
58 The Mall, Southgate, London N14, England

McCafferty, Donald F (Don), Jr — *Football Coach*
167 E Shore Rd, Huntington Bay, NY 11743, USA

McCaffrey, Barry R — *Army General*
CinC, US Southern Command, Quarry Heights Panama, APO, AA 34003, USA

McCaffrey, Robert H, Jr — *Businessman*
%C R Bard Inc, 730 Central Ave, Murray Hill, NJ 07974, USA

McCain, James A — *Educator*
1711 Sunny Slope Lane, Manhattan, KS 66502, USA

McCain, Warren E — *Businessman*
%Albertson's Inc, 250 Parkcenter Blvd, Boise, ID 83706, USA

McCall, Henry C — *Businessman*
%CUC International, 707 Summer St, Stamford, CT 06901, USA

McCall, Robert T — *Artist*
4816 E Moonlight Way, Paradise Valley, AZ 85253, USA

McCalla, Irish — *Actress*
920 Oak Terrace, Prescott, AZ 86301, USA

McCallister, Lon — *Actor*
PO Box 6040, Stateline, NV 89449, USA

McCallum, David — *Actor*
%The Agency, 1800 Ave of Stars, #400, Los Angeles, CA 90067, USA

McCambridge, Mercedes — *Actress*
2500 Torrey Pines Rd, #1203, La Jolla, CA 92037, USA

McCammon, Bob — *Hockey Coach*
%Vancouver Canucks, 100 N Renfrew St, Vancouver BC V5K 3N7, Canada

McCampbell, David — *WW II Navy Hero (CMH)*
725 Wright Dr, Lake Worth, FL 33461, USA

McCandless, Bruce, II — *Astronaut*
21852 Pleasant Park Dr, Conifer, CO 80433, USA

McCann, Chuck — *Comedian*
2941 Briar Knoll Dr, Los Angeles, CA 90046, USA

McCann, David A — *Publisher*
%Town & Country Magazine, 1700 Broadway, New York, NY 10019, USA

McCann, Les — *Jazz Pianist, Composer*
501 S Beverly Dr, #200, Beverly Hills, CA 90212, USA

McCants, Keith — *Football Player*
%St Louis Rams, 100 N Broadway, #2100, St Louis, MO 63102, USA

McCarron, Chris — *Thoroughbred Racing Jockey*
3328 Clarendon Dr, Beverly Hills, CA 90210, USA

McCarthy, Andrew — *Actor*
4708 Vesper Ave, Sherman Oaks, CA 91403, USA

McCarthy, Cormac — *Writer*
%Random House Inc, 201 E 50th St, New York, NY 10022, USA

McCarthy, Donald W — *Astronomer*
%Stewart Observatory, University of Arizona, Tucson, AZ 85721, USA

McCarthy, Eugene J — *Senator, MN*
PO Box 22, Sperryville, VA 22740, USA

McCarthy, Fred — *Cartoonist (Brother Juniper)*
%Field Newspaper Syndicate, 1703 Kaiser Ave, Irvine, CA 92714, USA

McCarthy, John — *Computer Scientist*
%Stanford University, Computer Science Dept, Stanford, CA 94305, USA

McCarthy, Joseph J — *WW II Marine Corps Hero (CMH), General*
2305 Lowson Rd, #D, Delray Beach, FL 33445, USA

McCarthy, Kevin — *Actor*
14854 Sutton St, Sherman Oaks, CA 91403, USA

McCarthy, Mary Frances — *Writer, Educator*
%Trinity College, English Dept, Washington, DC 20017, USA

McCarthy, Nobu — *Actress*
372 N Encinitas, Monrovia, CA 91016, USA

McCarthy, Paul F, Jr — *Navy Admiral*
16457 Saddle Creek Rd, Clarkson Valley, MO 63005, USA

McCartney, Bill — *Football Coach*
%Promise Keepers, PO Box 18376, Boulder, CO 80308, USA

McCartney, Linda — *Singer, Photographer*
Waterfall Estate, Peamarsh, St Leonard-on-Sea, Sussex, England

McCartney, O Kenton — *Financier*
%Jefferson Bankshares, 123 E Main St, Charlottesville, VA 22902, USA

McCartney, Paul — *Singer (Beatles), Songwriter*
Waterfall Estate, Peamarsh, St Leonard-on-Sea, Sussex, England

McCarty, Maclyn — *Bacteriologist, Immunologist*
%Rockefeller University, 66th St & York Ave, New York, NY 10021, USA

McCarver, J Timothy (Tim) — *Baseball Player, Sportscaster*
1518 Youngford Rd, Gladwynne, PA 19035, USA

McCary, Michael — *Singer (Boyz II Men)*
%BIV Entertainment, 5 Bishop Rd, Vincentown, NJ 08088, USA

McCashin, Constance — *Actress*
2037 Desford Dr, Beverly Hills, CA 90210, USA

McCaskey, Michael B (Mike) — *Football Executive*
%Chicago Bears, Halas Hall, 250 N Washington Rd, Lake Forest, IL 60045, USA

McCaskill, Kirk E — *Baseball Player*
927 Ash St, Winnetka, IL 60093, USA

McCauley, Barry — *Opera Singer*
8 Pershing St, Emerson, NJ 07630, USA

McCauley, Donald F (Don), Jr — *Football Player*
167 E Shore Rd, Huntington Bay, NY 11743, USA

McCausland, Peter — *Businessman*
%Airgas Inc, 5 Radnor Corporate Center, 100 Matsonford Rd, Radnor, PA 19087, USA

McCausland, Thomas J, Jr *Financier*
%Chicago Corp, 208 S LaSalle St, Chicago, IL 60604, USA

McCay, Peggy *Actress*
8811 Wonderland Ave, Los Angeles, CA 90046, USA

McClanahan, Rue *Actress*
%Agency For Performing Arts, 9000 Sunset Blvd, #1200, Los Angeles, CA 90069, USA

McClane, Robert S *Financier*
%Cullen/Frost Bankers Inc, 100 W Houston St, San Antonio, TX 78205, USA

McClatchy, James B *Publisher*
%McClatchy Newspapers, 2100 "Q" St, Sacramento, CA 95816, USA

McCleery, Finnis D *Vietnam War Army Hero (CMH)*
826 Veck St, #F, San Angelo, TX 76903, USA

McClelland, David C *Psychologist*
81 Washington Ave, Cambridge, MA 02140, USA

McClelland, W Craig *Businessman*
%Union Camp Corp, 1600 Valley Rd, Wayne, NJ 07470, USA

McClendon, Sarah N *Writer, Journalist*
2933 28th St NW, Washington, DC 20008, USA

McClinton, Delbert *Singer*
%Harriet Sternberg Mgmt, 15250 Ventura Blvd, #1215, Sherman Oaks, CA 91403, USA

McCloskey, J Michael *Environmentalist*
%Sierra Club, 408 "C" St NE, Washington, DC 20002, USA

McCloskey, Jack *Basketball Coach, Executive*
%Minnesota Timberwolves, Target Center, 600 1st Ave N, Minneapolis, MN 55403, USA

McCloskey, Jim *Social Activist*
32 Nassau St, #3, Princeton, NJ 08542, USA

McCloskey, Leigh *Actor*
6032 Philip Ave, Malibu, CA 90265, USA

McCloskey, Robert J *Diplomat*
111 Hesketh St, Chevy Chase, MD 20815, USA

McCluggage, Kerry *Television Executive*
%Paramount Television, 5555 Melrose Ave, Los Angeles, CA 90038, USA

McClure, Donald F *Financier*
%LMSC Federal Credit Union, PO Box 3643, Sunnyvale, CA 94088, USA

McClure, Donald S *Chemist*
23 Hemlock Circle, Princeton, NJ 08540, USA

McClure, James A *Senator, ID*
PO Box 2029, McCall, ID 83638, USA

McClurg, Edie *Actress*
3306 Wonderview Plaza, Los Angeles, CA 90068, USA

McColgan, Edward J *Financier*
%Collective Bancorp, 158 Philadelphia Ave, Egg Harbor, NJ 08215, USA

McColl, Hugh L, Jr *Financier*
%NationsBank, 1 NationsBank Plaza, Charlotte, NC 28255, USA

McColl, William (Bill) *Football Player*
5166 Chelsea St, La Jolla, CA 92037, USA

McComas, Murray K *Businessman*
%Blair Corp, 220 Hickory St, Warren, PA 16366, USA

McConnell, Harden M *Chemist*
%Stanford University, Chemistry Dept, Stanford, CA 94305, USA

McConnell, John H *Businessman*
%Worthington Industries, 1205 Dearborn Dr, Columbus, OH 43085, USA

McConnell, John P *Businessman*
%Worthington Industries, 1205 Dearborn Dr, Columbus, OH 43085, USA

McConnell, Robert *Publisher*
%The Gazette, 250 St Antoine St W, Montreal PQ H2Y 3R7, Canada

McConnell, Thomas R *Educator*
Grand Lake Gardens, 401 Santa Cruz Ave, #214, Oakland, CA 94610, USA

McConville, Frank *Labor Leader*
%Union of Plant Guard Workers of America, 25510 Kelly Rd, Roseville, MI 48066, USA

McCoo, Marilyn *Singer*
%Davis, 9911 Mark Place, Beverly Hills, CA 90210, USA

McCook, John *Actor*
4154 Colbath Ave, Sherman Oaks, CA 91423, USA

McCool, Richard M *WW II Navy Hero (CMH)*
PO Box 11347, Bainbridge Island, WA 98110, USA

McCord, Catherine *Model*
%Elite Model Mgmt, 111 E 22nd St, #200, New York, NY 10010, USA

M

McCausland - McCord

McCord, Darris *Football Player*
725 Vaughan Rd, Bloomfield Hills, MI 48304, USA

McCord, Kent *Actor*
%David Shapira Assoc, 15301 Ventura Blvd, #345, Sherman Oaks, CA 91403, USA

McCorkindale, Douglas H *Businessman*
%Gannett Co, 1100 Wilson Blvd, Arlington, VA 22209, USA

McCormack, Mark H *Attorney, Sports Executive*
%Mark McCormack Enterprises, 1 Erieview Plaza, #1300, Cleveland, OH 44114, USA

McCormack, Mike *Football Coach, Executive*
%Seattle Seahawks, 11220 NE 53rd St, Kirkland, WA 98033, USA

McCormack, Patricia *Actress*
%Paradigm Agency, 10100 Santa Monica Blvd, #2500, Los Angeles, CA 90067, USA

McCormack, Patty *Actress, Model*
14723 Magnolia Blvd, Sherman Oaks, CA 91403, USA

McCormick, Charles P, Jr *Businessman*
%McCormick & Co, 18 Loveton Circle, Sparks, MD 21152, USA

McCormick, Kevin *Cartoonist (Arnold)*
%News America Syndicate, 1703 Kaiser Ave, Irvine, CA 92714, USA

McCormick, Maureen *Actress, Singer*
2812 Shellcreek Place, Westlake Village, CA 91361, USA

McCormick, Michael F (Mike) *Baseball Player*
22330 Homestead Rd, #305, Cupertino, CA 95014, USA

McCormick, Pat *Diver*
PO Box 259, Seal Beach, CA 90740, USA

McCormick, Richard D *Businessman*
%US West Inc, 7800 E Orchard Rd, Englewood, CO 80111, USA

McCormick, Tim *Basketball Player*
%Atlanta Hawks, 1 CNN Center, South Tower, Atlanta, GA 30303, USA

McCormick, William C *Businessman*
%Precision Castparts Corp, 4600 SE Harney Dr, Portland, OR 97206, USA

McCormick, William E *Publisher*
%Pittsburgh Post-Gazette & Press, 34 Blvd of Allies, Pittsburgh, PA 15230, USA

McCormick, William T, Jr *Businessman*
%CMS Energy Corp, Fairlane Plaza South, 330 Town Center Dr, Dearborn, MI 48126, USA

McCosky, W Barney *Baseball Player*
764 Village Circle, #120, Venice, FL 34292, USA

McCovey, Willie L *Baseball Player*
%San Francisco Giants, Candlestick Park, San Francisco, CA 94124, USA

McCowen, Alec *Actor*
%Conway Van Gelder Robinson, 18-21 Jermyn St, London SW1Y 6HB, England

McCoy, Dave *Ski Resort Builder*
%Mammoth Mountain Chairlifts, PO Box 24, Mammoth Lakes, CA 93546, USA

McCoy, John B *Financier*
%Banc One Corp, 100 E Broad St, Columbus, OH 43215, USA

McCoy, Matt *Actor*
%Metropolitan Talent Agency, 4526 Wilshire Blvd, Los Angeles, CA 90010, USA

McCoy, Michael P (Mike) *Football Player*
551 Exam Court, Lawrenceville, GA 30244, USA

McCoy, Neal *Singer*
3878 Oak Lawn Ave, #620, Dallas, TX 75219, USA

McCracken, Edward R *Businessman*
%Silicon Graphics, 2011 N Shoreline Blvd, Mountain View, CA 94043, USA

McCracken, Paul W *Economist, Government Official*
2564 Hawthorne Rd, Ann Arbor, MI 48104, USA

McCraig, Joseph J *Businessman*
%Grand Union Co, 201 Willowbrook Blvd, Wayne, NJ 07470, USA

McCraw, Leslie G *Businessman*
%Fluor Corp, 3333 Michelson Dr, Irvine, CA 92730, USA

McCray, Curtis L *Educator*
%Millikin University, President's Office, Decatur, IL 62522, USA

McCrea, William H *Astrophysicist, Mathematician*
87 Houdean Rise, Lewes, Sussex BN7 1EJ, England

McCready, Mike *Guitarist (Pearl Jam)*
%Curtis Mgmt, 207 1/2 1st Ave S, #300, Seattle, WA 98104, USA

McCree, Donald H, Jr *Financier*
%IBJ Schroder Bank & Trust, 1 State St, New York, NY 10004, USA

McCrillis, John W *Skiing Executive, Writer*
%McCrillis & Eldredge Insurance, 17 Depot St, Newport, NH 03773, USA

McCrimmon, Brad *Hockey Player*
%Hartford Whalers, Coliseum, 242 Trumbell St, #800, Hartford, CT 06103, USA

McCrone, Walter C *Microscopologist*
%McCrone Institute, 2820 S Michigan Ave, Chicago, IL 60616, USA

McCrory, Glenn *Boxer*
Holborn, 35 Station Rd, County Durham, England

McCrory, Milt *Boxer*
%Escot Boxing Enterprises, 19600 W McNichols, Detroit, MI 48219, USA

McCrossen, Richard G *Financier*
%Citibank (South Dakota), 701 E 60th St N, Sioux Falls, SD 57104, USA

McCulley, Michael J *Astronaut*
108 Yacht Haven Dr, Cocoa Beach, FL 32931, USA

McCullin, Donald *Photographer*
Holly Hill House, Batcombe, Shepton Mallet, Somerset BA4 6BL, England

McCulloch, Frank W *Attorney, Educator, Arbitrator*
2401 Old Ivy Rd, #2307, Charlottesville, VA 22903, USA

McCulloch, Frank W *Editor*
%San Francisco Examiner, Editorial Dept, 110 5th St, San Francisco, CA 94103, USA

McCullough, Colleen *Writer*
Out Yenna, Norfolk Island 2899, Oceania, Australia

McCullough, David *Writer*
%Janklow & Nesbit Assoc, 598 Madison Ave, New York, NY 10022, USA

McCullough, Eugene F, Jr *Financier*
%BOT Financial Corp, 125 Summer St, Boston, MA 02110, USA

McCullough, Julie *Actress*
8033 Sunset Blvd, #353, Los Angeles, CA 90046, USA

McCullough, Samuel A *Financier*
%Meridian Bancorp, 35 N 6th St, Reading, PA 19601, USA

McCumber, Mark *Golfer*
%Professional Golfer's Assn, PO Box 109601, Palm Beach Gardens, FL 33410, USA

McCune, Don *Bowler*
%Professional Bowlers Assn, 1720 Merriman Rd, Akron, OH 44313, USA

McCurley, F Cedric *Businessman*
%American States Insurance, 500 N Meridian St, Indianapolis, IN 46204, USA

McCutcheon, Bill *Actor*
65 Park Terrace W, New York, NY 10034, USA

McDaniel Singleton, Mildred *Track Athlete*
211 W Poppy Field Dr, Altadena, CA 91001, USA

McDaniel, Boyce D *Physicist*
26 Woodcrest Ave, Ithaca, NY 14850, USA

McDaniel, Lyndall D (Lindy) *Baseball Player*
225 Wake Rd, #323, El Centro, CA 92243, USA

McDaniel, Mel *Singer*
106 Cranwell Dr, Hendersonville, TN 37075, USA

McDaniel, Randall *Football Player*
%Minnesota Vikings, 9520 Viking Dr, Eden Prairie, MN 55344, USA

McDaniels (Darryl M), Darryl *Rapper (Run-DMC)*
%Rush Artists Mgmt, 1600 Varick St, New York, NY 10013, USA

McDermott, Edward A *Government Official*
Lake House South, 875 E Camino Real, Boca Raton, FL 33432, USA

McDivitt, James A *Astronaut, Air Force General*
9146 Cherry Ave, Rapid City, MI 49676, USA

McDonald, Audra *Actress*
%Peter Strain Assoc, 1500 Broadway, #2001, New York, NY 10036, USA

McDonald, Charles C *Air Force General*
Commader, AF Logistics Command, Wright-Patterson Air Force Base, OH 45433, USA

McDonald, Country Joe *Singer*
PO Box 7054, Berkeley, CA 94707, USA

McDonald, Forrest *Historian*
PO Box 155, Coker, AL 35452, USA

McDonald, Gail C *Government Official*
%Interstate Commerce Commission, 12th & Constitution NW, Washington, DC 20423, USA

Mcdonald, Gregory C *Writer*
%Arthur Greene, 101 Park Ave, New York, NY 10178, USA

McDonald, James F *Businessman*
%Scientific-Atlanta Inc, 1 Technology Parkway S, Norcross, GA 30092, USA

McDonald, John W *Government Official*
3800 N Fairfax Dr, Arlington, VA 22203, USA

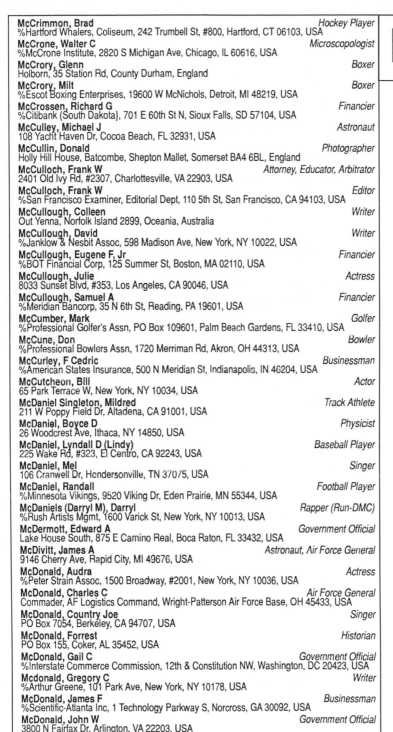

M

McCrimmon - McDonald

M

McDonald, Mackey J — *Businessman*
%VF Corp, 1047 N Park Rd, Wyomissing, PA 19610, USA

McDonald, Malcolm S — *Financier*
%Signet Banking Corp, 7 N 8th St, Richmond, VA 23219, USA

McDonald, Michael — *Singer, Songwriter*
%HK Mgmt, 8900 Wilshire Blvd, #300, Beverly Hills, CA 90211, USA

McDonald, Paul — *Football Player*
1815 Tradewinds Lane, Newport Beach, CA 92660, USA

McDonald, Robert B — *Businessman*
%Great Lakes Chemical Corp, 1 Great Lakes Blvd, West Lafayette, IN 47906, USA

McDonald, Thomas F (Tommy) — *Football Player*
537 W Valley Forge Rd, King of Prussia, PA 19406, USA

McDonald, Tim — *Football Player*
%San Francisco 49ers, 4949 Centennial Blvd, Santa Clara, CA 95054, USA

McDonnell, John F — *Businessman*
%McDonnell Douglas Corp, PO Box 516, St Louis, MO 63166, USA

McDonnell, Mary — *Actress*
%William Morris Agency, 151 S El Camino Dr, Beverly Hills, CA 90212, USA

McDonnell, Patrick — *Cartoonist (Mutts)*
%King Features Syndicate, 216 E 45th St, New York, NY 10017, USA

McDonough, John J — *Businessman*
%DENTSPLY International, 570 W College Ave, York, PA 17404, USA

McDonough, Sean — *Sportscaster*
%CBS-TV, Sports Dept, 51 W 52nd St, New York, NY 10019, USA

McDonough, Will — *Sportswriter*
4 Malcolm St, Hingham, MA 02043, USA

McDonough, William — *Architect*
410 E Water St, Charlottesvle, VA 22902, USA

McDormand, Frances — *Actress*
%William Morris Agency, 1325 Ave of Americas, New York, NY 10019, USA

McDougal, Jerome R — *Financier*
%River Bank America, 145 Huguenot St, New Rochelle, NY 10801, USA

McDougald, Gilbert J (Gil) — *Baseball Player*
10 Warren Ave, Spring Lake, NJ 07762, USA

McDougall, Ronald A — *Businessman*
%Brinker International, 6830 LBJ Freeway, Dallas, TX 75240, USA

McDougall, Walter A — *Historian*
%University of Pennsylvania, History Dept, Philadelphia, PA 19104, USA

McDowall, Roddy — *Actor*
3110 Brookdale Rd, Studio City, CA 91604, USA

McDowell, David E — *Businessman*
%McKesson Corp, 1 Post St, San Francisco, CA 94104, USA

McDowell, Frank — *Plastic Surgeon*
100 N Kalaheo, #F, Kailua, HI 96734, USA

McDowell, J Walter — *Financier*
%Wachovia Bank of North Carolina, PO Box 3099, Winston-Salem, NC 27102, USA

McDowell, Jack B — *Baseball Player*
5443 Van Noord Ave, Van Nuys, CA 91401, USA

McDowell, Malcolm — *Actor*
%Markham & Froggett, 4 Windmill St, London W1P 1HF, England

McDowell, Samuel E (Sam) — *Baseball Player*
7479 McClure Ave, Pittsburgh, PA 15218, USA

McDuffie, Robert — *Concert Violinist*
111 E 85th St, New York, NY 10028, USA

McDyess, Antonio — *Basketball Player*
%Denver Nuggets, McNichols Arena, 1635 Clay St, Denver, CO 80204, USA

McEachran, Angus — *Editor*
%Memphis Commercial Appeal, Editorial Dept, 495 Union Ave, Memphis, TN 38103, USA

McEldowney, Brooke — *Cartoonist (9 Chickwood Lane)*
%United Feature Syndicate, 200 Park Ave, New York, NY 10166, USA

McElhenny, Hugh — *Football Player*
4023 171st Ave SE, Bellevue, WA 98008, USA

McElravey, R C — *Financier*
%LMSC Federal Credit Union, PO Box 3643, Sunnyvale, CA 94088, USA

McElroy, Joseph P — *Writer*
%Georges Borchandt, 136 E 57th St, New York, NY 10022, USA

McElroy, William D — *Biochemist*
%University of California, Biology Dept, La Jolla, CA 92067, USA

McDonald - McElroy

McElwaine, Guy — *Businessman*
%Columbia Pictures Industries, 711 5th Ave, New York, NY 10022, USA

McEnroe, John P, Jr — *Tennis Player*
23712 Malibu Colony Rd, Malibu, CA 90265, USA

McEntee, Gerald W — *Labor Leader*
%State County Muncipal Employees Union, 1625 "L" St NW, Washington, DC 20036, USA

McEntire, Reba — *Singer*
%Starstruck Talent, PO Box 121966, Nashville, TN 37212, USA

McEuen, John — *Banjo Player (Nitty Gritty Dirt Band)*
%World Class Talent, 1522 Demonbreun St, Nashville, TN 37203, USA

McEvoy, Marian — *Editor*
%Elle Decor Magazine, Editorial Dept, 1633 Broadway, New York, NY 10019, USA

McEwan, Geraldine — *Actress*
%Marmont Mgmt, Langham House, 302-08 Regent St, London W1R 5AL, England

McEwan, Ian — *Writer*
%Jonathan Cape, 20 Vauxhall Bridge Rd, London SW1V 2SA, England

McEwen, Mark — *Commentator*
%"America Tonight" Show, CBS-TV, News Dept, 51 W 52nd St, New York, NY 10019, USA

McEwen, Mike — *Hockey Player*
%Hartford Whalers, Coliseum, 242 Trumbell St, #800, Hartford, CT 06103, USA

McEwen, Tom — *Drag Racing Driver*
17368 Buttonwood St, Fountain Valley, CA 92708, USA

McEwen, Tom — *Sportswriter*
%Tampa Tribune, 202 S Parker St, Tampa, FL 33606, USA

McFadden, Gates — *Actress*
2332 E Allview Terrace, Los Angeles, CA 90068, USA

McFadden, James (Banks) — *Football Player*
253 Riggs Dr, Clemson, SC 29631, USA

McFadden, Mary J — *Fashion Designer*
240 W 35th St, #1700, New York, NY 10001, USA

McFadin, Lewis (Bud) — *Football Player*
428 Springwood Dr, Victoria, TX 77905, USA

McFarland, Duncan M — *Financier*
%Wellington Management Co, 75 State St, Boston, MA 02109, USA

McFarlane, Robert C — *Government Official*
2010 Prospect St NW, Washington, DC 20037, USA

McFeeley, William S — *Historian*
445 Franklin St, #25, Athens, GA 30606, USA

McFerrin, Bobby — *Singer, Songwriter*
%Original Artists, 853 Broadway, #1901, New York, NY 10003, USA

McFerson, D Richard — *Businessman*
%Nationwide Life Insurance, 1 Nationwide Plaza, Columbus, OH 43215, USA

McGahey, James C — *Labor Leader*
%Plant Guard Workers Union, 25510 Kelly Rd, Roseville, MI 48066, USA

McGarity, Vernon — *WW II Army Hero (CMH)*
4522 Quince Ave, Memphis, TN 38117, USA

McGaugh, James L — *Psychobiologist*
2327 Aralia St, Newport Beach, CA 92660, USA

McGavin, Darren — *Actor*
PO Box 2939, Beverly Hills, CA 90213, USA

McGeady, Sister Mary Rose — *Social Activist*
%Covenant House, 460 W 41st St, New York, NY 10036, USA

McGee, Mike — *Football Player, Administrator*
%University of South Carolina, Athletic Dept, Columbia, SC 29208, USA

McGee, Willie D — *Baseball Player*
668 Turquoise Dr, Hercules, CA 94547, USA

McGeehan, Robert L — *Businessman*
%Kennametal Inc, State Rt 981 S, Latrobe, PA 15650, USA

McGhee, Brownie — *Singer*
688 43rd St, Oakland, CA 94609, USA

McGhee, George C — *Government Official*
36276 Mountville Rd, Middleburg, VA 22117, USA

McGill, Archie J, Jr — *Financier*
50 Belmont Ave, Bela Cynwyd, PA 19004, USA

McGill, William J — *Educator*
2624 Costebelle Dr, La Jolla, CA 92037, USA

McGillis, Kelly — *Actress*
303 Whitehead St, Key West, FL 33040, USA

M

McElwaine - McGillis

M

McGinest, Willie — *Football Player*
%New England Patriots, Foxboro Stadium, Rt 1, Foxboro, MA 02035, USA

McGinley, Ted — *Actor*
662 N Van Ness Ave, #305, Los Angeles, CA 90004, USA

McGinnis, Joe — *Writer*
%Morton Janklow Assoc, 598 Madison Ave, New York, NY 10022, USA

McGinty, John J, III — *Vietnam War Marine Corps Hero (CMH)*
75 Eastern Ave, Lynn, MA 01902, USA

McGinty, Kathleen A — *Government Official*
%Environmental Policy, White House, 1600 Pennsylvania Ave, Washington, DC 20500, USA

McGirt, James (Buddy) — *Boxer*
%Madison Square Garden Boxing, 4 Pennsylvania Plaza, New York, NY 10001, USA

McGlaughlin, Daniel W — *Businessman*
%Equifax Inc, 1600 Peachtree St NW, Atlanta, GA 30309, USA

McGlockin, Jon — *Basketball Player*
%Bando-McGlocklin Investment Co, 13555 Bishops Court, #205, Brookfield, WI 53005, USA

McGonagle, William L — *Mediterrean Action Navy Hero (CMH)*
500 E Amado Rd, #612, Palm Springs, CA 92262, USA

McGoohan, Patrick — *Actor*
16808 Bollinger Dr, Pacific Palisades, CA 90272, USA

McGoon, Dwight C — *Surgeon*
706 12th Ave SW, Rochester, MN 55902, USA

McGough, George — *Financier*
%Sutro Co, 201 California St, San Francisco, CA 94111, USA

McGovern, Elizabeth — *Actress*
9161 Hazen Dr, Beverly Hills, CA 90210, USA

McGovern, George S — *Senator, SD*
Friendship Station, Box 5591, Washington, DC 20016, USA

McGovern, Maureen — *Singer*
%Barron Mgmt, 163 Amsterdam Ave, #174, New York, NY 10023, USA

McGranahan, Donald V — *Social Scientist*
47 Chemin Moise Duboule, 1209 Geneva, Switzerland

McGrath, Don J — *Financier*
%Bank of the West, 1450 Treat Blvd, Walnut Creek, CA 94596, USA

McGrath, Eugene R — *Businessman*
%Consolidated Edison of New York, 4 Irving Place, New York, NY 10003, USA

McGrath, Mike — *Bowler*
%Professional Bowlers Assn, 1720 Merriman Rd, Akron, OH 44313, USA

McGraw, Frank E (Tug) — *Baseball Player*
1518 Grace Lake Circle, Longwood, FL 32750, USA

McGraw, Harold W, III — *Businessman*
%McGraw-Hill Inc, 1221 Ave of Americas, New York, NY 10020, USA

McGraw, Harold W, Jr — *Publisher*
%McGraw-Hill Inc, 1221 Ave of Americas, New York, NY 10020, USA

McGraw, Tim — *Singer*
%Image Management Group, 27 Music Square E, Nashville, TN 37203, USA

McGregor, Douglas J — *Businessman*
%M A Hanna Co, 200 Public Square, Cleveland, OH 44114, USA

McGregor, Maurice — *Cardiologist*
%Royal Victoria Hospital, 687 Pine Ave W, Montreal PQ H3A 1A1, Canada

McGregor, Scott H — *Baseball Player*
Star Rt 1, Box 2800-1300, Tehachapi, CA 93561, USA

McGriff, Frederick S (Fred) — *Baseball Player*
16314 Millan De Avila, Tampa, FL 33613, USA

McGriff, Hershel — *Auto Racing Driver*
%General Delivery, Green Valley, AZ 85622, USA

McGriff, Jimmy — *Musician*
%Hands On PR, 3424 Primera Ave, Los Angeles, CA 90068, USA

McGrory, Mary — *Columnist*
%Washington Post, Editorial Dept, 1150 15th St NW, Washington, DC 20071, USA

McGuane, Thomas F, III — *Writer*
PO Box 25, McLeod, MT 59052, USA

McGuff, Joe — *Sportswriter*
%Kansas City Star, 1729 Grand Ave, Kansas City, MO 64108, USA

McGuinn, Martin G — *Financier*
%Mellon Bank Corp, 1 Mellon Bank Center, 500 Grant St, Pittsburgh, PA 15219, USA

McGuinn, Roger — *Singer, Guitarist (Byrds), Songwriter*
%Elizabeth Rush Agency, PO Box 99, Newton, MA 02258, USA

McGinest - McGuinn

McGuire, Alfred J (Al) *Basketball Coach, Sportscaster*
%NBC-TV, Sports Dept, 30 Rockefeller Plaza, New York, NY 10112, USA

McGuire, Biff *Actor*
315 W 57th St, #4-H, New York, NY 10019, USA

McGuire, Christine *Singer (McGuire Sisters)*
100 Rancho Circle, Las Vegas, NV 89107, USA

McGuire, Dick *Basketball Player, Coach*
%New York Knicks, Madison Square Garden, 4 Penn Plaza, New York, NY 10001, USA

McGuire, Dorothy *Actress*
121 Copley Place, Beverly Hills, CA 90210, USA

McGuire, Dorothy *Singer (McGuire Sisters)*
100 Rancho Circle, Las Vegas, NV 89107, USA

McGuire, Patricia A *Educator*
%Trinity College, President's Office, Washington, DC 20017, USA

McGuire, Phyllis *Singer (McGuire Sisters)*
100 Rancho Circle, Las Vegas, NV 89107, USA

McGuire, Willard H *Labor Leader*
%National Education Assn, 1201 16th St NW, Washington, DC 20036, USA

McGuire, William W *Businessman*
%United HealthCare, Opus Center, #300, 9900 Bren Rd E, Minnetonka, MN 55343, USA

McGwire, Mark D *Baseball Player*
%Oakland Athletics, Oakland Coliseum, Oakland, CA 94621, USA

McHale, Kevin *Basketball Player, Executive*
7723 McCarthy Beach Rd, Hibbing, MN 55746, USA

McHarg, Ian L *Landscape Architect*
PO Box 778, Rt 82, Unionsville, PA 19375, USA

McHenry, Dean E *Educator*
%University of California, McHenry Library, Santa Cruz, CA 95064, USA

McHenry, Donald F *Diplomat*
%Georgetown University, Foreign Service School, Washington, DC 20057, USA

McInally, Pat *Football Player*
PO Box 17791, Fort Mitchell, KY 41017, USA

McInerney, Thomas G (Tom) *Air Force General*
Assistant Vice Chief of Staff, HqUSAF, Pentagon, Washington, DC 20330, USA

McInnes, Harold A *Businessman*
%AMP Inc, 470 Friendship Rd, Harrisburg, PA 17111, USA

McIntyre, Donald C *Opera Singer*
Foxhill Farm, Jackass Lane, Keston, Bromley, Kent BR2 6AN, England

McIntyre, Guy *Football Player*
%San Francisco 49ers, 4949 Centennial Blvd, Santa Clara, CA 95054, USA

McIntyre, James A *Businessman*
%Fremont General Corp, 2020 Santa Monica Blvd, Santa Monica, CA 90404, USA

McIntyre, James T, Jr *Government Official*
%Hansell Post Brandon Dorsey, 1747 Pennsylvania Ave, Washington, DC 20006, USA

McKagan, Duff *Bassist (Guns 'n' Roses)*
15250 Ventura Blvd, #900, Sherman Oaks, CA 91403, USA

McKay, Gardner *Actor*
252 Lumahai Place, Honolulu, HI 96825, USA

McKay, Heather *Squash, Racquetball Player*
48 Nesbitt Dr, Toronto ON M4W 2G3, Canada

McKay, Janet H *Educator*
%Mills College, President's Office, Oakland, CA 94613, USA

McKay, Jim *Sportscaster*
Battlefield Farm, 2805 Shepperd Rd, Monkton, MD 21111, USA

McKay, John A *Businessman*
%Harnischfeger Corp, 13400 Bishops Lane, Brookfield, WI 53005, USA

McKean, John R *Financier*
%Bay View Federal Bank, 2121 S El Camino Real, San Mateo, CA 94403, USA

McKechnie, Donna *Dancer, Actress*
127 Broadway, #220, Santa Monica, CA 90401, USA

McKee, Frank S *Labor Leader*
%United Steelworkers Union, 5 Gateway Center, Pittsburgh, PA 15222, USA

McKee, Kinnaird R *Navy Admiral*
214 Morris St, Oxford, MD 21654, USA

McKee, Lewis K *Businessman*
%Holly Farms, 1744 Lynnfield, #D, Memphis, TN 38119, USA

McKee, Maria *Singer*
%Premier Talent Agency, 3 E 54th St, #1400, New York, NY 10022, USA

M

McKee, Todd — *Actor*
32362 Lake Pleasant Dr, Westlake Village, CA 91361, USA

McKee, W W — *Businessman*
%Pitt-Des Moines Inc, 3400 Grand Ave, Pittsburgh, PA 15225, USA

McKeel, Sam S — *Publisher*
%Chicago Sun-Times, 401 N Wabash Ave, Chicago, IL 60611, USA

McKeever, Jeffrey D — *Businessman*
%MicroAge Inc, 2308 S 55th St, Tempe, AZ 85280, USA

McKeever, Marlin — *Football Player*
332 Evening Canyon Rd, Corona del Mar, CA 92625, USA

McKeithen, John J — *Governor, LA*
%McKeithen Wear Ryland Woodard, 221 Wall St, Columbia, LA 71418, USA

McKellar, Danica — *Actress*
%Agency For Performing Arts, 9000 Sunset Blvd, #1200, Los Angeles, CA 90069, USA

McKellen, Ian — *Actor*
25 Earl's Terrace, London W8, England

McKenna, Quentin C — *Businessman*
%Kennametal Inc, State Rt 981 S, Latrobe, PA 15650, USA

McKenna, William J — *Businessman*
%Kellwood Co, 600 Kellwood Parkway, Chesterfield, MO 63017, USA

McKennon, Keith R — *Businessman*
%PacifiCorp, 700 NE Multnomah, Portland, OR 97232, USA

McKenzie, Andrew — *Labor Leader*
%Leathers Goods Plastics Novelty Union, 265 W 14th St, New York, NY 10011, USA

McKenzie, Kevin — *Ballet Dancer*
%American Ballet Theatre, 890 Broadway, New York, NY 10003, USA

McKenzie, Reginald (Reggie) — *Football Player*
1334 100th Ave NE, Bellevue, WA 98004, USA

McKeon, Nancy — *Actress*
PO Box 1873, Studio City, CA 91614, USA

McKeown, Bob — *Commentator*
%CBS-TV, News Dept, 51 W 52nd St, New York, NY 10019, USA

McKern, Leo — *Actor*
%Richard Hatton, 29 Roehampton Lane, London SW15 5JR, England

McKernan, Leo J — *Businessman*
%Clark Equipment Co, 100 N Michigan St, South Bend, IN 46601, USA

McKey, Derrick — *Basketball Player*
%Indiana Pacers, Market Square Arena, 300 E Market St, Indianapolis, IN 46204, USA

McKiernan, John S — *Governor, RI*
95 Hilltop Dr, East Greenwich, RI 02818, USA

McKinney, John R — *WW II Army Hero (CMH)*
209 Singleton Ave, Sylvania, GA 30467, USA

McKinney, Joseph F — *Businessman*
%Tyler Corp, San Jacinto Tower, 2121 San Jacinto St, Dallas, TX 75201, USA

McKinney, Kennedy — *Boxer*
7127 Gleneagles Dr, Memphis, TN 38141, USA

McKinney, Rick — *Archer*
%Hoyt/Easton USA, 549 E Silver Creek, Gilbert, AZ 85296, USA

McKinney, Robert M — *Publisher, Diplomat*
Wind Fields, 39850 Snickersville Turnpike, Middleburg, VA 22117, USA

McKinney, Tamara — *Skier*
4935 Parkers Mill Rd, Lexington, KY 40513, USA

McKinnon, Bruce — *Editorial Cartoonist*
%Halifax Herald, Editorial Dept, PO Box 610, Halifax NS B3J 2T2, Canada

McKinzie, Gordon — *Aviation Engineer*
%Boeing Co, 777 Program, PO Box 3707, Seattle, WA 98124, USA

McKone, Francis L — *Businessman*
%Albany International Corp, PO Box 1907, Albany, NY 12201, USA

McKuen, Rod — *Poet, Singer*
1155 Angelo Dr, Beverly Hills, CA 90210, USA

McKusick, Victor A — *Clinical Geneticist*
%Johns Hopkins Hospital, Genetics Dept, 600 N Wolfe St, Baltimore, MD 21205, USA

McLachlan, Sarah — *Singer, Songwriter*
%Nettwerk Productions, 1250 W 6th Ave, Vancouver BC V6H 1A5, Canada

McLaglen, Andrew V — *Movie Director*
%Stanmore Productions, PO Box 1056, Friday Harbor, WA 98250, USA

McLain, Dennis D (Denny) — *Baseball Player*
11994 Hyne Rd, Brighton, MI 48116, USA

McKee - McLain

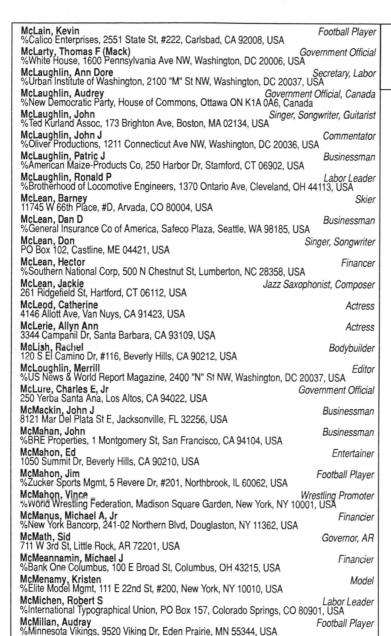

McLain, Kevin *Football Player*
%Calico Enterprises, 2551 State St, #222, Carlsbad, CA 92008, USA

McLarty, Thomas F (Mack) *Government Official*
%White House, 1600 Pennsylvania Ave NW, Washington, DC 20006, USA

McLaughlin, Ann Dore *Secretary, Labor*
%Urban Institute of Washington, 2100 "M" St NW, Washington, DC 20037, USA

McLaughlin, Audrey *Government Official, Canada*
%New Democratic Party, House of Commons, Ottawa ON K1A 0A6, Canada

McLaughlin, John *Singer, Songwriter, Guitarist*
%Ted Kurland Assoc, 173 Brighton Ave, Boston, MA 02134, USA

McLaughlin, John J *Commentator*
%Oliver Productions, 1211 Connecticut Ave NW, Washington, DC 20036, USA

McLaughlin, Patric J *Businessman*
%American Maize-Products Co, 250 Harbor Dr, Stamford, CT 06902, USA

McLaughlin, Ronald P *Labor Leader*
%Brotherhood of Locomotive Engineers, 1370 Ontario Ave, Cleveland, OH 44113, USA

McLean, Barney *Skier*
11745 W 66th Place, #D, Arvada, CO 80004, USA

McLean, Dan D *Businessman*
%General Insurance Co of America, Safeco Plaza, Seattle, WA 98185, USA

McLean, Don *Singer, Songwriter*
PO Box 102, Castline, ME 04421, USA

McLean, Hector *Financer*
%Southern National Corp, 500 N Chestnut St, Lumberton, NC 28358, USA

McLean, Jackie *Jazz Saxophonist, Composer*
261 Ridgefield St, Hartford, CT 06112, USA

McLeod, Catherine *Actress*
4146 Allott Ave, Van Nuys, CA 91423, USA

McLerie, Allyn Ann *Actress*
3344 Campanil Dr, Santa Barbara, CA 93109, USA

McLish, Rachel *Bodybuilder*
120 S El Camino Dr, #116, Beverly Hills, CA 90212, USA

McLoughlin, Merrill *Editor*
%US News & World Report Magazine, 2400 "N" St NW, Washington, DC 20037, USA

McLure, Charles E, Jr *Government Official*
250 Yerba Santa Ana, Los Altos, CA 94022, USA

McMackin, John J *Businessman*
8121 Mar Del Plata St E, Jacksonville, FL 32256, USA

McMahan, John *Businessman*
%BRE Properties, 1 Montgomery St, San Francisco, CA 94104, USA

McMahon, Ed *Entertainer*
1050 Summit Dr, Beverly Hills, CA 90210, USA

McMahon, Jim *Football Player*
%Zucker Sports Mgmt, 5 Revere Dr, #201, Northbrook, IL 60062, USA

McMahon, Vince *Wrestling Promoter*
%World Wrestling Federation, Madison Square Garden, New York, NY 10001, USA

McManus, Michael A, Jr *Financier*
%New York Bancorp, 241-02 Northern Blvd, Douglaston, NY 11362, USA

McMath, Sid *Governor, AR*
711 W 3rd St, Little Rock, AR 72201, USA

McMeannamin, Michael J *Financier*
%Bank One Columbus, 100 E Broad St, Columbus, OH 43215, USA

McMenamy, Kristen *Model*
%Elite Model Mgmt, 111 E 22nd St, #200, New York, NY 10010, USA

McMichen, Robert S *Labor Leader*
%International Typographical Union, PO Box 157, Colorado Springs, CO 80901, USA

McMillan, Audray *Football Player*
%Minnesota Vikings, 9520 Viking Dr, Eden Prairie, MN 55344, USA

McMillan, Ernie *Football Player*
3835 Windsor Place, St Louis, MO 63113, USA

McMillan, Howard L, Jr *Financier*
%Deposit Guaranty Corp, 210 E Capitol St, Jackson, MS 39201, USA

McMillan, John A *Businessman*
%Nordstrom Inc, 1501 5th Ave, Seattle, WA 98101, USA

McMillan, Roy D *Baseball Player*
1200 E 9th St, Bonham, TX 75418, USA

McMillan, Terry *Writer*
PO Box 2408, Danville, CA 94526, USA

M

McLain - McMillan

McMillen, C Thomas (Tom) *Basketball Player; Representative, MD*
%Physical Fitness-Sports Council, 701 Pennsylvania Ave NW, Washington, DC 20004, USA

McMonagle, Donald R *Astronaut*
%NASA, Johnson Space Center, 2101 NASA Rd, Houston, TX 77058, USA

McMullen, Donald A, Jr *Financier*
%American Capital Management-Research, 2800 Post Oak Blvd, Houston, TX 77056, USA

McMullen, John J *Baseball, Hockey Executive*
%New Jersey Devils, Meadowlands Arena, PO Box 504, East Rutherford, NJ 07073, USA

McMullian, Amos R *Businessman*
%Flowers Industries, 200 US Highway 19 S, Thomasville, GA 31792, USA

McMurray, Joseph P B *Economist*
College Harbor, 4650 5th Ave S, St Petersburg, FL 33711, USA

McMurray, W Grant *Religious Leader*
%Reorganized Church of Latter Day Saints, PO Box 1059, Independence, MO 64051, USA

McMurtry, Larry *Writer*
PO Box 552, Archer City, TX 76351, USA

McNair, Barbara *Singer*
%Roland Terry Productions, 909 Parkview Ave, Lodi, CA 95242, USA

McNair, Robert E *Governor, SC*
Rt 2, Box 310, Columbia, SC 29212, USA

McNair, Steve *Football Player*
%Houston Oilers, 6910 Fannin St, Houston, TX 77030, USA

McNair, Sylvia *Concert Singer*
%Colbert Artists, 111 W 57th St, New York, NY 10019, USA

McNall, Bruce *Hockey Executive*
%Los Angeles Kings, Forum, PO Box 17013, Inglewood, CA 90308, USA

McNally, Alan G *Financier*
%Harris Bankcorp, 111 W Monroe St, Chicago, IL 60603, USA

McNally, Andrew, III *Publisher*
%Rand McNally Co, PO Box 7600, Chicago, IL 60680, USA

McNally, Andrew, IV *Publisher*
%Rand McNally Co, PO Box 7600, Chicago, IL 60680, USA

McNally, David A (Dave) *Baseball Player*
3305 Ramada Dr, Billings, MT 59102, USA

McNally, Terrence *Playwright*
218 W 10th St, New York, NY 10014, USA

McNamara, Brian *Actor*
11730 National Blvd, #19, Los Angeles, CA 90064, USA

McNamara, John F *Baseball Manager*
1008 Wilson Pike, Brentwood, TN 37027, USA

McNamara, John F *Businessman*
%AmeriSource Corp, PO Box 959, Valley Forge, PA 19482, USA

McNamara, Julianne *Gymnast, Actress*
%Gold Marshak Assoc, 3500 W Olive Ave, #1400, Burbank, CA 91505, USA

McNamara, Kevin J *Businessman*
%Chemed Corp, Chemed Center, 225 E 5th St, Cincinnati, OH 45202, USA

McNamara, Robert S *Secretary, Defense*
2412 Tracy Place NW, Washington, DC 20008, USA

McNamara, William *Actor*
27040 Malibu Cove Colony Dr, Malibu, CA 90265, USA

McNary, Gene *Government Official*
%US Immigration & Naturalization Service, 425 "I" St NW, Washington, DC 20001, USA

McNaught, Judith *Writer*
%Pocket Books, 1230 Ave of Americas, New York, NY 10020, USA

McNaughton, Robert F, Jr *Computer Scientist*
2511 15th St, Troy, NY 12180, USA

McNealy, Scott G *Businessman*
%Sun Microsystems, 2550 Garcia Ave, Mountain Valley, CA 94043, USA

McNeer, Charles S *Businessman*
1111 N Edison St, Milwaukee, WI 53202, USA

McNeice, John A, Jr *Financier*
%Colonial Group, 1 Financial Center, Boston, MA 02111, USA

McNeil, Corbin A, Jr *Businessman*
%PECO Energy Co, 2301 Market St, Philadelphia, PA 19103, USA

McNeil, Frederick A (Fred) *Football Player*
12605 Hilloway Rd, Minnetonka, MN 55305, USA

McNeil, Gerald *Football Player*
%Cleveland Browns, 80 1st Ave, Berea, OH 44017, USA

McNeil, Kate *Actress*
5640 Rhodes Ave, North Hollywood, CA 91607, USA

McNeil, Lori *Tennis Player*
%International Management Group, 1 Erieview Plaza, #1300, Cleveland, OH 44114, USA

McNeill, Alfred T, Jr *Businessman*
%Turner Corp, 375 Hudson Ave, New York, NY 10014, USA

McNeill, Robert Duncan *Actor*
%Susan Smith Assoc, 121 N San Vicente Blvd, Beverly Hills, CA 90211, USA

McNeill, W Donald *Tennis Player*
670 Eugenia Rd, Vero Beach, FL 32963, USA

McNeish, Richard *Archeologist*
%Andover Archaeological Research Foundation, 1 Woodland Rd, Andover, MA 01810, USA

McNerney, David H *Vietnam War Army Hero (CMH)*
20322 New Moon Trail, Crosby, TX 77532, USA

McNichol, Kristy *Actress*
15060 Ventura Blvd, #350, Sherman Oaks, CA 91403, USA

McNicholas, John P *Businessman*
%Collins & Aikman Corp, 701 McCullough Dr, Charlotte, NC 28262, USA

McNichols, Stephen L R *Governor, CO*
3404 S Race St, Englewood, CO 80110, USA

McPartland, Marian *Jazz Pianist*
%Jazz Alliance, PO Box 515, Concord, CA 94522, USA

McPeak, Merrill A (Tony) *Air Force General*
%Chief of Staff, US Air Force, HqUSAF, Washington, DC 20330, USA

McPhee, John A *Writer*
475 Drake's Corner Rd, Princeton, NJ 08540, USA

McPherson, Frank A *Businessman*
%Kerr-McGee Corp, 123 Robert Kerr Ave, Oklahoma City, OK 73102, USA

McPherson, Harry C, Jr *Government Official*
10213 Montgomery Ave, Kensington, MD 20895, USA

McPherson, James M *Historian*
15 Randall Rd, Princeton, NJ 08540, USA

McPherson, John *Cartoonist (Close to Home)*
%Universal Press Syndicate, 4900 Main St, #900, Kansas City, KS 64112, USA

McPherson, M Peter *Educator*
%Michigan State University, President's Office, East Lansing, MI 48824, USA

McPherson, Mary Patterson *Educator*
%Bryn Mawr College, President's Office, Bryn Mawr, PA 19010, USA

McPherson, Melville P *Government Official*
%Bank of America, 555 California St, San Francisco, CA 94104, USA

McPherson, Rolf K *Religious Leader*
%Church of Foursquare Gospel, 1100 Glendale Blvd, Los Angeles, CA 90026, USA

McQueen, Butterfly *Actress*
3060 Dent St, #A, Augusta, GA 30906, USA

McQueen, Chad *Actor*
8306 Wilshire Blvd, #438, Beverly Hills, CA 90211, USA

McQuillian, Joseph M *Financier*
%Associates Corp of America, 250 Carpenter Freeway, Dallas, TX 75266, USA

McRaney, Gerald *Actor*
%Karg/Weissenbach Assoc, 329 N Wetherly Dr, #101, Beverly Hills, CA 90211, USA

McRee, Lisa *Commentator*
%ABC-TV, News Dept, 77 W 66th St, New York, NY 10023, USA

McReynolds, W Kevin *Baseball Player*
%Kansas City Royals, PO Box 419969, Kansas City, MO 64141, USA

McShane, Edward J *Mathematician*
209 Maury Ave, Charlottesville, VA 22903, USA

McShane, Ian *Actor*
%International Creative Mgmt, 76 Oxford St, London W1N 0AX, England

McSorley, Marty *Hockey Player*
%Los Angeles Kings, Forum, PO Box 17013, Inglewood, CA 90308, USA

McTeer, Robert D, Jr *Financier, Government Official*
%Federal Reserve Bank, 2200 N Pearl St, Dallas, TX 75201, USA

McTiernan, John *Movie Director*
%William Morris Agency, 151 S El Camino Dr, Beverly Hills, CA 90212, USA

McVie, Christine *Singer (Fleetwood Mac), Songwriter*
9744 Lloydcrest Dr, Beverly Hills, CA 90210, USA

McVie, John *Singer (Fleetwood Mac), Songwriter*
13486 Firth Dr, Beverly Hills, CA 90210, USA

M

McNeil - McVie

M

McVie, Tom — *Hockey Coach*
%Boston Bruins, Boston Garden, 150 Causeway St, Boston, MA 02114, USA

McWethy, John F — *Commentator*
%ABC-TV, News Dept, 1717 De Sales St NW, Washington, DC 20036, USA

McWherter, Ned R — *Governor, TN*
22 Bypass Building, Dresden, TN 38225, USA

McWhirter, Norris D — *Publisher*
Manor House, Kington Langley Near Chippenham, Wilts SN15 5NH, England

McWhorter, R Clayton — *Businessman*
%HealthTrust Inc, 4525 Harding Rd, Nashville, TN 37205, USA

McWilliam, Edward — *Sculptor*
8-A Holland Villas Rd, London W14 8DP, England

McWilliams, Brian — *Labor Leader*
%Longshoremen/Warehousemen Union, 1188 Franklin St, San Francisco, CA 94109, USA

McWilliams, Caroline — *Actress*
2195 Mandeville Canyon, Los Angeles, CA 90049, USA

McWilliams, David — *Football Coach, Administrator*
%University of Texas, Athletic Dept, Austin, TX 78712, USA

Mead, Dana G — *Businessman*
%Tenneco Inc, Tenneco Building, PO Box 2511, Houston, TX 77252, USA

Mead, George W — *Businessman*
%Consolidated Papers Inc, 231 1st Ave N, Wisconsin Rapids, WI 54495, USA

Mead, Shepherd — *Writer*
53 Rivermead Court, London SW6 3RY, England

Meade, Carl J — *Astronaut*
%NASA, Johnson Space Center, 2101 NASA Rd, Houston, TX 77058, USA

Meade, James E — *Nobel Economics Laureate*
40 High St, Little Shelford, Cambridge CB2 5ES, England

Meadlock, James W — *Businessman*
%Intergraph Corp, 1 Madison Industrial Park, Huntsville, AL 35894, USA

Meador, Eddie D (Ed) — *Football Player*
%Oro by Jon, PO Box 126, Natural Bridge, VA 24578, USA

Meadow, David L — *Religious Leader*
%Churches of God General Conference, 7176 Glenmeadow Dr, Frederick, MD 21703, USA

Meadows, Audrey — *Actress*
350 Trousdale Place, Beverly Hills, CA 90210, USA

Meadows, Bernard W — *Sculptor*
34 Belsize Grove, London NW3, England

Meadows, Jayne — *Actress*
16185 Woodvale Rd, Encino, CA 91436, USA

Meadows, Stephen — *Actor*
%Jook Box Corp, 4525 Alger St, Los Angeles, CA 90039, USA

Meagher, James P — *Editor*
%Barron's Magazine, Editorial Dept, 200 Liberty St, New York, NY 10281, USA

Meagher, John W — *WW II Army Hero (CMH)*
38 Hyannis St, Toms River, NJ 08757, USA

Meagher, Mary T — *Swimmer*
2503 Stuts Lane, Richmond, VA 23236, USA

Mealey, George A — *Businessman*
%Freeport-McMoRan Inc, 1615 Poydras St, New Orleans, LA 70112, USA

Meaney, Colm — *Actor*
%Gage Group, 9255 Sunset Blvd, #515, Los Angeles, CA 90069, USA

Means, Natrone — *Football Player*
%San Diego Chargers, Jack Murphy Stadium, San Diego, CA 92160, USA

Means, Russell — *Indian Activist*
444 Crazy Horse Dr, Porcupine, SD 57772, USA

Meara, Anne — *Comedienne*
118 Riverside Dr, #5-A, New York, NY 10024, USA

Mears, Gary H — *Air Force General*
Director, Logistics, J-4, Joint Staff, Pentagon, Washington, DC 20318, USA

Mears, Rick — *Auto Racing Driver*
204 Spyglass Lane, Jupiter, FL 33477, USA

Mears, Walter R — *Journalist*
%Associated Press, Editorial Dept, 2021 "K" St NW, Washington, DC 20006, USA

Meat Loaf (Marvin Lee Aday) — *Singer*
%Left Bank Mgmt, 6255 Sunset Blvd, #2100, Los Angeles, CA 90028, USA

Mebane, G Allen — *Businessman*
%Unifi Inc, 7201 W Friendly Rd, Greensboro, NC 27410, USA

McVie - Mebane

Mecham, Evan *Governor, AZ*
%Mecham Pontiac-AMC-Renault, 4510 W Glendale Ave, Glendale, AZ 85301, USA

Mechem, Charles S, Jr *Businessman, Golf Executive*
%United States Show Corp, 1 Eastwood Dr, Cincinnati, OH 45227, USA

Mechem, Edwin L *Governor/Senator, NM; Judge*
%US District Court, PO Box 97, Albuquerque, NM 87103, USA

Meciar, Vladimir *Prime Minister, Slovakia*
Urad Vlady SR, Nam Slobody 1, 81370 Bratislava, Slovakia

Mecir, Miloslav *Tennis Player*
Sevcenkova 9, 85102 Bratislava, Czech Republic

Mecklenburg, Karl *Football Player*
%Denver Broncos, 13655 E Dove Valley Parkway, Englewood, CO 80112, USA

Mecom, John W, Jr *Football Executive*
%New Orleans Saints, 1500 Poydras St, New Orleans, LA 70112, USA

Medak, Peter *Movie Director*
1712 Stanley Ave, Los Angeles, CA 90046, USA

Medaris, J Bruce *Clergyman, Army General*
PO Box 415, Fern Park, FL 32751, USA

Medavoy, Mike *Entertainment Executive*
9101 Hazen Dr, Beverly Hills, CA 90210, USA

Medearis, Donald N, Jr *Pediatrician*
%Massachusetts General Hospital, Children's Services Dept, Boston, MA 02114, USA

Medina, Patricia *Actress*
1993 Mesa Dr, Palm Springs, CA 92264, USA

Medley, Bill *Singer (Righteous Brothers)*
%Barry Rillera, 9841 Hot Springs Dr, Huntington Beach, CA 92646, USA

Medley, Charles R O *Artist*
Charterhouse, Charterhouse Square, London EC1M 6AN, England

Medlin, John G, Jr *Financier*
%Wachovia Corp, 301 N Main St, Winston-Salem, NC 27150, USA

Medoff, Mark H *Playwright*
PO Box 3072, Las Cruces, NM 88003, USA

Medved, Aleksandr V *Wrestler*
%Central Soviet Sports Federation, Skatertny p 4, Moscow, Russia

Medvedev, Andrei *Tennis Player*
6352 Ellmau/Tirol, Austria

Medvedev, Zhores A *Biologist*
4 Osborn Gardens, London NW7 1DY, England

Meehan, Thomas E *Writer*
Brook House, Obtuse Rd, Newtown, CT 06470, USA

Meek, Paul D *Businessman*
%FINA Inc, FINA Plaza, 8350 N Central Expressway, Dallas, TX 75206, USA

Meek, Phillip J *Publisher*
%Capital Cities/ABC Inc, 77 W 66th St, New York, NY 10023, USA

Meeks, Gary A *Financier*
%Alliance Mortgage Co, 4500 Salisbury Rd, Jacksonville, FL 32216, USA

Meese, Edwin, III *Attorney General*
1075 Springhill Rd, McLean, VA 22102, USA

Meggett, David *Football Player*
%New England Patriots, Foxboro Stadium, Rt 1, Foxboro, MA 02035, USA

Megson, Claude W *Architect*
27 Dingle Rd, St Hellers, Auckland 5, New Zealand

Mehl, Lance A *Football Player*
66766 Graham Rd, St Clairsville, OH 43950, USA

Mehlhaff, Harvey *Religious Leader*
%North American Baptist Conference, 210 Summit Ave, Oakbridge Terrace, IL 60181, USA

Mehrabian, Robert *Educator*
%Carnegie Mellon University, President's Office, Pittsburgh, PA 15213, USA

Mehregany, Mehran *Microbiotics Engineer*
%Case Western Reserve University, Electrical Engineer Dept, Cleveland, OH 44106, USA

Mehta, Shailesh J *Businessman*
%Providian Corp, 400 W Market St, Louisville, KY 40202, USA

Mehta, Ved *Writer*
139 E 79th St, New York, NY 10021, USA

Mehta, Zubin *Conductor*
%New York Philharmonic, Avery Fisher Hall, Lincoln Center, New York, NY 10023, USA

Meier, Raymond *Photographer*
%Raymond Meier Photography, 532 Broadway, New York, NY 10012, USA

M

Meier, Richard A *Architect*
%Richard Meier Partners, 475 10th Ave, New York, NY 10018, USA

Meier, Waltraud *Opera Singer*
%Festspielhugel 3, 95445 Bayreuth, Germany

Meigher, S Christopher, III *Publisher*
%Meigher Communications, 100 Ave of Americas, New York, NY 10003, USA

Meijer, Doug *Businessman*
%Meijer Inc, 2929 Walker NW, Grand Rapids, MI 49544, USA

Meijer, Hank *Businessman*
%Meijer Inc, 2929 Walker NW, Grand Rapids, MI 49544, USA

Meinwald, Jerrold *Chemist*
%Cornell University, Chemistry Dept, Ithaca, NY 14853, USA

Meisner, Joachim Cardinal *Religious Leader*
Kardinal-Frings-Str 10, 50668 Cologne, Germany

Meisner, Randy *Bassist, Singer (Eagles, Poco)*
%Geoffrey Blumenauer Artists, 11846 Balboa Blvd,#204, Granada Hills, CA 91344, USA

Meisner, Sanford *Actor, Director*
%Neighborhood Playhouse School, 340 E 54th St, New York, NY 10022, USA

Mejia, Paul *Choreographer*
%New York City Ballet, Lincoln Center Plaza, New York, NY 10023, USA

Mekka, Eddie *Actor*
3518 Cahuenga Blvd W, #216, Los Angeles, CA 90068, USA

Meksi, Alexander *Prime Minister, Albania*
%Prime Minister's Office, Keshilli i Ministrave, Tirana, Albania

Melamid, Aleksandr *Artist*
%Ronald Freeman Fine Arts, 31 Mercer St, New York, NY 10013, USA

Melanie *Singer*
%Fantasma Tours, 2000 S Dixie Highway, West Palm Beach, FL 33401, USA

Melato, Mariangela *Actress*
%William Morris Organization, Via G Carducchi 10, 00187 Rome, Italy

Melcher, John *Senator, MT*
%General Delivery, Forsyth, MT 59327, USA

Melchior, Ib *Writer*
8228 Marymount Lane, Los Angeles, CA 90069, USA

Melendez, Bill *Animator*
438 N Larchmont Blvd, Los Angeles, CA 90004, USA

Melinda (Saxe) *Illusionist*
%Lady Luck Casino Hotel, Showroom, 206 N 3rd St, Las Vegas, NV 89101, USA

Mellen, Harold J, Jr *Businessman*
%MDU Resources Group, 400 N 4th St, Bismarck, ND 58501, USA

Mellencamp, John *Singer*
Rt 1, Box 361, Nashville, IN 47448, USA

Melles, Carl *Conductor*
Grunbergstr 4, 1130 Vienna, Austria

Mellick, William L *Businessman*
%20th Century Insurance, 6301 Owensmouth Ave, Woodland Hills, CA 91367, USA

Mellinkoff, Sherman M *Physician, Educator*
%University of California Medical Center, Los Angeles, CA 90024, USA

Mellish of Bermondsey, Robert J *Government Official, England*
West India House, Millwall Dock, London E14 9TJ, England

Mellon, Paul *Foundation Executive, Museum Official*
1729 "H" St NW, Washington, DC 20006, USA

Mellor, David *Government Official, England*
%House of Commons, Westminster, London SW1A 0AA, England

Mellor, James R *Businessman*
%General Dynamics Corp, 3190 Fairview Park Dr, Falls Church, VA 22042, USA

Melmon, Kenneth L *Pharmacologist*
51 Cragmont Way, Redwood City, CA 94062, USA

Melnick, Bruce E *Astronaut*
%Lockheed Space Operations, 1100 Lockheed Way, Titusville, FL 32780, USA

Melnick, Daniel *Movie, Television Producer*
1123 Sunset Hills Dr, Los Angeles, CA 90069, USA

Melnikov, Vitaly V *Movie Director*
Bucharestskaya Str 23, Korp 1, #193, 192282 St Petersburg, Russia

Melone, Joseph J *Businessman*
%Equitable Life Assurance Society, 787 7th Ave, New York, NY 10019, USA

Melrose, Kendrick B *Businessman*
%Toro Co, 8111 Lyndale Ave S, Minneapolis, MN 55420, USA

Meier - Melrose

Melroy, Pamela A — *Astronaut*
%NASA, Johnson Space Center, 2101 NASA Rd, Houston, TX 77058, USA

Melton, Sid — *Actor*
5347 Cedros Ave, Van Nuys, CA 91411, USA

Meltzer, Allan L — *Economist*
%Carnegie Mellon University, Economics Dept, Pittsburgh, PA 15260, USA

Melvin, Allan — *Actor*
271 N Bowling Green Way, Los Angeles, CA 90049, USA

Melzer, Thomas C — *Financier*
%Federal Reserve Bank, 411 Locust St, St Louis, MO 63102, USA

Men Huifeng — *Taiji Master*
%Physical Education Institute, Martial Arts Dept, Beijing, China

Menard, Henry W — *Geologist*
%Scripps Institute of Oceanography, Geology Dept, La Jolla, CA 92093, USA

Menchu Tum, Rigoberta — *Nobel Peace Laureate*
%Vincente Menchu Foundation, PO Box 5274, Berkeley, CA 94705, USA

Mendelsohn, Robert V — *Businessman*
%Royal Indemnity, 9300 Arrowpoint Blvd, Charlotte, NC 28273, USA

Mendenhall, Steven C — *Businessman*
%American Brands Inc, 1700 E Putnam Ave, Old Greenwich, CT 06870, USA

Mendes, Sergio — *Musician*
4849 Encino Ave, Encino, CA 91316, USA

Mendoza, June — *Artist*
34 Inner Park Rd, London SW19 6DD, England

Mendoza, Roberto G — *Financier*
%J P Morgan Co, 60 Wall St, New York, NY 10005, USA

Menem, Carlos Saul — *President, Argentina*
%Casa de Gobierno, Balcarce 50, 1064 Buenos Aires, Argentina

Meneses, Antonio — *Concert Cellist*
%International Creative Mgmt, 40 W 57th St, New York, NY 10019, USA

Menges, Carl B — *Financier*
%Donaldson Lufkin Jenrette, 140 Broadway, New York, NY 10005, USA

Menges, Chris — *Cinematographer*
%Harmony Pictures, 2921 W Alameda Ave, Burbank, CA 91505, USA

Mennea, Pietro — *Track Athlete*
Via Cassia 1041, 00189 Rome, Italy

Meno, Chorepiscopus John — *Religious Leader*
263 Elm Ave, Teaneck, NJ 07666, USA

Menotti, Gian-Carlo — *Composer*
Gilford Haddington, E Lothian EH41 4JF, Scotland

Mentzer, Carl F — *Financier*
%SunBank/Miami, 777 Brickell Ave, Miami, FL 33131, USA

Menuhin, Yehudi — *Concert Violinist*
Chalet Chankly Bore, Buhlstr, 3780 Gstaad-Neuret, Switzerland

Menzel, Jiri — *Movie, Theater Director*
%Studio 989, KF A S Jlndrisska 34, 112 07 Prage 1, Czech Republic

Menzies, Heather — *Actress*
PO Box 5973-1006, Sherman Oaks, CA 91403, USA

Menzies, James P — *Financier*
%Key Bank of New York, 66 S Pearl St, Albany, NY 12207, USA

Meola, Eric — *Photographer*
535 Greenwich St, New York, NY 10013, USA

Merbold, Ulf — *Astronaut, Germany*
Am Sonnenhang 4, 53721 Siegburg, Germany

Mercer, D Scott — *Businessman*
%Western Digital Corp, 8105 Irvine Center Dr, Irvine, CA 92718, USA

Mercer, Marian — *Actress, Singer*
25901 Piuma Rd, Calabasas, CA 91302, USA

Merchant, Ismail N — *Movie Producer*
%Merchant-Ivory Productions, 46 Lexington St, London W1P 3LH, England

Merchant, Natalie — *Singer, Songwriter*
%New York End Ltd, 29 W 65th St, #4-A, New York, NY 10023, USA

Mercure, Alex P — *Government Official*
%Department of Agriculture, 14th & Independence SW, Washington, DC 20250, USA

Mercurio, Paul — *Actor, Singer*
%Beyond Films, 53-55 Brisbane St, Sunnyhills, Sydney NSW 2010, Australia

Meredith, Burgess — *Actor*
25 Malibu Colony Rd, Malibu, CA 90265, USA

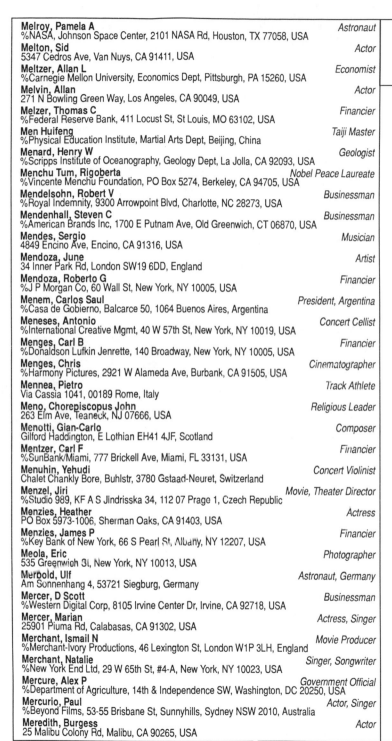

M

Melroy - Meredith

M

Meredith, Don — *Football Player, Sportscaster*
PO Box 597, Santa Fe, NM 87504, USA

Meredith, Edwin T, III — *Publisher*
%Meredith Corp, 1716 Locust St, Des Moines, IA 50309, USA

Meredith, James H — *Civil Rights Activist*
427 Eastview St, Jackson, MS 39209, USA

Meredith, Thomas C — *Educator*
%Western Kentucky University, President's Office, Bowling Green, KY 42101, USA

Meredith, William — *Poet*
6300 Bradley Blvd, Bethesda, MD 20817, USA

Meri, Lennart — *President, Estonia*
%President's Office, 39 Weizenberg St, 0100 Tallinn, Estonia

Merigan, Thomas C, Jr — *Medical Researcher*
148 Goya Rd, Portola Valley, CA 94028, USA

Meriwether, Lee — *Actress*
12139 Jeanette Place, Granada Hills, CA 91344, USA

Merle, Carole — *Skier*
74 Samoens, Haute Savoie, France

Merli, Gino J — *WW II Army Hero (CMH)*
605 Gino Merli Dr, Peckville, PA 18452, USA

Merlin, Jan — *Actor*
9016 Wonderland Ave, Los Angeles, CA 90046, USA

Merlo, Harry A — *Businessman*
%Louisiana-Pacific Corp, 111 SW 5th Ave, Portland, OR 97204, USA

Merrifield, R Bruce — *Nobel Medicine Laureate*
43 Mezzine Dr, Cresskill, NJ 07626, USA

Merrill, Dina — *Actress*
325 Dunemere Dr, La Jolla, CA 92037, USA

Merrill, John O — *Architect*
101 Gardner Place, Colorado Springs, CO 80906, USA

Merrill, Maurice H — *Attorney, Educator*
800 Elm Ave, Norman, OK 73069, USA

Merrill, Richard A — *Attorney, Educator*
501 Wellington Place, Charlottesville, VA 22903, USA

Merrill, Richard T — *Businessman*
740 Glendevon Court, Naples, FL 33999, USA

Merrill, Robert — *Opera Singer*
%Robert Merrill Assoc, 79 Oxford Rd, New Rochelle, NY 10804, USA

Merrill, Stephen (Steve) — *Governor, NH*
%Governor's Office, State House, Concord, NH 03301, USA

Merritt, C C I — *WW II Canadian Army Hero (VC)*
1255 58th Ave W, Vancouver BC V6P 1V9, Canada

Merritt, Jack N — *Army General*
%US Army Assn, 2425 Wilson Blvd, Arlington, VA 22201, USA

Merrow, Susan — *Association Executive*
%Sierra Club, 730 Polk St, San Francisco, CA 94109, USA

Merson, Michael — *Government Official*
%World Health Orgainzation, Ave Appia, 1211 Geneva 27, Switzerland

Merten, James A — *Financier*
%City Securities Corp, 135 N Pennsylvania St, Indianapolis, IN 46204, USA

Merten, Lauri — *Golfer*
%Ladies Professional Golf Assn, 2570 Volusia Ave, Daytona Beach, FL 32114, USA

Merton, Robert K — *Sociologist*
450 Riverside Dr, New York, NY 10027, USA

Mertz, Edwin T — *Biochemist*
%Montana State University, Plant Soil/Environmental Sci Dept, Bozeman, MT 59717, USA

Mertz, Francis J — *Educator*
%Farleigh Dickinson University, President's Office, Rutherford, NJ 07070, USA

Mertz, Martin F — *Financier*
%Republic Bank for Savings, 415 Madison Ave, New York, NY 10017, USA

Merwin, William Stanley — *Poet*
%Atheneum Publishers, 866 3rd Ave, New York, NY 10022, USA

Mese, John — *Actor*
%Century Artists, 9744 Wilshire Blvd, #308, Beverly Hills, CA 90212, USA

Meselson, Matthew S — *Biochemist*
%Harvard University, Fairchild Biochemistry Laboratories, Cambridge, MA 02138, USA

Meskill, Thomas J — *Governor, CT; Judge*
84 Randeckers Lane, Kensington, CT 06037, USA

Meredith - Meskill

Mesnil Du Buisson, Robert Du *Archaeologist*
Chateau de Champobert, Par 61310 Exmes, Orne, France

Messenger, George L *Businessman*
%Kemper Reinsurance Co, 1 Kemper Dr, Long Grove, IL 60047, USA

Messer, Thomas M *Museum Director*
1105 Park Ave, New York, NY 10128, USA

Messerschmid, Ernst *Astronaut, Germany*
Der Schone Weg 6, 72766 Reutlingen, Germany

Messerschmidt, J Alexander (Andy) *Baseball Player*
200 Lagunita Dr, Soquel, CA 95073, USA

Messick, Dale *Cartoonist (Brenda Starr)*
%Tribune Media Services, 435 N Michigan Ave, #1417, Chicago, IL 60611, USA

Messier, Mark *Hockey Player*
%New York Rangers, Madison Square Garden, 4 Penn Plaza New York, NY 10001, USA

Messina, Jim *Singer, Songwriter*
%Ira Fraitag, RD 1, Box 214, High Falls, NY 12440, USA

Messner, Reinhold *Explorer, Mountaineer*
Juval-Sudtirol, 39020 Stabel BZ, Italy

Metcalf, Eric *Football Player*
%Atlanta Falcons, 2745 Burnett Rd, Suwanee, GA 30174, USA

Metcalf, Laurie *Actress*
11845 Kling St, North Hollywood, CA 91607, USA

Metcalf, Robert L *Entomologist*
1902 Golfview Dr, Urbana, IL 61801, USA

Metcalf, Shelby *Basketball Coach*
%Texas A&M University, Athletic Dept, College Station, TX 77843, USA

Metheny, Pat *Jazz Musician, Composer*
%Ted Kurland Assoc, 173 Brighton Ave, Boston, MA 02134, USA

Metrano, Art *Actor*
1330 N Doheny Dr, Los Angeles, CA 90069, USA

Metzger, Henry *Medical Researcher*
3410 Taylor St, Chevy Chase, MD 20815, USA

Mey, Uwe-Jens *Speed Skater*
Vulkanstr 22, 10367 Berlin, Germany

Meyer Reyes, Debbie *Swimmer*
4840 Marconi Ave, Carmichael, CA 95608, USA

Meyer, Armin H *Diplomat*
4610 Reno Rd NW, Washington, DC 20008, USA

Meyer, Daniel J *Businessman*
%Cincinnati Milacron Inc, 4701 Marburg Ave, Cincinnati, OH 45209, USA

Meyer, Dina *Actress*
%Innovative Artists, 1999 Ave of Stars, #2850, Los Angeles, CA 90067, USA

Meyer, Jerome J *Businessman*
%Tektronix Inc, 26600 Southwest Parkway, Wilsonville, OR 97070, USA

Meyer, Joey *Basketball Coach*
%DePaul University, Athletic Dept, Chicago, IL 60614, USA

Meyer, Karl H *Biochemist*
642 Wyndham Rd, Teaneck, NJ 07666, USA

Meyer, Larry *Writer, Educator*
19811 Bushard St, Huntington Beach, CA 92646, USA

Meyer, Loren *Basketball Player*
%Dallas Mavericks, Reunion Arena, 777 Sports St, Dallas, TX 75207, USA

Meyer, Randall *Businessman*
407 Shadywood Rd, Houston, TX 77057, USA

Meyer, Raymond J (Ray) *Basketball Coach*
2518 Cedar Glen Dr, Arlington Heights, IL 60005, USA

Meyer, Robert K *Philosopher, Logician*
%Australian National University, I-Block, Canberra ACT 2801, Australia

Meyer, Ron *Entertainment Executive*
%MCA Inc, 100 Universal City Plaza, Universal City, CA 91608, USA

Meyer, Russ *Movie Producer, Photographer*
3121 Arrowhead Dr, Los Angeles, CA 90068, USA

Meyers Drysdale, Ann *Basketball Player, Sportscaster*
6621 Doral Dr, Huntington Beach, CA 92648, USA

Meyers, Ari *Actress*
%Dove Audio, 301 N Canon Dr, #203, Beverly Hills, CA 90210, USA

Meyers, John A *Publisher*
%Time Magazine, Time-Life Building, 1221 Ave of Americas, New York, NY 10020, USA

M

Meyerson, Martin — *Educator*
2016 Spruce St, Philadelphia, PA 19103, USA

Meyfarth, Ulrike Nasse- — *Track Athlete*
Buschweg 53, 51519 Odenthal, Germany

Mezentseva, Galina — *Ballerina*
%Kirov Ballet Theatre, 1 Ploshchad Iskusstr, St Petersburg, Russia

Miandad, Javed — *Cricketer*
%Cricket Board of Control, Gaddafi Stadium, Lahore, Pakistan

Micek, Ernest — *Businessman*
%Cargill Inc, PO Box 9300, Minneapolis, MN 55440, USA

Michael — *King, Romania*
Villa Serena, 77 Chemin Louis-Degallier, 1290 Versoix-Geneva, Switzerland

Michael (Shaheen), Archbishop — *Religious Leader*
%Antiochian Orthodox Christian Archdiocese, 358 Mountain Rd, Englewood, NJ 07631, USA

Michael, Eugene R (Gene) — *Baseball Manager, Executive*
49 Union Ave, Upper Saddle River, NJ 07458, USA

Michael, Gary G — *Businessman*
%Albertson's Inc, 250 Park Center Blvd, Boise, ID 83706, USA

Michael, George — *Singer, Songwriter*
2222 Mount Calvary Rd, Santa Barbara, CA 93105, USA

Michaels, Alan R (Al) — *Sportscaster*
%ABC-TV, Sports Dept, 77 W 66th St, New York, NY 10023, USA

Michaels, Brett — *Singer (Poison)*
%Levine/Schneider, 433 N Camden Dr, Beverly Hills, CA 90210, USA

Michaels, Corinne — *Actress*
%Allen Goldstein Assoc, 5015 Lemona Ave, Sherman Oaks, CA 91403, USA

Michaels, Eugene H — *Association Executive*
%Alzheimer's Disease Research, 15825 Shady Grove Rd, Rockville, MD 20850, USA

Michaels, Jack D — *Businessman*
%HON Industries, 414 E 3rd St, Muscatine, IA 52761, USA

Michaels, James W — *Editor*
%Forbes Magazine, Editorial Dept, 60 5th Ave, New York, NY 10011, USA

Michaels, Leonard — *Writer*
438 Beloit Ave, Kensington, CA 94708, USA

Michaels, Lisa — *Actress*
4942 Vineland Ave, #8, North Hollywood, CA 91601, USA

Michaels, Lorne — *Television Producer, Screenwriter*
88 Central Park West, New York, NY 10023, USA

Michaels, Louis A (Lou) — *Football Player*
69 Grace St, Swoyersville, PA 18704, USA

Michaels, Walter — *Football Player, Coach*
8127 Boca Rio Dr, Boca Raton, FL 33433, USA

Michaelsen, Kari — *Actress*
280 S Beverly Dr, #400, Beverly Hills, CA 90212, USA

Michals, Duane — *Photographer*
109 E 19th St, New York, NY 10003, USA

Michel, F Curtis — *Astronaut*
2101 University Blvd, Houston, TX 77030, USA

Michel, Hartmut — *Nobel Chemistry Laureate*
%Max Planck Biophysik Institut, 60437 Frankfurt/Main, Germany

Michel, Jean-Louis — *Underwater Scientist*
%IFREMER, Center de Toulon, 83500 La Seyne dur Mer, Toulon, France

Micheler, Elisabeth — *Kayak Athlete*
Gruntenstr 45, 86163 Augsburg, Germany

Michell, Keith — *Actor*
%London Mgmt, 2-4 Noel St, London W1V 3RB, England

Michelmore, Lawrence — *Government Official*
4924 Sentinel Dr, Bethesda, MD 20816, USA

Michels, Rinus — *Soccer Coach*
Hotel Breitenbacher Hof, H-Heine-Allee 36, 40213 Dusseldorf, Germany

Michener, Charles D — *Entomologist*
1706 W 2nd St, Lawrence, KS 66044, USA

Michener, James A — *Writer*
2706 Mountain Laurel Lane, Austin, TX 78703, USA

Michie, Donald — *Computer Scientist*
6 Inveralmond Grove, Cramond, dinburgh EH4 6RA, Scotland

Michiko — *Empress, Japan*
Imperial Palace, 1-1 Chiyoda-ku, Tokyo 100, Japan

Michnik, Adam — *Political Activist*
%Sejm, Parliament, Warsaw, Poland

Mickal, Abe — *Football Player, Physician*
774 Topaz St, New Orleans, LA 70124, USA

Middendorf, J William, II — *Secretary, Navy*
333 N Pitt St, Alexandria, VA 22314, USA

Middlecoff, Cary — *Golfer*
11765 Lost Tree Way, North Palm Beach, FL 33408, USA

Middleton, Rick — *Hockey Player*
47 Edgelawn Ave, #7, North Andover, MA 01845, USA

Midkiff, Dale — *Actor*
4640 Mary Ellen Ave, Sherman Oaks, CA 91423, USA

Midler, Bette — *Singer, Actress*
820 N San Vicente Blvd, #69-D, Los Angeles, CA 90069, USA

Midori — *Concert Violinist*
%Midori Foundation, 850 7th Ave, #705, New York, NY, 10019, USA

Miechur, Thomas F — *Labor Leader*
%Cement & Allied Workers Union, 2500 Brickdale, Elk Grove Village, IL 60007, USA

Mieto, Juha — *Cross Country Skier*
%General Delivery, Mieto, Finland

Mieuli, Franklin — *Basketball Executive*
%Golden State Warriors, Oakland Coliseum Arena, Oakland, CA 94621, USA

Mifsud Bonnici, Carmelo — *Prime Minister, Malta*
%House of Representatives, Valletta, Malta

Mifune, Toshiro — *Actor*
%Mifune Productions, 9-30-7 Siejyo-Machi, Setagayaku, Tokyo 157, Japan

Migenes, Julia — *Opera Singer*
%Robert Lombardo, 61 W 62nd St, #6-F, New York, NY 10023, USA

Miglio, Daniel J — *Businessman*
%Southern New England Telecommunications, 227 Church St, New Haven, CT 06510, USA

Miguel, Luis — *Singer*
%Ventura Productions, 11003 Rooks Rd, Pico Rivera, CA 90660, USA

Mihalik, Zigmund (Red) — *Basketball Referee*
307 O'Connor St, Ford City, PA 16226, USA

Mihaly, Andre — *Composer*
Verhalom Ter 9-B, 1025 Budapest II, Hungary

Mikan, George L — *Basketball Player, Executive*
7096 Cahill Rd, Minneapolis, MN 55439, USA

Mike-Mayer, Istvan (Steve) — *Football Player*
5277 Fairmead Circle, Raleigh, NC 27613, USA

Mikhalchenko, Alla A — *Ballerina*
%Bolshoi Theater, Teatralnaya Pl 1, 103009 Moscow, Russia

Mikhalkov, Nikita S — *Movie Director*
Malaya Gruzinskaya 28, #10, 123557 Moscow, Russia

Mikhalkov-Konchalovsky, Andrei S — *Movie Director*
Malaya Gruzinskaya 28, #10, 123557 Moscow, Russia

Mikita, Stan — *Hockey Player*
15 Windsor Dr, Oak Park, IL

Mikva, Abner J — *Judge*
%White House, 1600 Pennsylvania Ave NW, Washington, DC 20006, USA

Milano, Alyssa — *Actress*
12952 Woodbridge St, Studio City, CA 91604, USA

Milbury, Mike — *Hockey Player, Coach, Executive*
%New York Islanders, Veterans Memorial Coliseum, Uniondale, NY 11553, USA

Milch, David — *Screenwriter*
%International Creative Mgmt, 8942 Wilshire Blvd, Beverly Hills, CA 90211, USA

Miles, Joanna — *Actress*
2064 N Vine St, Los Angeles, CA 90068, USA

Miles, John C, II — *Businessman*
%DENTSPLY International, 570 W College Ave, York, PA 17404, USA

Miles, John W — *Geophysicist*
8448 Paseo del Ocaso, La Jolla, CA 92037, USA

Miles, Josephine — *Poet*
2275 Virginia St, Berkeley, CA 94709, USA

Miles, Mark — *Tennis Executive*
%Assn of Tennis Pros, 200 Tournament Players Rd, Ponte Vedra Beach, FL 32082, USA

Miles, Sarah — *Actress*
%Marina Martin Mgmt, 6-A Danbury St, London N1 8JU, England

Miles, Sylvia *Actress*
240 Central Park South, New York, NY 10019, USA

Miles, Vera *Actress*
PO Box 1704, Big Bear Lake, CA 92315, USA

Milford, Penelope *Actress*
219 Market St, Venice, CA 90291, USA

Milgram, Stanley *Social Psychologist*
%City University of New York, Graduate Center, New York, NY 10036, USA

Milius, John F *Movie Director*
888 Linda Flora Dr, Los Angeles, CA 90049, USA

Milken, Michael R *Financier*
4543 Tara Dr, Encino, CA 91436, USA

Milla, Roger *Soccer Player*
%Federation Camerounaise de Football, BP 1116, Yaounde, Cameroon

Millar, Jeffrey L (Jeff) *Cartoonist (Tank McNamara)*
%Universal Press Syndicate, 1301 Spring Oaks Circle, Houston, TX 77055, USA

Millard, Keith *Football Player*
%Minnesota Vikings, 9520 Viking Dr, Eden Prairie, MN 55344, USA

Millen, Matt *Football Player, Sportscaster*
%Fox-TV, Sports Dept, PO Box 900, Beverly Hills, CA 90213, USA

Miller, Alice *Golfer*
%Ladies Professional Golf Assn, 2570 Volusia Ave, Daytona Beach, FL 32114, USA

Miller, Ann *Actress, Dancer*
618 N Alta Dr, Beverly Hills, CA 90210, USA

Miller, Anthony *Football Player*
%San Diego Chargers, Jack Murphy Stadium, San Diego, CA 92160, USA

Miller, Arthur *Writer*
RR 1, Box 320, Tophet Rd, Roxbury, CT 06783, USA

Miller, C Arden *Pediatrician*
908 Greenwood Rd, Chapel Hill, NC 27514, USA

Miller, C Ray *Religious Leader*
%United Brethren in Christ, 302 Lake St, Huntington, IN 46750, USA

Miller, Charles D *Businessman*
%Avery Denninson Corp, 150 N Orange Grove Blvd, Pasadena, CA 91103, USA

Miller, Creighton *Football Player*
1610 Euclid Ave, Cleveland, OH 44115, USA

Miller, David *Cartoonist (Dave)*
%Tribune Media Services, 435 N Michigan Ave, #1417, Chicago, IL 60611, USA

Miller, Delvin *Harness Racing Driver*
PO Box 356, Meadow Lands, PA 15347, USA

Miller, Dennis *Entertainer*
814 N Mansfield Ave, Los Angeles, CA 90038, USA

Miller, Denny *Actor*
323 E Matilija St, #112, Ojai, CA 93023, USA

Miller, Donald E *Businessman*
%Gates Corp, 900 S Broadway St, Denver, CO 80209, USA

Miller, Edward D *Financier*
%Chemical Bank, 270 Park Ave, New York, NY 10017, USA

Miller, Elizabeth C *Medical Educator*
5517 Hammersely Rd, Madison, WI 53711, USA

Miller, Eugene A *Financier*
%Comerica Inc, 500 Woodward Ave, Detroit, MI 48226, USA

Miller, Frank *Radio Executive*
%CBS Radio Network, 51 W 52nd St, New York, NY 10019, USA

Miller, Franklin D *Vietnam War Army Hero (CMH)*
3693 Belle Vista Dr E, St Petersburg, FL 33706, USA

Miller, G William *Secretary, Treasury; Businessman*
%G William Miller Co, 1215 19th St NW, Washington, DC 20036, USA

Miller, Geoff *Publisher*
%Los Angeles Magazine, 1888 Century Park East, Los Angeles, CA 90067, USA

Miller, George A *Psychologist*
753 Prospect Ave, Princeton, NJ 08540, USA

Miller, George D *Air Force General*
Quincy Commons, 10 Arnold Rd, #28, North Quincy, MA 02171, USA

Miller, George T (Kennedy) *Movie Director*
30 Orwell St, King's Cross, Sydney 2011, Australia

Miller, Harold T *Publisher*
%Houghton Mifflin Co, 222 Berkeley St, Boston, MA 02116, USA

Miles - Miller

Miller, Harvey R — *Attorney*
%Weil Gotshal Manges, 767 5th Ave, New York, NY 10153, USA

Miller, Jack R — *Senator, IA; Judge*
6710 Maybole Place, Temple Terrace, FL 33617, USA

Miller, James A — *Oncologist*
5517 Hammersely Rd, Madison, WI 53711, USA

Miller, James C, III — *Government Official*
%Citizens for Sound Economy, 1250 "H" St NW, Washington, DC 20005, USA

Miller, Jason — *Playwright, Actor*
436 Spruce St, #600, Scranton, PA 18503, USA

Miller, Jeremy — *Actor*
%Gold Marshak Assoc, 3500 W Olive Ave, #1400, Burbank, CA 91505, USA

Miller, John E — *Army General*
Deputy CG Training & Doctrine Command, Fort Monroe, VA 23651, USA

Miller, John L (Johnny) — *Golfer*
%Johnny Miller Enterprises, PO Box 2260, Napa, CA 94558, USA

Miller, Jonathan W — *Stage, Movie Director*
63 Gloucester Crescent, London NW1, England

Miller, Joyce D — *Labor Leader*
%Amalgamated Clothing & Textile Workers, 15 Union Sq, New York, NY 10003, USA

Miller, Keith H — *Governor, AK*
3605 Arctic Blvd, #1001, Anchorage, AK 99503, USA

Miller, Lajos — *Opera Singer*
Balogh Adam Ut 28, 1026 Budapest, Hungary

Miller, Larry H — *Basketball Executive, Softball Player*
%Utah Jazz, 301 W South Temple, Salt Lake City, UT 84101, USA

Miller, Lennox — *Track Athlete*
1213 N Lake Ave, Pasadena, CA 91104, USA

Miller, Lenore — *Labor Leader*
%Retail/Wholesale/Department Store Union, 30 E 29th St, New York, NY 10016, USA

Miller, Leonard — *Businessman*
%Lennar Corp, 700 NW 107th Ave, Miami, FL 33172, USA

Miller, Lewis N, Jr — *Financier*
%Central Fidelity National Bank, 1021 E Cary St, Richmond, VA 23219, USA

Miller, Mark — *Singer (Sawyer Brown)*
%TKO Artist Mgmt, 4219 Hillsboro Rd, #318, Nashville, TN 37215, USA

Miller, Marvin J — *Labor Leader*
%Baseball Players Assn, 1370 Ave of Americas, New York, NY 10019, USA

Miller, Merton H — *Nobel Economics Laureate*
%University of Chicago, Graduate Business School, 1101 E 58th, Chicago, IL 60637, USA

Miller, Mildred — *Opera Singer*
PO Box 110108, Pittsburgh, PA 15232, USA

Miller, Mitch — *Musician*
345 W 58th St, New York, NY 10019, USA

Miller, Mulgrew — *Jazz Pianist*
3725 Farmersville Rd, Easton, PA 18045, USA

Miller, Neal E — *Psychologist*
%Yale University, Psychology Dept, New Haven, CT 06520, USA

Miller, Nicole J — *Fashion Designer*
780 Madison Ave, New York, NY 10021, USA

Miller, Paul D — *Navy Admiral*
Commander, US Atlantic Fleet, 1562 Mitscher Ave, Norfolk, VA 23551, USA

Miller, Penelope Ann — *Actress*
%Kincaid Personal Mgmt, 43 Navy St, #B, Venice, CA 90291, USA

Miller, Peter North — *Businessman*
%Lloyd's of London, Lime St, London EC3M 7HL, England

Miller, Reginald W (Reggie) — *Basketball Player*
%Indiana Pacers, Market Square Arena, 300 E Market St, Indianapolis, IN 46204, USA

Miller, Richard B — *Attorney*
%Miller Keeton, 909 Fannin, Houston, TX 77010, USA

Miller, Robert (Red) — *Football Coach*
%Dean Witter Reynolds, 4582 S Ulster Parkway, #300, Denver, CO 80237, USA

Miller, Robert G — *Businessman*
%Fred Meyer Co, 3800 SE 22nd Ave, Portland, OR 97202, USA

Miller, Robert J (Bob) — *Governor, NV*
%Governor's Office, State Capitol, Carson City, NV 89710, USA

Miller, Robert L — *Publisher*
%Berlitz Publishing Co, 257 Park Ave S, New York, NY 10010, USA

M

Miller - Miller

M

Miller, Samuel H *Businessman*
%Forest City Enterprises, 10800 Brookpark Rd, Cleveland, OH 44130, USA

Miller, Shannon *Gymnast*
715 S Kelley Ave, Edmond, OK 73003, USA

Miller, Sidney *Actor*
%First Artists Agency, 10000 Riverside Dr, #10, Toluca Lake, CA 91602, USA

Miller, Stanley L *Chemist*
%University of California, Chemistry Dept, La Jolla, CA 92093, USA

Miller, Steve *Singer, Songwriter, Band Leader*
PO Box 4127, Bellevue, WA 98009, USA

Miller, Stuart L (Stu) *Baseball Player*
3701 Ocaso Court, Cameron Park, CA 95682, USA

Miller, Ty *Actor*
450 1/2 Entrada Dr, Santa Monica, CA 90402, USA

Miller, Warren *Ski Photographer*
505 Pier Ave, Hermosa Beach, CA 90254, USA

Miller, Wiley *Cartoonist (Non Sequitur, Us & Them)*
7 Fairview Knolls NE, Iowa City, IA 52240, USA

Miller, William J *Businessman*
%Quantum Corp, 500 McCarthy Blvd, Milpitas, CA 95035, USA

Miller, Zell B *Governor, GA*
%Governor's Office, State Capitol Building, #203, Atlanta, GA 30334, USA

Millett, Kate *Feminist Leader, Writer*
20 Old Overlook Rd, Poughkeepsie, NY 12603, USA

Millett, Lewis L *Korean War Army Hero (CMH)*
%Korean War Memorial, Patriotic Hall, 1816 Figueroa, #700, Los Angeles, CA 90015, USA

Milligan, Terence A (Spike) *Movie Director*
%Spike Milligan Productions, 9 Orme Court, London W2 4RL, England

Milliken, William G *Governor, MI*
300 Grandview Parkway, Traverse City, MI 49684, USA

Milling, R King *Financier*
%Whitney National Bank, 228 St Charles Ave, New Orleans, LA 70130, USA

Millo, Aprile *Opera Singer*
%Columbia Artists Mgmt Inc, 165 W 57th St, New York, NY 10019, USA

Mills, Alley *Actress*
444 Carol Canal, Venice, CA 90291, USA

Mills, Billy *Track Athlete*
124 Pecos, Raton, NM 87740, USA

Mills, Curtis *Track Athlete*
328 Lake St, Lufkin, TX 75904, USA

Mills, Donna *Actress*
2260 Benedict Canyon Dr, Beverly Hills, CA 90210, USA

Mills, Hayley *Actress*
81 High St, Hampton, Middx, England

Mills, John *Actor*
Hill House, Denham Village, Buckinghamshire, England

Mills, Juliet *Actress*
2890 Hidden Valley Lane, Santa Barbara, CA 93108, USA

Mills, Mike *Bassist (REM)*
%REM/Athens Ltd, 250 W Clayton St, Athens, GA 30601, USA

Mills, Phoebe *Gymnast*
1247 Mariposa Ave, Miami, FL 33146, USA

Mills, Samuel D (Sam), Jr *Football Player*
%Carolina Panthers, 227 W Trade St, #1600, Charlotte, NC 28202, USA

Mills, Stephanie *Singer*
5807 Topanga Canyon Blvd, Woodland Hills, CA 91367, USA

Mills, Terry *Basketball Player*
%New Jersey Nets, Byrne Meadowlands Arena, East Rutherford, NJ 07073, USA

Millsaps, Knox *Aerospace Engineer*
PO Box 13857, Gainesville, FL 32604, USA

Milmoe, Caroline *Actress*
Martin-Smith, Half Moon Chambers, Chapel Walks, Manchester M2 1HN, England

Milne, John D *Businessman*
Chilton House, Chilton Candover Near Alresford, Hants SO24 9TX, England

Milner, Martin *Actor*
1846 Ocean Front, Santa Monica, CA 90401, USA

Milnes, Sherrill *Opera Singer*
%Herbert Barrett Mgmt, 1776 Broadway, #1800 New York, NY 10019, USA

Miller - Milnes

Milosevic, Slobodan   *President, Serbia*
%President's Office, Nemanjina 11, 11000 Belgrade, Serbia

Milosz, Czeslaw   *Nobel Literature Laureate*
%University of California, Slavic Languages Dept, Berkeley, CA 94720, USA

Milow, Keith   *Artist*
32 W 20th St, New York, NY 10011, USA

Milsap, Ronnie   *Singer, Songwriter*
PO Box 121831, Nashville, TN 37212, USA

Milstein, Cesar   *Nobel Medicine Laureate*
%Medical Research Council Center, Hills Rd, Cambridge CB2 2QH, England

Milstein, Elliott   *Educator*
%American University, President's Office, Washington, DC 20016, USA

Milstein, Howard P   *Financier*
%Emigrant Savings Bank, 5 E 42nd St, New York, NY 10017, USA

Milstein, Monroe G   *Businessman*
%Burlington Coat Factory Warehouse Corp, 1839 Rt 130, Burlington, NJ 08016, USA

Mimieux, Yvette   *Actress*
500 Perugia Way, Los Angeles, CA 90077, USA

Mimoun, Alain   *Marathon Runner*
27 Ave Edouard-Jenner, 94500 Champigny-sur-Marne, France

Min, Gao   *Diver*
%Olympic Committee, 9 Tiyuguan Rd, Beijing, China

Mincer, Jacob   *Economist*
448 Riverside Dr, New York, NY 10027, USA

Minehan, Cathy E   *Financier*
%Federal Reserve Bank, 600 Atlantic Ave, Boston, MA 02210, USA

Miner, Harold   *Basketball Player*
%Cleveland Cavaliers, 2923 Statesboro Rd, Richfield, OH 44286, USA

Miner, Jan   *Actress*
PO Box 293, Southbury, CT 06488, USA

Minisi, Anthony S (Skip)   *Football Player*
300 Continental Lane, Paoli, PA 19301, USA

Minix, F L   *Businessman*
%Crawford Co, 5620 Glenridge Dr NE, Atlanta, GA 30342, USA

Minnelli, Liza   *Actress, Singer*
%Black, 150 E 69th St, #21-G, New York, NY 10021, USA

Minnifield, Frank   *Football Player*
%Cleveland Browns, 80 1st Ave, Berea, OH 44017, USA

Minogue, Kylie   *Singer*
PO Box 292, Watford, Herts WD2 4ND, England

Minor, G Gilmer, III   *Businessman*
%Owens & Minor Inc, 4800 Cox Rd, Glen Allen, VA 23060, USA

Minor, Ronald R   *Religious Leader*
%Pentecostal Church of God, 4901 Pennsylvania, Joplin, MO 64804, USA

Minoso, Saturino O (Minnie)   *Baseball Player, Coach*
4250 Marin Dr, Chicago, IL 60613, USA

Minow, Newton N   *Government Official*
179 E Lake Shore Dr, #15-W, Chicago, IL 60611, USA

Minsky, Marvin L   *Computer Scientist*
%Massachusetts Institute of Technology, Computer Sci Dept, Cambridge, MA 02139, USA

Minter, Alan   *Boxer*
%Minter's Restaurant, 49 High St, Crawley, Sussex, England

Minter, Kelly   *Actress*
%Marshak-Wyckoff Assoc, 280 S Beverly Dr, #400, Beverly Hills, CA 90212, USA

Mintoff, Dominic   *Prime Minister, Malta*
The Olives, Xintill St, Tarxien, Malta

Minton, Dwight C   *Businessman*
%Church & Dwight Co, 469 N Harrison St, Princeton, NJ 08540, USA

Minton, Yvonne F   *Opera Singer*
%Ingpen & Williams, 14 Kensington Court, London W8, England

Mintz, Shlomo   *Concert Violinist*
%International Creative Mgmt, 40 W 57th St, New York, NY 10019, USA

Mir, Isabelle   *Skier*
65170 Saint-Lary, France

Mira, George   *Football Player*
19225 SW 128th Court, Miami, FL 33177, USA

Mirabella, Grace   *Editor, Publisher*
%Mirabella Magazine, 200 Madison Ave, New York, NY 10016, USA

M

Milosevic - Mirabella

M

Mirer, Rick — *Football Player*
%Seattle Seahawks, 11220 NE 53rd St, Kirkland, WA 98033, USA

Mirisch, Walter M — *Movie Producer*
647 Warner Ave, Los Angeles, CA 90024, USA

Mirren, Helen — *Actress*
2003 La Brea Terrace, Los Angeles, CA 90016, USA

Mirvish, Edwin (Ed) — *Comedian, Theater Producer*
%Honest Ed's Ltd, 581 Bloor St W, Toronto ON M6G 1K3, Canada

Mirzoev, Akbar — *Prime Minister, Tajikistan*
%Prime Minister's Office, Dushaube, Tajikistan

Mischke, Carl H — *Religious Leader*
1034 Buena Vista Dr, Sun Prairie, WI 53590, USA

Misersky, Antje — *Biathlete*
Grenzgraben 3-A, 98714 Stutzerbach, Germany

Mishin, Vasiliy P — *Space Engineer*
%Aviation Institute, Volokolamskoye Sh 4, 125080 Moscow, Russia

Mitchell, Andrea — *Commentator*
%NBC-TV, News Dept, 4001 Nebraska Ave NW, Washington, DC 20016, USA

Mitchell, Arthur — *Dance Director*
%Dance Theatre of Harlem, 215 E 94th St, New York, NY 10128, USA

Mitchell, Bradford W — *Businessman*
%Harleysville Mutual Insurance, 355 Maple Ave, Harleysville, PA 19438, USA

Mitchell, Brian — *Actor*
243 W 98th St, #5-C, New York, NY 10025, USA

Mitchell, Brian — *Football Player*
%Washington Redskins, 21300 Redskin Park Dr, Ashburn, VA 22011, USA

Mitchell, Broadus — *Economist*
49 Barrow St, New York, NY 10014, USA

Mitchell, Dan W — *Financier*
%Old National Bancorp, 420 Main St, Evansville, IN 47708, USA

Mitchell, Don — *Actor*
4139 Cloverdale Ave, Los Angeles, CA 90008, USA

Mitchell, Edgar D — *Astronaut*
242 Seaspray Ave, Palm Beach, FL 33480, USA

Mitchell, Edward E — *Businessman*
%Potomac Electric Power Co, 1900 Pennsylvania Ave NW, Washington, DC 20068, USA

Mitchell, George P — *Businessman*
%Mitchell Energy & Development, 2001 Timberloch Place, The Woodlands, TX 77380, USA

Mitchell, Gerald M — *Businessman*
%Cargill Inc, PO Box 9300, Minneapolis, MN 55440, USA

Mitchell, James F — *Prime Minister, St Vincent & Grenadines*
%Prime Minister's Office, Kingstown, St Vincent, St Vincent & Grenadines

Mitchell, Jerry R — *Businessman*
%Upjohn Co, 7000 Portage Rd, Kalamazoo, MI 49001, USA

Mitchell, John F — *Businessman*
%Motorola Inc, 1303 E Algonquin Rd, Schaumberg, IL 60196, USA

Mitchell, Johnny — *Football Player*
%New York Jets, 1000 Fulton Ave, Hempstead, NY 11550, USA

Mitchell, Joni — *Singer, Songwriter*
%Peter Asher Mgmt, 644 N Doheny Dr, Los Angeles, CA 90069, USA

Mitchell, Joseph Q — *Writer*
44 W 10th St, New York, NY 10011, USA

Mitchell, Kevin D — *Baseball Player*
3867 Ocean View Blvd, San Diego, CA 92113, USA

Mitchell, Leona — *Opera Singer*
%Columbia Artists Mgmt Inc, 165 W 57th St, New York, NY 10019, USA

Mitchell, Michele — *Diver*
10664 San Bernadino Way, Boca Raton, FL 33428, USA

Mitchell, Richard — *Businessman*
%Hy-Vee Food Stores, 1801 Osceola Ave, Chariton, IA 50049, USA

Mitchell, Robert C (Bobby) — *Football Player, Executive*
%Washington Redskins, 21300 Redskin Park Dr, Ashburn, VA 22011, USA

Mitchell, Sasha — *Actor*
%Flick East-West Talents, 9057 Nemo St, #A, West Hollywood, CA 90069, USA

Mitchell, Susan — *Poet*
%Florida Atlantic University, English Dept, Boca Raton, FL 33431, USA

Mitchell, William D — *Businessman*
%Texas Instruments, 13500 North Central Expressway, Dallas, TX 75243, USA

Mirer - Mitchell

Mitchelson, Marvin — *Attorney*
1486 N Sweetzer Ave, Los Angeles, CA 90069, USA

Mitchum, Carrie — *Actress*
%Abrams-Rubaloff Lawrence, 8075 W 3rd St, #303, Los Angeles, CA 90048, USA

Mitchum, Robert — *Actor*
PO Box 52516, Montecito, CA 93108, USA

Mitford, Jessica — *Writer*
6411 Regent St, Oakland, CA 94618, USA

Mitsotakis, Constantine — *Prime Minister, Greece*
%New Democracy Party, Odos Rigillis 18, 106 74 Athens, Greece

Mittermaier, Rosi — *Skier*
Winkelmoosalm, 83242 Reit Im Winkel, Germany

Mitterrand, Francois M M — *President, France*
22 Rue de Bievre, 75005 Paris, France

Mitzelfeld, Jim — *Journalist*
1905 Anderson Ave, Ann Arbor, MI 48104, USA

Mix, Ronald J (Ron) — *Football Player*
2317 Caminto Recodo, San Diego, CA 92107, USA

Mix, Steve — *Basketball Player*
%WPHL-TV, Sports Dept, 5001 Wynnefield Ave, Philadelphia, PA 19131, USA

Mixon, Alan — *Actor*
210 W 16th St, New York, NY 10011, USA

Mixon, Wayne — *Governor, FL*
2219 Demeron Rd, Tallahassee, FL 32312, USA

Miyamura, Hiroshi H — *Korean War Army Hero (CMH)*
1905 Mossman, Gallup, NM 87301, USA

Miyazaki, Yasuji — *Swimmer*
2-5-35 Izumicho, Hamamatsu, Postal #430, Shizuka Ken, Japan

Miyazawa, Kiichi — *Prime Minister, Japan*
6-34-1 Jingu-mae, Shibuyaku, Tokyo 150, Japan

Miyori, Kim — *Actress*
%Susan Smith Assoc, 121 N San Vicente Blvd, Beverly Hills, CA 90211, USA

Mize, Larry — *Golfer*
%Professional Golf Assn, PO Box 109601, Palm Beach Gardens, FL 33410, USA

Mize, Ola Lee — *Korean War Army Hero (CMH)*
211 Hartwood Dr, Gasden, AL 35901, USA

Mizel, Larry A — *Financier*
%Asset Investors Corp, 3600 S Yosemite St, Denver, CO 80237, USA

Mizell, Jason — *Rapper (Run-DMC)*
%Rush Artists Mgmt, 1600 Varick St, New York, NY 10013, USA

Mizerak, Steve — *Billiards Player*
140 Alfred St, Edison, NJ 08820, USA

Mizrahi, Isaac — *Fashion Designer*
104 Wooster St, New York, NY 10012, USA

Mladenov, Petar T — *President, Bulgaria*
10 Veliko Turnovo St, Sofia, Bulgaria

Mnouchkine, Ariane — *Theater Director*
%Theatre du Soleil, Cartoucherie, 75012 Paris, France

Mobley, Mary Ann — *Actress*
2751 Hutton Dr, Beverly Hills, CA 90210, USA

Mobley, William H — *Educator*
1 Reed Dr, College Station, TX 77843, USA

Mobutu Sese Seko — *President, Zaire; Army Marshal*
%President's Office, Mont Ngaliema, Kinshasa, Zaire

Moch, Jules — *Government Official, France*
La Griviere, Cabris, 06530 Peymeinade, France

Mochrie, Dottie — *Golfer*
%Ladies Professional Golf Assn, 2570 Volusia Ave, Daytona Beach, FL 32114, USA

Moco, Marcolino J Carlos — *Prime Minister, Angola*
%Prime Minister's Office, Council of Ministers, Luanda, Angola

Moctezuma, Edwardo Matos — *Archeologist*
%Great Temple Museum, Mexico City, Mexico

Modano, Mike — *Hockey Player*
%Dallas Stars, 211 Cowboys Parkway, Dallas, TX 75063, USA

Modell, Arthur B — *Football Executive*
%Cleveland Browns, 80 1st Ave, Berea, OH 44017, USA

Modell, Frank — *Cartoonist*
115 Three Mile Course, Guilford, CT 06437, USA

M

Mitchelson - Modell

M

Modena, Stefano *Auto Racing Driver*
%Alfa Corse, Via Enrico Fermi 7, 20019 Settimo Milanese, Italy

Modica, Frank A *Businessman*
%Showboat Inc, 2800 E Fremont St, Las Vegas, NV 89104, USA

Modigliani, Franco *Nobel Economics Laureate*
25 Clark St, Belmont, MA 02178, USA

Modine, Matthew *Actor*
9696 Culver Blvd, #203, Culver City, CA 90232, USA

Modl, Martha *Opera Singer*
Perlacherstr 19, 81539 Munich-Grunwald, Germany

Modrow, Hans *Prime Minister, East Germany*
Bundeskanzlerplatz 2-10, Bonn-Center, 53113 Bonn, Germany

Modrzejewski, Robert J *Vietnam War Marine Corps Hero (CMH)*
4725 Oporto Court, San Diego, CA 92124, USA

Modzelewski, Ed *Football Player*
PO Box 4207, 15 Last Wagon Dr, West Sedona, AZ 86340, USA

Modzelewski, Richard (Dick) *Football Player*
Pier Pointe #1, New Bern, NC 28562, USA

Moe, Douglas E (Doug) *Basketball Player, Coach*
%Philadelphia 76ers, Veterans Stadium, PO Box 25040, Philadelphia, PA 19147, USA

Moe, Thomas S (Tommy) *Skier*
%Shane Johnson, Moe Mentum Inc, 1821 Blake St, #3-B, Denver, CO 80202, USA

Moellering, John H *Army General*
1526 Shipsview Rd, Annapolis, MD 21401, USA

Moffatt, Katy *Singer, Songwriter*
PO Box 334, O'Fallon, IL 62269, USA

Moffett, D W *Actor*
450 N Rossmsore Ave, #401, Los Angeles, CA 90004, USA

Moffett, James R *Businessman*
%Freeport-McMoran Inc, 1615 Poydras St, New Orleans, LA 70112, USA

Moffitt, Donald E *Businessman*
%Consolidated Freightways, 3240 Hillview Ave, Palo Alto, CA 94304, USA

Moffo, Anna *Opera Singer*
%Carl Byoir Assoc, 420 Lexington Ave, #1000, New York, NY 10170, USA

Mogenburg, Dietmar *Track Athlete*
Frankenstr 59, 5000 Cologne 40, Germany

Mogilny, Alexander *Hockey Player*
%Vancouver Canucks, 100 N Renfrew St, Vancouver BC V5K 3N7, Canada

Mohn, Reinhard *Publisher*
%Bertelsmann AG, Carl-Bertelsmann-Str 270, 33311 Guetersloh, Germany

Mohn, Richard E *Financier*
%Soverign Bancorp, 1130 Berkshire Blvd, Wyomissing, PA 19610, USA

Mohri, Mamoru *Astronaut, Japan*
%NASDA, 2-1-1 Sengen, Tukubashi, Ibaraki 305, Japan

Moi, Daniel Arap *President, Kenya*
%President's Office, Harambee House, PO Box 30510, Nairobi, Kenya

Moiseyev, Igor A *Dance Director, Choreographer*
%Moiseyev Dance Co, 20 R, Triumfalnaya Pl, Moscow, Russia

Mokae, Zakes *Actor*
%Gersh Agency, 232 N Canon Dr, Beverly Hills, CA 90210, USA

Mokhehle, Ntsu *Prime Minister, Lesotho*
%Prime Minister's Office, Military Council, PO Box 527, Maseru, Lesotho

Mokrzynski, Jerzy *Architect*
Ul Marszalkowska 140 M 18, 00 061 Warsaw, Poland

Moldofsky, Philip J *Cancer Researcher*
%Fox Chase Cancer Center, 7701 Burholme Ave, Philadelphia, PA 19111, USA

Molen, Richard L *Businessman*
%Huffy Corp, PO Box 1204, Dayton, OH 45401, USA

Molina, Mario J *Physical Chemist*
8 Clematis Rd, Lexington, MA 02173, USA

Molinari, William R *Financier*
%Van Kampen/American Capital, 1 Parkview Plaza, Oakbrook Terrace, IL 60181, USA

Molinaro, Al *Actor*
PO Box 9218, Glendale, CA 91226, USA

Molitor, Paul L *Baseball Player*
%Toronto Blue Jays, 300 Bremner Blvd, Toronto ON M5V 3B3, Canada

Moll, Kurt *Opera Singer*
Billwerder Billdeich, 22033 Hamburg, Germany

Moll, Richard *Actor*
1119 Amalfi Dr, Pacific Palisades, CA 90272, USA

Mollemann, Jurgen W *Government Official, Germany*
Coesfeldweg 59, 48161 Munster, Germany

Moller, Hans *Artist*
2207 W Allen St, Allentown, PA 18104, USA

Moller-Gladisch, Silke *Track Athlete*
Lange Str 6, 18055 Rostock, Germany

Moloney, Paddy *Singer (The Chieftains)*
%S L Feldman Assoc, 1505 W 2nd Ave, #200, Vancouver BC V6H 3Y4, Canada

Molson, Hartland *Hockey Executive*
21 Rosemount, Westmount PQ, Canada

Molz, Otis *Businessman*
%Farmland Industries, 3315 Oak Trafficway, Kansas City, MO 64116, USA

Momaday, N Scott *Writer*
%University of Arizona, English Dept, Tucson, AZ 85721, USA

Monacelli, Amieto *Bowler*
%Professional Bowlers Assn, 1720 Merriman Rd, Akron, OH 44313, USA

Monaghan, Thomas L *Businessman, Baseball Executive*
%Domino's Pizza, 30 Frank Lloyd Wright Dr, Ann Arbor, MI 48105, USA

Monahan, Michael T *Financier*
%Comerica Inc, 500 Woodward Ave, Detroit, MI 48226, USA

Monan, J Donald *Educator*
%Boston College, President's Office, Chestnut Hill, MA 02167, USA

Monbouquette, William C (Bill) *Baseball Player*
PO Box 957, Dunedin, FL 34697, USA

Moncrief, Sidney *Basketball Player*
%Milwaukee Bucks, Bradley Center, 1001 N 4th St, Milwaukee, WI 53203, USA

Mondale, Walter F *Vice President, Diplomat*
%Dorsey & Whitney, 1st National Bank Plaza E, #2200, Minneapolis, MN 55411, USA

Mondavi, Robert G *Businessman*
%Robert Mondavi Winery, 7801 St Helena Highway, Oakville, CA 94562, USA

Monday, Robert J (Rick) *Baseball Player, Sportscaster*
10815 Olrtibello Dr, San Diego, CA 92124, USA

Money, Eddie *Singer*
%Bill Graham Mgmt, PO Box 1994, San Francisco, CA 94101, USA

Money, John W *Psychologist*
2104 E Madison St, Baltimore, MD 21205, USA

Money, Ken *Astronaut, Canada*
%Canadian Space Agency, PO Box 7014, Station V, Vanier ON K1A 8E2, Canada

Monicelli, Mario *Movie Director*
Via del Babuino 135, 00137 Rome, Italy

Monk, Art *Football Player*
%New York Jets, 1000 Fulton Ave, Hempstead, NY 11550, USA

Monk, Debra *Actress*
%Gage Group, 315 W 57th St, #4-H, New York, NY 10019, USA

Monk, Meredith *Choreographer, Composer*
%House Foundation for Arts, 131 Varick St, New York, NY 10013, USA

Monreal Luque, Alberto *Government Official, Spain*
Zurbaran 10, Madrid 28010, Spain

Monroe, A L (Mike) *Labor Leader*
%International Brotherhood of Painters, 1750 New York NW, Washington, DC 20006, USA

Monroe, Bill *Singer, Guitarist*
%Buddy Lee Attractions, 38 Music Square E, #300, Nashville, TN 37203, USA

Monroe, Earl *Basketball Player*
535 Boulevard, Kenilworth, NJ 07033, USA

Monroe, Haskell M, Jr *Educator*
3200 Westcreek Circle, Columbia, MO 65203, USA

Monroe, Richard *Publisher*
%Atlanta Journal-Constitution, 72 Marietta St, Atlanta, GA 30303, USA

Montagnier, Luc *Medical Researcher*
%Institut Pasteur, 25-28 Rue du Docteur-Roux, 75724 Paris Cedex 15, France

Montagu, Ashley *Anthropologist, Educator*
321 Cherry Hill Rd, Princeton, NJ 08540, USA

Montague, Diana *Opera Singer*
91 St Martin's Lane, London WC2, England

Montague-Smith, Patrick W *Editor*
%Brereton, 197 Park Rd, Kingston-upon-Thames, Surrey, England

M

Moll - Montague-Smith

M

Montalban, Ricardo — *Actor*
1423 Oriole Dr, Los Angeles, CA 90069, USA

Montana, Claude — *Fashion Designer*
131 Rue Saint-Denis, 75001 Paris, France

Montana, Joseph C (Joe), Jr — *Football Player, Sportscaster*
PO Box 7342, Menlo Park, CA 94026, USA

Montana, Monte — *Actor*
10326 Montana Lane, Aqua Dulce, CA 91350, USA

Montana, Patsy — *Singer*
%Country Lake, 21100 Highway 79, Sp 147, San Jacinto, CA 92383, USA

Montazeri, Ayatollah Hussein Ali — *Religious Leader*
%Madresseh Faizieh, Qom, Iran

Monteiro, Antonio M — *President, Cape Verde*
%President's Office, Cia de la Republica, Sao Tiago, Praia, Cape Verde

Monteith, Larry K — *Educator*
%North Carolina State University, President's Office, Raleigh, NC 27695, USA

Monteveecchi, Liliane — *Singer*
24 W 60th St, #1700, New York, NY 10023, USA

Montgomery, Anne — *Sportscaster*
%ESPN-TV, Sports Dept, ESPN Plaza, Bristol, CT 06010, USA

Montgomery, Belinda — *Actress*
335 N Maple Dr, #361, Beverly Hills, CA 90210, USA

Montgomery, Clifford (Cliff) — *Football Player*
362 I U Willets Rd, Roslyn Heights, NY 11577, USA

Montgomery, David — *Photographer*
11 Edith Grove, #B, London SW10, England

Montgomery, George — *Actor*
PO Box 2187, Rancho Mirage, CA 92270, USA

Montgomery, Greg — *Football Player*
%Houston Oilers, 6910 Fannin St, Houston, TX 77030, USA

Montgomery, Jack C — *WW II Army Hero (CMH)*
2701 Fort Davis Dr, Muskogee, OK 74403, USA

Montgomery, James F — *Financier*
%Great Western Financial Corp, 9200 Oakdale Ave, Chatsworth, CA 91311, USA

Montgomery, Jim — *Swimmer, Coach*
%Indiana University, Athletic Dept, Bloomington, IN 47405, USA

Montgomery, John Michael — *Singer*
%Wesco Music Group, PO Box 24281, Nashville, TN 37202, USA

Montgomery, John W — *Theologian*
2 Rue de Rome, 67000 Strasbourg, France

Montgomery, Julia — *Actress*
8380 Melrose Ave, #207, Los Angeles, CA 90069, USA

Montgomery, Thomas M — *Army General*
US Representative, NATO Military Committee, APO, AE 09724, USA

Montgomery, W Burton — *Businessman*
%Nationwide Life Insurance, 1 Nationwide Plaza, Columbus, OH 43215, USA

Montgoris, William J — *Financier*
%Bears Steans Co, 245 Park Ave, New York, NY 10167, USA

Montross, Eric — *Basketball Player*
%Boston Celtics, 151 Merrimac St, #500, Boston, MA 02114, USA

Montville, Leigh — *Sportswriter*
%Boston Globe, Editorial Dept, 135 Morrissey Blvd, Boston, MA 02128, USA

Moody, James L, Jr — *Businessman*
%Hannaford Bros Co, 145 Pleasant Hill Rd, Scarborough, ME 04074, USA

Moody, Orville — *Golfer*
%Professional Golfer's Assn, PO Box 109601, Palm Beach Gardens, FL 33410, USA

Moody, Robert L — *Businessman*
%American National Insurance Co, 1 Moody Plaza, Galveston, TX 77550, USA

Moody, Ron — *Actor*
%Eric Glass, 28 Berkeley Square, London W1X 6HD, England

Moody, Ross R — *Businessman*
%National Western Life Insurance, 850 E Anderson Lane, Austin, TX 78752, USA

Moomaw, Donn D — *Football Player*
3124 Corda Dr, Los Angeles, CA 90049, USA

Moon, Sun Myung — *Religious Leader*
%Unification Church, 4 W 43rd St, New York, NY 10036, USA

Moon, Wallace W (Wally) — *Baseball Player*
1415 Angelina Circle, College Station, TX 77840, USA

Moon, Warren *Football Player*
%Minnesota Vikings, 9520 Viking Dr, Eden Prairie, MN 55344, USA

Mooney, Edward J *Businessman*
%Nalco Chemical Co, 1 Nalco Center, Naperville, IL 60563, USA

Mooney, Harold A *Biologist*
2625 Ramona St, Palo Alto, CA 94306, USA

Mooney, Michael J *Educator*
%Lewis & Clark College, President's Office, Portland, OR 97219, USA

Moonves, Leslie *Television Executive*
%Warner Bros Television, 100 Television Plaza, Burbank, CA 91505, USA

Moore, Alvy *Actor*
487 Desert Falls Dr N, Palm Desert, CA 92211, USA

Moore, Arch A, Jr *Governor, WV*
507 Jefferson Ave, Glen Dale, WV 26038, USA

Moore, Archie *Boxer*
3517 East St, San Diego, CA 92102, USA

Moore, Arthur *Labor Leader*
%Sheet Metal Workers Int'l Assn, 1750 New York Ave NW, Washington, DC 20006, USA

Moore, Brian *Writer*
33958 Pacific Coast Highway, Malibu, CA 90265, USA

Moore, Chante *Singer*
%Silas/MCA Records, 1755 Broadway, New York, NY 10019, USA

Moore, Clayton *Actor*
4720 Park Olivo, Calabasas, CA 91302, USA

Moore, Clyde R *Businessman*
%Thomas & Betts Corp, 1555 Lynnfield Rd, Memphis, TN 38119, USA

Moore, Constance *Actress*
10450 Wilshire Blvd, #1-B, Los Angeles, CA 90024, USA

Moore, D Larry *Businessman*
%Honeywell Inc, PO Box 524, Minneapolis, MN 55440, USA

Moore, Demi *Actress*
1453 3rd St, #420, Santa Monica, CA 90401, USA

Moore, Dick *Cartoonist (Our Gang)*
%Dick Moore Assoc, 1560 Broadway, New York, NY 10036, USA

Moore, Dickie *Hockey Executive*
%Moore Equipments, 675 Montee de Liesse, St Laurent PQ H4T 1P5, Canada

Moore, Dudley *Comedian*
73 Market St, Venice, CA 90291, USA

Moore, Francis D *Surgeon*
10 Longwood Dr, #264, Westwood, MA 02090, USA

Moore, Gary V *Financier*
%Allied Finance Co, 250 E John Carpenter Freeway, Dallas, TX 75219, USA

Moore, George E *Surgeon*
12048 S Blackhawk Dr, Conifer, CO 80433, USA

Moore, Gordon E *Businessman*
%Intel Corp, 2200 Mission College Blvd, Santa Clara, CA 95054, USA

Moore, Herman *Football Player*
%Detroit Lions, Silverdome, 1200 Featherstone Rd, Pontiac, MI 48342, USA

Moore, J Jeremy *General, England*
%Lloyds Bank, Cox's & King's Branch, 7 Pall Mall, London SW1, England

Moore, Jackson W *Financier*
%Union Planters Corp, 7130 Goodlett Farms Parkway, Cordova, TN 38018, USA

Moore, James L, Jr *Businessman*
%Coca-Cola Bottling Consolidated, 1900 Rexford Rd, Charlotte, NC 28211, USA

Moore, Jesse W *Space Engineer*
%Ball Aerospace Corp, Boulder Industrial Park, Boulder, CO 80306, USA

Moore, John A *Biologist*
11522 Tulane Ave, Riverside, CA 92507, USA

Moore, John W *Educator*
%Indiana State University, President's Office, Terre Haute, IN 47809, USA

Moore, Johnny *Basketball Player*
%San Antonio Spurs, 600 E Market St, #102, San Antonio, TX 78205, USA

Moore, Joseph G (Joe) *Baseball Player*
PO Box 65, Gause, TX 77857, USA

Moore, Julianne *Actress*
%Bymel, 1724 N Vista St, Los Angeles, CA 90046, USA

Moore, Leonard E (Lenny) *Football Player*
8815 Stonehaven Rd, Randallstown, MD 21133, USA

M

Moore, M Thomas *Businessman*
%Cleveland-Cliffs Co, 1100 Superior Ave, Cleveland, OH 44114, USA

Moore, Malcolm A S *Medical Researcher*
%Memorial Sloan-Kettering Cancer Center, 1275 York Ave, New York, NY 10021, USA

Moore, Mary Tyler *Actress*
510 E 86th St, #21-A, New York, NY 10028, USA

Moore, Melba *Singer*
%Hush Productions, 231 W 58th St, New York, NY 10019, USA

Moore, Michael K *Prime Minister, New Zealand*
%Labor Party, House of Representatives, Wellington, New Zealand

Moore, Nathaniel (Nat) *Football Player*
%Nat Moore Assoc, 16911 NE 6th Ave, North Miami Beach, FL 33162, USA

Moore, Patrick *Astronomer, Writer*
Farthings, 39 West St, Selsey, Sussex, England

Moore, Paul, Jr *Religious Leader*
55 Bank St, New York, NY 10014, USA

Moore, Roger *Actor*
Chalet Le Fenil, 3783 Grund Bei Staad, Switzerland

Moore, Sam *Singer (Sam & Dave)*
%Geoffrey Blumenauer, 11846 Balboa Ave, #204, Granada Hills, CA 91344, USA

Moore, Steve *Cartoonist (In the Bleachers)*
%Tribune Media Services, 435 N Michigan Ave, #1417, Chicago, IL 60611, USA

Moore, Stevron *Football Player*
%Cleveland Browns, 80 1st Ave, Berea, OH 44017, USA

Moore, Terry *Actress*
833 Ocean Ave, #104, Santa Monica, CA 90403, USA

Moore, Thomas *Writer*
%Harper/Collins Publishers, 10 E 53rd St, New York, NY 10022, USA

Moore, Tom *Movie, Theater Director*
8283 Hollywood Blvd, Los Angeles, CA 90069, USA

Moore, W Edward C *Microbiologist*
1607 Boxwood Dr, Blacksburg, VA 24060, USA

Moorer, Michael *Boxer*
%Main Events, 811 Totowa Rd, #100, Totowa, NJ 07512, USA

Moorer, Thomas H *Navy Admiral, Businessman*
6901 Lupine Lane, McLean, VA 22101, USA

Moorman, Thomas S (Tom), Jr *Air Force General*
Vice Chief of Staff, HqUSAF, Pentagon, Washington, DC 20330, USA

Moos, Eugene *Financier, Government Official*
%Commodity Credit Corp, PO Box 2415, Washington, DC 20013, USA

Mora, James E (Jim) *Football Coach*
%New Orleans Saints, 1500 Poydras St, New Orleans, LA 70112, USA

Morales, Pablo *Swimmer*
%Cornell University, Law School, Ithaca, NY 14853, USA

Moran, Erin *Actress*
%The Agency, 1800 Ave of Stars, #400, Los Angeles, CA 90067, USA

Moran, Jim *Businessman*
%JM Family Enterprises, 100 NW 12th Ave, Deerfield Beach, FL 33442, USA

Moran, John *Religious Leader*
%Missionary Church, PO Box 9127, Fort Wayne, IN 46899, USA

Moran, Julie *Sportscaster*
%ABC-TV, Sports Dept, 77 W 66th St, New York, NY 10023, USA

Moran, Pat *Businesswoman*
%JM Family Enterprises, 100 NW 12th Ave, Deerfield Beach, FL 33442, USA

Moran, Peggy *Actress*
3101 Village, #3, Camarillo, CA 93012, USA

Moranis, Rick *Actor*
101 Central Park West, #12-B, New York, NY 10023, USA

Morath, Ingeborg H (Inge) *Photographer*
212 Tophet Rd, Roxbury, CT 06783, USA

Morby, Jeffrey L *Financier*
%Mellon Bank Corp, 1 Mellon Bank Center, 500 Grant St, Pittsburgh, PA 15219, USA

Morcott, Southwood J *Businessman*
%Dana Corp, PO Box 1000, Toledo, OH 43697, USA

Mordkovitch, Lydia *Concert Violinist*
25-A Belsize Ave, London NW3, England

Moreau, Gary L *Businessman*
%Oneida Inc, Kenwood Ave, Oneida, NY 13421, USA

Moreau, Jeanne *Actress*
103 Blvd Haussmann, 75008 Paris, France
Moreira Neves, Lucas Cardinal *Religious Leader*
CP 1907, Ave 7 de Setembro 309, Campo Grande, 40120 Salvador, Brazil
Moreno, Rita *Actress, Singer*
1620 Amalfi Dr, Pacific Palisades, CA 90272, USA
Moret, Rogelio (Roger) *Baseball Player*
RR 1, Box 6742, Guayama, PR 00784, USA
Morford, John A *Businessman*
%V T Inc, 8500 Shawnee Mission Parkway, Merriam, KS 66202, USA
Morgan, Barbara R *Astronaut*
%Oklahoma State University, Teacher in Space Program, Stillwater, OK 74078, USA
Morgan, Calvert A, Jr *Financier*
%PNC Bank Delaware, 222 Delaware Ave, Wilmington, DE 19899, USA
Morgan, Debbi *Actress*
1801 Ave of Stars, #1250, Los Angeles, CA 90067, USA
Morgan, Gil *Golfer*
%Professional Golfer's Assn, PO Box 109601, Palm Beach Gardens, FL 33410, USA
Morgan, Harry *Actor*
13172 Boca de Canon Lane, Los Angeles, CA 90049, USA
Morgan, James N *Economist*
1217 Bydding Rd, Ann Arbor, MI 48103, USA
Morgan, Jane *Singer*
27740 Pacific Coast Highway, Malibu, CA 90265, USA
Morgan, Jaye P *Singer, Actress*
1185 La Grange Ave, Newbury Park, CA 91320, USA
Morgan, Joseph L (Joe) *Baseball Player*
31650 Hayman St, Hayward, CA 94544, USA
Morgan, Joseph M (Joe) *Baseball Manager*
15 Oak Hill Dr, Walpole, MA 02081, USA
Morgan, Lorrie *Singer*
%PLA Media, 1303 16th Ave S, Nashville, TN 37212, USA
Morgan, Marabel *Writer*
%Total Woman Inc, 1300 NW 167th St, Miami, FL 33169, USA
Morgan, Michele *Actress, Singer*
5 Rue Jacques Dulud, 92200 Neuilly-sur-Seine, France
Morgan, Nancy *Actress*
8380 Melrose Ave, #207, Los Angeles, CA 90069, USA
Morgan, Robert B *Senator, NC*
PO Box 377, Lillington, NC 27546, USA
Morgan, Robert B *Financier*
%Cincinnati Financial Corp, PO Box 145496, Cincinnati, OH 45250, USA
Morgan, Robin E *Editor*
%Ms Magazine, Editorial Dept, 230 Park Ave, New York, NY 10169, USA
Morgan, Walter T, J *Biochemist*
57 Woodbury Dr, Sutton, Surrey, England
Morgenthau, Robert M *Attorney*
1085 Park Ave, New York, NY 10128, USA
Morgridge, John P *Businessman*
%Cisco Systems, 170 W Tasan Dr, San Jose, CA 95134, USA
Mori, Hanae *Fashion Designer*
17 Ave Montaigne, 75008 Paris, France
Moriarty, Cathy *Actress*
930 N Doheny Dr, #308, Los Angeles, CA 90069, USA
Moriarty, Michael *Actor*
200 W 58th St, #3-B, New York, NY 10019, USA
Moriarty, Phil *Swimming Coach*
%Harbour Village, #20-E, Branford, CT 06045, USA
Moriguchi, Takahiro *Financier*
%Union Bank, 350 California St, San Francisco, CA 94104, USA
Morikawa, Toshio *Financier*
%Sumitomo Bank Ltd, 3-2-1 Marunouchi, Chiyodaku, Tokyo 100, Japan
Morin, Jim *Editorial Cartoonist*
%Miami Herald, Editorial Dept, Herald Plaza, Miami, FL 33101, USA
Morin, William J *Businessman*
%Drake Beam Morin Inc, 100 Park Ave, New York, NY 10017, USA
Morini, Erica *Concert Violinist*
1200 5th Ave, New York, NY 10029, USA

M

Moreau - Morini

M

Morinigo, Higinio — *President, Paraguay; Army General*
Calle General Urguiza 625-Acassuso, Buenos Aires, Argentina

Morishita, Yoichi — *Businessman*
%Matsushita Electrical Industrial, 1006 Kadoma City, Osaka 571, Japan

Morison, Patricia — *Actress, Singer*
400 S Hauser Blvd, #9-L, Los Angeles, CA 90036, USA

Morissette, Alanis — *Singer, Songwriter*
%Maverick Entertainment, 75 Rockefeller Plaza, #2100, New York, NY 10019, USA

Morita, Akio — *Businessman*
%Sony Corp, 6-7-35 Kitashinagawa, Shinagawaku, Tokyo 141, Japan

Morita, Pat (Noriyuki) — *Actor*
4007 Sunswept Dr, Studio City, CA 91604, USA

Moritz, Charles F — *Editor*
%Current Biography, H W Wilson Co, 950 University Ave, Bronx, NY 10452, USA

Moritz, Louisa — *Actress*
%Beverly Hills St Moritz, 120 S Reeves St, Beverly Hills, CA 90212, USA

Moriya, Gakuji — *Businessman*
%Mitsubishu Heavy Industries, 2-5-1 Marunouchi, Chiyodaku, Tokyo, Japan

Moriyama, Raymond — *Architect*
32 Davenport Rd, Toronto ON M5R 1H3, Canada

Mork, Richard G — *Businessman*
%A M Castle Co, 3400 N Wolf Rd, Franklin Park, IL 60131, USA

Morley, Malcolm — *Artist*
%Pace Gallery, 32 E 57th St, New York, NY 10022, USA

Moro, Peter — *Architect*
20 Blackheath Park, London SE3 9RP, England

Moroder, Giorgio — *Composer*
9348 Civic Center Dr, #101, Beverly Hills, CA 90210, USA

Morrall, Earl E — *Football Player*
%Arrowhead Country Club, 8201 SW 24th St, Fort Lauderdale, FL 33324, USA

Morrey, Charles B, Jr — *Mathematician*
210 Yale Ave, Berkeley, CA 94708, USA

Morrice, Norman A — *Ballet Choreographer*
%Royal Ballet, Bow St, London WC2E 9DD, England

Morricone, Ennio — *Composer*
Piazza SS Giovanni e Paolo 8, 00184 Rome, Italy

Morrill, James L — *Educator*
1752 Ardleigh Rd, Columbus, OH 43221, USA

Morris Wingerter, Pam — *Synchronized Swimmer*
403 Boros Rd, New Bern, NC 28560, USA

Morris, Betty — *Bowler*
%Women's International Bowling Congress, 5301 S 76th St, Greendale, WI 53129, USA

Morris, Charles B — *Vietnam War Army Hero (CMH)*
1103 Riverside Circle, Spring Lake, NC 28390, USA

Morris, Chris — *Basketball Player*
%Utah Jazz, 301 W South Temple, Salt Lake City, UT 84101, USA

Morris, David H — *Businessman*
%Toro Co, 8111 Lyndale Ave S, Bloomington, MN 55420, USA

Morris, Desmond J — *Writer, Zoologist*
%Jonathan Cape Ltd, 20 Vauxhall Bridge Rd, London SW1V 2SA, England

Morris, Garrett — *Actor, Singer*
3740 Barham Blvd, #E-116, Los Angeles, CA 90068, USA

Morris, Gary — *Singer*
%Gurley Co, 3322 W End Ave, #11, Nashville, TN 37203, USA

Morris, George — *Football Player*
6075 Roswell Rd NE, #112, Atlanta, GA 30328, USA

Morris, George N — *Businessman*
%General Accident Insurance Group, 436 Walnut St, Philadelphia, PA 19106, USA

Morris, Greg — *Actor*
700 E Flamingo Rd, #C-205, Las Vegas, NV 89119, USA

Morris, Howard — *Comedian*
2723 Carmar Dr, Los Angeles, CA 90046, USA

Morris, James P — *Opera Singer*
%Colbert Artists Mgmt, 111 W 57th St, New York, NY 10019, USA

Morris, Jan — *Writer*
Trefan Morys, Llanystumdwy, Criccieth, Gwymedd, Wales

Morris, Joe — *Football Player*
%Cleveland Browns, 80 1st Ave, Berea, OH 44017, USA

Morinigo - Morris

Morris, John S (Jack) *Baseball Player*
4705 Old Orchard Trail, Orchard Lake, MI 48324, USA

Morris, Johnny *Football Player*
%WBBM-TV, Sports Dept, 620 N McClurg Court, Chicago, IL 60611, USA

Morris, Mark W *Choreographer*
%Mark Morris Dance Group, 225 Lafayette St, #504, New York, NY 10012, USA

Morris, Nathan *Singer (Boyz II Men)*
%BIV Entertainment, 5 Bishop Rd, Vincentown, NJ 08088, USA

Morris, Oswald *Cinematographer*
Holbrook, Church St, Fontmell Magna, Dorset, England

Morris, Robert *Sculptor*
%Hunter College, Art Dept, New York, NY 10021, USA

Morris, Seth Irvin *Architect*
2 Waverly Court, Houston, TX 77005, USA

Morris, Wayna *Singer (Boyz II Men)*
%BIV Entertainment, 5 Bishop Rd, Vincentown, NJ 08088, USA

Morris, William C *Financier*
%J&W Seligman Co, 100 Park Ave, New York, NY 10017, USA

Morris, William S, III *Publisher*
%Florida Times-Union, 1 Riverside Ave, Jacksonville, FL 32202, USA

Morris, Wright *Writer*
341 Laurel Way, Mill Valley, CA 94941, USA

Morrison, Philip *Astronomer*
%Massachusetts Institute of Technology, Astronomy Dept, Cambridge, MA 02139, USA

Morrison, Toni *Nobel Literature Laureate*
%Princeton University, Dickinson Hall, Princeton, NJ 08544, USA

Morrison, Van *Singer, Songwriter*
%Polydor Records, 11150 Santa Monica Blvd, #1100, Los Angeles, CA 90025, USA

Morrissey *Singer, Songwriter*
%International Creative Mgmt, 40 W 57th St, New York, NY 10019, USA

Morrissey, Bill *Singer, Songwriter*
%Sage Productions, 258 Harvard St, #283, Brookline, MA 02146, USA

Morrow (Cousin Brucie), Bruce *Radio Entertainer*
%CBS Radio Network, 51 W 52nd St, New York, NY 10019, USA

Morrow, Bobby *Track Athlete*
Rt 4, Box 57, San Benito, TX 78586, USA

Morrow, Byron *Actor*
%Ricky Barr Agency, PO Box 69590, Los Angeles, CA 90069, USA

Morrow, Rob *Actor*
%William Morris Agency, 151 S El Camino Dr, Beverly Hills, CA 90212, USA

Morse, David *Actor*
%Yvette Bikoff Agency, 8721 Santa Monica Blvd, #21, West Hollywood, CA 90069, USA

Morse, David E *Publisher*
%Christian Science Monitor, 1 Norway St, Boston, MA 02115, USA

Morse, Edward J *Businessman*
%Morse Operations, 6363 NW 6th Way, Fort Lauderdale, FL 33309, USA

Morse, Ella Mae *Singer*
3232 W 152nd Place, Gardena, CA 90249, USA

Morse, Philip M *Physicist*
126 Wildwood St, Winchester, MA 01890, USA

Morse, Robert *Actor*
13830 Davana Terrace, Sherman Oaks, CA 91423, USA

Morse, Ted *Businessman*
%Morse Operations, 6363 NW 6th Way, Fort Lauderdale, FL 33309, USA

Mortensen, J D *Surgeon*
%Cardipulmonics Inc, 5060 W Amelia Earhart Dr, Salt Lake City, UT 84116, USA

Mortier, Gerard *Opera Director*
%Opera National de la Monnaie, 4 Rue Leopold, 1000 Brussels, Belgium

Mortimer Barrett, Angela *Tennis Player*
The Oaks, Coombe Hill, Beverly Lane, Kingston-on-Thames, Surrey, England

Mortimer, John C *Writer*
Turville Heath Cottage, Henley-on-Thames, Oxon, England

Mortimer, Kenneth P *Educator*
%University of Hawaii at Manoa, President's Office, Honolulu, HI 96822, USA

Mortimer, Penelope R *Writer*
19 St Gabriel's Rd, London NW2 4DS, England

Morton, Bruce A *Commentator*
%Cable News Network, News Dept, 820 1st St NE, Washington, DC 20002, USA

M

M

Morton, Gary *Comedian*
40241 Clubview Dr, Rancho Mirage, CA 92270, USA

Morton, Joe *Actor*
%Judy Schoen Assoc, 606 N Larchmont Blvd, #309, Los Angeles, CA 90004, USA

Morton, John, III *Financier*
%Boatmen's National Bank (St Louis), 800 Market St, St Louis, MO 63101, USA

Morton, Johnnie *Football Player*
%Detroit Lions, Silverdome, 1200 Featherstone Rd, Pontiac, MI 48342, USA

Morton, Rogers C B *Secretary, Commerce & Interior*
Rt 1, Easton, MD 21601, USA

Morton, T Ron *Financier*
%PACCAR Financial Corp, 777 106th Ave NE, Bellevue, WA 98004, USA

Mosbacher, Robert A *Secretary, Commerce*
%Mosbacher Energy Co, 712 Main St, #2200, Houston, TX 77002, USA

Moschen, Michael *Juggler*
41 Popple Swamp Rd, Cornwall Bridge, CT 06754, USA

Moschitta, John, Jr *Comedian*
8033 Sunset Blvd, #41, Los Angeles, CA 90046, USA

Moschner, Albin F *Businessman*
%Zenith Electronics Corp, 1000 Milwaukee Ave, Glenview, IL 60025, USA

Mosconi, Alain *Swimmer*
%French Swimming Federation, 148 Ave Gambetta, 75020 Paris, France

Mosebar, Donald H (Don) *Football Player*
%Oakland Raiders, Oakland Coliseum, Oakland, CA 94621, USA

Mosel, Tad *Playwright*
149 East Side Dr, Box 249, #26-B, Concord, NH 03302, USA

Moseley, Mark D *Football Player*
16001 Berkeley Dr, Haymarket, VA 22069, USA

Moser, Donald B *Editor*
%Smithsonian Magazine, Editorial Dept, 900 Jefferson SW, Washington, DC 20560, USA

Moser, Jurgen K *Mathematician*
%Eidgenossische Technische Hochschule, Ramistr, 8092 Zurich, Switzerland

Moser-Proll, Annemarie *Skier*
5602 Kleinarl 115, Austria

Moses, Edwin *Track Athlete*
PO Box 18600, Atlanta, GA 31126, USA

Moses, Haven C *Football Player*
7052 S Owens St, Littleton, CO 80127, USA

Moses, Lincoln E *Statistician*
%Stanford University, Statistics Dept, Stanford, CA 94305, USA

Moses, Rick *Actor, Singer*
%Calder Agency, 19919 Redwing St, Woodland Hills, CA 91364, USA

Moses, Yolanda T *Educator*
%City College of New York, President's Office, New York, NY 10031, USA

Mosimann, Anton *Chef*
46 Abingdon Villas, London W8, England

Moskow, Michael *Financier*
%Federal Reserve Bank, 230 S LaSalle St, Chicago, IL 60604, USA

Moskowitz, Robert *Artist*
81 Leonard St, New York, NY 10013, USA

Mosley, J Brooke *Religious Leader*
1604 Foulkeways, Gwynedd, PA 19436, USA

Mosley, Roger E *Actor*
3756 Prestwick Dr, Los Angeles, CA 90027, USA

Mosley, Walter *Writer*
37 Carmine St, #275, New York, NY 10014, USA

Mosmiller, Joseph W *Financier*
%Loyola Federal Savings Bank, 1300 N Charles St, Baltimore, MD 21201, USA

Moss, Cynthia *Elephant Conservationist*
%African Wildlife Foundation, Mara Rd, PO Box 48177, Nairobi, Kenya

Moss, Elza *Religious Leader*
%Primitive Advent Christian Church, 395 Frame Rd, Elkview, WV 25071, USA

Moss, Frank E *Senator, UT*
1848 S Wasatch Dr, Salt Lake City, UT 84108, USA

Moss, Geoffrey *Cartoonist, Illustrator*
315 E 68th St, New York, NY 10021, USA

Moss, Jerry *Record Company Executive*
%A&M Records, 1416 N La Brea Ave, Los Angeles, CA 90028, USA

Morton - Moss

Moss, Kate *Model*
%Women Model Mgmt, 107 Greene St, #200, New York, NY 10012, USA

Moss, Ronn *Actor*
%Yvette Bikoff Agency, 8721 Santa Monica Blvd, #21, West Hollywood, CA 90069, USA

Mossbauer, Rudolf *Nobel Physics Laureate*
Stumpflingstr 6-A, 82031 Grunwald, Germany

Mossi, Donald L (Don) *Baseball Player*
1340 Sanford Ranch Rd, Ukiah, CA 95482, USA

Most, Donald *Actor*
6643 Buttonwood Ave, Agoura, CA 91301, USA

Mosteller, Frederick *Statistician*
%Harvard University, Statistics Dept, Cambridge, MA 02138, USA

Mostow, George D *Mathematician*
25 Beechwood Rd, Woodbridge, CT 06525, USA

Mota Pinto, Carlos *Prime Minister, Portugal*
Rua Gil Vicente 83, 3000 Coimbra, Portugal

Mota, Manuel R (Manny) *Baseball Player, Coach*
3926 Los Olivos Lane, La Crescenta, CA 91214, USA

Mota, Rosa *Marathon Athlete*
R Teatro 194 4 Esq, 4100 Porto, Portugal

Motelson, Benjamin *Nobel Physics Laureate*
Nordita, Blegdamsvej 17, 2100 Copenhagen 0, Denmark

Motherway, Thomas J *Financier*
%McDonnell Douglas Finance Corp, 4060 Lakewood Blvd, Long Beach, CA 90808, USA

Motley, Marion *Football Player*
6801 Lucerne, Cleveland, OH 44103, USA

Motoyama, Hideyo *Businessman*
%Kirin Brewery, 6-26-1 Jingumae, Shibuyaku, Tokyo 150, Japan

Mott, Nevill F *Nobel Physics Laureate*
63 Mount Pleasant, Aspley Guise, Milton Keynes MK17 8JX, England

Mott, Stewart R *Political Activist*
515 Madison Ave, New York, NY 10022, USA

Motta, Dick *Basketball Coach*
%Dallas Mavericks, Reunion Arena, 777 Sports St, Dallas, TX 75207, USA

Motulsky, Arno G *Geneticist*
4347 53rd St NE, Seattle, WA 98105, USA

Moulton, Alexander E *Bicycle Engineer*
The Hall, Bradford-on-Avon, Wilts, England

Mounsey, Yvonne *Ballerina*
%Westside School of Ballet, 1711 Stewart St, Santa Monica, CA 90404, USA

Mount, Rick *Basketball Player*
904 Hopkins Rd, Lebanon, IN 46052, USA

Mountcastle, Vernon B, Jr *Neurophysiologist*
15601 Carroll Rd, Monkton, MD 21111, USA

Mourning, Alonzo *Basketball Player*
%Charlotte Hornets, 1 Hive Dr, Charlotte, NC 28217, USA

Mouskouri, Nana *Singer, Songwriter*
12 Rue Gutemberg, 92000 Boulogne, France

Mowat, Farley M *Writer, Naturalist*
25 St John St, Port Hope ON, Canada

Mowerson, Robert *Swimmer*
3417 Downers Dr, Minneapolis, MN 55418, USA

Moxley, John H, III *Physician, Businessman*
8180 Manitoba St, #210, Playa del Rey, CA 90293, USA

Moyer, Alan D *Editor*
%Phoenix Newspaper Inc, Editorial Dept, 120 E Van Buren St, Phoenix, AZ 85004, USA

Moyer, Paul *Commentator*
12742 Highwood St, Los Angeles, CA 90049, USA

Moyers, Bill D *Commentator*
76 4th St, Garden City, NY 11530, USA

Moyet, Alison *Singer*
%Solo, 55 Fulham High St, London SW6 6BB, England

Moynihan, Colin B *Government Official, England*
Crown Reach, 16 Grosvenor Rd, London SW1V 3JV, England

Moyola of Castledawson, Baron *Prime Minister, Northern Ireland*
Moyola Park, Castledawson, County Derry, Northern Ireland

Mozilo, Angelo R *Financier*
%Countrywide Credit Industries, 1555 N Lake Ave, Pasadena, CA 91104, USA

M

M

Mphahlele, Ezekiel *Writer*
5444 Zone 5, Pimville, Johannesburg, South Africa

Mswati III *King, Swaziland*
%Royal Palace, PO Box 1, Mbabane, Swaziland

Mu'alla, Sheikh Rashid bin Ahmed Al- *Ruler, Umm al Quwain*
%Royal Palace, Umm Al Quwain, United Arab Emirates

Mubarak, Muhammad Hosni *President, Egypt; Army General*
%Presidential Palace, Abdeen, Cairo, Egypt

Muckler, John *Hockey Coach, Executive*
%Buffalo Sabres, Memorial Stadium, 140 Main St, Buffalo, NY 14202, USA

Mudd, Howard *Football Player, Coach*
%Seattle Seahawks, 11220 NE 53rd St, Kirkland, WA 98033, USA

Mudd, Jodie *Golfer*
%Professional Golfer's Assn, PO Box 109601, Palm Beach Gardens, FL 33410, USA

Mudd, Roger H *Commentator*
7167 Old Dominion Dr, McLean, VA 22101, USA

Mueller, Carl M *Financier*
%BT Capital Corp, 280 Park Ave, New York, NY 10017, USA

Mueller, Charles W *Businessman*
%Union Electric Co, 1901 Chouteau Ave, St Louis, MO 63103, USA

Mueller, George E *Electrical Engineer, Missile Scientist*
PO Box 5856, Santa Barbara, CA 93150, USA

Mueller, Gerd D *Businessman*
%Bayer Corp, Mellon Center, 500 Grant St, Pittsburgh, PA 15219, USA

Mueller-Stahl, Armin *Actor*
Gartenweg 31, 23730 Sierksdorf, Germany

Muench, David *Photographer*
PO Box 30500, Santa Barbara, CA 93130, USA

Muench, John *Artist*
Flying Point, Freeport, ME 04032, USA

Muetterties, Earl L *Chemist*
%University of California, Chemistry Dept, Berkeley, CA 94720, USA

Muetzelfeldt, Bruno *Religious Leader*
%Lutheran World Federation, 150 Rt de Ferney, 1211 Geneva 20, Switzerland

Mugabe, Robert G *President, Zimbabwe*
%President's Office, Munhumutapa Bldg, Samora Machel Ave, Harare, Zimbabwe

Mugler, Thierry *Fashion Designer*
4-6 Rue Aux Ours, 75003 Paris, France

Muhammad, Wallace D *Religious Leader*
%American Muslim Mission, 7351 S Stony Island Blvd, Chicago, IL 60649, USA

Muir DeGraad, Karen *Swimmer*
%Applebosch State Hospital, Ozwatini, Natal, South Africa

Muir, J Gordon, Jr *Financier*
%Cullen/Frost Bankers Inc, 100 W Houston St, San Antonio, TX 78205, USA

Muirsheil of Kilmacolm, Viscount *Government Official, England*
Knapps, Kilmacolm, Renfrewshire, Scotland

Mukai, Chiaki Naito- *Astronaut, Japan*
15836 Seahorse Dr, Houston, TX 77062, USA

Mukhamedov, Irek J *Ballet Dancer*
%Royal Ballet, Bow St, London WC2E 9DD, England

Mukherjee, Bharati *Writer*
%Grove Weidenfeld, 841 Broadway, New York, NY 10003, USA

Mulari, Tarja *Speed Skier*
%Motion Oy, Vanhan Mankkaantie 33, 02180 Espoo, Finland

Muldaur, Diana *Actress*
259 Quadro Vecchio Dr, Pacific Palisades, CA 90272, USA

Muldaur, Maria *Singer, Songwriter*
PO Box 5535, Mill Valley, CA 94942, USA

Muldoon, Paul *Poet*
%Farrar Straus Giroux, 19 Union Square W, New York, NY 10003, USA

Muldowney, Shirley *Drag Racing Driver*
79559 North Ave, Armada, MI 48005, USA

Mulgrew, Kate *Actress*
11938 Foxboro Dr, Los Angeles, CA 90049, USA

Mulhare, Edward *Actor*
6045 Sunnyslope Ave, Van Nuys, CA 91401, USA

Mulhern, Matt *Actor*
9171 Wilshire Blvd, #436, Beverly Hills, CA 90210, USA

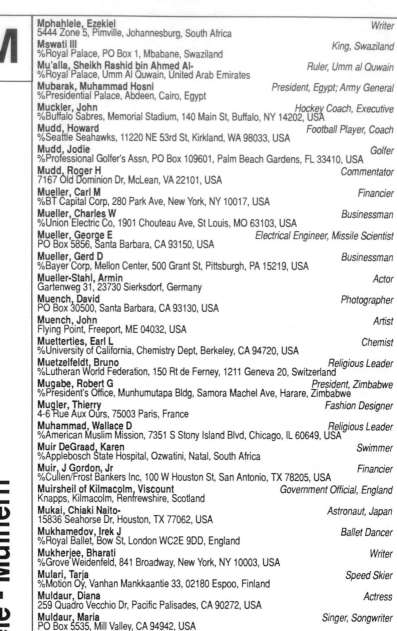

Mphahlele - Mulhern

Mulholland, Robert E — *Television Executive*
%Northwestern University, Journalism Dept, Evanston, IL 60208, USA

Mull, Martin — *Actor*
338 Chadbourne Ave, Los Angeles, CA 90049, USA

Mullane, Richard M (Mike) — *Astronaut*
1301 Las Lomas Rd NE, Albuquerque, NM 87106, USA

Mullaney, Joseph E — *Businessman*
%Gillette Co, Prudential Tower Building, Boston, MA 02199, USA

Mullavey, Greg — *Actor*
4640 Danza St, Woodland Hills, CA 91364, USA

Mullen, Joseph P (Joe) — *Hockey Player*
%Boston Bruins, Boston Garden, 150 Causeway St, Boston, MA 02114, USA

Mullen, Larry, Jr — *Drummer (U-2)*
%Principle Mgmt, 30-32 Sir John Rogerson Quay, Dublin 2, Ireland

Muller, Egon — *Motorcycle Racing Rider*
Dorfstr 17, 24247 Rodenbek/Kiel, Germany

Muller, Gerd — *Soccer Player*
Noestr 21, 81479 Munich, Germany

Muller, Henry J — *Editor*
%Time Warner Inc, Magazines Division, Rockefeller Center, New York, NY 10020, USA

Muller, Jennifer — *Dancer, Choreographer*
%The Muller/Works Foundation, 131 W 24th St, New York, NY 10011, USA

Muller, K Alex — *Nobel Physics Laureate*
%IBM Research Laboratory, Saumerstr 4, 8803 Ruschlikon, Switzerland

Muller, Kirk — *Hockey Player*
%New York Islanders, Veterans Memorial Coliseum, Uniondale, NY 11553, USA

Muller, Peter — *Skier*
Haldenstr 18, 8134 Adliswil, Switzerland

Muller, Peter — *Architect*
3 Rue Rene Boylesve, 37600 Loches, France

Muller, Richard S — *Microbiotics Engineer*
%University of California, Sensor/Acutator Center, Berkeley, CA 94720, USA

Muller, Robby — *Cinematographer*
%Smith/Gosnell, 1515 Palisades Dr, #N, Pacific Palisades, CA 90272, USA

Muller, Steven — *Educator*
%21st Century Foundation, 919 18th St NW, #800, Washington, DC 20006, USA

Mulley of Manor Park, Frederick W — *Government Official, England*
%House of Lords, Westminster, London SW1A 0PW, England

Mulligan, Gerald J (Gerry) — *Jazz Saxophonist*
%Namco Booking, 165 W 46th St, #1202, New York, NY 10036, USA

Mulligan, Richard — *Actor*
419 N Larchmont Blvd, #129, Los Angeles, CA 90004, USA

Mulligan, Richard C — *Molecular Biologist*
11 Sumner Rd, Cambridge, MA 02138, USA

Mulligan, Robert P — *Movie Director*
%J V Broffman, 5150 Wilshire Blvd, #505, Los Angeles, CA 90036, USA

Mulliken, Bill — *Swimmer*
7050 W 71st St, Chicago, IL 60638, USA

Mullin, Christopher P (Chris) — *Basketball Player*
%Golden State Warriors, Oakland Coliseum Arena, Oakland, CA 94621, USA

Mullin, J Stanley — *Skier*
%Sheppard Mullin Richter Hampton, 333 S Hope St, Los Angeles, CA 90071, USA

Mullin, Leo F — *Financier*
%American National Bank & Trust, 33 N LaSalle St, Chicago, IL 60602, USA

Mullins, Jeff — *Basketball Player, Coach*
%University of North Carolina Charlotte, Athletic Dept, Charlotte, NC 28223, USA

Mullis, Kary B — *Nobel Chemistry Laureate*
6767 Neptune Place, #4, La Jolla, CA 92037, USA

Mullova, Viktoria Y — *Concert Violinist*
%Harold Holt Ltd, 31 Sinclair Rd, London W14 ONS, England

Mulroney, M Brian — *Prime Minister, Canada*
%Ogilvy Renault, 1981 McGill College Ave, Montreal PQ H3A 3C1, Canada

Mulumba, Etienne Tshisekedi Wa — *Prime Minister, Zaire*
%Prime Minister's Office, Kinshasa, Zaire

Muluzi, Bakili — *President, Malawi*
%President's Office, Private Bag 361, Capitol City, Lilongwe 3, Malawi

Mulva, James J — *Businessman*
%Phillips Petroleum Co, Phillips Building, 4th & Keeler Sts, Bartlesville, 74004, USA

M

Mulholland - Mulva

M

Mulvoy, Mark *Editor, Publisher*
%Sports Illustrated Magazine, Rockefeller Center, New York, NY 10020, USA

Mumford, David B *Mathematician*
26 Gray St, Cambridge, MA 02138, USA

Mumy, Billy *Actor*
2419 Laurel Pass Ave, Los Angeles, CA 90046, USA

Muna, Solomon Tandeng *Prime Minister, Cameroon*
PO Box 15, Mbengwi, Mono Division, North West Province, Cameroon

Munch, Guido *Astronomer*
%Max Planck Institute, Konigstuhl 17, 69117 Heidelberg, Germany

Munchak, Michael A (Mike) *Football Player*
%Houston Oilers, 6910 Fannin St, Houston, TX 77030, USA

Mundt, Ray B *Businessman*
%Alco Standard Corp, 825 Duportail Rd, Wayne, PA 19087, USA

Munger, Charles T *Businessman*
%Berkshire Hathaway Inc, 1440 Kiewit Plaza, Omaha, NE 68131, USA

Munitz, Barry A *Educator*
%California State University System, 400 Golden Shore St, Long Beach, CA 90802, USA

Munk, Walter H *Geophysicist*
9530 La Jolla Shores Dr, La Jolla, CA 92037, USA

Munn, Stephen P *Businessman*
%Carlisle Corp, 250 S Clinton, Syracuse, NY 13202, USA

Munnell, Alicia *Economist, Government Official*
%Council of Economic Advisers, Old Government Office Bldg, Washington, DC 20500, USA

Munoz Vega, Paolo Cardinal *Religious Leader*
Casa del Sagrado Corazon, Casilla 17-02-5222, Suc 2, Quito, Ecuador

Munoz, Anthony *Football Player, Sportscaster*
%Fox TV, Sports Dept, PO Box 900, Beverly Hills, CA 90213, USA

Munro, Alice *Writer*
PO Box 1133, Clinton ON N0M 1L0, Canada

Munro, Caroline *Actress*
%International Creative Mgmt, 76 Oxford St, London W1N 0AX, England

Munro, Dana G *Diplomat*
PO Box 317, Media, PA 19063, USA

Munro, Ian *Editor*
%Annals of Internal Medicine, Editorial Dept, 34 Beacon St, Boston, MA 02108, USA

Munro, J Richard *Publisher*
%Time Warner Inc, Rockefeller Plaza, New York, NY 10020, USA

Munsel, Patrice *Opera Singer*
PO Box 472, Schroon Lake, NY 12870, USA

Munson, William A (Bill) *Football Player*
1212 Lakeside, Birmingham, MI 48009, USA

Muntyan, Mikhail *Opera Singer*
16 N Iorga Str, #13, 277012 Kishinev, Moldova

Muradov, Sakhat A *Head of Government, Turkmenistan*
%Turkmenistan Mejlis, 17 Gogol St, Ashkhabad, Turkmenistan

Murayama, Makio *Biochemist*
5010 Benton Ave, Bethesda, MD 20814, USA

Murayama, Tomiichi *Prime Minister, Japan*
%Prime Minister's Office, 1-6-1 Nagato-cho, Chiyodaku, Tokyo 100, Japan

Murdoch, J Iris *Writer*
Cedar Lodge, Steeple Aston, Oxon, England

Murdoch, K Rupert *Publisher*
%News America Publishing, 1211 Ave of Americas, New York, NY 10036, USA

Murdoch, Robert J (Bob) *Hockey Coach*
%Winnipeg Jets, Arena, 15-1430 Maroons Rd, Winnipeg MB R3G 0L5, Canada

Murdock, David H *Businessman*
%Dole Food Co, 31355 Oak Crest, Westlake Village, CA 91361, USA

Murdock, George *Actor*
5733 Sunfield Ave, Lakewood, CA 90712, USA

Murdock, George P *Anthropologist*
Wynnewood Plaza, #107, Wynnewood, PA 19096, USA

Murphey, Michael Martin *Singer, Songwriter*
PO Box 555, Taos, NM 87571, USA

Murphy, Austin S *Financier*
%River Bank America, 145 Huguenot St, New Rochelle, NJ 10801, USA

Murphy, Barth T *Financier*
%Bankers Life & Casualty, 222 Merchandise Mart Plaza, Chicago, IL 60654, USA

Mulvoy - Murphy

Murphy, Ben *Actor*
3601 Vista Pacifica, #17, Malibu, CA 90265, USA

Murphy, Calvin *Basketball Player, Executive*
%Houston Rockets, Summit, Greenway Plaza, #10, Houston, TX 77277, USA

Murphy, Caryle M *Journalist*
%Washington Post, Editorial Dept, 1150 15th St NW, Washington, DC 20071, USA

Murphy, Charles H, Jr *Businessman*
%Murphy Oil Corp, 200 E Peach St, El Dorado, AK 71730, USA

Murphy, Charles S *Government Official*
100 Bluff View Dr, #503-C, Belleair Bluffs, FL 34640, USA

Murphy, Dale B *Baseball Player*
1603 W Grantville, Grantville, GA 30220, USA

Murphy, Donna *Actress*
%Silver Kass Massetti Agency, 145 W 45th St, #1204, New York, NY 10036, USA

Murphy, Ed *Basketball Coach*
%University of Mississippi, Smith Coliseum, University, MS 38677, USA

Murphy, Eddie *Comedian, Actor*
%Eddie Murphy Productions, Carnegie Tower, 152 W 57th St, #4700, New York, 10019, USA

Murphy, John Cullen *Cartoonist (Prince Valiant)*
%King Features Syndicate, 216 E 45th St, New York, NY 10017, USA

Murphy, John J *Businessman*
%Dresser Industries, PO Box 718, Dallas, TX 75221, USA

Murphy, Lawrence T (Larry) *Hockey Player*
%Toronto Maple Leafs, 60 Carlton St, Toronto ON M5B 1L1, Canada

Murphy, Michael *Actor*
%International Creative Mgmt, 8942 Wilshire Blvd, Beverly Hills, CA 90211, USA

Murphy, Michael E *Businessman*
%Sara Lee Corp, 3 First National Plaza, Chicago, IL 60602, USA

Murphy, R Madison *Businessman*
%Murphy Oil Corp, 200 Peach St, El Dorado, AR 71730, USA

Murphy, Raymond G *Korean War Marine Corps Hero (CMH)*
4677 Sutton St NW, Albuquerque, NM 87114, USA

Murphy, Reg *Editor, Publisher*
%National Geographic Society, 1145 17th St NW, Washington, DC 20036, USA

Murphy, Richard W *Diplomat*
16 Sutton Place, #9-A, New York, NY 10022, USA

Murphy, Rosemary *Actress*
220 E 73rd St, New York, NY 10021, USA

Murphy, Terry *Entertainer*
%"Hard Copy" Show, ABC-TV, 77 W 66th St, New York, NY 10023, USA

Murphy, Thomas S *Businessman*
%Capital Cities/ABC Inc, 77 W 66th St, New York, NY 10023, USA

Murray of Epping Forest, Lionel (Len) *Union Official*
29 The Crescent, Loughton, Essex, England

Murray, A Brean *Financer*
%Brean Murray Foster Securities, 633 3rd Ave, New York, NY 10017, USA

Murray, Anne *Singer*
%Balmur Ltd, 4950 Yonge St, #2400, Toronto ON M2N 6K1, Canada

Murray, Barbara *Actress*
%Barry Burnett, Grafton House, 2-3 Golden Sq, London W1R 3AD, England

Murray, Bill *Comedian*
RD 1, PO Box 573, Washington Springs Rd, Palisades, NY 10964, USA

Murray, Bruce C *Planetary Scientist*
%Jet Propulsion Laboratory, 4800 Oak Grove Dr, Pasadena, CA 91109, USA

Murray, Bryan C *Hockey Coach, Executive*
%Florida Panthers, 100 NE 3rd Ave, #1000, Fort Lauderdale, FL 33301, USA

Murray, Charles P, Jr *WW II Army Hero (CMH)*
5906 Northridge Rd, Columbia, SC 29206, USA

Murray, Don *Actor*
1201 La Patera Canyon Rd, Goleta, CA 93117, USA

Murray, Doug *Cartoonist (The 'Nam)*
%Marvel Comic Group, 387 Park Ave S, New York, NY 10016, USA

Murray, Eddie *Football Player*
%Washington Redskins, 21300 Redskin Park Dr, Ashburn, VA 22011, USA

Murray, Eddie C *Baseball Player*
2330 W Joppa Rd, #155, Lutherville, MD 21093, USA

Murray, Iain *Yachtsman*
%International Management Group, 75490 Fairway Dr, Indian Wells, CA 92210, USA

M

Murray, J Alec G	*Businessman*
%Standard Commerical Corp, 2301 Miller Rd, Wilson, NC 27894, USA	
Murray, Jan	*Comedian*
1157 Calle Vista Dr, Beverly Hills, CA 90210, USA	
Murray, Jim	*Sportswriter*
430 Bellagio Terrace, Los Angeles, CA 90049, USA	
Murray, John E, Jr	*Educator*
%Duquesne University, President's Office, Pittsburgh, PA 15282, USA	
Murray, John L	*Businessman*
%Universal Foods Corp, 433 E Michigan St, Milwaukee, WI 53202, USA	
Murray, Joseph E	*Nobel Medicine Laureate*
108 Abbott Rd, Wellesley Hills, MA 02181, USA	
Murray, Kathryn	*Dancer*
2877 Kalakaua Ave, Honolulu, HI 96815, USA	
Murray, Michael	*Concert Organist*
1876 Northwest Blvd, #B, Columbus, OH 43212, USA	
Murray, Paul B	*Financier*
%East New York Savings Bank, 350 Park Ave, New York, NY 10022, USA	
Murray, Peg	*Actress*
800 Light House Rd, Southold, NY 11971, USA	
Murray, Terence R (Terry)	*Hockey Coach*
%Philadelphia Flyers, Spectrum, Pattison Place, Philadelphia, PA 19148, USA	
Murray, Terrence	*Financier*
%Fleet Financial Group, 50 Kennedy Plaza, Providence, RI 02903, USA	
Murray, Troy	*Hockey Player*
%Pittsburgh Penguins, Civic Arena, Centre Ave, Pittsburgh, PA 15219, USA	
Murray, Ty	*Rodeo Rider*
Rt 6, Box 320, Stephenville, TX 76401, USA	
Murschel, William H	*Businessman*
%Skyline Corp, 2520 By-Pass Rd, Elkhart, IN 46514, USA	
Murtagh, Kate	*Actress*
15146 Moorpark St, Sherman Oaks, CA 91403, USA	
Musante, Tony	*Actor*
38 Bedford St, New York, NY 10014, USA	
Musburger, Brent W	*Sportscaster*
%ABC-TV, Sports Dept, 77 W 66th St, New York, NY 10023, USA	
Muse, William V	*Educator*
%Auburn University, President's Office, Auburn University, AL 36849, USA	
Museveni, Yoweri K	*President, Uganda*
%President's Office, State House, PO Box 7006, Kampala, Uganda	
Musgrave, F Story	*Astronaut*
426 Biscayne Blvd, Seabrook, TX 77586, USA	
Musgrave, R Kenton	*Judge*
%US Court of International Trade, 1 Federal Plaza, New York, NY 10278, USA	
Musgrave, Thea	*Composer, Conductor*
%Virginia Opera Assn, PO Box 2580, Norfolk, VA 23501, USA	
Musial, Stanley F (Stan)	*Baseball Player*
1655 Des Peres Rd, #125, St Louis, MO 63131, USA	
Muskie, Edmund S	*Secretary, State; Governor/Senator, ME*
%Chadborne & Parke, 1101 Vermont Ave NW, Washington, DC 20005, USA	
Mussa, Michael	*Economist*
%International Monetary Fund, 700 19th St NW, Washington, DC 20431, USA	
Musser, Warren V	*Businessman*
%Safeguard Scientifics, 435 Devon Park Dr, Wayne, PA 19087, USA	
Mussina, Michael C (Mike)	*Baseball Player*
1302 Spruce St, Montoursville, PA 17754, USA	
Musso, George F	*Football Player*
604 W High St, Edwardsville, IL 62025, USA	
Muster, Brad	*Football Player*
%New Orleans Saints, 1500 Poydras St, New Orleans, LA 70112, USA	
Muster, Thomas	*Tennis Player*
8430 Leibnitz, Austria	
Mutalov, Abdulkhashim	*Prime Minister, Uzbekistan*
%Prime Minister's Office, Tashkent, Uzbekistan	
Muth, Rene	*Basketball Coach*
%Pennsylvania State University, Athletic Dept, University Park, PA 16802, USA	
Muti, Ornella	*Actress*
%Tony Ruggero Initiative, Via Giovanni Bettolo 3, 00195 Rome, Italy	

Murray - Muti

Muti, Riccardo *Conductor*
Via Corti Alle Mura 25, 48100 Ravenna, Italy

Mutombo, Dikembe *Basketball Player*
%Denver Nuggets, McNichols Arena, 1635 Clay St, Denver, CO 80204, USA

Mutschler, Carlfried *Architect*
E-7, 7, 68159 Mannheim, Germany

Mutter, Anne-Sophie *Concert Violinist*
Effnerstr 48, 81925 Munich, Germany

Mwanawasa, Levy P *Vice President, Zambia*
%Vice President's Office, PO Box 30208, Lusaka, Zambia

Mwinyi, Ali Hassam *President, Tanzania*
%President's Office, State House, PO Box 9120, Dar es Salaam, Tanzania

Myatt, L David *Businessman*
%Quaker State Corp, 255 Elm St, Oil City, PA 16301, USA

Mydans, Carl *Photographer*
%Time Inc Magazines, Time & Life Bldg, Rockefeller Center, New York, NY 10020, USA

Myers Tikalsky, Linda *Skier*
RR 5, Box 265-T, Santa Fe, NM 87501, USA

Myers, A Maurice *Businessman*
%American West Airlines, 51 W 3rd St, Tempe, AZ 85281, USA

Myers, Anne M *Religious Leader*
%Church of the Brethren, 1451 Dundee Ave, Elgin, IL 60120, USA

Myers, Barton *Architect*
%Barton Myers Assoc, 9348 Civic Center Dr, Beverly Hills, CA 90210, USA

Myers, Dale D *Space Engineer*
%Dale Myers Assoc, PO Box 232518, Leucadia, CA 92023, USA

Myers, Dee Dee *Government Official*
%"Equal Time" Show, CNBC-TV, 30 Rockefeller Plaza, New York, NY 10112, USA

Myers, Harry J, Jr *Publisher*
46 W Ranch Trail, Morrison, CO 80465, USA

Myers, Jack D *Physician*
%University of Pittsburgh, Scaife Hall, #1291, Pittsburgh, PA 15261, USA

Myers, Lisa *Commentator*
%NBC-TV, News Dept, 4001 Nebraska Ave NW, Washington, DC 20016, USA

Myers, Mike *Comedian*
%Brillstein Co, 9150 Wilshire Blvd, #350, Beverly Hills, CA 90212, USA

Myers, Minor, Jr *Educator*
%Illinois Wesleyan University, President's Office, Bloomington, IL 61702, USA

Myers, Norman *Environmental Scientist, Conservationist*
Upper Meadow, Old Road, Headington, Oxford OX3 8SZ, England

Myers, Norman A *Businessman*
%Browning-Ferris Industries, 757 N Eldridge Parkway, Houston, TX 77079, USA

Myers, Reginald R *Korean War Marine Corps Hero (CMH)*
PO Box 803, Annandale, VA 22003, USA

Myers, Richard B (Dick) *Air Force General*
Commander, US Forces Japan, Unit 5068, APO, AP 96328, USA

Myers, Rochelle *Writer*
3827 California St, San Francisco, CA 94118, USA

Myers, Roy A *Businessman*
%Curtice Burns Foods, 90 Linden Place, Rochester, NY 14603, USA

Myers, Russell *Cartoonist (Broom Hilda)*
%Tribune Media Services, 435 N Michigan Ave, #1417, Chicago, IL 60611, USA

Myers, Stephen E *Businessman*
%Myers Industries, 1293 S Main St, Akron, OH 44301, USA

Myerson, Bess *Consumer Advocate*
2 E 71st St, New York, NY 10021, USA

Myerson, Harvey *Attorney*
%Finley Kumble Wagner Assoc, 425 Park Ave, New York, NY 10022, USA

Myles, Alannah *Singer*
%Levine/Schneider, 433 N Camden Dr, Beverly Hills, CA 90210, USA

Mylod, Robert J *Financier*
%Michigan National Corp, 27777 Inkster Rd, Farmington Hills, MI 48334, USA

Myrick, Goodwin L *Businessman*
%Alfa Corp, 2108 E South Blvd, Montogmery, AL 36191, USA

Mysen, Bjorn O *Geochemist*
%Carnegie Institution, 5221 Broad Branch Rd, Washington, DC 20015, USA

Myslowka, Myron W (Ron) *Labor Leader*
%United Textile Workers, 2 Echelon Plaza, Laurel Rd, Voorhees, NJ 08043, USA

M

Muti - Myslowka

N'Dour, Youssou	*Singer*
%Soundscape, 799 Greenwich St, New York, NY 10014, USA	
Naber, John	*Swimmer*
PO Box 50107, Pasadena, CA 91115, USA	
Nabers, Drayton, Jr	*Businessman*
%Protective Life Corp, 2801 Highway 280 S, Birmingham, AL 35223, USA	
Nabors, Jim	*Actor, Singer*
215 Kulamanu, Honolulu, HI 96816, USA	
Nachmansohn, David	*Biochemist*
560 Riverside Dr, New York, NY 10027, USA	
Nader, George	*Actor*
893 Camino del Sur, Palm Springs, CA 92262, USA	
Nader, Michael	*Actor*
%Paradigm Agency, 10100 Santa Monica Blvd, #2500, Los Angeles, CA 90067, USA	
Nader, Ralph	*Consumer Activist*
%Center for Study of Responsive Law, PO Box 19367, Washington, DC 20036, USA	
Nagako Kuni	*Empress Mother, Japan*
%Imperial Palace, 1-1 Chiyoda, Chiyoda-ku, Tokyo, Japan	
Nagamo, Takeshi	*Businessman*
%Mitsubishi Metal Corp, 1-5-2 Otemachi, Chiyodaku, Tokyo 100, Japan	
Nagamo, Wakichi	*Businessman*
%Mitsubishi Gas & Chemical, 2-5-2 Marunouchi, Chiyodaku, Tokyo 100, Japan	
Nagano, Kent	*Conductor*
%Berkeley Symphony Orchestra, 2322 Shattuck Ave, Berkeley, CA 94704, USA	
Nagel, Steven R	*Astronaut*
%NASA, Johnson Space Center, 2101 NASA Rd, Houston, TX 77058, USA	
Nagorske, Lynn A	*Financier*
%TCF Financial Corp, 801 Marquette Ave, Minneapolis, MN 55402, USA	
Nahan, Stu	*Sportscaster*
11274 Canton Dr, Studio City, CA 91604, USA	
Naharin, Ohad	*Choreographer*
%Dance Theater, Scheldeldoekshaven 60, 2511 EN Gravenhage, Netherlands	
Naifeh, Steven W	*Writer*
%Connie Clausen Assoc, 250 E 87th St, New York, NY 10128, USA	
Naipaul, V S	*Writer*
%Aitken & Stone Ltd, 29 Fernshaw Rd, London SW10 0TG, England	
Nair, Mira	*Movie Director*
%International Creative Mgmt, 8942 Wilshire Blvd, Beverly Hills, CA 90211, USA	
Naisbitt, John	*Writer*
%Universal Press Syndicate, 4900 Main St, #900, Kansas City, KS 64112, USA	
Najarian, John S	*Surgeon*
%University of Minnesota Health Center, Surgery Dept, Minneapolis, MN 55455, USA	
Najimy, Kathy	*Actress*
120 W 45th St, #3601, New York, NY 10036, USA	
Nakahara, Shin	*Financier*
%Bank of Tokyo Trust, 1251 Ave of Americas, New York, NY 10116, USA	
Nakama, Keo	*Swimmer*
1788 Laukahi St, Honolulu, HI 96821, USA	
Nakamura, Tameaki	*Businessman*
%Sumitomo Metal Industries, 5-33-4 Kitahama, Chuoku, Osaka 541, Japan	
Nakano, Kiyonori	*Businessman*
%Mitsui Petrochemical Industries, 2-5 Kasumigaseki, Tokyo 100, Japan	
Nakasone, Robert C	*Businessman*
%Toys "R" Us Inc, 461 From Rd, Paramus, NJ 07652, USA	
Nakasone, Yasuhiro	*Prime Minister, Japan*
3-22-7 Kamikitazawa, Setagayaku, Tokyo, Japan	
Nalder, Eric C	*Journalist*
%Seattle Times, Editorial Dept, Fairview Ave N & John St, Seattle, WA 98111, USA	
Nalty, Donald J	*Financier*
%Hibernia Corp, 313 Carondelet St, New Orleans, LA 70130, USA	
Nam Duck-Woo	*Prime Minister, South Korea*
395-101 Soekyo-Dong, Mapo-ku Seoul, South Korea	
Namath, Joseph W (Joe)	*Football Player*
%Namanco Productions, 300 E 51st St, #11-A, New York, NY 10022, USA	
Namias, Jerome	*Meteorologist*
%Scripps Institute of Oceanography, Sverdrup Hall, La Jolla, CA 92093, USA	
Nance, Jack	*Actor*
5625 Del Amo Blvd, Torrance, CA 90503, USA	

Nanne, Louis V (Lou) — *Hockey Executive*
5801 Hidden Lane, Minneapolis, MN 55436, USA

Nannen, Henri — *Editor*
Hinter dem Rahmen 13, 26721 Emden, Germany

Nannini, Alessandro — *Auto Racing Driver*
Via del Paradiso 4, 53100 Siena, Italy

Nantz, Jim — *Sportscaster*
%CBS-TV, Sports Dept, 51 W 52nd St, New York, NY 10019, USA

Napier, Charles — *Actor*
Star Route, Box 60-H, Caliente, CA 93518, USA

Napier, James V — *Businessman*
%Scientific-Atlanta Inc, 1 Technology Parkway, Norcross, GA 30092, USA

Napier, John — *Stage Designer*
%MLR, 200 Fulham Rd, London SW10, England

Napier, Wilfrid F Cardinal — *Religious Leader*
%Archdiocese, 97 St John's St, PO Box 65, 4700 Kokstad, South Africa

Narasimha Rao, P V — *Prime Minister, India*
9 Moti Lal Nehru Marg, New Delhi 11, India

Narayan, R K — *Writer*
Soundarya Apts, 1 Eldams Rd, #164-A, Alwarpet, Madras 600 018, India

Narizzano, Silvio — *Movie Director*
%Al Parker, 55 Park Lane, London, England

Narleski, Raymond E (Ray) — *Baseball Player*
1183 Chews Landing Rd, Laurel Springs, NJ 08021, USA

Naruhito — *Crown Prince, Japan*
%Imperial Palace, 1-1 Chiyoda, Chiyoda-ku, Tokyo, Japan

Narvekar, Prabhakar R — *Financier*
%International Monetary Fund, 700 19th St NW, Washington, DC 20431, USA

Narz, Jack — *Television Host*
1905 Beverly Place, Beverly Hills, CA 90210, USA

Nascimento, Milton — *Singer, Songwriter*
%Quilombo, Rua Padre Rolim 769, Bela Horizonte MG, CEP 30130, Brazil

Nash, Graham — *Singer, Songwriter*
%Siddons Assoc, 584 N Larchmont Blvd, Los Angeles, CA 90004, USA

Nash, Jack — *Financier*
%Odyssey Partners, 31 W 52nd St, New York, NY 10019, USA

Nash, John F — *Nobel Economics Laureate*
%Princeton University, Economics Department, Princeton, NJ 08544, USA

Nason, John W — *Educator*
Rocky Point, Keene, NY 12942, USA

Nastase, Ilie — *Tennis Player*
15 E 169th St, New York, NY 10021, USA

Nasution, Abdul Haris — *Army General, Indonesia*
Jl Touku Umar 40, Jakarta Pusat, Indonesia

Natalicio, Diana S — *Educator*
%University of Texas at El Paso, President's Office, El Paso, TX 79968, USA

Nathan, Tony C — *Football Player, Coach*
15110 Dunbarton Place, Miami Lakes, FL 33016, USA

Nathaniel (Popp), Bishop — *Religious Leader*
%Romanian Orthodox Episcopate, 2522 Grey Tower Rd, Jackson, MI 49201, USA

Nathans, Daniel — *Nobel Medicine Laureate*
%Johns Hopkins School of Medicine, Microbiology Dept, Baltimore, MD 21205, USA

Natkin, Robert — *Artist*
24 Mark Twain Lane, West Redding, CT 06896, USA

Natori, Josie C — *Fashion Designer*
%Natori Co, 40 E 34th St, New York, NY 10016, USA

Naude, C F Beyers — *Religious Leader*
%Ecumenical Advice Bureau, 185 Smit St, Braamfontein 2001, South Africa

Naughton, David — *Actor*
%Gold Marshak Assoc, 3500 W Olive Ave, #1400, Burbank, CA 91505, USA

Naughton, James — *Actor*
3100 Arrowhead Dr, Los Angeles, CA 90068, USA

Naulls, Willie — *Basketball Player*
%Chuck & Willie's Auto Agency, 13900 Hawthorne Blvd, Hawthorne, CA 90250, USA

Nauman, Bruce — *Artist*
%Leo Castelli Gallery, 420 W Broadway, New York, NY 10012, USA

Navasky, Victor S — *Editor*
%Nation Magazine, Editorial Dept, 72 5th Ave, New York, NY 10011, USA

N

Nanne - Navasky

N

Navon, Itzhak — *President, Israel*
%Education & Culture Ministry, Jerusalem, Israel

Navratilova, Martina — *Tennis Player*
%Women's Tennis Assn, 133 1st St NE, St Petersburg, FL 33701, USA

Nayden, Denis J — *Businessman*
%Kidder Peabody Co, 10 Hanover Square, New York, NY 10005, USA

Naylor, Gloria — *Writer*
%One Way Productions, 638 2nd St, Brooklyn, NY 11215, USA

Nazam, Hisham — *Government Official, Saudi Arabia*
%Ministry of Petroleum & Mineral Resources, Riyadh, Saudi Arabia

Nazarbayev, Nursultan A — *President, Kazakhstan*
%President's Office, Pl Respubliki 4, 480091 Alma Ata, Kazakhstan

Nduwayo, Antoine — *Prime Minister, Burundi*
%Prime Minister's Officer, Bujumbura, Burundi

Neal, James F — *Attorney*
%Neal & Harwell, 3rd National Bank Bldg, #800, Nashville, TN 37219, USA

Neal, John E — *Financier*
%Kemper Financial Services, 120 S LaSalle St, Chicago, IL 60603, USA

Neal, Patricia — *Actress*
45 East End Ave, #4-C, New York, NY 10028, USA

Neal, Philip M — *Businessman*
%Avery Dennison Corp, 150 N Orange Grove Blvd, Pasadena, CA 91109, USA

Neale, Gary L — *Businessman*
%Northern Indiana Public Service Co, 5265 Hohman Ave, Hammond, IN 46320, USA

Neame, Ronald — *Movie Director*
%Kimridge Corp, 2317 Kimridge Ave, Beverly Hills, CA 90210, USA

Near, Holly — *Singer*
560 Key Blvd, Richmond, CA 94805, USA

Near, James W — *Businessman*
%Wendy's International, 4288 W Dublin Granville Rd, Dublin, OH 43017, USA

Nebel, Dorothy Hoyt — *Skier*
19 Garwood Trail, Denville, NJ 07834, USA

Neblett, Carol — *Opera Singer*
%Robert Lombardo Assoc, 61 W 62nd St, #F, New York, NY 10023, USA

Nederlander, James M — *Theater Producer*
%Nederlander Organization, 810 7th Ave, New York, NY 10019, USA

Nedley, Robert E — *Businessman*
%St Joe Paper Co, 1650 Prudential Dr, Jacksonville, FL 32207, USA

Nedved, Petr — *Hockey Player*
%Pittsburgh Penguins, Civic Arena, Centre Ave, Pittsburgh, PA 15219, USA

Needham, Connie — *Actress*
%Twentieth Century Artists, 15315 Magnolia Blvd, #429, Sherman Oaks, CA 91403, USA

Needham, Hal — *Movie Director*
%Bandit Productions, 3518 Cahuenga Blvd W, #110, Los Angeles, CA 90068, USA

Needham, Tracey — *Actress*
%Badgley Connor, 9229 Sunset Blvd, #311, Los Angeles, CA 90069, USA

Needleman, Jacob — *Philosopher*
25 San Andreas Way, San Francisco, CA 94127, USA

Neel, James V G — *Geneticist*
2235 Belmont Rd, Ann Arbor, MI 48104, USA

Neel, Louis Boyd — *Conductor*
%York Club, 135 St George St, Toronto ON M5B 2L8, Canada

Neel, Louis E F — *Nobel Physics Laureate*
15 Rue Marcel Allegot, 92190 Meudon, France

Neely, Cam — *Hockey Player*
%Boston Bruins, Boston Garden, 150 Causeway St, Boston, MA 02114, USA

Neely, Mark E, Jr — *Historian*
%Oxford University Press, 200 Madison Ave, New York, NY 10016, USA

Neely, Ralph E — *Football Player*
806 Patricia Circle, Quitman, TX 75783, USA

Neeson, Liam — *Actor*
%Susan Culley Assoc, 150 S Rodeo Dr, #220, Beverly Hills, CA 90212, USA

Nef, John U — *Historian*
2726 "N" St NW, Washington, DC 20007, USA

Neff, Francine I — *Government Official*
1509 Sagebrush Trail SE, Albuquerque, NM 87123, USA

Neff, William D — *Psychologist*
2080 Hideaway Court, Morris, IL 60450, USA

Navon - Neff

Neher, Erwin   *Nobel Medicine Laureate*
%Max'Planck Biophysical Chemistry Institute, 37083 Gottingen, Germany

Nehlen, Don   *Football Coach*
%West Virginia University, Athletic Dept, Morgantown, WV 26506, USA

Neil, Andrew F   *Editor*
%Sunday Times, Editorial Dept, 1 Pennington St, London E1 9XN, England

Neill, Mary Gardner   *Museum Director*
%Seattle Art Museum, Volunteer Park, Seattle, WA 98112, USA

Neill, Noel   *Actress*
331 Sage Lane, Santa Monica, CA 90402, USA

Neill, Rolfe   *Publisher*
%Charlotte News-Observer, 600 S Tryon St, Charlotte, NC 28202, USA

Neill, Sam   *Actor*
PO Box 153, Noble Park, VIC 3174, Australia

Neilson, Roger   *Hockey Coach*
1796 Westover Point Rd, RR 3, Lakefield ON K0L 2HO, Canada

Neilson-Bell, Sandra   *Swimmer*
3101 Mistyglen Circle, Austin, TX 78746, USA

Neiman, LeRoy   *Artist*
1 W 67th St, New York, NY 10023, USA

Neinas, Charles M (Chuck)   *Football Executive*
%College Football Assn, 6688 Gunpark Dr, Boulder, CO 80301, USA

Nelligan, Kate   *Actress*
%Larry Dalzell Assoc, 17 Broad Court, London WC2B 5QN, England

Nelms, Mike   *Football Player*
%Washington Redskins, 21300 Redskin Park Dr, Ashburn, VA 22011, USA

Nelson, Barry   *Actor*
134 W 58th St, New York, NY 10019, USA

Nelson, Byron   *Golfer*
Fairway Ranch, Litsey Rd, Box 5, Roanoke, TX 76262, USA

Nelson, Cindy   *Skier*
%US Ski Assn, PO Box 100, Park City, UT 84060, USA

Nelson, Craig T   *Actor*
288/2 Boniface Dr, Malibu, CA 90265, USA

Nelson, Daniel R   *Financier*
%West One Bancorp, 101 S Capitol Blvd, Boise, ID 83702, USA

Nelson, Darrin   *Football Player*
%San Diego Chargers, Jack Murphy Stadium, San Diego, CA 92160, USA

Nelson, David   *Actor, Television Director*
8544 Sunset Blvd, Los Angeles, CA 90069, USA

Nelson, Donald A (Nellie)   *Basketball Player, Coach*
%New York Knicks, Madison Square Garden, 4 Penn Plaza, New York, NY 10001, USA

Nelson, Ed   *Actor*
124 Old Pecan Grove Lane, Waveland, MS 39576, USA

Nelson, Gaylord A   *Governor/Senator, WI; Environmentalist*
%Wilderness Society, 900 17th St NW, Washington, DC 20006, USA

Nelson, Gene   *Actor, Dancer*
14155 Magnolia Blvd, #1, Sherman Oaks, CA 91423, USA

Nelson, George D   *Astronaut*
%University of Washington, Astronomy Dept, Seattle, WA 98195, USA

Nelson, J Russell   *Educator*
%University of Colorado, Business Administration College, Boulder, CO 80309, USA

Nelson, James E   *Religious Leader*
%Baha'i Faith, 536 Sheridan Rd, Wilmette, IL 60091, USA

Nelson, John Allen   *Actor*
%Paradigm Agency, 10100 Santa Monica Blvd, #2500, Los Angeles, CA 90067, USA

Nelson, John C   *Financier*
%Norwest Bank Colorado, 1740 Broadway, Denver, CO 80274, USA

Nelson, John W   *Conductor*
%IMG Artists, Media House, 3 Burlington Lane, London W4 2TH, England

Nelson, Judd   *Actor*
2934 1/2 N Beverly Glen Circle, #57, Los Angeles, CA 90077, USA

Nelson, Judith   *Opera Singer*
2600 Buena Vista Way, Berkeley, CA 94708, USA

Nelson, Kent C   *Businessman*
%United Parcel Service, 55 Glenlake Parkway NE, Atlanta, GA 30328, USA

Nelson, Kirk N   *Businessman*
%Federated Mutual Insurance, 121 E Park Square, Owatonna, MN 55060, USA

N

Neher - Nelson

Nelson, Larry *Golfer*
%Professional Golfer's Assn, PO Box 109601, Palm Beach Gardens, FL 33410, USA

Nelson, Marilyn Carlson *Businesswoman*
%Carlson Companies, Carlson Parkway, PO Box 59159, Minneapolis, MN 55459, USA

Nelson, Ralph A *Nutritionist*
%Carle Foundation Hospital, 611 W Park St, Urbana, IL 61801, USA

Nelson, Robert T *Admiral, Coast Guard*
%Vice Commandant's Office, Coast Guard Hdq, 2100 2nd SW, Washington, DC 20593, USA

Nelson, Steve *Football Player, Coach*
%New England Patriots, Foxboro Stadium, Rt 1, Foxboro, MA 02035, USA

Nelson, Ted *Computer Inventor (Xanadu)*
%Autodesk Inc, 2320 Marinship Way, Sausalito, CA 94965, USA

Nelson, Tracy *Actress*
407 Sycamore Rd, Santa Monica, CA 90402, USA

Nelson, William (Bill) *Representative, FL; Astronaut*
3000 Rocky Point Rd, Melbourne, FL 32905, USA

Nelson, William C *Financier*
%Boatmen's First National (Kansas City), 10th & Baltimore, Kansas City, MO 64114, USA

Nelson, Willie *Singer, Songwriter*
%Pedernails Studio, Rt 1, Briarcliff TT, Spicewood, TX 78669, USA

Nemecheck, Joe *Auto Racing Driver*
%Nemco Motorsports, PO Box 1131, Mooresville, NC 28115, USA

Nemeth, Miklos *Prime Minister, Hungary*
%European Reconstruction Bank, 175 Bishopgate, London EC2A 2EH, England

Nemirow, Arnold M *Businessman*
%Bowater Inc, 55 E Campendown Way, Greenville, SC 29601, USA

Nenneman, Richard A *Editor*
PO Box 992, East Brunswick, NJ 08816, USA

Nepote, Jean *Law Enforcement Official*
26 Rue Armengaud, 92210 Saint-Cloud, Hauts-de-Seine, France

Nerette, Joseph *President, Haiti; Judge*
%Supreme Court, Chief Justice's Office, Port-au-Prince, Haiti

Neri Vela, Rodolfo *Astronaut, Mexico*
Playa Copacabana 131, Col Marte, Mexico City DF 08830, Mexico

Neri, Manuel *Artist*
%Anne Kohs Assoc, 251 Post St, #540, San Francisco, CA 94108, USA

Nerlove, Marc L *Economist*
%University of Maryland, Agricultural/Resource Economics, College Park, MD 20742, USA

Nero, Peter *Pianist, Conductor*
4114 Royal Crest Place, Encino, CA 91436, USA

Nerud, John *Thoroughbred Racing Executive*
%Tartan Farms, 6775 SW 43rd Ave, Ocala, FL 34476, USA

Nesbitt, Gregory L *Businessman*
%Central Louisiana Electric Co, 2030 Donahue Ferry Rd, Pineville, LA 71360, USA

Nesmith, Michael *Singer, Guitarist (The Monkees)*
%Pacific Arts Video, 11858 LaGrange Ave, Los Angeles, CA 90025, USA

Nespral, Jackie *Commentator*
%NBC-TV, News Dept, 30 Rockefeller Plaza, New York, NY 10112, USA

Ness, Norman F *Astrophysicist*
9 Wilkinson Dr, Landenberg, PA 19350, USA

Nessen, Ronald H (Ron) *Government Official, Commentator*
6409 Walhonding Rd, Bethesda, MD 20816, USA

Nesterenko, Yevgeny Y *Opera Singer*
Fruzenskaya Nab 24/1-78, 119146 Moscow, Russia

Netanyahu, Benjamin *Government Leader, Israel*
%Likud Party, 38 Rehov King George, Tel-Aviv 61231, Israel

Nett, Robert B *WW II Army Hero (CMH)*
5417 Kessington Dr, Columbus, GA 31907, USA

Nettles, Graig *Baseball Player*
13 North Lane, Del Mar, CA 92014, USA

Nettleton, Lois *Actress*
%Susan Mann, 11762 Moorpark St, #G, Studio City, CA 91604, USA

Neubauer, Franz *Financier*
%Bayerische Landesbank, 80277 Munich, Germany

Neufeld, Elizabeth F *Biochemist*
%University of California Medical School, Biology Dept, Los Angeles, CA 90024, USA

Neugarten, Bernice L *Social Scientist*
5801 Dorchester Ave, Chicago, IL 60637, USA

Neuharth, Allen H *Publisher*
%Freedom Forum, 1101 Wilson Blvd, Arlington, VA 22209, USA

Neuhaus, Max *Artist, Composer*
350 5th Ave, #3304, New York, NY 10118, USA

Neuhaus, Richard J *Religious Leader*
%Center on Religion & Society, 152 Madison Ave, New York, NY 10016, USA

Neuhauser, Duncan V B *Epidemiologist*
2655 N Park Ave, Cleveland Heights, OH 44106, USA

Neumann, Gerhard *Aeronautical Engineer*
%General Electric Co, 1000 Western Ave, West Lynn, MA 01905, USA

Neumann, Robert G *Diplomat, Educator*
4986 Sentinel Dr, #301, Bethesda, MD 20816, USA

Neumann, Wolfgang *Opera Singer*
%Metropolitan Opera Assn, Lincoln Center Plaza, New York, NY 10023, USA

Neumeier, John *Choreographer*
%Hamburg Ballet, 54 Caspar-Voght-Str, 20535 Hamburg, Germany

Neuner, Doris *Luge Athlete*
6024 Innsbruck, Austria

Neurath, Hans *Biochemist*
5752 60th NE, Seattle, WA 98105, USA

Neustadt, Richard E *Political Scientist, Educator*
1010 Memorial Dr, Cambridge, MA 02138, USA

Neuwirth, Bebe *Actress, Dancer*
212 1/2 S Poinsettia Place, Los Angeles, CA 90036, USA

Neves, Lucas Moreira Cardinal *Religious Leader*
Av Sefa de Setembro 1682, 40080-001 Salvador, Bahia, Brazil

Neville, Aaron *Singer*
5771 Eastover Dr, New Orleans, LA 70128, USA

Neville, John *Actor*
99 Norman St, Stratford ON N5A 5R8, Canada

Neville, Robert C *Theologian*
%Boston University, Theology School, Boston, MA 02215, USA

Nevins, Claudette *Actress*
%Gold Marshak Assoc, 3500 W Olive Ave, #1400, Burbank, CA 91505, USA

Newberry, Tom *Football Player*
%St Louis Rams, 100 N Broadway, #2100, St Louis, MO 63102, USA

Newbigging, William *Publisher*
%Edmonton Journal, 10006 101st St, Edmonton AB T5J 2S6, Canada

Newbury, Mickey *Songwriter, Singer*
128 River Rd, Hendersonville, TN 37075, USA

Newcomb, Jonathan *Publisher*
35 Pierrepont St, Brooklyn, NY 11201, USA

Newcombe, Donald (Don) *Baseball Player*
3420 Ocean Park Blvd, #3000, Santa Monica, CA 90405, USA

Newcombe, John D *Tennis Player*
%John Newcombe's Tennis Ranch, PO Box 310469, New Braunfels, TX 78131, USA

Newell, Homer E *Physicist*
2567 Nicky Lane, Alexandria, VA 22311, USA

Newell, Norman D *Palaeontologist, Geologist*
%American Museum of Natural History, Central Park W & 79th, New York, NY 10023, USA

Newell, Peter F (Pete) *Basketball Coach*
%Naismith Basketball Hall of Fame, 1150 W Columbus Ave, Springfield, MA 01105, USA

Newgard, Christopher *Biochemist*
%Southwestern Medical Center, Biochemistry Dept, Dallas, TX 75237, USA

Newhart, Bob *Comedian*
420 Amapola Lane, Los Angeles, CA 90077, USA

Newhouse, Donald E *Publisher*
%Advance Publications, 950 Fingerboard Rd, Staten Island, NY 10305, USA

Newhouse, Samuel I, Jr *Publisher*
%Conde Nast Publications, Conde Nast Bldg, 350 Madison Ave, New York, NY 10017, USA

Newhouser, Harold (Hal) *Baseball Player*
2584 Marcy Court, Bloomfield Hills, MI 48302, USA

Newley, Anthony *Singer*
%Peter Charlesworth, 60 Old Brompton Rd, London SW7 3LQ, England

Newman, Andrew E *Businessman*
%Edison Brothers Stores, 501 N Broadway, St Louis, MO 63102, USA

Newman, Arnold *Photographer*
33 W 67th St, New York, NY 10023, USA

N

Newman, Barry — *Actor*
425 N Oakhurst Dr, Beverly Hills, CA 90210, USA

Newman, Bernard — *Judge*
%US Court of International Trade, 1 Federal Plaza, New York, NY 10278, USA

Newman, Beryl R — *WW II Army Hero (CMH)*
HC 67, Box 843, Urbanna, VA 23175, USA

Newman, Edward K (Ed) — *Football Player*
10100 SW 140th St, Miami, FL 33176, USA

Newman, Edwin H — *Commentator*
870 United Nations Plaza, #18-D, New York, NY 10017, USA

Newman, Frank A — *Businessman*
%Eckerd Corp, PO Box 4689, Clearwater, FL 34618, USA

Newman, Frank N — *Businessman*
%Bankers Trust New York Corp, 280 Park Ave, New York, NY 10017, USA

Newman, Harry L — *Football Player*
3145 Palm Aire Dr N, #102, Pompano Beach, FL 33069, USA

Newman, James H — *Astronaut*
%NASA, Johnson Space Center, 2101 NASA Rd, Houston, TX 77058, USA

Newman, Johnny — *Basketball Player*
%New Jersey Nets, Byrne Meadowlands Arena, East Rutherford, NJ 07073, USA

Newman, Laraine — *Comedienne*
10480 Ashton Ave, Los Angeles, CA 90024, USA

Newman, Melvin S — *Organic Chemist*
2239 Onandaga Dr, Columbus, OH 43221, USA

Newman, Nanette — *Actress*
Seven Pines, Wentworth, Surrey GU25 4QP, England

Newman, Oscar — *Architect, Urban Planner*
%Washington University, Architecture Dept, St Louis, MO 63130, USA

Newman, Paul — *Actor*
9056 Santa Monica Blvd, #100, Los Angeles, CA 90069, USA

Newman, Phyllis — *Singer, Actress*
529 W 42nd St, #7-F, New York, NY 10036, USA

Newman, Randy — *Singer, Songwriter*
2174 Banyan Dr, Los Angeles, CA 90049, USA

Newmar, Julie — *Actress*
204 S Carmelina Ave, Los Angeles, CA 90049, USA

Newmarch, Michael G — *Businessman*
%Jackson National Life Insurance, 5901 Executive Dr, Lansing, MI 48911, USA

Newsom, David D — *Diplomat*
4990 Sentinel Dr, #102, Bethesda, MD 20816, USA

Newsome, Ozzie — *Football Player, Executive*
%Cleveland Browns, 80 1st Ave, Berea, OH 44017, USA

Newton, C M — *Basketball Coach, Administrator*
%University of Kentucky, Athletic Dept, Lexington, KY 40536, USA

Newton, Christopher — *Theater Director*
%Shakespeare Festival, PO Box 774, Niagara-on-the-Lake ON L0S 1J0, Canada

Newton, Helmut — *Photographer*
7 Ave St Roman, #T-1008, Monte Carlo, Monaco

Newton, John T — *Businessman*
%KU Energy Corp, 1 Quality St, Lexington, KY 40507, USA

Newton, Juice — *Singer, Songwriter*
PO Box 293323, Lewisville, TX 75029, USA

Newton, Nate — *Football Player*
%Dallas Cowboys, 1 Cowboys Parkway, Irving, TX 75063, USA

Newton, Russell B, Jr — *Financier*
%Alliance Mortgage Co, 4500 Salisbury Rd, Jacksonville, FL 32216, USA

Newton, Wayne — *Singer*
6629 S Pecos Rd, Las Vegas, NV 89120, USA

Newton-John, Olivia — *Singer*
PO Box 2710, Malibu, CA 90265, USA

Ney, Edward N — *Businessman, Diplomat*
%Young & Rubicam-Marsteller, 230 Park Ave S, New York, NY 10003, USA

Ney, Edward P — *Physicist*
1925 Penn Ave S, Minneapolis, MN 55405, USA

Ney, Richard — *Actor*
800 S San Rafael Ave, Pasadena, CA 91105, USA

Nezhat, Camran — *Endocrinologist*
%Fertility/Endocrinology Ctr, 5555 Peachtree Dunwoody Rd NE, Atlanta, GA 30342, USA

Ngor, Haing S *Actor*
945 N Beaudry Ave, Los Angeles, CA 90012, USA

Nguyen Van Linh *Chairman, Vietnam*
%Communist Party, Hoang Hoa Tham, Hanoi, Vietnam

Nguyen Van Thieu *President, South Vietnam; Army General*
White House, Coombe Park, Kingston-Upon-Thames, Surrey, England

Nguyen, Dustin *Actor*
465 N Sierra Bonita Ave, #8, Los Angeles, CA 90036, USA

Nicandros, Constantine S *Businessman*
%E I Du Pont de Nemours Co, 1007 Market St, Wilmington, DE 19801, USA

Nicely, Olza M (Tony) *Businessman*
%Geico Corp, 1 Geico Plaza, 5260 Western Ave NW, Washington, DC 20076, USA

Nicholas (Smisko), Bishop *Religious Leader*
%American Carpatho, 312 Garfield St, Johnstown, PA 15906, USA

Nicholas, Denise *Actress*
932 Longwood Ave, Los Angeles, CA 90019, USA

Nicholas, Fayard *Dancer*
23388 Mulholland Dr, #58, Woodland Hills, CA 91364, USA

Nicholas, Harold *Dancer*
789 West End Ave, #9-D, New York, NY 10025, USA

Nicholas, Henry *Labor Leader*
%Hospital & Health Care Union, 330 W 42nd St, #1905, New York, NY 10036, USA

Nicholas, Nicholas J, Jr *Publisher*
%Pluggers Inc, 10065 NW Ash St, Portland, OR 97229, USA

Nicholls, Bernie *Hockey Player*
%Chicago Blackhawks, Chicago Stadium, 1800 W Madison St, Chicago, IL 60612, USA

Nichols, Bobby *Golfer*
8681 Glenlyon Court, Fort Myers, FL 33912, USA

Nichols, David L *Businessman*
%Mercantile Stores Co, 9450 Seward Rd, Fairfield, OH 45014, USA

Nichols, Dorothy L *Financier*
%Farm Credit Administration, 1501 Farm Credit Dr, McLean, VA 22102, USA

Nichols, John D *Businessman*
%Illinois Tool Works, 3600 W Lake Ave, Glenview, IL 60025, USA

Nichols, Kyra *Ballerina*
%New York City Ballet, Lincoln Center Plaza, New York, NY 10023, USA

Nichols, Larry *Rubik Cube Designer*
%Moleculon Research Corp, 139 Main St, Cambridge, MA 02142, USA

Nichols, Mike *Movie Director, Comedian*
%Westbury Hotel, 15 E 69th St, New York, NY 10021, USA

Nichols, Nichelle *Actress*
23281 Leonora Dr, Woodland Hills, CA 91367, USA

Nichols, Peter R *Writer*
%Rochelle Stevens, 2 Terrett's Place, Upper St, London N1 19Z, England

Nichols, Stephen *Actor*
3176 Federal Ave, Los Angeles, CA 90066, USA

Nicholson, Jack *Actor*
9911 W Pico Blvd, #PH-A, Los Angeles, CA 90035, USA

Nicholson, William B (Bill) *Baseball Player*
RR 3, Chestertown, MD 21620, USA

Nickel, Herman W *Diplomat*
%US Institute for Peace, 4701 Willard Ave, #1216, Bethesda, MD 20815, USA

Nickerson, Donald A, Jr *Religious Leader*
%Episcopal Church, 815 2nd Ave, New York, NY 10017, USA

Nickerson, Hardy *Football Player*
%Tampa Bay Buccaneers, 1 Buccaneer Place, Tampa, FL 33607, USA

Nicklaus, Jack W *Golfer*
%Golden Bear International, 11780 US Highway 1, North Palm Beach, FL 33408, USA

Nicks, John *Figure Skating Coach*
%Ice Capades Chalet, 2701 Harbor Blvd, Costa Mesa, CA 92626, USA

Nicks, Michelle *Model*
%Wilhelmina Models, 300 Park Ave S, New York, NY 10010, USA

Nicks, Stevie *Singer, Songwriter*
%Front Line Mgmt, 8900 Wilshire Blvd, #300, Beverly Hills, CA 90211, USA

Nickson, David W *Businessman*
%Scottish & Newcastle Breweries, Holrood Rd, Edinburgh EH8 8YS, Scotland

Nickson-Soul, Julia *Actress*
2232 Moreno Dr, Los Angeles, CA 90039, USA

Nicol, Alex *Actor*
1496 San Leandro Park, Santa Barbara, CA 93108, USA

Nicol, Donald *Publisher*
%Winnipeg Free Press, 300 Carlton St, Winnipeg MB R3C 3A7, Canada

Nicolin, Curt *Businessman*
%ASEA AB, Box 7373, 103 91 Stockholm, Sweden

Nicollier, Claude *Astronaut, Switzerland*
18710 Martinique Dr, Houston, TX 77058, USA

Nicolson, Nigel *Writer*
Sissinghurst Castle, Kent, England

Nidetch, Jean *Businesswoman*
%Weight Watchers International, 3860 Crenshaw Blvd, Los Angeles, CA 90008, USA

Nieder, Bill *Track Athlete*
%General Delivery, Mountain Ranch, CA 95246, USA

Niederhoffer, Victor *Squash Player*
%Niederhoffer Cross Zeckhauser, 757 3rd Ave, New York, NY 10017, USA

Niekro, Joseph F (Joe) *Baseball Player*
38 Shadow Lane, Lakeland, FL 33813, USA

Niekro, Philip H (Phil) *Baseball Player*
6382 Nichols Rd, Flowery Branch, GA 30542, USA

Nielsen, Brigitte *Actress, Model*
%Bartels, PO Box 57593, Sherman Oaks, CA 91413, USA

Nielsen, Gifford *Football Player*
3665 Maranatha Dr, Sugar Land, TX 77479, USA

Nielsen, Leslie *Actor*
1622 Viewmont Dr, Los Angeles, CA 90069, USA

Nielsen, Rick *Singer, Guitarist (Cheap Trick)*
1818 Parmenter St, #202, Middleton, WI 53562, USA

Niemann, Gunda *Speed Skater*
E Hackel Str 6, 99097 Erfurt, Germany

Niemeyer, Gerhart *Political Scientist*
806 E Angela Blvd, South Bend, IN 46617, USA

Niemi, Lisa *Actress*
10960 Dickens St, #302, Sherman Oaks, CA 91423, USA

Nieminen, Toni *Ski Jumper*
%Landen Kanava 99, Vesijarvenkatu 74, 15140 Lahti, Finland

Nierenberg, William A *Physicist*
9581 La Jolla Farms Rd, La Jolla, CA 92037, USA

Nierman, Leonardo *Artist*
Amsterdam 43 PH, Mexico City 11 DF, Mexico

Niewendyk, Joe *Hockey Player*
%Calgary Flames, PO Box 1540, Station "M", Calgary AB T2P 389, Canada

Nigh, George P *Governor, OK; Educator*
%University of Central Oklahoma, 100 N University Dr, Edmond, OK 73034, USA

Nigrelli, Ross F *Pathologist*
29 Barracuda Rd, East Quogue, NY 11942, USA

Nikolayev, Andrian G *Cosmonaut, Air Force General*
%Potchta Kosmonavtov, 141 160 Svyosdny Gorodok, Moskovskoi Oblasti, Russia

Niles, Nicholas H *Publisher*
%Sportng News Publishing Co, 1212 N Lindbergh Blvd, St Louis, MO 63132, USA

Niles, Thomas M T *Diplomat*
PSC 108, Box 560, APO, AE 09842, USA

Nilsson, Birgit *Opera Singer*
Hammenhogs, 270 50 Hammenhog, Sweden

Nilsson, Lars-Goran *Businessman*
%Home Insurance, 59 Maiden Lane, New York, NY 10038, USA

Nilsson, Lennart *Photographer*
%Pantheon Books, 201 E 50th St, New York, NY 10022, USA

Nimoy, Leonard *Actor*
17 Gateway Dr, Batavia, NY 14020, USA

Nin-Culmell, Joaquin M *Composer*
5830 Clover Dr, Oakland, CA 94618, USA

Nininger, Harvey H *Meteoriticist*
PO Box 420, Sedona, AZ 86339, USA

Nipar, Yvette *Actress*
9300 Wilshire Blvd, #410, Beverly Hills, CA 90212, USA

Nipon, Albert *Fashion Designer*
%Leslie Faye Co, Albert Nipon Div, 1400 Broadway, #1600, New York, NY 10018, USA

Nirenberg, Charles — *Businessman*
%Dairy Mart Convenience Stores, 1 Vision Dr, Enfield, CT 06082, USA

Nirenberg, Louis — *Mathematician*
221 W 82nd St, New York, NY 10024, USA

Nirenberg, Marshall W — *Nobel Medicine Laureate*
%National Heart Institute, Biochemical Genetics Lab, Bethesda, MD 20014, USA

Nisbet, Robert A — *Historian, Sociologist*
2828 Wisconsin Ave NW, #102, Washington, DC 20007, USA

Nishio, Suehiro — *Government Official, Japan*
1 Shiba Sakuragawacho, Minatoku, Tokyo, Japan

Nishizawa, Junichi — *Electronics Inventor*
%Semiconductor Research Institute, Sendai, Japan

Nishizuka, Yassutomi — *Pharmacologist*
%Kobe University School of Medicine, Pharmacology Dept, Kobe, Japan

Nishkian, Byron — *Skier*
150 4th St, #PH, San Francisco, CA 94103, USA

Niskanen, William A, Jr — *Government Official, Economist*
%Cato Institute, 1000 Massachusetts Ave NW, #6, Washington, DC 20001, USA

Nitschke, Raymond E (Ray) — *Football Player*
411 Peppermint Court, RR 1, Oneida, WI 54155, USA

Nitze, Paul H — *Secretary, Navy; Diplomat*
1619 Massachusetts Ave NW, #811, Washington, DC 20036, USA

Nitzschke, Dale F — *Educator*
%University of New Hampshire, President's Office, Durham, NH 03824, USA

Niven, Kip — *Actor*
20781 Big Rock Dr, Malibu, CA 90265, USA

Niven, Laurence (Larry) — *Writer*
136 El Camino Dr, Beverly Hills, CA 90212, USA

Niwano, Nikkyo — *Religious Leader*
Rissho Kosei-kai, 2-11-1 Wada Suginamiku, Tokyo 166, Japan

Nixon, Agnes E — *Television Producer, Screenwriter*
774 Conestoga Rd, Rosemont, PA 19010, USA

Nixon, Gary — *Motorcycle Racing Rider*
%Gary Nixon Enterprises, 2408 Carroll Mill Rd, Phoenix, MD 21131, USA

Nixon, Marni — *Singer*
1747 Van Buren St, #790, Hollywood, FL 33020, USA

Nixon, Norm — *Basketball Player*
607 Marguerita Ave, Santa Monica, CA 90402, USA

Niyazov, Saparmurad — *President, Turkmenistan*
%President's Office, Askkhabad, Turkmenistan

Nkomo, Joshua — *Political Leader, Zimbabwe*
%House of Assembly, Salisbury, Zimbabwe

Noah, Yannick — *Tennis Player, Coach*
%ProServe Europe, 20 Rue Billancourt, 92100 Boulogne, France

Noakes, Michael — *Artist*
146 Hamilton Terrace, St John's Wood, London NW8 9UX, England

Nobis, Thomas H (Tommy), Jr — *Football Player, Executive*
40 S Battery Place NE, Atlanta, GA 30342, USA

Noble, Adrian K — *Theater Director*
%Royal Shakespeare Co, Barbican Theater, London EC2, England

Noble, Chelsea — *Actress*
PO Box 8665, Calabasas, CA 91372, USA

Noble, David J — *Businessman*
%Statesman Group, 1400 Des Moines Building, Des Moines, IA 50316, USA

Nobles, Bruce R — *Businessman*
%Hawaiian Airlines, 531 Ohohia St, Honolulu, HI 96819, USA

Nobuhara, Hiroya — *Financier*
%Sanwa Bank California, 444 Market St, San Francisco, CA 94111, USA

Noda, Minoru — *Financier*
%Bank of California, 400 California St, San Francisco, CA 94104, USA

Noe, Vergilius Cardinal — *Religious Leader*
St Peter's Basilica, Vatican City, Rome, Italy

Noel, Philip W — *Governor, RI*
21 Kirby Ave, Warwick, RI 02889, USA

Noguchi, Thomas T — *Pathologist*
1110 Avoca Ave, Pasadena, CA 91105, USA

Noha, Edward J — *Businessman*
%CNA Financial Corp, CNA Plaza, Chicago, IL 60685, USA

Noia, Alan J *Businessman*
%Allegheny Power System, 12 E 49th St, #4900, New York, NY 10017, USA

Noiret, Philippe *Actor*
104 Rue des Sablons, 78750 Mareil-Marly, France

Nojima, Minoru *Concert Pianist*
%Hillyer Kazuko International, 250 W 57th St, New York, NY 10107, USA

Nokes, Matthew D (Matt) *Baseball Player*
%New York Yankees, Yankee Stadium, 161st St & River Ave, Bronx, NY 10451, USA

Nolan, Christopher *Writer*
158 Vernon Ave, Clontanf, Dublin 3, Ireland

Nolan, Jeanette *Actress*
940 Locust Ave, Charlottesville, VA 22901, USA

Nolan, Kathleen *Actress*
360 E 55th St, #PH, New York, NY 10022, USA

Nolan, Kenneth C *Artist*
PO Box 125, South Salem, NY 10590, USA

Nolan, Martin F *Editor*
%Boston Globe, Editorial Dept, 135 Morrissey Blvd, Boston, MA 02128, USA

Nolan, Richard J, Jr *Financier*
%Chemical Bank Delaware, 1201 Market St, Wilmington, DE 19801, USA

Nolan, Ted *Hockey Coach*
%Hartford Whalers, Coliseum, 242 Trumbell St, #800, Hartford, CT 06103, USA

Nolan, Thomas B *Geologist*
2219 California St NW, Washington, DC 20008, USA

Noland, Kenneth *Artist*
RR 2, Box 125, Kitchawan Rd, South Salem, NY 10590, USA

Nolte, Nick *Actor*
6174 Bonsall Dr, Malibu, CA 90265, USA

Nolting, Paul F *Religious Leader*
%Church of Lutheran Confession, 620 E 50th St, Loveland, CO 80538, USA

Nomellini, Leo *Football Player*
520 St Claire Dr, Palo Alto, CA 94306, USA

Noonan, Peggy *Writer*
%Random House Inc, 201 E 50th St, New York, NY 10022, USA

Noonan, Thomas M *Financier*
%Commerce Bank, 8000 Forsyth Blvd, Clayton, MO 63105, USA

Noone, Peter *Singer, Actor*
9265 Robin Lane, Los Angeles, CA 90069, USA

Noor Al-Hussein *Queen, Jordan*
%Royal Palace, Amman, Jordan

Nordenstrom, Bjorn *Cancer Radiologist*
%Karolinska Institute, Radiology Dept, Stockholm, Sweden

Nordli, Odvar *Prime Minister, Norway*
Snarveien 4, 2312 Ottestad, Norway

Nordsieck, Kenneth H *Astronaut*
%University of Wisconsin, Space Astronomy Lab, Madison, WI 53706, USA

Nordstrom, Bruce A *Businessman*
%Nordstrom Inc, 1501 5th Ave, Seattle, WA 98101, USA

Nordstrom, James F *Businessman*
%Nordstrom Inc, 1501 5th Ave, Seattle, WA 98101, USA

Nordstrom, John N *Businessman*
%Nordstrom Inc, 1501 5th Ave, Seattle, WA 98101, USA

Noren, Irving A (Irv) *Baseball Player*
3215 Valley Glen Rd, Oceanside, CA 92056, USA

Norman, Greg *Golfer*
%Great White Shark Enterprises, PO Box 1189, Hobe Sound, FL 33475, USA

Norman, Jack, Sr *Attorney*
3723 West End Ave, Nashville, TN 37205, USA

Norman, Jessye *Concert Singer*
%Shaw Concerts, Lincoln Plaza, 1900 Broadway, #200, New York, NY 10023, USA

Norman, Ken *Basketball Player*
%Atlanta Hawks, 1 CNN Center, South Tower, Atlanta, GA 30303, USA

Norodom Sihanouk, Prince Samdech Preah *King, Cambodia*
%Khemarindra Palace, Phnom Penh, Cambodia

Norrington, Roger A C *Conductor*
%Byers Schwalbe Assoc, 1 5th Ave, New York, NY 10003, USA

Norris, Christopher *Actress*
12747 Riverside Dr, #208, Valley Village, CA 91607, USA

Noia - Norris

Norris, Chuck *Actor*
PO Box 872, Navasota, TX 77868, USA

Norris, Michael K (Mike) *Baseball Player*
1003 Imperial Dr, Hayward, CA 94541, USA

Norris, T C *Businessman*
%P H Glatfelter Co, 228 S Main St, Spring Grove, PA 17362, USA

Norris, Thomas R *Vietnam War Navy Hero (CMH)*
Rt 2, Box 202-A, Hayden Lake, ID 83835, USA

Norsworthy, Lamar *Businessman*
%Holly Corp, 100 Crescent Court, Dallas, TX 75201, USA

North, Andy *Golfer*
%Professional Golfer's Assn, PO Box 109601, Palm Beach Gardens, FL 33410, USA

North, Douglass C *Nobel Economics Laureate*
7569 Homestead Rd, Benzonia, MI 49616, USA

North, Jay *Actor*
290 NE 1st Ave, Lake Butler, FL 32054, USA

North, Oliver L *Government Official, Marine Officer*
RR 1, Box 560, Bluemont, VA 22012, USA

North, Sheree *Actress*
1467 Palisades Dr, Pacific Palisades, CA 90272, USA

Northrip, Richard A *Labor Leader*
%Cement & Allied Workers Union, 2500 Brickdale, Elk Grove Village, IL 60007, USA

Northrop, Wayne *Actor*
21919 W Canon Dr, Topanga, CA 90290, USA

Northrup, James T (Jim) *Baseball Player*
%Freeman-Bocci, 4320 Delemere, Royal Oak, MI 48073, USA

Norton, Gerard Ross (Toys) *WW II Rhodesian Army Hero (VC)*
Box 112, PO Banket, Zimbabwe

Norton, James J *Labor Leader*
%Graphic Communications International, 1900 "L" St NW, Washington, DC 20036, USA

Norton, Ken *Boxer*
16 S Peck Dr, Laguna Niguel, CA 92677, USA

Norton, Ken, Jr *Football Player*
%San Francisco 49ers, 4949 Centennial Blvd, Santa Clara, CA 95054, USA

Norton, Peter *Computer Software Designer*
225 Arizona Ave, #200-W, Santa Monica, CA 90401, USA

Norton, Robert *Businessman*
%Fabri-Centers of America, 5555 Darrow Rd, Hudson, OH 44236, USA

Norton-Taylor, Judy *Actress*
6767 Forest Lawn Dr, #115, Los Angeles, CA 90068, USA

Norville, Deborah *Commentator*
PO Box 426, Mill Neck, NY 11765, USA

Norvo, Kenneth N (Red) *Jazz Vibraphonist*
420 Alta Ave, Santa Monica, CA 90402, USA

Nosseck, Noel *Movie Director*
24124 Malibu Rd, Malibu, CA 90265, USA

Notebaert, Richard C *Businessman*
%Ameritech, 30 S Wacker Dr, Chicago, IL 60606, USA

Noth, Chris *Actor*
%United Talent Agency, 9560 Wilshire Blvd, #500, Beverly Hills, CA 90212, USA

Notkins, Abner L *Virologist*
%National Institute of Dental Research, 9000 Rockville Pike, Bethesda, MD 20205, USA

Noto, Lore *Theater Producer, Actor*
%Sullivan Street Playhouse, 181 Sullivan St, New York, NY 10012, USA

Noto, Lucio A *Businessman*
%Mobil Corp, 3225 Gallows Rd, Fairfax, VA 22037, USA

Nott, John W F *Government Official, England*
%Hillsdown Holdings PLC, 32 Hampstead High St, London NW3 1QD, England

Nottingham, R Kendall *Businessman*
%American Life Insurance Co, 1 Alico Plaza, 600 King St, Wilmington, DE 19801, USA

Nouhak Phoumsavanh *President, Laos*
%President's Office, Presidential House, Vientiane, Laos

Nouri, Michael *Actor*
108 Mira Mesa, Rancho Santa Margarita, CA 92688, USA

Novacek, Jay M *Football Player*
%Dallas Cowboys, 1 Cowboys Parkway, Irving, TX 75063, USA

Novak Popper, Ilona *Swimmer*
Il-Orso-U 23, Budapest, Hungary

N

Novak, John R — *Inventor (Air Cleaning Radiator)*
%Engelhard Corp, Automotive Emissions Systems, 101 Wood Ave, Iselin, NJ 08830, USA

Novak, Kim — *Actress*
PO Box 339, Chiloquin, OR 97624, USA

Novak, Michael — *Theologian*
%American Enterprise Institute, 1150 17th St NW, Washington, DC 20036, USA

Novak, Robert D S — *Columnist*
1750 Pennsylvania Ave NW, #1312, Washington, DC 20006, USA

Novello (Fr Guido Sarducci), Don — *Comedian*
%Vesuvio Olive Oil Co, PO Box 245, Fairfax, CA 94978, USA

Novello, Antonia C — *Medical Administrator*
1315 31st St NW, Washington, DC 20007, USA

Novosel, Michael J — *Vietnam War Army Hero (CMH)*
202 Oakwood Dr, Enterprise, AL 36330, USA

Novotna, Jana — *Tennis Player*
%Women's Tennis Assn, 133 1st St NE, St Petersburg, FL 33701, USA

Nowak, John M — *Air Force General*
Deputy Chief of Staff, Logistics, HqUSAF, Pentagon, Washington, DC 20330, USA

Noyce, Phillip — *Movie Director*
%International Creative Mgmt, 8942 Wilshire Blvd, Beverly Hills, CA 90211, USA

Noyd, R Allen — *Religious Leader*
%General Council, Christian Church, Box 141-A, RD 1, Transfer, PA 16154, USA

Noyes, Albert, Jr — *Chemist*
5102 Fairview Dr, Austin, TX 78731, USA

Noyes, George W — *Financier*
%Standish Ayer & Wood, 1 Financial Center, Boston, MA 02111, USA

Noyes, Richard M — *Chemist*
2014 Elk Ave, Eugene, OR 97403, USA

Noyo Sanchez, Aristides — *President, Panama*
PO Box 3333, Panama City, Panama

Nozawa, Hiroo — *Financier*
%Bank of California, 400 California St, San Francisco, CA 94104, USA

Nozick, Robert — *Philosopher*
%Harvard University, Emerson Hall, Cambridge, MA 02138, USA

Nsengiyremeye, Dismas — *Prime Minister, Rwanda*
%Prime Minister's Office, Kigali, Rwanda

Ntombi — *Queen, Swaziland*
%Royal Residence, PO Box 1, Lobamba, Swaziland

Nuami, Sheikh Humaidbin Rashid al- — *Ruler, Ajman*
%Royal Palace, Ajman, United Arab Emirates

Nucatola, John P — *Basketball Referee*
61-47 210th St, Bayside, NY 11364, USA

Nucci, Leo — *Opera Singer*
%Herbert Breslin Inc, 119 W 57th St, New York, NY 10019, USA

Nugent, Nelle — *Theater Producer*
%Foxboro Entertainment, 133 E 58th St, #301, New York, NY 10022, USA

Nugent, Ted — *Singer, Guitarist*
%Madhouse Mgmt, PO Box 15108, Ann Arbor, MI 48106, USA

Nujoma, Sam S — *President, Namibia*
%President's Office, State House, Mugabe Ave, 9000 Windhoek, Namibia

Nunley, Frank — *Football Player*
24632 Olive Tree Lane, Los Altos Hills, CA 94024, USA

Nunn, Louie B — *Governor, KY*
RR 3, Park, KY 42749, USA

Nunn, Trevor R — *Theater Director*
%Royal Shakespeare Theater, Stratford-upon-Avon, Warwickshire, England

Nurmi (Vampira), Maila — *Actress*
844 1/2 N Hudson, Los Angeles, CA 90038, USA

Nussbaum, Karen — *Labor Activist*
%9 to 5 National Assn of Working Women, 614 Superior Ave, Cleveland, OH 44113, USA

Nusslein-Volhard, Christiane — *Nobel Medicine Laureatet*
%Max Planck Biology Institute, Spenmammstr 35/111, 72076 Tubingen, Germany

Nutt, Jim — *Artist*
1035 Greenwood Ave, Wilmette, IL 60091, USA

Nutting, H Anthony — *Government Official, England*
7 Ashchurch Park Villas, London W12 9SP, England

Nutting, Wallace H — *Army General*
PO Box 96, Biddeford Pool, ME 04006, USA

Novak - Nutting

N

Nutzle, Futzie *Artist, Cartoonist*
PO Box 325, Aromas, CA 95004, USA

Nuwer, Hank *Writer, Journalist*
%Arts Indiana Magazine, 47 S Pennsylvania St, Indianapolis, IN 46204, USA

Nuxhall, Joseph H (Joe) *Baseball Player*
5706 Lindenwood Lane, Fairfield, OH 45014, USA

Nuyen, France *Actress*
1800 Franklin Canyon Terrace, Beverly Hills, CA 90210, USA

Nyad, Diana *Swimmer, Sportscaster*
%Uptown Racquet Club, 151 E 86th St, New York, NY 10028, USA

Nye, Carrie *Actress*
200 W 57th St, #900, New York, NY 10019, USA

Nye, Eric *Businessman*
%Texas Utilities Co, 1601 Bryan St, Dallas, TX 75201, USA

Nye, Joseph S, Jr *Political Scientist*
%Harvard University, John Kennedy Government School, Cambridge, MA 02138, USA

Nye, Louis *Actor*
1241 Corsica Dr, Pacific Palisades, CA 90272, USA

Nye, Robert *Writer*
2 Westbury Crescent, Wilton, Cork, Ireland

Nyerere, Julius K *President, Tanzania*
%Sokiene University, PO Box 3000, Chuo Kikuu, Morogoro, Tanzania

Nyers, Rezso *Secretary General, Hungary*
%Representatives House, Szechenyi Rakpart 19, 1054 Budapest, Hungary

Nygren, Carrie *Model*
%Elite Model Mgmt, 111 E 22nd St, #200, New York, NY 10010, USA

Nykvist, Sven *Cinematographer*
%Dove Films, 6387 Ivarene Ave, Los Angeles, CA 90068, USA

Nyman, Michael *Composer*
%Michael Nyman Ltd, PO Box 430, High Wycombe HP13 5QT, England

Nyro, Laura *Singer, Songwriter*
PO Box 186, Shoreham, NY 11786, USA

Nystrom, Joakim *Tennis Player*
Torsgatan 194, 931 00 Skellefteaa, Sweden

Nutzle - Nystrom

O

O'Bannon, Ed *Basketball Player*
%New Jersey Nets, Byrne Meadowlands Arena, East Rutherford, NJ 07073, USA

O'Berry, Carl G *Air Force General*
Deputy CofS, Command Control Communications, HqUSAF, Washington, DC 20330, USA

O'Boyle, Maureen *Entertainer*
%"A Current Affair" Show, Fox-TV, PO Box 900, Beverly Hills, CA 90213, USA

O'Brasky, David *Publisher*
%Vanity Fair Magazine, 350 Madison Ave, New York, NY 10017, USA

O'Brian, Hugh *Actor*
%Hugh O'Brian Youth Foundation, 10880 Wilshire Blvd, #900, Los Angeles, CA 90024, USA

O'Brian, Patrick *Writer*
19536 Crystal Rock Dr, Germantown, MD 20874, USA

O'Brien, Brian *Physicist*
PO Box 166, North Hollywood, CT 06281, USA

O'Brien, Cathy *Track Athlete*
19 Foss Farm Rd, Durham, NH 03824, USA

O'Brien, Conan *Entertainer*
125 N Wetherly Dr, Los Angeles, CA 90048, USA

O'Brien, Conor Cruise *Writer; Diplomat, Ireland*
Whitewater, The Summit, Howth, Dublin, Ireland

O'Brien, Dan *Track Athlete*
PO Box 9244, Moscow, ID 83843, USA

O'Brien, Edna *Writer*
%Weidenfeld & Nicolson, Orion House, 5 Upper St, London WC2H 9EA, England

O'Brien, G Dennis *Educator*
PO Box 510, RD 3, Middlebury, VT 05753, USA

O'Brien, George H, Jr *Korean War Marine Corps Hero (CMH)*
2001 Douglas St, Midland, TX 79701, USA

O'Brien, Gregory M *Educator*
%University of New Orleans, Chancellor's Office, New Orleans, LA 70148, USA

O'Brien, Ian *Swimmer*
PO Box 36, Forestville NSW 2087, Australia

O'Brien, Ken *Football Player*
%New York Jets, 1000 Fulton Ave, Hempstead, NY 11550, USA

O'Brien, L Douglas *Financier*
%Bank of Ireland First Holdings, 1000 Elm St, Manchester, NH 03101, USA

O'Brien, M Vincent *Thoroughbred Racing Trainer*
Ballydoyle House, Cashel, County Tipperary, Ireland

O'Brien, Margaret *Actress*
1250 La Peresa Dr, Thousand Oaks, CA 91362, USA

O'Brien, Parry *Track Athlete*
73285 Goldflower St, Palm Desert, CA 92260, USA

O'Brien, Pat *Sportscaster*
%CBS-TV, Sports Dept, 51 W 52nd St, New York, NY 10019, USA

O'Brien, Raymond F *Businessman*
%Consolidated Freightways, 3240 Hillview Ave, Palo Alto, CA 94304, USA

O'Brien, Thomas H *Financier*
%PNC Bank Corp, 5th Ave & Wood St, Pittsburgh, PA 15222, USA

O'Brien, Thomas M *Financier*
%North Side Savings Bank, 185 W 231st St, Bronx, NY 10463, USA

O'Brien, Tim *Writer*
17 Partride Lane, Boxford, MA 01921, USA

O'Brien, Virginia *Actress*
PO Box 456, Wrightwood, CA 92397, USA

O'Byrne, Bryan *Actor*
9200 Sunset Blvd, #801, Los Angeles, CA 90069, USA

O'Callaghan, Mike *Governor, NV*
%Las Vegas Sun, 121 S Martin Luther King Blvd, Las Vegas, NV 89106, USA

O'Connell, Maura *Singer*
%Monterey Artists, 901 18th Ave S, Nashville, TN 37212, USA

O'Connor, Bryan D *Astronaut*
%NASA, Johnson Space Center, 2101 NASA Rd, Houston, TX 77058, USA

O'Connor, Carroll *Actor*
30826 Broad Beach Rd, Malibu, CA 90265, USA

O'Connor, Donald *Actor, Dancer*
PO Box 20204, Sedona, AZ 86341, USA

O'Connor, Glynnis *Actress*
%Bill Treusch Assoc, 853 7th Ave, #9-A, New York, NY 10019, USA

O'Bannon - O'Connor

O

O'Connor, J Dennis — *Educator*
%University of Pittsburgh, President's Office, Pittsburgh, PA 15260, USA

O'Connor, James J — *Businessman*
%Commonwealth Edison Co, 1 First National Plaza, PO Box 767, Chicago, IL 60690, USA

O'Connor, John J Cardinal — *Religious Leader*
%Archdiocese of New York, 452 Madison Ave, New York, NY 10022, USA

O'Connor, Martin J — *Religious Leader*
Palazzo San Carlo, 00120 Vatican City, Rome, Italy

O'Connor, Sandra Day — *Supreme Court Justice*
%US Supreme Court, 1 1st St NE, Washington, DC 20543, USA

O'Connor, Sinead — *Singer*
35 Harwood Rd, Fulham, London W1V 3AT, England

O'Connor, Thom — *Artist*
Moss Rd, Voorheesville, NY 12186, USA

O'Connor, Timothy J — *Actor*
%Artists Agency, 10000 Santa Monica Blvd, #305, Los Angeles, CA 90067, USA

O'Day, Anita — *Singer*
%Alan Eichler, 1524 LaBaig Ave, Los Angeles, CA 90028, USA

O'Day, Molly — *Singer*
PO Box 2123, Avila Beach, CA 93424, USA

O'Donnell, Chris — *Actress*
1724 N Vista St, Los Angeles, CA 90046, USA

O'Donnell, John J — *Labor Leader*
%Air Line Pilots Assn, 1625 Massachusetts Ave NW, Washington, DC 20036, USA

O'Donnell, Rosie — *Actress*
%Bernie Young Agency, 9800 Topanga Canyon Blvd, #D, Chatsworth, CA 91311, USA

O'Donnell, Thomas M — *Financier*
%McDonald Co Investments, 800 Superior Ave, Cleveland, OH 44114, USA

O'Donnell, William — *Harness Racing Driver*
%O'Donnell Stable, PO Box 165, Cranbury, NJ 08512, USA

O'Donnell, William T — *Labor Leader*
%United Garment Workers, PO Box 239, Hermitage, TN 37076, USA

O'Donovan, Leo J — *Educator*
%Georgetown University, President's Office, Washington, DC 20057, USA

O'Driscoll, Martha — *Actress*
22 Indian Circle Dr, Indian Creek Village, Miami Beach, FL 33154, USA

O'Grady, Gail — *Actress*
%Badgley Connor, 9229 Sunset Blvd, #311, Los Angeles, CA 90069, USA

O'Grady, Lani — *Actress*
%First Artists Agency, 10000 Riverside Dr, #10, Toluca Lake, CA 91602, USA

O'Grady, Mac — *Golfer*
%Professional Golfer's Assn, PO Box 109601, Palm Beach Gardens, FL 33410, USA

O'Grady, Scott — *Air Force Pilot*
3519 Wallingford Ave N, Seattle, WA 98103, USA

O'Grady, Sean — *Boxer*
%"Tuesday Night Fights" Show, USA-TV, 1230 Ave of Americas, New York, NY 10020, USA

O'Hair, Madalyn Murray — *Social Activist*
2210 Hancock Dr, Austin, TX 78756, USA

O'Hara, Jenny — *Actress*
8663 Wonderland Ave, Los Angeles, CA 90046, USA

O'Hara, Maureen — *Actress*
PO Box 1400, Christeansted, St Croix, VI 00821, USA

O'Hara, Terrence J — *Movie Director*
%Armstrong/Hirsch, 1888 Century Park East, #1800, Los Angeles, CA 90067, USA

O'Hare, Dean R — *Businessman*
%Chubb Corp, 15 Mountain View Rd, Warren, NJ 07059, USA

O'Hare, Don R — *Businessman*
%Sundstrand Corp, 4949 Harrison Ave, Rockford, IL 61108, USA

O'Hare, Joseph A — *Educator*
%Fordham University, President's Office, Bronx, NY 10458, USA

O'Herlihy, Daniel — *Actor*
%Artists Group, 10100 Santa Monica Blvd, #2490, Los Angeles, CA 90067, USA

O'Horgan, Thomas F (Tom) — *Composer, Director*
%William Morris Agency, 1325 Ave of Americas, New York, NY 10019, USA

O'Keefe, Michael — *Actor*
25150 Malibu Rd, Malibu, CA 90265, USA

O'Keefe, Miles — *Actor*
%Paige Management Group, PO Box 2132, Malibu, CA 90265, USA

O'Connor - O'Keefe

O

O'Koren, Mike *Basketball Player*
%New Jersey Nets, Byrne Meadowlands Arena, East Rutherford, NJ 07073, USA

O'Leary, Brian T *Astronaut*
1993 S Kihei Rd, #21200, Kihei, HI 96753, USA

O'Leary, Hazel R *Secretary, Energy*
%Energy Department, 1000 Independence Ave SW, Washington, DC 20585, USA

O'Leary, Robert W *Businessman*
%American Medical Holdings, 14001 Dallas Parkway, Dallas, TX 75240, USA

O'Leary, Thomas H *Businessman*
%Burlington Resources Inc, PO Box 4239, Houston, TX 77210, USA

O'Loughlin, Gerald S *Actor*
PO Box 340832, Arleta, CA 91334, USA

O'Maley, David B *Businessman*
%Ohio National Life Insurance, 237 William H Taft Rd, Cincinnati, OH 45215, USA

O'Malley, Karina *Sociologist*
%St Norbert College, Sociology Dept, De Pere, WI 54115, USA

O'Malley, Peter *Baseball Executive*
%Los Angeles Dodgers, 1000 Elysian Park Ave, Los Angeles, CA 90012, USA

O'Malley, Robert E *Vietnam War Marine Corps Hero (CMH)*
PO Box 775, Goldthwaite, TX 76844, USA

O'Malley, Susan *Basketball Executive*
%Washington Bullets, Capital Centre, 1 Truman Dr, Landover, MD 20785, USA

O'Malley, Thomas D *Businessman*
%Tosco Inc, 72 Cummings Point Rd, Stamford, CT 06902, USA

O'Malley, Thomas P *Educator*
%Loyola Marymount University, President's Office, Los Angeles, CA 90045, USA

O'Mara, Donald J *Businessman*
%Hexcel Corp, 5794 W Las Positas Blvd, Pleasanton, CA 94588, USA

O'Mara, Mark *Harness Racing Driver, Trainer*
6882 NW 65th Terrace, Pompano Beach, FL 33067, USA

O'Meara, Mark *Golfer*
%International Management Group, 1 Erieview Plaza, #1300, Cleveland, OH 44114, USA

O'Neal, A Daniel, Jr *Government Official*
1613 Forest Lane, McLean, VA 22101, USA

O'Neal, Alexander *Singer, Songwriter*
%Famous Artists Agency, 1700 Broadway, #500, New York, NY 10019, USA

O'Neal, Bob H *Businessman*
%Stewart & Stevenson Services, 2707 North Loop W, Houston, TX 77008, USA

O'Neal, Edward A *Financier*
%Bank of Boston Corp, 100 Federal St, Boston, MA 02110, USA

O'Neal, Griffin *Actor*
14209 Riverside Dr, Van Nuys, CA 91423, USA

O'Neal, Leslie *Football Player*
%San Diego Chargers, Jack Murphy Stadium, San Diego, CA 92160, USA

O'Neal, Ryan *Actor*
21368 Pacific Coast Highway, Malibu, CA 90265, USA

O'Neal, Shaquille R *Basketball Player*
%Orlando Magic, Orlando Arena, 1 Magic Place, Orlando, FL 32801, USA

O'Neal, Tatum *Actress*
200 East End Ave, #16-H, New York, NY 10128, USA

O'Neil, F J *Actor*
12228 Cantura St, Studio City, CA 91604, USA

O'Neil, Thomas F *Businessman*
%General Tire & Rubber Co, 1 General St, Akron, OH 44329, USA

O'Neil, Tricia *Actress*
%David Shapira Assoc, 15301 Ventura Blvd, #345, Sherman Oaks, CA 91403, USA

O'Neill, Brian F *Hockey Executive*
%Hockey Hall of Fame, Exhibition Place, Toronto ON M6K 3C3, Canada

O'Neill, Dick *Actor*
230 S Lasky Dr, Beverly Hills, CA 90212, USA

O'Neill, Ed *Actor*
2607 Grand Canal, Venice, CA 90291, USA

O'Neill, Eugene F *Communications Engineer*
17 Dellwood Court, Middletown, NJ 07748, USA

O'Neill, Gail *Model*
%Click Model Mgmt, 881 7th Ave, New York, NY 10019, USA

O'Neill, Jennifer *Actress, Model*
%Oscar Productions, 32356 Mulholland Highway, Malibu, CA 90265, USA

O'Koren - O'Neill

O'Neill, Malcolm R *Army General*
Ballistic Missile Defense Organization, HqUSArmy, Pentagon, Washington, 20301, USA

O'Neill, Michael J *Editor*
23 Cayuga Rd, Scarsdale, NY 10583, USA

O'Neill, Paul H *Businessman, Baseball Executive*
%Aluminum Co of America, 1501 Alcoa Building, Pittsburgh, PA 15219, USA

O'Neill, Shane *Television Executive*
%RKO General Inc, 1440 Broadway, New York, NY 10018, USA

O'Neill, Terence P *Photographer*
8 Warwick Ave, London W2 1XB, England

O'Neill, William A *Governor, CT*
Meeks Point, East Hampton, CT 06424, USA

O'Quinn, John M *Attorney*
%O'Quinn Kerensky McAnich, 2300 Lyric Center, 440 Louisiana, Houston, TX 77002, USA

O'Reilly, Anthony J F *Businessman, Publisher*
%H J Heinz Co, 600 Grant St, Pittsburgh, PA 15219, USA

O'Rourke Keiski, Heidi *Synchronized Swimmer*
400 NE 13th Ave, Gainesville, FL 32601, USA

O'Rourke, Charles *Football Player*
220 Bedford St, Bridgewater, MA 02324, USA

O'Rourke, J Tracy *Businessman*
%Varian Assoc, 3050 Hansen Way, Palo Alto, CA 94304, USA

O'Shea, Kevin *Basketball Player*
%Marovich & O'Shea, 215 Leidesdorff St, San Francisco, CA 94111, USA

O'Shea, Milo *Actor*
%Bancroft Hotel, 40 W 72nd St, #17-A, New York, NY 10023, USA

O'Sullivan, Maureen *Actress*
1839 Union St, Schenectady, NY 12309, USA

O'Sullivan, Peter *Editor*
%Houston Post, Editorial Dept, 4747 Southwest Freeway, Houston, TX 77027, USA

O'Toole, Annette *Actress*
%William Morris Agency, 151 S El Camino Dr, Beverly Hills, CA 90212, USA

O'Toole, Peter *Actor*
%Veerline Ltd, 8 Baker St, London W1A 1DA, England

O'Toole, Robert J *Businessman*
%A O Smith Corp, 11270 W Park Place, Milwaukee, WI 53224, USA

Oakes, John B *Editor*
1120 5th Ave, New York, NY 10128, USA

Oakley, Charles *Basketball Player*
%New York Knicks, Madison Square Garden, 4 Penn Plaza, New York, NY 10001, USA

Oaks, Robert C (Bob) *Air Force General, Businessman*
%USAir Group Inc, 2345 Crystal Dr, Arlington, VA 22227, USA

Oates, Adam R *Hockey Player*
%Boston Bruins, Boston Garden, 150 Causeway St, Boston, MA 02114, USA

Oates, John *Singer (Hall & Oates), Songwriter*
%Horizon Entertainment, 130 W 57th St, #12-B, New York, NY 10019, USA

Oates, Johnny L *Baseball Manager*
3718 Pertshire Lane, Colonial Heights, VA 23834, USA

Oates, Joyce Carol *Writer*
%Princeton University, English Dept, Princeton, NJ 08540, USA

Oates, Simon *Actor*
%International Artistes, 235 Regent St, London W1R 8AX, England

Obando Bravo, Miguel Cardinal *Religious Leader*
Arzobispado, Apartado 3050, Managua, Nicaragua

Obasanjo, Olusegun *President, Nigeria; Army General*
%Obasanjo Farms Nigeria Ltd, PO Box 90, Otta, Ogun State, Nigeria

Obato, Gyo *Architect*
%Hellmuth Obato Kassabaum, 1831 Chestnut St, St Louis, MO 63103, USA

Ober, Eric W *Television Executive*
%CBS-TV, News Division, 524 W 57th St, New York, NY 10019, USA

Oberding, Mark *Basketball Player*
%Sacramento Kings, 1 Sports Parkway, Sacramento, CA 95834, USA

Oberg, Margo *Surfer*
RR1, Box 73, Koloa, Kaui HI 96756, USA

Oberlin, David W *Government Official*
800 Independence Ave SW, #814, Washington, DC 20591, USA

Obermeyer, Klaus F *Fashion Designer*
%Sport Obermeyer, 115 Atlantic Ave, Aspen, CO 81611, USA

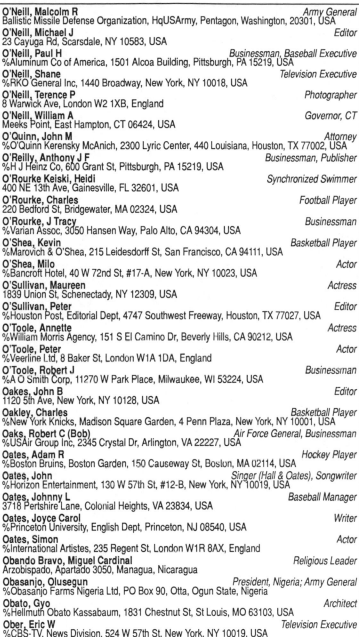

O

O'Neill - Obermeyer

O

Obote, A Milton — *President, Uganda*
%Uganda People's Congress, PO Box 1951, Kampala, Uganda

Obraztsova, Elena V — *Opera Singer*
%Bolshoi Theater, Teatralnaya Pl 1, 103009 Moscow, Russia

Ocean, Billy — *Singer, Songwriter*
%Arista Records, 6 W 57th St, New York, NY 10019, USA

Ochiltree, Ned A, Jr — *Businessman*
74 Briarwood Circle, Hinsdale, IL 60521, USA

Ochirbat, Punsalmaagiyn — *President, Mongolia*
%Presidential Palace, Ulan Bator, Mongolia

Ochman, Wieslaw — *Opera Singer*
Ul Miaczynska 46-B, 02-637 Warsaw, Poland

Ochoa, Ellen — *Astronaut*
%NASA, Johnson Space Center, 2101 NASA Rd, Houston, TX 77058, USA

Ockels, Wubbo — *Astronaut, Netherlands*
%ESTEC, Postbus 299, 2200 AG Noordwijk, Netherlands

Oddi, Silvio Cardinal — *Religious Leader*
Via Pompeo Magno 21, 00192 Rome, Italy

Oddsson, David — *Prime Minister, Iceland*
%Prime Minister's Office, Stjo'rnaaroshusio, 150 Reykjavik, Iceland

Odegaard, Charles E — *Educator*
%University of Washington, Education College, Seattle, WA 98195, USA

Odell, Bob — *Football Player, Coach*
35 Beth Ellen Dr, Lewisburg, PA 17837, USA

Odell, Noel E — *Geological Researcher, Mountaineer*
5 Dean Court, Cambridge, England

Odermatt, Robert A — *Architect*
39 Drury Lane, Berkeley, CA 94705, USA

Odetta — *Singer*
%Douglas Yeager Productions, 300 W 55th St, New York, NY 10019, USA

Odjig, Daphne — *Artist*
PO Box 111, Anglemont BC V0E 1A0, Canada

Odom, William E — *Army General*
%Hudson Institute, 1015 18th St NW, #200, Washington, DC 20036, USA

Odom, William E — *Financier*
%Ford Motor Credit Co, American Rd, Dearborn, MI 48121, USA

Odomes, Nate — *Football Player*
%Seattle Seahawks, 11220 NE 53rd St, Kirkland, WA 98033, USA

Oduber, Nelson O — *Prime Minister, Aruba*
%Prime Minister's Office, Oranjestad, Aruba

Odum, Eugene P — *Ecologist*
30602 Beech Creek Rd, Athens, GA 30606, USA

Oe, Kenzaburo — *Nobel Literature Laureate*
585 Seijo-machi, Setagayaku, Tokyo, Japan

Oenish, Dean — *Physician*
%Preventive Medical Research Inst, 900 Bridgeway, #2, Sausalito, CA 94965, USA

Oerter, Alfred A (Al) — *Track Athlete*
19435 Doewood Dr, Monument, CO 80132, USA

Oesterreicher, James E — *Businessman*
%J C Penney Co, PO Box 10001, Dallas, TX 75301, USA

Ogasawara, Isamu — *Financier*
%Yamaichi International, 2 World Trade Center, New York, NY 10048, USA

Ogden, Carlos C — *WW II Army Hero (CMH)*
8786 Grape Wagon Circle, San Jose, CA 95135, USA

Ogden, Ralph L — *Businessman*
%Liberty Life Insurance, PO Box 789, Greenville, SC 29602, USA

Ogi, Adolf — *President, Switzerland*
Bundesjause-Nord, Kochergasse 10, 3003 Berne, Switzerland

Ogilvie, Lana — *Model*
%Company Models, 270 Lafayette St, #1400, New York, NY 10012, USA

Ogilvy, David M — *Businessman*
Chateau de Touffou, 86300 Bonnes, France

Oglivie, Benjamin A (Ben) — *Baseball Player*
2019 E Myrna Lane, Tempe, AZ 85284, USA

Ogrodnick, John — *Hockey Player*
%New York Rangers, Madison Square Garden, 4 Penn Plaza New York, NY 10001, USA

Oh, Sadaharu — *Baseball Player*
%Yomiuri Giants, 1-7-1 Otemachi, Chiyodaku, Tokyo 100, Japan

Ohara, Elichi *Businessman*
%Fuji Heavy Industries, 1-7-2 Nishi-Shinjuku, Shinjukuku, Tokyo 160, Japan

Ohara, Sakae *Businessman*
%Daihatsu Motor Co, 1-1 Daihatsucho, Ikeda City 563, Japan

Ohira, Masayoshi *Prime Minister, Japan*
105 Komagome Hayashicho, Bunkyoku, Tokyo, Japan

Ohlmeyer, Donald W, Jr *Television Executive*
%NBC West Coast, NBC-TV, 30 Rockefeller Plaza, New York, NY 10112, USA

Ohlsson, Garrick *Concert Pianist*
%Vincent Ryan, 135 W 16th St, New York, NY 10011, USA

Ohman, Jack *Editorial Cartoonist (Mixed Media)*
%Portland Oregonian, Editorial Dept, 1320 SW Broadway, Portland, OR 97201, USA

Ohnishi, Minoru *Businessman*
%Fuji Photo Film Co, 26-30 Nishiazabu, Minatoku, Tokyo 106, Japan

Ohno, Susumu *Geneticist*
7329 Oak Dr, Glendora, CA 91741, USA

Ohtani, Ichiji *Businessman*
%Toyobo Co, 2-2-8 Dojimahama, Kitaku, Osaka 530, Japan

Ohtani, Monshu Koshin *Religious Leader*
Horikawa-dori, Hanayachosagaru, Shimogyoku, Kyoto 600, Japan

Ohyama, Heiichiro *Conductor*
2878 Angelo Dr, Los Angeles, CA 90077, USA

Oimeon, Casper *Skier*
540 S Mountain Ave, Ashland, OR 97520, USA

Oistrakh, Igor *Concert Violinist*
Novolesnaya Str 3, Korp 2, #10, Moscow, Russia

Ojukwu, Chukwuemeka O *Head of State, Biafra; Army General*
75 Marine Rd, Apapa, Lagos, Nigeria

Okamoto, Ayako *Golfer*
%Ladies Professional Golf Assn, 2570 Volusia Ave, Daytona Beach, FL 32114, USA

Okamoto, Tochiro *Businessman*
%Isuzu Motors Ltd, 6-22-10 Minamioi, Shinagawaku, Tokyo 140, Japan

Okamura, Arthur *Artist*
210 Kale St, Bolinas, CA 94924, USA

Okhotnikoff, Nikolai P *Opera Singer*
Canal Griboedova 109, 190068 St Petersburg, Russia

Okubo, Susumu *Physicist*
1209 East Ave, Rochester, NY 14607, USA

Okuda, Hiroshi *Businessman*
%Toyota Motor Corp, 1 Toyotacho, Toyota City, Aicji Prefecture 471, Japan

Olafsson, Olafur J *Publisher*
%Sony Electronics Publishing Co USA, 9 W 57th St, New York, NY 10019, USA

Olah, George A *Nobel Chemistry Laureate*
2252 Gloaming Way, Beverly Hills, CA 90210, USA

Olajuwon, Hakeem A *Basketball Player*
%Houston Rockets, Summit, Greenway Plaza, #10, Houston, TX 77277, USA

Olberman, Keith *Sportscaster*
%ESPN-TV, Sports Dept, ESPN Plaza, Bristol, CT 06010, USA

Olczyk, Ed *Hockey Player*
%Winnipeg Jets, Arena, 15-1430 Maroons Rd, Winnipeg MB R3G 0L5, Canada

Old, Lloyd J *Cancer Biologist*
%Ludwig Institute of Cancer Research, 1345 Ave of Americas, New York, NY 10105, USA

Oldenburg, Claes T *Sculptor*
556 Broome St, New York, NY 10013, USA

Oldenburg, Richard E *Museum Director*
%Museum of Modern Art, 11 W 53rd St, New York, NY 10019, USA

Oldendorf, William *Physician*
%University of California Medical Center, Neurology Dept, Los Angeles, CA 90024, USA

Oldfield, Bruce *Fashion Designer*
27 Beauchamp Place, London SW3, England

Oldfield, Mike *Singer, Songwriter*
%Management Works, 32 Galena Rd, Singes House, London W6 OLT, England

Oldham, Todd *Fashion Designer*
499 7th Ave, #800, New York, NY 10018, USA

Oldman, Gary *Actor*
%International Creative Mgmt, 76 Oxford St, London W1N 0AX, England

Olds, Robin *WW II Air Force Hero, Football Player*
PO Box 1478, Steamboat Springs, CO 80477, USA

O

Ohara - Olds

O

Oleksy, Jozef *Prime Minister, Poland*
%Ul Ursad Rady Ministrow, Ul Wiejska 4/8, 00-583 Warsaw, Poland

Olerud, John G *Baseball Player*
1310 180th Ave NE, Bellevue, WA 98008, USA

Olevsky, Julian *Concert Violinist*
68 Blue Hills Rd, Amherst, MA 01002, USA

Oliansky, Joel *Movie Director, Writer*
%Creative Artists Agency, 9830 Wilshire Blvd, Beverly Hills, CA 90212, USA

Olin, Ken *Actor*
522 Arbamar Place, Pacific Palisades, CA 90272, USA

Olin, Lena *Actress*
Strindbergsgatan 49, 115 31 Stockholm, Sweden

Oliphant, Patrick *Editorial Cartoonist*
%Universal Press Syndicate, 4900 Main St, #900, Kansas City, KS 64112, USA

Olitski, Jules *Artist*
PO Box 440, Marlboro, VT 05344, USA

Oliva, L Jay *Educator*
%New York University, President's Office, New York, NY 10012, USA

Oliva, Pedro (Tony) *Baseball Player*
212 Spring Valley Dr, Bloomington, MN 55420, USA

Oliva, Sergio *Body Builder*
%Oliva's Gym, 7383 Rogers Ave, Chicago, IL 60626, USA

Olivares, Ruben *Boxer*
%Geno Productions, PO Box 113, Montebello, CA 90640, USA

Oliveira, Elmar *Concert Violinist*
%Shaw Concerts, Lincoln Plaza, 1900 Broadway, #200, New York, NY 10023, USA

Oliveira, Nathan *Artist*
785 Santa Maria Ave, Palo Alto, CA 94305, USA

Oliver, Albert (Al) *Baseball Player*
%Shawnee State University, Athletic Dept, Portsmouth, OH 45662, USA

Oliver, Covey T *Attorney, Diplomat*
Ingleton-on-Miles, RFD 1, Box 194, Easton, MD 21601, USA

Oliver, Daniel *Government Official*
%Heritage Foundation, 214 Massachusetts Ave NW, Washington, DC 20002, USA

Oliver, Edith *Theater Critic*
%New Yorker Magazine, Editorial Dept, 20 W 43rd St, New York, NY 10036, USA

Olivero, Magda *Opera Singer*
%Matthews/Napal Ltd, 270 West End Ave, New York, NY 10023, USA

Olivor, Jane *Singer*
%William Morris Agency, 151 S El Camino Dr, Beverly Hills, CA 90212, USA

Olmedo, Alex *Tennis Player*
5067 Woodley Ave, Encino, CA 91436, USA

Olmos, Edward James *Actor*
18034 Ventura Blvd, #228, Encino, CA 91316, USA

Olney, Claude W *Educator*
%Olney 'A' Seminars, PO Box 686, Scottsdale, AZ 85252, USA

Olscamp, Paul J *Educator*
%Bowling Green State University, President's Office, Bowling Green, OH 43403, USA

Olsen, Jack *Writer*
7954 NE Baker Hill Rd, Bainbridge Island, WA 98110, USA

Olsen, Merlin J *Football Player, Sportscaster*
714 E California Blvd, Pasadena, CA 91106, USA

Olsen, Paul E *Geologist*
%Columbia University, Lamont-Doherty Geoigical Laboratory, New York, NY 10027, USA

Olson, Allen I *Governor, ND*
6951 Raven Court, Eden Prairie, MN 55346, USA

Olson, Gary G *Financier*
%Norwest Bank South Dakota, PO Box 5128, Sioux Falls, SD 57117, USA

Olson, James *Actor*
250 W 57th St, #2223, New York, NY 10107, USA

Olson, Lute *Basketball Coach*
%University of Arizona, McKale Memorial Center, Tucson, AZ 85721, USA

Olson, Nancy *Actress*
945 N Alpine Dr, Beverly Hills, CA 90210, USA

Olsson, Curt G *Financier*
%Skandinaviska Enskilda Banken, 106 40, Stockholm, Sweden

Olsten, Stuart P *Businessman*
%Olsten Corp, 175 Broad Hollow Rd, Melville, NY 11747, USA

Olszewski, Jan — *Prime Minister, Poland*
Biuro Poselskie, Al Ujazdowskie 13, 00-567 Warsaw, Poland

Olszewski, John — *Football Player*
1534 Grand Ave, Long Beach, CA 90804, USA

Olter, Bailey — *President, Micronesia*
%President's Office, Palikia, Pohnepei FM, 96941 Kolonia, Micronesia

Olum, Paul — *Educator*
156 Massapoag Ave, Sharon, MA 02067, USA

Onanian, Edward — *Religious Leader*
%Diocese of Armenian Church, 630 2nd Ave, New York, NY 10016, USA

Ondaatje, Michael — *Writer*
%Glendon College, English Dept, 2275 Bayview, Toronto ON M4N 3M6, Canada

Ong Teng Cheong — *President, Singapore*
%President's Office, Orchard Rd, Istana, Singapore 0922, Singapore

Ong, John D — *Businessman*
%B F Goodrich Co, 3925 Embassy Parkway, Akron, OH 44333, USA

Ongais, Danny — *Auto Racing Driver*
3031 Orange Ave, Santa Ana, CA 92707, USA

Ono, Yoko — *Filmmaker, Artist*
%Dakota Hotel, 1 W 72nd St, New York, NY 10023, USA

Onorati, Peter — *Actor*
4191 Stansbury St, Sherman Oaks, CA 91423, USA

Ontkean, Michael — *Actor*
7120 Grasswood Ave, Malibu, CA 90265, USA

Oosterhuis, Peter — *Golfer*
%Riviera Country Club, 1250 Capri Dr, Pacific Palisades, CA 90272, USA

Opalinski-Harrer, Janice — *Volleyball Player*
%Women's Pro Volleyball Assn, 1730 Oak St, Santa Monica, CA 90405, USA

Opatoshu, David — *Actor*
4161 Dixie Canyon Ave, Sherman Oaks, CA 91423, USA

Ophuls, Marcel — *Movie Director*
10 Rue Ernest Deloison, 92200 Neuilly-sur-Seine, France

Opik, Ernst J — *Astronomer*
%University of Maryland, Physics-Astronomy Dept, College Park, MD 20742, USA

Oppel, Richard A — *Editor*
%Knight-Ridder, 700 National Press Bldg, 529 14th St NW, Washington, DC 20045, USA

Oppenheim, Dennis A — *Artist*
54 Franklin St, New York, NY 10013, USA

Oppenheim-Barnes, Sally — *Government Official, England*
Quietways, The Highlands, Painswick, Glos, England

Opperman, Jan — *Auto Racing Driver*
4630 Minnesota, Fair Oaks, CA 95628, USA

Orbach, Jerry — *Actor, Singer*
301 W 53rd St, New York, NY 10019, USA

Orbach, Raymond L — *Educator*
%University of California, Chancellor's Office, Riverside, CA 92521, USA

Orbelian, Konstantin A — *Composer*
Demirchyan Str 27, #12, 3750002 Yerevan, Armenia

Ord, Robert L, III — *Army General*
Commanding General, US Army Pacific, Fort Shafter, HI 96858, USA

Ordovos, Jose M — *Medical Researcher*
%Tufts University, Nutrition Research Center, Medford, MA 02155, USA

Oresko, Nicholas — *WW II Army Hero (CMH)*
31 Benjamin Rd, Tenafly, NJ 07670, USA

Org, John D — *Businessman*
%B F Goodrich Co, 3925 Embassy Parkway, Akron, OH 44333, USA

Orgad, Ben Zion — *Composer*
14 Bloch St, Tel-Aviv 64161, Israel

Organ, H Bryan — *Artist*
%Redfern Gallery, 20 Cork St, London W1, England

Orlando, George J — *Labor Leader*
%Distillery Wine & Allied Workers, 66 Grand Ave, Englewood, NJ 07631, USA

Orlando, Tony — *Singer*
PO Box 7710, Branson, MO 65615, USA

Orme, Stanley — *Government Official, England*
8 Northwood Grove, Sale, Cheshire, England

Ormond, Julia — *Actress*
%Marmont Mgmt, Langham House, 302/308 Regent St, London W1R 5AL, England

O

Olszewski - Ormond

O

Ornstein, Donald S — *Mathematician*
857 Tolman Dr, Stanford, CA 94305, USA

Orr, James E (Jim), Jr — *Football Player*
6059 E Butterfield Lane, Anaheim, CA 92807, USA

Orr, James F, III — *Businessman*
%UNUM Corp, 2211 Congress St, Portland, ME 04122, USA

Orr, Johnny — *Basketball Coach, Administrator*
%Iowa State University, Athletic Dept, Ames, IA 50011, USA

Orr, Kay — *Governor, NE*
%Governor's Office, State Capitol, Lincoln, NE 68509, USA

Orr, Michael P — *Financier*
%John Deere Credit Co, John Deere Rd, Moline, IL 61265, USA

Orr, Robert D — *Governor, IN; Diplomat*
%US Embassy, 30 Hill St, Singapore, Singapore

Orr, Robert G (Bobby) — *Hockey Player*
1800 W Madison St, Chicago, IL 60612, USA

Orr, Terrence S — *Ballet Dancer*
%American Ballet Theatre, 890 Broadway, New York, NY 10003, USA

Orr, Verne — *Government Official*
%Air Force Department, Pentagon, Washington, DC 20330, USA

Orr-Cahall, Christina — *Museum Director*
%Norton Gallery of Art, 1451 S Olive Ave, West Palm Beach, FL 33401, USA

Orrall, Robert Ellis — *Singer*
3 E 54th St, #1400, New York, NY 10022, USA

Orser, Brian — *Figure Skater*
1600 James Naismith Dr, Gloucester ON L1B 5N4, Canada

Ortega Saavedra, Daniel — *President, Nicaragua*
%Frente Sandinista de Liberacion National, Managua, Nicaragua

Ortenberg, Arthur — *Businessman*
%Liz Claiborne Inc, 1441 Broadway, New York, NY 10018, USA

Ortiz, Christina — *Concert Pianist*
%Harrison-Parrott Ltd, 12 Penzance Place, London W11 4PA, England

Ortiz, Frank V, Jr — *Diplomat*
663 Garcia St, Santa Fe, NM 87501, USA

Ortlieb, Patrick — *Skier*
%Hotel Montana, Oberlech, 6764 Lech, Austria

Ortoli, Francois-Xavier — *Businessman*
18 Rue de Bourgogne, 75007 Paris, France

Orum, Stephen A — *Businessman*
%Lands' End Inc, 1 Lands' End Lane, Dodgeville, WI 53595, USA

Orvick, George M — *Religious Leader*
%Evangelical Lutheran Synod, 447 N Division St, Mankato, MN 56001, USA

Osada, Tadao — *Financier*
%Nikko Securities, 1 World Financial Center, 200 Liberty St, New York, NY 10281, USA

Osborn, David V (Dave) — *Football Player*
18067 Judicial Way N, Lakeville, MN 55044, USA

Osborn, Guy A — *Businessman*
%Universal Foods Corp, 433 E Michigan St, Milwaukee, WI 53202, USA

Osborn, William A — *Financier*
%Northern Trust Corp, 50 S LaSalle St, Chicago, IL 60603, USA

Osborne DuPont, Margaret — *Tennis Player*
415 Camino Real, El Paso, TX 79922, USA

Osborne, Burl — *Editor, Publisher*
%Dallas Morning News, Editorial Dept, Communications Center, Dallas, TX 75265, USA

Osborne, James A — *Religious Leader*
%Salvation Army, 799 Bloomfield Ave, Verona, NJ 07044, USA

Osborne, Jeffrey — *Singer, Songwriter*
%Jack Nelson Inc, 5800 Valley Oak Dr, Los Angeles, CA 90068, USA

Osborne, Joan — *Singer, Songwriter*
%Artists & Audience Entertainment, 83 Riverside Dr, New York, NY 10024, USA

Osborne, Richard de J — *Businessman*
%Asarco Inc, 180 Maiden Lane, New York, NY 10038, USA

Osborne, Tom — *Football Coach*
%University of Nebraska, Athletic Dept, South Stadium, Lincoln, NE 68588, USA

Osbourne, Ozzy — *Singer, Songwriter*
PO Box 15397, Beverly Hills, CA 90209, USA

Osgood, Charles — *News Commentator*
%CBS-TV, News Dept, 524 W 57th St, New York, NY 10019, USA

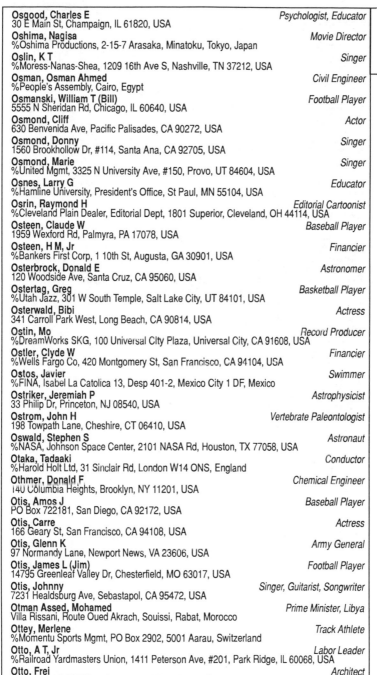

Osgood, Charles E — *Psychologist, Educator*
30 E Main St, Champaign, IL 61820, USA

Oshima, Nagisa — *Movie Director*
%Oshima Productions, 2-15-7 Arasaka, Minatoku, Tokyo, Japan

Oslin, K T — *Singer*
%Moress-Nanas-Shea, 1209 16th Ave S, Nashville, TN 37212, USA

Osman, Osman Ahmed — *Civil Engineer*
%People's Assembly, Cairo, Egypt

Osmanski, William T (Bill) — *Football Player*
5555 N Sheridan Rd, Chicago, IL 60640, USA

Osmond, Cliff — *Actor*
630 Benvenida Ave, Pacific Palisades, CA 90272, USA

Osmond, Donny — *Singer*
1560 Brookhollow Dr, #114, Santa Ana, CA 92705, USA

Osmond, Marie — *Singer*
%United Mgmt, 3325 N University Ave, #150, Provo, UT 84604, USA

Osnes, Larry G — *Educator*
%Hamline University, President's Office, St Paul, MN 55104, USA

Osrin, Raymond H — *Editorial Cartoonist*
%Cleveland Plain Dealer, Editorial Dept, 1801 Superior, Cleveland, OH 44114, USA

Osteen, Claude W — *Baseball Player*
1959 Wexford Rd, Palmyra, PA 17078, USA

Osteen, H M, Jr — *Financier*
%Bankers First Corp, 1 10th St, Augusta, GA 30901, USA

Osterbrock, Donald E — *Astronomer*
120 Woodside Ave, Santa Cruz, CA 95060, USA

Ostertag, Greg — *Basketball Player*
%Utah Jazz, 301 W South Temple, Salt Lake City, UT 84101, USA

Osterwald, Bibi — *Actress*
341 Carroll Park West, Long Beach, CA 90814, USA

Ostin, Mo — *Record Producer*
%DreamWorks SKG, 100 Universal City Plaza, Universal City, CA 91608, USA

Ostler, Clyde W — *Financier*
%Wells Fargo Co, 420 Montgomery St, San Francisco, CA 94104, USA

Ostos, Javier — *Swimmer*
%FINA, Isabel La Catolica 13, Desp 401-2, Mexico City 1 DF, Mexico

Ostriker, Jeremiah P — *Astrophysicist*
33 Philip Dr, Princeton, NJ 08540, USA

Ostrom, John H — *Vertebrate Paleontologist*
198 Towpath Lane, Cheshire, CT 06410, USA

Oswald, Stephen S — *Astronaut*
%NASA, Johnson Space Center, 2101 NASA Rd, Houston, TX 77058, USA

Otaka, Tadaaki — *Conductor*
%Harold Holt Ltd, 31 Sinclair Rd, London W14 ONS, England

Othmer, Donald F — *Chemical Engineer*
140 Columbia Heights, Brooklyn, NY 11201, USA

Otis, Amos J — *Baseball Player*
PO Box 722181, San Diego, CA 92172, USA

Otis, Carre — *Actress*
166 Geary St, San Francisco, CA 94108, USA

Otis, Glenn K — *Army General*
97 Normandy Lane, Newport News, VA 23606, USA

Otis, James L (Jim) — *Football Player*
14795 Greenleaf Valley Dr, Chesterfield, MO 63017, USA

Otis, Johnny — *Singer, Guitarist, Songwriter*
7231 Healdsburg Ave, Sebastapol, CA 95472, USA

Otman Assed, Mohamed — *Prime Minister, Libya*
Villa Rissani, Route Oued Akrach, Souissi, Rabat, Morocco

Ottey, Merlene — *Track Athlete*
%Momentu Sports Mgmt, PO Box 2902, 5001 Aarau, Switzerland

Otto, A T, Jr — *Labor Leader*
%Railroad Yardmasters Union, 1411 Peterson Ave, #201, Park Ridge, IL 60068, USA

Otto, Frei — *Architect*
Berghalde 19, 7250 Leonberg, 71229 Warmbroun, Germany

Otto, James E (Jim) — *Football Player*
00 Estates Dr, Auburn, CA 95603, USA

Otto, Joel — *Hockey Player*
%Philadelphia Flyers, Spectrum, Pattison Place, Philadelphia, PA 19148, USA

O

Otto, Kristin *Swimmer*
%SC DHFK Leipzig, Friedrich-Ebert-Str 130, 04105 Leipzig, Germany
Otto, Michael *Businessman*
%Spiegel Inc, 3500 Lacey Rd, Downers Grove, IL 60515, USA
Otto, Philip G *Businessman*
%Venture Stores, 2001 E Terra Lane, O'Fallon, MO 63366, USA
Otumfuo Nana Opoku Ware II *Ruler, Ghana*
%Asantehene's Palace, Manhyia, Kumasi, Ashanti, Ghana
Otunga, Maurice Cardinal *Religious Leader*
%Cardinal's Residence, PO Box 14231, Nairobi, Kenya
Otwell, Ralph M *Editor*
2750 Hurd Ave, Evanston, IL 60201, USA
Ouattara, Alassane D *Prime Minister, Cote D'Ivoire; Financier*
%International Monetary Fund, 700 19th St NW, Washington, DC 20431, USA
Ouchi, William G *Educator*
%University of California, Management School, Los Angeles, CA 90024, USA
Ouedraogo, Gerard Kango *Prime Minister, Burkina Faso*
01-BP 347, Ouagadougou, Burkina Faso
Ousmane, Mahamane *President, Niger*
%President's Office, Niamey, Niger
Ovchinikov, Vladimir P *Concert Pianist*
%Manygate, 13 Cotswold Mews, 30 Battersea Square, London SW11 3RA, England
Overall, Park *Actress*
4904 Sancola Ave, North Hollywood, CA 91601, USA
Overgard, Robert M *Religious Leader*
%Church of Lutheran Brethren, PO Box 655, Fergus Falls, MN 56538, USA
Overgard, William *Cartoonist (Rudy)*
%United Feature Syndicate, 200 Park Ave, New York, NY 10166, USA
Overhauser, Albert W *Physicist*
236 Pawnee Dr, West Lafayette, IN 47906, USA
Overholser, Geneva *Editor*
%Des Moines Register, Editorial Dept, Box 957, Des Moines, IA 50304, USA
Overmyer, Robert F *Astronaut*
%McDonnell Douglas Space Div, 13100 Space Center Blvd, Houston, TX 77059, USA
Overstreet, Paul *Singer, Songwriter*
PO Box 121975, Nashville, TN 37212, USA
Overstrom, Gunnar S, Jr *Financier*
%Shawmut National Corp, 1 Federal St, Boston, MA 02110, USA
Ovitz, Michael S *Entertainment Executive*
%Walt Disney Productions, 500 S Buena Vista St, Burbank, CA 91521, USA
Ovshinsky, Stanford R *Ovionics Engineer, Inventor*
%Energy Conversion Devices, 1675 W Maple Rd, Troy, MI 48084, USA
Owen, Claude B, Jr *Businessman*
%Richfood Holdings, 2000 Richfood Rd, Richmond, VA 23261, USA
Owen, David *Government Official, England*
%House of Commons, Westminster, London SW1A 0AA, England
Owen, Henry *Diplomat*
%Brookings Institute, 1775 Massachusetts Ave NW, Washington, DC 20036, USA
Owen, Randy *Singer, Guitarist (Alabama)*
PO Box 529, Fort Payne, AL 35967, USA
Owen, Ray D *Biologist*
1583 Rose Villa St, Pasadena, CA 91106, USA
Owens, Billy *Basketball Player*
%Golden State Warriors, Oakland Coliseum Arena, Oakland, CA 94621, USA
Owens, Buck *Singer, Songwriter*
%Buck Owens Production Co, 3223 Sillect Ave, Bakersfield, CA 93308, USA
Owens, Gary *Entertainer*
17856 Via Vallarta, Encino, CA 91316, USA
Owens, James D (Jim) *Football Player, Coach*
%Rowan Companies, 2470 First City Tower, 1001 Fannin, Houston, TX 77002, USA
Owens, Stewart K *Businessman*
%Bob Evans Farms, 3776 S High St, Columbus, OH 43207, USA
Owens, William A *Navy Admiral*
Vice Chairman, Joint Chiefs of Staff, Pentagon, Washington, DC 20318, USA
Owensby, Earl *Movie, Television Producer*
1 Motion Picture Blvd, Shelby, NC 28152, USA
Owlsey, Alvin *Businessman*
%Ball Corp, 345 S High St, Muncie, IN 47305, USA

Otto - Owlsey

Oxenberg, Catherine *Actress*
PO Box 5514, Beverly Hills, CA 90209, USA

Oyakawa, Yoshi *Swimmer*
4171 Hutchinson Rd, Cincinnati, OH 45248, USA

Oz, Amos *Writer*
Arad 80700, Arad, Israel

Oz, Frank R *Puppeteer, Movie Director*
PO Box 20750, New York, NY 10023, USA

Ozark, Daniel L (Danny) *Baseball Executive*
PO Box 6666, Vero Beach, FL 32961, USA

Ozawa, Ichiro *Government Official, Japan*
%Liberal Democratic Party, 1-11-23 Nagatacho, Chiyodaku, Tokyo 100, Japan

Ozawa, Seiji *Conductor*
%Boston Symphony, Symphony Hall, 301 Massachusetts Ave, Boston, MA 02115, USA

Ozbek, Rifat *Fashion Designer*
%Ozbek Ltd, 18 Haunch of Venison Yard, London W1Y 1AF, England

Ozbun, Jim L *Educator*
%North Dakota State University, President's Office, Fargo, ND 58105, USA

Ozick, Cynthia *Writer*
%Alfred A Knopf Inc, 201 E 50th St, New York, NY 10022, USA

Ozim, Igor *Concert Violinist*
Briebergstr 6, 50939 Colgone, Germany

Ozio, David *Bowler*
%Professional Bowlers Assn, 1720 Merriman Rd, Akron, OH 44313, USA

Ozolinsh, Sandis *Hockey Player*
%San Jose Sharks, 525 W Santa Clara St, San Jose, CA 95113, USA

Ozorkiewicz, Ralph L *Businessman*
%Wyle Electronics, 15370 Barranca Parkway, Irvine, CA 92718, USA

Ozzie, Raymond *Computer Software Designer (Notes)*
33 Harbor St, Manchester-by-the-Sea, MA 01944, USA

O

Oxenberg - Ozzie

P

Paar, Jack — *Entertainer*
9 Chateau Ridge Dr, Greenwich, CT 06831, USA

Pace, Judy — *Actress*
4139 Cloverdale Ave, Los Angeles, CA 90008, USA

Pace, Stanley C — *Businessman*
75-735 Topaz Lane, Indian Wells, CA 92210, USA

Pace, Wayne H — *Businessman*
%Turner Broadcasting System, 1 CNN Center, Atlanta, GA 30303, USA

Pacheco, Ferdie — *Sportscaster*
%NBC-TV, Sports Dept, 30 Rockefeller Plaza, New York, NY 10112, USA

Pacheco, Manuel T — *Educator*
%University of Arizona, President's Office, Tucson, AZ 85721, USA

Pacino, Al — *Actor*
%Chal Productions, 301 W 57th St, #16-C, New York, NY 10019, USA

Packard, David — *Businessman*
%Hewlett-Packard Co, 3000 Hanover St, Palo Alto, CA 94304, USA

Packard, Vance O — *Writer*
87 Mill Rd, New Canaan, CT 06840, USA

Packer, A William (Billy) — *Sportscaster*
105 Tescue Dr, Advance, NC 27001, USA

Packer, Kerry F B — *Businessman*
%Consolidated Press Holdings, 54 Park St, Sydney NSW 2000, Australia

Pacquer, Michel — *Businessman*
%Elf-Aquitaine Societe Nationale, 75739 Paris Cedex 15, France

Pacula, Joanna — *Actress*
%Gersh Agency, 232 N Canon Dr, Beverly Hills, CA 90210, USA

Paddock, John — *Hockey Coach, Executive*
%Winnipeg Jets, Arena, 15-1430 Maroons Rd, Winnipeg MB R3G 0L5, Canada

Padilla, Doug — *Track Athlete*
%General Delivery, Orem, UT 84057, USA

Padiyara, Anthony Cardinal — *Religious Leader*
Archdiocese Curia, Post Bag 2580, Ernakulam, Cochin-68201, Kerala, India

Paeniu, Bikenibeu — *Prime Minister, Tuvalu*
%Prime Minister's Office, Vaiaku, Funafuti, Tuvalu

Paez, Jorge (Maromero) — *Boxer*
%Decor Depot, 677 Anita St, #D, Chula Vista, CA 91911, USA

Pafko, Andrew (Andy) — *Baseball Player*
1420 Blackhawk Dr, Mount Prospect, IL 60056, USA

Paganelli, Robert P — *Diplomat*
331 S Main St, Albion, NY 14411, USA

Page, Alan C — *Football Player, Judge*
1732 Knox Ave S, Minneapolis, MN 55403, USA

Page, Anita — *Actress*
929 Rutland Ave, Los Angeles, CA 90042, USA

Page, David C — *Geneticist*
%Whitehead Institute, 9 Cambridge Center, Cambridge, MA 02142, USA

Page, Genevieve — *Actress*
52 Rue de Vaugirard, 75006 Paris, France

Page, Greg — *Boxer*
%Don King Promotions, 968 Pinehurst Dr, Las Vegas, NV 89109, USA

Page, Jimmy — *Singer (Yardbirds, Led Zeppelin)*
57-A Great Titchfield St, London W1P 7FL, England

Page, LaWanda — *Actress*
1056 W 84th St, Los Angeles, CA 90044, USA

Page, Oscar C — *Educator*
%Austin College, President's Office, Sherman, TX 75090, USA

Page, Patti — *Singer, Actress*
1412 San Lucas Court, Solana Beach, CA 92075, USA

Page, Pierre — *Hockey Coach, Executive*
%Calgary Flames, PO Box 1540, Station "M", Calgary AB T2P 389, Canada

Page, Stephen F — *Businessman*
%United Technologies Corp, United Technologies Building, Hartford, CT 06101, USA

Page, Thomas A — *Businessman*
%San Diego Gas & Electric Co, 101 Ash St, San Diego, CA 92101, USA

Pagels, Elaine H — *Educator*
%Barnard College, Religion Dept, New York, NY 10027, USA

Paget, Debra — *Actress*
737 Kuhlman Rd, Houston, TX 77024, USA

Pagett, Nicola — *Actress*
22 Victoria Rd, Mortlake, London SW14, England

Paglia, Camille — *Writer, Educator*
%University of the Arts, Humanities Dept, 320 S Broad St, Philadelphia, PA 19102, USA

Pagliarulo, Michael T (Mike) — *Baseball Player*
12100 Marin, #6309, Minnetonka, MN 55343, USA

Pagonis, William G — *Army General*
25190 N Pawnee Rd, Barrington, IL 60010, USA

Paige, Elaine — *Singer*
DeWalden Court, 85 New Cavendish St, London W1M 7RA, England

Paige, Janis — *Actress*
1700 Rising Glen Rd, Los Angeles, CA 90069, USA

Paige, Mitchell — *WW II Marine Corps Hero (CMH)*
PO Box 2358, Palm Desert, CA 92261, USA

Paik, Kun Woo — *Concert Pianist*
%Worldwide Artists, 6 Petersfield Crescent, Coulsdon, Surrey CR5 2JP, England

Paik, Nam June — *Video Artist*
%Galerie Bonino, 48 Great Jones St, New York, NY 10012, USA

Pailes, William A — *Astronaut*
8305 Ridge Crossing Lane, Springfield, VA 22152, USA

Pais, Abraham — *Physicist*
450 E 63rd St, New York, NY 10021, USA

Paisley, Ian R K — *Political Leader, Northern Ireland*
%Parsonage, 17 Cyprus Ave, Belfast BT5 5NT, Northern Ireland

Pajor, Robert E — *Businessman*
%Valspar Corp, 1101 3rd St S, Minneapolis, MN 55415, USA

Pak, Charles — *Medical Researcher*
%University of Texas, Health Sciences Center, Dallas, TX 75235, USA

Pake, George E — *Physicist*
2 Yerba Buena Ave, Los Altos, CA 94022, USA

Pakula, Alan J — *Movie Director*
%Pakula Co, 330 W 58th St, #508, New York, NY 10019, USA

Palade, George E — *Nobel Medicine Laureate*
%University of California, Cellular & Molecular Division, La Jolla, CA 92093, USA

Palance, Jack — *Actor*
PO Box 6201, Tehachapi, CA 93561, USA

Palau, Luis — *Evangelist*
1500 NW 167th Place, Beaverton, OR 97006, USA

Palazzini, Pietro Cardinal — *Religious Leader*
Via Proba Petronia 83, 00136 Rome, Italy

Palermo, Stephen M — *Baseball Umpire*
7921 W 118th, Overland Park, KS 66210, USA

Palevsky, Max — *Businessman*
924 Westwood Blvd, #700, Los Angeles, CA 90024, USA

Paley, Albert R — *Sculptor*
%Paley Studio, 25 N Washington St, Rochester, NY 14614, USA

Paley, Grace — *Writer*
PO Box 620, Thetford Hill, VT 05074, USA

Palfrey Danzig, Sarah — *Tennis Player*
993 Park Ave, New York, NY 10028, USA

Palillo, Ron — *Actor*
5400 Newcastle Ave, #26, Encino, CA 91316, USA

Palin, Michael — *Actor, Writer (Monty Python)*
%Gumby Corp, 68-A Delancey St, Camden Town, London NW1 7RY, England

Pall, Olga — *Skier*
Fahrenweg 28, 6060 Absam, Austria

Palladino, Vincent — *Labor Leader*
%National Assn of Postal Supervisors, 1727 King St, Alexandria, VA 22314, USA

Palley, Stephen W — *Television Executive*
%King World Productions, 1700 Broadway, New York, NY 10019, USA

Palmeiro, Rafael C — *Baseball Player*
5216 Reims Court, Colleyville, TX 76034, USA

Palmer, Arnold D — *Golfer*
PO Box 52, Youngstown, PA 15696, USA

Palmer, Betsy — *Actress*
4040 Farmdale Ave, Studio City, CA 91604, USA

Palmer, C R — *Businessman*
%Rowan Companies, Transco Tower, 2800 Post Oak Blvd, Houston, TX 77056, USA

P

Pagett - Palmer

Palmer, Geoffrey W R *Prime Minister, New Zealand*
85 Elizabeth St, #7, Wellington, New Zealand

Palmer, James D (Jim) *Baseball Player, Sportscaster*
PO Box 145, Brooklandville, MD 21022, USA

Palmer, Paul *Football Player*
%Cincinnati Bengals, 200 Riverfront Stadium, Cincinnati, OH 45202, USA

Palmer, Reginald Oswald *Governor General, Grenada*
Government House, St George's, Grenada

Palmer, Robert *Singer, Songwriter*
2-A Chelsea Manor, Blood St, London SW3, England

Palmer, Robert B *Businessman*
%Digital Equipment Corp, 111 Powdermill Rd, Maynard, MA 01754, USA

Palmer, Russell E *Educator*
%University of Pennsylvania, Business School, Philadelphia, PA 19104, USA

Palmer, Sandra *Golfer*
PO Box 986, La Quinta, CA 92253, USA

Palmer, William R *Publisher*
%Detroit News, 615 Lafayette Blvd, Detroit, MI 48226, USA

Palmieri, Paul *Religious Leader*
%Church of Jesus Christ, 6th & Lincoln Sts, Monongahela, PA 15063, USA

Palmieri, Peter C *Financier*
%First Fidelity Bancorp, 2673 Main St, Lawrenceville, NJ 08648, USA

Palminteri, Chazz *Actor*
375 Greenwich St, New York, NY 10013, USA

Palms, John M *Educator*
%University of South Carolina, President's Office, Columbia, SC 29208, USA

Paltrow, Bruce W *Television Producer*
304 21st St, Santa Monica, CA 90402, USA

Palu, Robert G *Businessman*
%Allen Group, 25101 Chagrin Blvd, Beachwood, OH 44122, USA

Pan Hong *Actress*
%Omei Film Studio, Tonghui Menwai, Chengdu City, Sichuan Province, China

Panasci, David H *Businessman*
%Fay's Inc, 7245 Henry Clay Blvd, Liverpool, NY 13088, USA

Panasci, Henry A, Jr *Businessman*
%Fay's Inc, 7245 Henry Clay Blvd, Liverpool, NY 13088, USA

Pancetti, John A *Financier*
%Republic Bank for Savings, 415 Madison Ave, New York, NY 10017, USA

Pandit, Korla *Organist*
PO Box 11614, Santa Rosa, CA 95406, USA

Panetta, Leon E *Government Official*
%White House, 1600 Pennsylvania Ave NW, Washington, DC 20006, USA

Panettiere, John M *Businessman*
%Blount Inc, 4520 Executive Park Dr, Montgomery, AL 36116, USA

Panhofer, Walter *Concert Pianist*
Erdbergstr 35/9, 1030 Vienna, Austria

Panic, Milan *Prime Minister, Yugoslavia; Businessman*
%ICN Pharmaceuticals, 3300 Hyland Ave, Costa Mesa, CA 92626, USA

Panichas, George A *Writer*
PO Box AB, College Park, MD 20741, USA

Panitch, Michael B *Financier*
%Smith Barney Inc, 1345 Ave of Americas, New York, NY 10105, USA

Pankey, Irv *Football Player*
%Indianapolis Colts, 7001 W 56th St, Indianapolis, IN 46254, USA

Pankow, James *Trumpeter (Chicago)*
%Front Line Mgmt, 8900 Wilshire Blvd, #300, Beverly Hills, CA 90211, USA

Panoff, Robert *Nuclear Engineer*
1140 Connecticut Ave NW, Washington, DC 20036, USA

Panofsky, Wolfgang K H *Physicist*
25671 Chapin Rd, Los Altos, CA 94022, USA

Panov, Valery M *Ballet Dancer*
%Carson Office, 119 W 57th St, #903, New York, NY 10019, USA

Panova, Galina *Ballerina*
%Carson Office, 119 W 57th St, #903, New York, NY 10019, USA

Panton, Verner *Architect*
Kohlenberggasse 21, 4051 Basle, Switzerland

Panza di Biumo, Giuseppe *Art Patron*
Sentiero Vinorum 2, 6900 Massagno, Switzerland

Paola *Queen, Belgium*
%Koninklijk Palais, Rue de Brederode, 1000 Brussels, Belgium

Paolozzi, Eduardo L *Sculptor*
107 Dovehouse, London SW3, England

Papandreou, Andreas *Prime Minister, Greece*
Papaia Anaktora, Athens, Greece

Papart, Max *Artist*
10 Rue Pernety, 75014 Paris, France

Papas, Irene *Actress*
Xenokratous 39, Athens-Kolonaki, Greece

Papert, Seymour *Mathematician*
%Massachusetts Institute of Technology, 20 Ames St, Cambridge, MA 02142, USA

Papp, Lazlo *Boxer*
Ora-Ut 6, 1125 Budapest, Hungary

Pappalardo, Salvatore Cardinal *Religious Leader*
%Arcivescovado, Corso Vittorio Emanuele 461, 90134 Palermo, Italy

Pappas, George *Bowler*
%George Pappas's Park Lanes, 1700 Montford Dr, Charlotte, NC 28209, USA

Pappas, Milton S (Milt) *Baseball Player*
RR 1, Box 154, Ashland Ave, Beecher, IL 60401, USA

Pappenheimer, John R *Physiologist*
15 Fayerweather St, Cambridge, MA 02138, USA

Paquet, Jean Guy *Educator*
%Laval University, Rector's Office, Quebec PQ G1K 7P4, Canada

Paquette, Joseph F, Jr *Businessman*
%PECO Energy Co, 2301 Market St, Philadelphia, PA 19103, USA

Paquin, Anna *Actress*
%Double Happy, PO Box 9585, Wellington, New Zealand

Paradis, Vanessa *Model, Singer*
BP 138, 75223 Paris Cedex 05, France

Parayre, Jean-Paul C *Businessman*
%Lyonnaise des Eaux-Dumez, 32 Ave Pablo Picasso, 92022 Nanterre, France

Parazaider, Walt *Woodwindist (Chicago)*
%Front Line Mgmt, 8900 Wilshire Blvd, #300, Beverly Hills, CA 90211, USA

Parazynski, Scott E *Astronaut*
%NASA, Johnson Space Center, 2101 NASA Rd, Houston, TX 77058, USA

Parcells, Duane C (Bill) *Football Coach*
%New England Patriots, Foxboro Stadium, Rt 1, Foxboro, MA 02035, USA

Pardee, Arthur B *Biochemist*
30 Codman Rd, Brookline, MA 02146, USA

Pardus, Donald G *Businessman*
%Eastern Utilities Assoc, 1 Liberty Square, Boston, MA 02109, USA

Pare, Michael *Actor*
2804 Pacific Ave, Venice, CA 90291, USA

Parent, Bernie *Hockey Player*
%Philadelphia Flyers, Spectrum, Pattison Place, Philadelphia, PA 19148, USA

Paret, Peter *Historian*
%Institute for Advanced Studies, Historical Studies School, Princeton, NJ 08540, USA

Paretsky, Sara N *Writer*
5831 S Blackstone Ave, Chicago, IL 60637, USA

Parfet, William U *Businessman*
%Upjohn Co, 7000 Portage Rd, Kalamazoo, MI 49001, USA

Parillaud, Anne *Actress*
%Artmedia, 10 Ave George V, 75008 Paris, France

Parilli, Vito (Babe) *Football Player, Coach*
545 Downing St, Denver, CO 80218, USA

Paris, Johnny *Singer*
%Wolfman Jack Entertainment, Rt 1, PO Box 56, Belvidere, NC 27919, USA

Paris, Mica *Singer*
%Garfield Group, 325 W Lafayette St, #200, New York, NY 10012, USA

Parise, Louis *Labor Leader*
%National Maritime Union, 1125 15th St NW, Washington, DC 20005, USA

Parise, Ronald A *Astronaut*
15419 Good Hope Rd, Silver Spring, MD 20905, USA

Parish, Robert L *Basketball Player*
%Charlotte Hornets, 1 Hive Dr, Charlotte, NC 28217, USA

Parizeau, Jacques *Political Leader, Canada*
%Gouvernement du Quebec, 885 Grand-Allee Est, Quebec PC G1A 1A2, Canada

P

Paola - Parizeau

P

Park Choong-Hoon — *President, South Korea; General*
1-36 Seongbuk-dong, Seonbuk-ku, Seoul, South Korea

Park Yung-Wok — *Businessman*
%Hyundai Corp, 140-2 Kyedong, Chongroku, Seoul, South Korea

Park, Brad — *Hockey Player, Coach*
%Bradan Corp, 22-B Cranes Ct, Woburn, MA 01801, USA

Park, Charles R — *Physiologist*
5325 Stanford Dr, Nashville, TN 37215, USA

Park, Merle F — *Ballerina*
21 Millers Court, Chiswick Mall, London W4 2PF, England

Park, W B — *Cartoonist (Off the Leash)*
%United Feature Syndicate, 200 Park Ave, New York, NY 10166, USA

Parkening, Christopher — *Concert Guitarist*
%Columbia Artists Mgmt Inc, 165 W 57th St, New York, NY 10019, USA

Parker, Alan W — *Movie Director*
%Parker Film Co, Pinewood Studios, Iver Heath, Bucks, England

Parker, Bob — *Skier*
408 Camino Don Miguel, Santa Fe, NM 87501, USA

Parker, Brant J — *Cartoonist (Wizard of Id)*
5668 Thorndyke Court, Centreville, VA 22020, USA

Parker, Bruce C — *Botanist*
841 Hutcheson Dr, Blacksburg, VA 24060, USA

Parker, Clarence M (Ace) — *Football Player*
210 Snead's Fairway, Portsmouth, VA 23701, USA

Parker, Corey — *Actor*
2516 5th St, Santa Monica, CA 90405, USA

Parker, David G (Dave) — *Baseball Player*
7864 Ridge Rd, Cincinnati, OH 45237, USA

Parker, Denise — *Archer*
4253 Yorkshire Circle, South Jordan, UT 84095, USA

Parker, Eleanor — *Actress*
2195 La Paz Way, Palm Springs, CA 92264, USA

Parker, Eugene N — *Physicist*
1323 Evergreen Rd, Homewood, IL 60430, USA

Parker, Fess — *Actor*
PO Box 898, Los Olivos, CA 93441, USA

Parker, Frank A — *Tennis Player*
600 N McClurg Court, #4001-A, Chicago, IL 60611, USA

Parker, Franklin — *Writer*
%Western Carolina University, Education & Psychology Dept, Cullowhee, NC 28723, USA

Parker, George M — *Labor Leader*
%Glass Workers Union, 1440 S Byrne Rd, Toledo, OH 43614, USA

Parker, Graham — *Singer, Guitarist*
%Chapman, 11 Old Lincoln's Inn, London WC2, England

Parker, Jackie — *Football Player*
%Edmonton Eskimo, 90211 111th Ave, Edmonton AB T5B 0C3, Canada

Parker, James (Jim) — *Football Player*
5448 Wingborne Court, Columbia, MD 21045, USA

Parker, Jameson — *Actor*
4354 Laurel Canyon Blvd, #306, Studio City, CA 91604, USA

Parker, Maceo — *Jazz Saxophonist*
%Verve Records, Worldwide Plaza, 825 8th Ave, New York, NY 10019, USA

Parker, Maynard M — *Editor*
%Newsweek Magazine, Editorial Dept, 251 W 57th St, New York, NY 10019, USA

Parker, Olivia — *Photographer*
%Brent Sikkema, 252 Lafayette St, #400, New York, NY 10012, USA

Parker, Patrick S — *Businessman*
%Parker Hannifin Corp, 17325 Euclid Ave, Cleveland, OH 44112, USA

Parker, Ray, Jr — *Singer, Guitarist*
1025 N Roxbury Dr, Beverly Hills, CA 90210, USA

Parker, Robert A R — *Astronaut*
%NASA Headquarters, Policy & Plans Division, Washington, DC 20546, USA

Parker, Robert B — *Writer*
555 W 57th St, #1230, New York, NY 10019, USA

Parker, Sarah Jessica — *Actress*
PO Box 611, Englewood, NJ 07631, USA

Parker, Scott — *Motorcyle Racing Rider*
6080 Grand Blanc Rd, Swartz Creek, MI 48473, USA

Parker, Suzy	*Model, Actress*
770 Hot Springs Rd, Santa Barbara, CA 93108, USA	
Parker, Willard	*Actor*
74580 Fairway Dr, Indian Wells, CA 92260, USA	
Parkinson, Dian	*Entertainer, Model*
4655 Natick Ave, #1, Sherman Oaks, CA 91403, USA	
Parkinson, Roger P	*Publisher*
%Minneapolis Star Tribune, 425 Portland Ave, Minneapolis, MN 55488, USA	
Parks, Cherokee	*Basketball Player*
%Dallas Mavericks, Reunion Arena, 777 Sports St, Dallas, TX 75207, USA	
Parks, Gordon R	*Movie Director, Photographer*
860 United Nations Plaza, New York, NY 10017, USA	
Parks, Hildy	*Actress*
225 W 44th St, New York, NY 10036, USA	
Parks, Michael	*Actor*
%Agency For Performing Arts, 9000 Sunset Blvd, #1200, Los Angeles, CA 90069, USA	
Parks, Rosa L	*Civil Rights Activist*
9336 Wildemere St, Detroit, MI 48206, USA	
Parks, Van Dyke	*Composer*
267 S Arden Blvd, Los Angeles, CA 90004, USA	
Parmelee, Harold J	*Businessman*
%Turner Corp, 375 Hudson St, New York, NY 10014, USA	
Parnell, Lee Roy	*Singer*
%Mike Robertson Mgmt, 1227 17th Ave S, #200, Nashville, TN 37212, USA	
Parnell, Melvin L (Mel)	*Baseball Player*
700 Turquoise St, New Orleans, LA 70124, USA	
Parr, Robert G	*Chemist*
701 Kenmore Rd, Chapel Hill, NC 27514, USA	
Parrish, Lance M	*Baseball Player*
22370 Starwood Dr, Yorba Linda, CA 92687, USA	
Parrish, Larry A	*Baseball Player*
1201 Hyde Park Blvd, Niagara Falls, NY 14301, USA	
Parry, Robert T	*Financier*
%Federal Reserve Bank, 101 Market St, San Francisco, CA 94105, USA	
Parseghian, Ara	*Football Coach, Sportscaster*
%St Joseph Bank Building, #1212, South Bend, IN 46601, USA	
Parsky, Gerald L	*Attorney*
%Aurora Capital Partners, 1800 Century Park East, Los Angeles, CA 90067, USA	
Parsons, Benny	*Auto Racing Driver*
1691 Old Harmony Dr, Concord, NC 28027, USA	
Parsons, David	*Choreographer*
%Parsons Dance Foundation, 476 Broadway, New York, NY 10013, USA	
Parsons, Estelle	*Actress*
505 West End Ave, New York, NY 10024, USA	
Parsons, Karyn	*Actress*
3208 Cahuenga Blvd W, #16, Los Angeles, CA 90068, USA	
Parsons, Richard D	*Financier*
%Time Warner Inc, 75 Rockefeller Plaza, New York, NY 10019, USA	
Part, Arvo	*Composer*
%Universal Editions, Warwick House, 9 Warrick St, London W1R 5RA, England	
Parton, Dolly	*Singer, Actress, Songwriter*
Crockett Rd, Rt 1, Brentwood, TN 37027, USA	
Partridge, John A	*Architect*
20 Old Pye St, Westminster, London SW1, England	
Parzybok, William G, Jr	*Businessman*
%Fluke Corp, 6920 Seaway Blvd, Everett, WA 98203, USA	
Pasanella, Marco	*Furniture Designer*
%Pasanella Co, 45 W 18th St, New York, NY 10011, USA	
Pasarell, Charles	*Tennis Player*
%Sportsworld, 8245 Ronson Rd, San Diego, CA 92111, USA	
Pasatieri, Thomas	*Composer*
500 West End Ave, New York, NY 10024, USA	
Pasco, Richard	*Actor*
%Michael Whitehall Ltd, 125 Gloucester Rd, London SW7 4TE, England	
Pascoal, Hermeto	*Jazz Musician*
%Brasil Universo Prod, RVN Vitor Guisard 209, Rio de Janerio 21832, Brazil	
Pascual, Camilo A	*Baseball Player*
7741 SW 32nd St, Miami, FL 33155, USA	

P

Parker - Pascual

P

Pasdar, Adrian — *Actor*
4250 Wilshire Blvd, Los Angeles, CA 90010, USA

Pasetti, Peter — *Actor*
Felitzschstr 34, 80802 Munich, Germany

Paskai, Laszlo Cardinal — *Religious Leader*
Uri Ut 62, 1014 Budapest, Hungary

Pasmore, E J Victor — *Artist*
Dar Gamri, Gudja, Malta

Passeau, Claude W — *Baseball Player*
113 London St, Lucedale, MS 39452, USA

Passer, Ivan — *Movie Director*
%Creative Road Corp, 8170 Beverly Blvd, #106, Los Angeles, CA 90048, USA

Pastore, John O — *Governor/Senator, RI*
81 Mountain Laurel Dr, Cranston, RI 02920, USA

Pastorelli, Robert — *Actor*
2751 Holly Ridge Dr, Los Angeles, CA 90068, USA

Pastrana Borrero, Misael — *President, Colombia*
Carrera 4, 92-10, Bogota DE, Colombia

Pataki, George E — *Governor, NY*
%Governor's Office, State Capitol, Albany, NY 12224, USA

Patane, Giuseppe — *Conductor*
Holbeinstr 6, 81679 Munich, Germany

Patat, Frederic — *Spatinaut, France*
%Faculte de Medecine, 2 Bis Blvd Tonnelle, 37032 Tours Cedex, France

Patch, Lauren N — *Financier*
%Ohio Casualty Corp, 136 N 3rd St, Hamilton, OH 45025, USA

Pate, James L — *Businessman*
%Pennzoil Co, Pennzoil Place, PO Box 2967, Houston, TX 77252, USA

Pate, Jerry — *Golfer*
530 Beacon Parkway W, #503, Birmingham, AL 35209, USA

Pate, Michael — *Actor*
21 Bukdarra Rd, Bellvue Hill NSW 2023, Australia

Patel, Homi B — *Businessman*
%Hartmarx Corp, 101 N Wacker Dr, Chicago, IL 60606, USA

Patera, Jack — *Football Player, Coach*
7305 172nd St SW, Edmonds, WA 98026, USA

Paterno, Joseph V (Joe) — *Football Coach*
%Pennsylvania State University, Greenberg Complex, University Park, PA 16802, USA

Paterson, Bill — *Actor*
%Kerry Gardner, 15 Kensington High St, London W8 5NP, England

Patin, Robert W — *Businessman*
%Washington National Insurace, 300 Tower Parkway, Lincolnshire, IL 60069, USA

Patinkin, Mandy — *Actor*
200 W 90th St, New York, NY 10024, USA

Patitz, Tatjana — *Model, Actress*
%Elite Model Mgmt, 111 E 22nd St, #200, New York, NY 10010, USA

Patkin, Max — *Baseball Clown*
2000 Valley Forge Circle, #837, King of Prussia, PA 19406, USA

Paton, T Angus L — *Civil Engineer*
L'Epervier, Rt Orange, St Brelade, Jersey, United Kingdom

Patrell, Oliver L — *Businessman*
%Colonial Penn Group, PO Box 1990, Valley Forge, PA 19482, USA

Patrese, Ricardo — *Auto Racing Driver*
Via Umberto 1, 35100 Padova, Italy

Patric, Jason — *Actor*
501 21st Place, Santa Monica, CA 90402, USA

Patrick, Dennis — *Movie Director, Actor*
%Arlene Dayton Mgmt, 10110 Empyrean Way, #304, Los Angeles, CA 90067, USA

Patrick, Joseph A — *Financier*
Baird Patrick Co, 20 Exchange Place, New York, NY 10005, USA

Patrick, Ruth — *Educator*
%Academy of Natural Sciences, 19th & Parkway, Philadelphia, PA 19103, USA

Patrick, Stuart K — *Financier*
%Baird Patrick Co, 20 Exchange Place, New York, NY 10005, USA

Patricof, Alan J — *Businessman*
%Patricof Co Ventures, 445 Park Ave, New York, NY 10022, USA

Patsatsia, Otar — *Prime Minister, Georgia*
%Prime Minister's Office, Government House, Ul Ingorokva, Tbilisi, Georgia

Patten, Christopher   *Governor General, Hong Kong*
%Government House, Upper Albert Rd, Hong Kong

Patterson, Aubrey B   *Financier*
%BancorpSouth, 1 Mississippi Plaza, Tupelo, MS 38802, USA

Patterson, Dick   *Actor*
%Pat Lynn, 10525 Strathmore Dr, Los Angeles, CA 90024, USA

Patterson, Elvis   *Football Player*
%Oakland Raiders, Oakland Coliseum, Oakland, CA 94621, USA

Patterson, Floyd   *Boxer*
PO Box 336, Springtown Rd, New Paltz, NY 12561, USA

Patterson, Francine G (Penny)   *Animal Psychologist (Koko Trainer)*
%Gorilla Foundation, PO Box 620-640, Woodside, CA 94062, USA

Patterson, Gardner   *Economist*
1517 Vermont Ave NW, Washington, DC 20005, USA

Patterson, Gary   *Cartoonist (Cats)*
%Patterson International, 25208 Malibu Rd, Malibu, CA 90265, USA

Patterson, John M   *Governor, AL*
%Court of Judiciary, PO Box 30155, Montgomery, AL 36101, USA

Patterson, Lorna   *Actress*
12831 Mulholland Dr, Beverly Hills, CA 90210, USA

Patterson, Percival J   *Prime Minister, Jamaica*
%Prime Minister's Office, 1 Devon Rd, PO Box 272, Kingston 6, Jamaica

Patterson, Richard North   *Writer*
%McCutchen Doyle Brown Enersen, 3 Embarcadero Center, San Francisco, CA 94111, USA

Patterson, Robert M   *Vietnam War Army Air Hero (CMH)*
203 Avenida Las Brisas, Evansville, IN 47712, USA

Patti, Sandi   *Singer*
2200 Madison Square, Anderson, IN 46011, USA

Pattillo, Linda   *News Correspondent*
%ABC-TV, News Dept, 77 W 66th St, New York, NY 10023, USA

Patty, J Edward (Budge)   *Tennis Player*
La Marne, 14 Ave de Jurigoz, 1006 Lausanne, Switzerland

Patulski, Walter G (Walt)   *Football Player*
4899 Abbottsbury Lane, Syracuse, NY 13215, USA

Patz, Arnall   *Ophthalmologist*
%Johns Hopkins Hospital, Wilmer Eye Institute, 600 N Wolfe, Baltimore, MD 21205, USA

Patzaichan, Ivan   *Canoeist*
SC Sportiv, Unirea Tricolor, Soseaua Stefan Cel Mare 9, Bucharest, Romania

Paul, Adrian   *Actor*
16027 Ventura Blvd, #206, Encino, CA 91436, USA

Paul, Alan   *Musician, Singer (Manhattan Transfer)*
%AVNET, 3815 W Olive Ave, Burbank, CA 91505, USA

Paul, Alexandra   *Actress*
11936 Gorham Ave, #104, Los Angeles, CA 90049, USA

Paul, Arthur   *Magazine Designer*
17 E Delaware Place, Chicago, IL 60611, USA

Paul, Donald (Don)   *Football Player*
23801 Calabasas Rd, #1023, Calabasas, CA 91302, USA

Paul, Gyorgy   *Concert Violinist*
27 Armitage Rd, London NW11, England

Paul, Les   *Musician, Inventor (Recording Methods)*
78 Deerhaven Rd, Mahwah, NJ 07430, USA

Paul, Robert   *Figure Skater*
10675 Rochester Ave, Los Angeles, CA 90024, USA

Paul, Wolfgang   *Soccer Player*
Postfach 1324, 59939 Olsberg-Bigge, Germany

Paula, Alejandro F (Jandi)   *Prime Minister, Netherlands Antilles*
%Premier's Office, Fort Amsterdam 17, Willemstad, Netherlands Antilles

Pauley, Jane   *Commentator*
271 Central Park West, #10-E, New York, NY 10024, USA

Pauls, Raymond   *Jazz Pianist, Composer*
Veidenbaum Str 41/43, #26, 226001 Riga, Latvia

Paulsen, Albert   *Actor*
%H David Moss Assoc, 733 N Seward St, #PH, Los Angeles, CA 90038, USA

Paulson, Henry M, Jr   *Financier*
%Goldman Sachs Co, 85 Broad St, New York, NY 10004, USA

Pavan, Marisa   *Actress*
Lorcaster Lola Mouloudji, 27 Rue de Richelieu, 75001 Paris, France

P

Patten - Pavan

Pavarotti, Luciano *Opera Singer*
Via Giardini 941, 41040 Saliceta San Giuliano, Modena, Italy

Pavin, Corey *Golfer*
%International Management Group, 1 Erieview Plaza, #1300, Cleveland, OH 44114, USA

Paxton, John *Editor*
%St Martin's Press, 175 5th Ave, New York, NY 10010, USA

Paxton, Tom *Singer, Songwriter*
%Pax Records, 19 Railroad Ave, East Hampton, NY 11937, USA

Paycheck, Johnny *Singer, Songwriter*
%Talent Group International, 1321 Murfreesboro Rd, Nashville, TN 37217, USA

Payden, Joan A *Financier*
%Payden & Pagel, 333 S Grand Ave, Los Angeles, CA 90071, USA

Paymer, David *Actor*
1506 Pacific St, Santa Monica, CA 90405, USA

Payne, Anthony E *Composer*
2 Wilton Square, London N1 3DL, England

Payne, David L *Financier*
%Westamerica Bancorp, 1108 5th Ave, San Rafael, CA 94901, USA

Payne, Freda *Singer*
10160 Cielo Dr, Beverly Hills, CA 90210, USA

Payne, Harry C *Educator*
%Williams College, President's Office, Williamstown, MA 01267, USA

Payne, Keith *Vietnam War Australian Army Hero (VC)*
2 St Bee's Ave, Bucasia, QLD 4740, Australia

Payne, Ladell *Educator*
%Randolph-Macon College, President's Office, Ashland, VA 23005, USA

Payne, William (Billy) *Sports Executive*
%1996 Olympic Games Committee, 150 Williams St, #6000, Atlanta, GA 30303, USA

Pays, Amanda *Actress*
3541 N Knoll Dr, Los Angeles, CA 90068, USA

Payton, Benjamin F *Educator*
%Tuskegee Institute, President's Office, Tuskegee, AL 36088, USA

Payton, Gary *Basketball Player*
%Seattle Supersonics, 190 Queen Ave N, PO Box C-900911, Seattle, WA 98109, USA

Payton, Gary E *Astronaut*
7835 Belleflower Dr, Springfield, VA 22152, USA

Payton, Walter *Football Player*
300 N Martingale, #340, Schaumburg, IL 60173, USA

Paz, Octavio *Nobel Literature Laureate, Diplomat*
%Revista Vuelta, Leonardo da Vinci 17, Mexico City 03910 DF, Mexico

Pazienza, Vinny *Boxer*
64 Waterman Ave, Cranston, RI 02910, USA

Peabody, Endicott (Chub), III *Governor, MA; Football Player*
PO Box 803, Hollis, NH 03049, USA

Peacock, Andrew S *Government Official, Australia*
30 Monomeath Ave, Canterbury, VIC 3126, Australia

Peacock, Eulace *Track Athlete*
100 Cook Ave, Yonkers, NY 10701, USA

Peaker, E J *Actress*
4935 Densmore Ave, Encino, CA 91436, USA

Pearce, Austin W *Businessman*
%British Aerospace, Brooklands Rd, Weybridge, Surrey KT13 0SJ, England

Pearce, Harry J *Businessman*
%Tyco Toys Inc, 6000 Midlantic Dr, Mount Laurel, NJ 08054, USA

Pearl, Minnie *Comedienne*
PO Box 158949, Nashville, TN 37215, USA

Pearl, Neil *Drummer (Rush)*
%SRO Mgmt, 189 Carlton St, Toronto ON M5A 2K7, Canada

Pearlman, Jerry K *Businessman*
%Zenith Electronics Corp, 1000 Milwaukee Ave, Glenview, IL 60025, USA

Pearlstein, Philip *Artist*
361 W 36th St, New York, NY 10018, USA

Pearlstine, Norman *Editor*
%Time Warner Inc, Magazines Division, Rockefeller Plaza, New York, NY 10020, USA

Pearson, David *Auto Racing Driver*
PO Box 8099, Spartanburg, SC 29305, USA

Pearson, James B *Senator, KS*
%Stroock Stroock & Lavan, 1150 17th St NW, Washington, DC 20036, USA

Pearson, Louis — *Sculptor*
224 12th St, San Francisco, CA 94103, USA

Pearson, Paul G — *Educator*
5110 Bonham Rd, Oxford, OH 45056, USA

Pearson, Preston — *Football Player*
%Pro Style Assoc, 16990 N Dallas Parkway, #212, Dallas, TX 75248, USA

Pearson, Ralph G — *Chemist*
715 Grove Lane, Santa Barbara, CA 93105, USA

Pearson, Richard J — *Businessman*
1046 Oak Grove Pl, San Marino, CA 91108, USA

Pearson, Ronald D — *Businessman*
%Hy-Vee Food Stores, 1801 Osceola Ave, Chariton, IA 50049, USA

Peart, Neal — *Musician (Rush)*
%SRO Mgmt, 189 Carlton St, Toronto ON M5A 2K7, Canada

Pease, Patsy — *Actress*
13413 Chandler Blvd, Van Nuys, CA 91401, USA

Pease, Rendel S — *Physicist*
The Poplars, West Isley, Newbury, Berks RG16 0AW, England

Peay, Francis — *Football Player, Coach*
PO Box 53877, Indianapolis, IN 46253, USA

Peay, J H Binford, III — *Army General*
Commander in Chief, US Central Command, MacDill Air Force Base, FL 33621, USA

Pechstein, Claudia — *Speed Skater*
%Pollinger Consulting, Wartenberger Str 24, 13053 Berlin, Germany

Peck, Gregory — *Actor*
PO Box 837, Beverly Hills, CA 90213, USA

Peck, M Scott — *Psychiatrist, Writer*
New Preston Marble Bliss Rd, RFD 1, Washington Depot, CT 06793, USA

Peck, Richard E — *Educator*
%University of New Mexico, President's Office, Albuquerque, NM 87131, USA

Pecker, David J — *Publisher*
%Hachette Filipacchi, 1633 Broadway, New York, NY 10019, USA

Pecker, Jean-Claude — *Astronomer*
Pusat-Tasek, 85350 Les Corbeaux, Ile d'Yeu, France

Pecqueur, Michel A F — *Businessman*
%Sanofi, 39 Ave Pierre 1er de Serbie, 75008 Paris, France

Peddle, Chuck — *Computer Designer*
PO Box 91346, Mission Hill, CA 91345, USA

Pedersen, Calvin J — *Financier*
%Duff & Phelps Corp, 55 E Monroe St, Chicago, IL 60603, USA

Pedersen, Richard F — *Diplomat*
Twilight Park, Haines Falls, NY 12436, USA

Pedersen, William — *Architect*
%Kohn Pedersen Fox Assoc, 111 W 57th St, New York, NY 10019, USA

Pederson, Donald O — *Electrical Engineer*
1436 Via Loma, Walnut Creek, CA 94598, USA

Pederson, Jerold P — *Businessman*
%Montana Power Co, 40 E Broadway, Butte, MT 59707, USA

Peebles, Ann — *Singer*
%Rounder/Bullseye Blues, 1 Camp St, Cambridge, MA 02140, USA

Peebles, P J E — *Physicist, Educator*
%Princeton University, Physics Dept, Princeton, NJ 08544, USA

Peeples, Nia — *Actress, Singer*
26012 Trana Circle, Calabasas, CA 91302, USA

Peerce, Larry — *Movie Director*
225 W 34th St, #1012, New York, NY 10122, USA

Peery, Troy A, Jr — *Businessman*
%Heilig-Meyers Co, 2235 Staples Mill Rd, Richmond, VA 23230, USA

Peete, Calvin — *Golfer*
%Calvin Peete Enterprises, 2050 Collier Ave, Fort Myers, FL 33901, USA

Peete, Rodney — *Football Player*
%Detroit Lions, Silverdome, 1200 Featherstone Rd, Pontiac, MI 48342, USA

Peeters, Pete — *Hockey Player*
%Boston Bruins, Boston Garden, 150 Causeway St, Boston, MA 02114, USA

Pei, I M — *Architect*
%Pei Cobb Freed Partners, 600 Madison Ave, New York, NY 10022, USA

Pei-Yuan Chia — *Financier*
%Citicorp, 399 Park Ave, New York, NY 10022, USA

P

Pekarkova, Iva *Writer*
%Farrar Straus Giroux, 19 Union Square W, New York, NY 10003, USA

Peladeau, Pierre *Editor*
%Quebecor Inc, 612 St Jacques St, Montreal PQ H3C 4M8, Canada

Pele (Edison Arantes do Nascimento) *Soccer Player*
Praca dos Tres Poderes, Palacio de Planalto 50150900 Brasilia DF, Brazil

Pelen, Perrine *Skier*
31 Ave de l'Eygala, 38700 Corens Mont Fleury, France

Pelikan, Jaroslav J *Historian*
156 Chestnut Lane, Hamden, CT 06518, USA

Pelikan, Lisa *Actress*
%Kathy Bartels, PO Box 57333, Sherman Oaks, CA 91413, USA

Pell, Wilbur F, Jr *Judge*
%US Court of Appelas, US Courthouse, 219 S Dearborn St, Chicago, IL 60604, USA

Pellegrini, Bob *Football Player*
7504 Heather Knoll Circle, Las Vegas, NV 89129, USA

Pellegrino, Edmund D *Physician*
6 Chalfont Court, Bethesda, MD 20816, USA

Pelletreau, Robert H, Jr *Diplomat*
%State Department, 2201 "C" St NW, Washington, DC 20520, USA

Pelli, Cesar *Architect*
%Cesar Pelli Assoc, 1056 Chapel St, New Haven, CT 06510, USA

Pelson, Victor A *Businessman*
%American Telephone & Telegraph Co, 32 Ave of Americas, New York, 10013, USA

Peltason, Jack W *Educator*
70 Rincon Rd, Kensington, CA 94707, USA

Peltz, Nelson *Businessman*
%Triarc Companies, 900 3rd Ave, New York, NY 10022, USA

Peluso, Lisa *Actress*
%Shauna Sickenger, PO Box 301, Ramona, CA 92065, USA

Pemberton, Brian *Businessman*
%Cable & Wireless PLC, Mercury House, Theobald's Rd, London WC1, England

Pena, Alejandro *Baseball Player*
PO Box 2176, Roswell, GA 30077, USA

Pena, Elizabeth *Actress*
%Paradigm Agency, 10100 Santa Monica Blvd, #2500, Los Angeles, CA 90067, USA

Pena, Federico F *Secretary, Transportation*
%Transportation Department, 400 7th St SW, Washington, DC 20004, USA

Pena, Paco *Concert Guitarist*
%Karin Vaessen, 4 Boscastle Rd, London NW5 1EG, England

Penderecki, Krzysztof *Composer, Conductor*
Ul Cisowa 22, 30-229 Cracow, Poland

Pendergrass, Henry P *Physician, Educator*
%Vanderbilt University, Medical School, 1621 21st Ave S, Nashville, TN 37212, USA

Pendergrass, Teddy *Singer, Songwriter*
1505 Flat Rock Rd, Narberth, PA 19072, USA

Penders, Tom *Basketball Coach*
%University of Texas, Athletic Dept, Austin, TX 78713, USA

Pendleton, Moses *Dancer, Choreographer*
%Momix, PO Box 35, Washington, CT 06794, USA

Pendleton, Terry L *Baseball Player*
%Atlanta Braves, Atlanta-Fulton County Stadium, PO Box 4064, Atlanta, GA 30302, USA

Penghlis, Thaao *Actor*
7187 Macapo Dr, Los Angeles, CA 90068, USA

Peniston, CeCe *Singer*
%Famous Artists Agency, 1700 Broadway, #500, New York, NY 10019, USA

Penky, Joseph F *Chemical Engineer*
%Purdue University, Chemical Engineering Dept, West Lafayette, IN 47907, USA

Penn (Jillette) *Comedian, Illusionist (Penn & Teller)*
%Earth's Center, PO Box 1196, New York, NY 10185, USA

Penn, Arthur H *Movie Director*
%William Morris Agency, 151 S El Camino Dr, Beverly Hills, CA 90212, USA

Penn, Christopher *Actor*
6728 Zumirez Dr, Malibu, CA 90265, USA

Penn, Irving *Photographer*
%Irving Penn Studio, 89 5th Ave, New York, NY 10003, USA

Penn, Sean *Actor*
%Clyde Is Hungary Productions, 22333 Pacific Coast Highway, Malibu, CA 90265, USA

Pennario, Leonard *Concert Pianist*
1140 Calle Vista Dr, Beverly Hills, CA 90210, USA

Penney, Alexandra *Editor*
%Conde Nast Publications, Editorial Dept, 350 Madison Ave, New York, NY 10017, USA

Pennington, Weldon J *Publisher*
%Seattle Times, Fairview Ave N & John St, Seattle, WA 98109, USA

Pennington, William N *Businessman*
%Circus Circus Enterprises, 2880 Las Vegas Blvd S, Las Vegas, NV 89109, USA

Pennock of Norton, Raymond *Businessman*
%Morgan Grenfell Group, 23 Great Winchester St, London EC2P 2AX, England

Penny, Joe *Actor*
10453 Sarah St, North Hollywood, CA 91602, USA

Penny, Roger P *Businessman*
%Bethlehem Steel Corp, 1170 8th Ave, Bethlehem, PA 18018, USA

Penny, Sydney *Actress*
10112 Valley Circle Blvd, Chatsworth, CA 91311, USA

Penske, Roger S *Auto Racing Driver, Builder; Businessman*
%Penske Corp, 13400 Outer Dr W, Detroit, MI 48239, USA

Penzias, Arno A *Nobel Physics Laureate*
%AT&T Bell Laboratories, Radiophysics Research Dept, Holmdel, NJ 07733, USA

People, D Louis *Businessman*
%Orange & Rockland Utilities, 1 Blue Hill Plaza, Pearl River, NY 10965, USA

Peoples, John *Physicist*
%Fermi Nat Acceleration Lab, CDF Collaboration, PO Box 500, Batavia, IL 60510, USA

Pep, Willie *Boxer*
166 Bunce Rd, Wethersfield, CT 06109, USA

Pepitone, Joseph A (Joe) *Baseball Player*
32 Lois Lane, Farmingdale, NY 11735, USA

Pepper, John E, Jr *Businessman*
%Procter & Gamble Co, 1 Procter & Gamble Plaza, Cincinnati, OH 45202, USA

Peppler, Mary Jo *Volleyball Player*
2015 Garnet Ave, #R-136, San Diego, CA 92109, USA

Perahia, Murray *Concert Pianist*
%Fine Arts Mgmt, 146 W 82nd St, #1-C, New York, NY 10024, USA

Perak, Sultan of *Ruler, Malaysia*
%Sultan's Palace, Istana Bukit Serene, Kuala Lumpur, Malaysia

Peralta, Ricardo *Astronaut, Mexico*
%Ingeneria Instituto, Ciudad Universitaria, 04510 Mexico City DF, Mexico

Percy, Charles H *Senator, IL*
%Charles Percy Assoc, 900 19th St N, #700, Washington, DC 20006, USA

Perdue, Franklin P *Businessman*
%Perdue Farms, PO Box 1537, Salisbury, MD 21802, USA

Pereira, Aristides M *President, Cape Verde*
PO Box 172, Praia, Cape Verde

Perek, Lubos *Astronomer*
%Astronomical Institute, Budecska 6, Prague 2, Czech Republic

Perelman, Ronald O *Businessman*
%MacAndrews & Forbes Group, 36 E 63rd St, New York, NY 10021, USA

Perenchio, A Jerrold *Entertainment Executive*
%Chartwell Partnerships Group, 1901 Ave of Stars, #680, Los Angeles, CA 90067, USA

Perenyi, Miklos *Concert Violinist*
Erdoalja Ut 1/B, 1037 Budapest, Hungary

Peres, Shimon *Prime Minister, Israel; Nobel Laureate*
%Israel Labour Party, 10 Hayarkon St, Tel-Aviv 63571, Israel

Peretokin, Mark *Ballet Dancer*
%Bolshoi Theater, Teatralnaya Pl 1, 103009 Moscow, Russia

Perez Balladares, Ernesto *President, Panama*
%President's Office, Valija 50, Panama City 1, Panama

Perez de Cuellar, Javier *Secretary General, United Nations*
3 Sutton Place, New York, NY 10022, USA

Perez Esquivel, Adolfo *Nobel Peace Laureate*
%University of Peace, Apdo Postal 199, 1250 Escalzu, Costa Rica

Perez Fernandez, Pedro *Government Official, Spain*
%Ministerio de Economia, Hacieda y Comercio, Alcala 9, Madrid 14, Spain

Perez Godoy, Ricardo P *President, Peru; Army General*
Blasco Nunez de Balboa 225, Miraflores, Lima, Peru

Perez, Atanasio R (Tony) *Baseball Player, Manager*
Los Flores 113, Santurce, PR 00911, USA

Perez, Pascual   *Baseball Player*
%Salvador, Cucurulo #105, Santiago, Dominican Republic

Perez, Rosie   *Actress*
1135 Keniston Ave, Los Angeles, CA 90019, USA

Perez, Vincent   *Actor*
%Artmedia, 10 Ave George V, 75008 Paris, France

Perick, Christof   *Conductor*
%Shaw Concerts, Lincoln Plaza, 1900 Broadway, #200, New York, NY 10023, USA

Perier, Francois   *Actor*
%Artmedia, 10 Ave George V, 75008 Paris, France

Perini, David B   *Businessman*
PO Box 9160, Framingham, MA 01701, USA

Perkins, Carl   *Singer, Songwriter*
%Carl Perkins Ents, 27 Sunnymeade Dr, Jackson, TN 38305, USA

Perkins, David D   *Biologist, Geneticist*
345 Vine St, Menlo Park, CA 94025, USA

Perkins, Donald S   *Businessman*
%Kmart Corp, 3100 W Big Beaver Rd, Troy, MI 48084, USA

Perkins, Edward J   *Diplomat*
%State Department, 2201 "C" St NW, Washington, DC 20520, USA

Perkins, Elizabeth   *Actress*
%Creative Artists Agency, 9830 Wilshire Blvd, Beverly Hills, CA 90212, USA

Perkins, James A   *Educator*
94 North Rd, Princeton, NJ 08540, USA

Perkins, Kevin W   *Businessman*
%Sizzler International, 12655 W Jefferson Blvd, Los Angeles, CA 90066, USA

Perkins, Lawrence B, Jr   *Architect*
%Perkins Eastman Partners, 437 5th Ave, New York, NY 10016, USA

Perkins, Lucian   *Photographer*
%Washington Post, Editorial Dept, 1150 15th St NW, Washington, DC 20071, USA

Perkins, Millie   *Actress*
2511 Canyon Dr, Los Angeles, CA 90068, USA

Perkins, Ray   *Football Player, Coach*
%New England Patriots, Foxboro Stadium, Rt 1, Foxboro, MA 02035, USA

Perkins, Sam   *Basketball Player*
%Seattle Supersonics, 190 Queen Ave N, PO Box C-900911, Seattle, WA 98109, USA

Perkins, Thomas J   *Businessman*
%Tandem Computers, 19333 Vallco Parkway, Cupertino, CA 95014, USA

Perkoff, Gerald T   *Physician*
1300 Torrey Pines Dr, Columbia, MO 65203, USA

Perl, Martin L   *Nobel Physics Laureate*
3737 El Centro Ave, Palo Alto, CA 94306, USA

Perle, George   *Composer*
%Queens College, Music Dept, Flushing, NY 11367, USA

Perlemuter, Vlado   *Concert Pianist*
21 Rue Ampere, 75017 Paris, France

Perley, James   *Labor Leader*
%American Assn of University Professors, 1012 14th St NW, Washington, DC 20005, USA

Perlman, Itzhak   *Concert Violinist*
%International Creative Mgmt, 40 W 57th St, New York, NY 10019, USA

Perlman, Lawrence   *Businessman*
%Ceridian Corp, 8100 34th Ave S, Minneapolis, MN 55425, USA

Perlman, Rhea   *Actress*
31020 Broad Beach Rd, Malibu, CA 90265, USA

Perlman, Ron   *Actor*
335 N Maple Dr, #361, Beverly Hills, CA 90210, USA

Perlmutter, Norman   *Financier*
%Heitman Financial, 180 N LaSalle St, Chicago, IL 60601, USA

Pero, Joseph J   *Businessman*
%Motors Insurance Corp, 3044 W Grand Blvd, Detroit, MI 48202, USA

Peron, Isabelita Martinez de   *President, Argentina*
Moreto 3, Los Jeronimos, Madrid, Spain

Perot, H Ross   *Businessman*
%Perot Group, Lakeside Square, 12377 Merit Dr, #1700, Dallas, TX 75251, USA

Perranoski, Ronald P (Ron)   *Baseball Player*
3805 Indian River Dr, Vero Beach, FL 32963, USA

Perreau, Gigi   *Actress*
4258 Beeman Ave, Studio City, CA 91604, USA

Perreault, Gil — *Hockey Player*
%Buffalo Sabres, Memorial Stadium, 140 Main St, Buffalo, NY 14202, USA

Perrella, James E — *Businessman*
%Ingersoll-Rand Co, 20 Chestnut Ridge Rd, Woodcliff Lake, NJ 07675, USA

Perrin, Charles R — *Businessman*
%Durcell International, Bershire Corporate Park, Bethel, CT 06801, USA

Perrine, Valerie — *Actress*
14411 Riverside Dr, Sherman Oaks, CA 91423, USA

Perry, Charles O — *Sculptor*
20 Shorehaven Rd, Norwalk, CT 06855, USA

Perry, Felton — *Actor*
PO Box 931359, Los Angeles, CA 90093, USA

Perry, Fletcher (Joe) — *Football Player*
350 Moscow St, San Francisco, CA 94112, USA

Perry, Gaylord J — *Baseball Player*
PO Box 1958, Kill Devil Hill, NC 27948, USA

Perry, George L — *Economist*
%Brookings Institute, 1775 Massachusetts Ave NW, Washington, DC 20036, USA

Perry, James E (Jim) — *Baseball Player*
2608 S Ridgeview Way, Sioux Falls, SD 57105, USA

Perry, Joe — *Guitarist (Aerosmith), Songwriter*
%Collins Mgmt, 5 Bigelow St, Cambridge, MA 02139, USA

Perry, John Bennett — *Actor*
%Judy Schoen Assoc, 606 N Larchmont Blvd, #309, Los Angeles, CA 90004, USA

Perry, John R — *Philosopher*
%Stanford University, Philosophy Dept, Stanford, CA 94305, USA

Perry, Luke — *Actor*
19528 Ventura Blvd, #533, Tarzana, CA 91356, USA

Perry, Matthew — *Actor*
9911 W Pico Blvd, #PH-1, Los Angeles, CA 90035, USA

Perry, Michael Dean — *Football Player*
%Denver Broncos, 13655 E Dove Valley Parkway, Englewood, CO 80112, USA

Perry, Robert P — *Molecular Biologist*
1808 Bustleton Pike, Churchville, PA 18966, USA

Perry, Roger — *Actor*
4363 Ledge Avo, Toluca Lake, CA 91602, USA

Perry, Seymour M — *Physician*
%Georgetown Medical School, Community Medicine Dept, Washington, DC 20007, USA

Perry, Steve — *Singer (Journey)*
1401 Pathfinder Ave, Westlake Village, CA 91362, USA

Perry, Troy D — *Religious Leader*
%Metropolitan Churches Fellowship, 5300 Santa Monica Blvd, Los Angeles, CA 90029, USA

Perry, William J — *Secretary, Defense*
14 Wolfe St, Alexandria, VA 22314, USA

Persoff, Nehemiah — *Actor*
584/ Tampa Ave, Tarzana, CA 91356, USA

Person, Chuck — *Basketball Player*
%San Antonio Spurs, 600 E Market St, #102, San Antonio, TX 78205, USA

Persson, Jorgen — *Cinematographer*
Lievagen 23, 183 38 Taby, Sweden

Pertschuk, Michael — *Government Official, Political Activist*
%Advocacy Institute, 1730 "M" St NW, #600, Washington, DC 20036, USA

Perutz, Max F — *Nobel Chemistry Laureate*
42 Sedley Taylor Rd, Cambridge, England

Pesci, Joe — *Actor*
PO Box 6, Lavallette, NJ 08735, USA

Pescia, Lisa — *Actress*
280 S Beverly Dr, #400, Beverly Hills, CA 90212, USA

Pescow, Donna — *Actress*
2179 W 21st St, Los Angeles, CA 90018, USA

Pesek, Libor — *Conductor*
%IMG Artists, Media House, 3 Burlington Lane, London W4 2TH, England

Pesky, John M (Johnny) — *Baseball Player*
2201 Edison Ave, Fort Myers, FL 33901, USA

Peter, Valentine J — *Religious Leader, Educator*
%Father Flanagan's Boys Home, Boys Town, NE 68010, USA

Peterdi, Gabor — *Artist*
108 Highland Ave, Rowayton, CT 06853, USA

P

Perreault - Peterdi

P

Peters, Bernadette — *Actress, Singer*
323 W 80th St, New York, NY 10024, USA

Peters, Brock — *Actor*
PO Box 8156, North Hollywood, CA 91618, USA

Peters, Charles G, Jr — *Editor*
%Washington Monthly, 1611 Connecticut Ave NW, Washington, DC 20009, USA

Peters, Dan — *Drummer (Mudhoney)*
%Reprise Records, 3300 Warner Blvd, Burbank, CA 91505, USA

Peters, Floyd — *Football Player, Coach*
9222 Hyland Creek Rd, Bloomington, MN 55437, USA

Peters, Gary C — *Baseball Player*
7121 N Serenoa Dr, Sarasota, FL 34241, USA

Peters, Jean — *Actress*
507 N Palm Dr, Beverly Hills, CA 90210, USA

Peters, Jon — *Movie Producer*
9 Beverly Park, Beverly Hills, CA 90210, USA

Peters, Maria Liberia — *Prime Minister, Netherlands Antilles*
%Prime Minister's Office, Fort Amsterdam, Willemstad, Netherlands Antilles

Peters, Mary — *Track Athlete*
Willowtree Cottage, River Rd, Dunmurray, Belfast, Northern Ireland

Peters, Mike — *Editorial Cartoonist (Grimmy)*
1269 1st St, #8, Sarasota, FL 34236, USA

Peters, Richard J — *Businessman*
%Penske Corp, 13400 Outer Dr W, Detroit, MI 48239, USA

Peters, Roberta — *Opera Singer*
64 Garden Rd, Scarsdale, NY 10583, USA

Peters, Tom — *Management Consultant, Writer*
%Tom Peters Group, 555 Hamilton Ave, Palo Alto, CA 94301, USA

Peters, Tony — *Football Player*
13408 Sandrock Court, Chantilly, VA 22021, USA

Petersdorf, Robert G — *Physician*
1219 Parkside Dr E, Seattle, WA 98112, USA

Petersen, John M — *Businessman*
%Erie Insurance Group, 100 Erie Insurance Place, Erie, PA 16530, USA

Petersen, Paul — *Actor*
14530 Denker Ave, Gardena, CA 90247, USA

Petersen, Raymond J — *Publisher*
%Hearst Corp, 959 8th Ave, New York, NY 10019, USA

Petersen, Robert E — *Publisher*
%Petersen Publishing Co, 8490 Sunset Blvd, Los Angeles, CA 90069, USA

Petersen, Wolfgang — *Movie Director*
%Radiant Pictures, Tri-Star, 10202 W Washington Blvd, Culver City, CA 90232, USA

Peterson, Ben — *Wrestler*
%Camp of Champs, PO Box 438, Watertown, WI 53094, USA

Peterson, Bruce — *Test Pilot*
43665 21st St W, Lancaster, CA 93536, USA

Peterson, Chase N — *Educator*
66 Thaynes Canyon Dr, Park City, UT 84060, USA

Peterson, Dave — *Hockey Coach*
%US Hockey Team, 1750 E Boulder St, Colorado Springs, CO 80909, USA

Peterson, David C — *Photographer*
2024 35th St, Des Moines, IA 50310, USA

Peterson, Donald H — *Astronaut*
%Aerospace Operations Consultants, 427 Pebblebrook, Seabrook, TX 77586, USA

Peterson, Elly — *Women's Activist*
1515 "M" St NW, Washington, DC 20005, USA

Peterson, Esther — *Consumer Advocate*
3032 Stephenson Place NW, Washington, DC 20015, USA

Peterson, James R — *Businessman*
7762 Lochmere Terrace, Edina, MN 55439, USA

Peterson, John D — *Financier*
%City Securities Corp, 135 N Pennsylvania St, Indianapolis, IN 46204, USA

Peterson, Lars — *Surgeon*
%Sahlgrenska University Hospital, Goteborg, Sweden

Peterson, Max W — *Financier*
%America First Credit Union, PO Box 9199, Ogden, UT 84409, USA

Peterson, Norman L — *Financier*
%Advanced Financial Inc, 5425 Martindale, Shawnee, KS 66218, USA

Peters - Peterson

Peterson, Oscar *Jazz Pianist, Composer*
%Regal Recordings Ltd, 2421 Hammond Rd, Mississauga ON L5K 1T3, Canada

Peterson, Paul E *Political Scientist*
5 Midland Rd, Wellesley, MA 02181, USA

Peterson, Peter G *Financier, Secretary of Commerce*
%Blackstone Group, 345 Park Ave, New York, NY 10154, USA

Peterson, Robert L *Businessman*
%IBP Inc, IBP Ave, Dakota City, NE 68731, USA

Peterson, Roger Tory *Ornithologist, Artist*
125 Neck Rd, Old Lyme, CT 06371, USA

Peterson, Russell W *Governor, DE*
1613 N Broom St, Wilmington, DE 19806, USA

Peterson, Thomas R *Educator*
%Seton Hall University, President's Office, South Orange, NJ 07079, USA

Peterson, Walter *Governor, NH; Educator*
19 East Mountain Rd, Peterborough, NH 03458, USA

Petersson, Tom *Singer, Bassist (Cheap Trick)*
1818 Parmenter St, #202, Middleton, WI 53562, USA

Petherbridge, Edward *Actor*
%Jonathan Altaras Assoc, 2 Goodwins Court, London WC2N 4LL, England

Petibon, Richard A (Richie) *Football Player, Coach*
%Washington Redskins, 21300 Redskin Park Dr, Ashburn, VA 22011, USA

Petit, Philippe *High Wire Walker*
%Cathedral of Saint John the Devine, 1047 Amsterdam Ave, New York, NY 10025, USA

Petit, Richard G *Businessman*
%Colonial Penn Life Insurance, 1818 Market St, Philadelphia, PA 19103, USA

Petit, Roland *Ballet Dancer, Choreographer*
20 Blvd Gabes, 13008 Marseilles, France

Petraglia, Johnny *Bowler*
%Professional Bowlers Assn, 1720 Merriman Rd, Akron, OH 44313, USA

Petrassi, Goffrodo *Composer*
Via Ferdinando di Savoia 3, 00196 Rome, Italy

Petrecca, Vincent R *Businessman*
%Hubbell Inc, 584 Derby Milford Rd, Orange, CT 06477, USA

Petrello, Anthony G *Businessman*
%Nabors Industries, 515 W Greens Rd, Houston, TX 77067, USA

Petrenko, Viktor *Figure Skater*
%International Skating Center, 1375 Hopmeadow St, Simsbury, CT 06070, USA

Petri, Michala *Concert Recorder Player*
Nodde-Hegnet 30, Nodebo, 3480 Fredensborg, Denmark

Petrie, Daniel M, Jr *Movie Director*
%Richland/Wunsch/Hohman Agency, 9220 Sunset Blvd, #311, Los Angeles, CA 90069, USA

Petrie, Daniel M, Sr *Movie, Theater Director*
13201 Haney Place, Los Angeles, CA 90049, USA

Petrie, Geoff *Basketball Player, Executive*
%Sacramento Kings, 1 Sports Parkway, Sacramento, CA 95834, USA

Petrie, George O *Actor*
%Gage Group, 9255 Sunset Blvd, #515, Los Angeles, CA 90069, USA

Petrillo, Anthony R *Businessman*
%Kash n' Karry Food Stores, 6422 Harney Rd, Tampa, FL 33610, USA

Petrocelli, Americo P (Rico) *Baseball Player*
19 Townsend Rd, Lynnfield, MA 01940, USA

Petrone, Patrick J *Financier*
%Sovereign Bancorp, 1130 Berkshire Blvd, Wyomissing, PA 19610, USA

Petrone, Rocco A *Missile Engineer*
1329 Granvia Altamira, Palos Verdes Estates, CA 90274, USA

Petrov, Andrei P *Composer*
Petrovskaya Str 42, #75, 197046 St Petersburg, Russia

Petrov, Nikolai A *Concert Pianist*
Kutuzovsky Prosp 26, #23, 121 165 Moscow, Russia

Petrovics, Emil *Composer*
Attila Ut 29, 1013 Budapest, Hungary

Petry, Daniel J (Dan) *Baseball Player*
1808 Cartlen Dr, Placentia, CA 92670, USA

Petry, Thomas E *Businessman*
%Eagle-Picher Industries, 580 Walnut St, Cincinnati, OH 45202, USA

Pett, Joel *Editorial Cartoonist*
%Lexington Herald-Leader, Editorial Dept, Main & Midland, Lexington, KY 40507, USA

P

Peterson - Pett

P

Pettengill, Gordon H *Planetary Physicist*
%Massachusetts Institute of Technology, Space Research Center, Cambridge, 02139, USA

Petterson, Donald K *Diplomat*
American Embassy Khartoum, #63900, APO, AE 09829, USA

Pettet, Joanna *Actress*
%Paradigm Agency, 10100 Santa Monica Blvd, #2500, Los Angeles, CA 90067, USA

Pettibon, Raymond *Artist*
%Richard/Bennett Gallery, 10337 Wilshire Blvd, Los Angeles, CA 90024, USA

Pettigrew, L Eudora *Educator*
%State University of New York, President's Office, Old Westbury, NY 11568, USA

Pettijohn, Francis J *Geologist*
11630 Glen Arm Rd, #V-51, Glen Arm, MD 21057, USA

Pettit, T Christopher *Financier*
%Lehman Brothers, 3 World Financial Center, New York, NY 10285, USA

Pettit, W Thomas (Tom) *Commentator*
%NBC-TV, News Dept, 4001 Nebraska Ave NW, Washington, DC 20016, USA

Petty, Kyle *Auto Racing Driver*
4941 Finch Farm Rd, Trinity, NC 27370, USA

Petty, Lori *Actress*
15060 Ventura Blvd, #350, Sherman Oaks, CA 91403, USA

Petty, Richard *Auto Racing Driver*
PO Box 86, 311 Branson Mill Rd, Randleman, NC 27317, USA

Petty, Tom *Singer*
%Levine/Schneider, 433 N Camden Dr, Beverly Hills, CA 90210, USA

Peugeot, Roland *Businessman*
%Establissements Pergeot Ferres, 75 Ave Grande Armee, 75116 Paris, France

Peyser, Penny *Actress*
%Artists Agency, 10000 Santa Monica Blvd, #305, Los Angeles, CA 90067, USA

Peyton of Yeovil, John W W *Government Official, England*
Old Malt House, Hinton St George, Somerset TA17 8SE, England

Pezzano, Chuck *Bowling Writer*
%Professional Bowlers Assn, 1720 Merriman Rd, Akron, OH 44313, USA

Pfaff, Judy *Artist*
%Holly Solomon Gallery, 172 Mercer St, New York, NY 10012, USA

Pfann, George R *Football Player*
120 Warwick Place, Ithaca, NY 14850, USA

Pfeifer, Friedl *Skier*
6430 E Hummingbird Lane, Paradise Valley, AZ 85253, USA

Pfeiffer, Carl E *Businessman*
%Quanex Corp, 1900 W Loop S, Houston, TX 77027, USA

Pfeiffer, Doug *Ski Instructor, Editor*
PO Box 1806, Big Bear Lake, CA 92315, USA

Pfeiffer, Eckhard *Businessman*
%Compaq Computer Corp, 20555 State Highway 249, Houston, TX 77070, USA

Pfeiffer, Michelle *Actress*
2210 Wilshire Blvd, #998, Santa Monica, CA 90403, USA

Pfeiffer, Norman *Architect*
%Hardy Holzman Pfeiffer, 811 W 7th St, Los Angeles, CA 90017, USA

Pfenniger, Richard C, Jr *Businessman*
%IVAX Corp, 8800 NW 36th St, Miami, FL 33178, USA

Pfister, Peter A *Businessman*
%Adia Services, 100 Redwood Shores Parkway, Redwood City, CA 94065, USA

Pflimlin, Pierre *Prime Minister, France*
24 Ave de la Paix, 67000 Strasbourg, France

Pflug, Jo Ann *Actress*
118 Bowsprit Dr, North Palm Beach, FL 33408, USA

Pfund, Randy *Basketball Coach, Executive*
%Miami Heat, Miami Arena, Miami, FL 33136, USA

Phair, Liz *Singer, Songwriter*
%Matador Records, 676 Broadway, New York, NY 10012, USA

Phantog *Mountaineer*
%Wuxi Sports & Physical Culture Commission, Jiagnsu, China

Phelan, Jim *Basketball Coach*
%Mount St. Mary's College, Athletic Dept, Emmitsburg, MD 21727, USA

Phelps, Ashton, Jr *Publisher*
%New Orleans Times-Picayune, 3800 Howard Ave, New Orleans, LA 70140, USA

Phelps, Edmund S *Economist*
45 E 89th St, New York, NY 10128, USA

Pettengill - Phelps

Phelps, Michael E *Neuroscientist*
16720 Huerta Rd, Encino, CA 91436, USA

Philbin, Regis *Entertainer*
955 Park Ave, New York, NY 10028, USA

Philip *Crown Prince, England; Duke of Edinburgh*
%Buckingham Palace, London SW1A 1AA, England

Philip (Saliba), Primate *Religious Leader*
%Antiochian Orthodox Christian Church, 358 Mountain Rd, Englewood, NJ 07631, USA

Philippe *Crown Prince, Belgium*
%Koninklijk Palais, Rue de Brederode, 1000 Brussels, Belgium

Philips, Jesse *Businessman*
3870 Honey Hill Lane, Dayton, OH 45405, USA

Phillip, Andy *Basketball Player*
PO Box 385, Rancho Mirage, CA 92270, USA

Phillips, Caryl *Writer*
%Amherst College, English Dept, Amherst, MA 01002, USA

Phillips, Chynna *Singer, Actress*
938 2nd St, #302, Santa Monica, CA 90403, USA

Phillips, Grace *Actress*
%Gersh Agency, 232 N Canon Dr, Beverly Hills, CA 90210, USA

Phillips, Graham H *Businessman*
%Ogilvy & Mather Worldwide, Worldwide Plaza, 309 W 49th St, New York, NY 10019, USA

Phillips, Harry J, Sr *Businessman*
%Browning-Ferris Industries, 757 N Eldridge Parkway, Houston, TX 77079, USA

Phillips, Harvey *Concert Tuba Player*
%TubaRanch, 4769 S Harrell Rd, Bloomington, IN 47401, USA

Phillips, Howard *Public Policy Anaylst*
%Conservative Caucus, 47 West St, Boston, MA 02111, USA

Phillips, John *Singer (Mamas & Papas), Songwriter*
Marmont, Langham House, 308 Regent St, London W1R 5AL, England

Phillips, John D *Businessman*
%Actava Group, 4900 Georgia-Pacific Center, Atlanta, GA 30303, USA

Phillips, Julia *Movie Producer, Writer*
2534 Benedict Canyon Dr, Beverly Hills, CA 90210, USA

Phillips, Julianne *Actress*
2227 Mandeville Canyon Rd, Los Angeles, CA 90049, USA

Phillips, Kevin P *Political Anaylst*
%American Political Research Corp, 7316 Wisconsin Ave, Bethesda, MD 20814, USA

Phillips, Lou Diamond *Actor*
11766 Wilshire Blvd, #1470, Los Angeles, CA 90025, USA

Phillips, Mackenzie *Actress*
PO Box 396, Minisink Hills, PA 18341, USA

Phillips, Michael W *Financier*
%Sears Roebuck Acceptance Corp, 3711 Kennett Pike, Greenville, DE 19807, USA

Phillips, Michelle *Actress, Singer (Mamas & Papas)*
10557 Troon Ave, Los Angeles, CA 90064, USA

Phillips, Norma *Social Activist*
%Mothers Against Drunk Driving, PO Box 819100, Dallas, TX 75381, USA

Phillips, Owen M *Geophysical Engineer*
%Johns Hopkins University, Geophysical Mechanics Dept, Baltimore, MD 21218, USA

Phillips, Robert W *Astronaut*
%NASA Hdqs, Code D-4, Washington, DC 20546, USA

Phillips, Sian *Actress*
8 Alexa Court, 78 Lexham Gardens, London W8 6JL, England

Phillips, Stone *Commentator*
%NBC-TV, News Dept, 30 Rockefeller Plaza, New York, NY 10112, USA

Phillips, Susan M *Financier, Government Official*
%Federal Reserve Board, 20th St & Constitution Ave NW, Washington, DC 20551, USA

Phillips, Warren H *Publisher*
%Bridge Works Publications, PO Box 1798, Bridgehampton, NY 11932, USA

Phillips, Wendy *Actress*
3231 Greenfield Ave, Los Angeles, CA 90034, USA

Phillips, William *Editor, Writer*
%Partisan Review, Editorial Dept, 236 Bay State Rd, Boston, MA 02215, USA

Phipps, Howard, Jr *Financier*
%Bessemer Group, 100 Woodbridge Center Dr, Woodbridge, NJ 07095, USA

Phipps, Michael E (Mike) *Football Player*
20912 Pinar Trail, Boca Raton, FL 33433, USA

P

Phipps, Ogden M   *Financier, Thoroughbred Racing Executive*
%Bessemer Group, 100 Woodbridge Center Dr, Woodbridge, NJ 07095, USA

Piaget, Jean   *Psychologist*
%Geneva University, Psychology & Education Dept, Geneva, Switzerland

Piano, Renzo   *Architect*
Via Rubens 29, 16158 Genoa, Italy

Piazza, Marguerite   *Opera Singer*
5400 Park Ave, #301, Memphis, TN 38119, USA

Picachy, Lawrence Cardinal   *Religious Leader*
%Archbishop's House, 32 Park St, Calcutta 700016, India

Picard, Dennis J   *Businessman*
%Raytheon Co, 141 Spring St, Lexington, MA 02173, USA

Picard, Henry   *Golfer*
13 Formosa Dr, Charleston, SC 29407, USA

Picardo, Robert   *Actor*
4926 Commonwealth Ave, La Canada, CA 91011, USA

Picasso, Paloma   *Jewelry Designer*
%Lopez-Cambil Ltd, 37 W 57th St, New York, NY 10019, USA

Piccard, Franck   *Skier*
%General Delivery, Les Sailses, France

Piccard, Jacques E J   *Underwater Scientist*
Place d'Armes, 1096 Cully, Switzerland

Piccinini, Robert   *Businessman*
%Save Mart Supermarkets, 1800 Standiford Ave, Modesto, CA 95350, USA

Piccoli, Michel   *Actor*
11 Rue Des Lions St Paul, 75004 Paris, France

Piccone, Robin   *Fashion Designer*
%Piccone Apparel Corp, 1424 Washington Blvd, Venice, CA 90291, USA

Picerni, Paul   *Actor*
19119 Wells Dr, Tarzana, CA 91356, USA

Pichler, Joseph A   *Businessman*
%Kroger Co, 1014 Vine St, Cincinnati, OH 45202, USA

Pickard, Nancy   *Writer*
2502 W 71st Terrace, Prairie Village, KS 66208, USA

Pickens, Carl   *Football Player*
%Cincinnati Bengals, 200 Riverfront Stadium, Cincinnati, OH 45202, USA

Pickens, Jo Ann   *Opera Singer*
%Norman McCann Artists, 56 Lawrie Park Gardens, London SE26 6XJ, England

Pickens, T Boone, Jr   *Businessman*
%Mesa Inc, Trammell Crow Center, 2001 Ross Ave, Dallas, TX 75201, USA

Pickering, James H   *Educator*
%University of Houston, President's Office, Houston, TX 77204, USA

Pickering, Thomas R   *Diplomat*
%State Department, 2201 "C" St NW, Washington, DC 20520, USA

Pickering, William H   *Scientist, Educator*
292 St Katherine Dr, Flintridge, CA 91011, USA

Pickett, Bobby   *Singer*
%Stuart Hersh Entertainment, PO Box 310, Hartsdale, NY 10530, USA

Pickett, Cindy   *Actress*
662 N Van Ness Ave, #305, Los Angeles, CA 90004, USA

Pickett, Michael D   *Businessman*
%Merisel Inc, 200 Continental Blvd, El Segundo, CA 90245, USA

Pickett, Wilson   *Singer*
%Talent Source, 1560 Broadway, #1308, New York, NY 10036, USA

Pickitt, John L   *Air Force General*
38 Sunrise Point Rd, Lake Wylie, SC 29710, USA

Pickles, Christina   *Actress*
137 S Westgate Ave, Los Angeles, CA 90049, USA

Piech, Ferdinand   *Businessman*
%Volkswagenwerk AG, 38434 Wolfsburg, Germany

Piel, Gerard   *Editor, Publisher*
%Scientific American Magazine, 415 Madison Ave, New York, NY 10017, USA

Piel, Jonathan   *Editor*
%Scientific American Magazine, 415 Madison Ave, New York, NY 10017, USA

Pieper, W Bernard   *Businessman*
%Halliburton Co, Lincoln Plaza, 500 N Akard St, Dallas, TX 75201, USA

Pierce, Daniel   *Financier*
%Scudder Stevens Clark, 345 Park Ave, New York, NY 10154, USA

Phipps - Pierce

Pierce, David Hyde *Actor*
%J Michael Bloom Ltd, 9255 Sunset Blvd, #710, Los Angeles, CA 90069, USA

Pierce, Harvey R *Businessman*
%American Family Insurance Group, 6000 American Parkway, Madison, WI 53783, USA

Pierce, John R *Electrical Engineer*
4008 El Cerrito Rd, Palo Alto, CA 94306, USA

Pierce, Mary *Tennis Player*
%Nick Bollettieri Tennis Academy, 5500 34th St W, Bradenton, FL 34210, USA

Pierce, Ricky C *Basketball Player*
%Indiana Pacers, Market Square Arena, 300 E Market St, Indianapolis, IN 46204, USA

Pierce, Samuel R, Jr *Secretary, Housing & Urban Development*
16 W 77th St, New York, NY 10024, USA

Pierce, W William (Billy) *Baseball Player*
9000 S Francisco, Evergreen Park, IL 60805, USA

Piercy, Marge *Writer*
%Moddlemarsh Inc, PO Box 1473, Wellfleet, MA 02667, USA

Pierpoint, Eric *Actor*
10929 Morrison St, #14, North Hollywood, CA 91601, USA

Pierpoint, Robert *Commentator*
%CBS-TV, News Dept, 2020 "M" St NW, Washington, DC 20036, USA

Pierre, Andrew J *Political Scientist*
%Carnegie Endowment for Peace, 2400 "N" St NW, Washington, DC 20037, USA

Pierson, Eric *Businessman*
%Willcox & Gibbs Inc, 150 Alhambra Circle, Coral Gables, FL 33134, USA

Pierson, Frank R *Movie, Television Director, Writer*
1223 Amalfi Dr, Pacific Palisades, CA 90272, USA

Pierson, Jean *Businessman*
%Airbus-Industrie, 5 Ave de Villiers, 75017 Paris, France

Pierson, Markus *Sculptor*
%OutWest, 7216-F Washington NE, Albuquerque, NM 87109, USA

Pietrangeli, Nicola *Tennis Player*
Via Eustachio Manfredi 15, Rome, Italy

Piggty, Leo J *Army General*
DCG, Material Readiness, 5001 Eisenhower Ave, Arlington, VA 22333, USA

Pigford, Robert L *Chemical Engineer*
300 Wilson Rd, Newark, DE 19711, USA

Piggott, Lester K *Thoroughbred Racing Jockey*
Florizel, Newmarket, Suffolk, England

Pigliucci, Riccardi *Businessman*
%Perkin-Elmer Corp, 761 Main Ave, Norwalk, CT 06859, USA

Pigott, Charles M *Businessman*
%Paccar Inc, 777 106th Ave NE, Bellevue, WA 98004, USA

Pigott-Smith, Tim *Actor*
%Michael Whitehall, 125 Gloucester Rd, London SW7 4TE, England

Pihos, Peter L (Pete) *Football Player*
%Home Improvement, 112 E Little Creek Rd, Norfolk, VA 23505, USA

Pike, Larry R *Businessman*
%Union Central Life Insurance, 1876 Waycross Rd, Cincinnati, OH 45240, USA

Pilarczyk, Daniel E *Religious Leader*
100 E 8th St, Cincinnati, OH 45202, USA

Pilgrim, Lindy M *Businessman*
%Pilgrim's Pride Corp, 110 S Texas St, Pittsburg, TX 75686, USA

Pilgrim, Lonnie A (Bo) *Businessman*
%Pilgrim's Pride Corp, 110 S Texas St, Pittsburg, TX 75686, USA

Pilic, Nicki *Tennis Player*
Neckarstr 2, 81677 Munich, Germany

Pilkis, Simon J *Physiologist, Biophysicist*
%State University of New York, Health Sciences Center, Stony Brook, NY 11794, USA

Pillard, Charles H *Labor Leader*
%Electrical Workers Union, 1125 15th St NW, Washington, DC 20005, USA

Pilliod, Charles J, Jr *Businessman, Diplomat*
494 Saint Andrews Dr, Akron, OH 44303, USA

Pillow, Ray *Singer*
%Joe Taylor Artist Agency, 2802 Columbine Place, Nashville, TN 37204, USA

Pillsbury, Edmund P *Museum Director*
%Kimbell Art Museum, 3333 Camp Bowie Blvd, Fort Worth, TX 76107, USA

Pilson, Neal H *Television Executive*
%CBS-TV, Sports Dept, 51 W 52nd St, New York, NY 10019, USA

P

Pimenta, Simon I Cardinal — *Religious Leader*
%Archbishop's House, 21 Nathalal Parekh Marg, Bombay 400 039, India

Pimentel, Albert A — *Businessman*
%LSI Logic Corp, 1551 McCarthy Blvd, Milpitas, CA 95035, USA

Pinchot, Bronson — *Actor*
%Brillstein Co, 9150 Wilshire Blvd, #350, Beverly Hills, CA 90212, USA

Pinckney, Ed — *Basketball Player*
%Toronto Raptors, 20 Bay St, #1702, Toronto ON M5J 2N8, Canada

Pincus, Lionel I — *Financier*
%E M Warburg Pincus Co, 466 Lexington Ave, New York, NY 10017, USA

Pine, Robert — *Actor*
11923 Addison St, Valley Village, CA 91607, USA

Pinera, Mike — *Singer*
4300 Bayview Dr, Fort Lauderdale, FL 33308, USA

Pingel, John — *Football Player*
582 Peach Tree Lane, Grosse Pointe Woods, MI 48236, USA

Pingree, David — *Educator*
%Brown University, Math History Dept, Providence, RI 02912, USA

Piniella, Louis V (Lou) — *Baseball Player, Manager*
1005 Taray De Avila, Tampa, FL 33613, USA

Pinkel, Donald P — *Pediatrician*
2501 Addison Rd, Houston, TX 77030, USA

Pinkerton, Guy C — *Financier*
%Washington Federal Savings, 425 Pike St, Seattle, WA 98101, USA

Pinkett, Jada — *Actress*
10683 Santa Monica Blvd, Los Angeles, CA 90025, USA

Pinkston, Kenneth H — *Businessman*
%Willis Corroon Corp, 26 Century Blvd, Nashville, TN 37214, USA

Pinnock, Trevor — *Conductor*
35 Gloucester Crescent, London NW1 7DL, England

Pinochet Ugarte, Augusto — *President, Chile*
%Commander in Chief's Office, Military Affairs Office, Santiago, Chile

Pinson, Vada E — *Baseball Player*
710 31st St, Oakland, CA 94609, USA

Pintasilgo, Maria de Lourdes — *Premier, Portugal*
Almeda Santo Antonio dos Capuchos 4-5, 1100 Lisbon, Portugal

Pintauro, Danny — *Actor*
%Agency For Performing Arts, 9000 Sunset Blvd, #1200, Los Angeles, CA 90069, USA

Pinter, Harold — *Writer*
%Judy Daish Assoc, 83 Eastbourne Mews, London W2 6LQ, England

Pinter, Michael R — *Businessman*
%Kemper Reinsurance Co, 1 Kemper Dr, Long Grove, IL 60047, USA

Piore, Emanuel R — *Physicist*
2 5th Ave, New York, NY 10011, USA

Piovanelli, Silvano Cardinal — *Religious Leader*
Piazzi S Giovanni 3, 50129 Florence, Italy

Pipes, R Byron — *Educator*
%Rensselaer Polytechnic Institute, President's Office, Troy, NY 12180, USA

Pippard, A Brian — *Physicist*
30 Porson Rd, Cambridge CB2 2EU, England

Pippen, Scottie — *Basketball Player*
%Chicago Bulls, 1901 W Madison St, Chicago, IL 60612, USA

Piquet, Nelson — *Auto Racing Driver*
9 Ave des Papauns Fontvieille, Monte Carlo, Monaco

Piraro, Dan — *Cartoonist (Bizarro)*
%Chronicle Features, 870 Market St, San Francisco, CA 94102, USA

Pirelli, Leopoldo — *Businessman*
Piazzle Cadorna 5, 20123 Milan, Italy

Pires de Miranda, Pedro — *Businessman*
%Petroleos de Portugal, Rua das Flores 7, 1200 Lisbon, Portugal

Pires, Pedro V R — *Prime Minister, Cape Verde; Army General*
%PAICV, CP 22, Sao Tiago, Cape Verde

Pironio, Eduardo Cardinal — *Religious Leader*
Piazza del S Uffizio 11, 00193 Rome, Italy

Pischetsrider, Bernd — *Businessman*
%Bayerishe Motoren Werke AG (BMW), Petuelring 130, 80809 Munich, Germany

Piscopo, Joe — *Actor*
122 E 42nd St, #210, New York, NY

Pisier, Marie-France *Actress*
%Gaumont International, 30 Ave Charles de Gaulle, 92200 Neuilly, France

Pister, Karl S *Educator*
%University of California, Chancellor's Office, Santa Cruz, CA 95064, USA

Pitillo, Maria *Actress*
%William Morris Agency, 151 S El Camino Dr, Beverly Hills, CA 90212, USA

Pitino, Richard (Rick) *Basketball Coach*
%University of Kentucky, Memorial Coliseum, Lexington, KY 40506, USA

Pitman, Charles H *Marine Corps General*
%Deputy Chief Staff Aviation, Marine Corps Headquarters, Washington, DC 20380, USA

Pitney, Gene *Singer*
8901 6 Mile Rd, Caledonia, WI 53108, USA

Pitou Zimmerman, Penny *Skier*
%Penny Pitou Travel, 55 Canal St, Laconia, NH 03246, USA

Pitt, Brad *Actor*
%Creative Artists Agency, 9830 Wilshire Blvd, Beverly Hills, CA 90212, USA

Pittendrigh, Colin S *Biologist*
2309 Fairway Dr, Bozeman, MT 59715, USA

Pittman, James A, Jr *Endocrinologist*
5 Ridge Dr, Birmingham, AL 35213, USA

Pittman, John A *Korean War Army Hero (CMH)*
303 Grand Ave, Box 331, Greenwood, MS 38935, USA

Pittman, R F *Publisher*
%Tampa Tribune, 202 S Parker St, Tampa, FL 33606, USA

Pittman, Richard A *Vietnam War Marine Corps Hero (CMH)*
3758 Mulberry St, Oceanside, CA 92054, USA

Pittman, Robert W *Television Executive*
%Time Warner Enterprises, 75 Rockefeller Plaza, New York, NY 10019, USA

Pitts, Keith B *Businessman*
%OrNda HealthCorp, 3401 West End Ave, Nashville, TN 37203, USA

Pitts, Ron *Sportscaster*
%Fox-TV, Sports Dept, 205 E 67th St, New York, NY 10021, USA

Pitts, Tyrone S *Religious Leader*
%Progressive National Baptist Convention, 601 50th St NE, Washington, DC 20019, USA

Pitzer, Kenneth S *Chemist*
12 Eagle Hill, Kensington, CA 94707, USA

Piza, Arthur Luiz de *Artist*
16 Rue Dauphine, 75006 Paris, France

Place, Mary Kay *Actress*
2739 Motor Ave, Los Angeles, CA 90064, USA

Plachta, Leonard *Educator*
%Central Michigan University, President's Office, Mt Pleasant, MI 48859, USA

Plager, Bob *Hockey Coach, Executive*
%St Louis Blues, St Louis Arena, 5700 Oakland Ave, St Louis, MO 63110, USA

Plain, Belva *Writer*
%Delacorte Press, 1540 Broadway, New York, NY 10036, USA

Plakson, Suzie *Actress*
152 S Sycamore Ave, #301, Los Angeles, CA 90036, USA

Planchon, Roger *Theater Director, Playwright*
%Artmedia, 10 Ave George V, 75008 Paris, France

Planinc, Milka *Prime Minister, Yugoslavia*
%Federal Executive Council, Bul Lenjina 2, 11075 Novl Belgrad, Yugoslavia

Plank, Raymond *Businessman*
%Apache Corp, 2000 Post Oak Blvd, Houston, TX 77056, USA

Plano, Richard J *Physicist*
PO Box 5306, Somerset, NJ 08875, USA

Plant, Robert *Singer, Songwriter*
484 Kings Rd, London SW10 0LF, England

Plante, William M *Commentator*
%CBS-TV, News Dept, 2020 "M" St NW, Washington, DC 20036, USA

Plantu (Jean H Plamtureux) *Editorial Cartoonist*
%Le Monde, Editorial Dept, 7 Rue Falguiere, 75015 Paris, France

Platini, Michel *Soccer Player*
%Comite d'Org, 90 Ave des Champs-Elysees, 75008 Paris, France

Platon, Nicolas *Archaeologist*
Leof Alexandras 126, 11471 Athens, Greece

Platt, Kenneth A *Physician*
11435 Quivas Way, Westminster, CO 80234, USA

P

Pisier - Platt

P

Platt, Nicholas — *Diplomat*
131 E 69th St, New York, NY 10021, USA

Platten, Peter M, III — *Financier*
%Marshall & Ilsley Corp, 770 N Water St, Milwaukee, WI 53202, USA

Plavinsky, Dmitri — *Artist*
Arbat Str 51, Kotp 2, #97, 121002 Moscow, Russia

Player, Gary J — *Golfer*
PO Box 785629, Sandton 2146, South Africa

Playten, Alice — *Actress*
33 5th Ave, New York, NY 10003, USA

Pleau, Larry — *Hockey Coach*
%Hartford Whalers, Coliseum, 242 Trumbell St, #800, Hartford, CT 06103, USA

Pleshette, Suzanne — *Actress*
PO Box 1492, Beverly Hills, CA 90213, USA

Pletcher, Eldon — *Editorial Cartoonist*
210 Canberra Court, Slidell, LA 70458, USA

Pletnev, Mikhail V — *Conductor*
Starpkonyushenny Per 33, #16, Moscow, Russia

Plettner, Bernhard — *Businessman*
%Siemens A G, Wittelsbacherplatz 2, 80333 Munich, Germany

Plettner, Helmut — *Businessman*
%Bosch-Siemens Hausgerate, Hochstr 17, 81541 Munich, Germany

Plimpton, Calvin H — *Physician*
%Downstate Medical Center, 450 Clarkson Ave, Brooklyn, NY 11203, USA

Plimpton, George A — *Writer*
%Paris Review, 541 E 72nd St, New York, NY 10021, USA

Plimpton, Martha — *Actress*
502 Park Ave, #15-G, New York, NY 10022, USA

Plisetskaya, Maiya M — *Ballerina*
Tverskaya 25/9, #31, 103050 Moscow, Russia

Pliska, Paul — *Opera Singer*
%Metropolitan Opera Assn, Lincoln Center Plaza, New York, NY 10023, USA

Plitt, Henry G — *Entertainment Executive*
%Showscan Film Corp, 3939 Landmark St, Culver City, CA 90232, USA

Plotkin, Stanley A — *Virologist*
3940 Delancey St, Philadelphia, PA 19104, USA

Plowright, Joan — *Actress*
%Write on Cue, 15 New Row, #300, London WC2N 4LA, England

Plowright, Rosalind — *Opera Singer*
%Columbia Artists Mgmt Inc, 165 W 57th St, New York, NY 10019, USA

Plum, Milton R (Milt) — *Football Player*
1104 Oakside Court, Raleigh, NC 27609, USA

Plumb, Eve — *Actress*
145 S Fairfax Ave, #310, Los Angeles, CA 90036, USA

Plumeri, Joseph J — *Businessman*
%Travelers Inc, 65 E 55th St, New York, NY 10022, USA

Plummer, Amanda — *Actress*
49 Wampum Hill Rd, Weston, CT 06883, USA

Plummer, Christopher — *Actor*
49 Wampum Hill Rd, Weston, CT 06883, USA

Plunkett, James W (Jim), Jr — *Football Player*
51 Kilroy Way, Atherton, CA 94027, USA

Plyushch, Ivan S — *Head of State, Ukraine*
%Supreme Soviet, Government Bldg, Bankivska Ul 11, Kiev 252009, Ukraine

Pocklington, Peter H — *Hockey Executive*
%Edmonton Oilers, Northlands Coliseum, Edmonton AB T5B 4M9, Canada

Podewell, Cathy — *Actress*
17328 S Crest Dr, Los Angeles, CA 90035, USA

Podhoretz, Norman — *Editor, Writer*
%Commentary Magazine, Editorial Dept, 165 E 56th St, New York, NY 10022, USA

Podres, John J (Johnny) — *Baseball Player*
1 Colonial Court, Glens Falls, NY 12804, USA

Poe, Gregory — *Fashion Designer*
%Dutch Courage, 1950 S Santa Fe Ave, Los Angeles, CA 90021, USA

Poelker, John S — *Financier*
%Fleet Finance Inc, 211 Perimeter Center Parkway, Atlanta, GA 30346, USA

Pogorelich, Ivo — *Concert Pianist*
%Kantor Concert Mgmt, 67 Teignmouth Rd, London NW2 4EA, England

Platt - Pogorelich

Pogrebin, Letty Cottin *Editor, Writer*
33 W 67th St, New York, NY 10023, USA

Pogue, L Welch *Attorney*
5204 Kenwood Ave, Chevy Chase, MD 20815, USA

Pogue, William R *Astronaut*
%Vutuara Assoc, 1101 S Old Missouri Rd, #30, Springdale, AR 72764, USA

Pohl, Dan *Golfer*
11609 S Tusaye Court, Phoenix, AZ 85044, USA

Pohl, Karl Otto *Financier*
%Oppenheim Jr Cie, Bockenheimer Landstr 20, 60325 Frankfurt/Main, Germany

Pohlad, Carl R *Baseball Executive*
%Minnesota Twins, 501 Chicago Ave S, Minneapolis, MN 55415, USA

Poile, N R (Bud) *Hockey Executive*
1509-2004 Fullerton Ave, North Vancouver BC V7P 3G8, Canada

Poindexter, Christian H *Businessman*
%Baltimore Gas & Electric, 39 W Lexington St, Baltimore, MD 21201, USA

Poindexter, John M *Navy Admiral, Government Official*
1322 Merry Ridge Rd, #400, Washington, DC 20036, USA

Pointer, Anita *Singer (Pointer Sisters)*
12060 Crest Court, Beverly Hills, CA 90210, USA

Pointer, Priscilla *Singer (Pointer Sisters)*
213 16th St, Santa Monica, CA 90402, USA

Pointer, Ruth *Singer (Pointer Sisters)*
6408 Trancas Canyon Rd, Malibu, CA 90265, USA

Poitier, Sidney *Actor*
9255 Doheny Rd, West Hollywood, CA 90069, USA

Pokelwaldt, Robert N *Businessman*
%York International, 631 S Richland Ave, York, PA 17403, USA

Polanski, Roman *Movie Director*
%Georges Beaume, 201 Rue de Faubourg St Honore, 75008 Paris, France

Polanyi, John C *Nobel Chemistry Laureate*
%University of Toronto, Chemistry Dept, Toronto ON M5S 1A1, Canada

Poletti, Ugo Cardinal *Religious Leader*
Vicario di Roma, Piazza S Giovanni in Laterano 6, 00184 Rome, Italy

Polgar, Laszlo *Opera Singer*
Abel Jeno Ut 12, 1113 Budapest, Hungary

Polke, Sigmar *Artist*
%Michael Werner, 21 E 67th St, New York, NY 10021, USA

Poll, Martin H *Movie Producer*
%Martin Poll Productions, 8961 Sunset Blvd, #E, Los Angeles, CA 90069, USA

Polla, Dennis L *Microbiotics Engineer*
%University of Minnesota, Electrical Engineering Dept, Minneapolis, MN 55455, USA

Pollack, Daniel *Concert Pianist*
28 Canterbury Lane, Short Hills, NJ 07078, USA

Pollack, Jim *Actor*
%Ericka Wain Agency, 1418 N Highland Ave, #102, Los Angeles, CA 90028, USA

Pollack, Joseph *Labor Leader*
%Insurance Workers Union, 1017 12th St NW, Washington, DC 20005, USA

Pollack, Lester *Financier*
%Centre Partners, 1 Rockefeller Center, New York, NY 10020, USA

Pollack, Sydney *Movie Director*
13525 Lucca Dr, Pacific Palisades, CA 90272, USA

Pollak, Cheryl A *Actress*
%Gersh Agency, 232 N Canon Dr, Beverly Hills, CA 90210, USA

Pollan, Tracy *Actress*
Lottery Hill Farm, South Woodstock, VT 05071, USA

Pollard, C William *Businessman*
%ServiceMaster Industries, 1 ServiceMaster Rd, Downers Grove, IL 60515, USA

Pollard, Michael J *Actor*
29652 Cuthbert Rd, Malibu, CA 90265, USA

Pollard, Richard F *Financier*
%BayBanks Inc, 175 Federal St, Boston, BA 02110, USA

Pollay, Richard L *Financier*
%Chicago Title & Trust, 171 N Clark St, Chicago, IL 60601, USA

Pollen, Arabella R H *Fashion Designer*
Canham Mews, #8, Canham Rd, London W3 7SR, England

Pollicino, Joseph A *Financier*
%CIT Group Holdings, 650 CIT Dr, Livingston, NJ 07039, USA

Pollin, Abe *Basketball, Hockey Executive*
%Centre Group, Capital Centre, 1 Truman Dr, Landover, MD 20785, USA

Pollini, Maurizio *Concert Pianist*
%RESIA, Via Manzoni 31, 20120 Milan, Italy

Pollock, Alex J *Businessman*
%Federal Home Loan Bank, 111 E Wacker Dr, Chicago, IL 60601, USA

Pollock, Michael P *Navy Fleet Admiral, England*
Ivy House, Churchstoke, Montgomery, Powys SY15 6DU, Wales

Pollock, Thomas P *Entertainment Executive*
%MCA Inc, 100 Universal City Plaza, Universal City, CA 91608, USA

Polyakov, Valery *Cosmonaut*
%Health Ministry, Choroshevskoye Chaussee 76-A, 123 007 Moscow, Russia

Polynice, Olden *Basketball Player*
%Sacramento Kings, 1 Sports Parkway, Sacramento, CA 95834, USA

Pomerantz, John J *Businessman*
%Leslie Fay Co, 1400 Broadway, New York, NY 10018, USA

Pomerantz, Marvin A *Businessman*
%Gaylord Container Corp, 500 Lake Cook Rd, Deerfield, IL 60015, USA

Pomeroy, Wardell B *Psychotherapist*
1611 Vallejo St, San Francisco, CA 94123, USA

Pommier, Jean Bernard *Concert Pianist*
2 Chemin Des Cotes de Montmoiret, 1012 Lausanne, Switzerland

Pomodora, Arnaldo *Sculptor*
Via Vigevano 5, 20144 Milan, Italy

Ponazecki, Joe *Actor*
%Don Buchwald Assoc, 10 E 44th St, #500, New York, NY 10017, USA

Ponce Enrile, Juan *Government Official, Philippines*
2305 Morado St, Dasmarinas Village, Makati, Metro Manila, Philippines

Ponce, LuAnne *Actress*
3205 W Jeffries Ave, Burbank, CA 91505, USA

Pond, Byron O *Businessman*
%Arvin Industries, Noblitt Plaza, PO Box 3000, Columbus, IN 47202, USA

Pond, Kirk P *Businessman*
%National Semiconductor Corp, 2900 Semiconductor Dr, Santa Clara, CA 95051, USA

Ponder, Henry *Educator*
%Fisk University, President's Office, Nashville, TN 37208, USA

Pons, B Stanley *Chemist*
%University of Utah, Chemistry Dept, Eyring Bldg, Salt Lake City, UT 84112, USA

Pons, Juan *Opera Singer*
%Columbia Artists Mgmt Inc, 165 W 57th St, New York, NY 10019, USA

Pont, John *Football Coach*
482 White Oak Dr, Oxford, OH 45056, USA

Ponti, Carlo *Movie Producer*
Chalet Daniel, Burgenstock, Nidwalden, Switzerland

Ponti, Michael *Concert Pianist*
Heubergstr 32, 83565 Eschenlohe, Germany

Ponty, Jean-Luc *Jazz Violinist, Composer*
12304 Santa Monica Blvd, #119, Los Angeles, CA 90025, USA

Ponzini, Anthony *Actor*
%Gold Marshak Assoc, 3500 W Olive Ave, #1400, Burbank, CA 91505, USA

Pool, John L *Cancer Surgeon*
560 Belden Hill Rd, Wilton, CT 06897, USA

Poole, G Barney *Football Player*
111 Saratoga Circle, Hattisburg, MS 39401, USA

Poole, Shawn W *Businessman*
%Carolina Freight Corp, 1201 E Church St, Cherryville, NC 28021, USA

Poole, William *Government Official, Economist*
%Brown University, Economics Dept, Providence, RI 01912, USA

Pooley, Don *Golfer*
PO Box 35352, Tucson, AZ 85740, USA

Poons, Larry *Artist*
831 Broadway, New York, NY 10003, USA

Poore, Edgar E *Businessman*
%Richfood Holdings, 2000 Richfood Rd, Richmond, VA 23261, USA

Pop, Iggy *Singer, Songwriter*
%Floyd Peluce, 449 S Beverly Dr, #102, Beverly Hills, CA 90212, USA

Popcorn, Faith *Businesswoman*
%Brain Reserve Inc, 1 Madison Ave, New York, NY 10010, USA

Pope, Clarence C, Jr *Religious Leader*
%Diocese of Fort Worth Episcopal Church, 6300 Ridlea Pl, Fort Worth, TX 76116, USA

Pope, Edwin *Sportswriter*
%Miami Herald, 1 Herald Plaza, Miami, FL 33132, USA

Pope, Everett P *WW II Marine Corps Hero (CMH)*
Amelia Island Plantation, 4 Water Oak, Fernandina Beach, FL 32034, USA

Pope, Paula Jean Myers *Diver*
415 Del Norte Rd, Ojai, CA 93023, USA

Pope, Peter T *Businessman*
%Pope & Talbot Inc, 1500 SW 1st Ave, Portland, OR 97201, USA

Popoff, Frank P *Businessman*
%Dow Chemical Co, 2030 Dow Center, Midland, MI 48674, USA

Popov, Leonid I *Cosmonaut*
%Potchta Kosmonavtov, 141 160 Svyosdny Gorodok, Moskovskoi Oblasti, Russia

Popov, Oleg *Actor*
%Organization of State Circues, Pushecnaya 4, Moscow, Russia

Popovich, Pavel R *Cosmonaut, Air Force General*
AIUS-Agroressurs, VNIZ, Bolshevitskij Per 11, 101 000 Moscow, Russia

Poppa, Ryal R *Businessman*
%Storage Technology Corp, 2270 S 88th St, Louisville, CO 80028, USA

Popwell, Albert *Actor*
1427 3rd St, #205, Santa Monica, CA 90401, USA

Porizkova, Paulina *Model, Actress*
331 Newbury St, Boston, MA 02115, USA

Porsche, Ferdinand *Businessman*
%Porsche Dr Ing HCF, Porschenstr 42, 70435 Stuttgart, Germany

Portale, Carl *Publisher*
%Elle Magazine, Hachette Filipacchi, 1633 Broadway, New York, NY 10019, USA

Porteous, Patrick A *WW II British Army Hero (VC)*
Christmas Cottage, Church Lane, Funtington, West Sussex PO 18 9LQ, England

Porter of Luddenham, George *Nobel Chemistry Laureate*
%Imperial College, Photomolecular Sciences Center, London SW7 2BB, England

Porter, Charles E *Businessman*
%Shoney's Inc, 1727 Elm Hill Pike, Nashville, TN 37210, USA

Porter, David H *Educator*
%Skidmore College, President's Office, Saratoga Springs, NY 12866, USA

Porter, Don *Actor*
%William Morris Agency, 151 S El Camino Dr, Beverly Hills, CA 90212, USA

Porter, John A *Businessman*
%LDDS Communications, 515 E Amite St, Jackson, MS 39201, USA

Porter, Keith R *Cytologist, Educator*
%University of Colorado, Molecular Cellular Dept, Boulder, CO 80309, USA

Porter, Richard W *Electrical Engineer*
88 Notch Hill Rd, #369, North Branford, CT 06471, USA

Portera, Vito S *Financier*
%Republic Bank for Savings, 415 Madison Ave, New York, NY 10017, USA

Portis, Charles *Writer*
7417 Kingwood Rd, Little Rock, AR 72207, USA

Portman, John C, Jr *Architect*
%Charles Portman Assoc, 225 Peachtree St NE, #200, Atlanta, GA 30303, USA

Porto, James *Photographer*
480 Canal St, New York, NY 10013, USA

Posner, Roy E *Businessman*
%Loews Corp, 607 Madison Ave, New York, NY 10022, USA

Posnick, Adolph *Businessman*
%Ferro Corp, 1000 Lakeslde Ave, Cleveland, OH 44114, USA

Post, Avery D *Religious Leader*
PO Box 344, Meadowbrook Rd, Norwich, VT 05055, USA

Post, Glen F, III *Businessman*
%Century Telephone Enterprises, 100 Century Park Dr, Monroe, LA 71203, USA

Post, Markie *Actress*
10153 1/2 Riverside Dr, #333, Toluca Lake, CA 91602, USA

Post, Mike *Composer*
%Mike Post Productions, 1007 W Olive Ave, Burbank, CA 91506, USA

Post, Sandra *Golfer*
%Ladies Professional Golf Assn, 2570 Volusia Ave, Daytona Beach, FL 32114, USA

Post, Ted *Movie Director*
%Norman Blumenthal, 11030 Santa Monica Blvd, Los Angeles, CA 90025, USA

P

Pope - Post

P

Poster, Steve *Cinematographer*
%Smith/Gosnell, 1515 Palisades Dr, #N, Pacific Palisades, CA 90272, USA

Postlethwaite, Pete *Actor*
%Markham & Froggat, 4 Windmill St, London W1P 1HF, England

Postlewait, Kathy *Golfer*
%Ladies Professional Golf Assn, 2570 Volusia Ave, Daytona Beach, FL 32114, USA

Postman, Marc *Astronomer*
3311 Greenvale Rd, Pikesville, MD 21208, USA

Poston, Tom *Actor*
2930 Deep Canyon Dr, Beverly Hills, CA 90210, USA

Potok, Chaim *Writer, Artist*
%Alfred A Knopf Inc, 201 E 50th St, New York, NY 10022, USA

Potter, Cynthia *Diver, Sportscaster*
1151 N Saddlewood Ranch Dr, Tucson, AZ 85745, USA

Potter, Dan M *Religious Leader*
PO Box 66052, Albany, NY 12206, USA

Potter, Huntington *Medical Researcher*
%Harvard Medical School, 25 Shattuck St, Boston, MA 02115, USA

Potter, Michael J *Businessman*
%Consolidated Stores, 1105 N Market St, Wilmington, DE 19801, USA

Potter, Philip A *Religious Leader*
3-A York Castle Ave, Kingston 6, Jamaica

Pottruck, David S *Financier*
%Charles Schwab Corp, 101 Montgomery St, San Francisco, CA 94104, USA

Potts, Annie *Actress*
%Erwin Stoff, 7920 Sunset Blvd, #350, Los Angeles, CA 90046, USA

Potts, Cliff *Actor*
PO Box 131, Topanga, CA 90290, USA

Potts, Erwin *Businessman*
%McClatchy Newspapers, 2100 "Q" St, Sacramento, CA 95816, USA

Potts, Thomas H *Financier*
%Resource Mortgage Capital, 10500 Little Patuxent Parkway, Columbia, MD 21044, USA

Potvin, Denis *Hockey Player*
%David Cogan Mgmt, Empire State Building, New York, NY 10118, USA

Potvin, Felix *Hockey Player*
%Toronto Maple Leafs, 60 Carlton St, Toronto ON M5B 1L1, Canada

Poulin, Dave *Hockey Player, Coach*
%University of Notre Dame, Athletic Dept, Notre Dame, IN 46556, USA

Pound, Richard W D *Olympics Official*
87 Arlington Ave, Westmount PQ H3Y 2W5, Canada

Pound, Robert V *Physicist*
87 Pinehurst Rd, Belmont, MA 02178, USA

Pounder, C C H *Actress*
%Susan Smith Assoc, 121 N San Vicente Blvd, Beverly Hills, CA 90211, USA

Poundstone, Paula *Comedienne*
1223 Broadway, #162, Santa Monica, CA 90404, USA

Poupard, Paul Cardinal *Religious Leader*
%Pontificium Consilium Pro Dialogo, 00120 Vatican City, Rome, Italy

Pousette, Lena *Actress*
30766 Lakefront Dr, Agoura Hills, CA 91301, USA

Poussaint, Alvin F *Psychiatrist, Educator*
%Judge Baker Guidance Center, 295 Longwood Ave, Boston, MA 02115, USA

Poutsiaka, William J *Businessman*
%Arkwright Mutual Insurance, 225 Wyman St, Waltham, MA 02154, USA

Povich, Maury R *Commentator, Entertainer*
%Maury Povich Show, 221 W 26th St, New York, NY 10001, USA

Povich, Shirley L *Sportswriter*
%Washington Post, 1150 15th St NW, Washington, DC 20071, USA

Powell, A J Philip *Architect*
%Powell Moya Partners, 21 Upper Cheyne Row, London SW3, England

Powell, Anthony *Writer*
Chantry Near Frome, Somerset BA11 3LJ, England

Powell, Colin L *Army General*
310 S Henry St, Alexandria, VA 22314, USA

Powell, Don G *Financier*
%Van Kampen/American Capital, 1 Parkview Plaza, Oakview Terrace, IL 60181, USA

Powell, Earl A (Rusty), III *Museum Official*
%National Gallery of Art, Constitution Ave & 4th St NW, Washington, DC 20565, USA

Powell, George E, III — *Businessman*
%Yellow Corp, 10777 Barkley, Overland Park, KS 66211, USA

Powell, George E, Jr — *Businessman*
%Yellow Corp, 10777 Barkley, Overland Park, KS 66211, USA

Powell, J Enoch — *Government Official, England*
33 S Eaton Place, London SW1, England

Powell, James B — *Businessman*
%Laboratory Corp of America Holdings, 358 S Main St, Burlington, NC 27215, USA

Powell, James R — *Inventor (Magnetic Levitation Vehicle)*
%Brookhaven National Laboratory, Upton, NY 11973, USA

Powell, Jane — *Singer, Actress*
150 West End Ave, #26-C, New York, NY 10023, USA

Powell, John — *Track Athlete*
%John Powell Assoc, 10445 Mary Ave, Cupertino, CA 95014, USA

Powell, John W (Boog) — *Baseball Player*
333 W Camden St, Baltimore, MD 21201, USA

Powell, Joseph L (Jody) — *Government Official, Journalist*
%Powell Tate, 700 13th St NW, #1000, Washington, DC 20005, USA

Powell, Lewis F, Jr — *Supreme Court Justice*
%US Supreme Court, 1 1st St NE, Washington, DC 20543, USA

Powell, Marvin — *Football Player*
17330 Burbank Blvd, #5, Encino, CA 91316, USA

Powell, Mel — *Composer*
%California School of Arts, Composition Dept, Santa Clarita, CA 91355, USA

Powell, Mike — *Track Athlete*
%Team Powell, PO Box 8000-354, Alta Loma, CA 91701, USA

Powell, Robert — *Actor*
%Jonathan Altaras Assoc, 2 Goodwins Ct, London WC2N 4LL, England

Powers, Alexandra — *Actress*
12142 Burbank Blvd, #2, Valley Village, CA 91607, USA

Powers, Brian M — *Businessman*
%Valassis Communications, 36111 Schoolcraft Rd, Livonia, MI 48150, USA

Powers, J F — *Writer*
%Alfred A Knopf Inc, 201 E 50th St, New York, NY 10022, USA

Powers, James B — *Religious Leader*
%American Baptist Assn, 4605 N State Line, Texarkana, TX 75503, USA

Powers, Mala — *Actress*
10543 Valley Spring Lane, North Hollywood, CA 91602, USA

Powers, Paul J — *Businessman*
%Commerical Intertech Corp, 1775 Logan Ave, Youngstown, OH 44505, USA

Powers, Stefanie — *Actress*
PO Box 67981, Los Angeles, CA 90067, USA

Powter, Susan — *Physical Fitness Instructor*
%Susan Powter Corp, 2220 Colorado Ave, #1, Santa Monica, CA 90404, USA

Pozsgay, Imre — *Government Official, Hungary*
%Parliament Buildings, Kossuth Lajos Ter 1, 1055 Budapest, Hungary

Pramoj, Mom Rachawongse Seni — *Prime Minister, Thailand*
219 Egamai Rd, Bangkok, Thailand

Prance, Ghillean T — *Botanist*
%Kew Royal Botanic Gardens, Richmond, Surrey TW9 3AE, England

Prange, Laurie — *Actress*
1519 Sargent Place, Los Angeles, CA 90026, USA

Prather, Joan — *Actress*
31647 Sea Level Dr, Malibu, CA 90265, USA

Pratiwi Sudarmono — *Astronaut, Indonesia*
Jalan Pegangsaan, Timur 16, Jakarta, Indonesia

Pratt, Donald H — *Businessman*
%Butler Manufacturing Co, BMA Tower, Penn Valley Park, Kansas City, MO 64141, USA

Pratt, Edward T, Jr — *Businessman*
%Pratt Hotel Corp, 2 Galleria Tower, 13455 Noel Rd, Dallas, TX 75240, USA

Pratt, Jack E, Sr — *Businessman*
%Pratt Hotel Corp, 2 Galleria Tower, 13455 Noel Rd, Dallas, TX 75240, USA

Pratt, Richard D — *Businessman*
%Intelligent Electronics, 411 Eagleview Blvd, Exton, PA 19341, USA

Preate, Ernest, Jr — *Attorney, Government Official*
%Attorney General's Office, 4th & Walnut St, Harrisburg, PA 17120, USA

Precourt, Charles J — *Astronaut*
%NASA, Johnson Space Center, 2101 NASA Rd, Houston, TX 77058, USA

P

Preer, John R, Jr — *Biologist*
1414 E Maxwell Lane, Bloomington, IN 47401, USA

Pregulman, Merv — *Football Player*
%Siskin Steel & Supply Co, PO Box 1191, Chattanooga, TN 37401, USA

Prelog, Vladimir — *Nobel Chemistry Laureate*
Bellariastr 33, 8002 Zurich, Switzerland

Prendergast, G Joseph — *Financier*
%Wachovia Bank of Georgia, 191 Peachtree St NE, Atlanta, GA 30303, USA

Prentice of Daventry, Reginald — *Government Official, England*
Wansdyke, Church Lane, Mildenhall, Marlborough, Wilts, England

Prentice, Dean — *Hockey Player*
13-220 Salisbury Ave, Cambridge ON N1S 1K5, Canada

Prentiss, Paula — *Actress, Comedienne*
719 N Foothill Rd, Beverly Hills, CA 90210, USA

Prescott, John L — *Government Official, England*
365 Saltshouse Rd, Sutton-on-Hull, North Humberside, England

Presle, Micheline — *Actress*
6 Rue Antoine Dubois, 75006 Paris, France

Presley, Priscilla — *Actress*
1167 Summit Dr, Beverly Hills, CA 90210, USA

Press, Frank — *Geophysicist*
%Carnegie Institution, 5241 Broad Branch Rd, Washington, DC 20015, USA

Pressey, Paul — *Basketball Player, Coach*
%Golden State Warriors, Oakland Coliseum Arena, Oakland, CA 94621, USA

Pressler, H Paul — *Attorney, Judge*
2133 Pine Valley Dr, Houston, TX 77019, USA

Pressman, Edward R — *Movie Producer*
%Edward R Pressman Films, 445 N Bedford Dr, #PH, Beverly Hills, CA 90210, USA

Pressman, Lawrence — *Actor*
15033 Encanto Dr, Sherman Oaks, CA 91403, USA

Pressman, Michael — *Movie Director*
%Twentieth Century Fox Studios, 10201 W Pico Blvd, Los Angeles, CA 90064, USA

Preston, Billy — *Singer, Songwriter*
%Murray & Andriolo, 156 5th Ave, #434, New York, NY 10010, USA

Preston, Kelly — *Actress, Model*
12522 Moorpark St, #109, Studio City, CA 91604, USA

Preston, Mike — *Actor*
%Artists Group, 10100 Santa Monica Blvd, #2490, Los Angeles, CA 90067, USA

Preston, Simon J — *Concert Organist, Choirmaster*
Little Hardwick, Langton Green, Tunbridge Wells, Kent TN3 0EY, England

Pretre, Georges — *Conductor*
Chateau de Vaudricourt, A Naves, Par Castres 81100, France

Preus, David W — *Religious Leader*
2481 Como Ave, St Paul, MN 55108, USA

Previn, Andre G — *Conductor, Composer*
%Sherwood Stables, 8 Sherwood Lane, Bedford Hills, NY 10507, USA

Previn, Dory — *Singer, Songwriter*
2533 Zorada Dr, Los Angeles, CA 90046, USA

Previte, Richard — *Businessman*
%Advanced Micro Devices, 1 AMD Pl, PO Box 3453, Sunnyvale, CA 94088, USA

Prew, William A — *Swimmer, Businessman*
1920 S Ocean Blvd, #A, Delray Beach, FL 33483, USA

Prey, Hermann — *Opera, Concert Singer*
Fichtenstr 14, 82152 Krailling, Germany

Price, Alan — *Singer (Animals); Songwriter*
%Crowell Mgmt, 4/5 High St, Huntingdon, Cambs PE18 6TE, England

Price, Antony — *Fashion Designer*
34 Brook St, London W1, England

Price, Charles H, II — *Businessman, Diplomat*
1 W Armour Blvd, #300, Kansas City, MO 64111, USA

Price, Frank — *Entertainment Executive*
%Price Entertainment, 2425 Olympic Blvd, Santa Monica, CA 90404, USA

Price, Frederick K C — *Religious Leader*
%Crenshaw Christian Church, 7901 S Vermont Ave, Los Angeles, CA 90044, USA

Price, George C — *Prime Minister, Belize*
%House of Representatives, Belmopan, Belize

Price, Hugh B — *Association Executive*
%Rockefeller Foundation, 420 5th Ave, New York, NY 10018, USA

Price, Kenneth — *Artist*
PO Box 1356, Taos, NM 87571, USA

Price, Larry C — *Photographer*
%Philadelphia Inquirer, 400 N Broad St, Philadelphia, PA 19130, USA

Price, Leontyne — *Opera Singer*
%Columbia Artists Mgmt Inc, 165 W 57th St, New York, NY 10019, USA

Price, Lloyd — *Singer, Pianist, Songwriter*
%Wolfman Jack Entertainment, Rt 1, PO Box 56, Belvidere, NC 27919, USA

Price, Marc — *Actor*
8444 Magnolia Dr, Los Angeles, CA 90046, USA

Price, Margaret B — *Opera Singer*
%Harrison/Parrott Ltd, 12 Penzance Place, London W11 4PA, England

Price, Mark — *Basketball Player*
%Philadelphia 76ers, Veterans Stadium, PO Box 25040, Philadelphia, PA 19147, USA

Price, Nick — *Golfer*
%Professional Golfer's Assn, PO Box 109601, Palm Beach Gardens, FL 33410, USA

Price, Paul B — *Physicist*
1056 Overlook Rd, Berkeley, CA 94708, USA

Price, Ray — *Singer*
%Ray Price Agency, PO Box 1986, Mount Pleasant, TX 75456, USA

Price, Reynolds — *Writer*
PO Box 99014, Durham, NC 27708, USA

Price, Richard — *Writer*
%Janklow & Nesbit Assoc, 598 Madison Ave, New York, NY 10022, USA

Price, S H — *Publisher*
%Newsweek Inc, 444 Madison Ave, New York, NY 10022, USA

Price, W Mark — *Basketball Player*
%Cleveland Cavaliers, 2923 Statesboro Rd, Richfield, OH 44286, USA

Price, Westcott W, III — *Businessman*
%FHP International Corp, 9900 Talbert Ave, Fountain Valley, CA 92708, USA

Price, Willard D — *Explorer*
814 Via Alhambra, #N, Laguna Hills, CA 92653, USA

Prichard, Peter S — *Editor*
%USA Today, Editorial Dept, 1000 Wilson Blvd, Arlington, VA 22209, USA

Priddy, Nancy — *Actress*
%Cunningham-Escott-Dipene, 10635 Santa Monica Blvd, Los Angeles, CA 90025, USA

Pride, Charlie — *Singer*
%Chardon Inc, 3198 Royal Lane, #204, Dallas, TX 75229, USA

Priesand, Sally J — *Religious Leader*
10 Wedgewood Circle, Eatontown, NJ 07724, USA

Priest, Pat — *Actress*
PO Box 1298, Hatley, ID 83333, USA

Priestley, Jason — *Actor*
1811 Whitley Ave, Los Angeles, CA 90028, USA

Prigogine, V Ilya — *Nobel Chemistry Laureate*
67 Ave Fond'Roy, 1180 Drussels, Belgium

Primatesta, Raul Francisco Cardinal — *Religious Leader*
Arzobispado, Ave H Irigoyen 98, 5000 Cordoba, Argentina

Primis, Lance R — *Publisher*
%New York Times Co, 229 W 43rd St, New York, NY 10036, USA

Prince (Rogers Nelson) — *Singer, Songwriter*
%Paisley Park Enterprises, 7801 Audubon Rd, Chanhassen, MN 55317, USA

Prince, Gregory S, Jr — *Educator*
%Hampshire College, President's Office, Amherst, MA 01002, USA

Prince, Harold S — *Theater Producer, Director*
%Harold Prince Organization, 10 Rockefeller Plaza, #1009, New York, NY 10020, USA

Prince, Larry L — *Businessman*
%Genuine Parts Co, 2999 Circle 75 Parkway, Atlanta, GA 30339, USA

Prince, William — *Actor*
750 N Kings Rd, #307, Los Angeles, CA 90069, USA

Principal, Victoria — *Actress*
814 Cynthia St, Beverly Hills, CA 90210, USA

Prine, Andrew — *Actor*
3264 Longridge Ave, Sherman Oaks, CA 91423, USA

Prine, John — *Singer, Songwriter*
%Al Bunetta Mgmt, 33 Music Square W, #102-A, Nashville, TN 37203, USA

Pringle, Joan — *Actress*
740 S Burnside Ave, Los Angeles, CA 90036, USA

P

Price - Pringle

P

Prinz, Dianne K *Astronaut*
%US Naval Research Lab, Code 7660, 4555 Overlook Ave, Washington, DC 20375, USA

Prior of Brampton, James M L *Government Official, England*
36 Morpeth Mansions, London SW1, England

Priory, Richard B *Businessman*
%Duke Power Co, 422 S Church St, Charlotte, NC 28242, USA

Pritchard, David E *Physicist*
%Massachusetts Institute of Technology, Physics Dept, Cambridge, MA 02139, USA

Pritchett, James *Actor*
53 W 74th St, New York, NY 10023, USA

Pritchett, Matt *Cartoonist (Matt)*
%London Daily Telegraph, 181 Marsh Wall, London E14 9SR, England

Pritchett, Victor S *Writer*
12 Regent's Park Terrace, London NW1, England

Pritkin, Roland I *Eye Surgeon*
Independence Village, 3655 N Alpine Rd, B-302, Rockford, IL 61114, USA

Pritzker, Jay A *Businessman*
%Marmon Holdings, 225 W Washington St, Chicago, IL 60606, USA

Pritzker, Robert A *Businessman*
%Marmon Group, 225 W Washington St, Chicago, IL 60606, USA

Prix, Wolf *Architect*
%Coop Himmelblau, 8561 Higuera St, Culver City, CA 90232, USA

Probert, Bob *Hockey Player*
%Chicago Blackhawks, Chicago Stadium, 1800 W Madison St, Chicago, IL 60612, USA

Prochnow, Jurgen *Actor*
Lamontstr 98, 81679 Munich, Germany

Proctor, Charles N *Skier*
6 Oak Rd, Santa Cruz, CA 95060, USA

Profumo, John D *Government Official, England*
28 Commercial St, London E1 6LS, England

Prokhorov, Aleksandr M *Nobel Physics Laureate*
%General Physics Institute, 38 Vavilov Str, 117942 Moscow, Russia

Proops, Jay D *Businessman*
%Vigoro Corp, 225 N Michigan Ave, Chicago, IL 60601, USA

Prophet, Elizabeth Clare *Religious Leader*
%Church Universal & Triumphant, Box A, Livingston, MT 59047, USA

Propp, Brian *Hockey Player*
%Philadelphia Flyers, Spectrum, Pattison Place, Philadelphia, PA 19148, USA

Props, Rene *Actress*
%J Michael Bloom Ltd, 233 Park Ave S, #1000, New York, NY 10017, USA

Prosky, Robert *Actor*
381 2nd St, #3-R, Jersey City, NJ 07302, USA

Prosser, C Ladd *Physiologist*
101 W Windsor Rd, #2106, Urbana, IL 61801, USA

Prosser, Robert *Religious Leader*
%Cumberland Presbyterian Church, 1978 Union Ave, Memphis, TN 38104, USA

Prost, Alain M P *Auto Racing Driver*
%Star Racing Promotion, 2 Rue Neuve, 1450 Sainte-Croix, France

Protopopov, Oleg *Figure Skater*
Chalet Hubel, 3818 Grindelwald, Switzerland

Prough, Stephen W *Financier*
%Downey Savings & Loan, 3501 Jamboree Rd, Newport Beach, CA 92660, USA

Proulx, E Annie *Writer*
General Delivery, Vershire, VT 05079, USA

Prout, Patrick M *Financier*
%Bank One Corp Cleveland, 600 Superior Ave, Cleveland, OH 44114, USA

Prowse, Dave *Actor*
%David Prowse Fitness Centre, 12 Marshalsea Rd, London SE1 4YB, England

Prowse, Juliet *Dancer, Actress*
343 S Beverly Glen Blvd, Los Angeles, CA 90024, USA

Prudhomme, Don *Drag Racing Driver*
PO Box 33907, Granada Hills, CA 91394, USA

Prudhomme, Paul *Chef*
527 Mandeville St, New Orleans, LA 70117, USA

Prueher, Joseph W *Navy Admiral*
Commander, 6th Fleet, Unit 50148, FPO, AE 09501, USA

Pruett, Jeanne *Singer, Songwriter*
%Eddie Fulton, Rt 1, Franklin, TN 37064, USA

Prinz - Pruett

Pruett, Scott — *Auto Racing Driver*
%SPD Motorsports Ltd, PO Box 7243, Citrus Heights, CA 95621, USA

Pruitt, Basil A, Jr — *Burn Surgeon*
%US Army Institute of Surgical Research, Fort Sam Houston, TX 78234, USA

Pruitt, Gregory D (Greg) — *Football Player*
13851 Larchmere Blvd, Shaker Heights, OH 44120, USA

Prunariu, Dumitru D — *Cosmonaut, Romania*
Str Sf Spiridon 12, #4, 70231 Bucharest, Romania

Prunskiene, Kazimiera — *Council of Ministers Chairman, Lithuania*
Blindzui 19-11, 2004 Vilnius, Lithuania

Prusiner, Stanley B — *Neurologist, Biochemist*
%University of San Francisco, Neurology Dept, San Francisco, CA 94143, USA

Pryce, Jonathan — *Actor*
%James Sharkey Assoc, 21 Golden Square, London W1R 3PA, England

Pryor, Hubert — *Editor, Publisher*
3560 S Ocean Blvd, #607, Palm Beach, FL 33480, USA

Pryor, Nicholas — *Actor*
%Century Artists, 9744 Wilshire Blvd, #308, Beverly Hills, CA 90212, USA

Pryor, Peter P — *Editor*
%Daily Variety, Editorial Dept, 5700 Wilshire Blvd, #120, Los Angeles, CA 90036, USA

Pryor, Richard — *Comedian*
16030 Ventura Blvd, #380, Encino, CA 91436, USA

Pryor, Thomas M — *Editor*
%Daily Variety, Editorial Dept, 5700 Wilshire Blvd, #120, Los Angeles, CA 90036, USA

Ptashne, Mark S — *Molecular Biologist*
%Harvard University, Biochemistry Dept, Cambridge, MA 02138, USA

Pucci, Bert — *Publisher*
%Los Angeles Magazine, 1888 Century Park East, Los Angeles, CA 90067, USA

Puck, Theodore T — *Biophysicist*
10 S Albion St, Denver, CO 80222, USA

Puck, Wolfgang — *Chef*
%Spago Restaurant, 8795 W Sunset Blvd, Los Angeles, CA 90069, USA

Puckett, Gary — *Singer, Songwriter*
11088 Indian Lore Court, San Diego, CA 92127, USA

Puckett, Kirby — *Baseball Player*
6625 West Trail, Minneapolis, MN 55439, USA

Puente, Tito — *Orchestra Leader*
%Ralph Mercado Mgmt, 568 Broadway, #806, New York, NY 10012, USA

Puenzo, Luis A — *Movie Director*
%Cinematografia Nacional Instituto, Lima 319, 1073 Buenos Aires, Argentina

Puett, Clay — *Thoroughbred Racing Gate Inventor*
%True Center Gate Co, PO Box 32221, Phoenix, AZ 85064, USA

Puett, Tommy — *Actor*
23441 Golden Springs, #199, Diamond Bar, CA 91765, USA

Pugh, Jethro — *Football Player*
%Gifts Inc, 5616 Gaston Ave, Dallas, TX 75214, USA

Pugh, Lawrence R — *Businessman*
%VF Corp, 1047 N Park Rd, Wyomissing, PA 19610, USA

Pugsley, Don — *Actor*
6305 Yucca St, #214, Los Angeles, CA 90028, USA

Pulford, Bob — *Hockey Player, Executive*
%Chicago Blackhawks, Chicago Stadium, 1800 W Madison St, Chicago, IL 60612, USA

Pullen, Gregory J — *Financier*
%TCF Financial Corp, 801 Marquette Ave, Minneapolis, MN 55402, USA

Pulliam, Eugene S — *Publisher*
%Indianapolis Star, 307 N Pennsylvania St, Indianapolis, IN 46204, USA

Pulte, William J — *Businessman*
%Pulte Corp, 33 Bloomfield Hills Parkway, Bloomfield Hills, MI 48304, USA

Pulver, Liselotte — *Actress*
%Lilly M Gibbs, 16 Ave Callas, 1206 Geneva, Switzerland

Punsley, Bernard — *Actor*
1415 Granvia Altemeia, Rancho Palos Verdes, CA 90274, USA

Puppa, Daren — *Hockey Player*
%Toronto Maple Leafs, 60 Carlton St, Toronto ON M5B 1L1, Canada

Purcell, Edward M — *Nobel Physics Laureate*
5 Wright St, Cambridge, MA 02138, USA

Purcell, James N — *Government Official*
10 Parc Chateau-Banquet, 1202 Geneva, Switzerland

P

Pruett - Purcell

P

Purcell, Lee *Actress*
1317 N San Fernando Rd, #167, Burbank, CA 91504, USA

Purcell, Patrick B *Publisher, Entertainment Executive*
%News America Publishing Inc, 210 South St, New York, NY 10002, USA

Purcell, Philip J *Businessman*
%Dean Witter Discover Co, 2 World Trade Center, New York, NY 10048, USA

Purcell, Sarah *Actress*
6525 Esplanade St, Playa del Rey, CA 90293, USA

Purdee, Nathan *Actor*
56 W 66th St, New York, NY 10023, USA

Purdum, Robert L *Businessman*
26 Horizon Dr, Mendham, NJ 07945, USA

Purdy, James *Writer*
236 Henry St, Brooklyn, NY 11201, USA

Purkey, Robert T (Bob) *Baseball Player*
5767 King School Rd, Bethel Park, PA 15102, USA

Purl, Linda *Actress*
431 Alma Real Dr, Pacific Palisades, CA 90272, USA

Purpura, Dominick P *Neuroscientist*
%Albert Einstein College of Medicine, 1300 Morris Park Ave, Bronx, NY 10461, USA

Purpura, Vincent M *Financier*
%D A Davidson Co, 8 3rd St N, Great Falls, MT 59401, USA

Purvis, G Frank, Jr *Businessman*
%Pan-American Life Insurance, 601 Poydras St, New Orleans, LA 70130, USA

Puryear, Martin *Artist*
%Nancy Drysdale Gallery, 2103 "O" St NW, Washington, DC 20037, USA

Pusch, Alexander *Fencer*
Lindenweg 39, 97941 Tauberbischofsheim, Germany

Pusey, Nathan M *Educator*
200 E 66th St, New York, NY 10021, USA

Putnam, Ashley *Opera Singer*
%Colbert Artists Mgmt, 111 W 57th St, New York, NY 10019, USA

Putnam, George *Financier*
%Putnam Investments, 1 Post Office Square, Boston, MA 02109, USA

Putnam, Hilary *Philosopher*
116 Winchester Rd, Arlington, MA 02174, USA

Puttnam, David T *Movie Producer*
%Enigma Productions, 13/15 Queens Gate Place Mews, London SW7 5BG, England

Puyana, Rafael *Concert Harpsichordist*
88 Rue de Grenelle, 75007 Paris, France

Puzo, Mario *Writer*
866 Manor Lane, Bay Shore, NY 11706, USA

Pye, William B *Sculptor*
43 Hambalt Rd, Clapham, London SW4 9EQ, England

Pyle, Andy *Bassist (The Kinks)*
%Larry Page, 29 Ruston Mews, London W11 1RB, England

Pyle, Denver *Actor*
%Tri Island Land & Cattle Co, 10614 Whipple St, North Hollywood, CA 91602, USA

Pyle, Michael J (Mike) *Football Player*
1260 Spruce St, Winnetka, IL 60093, USA

Pym of Sandy, Francis L *Government Official, England*
Everton Park, Sandy, Beds, England

Pynchon, Thomas *Writer*
%Little Brown Co, 34 Beacon St, Boston, MA 02108, USA

Pyne, Natasha *Actress*
%Kate Feast Mgmt, 43-A Princess Rd, Regent's Park, London NW1 8JS, England

Pyne, Stephen J *Historian*
%University of Iowa, History Dept, Iowa City, IA 52242, USA

Pytka, Joseph *Commercials Director*
%Suellen Wagner, 916 Main St, Venice, CA 90291, USA

Purcell - Pytka

Qaboos Bin Said *Sultan, Oman*
%Royal Palace, PO Box 252, Muscat, Oman

Qasimi, Sheikh Saqr bin Muhammad Al- *Ruler, Ras al Khaimah*
%Royal Palace, Ras Al Khaimah, United Arab Emirates

Qasimi, Sheikh Sultan bin Muhammad Al- *Ruler, Sharjah*
%Royal Palace, Sharjah, United Arab Emirates

Qin Jiwei *Army General, China*
%Defense Minister's Office, Communist Party, Beijing, China

Quackenbush, H Q (Bill) *Hockey Player*
18 Washington St, Rocky Hill, NJ 08553, USA

Quade, John *Actor*
%Alex Brewis Agency, 12429 Laurel Terrace Dr, Studio City, CA 91604, USA

Quadflieg, Will *Actor*
27711 Osterholz-Scharmbeck, Germany

Quaid, Dennis *Actor*
11718 Barrington Court, #508, Los Angeles, CA 90049, USA

Quaid, Randy *Actor*
PO Box 17372, Beverly Hills, CA 90209, USA

Quaife, Pete *Bassist (The Kinks)*
%Larry Page, 29 Ruston Mews, London W11 1RB, England

Qualls, R L *Businessman*
%Baldor Electric Co, 5711 R S Boreham Jr St, Fort Smith, AR 72901, USA

Quant, Mary *Fashion Designer*
%Mary Quant Ltd, 3 Ives St, London SW3 2NE, England

Quarracino, Antonio Cardinal *Religious Leader*
%Archdiocese of Buenos Aires, Buenos Aires, Argentina

Quarrie, Donald (Don) *Track Athlete*
1867 Rainbow Terrace Lane, Montebello, CA 90640, USA

Quarry, Jerry *Boxer*
11382 Orange Park Blvd, Orange, CA 92669, USA

Quaohq, Alan G *Businessman*
%Hanover Direct Inc, 1509 Harbor Blvd, Weehawken, NJ 07087, USA

Quastel, J Hirsch *Biochemist*
4585 Langara Ave, Vancouver BC V6R 1C9, Canada

Quatro, Suzl *Singer*
Hellkamp 17, 20255 Hamburg, Germany

Quayle, J Danforth (Dan) *Vice President*
201 N Illinois St, #2240, Indianapolis, IN 46204, USA

Queen Latifah (Dana Owens) *Rapper, Actress*
%Flavor Unit Mgmt, 155 Morgan St, Jersey City, NJ 07302, USA

Queffelec, Anne *Concert Pianist*
15 Ave Corneille, 78600 Maisons-Laffitte, France

Queler, Eve *Conductor*
%Opera Orchestra of New York, 239 W 72nd St, #2-R, New York, NY 10023, USA

Quesnel, Gregory L *Businessman*
%Consolidated Freightways Inc, 3240 Hillview Ave, Palo Alto, CA 94304, USA

Questel, Mae *Actress*
27 E 65th St, New York, NY 10021, USA

Questrom, Allen I *Businessman*
%Federated Department Stores, 7 W 7th St, Cincinnati, OH 45202, USA

Quick, Diana *Actress*
39 Seymour Walk, London SW10, England

Quick, Leslie C, Jr *Finnacier*
%Quick & Reilly Group, 26 Broadway, New York, NY 10004, USA

Quick, Michael A (Mike) *Football Player*
13 Slab Branch Rd, Marlton, NJ 08053, USA

Quick, Peter *Financier*
%Quick & Reilly Group, 26 Broadway, New York, NY 10004, USA

Quick, Richard *Swimming Coach*
%Stanford University, Athletic Dept, Stanford, CA 94305, USA

Quicke, John J *Businessman*
%Sequa Corp, 200 Park Ave, New York, NY 10166, USA

Quie, Albert H *Governor, MN*
Rt 5, Box 231-A, Faribault, MN 55021, USA

Quigley, Linnea *Actress*
13659 Victory Blvd, #467, Van Nuys, CA 91401, USA

Quigley, Philip J *Businessman*
%Pacific Telesis Group, 130 Kearny St, San Francisco, CA 94108, USA

Q

Qaboos Bin Said - Quigley

Q

Quill, Leonard W — *Financier*
%Wilmington Trust Corp, Rodney Square N, 1100 N Market St, Wilmington, DE 19890, USA

Quilley, Denis — *Actor*
%Bernard Hunter Assoc, 13 Spencer Gardens, London SW14 7AH, England

Quin, J Marvin — *Businessman*
%Ashland Oil Inc, 1000 Ashland Dr, Russell, KY 41169, USA

Quindlen, Anna — *Columnist*
%New York Times, Editorial Dept, 229 W 43rd St, New York, NY 10036, USA

Quine, Willard V O — *Philosopher*
38 Chestnut St, Boston, MA 02108, USA

Quinlan, Kathleen — *Actress*
PO Box 2465, Malibu, CA 90265, USA

Quinlan, Michael R — *Businessman*
%McDonald's Corp, McDonald's Plaza, 1 Kroc Dr, Oak Brook, IL 60521, USA

Quinn, Aidan — *Actor*
%Creative Artists Agency, 9830 Wilshire Blvd, Beverly Hills, CA 90212, USA

Quinn, Anthony — *Actor*
60 East End Ave, New York, NY 10028, USA

Quinn, Carmel — *Singer*
456 Park Ave, Leonia, NJ 07605, USA

Quinn, David W — *Businessman*
%Centex Corp, 3333 Lee Parkway, Dallas, TX 75219, USA

Quinn, J B Patrick (Pat) — *Hockey Executive*
%Vancouver Canucks, 100 N Renfrew St, Vancouver BC V5K 3N7, Canada

Quinn, Jack J — *Hockey Executive*
%St Louis Blues, St Louis Arena, 5700 Oakland Ave, St Louis, MO 63110, USA

Quinn, Jane Bryant — *Columnist*
%Newsweek Magazine, Editorial Dept, 251 W 57th St, New York, NY 10019, USA

Quinn, John C — *Editor*
%Freedom Forum, 1101 Wilson Blvd, Arlington, VA 22209, USA

Quinn, Martha — *Actress*
13903 Hesby St, Sherman Oaks, CA 91423, USA

Quinn, Sally — *Journalist*
3014 "N" St NW, Washington, DC 20007, USA

Quinn, William F — *Governor, HI*
1365 Laukahi St, Honolulu, HI 96821, USA

Quinn, William J — *Businessman*
1420 Sheridan Rd, #4-D, Wilmette, IL 60091, USA

Quintero, Jose — *Theater Director*
%Thomas Andrews, 39 E 72nd St, #500, New York, NY 10021, USA

Quiroga, Elena — *Writer*
%Agencia Balcells, Diagonal 580, 08021 Barcelona, Spain

Quisenberry, Daniel R (Dan) — *Baseball Player*
12208 Buena Vista, Leawood, KS 66209, USA

Quivar, Florence — *Opera Singer*
%Metropolitan Opera Assn, Lincoln Center Plaza, New York, NY 10023, USA

Qureshey, Safi U — *Businessman*
%AST Research Inc, 16215 Alton Parkway, Irvine, CA 92718, USA

Quill - Qureshey

Raab, Walter F — *Businessman*
%AMP Inc, 470 Friendship Rd, Harrisburg, PA 17111, USA

Raaum, Gustav — *Skier*
PO Box 700, Mercer Island, WA 98040, USA

Rabassa, Gregory — *Educator*
136 E 72nd St, New York, NY 10021, USA

Rabb, Maxwell M — *Diplomat*
Wilson Hill Rd, Colrain, MA 01340, USA

Rabbani, Burhanuddin — *President, Afghanistan*
%President's Office, Shar Rahi Sedarat, Kabul, Afghanistan

Rabbitt, Eddie — *Singer, Songwriter*
%Moress Nanas Shea, 1209 16th Ave S, Nashville, TN 37212, USA

Rabin, Stanley A — *Businessman*
%Commercial Metals Co, 7800 N Stemmons Freeway, Dallas, TX 75247, USA

Rabinow, Jacob — *Electrical Engineer*
6920 Selkirk Dr, Bethesda, MD 20817, USA

Rabinowitz, Harry — *Conductor, Composer*
%Honor Music, Walking Bottom, Peaslake, Surrey GU5 9RR, England

Rabinowitz, Jesse C — *Biochemist*
%University of California, Molecular & Cell Biology Dept, Berkeley, CA 94720, USA

Rabkin, Mitchell T — *Physician*
124 Canton Ave, Milton, MA 02186, USA

Raboy, S Caesar — *Businessman*
4 Seasons Place, 220 Boylston St, #1010, Boston, MA 02116, USA

Rabuka, Sitiveni — *Prime Minister, Fiji; Army General*
%Prime Minister's Office, Victoria Parade, 6 Berkeley Parade, Suva, Fiji

Raby, Stuart — *Physicist*
%Ohio State University, Physics Dept, Columbus, OH 43210, USA

Rachins, Alan — *Actor*
1274 Capri Dr, Pacific Palisades, CA 90272, USA

Racicot, Marc F — *Governor, MT*
%Governor's Office, State Capitol, Helena, MT 59620, USA

Racimo, Victoria — *Actress*
%Marion Rosenberg Office, 8428 Melrose Place, #C, Los Angeles, CA 90069, USA

Radatz, Richard R (Dick) — *Baseball Player*
%Atlantic Container, PO Box 348, Braintree, MA 02184, USA

Rademacher, Pete — *Boxer*
5585 River Styx Rd, Medina, OH 44256, USA

Rader, Douglas L (Doug) — *Baseball Manager*
112-7 Cedar Point, Stuart, FL 33494, USA

Rader, Randall R — *Judge*
%US Claims Court, 717 Madison Place NW, Washington, DC 20005, USA

Radford, Michael — *Movie Director*
3-B Rickering Mews, London W2 5AD, England

Radner, Roy — *Economist*
1 Park Place, Short Hills, NJ 07078, USA

Radojevic, Danilo — *Ballet Dancer*
%American Ballet Theatre, 890 Broadway, New York, NY 10003, USA

Radwanski, George — *Editor*
%Toronto Star, Editorial Dept, 1 Yonge St, Toronto ON M5E 1E6, Canada

Rady, Ernest S — *Businessman*
%WestCorp, 23 Pasteur Rd, Irvine, CA 92718, USA

Rae, Charlotte — *Actress*
1413 Allenford Ave, Los Angeles, CA 90049, USA

Rae, Robert K — *Political Leader, Canada*
%Premier's Office, Queen's Park, Toronto ON M7A 1A1, Canada

Rafelson, Bob — *Movie Director*
12899 Mulholland Dr, Beverly Hills, CA 90210, USA

Rafferty, Thomas M (Tom) — *Football Player*
10539 Mapleridge Dr, Dallas, TX 75238, USA

Raffi (Cavoukian) — *Singer*
%Jensen Communications, 230 E Union St, Pasadena, CA 91101, USA

Raffin, Deborah — *Actress*
2630 Eden Place, Beverly Hills, CA 90210, USA

Rafsanjani, Hojatoleslam H — *President, Iran*
%Islamic Republican Party, Dr Ali Shariati Ave, Teheran, Iran

Raftery, S Frank — *Labor Leader*
%Painters & Allied Trades Union, 1750 New York Ave NW, Washington, DC 20006, USA

R

Raab - Raftery

Ragin, John S — *Actor*
5708 Briarcliff Rd, Los Angeles, CA 90068, USA

Rahal, Bobby — *Auto Racing Driver*
%Bobby Rahal Co, PO Box 39, Hilliard, OH 43026, USA

Rahman Khan, Ataur — *Prime Minister, Bangladesh*
%Bangladesh Jatiya League, 500-A Dhanmondi R/A, Road 7, Dhaka, Bangladesh

Rahn, Helmut — *Soccer Player*
Dittmarstr 1, 45144 Essen, Germany

Raichle, Marcus E — *Neurologist, Radiologist*
%Washington University Medical School, Neurology Dept, St Louis, MO 63130, USA

Railsback, Steve — *Actor*
PO Box 1308, Los Angeles, CA 90078, USA

Raimond, Jean-Bernard — *Government Official, France*
203 Ave Daumesnil, 75012 Paris, France

Raimondi, Ruggero — *Opera Singer*
%Columbia Artists Mgmt Inc, 165 W 57th St, New York, NY 10019, USA

Raine, Craig A — *Poet*
%New College, English Dept, Oxford OX1 3BN, England

Raine, Kathleen J — *Poet*
47 Paultons Square, London SW3, England

Rainer, Jack H — *Financier*
%Colonial BancGroup, 1 Commerce St, Montgomery, AL 36104, USA

Rainer, Luise — *Actress*
%Knittel, Vico Morcote, 6911 Lugano, Switzerland

Raines, Franklin D — *Financier*
%Lazzard Freres, 1 Rockefeller Plaza, New York, NY 10020, USA

Raines, Howell — *Journalist*
%New York Times, Editorial Dept, 229 W 43rd St, New York, NY 10036, USA

Raines, Timothy (Tim) — *Baseball Player*
2316 Airport Blvd, Sanford, FL 32773, USA

Rainey, Ford — *Actor*
3821 Carbon Canyon Rd, Malibu, CA 90265, USA

Rainey, Wayne — *Motorcyle Racing Rider*
1660 Akron Peninsula Rd, #201, Akron, OH 44313, USA

Rainier III — *Prince, Monaco*
%Palais de Monaco, Boite Postale 518, 98015 Monte Carlo Cedex, Monaco

Rainwater, Gregg — *Actor*
PO Box 291836, Los Angeles, CA 90029, USA

Raisian, John — *Educator*
%Stanford University, Hoover Institution, Stanford, CA 94305, USA

Raitt, Bonnie — *Singer*
1344 N Spaulding Ave, Los Angeles, CA 90046, USA

Raitt, John — *Singer, Actor*
%Lew Sherrell Agency, 1354 Los Robles, Palm Springs, CA 92262, USA

Rajna, Thomas — *Concert Pianist, Composer*
10 Wyndover Rd, Claremont, Cape 7700, South Africa

Rakhmonov, Emomali — *President, Tajikistan*
%President's Office, Supreme Soviet, Dushanbe, Tajikistan

Rakowski, Mieczyslaw F — *Prime Minister, Poland*
Miesiecznik Dzis, Ul Poznanska 3, 00-680 Warsaw, Poland

Raksin, David — *Composer*
6519 Aldea Ave, Van Nuys, CA 91406, USA

Rales, Mitchell P — *Businessman*
%Danaher Corp, 1250 24th St NW, Washington, DC 20037, USA

Rales, Steven M — *Businessman*
%Danaher Corp, 1250 24th St NW, Washington, DC 20037, USA

Rall, David P — *Toxicologist, Pharmacologist*
5302 Reno Rd NW, Washington, DC 20015, USA

Rall, J Edward — *Physician*
3947 Baltimore St, Kensington, MD 20895, USA

Rallis, George J — *Prime Minister, Greece*
4 Kanari St, Athens, Greece

Ralph, Sheryl Lee — *Actress, Singer*
938 S Longwood Ave, Los Angeles, CA 90019, USA

Ralston, Dennis — *Tennis Player*
%US Tennis Assn, 1212 Ave of Americas, New York, NY 10036, USA

Ralston, Vera Hruba — *Actress*
4121 Crescienta Dr, Santa Barbara, CA 93110, USA

Ram, C Venkata *Physician*
%Texas Southwestern Medical Center, 5323 Harry Hines Blvd, Dallas, TX 75235, USA

Rama Rau, Santha *Writer*
RR 1, Box 200, Leedsville Rd, Amenia, NY 12501, USA

Ramage, Rob *Hockey Player*
%Tampa Bay Lightning, Mack Center, 501 E Kennedy Blvd, Tampa, FL 33602, USA

Rambahadur Limbu *Vietnam War Sarawak Army Hero (VC)*
Box 420, Bandar Seri Begawan, Negara Brunei Darussalam, Brunei

Rambert, Charles J J *Architect*
179 Rue de Courcelles, 75017 Paris, France

Rambis, Kurt *Basketball Player*
%Los Angeles Lakers, Forum, PO Box 10, Inglewood, CA 90306, USA

Rambo, David L *Religious Leader*
%Christian & Missionary Alliance, PO Box 35000, Colorado Springs, CO 80935, USA

Ramey, Samuel E *Opera Singer*
320 Central Park West, New York, NY 10025, USA

Ramgoolam, Seewosagur *Prime Minister, Mauritius*
85 Desforges St, Port Louis, Mauritius

Ramirez Vazquez, Pedro *Architect*
Ave de la Fuentes 170, Mexico City 20 DF, Mexico

Ramirez, Michael P *Editorial Cartoonist*
%Memphis Commercial Appeal, Editorial Dept, 495 Union Ave, Memphis, TN 38103, USA

Ramirez, Raul *Tennis Player*
Avenida Ruiz, 65 Sur Ensenada, Baja California, Mexico

Ramis, Harold A *Actor, Movie Director*
12921 Evanston St, Los Angeles, CA 90049, USA

Ramos, Fidel V *President, Philippines; Army General*
%President's Office, Malacanang Palace, J P Laurel St, Manila, Philippines

Ramos, Mando *Boxer*
16032 Springdale St, #415, Huntington Beach, CA 92649, USA

Ramos, Mel *Artist*
5941 Ocean View Dr, Oakland, CA 94618, USA

Rampal, Jean-Pierre *Concert Flutist*
15 Ave Mozart, 75016 Paris, France

Rampino, Louis J *Businessman*
%Fremont General Corp, 2020 Santa Monica Blvd, Santa Monica, CA 90404, USA

Rampling, Charlotte *Actress*
1 Ave Emile Augier, 78290 Croissy-sur-Seine, France

Rampton, Calvin L *Governor, UT*
2550 Elizabeth St, Salt Lake Cty, UT 84106, USA

Ramsay, Garrard (Buster) *Football Player*
4102 Highway 411-S, Maryville, TN 37801, USA

Ramsey, Frank V, Jr *Basketball Player*
Buckner Ridge Lane, Box 363, Madisonville, KY 42431, USA

Ramsey, Logan *Actor*
12923 Killion St, Van Nuys, CA 91401, USA

Ramsey, Mike *Hockey Player*
%Detroit Red Wings, Joe Louis Arena, 600 Civic Center Dr, Detroit, MI 48226, USA

Ramsey, Norman F, Jr *Nobel Physics Laureate*
24 Monmouth Court, Brookline, MA 02146, USA

Ramsey, William *Singer, Songwriter*
Biebricher Allee 37, 65187 Wiesbaden, Germany

Ran, Shulamit *Composer*
%University of Chicago, Music Dept, 5845 S Ellis Ave, Chicago, IL 60637, USA

Ranck, Bruce E *Businessman*
%Browning-Ferris Industries, 757 N Eldridge Parkway, Houston, TX 77079, USA

Rand, Robert W *Neurosurgeon, Educator*
%Good Samaritan Hospital, Neurosciences Institute, Los Angeles, CA 90017, USA

Randall, Carolyn D *Judge*
%US Court of Appeals, 515 Rusk St, Houston, TX 77002, USA

Randall, Claire *Religious Leader*
13427 Countryside Dr, Sun City West, AZ 85375, USA

Randall, James R *Businessman*
%Archer Daniels Midland Co, 4666 E Faries Parkway, Decatur, IL 62526, USA

Randall, Tony *Actor*
%Beresford, 1 W 81st St, #6-D, New York, NY 10024, USA

Randall, W D (Bo), Jr *Knife Maker*
%Randall Made Knives, PO Box 1988, Orlando, FL 32802, USA

R

Ram - Randall

R

Randall, William S — *Financier*
%First Interstate Bancorp, 633 W 5th St, Los Angeles, CA 90071, USA

Randi, James — *Illusionist*
12000 NW 8th St, Fort Lauderdale, FL 33325, USA

Randle, John — *Football Player*
%Minnesota Vikings, 9520 Viking Dr, Eden Prairie, MN 55344, USA

Randolph, A Raymond — *Judge*
%US Court of Appeals, 3rd & Constitution Ave NW, Washington, DC 20001, USA

Randolph, Boots — *Jazz Saxophonist*
PO Box 110379, Nashville, TN 37222, USA

Randolph, Francis E, Jr — *Businessman*
%Cablevision Systems Corp, 1 Media Crossways, Woodbury, NY 11797, USA

Randolph, Jackson H — *Businessman*
%CINergy Corp, 139 E 4th St, Cincinnati, OH 45202, USA

Randolph, Jennings — *Senator, WV*
300 3rd St, Elkins, WV 26241, USA

Randolph, John — *Actor*
1850 N Whitney Place, Los Angeles, CA 90028, USA

Randolph, Joyce — *Actress*
295 Central Park W, #18-A, New York, NY 10024, USA

Randolph, Judson G — *Pediatric Surgeon*
111 Michigan Ave NW, Washington, DC 20010, USA

Randolph, Leo — *Boxer*
2012 S "K" St, Tacoma, WA 98405, USA

Randolph, Willie L — *Baseball Player*
648 Juniper Place, Franklin Lakes, NJ 07417, USA

Randrup, Michael — *Test Pilot*
10 Fairlawn Rd, Lytham, Lanc, England

Rands, Bernard — *Composer*
%Harvard University, Music Dept, Cambridge, MA 02138, USA

Ranford, Bill — *Hockey Player*
%Edmonton Oilers, Northlands Coliseum, Edmonton AB T5B 4M9, Canada

Rangos, Alexander W — *Businessman*
%Chambers Development Co, 10700 Frankstown Rd, Pittsburgh, PA 15235, USA

Rangos, John G, Jr — *Businessman*
%Chambers Development Co, 10700 Frankstown Rd, Pittsburgh, PA 15235, USA

Rangos, John G, Sr — *Businessman*
%Chambers Development Co, 10700 Frankstown Rd, Pittsburgh, PA 15235, USA

Ranieri, Lewis S — *Financier*
%Bank United of Texas, 3200 Southwest Freeway, Houston, TX 77027, USA

Ranis, Gustav — *Economist*
7 Mulberry Rd, Woodbridge, CT 06525, USA

Ranki, Dezso — *Concert Pianist*
Kertesz-Ut 50, 1073 Budapest, Hungary

Rankin, Alfred M, Jr — *Businessman*
%NACCO Industries, 5875 Landerbrook Dr, Mayfield Heights, OH 44124, USA

Rankin, Judy — *Golfer*
%Kingsmill-on-the-James Golf Course, Williamsburg, VA 23185, USA

Rankin, Kenny — *Singer*
8033 Sunset Blvd, #1037, Los Angeles, CA 90046, USA

Ranks, Shabba — *Singer*
%Famous Artists Agency, 1700 Broadway, #500, New York, NY 10019, USA

Ranney, Helen M — *Physician*
6229 La Jolla Mesa Dr, La Jolla, CA 92037, USA

Ransohoff, Joseph — *Neurosurgeon*
%New York University Medical School, Neurosurgery Dept, New York, NY 10016, USA

Rao, P V Narasimha — *Prime Minister, India*
%Prime Minister's Office, 1 Safdarjung Rd, New Delhi 11011, India

Rao, Paul P — *Judge*
%US Court of International Trade, 1 Federal Plaza, New York, NY 10007, USA

Raoul, Alfred — *Prime Minister, Congo; Army Officer*
%Foreign Affairs Ministry, Brazzaville, Congo

Raper, Kenneth B — *Bacteriologist*
602 N Segoe Rd, Madison, WI 53705, USA

Raphael (Martos) — *Singer*
%Kaduri Agency, 16125 NE 18th Ave, North Miami Beach, FL 33162, USA

Raphael, Fredric M — *Writer*
Largadelle, St Lauraent la Vallee, 24170 Belves, France

Randall - Raphael

Raphael, Sally Jessy — *Entertainer*
%MultiMedia Entertainment, 8 Elm St, New Haven, CT 06510, USA

Rappaport, Norman L — *Financier*
%Pentagon Federal Credit Union, PO Box 1532, Arlington, VA 22210, USA

Rappuoli, Rino — *Medical Researcher*
%Sclavo Research Center, Via Fiorentina 1, 53100, Siena, Italy

Rapson, Ralph — *Architect*
1 Seymour Ave, Minneapolis, MN 55414, USA

Rarick, Cindy — *Golfer*
%Ladies Professional Golf Assn, 2570 Volusia Ave, Daytona Beach, FL 32114, USA

Rasche, David — *Actor*
687 Grove Lane, Santa Barbara, CA 93105, USA

Rashad, Ahmad — *Football Player, Sportscaster*
%NBC-TV, Sports Dept, 30 Rockefeller Plaza, New York, NY 10112, USA

Rashad, Phylicia — *Actress*
130 W 42nd St, #2400, New York, NY 10036, USA

Rasmuson, Edward B — *Financier*
%National Bancorp of Alaska, 301 W Northern Lights Blvd, Anchorage, AK 99503, USA

Rasmussen, Norman C — *Nuclear Engineer*
80 Winsor Rd, Sudbury, MA 01776, USA

Rasmussen, Poul N — *Prime Minister, Denmark*
Christiansborg Palace, Prins Jorgens Ganard II, 1218 Copenhagen K, Denmark

Raspberry, William J — *Journalist*
%Washington Post, Editorial Dept, 1150 15th St NW, Washington, DC 20071, USA

Ratcliffe, G Jackson, Jr — *Businessman*
%Hubbell Inc, 584 Derby Milford Rd, Orange, CT 06477, USA

Ratcliffe, John A — *Radio Astronomer*
193 Huntingdon Rd, Cambridge CB3 0DL, England

Ratelle, Jean — *Hockey Player*
%Boston Bruins, Boston Garden, 150 Causeway St, Boston, MA 02114, USA

Rathbone, Perry T — *Museum Director*
130 Mt Auburn St, #506, University Green, Cambridge, MA 02138, USA

Rather, Dan — *Commentator*
%CBS-TV, News Dept, 524 W 57th St, New York, NY 10019, USA

Rathmann, Jim — *Auto Racing Driver*
3950 N Riverside Dr, Indialantic, FL 32903, USA

Ratliff, Floyd — *Biophysicist*
2215 Calle Cacique, Santa Fe, NM 87505, USA

Ratliff, Robert J — *Businessman*
%AGCO Corp, 4830 River Green Parkway, Duluth, GA 30136, USA

Ratliff, Theo — *Basketball Player*
%Detroit Pistons, Palace, 2 Championship Dr, Auburn Hills, MI 48057, USA

Ratner, Albert B — *Businessman*
%Forest City Enterprises, 10800 Brookpart Rd, Cleveland, OH 44130, USA

Ratner, Charles A — *Businessman*
%Forest City Enterprises, 10800 Brookpark Rd, Cleveland, OH 44130, USA

Ratnoff, Oscar D — *Physician*
2916 Sedgewick Rd, Shaker Heights, OH 44120, USA

Ratterman, George — *Football Player*
750 Crescent Lane, Lakewood, CO 80215, USA

Rattle, Simon — *Conductor*
%Birmingham Symphony, Paradise Place, Brimingham B3 3RP, England

Ratushinskaya, Irina B — *Poet*
15 Crothall Close, Palmers Green, London N13, England

Ratzenberger, John — *Actor*
7080 Hollywood Blvd, #1118, Los Angeles, CA 90028, USA

Ratzinger, Joseph Cardinal — *Religious Leader*
Piazza del Santuffizio 11, 00120 Vatican City, Rome, Italy

Rau, Johannes — *Government Official, West Germany*
Haroldstr 2, 47057 Dusseldorf, Germany

Rau, Robert H — *Businessman*
%Rohr Inc, 850 Lagoon Dr, Chula Vista, CA 91910, USA

Rauch, Johnny — *Football Player, Coach*
%San Jose State University, Athletic Dept, San Jose, CA 95192, USA

Raum, Arnold — *Judge*
%US Tax Court, 400 2nd St NW, Washington, DC 20217, USA

Rauschenberg, Robert — *Artist*
%M Knoedler Co, 19 E 70th St, New York, NY 10021, USA

R

Raveling, George H — *Basketball Coach, Administrator*
%University of Southern California, Heritage Hall, Los Angeles, CA 90089, USA

Raven, Eddy — *Singer, Guitarist*
PO Box 2476, Hendersonville, TN 37077, USA

Raven, Peter H — *Botanist*
%Missouri Botanical Garden, PO Box 299, St Louis, MO 63166, USA

Raven, Robert D — *Attorney*
%Morrison & Foerster, 345 California St, #3500, San Francisco, CA 94104, USA

Ravitch, Diane S — *Historian*
%New York University, Press Building, Washington Pl, New York, NY 10003, USA

Ravony, Francisque — *Prime Minister, Madagascar*
%Prime Minister's Office, Mahazoarivo, Antananarivo, Madagascar

Rawlings, Hunter R, III — *Educator*
%Cornell University, President's Office, Ithaca, NY 14853, USA

Rawlings, Jerry J — *President, Ghana; Air Force Officer*
%Head of State's Office, The Castle, PO Box 1627, Accra, Ghana

Rawlins, Benjamin W, Jr — *Financier*
%Union Planters Corp, 7130 Goodlett Farms Parkway, Cordova, TN 38018, USA

Rawlins, V Lane — *Educator*
%University of Memphis, President's Office, Memphis, TN 38152, USA

Rawlinson of Ewell, Peter — *Government Official, England*
9 Priory Walk, London SW10 9SP, England

Rawls, Betsy — *Golfer*
%Ladies Professional Golf Assn, 2570 Volusia Ave, Daytona Beach, FL 32114, USA

Rawls, Eugenia — *Actress*
510 E 84th St, New York, NY 10028, USA

Rawls, John — *Philosopher*
9 Winthrop Rd, Lexington, MA 02173, USA

Rawls, Lou — *Singer*
109 Fremont Place W, Los Angeles, CA 90005, USA

Ray, Donald P — *Political Economist, Editor*
1505 28th St S, Arlington, VA 22206, USA

Ray, Gene Anthony — *Actor*
104-60 Queens Blvd, #1-D, Forest Hills, NY 11375, USA

Ray, Marguerite — *Actress*
1329 N Vista St, #106, Los Angeles, CA 90046, USA

Ray, Michael L — *Educator*
%Stanford University, Business School, Stanford, CA 94305, USA

Ray, Norman W — *Navy Admiral*
Deputy Chairman, NATO, PSC 80, Box 300, APO, AE 09724, USA

Ray, Robert D — *Governor, IA*
%Blue Cross/Blue Shield of Iowa, 636 Grand Ave, Des Moines, IA 50309, USA

Ray, Ronald E — *Vietnam War Army Hero (CMH)*
6901 Lemon Rd, McLean, VA 22101, USA

Rayburn, Gene — *Entertainer*
Seaview Ave, Osterville, ME 02655, USA

Raymond, Arthur E — *Airplane Designer*
73 Oakmont Dr, Los Angeles, CA 90049, USA

Raymond, Gene — *Actor*
250 Trino Way, Pacific Palisades, CA 90272, USA

Raymond, Guy — *Actor*
550 Erskine Dr, Pacific Palisades, CA 90272, USA

Raymond, Lee R — *Businessman*
%Exxon Corp, 225 E John W Carpenter Freeway, Irving, TX 75062, USA

Raymond, Paula — *Actress*
PO Box 86, Beverly Hills, CA 90213, USA

Raymond, Steven A — *Businessman*
%Tech Data Corp, 5350 Tech Data Dr, Clearwater, FL 34620, USA

Rayner, E Charles (Chuck) — *Hockey Player*
116-5710 201st St, Langley BC V3A 8A8, Canada

Raynor, John P — *Educator*
%Marquette University, Chancellor's Office, Milwaukee, WI 53233, USA

Raz, Kavi — *Actor*
%Dale Garrick International, 8831 Sunset Blvd, #402, Los Angeles, CA 90069, USA

Razafimahatratra, Victor Cardinal — *Religious Leader*
Archeveche, Andohalo, 101 Antananarivo, Madagascar

Razanamasy, Guy — *Prime Minister, Madagascar*
%Prime Minister's Office, Mahazoarivo, Antananarivo, Madagascar

Razumovsky, Georgy P — *Government Official, USSR*
%Russian Parliament, Moscow, Russia

Re, Edward D — *Judge*
%US Court of International Trade, 1 Federal Plaza, New York, NY 10278, USA

Rea, Peggy — *Actress*
8822 Rosewood Ave, Los Angeles, CA 90048, USA

Rea, Stephen — *Actor*
108 Leonard St, London EC2A 4RH, England

Read, James — *Actor*
%Gersh Agency, 232 N Canon Dr, Beverly Hills, CA 90210, USA

Read, William E — *Financier*
%Bank One Milwaukee, 111 E Wisconsin Ave, Milwaukee, WI 53202, USA

Readdy, William F — *Astronaut*
%NASA, Johnson Space Center, 2101 NASA Rd, Houston, TX 77058, USA

Reagan, Nancy — *Wife of US President*
668 St Cloud Rd, Bel Air, CA 90077, USA

Reagan, Ronald — *President, USA*
668 St Cloud Rd, Bel Air, CA 90077, USA

Reagon, Bernice Johnson — *Singer (Sweet Honey in the Rock)*
%American University, History Dept, Washington, DC 20016, USA

Reamer, Norton H — *Financier*
%United Asset Management Corp, 1 International Plaza, Boston, MA 02110, USA

Reams, Lee Roy — *Actor, Singer*
%Ligeti, 415 W 55th St, New York, NY 10019, USA

Reardon, Jay — *Financier*
%Commerce Bank Kansas City, 1000 Walnut St, Kansas City, MO 64106, USA

Reardon, Jeffrey J (Jeff) — *Baseball Player*
5 Marlwood Lane, Palm Beach Gardens, FL 33418, USA

Reason, J Paul — *Navy Admiral*
%Plans Policy & Operations, Navy Department, Pentagon, Washington, DC 20350, USA

Reason, Rex — *Actor*
%Roadside Productions, 20105 Rhapsody Rd, Walnut Creek, CA 91789, USA

Reaves, T Johnson (John) — *Football Player, Coach*
4830 NW 43rd St, #A-3, Gainesville, FL 32606, USA

Reavley, Thomas M — *Judge*
%US Court of Appeals, 903 San Jacinto St, Austin, TX 78701, USA

Rebek, Julius, Jr — *Chemist*
100 Memorial Dr, #53-A, Cambridge, MA 02142, USA

Recchi, Mark — *Hockey Player*
%Philadelphia Flyers, Spectrum, Pattison Place, Philadelphia, PA 19148, USA

Rechin, Bill — *Cartoonist (Crock)*
%North America Syndicate, 235 E 45th St, New York, NY 10017, USA

Rechter, Yacov — *Architect*
150 Arlozorov St, Tel Aviv 62098, Israel

Reckell, Peter — *Actor*
%Paradigm Agency, 10100 Santa Monica Blvd, #2500, Los Angeles, CA 90067, USA

Rector, Milton G — *Association Executive*
%National Council on Crime & Delinquency, 288 Monroe, River Edge, NJ 07661, USA

Redbone, Leon — *Singer*
%Red Shark Inc, 179 Aquetong Rd, New Hope, PA 18938, USA

Reddicliffe, Steven — *Editor*
%TV Guide Magazine, Editorial Dept, 100 Matsonford Rd, Radnor, PA 19080, USA

Redding, Peter S — *Businessman*
%Standard Register Co, 600 Albany St, Dayton, OH 45408, USA

Reddy, D Raj — *Computer Scientist*
%Robotics Institute, Carnegie-Mellon University, Pittsburgh, PA 15213, USA

Reddy, Helen — *Singer*
%Helen Reddy Inc, 820 Stanford St, Santa Monica, CA 90403, USA

Reddy, Neelam Sanjiva — *President, India*
Illure, Anatapur, Andra Pradesh, India

Redfern, John D — *Businessman*
%Lafarge Corp, 11130 Sunrise Valley Dr, Reston, VA 22091, USA

Redford, Robert — *Actor, Movie Director*
Rt 3, Box 837, Provo, UT 84604, USA

Redgrave, Lynn — *Actress*
21342 Colina Dr, Topanga, CA 90290, USA

Redgrave, Martyn R — *Businessman*
%Carlson Companies, Carlson Parkway, PO Box 59159, Minneapolis, MN 55459, USA

R

Razumovsky - Redgrave

Redgrave, Vanessa *Actress*
%James Sharkey Assoc, 21 Golden Square, London W1R 3PA, England

Reding, Juli *Actress*
PO Box 1806, Beverly Hills, CA 90213, USA

Reding, Nicholas L *Businessman*
%Monsanto Co, 800 N Lindbergh Blvd, St Louis, MO 63141, USA

Redington, Joe, Sr *Dog Sled Racer*
%Joe Redington Sled Dog Institute, HC 30, Box 5460, Wasilla, AK 99654, USA

Redman, Joshua *Jazz Saxophonist, Composer*
%Jazz Tree, 211 Thompson St, #1-D, New York, NY 10012, USA

Redman, Peter *Financer*
%Cessna Finance Corp, 5800 E Pawnee, Wichita, KS 67218, USA

Redman, Richard C (Rick) *Football Player*
153 Prospect St, Seattle, WA 98109, USA

Redmond, Marge *Actress*
101 Central Park West, New York, NY 10023, USA

Redmond, Paul A *Businessman*
%Washington Water Power Co, East 1411 Mission Ave, Spokane, WA 99220, USA

Redpath, Jean *Singer*
Sunny Knowe, The Promenade, Leven, Fife, Scotland

Redstone, Sumner M *Theater Executive*
%Viacom Inc, 1515 Broadway, New York, NY 10036, USA

Redwine, Jarvis J *Football Player*
2707 W 79th St, Inglewood, CA 90305, USA

Reece, Beasley *Football Player, Sportscaster*
%Premier Sports, 110 E 59th St, #800, New York, NY 10022, USA

Reece, Thomas L *Businessman*
%Dover Corp, 280 Park Ave, New York, NY 10017, USA

Reed Donald B *Businessman*
%Nynex Corp, 1095 Ave of Americas, New York, NY 10036, USA

Reed, Andre D *Football Player*
%Buffalo Bills, 1 Bills Dr, Orchard Park, NY 14127, USA

Reed, Carlton D, Jr *Businessman*
%Central Main Power Co, Edison Dr, Augusta, ME 04336, USA

Reed, Charles B *Educator*
%State University System of Florida, Chancellor's Office, Tallahassee, FL 32399, USA

Reed, Ishmael S *Writer*
1446 6th St, #C, Berkeley, CA 94710, USA

Reed, James M *Businessman*
%Union Camp Corp, 1600 Valley Rd, Wayne, NJ 07470, USA

Reed, James W *Educator*
%Rutgers State University, President's Office, New Brunswick, NJ 08903, USA

Reed, Jerry *Singer*
153 Rue De Grande, Brentwood, TN 37027, USA

Reed, Joel L *Businessman*
1608 Stanolind Ave, Midland, TX 79705, USA

Reed, John E *Businessman*
%Mestek Inc, 200 N Elm St, Westfield, MA 01085, USA

Reed, John H *Governor, ME; Diplomat*
410 "O" St SW, Washington, DC 20024, USA

Reed, John S *Financier*
%Citicorp, 399 Park Ave, New York, NY 10022, USA

Reed, Lou *Singer, Songwriter (Velvet Undergound)*
%Sister Ray Enterprises, 584 Broadway, #609, New York, NY 10012, USA

Reed, Mark A *Physicist*
%Yale University, Electrical Engineering Dept, PO Box 2157, New Haven, CT 06520, USA

Reed, Oliver *Actor*
Houmit Lane, Houmit Vale, Guernsey, Channel Islands, England

Reed, Pamela *Actress*
1875 Century Park East, #1300, Los Angeles, CA 90067, USA

Reed, Rex *Entertainment Critic*
1 W 72nd St, #86, New York, NY 10023, USA

Reed, Richard J *Meteorologist*
%University of Washington, Atmospheric Sciences Dept, Seattle, WA 98195, USA

Reed, Shanna *Actress*
3711 Fredonia Dr, Los Angeles, CA 90068, USA

Reed, Thomas C *Government Official*
%Quaker Hill Development Corp, PO Box 2240, Healdsburg, CA 95448, USA

Reed, Willis, Jr *Basketball Player, Coach, Executive*
%New Jersey Nets, Byrne Meadowlands Arena, East Rutherford, NJ 07073, USA

Reedy, George E, Jr *Educator, Journalist*
925 E Wells St, #625, Milwaukee, WI 53202, USA

Rees, Clifford H (Ted), Jr *Air Force General*
3114 Barbard Court, Fairfax, VA 22031, USA

Rees, Merlyn *Government Official, England*
%House of Commons, Westminster, London SW1A 0AA, England

Rees, Mina *Mathematician*
301 E 66th St, New York, NY 10021, USA

Rees, Norma S *Educator*
%California State University, President's Office, Hayward, CA 94542, USA

Rees, Roger *Actor*
%International Creative Mgmt, 76 Oxford St, London W1N 0AX, England

Rees-Mogg of Hinton Blewett, William *Publisher*
3 Smith Square, London SW1, England

Reese, Della *Singer, Actress*
1910 Bel Air Rd, Los Angeles, CA 90077, USA

Reese, Eddie *Swimming Coach*
%University of Texas, Athletic Dept, Austin, TX 78712, USA

Reese, Harold H (Pee Wee) *Baseball Player*
1400 Willow Ave, Louisville, KY 40204, USA

Reese, Miranda *Ballerina*
%New York City Ballet, Lincoln Center Plaza, New York, NY 10023, USA

Reeve, Christopher *Actor*
121 Treadwell Hollow Rd, Williamstown, MA 01267, USA

Reeves, Bryant *Basketball Player*
%Vancouver Grizzlies, 788 Beatty St, #300, Vancouver BC V6B 2M1, Canada

Reeves, Daniel E (Dan) *Football Player, Coach*
%New York Giants, Giants Stadium, East Rutherford, NJ 07073, USA

Reeves, Del *Singer, Songwriter*
%Playgold Media, 3220 Ellington Circle, Nashville, TN 37211, USA

Reeves, Donna A *Golfer*
%Ladies Professional Golf Assn, 2570 Volusla Ave, Daytona Beach, FL 32114, USA

Reeves, Keanu *Actor*
%Creative Artists Agency, 9830 Wilshire Blvd, Beverly Hills, CA 90212, USA

Reeves, Martha *Singer (Martha & The Vandellas)*
PO Box 1987, Paramount, CA 90723, USA

Reeves, Richard *Columnist*
%Universal Press Syndicate, 4900 Main St, #900, Kansas City, KS 64112, USA

Reeves, Scott *Actor*
23643 Califa St, Woodland Hills, CA 91367, USA

Reeves, Steve *Actor, Bodybuilder*
%Classic Images Enterprises, PO Box 807, Valley Center, CA 92082, USA

Regalbuto, Joe *Actor*
724 24th St, Santa Monica, CA 90402, USA

Regan, Donald T *Secretary, Treasury; Financier*
240 Mclaws Circle, #142, Williamsburg, VA 23185, USA

Regan, Gerald A *Government Official, Canada*
PO Box 828, Station B, Ottawa ON K1P 5P9, Canada

Regan, Philip R *Baseball Player, Manager*
1375 108th St, Byron Center, MI 49315, USA

Regazzoni, Clay *Auto Racing Driver*
Via Monzoni 13, 6900 Lugano, Switzerland

Regehr, Duncan *Actor*
2401 Main St, Santa Monica, CA 90405, USA

Reggiani, Serge *Singer, Actor*
%Charley Marouani, 4 Ave Hoche, 75008 Paris, France

Regine *Restauranteur*
502 Park Ave, New York, NY 10022, USA

Regis, John *Track Athlete*
67 Fairby Rd, London SE12, England

Regnier, Charles *Actor, Theater Director*
Seestr 6, 82541 Munsing, Germany

Rehm, Jack D *Publisher*
%Meredith Corp, 1716 Locust St, Des Moines, IA 50309, USA

Rehnquist, William H *Supreme Court Chief Justice*
%US Supreme Court, 1 1st St NE, Washington, DC 20543, USA

R

Reich, John *Theater Director*
724 Bohemia Parkway, Sayville, NY 11782, USA

Reich, Robert B *Secretary, Labor*
%Labor Department, 200 Constitution Ave NW, Washington, DC 20210, USA

Reich, Steve *Composer*
%Helene Cann Reich Music Foundation, 175 5th Ave, #2396, New York, NY 10010, USA

Reichert, Jack F *Businessman*
%Brunswick Corp, 1 N Field Court, Lake Forest, IL 60045, USA

Reichman, Fred *Artist*
1235 Stanyan St, San Francisco, CA 94117, USA

Reichmann, Paul *Businessman*
%Olympia & York Ltd, 2 First Canadian Place, Toronto ON M5X 1B5, Canada

Reichstein, Tadeus *Nobel Medicine Laureate*
Weissensteinstr 22, 4059 Basel, Switzerland

Reid, Antonio (L A) *Songwriter*
%Kear Music, Carter Turner Co, 9229 W Sunset Blvd, West Hollywood, CA 90069, USA

Reid, Daphne Maxwell *Actress*
11342 Dona Lisa Dr, Studio City, CA 91604, USA

Reid, Don S *Singer (Statler Brothers), Songwriter*
PO Box 2703, Staunton, VA 24402, USA

Reid, Frances *Actress*
%Brooke Dunn Oliver, 9169 Sunset Blvd, #202, Los Angeles, CA 90069, USA

Reid, Harold W *Singer (Statler Brothers), Songwriter*
PO Box 2703, Staunton, VA 24402, USA

Reid, J R *Basketball Player*
%San Antonio Spurs, 600 E Market St, #102, San Antonio, TX 78205, USA

Reid, James S, Jr *Businessman*
%Standard Products Co, 2130 W 110th St, Cleveland, OH 44102, USA

Reid, Michael B (Mike) *Football Player, Songwriter*
825 Overton Lane, Nashville, TN 37220, USA

Reid, Norman R *Museum Director*
50 Brabourne Rise, Park Langley, Beckenham, Kent, England

Reid, Ogden R *Journalist, Diplomat*
Ophir Hill, Purchase, NY 10577, USA

Reid, Robert *Basketball Player, Coach*
%Washington Bullets, Capital Centre, 1 Truman Dr, Landover, MD 20785, USA

Reid, Robert *Skier*
%Dixfield Health Care Center, Dixfield, ME 04224, USA

Reid, Stephen E (Steve) *Football Player, Physician*
262 Graemere, Northfield, IL 60093, USA

Reid, Tim *Actor*
11342 Dona Lisa, Studio City, CA 91604, USA

Reid, William R *WW II British Royal Air Force Hero (VC)*
Cranford, Ferntower Place, Crieff, Perthshire PH7 3DD, Scotland

Reidy, Carolyn K *Publisher*
%Simon & Schuster Inc, 1230 Ave of Americas, New York, NY 10020, USA

Reier, John D *Businessman*
%Family Dollar Stores, 10401 Old Monroe Rd, Charlotte, NC 28201, USA

Reig, Oscar Ribas *Head of Government, Andorra*
%Governmental Offices, Andorra la Vella, Andorra

Reightler, Kenneth S, Jr *Astronaut*
%NASA, Johnson Space Center, 2101 NASA Rd, Houston, TX 77058, USA

Reilly, Charles Nelson *Actor*
2341 Gloaming Way, Beverly Hills, CA 90210, USA

Reilly, John *Actor*
%Innovative Artists, 1999 Ave of Stars, #2850, Los Angeles, CA 90067, USA

Reilly, John P *Businessman*
%Figgie International Inc, 4420 Sherwin Rd, Willoughby, OH 44094, USA

Reilly, William K *Government Official*
%Stanford University, International Studies Institute, Stanford, CA 94305, USA

Reimer, Dennis J *Army General*
%Chief of Staff, HqUSA, Pentagon, Washington, DC 20310, USA

Reimer, Roland *Religious Leader*
%Mennonite Brethren Churches Conference, 8000 W 21st, Wichita, KS 67205, USA

Rein, Harry T *Businessman*
%Canaan Partners, 105 Rowayton Ave, Rowayton, CT 06853, USA

Reina, Carlos Roberto *President, Honduras*
%President's Office, 6 Avda La Calle, Tegucigalpa, Honduras

Reich - Reina

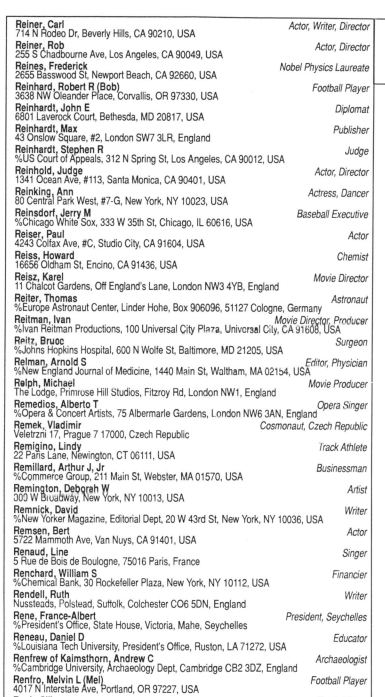

Reiner, Carl *Actor, Writer, Director*
714 N Rodeo Dr, Beverly Hills, CA 90210, USA

Reiner, Rob *Actor, Director*
255 S Chadbourne Ave, Los Angeles, CA 90049, USA

Reines, Frederick *Nobel Physics Laureate*
2655 Basswood St, Newport Beach, CA 92660, USA

Reinhard, Robert R (Bob) *Football Player*
3638 NW Oleander Place, Corvallis, OR 97330, USA

Reinhardt, John E *Diplomat*
6801 Laverock Court, Bethesda, MD 20817, USA

Reinhardt, Max *Publisher*
43 Onslow Square, #2, London SW7 3LR, England

Reinhardt, Stephen R *Judge*
%US Court of Appeals, 312 N Spring St, Los Angeles, CA 90012, USA

Reinhold, Judge *Actor, Director*
1341 Ocean Ave, #113, Santa Monica, CA 90401, USA

Reinking, Ann *Actress, Dancer*
80 Central Park West, #7-G, New York, NY 10023, USA

Reinsdorf, Jerry M *Baseball Executive*
%Chicago White Sox, 333 W 35th St, Chicago, IL 60616, USA

Reiser, Paul *Actor*
4243 Colfax Ave, #C, Studio City, CA 91604, USA

Reiss, Howard *Chemist*
16656 Oldham St, Encino, CA 91436, USA

Reisz, Karel *Movie Director*
11 Chalcot Gardens, Off England's Lane, London NW3 4YB, England

Reiter, Thomas *Astronaut*
%Europe Astronaut Center, Linder Hohe, Box 906096, 51127 Cologne, Germany

Reitman, Ivan *Movie Director, Producer*
%Ivan Reitman Productions, 100 Universal City Plaza, Universal City, CA 91608, USA

Reitz, Bruce *Surgeon*
%Johns Hopkins Hospital, 600 N Wolfe St, Baltimore, MD 21205, USA

Relman, Arnold S *Editor, Physician*
%New England Journal of Medicine, 1440 Main St, Waltham, MA 02154, USA

Relph, Michael *Movie Producer*
The Lodge, Primrose Hill Studios, Fitzroy Rd, London NW1, England

Remedios, Alberto T *Opera Singer*
%Opera & Concert Artists, 75 Albermarle Gardens, London NW6 3AN, England

Remek, Vladimir *Cosmonaut, Czech Republic*
Veletrzni 17, Prague 7 17000, Czech Republic

Remigino, Lindy *Track Athlete*
22 Paris Lane, Newington, CT 06111, USA

Remillard, Arthur J, Jr *Businessman*
%Commerce Group, 211 Main St, Webster, MA 01570, USA

Remington, Deborah W *Artist*
300 W Broadway, New York, NY 10013, USA

Remnick, David *Writer*
%New Yorker Magazine, Editorial Dept, 20 W 43rd St, New York, NY 10036, USA

Remsen, Bert *Actor*
5722 Mammoth Ave, Van Nuys, CA 91401, USA

Renaud, Line *Singer*
5 Rue de Bois de Boulogne, 75016 Paris, France

Renchard, William S *Financier*
%Chemical Bank, 30 Rockefeller Plaza, New York, NY 10112, USA

Rendell, Ruth *Writer*
Nussteads, Polstead, Suffolk, Colchester CO6 5DN, England

Rene, France-Albert *President, Seychelles*
%President's Office, State House, Victoria, Mahe, Seychelles

Reneau, Daniel D *Educator*
%Louisiana Tech University, President's Office, Ruston, LA 71272, USA

Renfrew of Kaimsthorn, Andrew C *Archaeologist*
%Cambridge University, Archaeology Dept, Cambridge CB2 3DZ, England

Renfro, Melvin L (Mel) *Football Player*
4017 N Interstate Ave, Portland, OR 97227, USA

Renk, Silke *Track Athlete*
Erhard-Hubner-Str 13, 06132 Halle/S, Germany

Renko, Steven (Steve) *Baseball Player*
3408 W 35th St, Leawood, KS 68209, USA

R

Reiner - Renko

R

Rennebohm, J Fred *Religious Leader*
%Congregational Christian Churches National Assn, Box 1620, Oak Creek, MI 53154, USA

Rennert, Gunther *Opera Director*
Schwalbenweg 11-A, 82152 Krailling, Oberbayem, Germany

Rennert, Laurence H (Dutch) *Baseball Umpire*
2560 46th Rd, Vero Beach, FL 32966, USA

Rennert, Wolfgang *Conductor*
Holbeinstr 58, 12203 Berlin, Germany

Reno, Janet *Attorney General*
%Justice Department, Constitution Ave & 10th St NW, Washington, DC 20530, USA

Reno, John F *Businessman*
%Dynatech Corp, 3 New England Executive Park, Burlington, MA 01803, USA

Reno, Nancy *Volleyball Player*
%Assn of Volleyball Pros, 15260 Ventura Blvd, #2250, Sherman Oaks, CA 91403, USA

Reno, William H *Army General*
Deputy Chief of Staff for Personnel, HqUSA, Washington, DC 20310, USA

Rense, Paige *Editor*
%Architectural Digest, 5900 Wilshire Blvd, Los Angeles, CA 90036, USA

Rensi, Edward H *Businessman*
%McDonald's USA, McDonald's Plaza, 1 Kroc Dr, Oak Brook, IL 60521, USA

Rentmeester, Co *Photographer*
4479 Douglas Ave, Bronx, NY 10471, USA

Renton, R Timothy *Government Official, England*
%House of Commons, Westminster, London SW1A 0AA, England

Rentzepis, Peter M *Chemist*
%University of California, Chemistry Dept, Irvine, CA 92717, USA

Renvall, Johan *Ballet Dancer*
%American Ballet Theatre, 890 Broadway, New York, NY 10003, USA

Renyi, Thomas A *Financier*
%Bank of New York Co, 48 Wall St, New York, NY 10005, USA

Repin, Vadim V *Concert Violinist*
Eckholdtweg 2-A, 23566 Lubeck, Germany

Rescigno, Nicola *Conductor*
%Robert Lombardo, 61 W 62nd St, #6-F, New York, NY 10023, USA

Resnais, Alain *Movie Director*
70 Rue Des Plantes, 75014 Paris, France

Resnick, Milton *Artist*
87 Eldridge St, New York, NY 10002, USA

Resnik, Regina *Opera Singer*
50 W 56th St, New York, NY 10019, USA

Respert, Shawn *Basketball Player*
%Milwaukee Bucks, Bradley Center, 1001 N 4th St, Milwaukee, WI 53203, USA

Ressler, Glenn E *Football Player*
328 Blacklatch Lane, Camp Hill, PA 17011, USA

Restani, Jane A *Judge*
%US Court of International Trade, 1 Federal Plaza, New York, NY 10278, USA

Reston, James B *Columnist*
1804 Kallorama Square NW, Washington, DC 20008, USA

Reswick, James B *Engineer*
1003 Dead Run Dr, McLean, VA 22101, USA

Rettig, Tommy *Actor*
2532 Lincoln Blvd, #110, Marina del Rey, CA 90291, USA

Retton, Mary Lou *Gymnast*
%Proper Marketing, 322 Vista Del Mar, Redondo Beach, CA 90277, USA

Retzlaff, Palmer (Pete) *Football Player*
%Sports Film, 511 Old Lancaster Pike, Berwyn, PA 19312, USA

Reuben, David R *Psychiatrist, Writer*
%Scott Meredith, 845 3rd Ave, New York, NY 10022, USA

Reum, W Robert *Businessman*
%Interlake Corp, 550 Warrenville Rd, Lisle, IL 60532, USA

Reuschel, Ricky E (Rick) *Baseball Player*
618 E Maude Ave, Arlington Heights, IL 60004, USA

Reuss, Jerry *Baseball Player*
9428 Churchill Downs Dr, Las Vegas, NV 89117, USA

Reuter, Edzard *Businessman*
%Daimler-Benz AG, Mercedesstr 136, 70327 Stuttgart, Germany

Reutersward, Carl Fredrik *Artist*
6 Rue Montolieu, 1030 Bussigny/Lausanne, Switzerland

Rennebohm - Reutersward

Reveiz, Fuad *Football Player*
%Minnesota Vikings, 9520 Viking Dr, Eden Prairie, MN 55344, USA

Revel, Jean-Francois *Writer*
55 Quai de Bourbon, 75004 Paris, France

Revere, Paul *Singer (Paul Revere & the Raiders)*
PO Box 544, Grangeville, ID 83530, USA

Revill, Clive *Actor*
15029 Encanto Dr, Sherman Oaks, CA 91403, USA

Revollo Bravo, Mario Cardinal *Religious Leader*
Arzobispado, Carrera 7-A N 10-20, Bogota DE, Colombia

Rewak, William J *Educator*
%Spring Hill College, President's Office, Mobile, AL 36608, USA

Reynolds Booth, Nancy *Skier*
3197 Padaro Lane, Carpinteria, CA 93013, USA

Reynolds, A William *Businessman*
%GenCorp, 175 Ghent Rd, Fairlawn, OH 44333, USA

Reynolds, Albert *Prime Minister, Ireland*
Mount Carmel House, Dublin Rd, Longford, Ireland

Reynolds, Anna *Opera Singer*
Peesten 9, 8656 Kasendorf, Germany

Reynolds, Burt *Actor*
16133 Jupiter Farms Rd, Jupiter, FL 33478, USA

Reynolds, David P *Businessman*
%Reynolds Metals Co, 6601 Broad Street Rd, Richmond, VA 23261, USA

Reynolds, Dean *Commentator*
%ABC-TV, News Dept, 1717 De Sales St NW, Washington, DC 20036, USA

Reynolds, Debbie *Actress, Singer*
305 Convention Center Dr, Las Vegas, NV 89109, USA

Reynolds, Frank *Commentator*
1124 Connecticut Ave NW, Washington, DC 20036, USA

Reynolds, Gene *Actor, Television Producer*
2034 Castillian Dr, Los Angeles, CA 90068, USA

Reynolds, Glenn F *Inventor (Proscar Drug)*
242 Edgewood Ave, Westfield, NJ 07090, USA

Reynolds, Harry (Butch) *Track Athlete*
%Advantage International, 1025 Thomas Jefferson St NW, #450, Washington 20007, USA

Reynolds, Herbert H *Educator*
%Baylor University, President's Office, Waco, TX 76798, USA

Reynolds, J Louis *Businessman*
2000 W Club Lane, #A, Richmond, VA 23226, USA

Reynolds, Jerry O *Basketball Coach, Executive*
%Sacramento Kings, 1 Sports Parkway, Sacramento, CA 95834, USA

Reynolds, John H *Physicist, Educator*
%University of California, Physics Dept, Berkeley, CA 94720, USA

Reynolds, John T *Television Executive*
PO Box 1738, Beverly Hills, CA 90213, USA

Reynolds, John W *Governor, WI; Judge*
%US District Court, 517 E Wisconsin Ave, Milwaukee, WI 53202, USA

Reynolds, Robert *Bassist (Mavericks)*
%AristoMedia, 1620 16th Ave S, Nashville, TN 37212, USA

Reynolds, Thomas A, Jr *Attorney*
%Winston & Strawn, 1 First National Plaza, 45 W Wacker Dr, Chicago, IL 60601, USA

Reynolds, W Ann *Educator*
%City University of New York, Chancellor's Office, New York, NY 10021, USA

Reznicek, Bernard W *Businessman*
%Boston Edison Co, 800 Boylston St, Boston, MA 02199, USA

Reznor, Trent *Singer (Nine Inch Nails)*
%Artists & Audience Entertainment, 83 Riverside Dr, New York, NY 10024, USA

Rhame, Thomas G *Army General*
%Defense Security Assistance Agency, 1111 J Davis Highway, Arlington, VA 22202, USA

Rheaume, Manon *Hockey Player*
%Atlanta Knights, 100 Techwood Dr NW, Atlanta, GA 30303, USA

Rhines, Peter B *Oceanographer*
5753 61st Ave NE, Seattle, WA 98105, USA

Rhoades, Barbara *Actress*
90 Old Redding Rd, Weston, CT 06883, USA

Rhoads, George *Sculptor*
1478 Mecklenburg Rd, Ithaca, NY 14850, USA

R

R

Rhoads, James B — *Archivist*
3613 E Illinois Lane, Bellingham, WA 98226, USA

Rhoden, Richard A (Rick) — *Baseball Player*
PO Box 546, Crescent City, FL 32112, USA

Rhodes, Cynthia — *Actress, Dancer*
15250 Ventura Blvd, #900, Sherman Oaks, CA 91403, USA

Rhodes, Donnelly — *Actor*
%Century Artists, 9744 Wilshire Blvd, #308, Beverly Hills, CA 90212, USA

Rhodes, James A — *Governor, OH*
2375 Tremont Rd, Columbus, OH 43221, USA

Rhodes, Ray — *Football Coach*
%Philadelphia Eagles, 3501 S Broad St, Philadelphia, PA 19148, USA

Rhodes, Richard L — *Writer*
%Janklow & Assoc, 598 Madison Ave, New York, NY 10022, USA

Rhodes, William R — *Financier*
%Citibank, 399 Park Ave, New York, NY 10022, USA

Rhodes, Zandra — *Fashion Designer*
64 Porchester Rd, London W2, England

Rhome, Gerald B (Jerry) — *Football Player, Coach*
%Minnesota Vikings, 9520 Viking Dr, Eden Prairie, MN 55344, USA

Rhue, Madlyn — *Actress*
%Gold Marshak Assoc, 3500 W Olive Ave, #1400, Burbank, CA 91505, USA

Rhys-Davies, John — *Actor*
1933 Cold Canyon Rd, Calabasas, CA 91302, USA

Riady, Mochtar — *Financier*
%Bank Central Asia, 25/26 Jalan Asemka, Jakarta Barat 01, Indonesia

Ribbs, Willy T — *Auto Racing Driver*
%International Motor Sports Assn, PO Box 3465, Bridgeport, CT 06605, USA

Ribeiro, Antonio Cardinal — *Religious Leader*
Campo Martires da Patria 45, 1198 Lisbon Codex, Portugal

Ribicoff, Abraham A — *Secretary, Health Education Welfare*
%Kaye Scholer Fierman Hays Handler, 425 Park Ave, New York, NY 10022, USA

Ricardo-Campbell, Rita — *Economist*
26915 Alejandro Dr, Los Altos Hills, CA 94022, USA

Ricci, Christina — *Actress*
PO Box 866, Teaneck, NJ 07666, USA

Ricci, Ruggiero — *Concert Violinist*
2930 E Delhi Rd, Ann Arbor, MI 48103, USA

Ricciarelli, Katia — *Opera Singer*
Via Magellana 2, 20097 Corsica, Italy

Rice, Anne — *Writer*
1239 1st St, New Orleans, LA 70130, USA

Rice, Charles E — *Financier*
%Barnett Banks, 50 N Laura St, Jacksonville, FL 32202, USA

Rice, Donald B — *Businessman, Government Official*
%Teledyne Inc, 2049 Century Park East, Los Angeles, CA 90067, USA

Rice, Dorothy P — *Medical Economist*
13895 Campus Dr, Oakland, CA 94605, USA

Rice, Gene D — *Religious Leader*
%Church of God, PO Box 2430, Cleveland, TN 37320, USA

Rice, Glen — *Basketball Player*
%Miami Heat, Miami Arena, Miami, FL 33136, USA

Rice, James E (Jim) — *Baseball Player*
96 Castlemere Place, North Andover, MA 01845, USA

Rice, Jerry L — *Football Player*
%San Francisco 49ers, 4949 Centennial Blvd, Santa Clara, CA 95054, USA

Rice, Joseph L, III — *Financier*
%Clayton Dubilier Rice Inc, 126 E 56th St, New York, NY 10022, USA

Rice, Stuart A — *Chemist*
5421 Greenwood Ave, Chicago, IL 60615, USA

Rice, Timothy M B (Tim) — *Lyricist*
196 Shaftesbury Ave, London WC2, England

Rice, Victor A — *Businessman*
%Varity Corp, 672 Delaware Ave, Buffalo, NY 14209, USA

Rich, Adam — *Actor*
1450 Belfast Dr, Los Angeles, CA 90069, USA

Rich, Adrienne — *Poet*
%Stanford University, English Dept, Stanford, CA 94305, USA

Rich, Alexander *Molecular Biologist*
2 Walnut Ave, Cambridge, MA 02140, USA

Rich, Ben R *Aeronautical Engineer, Designer*
%Lockheed Corp, 4500 Park Granada Blvd, Calabasas, CA 91302, USA

Rich, Clayton *Physician*
%University of Oklahoma, Health Services Center, Oklahoma City, OK 73190, USA

Rich, Frank H *Drama Critic*
%New York Times, 229 W 43rd St, New York, NY 10036, USA

Rich, Giles S *Judge*
%US Court of Appeals, 717 Madison Place NW, Washington, DC 20439, USA

Rich, Larry *Businessman*
%JM Family Enterprises, 100 NW 12th Ave, Deerfield Beach, FL 33442, USA

Rich, Lee *Entertainment Executive*
%Lee Rich Productions, Warner, 75 Rockefeller Plaza, New York, NY 10019, USA

Rich, Norman S *Businessman*
%Weis Markets, 1000 S 2nd St, Subnury, PA 17801, USA

Rich, Robert G, Jr *Diplomat*
%Spelman College, International Affairs Center, Atlanta, GA 30314, USA

Richard, Cliff *Singer*
St George's Hill, Weybridge, England

Richard, Henri *Hockey Player*
4300 Place de Cageux, #905, Ile Paton Laval PQ H7W 4Z3, Canada

Richard, Ivor S *Government Official, England*
11 South Square, Gray's Inn, London WC1R 5EU, England

Richard, James Rodney (J R) *Baseball Player*
10701 Sabo Rd, #2108, Houston, TX 77089, USA

Richard, Maurice *Hockey Player*
10950 Rue Peloquin, Montreal PQ H2C 2K8, Canada

Richard, Oliver G, III *Businessman*
%New Jersey Resources Corp, 1415 Wyckoff Rd, Wall, NJ 07719, USA

Richards, Ann W *Governor, TX*
PO Box 684746, Austin, TX 78768, USA

Richards, Beah *Actress*
PO Box 191515, Los Angeles, CA 90019, USA

Richards, Bob *Track Athlete*
1616 Estates Dr, Waco, TX 76712, USA

Richards, Frank *Actor*
%William Carroll Agency, 139 N San Fernando Rd, #A, Burbank, CA 91502, USA

Richards, Frederic M *Biochemist*
69 Andrews Rd, Guilford, CT 06437, USA

Richards, James C *Businessman*
%Southwire Co, 1 Southwire Dr, Carrollton, GA 30117, USA

Richards, John M *Businessman*
%Potlatch Corp, 1 Maritime Plaza, San Francisco, CA 04111, USA

Richards, Keith *Singer, Guitarist (Rolling Stones)*
Redlands, West Wittering Near Chichester, Sussex, England

Richards, Lloyd G *Theatre Director*
18 W 95th St, New York, NY 10025, USA

Richards, Mark *Surfer*
755 Hunter St, Newcastle NSW 2302, Australia

Richards, Michael *Actor*
%Agency For Performing Arts, 9000 Sunset Blvd, #1200, Los Angeles, CA 90069, USA

Richards, Paul G *Theoretical Seismologist*
%Lamont-Doherty Geological Observatory, Palisades, NY 10964, USA

Richards, Renee *Tennis Player*
40 Park Ave, New York, NY 10016, USA

Richards, Reuben F *Businessman*
%Terra Industries, 600 4th St, Sioux City, IA 51101, USA

Richards, Richard N *Astronaut*
%NASA, Johnson Space Center, 2101 NASA Rd, Houston, TX 77058, USA

Richards, Robert W *Financier*
%Source One Mortgage Services, 27555 Farmington Rd, Farmington Hills, MI 48334, USA

Richards, Roy *Businessman*
%Southwire Co, 1 Southwire Dr, Carrollton, GA 30117, USA

Richards, Thomas C *Air Force General, Government Official*
%Federal Aviation Administration, 800 Independence Ave SW, Washington, DC 20591, USA

Richardson of Duntisbourne, William H *Financier*
Kingsley House, 1-A Wimpole St, London W1M 7AA, England

Richardson of Lee, John S — *Physician*
Windcutter, Lee, North Devon, England

Richardson, Cheryl — *Actress*
16919 Gault St, Van Nuys, CA 91406, USA

Richardson, Elliot L — *Secretary, Defense & HEW*
%Milbank Tweed Hadley McCloy, 1825 "I" St NW, Washington, DC 20006, USA

Richardson, F C — *Educator*
152 Lincoln Parkway, Buffalo, NY 14222, USA

Richardson, Gordon W H — *Financier*
%Bank of England, London EC2R 8AH, England

Richardson, Hamilton — *Tennis Player*
920 Park Ave, New York, NY 10028, USA

Richardson, Howard — *Playwright*
207 Columbus Ave, New York, NY 10023, USA

Richardson, Ian — *Actor*
131 Lavender Sweep, London SW 11, England

Richardson, Jerome J — *Businessman*
%Flagstar Companies, 203 E Main St, Spartanburg, SC 29319, USA

Richardson, Joely — *Actress*
%International Creative Mgmt, 76 Oxford St, London W1N 0AX, England

Richardson, John T — *Educator*
2233 N Kenmore Ave, Chicago, IL 60614, USA

Richardson, Margaret M — *Government Official*
%Internal Revenue Service, 1111 Constitution Ave NW, Washington, DC 20224, USA

Richardson, Midge T — *Editor*
%Seventeen Magazine, Editorial Dept, 850 3rd Ave, New York, NY 10022, USA

Richardson, Miranda — *Actress*
%Kerry Gardner Mgmt, 15 Kensington High St, London W8 5NP, England

Richardson, Natasha — *Actress*
30 Brackenburg Ave, London W6, England

Richardson, Nolan — *Basketball Coach*
%University of Arkansas, Broyles Athletic Complex, Fayetteville, AR 72701, USA

Richardson, Patricia — *Actress*
253 26th St, #A-312, Santa Monica, CA 90402, USA

Richardson, Pooh — *Basketball Player*
%Los Angeles Clippers, Sports Arena, 3939 S Figueroa St, Los Angeles, CA 90037, USA

Richardson, Robert C (Bobby) — *Baseball Player*
47 Adams Ave, Sumter, SC 29150, USA

Richardson, Sam — *Sculptor*
4121 Sequoyah Rd, Oakland, CA 94605, USA

Richardson, Susan — *Actress*
6331 Hollywood Blvd, #924, Los Angeles, CA 90028, USA

Richardson, W Franklyn — *Religious Leader*
%National Baptist Convention, 52 S 6th Ave, Mt Vernon, NY 10550, USA

Richardson, William C — *Educator*
%Johns Hopkins University, President's Office, Baltimore, MD 21218, USA

Richer, Stephane — *Hockey Player*
%New Jersey Devils, Meadowlands Arena, PO Box 504, East Rutherford, NJ 07073, USA

Richey, Donald L — *Businessman*
%Fabri-Centers of America, 5555 Darrow Rd, Hudson, OH 44236, USA

Richey, Ronald K — *Businessman*
%Torchmark Corp, 2001 3rd Ave S, Birmingham, AL 35233, USA

Richie, Lionel — *Singer, Songwriter*
%DeMann Entertainment, 8000 Beverly Blvd, Los Angeles, CA 90048, USA

Richler, Mordecai — *Writer*
1321 Sherbroke St W, #80-C, Montreal PQ H3Y 1J4, Canada

Richman, Caryn — *Actress*
12304 Santa Monica Blvd, #104, Los Angeles, CA 90025, USA

Richman, Peter Mark — *Actor*
5114 Del Moreno Dr, Woodland Hills, CA 91364, USA

Richmond, Julius B — *Physician*
79 Beverly Rd, Chestnut Hill, MA 02167, USA

Richmond, Mitch — *Basketball Player*
%Sacramento Kings, 1 Sports Parkway, Sacramento, CA 95834, USA

Richter, Burton — *Nobel Physics Laureate*
%Stanford University, Linear Accelerator Center, PO Box 4349, Stanford, CA 94309, USA

Richter, Earl E — *Businessman*
%Modine Manufacturing Co, 1500 DeKoven Ave, Racine, WI 53403, USA

Richter, Gerhard *Artist*
Bismarckstr 50, 50672 Cologne, Germany

Richter, Leslie A *Football Player*
%National Assn of Stock Car Racing, 1801 Speedway Blvd, Daytona Beach, FL 32015, USA

Richter, Michael T (Mike) *Hockey Player*
%New York Rangers, Madison Square Garden, 4 Penn Plaza New York, NY 10001, USA

Richter, Pat *Football Player, Administrator*
45 Cambridge Rd, Madison, WI 53704, USA

Richter, Sviatoslav T *Concert Pianist*
%Moscow State Philharmonic Society, 31 Ul Gorkogo, Moscow, Russia

Richter, Ulrike *Swimmer*
Goethestr 65, 08297 Zwonitz, Germany

Rick, Charles M, Jr *Geneticist*
8 Parkside Dr, Davis, CA 95616, USA

Ricker, Robert S *Religious Leader*
%Baptist General Conference, 2002 S A Heights Rd, Arlington Heights, IL 60005, USA

Rickershauser, Charles E, Jr *Businessman*
%PS Group, 4307 La Jolla Village Dr, San Diego, CA 92122, USA

Ricketts, Thomas R *Financier*
%Standard Federal Bank, 2600 W Big Beaver Rd, Troy, MI 48084, USA

Rickey, George W *Sculptor*
Rt 2, Box 235, East Chatham, NY 12060, USA

Rickles, Don *Comedian*
925 N Alpine Dr, Beverly Hills, CA 90210, USA

Rickman, Alan *Actor*
%International Creative Mgmt, 76 Oxford St, London W1N 0AX, England

Ridder, Bernard H, Jr *Publisher*
%St Paul Pioneer Press, 345 Cedar St, St Paul, MN 55101, USA

Ridder, Eric *Publisher*
%Knight-Ridder Newspapers, 1 Herald Plaza, Miami, FL 33132, USA

Ridder, P Anthony *Publisher*
%Knight-Ridder Inc, 1 Herald Plaza, Miami, FL 33132, USA

Riddick, Frank A, Jr *Physician*
1923 Octavia St, New Orleans, LA 70115, USA

Riddick, Steve *Track Athlete*
7601 Crittenden, #F-2, Philadelphia, PA 19118, USA

Riddle, D Raymond *Businessman*
%First National Bank of Atlanta, 2 Peachtree St NW, Atlanta, GA 30303, USA

Riddles, Libby *Dog Sled Racer*
PO Box 872901, Wasilla, AK 99687, USA

Ride, Sally K *Astronaut*
%California Space Institute, PO Box 0221, 9500 Gilman Dr, La Jolla, CA 92038, USA

Rider, Isaiah (J R) *Basketball Player*
%Minnesota Timberwolves, Target Center, 600 1st Ave N, Minneapolis, MN 55400, USA

Ridge, Thomas J *Governor, Representative, PA*
%Governor's Office, Main Capitol Building, Harrisburg, PA 17120, USA

Ridgley, Bob *Actor*
%Twentieth Century Artists, 15315 Magnolia Blvd, #429, Sherman Oaks, CA 91403, USA

Ridgway, Brunilde S *Archaeologist*
%Bryn Mawr College, Archaeology Dept, Bryn Mawr, PA 19010, USA

Riederer, Richard K *Businessman*
%Weirton Steel Corp, 400 Three Springs Dr, Weirton, WV 26062, USA

Riefenstahl, Leni *Movie Director*
Tengstr 20, 80798 Munich, Germany

Riegert, Peter *Actor*
%United Talent Agency, 9560 Wilshire Blvd, #500, Beverly Hills, CA 90212, USA

Riessen, Marty *Tennis Player*
%US Tennis Assn, 1212 Ave of Americas, New York, NY 10036, USA

Rifkin, Jeremy *Writer, Social Activist*
1660 "L" St NW, #216, Washington, DC 20036, USA

Rifkin, Joshua *Concert Pianist*
61 Dana St, Cambridge, MA 02138, USA

Rifkin, Ron *Actor*
500 S Sepulveda Blvd, Los Angeles, CA 90049, USA

Rifkind, Malcolm M *Government Official, England*
%House of Commons, Westminster, London SW1A 0AA, England

Rigby McCoy, Cathy *Gymnast, Actress*
2695 Camino del Sol, Fullerton, CA 92633, USA

R

Richter - Rigby McCoy

Rigby, Jean P *Opera Singer*
31 Sinclair Rd, London W14 0NS, England

Rigg, Diana *Actress*
%London Mgmt, 2-4 Noel St, London W1V 3RB, England

Riggin Soule, Aileen *Diver*
2943 Kalakaua Ave, #1007, Honolulu, HI 96815, USA

Riggin, Paul *Hockey Player*
%Washington Capitals, USAir Arena, Landover, MD 20785, USA

Riggs, Barton M *Financier*
%Morgan Stanley Co, 1251 Ave of Americas, New York, NY 10020, USA

Riggs, Bobby *Tennis Player*
1834 Parliament Rd, Encinitas, CA 92024, USA

Riggs, Gerald *Football Player*
%Washington Redskins, 21300 Redskin Park Dr, Ashburn, VA 22011, USA

Riggs, Henry E *Educator*
%Harvey Mudd College, President's Office, Claremont, CA 91711, USA

Riggs, Lorrin A *Psychologist*
%Brown University, Psychology Laboratory, Providence, RI 02912, USA

Righetti, David A (Dave) *Baseball Player*
552 Magdalena Ave, Los Altos, CA 94024, USA

Righi-Lambertini, Egano Cardinal *Religious Leader*
Piazza della Citta Leonina 9, 00193 Rome, Italy

Rights, Graham H *Religious Leader*
%Moravian Church, Southern Province, 459 S Church St, Winston-Salem, NC 27101, USA

Rigney, William J (Bill) *Baseball Manager*
3136 Round Hill Rd, Alamo, CA 94507, USA

Riker, Albert J *Plant Pathologist*
2760 E 8th St, Tucson, AZ 85716, USA

Riklis, Meshulam *Businessman*
%Riklis Family Corp, 2901 Las Vegas Blvd S, Las Vegas, NV 89109, USA

Riles, Wilson C *Educator*
%Wilson Riles Assoc, 400 Capitol Mall, #1540, Sacramento, CA 95814, USA

Riley, Bridget *Artist*
%Mayor Rowan Gallery, 31-A Bruton Place, London W1X 7A8, England

Riley, H John, Jr *Businessman*
%Cooper Industries, First City Tower, 1001 Fannin St, Houston, TX 77002, USA

Riley, Jack *Actor*
%Artists Agency, 10000 Santa Monica Blvd, #305, Los Angeles, CA 90067, USA

Riley, Jack *Hockey Coach*
%US Military Academy, Athletic Dept, West Point, NY 10996, USA

Riley, Jeannie C *Singer*
%Jeannie C Riley Enterprises, PO Box 23256, Nashville, TN 37202, USA

Riley, Patrick J (Pat) *Basketball Player, Coach, Executive*
%Miami Heat, Miami Arena, Miami, FL 33136, USA

Riley, Richard W *Secretary, Education*
%Education Department, 400 Maryland Ave SW, Washington, DC 20202, USA

Riley, Robert F *Financier*
%Dreyfus Corp, 200 Park Ave, New York, NY 10166, USA

Riley, Teddy *Songwriter, Singer*
%Future Enterprise Records, MCA, 70 Universal City Plz, Universal City, CA 91608, USA

Riley, Terry M *Composer, Musician*
%Shri Moonshine Ranch, 13699 Moonshine Rd, Camptonville, CA 95922, USA

Riley, Victor J, Jr *Financier*
%KeyCorp, 127 Public Square, Cleveland, OH 44114, USA

Rilling, Helmuth *Conductor*
Johann-Sebastian-Bach-Platz, 70178 Stuttgart, Germany

Rimmel, James E *Religious Leader*
%Evangelical Presbyterian Church, 26049 Five Mile Rd, Detroit, MI 48239, USA

Rinaldi, Kathy *Tennis Player*
%Advantage International, 1025 Thomas Jefferson St NW, #450, Washington 20007, USA

Rinaldo, Benjamin *Skier*
%Ski World, 3680 Buena Park Dr, North Hollywood, CA 91604, USA

Rindlaub, John V *Financier*
%Seafirst Corp, 701 5th Ave, Seattle, WA 98104, USA

Rinearson, Peter M *Journalist*
%Seattle Times, Editorial Dept, Fairview Ave N & John St, Seattle, WA 98111, USA

Rinehart, Charles R *Publisher*
%Ashai Shimbun, 2-6-1 Yuraku-Cho, Chiyoda-Ku, Tokyo 100, Japan

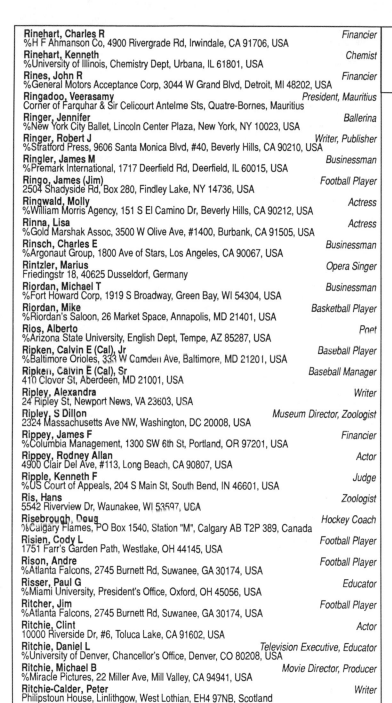

Rinehart, Charles R — *Financier*
%H F Ahmanson Co, 4900 Rivergrade Rd, Irwindale, CA 91706, USA

Rinehart, Kenneth — *Chemist*
%University of Illinois, Chemistry Dept, Urbana, IL 61801, USA

Rines, John R — *Financier*
%General Motors Acceptance Corp, 3044 W Grand Blvd, Detroit, MI 48202, USA

Ringadoo, Veerasamy — *President, Mauritius*
Corner of Farquhar & Sir Celicourt Antelme Sts, Quatre-Bornes, Mauritius

Ringer, Jennifer — *Ballerina*
%New York City Ballet, Lincoln Center Plaza, New York, NY 10023, USA

Ringer, Robert J — *Writer, Publisher*
%Stratford Press, 9606 Santa Monica Blvd, #40, Beverly Hills, CA 90210, USA

Ringler, James M — *Businessman*
%Premark International, 1717 Deerfield Rd, Deerfield, IL 60015, USA

Ringo, James (Jim) — *Football Player*
2504 Shadyside Rd, Box 280, Findley Lake, NY 14736, USA

Ringwald, Molly — *Actress*
%William Morris Agency, 151 S El Camino Dr, Beverly Hills, CA 90212, USA

Rinna, Lisa — *Actress*
%Gold Marshak Assoc, 3500 W Olive Ave, #1400, Burbank, CA 91505, USA

Rinsch, Charles E — *Businessman*
%Argonaut Group, 1800 Ave of Stars, Los Angeles, CA 90067, USA

Rintzler, Marius — *Opera Singer*
Friedingstr 18, 40625 Dusseldorf, Germany

Riordan, Michael T — *Businessman*
%Fort Howard Corp, 1919 S Broadway, Green Bay, WI 54304, USA

Riordan, Mike — *Basketball Player*
%Riordan's Saloon, 26 Market Space, Annapolis, MD 21401, USA

Rios, Alberto — *Poet*
%Arizona State University, English Dept, Tempe, AZ 85287, USA

Ripken, Calvin E (Cal), Jr — *Baseball Player*
%Baltimore Orioles, 333 W Camden Ave, Baltimore, MD 21201, USA

Ripken, Calvin E (Cal), Sr — *Baseball Manager*
410 Clover St, Aberdeen, MD 21001, USA

Ripley, Alexandra — *Writer*
24 Ripley St, Newport News, VA 23603, USA

Ripley, S Dillon — *Museum Director, Zoologist*
2324 Massachusetts Ave NW, Washington, DC 20008, USA

Rippey, James F — *Financier*
%Columbia Management, 1300 SW 6th St, Portland, OR 97201, USA

Rippey, Rodney Allan — *Actor*
4900 Clair Del Ave, #113, Long Beach, CA 90807, USA

Ripple, Kenneth F — *Judge*
%US Court of Appeals, 204 S Main St, South Bend, IN 46601, USA

Ris, Hans — *Zoologist*
5542 Riverview Dr, Waunakee, WI 53597, USA

Risebrough, Doug — *Hockey Coach*
%Calgary Flames, PO Box 1540, Station "M", Calgary AB T2P 389, Canada

Risien, Cody L — *Football Player*
1751 Farr's Garden Path, Westlake, OH 44145, USA

Rison, Andre — *Football Player*
%Atlanta Falcons, 2745 Burnett Rd, Suwanee, GA 30174, USA

Risser, Paul G — *Educator*
%Miami University, President's Office, Oxford, OH 45056, USA

Ritcher, Jim — *Football Player*
%Atlanta Falcons, 2745 Burnett Rd, Suwanee, GA 30174, USA

Ritchie, Clint — *Actor*
10000 Riverside Dr, #6, Toluca Lake, CA 91602, USA

Ritchie, Daniel L — *Television Executive, Educator*
%University of Denver, Chancellor's Office, Denver, CO 80208, USA

Ritchie, Michael B — *Movie Director, Producer*
%Miracle Pictures, 22 Miller Ave, Mill Valley, CA 94941, USA

Ritchie-Calder, Peter — *Writer*
Philipstoun House, Linlithgow, West Lothian, EH4 97NB, Scotland

Ritenour, Lee — *Singer, Guitarist*
PO Box 6774, Malibu, CA 90264, USA

Ritger, Dick — *Bowler*
%Professional Bowlers Assn, 1720 Merriman Rd, Akron, OH 44313, USA

R

Rinehart - Ritger

Ritter, C Dowd — *Financier*
%AmSouth Bancorp, 1900 5th Ave N, Birmingham, AL 35203, USA

Ritter, Jerry E — *Businessman*
%Anheuser-Busch Companies, 1 Busch Place, St Louis, MO 63118, USA

Ritter, John — *Actor*
%William Morris Agency, 151 S El Camino Dr, Beverly Hills, CA 90212, USA

Rittereiser, Robert P — *Financier*
%Nationar, 330 Madison Ave, New York, NY 10017, USA

Ritts, Herb — *Photographer*
7927 Hillside Ave, Los Angeles, CA 90046, USA

Ritts, Jim — *Golf Executive*
%Ladies Professional Golf Assn, 2570 Volusia Ave, Daytona Beach, FL 32114, USA

Rivera, Chita — *Actress, Singer, Dancer*
99 S Greenbush, Blauvelt, NY 10913, USA

Rivera, Geraldo — *Entertainer*
%Geraldo Investigative News Group, 555 W 57th St, #1100, New York, NY 10019, USA

Rivers, Glenn (Doc) — *Basketball Player*
%San Antonio Spurs, 600 E Market St, #102, San Antonio, TX 78205, USA

Rivers, Joan — *Entertainer*
1 E 62nd St, New York, NY 10021, USA

Rivers, Johnny — *Singer, Songwriter*
3141 Coldwater Canyon Lane, Beverly Hills, CA 90210, USA

Rivers, Larry — *Artist*
404 E 14th St, New York, NY 10009, USA

Rivette, Jacques — *Movie Director*
20 Blvd de la Bastille, 75012 Paris, France

Rivkin, Jack L — *Financier*
%Smith Barney Inc, 1345 Ave of Americas, New York, NY 10105, USA

Rivlin, Alice M — *Government Official*
2842 Chesterfield Place, Washington, DC 20008, USA

Rizzuto, Philip F (Phil) — *Baseball Player, Sportscaster*
912 Westminster Ave, Hillside, NJ 07205, USA

Roach, John R — *Religious Leader*
%Archdiocese of St Paul, 226 Summit Ave, St Paul, MN 55102, USA

Roach, John V, II — *Businessman*
%Tandy Corp, 1 Tandy Center, #1800, Fort Worth, TX 76102, USA

Roach, Max — *Jazz Percussionist*
%Max Roach Productions, 415 Central Park West, #14-E, New York, NY 10025, USA

Roark, Terry P — *Educator*
%University of Wyoming, President's Office, Laramie, WY 82071, USA

Roath, S D — *Businessman*
%Longs Drug Stores, 141 N Civic Dr, Walnut Creek, CA 94596, USA

Robards, Jason — *Actor*
%Don Buchwald Assoc, 10 E 44th St, #500, New York, NY 10017, USA

Robbe-Grillet, Alain — *Movie Director*
18 Blvd Maillot, 92200 Neuilly-sur-Seine, France

Robbins, D Walter, Jr — *Businessman*
%W R Grace Co, 1 Town Center Rd, Boca Raton, FL 33486, USA

Robbins, Frederick C — *Nobel Medicine Laureate*
2626 W Park Blvd, Shaker Heights, OH 44120, USA

Robbins, Harold — *Writer*
601 W Camino Sur, Palm Springs, CA 92262, USA

Robbins, Herbert E — *Mathematician*
%Rutgers University, Mathematics Dept, New Brunswick, NJ 08903, USA

Robbins, Tim — *Actor*
%International Creative Mgmt, 40 W 57th St, New York, NY 10019, USA

Robbins, Tom — *Writer*
PO Box 338, La Conner, WA 98257, USA

Robens of Woldingham, Alfred — *Government Official, England*
2 Laleham Abbey, Staines, Middx TW18 1SZ, England

Robert, Gilbert O — *Financier*
%ALBANK Financial Corp, 10 N Pearl St, Albany, NY 12207, USA

Roberts, Bernard — *Concert Pianist*
Uwchlaw'r Coed, Llanbedr, Gwynedd LL45 2NA, Wales

Roberts, Bert C, Jr — *Businessman*
%MCI Communications Corp, 1801 Pennsylvania Ave NW, Washington, DC 20006, USA

Roberts, Brian L — *Businessman*
%Storer Communications, 12000 Biscayne Blvd, Miami, FL 33181, USA

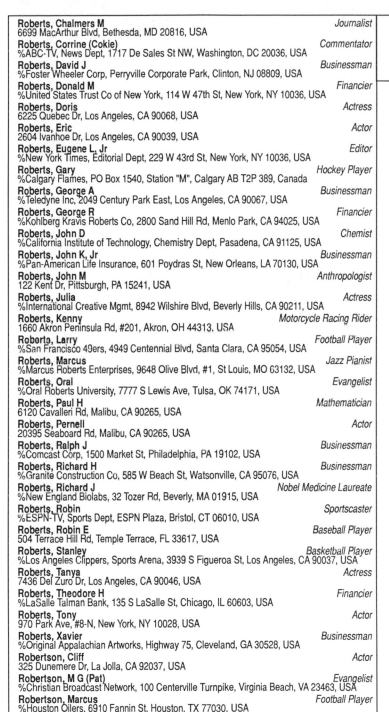

Roberts, Chalmers M — *Journalist*
6699 MacArthur Blvd, Bethesda, MD 20816, USA

Roberts, Corrine (Cokie) — *Commentator*
%ABC-TV, News Dept, 1717 De Sales St NW, Washington, DC 20036, USA

Roberts, David J — *Businessman*
%Foster Wheeler Corp, Perryville Corporate Park, Clinton, NJ 08809, USA

Roberts, Donald M — *Financier*
%United States Trust Co of New York, 114 W 47th St, New York, NY 10036, USA

Roberts, Doris — *Actress*
6225 Quebec Dr, Los Angeles, CA 90068, USA

Roberts, Eric — *Actor*
2604 Ivanhoe Dr, Los Angeles, CA 90039, USA

Roberts, Eugene L, Jr — *Editor*
%New York Times, Editorial Dept, 229 W 43rd St, New York, NY 10036, USA

Roberts, Gary — *Hockey Player*
%Calgary Flames, PO Box 1540, Station "M", Calgary AB T2P 389, Canada

Roberts, George A — *Businessman*
%Teledyne Inc, 2049 Century Park East, Los Angeles, CA 90067, USA

Roberts, George R — *Financier*
%Kohlberg Kravis Roberts Co, 2800 Sand Hill Rd, Menlo Park, CA 94025, USA

Roberts, John D — *Chemist*
%California Institute of Technology, Chemistry Dept, Pasadena, CA 91125, USA

Roberts, John K, Jr — *Businessman*
%Pan-American Life Insurance, 601 Poydras St, New Orleans, LA 70130, USA

Roberts, John M — *Anthropologist*
122 Kent Dr, Pittsburgh, PA 15241, USA

Roberts, Julia — *Actress*
%International Creative Mgmt, 8942 Wilshire Blvd, Beverly Hills, CA 90211, USA

Roberts, Kenny — *Motorcycle Racing Rider*
1660 Akron Peninsula Rd, #201, Akron, OH 44313, USA

Roberts, Larry — *Football Player*
%San Francisco 49ers, 4949 Centennial Blvd, Santa Clara, CA 95054, USA

Roberts, Marcus — *Jazz Pianist*
%Marcus Roberts Enterprises, 9648 Olive Blvd, #1, St Louis, MO 63132, USA

Roberts, Oral — *Evangelist*
%Oral Roberts University, 7777 S Lewis Ave, Tulsa, OK 74171, USA

Roberts, Paul H — *Mathematician*
6120 Cavalleri Rd, Malibu, CA 90265, USA

Roberts, Pernell — *Actor*
20395 Seaboard Rd, Malibu, CA 90265, USA

Roberts, Ralph J — *Businessman*
%Comcast Corp, 1500 Market St, Philadelphia, PA 19102, USA

Roberts, Richard H — *Businessman*
%Granite Construction Co, 585 W Beach St, Watsonville, CA 95076, USA

Roberts, Richard J — *Nobel Medicine Laureate*
%New England Biolabs, 32 Tozer Rd, Beverly, MA 01915, USA

Roberts, Robin — *Sportscaster*
%ESPN-TV, Sports Dept, ESPN Plaza, Bristol, CT 06010, USA

Roberts, Robin E — *Baseball Player*
504 Terrace Hill Rd, Temple Terrace, FL 33617, USA

Roberts, Stanley — *Basketball Player*
%Los Angeles Clippers, Sports Arena, 3939 S Figueroa St, Los Angeles, CA 90037, USA

Roberts, Tanya — *Actress*
7436 Del Zuro Dr, Los Angeles, CA 90046, USA

Roberts, Theodore H — *Financier*
%LaSalle Talman Bank, 135 S LaSalle St, Chicago, IL 60603, USA

Roberts, Tony — *Actor*
970 Park Ave, #8-N, New York, NY 10028, USA

Roberts, Xavier — *Businessman*
%Original Appalachian Artworks, Highway 75, Cleveland, GA 30528, USA

Robertson, Cliff — *Actor*
325 Dunemere Dr, La Jolla, CA 92037, USA

Robertson, M G (Pat) — *Evangelist*
%Christian Broadcast Network, 100 Centerville Turnpike, Virginia Beach, VA 23463, USA

Robertson, Marcus — *Football Player*
%Houston Oilers, 6910 Fannin St, Houston, TX 77030, USA

Robertson, Oscar P — *Basketball Player*
%Orchem, 4293 Mulhauser Rd, Fairfield, OH 45014, USA

R

Roberts - Robertson

R

Robertson, Robbie — *Singer, Guitarist (The Band); Songwriter*
323 14th St, Santa Monica, CA 90402, USA

Robertson, William R — *Financier*
%National City Corp, 1900 E 9th St, Cleveland, OH 44114, USA

Robes, Ernest C (Bill) — *Ski Jumper*
3 Mile Rd, Etna, NH 03750, USA

Robie, Carl — *Swimmer*
2828 S Tamiami Trail, Sarastota, FL 34239, USA

Robinette, Larry R — *Businessman*
%Morgan Products, 75 Tri-State International Building, Lincolnshire, IL 60069, USA

Robinowitz, Joseph R — *Editor, Publisher*
%TV Guide Magazine, Editorial Dept, 100 Matsonford Rd, Radnor, PA 19087, USA

Robinson of Woolwich, John — *Religious Leader*
%Trinity College, Cambridge CB2 1TQ, England

Robinson, Alexia — *Actress*
%Gold Marshak Assoc, 3500 W Olive Ave, #1400, Burbank, CA 91505, USA

Robinson, Andrew — *Actor*
2671 Byron Place, Los Angeles, CA 90046, USA

Robinson, Arnie — *Track Athlete*
2904 Ocean View Blvd, San Diego, CA 92113, USA

Robinson, Arthur H — *Cartographer*
7438 Cedar Creek Trail, Madison, WI 53717, USA

Robinson, Brooks C — *Baseball Player*
PO Box 1168, Baltimore, MD 21203, USA

Robinson, Charles E — *Businessman*
%Pacific Telecom, 805 Broadway, Vancouver, WA 98660, USA

Robinson, Chip — *Auto Racing Driver*
1205 Huntsdale Rd, Reidsville, NC 27320, USA

Robinson, Chris — *Actor*
%CBR Mgmt, PO Box 85007, Los Angeles, CA 90072, USA

Robinson, Cliff — *Basketball Player*
%Portland Trail Blazers, 700 NE Multnomah St, #600, Portland, OR 97232, USA

Robinson, Dave — *Football Player*
406 S Rose Blvd, Akron, OH 44320, USA

Robinson, David — *Basketball Player*
%San Antonio Spurs, 600 E Market St, #102, San Antonio, TX 78205, USA

Robinson, David B — *Navy Admiral*
Commander, Naval Surface Force, Naval Air Base, Coronado, CA 92155, USA

Robinson, Dawn — *Singer (En Vogue)*
%William Morris Agency, 1325 Ave of Americas, New York, NY 10019, USA

Robinson, Dwight P — *Financier*
%Government National Mortgage Assn, 451 7th St SW, Washington, DC 20410, USA

Robinson, E B, Jr — *Financier*
%Deposit Guaranty Corp, 210 E Capitol St, Jackson, MS 39201, USA

Robinson, Eddie G — *Football Coach*
%Grambling State University, Athletic Dept, Grambling, LA 71245, USA

Robinson, Edward J — *Businessman*
%Avon Products, 9 W 57th St, New York, NY 10019, USA

Robinson, Eugene — *Football Player*
%Seattle Seahawks, 11220 NE 53rd St, Kirkland, WA 98033, USA

Robinson, Frank — *Baseball Player, Manager*
15557 Aqua Verde Dr, Los Angeles, CA 90077, USA

Robinson, Gerald — *Football Player*
%Minnesota Vikings, 9520 Viking Dr, Eden Prairie, MN 55344, USA

Robinson, Glenn — *Basketball Player*
%Milwaukee Bucks, Bradley Center, 1001 N 4th St, Milwaukee, WI 53203, USA

Robinson, Holly — *Actress*
%Dolores Robinson Mgmt, 10683 Santa Monica Blvd, Los Angeles, CA 90025, USA

Robinson, James H — *Financier*
%SunBank/South Florida, 501 E Las Olas Blvd, Fort Lauderdale, FL 33301, USA

Robinson, Jay — *Actor*
13757 Milbank Ave, Sherman Oaks, CA 91423, USA

Robinson, Jerry — *Football Player*
%Oakland Raiders, Oakland Coliseum, Oakland, CA 94621, USA

Robinson, John — *Football Coach*
%University of Southern California, Heritage Hall, Los Angeles, CA 90089, USA

Robinson, John C — *Businessman*
%Bearings Inc, 3600 Euclid Ave, Cleveland, OH 44115, USA

Robertson - Robinson

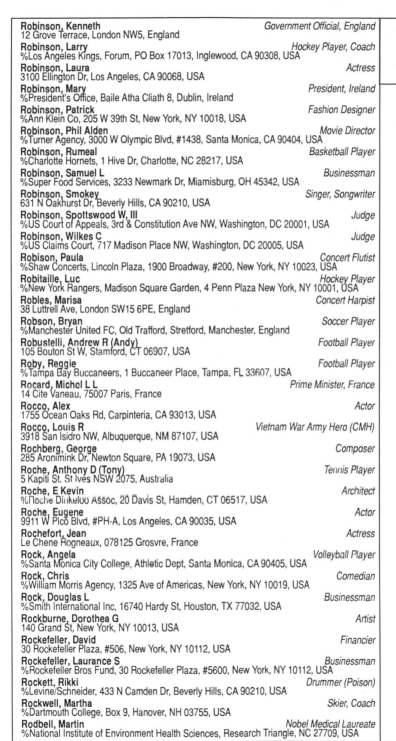

Robinson, Kenneth — *Government Official, England*
12 Grove Terrace, London NW5, England

Robinson, Larry — *Hockey Player, Coach*
%Los Angeles Kings, Forum, PO Box 17013, Inglewood, CA 90308, USA

Robinson, Laura — *Actress*
3100 Ellington Dr, Los Angeles, CA 90068, USA

Robinson, Mary — *President, Ireland*
%President's Office, Baile Atha Cliath 8, Dublin, Ireland

Robinson, Patrick — *Fashion Designer*
%Ann Klein Co, 205 W 39th St, New York, NY 10018, USA

Robinson, Phil Alden — *Movie Director*
%Turner Agency, 3000 W Olympic Blvd, #1438, Santa Monica, CA 90404, USA

Robinson, Rumeal — *Basketball Player*
%Charlotte Hornets, 1 Hive Dr, Charlotte, NC 28217, USA

Robinson, Samuel L — *Businessman*
%Super Food Services, 3233 Newmark Dr, Miamisburg, OH 45342, USA

Robinson, Smokey — *Singer, Songwriter*
631 N Oakhurst Dr, Beverly Hills, CA 90210, USA

Robinson, Spottswood W, III — *Judge*
%US Court of Appeals, 3rd & Constitution Ave NW, Washington, DC 20001, USA

Robinson, Wilkes C — *Judge*
%US Claims Court, 717 Madison Place NW, Washington, DC 20005, USA

Robison, Paula — *Concert Flutist*
%Shaw Concerts, Lincoln Plaza, 1900 Broadway, #200, New York, NY 10023, USA

Robitaille, Luc — *Hockey Player*
%New York Rangers, Madison Square Garden, 4 Penn Plaza New York, NY 10001, USA

Robles, Marisa — *Concert Harpist*
38 Luttrell Ave, London SW15 6PE, England

Robson, Bryan — *Soccer Player*
%Manchester United FC, Old Trafford, Stretford, Manchester, England

Robustelli, Andrew R (Andy) — *Football Player*
105 Bouton St W, Stamford, CT 06907, USA

Roby, Reggie — *Football Player*
%Tampa Bay Buccaneers, 1 Buccaneer Place, Tampa, FL 33607, USA

Rocard, Michel L L — *Prime Minister, France*
14 Cite Vaneau, 75007 Paris, France

Rocco, Alex — *Actor*
1755 Ocean Oaks Rd, Carpinteria, CA 93013, USA

Rocco, Louis R — *Vietnam War Army Hero (CMH)*
3918 San Isidro NW, Albuquerque, NM 87107, USA

Rochberg, George — *Composer*
285 Aronimink Dr, Newton Square, PA 19073, USA

Roche, Anthony D (Tony) — *Tennis Player*
5 Kapiti St. St Ives NSW 2075, Australia

Roche, E Kevin — *Architect*
%Roche Dinkeloo Assoc, 20 Davis St, Hamden, CT 06517, USA

Roche, Eugene — *Actor*
9911 W Pico Blvd, #PH-A, Los Angeles, CA 90035, USA

Rochefort, Jean — *Actress*
Le Chene Rogneaux, 078125 Grosvre, France

Rock, Angela — *Volleyball Player*
%Santa Monica City College, Athletic Dept, Santa Monica, CA 90405, USA

Rock, Chris — *Comedian*
%William Morris Agency, 1325 Ave of Americas, New York, NY 10019, USA

Rock, Douglas L — *Businessman*
%Smith International Inc, 16740 Hardy St, Houston, TX 77032, USA

Rockburne, Dorothea G — *Artist*
140 Grand St, New York, NY 10013, USA

Rockefeller, David — *Financier*
30 Rockefeller Plaza, #506, New York, NY 10112, USA

Rockefeller, Laurance S — *Businessman*
%Rockefeller Bros Fund, 30 Rockefeller Plaza, #5600, New York, NY 10112, USA

Rockett, Rikki — *Drummer (Poison)*
%Levine/Schneider, 433 N Camden Dr, Beverly Hills, CA 90210, USA

Rockwell, Martha — *Skier, Coach*
%Dartmouth College, Box 9, Hanover, NH 03755, USA

Rodbell, Martin — *Nobel Medical Laureate*
%National Institute of Environment Health Sciences, Research Triangle, NC 27709, USA

R

Robinson - Rodbell

R

Rodd, Marcia — *Actress*
11738 Moorpark St, #C, Studio City, CA 91604, USA

Rodgers of Quarry Bank, William T — *Government Official, England*
48 Patshull Rd, London NW3 2LD, England

Rodgers, Jimmie — *Singer, Songwriter*
PO Box 685, Forsyth, MO 65653, USA

Rodgers, Joan — *Opera Singer*
113 Sotheby Rd, London N5 2UT, England

Rodgers, Joe M — *Diplomat*
%JMR Investments, Vanderbilt Plaza, 2100 West End Ave, Nashville, TN 37203, USA

Rodgers, John — *Geologist*
%Yale University, Geology Dept, New Haven, CT 06520, USA

Rodgers, Robert L (Buck) — *Baseball Player, Manager*
5181 West Knoll Dr, Yorba Linda, CA 92686, USA

Rodgers, T J — *Businessman*
%Cypress Semiconductor Corp, 3901 N 1st St, San Jose, CA 95134, USA

Rodgers, William H (Bill) — *Marathon Runner*
%Bill Rodgers Running Center, 353 N Marketplace, Fanueil Hall, Boston, MA 02109, USA

Rodin, Judith S — *Psychiatrist, Educator*
%University of Pennsylvania, President's Office, Philadelphia, PA 19104, USA

Rodin, Robert — *Businessman*
%Marshall Industries, 9320 Telstar Ave, El Monte, CA 91731, USA

Rodman, Dennis — *Basketball Player*
%Chicago Bulls, 1901 W Madison St, Chicago, IL 60612, USA

Rodrigue, George — *Journalist*
%Dallas News, Editorial Dept, Communications Center, Dallas, TX 75265, USA

Rodriguez, Andres — *President, Paraguay; Army General*
Bostra Senora del Carmen y San Rafael, Asuncion, Paraguay

Rodriguez, Arturo — *Labor Leader*
%United Farm Workers of America, 29700 Woodfoel Tehachapi Rd, Keene, CA 93531, USA

Rodriguez, Beatriz — *Ballerina*
%Joffrey Ballet, 130 W 56th St, New York, NY 10019, USA

Rodriguez, Johnny — *Singer, Songwriter*
PO Box 120725, Nashville, TN 37212, USA

Rodriguez, Joseph C — *Korean War Army Hero (CMH)*
1736 Tommy Aaron Dr, El Paso, TX 79936, USA

Rodriguez, Juan (Chi Chi) — *Golfer*
%Eddie Elias Enterprises, 1720 Merriam Rd, #5118, Akron, OH 44334, USA

Rodriguez, Larry — *Religious Leader*
%Metropolitan Churches Fellowship, 5300 Santa Monica Blvd, Los Angeles, CA 90029, USA

Rodriguez, Paul — *Actor*
8730 Sunset Blvd, #600, Los Angeles, CA 90069, USA

Rodriguez, Raul — *Float Designer*
%Fiesta Floats, 9362 Lower Azusa Rd, Temple City, CA 91780, USA

Rodriguez, Rita M — *Financier*
%Export-Import Bank, 811 Vermont Ave NW, Washington, DC 20571, USA

Rodstein, Richard M — *Businessman*
%Anthony Industries, 4900 S Eastern Ave, Los Angeles, CA 90040, USA

Roe, Elwin C (Preacher) — *Baseball Player*
204 Wildwood Terrace, White Plains, MO 65775, USA

Roe, John H — *Businessman*
%Bemis Co, Northstar Center, 222 S 9th St, Minneapolis, MN 55402, USA

Roe, Tommy — *Singer*
%DHM-Dave Hoffman Mgmt, PO Box 26037, Minneapolis, MN 55426, USA

Roedel, Paul R — *Businessman*
416 Wheatland Ave, Reading, PA 19607, USA

Roeder, Kenneth D — *Physiologist*
454 Monument St, Concord, MA 01742, USA

Roeg, Nicolas J — *Movie Director*
2 Oxford & Cambridge Mansions, Old Marylebone Rd, London NW1, England

Roehm, Carolyne J — *Fashion Designer*
%Carolyn Roehm Inc, 257 W 39th St, #400, New York, NY 10018, USA

Roemer, Charles E (Buddy), III — *Governor, LA*
%Governor's Office, State Capitol Building, Baton Rouge, LA 70804, USA

Roemer, William F — *Financier*
%Integra Financial, 4 PPG Place, Pittsburgh, PA 15222, USA

Roenick, Jeremy — *Hockey Player*
%Chicago Blackhawks, Chicago Stadium, 1800 W Madison St, Chicago, IL 60612, USA

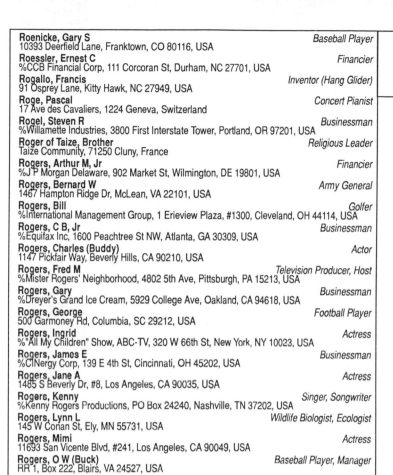

Roenicke, Gary S — *Baseball Player*
10393 Deerfield Lane, Franktown, CO 80116, USA

Roessler, Ernest C — *Financier*
%CCB Financial Corp, 111 Corcoran St, Durham, NC 27701, USA

Rogallo, Francis — *Inventor (Hang Glider)*
91 Osprey Lane, Kitty Hawk, NC 27949, USA

Roge, Pascal — *Concert Pianist*
17 Ave des Cavaliers, 1224 Geneva, Switzerland

Rogel, Steven R — *Businessman*
%Willamette Industries, 3800 First Interstate Tower, Portland, OR 97201, USA

Roger of Taize, Brother — *Religious Leader*
Taize Community, 71250 Cluny, France

Rogers, Arthur M, Jr — *Financier*
%J P Morgan Delaware, 902 Market St, Wilmington, DE 19801, USA

Rogers, Bernard W — *Army General*
1467 Hampton Ridge Dr, McLean, VA 22101, USA

Rogers, Bill — *Golfer*
%International Management Group, 1 Erieview Plaza, #1300, Cleveland, OH 44114, USA

Rogers, C B, Jr — *Businessman*
%Equifax Inc, 1600 Peachtree St NW, Atlanta, GA 30309, USA

Rogers, Charles (Buddy) — *Actor*
1147 Pickfair Way, Beverly Hills, CA 90210, USA

Rogers, Fred M — *Television Producer, Host*
%Mister Rogers' Neighborhood, 4802 5th Ave, Pittsburgh, PA 15213, USA

Rogers, Gary — *Businessman*
%Dreyer's Grand Ice Cream, 5929 College Ave, Oakland, CA 94618, USA

Rogers, George — *Football Player*
500 Garmoney Rd, Columbia, SC 29212, USA

Rogers, Ingrid — *Actress*
%"All My Children" Show, ABC-TV, 320 W 66th St, New York, NY 10023, USA

Rogers, James E — *Businessman*
%CINergy Corp, 139 E 4th St, Cincinnati, OH 45202, USA

Rogers, Jane A — *Actress*
1485 S Beverly Dr, #8, Los Angeles, CA 90035, USA

Rogers, Kenny — *Singer, Songwriter*
%Kenny Rogers Productions, PO Box 24240, Nashville, TN 37202, USA

Rogers, Lynn L — *Wildlife Biologist, Ecologist*
145 W Conan St, Ely, MN 55731, USA

Rogers, Mimi — *Actress*
11693 San Vicente Blvd, #241, Los Angeles, CA 90049, USA

Rogers, O W (Buck) — *Baseball Player, Manager*
RR 1, Box 222, Blairs, VA 24527, USA

Rogers, Paul — *Actor*
9 Hillside Gardens, Highgate, London N6 5SU, England

Rogers, Ralph B — *Businessman*
%Texas Industries, 1341 W Mockingbird Lane, Dallas, TX 75247, USA

Rogers, Ray — *Labor Leader*
%Corporate Campaign Inc, 80 8th Ave, New York, NY 10011, USA

Rogers, Richard G — *Architect*
%R Rogers Partnership, Thames Wharf, Rainville Rd, London W6 9HA, England

Rogers, Rob — *Editorial Cartoonist*
%Pittsburgh Press, Editorial Dept, 34 Blvd of Allies, Pittsburgh, PA 15230, USA

Rogers, Robert D — *Businessman*
%Texas Industries, 1341 W Mockingbird Lane, Dallas, TX 75247, USA

Rogers, Rodney — *Basketball Player*
%Denver Nuggets, McNichols Arena, 1635 Clay St, Denver, CO 80204, USA

Rogers, Rosemary — *Writer*
%Avon Books, 959 8th Ave, New York, NY 10019, USA

Rogers, Roy — *Actor, Singer*
15650 Seneca Rd, Victorville, CA 92392, USA

Rogers, Stephen D (Steve) — *Baseball Player*
3746 S Madison Ave, Tulsa, OK 74105, USA

Rogers, Suzanne — *Actress*
11266 Canton Dr, Studio City, CA 91604, USA

Rogers, Tristan — *Actor*
8550 Holloway Dr, #301, Los Angeles, CA 90069, USA

Rogers, Wayne — *Actor*
11828 La Grange Ave, Los Angeles, CA 90025, USA

R

Rogers, William P *Secretary, State; Attorney General*
%Rogers & Wells, 607 14th St NW, #900, Washington, DC 20005, USA

Rogerson, Kate *Golfer*
%Ladies Professional Golf Assn, 2570 Volusia Ave, Daytona Beach, FL 32114, USA

Roggin, Fred *Sportscaster*
%"Roggin's Heroes" Show, NBC-TV, 3000 W Alameda Ave, Burbank, CA 91523, USA

Rogin, Gilbert L *Editor*
43 W 10th St, New York, NY 10011, USA

Rogoff, Ilan *Concert Pianist*
Villa La Puerta, 07170 Valldemosa, Majorca, Baleares, Spain

Rogovin, Saul W *Baseball Player*
420 W 24th Dr, New York, NY 10011, USA

Roh Tae Woo *President, South Korea*
Chong Wa Dae, 1 Sejongno, Chongnogu, Seoul 110-050, South Korea

Rohmer, Eric *Movie Director*
%Les Films du Losange, 26 Ave Pierre-de-Serbie, 75116 Paris, France

Rohr, James E *Financier*
%PNC Bank Corp, 5th Ave & Wood St, Pittsburgh, PA 15222, USA

Rohrbasser, Markus *Financier*
%UBS North America, 299 Park Ave, New York, NY 10171, USA

Rohrer, Heinrich *Nobel Physics Laureate*
%IBM Research Laboratory, Saumerstr 4, 8803 Ruschlikon, Switzerland

Rohrmann, Gunter *Businessman*
%Air Express International, 120 Tokenecke Rd, Darien, CT 06820, USA

Roizman, Bernard *Virologist*
5555 S Everett Ave, Chicago, IL 60637, USA

Roizman, Owen *Cinematographer*
17533 Magnolia Blvd, Encino, CA 91316, USA

Roker, Al *Entertainer*
%CNBC-TV, 2200 Fletcher Ave, Fort Lee, NJ 07024, USA

Roker, Roxie *Actress*
4061 Cloverdale Ave, Los Angeles, CA 90008, USA

Roland, Johnny E *Football Player, Coach*
%St Louis Rams, 100 N Broadway, #2100, St Louis, MO 63102, USA

Rolandi, Gianna *Opera Singer*
%Columbia Artists Mgmt Inc, 165 W 57th St, New York, NY 10019, USA

Rolfe Johnson, Anthony *Opera Singer*
%Lies Askonas Ltd, 6 Henrietta St, London WC2E 8LA, England

Rolland, Ian M *Businessman*
%Lincoln National Corp, 200 E Berry St, Fort Wayne, IN 46802, USA

Rollans, James O *Businessman*
%Fluor Corp, 3333 Michelson Dr, Irvine, CA 92730, USA

Rolle, Esther *Actress*
4421 Don Felipe Dr, Los Angeles, CA 90008, USA

Rollin, Betty *Writer, Commentator*
%NS Bienstack Inc, 1740 Broadway, New York, NY 10019, USA

Rollins, Gary W *Businessman*
%Rollins Inc, 2170 Piedmont Rd NE, Atlanta, GA 30324, USA

Rollins, Henry *Singer, Songwriter*
%Three Artists Mgmt, 1727 1/2 N Sycamore Ave, Los Angeles, CA 90028, USA

Rollins, Howard E, Jr *Actor*
%Michael Thomas Agency, 305 Madison Ave, New York, NY 10165, USA

Rollins, Jack *Movie Producer*
%Rollins Joffe Morra Brezner Productions, 130 W 57th St, New York, NY 10019, USA

Rollins, John W *Businessman*
%Rollins Truck Leasing Corp, 1 Rollins Plaza, Wilmington, DE 19803, USA

Rollins, John W, Jr *Businessman*
%Rollins Truck Leasing Corp, 1 Rollins Plaza, Wilmington, DE 19803, USA

Rollins, R Randall *Businessman*
%Rollins Inc, 2170 Piedmont Rd NE, Atlanta, GA 30324, USA

Rollins, Reed C *Botanist*
19 Chauncy St, Cambridge, MA 02138, USA

Rollins, Sonny *Jazz Saxophonist, Composer*
Route 9-G, Germantown, NY 12526, USA

Rollins, Tree *Basketball Player, Coach*
%Orlando Magic, Orlando Arena, 1 Magic Place, Orlando, FL 32801, USA

Rolls, John A *Financier*
%Deutsche Credit Corp, 2333 Waukegan Rd, Deerfield, IL 60015, USA

Rogers - Rolls

Rolston, Matthew *Photographer*
%Bulfinch Press, Little Brown Co, 34 Beacon St, Boston, MA 02108, USA

Roman, Joseph *Labor Leader*
%Glass & Ceramic Workers Union, 556 E Town St, Columbus, OH 43215, USA

Roman, Petre *Prime Minister, Romania*
Str Gogol 2, Sector 1, Bucharest, Romania

Roman, Ruth *Actress*
%Curtis Roberts Enterprises, 9056 Santa Monica Blvd, Los Angeles, CA 90069, USA

Romanenko, Yuri V *Cosmonaut*
%Potchta Kosmonavtov, 141 160 Svyosdny Gorodok, Moskovskoi Oblasti, Russia

Romano, John *Psychiatrist*
240 Chelmsford Rd, Rochester, NY 14618, USA

Romano, Umberto *Artist*
162 E 83rd St, New York, NY 10028, USA

Romanos, John J (Jack), Jr *Publisher*
%Pocket Books, 1230 Ave of Americas, New York, NY 10020, USA

Romansky, Monroe J *Physician*
5600 Wisconsin Ave, Chevy Chase, MD 20815, USA

Romario (de Souza Faria) *Soccer Player*
%Futebol Confederacao, Rua da Alfandega 70, 20.070 Rio de Janeiro, Brazil

Romelfanger, Charles *Labor Leader*
%Pattern Makers League, 4106 34th Ave, Moline, IL 61265, USA

Romeo, Robin *Bowler*
%Ladies Professional Bowlers Tour, 7171 Cherryvale Blvd, Rockford, IL 61112, USA

Romer, Roy R *Governor, CO*
%Governor's Office, State Capitol Building, #136, Denver, CO 80203, USA

Romer, Suzanne F C *Prime Minister, Netherlands Antilles*
%Prime Minister's Office, Willemstad, Curacao, Netherlands Antilles

Romero, Ned *Actor*
19438 Lassen Ave, Northridge, CA 91324, USA

Romero, Pepe *Concert Guitarist*
%Columbia Artists Mgmt Inc, 165 W 57th St, New York, NY 10019, USA

Romig, Joseph (Joe) *Football Player*
1300 Plaza Court N, Lafayette, CO 80026, USA

Romijn, Rebecca *Model*
%Next Model Mgmt, 115 E 57th St, #1540, New York, NY 10022, USA

Rominger, Richard E *Financier, Government Official*
%Commodity Credit Corp, PO Box 2415, Washington, DC 20013, USA

Romiti, Cesare *Businessman*
%Fiat SpA, Corso Marconi 10, 10125 Turin, Italy

Rompala, Richard M *Businessman*
%Valsapar Corp, 1101 3rd St S, Minneapolis, MN 55415, USA

Ronan, William J *Railway Engineer*
525 S Flagler Dr, West Palm Beach, FL 33401, USA

Roney, Paul H *Judge*
%US Court of Appeals, Federal Building, 144 1st Ave S, St Petersburg, FL 33701, USA

Ronningen, Jon *Yachtsman*
Mellomasveien 132, 1414 Trollasen, Norway

Rono, Peter *Track Athlete*
%Mount Saint Mary's College, Athletic Dept, Emmitsburg, MD 21727, USA

Ronstadt, Linda *Singer*
%Peter Asher Mgmt, 644 N Doheny Dr, Los Angeles, CA 90069, USA

Rook, Susan *Commentator*
%Cable News Network, News Dept, 1050 Techwood Dr NW, Atlanta, GA 30318, USA

Rooney, Andrew A (Andy) *Commentator*
254 Rowayton Ave, Rowayton, CT 06853, USA

Rooney, Daniel M *Football Executive*
%Pittsburgh Steelers, 3 Rivers Stadium, 300 Stadium Circle, Pittsburgh, PA 15212, USA

Rooney, Mickey *Actor*
31351 Via Colinas, Westlake Village, CA 91362, USA

Rooney, Patrick W *Businessman*
%Cooper Tire & Rubber Co, Lima & Western Aves, Findlay, OH 45840, USA

Rooney, Phillip B *Businessman*
%WMX Technologies Inc, 3003 Butterfield Rd, Oak Brook, IL 60521, USA

Roots, Melvin H *Labor Leader*
%Plasters & Cement Workers Union, 1125 17th St NW, Washington, DC 20036, USA

Roper, Dee Dee (Spinderella) *Singer (Salt-N-Pepa)*
%International Creative Mgmt, 8942 Wilshire Blvd, Beverly Hills, CA 90211, USA

R

Rolston - Roper

R

Rorem, Ned *Composer, Writer*
PO Box 764, Nantucket, MA 02554, USA

Rorty, Richard M *Philosopher*
402 Peacock Dr, Charlottesville, VA 22903, USA

Rosato, Genesia *Ballerina*
%Royal Ballet, Bow St, London WC2E 9DD, England

Rosberg, Keke *Auto Racing Driver*
%Opel Team Rosberg, Nactweide 35, 67433 Neustadt/Weinstr, Germany

Roschkov, Victor *Editorial Cartoonist*
1 Yonge St, Toronto ON, Canada 90068, USA

Rose Marie *Actress*
6916 Chisholm Ave, Van Nuys, CA 91406, USA

Rose, Axl *Singer (Guns & Roses), Songwriter*
%Artists & Audience Entertainment, 83 Riverside Dr, New York, NY 10024, USA

Rose, Charles (Charlie) *Commentator*
%WNET-TV, News Dept, 356 W 58th St, #1000, New York, NY 10019, USA

Rose, H Michael *Army General, England*
%Coldstream Guards, Wellington Barracks, London SW1E 6HQ, England

Rose, Jalen *Basketball Player*
%Denver Nuggets, McNichols Arena, 1635 Clay St, Denver, CO 80204, USA

Rose, Jamie *Actress*
13268 Mulholland Dr, Beverly Hills, CA 90210, USA

Rose, Lee *Basketball Coach*
%University of South Florida, Athletic Dept, Tampa, FL 33620, USA

Rose, Michael D *Businessman*
%Promus Companies, 1023 Cherry Rd, Memphis, TN 38117, USA

Rose, Michel *Businessman*
%LaFarge Inc, 11130 Sunrise Valley Dr, Reston, VA 22091, USA

Rose, Murray *Swimmer*
3305 Carse Dr, Los Angeles, CA 90068, USA

Rose, Peter E (Pete) *Baseball Player*
6248 NW 32nd Terrace, Boca Raton, FL 33496, USA

Rose, Richard *Political Scientist*
Bennochy, 1 E Abercromby St, Helensburgh, Dunbartonshire G84 7SP, Scotland

Rose, Thomas L *Businessman*
%Dean Foods Co, 3600 N River Rd, Franklin Park, IL 60131, USA

Roseanne *Comedienne*
%"Roseanne" Show, Carsey Werner, 4024 Radford Ave, Studio City, CA 91604, USA

Rosellini, Albert D *Governor, WA*
5936 6th Ave S, Seattle, WA 98108, USA

Roseman, Saul *Biochemist*
8206 Cranwood Court, Baltimore, MD 21208, USA

Rosen, Al *Conductor*
%Music International, 13 Ardilaun Rd, London N5 2QR, England

Rosen, Albert *Conductor*
Pod Lysinami 21, 14700 Prague 4, Czech Republic

Rosen, Benjamin M *Businessman*
%Compaq Computer Corp, 20555 State Highway 249, Houston, TX 77070, USA

Rosen, Charles W *Concert Pianist*
101 W 78th St, New York, NY 10024, USA

Rosen, Milton W *Engineer, Physicist*
5610 Alta Vista Rd, Bethesda, MD 20817, USA

Rosen, Nathaniel *Concert Cellist*
36 Clinton Ave, Nyack, NY 10960, USA

Rosenbach, Timm *Football Player*
%Hamilton Tiger-Cats, PO Box 172, Hamilton ON L8N 0C3, Canada

Rosenbaum, Edward E *Physician*
333 NW 23rd St, Portland, OR 97210, USA

Rosenberg, Alan *Actor*
%Gersh Agency, 232 N Canon Dr, Beverly Hills, CA 90210, USA

Rosenberg, Claude N, Jr *Financier*
%RCM Capital Management, 4 Embarcadero Center, San Francisco, CA 94111, USA

Rosenberg, Henry A, Jr *Businessman*
%Crown Central Petroleum Corp, 1 N Charles St, Baltimore, MD 21201, USA

Rosenberg, Howard *Television Critic*
5859 Larboard Lane, Agoura Hills, CA 91301, USA

Rosenberg, Pierre M *Museum Director*
%Musee du Louvre, 34-36 Quai du Louvre, 75068 Paris, France

Rorem - Rosenberg

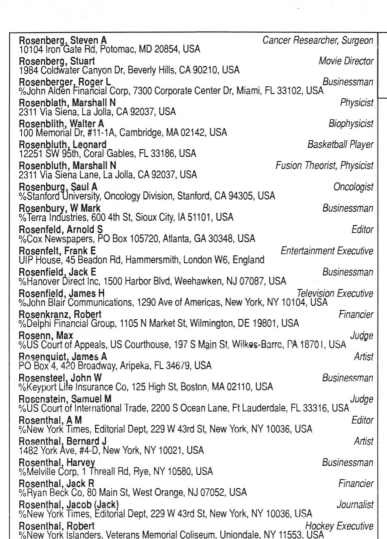

Rosenberg, Steven A — *Cancer Researcher, Surgeon*
10104 Iron Gate Rd, Potomac, MD 20854, USA

Rosenberg, Stuart — *Movie Director*
1984 Coldwater Canyon Dr, Beverly Hills, CA 90210, USA

Rosenberger, Roger L — *Businessman*
%John Alden Financial Corp, 7300 Corporate Center Dr, Miami, FL 33102, USA

Rosenblath, Marshall N — *Physicist*
2311 Via Siena, La Jolla, CA 92037, USA

Rosenblith, Walter A — *Biophysicist*
100 Memorial Dr, #11-1A, Cambridge, MA 02142, USA

Rosenbluth, Leonard — *Basketball Player*
12251 SW 95th, Coral Gables, FL 33186, USA

Rosenbluth, Marshall N — *Fusion Theorist, Physicist*
2311 Via Siena Lane, La Jolla, CA 92037, USA

Rosenburg, Saul A — *Oncologist*
%Stanford University, Oncology Division, Stanford, CA 94305, USA

Rosenbury, W Mark — *Businessman*
%Terra Industries, 600 4th St, Sioux City, IA 51101, USA

Rosenfeld, Arnold S — *Editor*
%Cox Newspapers, PO Box 105720, Atlanta, GA 30348, USA

Rosenfelt, Frank E — *Entertainment Executive*
UIP House, 45 Beadon Rd, Hammersmith, London W6, England

Rosenfield, Jack E — *Businessman*
%Hanover Direct Inc, 1500 Harbor Blvd, Weehawken, NJ 07087, USA

Rosenfield, James H — *Television Executive*
%John Blair Communications, 1290 Ave of Americas, New York, NY 10104, USA

Rosenkranz, Robert — *Financier*
%Delphi Financial Group, 1105 N Market St, Wilmington, DE 19801, USA

Rosenn, Max — *Judge*
%US Court of Appeals, US Courthouse, 197 S Main St, Wilkes-Barre, PA 18701, USA

Rosenquist, James A — *Artist*
PO Box 4, 420 Broadway, Aripeka, FL 34679, USA

Rosensteel, John W — *Businessman*
%Keyport Life Insurance Co, 125 High St, Boston, MA 02110, USA

Rosenstein, Samuel M — *Judge*
%US Court of International Trade, 2200 S Ocean Lane, Ft Lauderdale, FL 33316, USA

Rosenthal, A M — *Editor*
%New York Times, Editorial Dept, 229 W 43rd St, New York, NY 10036, USA

Rosenthal, Bernard J — *Artist*
1482 York Ave, #4-D, New York, NY 10021, USA

Rosenthal, Harvey — *Businessman*
%Melville Corp, 1 Threall Rd, Rye, NY 10580, USA

Rosenthal, Jack R — *Financier*
%Ryan Beck Co, 80 Main St, West Orange, NJ 07052, USA

Rosenthal, Jacob (Jack) — *Journalist*
%New York Times, Editorial Dept, 229 W 43rd St, New York, NY 10036, USA

Rosenthal, Robert — *Hockey Executive*
%New York Islanders, Veterans Memorial Coliseum, Uniondale, NY 11553, USA

Rosenthal, Tony — *Sculptor*
173 E 73rd St, New York, NY 10021, USA

Rosenwald, E John, Jr — *Financier*
%Bear Stearns Co, 245 Park Ave, New York, NY 10167, USA

Rosenzweig, Barney — *Television Producer*
%Rosenzweig Productions, 130 S Hewitt St, Los Angeles, CA 90012, USA

Rosenzweig, Mark R — *Physiological Psychologist*
%University of California, Psychology Dept, Berkeley, CA 94720, USA

Roses, Allen D — *Neurologist*
%Duke University, Medical Center, Bryan Research Center, Durham, NC 27706, USA

Rosewall, Ken — *Tennis Player*
111 Pentacost Ave, Turramurra NSW 2074, Australia

Rosin, Walter L — *Religious Leader*
%Lutheran Church Missouri Synod, 1333 S Kirkwood Rd, St Louis, MO 63122, USA

Roskill of Newtown, Eustace W — *Judge*
New Court, Temple, London EC4, England

Roskovensky, Elmer A — *Businessman*
%Robertson-Ceco Corp, 222 Berkeley St, Boston, MA 02116, USA

Ross Fairbanks, Anne — *Swimmer*
10 Grandview Ave, Troy, NY 12180, USA

R

Rosenberg - Ross Fairbanks

R

Ross, Al — Cartoonist
2185 Bolton St, Bronx, NY 10462, USA

Ross, Betsy — Sportscaster
%Madison Square Garden Network, 4 Pennsylania Plaza, New York, NY 10001, USA

Ross, Charlotte — Actress
%Yorke, 7223 Beverly Blvd, #201, Los Angeles, CA 90036, USA

Ross, David A — Museum Director
%Whitney Museum of American Art, 945 Madison Ave, New York, NY 10021, USA

Ross, Diana — Singer, Actress
%RTC Mgmt, PO Box 1683, New York, NY 10185, USA

Ross, Don — Body Builder
PO Box 981, Venice, CA 90294, USA

Ross, Donald R — Judge
%US Court of Appeals, Federal Building, PO Box 307, Omaha, NE 68101, USA

Ross, Douglas T — Computer Scientist
%Softech Inc, 460 Totten Pond Rd, Waltham, MA 02154, USA

Ross, Herbert D — Movie Director
30900 Broad Beach Rd, Malibu, CA 90265, USA

Ross, Ian M — Electrical Engineer
%AT&T Bell Laboratories, 101 Crawfords Corner Rd, Holmdel, NJ 07733, USA

Ross, Jerry L — Astronaut
%NASA, Johnson Space Center, 2101 NASA Rd, Houston, TX 77058, USA

Ross, Jimmy D — Army General
9208 Cross Oaks Court, Fairfax Station, VA 22039, USA

Ross, Joseph J — Businessman
%Federal Signal Corp, 1415 W 22nd St, Oak Brook, IL 60521, USA

Ross, Karie — Sportscaster
%ESPN-TV, Sports Dept, ESPN Plaza, Bristol, CT 06010, USA

Ross, Katherine — Actress
33050 Pacific Coast Highway, Malibu, CA 90265, USA

Ross, Louis R — Businessman
%Ford Motor Co, American Rd, Dearborn, MI 48121, USA

Ross, Marion — Actress
14159 Riverside Dr, #101, Sherman Oaks, CA 91423, USA

Ross, Raymond E — Businessman
%Cincinnati Milacron Inc, 4701 Marburg Ave, Cincinnati, OH 45209, USA

Ross, Robert — Foundation Executive
%Muscular Dystrophy Assn, 3300 E Sunrise Dr, Tucson, AZ 85718, USA

Ross, Robert J (Bobby) — Football Coach
%San Diego Chargers, Jack Murphy Stadium, San Diego, CA 92160, USA

Ross, Wilburn K — WW II Army Hero (CMH)
PO Box 355, Dupont, WA 98327, USA

Rosse, James N — Publisher
%Freedom Newspapers Inc, PO Box 19549, Irvine, CA 92713, USA

Rossellini, Isabella — Model, Actress
745 5th Ave, #814, New York, NY 10151, USA

Rossen, Carol — Actress
7 E 88th St, #4-A, New York, NY 10128, USA

Rosser, James M — Educator
%California State University, President's Office, Los Angeles, CA 90032, USA

Rosser, Ronald E — WW II Army Hero (CMH)
36 James St, Roseville, OH 43777, USA

Rosset, Barnet L, Jr — Publisher
%Rosset Co, 61 4th Ave, New York, NY 10003, USA

Rosset, Marc — Tennis Player
%Michel Rosset, Rue Albert Gos 16, 1206 Geneva, Switzerland

Rossi, Opilio Cardinal — Religious Leader
Via Della Scrofa 70, 00186 Rome, Italy

Rossi, Paolo — Soccer Player
%Juventus FC Turin, Piazza Crimea 7, 10131 Turin, Italy

Rossi, Tino — Singer, Actor
40 Blvd Maillot, 92200 Neuilly/Seine, France

Rossini, Frederick D — Chemist
605 S Highway 1, #T-900, Juno Beach, FL 33408, USA

Rosskamm, Alan — Businessman
%Fabri-Centers of America, 5555 Darrow Rd, Akron, OH 44236, USA

Rossner, Judith — Writer
263 West End Ave, New York, NY 10023, USA

Ross - Rossner

Rossner, Petra *Cyclist*
Goethstr 9, 72124 Pliezhausen, Germany

Rosso, Louis T *Businessman*
%Beckman Instruments, 2500 Harbor Blvd, Fullerton, CA 92635, USA

Rossovich, Timothy J (Tim) *Football Player, Actor*
%Artists Group, 10100 Santa Monica Blvd, #2490, Los Angeles, CA 90067, USA

Rosten, Irwin *Writer, Producer, Director*
2217 Chelan Dr, Los Angeles, CA 90068, USA

Rostow, Eugene V *Economist*
1315 4th St SW, Washington, DC 20024, USA

Rostow, Walt W *Economist, Government Official*
1 Wildwind Point, Austin, TX 78746, USA

Rostropovich, Mstislav L *Concert Cellist, Conductor*
%National Symphony Orchestra, Kennedy Center, Washington, DC 20566, USA

Rostvold, Gerhard N *Economist*
19712 Oceanaire, Huntington Beach, CA 92648, USA

Roszell, Stephen W *Financier*
%IDA Advisory Group, 80 S 8th St, Minneapolis, MN 55402, USA

Rota, Gian-Carlo *Applied Mathematician*
1105 Massachusetts Ave, #8-F, Cambridge, MA 02138, USA

Rote, Kyle W *Football Player*
24700 Deepwater Point Dr, #14, St Michaels, MD 21663, USA

Rote, Tobin C *Football Player*
7590 Lighthouse Rd, Port Hope, MI 48468, USA

Roten, Robert W *Businessman*
%Sterling Chemicals, 1200 Smith St, Houston, TX 77002, USA

Rotenstreich, Jon *Businessman*
%TIG Insurance, 5205 N O'Connor Blvd, Irving, TX 75039, USA

Roth, Ann *Costume Designer*
Road 3, Box 3124, Bangor, PA 18013, USA

Roth, Arnold *Cartoonist*
%National Cartoonists Society, 9 Ebony Court, Brooklyn, NY 11229, USA

Roth, David Lee *Singer, Songwriter (Van Halen)*
%Angelus Entertainment, 9016 Wilshire Blvd, #346, Beverly Hills, CA 90211, USA

Roth, Dick *Swimmer*
Big Spring Ranch, Wells, NV 89835, USA

Roth, Henry *Writer*
300 Hendrix Rd NW, Albuquerque, NM 87107, USA

Roth, Jesse *Endocrinologist*
%National Institute of Arthritis, 9000 Rockville Pike, Bethesda, MD 20205, USA

Roth, Joe *Television Executive*
%Walt Disney Pictures, 500 S Buena Vista Blvd, Burbank, CA 91521, USA

Roth, Mark *Bowler*
%Professional Bowlers Assn, 1720 Merriman Rd, Akron, OH 44313, USA

Roth, Michael I *Financier*
%Mutual Life Insurance, 1740 Broadway, New York, NY 10019, USA

Roth, Philip *Writer*
%Houghton Mifflin Co, 215 Park Ave S, New York, NY 10003, USA

Roth, Tim *Actor, Director*
%Markham & Froggatt, Julian House, 4 Windmill St, London W1P 1HF, England

Roth, William G *Businessman*
%Dravo Corp, 1 Oliver Plaza, Pittsburgh, PA 15222, USA

Rothenberg, Alan I *Soccer, Basketball Executive*
%US Soccer Federation, 1801-11 S Prairie Ave, Chicago, IL 60616, USA

Rothenberg, Susan *Artist*
%Sperone Westwater Gallery, 142 Green St, New York, NY 10012, USA

Rothenberger, Anneliese *Opera Singer*
Quellenhof, 8268 Salenstein/TG, Switzerland

Rothermere of Hemsted, V Harold *Publisher*
New Carmelite House, Carmelite St, London EC4, England

Rothman, Frank *Entertainment Executive*
10555 Rocca Place, Los Angeles, CA 90077, USA

Rothschild, David de *Financier*
%Rothschild Inc, 1251 Ave of Americas, New York, NY 10020, USA

Rothschild, Miriam *Naturalist*
%Ashton World, Peterborough, Northants, England

Rothstein, Ronald (Ron) *Basketball Coach*
%Cleveland Cavaliers, 2923 Statesboro Rd, Richfield, OH 44286, USA

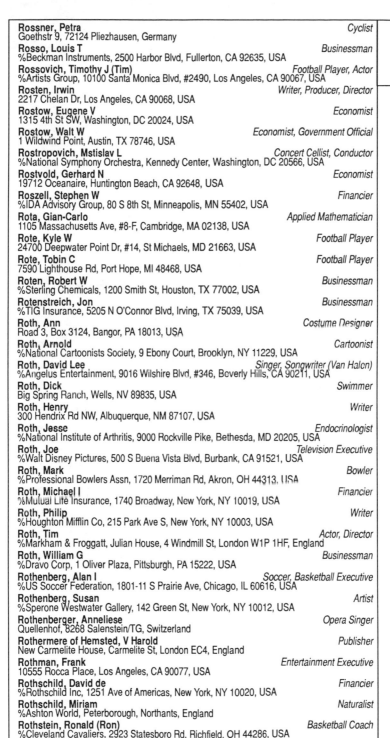

R

Rossner - Rothstein

Roubos, Gary L — *Businessman*
%Dover Corp, 280 Park Ave, New York, NY 10017, USA

Rouleau, Joseph-Alfred — *Opera Singer*
32 Lakeshore Rd, Beaconsfield PQ H9W 4H3, England

Roundtree, Richard — *Actor*
4528 Camelia Ave, North Hollywood, CA 91602, USA

Rourke, Mickey — *Actor*
1020 Benedict Canyon Rd, Beverly Hills, CA 90210, USA

Rouse, Christopher — *Composer*
%University of Rochester, Eastman School of Music, Rochester, NY 14604, USA

Rouse, Irving — *Anthropologist*
12 Ridgewood Terrace, North Haven, CT 06473, USA

Roux, Albert H — *Chef*
%Le Gavroche, 43 Upper Brook St, London W1Y 1PF, England

Roux, Jean-Louis — *Theater Director*
4145 Blueridge Crescent, #2, Montreal PQ H3H 1S7, Canada

Roux, Michel A — *Chef*
%Waterside Inn, Ferry Rd, Bray, Berks SL6 2AT, England

Rowan, Carl T — *Columnist*
%CTR Productions, 3251 Sutton Place NW, #C, Washington, DC 20016, USA

Rowden, William H — *Navy Admiral*
RR 1, Box 818, Lancaster, VA 22503, USA

Rowe, James W — *Businessman*
%Great Atlantic & Pacific Tea Co, 2 Paragon Dr, Montvale, NJ 07645, USA

Rowe, John W — *Businessman*
%New England Electric System, 25 Research Dr, Westborough, MA 01582, USA

Rowe, Misty — *Actress*
50 Pierrepont Dr, Ridgefield, CT 06877, USA

Rowell, Lester J, Jr — *Businessman*
%Provident Mutual Life Insurance, 1600 Market St, Philadelphia, PA 19103, USA

Rowell, Victoria — *Actress*
%Days Ferry Productions, 7800 Beverly Blvd, Los Angeles, CA 90036, USA

Rowen, Robert G — *Financier*
%Bell Federal Savings & Loan, 79 W Monroe St, Chicago, IL 60603, USA

Rowland, F Sherwood — *Chemist*
4807 Dorchester Rd, Corona del Mar, CA 92625, USA

Rowland, James A — *Royal Air Force Marshal, Australia*
21/171 Walker St, North Sydney 2060, Australia

Rowland, John G — *Governor, CT*
%Governor's Office, State Capitol, 210 Capitol Ave, Hartford, CT 06106, USA

Rowland, John W — *Labor Leader*
%Amalgamated Transit Union, 5025 Wisconsin Ave NW, Washington, DC 20016, USA

Rowland, Landon H — *Businessman*
%Kansas City Southern Industries, 114 W 11th St, Kansas City, MO 64105, USA

Rowland, Robert A — *Government Official*
%Occupational Safety Commission, 1825 "K" St NW, Washington, DC 20006, USA

Rowland, Roland W (Tiny) — *Businessman*
%Lonrho Ltd, Cheapside House, 138 Cheapside, London EC2V 6BL, England

Rowlands, Gena — *Actress*
7917 Woodrow Wilson Dr, Los Angeles, CA 90046, USA

Rowling, Wallace E — *Prime Minister, New Zealand*
PO Box 78, Motueka, Nelson, New Zealand

Roy (Uwe Ludwig Horn) — *Animal Illusionist (Siegfried & Roy)*
%Beyond Belief, 1639 N Valley Dr, Las Vegas, NV 89108, USA

Roy, James D — *Financier*
%Federal Home Loan Bank, 601 Grant St, Pittsburgh, PA 15219, USA

Roy, Patrick — *Hockey Player*
%Montreal Canadiens, 2313 St Catherine St W, Montreal PQ H3H 1N2, Canada

Roy, Vesta M — *Governor, NH*
%State Senate, State House, Concord, NH 03301, USA

Royal, Billy Joe — *Singer, Songwriter*
%Mark Ketchum Mgmt, 48 Music Square E, Nashville, TN 37203, USA

Royal, Darrell K — *Football Coach*
10507 La Costa Dr, Austin, TX 78747, USA

Royko, Mike — *Columnist*
%Chicago Tribune, 435 N Michigan Ave, Chicago, IL 60611, USA

Royo Sanchez, Aristides — *President, Panama*
PO Box 3333, Panama City, Panama

Royse, John N   *Financier*
%Old National Bancorp, 420 Main St, Evansville, IN 47708, USA
Royster, Vermont C   *Editor*
3450 Springmoor Circle, Raleigh, NC 27615, USA
Rozanov, Evgeny G   *Architect*
24 Pushkinskaya Ul, 103824 Moscow, Russia
Rozelle, Alvin R (Pete)   *Football Executive*
%National Football League, 410 Park Ave, New York, NY 10022, USA
Rozhdestvensky, Gennady N   *Conductor*
%Victor Hochhauser Ltd, 4 Oak Hill Way, London NW3, England
Rozhdestvensky, Valery I   *Cosmonaut*
%Potchta Kosmonavtov, 141 160 Svyosdny Gorodok, Moskovskoi Oblasti, Russia
Rozier, Clifford   *Basketball Player*
%Golden State Warriors, Oakland Coliseum Arena, Oakland, CA 94621, USA
Rozier, Mike   *Football Player*
PO Box 1516, Houston, TX 77251, USA
Rubbia, Carlo   *Nobel Physics Laureate*
%Harvard University, Physics Dept, Cambridge, MA 02138, USA
Ruben, Joseph P   *Movie Director*
%United Talent Agency, 9560 Wilshire Blvd, #500, Beverly Hills, CA 90212, USA
Rubenstein, Ann   *Commentator*
%NBC-TV, News Dept, 30 Rockefeller Plaza, New York, NY 10112, USA
Rubenstein, Edward   *Physician*
%Stanford University Medical School, Surgery Dept, Stanford, CA 94305, USA
Rubik, Erno   *Inventor (Rubik Cube)*
Rubik Studio, Varosmajor U 74, 1122 Budapest, Hungary
Rubin, Benjamin A   *Inventor (Bifurcated Needle)*
50 Belmont Ave, #601, Bala Cynwyd, PA 19004, USA
Rubin, Ellis   *Attorney*
333 NE 23rd St, Miami, FL 33137, USA
Rubin, Harry   *Biologist*
%University of California, Molecular Biology Dept, Berkeley, CA 94720, USA
Rubin, Lewis   *Businessman*
%XTRA Corp, 60 State St, Boston, MA 02109, USA
Rubin, Louis D, Jr   *Writer*
702 Ginghoul Rd, Chapel Hill, NC 27514, USA
Rubin, Robert   *Medical Researcher*
%Massachusetts General Hospital, 32 Fruit St, Boston, MA 02114, USA
Rubin, Robert E   *Secretary, Treasury*
%Treasury Department, 1500 Pennsylvania Ave NW, Washington, DC 20005, USA
Rubin, Stephen E   *Publisher*
%Doubleday Co, 1540 Broadway, New York, NY 10036, USA
Rubin, Theodore I   *Psychiatrist*
219 E 62nd St, New York, NY 10021, USA
Rubin, Vanessa   *Singer*
%Live Jazz Booking, PO Box 9409, Washington, DC 20016, USA
Rubin, Vera C   *Astronomer*
%Carnegie Institute, 5241 Broad Branch Rd NW, Washington, DC 20015, USA
Rubin, William   *Museum Curator*
%Museum of Modern Art, 11 W 53rd St, New York, NY 10019, USA
Rubino, Frank A   *Attorney*
2601 S Bayshore Dr, Miami, FL 33133, USA
Rubinstein, John   *Actor*
200 W 57th St, #900, New York, NY 10019, USA
Ruby, Michael   *Editor*
%US News & World Report Magazine, 2400 "N" St NW, Washington, DC 20037, USA
Ruch, Richard H   *Businessman*
%Herman Miller Inc, 855 E Main St, Zeeland, MI 49464, USA
Ruckelshaus, William D   *Businessman, Government Official*
%Browning-Ferris Industries, 757 N Eldridge, Houston, TX 77079, USA
Ruckriem, Ulrich   *Sculptor*
%C Grimaldis Gallery, 1006 Morton St, Baltimore, MD 21201, USA
Rudbottom, Roy R, Jr   *Diplomat*
3429 University Blvd, Dallas, TX 75205, USA
Rudd, Paul   *Actor*
%Gersh Agency, 232 N Canon Dr, Beverly Hills, CA 90210, USA
Rudd, Ricky   *Auto Racing Driver*
%Sports Management Group, PO Box 1857, Davidson, NC 28036, USA

R

Royse - Rudd

R

Ruddle, Francis H — *Biologist, Geneticist*
%Yale University, Biology Dept, New Haven, CT 06511, USA

Rudel, Julius — *Conductor*
101 Central Park West, #11-A, New York, NY 10023, USA

Rudenstine, Neil L — *Educator*
%Harvard University, President's Office, Cambridge, MA 02138, USA

Ruder, David S — *Government Official, Educator*
%Baker & McKenzie, 1 Prudential Plaza, 130 E Randolph Dr, Chicago, IL 60601, USA

Rudi, Joseph O (Joe) — *Baseball Player*
RR 1, Box 186, Baker City, OR 97814, USA

Rudie, Evelyn — *Actress*
%Santa Monica Playhouse, 1211 4th St, Santa Monica, CA 90401, USA

Ruding, H Onno — *Financier*
%Citibank, 399 Park Ave, New York, NY 10022, USA

Rudman, Warren B — *Senator, NH*
41 Indian Rock Rd, Nashua, NH 03063, USA

Rudner, Rita — *Comedienne*
2447 Benedict Canyon Dr, Beverly Hills, CA 90210, USA

Rudnick, Paul — *Playwright*
%Creative Artists Agency, 9830 Wilshire Blvd, Beverly Hills, CA 90212, USA

Rudoff, Sheldon — *Religious Leader*
%Union of Orthodox Jewish Congregations, 333 7th Ave, New York, NY 10001, USA

Rudolph, Alan S — *Movie Director*
15760 Ventura Blvd, #16, Encino, CA 91436, USA

Rudolph, Donald E — *WW II Army Hero (CMH)*
497 Shamrock Dr, Bovey, MN 55709, USA

Rudolph, Frederick — *Historian*
234 Ide Rd, Williamstown, MA 01267, USA

Rudolph, Paul M — *Architect*
%Paul Rudolph Architects, 23 Beekman Place, #5, New York, NY 10022, USA

Rudolph, Robert R — *Financier*
%Chicago Corp, 208 S LaSalle Ave, Chicago, IL 60604, USA

Rue, Sara — *Actress, Comedienne*
%Innovative Artists, 1999 Ave of Stars, #2850, Los Angeles, CA 90067, USA

Ruehe, Volker — *Government Official, Germany*
%Bundesministerium Der Verteidigung, Hardthoehe, 53125 Bonn, Germany

Ruehl, Mercedes — *Actress*
129 McDougal St, New York, NY 10012, USA

Ruether, Rosemary R — *Theologian*
1426 Hinman Ave, Evanston, IL 60201, USA

Ruettgers, Ken — *Football Player*
%Green Bay Packers, 1265 Lombardi Ave, Green Bay, WI 54304, USA

Ruettgers, Michael C — *Businessman*
%EMC Corp, 171 South St, Hopkinton, MA 01748, USA

Ruffini, Attilio — *Government Official, Italy*
Camera dei Deputati, 00187 Rome, Italy

Rugambwa, Laurian Cardinal — *Religious Leader*
%Archbishop's House, St Joseph, PO Box 167, Dar es Salaam, Tanzania

Ruge, John A — *Cartoonist*
240 Bronxville Rd, #B-4, Bronxville, NY 10708, USA

Rugers, Martin — *Astronomer*
%University of Washington, Astronomy Dept, Seattle, WA 98195, USA

Ruijssenaars, Andries — *Businessman*
%Eagle-Picher Industries, 580 Walnut St, Cincinnati, OH 45202, USA

Ruisi, Christopher S — *Businessman*
%USLIFE Corp, 125 Maiden Lane, New York, NY 10038, USA

Ruiz Garcia, Samuel — *Religious Leader*
%San Cristobal Diocese, 20 De Noviembre 1, San Cristobal de Casas, Mexico

Ruiz, Alejandro R — *WW II Army Hero (CMH)*
32146 Road 124, Visalia, CA 93291, USA

Rukavishnikov, Nikolai N — *Cosmonaut*
%Potchta Kosmonavtov, 141 160 Svyosdny Gorodok, Moskovskoi Oblasti, Russia

Rukeyser, Louis R — *Commentator*
PO Box 25527, Alexandria, VA 22313, USA

Rukeyser, William S — *Publisher*
1509 Rudder Lane, Knoxville, TN 37919, USA

Ruland, Jeff — *Basketball Player, Coach*
%Philadelphia 76ers, Veterans Stadium, PO Box 25040, Philadelphia, PA 19147, USA

Ruddle - Ruland

Rule, Janice _Actress_
105 W 72nd St, #12-B, New York, NY 10023, USA

Rummenigge, Karl-Heinz _Soccer Player_
Eichleite 4, 80231 Grunwald, Germany

Rumsfeld, Donald H _Secretary, Defense; Businessman_
400 N Michigan Ave, #405, Chicago, IL 60611, USA

Runcie of Cuddesdon, Robert A K _Archbishop, Canterbury_
26-A Jennings Rd, St Albans, Herts AL1 4PD, England

Runco, Mario, Jr _Astronaut_
%NASA, Johnson Space Center, 2101 NASA Rd, Houston, TX 77058, USA

Rundgren, Todd _Singer_
%Panacea Entertainment, 2705 Glendower Rd, Los Angeles, CA 90027, USA

Runge, Edward P (Ed) _Baseball Umpire_
4949 Cresita Dr, San Diego, CA 92115, USA

Runnells, Charles _Educator_
%Pepperdine University, Chancellor's Office, Malibu, CA 90265, USA

Runnells, Thomas W (Tom) _Baseball Manager_
1942 29th Ave, Greeley, CO 80631, USA

Runyan, Joe _Dog Sled Racer_
%Rt 1, 314.5 Parks Highway, Nenana, AK 99760, USA

Runyon, Edwin _Religious Leader_
%General Assn of General Baptists, 100 Stinson Dr, Popular Bluff, MO 63901, USA

Runyon, Marvin T, Jr _Government Official_
%US Postal Service, 475 L'Enfant Plaza SW, Washington, DC 20260, USA

RuPaul _Entertainer_
902 Broadway, #1300, New York, NY 10010, USA

Rupp, George E _Educator_
%Columbia University, President's Office, New York, NY 10027, USA

Ruscha, Edward _Artist_
13775 Valley Vista Blvd, Sherman Oaks, CA 91423, USA

Rush, Barbara _Actress_
1708 Tropical Ave, Beverly Hills, CA 90210, USA

Rush, Jennifer _Singer_
%William Morris Agency, 1325 Ave of Americas, New York, NY 10019, USA

Rush, Richard W _Movie Director, Producer_
821 Stradella Rd, Los Angeles, CA 90077, USA

Rush, Robert J (Bob) _Football Player_
8291 Scruggs, Germantown, TN 38138, USA

Rushdie, A Salman _Writer_
%Deborah Rodgers Ltd, 49 Blenhiem Crescent, London W11, England

Ruskin, Uzi _Businessman_
%United Merchants & Manufacturers Inc, 1650 Palisade Ave, Teaneck, NJ 07666, USA

Russ, William _Actor_
2973 Passmore Dr, Los Angeles, CA 90068, USA

Russell, Betsy _Actress_
12026 Magnolia Blvd, Sherman Oaks, CA 91423, USA

Russell, Brenda _Singer_
%Jensen Communications, 230 E Union St, Pasadena, CA 91101, USA

Russell, C Andrew (Andy) _Football Player_
2400 Trimont Lane, #A, Pittsburgh, PA 15222, USA

Russell, Charles T _Businessman_
%Visa International Service Assn, 3125 Clearview Way, San Mateo, CA 94402, USA

Russell, Donald Stuart _Governor/Senator, SC; Judge_
%US Court of Appeals, PO Box 1985, Spartenburg, SC 29304, USA

Russell, Frank E _Businessman_
%Central Newspapers, 135 N Pennsylvania Ave, Indianapolis, IN 46204, USA

Russell, Fred M _Sportswriter_
500 Elmington Ave, #525, Nashville, TN 37205, USA

Russell, George A _Jazz Drummer, Pianist, Composer_
%Joel Chriss Co, 300 Mercer St, #3-J, New York, NY 10003, USA

Russell, George A _Educator_
%University of Missouri, President's Office, Columbia, MO 65205, USA

Russell, Harold _Actor, Government Official_
34 Old Town Rd, Hyannis, MA 02601, USA

Russell, James S _Navy Admiral, Hero_
7734 Walnut Ave SW, Tacoma, WA 98498, USA

Russell, Jane _Actress_
2935 Torito Rd, Montecito, CA 93108, USA

R

Russell, Keith P *Financier*
%Mellon Bank Corp, 1 Mellon Bank Center, 500 Grant St, Pittsburgh, PA 15219, USA

Russell, Ken *Movie Director*
16 Salisbury Place, London W1H 1FH, England

Russell, Kurt *Actor*
229 E Gainsborough Rd, Thousand Oaks, CA 91360, USA

Russell, Leon *Singer, Songwriter*
%Brad Davis, PO Box 158125, Nashville, TN 37215, USA

Russell, Mark *Comedian*
2800 Wisconsin Ave NW, Washington, DC 20007, USA

Russell, Nipsy *Comedian*
353 W 57th St, New York, NY 10019, USA

Russell, Theresa *Actress*
9454 Lloydcrest Dr, Beverly Hills, CA 90210, USA

Russell, William F (Bill) *Basketball Player, Coach*
PO Box 1200, Mercer Island, WA 98040, USA

Russell, William L *Geneticist*
130 Tabor Rd, Oak Ridge, TN 37830, USA

Russert, Timothy J (Tim) *Commentator*
%"Meet the Press" Show, NBC-TV, 4001 Nebraska Ave NW, Washington, DC 20016, USA

Russi, Bernhard *Skier*
Postfach, 6490 Andermatt, Switzerland

Russo, Rene *Actress*
%Progressive Artists Agency, 400 S Beverly Dr, #216, Beverly Hills, CA 90212, USA

Russo, Thomas J *Businessman*
2650 Edgewater Dr, Fort Lauderdale, FL 33332, USA

Rust, Edward B, Jr *Businessman*
%State Farm Mutual Auto Insurance, 1 State Farm Plaza, Bloomington, IL 61710, USA

Rutan, Elbert L (Burt) *Airplane Designer*
%Scaled Composites, Mojave Airport, Hangar 78, Mojave, CA 93501, USA

Rutan, Richard G *Experimental Airplane Pilot, Designer*
%Voyager Aircraft Inc, Mojave Airport, Hangar 77, Mojave, CA 93501, USA

Ruthenberg, Donald B *Educator*
%Columbia College, President's Office, Columbia, MO 65216, USA

Rutherford, Ann *Actress*
826 Greenway Dr, Beverly Hills, CA 90210, USA

Rutherford, John S (Johnny), III *Auto Racing Driver*
4919 Black Oak Lane, Fort Worth, TX 76114, USA

Rutherford, Kelly *Actress*
PO Box 492266, Los Angeles, CA 90049, USA

Rutherford, Mike *Guitarist (Genesis)*
%Hit & Run Music, 25 Ives St, London SW3 2ND, England

Rutherford, Robert L (Skip) *Air Force General*
CinC, Pacific Air Forces, 25 "E" St, Hickam Air Force Base, HI 96853, USA

Rutigliano, Sam *Football Coach*
%Liberty University, Athletic Dept, Lynchburg, VA 24506, USA

Rutledge, John *Economist*
%Claremont Economics Institute, Claremont, CA 91711, USA

Rutledge, William P *Businessman*
%Teledyne Inc, 2049 Century Park East, Los Angeles, CA 90067, USA

Rutstein, David D *Educator, Physician*
98 Winthrop St, Cambridge, MA 02138, USA

Ruttan, Susan *Actresss*
2677 La Cuesta Dr, Los Angeles, CA 90046, USA

Rutter, John M *Composer, Conductor*
Old Lacey's, St John's St, Duxford, Cambridge, England

Ruud, Birger *Skier, Ski Jumper*
Munstersvei 20, 3600 Kongsberg, Norway

Ruud, Sigmund *Skier, Ski Jumper*
Kirkeveien 57, Oslo 3, Norway

Ruuska Percy, Sylvia *Swimmer*
4216 College View Way, Carmichael, CA 95608, USA

Ruusuvuori, Aarno E *Architect*
Annankatu 15 B 10, 00120 Helsinki 12, Finland

Ruuttu, Christian *Hockey Player*
%Buffalo Sabres, Memorial Stadium, 140 Main St, Buffalo, NY 14202, USA

Ruwe, Robert P *Judge*
%US Tax Court, 400 2nd St NW, Washington, DC 20217, USA

Russell - Ruwe

Rwigema, Pierre Claver *Prime Minister, Rwanda*
%Prime Minister's Office, Assembly Building, Church St, Kigali, Rwanda

Ryan, Arthur F *Businessman*
%Prudential Insurance, Prudential Plaza, 751 Broad St, Newark, NJ 07102, USA

Ryan, Ashton J, Jr *Financier*
%First National Bank of Commerce, 210 Baronne St, New Orleans, LA 70112, USA

Ryan, Debbie *Basketball Coach*
%University of Virginia, Athletic Dept, PO Box 3785, Charlottesville, VA 22903, USA

Ryan, Fran *Actress*
22440 Clarendon St, #102, Woodland Hls, CA 91367, USA

Ryan, Frank B *Football Player*
282 Prospect St, New Haven, CT 06511, USA

Ryan, James (Buddy) *Football Coach*
%Arizona Cardinals, 8701 S Hardy Dr, Tempe, AZ 85284, USA

Ryan, James L *Judge*
%US Court of Appeals, US Courthouse, 231 W Lafayette Blvd, Detroit, MI 48226, USA

Ryan, John E *Financier*
%Resolution Trust Corp, 801 17th St NW, Washington, DC 20434, USA

Ryan, John T, III *Businessman*
%Mine Safety Appliances Co, 121 Gamma Dr, Pittsburgh, PA 15238, USA

Ryan, L Nolan *Baseball Player*
PO Box 670, Alvin, TX 77512, USA

Ryan, Martin J, Jr *Air Force General*
Commander, 8th Air Force, Barksdale Air Force Base, LA 71110, USA

Ryan, Meg *Actress*
11718 Barrington Court, #508, Los Angeles, CA 90049, USA

Ryan, Michael E (Mike) *Air Force General*
Assistant to Chairman, Joint Chiefs of Staff, Pentagon, Washington, DC 20318, USA

Ryan, Michael M *Actor*
48 E 3rd St, New York, NY 10003, USA

Ryan, Mitchell *Actor*
30355 Mulholland Dr, Cornell, CA 91301, USA

Ryan, Patrick G *Businessman*
%Aon Corp, 123 N Wacker Dr, Chicago, IL 60606, USA

Ryan, Tim *Sportscaster*
%CBS TV, Sports Dept, 51 W 52nd St, New York, NY 10019, USA

Ryan, Tim *Football Player*
%Chicago Bears, Halas Hall, 250 N Washington Rd, Lake Forest, IL 60045, USA

Ryan, Tom K *Cartoonist (Tumbleweeds)*
%North America Syndicate, 235 E 45th St, New York, NY 10017, USA

Ryan, William J *Financier*
%People Heritage Financial Group, 1 Portland Square, Portland, ME 04101, USA

Rydell, Bobby *Singer*
917 Bryn Mawr Ave, Narbeth, PA 19072, USA

Rydell, Mark *Movie Director*
1 Topsail St, Marina del Rey, CA 90292, USA

Ryder, Winona *Actress*
240 Centre St, New York, NY 10013, USA

Rykiel, Sonia F *Fashion Designer*
175 Blvd St Germain, 75006 Paris, France

Ryman, Robert T *Artist*
17 W 16th St, New York, NY 10011, USA

Rymer, Pamela Ann *Judge*
%US Court of Appeals, 125 S Grand Ave, Pasadena, CA 91105, USA

Rypdal, Terje *Musician*
Rypdal, 6380 Tresfjord, Norway

Rypien, Mark R *Football Player*
%St Louis Rams, 100 N Broadway, #2100, St Louis, MO 63102, USA

Rysanek, Leonie *Opera Singer*
83115 Neubeurern, Germany

Ryumin, Valery V *Cosmonaut*
%Potchta Kosmonavtov, 141 160 Svyosdny Gorodok, Moskovskoi Oblasti, Russia

Ryun, Jim *Track Athlete*
Rt 3, PO Box 62-B, Lawrence, KS 66044, USA

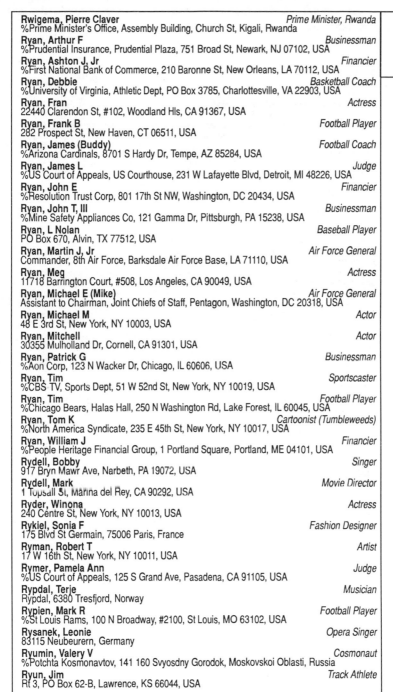

R

Rwigema - Ryun

Saam, Byrum *Sportscaster*
%Philadelphia Phillies, Veterans Stadium, PO Box 7575, Philadelphia, PA 19101, USA

Saar, Bettye *Artist*
8074 Willow Glen Rd, Los Angeles, CA 90046, USA

Saari, Roy *Swimmer*
PO Box 7086, Mammoth Lakes, CA 93546, USA

Saatchi, Charles *Businessman*
%Saatchi & Saatchi Co, 80 Charlotte St, London W1A 1AQ, England

Sabah, Sheikh Jaber Al-Ahmad Al-Jaber Al *Emir, Kuwait*
%Sief Palace, Amiry Diwan, Kuwait

Sabah, Sheikh Saad Al-Abdullah Al-Salem *Crown Prince & Prime Minister, Kuwait*
%Prime Minister's Office, PO Box 4, Safat, 13001 Kuwait City, Kuwait

Saban, Louis H (Lou) *Football Player, Coach*
1020 N Broadway, Milwaukee, WI 53202, USA

Saban, Nick *Football Coach*
%Michigan State University, Daugherty Football Building, East Lansing, MI 48824, USA

Sabatini, Gabriela *Tennis Player*
217 E Redwood St, #1800, Baltimore, MD 21202, USA

Sabato, Antonio, Jr *Actor*
13029 Mindanao Way, #5, Marina del Rey, CA 90292, USA

Sabato, Ernesto *Writer*
Severino Langeri 3135, Santos Lugares, Argentina

Sabattani, Aurelio Cardinal *Religious Leader*
Palazzo del Tribunale, Piazza S Marta, 00120 Vatican City, Rome, Italy

Saberhagen, Bret W *Baseball Player*
5535 Amber Cir, Calabasas, CA 91302, USA

Sabiston, David C, Jr *Surgeon*
1528 Pinecrest Rd, Durham, NC 27705, USA

Sabo, Christopher A (Chris) *Baseball Player*
141 Bewing Dr, Fairfield, OH 45014, USA

Sabonis, Arvydas *Basketball Player*
%Portland Trail Blazers, 700 NE Multnomah St, #600, Portland, OR 97232, USA

Sacco, Michael *Labor Leader*
%Seafarers International Union, 5201 Auth Way, Camp Springs, MO 20746, USA

Sacher, Paul *Conductor*
Schonenberg, 4133 Prattain, BL Basel, Switzerland

Sachs, Gloria *Fashion Designer*
%Gloria Sachs Designs Ltd, 550 7th Ave, New York, NY 10018, USA

Sachs, Jeffrey *Economist*
%Harvard University, Economics Dept, Cambridge, MA 02138, USA

Sachs, Richard *Surgeon*
6 St Ronan Terrace, New Haven, CT 06511, USA

Sachs, Robert G *Physicist*
5490 South Shore Dr, Chicago, IL 60615, USA

Sack, Steve *Cartoonist (Professor Doodle's)*
%Minneapolis Star & Tribune, 425 Portland Ave, Minneapolis, MN 55488, USA

Sacks, Jonathan *Religious Leader*
%Adler House, Tavistock Square, London WC1H 9HN, England

Sacks, Oliver W *Physician, Neurologist*
299 W 12th St, New York, NY 10014, USA

Sadat, Jehan El- *Social Activist*
%University of Maryland, Int'l Development Center, College Park, M 20742, USA

Saddler, Donald E *Choreographer, Dancer*
%Coleman-Rosenberg Agency, 210 E 58th St, New York, NY 10022, USA

Sade (Adu) *Singer, Songwriter*
%Roger Davies Mgmt, 37 Limerston St, London SW10, England

Sadecki, Raymond M (Ray) *Baseball Player*
4237 E Clovis Ave, Mesa, AZ 85206, USA

Sadik, Nafis *Government Official, Pakistan*
%United Nations Population Fund, 220 E 42nd St, New York, NY 10017, USA

Sadler, Robert L *Financier*
%Old Kent Financial Corp, 1 Vandenberg Center, Grand Rapids, MI 49503, USA

Saeki, Akira *Businessman*
%Sharp Corp, 22-22 Nagaikecho, Abenoku, Osaka 543, Japan

Safar, Peter *Surgeon*
%University of Pittsburgh Medical Center, Surgery Dept, Pittsburgh, PA 15260, USA

Safdie, Moshe *Architect*
100 Properzi Way, Somerville, MA 02143, USA

Safer, Morley — *Commentator*
%"Sixty Minutes" Show, CBS-TV, 555 W 57th St, New York, NY 10019, USA

Saffiotti, Umberto — *Pathologist*
5114 Wissioming Rd, Bethesda, MD 20816, USA

Safire, William — *Journalist, Writer*
6200 Elmwood Rd, Chevy Chase, MD 20815, USA

Safra, Edmond J — *Financier*
%Republic New York Corp, 452 5th Ave, New York, NY 10018, USA

Sagal, Katey — *Actress*
7095 Hollywood Blvd, #792, Los Angeles, CA 90028, USA

Sagan, Carl E — *Astronomer, Educator*
%Cornell University, Planetary Studies Laboratory, Ithaca, NY 14853, USA

Sagan, Francoise — *Writer*
%Equemauville, 14600 Honfleur, France

Sagansky, Jeff — *Entertainment Executive*
35 E 76th St, New York, NY 10021, USA

Sagdeev, Roald Z — *Physicist*
%Space Research Institute, Profsoyuznaya 84/32, 11780 Moscow B-485, Russia

Sage, Andrew G C, II — *Businessman*
%Robertson-Ceco Corp, 222 Berkeley St, Boston, MA 02116, USA

Sagebrecht, Marianne — *Actress*
Kaulbachstr 61, Ruckgeb, 80539 Munich, Germany

Sager, Carole Bayer — *Singer, Songwriter*
280 N Carolwood Dr, Los Angeles, CA 90077, USA

Sager, Ruth — *Geneticist*
%Dana-Farber Cancer Institute, 44 Binney St, Boston, MA 02115, USA

Saget, Bob — *Actor*
%International Creative Mgmt, 8942 Wilshire Blvd, Beverly Hills, CA 90211, USA

Sahl, Mort — *Comedian*
2325 San Ysidro Dr, Beverly Hills, CA 90210, USA

Said Mohamed Djohar — *President, Comoros Islands*
%President's Office, Boite Postale 421, Moroni, Comoros Islands

Said, Edward W — *Educator*
%Columbia University, English Dept, Hamilton Hall, New York, NY 10027, USA

Sailer, Toni — *Skier*
%Guthabing, 7370 Kitzbuhel, Tirol, Austria

Saimes, George — *Football Player, Executive*
%Washington Redskins, 21300 Redskin Park Dr, Ashburn, VA 22011, USA

Sain, John F (Johnny) — *Baseball Player*
2 S 707 Ave Latour, Oakbrook, IL 60521, USA

Saint James, Susan — *Actress*
%Marlene Fait, 854 N Genesee Ave, Los Angeles, CA 90046, USA

Saint Laurent, Yves — *Fashion Designer*
5 Ave du Marceau, 75016 Paris

Saint, Eva Marie — *Actress*
%Paul Kohner Inc, 9300 Wilshire Blvd, #555, Beverly Hills, CA 90212, USA

Saint-Subber, Arnold — *Theater Producer*
116 E 64th St, New York, NY 10021, USA

Sainte-Marie, Buffy — *Singer, Songwriter*
RR 1, Box 368, Kapaa, Kauai, HI 96746, USA

Saito, Eishiro — *Businessman*
%Nippon Steel Corp, 2-6-3 Otemachi, Chiyodaku, Tokyo, Japan

Sajak, Pat — *Entertainer*
%"Wheel of Fortune" Show, 3400 Riverside Dr, #201, Burbank, CA 91505, USA

Sakabe, Takeo — *Businessman*
%Ashai Glass Co, 2-1-1 Marunouchi, Chiyodaku, Tokyo 100, Japan

Sakai, Shinji — *Financier*
%Toyota Motor Credit Corp, 19001 S Western Ave, Torrance, CA 90501, USA

Sakamoto, Ryuichi — *Composer*
111 4th Ave, #11-K, New York, NY 10003, USA

Sakamoto, Soichi — *Swimming Coach*
768 McCully St, Honolulu, HI 96826, USA

Sakamura, Ken — *Computer Inventor*
%University of Tokyo, Information Science Dept, Tokyo, Japan

Saker, Joseph J — *Businessman*
%Foodarama Supermarkets, 922 Highway 33, Freehold, NJ 07728, USA

Sakic, Joe — *Hockey Player*
%Colorado Avalanche, McNichols Arena, 1635 Clay St, Denver, CO 80204, USA

S

Safer - Sakic

Sakmann, Bert   *Nobel Medicine Laureate*
%Max Planck Institute, Jahnstr 39, 69120 Heidelberg, Germany

Saks, Gene   *Theater Director, Actor*
7095 Hollywood Blvd, Hollywood, CA 90028, USA

Salaam, Rashaan   *Football Player*
%Chicago Bears, Halas Hall, 250 N Washington Rd, Lake Forest, IL 60045, USA

Salam, Abdus   *Nobel Physics Laureate*
%Imperial College of Science, Prince Consort Rd, London SW7, England

Salam, Saeb   *Prime Minister, Lebanon*
32 Rt de Malagnou, 1208 Geneva, Switzerland

Salans, Lester B   *Physician*
%Sandoz Research Institute, Rt 10, Hanover, NJ 07936, USA

Salazar, Alberto   *Marathon Runner*
%International Management Group, 1 Erieview Plaza, #1300, Cleveland, OH 44114, USA

Saldana, Theresa   *Actress*
%David Shapira Assoc, 15301 Ventura Blvd, #345, Sherman Oaks, CA 91403, USA

Saldich, Robert J   *Businessman*
%Raychem Corp, 300 Constitution Dr, Menlo Park, CA 94025, USA

Saleh, Ali Abdullah   *President, Yemen Arab Republic; General*
%President's Office, Zubairy St, Sana'a, Yemen Arab Republic

Saleh, Jaime   *Governor, Netherlands Antilles*
Fort Amsterdam 2, Willemstad, Curacao, Netherlands Antilles

Salenger, Meredith   *Actress*
12700 Ventura Blvd, #100, Studio City, CA 91604, USA

Salerno, Frederic V   *Businessman*
%NYNEX Corp, 1095 Ave of Americas, New York, NY 10036, USA

Salerno-Sonnenberg, Nadja   *Concert Violinist*
%Columbia Artists Mgmt Inc, 165 W 57th St, New York, NY 10019, USA

Sales, Eugenio de Araujo Cardinal   *Religious Leader*
Palacio Sao Joaquim, Rua da Gloria 446, 20241 Rio de Janeiro RJ, Brazil

Sales, Soupy   *Comedian*
245 E 35th St, New York, NY 10016, USA

Salhany, Lucille S   *Television Executive*
%Twentieth Century Fox TV, 10201 W Pico Blvd, Los Angeles, CA 90064, USA

Saliba, Metropolitan Primate Philip   *Religious Leader*
%Antiochian Orthodox Christian Diocese, 358 Mountain Rd, Englewood, NJ 07631, USA

Salim, Salim Ahmed   *Prime Minister, Tanzania*
%Organization of African Unity, PO Box 3243, Addis Ababa, Ethiopia

Salinger, J D   *Writer*
RR 3, Box 176, Cornish Flat, NH 03745, USA

Salinger, Pierre E G   *Senator, CA; Journalist*
%Burson Marsteller, 1850 "M" St NW, #900, Washington, DC 20036, USA

Salizzoni, Frank L   *Businessman*
%USAir Group, 2345 Crystal Dr, Arlington, VA 22227, USA

Salkind, Alexander   *Movie Producer*
Pinewood Studios, Iver Heath, Iver, Bucks SLO ONH, England

Salkind, Ilya   *Movie Producer*
Pinewood Studios, Iver Heath, Iver, Bucks SLO ONH, England

Salle, David   *Artist*
%Larry Gagosian Gallery, 980 Madison Ave, #PH, New York, NY 10021, USA

Salley, John   *Basketball Player*
%Toronto Raptors, 20 Bay St, #1702, Toronto ON M5J 2N8, Canada

Sallinen, Aulis H   *Composer*
Runneberginkatu 37-A, 00100 Helsinki 10, Finland

Salminen, Matti   *Opera Singer*
%Mariedi Anders Artists Mgmt, 535 El Camino del Mar, San Francisco, CA 94121, USA

Salming, Borje   *Hockey Player*
%Detroit Red Wings, Joe Louis Arena, 600 Civic Center Dr, Detroit, MI 48226, USA

Salmon, Thomas P   *Governor, VT; Educator*
%University of Vermont, President's Office, Burlington, VT 05405, USA

Salomon, Leon E   *Army General*
CG, US Army Material Command, 5001 Eisenhower Ave, Alexandria, VA 22304, USA

Salomon, Mikael   *Cinematographer*
PO Box 2230, Los Angeles, CA 90078, USA

Salonen, Esa-Pekka   *Conductor*
%Los Angeles Philharmonic, Music Center, 135 N Grand, Los Angeles, CA 90012, USA

Salonga, Lea   *Singer, Actress*
%Atlantic Records, 75 Rockefeller Plaza, New York, NY 10019, USA

Salpeter, Edwin E *Physicist*
116 Westbourne Lane, Ithaca, NY 14850, USA

Salt, Jennifer *Actress*
9045 Elevado St, West Hollywood, CA 90069, USA

Saltykov, Aleksey A *Movie Director*
%Institute Mosfilmosvsky Per 4-A #104, 119285 Moscow, Russia

Saltzman, Robert P *Businessman*
%Jackson National Life Insurance, 5901 Executive Dr, Lansing, MI 48911, USA

Salvador, Sal *Jazz Guitarist, Composer*
315 W 53rd St, New York, NY 10019, USA

Salzman, Pnina *Concert Pianist*
20 Dubnov St, Tel-Aviv, Israel

Sam the Sham (Domingo S Samudio) *Singer*
3667 Tutwiler Ave, Memphis, TN 38122, USA

Samaranch Torello, Juan Antonio *International Olympics Official*
Avenida Pau Casals 24, 08021 Barcelona 6, Spain

Samaras, Lucas *Sculptor, Photographer*
%Pace Gallery, 32 E 57th St, New York, NY 10022, USA

Samartini, James R *Businessman*
%Whirlpool Corp, 2000 N State St, Rt 63, Benton Harbor, MI 49022, USA

Sambora, Richie *Singer, Songwriter (Bon Jovi)*
%Bon Jovi Mgmt, 205 W 57th St, #603, New York, NY 10019, USA

Samios, Nicholas P *Science Administrator, Physicist*
%Brookhaven National Laboratory, Director's Office, Upton, NY 11973, USA

Samms, Emma *Actress*
2934 1/2 N Beverly Glen Circle, #417, Los Angeles, CA 90077, USA

Samoilova, Tatyana Y *Actress*
Kutuzovski Prosp 23, #26, 121151 Moscow, Russia

Sample, Steven B *Educator*
%University of Southern California, President's Office, Los Angeles, CA 90089, USA

Sampras, Pete *Tennis Player*
6352 MacLaurin Dr, Tampa, FL 33647, USA

Sampson, Kelvin *Basketball Coach*
%University of Oklahoma, Lloyd Noble Complex, Norman, OK 73019, USA

Sampson, Patsy H *Educator*
%Stephens College, President's Office, Columbia, MO 65215, USA

Sampson, Ralph *Basketball Player, Coach*
%James Madison University, Convocation Center, Harrisonburg, VA 22807, USA

Sampson, Robert *Actor*
%Paradigm Agency, 10100 Santa Monica Blvd, #2500, Los Angeles, CA 90067, USA

Sams, David E, Jr *Businessman*
%Connecicut Mutual Life Insurance, 140 Garden St, Hartford, CT 06154, USA

Samuelson, Don *Governor, ID*
Rt 3, PO Box 300, Sandpoint, ID 83864, USA

Samuelson, Paul A *Nobel Economics Laureate*
94 Somerset St, Belmont, MA 02178, USA

Samuelsson, Bengt I *Physician*
%Karolinska Institute, Chemistry Dept, 171 77 Stockholm, Sweden

Samuelsson, Kjell *Hockey Player*
%Philadelphia Flyers, Spectrum, Pattison Place, Philadelphia, PA 19148, USA

Samuelsson, Ulf *Hockey Player*
%New York Rangers, Madison Square Garden, 4 Penn Plaza New York, NY 10001, USA

San Giacomo, Laura *Actress*
13035 Woodbridge St, Studio City, CA 91604, USA

San Juan, Olga *Actress*
4845 Willowcrest Ave, Studio City, CA 91601, USA

Sanborn, David *Jazz Saxophonist*
%International Creative Mgmt, 8942 Wilshire Blvd, Beverly Hills, CA 90211, USA

Sanchez de Lozada, Gonzalo *President, Bolivia*
%President's Office, Palacio de Gobierno, Plaza Murilla, La Paz, Bolivia

Sanchez Vicario, Arantxa *Tennis Player*
%International Management Group, 22 E 71st St, New York, NY 10021, USA

Sanchez, Emilio *Artist*
333 E 30th St, New York, NY 10016, USA

Sanchez, Emilio *Tennis Player*
Sabiono de Avena 28, Barcelona 46, Spain

Sanchez, Jose Cardinal *Religious Leader*
%Congregation for Evangelization of Peoples, Vatican City, Rome, Italy

S

Salpeter - Sanchez

Sanchez, Poncho — *Jazz Drummer*
PO Box 59236, Norwalk, CA 90652, USA

Sanchez-Vilella, Roberto — *Governor, PR*
414 Munoz Rivera Ave #7-A, Stop 31-1/2, Hato Rey, PR 00918, USA

Sand, Paul — *Actor*
%Writers & Artists Agency, 924 Westwood Blvd, #900, Los Angeles, CA 90024, USA

Sanda, Dominique — *Actress*
%Artmedia, 10 Ave George V, 75008 Paris, France

Sandage, Allan R — *Astronomer*
%Hale Observatories, 813 Santa Barbara St, Pasadena, CA 91101, USA

Sandberg, Michael G R — *Financier*
54-A Hyde Park Gate, London SW7 5EB, England

Sandberg, Ryne D — *Baseball Player*
11809 S Montezuma Court, Phoenix, AZ 85044, USA

Sandbulte, Arend J — *Businessman*
%Minnesota Power, 30 W Superior St, Duluth, MN 55802, USA

Sander, Jil — *Fashion Designer*
Osterfeldstr 32-34, 22529 Hamburg, Germany

Sanderling, Kurt — *Conductor*
Am Iderfenngraben 47, 13156 Berlin, Germany

Sanders, Barry — *Football Player*
%Detroit Lions, Silverdome, 1200 Featherstone Rd, Pontiac, MI 48342, USA

Sanders, Bill — *Cartoonist*
PO Box 661, Milwaukee, WI 53201, USA

Sanders, Carl E — *Governor, GA*
1400 Candler Building, Atlanta, GA 30043, USA

Sanders, Charles A (Charlie) — *Football Player, Coach*
%Detroit Lions, Silverdome, 1200 Featherstone Rd, Pontiac, MI 48342, USA

Sanders, Deion L — *Football, Baseball Player*
125 W Meadow Court, Alpharetta, GA 30201, USA

Sanders, Doug — *Golfer*
8828 Sandringham Dr, Houston, TX 77024, USA

Sanders, James C — *Government Official*
%Small Business Administration, 1441 "C" St NW, Washington, DC 20416, USA

Sanders, Jon — *Yachtsman*
28 Portland St, Redlands 6009 WA, Australia

Sanders, Lawrence — *Writer*
%G P Putnam's Sons, 200 Madison Ave, New York, NY 10016, USA

Sanders, Lewis A — *Financier*
%Sanford C Bernstein Co, 767 5th Ave, New York, NY 10153, USA

Sanders, Marlene — *Commentator*
%WNET-TV, News Dept, 356 W 58th St, New York, NY 10019, USA

Sanders, Richard — *Actor*
PO Box 1644, Woodinville, WA 98072, USA

Sanders, Ricky W — *Football Player*
%Miami Dolphins, 7500 SW 30th St, Davie, FL 33329, USA

Sanders, Steve — *Singer (Oak Ridge Boys)*
329 Rockland Rd, Hendersonville, TN 37075, USA

Sanders, Summer — *Swimmer*
730 Sunrise Ave, Roseville, CA 95661, USA

Sanders, Tom (Satch) — *Basketball Player*
%National Basketball Assn, Olympic Tower, 645 5th Ave, New York, NY 10022, USA

Sanders, W J (Jerry), III — *Businessman*
%Advanced Micro Devices Inc, 1 AMD Place, PO Box 3453, Sunnyvale, CA 94088, USA

Sanders, Wayne R — *Businessman*
%Kimberly-Clark Corp, PO Box 619100, Dallas, TX 75261, USA

Sanderson, Geoff — *Hockey Player*
%Hartford Whalers, Coliseum, 242 Trumbell St, #800, Hartford, CT 06103, USA

Sanderson, Tessa — *Track Athlete*
%Tee-Dee Promotion, Atlas Bus Center, Oxgate Lane, London NW2 7HU, England

Sanderson, William — *Actor*
13047 Bloomfield St, Studio City, CA 91604, USA

Sanderson, Wimp — *Basketball Coach*
%University of Arkansas at Little Rock, Athletic Dept, Little Rock, AR 72204, USA

Sandeson, William S — *Editorial Cartoonist*
119 W Sherwood Terrace, Fort Wayne, IN 46807, USA

Sandiford, L Erskine — *Prime Minister, Barbados*
%Prime Minister's Office, Government Hdq, Bay St, Bridgetown, Barbados

Sandler, Herbert M *Financier*
%Golden West Financial Corp, 1901 Harrison St, Oakland, CA 94612, USA

Sandler, Marion O *Financier*
%Golden West Financial Corp, 1901 Harrison St, Oakland, CA 94612, USA

Sandlund, Debra *Actress*
%Innovative Artists, 1999 Ave of Stars, #2850, Los Angeles, CA 90067, USA

Sandoval, Arturo *Jazz Trumpeter*
%Turi's Music Enterprises, 101 S Royal Poinciana Blvd, Miami Springs, FL 33166, USA

Sandoval, Hope *Singer (Mazzy Star)*
%Creative Artists Agency, 9830 Wilshire Blvd, Beverly Hills, CA 90212, USA

Sandrelli, Stefania *Actress*
%TNA, Viale Parioli 41, 00197 Rome, Italy

Sandrich, Jay H *Television Director*
610 N Maple Dr, Beverly Hills, CA 90210, USA

Sands, Julian *Actor*
%Conway Van Gelder Robinson, 18-21 Jermyn St, London SW1Y 6HB, England

Sands, Tommy *Singer*
4312 Troost Ave, North Hollywood, CA 91604, USA

Sandstrom, Sven *Financier*
%World Bank Group, 1818 "H" St NW, Washington, DC 20433, USA

Sandstrom, Tomas *Hockey Player*
%Pittsburgh Penguins, Civic Arena, Centre Ave, Pittsburgh, PA 15219, USA

Sandusky, Alexander B (Alex) *Football Player*
30 Floral Ave, Key West, FL 33040, USA

Sandy, Gary *Actor*
12810 Waddell St, North Hollywood, CA 91607, USA

Sanford, Charles S, Jr *Financier*
%Bankers Trust New York Corp, 280 Park Ave, New York, NY 10017, USA

Sanford, Isabel *Actress*
%Agency For Performing Arts, 9000 Sunset Blvd, #1200, Los Angeles, CA 90069, USA

Sanford, Lucius M *Football Player*
8746 Carriage Hill Dr, Columbia, MD 21046, USA

Sanford, Richard D *Businessman*
%Intelligent Electronics, 411 Eagleview Blvd, Exton, PA 19341, USA

Sanford, Terry *Governor/Senator, NC; Educator*
1508 Pinecrest Rd, Durham, NC 27705, USA

Sanger, David J *Concert Organist*
Old Wesleyan Chapel, Embleton Near Cockermouth, Cumbria CA13 9YA, England

Sanger, Frederick *Nobel Chemistry Laureate*
Far Leys, Fen Lane, Swaffham Bulbeck, Cambridge CB5 0NJ, England

Sanger, Stephen W *Businessman*
%General Mills Inc, PO Box 1113, Minneapolis, MN 55440, USA

Sangueli, Andrei *Prime Minister, Moldova*
%Prime Minister's Office, Piaca Maril Atuner, 277033 Kishineu, Moldova

Sano, Kenjiro *Businessman*
%Isuzu Motors Ltd, 6-26-1 Minamioi, Shinagawaku, Tokyo 140, Japan

Sansom, Chip *Cartoonist (Born Loser)*
1050 Erie Cliff Dr, Cleveland, OH 44107, USA

Santamaria, Mongo *Congo Drummer*
%Jack Hooke, 78-08 223rd St, Bayside, NY 11364, USA

Santana, Carlos *Guitarist, Singer*
%Bill Graham Productions, 201 11th St, San Francisco, CA 94103, USA

Santana, Manuel *Tennis Player*
%International Tennis Hall of Fame, 194 Bellevue Ave, Newport, RI 02840, USA

Santer, Jacques *Premier, Luxembourg*
%Premier's Office, 4 Rue de la Congregation, 2910 Luxembourg

Santiago, Benito R *Baseball Player*
566 Port Halwick, Chula Vista, CA 91913, USA

Santiago, Saundra *Actress*
%Don Buchwald Assoc, 10 E 44th St, #500, New York, NY 10017, USA

Santmyer, Helen Hoover *Social Worker*
%Hospitality Home East, N Monroe Dr, Xenia, OH 45385, USA

Santo, Ronald E (Ron) *Baseball Player*
1721 Meadow Lane, Bannockburn, IL 60015, USA

Santoni, Reni *Actor*
247 S Beverly Dr, #102, Beverly Hills, CA 90212, USA

Santorini, Paul E *Physicist, Engineer*
PO Box 49, Athens, Greece

Santoro, Carmelo J *Businessman*
%AST Research Inc, 16215 Alton Parkway, Irvine, CA 92718, USA

Santos, Joe *Actor*
%Paradigm Agency, 10100 Santa Monica Blvd, #2500, Los Angeles, CA 90067, USA

Sara, Mia *Actress*
222 N Norton Ave, Los Angeles, CA 90004, USA

Sarafanov, Gennady V *Cosmonaut*
%Potchta Kosmonavtov, 141 160 Svyosdny Gorodok, Moskovskoi Oblasti, Russia

Sarandon, Chris *Actor*
107 Glasco Turnpike, Woodstock, NY 12498, USA

Sarandon, Susan *Actress*
%International Creative Mgmt, 40 W 57th St, New York, NY 10019, USA

Sarazen, Gene *Golfer*
%Emerald Beach Apartments, PO Box 667, Marco Island, FL 33969, USA

Sardi, Vincent, Jr *Restauranteur*
%Sardi's Restaurant, 234 W 44th St, New York, NY 10036, USA

Sarfati, Alain *Architect*
28 Rue Barbet Du Jouy, 75007 Paris, France

Sargent, Ben *Editorial Cartoonist*
%Austin American-Statesman, 166 E Riverside Dr, Austin, TX 78704, USA

Sargent, Francis W *Governor, MA*
Farm St, Dover, MA 02030, USA

Sargent, John T *Publisher*
Halsey Lane, Watermill, NY 11976, USA

Sargent, Joseph D *Movie Producer, Director*
33740 Pacific Coast Highway, Malibu, CA 90265, USA

Sargent, Joseph D *Financier*
%Conning Corp, City Place II, 185 Asylum St, Hartford, CT 06103, USA

Sarinic, Hrvoje *Prime Minister, Croatia*
%Prime Minister's Office, Opaticka 2, Zagreb, Croatia

Sarles, H Jay *Financier*
%Fleet Financial Group, 50 Kennedy Plaza, Providence, RI 02903, USA

Sarni, Vincent A *Baseball Executive*
%Pittsburgh Pirates, Three Rivers Stadium, Pittsburgh, PA 15212, USA

Sarnoff, William *Publisher*
%Warner Publishing Inc, 1325 Ave of Americas, New York, NY 10019, USA

Sarofim, Fayez S *Financier*
%Fayez Sarofim Co, 2 Houston Center, Houston, TX 77010, USA

Sarosi, Imre *Swimming Coach*
1033 Bp Harrer Dal Ut 4, Hungary

Sarraute, Nathalie *Writer*
12 Ave Pierre 1 de Serbie, 75116 Paris, France

Sarrazin, Michael *Actor*
9920 Beverly Grove Dr, Beverly Hills, CA 90210, USA

Sartzetakis, Christos *President, Greece*
%Presidential Palace, 7 Vas Georgiou B', Athens, Greece

Sasaki, Sadamichi *Businessman*
%Fuji Heavy Industries, 1-7-2 Nishi-Shinjuku, Shinjukuku, Tokyo 160, Japan

Sass, Sylvia *Opera Singer*
%Dido Senger Artists, The Garden, 103 Randolph Ave, London W9 1DL, England

Sasser, Clarence E *Vietnam War Army Hero (CMH)*
13414 FM 521, Rosharon, TX 77583, USA

Sasser, E Rhone *Financier*
%United Carolina Bancshares, 127 W Webster St, Whiteville, NC 28472, USA

Sassoon, Beverly *Model*
1923 Selby Ave, #203, Los Angeles, CA 90025, USA

Sassoon, David *Fashion Designer*
%Bellville Sassoon, 18 Culford Gardens, London SW3 2ST, England

Sassoon, Vidal *Hair Stylist*
1163 Calle Vista Dr, Beverly Hills, CA 90210, USA

Satanowski, Robert *Conductor*
Ul Madalinskiego 50/52 M 1, 02-581 Warsaw, Poland

Satcher, David *Medical Administrator*
%Centers for Disease Control, 1600 Clifton Rd NE, Atlanta, GA 30329, USA

Sather, Glen C *Hockey Coach, Executive*
%Edmonton Oilers, Northlands Coliseum, Edmonton AB T5B 4M9, Canada

Sato, Haruo *Financier*
%Yamaichi International, 2 World Trade Center, New York, NY 10048, USA

Sato, Kazuo *Economist*
300 E 71st St, #15-H, New York, NY 10021, USA

Sator, Ted *Hockey Coach*
%Hartford Whalers, Coliseum, 242 Trumbell St, #800, Hartford, CT 06103, USA

Satowaki, Joseph Cardinal *Religious Leader*
%Archbishop's House, 5-3 Minami Yametecho, Nagasaki 850, Japan

Satre, Philip G *Businessman*
%Promus Companies, 1023 Cherry Rd, Memphis, TN 38117, USA

Satriani, Joe *Singer, Guitarist*
%International Talent Group, 729 7th Ave, #1600, New York, NY 10019, USA

Satrum, Jerry R *Businessman*
%Georgia Gulf Corp, 400 Perimeter Center Terrace, Atlanta, GA 30346, USA

Satterfield, Paul *Actor*
PO Box 6945, Beverly Hills, CA 90212, USA

Saudners, Ernest W *Businessman*
%Arthur Guinness & Sons, 10 Albermarle St, London W1X 4AJ, England

Sauer, Henry J (Hank) *Baseball Player*
207 Vallejo Court, Millbrae, CA 94030, USA

Sauer, Louis *Architect*
3472 Marlowe St, Montreal PQ H4A 3L7, Canada

Sauer, Richard J *Educator, Association Executive*
%National 4-H Council, 7100 Connecticut Ave, Bethesda, MD 20815, USA

Saul, B Francis, II *Financier*
%Chevy Chase Bank, 8401 Connecticut Ave, Chevy Chase, MD 20815, USA

Saul, Richard R (Rich) *Football Player*
18465 Jocotal Ave, Villa Park, CA 92667, USA

Saul, Stephanie *Journalist*
%Newsday, Editorial Dept, 235 Pinelawn Rd, Melville, NY 11747, USA

Sauls, Don *Religious Leader*
%Pentecostal Free Will Baptist Church, PO Box 1568, Dunn, NC 28335, USA

Saunders, Arlene *Opera Singer*
535 E 86th St, New York, NY 10028, USA

Saunders, Cicely *Hospice Movement Founder*
%St Christopher's Hospice, 51-53 Lawreie Park Rd, Sydenham 6DZ, England

Saunders, George L, Jr *Attorney*
179 E Lake Shore Dr, Chicago, IL 60611, USA

Saunders, Jennifer *Actress*
%Peters Fraser Dunlop, Chelsea Harbour, Lots Rd, London SW10 0XF, England

Saunders, John *Cartoonist (Mary Worth)*
%King Features Syndicate, 216 E 45th St, New York, NY 10017, USA

Saunders, John *Sportscaster*
%ESPN-TV, Sports Dept, ESPN Plaza, Bristol, CT 06010, USA

Saura, Carlos *Movie Director*
%Direccion General del Libro, Paseo De la Casrellana 109, Madrid 16, Spain

Sauter, Van Gordon *Television Executive*
1815 Garden Highway, Sacramento, CA 95833, USA

Sauve, Bob *Hockey Player*
%New Jersey Devils, Meadowlands Arena, PO Box 504, East Rutherford, NJ 07073, USA

Savage, Fred *Actor*
1450 Belfast Dr, Los Angeles, CA 90069, USA

Savage, John *Actor*
%Artists Agency, 10000 Santa Monica Blvd, #305, Los Angeles, CA 90067, USA

Savage, Randy (Macho Man) *Wrestler*
%World Wrestling Federation, 1055 Summer St, Greenwich, CT 06905, USA

Savage, Richard T *Businessman*
%Modine Manufacturing Co, 1500 DeKovern Ave, Racine, WI 53403, USA

Savage, Rick *Bassist (Def Leppard)*
%Q Prime Mgmt, 729 7th Ave, #1400, New York, NY 10019, USA

Savant, Doug *Actor*
%J Michael Bloom Ltd, 9255 Sunset Blvd, #710, Los Angeles, CA 90069, USA

Savard, Denis *Hockey Player*
%Chicago Blackhawks, Chicago Stadium, 1800 W Madison St, Chicago, IL 60612, USA

Savard, Serge *Hockey Player, Executive*
%Montreal Canadiens, 2313 St Catherine St W, Montreal PQ H3H 1N2, Canada

Savary, Jerome *Theater Director*
%Theatre National de Chaillot, 1 Place du Trocadero, 75116 Paris, France

Saveleva, Lyudmila M *Actress*
Tverskaya Str 19, #76, 103050 Moscow, Russia

S

Savidge, Jennifer *Actress*
2705 Glenower Ave, Los Angeles, CA 90027, USA

Saville, Curtis *Long Distance Rower, Explorer*
RFD Box 44, West Charleston, VT 05872, USA

Saville, Kathleen *Long Distance Rower, Explorer*
RFD Box 44, West Charleston, VT 05872, USA

Savimbi, Jonas *Political Leader, Angola*
%Black Manafort Stone Kelly, 1111 N Fairfax St, Alexandria, VA 22314, USA

Savinykh, Viktor P *Cosmonaut*
%Moscow State University, Gorochovskii 4, 103 064 Moscow, Russia

Savio, Mario *Student Activist*
%San Francisco State University, Physics Dept, San Francisco, CA 94132, USA

Savitskaya, Svetlana Y *Cosmonaut*
%Russian Association, Khovanskaya Str 3, 129 515 Moscow, Russia

Savitske, Michael B *Businessman*
%National-Standard Co, 1618 Terminal Rd, Niles, MI 49120, USA

Savitsky, George *Football Player*
350 E Seabright Rd, Ocean City, NJ 08226, USA

Savitt, Richard *Tennis Player*
19 E 80th St, New York, NY 10021, USA

Savoy, Guy *Chef*
%Restaurant Guy Savoy, 18 Rue Troyon, 75017 Paris, France

Savvina, Iya S *Actress*
%Bolshaya Grunzinskaya St 12, #43, 123242 Moscow, Russia

Saw Maung *Prime Minister, Myanmar; Army General*
%Prime Minister's Office, Yangon, Myanmar

Sawalha, Julia *Actress*
%Associated International Mgmt, 5 Denmark St, London WC2H 8LP, England

Sawallisch, Wolfgang *Conductor*
Hinterm Bichl 2, 83224 Grassau, Germany

Sawaragi, Osamu *Businessman*
%National Steel Corp, 4100 Edison Lakes Parkway, Mishawaka, IN 46545, USA

Sawhill, John C *Government, Association Official*
%Nature Conservancy, 1815 N Lynn St, Arlington, VA 22209, USA

Sawyer, Amos *President, Liberia*
%President's Office, Executive Mansion, PO Box 9001, Monrovia, Liberia

Sawyer, Diane *Commentator*
%ABC-TV, News Dept, 77 W 66th St, New York, NY 10023, USA

Sawyer, Forrest *Commentator*
%"Day One" Show, 147 Columbus Ave, #800, New York, NY 10023, USA

Sawyer, Grant *Governor, NV*
%Lionel Sawyer Collins, Valley Bank Plaza, 300 S 4th St, Las Vegas, NV 89101, USA

Sawyer, James L *Labor Leader*
%Leather Workers Union, 11 Peabody Square, Peabody, MA 01960, USA

Sax, Stephen L (Steve) *Baseball Player*
7791 Park Dr, Fair Oaks, CA 95628, USA

Saxbe, William H *Attorney General; Senator, OH*
1171 N Ocean Blvd, Gulfstream, FL 33483, USA

Saxe, Adrian *Artist*
4835 N Figueroa St, Los Angeles, CA 90042, USA

Saxon, John *Actor*
2432 Banyan Dr, Los Angeles, CA 90049, USA

Sayed, Mostafa Amr El *Chemist*
2631 Northside Dr NW, Atlanta, GA 30305, USA

Sayers, E Roger *Educator*
%University of Alabama, President's Office, Tuscaloosa, AL 35487, USA

Sayers, Gale E *Football Player*
624 Birch Rd, Northbrook, IL 60062, USA

Sayles, John T *Movie Director*
225 Lafayette St, #1109, New York, NY 10012, USA

Sayles, Thomas D, Jr *Financier*
%Summit Bancorp, 1 Main St, Chatham, NJ 07928, USA

Scaasi, Arnold *Fashion Designer*
681 5th Ave, New York, NY 10022, USA

Scacchi, Greta *Actress*
%Susan Smith Assoc, 121 N San Vicente Blvd, Beverly Hills, CA 90211, USA

Scaggs, William R (Boz) *Singer, Songwriter*
%Howard Rose Agency, 8900 Wilshire Blvd, #320, Beverly Hills, CA 90211, USA

Scales, Prunella M — *Actress*
%Conway Van Gelder Robinson, 18-21 Jermyn St, London SW1Y 6HB, England

Scalfaro, Oscar L — *President, Italy*
%President's Office, Palazzo del Quirinale, 00187 Rome, Italy

Scalia, Antonin — *Supreme Court Justice*
%US Supreme Court, 1 1st St NE, Washington, DC 20543, USA

Scalia, Jack — *Actor*
%Wallack Assoc, 6202 Mary Ellen Ave, Van Nuys, CA 91401, USA

Scammon, Richard M — *Political Scientist*
5508 Greystone St, Chevy Chase, MD 20815, USA

Scancarelli, Jim — *Cartoonist (Gasoline Alley)*
%Tribune Media Services, 435 N Michigan Ave, #1417, Chicago, IL 60611, USA

Scanga, Italo — *Artist*
7127 Olivetas, La Jolla, CA 92037, USA

Scanlan, Hugh P S — *Labor Leader*
23 Seven Stones Dr, Broadstairs, Kent, England

Scarabelli, Michele — *Actress*
4720 Vineland Ave, #216, North Hollywood, CA 91602, USA

Scarbath, John C (Jack) — *Football Player*
736 Calvert Rd, Rising Sun, MD 21911, USA

Scarbrough, W Carl — *Labor Leader*
%Furniture Workers Union, 1910 Airlane Dr, Nashville, TN 37210, USA

Scardelletti, Robert A — *Labor Leader*
%Transportation Communications Int'l, 3 Research Place, Rockville, MD 20850, USA

Scardino, Albert J — *Journalist*
15 Empire House, Thurloe Place, London SW7 2RV, England

Scarf, Herbert E — *Economist*
88 Blake Rd, Hamden, CT 06517, USA

Scarfe, Gerald A — *Cartoonist*
10 Cheyne Walk, London SW3, England

Scargill, Arthur — *Labor Leader*
%National Union of Mineworkers, Holly St, Sheffield S1 2GT, England

Scarlata, Richard M — *Financier*
%Rockefeller Center Properties, 1270 Ave of Americas, New York, NY 10020, USA

Scarwid, Diana — *Actress*
PO Box 3614, Savannah, GA 31414, USA

Scates, Al — *Volleyball Coach*
%University of California, Athletic Dept, Los Angeles, CA 90024, USA

Scavullo, Francesco — *Photographer*
212 E 63rd St, New York, NY 10021, USA

Schaal, Richard — *Actor*
%Atkins Assoc, 303 S Crescent Heights Blvd, Los Angeles, CA 90048, USA

Schaap, Richard J — *Journalist*
%ABC-TV, Sports Dept, 77 W 66th St, New York, NY 10023, USA

Schachman, Howard K — *Molecular Biochemist*
%University of California, Molecular Biology Dept, Berkeley, CA 94720, USA

Schacht, Henry B — *Businessman*
%Cummins Engine Co, PO Box 3005, Columbus, IN 47202, USA

Schachter, Norm — *Football Referee*
7716 Westlawn Ave, Los Angeles, CA 90045, USA

Schadt, James P — *Publisher*
%Reader's Digest Assn, Reader's Digest Rd, Pleasantville, NY 10570, USA

Schaefer, Ernst J — *Medical Researcher*
%Tufts University, Nutrition Research Center, Medford, MA 02155, USA

Schaefer, George A, Jr — *Financier*
%Fifth Third Bancorp, 38 Fountain Square Plaza, Cincinnati, OH 45202, USA

Schaefer, George L — *Movie Director*
1040 Woodland Dr, Beverly Hills, CA 90210, USA

Schaefer, Glenn S — *Businessman*
%Pacific Mutual Life Insurance, 700 Newport Center Dr, Newport Beach, CA 92660, USA

Schaefer, Henry F, III — *Chemist*
%University of Georgia, Computational Quantum Chemistry Center, Athens, GA 30602, USA

Schaefer, Thomas J — *Financier*
%Columbia First Bank, 1560 Wilson Blvd, Arlington, VA 22209, USA

Schaeffer, Susan F — *Writer*
%Alfred A Knopf Inc, 201 E 50th St, New York, NY 10022, USA

Schaeffler, Johann — *Businessman*
%Airbus-Industrie, 5 Ave de Villiers, 75017 Paris, France

Schaeneman, Lewis G, Jr *Businessman*
%Stop & Shop Companies, PO Box 1942, Quincy, MA 02105, USA

Schaetzel, John R *Writer*
2 Bay Tree Lane, Bethesda, MD 20816, USA

Schafer, Edward *Governor, ND*
%Governor's Office, State Capitol, 600 "E" Blvd, Bismarck, ND 58501, USA

Schaffel, Lewis *Basketball Executive*
%Miami Heat, Miami Arena, Miami, FL 33136, USA

Schaffer, Peter L *Playwright*
%McNaughton-Lowe Representation, 200 Fulham Rd, London SW10, England

Schairer, George S *Aerospace Design Engineer*
4242 Hunts Point Rd, Bellevue, WA 98004, USA

Schaller, George B *Zoologist*
%Animal Research Ctr, New York Zoological Society, Bronx Park, Bronx, NY 10460, USA

Schallert, William *Actor*
14920 Ramos Place, Pacific Palisades, CA 90272, USA

Schally, Andrew V *Nobel Medicine Laureate*
%Veterans Administration Hospital, 1601 Perdido St, New Orleans, LA 70146, USA

Schama, Simon M *Historian*
%Minda de Gunzburg European Studies Center, Adolphus Hall, Cambridge, MA 02138, USA

Schanberg, Sydney H *Journalist*
164 W 79th St, Apt 12-D, New York, NY 10024, USA

Schank, Roger C *Computer Scientist, Psychologist*
%Northwestern University, Learning Sciences Institute, Evanston, IL 60201, USA

Schar, Dwight C *Businessman*
%NVR Inc, 7601 Lewinsville Rd, McLean, VA 22102, USA

Scharansky, Natan *Social Activist, Computer Scientist*
%Brandeis University, 415 South St, Waltham, MA 02154, USA

Scharer, Erich *Bobsled Athlete*
Grutstrasse 63, 8074 Herrliberg, Switzerland

Scharping, Rudolf *Government Official, Germany*
Wilhelmstr 5, 56112 Lahnstein, Germany

Schatz, Albert *Microbiologist*
%Rutgers Univesity, Research/Endowment Foundation, New Brunswick, NJ 08903, USA

Schatz, Gottfried *Biochemist*
%Basle University, Klingelbergstr 70 4056 Basle, Switzerland

Schatzberg, Jerry N *Movie Director*
%International Creative Mgmt, 8942 Wilshire Blvd, Beverly Hills, CA 90211, USA

Schauer, Henry *WW II Army Hero (CMH)*
840 Madrona Ave S, Salem, OR 97302, USA

Schaufuss, Peter *Ballet Dancer, Director*
%Papoutsis Representation Ltd, 18 Sundial Ave, London SE25 4BX, England

Schawlow, Arthur L *Nobel Physics Laureate*
849 Esplanada Way, Stanford, CA 94305, USA

Schayes, Dan *Basketball Player*
%Los Angeles Lakers, Forum, PO Box 10, Inglewood, CA 90306, USA

Scheckter, Jody D *Auto Racing Driver*
39 Ave Princess Grace, Monte Carlo, Monaco

Schedeen, Anne *Actress*
%Metropolitan Talent Agency, 4526 Wilshire Blvd, Los Angeles, CA 90010, USA

Scheel, Walter *President, West Germany*
Lindenallee 22, 50968 Cologne-Marienburg, Germany

Scheffer, Victor B *Zoologist*
14806 SE 54th St, Bellevue, WA 98006, USA

Scheffler, Israel *Philosopher*
%Harvard University, Larsen Hall, Cambridge, MA 02138, USA

Scheibel, Arnold B *Medical Researcher*
16231 Morrison St, Encino, CA 91436, USA

Scheider, Roy *Actor*
PO Box 364, Sagaponack, NY 11962, USA

Scheider, Wilhelm *Businessman*
%Freid Krupp GmbH, Altendorferstr 103, 45143 Essen, Germany

Schein, Philip S *Physician*
6212 Robinwood Rd, Bethesda, MD 20817, USA

Schell, Maria *Actress*
%Gertrud Rother, Nordstr 5, 83512 Reitmehring, Germany

Schell, Maximilian *Actor*
%Management Baumbauer, Keplestra 2, 81679 Munich, Germany

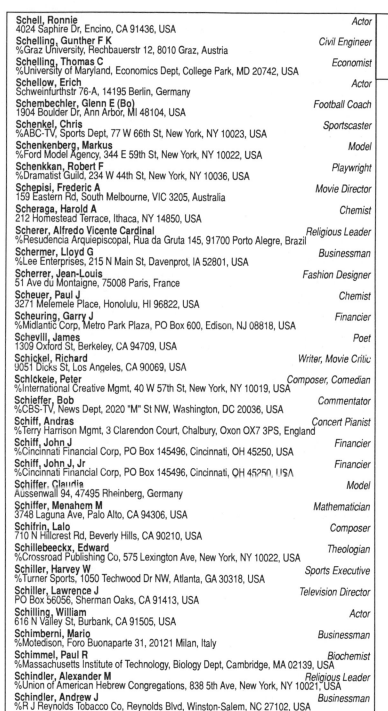

Schell, Ronnie — *Actor*
4024 Saphire Dr, Encino, CA 91436, USA

Schelling, Gunther F K — *Civil Engineer*
%Graz University, Rechbauerstr 12, 8010 Graz, Austria

Schelling, Thomas C — *Economist*
%University of Maryland, Economics Dept, College Park, MD 20742, USA

Schellow, Erich — *Actor*
Schweinfurthstr 76-A, 14195 Berlin, Germany

Schembechler, Glenn E (Bo) — *Football Coach*
1904 Boulder Dr, Ann Arbor, MI 48104, USA

Schenkel, Chris — *Sportscaster*
%ABC-TV, Sports Dept, 77 W 66th St, New York, NY 10023, USA

Schenkenberg, Markus — *Model*
%Ford Model Agency, 344 E 59th St, New York, NY 10022, USA

Schenkkan, Robert F — *Playwright*
%Dramatist Guild, 234 W 44th St, New York, NY 10036, USA

Schepisi, Frederic A — *Movie Director*
159 Eastern Rd, South Melbourne, VIC 3205, Australia

Scheraga, Harold A — *Chemist*
212 Homestead Terrace, Ithaca, NY 14850, USA

Scherer, Alfredo Vicente Cardinal — *Religious Leader*
%Resudencia Arquiepiscopal, Rua da Gruta 145, 91700 Porto Alegre, Brazil

Schermer, Lloyd G — *Businessman*
%Lee Enterprises, 215 N Main St, Davenprot, IA 52801, USA

Scherrer, Jean-Louis — *Fashion Designer*
51 Ave du Montaigne, 75008 Paris, France

Scheuer, Paul J — *Chemist*
3271 Melemele Place, Honolulu, HI 96822, USA

Scheuring, Garry J — *Financier*
%Midlantic Corp, Metro Park Plaza, PO Box 600, Edison, NJ 08818, USA

Schevill, James — *Poet*
1309 Oxford St, Berkeley, CA 94709, USA

Schickel, Richard — *Writer, Movie Critic*
9051 Dicks St, Los Angeles, CA 90069, USA

Schickele, Peter — *Composer, Comedian*
%International Creative Mgmt, 40 W 57th St, New York, NY 10019, USA

Schieffer, Bob — *Commentator*
%CBS-TV, News Dept, 2020 "M" St NW, Washington, DC 20036, USA

Schiff, Andras — *Concert Pianist*
%Terry Harrison Mgmt, 3 Clarendon Court, Chalbury, Oxon OX7 3PS, England

Schiff, John J — *Financier*
%Cincinnati Financial Corp, PO Box 145496, Cincinnati, OH 45250, USA

Schiff, John J, Jr — *Financier*
%Cincinnati Financial Corp, PO Box 145496, Cincinnati, OH 45250, USA

Schiffer, Claudia — *Model*
Aussenwall 94, 47495 Rheinberg, Germany

Schiffer, Menahem M — *Mathematician*
3748 Laguna Ave, Palo Alto, CA 94306, USA

Schifrin, Lalo — *Composer*
710 N Hillcrest Rd, Beverly Hills, CA 90210, USA

Schillebeeckx, Edward — *Theologian*
%Crossroad Publishing Co, 575 Lexington Ave, New York, NY 10022, USA

Schiller, Harvey W — *Sports Executive*
%Turner Sports, 1050 Techwood Dr NW, Atlanta, GA 30318, USA

Schiller, Lawrence J — *Television Director*
PO Box 56056, Sherman Oaks, CA 91413, USA

Schilling, William — *Actor*
616 N Valley St, Burbank, CA 91505, USA

Schimberni, Mario — *Businessman*
%Motedison, Foro Buonaparte 31, 20121 Milan, Italy

Schimmel, Paul R — *Biochemist*
%Massachusetts Institute of Technology, Biology Dept, Cambridge, MA 02139, USA

Schindler, Alexander M — *Religious Leader*
%Union of American Hebrew Congregations, 838 5th Ave, New York, NY 10021, USA

Schindler, Andrew J — *Businessman*
%R J Reynolds Tobacco Co, Reynolds Blvd, Winston-Salem, NC 27102, USA

Schine, G David — *Businessman*
PO Box 2181, Beverly Hills, CA 90213, USA

Schirra, Walter M, Jr — *Astronaut*
16834 Via de Santa Fe, PO Box 73, Rancho Santa Fe, CA 92067, USA

Schisgal, Murray J — *Playwright*
%International Creative Mgmt, 40 W 57th St, New York, NY 10019, USA

Schlafly, Phyllis S — *Women's Activist*
68 Fairmount, Alton, IL 62002, USA

Schlag, Edward W — *Chemist*
Osterwaldstr 91, 80805 Munich, Germany

Schlanger, Marvin G — *Businessman*
%ARCO Chemical Co, 3801 Westchester Pike, Newtown Square, PA 19073, USA

Schlatter, Charlie — *Actor*
13501 Contour Dr, Sherman Oaks, CA 91423, USA

Schlegel, Hans W — *Astronaut, Germany*
DLR, Astronautenburo, Postfach 906058, Linder Hohe, 51140 Cologne, Germany

Schlegel, John P — *Educator*
%University of San Francisco, President's Office, San Francisco, CA 94117, USA

Schlein, Dov C — *Financier*
%Republic New York Corp, 452 5th Ave, New York, NY 10018, USA

Schlenke, B Michael — *Businessman*
%American Home Assurance, 70 Pine Ave, New York, NY 10270, USA

Schlesinger, Arthur M, Jr — *Writer, Educator*
4 E 62nd St, #1, New York, NY 10021, USA

Schlesinger, Helmut — *Financier*
%Deutsche Bundesbank, W-Epstein-Str 14, 60431 Frankfurt/Main, Germany

Schlesinger, James R — *Secretary, Defense & Energy*
%Lehman Bros, 1627 "I" St NW, Washington, DC 20006, USA

Schlesinger, John R — *Movie Director*
1210 N Kings Rd, #102, Los Angeles, CA 90069, USA

Schlessinger, Laura — *Radio Psychologist*
%KFI-Radio, 610 S Ardmore Ave, Los Angeles, CA 90005, USA

Schleyer, Paul Von R — *Chemist*
%Friedrich-Alexander-Universitat, Henkestr 41, 91469 Erlangen, Germany

Schlondorff, Volker O — *Movie Director*
Obermaierstr 1, 80538 Munich, Germany

Schloredt, Robert (Bob) — *Football Player*
%Nestle-Beich, 1827 N 167th St, Seattle, WA 98133, USA

Schlosberg, Richard T, III — *Publisher*
%Los Angeles Times, Times Mirror Square, Los Angeles, CA 90053, USA

Schlumberger, Jean — *Jewelry Designer*
%Tiffany's, 727 5th Ave, New York, NY 10022, USA

Schluter, Poul H — *Prime Minister, Denmark*
%Prime Minister's Office, Prins Jorgens Gaard II, 1218 Copenhagen, Denmark

Schmeling, Max — *Boxer*
Sonnenweg 1, 21279 Hollenstedt, Germany

Schmemann, Serge — *Journalist*
%New York Times, Editorial Dept, 229 W 43rd St, New York, NY 10036, USA

Schmid, Rudi — *Physician*
211 Woodland Rd, Kentfield, CA 94904, USA

Schmidt, Benno C, Jr — *Educator*
%Edison Project, 375 Park Ave, New York, NY 10152, USA

Schmidt, Birgit — *Kayak Athlete*
Kuckuckswald 11, 14532 Kleinmachnow, Germany

Schmidt, Carl F — *Pharmacologist, Physiologist*
%Thomas Wynne Apartments, #1/3-B, Wynne, PA 19096, USA

Schmidt, Chauncey E — *Financier*
234 Albion Rd, Redwood City, CA 94062, USA

Schmidt, Helmut — *Chancellor, West Germany*
%Die Zeit, Speersport 1, 20095 Hamburg, Germany

Schmidt, Joseph (Joe) — *Football Player*
29600 Northwestern Highway, Southfield, MI 48034, USA

Schmidt, Kate — *Track Athlete*
1447 Ave de Cortez, Pacific Palisades, CA 90272, USA

Schmidt, Maarten — *Astronomer*
%California Institute of Technology, Astronomy Dept, Pasadena, CA 91125, USA

Schmidt, Michael J (Mike) — *Baseball Player*
373 Eagle Dr, Jupiter, FL 33477, USA

Schmidt, Milt — *Hockey Player*
%Boston Bruins, Boston Garden, 150 Causeway St, Boston, MA 02114, USA

Schmidt, Ole — *Conductor, Composer*
Puggaardsgade 17, 1573 Copenhagen, Norway

Schmidt, Richard — *Orthopedic Surgeon*
%University of Pennsylvania Hospital, 3400 Spruce St, Philadelphia, PA 19104, USA

Schmidt, Wolfgang — *Track Athlete*
Birkheckenstr 116-B, 70599 Stuttgart, Germany

Schmidt-Nielsen, Knut — *Physiologist*
%Duke University, Zoology Dept, Durham, NC 27706, USA

Schmiege, Robert W — *Businessman*
%Chicago & North Western Transportation, 165 N Canal St, Chicago, IL 60606, USA

Schmitt, Arnd — *Fencer*
Rheinuferweg 59-B, 47495 Bornheim, Germany

Schmitt, Harrison H (Jack) — *Senator, NM; Astronaut*
6053 McKinney Dr NE, Albuquerque, NM 87109, USA

Schmitt, Wolfgang R — *Businessman*
%Rubbermaid Inc, 1147 Akron Rd, Wooster, OH 44691, USA

Schnabel, Julian — *Artist*
%Pace Gallery, 32 E 57th St, New York 10022, USA

Schnabel, Karl Ulrich — *Concert Pianist*
305 West End Ave, New York, NY 10023, USA

Schnabel, Stefan — *Actor*
Rogaro Di Tremezzo, 22019 Como, Italy

Schnackenberg, Roy L — *Artist*
1919 N Orchard St, Chicago, IL 60614, USA

Schnarre, Monika — *Model*
%Ford Model Agency, 344 E 59th St, New York, NY 10022, USA

Schneider, Andrew — *Journalist*
%Pittsburgh Press, Editorial Dept, 34 Blvd of Allies, Pittsburgh, PA 15230, USA

Schneider, John — *Actor, Singer*
12451 Jacqueline Place, Granada Hills, CA 91344, USA

Schneider, Leann — *Financier*
%Showboat Inc, 2800 E Fremont St, Las Vegas, NV 89104, USA

Schneider, Vrenl — *Skier*
Dorf, 8767 Elm, Switzerland

Schneider, William G — *Physical Chemist*
%National Research Council, 65 Whitemarl Dr, #2, Ottawa ON K1L 8J9, Canada

Schneider, William H — *Army General*
526 Country Lane, San Antonio, TX 78209, USA

Schneiderhan, Wolfgang — *Concert Violinist*
Kaasgrabengasse 98-A, 1190 Vienna, Austria

Schnelldorfer, Manfred — *Figure Skater*
Seydlitzstr 55, 80993 Munich, Germany

Schnellenberger, Howard — *Football Coach*
%Oklahoma University, Athletic Dept, 108 W Brooks St, Norman, OK 73069, USA

Schnittke, Alfred — *Composer*
Beim Andreasbrunnen 5, 20249 Hamburg, Germany

Schnuck, Craig D — *Businessman*
%Schnuck Markets, 11420 Lackland Rd, St Louis, MO 63146, USA

Schnuck, Scott C — *Businessman*
%Schnuck Markets, 11420 Lackland Rd, St Louis, MO 63146, USA

Schochet, Bob — *Cartoonist*
Sunset Rd, Highland Mills, NY 10930, USA

Schockemohle, Alwin — *Equestrian Rider*
Munsterlandstr 51, 49439 Muhlen, Germany

Schoelen, Jill — *Actress*
%Gold Marshak Assoc, 3500 W Olive Ave, #1400, Burbank, CA 91505, USA

Schoellkopf, Wolfgang — *Financier*
%First Fidelity Bancorp, 2673 Main St, Lawrenceville, NJ 08648, USA

Schoen, Max H — *Dentist*
5818 S Sherbourne Dr, Los Angeles, CA 90056, USA

Schoendienst, Albert F (Red) — *Baseball Player, Manager*
331 Ladue Woods Court, Creve Coeur, MO 63141, USA

Schoenfeld, Gerald — *Theater Producer*
%Shubert Organization Inc, 225 W 44th St, New York, NY 10036, USA

Schoenfeld, Jim — *Hockey Coach*
%Washington Capitals, USAir Arena, Landover, MD 20785, USA

Schoenfeld, Peter — *Financier*
%Wertheim Schroder Co, Equitable Center, 787 7th Ave, New York, NY 10019, USA

S

Schmidt - Schoenfeld

Schoenfield - Schreyer

Schoenfield, Al *Swimming Administrator*
2731 Pecho Rd, Los Osos, CA 93402, USA

Schoffer, Nicolas *Sculptor*
Villa Des Arts, 15 Rue Hegesippe-Moreau, 75018 Paris, France

Schofield, George H *Businessman*
%Zurn Industries, 1 Zurn Place, Erie, PA 16505, USA

Schofield, Seth E *Businessman*
%USAir Group Inc, 2345 Crystal Dr, Arlington, VA 22227, USA

Scholder, Fritz *Artist*
118 Cattletrack Rd, Scottsdale, AZ 85251, USA

Scholes, Clarke *Swimmer*
1360 Somerset, Grosse Pointe Park, MI 48230, USA

Scholes, Myron S *Economist*
%Stanford University, Graduate Business School, Stanford, CA 94305, USA

Schollander, Don *Swimmer*
3576 Lakeview Blvd, Lake Oswego, OR 97035, USA

Scholten, Jim *Singer (Sawyer Brown)*
%TKO Artist Mgmt, 4219 Hillsboro Rd, #318, Nashville, TN 37215, USA

Schonberg, Claude-Michel *Composer*
%Theatre Royal Drury Lane, Catherine St, London WC2, England

Schonberg, Harold C *Music Critic*
160 Riverside Dr, New York, NY 10024, USA

Schonhuber, Franz *Commentator*
%Europaburo, Fraunhoferstr 23, 80469 Munich, Germany

Schonzeler, Hans-Hubert *Conductor*
%Savage Club, 9 Fitzmaurice Place, London W1, England

Schoolnik, Gary *Medical Researcher*
%Stanford University Medical School, Microbiology Dept, Stanford, CA 94305, USA

Schorer, Jane *Journalist*
%Des Moines Register, Editorial Dept, Box 957, Des Moines, IA 50304, USA

Schorr, Bill *Cartoonist (Phoebe's Place)*
%Kansas City Star, Editorial Dept, 1729 Grand Ave, Kansas City, MO 64108, USA

Schorr, Daniel L *Journalist, Writer*
3113 Woodley Rd, Washington, DC 20008, USA

Schorsch, Ismar *Educator*
%Jewish Theological Seminary, Chancellor's Office, New York, NY 10027, USA

Schott, Marge *Baseball Executive*
%Cincinnati Reds, 100 Riverfront Stadium, Cincinnati, OH 45202, USA

Schottenheimer, Martin E (Marty) *Football Coach*
%Kansas City Chiefs, 1 Arrowhead Dr, Kansas City, KS 64129, USA

Schou, Mogens *Psychiatrist*
%Aarhus University, Institute of Psychiatry, Aarhus, Denmark

Schowalter, Edward R, Jr *Korean War Army Hero (CMH)*
913 Bibb Ave, Auburn, AL 36830, USA

Schrader, Ken *Auto Racing Driver*
PO Box 599, Licking, MO 65542, USA

Schrader, Paul J *Movie Director*
9696 Culver Blvd, #203, Culver City, CA 90232, USA

Schrag, Karl *Artist*
127 E 95th St, New York, NY 10128, USA

Schramm, David N *Astrophysicist*
150 Pitkin Mesa Dr, Aspen, CO 81611, USA

Schramm, Texas E (Tex) *Football Executive*
6116 N Central Expressway, #518, Dallas, TX 75206, USA

Schramm, Wilbur *Educator*
1650 Ala Moana, #3009, Honolulu, CA 96815, USA

Schreiber, Avery *Actor*
6612 Ranchito Ave, Van Nuys, CA 91405, USA

Schreiber, Martin J *Governor, WI*
2700 S Shore Dr, #B, Milwaukee, WI 53207, USA

Schreier, Peter *Opera Singer*
Giesener Str 5, 31157 Sarstedt/Hanover, Germany

Schrempf, Detlef *Basketball Player*
%Seattle Supersonics, 190 Queen Ave N, PO Box C-900911, Seattle, WA 98109, USA

Schrempp, Jurgen E *Businessman*
%Daimler-Benz AG, Mercedestr 136, 70327 Stuttgart, Germany

Schreyer, Edward R *Governor-General, Canada*
401-250 Wellington Crescent, Winnipeg MB R3M 0B3, Canada

S

Schrieffer, John R *Nobel Physics Laureate*
%Florida State University, Physics Dept, Tallahassee, FL 32306, USA

Schriesheim, Alan *Applied Chemist*
1440 N Lake Shore Dr, #31-AC, Chicago, IL 60610, USA

Schriever, Bernard A *Air Force General*
2300 "M" St NW, #900, Washington, DC 20037, USA

Schrimshaw, Nevin S *Nutritionist*
Sandwich Notch Farm, Thornton, NH 03223, USA

Schrock, Richard R *Chemist*
%Massachusetts Institute of Technology, Chemistry Dept, Cambridge, MA 02139, USA

Schroder, Ernst A *Actor*
Podere Montalto, Castellina In Chianti, 53011 Siena, Italy

Schroeder, Barbet G *Movie Director*
8033 W Sunset Blvd, #51, Los Angeles, CA 90046, USA

Schroeder, Frederick R (Ted), Jr *Tennis Player*
1010 W Muirlands Dr, La Jolla, CA 92037, USA

Schroeder, Jim *Bowler*
3 Greenhaven Terrace, Tonawanda, NY 14150, USA

Schroeder, John H *Educator*
%University of Wisconsin, Chancellor's Office, Milwaukee, WI 53211, USA

Schroeder, Mary M *Judge*
%US Court of Appeals, 230 N 1st Ave, Phoenix, AZ 85025, USA

Schroeder, Paul W *Historian*
%University of Illinois, History Dept, 810 S Wright St, Urbana, IL 61801, USA

Schroeder, Terry *Water Polo Player, Coach*
4901 Lewis Rd, Agoura Hills, CA 91301, USA

Schrom, Kenneth M (Ken) *Baseball Player*
713 Roisante, El Paso, TX 79922, USA

Schruefer, John J *Physician*
%Georgetown University Hospital, Ob-Gyn Dept, Washington, DC 20007, USA

Schubert, Mark *Swimming Coach*
%University of Southern California, Athletic Dept, Los Angeles, CA 90089, USA

Schubert, Richard F *Association Executive*
7811 Old Dominion Dr, McLean, VA 22102, USA

Schuchart, John A *Businessman*
%MDU Resources Group, 400 N 4th St, Bismarck, ND 58501, USA

Schuck, John *Actor*
702 California Ave, Venice, CA 90291, USA

Schueler, Jon R *Artist*
40 W 22nd St, New York, NY 10010, USA

Schuermann, Fred L, Jr *Businessman*
%LADD Furniture, 1 Plaza Center, High Point, NC 27261, USA

Schuh, Harry F *Football Player*
2309 Massey Rd, Memphis, TN 38119, USA

Schul, Bob *Track Athlete*
27 E Dixon Ave, Dayton, OH 45419, USA

Schulberg, Budd *Writer*
Brookside, PO Box 707, Westhampton Beach, NY 11978, USA

Schulhof, Michael P *Entertainment Executive*
%Sony Pictures Entertainment, 10202 W Washington Blvd, Culver City, CA 90232, USA

Schuller, Grete *Sculptor*
8 Barstow Rd, #7-G, Great Neck, NY 11021, USA

Schuller, Gunther *Composer, Conductor*
%Margun Music, 167 Dudley Rd, Newton Centre, MA 02159, USA

Schuller, Robert H *Evangelist*
464 S Esplanade, Orange, CA 92669, USA

Schult, Jurgen *Track Athlete*
Herrmann Duncker Str 49, 15755 Schwerin, Germany

Schulte, David *Financier*
%Chilmark Partners, 2 N Riverside Plaza, Chicago, IL 60606, USA

Schultes, Richard E *Ethnobotanist*
%Harvard University Botanical Museum, 26 Oxford St, Cambridge, MA 02138, USA

Schultz, Dave *Wrestler*
4338 Upland Dr, Madison, WI 53705, USA

Schultz, Dean *Financier*
%Federal Home Loan Bank, PO Box 7948, San Francisco, CA 94120, USA

Schultz, Dwight *Actor*
%Paul Kohner Inc, 9300 Wilshire Blvd, #555, Beverly Hills, CA 90212, USA

Schultz, Frank J *Financier*
%ITT Financial Corp, 645 Maryville Centre Dr, St Louis, MO 63141, USA

Schultz, Frederick H *Government Official*
PO Box 1200, Jacksonville, FL 32201, USA

Schultz, Michael A *Movie Director*
%Chrystalite Productions, PO Box 1940, Santa Monica, CA 90406, USA

Schultz, Peter C *Inventor (Silica Optical Waveguide)*
%Heraeus Amersil Inc, 3473 Satellite Blvd, #300, Duluth, GA 30136, USA

Schultz, Peter G *Chemist*
%University of California, Chemistry Dept, Berkeley, CA 94720, USA

Schultz, Richard D *Association Executive*
%US Olympic Committee, 1750 E Boulder St, Colorado Springs, CO 80909, USA

Schultz, Theodore W *Nobel Economics Laureate*
5620 S Kimbark Ave, Chicago, IL 60637, USA

Schultze, Charles L *Government Official*
%Brookings Institute, 1775 Massachusetts Ave NW, Washington, DC 20036, USA

Schulz, Charles M *Cartoonist (Peanuts)*
1 Snoopy Pl, Santa Rosa, CA 95403, USA

Schulze, Horst H *Businessman*
%Ritz-Carlton Hotels, 3414 Peachtree Rd NE, Atlanta, GA 30326, USA

Schulze, John B *Businessman*
%Lamson & Sessions Co, 25701 Science Park Dr, Cleveland, OH 44122, USA

Schulze, Richard M *Businessman*
%Best Buy Co, PO Box 9312, Minneapolis, MN 55440, USA

Schumacher, Michael *Auto Racing Driver*
Forsthausstr 92, 54578 Kerpen-Manheim, Germany

Schuman, Allan L *Businessman*
%Ecolab Inc, Ecolab Center, 370 N Wabasha St, St Paul, MN 55102, USA

Schumann, Maurice *Government Official, France*
53 Ave Marechal-Lyautey, 75016 Paris, France

Schumann, Ralf *Pistol Marksman*
Auf'm Hollerstock 32, 66589 Merchweiler, Germany

Schurmann, Petra *Swimmer*
Max-Emanuel-Str 7, 82319 Starnberg, Germany

Schussler Fiorenza, Elisabeth *Writer, Educator*
%Notre Dame University, Theology Dept, Notre Dame, IN 46556, USA

Schutz, Stephen *Graphic Artist*
%Blue Mountain Arts Inc, PO Box 4549, Boulder, CO 80306, USA

Schutz, Susan Polis *Poet*
%Blue Mountain Arts Inc, PO Box 4549, Boulder, CO 80306, USA

Schuur, Diane *Singer*
31916 162nd Ave SE, Auburn, WA 98092, USA

Schuyler, Robert L *Businessman*
621 Pacific Ave, #214, Tacoma, WA 98402, USA

Schwab, Charles R *Financier*
%Charles Schwab Co, 101 Montgomery St, San Francisco, CA 94104, USA

Schwab, John J *Psychiatrist*
6217 Innes Trace Rd, Louisville, KY 40222, USA

Schwantner, Joseph *Composer*
%Eastman School of Music, 26 Gibbs St, Rochester, NY 14604, USA

Schwartz, David *Businessman*
%Bio-Rad Laboratories, 1000 Alfred Nobel Dr, Hercules, CA 94547, USA

Schwartz, Gerard *Conductor*
575 West End Ave, #4-B, New York, NY 10024, USA

Schwartz, Jacob T *Computer Scientist*
%New York University, Courant Math Sciences Institute, New York, NY 10012, USA

Schwartz, Linda *Sociologist*
%University of Washington, Sociology Dept, Seattle, WA 98195, USA

Schwartz, Lloyd *Music Critic*
27 Pennsylvania Ave, Somerville, MA 02145, USA

Schwartz, Maxime *Medical Administrator*
%Institut Pasteur, 25-28 Rue du Docteur-Roux, 75724 Paris Cedex 15, France

Schwartz, Melvin *Nobel Physics Laureate*
61 S Howells Point RD, Bellport, NY 11713, USA

Schwartz, Michael *Educator*
%Kent State University, White Hall, Kent, OH 44242, USA

Schwartz, Neil J *Actor*
9809 Virginia Woods Circle, Las Vegas, NV 89117, USA

Schwartz, Paul N — *Businessman*
%MAXXAM Inc, PO Box 572887, Houston, TX 77257, USA

Schwartz, Richard J — *Businessman*
%Jonathan Logan Co, 980 Ave of Americas, New York, NY 10018, USA

Schwartz, Stephen L — *Composer, Lyricist*
%Paramuse Assoc, 1414 Ave of Americas, New York, NY 10019, USA

Schwartz, Tony — *Communications Specialist*
455 W 56th St, New York, NY 10019, USA

Schwarz, Gerard R — *Conductor*
575 West End Ave, #4-B, New York, NY 10024, USA

Schwarz, H Marshall — *Financier*
%United States Trust Co of New York, 114 W 47th St, New York, NY 10036, USA

Schwarz, John H — *Physicist*
%California Institute of Technology, Physics Dept, Pasadena, CA 91125, USA

Schwarz, Wolfgang — *Figure Skater*
Program Zeitschriftenverlag, Parkring 12, Stiege 9/9, 1010 Vienna, Austria

Schwarz-Schilling, Christian — *Government Official, Germany*
%Post-Telecomm Ministry, Heinrich-von-Stephanstr 1, 53175 Bonn, Germany

Schwarzenegger, Arnold — *Body Builder, Actor*
3110 Main St, #300, Santa Monica, CA 90405, USA

Schwarzkopf, Elisabeth — *Opera Singer*
Rebhusstra 29, 8126 Zunnikon, Zurich, Switzerland

Schwarzkopf, H Norman — *Army General*
400 N Ashley Dr, #3050, Tampa, FL 33602, USA

Schwarzman, Stephen A — *Financier*
%Blackstone Group, 345 Park Ave, New York, NY 10154, USA

Schwarzschild, Martin — *Astronomer*
12 Ober Rd, Princeton, NJ 08540, USA

Schwebel, Stephen M — *Judge*
%Int'l Court of Justice, Peace Palace, 2517 KJ The Hague, Netherlands

Schweickart, Russell L — *Astronaut*
2125 Red Hill Cir, Belvedere, Tiburon, CA 94920, USA

Schweiker, Richard S — *Secretary, Health & Human Services*
%American Council of Life Insurance, 1001 Pennsylvania Ave, Washington, DC 20004, USA

Schweikert, J E — *Religious Leader*
%Old Roman Catholic Church, 4200 N Kedvale Ave, Chicago, IL 60641, USA

Schweikher, Paul — *Architect*
3222 E Missouri Ave, Phoenix, AZ 85018, USA

Schwery, Henri Cardinal — *Religious Leader*
%Bishoporic of Sion, CP 2068, 1950 Sion 2, Switzerland

Schwimmer, David — *Actor*
%Gersh Agency, 232 N Canon Dr, Beverly Hills, CA 90210, USA

Schwinden, Ted — *Governor, MT*
1335 Highland St, Helena, MT 59601, USA

Schygulla, Hanna — *Actress*
%ZBF Agentur, Leopoldstr 19, 80802 Munich, Germany

Sciarra, John M — *Football Player*
4420 Woodleigh Lane, La Canada-Flintridge, CA 91011, USA

Sciorra, Anabella — *Actress*
%Wolf/Kasteller, 1033 Gayley Ave, #208, Los Angeles, CA 90024, USA

Scirica, Anthony J — *Judge*
%US Court of Appeals, US Courthouse, 601 Market St, Philadelphia, PA 19106, USA

Scitovsky, Anne A — *Economist*
161 Erica Way, Menlo Park, CA 94028, USA

Scitovsky, Tibor — *Economist*
1175 N Lemon Ave, Menlo Park, CA 94025, USA

Sciutti, Graziella — *Opera Singer*
%RCA Records, 1540 Broadway, #900, New York, NY 10036, USA

Scofield, Dino — *Actor*
3330 Barham Blvd, #103, Los Angeles, CA 90068, USA

Scofield, Paul — *Actor*
Gables, Balcombe, Sussex RH17 6ND, England

Scofield, Richard M (Dick) — *Air Force General*
Commander, Space/Missile Systems, Los Angeles Air Force Base, CA 90245, USA

Scoggins, Matt — *Swimmer*
12802 Oak Bend Cove, Austin, TX 78727, USA

Scoggins, Tracy — *Actress*
1131 Alta Loma Rd, #515, Los Angeles, CA 90069, USA

S

Schwartz - Scoggins

Scola, Ettore *Movie Director*
Via Bertoloni 1/E, 00197 Rome, Italy

Scolari, Peter *Actor*
1104 Foothill Blvd, Ojai, CA 93023, USA

Scolnick, Edward *Cancer Researcher*
%Merck & Co, Research & Development, PO Box 2000, Rahway, NJ 07065, USA

Score, Herbert J (Herb) *Baseball Player, Sportscaster*
%WKNR-Radio, 9446 Broadview Rd, Cleveland, OH 44147, USA

Scorsese, Martin *Movie Director*
445 Park Ave, #700, New York, NY 10022, USA

Scott Thomas, Kristin *Actress*
%International Creative Mgmt, 76 Oxford St, London W1N 0AX, England

Scott, Andrew *Businessman*
%Cray Research Inc, 655 Lone Oak Dr, #A, Eagan, MN 55121, USA

Scott, Byron *Basketball Player*
31815 Camino Capistrano, #C, San Juan Capistrano, CA 92675, USA

Scott, Clyde L (Smackover) *Football Player*
12840 Rivercrest Dr, Little Rock, AR 72212, USA

Scott, David K *Educator*
%University of Massachusetts, President's Office, Amherst, MA 01003, USA

Scott, David R *Astronaut*
1300 Manhatten Ave, #B, Manhattan Beach, CA 90266, USA

Scott, Debralee *Actress*
%Fifi Oscard Assoc, 24 W 40th St, #1700, New York, NY 10018, USA

Scott, Dennis *Basketball Player*
%Orlando Magic, Orlando Arena, 1 Magic Place, Orlando, FL 32801, USA

Scott, Dick *Football Player*
9606 Falls Rd, Potomac, MD 20854, USA

Scott, Donovan *Actor*
%Gold Marshak Assoc, 3500 W Olive Ave, #1400, Burbank, CA 91505, USA

Scott, George *Baseball Player*
1316 Goodrich St, Greenville, MS 38701, USA

Scott, George C *Actor*
11766 Wilshire Blvd, #760, Los Angeles, CA 90025, USA

Scott, Irene F *Judge*
%US Tax Court, 400 2nd St NW, Washington, DC 20217, USA

Scott, Jacqueline *Actress*
PO Box 69405, Los Angeles, CA 90069, USA

Scott, James T (Terry) *Army General*
Commanding General, Special Operations Command, Fort Bragg, NC 28307, USA

Scott, Jane *Jazz Critic*
%Cleveland Plain Dealer, 1801 Superior Ave, Cleveland, OH 44114, USA

Scott, Jean Bruce *Actress*
144 N Westerly Dr, Los Angeles, CA 90048, USA

Scott, Jerry *Cartoonist (Baby Blues)*
%Creators Syndicate, 5777 W Century Blvd, #700, Los Angeles, CA 90045, USA

Scott, John A *Publisher*
%Playboy Enterprises, 680 N Lake Shore Dr, Chicago, IL 60611, USA

Scott, John B *Businessman*
%Kemper Investors Life Insurance, 1 Kemper Dr, Long Grove, IL 60047, USA

Scott, Judson *Actor*
%Artists Agency, 10000 Santa Monica Blvd, #305, Los Angeles, CA 90067, USA

Scott, Larry *Body Builder*
PO Box 162, North Salt Lake City, UT 84011, USA

Scott, Larry R *Businessman*
%Carolina Freight Corp, 1201 E Church St, Cherryville, NC 28021, USA

Scott, Lizabeth *Actress*
PO Box 69405, Los Angeles, CA 90069, USA

Scott, Martha *Actress*
14054 Chandler Blvd, Van Nuys, CA 91401, USA

Scott, Melody Thomas *Actress*
%Save the Earth, 4881 Topanga Canyon Blvd, #201, Woodland Hills, CA 91364, USA

Scott, Michael W (Mike) *Baseball Player*
28355 Chat Dr, Laguna Nigel, CA 92677, USA

Scott, Paul *Writer*
33 Drumsheugh Gardens, Edinburgh, Scotland

Scott, Pippa *Actress*
10 Ocean Park Blvd, #1, Santa Monica, CA 90405, USA

Scott, Richard L — *Businessman*
%Columbia/HCA Healthcare Corp, 201 W Main St, Louisville, KY 40202, USA

Scott, Ridley — *Movie Director*
%Percy Mann Productions, 5555 Melrose Ave, #117, Los Angeles, CA 90038, USA

Scott, Robert L, Jr — *WW II Army Air Corps Hero, Writer*
96 Ridgecrest Place, Warner Robins, GA 31088, USA

Scott, Robert S — *WW II Army Hero (CMH)*
312 Camino Encatado, Santa Fe, NM 87501, USA

Scott, Robert W — *Governor, NC; Educator*
%North Carolina Community College System, 200 W Jones St, Raleigh, NC 27603, USA

Scott, Ronald (Ronnie) — *Musician*
47 Firth St, London W1V 5TE, England

Scott, Shelby — *Labor Leader*
%American Federation of TV/Radio Artists, 260 Madison Ave, New York, NY 10016, USA

Scott, Steve — *Track Athlete*
1428 Eolus St, Leucadia, CA 92024, USA

Scott, Thomas C — *Football Player*
215 Lexington Ave, New York, NY 10016, USA

Scott, Tony — *Movie Director*
%Totem Productions, 8009 Santa Monica Blvd, West Hollywood, CA 90046, USA

Scott, W Richard — *Sociologist*
940 Lathrop Place, Stanford, CA 94305, USA

Scott, Walter, Jr — *Businessman*
%Peter Kiewit Sons, 1000 Kiewit Plaza, Omaha, NE 68131, USA

Scott, Willard H — *Entertainer*
%NBC-TV, News Dept, 30 Rockefeller Plaza, New York, NY 10112, USA

Scotti, Vito — *Actor*
5456 Vanalden Ave, Tarzana, CA 91356, USA

Scotto, Renata — *Opera Singer*
%Robert Lombardo Assoc, 61 W 62nd St, #6-F, New York, NY 10023, USA

Scovil, Samuel K — *Businessman*
%Cleveland-Cliffs Co, 1100 Superior Ave, Cleveland, OH 44114, USA

Scowcroft, Brent — *Air Force General, Government Official*
1750 "K" St NW, #800, Washington, DC 20006, USA

Scranton, William W — *Governor, PA; Ambassador to UN*
%Northeastern National Bank Bldg, #231, Penn & Spruce, Scranton, PA 18503, USA

Scribner, Charles, Jr — *Publisher*
211 E 70th St, New York, NY 10021, USA

Scrimm, Angus — *Actor*
PO Box 5193, North Hollywood, CA 91616, USA

Scrimshaw, Nevin S — *Nutritionist*
Sandwich Mountain Farm, PO Box 330, Thornton, NH 03223, USA

Scripps, Charles E — *Publisher*
10 Grandin Lane, Cincinnati, OH 45208, USA

Scruggs, Earl — *Singer, Banjoist, Songwriter*
201 Donna Dr, Madison, TN 37115, USA

Scudamore, Peter — *Thoroughbred Racing Jockey*
Mucky Cottage, Grangehill, Naunton, Cheltenham, Glos GL54 3AY, England

Scuduto, Al — *Cartoonist*
%King Features Syndicate, 216 E 45th St, New York, NY 10017, USA

Scully, Joseph C — *Financier*
%St Paul BanCorp, 6700 W North Ave, Chicago, IL 60635, USA

Scully, Sean P — *Artist*
%David McKee, 745 5th Ave, New York, NY 10151, USA

Scully, Vincent E (Vin) — *Sportscaster*
1555 Capri Dr, Pacific Palisades, CA 90272, USA

Scully-Power, Paul D — *Astronaut*
919 River Rd, Mystic, CT 06355, USA

Sculthorpe, Peter J — *Composer*
91 Holdsworth St, Woollahra, NSW 2025, Australia

Scutt, Der — *Architect*
%Der Scutt Architect, 44 W 28th St, New York, NY 10001, USA

Seaborg, Glenn T — *Nobel Chemistry Laureate*
%University of California, Lawrence Laboratory, Cyclotron Rd, Berkeley, CA 94720, USA

Seaforth-Hayes, Susan — *Actress*
4528 Beck Ave, North Hollywood, CA 91602, USA

Seaga, Edward P G — *Prime Minister, Jamaica*
Vale Royal, Kingston, Jamaica

S

Scott - Seaga

Seagal, Steven *Actor*
Box 727, Los Olivos, CA 93441, USA

Seagrave, Jocelyn *Actress*
%"Guiding Light" Show, CBS-TV, 222 E 44th St, New York, NY 10017, USA

Seagrove, Jenny *Actress*
%Marmont Mgmt, Langham House, 302-308 Regent St, London W1R 5AL, England

Seal (Sealhenry Samuels) *Singer, Songwriter*
%Beethoven Street Mgmt, 56 Beethoven St, London W1O 4LG, England

Seale, Bobby *Political Activist (Black Panthers)*
%Cafe Society, 302 W Chelton Ave, Philadelphia, PA 19144, USA

Seale, John *Cinematographer*
%Smith/Gosnell, 1515 Palisades Dr, #N, Pacific Palisades, CA 90272, USA

Seals, Dan *Singer, Songwriter*
PO Box 1770, Hendersonville, TN 37077, USA

Seals, Son *Singer*
%JQ Mgmt, 2873 E 91st St, Chicago, IL 60617, USA

Sealy, Malik *Basketball Player*
%Los Angeles Clippers, Sports Arena, 3939 S Figueroa St, Los Angeles, CA 90037, USA

Seaman, Christopher *Conductor*
25 Westfield Dr, Glasgow G52 2SG, Scotland

Seamans, Robert C, Jr *Aeronautical Engineer*
675 Hale St, Beverly Farms, MA 01915, USA

Searfoss, Richard A *Astronaut*
%NASA, Johnson Space Center, 2101 NASA Rd, Houston, TX 77058, USA

Searle, John *Philosopher*
109 Yosemite Rd, Berkeley, CA 94707, USA

Searle, Ronald *Artist*
%John Locke Studio, 15 E 76th St, New York, NY 10021, USA

Searock, Charles J, Jr *Air Force General*
Vice Commander, AF Material Command, Wright-Patterson Air Force Base, OH 45433, USA

Sears, Paul B *Ecologist*
17 Las Milpas, Taos, NM 87571, USA

Sears, Victor W (Vic) *Football Player*
181 Ross Lane, Eugene, OR 97404, USA

Seau, Tiana (Junior), Jr *Football Player*
%San Diego Chargers, Jack Murphy Stadium, San Diego, CA 92160, USA

Seaver, G Thomas (Tom) *Baseball Player*
Larkspur Lane, Greenwich, CT 06830, USA

Seavey, David *Editorial Cartoonist*
%USA Today, Editorial Dept, 1000 Wilson Blvd, Arlington, VA 22209, USA

Seawright, G William *Businessman*
%Stanhome Inc, 333 Western Ave, Westfield, MA 01085, USA

Sebastian, John *Singer, Songwriter*
%Bendett, 2431 Briarcrest Rd, Beverly Hills, CA 90210, USA

Secada, Jon *Singer*
425 E Rivo Alto Dr, Miami Beach, FL 33139, USA

Secchia, Peter *Diplomat*
%US Embassy, Via Veneto 1119-A, Rome, Italy

Secombe, Harry *Actor*
%Willinghurst Ltd, 46 St James's St, London SW1, England

Secord, John *Singer*
%Making Texas Music, PO Box 1971, Longview, TX 75606, USA

Sedaka, Neil *Singer, Songwriter*
%Neil Sedaka Music, 888 7th Ave, #1905, New York, NY 10106, USA

Seddon, Margaret Rhea *Astronaut*
%NASA, Johnson Space Center, 2101 NASA Rd, Houston, TX 77058, USA

Sedelmaier, J Josef (Joe) *Movie, Television Director; Animator*
%Sedelmaier Film Productions, 221 W Ohio St, Chicago, IL 60610, USA

Sedgman, Frank A *Tennis Player*
26 Bolton Ave, Hampton, VIC 3188, Australia

Sedgwick, Kyra *Actress*
1724 N Vista Pl, Los Angeles, CA 90046, USA

Sedney, Jules *Prime Minister, Suriname*
%Trade & Industry Assn, PO Box 111, Paramaribo, Suriname

Sedykh, Yuri *Track Athlete*
%Sports Council, 4 Skatertny Pereulok, Moscow, Russia

See, Carolyn *Writer*
PO Box 107, Topanga, CA 90290, USA

Seear, Beatrice N S	*Government Official, England*
189-B Kennington Rd, London SE11 6ST, England	
Seefehlner, Egon H	*Opera Director*
Weyrgasse 3/10, 1030 Vienna, Austria	
Seefelder, Matthias	*Businessman*
%BASF, Carl-Bosch-Str 38, 78351 Ludwigshafen, Germany	
Seegal, Frederick M	*Financier*
%Wasserstein Perella Group, 31 W 52nd St, New York, NY 10019, USA	
Seeger, Pete	*Singer, Songwriter*
PO Box 431, Dutchess Junction, Beacon, NY 12508, USA	
Seeherman, Julian M	*Businessman*
%Venture Stores, 2001 E Terra Lane, O'Fallon, MO 63366, USA	
Seelenfreund, Alan	*Businessman*
%McKesson Corp, 1 Post St, San Francisco, CA 94104, USA	
Seeler, Uwe	*Soccer Player*
Gutenbergring 71, 25868 Norderstedt, Germany	
Seely, Jeannie	*Singer*
%Tessier-Marsh, 505 Canton Pass, Madison, TN 37115, USA	
Seelye, Talcott W	*Diplomat*
5510 Pembroke Rd, Bethesda, MD 20817, USA	
Seeman, John	*Football Referee*
%National Football League, Referees Office, 410 Park Ave, New York, NY 10022, USA	
Sega, Ronald M	*Astronaut*
%NASA, Johnson Space Center, 2101 NASA Rd, Houston, TX 77058, USA	
Segal, Erich	*Writer*
%Wolfson College, English School, Oxford OX2 6UD, England	
Segal, Fred	*Fashion Designer*
%Fred Segal Jeans, 8100 Melrose Ave, Los Angeles, CA 90046, USA	
Segal, George	*Sculptor*
Davidson Mill Rd, New Brunswick, NJ 08901, USA	
Segal, George	*Actor*
10601 Wilshire Blvd, #1501, Los Angeles, CA 90024, USA	
Segal, Irving E	*Mathematician*
25 Moon Hill Rd, Lexington, MA 02173, USA	
Segal, Uri	*Conductor*
%Terry Harrison Mgmt, 3 Clarendon Court, Chalbury, Oxon OX7 3PS, England	
Segal, Zalman	*Financier*
%Bank Leumi Trust, 579 5th Ave, New York, NY 10017, USA	
Segall, Joel	*Educator*
%City University of New York, President's Office, New York, NY 10010, USA	
Segelstein, Irwin S	*Television Executive*
%National Broadcasting Co, 30 Rockfeller Plaza, New York, NY 10020, USA	
Seger, Bob	*Singer, Songwriter*
%Punch Enterprises, 567 Purdy St, Birmingham, MI 48009, USA	
Seglem, Christopher K	*Businessman*
%Westmoreland Coal Co, Bellvue, 200 S Broad St, Philadelphia, PA 19102, USA	
Segui, Diego P	*Baseball Player*
7520 King St, #J, Shawnee Mission, KS 66214, USA	
Segura, Francisco (Pancho)	*Tennis Player*
%La Costa Resort Hotel & Spa, Costa del Mar Rd, Carlsbad, CA 92009, USA	
Seguso, Robert	*Tennis Player*
%Advantage International, 1025 Thomas Jefferson St NW, #450, Washington 20007, USA	
Seibert, Peter	*Skier*
PO Box 98, Vail, CO 81658, USA	
Seibou, Ali	*President, Niger; Army General*
%Chairman of Higher Council for National Orientation, Niamey, Niger	
Seidelman, Susan	*Movie Director*
%Michael Shedler, 225 W 34th St, #1012, New York, NY 10122, USA	
Seidenberg, Ivan G	*Businessman*
%NYNEX Corp, 1095 Ave of Americas, New York, NY 10036, USA	
Seidler, Harry	*Architect*
13 Kalang Ave, Killara, NSW 2071, Australia	
Seidman, L William	*Government Official, Businessman*
1694 31st St NW, Washington, DC 20007, USA	
Seifert, George	*Football Coach*
%San Francisco 49ers, 4949 Centennial Blvd, Santa Clara, CA 95054, USA	
Seifert, Richard (Robin)	*Architect*
Eleventrees, Milespit Hill, Mill Hill, London NW7 2RS, England	

S

Seear - Seifert

S

Seigenthaler, John L *Publisher*
%Tennessean, 1100 Broadway, Nashville, TN 37203, USA

Seigner, Emmanuelle *Actress*
%Agents Artistiques Beaume/Bonnet, 4 Rue De Ponthieu, 75008 Paris, France

Seignoret, Clarence H A *President, Dominica*
%President's Office, Government House, Victoria St, Roseau, Dominica

Seikaly, Ron *Basketball Player*
%Golden State Warriors, Oakland Coliseum Arena, Oakland, CA 94621, USA

Seinfeld, Jerry *Comedian*
147 S Beverly Dr, #205, Beverly Hills, CA 90212, USA

Seitz, Collins J *Judge*
%US Court of Appeals, 844 N King St, Wilmington, DE 19801, USA

Seitz, Frederick *Physicist, Educator*
%Rockefeller University, Physics Dept, 1230 York Ave, New York, NY 10021, USA

Seitz, Peter J *Financier*
%Bethpage Federal Credit Union, 899 S Oyster Bay Rd, Bethpage, NY 11714, USA

Seitz, Raymond G H *Diplomat*
%United States Embassy, 24 Grosvenor Square, London S1A 1AE, England

Seixas, E Victor (Vic), Jr *Tennis Player*
716 N Beau Chene Dr, Mandeville, LA 70471, USA

Seizinger, Katja *Skier*
Rudolf-Epp-Str 48, 69412 Eberbach, Germany

Selanne, Teemu *Hockey Player*
%Winnipeg Jets, Arena, 15-1430 Maroons Rd, Winnipeg MB R3G 0L5, Canada

Selby, David *Actor*
%International Creative Mgmt, 8942 Wilshire Blvd, Beverly Hills, CA 90211, USA

Selby, Philip *Composer*
Hill Cottage, Via 1 Maggio 93, 00068 Rignano Flaminio, Rome, Italy

Seldin, Donald W *Physician*
%Texas Southwest Medical Center, 5323 Harry Hines Blvd, Dallas, TX 75235, USA

Selecman, Charles E *Businessman*
3433 Southwestern Blvd, Dallas, TX 75225, USA

Seles, Monica *Tennis Player*
%Laurel Oak Estates, 7751 Beeridge Rd, Sarasota, FL 34241, USA

Seley, Jason *Sculptor*
%Cornell University, Art Dept, Ithaca, NY 14853, USA

Selig, Allan H (Bud) *Baseball Executive*
%Milwaukee Brewers, County Stadium, 201 S 46th St, Milwaukee, WI 53214, USA

Seligman, Martin E P *Psychologist*
%University of Pennsylvania, Psychology Dept, Philadelphia, PA 19104, USA

Selkirk, George N *Government Official, England*
Rose Lawn Coppice, Wimborne, Dorset, England

Selkoe, Dennis J *Neurologist*
%Brigham & Women's Hospital, 221 Longwood Ave, Boston, MA 02115, USA

Sellars, Peter *Theater Director*
%Creative Artists Agency, 9830 Wilshire Blvd, Beverly Hills, CA 90212, USA

Selleca, Connie *Actress*
%William Morris Agency, 151 S El Camino Dr, Beverly Hills, CA 90212, USA

Selleck, Tom *Actor*
331 Sage Lane, Santa Monica, CA 90402, USA

Seller, Peg *Sychronized Swimmer, Coach*
72 Monkswood Crescent, Newmarket ON L3Y 2K1, Canada

Sellers, Franklin *Religious Leader*
%Reformed Episcopal Church, 2001 Frederick Rd, Baltimore, MD 21228, USA

Sellers, Ron *Football Player*
%Ron Sellers Assoc, 1615 Forum Pl, #4-C, West Palm Beach, FL 33401, USA

Sellick, Phyllis *Concert Pianist*
Beverley House, 29-A Ranelagh Ave, Barnes, London SW13 0BN, England

Sells, Harold E *Businessman*
%Woolworth Corp, Woolworth Building, 233 Broadway, New York, NY 10279, USA

Selmon, Lee Roy *Football Player*
18255 Wayne Rd, Odessa, FL 33556, USA

Selten, Reinhold *Nobel Economics Laureate*
Hardtweg 23, 53639 Konigswinter, Germany

Selya, Bruce M *Judge*
%US Court of Appeals, US Courthouse, Providence, RI 02903, USA

Selzer, Milton *Actor*
%LA Artists Talent Agency, 2566 Overland Ave, #600, Los Angeles, CA 90064, USA

Seigenthaler - Selzer

Selzer, Richard — *Writer, Surgeon*
6 St Roman Terrace N, Hartford, CT 06511, USA

Semak, Michael W — *Photographer*
1796 Spruce Hill Rd, Pickering ON L1V 1S4, Canada

Sembene, Ousmane — *Theater Director*
PO Box 8087, Yoff, Senegal

Sembler, Melvin F — *Diplomat*
%Sembler Co, 5858 Central Ave, St Petersburg, FL 33707, USA

Semel, Terry S — *Movie Executive*
%Warner Bros, 4000 Warner Blvd, Burbank, CA 91522, USA

Semenov, Anatoli — *Hockey Player*
%Florida Panthers, 100 NE 3rd Ave, #1000, Fort Lauderdale, FL 33301, USA

Semenyaka, Lyudmila — *Ballerina*
%Bolshoi Theater, Teatralnaya Pl 1, 103009 Moscow, Russia

Semiz, Teata — *Bowler*
27 Burnside Place, Haskell, NJ 07420, USA

Semizorova, Nina L — *Ballerina*
%Bolshoi Theater, Teatralnaya Pl 1, 103009 Moscow, Russia

Semkow, Jerzy G — *Conductor*
Ul Dynasy 6 M 1, 00-354 Warsaw, Poland

Semler, Jerry D — *Businessman*
%American United Life Insurance, 1 American Square, Indianapolis, IN 46282, USA

Sempe, Jean-Jacques — *Cartoonist*
4 Rue Du Moulin-Vert, 75014 Paris, France

Semyonov, Vladilen G — *Ballet Dancer*
15/17-504 Roubinshteina St, 191002 St Petersburg, Russia

Sen, Amartya K — *Economist*
%Harvard University, Economics Dept, Cambridge, MA 02138, USA

Sen, Mrinal — *Movie Director*
14 Beltola Rd, Calcutta 700026, India

Sendak, Maurice B — *Writer, Illustrator*
200 Chestnut Hill Rd, Ridgefield, CT 06877, USA

Senderens, Alain — *Chef*
%Restaurant Lucas Carton, 9 Place De La Madeleine, 75008 Paris, France

Senff, Nida — *Swimmer*
%D W Couturier-Senff, Praam 122, 1186-TL Amstelveen, Netherlands

Senge, Peter — *Management Consultant*
%Organization Learning Institute, MIT, Cambridge, MA 02139, USA

Senghor, Leopold Sedar — *President, Senegal; Poet*
1 Square de Tocqueville, 75015 Paris, France

Sengstacke, John H H — *Publisher*
%Sengstacke Enterprises, 2400 S Michigan Ave, Chicago, IL 60616, USA

Senkler, Robert L — *Businessman*
%Minnesota Mutual Life Insurance, 400 N Robert St, St Paul, MN 55101, USA

Sensi, Giuseppe Cardinal — *Religious Leader*
16 Piazza S Calisto, 00153 Rome, Italy

Sentelle, David B — *Judge*
%US Court of Appeals, 333 Constitution Ave NW, Washington, DC 20001, USA

Seow, Yit Kin — *Concert Pianist*
8 North Terrace, London SW3 2BA, England

Sepulveda, Charlie — *Jazz Musician*
%Patricia Doyle, 1994 3rd Ave, New York, NY 10029, USA

Sequeira, Luis — *Plant Pathologist*
10 Appomattox Court, Madison, WI 53705, USA

Serafini, Tito A — *Neurobiologist*
%University of California, Neurobiology Dept, San Francisco, CA 94143, USA

Seramur, John C — *Financier*
%First Financial Corp, 1305 Main St, Stevens Point, WI 54481, USA

Seraphim, His Beatitude Archbishop — *Religious Leader*
%Holy Synod of Church of Greece, Athens, Greece

Seraphin, Oliver — *Prime Minister, Dominica*
44 Green's Lane, Goodwill, Dominica

Serber, Robert — *Physicist*
450 Riverside Dr, New York, NY 10027, USA

Serebrier, Jose — *Conductor, Composer*
20 Queensgate Gardens, London SW7 5LZ, England

Serebrov, Alexander A — *Cosmonaut*
%Potchta Kosmonavtov, 141 160 Svyosdny Gorodok, Moskovskoi Oblasti, Russia

Serembus, John — *Labor Leader*
%Upholsterers Union, 25 N 4th St, Philadelphia, PA 19106, USA

Sereni, Mario — *Opera Singer*
%Eric Semon Assoc, 111 W 57th St, New York, NY 10019, USA

Serious, Yahoo — *Actor*
12/33 E Crescent St, McMahons Point, NSW 2060, Australia

Serkin, Peter A — *Concert Pianist*
RFD 3, Brattleboro, VT 05301, USA

Serlemitsos, Peter J — *Astronomer*
%BBXRT Project, Goddard Space Flight Center, Greenbelt, MD 20771, USA

Serna, Assumpta — *Actress*
8306 Wilshire Blvd, #438, Beverly Hills, CA 90211, USA

Serna, Pepe — *Actor*
2321 Hill Dr, Los Angeles, CA 90041, USA

Serota, Nicholas A — *Museum Director*
%Tate Gallery, Millbank, London SW1P 4RG, England

Serra, Richard — *Sculptor*
173 Duane St, New York, NY 10013, USA

Serrano, Diego — *Actor*
%"Another World" Show, NBC-TV, 79 Madison Ave, #500, New York, NY 10016, USA

Serrano, Juan — *Concert Guitarist*
%Prince/SF Productions, 1135 Francisco St, #7, San Francisco, CA 94109, USA

Serrault, Michel L — *Actor, Singer*
%MS Productions, 12 Rue Greuze, 75116 Paris, France

Serrin, James B — *Mathematician*
4422 Dupont Ave, S Minneapolis, MN 55409, USA

Servan-Schreiber, Jean-Claude — *Journalist*
147 Bis Rue d'Alesia, 75014 Paris, France

ServVass, Cory J — *Editor*
%Saturday Evening Post Magazine, 1100 Waterway Blvd, Indianapolis, IN 46202, USA

Sessions, William S — *Judge, Law Enforcement Official*
3920 Argyle Terrace NW, Washington, DC 20011, USA

Seter, Mordecai — *Composer*
1 Karny St, Ramat Aviv, Tel Aviv, Israel

Seth, Oliver — *Judge*
%US Court of Appeals, PO Drawer 1, Santa Fe, NM 87504, USA

Seth, Vikram — *Writer*
%Phoenix House, Orion House, 5 Upper St, London WC2H 9EA, England

Sethna, Homi N — *Engineer*
Old Yacht Club, Chatrapati Shrivaji Maharaj, Bombay 400 038, India

Setlow, Richard B — *Biophysicist*
4 Beachland Ave, East Quogue, NY 11942, USA

Sevastyanov, Vitayl I — *Cosmonaut*
%Potchta Kosmonavtov, 141 160 Svyosdny Gorodok, Moskovskoi Oblasti, Russia

Seven, Johnny — *Actor*
11213 McLennan Ave, Granada Hills, CA 91344, USA

Severance, Joan — *Model, Actress*
%Agency For Performing Arts, 9000 Sunset Blvd, #1200, Los Angeles, CA 90069, USA

Severeid, Susanne — *Model, Actress*
%Barry Freed Co, 2029 Century Park East, #600, Los Angeles, CA 90067, USA

Severino, John C — *Television Executive*
%Prime Ticket Network, 401 S Prairie St, Inglewood, CA 90301, USA

Severinsen, Carl H (Doc) — *Jazz Trumpeter, Band Leader*
4275 White Pine Lane, Santa Ynez, CA 93460, USA

Sevin, Irik P — *Businessman*
%Petroleum Heat & Power, 2187 Atlantic St, Stamford, CT 06902, USA

Seward, George C — *Attorney*
%Seward & Kissel, 1 Battery Park Plaza, New York, NY 10004, USA

Sewell, Cecil W, Jr — *Financier*
%Centura Banks, 134 N Church St, Rocky Mount, NC 27804, USA

Sewell, Rufus — *Actor*
%Julian Belfrage, 46 Albermarle St, London W1X 4PP, England

Seybold, Jonathan — *Businessman*
%Seybold Seminars, 303 Vintage Park Dr, Fosters, CA 94404, USA

Seyler, Athene — *Actress*
Coach House, 26 Upper Mall, Hammersmith, London W8, England

Seymour, Caroline — *Actress*
%Gage Group, 9255 Sunset Blvd, #515, Los Angeles, CA 90069, USA

Seymour, Jane	*Actress*
PO Box 548, Agoura, CA 91376, USA	
Seymour, Lynn	*Ballerina*
%Artistes in Action, 16 Balderton St, London W1Y 1TF, England	
Seymour, Paul C	*Football Player*
4185 Shoals Dr, Okemos, MI 48864, USA	
Seymour, Stephanie	*Model*
12828 High Bluff Dr, #200, San Diego, CA 92130, USA	
Seymour, Stephanie K	*Judge*
%US Court of Appeals, US Courthouse, 333 W 4th St, Tulsa, OK 74103, USA	
Seynhaeve, Ingrid	*Model*
%Elite Model Mgmt, 111 E 22nd St, New York, NY 10010, USA	
Sfar, Rachid	*Prime Minister, Tunisia*
278 Ave de Tervuren, 1150 Brussels, Belgium	
Sgouros, Dimitris	*Concert Pianist*
Tompazi 28 Str, Piraeus 18537, Greece	
Shaara, Michael	*Writer*
2074 Robinhood Dr, Melbourne, FL 32935, USA	
Shabat, Oscar	*Educator*
%City Colleges of Chicago, Chancellor's Office, Chicago, IL 60601, USA	
Shack, William A	*Anthropologist*
2597 Hilgard Ave, Berkeley, CA 94709, USA	
Shackelford, Ted	*Actor*
12305 Valley Heart Dr, Studio City, CA 91604, USA	
Shackleford, Charles	*Basketball Player*
%Minnesota Timberwolves, Target Center, 600 1st Ave N, Minneapolis, MN 55403, USA	
Shafer, R Donald	*Religious Leader*
%Brethren in Christ Church, PO Box 290, Grantham, PA 17027, USA	
Shafer, Raymond P	*Governor, PA*
%Dunaway & Cross, 1146 19th St, Washington, DC 20036, USA	
Shaffer, David H	*Publisher*
%MacMillan Inc, 866 3rd Ave, New York, NY 10022, USA	
Shaffer, Paul	*Orchestra Leader*
%Panacea Entertainment, 2705 Glendower Ave, Los Angeles, CA 90027, USA	
Shaffer, Peter L	*Playwright*
173 Riverside Dr, New York, NY 10024, USA	
Shaffer, Thomas	*Financier*
%First Los Angeles Bank, 2049 Century Park East, Los Angeles, CA 90067, USA	
Shafran, Nathan	*Businessman*
%Forest City Enterprises, 10800 Brookpark Rd, Cleveland, OH 44130, USA	
Shafto, Robert A	*Businessman*
%New England Mutual Life Insurance, 501 Boylston St, Boston, MA 02116, USA	
Shagan, Steve	*Writer*
285 W Via Lola, Palm Springs, CA 92262, USA	
Shagari, Alhaji Shehu Usman Aliu	*President, Nigeria*
22 Shehu Crescent, PO Box 162, Adarawa, Sokoto State, Nigeria	
Shah Reza Pahlavi II	*Crown Prince, Iran*
%Kubbeh Palace, Heliopolis, Cairo, Egypt	
Shah, Idries	*Writer*
%A P Watt Ltd, 26/28 Bedford Row, London WC1R 4HL, England	
Shahabuddin Ahmed	*President, Bangladesh; Judge*
%Supreme Court, Office of Chief Justice, Dhaka, Bangladesh	
Shaiman, Marc	*Composer*
8476 Brier Dr, West Hollywood, CA 90046, USA	
Shain, Harold	*Publisher*
%Newsweek Magazine, 251 W 57th St, New York, NY 10019, USA	
Shain, Irving	*Educator*
2820 Marshall Court, #8, Madison, WI 53705, USA	
Shakespeare, Frank J, Jr	*Television Executive, Diplomat*
303 Coast Blvd, La Jolla, CA 92037, USA	
Shalala, Donna E	*Secretary, Health & Human Services*
%Health & Human Services Dept, 200 Independence Ave SW, Washington, DC 20201, USA	
Shales, Thomas W	*Journalist*
%Washington Post, Editorial Dept, 1150 15th St NW, Washington, DC 20071, USA	
Shalikashvili, John M	*Army General*
Chairman's Office, Joint Chiefs of Staff, Pentagon, Washington, DC 20318, USA	
Shalit, Gene	*Movie Critic*
225 E 79th St, New York, NY 10021, USA	

S

Seymour - Shalit

Shamask, Ronaldus *Fashion Designer*
%Moss Shamask, 39 W 37th St, New York, NY 10018, USA

Shamir, Yitzhak *Prime Minister, Israel*
Kiriyat Ben Gurian, Jerusalem 91919, Israel

Shamoon, Alan *Financier*
%Apple Bank for Savings, 205 E 42nd St, New York, NY 10017, USA

Shanahan, Edmond M *Financier*
%Bell Federal Savings & Loan, 79 W Monroe St, Chicago, IL 60603, USA

Shanahan, Michael F *Hockey Executive*
%St Louis Blues, St Louis Arena, 5700 Oakland Ave, St Louis, MO 63110, USA

Shanahan, Mike *Football Coach*
%Denver Broncos, 13655 E Dove Valley Parkway, Englewood, CO 80112, USA

Shanahan, R Michael *Financier*
%Capital Research & Management Co, 333 S Hope St, Los Angeles, CA 90071, USA

Shanahan, William S *Businessman*
%Colgate-Palmolive Co, 300 Park Ave, New York, NY 10022, USA

Shandling, Garry *Comedian*
%Brillstein Co, 9150 Wilshire Blvd, #350, Beverly Hills, CA 90212, USA

Shane, Bob *Singer (Kingston Trio)*
9410 S 46th St, Phoenix, AZ 85044, USA

Shane, Rita *Opera Singer*
%Daniel Tritter, 545 5th Ave, New York, NY 10017, USA

Shanice *Singer*
%Famous Artists Agency, 1700 Broadway, #500, New York, NY 10019, USA

Shank, Bud *Jazz Musician*
PO Box 948, Port Townsend, WA 98368, USA

Shank, Roger C *Computer Scientist*
%Northwestern University, Learning Sciences Institute, Evanston, IL 60201, USA

Shankar, Ravi *Sitar Player*
%Christopher Tennant Mgmt, 39 Tadema Rd, #2, London SW10 0PY, England

Shanker, Albert *Labor Leader*
%American Federation of Teachers, 555 New Jersey Ave NW, Washington, DC 20001, USA

Shanks, Eugene B (Gene), Jr *Financier*
%Bankers Trust New York Corp, 280 Park Ave, New York, NY 10017, USA

Shanks, Michael *Economist*
703 Mountjoy, Barbicon, London EC2, England

Shannon, Claude E *Applied Mathematician*
5 Cambridge St, Winchester, MA 01890, USA

Shannon, Michael E *Businessman*
%Ecolab Inc, Ecolab Center, 370 N Wabasha St, St Paul, MN 55102, USA

Shantz, Robert C (Bobby) *Baseball Player*
152 Mount Pleasant Ave, Ambler, PA 19002, USA

Shapar, Howard K *Government Official*
4610 Langdrum Lane, Chevy Chase, MD 20815, USA

Shapiro, Ascher H *Mechanical Engineer*
111 Perkins St, Jamaica Plain, MA 02130, USA

Shapiro, Debbie *Actress*
%Agency For Performing Arts, 9000 Sunset Blvd, #1200, Los Angeles, CA 90069, USA

Shapiro, Eli *Economist*
180 Beacon St, Boston, MA 02116, USA

Shapiro, Harold T *Educator*
%Princeton University, President's Office, Princeton, NJ 08544, USA

Shapiro, Irving S *Businessman, Attorney*
%Skadden Arps Slate Meagher Flom, 919 3rd Ave, New York, NY 10022, USA

Shapiro, Irwin I *Physicist*
17 Lantern Lane, Lexington, MA 02173, USA

Shapiro, Joel E *Artist*
280-290 Lafayette St,, #3-D, New York, NY 10012, USA

Shapiro, Karl J *Poet*
211 W 106th St, #11-C, New York, NY 10025, USA

Shapiro, Marc J *Financier*
%Texas Commerce Bank, 712 Main St, Houston, TX 77002, USA

Shapiro, Mary L *Government Official*
%Securities & Exchange Commission, 450 5th St NW, Washington, DC 20549, USA

Shapiro, Maurice M *Astrophysicist*
205 S Yoakum Parkway, #1514, Alexandria, VA 22304, USA

Shapiro, Mel *Playwright*
%University of California, Theater Film & TV Dept, Los Angeles, CA 90024, USA

Shapiro, Robert B *Businessman*
%Monsanto Co, 800 N Lindbergh Blvd, St Louis, MO 63167, USA

Shapiro, Robert L *Attorney*
2121 Ave of Stars, #1900, Los Angeles, CA 90067, USA

Shapley, Lloyd S *Mathematician, Economist*
%University of California, Economics Dept, Los Angeles, CA 90024, USA

Sharer, Kevin W *Businessman*
%Amgen Inc, 1840 DeHavilland Dr, Thousand Oaks, CA 91320, USA

Sharif Zaid Ibin Shaker *Prime Minister, Jordan*
%Prime Minister's Office, PO Box 80, 35215 Amman, Jordan

Sharif, M M Nawaz *Prime Minister, Pakistan*
%Pakistan Muslim League, Parliament, Islamabad, Pakistan

Sharif, Omar *Actor*
%Anne Alvares Correa, 18 Rue Troyon, 75017 Paris, France

Sharma, Rakesh *Cosmonaut, India*
%Hindustan Aeronautics Ltd, Bangalore 560 037, India

Sharman, Helen *Cosmonaut*
12 Stratton Court, Adelaide Rd, Surbiton, Surrey, England

Sharman, William W (Bill) *Basketball Player, Coach, Executive*
4511 Roma Court, Marina del Rey, CA 90292, USA

Sharon, Ariel *Government Official, Israel*
%Knesset, Jerusalem, Israel

Sharp, Linda *Basketball Coach*
%Southwest Texas State University, Athletic Dept, San Marcos, TX 78666, USA

Sharp, Marsha *Basketball Coach*
%Texas Tech University, Athletic Dept, Lubbock, TX 79409, USA

Sharp, Mitchell W *Government Official, Canada*
33 Monkland Ave, Ottawa ON K1S 1Y8, Canada

Sharp, Phillip A *Nobel Medicine Laureate*
36 Fairmont Ave, Newton, MA 02158, USA

Sharp, Richard L *Businessman*
%Circuit City Stores, 9950 Maryland Dr, Richmond, VA 23233, USA

Sharp, Robert P *Geologist*
1901 Gibraltar Rd, Santa Barbara, CA 93105, USA

Sharpe, Luis *Football Player*
%Arizona Cardinals, 8701 S Hardy Dr, Tempe, AZ 85284, USA

Sharpe, Rochelle P *Journalist*
2500 "Q" St NW, #315, Washington, DC 20007, USA

Sharpe, Shannon *Football Player*
%Denver Broncos, 13655 E Dove Valley Parkway, Englewood, CO 80112, USA

Sharpe, Tom *Writer*
%Richard Scott Simon Ltd, 43 Doughty St, London WC1N 2LF, England

Sharpe, William F *Nobel Economics Laureate*
25 Doud Dr, Los Altos, CA 94022, USA

Sharpton, Al *Religious Leader, Social Activist*
1133 Bedford Ave, Brooklyn, NY 11216, USA

Sharqi, Sheikh Hamad Bin Muhammad Al- *Ruler, Fujairah*
%Royal Palace, Fujairah, United Arab Emirates

Sharra, Donald D *Businessman, Publisher*
%Multimedia Inc, 305 S Main St, Greenville, SC 29601, USA

Shatalov, Valdimir A *Cosmonaut*
%Potchta Kosmonavtov, 141 160 Svyosdny Gorodok, Moskovskoi Oblasti, Russia

Shatkin, Aaron J *Scientist*
%Center for Advanced Biotechnology, 679 Hoes Lane, Piscataway, NJ 08854, USA

Shatner, William *Actor*
3674 Berry Ave, Studio City, CA 91604, USA

Shattuck, Mayo A, III *Financier*
%Alex Brown & Sons, 135 E Baltimore St, Baltimore, MD 21202, USA

Shaud, Grant *Actor*
8738 Appian Way, Los Angeles, CA 90046, USA

Shaud, John A *Air Force General, Association Executive*
%Air Force Aid Society, 1745 Jefferson Davis Highway, #202, Arlington, VA 22202, USA

Shaughnessy, Charles *Actor*
2215 Malcolm Ave, Los Angeles, CA 90064, USA

Shavelson, Melville *Producer, Writer*
11947 Sunshine Terrace, North Hollywood, CA 91604, USA

Shaver, Billy Joe *Singer, Songwriter*
%Praxis International, 1700 Hayes St, #302, Nashville, TN 37203, USA

S

Shapiro - Shaver

Shaver, Helen *Actress*
%Litke/Gale, 10390 Santa Monica Blvd, #300, Los Angeles, CA 90025, USA

Shaw, Artie *Jazz Clarinetist*
2127 W Palos Court, Newbury Park, CA 91320, USA

Shaw, Bernard *Commentator*
%Cable News Network, News Dept, 820 1st St NE, Washington, DC 20002, USA

Shaw, Brewster H, Jr *Astronaut*
%NASA, Johnson Space Center, 2101 NASA Rd, Houston, TX 77058, USA

Shaw, Brian *Basketball Player*
%Orlando Magic, Orlando Arena, 1 Magic Place, Orlando, FL 32801, USA

Shaw, Carolyn Hagner *Publisher*
%Social Register, 2620 "P" St NW, Washington, DC 20007, USA

Shaw, David L *Journalist*
%Los Angeles Times, Editorial Dept, Times-Mirror Square, Los Angeles, CA 90053, USA

Shaw, Fiona *Actress*
%International Creative Mgmt, 76 Oxford St, London W1N 0AX, England

Shaw, George H *Football Player*
714 NE 174th Ave, Portland, OR 97230, USA

Shaw, Kenneth A *Educator*
%Syracuse University, President's Office, Syracuse, NY 13244, USA

Shaw, Martin *Actor*
204 Belswin's Lane, Hemel, Hempstead, Herts, England

Shaw, Robert E *Businessman*
%Shaw Industries, 616 E Walnut Ave, Dalton, GA 30721, USA

Shaw, Robert J (Bob) *Baseball Player*
10 Ocean Dr, Jupiter, FL 33469, USA

Shaw, Robert L *Conductor*
%Atlanta Symphony, 1280 Peachtree St NE, Atlanta, GA 30309, USA

Shaw, Run Run *Movie Producer*
Shaw House, Lot 220 Clear Water Bay Rd, Kowloon, Hong Kong

Shaw, Scott *Photographer*
%Odessa American, Editorial Dept, 222 E 4th, Odessa, TX 79761, USA

Shaw, Stan *Actor*
%Innovative Artists, 1999 Ave of Stars, #2850, Los Angeles, CA 90067, USA

Shaw, William *Businessman*
%Volt Information Services, 1221 Ave of Americas, New York, NY 10020, USA

Shawcross of Friston, H William *Judge; Government Official, England*
Friston Pl, Sussex, I-1 Albany, Piccadilly, London W1V 9RP, England

Shawn, Wallace *Playwright, Actor*
%Rosenstone/Wender, 3 E 48th St, New York, NY 10017, USA

Shaye, Robert *Movie Executive*
%New Line Cinema, 578 8th Ave, New York, NY 10018, USA

Shea, Jack *Speed Skater*
28 Forest St, Lake Placid, NY 12946, USA

Shea, John *Actor*
1495 Orlando Rd, Pasadena, CA 91106, USA

Shea, John J *Businessman*
%Spiegel Inc, 3500 Lacey Rd, Downers Grove, IL 60515, USA

Shea, Joseph F *Space Scientist*
15 Dogwood Rd, Weston, MA 02193, USA

Shea, Judith *Artist*
%Barbara Krakow Gallery, 10 Newbury St, Boston, MA 02116, USA

Shea, Terry *Football Coach*
%San Jose State University, Athletic Dept, San Jose, CA 95192, USA

Shea, William J *Financier*
%Bank of Boston Corp, 100 Federal St, Boston, MA 02110, USA

Shear, Rhonda *Comedienne*
PO Box 67838, Los Angeles, CA 90067, USA

Shearer, Moira *Ballerina, Actress*
%Rogers Coleridge White, 2 Powis Mews, London W11 1JN, England

Shearing, George *Jazz Pianist, Composer*
120 Montgomery St, #2400, San Francisco, CA 94104, USA

Sheed, Wilfrid J J *Writer*
%General Delivery, Sag Harbor, NY 11963, USA

Sheedy, Ally *Actress*
11755 Wilshire Blvd, #2270, Los Angeles, CA 90025, USA

Sheehan, Neil *Journalist*
4505 Klingle St NW, Washington, DC 20016, USA

Sheehan, Patty *Golfer*
%RLG ProImage, PO Box 11675, Reno, NV 89510, USA

Sheehan, Susan *Writer*
4505 Klingle St NW, Washington, DC 20016, USA

Sheehy, Gail H *Writer*
300 E 57th St, #18-D, New York, NY 10022, USA

Sheen, Martin *Actor*
6916 Dune Dr, Malibu, CA 90265, USA

Sheene, Barry *Motorcycle Racing Rider*
83 Clouchester Place, London W1, England

Sheffield, Gary A *Baseball Player*
6731 30th St S, St Petersburg, FL 33712, USA

Sheffield, John M *Actor*
834 1st Ave, Chula Vista, CA 91911, USA

Sheffield, William *Governor, AK*
PO Box 91476, Anchorage, AK 99509, USA

Sheh, Robert B *Businessman*
%International Technology Corp, 23456 Hawthorne Blvd, Torrance, CA 90505, USA

Sheikh Humaid Bin Rashid Al-Nuami *Ruler, Ajman*
%Royal Palace, Ajman, United Arab Emirates

Sheikh Martoum Bin Rashid Al-Maktoum *Ruler, Dubai*
%Royal Palace, Dubai, United Arab Emirates

Sheikh Rashid Bin Ahmed Al-Mu'alla *Ruler, Umm Al Quwain*
%Ruler's Palace, Umm Al Quwain, United Arab Emirates

Sheikh Saqr Bin Muhammad al-Qasimi *Ruler, Ras Al Khaimah*
%Ruler's Palace, Ras Al Khaimah, United Arab Emirates

Sheikh Sultan Bin Muhammad Al-Qasimi *Ruler, Sharjah*
%Royal Palace, Sharjah, United Arab Emirates

Sheikh Zayed Bin Slutan Al-Nahayan *President, United Arab Emirates*
%President's Office, Manhal Palace, Abu Dhabi, United Arab Emirates

Sheinberg, Sidney J *Entertainment Executive*
%MCA Inc, 100 Universal City Plaza, Universal City, CA 91608, USA

Sheiner, David S *Actor*
1827 Veteran Ave, #5, Los Angeles, CA 90025, USA

Sheinfeld, David *Composer*
1458 24th Ave, San Francisco, CA 94122, USA

Sheinkman, Jack *Labor Leader*
%Amalgamated Clothing & Textile Workers Union, 15 Union Sq, New York, NY 10003, USA

Sheinwold, Alfred *Bridge Expert, Columnist*
2625 Angelo Dr, Los Angeles, CA 90077, USA

Shelby, Carroll *Auto Racing Driver, Builder*
%Shelby Industries, 19021 S Figueroa St, Gardena, CA 90248, USA

Sheldon, Sidney *Writer*
10250 W Sunset Blvd, Los Angeles, CA 90077, USA

Shell, Art *Football Player, Coach*
13108 W 130th St, Overland Park, KS 66213, USA

Shell, Donnie *Football Player*
2945 Shandon Rd, Rock Hill, SC 29730, USA

Shelley, Carole *Actress*
333 W 56th St, New York, NY 10019, USA

Shelley, Elbert V *Football Player*
%Atlanta Falcons, 2745 Burnett Rd, Suwanee, GA 30174, USA

Shelley, Howard G *Concert Pianist, Conductor*
38 Cholmeley Park, London N6 5ER, England

Shelling, Thomas C *Economist*
%University of Maryland, Economics Dept, College Park, MD 20742, USA

Shelton, Chuck *Football Coach*
%University of Pacific, Athletic Dept, Stockton, CA 95211, USA

Shelton, Deborah *Actress*
%Levy, 1690 Coldwater Canyon Dr, Beverly Hills, CA 90210, USA

Shelton, E Kirk *Businessman*
%CUC International, 707 Summer St, Stanford, CT 06901, USA

Shelton, Henry H (Hugh) *Army General*
Commanding General, XVIII Airborne Corps, Fort Bragg, NC 28307, USA

Shelton, Lonnie *Basketball Player*
%Cleveland Cavaliers, 2923 Statesboro Rd, Richfield, OH 44286, USA

Shelton, Ricky Van *Singer, Songwriter*
Rt 12, PO Box 95, Lebanon, TN 37090, USA

Shelton, Robert M *Religious Leader*
%Cumberland Presbyterian Church, 1978 Union Ave, Memphis, TN 38104, USA

Shelton, Ronald W *Movie Director*
%Sanford/Skouras, 1015 Gayley Ave, Los Angeles, CA 90024, USA

Shelton, William E *Educator*
%Eastern Michigan University, President's Office, Ypsilanti, MI 48197, USA

Shenkarow, Barry L *Hockey Executive*
%Winnipeg Jets, Arena, 15-1430 Maroons Rd, Winnipeg MB R3G 0L5, Canada

Shepard, Alan B, Jr *Astronaut; Navy Admiral*
1512 Bonifacio Lane, Pebble Beach, CA 93953, USA

Shepard, Donald J *Financier*
%AEGON USA, 1111 N Charles St, Baltimore, MD 21201, USA

Shepard, Jean *Singer*
%AcoustiWorks, 802 18th Ave S, Nashville, TN 37203, USA

Shepard, Robert N *Psychologist*
%Stanford University, Psychology Dept, Stanford, CA 94305, USA

Shepard, Sam *Actor, Writer*
%Lois Berman, 21 W 26th St, New York, NY 10010, USA

Shephard, Stephen B *Editor*
%Business Week Magazine, 1221 Ave of Americas, New York, NY 10020, USA

Shepheard, Peter F *Architect*
21 Well Rd, London NW3 1LH, England

Shepherd, Cybill *Model, Actress*
16037 Royal Oak Rd, Encino, CA 91436, USA

Shepherd, Donald R *Financier*
%Loomis Sayles Co, 1 Financial Center, Boston, MA 02111, USA

Shepherd, Malcolm N *Government Official, England*
29 Kennington Palace Court, Sancroft St, London SE11, England

Shepherd, Morgan *Auto Racing Driver*
PO Box 623, Conover, NC 28613, USA

Shepherd, Sherrie *Cartoonist (Francie)*
%United Feature Syndicate, 200 Park Ave, New York, NY 10166, USA

Shepherd, William C *Businessman*
%Allergan Inc, 2525 Dupont Dr, Irvine, CA 92715, USA

Shepherd, William M *Astronaut*
12117 Ticonderoga Rd, Houston, TX 77044, USA

Sheppard, Jonathan *Steeplechase Racing Trainer*
%Ashwell Stables, 297 Lamborntown Rd, West Grove, PA 19390, USA

Sheppard, T G *Singer*
%R J Kaltenbach, 641 Lindsay Court, Dundee, IL 60118, USA

Sheps, Cecil G *Epidemiologist*
1304 Arboretum Dr, Chapel Hill, NC 27514, USA

Sher, Antony *Actor*
%Hope & Lyne, 108 Leonard St, London EC2A 4RH, England

Shera, Mark *Actor*
329 N Wetherly Dr, #101, Beverly Hills, CA 90211, USA

Sheridan, Bonnie Bramlett *Singer (Delaney & Bonnie), Actress*
18011 Martha St, Encino, CA 91316, USA

Sheridan, Jamey *Actor*
%Sames/Rollnick Assoc, 250 W 57th St, New York, NY 10107, USA

Sheridan, Jim *Movie Director*
%Creative Artists Agency, 9830 Wilshire Blvd, Beverly Hills, CA 90212, USA

Sheridan, Nicolette *Actress*
%Creative Artists Agency, 9830 Wilshire Blvd, Beverly Hills, CA 90212, USA

Sherimkulov, Medetkan *Supreme Soviet Chairman, Kryrgystan*
%Supreme Soviet, Uluk Kenesh, Bishkek, Kyrgystan

Sherlock, Nancy J *Astronaut*
%NASA, Johnson Space Center, 2101 NASA Rd, Houston, TX 77058, USA

Sherman, Bobby *Singer*
1870 Sunset Plaza Dr, Los Angeles, CA 90069, USA

Sherman, Cindy *Photographer*
%Metro Pictures, 150 Greene St, New York, NY 10012, USA

Sherman, George M *Businessman*
%Danaher Corp, 1250 24th St NW, Washington, DC 20037, USA

Sherman, Paddy *Publisher*
%Citizen, Box 5020, Ottawa ON K2C 3M4, Canada

Sherman, Richard M *Composer, Lyricist*
808 N Crescent Dr, Beverly Hills, CA 90210, USA

Sherman, Robert B	*Songwriter, Writer*
1032 Hilldale Ave, Los Angeles, CA 90069, USA	
Sherman, Vincent	*Movie Director*
6355 Sycamore Meadows Dr, Malibu, CA 90265, USA	
Sherman, William	*Religious Leader*
%Woodmont Baptist Church, 2100 Woodmont Blvd, Nashville, TN 37215, USA	
Shernoff, William M	*Attorney*
600 S Indian Hill Blvd, Claremont, CA 91711, USA	
Sherrard, Mike	*Football Player*
%New York Giants, Giants Stadium, East Rutherford, NJ 07073, USA	
Sherrill, Jackie	*Football Coach*
%Mississippi State University, Athletic Dept, Mississippi State, MS 39762, USA	
Sherrod, Blackie	*Sportswriter*
%Dallas Morning News, Editorial Dept, Communications Center, Dallas, TX 75265, USA	
Sherry, Paul H	*Religious Leader*
%United Church of Christ, 700 Prospect Ave, Cleveland, OH 44115, USA	
Sherwood, B P, III	*Financier*
%Old Kent Financial Corp, 1 Vandenberg Center, Grand Rapids, MI 49503, USA	
Sherwood, Madeline Thornton	*Actress*
32 Leroy St, New York, NY 10014, USA	
Shesol, Jeff	*Cartoonist (Thatch)*
%Creators Syndicate, 5777 W Century Blvd, #700, Los Angeles, CA 90045, USA	
Shestakova, Tatyana B	*Actress*
%Maly Drama Theatre, Rubinstein St 18, St Petersburg, Russia	
Shettles, Landrum B	*Obstetrician, Gynecologist*
2209 Pardee Place, Las Vegas, NV 89104, USA	
Shevardnadze, Eduard A	*President, Georgia*
%President's Office, State Council, Tbilisi, Georgia	
Shevchenko, Arkady N	*Government Official, Russia*
%Alfred A Knopf Inc, 201 E 50th St, New York, NY 10022, USA	
Shi, David E	*Educator*
%Furman University, President's Office, Greenville, SC 29613, USA	
Shields, Brooke	*Model, Actress*
%Christa Inc, 2300 W Sahara Ave, #630, Las Vegas, NV 89102, USA	
Shields, Carol	*Writer*
701-237 Wellington Crescent, Winnipeg MB R3M 0A1, Canada	
Shields, Perry	*Judge*
%US Tax Court, 400 2nd St NW, Washington, DC 20217, USA	
Shields, Robert	*Mime (Shields & Yarnell)*
%Arthur Shafman International, 31 Harmony Hill Rd, Pawling, NY 12564, USA	
Shiely, John S	*Businessman*
%Briggs & Stratton, PO Box 702, Milwaukee, WI 53201, USA	
Shigeta, James	*Actor*
8917 Cynthia St, #1, Los Angeles, CA 90069, USA	
Shikler, Aaron	*Artist*
44 W 77th Ol, New York, NY 10024, USA	
Shiley Newhouse, Jean	*Track Athlete*
3189 Barry Ave, Los Angeles, CA 90066, USA	
Shilton, Peter	*Soccer Player*
%Plymouth Argyll Football Club, Plymouth, England	
Shimerman, Armin	*Actor*
4912 Carpenter Ave, Valley Village, CA 91607, USA	
Shimkus, Joanna	*Actress*
1007 Cove Way, Beverly Hills, CA 90210, USA	
Shimmerman, Armin	*Actor*
%Silver/Kass, 8730 Sunset Blvd, #480, Los Angeles, CA 90069, USA	
Shimono, Sab	*Actor*
1661 Angelus Ave, Los Angeles, CA 90026, USA	
Shindo, Sadakazu	*Businessman*
%Mitsubishi Electric Corp, 2-2-3 Marunouchi, Chiyodaku, Tokyo 100, Japan	
Shinefield, Henry R	*Pediatrician*
2705 Larkin St, San Francisco, CA 94109, USA	
Shinn, George	*Basketball Executive*
%Charlotte Hornets, 1 Hive Dr, Charlotte, NC 28217, USA	
Shipler, David K	*Journalist*
4005 Thornapple St, Bethesda, MD 20815, USA	
Shipley, Walter V	*Financier*
%Chase Manhattan Corp, 270 Park Ave, New York, NY 10017, USA	

S

Sherman - Shipley

Shipp, John Wesley *Actor*
%Gersh Agency, 232 N Canon Dr, Beverly Hills, CA 90210, USA

Shire, David L *Composer*
14820 Valley Vista Blvd, Sherman Oaks, CA 91403, USA

Shire, Talia *Actress*
%Ed Astrim, 16633 Ventura Blvd, #1450, Encino, CA 91436, USA

Shirley, George *Opera Singer*
%University of Michigan, Music School, Ann Arbor, MI 48109, USA

Shirley, J Dallas *Basketball Referee*
5324 Pommel Dr, Mount Airy, MD 21771, USA

Shirley-Quirk, John *Opera Singer*
6062 Red Clover Lane, Clarksville, MD 21029, USA

Shivley, Albert *Businessman*
%Farmland Industries, 3315 Oak Trafficway, Kansas City, MO 64116, USA

Shlaudeman, Harry W *Diplomat*
3531 Winfield Lane NW, Washington, DC 20007, USA

Shlyapina, Galina A *Ballerina*
%Bolshoi Theater, Teatralnaya Pl 1, 103009 Moscow, Russia

Shnayerson, Robert B *Editor*
118 Riverside Dr, New York, NY 10024, USA

Shobert, Bubba *Motorcycle Racing Rider*
PO Box 1726, Carmel Valley, CA 93924, USA

Shock, Ernest F *Labor Leader*
%United Steelworkers Upholstery Division, 25 N 4th St, Philadelphia, PA 19106, USA

Shocked, Michelle *Singer*
%William Morris Agency, 1325 Ave of Americas, New York, NY 10019, USA

Shockley, William *Actor*
2062 Glencoe Way, Los Angeles, CA 90068, USA

Shoecraft, John A *Balloonist*
%Shoecraft Contracting Co, 7430 E Stetson Dr, Scottsdale, AZ 85251, USA

Shoemaker, Carolyn *Geologist, Astronomer*
%Mt Palomar Observatory, Palomar Mountain, Mt Palomar, CA 92060, USA

Shoemaker, Edwin J *Businessman*
%La-Z-Boy Chair Co, 1284 N Telegraph Rd, Monroe, MI 48162, USA

Shoemaker, Eugene M *Geologist*
%Mt Palomar Observatory, Palomar Mountain, Mt Palomar, CA 92060, USA

Shoemaker, Robert M *Army General*
Rt 4, Box 4510-K, Belton, TX 76513, USA

Shoemaker, William L (Willie) *Thoroughbred Racing Jockey, Trainer*
%Vincent Andrews Mgmt, 315 S Beverly Dr #216, Beverly Hills, CA 90212, USA

Shoemate, C Richard *Businessman*
%CPC International, International Plaza, Englewood Cliffs, NJ 07632, USA

Shonekan, Ernest A O *President, Nigeria*
12 Alexander Ave, Ikoyi, Lagos, Nigeria

Shonin, Georgi S *Cosmonaut, Air Force General*
%Potchta Kosmonavtov, 141 160 Svyosdny Gorodok, Moskovskoi Oblasti, Russia

Short, Alonzo E, Jr *Army General*
Director, Information Systems Agency, 701 S Courthouse Rd, Arlington, VA 22204, USA

Short, Bobby *Singer, Actor*
444 E 57th St, #9-E, New York, NY 10022, USA

Short, Leo N, Jr *Businessman*
%Mine Safety Appliances Co, 600 Penn Center Blvd, Pittsburgh, PA 15235, USA

Short, Martin *Comedian*
%William Morris Agency, 151 S El Camino Dr, Beverly Hills, CA 90212, USA

Shorter, Frank *Marathon Runner*
%Frank Shorter Sports Wear, 89 Willowbrook Rd, #D, Boulder, CO 80301, USA

Shorter, Wayne *Jazz Saxophonist*
%AGM Mgmt, 1680 N Vine St, #1101, Los Angeles, CA 90028, USA

Shortridge, Steve *Actor*
1707 Clearview Dr, Beverly Hills, CA 90210, USA

Shortway, Richard H *Publisher*
%Vogue Magazine, 350 Madison Ave, New York, NY 10017, USA

Shostakovich, Maxim D *Conductor*
173 Black Rock Turnpike, West Redding, CT 06896, USA

Show, Grant *Actor*
937 S Tremaine Ave, Los Angeles, CA 90019, USA

Showalter, Max *Actor*
5 Gilbert Hill Rd, Chester, CT 06412, USA

Showalter, William N (Buck), III 7501 Jefferson Ave, Century, FL 32535, USA	*Baseball Manager*
Shower, Kathy 300 W Lakeview Ave, Madison, WI 53716, USA	*Model, Actress*
Showfety, Robert E %Federal Home Loan Bank, 1475 Peachtree St NE, Atlanta, GA 30309, USA	*Financier*
Shreve, Susan R 3319 Newark St NW, Washington DC 20008, USA	*Author*
Shrimpton, Jean Abbey Hotel, Penzance, Cornwall, England	*Model, Actress*
Shriner, Kin 3915 Benedict Canyon Dr, Sherman Oaks, CA 91423, USA	*Actor*
Shriner, Wil 5313 Quakertown Ave, Woodland Hills, CA 91364, USA	*Entertainer*
Shriver, Donald W, Jr %Union Theological Seminary, President's Office, New York, NY 10027, USA	*Educator*
Shriver, Duward F 1100 Colfax St, Evanston, IL 60201, USA	*Chemist*
Shriver, Eunice Kennedy %Joseph P Kennedy Foundation, 1350 New York Ave, #500, Washington, DC 20005, USA	*Association Executive*
Shriver, Loren J %Space Transportation Systems Operation, Kennedy Space Center, FL 32899, USA	*Astronaut*
Shriver, Maria 3110 Main St, #300, Santa Monica, CA 90405, USA	*Commentator*
Shriver, Pamela H (Pam) %PHS Ltd, 2324 W Joppa Rd, #650, Timonium, MD 21093, USA	*Tennis Player*
Shriver, R Sargent, Jr %Fried Frank Harris Shriver Assoc, 1350 New Hampshire NW, Washington, DC 20036, USA	*Government Official*
Shrontz, Frank A %Boeing Co, 7755 E Marginal Way S, Seattle, WA 98108, USA	*Businessman*
Shtokolov, Boris T %Mariinsky Theater, Teatralnaya Pl 1, St Petersburg, Russia	*Opera Singer*
Shuart, James M %Hofstra University, President's Office, Hempstead, NY 11550, USA	*Educator*
Shubin, Neil H %Harvard University, Biology Dept, Cambridge, MA 02138, USA	*Biologist*
Shuck, Robert F %Raymond James Financial, 880 Carillon Parkway, St Petersburg, FL 33716, USA	*Financier*
Shudlick, Carol Ann %University of Minnesota, Athletic Dept, Minneapolis, MN 55455, USA	*Basketball Player*
Shue, Andrew %United Talent Agency, 9560 Wilshire Blvd, #500, Beverly Hills, CA 90212, USA	*Actor*
Shue, Elisabeth RR 1, PO Box 820, Brooks, ME 04921, USA	*Actress*
Shue, Gene %Philadelphia 76ers, Veterans Stadium, PO Box 25040, Philadelphia, PA 19147, USA	*Basketball Coach, Executive*
Shuey, John J %Amcast International Corp, 7887 Washington Village Dr, Dayton, OH 45459, USA	*Businessman*
Shugart, Alan F %Seagate Technologies, 920 Disc Dr, Scotts Valley, CA 95066, USA	*Inventor (Computer Disc Drive)*
Shukovsky, Joel %Shukovsky-English Ent, 4024 Radford Ave, Studio City, CA 91604, USA	*Screenwriter*
Shula, David D %Cincinnati Bengals, 200 Riverfront Stadium, Cincinnati, OH 45202, USA	*Football Coach*
Shula, Don F 16 Indian Creek Island, Miami, FL 33154, USA	*Football Coach*
Shuler, Ellie G, Jr 32 Willow Way W, Alexander City, AL 35010, USA	*Air Force General*
Shuler, Heath %Washington Redskins, 21300 Redskin Park Dr, Ashburn, VA 22011, USA	*Football Player*
Shuler, Mickey %New York Jets, 1000 Fulton Ave, Hempstead, NY 11550, USA	*Football Player*
Shull, Clifford G 4 Wingate Rd, Lexington, MA 02173, USA	*Nobel Physics Laureate*
Shull, Harrison %Naval Postgraduate School, Provost's Office, Code 01, Monterey, CA 93943, USA	*Educator, Chemist*
Shull, Richard B %Cheerieerie Ltd, 130 W 42nd St, #2400, New York, NY 10036, USA	*Actor*

S

Showalter - Shull

Shulman, Earl N *Financier*
%Seafirst Corp, 701 5th Ave, Seattle, WA 98104, USA

Shulman, Lawrence E *Biomedical Researcher*
6302 Swords Way, Bethesda, MD 20817, USA

Shulman, Marshall *Political Scientist*
450 Riverside Dr, New York, NY 10027, USA

Shulman, Robert G *Biophysicist*
333 Cedar St, New Haven, CT 06510, USA

Shultz, George P *Secretary, Treasury & Labor*
776 Dolores St, Stanford, CA 94305, USA

Shumejda, John M *Businessman*
%AGCO Corp, 4830 River Green Parkway, Duluth, GA 30136, USA

Shumsky, Oscar *Concert Violinist*
%Maxim Gershunoff Attractions, 502 Park Ave, New York, NY 10022, USA

Shumway, Norman E *Heart Surgeon*
%Stanford University Medical Center, 300 Pasteur Dr, Stanford, CA 94304, USA

Shyer, Charles R *Television Writer, Director*
4040 Stansburg Ave, Sherman Oaks, CA 91423, USA

Siart, William E B *Financier*
%First Interstate Bancorp, 633 W 5th St, Los Angeles, CA 90071, USA

Sias, John B *Publisher*
%Chronicle Publishing Co, 901 Mission St, San Francisco, CA'94103

Sibbett, Jane *Actress*
2144 Nichols Canyon Rd, Los Angeles, CA 90046, USA

Sibley, Antoinette *Ballerina*
%Royal Ballet, Bow St, London WC2E 9DD, England

Sichting, Jerry *Basketball Player, Executive*
%Minnesota Timberwolves, Target Center, 600 1st Ave N, Minneapolis, MN 55403, USA

Sidell, James V *Financier*
%UST Corp, 40 Court St, Boston, MA 02108, USA

Sidenbladh, Goran *Architect*
Narvagen 23, 114 60 Stockholm, Sweden

Sider, Harvey R *Religious Leader*
%Brethren in Christ Church, PO Box 290, Grantham, PA 17027, USA

Sidey, Hugh S *Journalist*
%Time Inc, Editorial Dept, 1050 Connecticut Ave NW, Washington, DC 20036, USA

Sidhu, Jay S *Financier*
%Soverign Bancorp, 1130 Berkshire Blvd, Wyomissing, PA 19610, USA

Sidi Mohammed *Crown Prince, Morocco*
%Royal Palace, Rabat, Morocco

Sidlik, Thomas W *Financier*
%Chrysler Financial Corp, 27777 Franklin Rd, Southfield, MI 48034, USA

Sidney, George *Movie Director*
910 N Rexford Dr, Beverly Hills, CA 90210, USA

Sidney, Sylvia *Actress*
%Century Artists, 9744 Wilshire Blvd, #308, Beverly Hills, CA 90212, USA

Sidorkiewicz, Peter *Hockey Player*
%Ottawa Senators, 301 Moodie Dr, #200, Nepean ON K2H 9C4, Canada

Siebert, Wilfred C (Sonny) *Baseball Player*
2555 Brush Creek, St Louis, MO 63129, USA

Sieff, Jean Loup *Photographer*
87 Rue Ampere, 75017 Paris, France

Siegbahn, Kai M B *Nobel Physics Laureate*
%University of Uppsala, Physics Institute, Uppsala, Sweden

Siegel, Bernie S *Surgeon, Writer*
61 Oxbow Lane, Woodbridge, CT 06525, USA

Siegel, Herbert J *Businessman*
%Chris-Craft Industries, 767 5th Ave, New York, NY 10153, USA

Siegel, Ira T *Publisher*
%Reed Reference Publishers, 121 Chanlon Rd, New Providence, NJ 07974, USA

Siegel, Janis *Singer (Manhattan Transfer)*
%AVNET, 3815 W Olive Ave, Burbank, CA 91505, USA

Siegel, L Pendleton *Businessman*
%Potlatch Corp, 1 Maritime Plaza, San Francisco, CA 94111, USA

Siegel, Milton P *Government Official*
2833 Sackett, Houston, TX 77098, USA

Siegel, Robert C *Commentator*
%National Public Radio, News Dept, 2025 "M" St NW, Washington, DC 20036, USA

Siegel, Robert C *Businessman*
%Stride Rite Corp, 5 Cambridge Center, Cambridge, MA 02142, USA

Siegel, Samuel *Businessman*
%Nucor Corp, 2100 Rexford Rd, Charlotte, NC 28211, USA

Siegfried (Fischbacher) *Animal Illusionist (Siegfried & Roy)*
%Beyond Belief, 1639 N Valley Dr, Las Vegas, NV 89108, USA

Siekevitz, Philip *Cell Biologist*
290 West End Ave, New York, NY 10023, USA

Siemon, Jeffrey G (Jeff) *Football Player*
5401 Londonderry, Edina, MN 55436, USA

Siepi, Cesare *Opera Singer*
12095 Brookfield Club Dr, Roswell, GA 30075, USA

Sierens, Gayle *Sportscaster*
%NBC-TV, Sports Dept, 30 Rockefeller Plaza, New York, NY 10112, USA

Sierra, Ruben A *Baseball Player*
%New York Yankees, Yankee Stadium, 161st St & River Ave, Bronx, NY 10451, USA

Siers, Kevin *Editorial Cartoonist*
%Charlotte Observer, Editorial Dept, 600 S Tryon St, Charlotte, NC 28202, USA

Sievers, Roy E *Baseball Player*
11505 Bellefontaine Rd, Spanish Lake, MO 63138, USA

Sieverts, Thomas C W *Architect*
Buschstr 20, 53113 Bonn, Germany

Sifford, Charlie *Golfer*
%Professional Golfer's Assn, PO Box 109601, Palm Beach Gardens, FL 33410, USA

Sigler, Andrew C *Businessman*
%Champion International Corp, 1 Champion Plaza, Stamford, CT 06921, USA

Sigman, Carl *Songwriter*
1036 NE 203rd Lane, North Miami Beach, FL 33179, USA

Sigwart, Ulrich *Heart Surgeon*
%Centre Hospitalier Universitaire Vaudois, Lausanne, Switzerland

Siilasvuo, Ensio *Army General, Finland*
Castrenikatu 6-A-17, 00530 Helsinki 53, Finland

Sikahema, Val *Football Player*
%Green Bay Packers, 1265 Lombardi Ave, Green Bay, WI 54304, USA

Sikes, Alfred C *Government Official*
%Hearst New Media/Technology Group, 959 8th Ave, New York, NY 10019, USA

Sikes, Cynthia *Actress*
250 N Delfern Dr, Los Angeles, CA 90077, USA

Sikking, James B *Actor*
258 S Carmelina Ave, Los Angeles, CA 90049, USA

Silas, Paul *Basketball Player, Coach*
%Phoenix Suns, 201 E Jefferson St, Phoenix, AZ 85004, USA

Silber, John R *Educator*
132 Carlton St, Brookline, MA 02146, USA

Silberman, Charles E *Writer*
535 E 86th St, New York, NY 10028, USA

Silberman, Laurence H *Judge*
%US Court of Appeals, 3rd & Constitution Ave NW, Washington, DC 20001, USA

Silberstein, Diane Wichard *Publisher*
%New Yorker Magazine, 20 W 43rd St, New York, NY 10036, USA

Silja, Anja *Opera Singer*
%Severence Hall, Cleveland, OH 44106, USA

Silk, George *Photographer*
Owenoke Park, Westport, CT 06880, USA

Silliphant, Stirling D *Movie Writer, Producer*
PO Box 351119, Los Angeles, CA 90035, USA

Sillitoe, Alan *Writer*
%Savage Club, 1 Whitehall Place, London SW1 2HD, England

Sills, Beverly *Opera Singer, Director*
Rural Farm Delivery, Lambert's Cove Rd, Vinegard Haven, MA 02568, USA

Sills, Lawrence I *Businessman*
%Standard Motor Products Inc, 37-18 Northern Blvd, Long Island City, NY 11101, USA

Sills, Nathaniel I *Businessman*
%Standard Motor Products Inc, 37-18 Northern Blvd, Long Island City, NY 11101, USA

Silva Henriquez, Raul Cardinal *Religious Leader*
Palacio Arzobispal, Casilla 30-D, Santiago, Chile

Silva, Henry *Actor*
5226 Beckford Ave, Tarzana, CA 91356, USA

..va, Jackie   *Volleyball Player*
%Marcia Esposito, PO Box 931416, Los Angeles, CA 90093, USA

Silver, Edward J   *Religious Leader*
%Bible Way Church, 5118 Clarendon Rd, Brooklyn, NY 11203, USA

Silver, Horace   *Jazz Pianist, Composer*
%Shore Fire Media, 193 Joralemon St, Brooklyn, NY 11201, USA

Silver, Joan Micklin   *Movie Director*
%Silverfilm Productions, 477 Madison Ave, New York, NY 10022, USA

Silver, Joel   *Movie Producer*
%Silver Pictures, 4000 Warner Blvd, Burbank, CA 91522, USA

Silver, Robert S   *Mechanical Engineer*
Oakbank, Breadalbane St, Tobermory, Isle of Mull, Scotland

Silver, Ron   *Actor*
6116 Tyndall Ave, Riverside, NY 10471, USA

Silver, William R   *Financier*
%Citicorp Bankers Leasing Corp, 2655 Campus Dr, San Mateo, CA 94403, USA

Silverman, Al   *Publisher*
%Book-of-the-Month Club Inc, Rockefeller Center, New York, NY 10020, USA

Silverman, Howard   *Financier*
%Gruntal Co, 14 Wall St, New York, NY 10005, USA

Silverman, Jeffrey S   *Businessman*
%Ply Gem Industries, 777 3rd Ave, New York, NY 10017, USA

Silverman, Jonathan   *Actor*
854 Birchwood Dr, Los Angeles, CA 90024, USA

Silverman, Syd   *Publisher*
%Variety, 154 W 46th St, New York, NY 10036, USA

Silvers, Robert J   *Publisher*
%Saturday Evening Post Magazine, 1100 Waterway Blvd, Indianapolis, IN 46202, USA

Silverstein, Abe   *Aeronautical Engineer*
21160 Seabury Ave, Fairview Park, OH 44126, USA

Silverstein, Elliott   *Movie Director*
%Gersh Agency, 232 N Canon Dr, Beverly Hills, CA 90210, USA

Silverstein, Joseph H   *Conductor*
%Utah Symphony Orchestra, 123 W South Temple, Salt Lake City, UT 84101, USA

Silverstein, Shel   *Cartoonist*
%Harper & Row Publishers, 10 E 53rd St, New York, NY 10022, USA

Silvia   *Queen, Sweden*
Kungliga Slottet, Stottsbacken, 111 30 Stockholm, Sweden

Silvia, Charles   *Swimming Contributor*
1974 Allen St, Springfield, MA 01118, USA

Simanek, Robert E   *Korean War Marine Corps Hero (CMH)*
25194 Westmoreland Dr, Farmington Hills, MI 48336, USA

Sime, David W   *Track Athlete, Physician*
240 Harbor Dr, Key Biscayne, FL 33149, USA

Simeon II   *King, Bulgaria*
Apartado de Correos 3135, 28080 Madrid, Spain

Simeoni, Sara   *Track Athlete*
Via Castello Rivoli Veronese, 37010 Verona, Italy

Simes, Dimitri K   *Political Scientist*
4430 Vacation Lane, Arlington, VA 22207, USA

Simic, Charles   *Poet*
PO Box 192, Strafford, NH 03884, USA

Simmonds, Kennedy A   *Prime Minister, St Kitts & Nevis*
%Prime Minister's Office, PO Box 196, Basseterre, St Kitts & Nevis

Simmons, Adele S   *Educator, Foundation Executive*
%Catherine T MacArthur Foundation, 140 S Dearborn St, Chicago, IL 60603, USA

Simmons, Clyde   *Football Player*
%Arizona Cardinals, 8701 S Hardy Dr, Tempe, AZ 85284, USA

Simmons, Gene   *Singer, Bassist (Kiss)*
%Ben Wages Agency, 5524 Claresholm St, Gautier, MS 39553, USA

Simmons, Glenn R   *Businessman*
%Valhi Inc, 3 Lincoln Center, 5430 LBJ Freeway, Dallas, TX 75240, USA

Simmons, Harold C   *Businessman*
%Valhi Inc, 3 Lincoln Center, 5430 LBJ Freeway, Dallas, TX 75240, USA

Simmons, Harris H   *Financier*
%1380 Kennecott Building, Salt Lake City, UT 84133, USA

Simmons, Jean   *Actress*
636 Adelaide Place, Santa Monica, CA 90402, USA

Silva - Simmons

Simmons, Joseph — *Rapper (Run-DMC)*
%Rush Artists Mgmt, 1600 Varick St, New York, NY 10013, USA

Simmons, Lionel — *Basketball Player*
%Sacramento Kings, 1 Sports Parkway, Sacramento, CA 95834, USA

Simmons, Richard — *Physical Fitness Instructor*
PO Box 5403, Beverly Hills, CA 90209, USA

Simmons, Richard D — *Publisher*
%International Herald Tribune, 181 Ave C de Gaulle, 92521 Neuilly, France

Simmons, Richard P — *Businessman*
%Allegheny Ludlum Corp, 1000 6 PPG Place, Pittsburgh, PA 15222, USA

Simmons, Roy W — *Financier*
%Zions Bancorp, 1380 Kennecott Building, Salt Lake City, UT 84133, USA

Simmons, Ted L — *Baseball Player*
PO Box 26, Chesterfield, MO 63006, USA

Simms, Kimberly — *Actress*
%Tobias Skouras Assoc, 1015 Gayley Ave, #300, Los Angeles, CA 90024, USA

Simms, Larry — *Actor*
PO Box 55, Grays River, WA 98621, USA

Simms, Phillip (Phil) — *Football Player, Sportscaster*
%David Fishof Productions, 252 W 71st St, New York, NY 10023, USA

Simms, Primate George Otto — *Religious Leader*
62 Cypress Grove Rd, Dublin 6, Ireland

Simon, Bob — *Commentator*
%CBS-TV, News Dept, 2020 "M" St NW, Washington, DC 20036, USA

Simon, Carly — *Singer, Songwriter*
135 Central Park W, #6-S, New York, NY 10023, USA

Simon, Claude — *Nobel Literature Laureate*
Place Vieille, Salses, 66600 Rivesaltes, France

Simon, George W — *Astronaut*
2308 Rancho Lane, Alamogordo, NM 88310, USA

Simon, Herbert A — *Nobel Economics Laureate*
%Carnegie-Mellon University, Psychology Dept, Pittsburgh, PA 15260, USA

Simon, John I — *Movie, Drama Critic*
%New York Magazine, Editorial Dept, 755 2nd Ave, New York, NY 10017, USA

Simon, Leonard S — *Financier*
%Rochester Community Savings Bank, 40 Franklin St, Rochester, NY 14604, USA

Simon, Neil — *Playwright*
10745 Chalon Rd, Los Angeles, CA 90077, USA

Simon, Paul — *Singer, Songwriter*
1619 Broadway, #500, New York, NY 10019, USA

Simon, Peter — *Actor*
%"Guiding Light" Show, CBS-TV, 222 E 44th St, New York, NY 10017, USA

Simon, Roger M — *Columnist*
%Baltimore Sun, 1627 "K" St NW, Washington, DC 20006, USA

Simon, Scott — *Commentator*
%NBC-TV, News Dept, 30 Rockefeller Plaza, New York, NY 10112, USA

Simon, Simone — *Actress*
5 Rue De Tilsitt, 75008 Paris, France

Simon, William E — *Secretary, Treasury*
Nomis Hill, Sandspring Rd, New Vernon, NJ 07976, USA

Simone, Albert J — *Educator*
%Rochester Institute of Technology, President's Office, Rochester, NY 14623, USA

Simone, Nina — *Singer, Songwriter*
7250 Franklin Ave, #115, Los Angeles, CA 90046, USA

Simonini, Edward (Ed) — *Football Player*
7471 S Marion Ave, Tulsa, OK 74136, USA

Simonis, Adrianus J Cardinal — *Religious Leader*
Aartsbisdom, BP 14019, Maliebaan, 3508 SB Utrecht, Netherlands

Simonon, Paul — *Bassist (Clash)*
%Clash, 268 Camden Rd, London NW1, England

Simonov, Yuriy I — *Conductor*
%Moscow Conservatory, Gertsema St 13, Moscow, Russia

Simons, Elwyn L — *Anthropologist*
%Duke University, Primate Center, 3705 Erwin Rd, Durham, NC 27705, USA

Simons, Lawrence B — *Government Official*
%Powell Goldstein Frazier, 1001 Pennsylvania Ave NW, Washington, DC 20004, USA

Simonsen, Renee — *Model*
%Ford Model Agency, 344 E 59th St, New York, NY 10022, USA

S

Simpkins, Ronald B (Ron) — *Football Player*
%Commitment to Character, PO Box 157151, Cincinnati, OH 45215, USA

Simplot, John R — *Businessman*
%J R Simplot Co, 1 Capital Center, Boise, ID 83707, USA

Simpson Stern, Carol — *Labor Leader*
%American Assn of University Professors, 1012 14th St NW, Washington, DC 20005, USA

Simpson, Charles R — *Judge*
%US Tax Court, 400 2nd St NW, Washington, DC 20217, USA

Simpson, Don — *Movie Producer*
685 Stone Canyon Rd, Los Angeles, CA 90077, USA

Simpson, John R — *Law Enforcement Official*
%US Secret Service, 1800 "G" St NW, Washington, DC 20223, USA

Simpson, Louis A — *Businessman*
%Geico Corp, 1 Geico Plaza, 5260 Western Ave NW, Washington, DC 20076, USA

Simpson, Louis A M — *Writer*
186 Old Field Rd, Setauket, NY 11733, USA

Simpson, Michael — *Businessman*
%A M Castle Co, 3400 N Wolf Rd, Franklin Park, IL 60131, USA

Simpson, O J — *Football Player, Actor, Sportscaster*
360 N Rockingham Ave, Los Angeles, CA 90049, USA

Simpson, Ralph — *Basketball Player*
%Metropolitan State College, Athletic Dept, Denver, CO 80204, USA

Simpson, Scott — *Golfer*
%Cornerstone Sports, 2515 McKinney, #940, Dallas, TX 75201, USA

Simpson, Terry — *Hockey Coach*
%Winnipeg Jets, Arena, 15-1430 Maroons Rd, Winnipeg MB R3G 0L5, Canada

Simpson, Tim — *Golfer*
%Jack P Simpson, 3031 Mornington Dr NW, Atlanta, GA 30327, USA

Simpson, Valerie — *Singer (Ashford & Simpson)*
%Hopsack & Silk Productions, 254 W 72nd St, #1-A, New York, NY 10023, USA

Simpson, Wayne K — *Baseball Player*
330 Collamer Dr, Carson, CA 90746, USA

Simpson, William A — *Businessman*
%USLIFE Corp, 125 Maiden Lane, New York, NY 10038, USA

Sims, J Richard — *Businessman*
%Woodmen of World Life Insurance Society, 1700 Farnam St, Omaha, NE 68102, USA

Sims, Joan — *Actress, Comedienne*
17 Esmond Court, Thackery St, London W8, England

Sims, Keith — *Football Player*
%Miami Dolphins, 7500 SW 30th St, Davie, FL 33329, USA

Sin, Jaime L Cardinal — *Religious Leader*
121 Arzobispo St, Entramuros, PO Box 132, Manila, Philippines

Sinatra, Frank — *Actor, Singer*
1729 E Palm Canyon Dr, #226, Palm Springs, CA 92264, USA

Sinatra, Frank, Jr — *Singer*
2211 Florian Place, Beverly Hills, CA 90210, USA

Sinatra, Nancy — *Singer*
PO Box 69453, Los Angeles, CA 90069, USA

SinBad (Atkins) — *Actor*
21704 Devonshire St, #13, Chatsworth, CA 91311, USA

Sinclair, Clive M — *Businessman, Inventor*
18 Shepherd House, 5 Shepherd St, London W1Y 7LD, England

Sinclair, Madge — *Actress*
566 Tamarac Dr, Pasadena, CA 91105, USA

Sindelar, Joey — *Golfer*
213 Prospect Hill Rd, Horseheads, NY 14845, USA

Sinden, Donald — *Actor*
Rats Castle, Isle of Oxney, Kent, England

Sinden, Harry — *Hockey Player, Executive*
%Boston Bruins, Boston Garden, 150 Causeway St, Boston, MA 02114, USA

Sinden, Jeremy — *Actor*
%International Creative Mgmt, 76 Oxford St, London W1N 0AX, England

Sindermann, Horst — *President, East Germany*
Volkskammer, Berlin, Germany

Sinfelt, John H — *Chemist*
%Exxon Research & Engineering, Clinton Township, Rt 22-E, Annandale, NJ 08801, USA

Singer, Isadore M — *Mathematician*
%Massachusetts Institute of Technology, Mathematics Dept, Cambridge, MA 02139, USA

Simpkins - Singer

Singer, Lori   *Actress*
%Creative Artists Agency, 9830 Wilshire Blvd, Beverly Hills, CA 90212, USA

Singer, Marc   *Actor*
11218 Canton Dr, Studio City, CA 91604, USA

Singer, Maxine F   *Biochemist*
5410 39th St NW, Washington, DC 20015, USA

Singer, Peter A D   *Philosopher*
%Monash University, Human Bioethics Center, Clayton Vic 3168, Australia

Singer, Robert W   *Businessman*
%Keystone Consolidated Industries, 5430 LBJ Freeway, Dallas, TX 75240, USA

Singer, S Fred   *Geophysicist*
4084 University Dr, #101, Fairfax, VA 22030, USA

Singer, William R (Bill)   *Baseball Player*
4572 Arrowhead Dr SE, Decatur, AL 35603, USA

Singh, Bipin   *Dancer, Choreographer*
%Manipuri Nartanalaya, 15-A Bipin Pal Rd, Calcutta 700026, India

Singh, Dinesh   *Government Official, India*
Raj Bhawan, PO Kalakankar UP 230203, India

Singh, Sukhmander   *Civil Engineer*
%Santa Clara University, Civil Engineering Dept, Santa Clara, CA 95053, USA

Singh, Vishwanath Pratap   *Prime Minister, India*
4 Askok Rd, Allahabad, India

Singletary, Michael (Mike)   *Football Player*
%Chicago Bears, Halas Hall, 250 N Washington Rd, Lake Forest, IL 60045, USA

Singleton, Henry E   *Businessman*
%Teledyne Inc, 2049 Century Park East, Los Angeles, CA 90067, USA

Singleton, John D   *Movie Director*
4223 Don Carlos Dr, Los Angeles, CA 90008, USA

Singleton, Kenneth W (Kenny)   *Baseball Player*
5 Tremblant Court, Lutherville, MD 21093, USA

Singleton, Penny   *Actress*
13419 Riverside Dr, #C, Sherman Oaks, CA 91423, USA

Singleton, Philip M   *Entertainment Executive*
%AMC Entertainment, 106 W 14th St, Kansas City, MO 64105, USA

Singleton, William D   *Publisher*
%Houston Post, 4747 Southwest Freeway, Houston, TX 77027, USA

Sington, Frederick W (Fred)   *Football Player*
3548 Douglas Rd, Birmingham, AL 35213, USA

Sinise, Gary   *Actor*
PO Box 6704, Malibu, CA 90264, USA

Sinner, George A   *Governor, ND*
101 N 3rd St, Moorhead, MN 56560, USA

Sinopoli, Giuseppe   *Conductor, Composer*
%Hannelore Tschope, Feilitzschstr 1, 80802 Munich, Germany

Sinowatz, Fred   *Chancellor, Austria*
Loewelstr 18, 1010 Vienna, Austria

Sinton, Nell   *Artist*
1020 Francisco St, San Francisco, CA 94109, USA

Siodmak, Curt   *Movie Producer, Director*
Old South Fork Ranch, 43422 S Fork Dr, Three Rivers, CA 93271, USA

Siouxsie Sioux   *Singer (Siouxsie & Banshees)*
127 Aldersgate St, London EC1, England

Siphandon, Khamtay   *Prime Minister, Laos; Army General*
%Prime Minister's Office, Vientiane, Laos

Sipinen, Arto K   *Architect*
Arkkitehtitoimistro Arto Sipinen Ky, Ahertajantie 3, 02100 Espoo, Finland

Siren, Heikki   *Architect*
Tiirasaarentie 35, 00200 Helsinki, Finland

Siren, Katri A H   *Architect*
Lounaisvayla 8-A, 00200 Helsinki, Finland

Siri Singh Sahib   *Religious Leader*
%Sikh, 1649 S Robertson Blvd, Los Angeles, CA 90035, USA

Sirikit   *Queen, Thailand*
%Chritrada Villa, Bangkok, Thailand

Sisco, Joseph J   *Educator, Government Official*
2517 Massachusetts Ave NW, Washington, DC 20008, USA

Sishido, Fukushige   *Businessman*
%Fuji Electric Co, 1-1 Tanabeshinden, Kawasakiku, Kawasaki 210, Japan

S

Singer - Sishido

S

Siskel, Gene — *Movie Critic*
%Chicago Tribune, 435 N Michigan Ave, Chicago, IL 60611, USA

Sissel, George A — *Businessman*
%Ball Corp, 345 S High St, Muncie, IN 47305, USA

Sissener, Einar W — *Businessman*
%A L Pharma Inc, 1 Executive Dr, Fort Lee, NJ 07024, USA

Sisson, C H — *Writer*
Moorfield Cottage, The Hill, Langport, Somerset TA10 9PU, England

Sister Max — *Fashion Designer*
%Mount Everest Centre for Buddhist Studies, Katmandu, Nepal

Sites, James W — *Publisher*
%American Legion Magazine, 700 N Pennsylvania St, Indianapolis, IN 46204, USA

Sithole, Ndabaningi — *Political Leader, Zimbabwe*
%ZANU Party, PO Box UA 525, Harare, Zimbabwe

Sitkovetsky, Dmitri — *Concert Violinist*
%Columbia Artists Mgmt Inc, 165 W 57th St, New York, NY 10019, USA

Sitter, Carl L — *Korean War Marine Corps Hero (CMH)*
3307 Quail Hill Dr, Midlothian, VA 23112, USA

Sitter, Charles R — *Businessman*
%Exxon Corp, 225 E John W Carpenter Freeway, Irving, TX 75062, USA

Sixx, Nikki — *Bassist, Drummer (Motley Crue)*
936 Vista Ridge Lane, Westlake Village, CA 91362, USA

Sizemore, Jerald G (Jerry) — *Football Player*
1730 Whipporwill Trail, Leander, TX 78641, USA

Sizer, Theodore R — *Educator*
%Brown University, Independent Schools Coalition, Providence, RI 02912, USA

Sizova, Alla I — *Ballerina*
%Universal Ballet School, 4301 Harewood Rd NE, Washington, DC 20017, USA

Sjoberg, Patrik — *Track Athlete*
Hokegatan 17, 416 66 Goteberg, Sweden

Sjogren, Kim — *Concert Violinist*
Edlevej 10, 2900 Hellerup, Denmark

Sjoman, Vilgot — *Movie Director*
PO Box 27126, 102 52 Stockholm, Sweden

Skaggs, L S (Sam) — *Businessman*
%American Stores Co, 709 E South Temple, Salt Lake City, UT 84102, USA

Skaggs, Ricky — *Singer, Guitarist*
380 Forest Retreat, Hendersonville, TN 37075, USA

Skala, Thomas J — *Financier*
%Fleet Bank-RI, 111 Westminster St, Providence, RI 02903, USA

Skarsgard, J Stellan — *Actor*
Hogersgatan 40, 118 26 Stockholm, Sweden

Skates, Ronald L — *Businessman*
%Data General Corp, 4400 Computer Dr, Westboro, MA 01580, USA

Skeggs, Leonard T, Jr — *Biochemist*
10212 Blair Lane, Kirtland, OH 44094, USA

Skelton, Byron G — *Judge*
%US Court of Appeals, Federal Building, Temple, TX 76501, USA

Skelton, Red — *Comedian*
37801 Thompson Rd, Rancho Mirage, CA 92270, USA

Skerritt, Tom — *Actor*
335 N Maple Dr, 360, Beverly Hills, CA 90210, USA

Skibbie, Lawrence F — *Army General*
%American Defense Preparedness Assn, 1700 N Moore St, #900, Arlington, VA 22209, USA

Skibniewska, Halina — *Architect*
Wydziat Architektury Politechniki , Ul Koszykowa 55, 00-659 Warsaw, Poland

Skilling, Hugh H — *Electrical Engineer*
1981 Montecito Ave, #128, Mountain View, CA 94043, USA

Skillington, Charles R — *Financier*
%Integra Financial Corp, 4 PPG Place, Pittsburgh, PA 15222, USA

Skinner, Jonty — *Swimmer, Coach*
%University of Alabama, Athletic Dept, Tuscaloosa, AL 35487, USA

Skinner, Samuel K — *Secretary, Transportation; Businessman*
%Commonweath Edison Co, 1 First National Plaza, PO Box 767, Chicago, IL 60690, USA

Skinner, Stanley T — *Businessman*
%Pacific Gas & Electric Co, PO Box 770000, San Francisco, CA 94177, USA

Skjvorecky, Josef — *Writer*
%Erindale College, English Dept, Toronto ON M5S 1A5, Canada

Siskel - Skjvorecky

Skladany, Thomas E (Tom) *Football Player*
6666 Highland Lakes Place, Westerville, OH 43082, USA

Sklenar, Herbert A *Businessman*
%Vulcan Materials Co, 1 Metroplex Dr, Birmingham, AL 35209, USA

Skoblikova, Lydia *Speed Skater*
B Chernizovskaya St 6-2-43, Moscow, Russia

Skol, Michael *Diplomat*
3033 Cleveland Ave NW, Washington, DC 20008, USA

Skold, Per *Businessman*
%Sventskt Stal, PO Box 16344, 103 28 Stockholm, Sweden

Skolimowski, Jerzy *Movie Director*
%Film Polski, Ul Mazowiecka 6/8, 00-048 Warsaw, Poland

Skolnick, Mark H *Geneticist*
%University of Utah Medical Center, Genetics Dept, Salt Lake City, UT 84112, USA

Skoog, Folke K *Physiologist*
2820 Marshall Court, Madison, WI 53705, USA

Skopil, Otto R, Jr *Judge*
%US Court of Appeals, Pioneer Courthouse, 555 SW Yamhill St, Portland, OR 97204, USA

Skoronski, Robert F (Bob) *Football Player*
N-8597 Firelane 9, Menasha, WI 54952, USA

Skotheim, Robert A *Museum Administrator*
%Huntington Library, 1151 Oxford Rd, San Marino, CA 91108, USA

Skrebneski, Victor *Photographer*
1350 N LaSalle Dr, Chicago, IL 60610, USA

Skrowaczewski, Stanislaw *Conductor, Composer*
%Minnesota Symphony, 1111 Nicollet Mall, Minneapolis, MN 55403, USA

Skrypnyk, Metropolitan Mstyslav S *Religious Leader*
%Ukranian Orthodox Church, PO Box 445, South Bound Brook, NJ 08880, USA

Skutt, Thomas J *Businessman*
%Mutual of Omaha Co, Mutual of Omaha Plaza, Omaha, NE 68175, USA

Skye, Ione *Actress*
8794 Lookout Mountain Ave, Los Angeles, CA 90046, USA

Slade, Bernard N *Playwright*
345 N Saltair Ave, Los Angeles, CA 90049, USA

Slade, Mark *Actor*
14332 Riverside Dr, #11, Sherman Oaks, CA 91423, USA

Slade, Roy *Artist, Museum Director*
%Cranbrook Academy Art Museum, 500 Lone Pine Rd, Bloomfield Hills, MI 48304, USA

Sladkevicius, Vicentas Cardinal *Religious Leader*
R Carno 31, 234230 Kaisiadorys, Lietuva, Lithuania

Slagle, James R *Computer Scientist*
2117 W Hoyt Ave, St Paul, MN 55108, USA

Slash (Saul Hudson) *Guitarist (Guns n' Roses)*
901 Dove St, #260, Newport Beach, CA 92660, USA

Slate, Jeremy *Actor*
1801 Ave of Stars #1250, Los Angeles, CA 90067, USA

Slater, Christian *Actor*
8007 Highland Terrace, Los Angeles, CA 90046, USA

Slater, Helen *Actress*
662 N Van Ness Ave, #305, Los Angeles, CA 90004, USA

Slater, Jackie *Football Player*
%St Louis Rams, 100 N Broadway, #2100, St Louis, MO 63102, USA

Slater, Joseph E *Educator*
%John J McCloy International Center, 680 5th Ave, #900, New York, NY 10019, USA

Slatkin, Leonard E *Conductor*
%St Louis Symphony, 1824 Garden St, Belleville, IL 62221, USA

Slaton, Tony *Football Player*
%Dallas Cowboys, 1 Cowboys Parkway, Irving, TX 75063, USA

Slattery, Richard X *Actor*
PO Box 2410, Avalon, CA 90704, USA

Slattvik, Simon *Nordic Skier*
Bankgata 22, 2600 Lillehammer, Norway

Slaughter, Enos B *Baseball Player*
RR 2, Box 159, Roxboro, NC 27573, USA

Slaughter, Frank G *Writer*
PO Box 14, Ortega Station, Jacksonville, FL 32210, USA

Slaughter, John B *Educator*
%Occidental College, President's Office, Los Angeles, CA 90041, USA

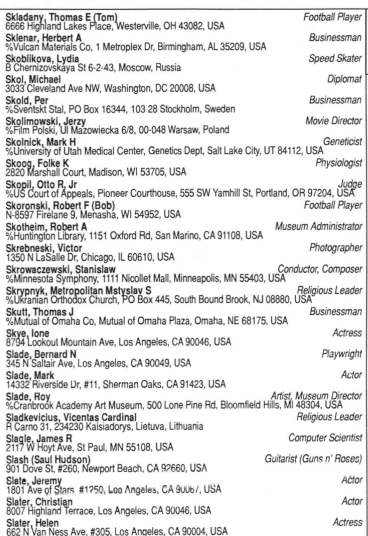

S

Skladany - Slaughter

Slaughter, Webster *Football Player*
%Kansas City Chiefs, 1 Arrowhead Dr, Kansas City, KS 64129, USA

Slavitt, David R *Author*
523 S 41st St, Philadelphia, PA 19104, USA

Slayton, Maurice W *Financier*
%Conning Corp, City Place II, 185 Asylum St, Hartford, CT 06103, USA

Sledge, Percy *Singer*
5524 Claresholm St, Gautier, MS 39553, USA

Sleep, Wayne *Dancer, Actor, Choreographer*
%London Mgmt, 2-4 Noel St, London W1V 3RB, England

Sleet, Moneta, Jr *Photographer*
%Ebony Magazine, Editorial Dept, 820 S Michigan Ave, Chicago, IL 60605, USA

Slevin, John N *Businessman*
%Comdisco Inc, 6111 N River Rd, Rosemont, IL 60018, USA

Slezak, Erika *Actress*
%International Creative Mgmt, 40 W 57th St, New York, NY 10019, USA

Slezevicius, Adolfas *Prime Minister, Lithuania*
%Prime Minister's Office, Tumo-Vaizganto 2, Vilnius, Lithuania

Slichter, Charles P *Physicist*
61 Chestnut Court, Champaign, IL 61821, USA

Slick, Grace *Singer, Songwriter*
2548 Laurel Pass, Los Angeles, CA 90046, USA

Sliwa, Curtis *Founder, Guardian Angels*
%Guardian Angels, 628 W 28th St, New York, NY 10001, USA

Sliwa, Lisa *President, Guardian Angels; Model*
%Guardian Angels, 628 W 28th St, New York, NY 10001, USA

Sloan, Gerald E (Jerry) *Basketball Player, Coach*
%Utah Jazz, 301 W South Temple, Salt Lake City, UT 84101, USA

Sloan, Norm *Basketball Coach*
%University of Florida, Athletic Dept, Gainesville, FL 32611, USA

Sloan, Robert L *Financier*
%Riggs National Corp, 808 17th St NW, Washington, DC 20006, USA

Sloan, Stephen C (Steve) *Football Coach, Administrator*
%University of Alabama, Athletic Dept, University, AL 35486, USA

Sloan, Stuart M *Businessman*
%Quality Food Centers, 10116 NE 8th St, Bellevue, WA 98004, USA

Slocum, R C *Football Coach*
%Texas A&M University, Athletic Dept, College Station, TX 77843, USA

Slonimsky, Nicolas *Composer*
2630 Midvale Ave, Los Angeles, CA 90064, USA

Slotnick, Bernard *Publisher*
%DC Comics Group, 355 Lexington Ave, New York, NY 10017, USA

Slotnick, Mortimer H *Artist*
43 Amherst Dr, Rochelle, NY 10804, USA

Slotnick, R Nathan *Surgeon*
%University of California Medical School, Prenatal Genetics, Davis, CA 95616, USA

Sloviter, Dolores Korman *Judge*
%US Court of Appeals, US Courthouse, 601 Market St, Philadelphia, PA 19106, USA

Sloyan, James *Actor*
13740 Albers St, Van Nuys, CA 91401, USA

Sluman, Jeff *Golfer*
%Professional Golfer's Assn, PO Box 109601, Palm Beach Gardens, FL 33410, USA

Slusarski, Tadeusz *Track Athlete*
Ul Atenska 2 M 154, 03-978 Warsaw, Poland

Slutsky, Lorie A *Foundation Executive*
%New York Community Trust, 2 Park Ave, New York, NY 10016, USA

Smagorinsky, Joseph *Meteorologist*
21 Duffield Place, Princeton, NJ 08540, USA

Smailes, E Jackson *Businessman*
%Hills Stores Co, 15 Dan Rd, Canton, MA 02021, USA

Smale, John G *Businessman*
%General Motors Corp, 3044 W Grand Blvd, Detroit, MI 48202, USA

Smale, Stephen *Mathematician*
68 Highgate Rd, Berkeley, CA 94707, USA

Small, Lawrence W *Financier*
%Federal National Mortgage Assn, 3900 Wisconsin Ave NW, Washington, DC 20016, USA

Small, William J *Television Executive*
%Fordham University, Business Administration Dept, New York, NY 10023, USA

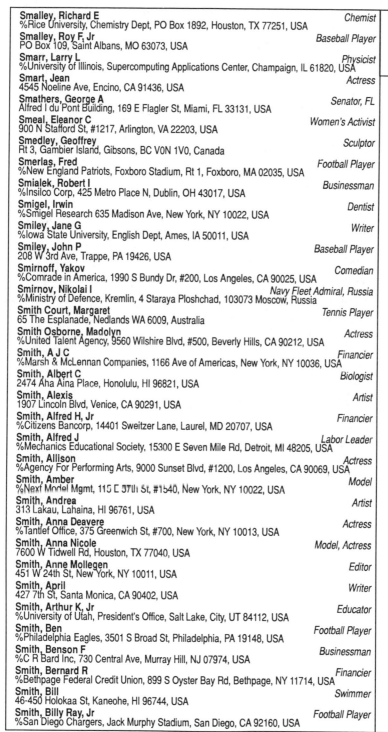

Smalley, Richard E — *Chemist*
%Rice University, Chemistry Dept, PO Box 1892, Houston, TX 77251, USA

Smalley, Roy F, Jr — *Baseball Player*
PO Box 109, Saint Albans, MO 63073, USA

Smarr, Larry L — *Physicist*
%University of Illinois, Supercomputing Applications Center, Champaign, IL 61820, USA

Smart, Jean — *Actress*
4545 Noeline Ave, Encino, CA 91436, USA

Smathers, George A — *Senator, FL*
Alfred I du Pont Building, 169 E Flagler St, Miami, FL 33131, USA

Smeal, Eleanor C — *Women's Activist*
900 N Stafford St, #1217, Arlington, VA 22203, USA

Smedley, Geoffrey — *Sculptor*
Rt 3, Gambier Island, Gibsons, BC V0N 1V0, Canada

Smerlas, Fred — *Football Player*
%New England Patriots, Foxboro Stadium, Rt 1, Foxboro, MA 02035, USA

Smialek, Robert I — *Businessman*
%Insilco Corp, 425 Metro Place N, Dublin, OH 43017, USA

Smigel, Irwin — *Dentist*
%Smigel Research 635 Madison Ave, New York, NY 10022, USA

Smiley, Jane G — *Writer*
%Iowa State University, English Dept, Ames, IA 50011, USA

Smiley, John P — *Baseball Player*
208 W 3rd Ave, Trappe, PA 19426, USA

Smirnoff, Yakov — *Comedian*
%Comrade in America, 1990 S Bundy Dr, #200, Los Angeles, CA 90025, USA

Smirnov, Nikolai I — *Navy Fleet Admiral, Russia*
%Ministry of Defence, Kremlin, 4 Staraya Ploshchad, 103073 Moscow, Russia

Smith Court, Margaret — *Tennis Player*
65 The Esplanade, Nedlands WA 6009, Australia

Smith Osborne, Madolyn — *Actress*
%United Talent Agency, 9560 Wilshire Blvd, #500, Beverly Hills, CA 90212, USA

Smith, A J C — *Financier*
%Marsh & McLennan Companies, 1166 Ave of Americas, New York, NY 10036, USA

Smith, Albert C — *Biologist*
2474 Aha Aina Place, Honolulu, HI 96821, USA

Smith, Alexis — *Artist*
1907 Lincoln Blvd, Venice, CA 90291, USA

Smith, Alfred H, Jr — *Financier*
%Citizens Bancorp, 14401 Sweitzer Lane, Laurel, MD 20707, USA

Smith, Alfred J — *Labor Leader*
%Mechanics Educational Society, 15300 E Seven Mile Rd, Detroit, MI 48205, USA

Smith, Allison — *Actress*
%Agency For Performing Arts, 9000 Sunset Blvd, #1200, Los Angeles, CA 90069, USA

Smith, Amber — *Model*
%Next Model Mgmt, 115 E 37th St, #1540, New York, NY 10022, USA

Smith, Andrea — *Artist*
313 Lakau, Lahaina, HI 96761, USA

Smith, Anna Deavere — *Actress*
%Tantlef Office, 375 Greenwich St, #700, New York, NY 10013, USA

Smith, Anna Nicole — *Model, Actress*
7600 W Tidwell Rd, Houston, TX 77040, USA

Smith, Anne Mollegen — *Editor*
451 W 24th St, New York, NY 10011, USA

Smith, April — *Writer*
427 7th St, Santa Monica, CA 90402, USA

Smith, Arthur K, Jr — *Educator*
%University of Utah, President's Office, Salt Lake, City, UT 84112, USA

Smith, Ben — *Football Player*
%Philadelphia Eagles, 3501 S Broad St, Philadelphia, PA 19148, USA

Smith, Benson F — *Businessman*
%C R Bard Inc, 730 Central Ave, Murray Hill, NJ 07974, USA

Smith, Bernard R — *Financier*
%Bethpage Federal Credit Union, 899 S Oyster Bay Rd, Bethpage, NY 11714, USA

Smith, Bill — *Swimmer*
46-450 Holokaa St, Kaneohe, HI 96744, USA

Smith, Billy Ray, Jr — *Football Player*
%San Diego Chargers, Jack Murphy Stadium, San Diego, CA 92160, USA

S

Smalley - Smith

Smith, Bruce P *Football Player*
4584 Winding Woods Lane, Hamburg, NY 14075, USA

Smith, Buffalo Bob *Actor*
500 Overlook Dr, Flat Rock, NC 28731, USA

Smith, Calvin *Track Athlete*
16703 Sheffield Park Dr, Lutz, FL 33549, USA

Smith, Carl R *Air Force General*
%Armed Forces Benefit Assn, 909 N Washington St, Alexandria, VA 22314, USA

Smith, Carleton *Foundation Executive, Art Expert*
Chalet le Stop, 1882 Gryon, Switzerland

Smith, Chad *Drummer (Red Hot Chili Peppers)*
%Lindy Goetz Mgmt, 11116 Aqua Vista, #39, Studio City, CA 91602, USA

Smith, Charles *Basketball Player*
%New York Knicks, Madison Square Garden, 4 Penn Plaza, New York, NY 10001, USA

Smith, Charles A (Bubba) *Football Player, Actor*
5178 Sunlight Place, Los Angeles, CA 90016, USA

Smith, Charles Martin *Actor*
31515 Germaine Lane, Westlake Village, CA 91361, USA

Smith, Charles Miller *Businessman*
%Imperial Chemical Industries, Millbank, London SW1P 3JF, England

Smith, Chesterfield *Attorney*
5915 Ponce de Leon Blvd, #63, Coral Gables, FL 33146, USA

Smith, Clifford V, Jr *Educator*
12 Valley View Rd, Newtown, CT 06470, USA

Smith, Connie *Singer*
%Joe Taylor Artists, 2302 Columbine Place, Nashville, TN 37204, USA

Smith, Cotter *Actor*
15332 Antioch St, #800, Pacific Palisades, CA 90272, USA

Smith, Dan F *Businessman*
%Lyondell Petrochemical Co, 1221 McKinney St, Houston, TX 77010, USA

Smith, Daniel R *Financier*
%First of American Bank Corp, 211 S Rose St, Kalmazoo, MI 49007, USA

Smith, Darwin E *Businessman*
PO Box 612547, Dallas, TX 75261, USA

Smith, Dean E *Basketball Coach*
%University of North Carolina, PO Box 2126, Chapel Hill, NC 27515, USA

Smith, Dennis *Football Player*
%Denver Broncos, 13655 E Dove Valley Parkway, Englewood, CO 80112, USA

Smith, Dennis *Businessman*
%Crawford Co, 5620 Glenridge Dr NE, Atlanta, GA 30342, USA

Smith, Dick *Diving Coach*
PO Box 304, The Woodlands, TX 77383, USA

Smith, Doug *Basketball Player*
%Dallas Mavericks, Reunion Arena, 777 Sports St, Dallas, TX 75207, USA

Smith, Edward S *Judge*
%US Court of Appeals, US Courthouse, 1729 5th Ave N, Birmingham, AL 35203, USA

Smith, Emil L *Biochemist, Biophysicist*
%University of California, Medical School, Los Angeles, CA 90024, USA

Smith, Emmitt J, III *Football Player*
%Dallas Cowboys, 1 Cowboys Parkway, Irving, TX 75063, USA

Smith, Francis G *Astronomer*
Old School House, Henbury, Macclesfield, Cheshire SK11 9PH, England

Smith, Frederick W *Businessman*
%Federal Express Corp, PO Box 727, Memphis, TN 38194, USA

Smith, Gerard *Publisher, Tennis Executive*
%World Tennis Assn, 133 1st St NE, St Petersburg, FL 33701, USA

Smith, Gerard C *Government Official*
2425 Tracy Place NW, Washington, DC 20008, USA

Smith, Godfrey Taylor (G T) *Educator*
2200 Lupine Dr, Ashland, OR 97520, USA

Smith, Gregory White *Writer*
129 1st Ave SW, Aiken, SC 29801, USA

Smith, Hamilton O *Nobel Medicine Laureate*
8222 Carrbridge Circle, Baltimore, MD 21204, USA

Smith, Harold B, Jr *Businessman*
%Illinois Tool Works, 3600 W Lake Ave, Glenview, IL 60025, USA

Smith, Harry *Commentator*
%CBS-News, 524 W 57th St, New York, NY 10019, USA

Smith, Harry — *Bowler*
%Professional Bowlers Assn, 1720 Merriman Rd, Akron, OH 44313, USA

Smith, Harry E (Blackjack) — *Football Player*
805 Leawood Terrace, Columbia, MO 65203, USA

Smith, Hedrick L — *Journalist*
4204 Rosemary St, Chevy Chase, MD 20815, USA

Smith, Henry N — *Educator*
2550 Dana St, #9-D, Berkeley, CA 94704, USA

Smith, Hoke L — *Educator*
%Towson State University, President's Office, Towson, MD 21204, USA

Smith, Howard G — *Publisher*
%Newsweek Magazine, 444 Madison Ave, New York, NY 10022, USA

Smith, Howard K — *Commentator*
6450 Brooks Lane, Washington, DC 20016, USA

Smith, Hulett C — *Governor, WV*
2105 Harper Rd, Beckley, WV 25801, USA

Smith, Ian D — *Prime Minister, Rhodesia*
Gwenoro Farm, Selukwe, Zimbabwe

Smith, J Albert, Jr — *Financier*
%Bank One Indianapolis, 111 Monument Circle, Indianapolis, IN 46204, USA

Smith, Jack C — *Journalist, Author*
4251 Camino Real, Los Angeles, CA 90065, USA

Smith, Jaclyn — *Actress*
10398 Sunset Blvd, Los Angeles, CA 90077, USA

Smith, James (Bonecrusher) — *Boxer*
PO Box 1385, Littleton, NC 27546, USA

Smith, James F, Jr — *Financier*
%First American Corp, First American Center, Nashville, TN 37237, USA

Smith, Jay R — *Publisher*
%Atlanta Journal-Constitution, 72 Marietta St, Atlanta, GA 30303, USA

Smith, Jeff — *Writer, Food Expert*
%Frugal Gourmet, 88 Virginia Ave, #2, Seattle, WA 98101, USA

Smith, Jeffrey P — *Businessman*
%Smith's Food & Drug Centers, 1550 S Redwood Rd, Salt Lake City, UT 84104, USA

Smith, Jerry E — *Judge*
%US Court of Appeals, 515 Rusk Ave, Houston, TX 77002, USA

Smith, Jim Ray — *Football Player*
7049 Cliffbrook Dr, Dallas, TX 75240, USA

Smith, Jimmy — *Jazz Organist*
2125 Kincaid Way, Sacramento, CA 95825, USA

Smith, Joe — *Basketball Player*
%Golden State Warriors, Oakland Coliseum Arena, Oakland, CA 94621, USA

Smith, John — *Track Athlete*
%University of California, Athletic Dept, Los Angeles, CA 90024, USA

Smith, John Coventry — *Religious Leader*
%World Council of Churches, 150 Rt de Ferbey, 1211 Geneva 20, Switzerland

Smith, John F, Jr — *Businessman*
%General Motors Corp, 3044 W Grand Blvd, Detroit, MI 48202, USA

Smith, John J — *Businessman*
%Sparton Corp, 2400 E Ganson St, Jackson, MI 49202, USA

Smith, John W — *Wrestler, Coach*
1509 Fairway Dr, Stillwater, OK 74074, USA

Smith, Kathy — *Physical Fitness Instructor*
11601 Wilshire Blvd, #500, Los Angeles, CA 90025, USA

Smith, Kenny — *Basketball Player*
%Houston Rockets, Summit, Greenway Plaza, #10, Houston, TX 77277, USA

Smith, Lane — *Actor*
%Innovative Artists, 1999 Ave of Stars, #2850, Los Angeles, CA 90067, USA

Smith, Lawrence Leighton — *Conductor*
%Louisville Symphony, 611 W Main St, Louisville, KY 40202, USA

Smith, Lee A — *Baseball Player*
%Baltimore Orioles, 333 W Camden Ave, Baltimore, MD 21201, USA

Smith, Leonard — *Football Player*
%Arizona Cardinals, 8701 S Hardy Dr, Tempe, AZ 85284, USA

Smith, Leslie E — *Businessman*
%BOC Group, Hammersmith House, Hammersmith W6 9DX, England

Smith, Ley S — *Businessman*
%Upjohn Co, 7000 Portage Rd, Kalamazoo, MI 49001, USA

Smith, Loren A — *Judge*
%US Claims Court, 717 Madison Place NW, Washington, DC 20005, USA

Smith, M Elizabeth (Liz) — *Columnist*
160 E 38th St, New York, NY 10016, USA

Smith, Maggie — *Actress*
%International Creative Mgmt, 76 Oxford St, London W1N 0AX, England

Smith, Martha — *Actress, Model*
9690 Heather Rd, Beverly Hills, CA 90210, USA

Smith, Martin Cruz — *Writer*
%Random House Inc, 201 E 50th St, New York, NY 10022, USA

Smith, Marty W — *Businessman*
%Thrifty Payless, 9275 SW Peyton Lane, Wilsonville, OR 97070, USA

Smith, Mary Louise — *Government Official*
654 59th St, Des Moines, IA 50312, USA

Smith, Mel — *Comedian*
%Talkback, 33 Percy St, London W1P 9FG, England

Smith, Michael — *Nobel Chemistry Laureate*
300-2455 W 3rd Ave, Vancouver BC V6K 1L8, Canada

Smith, Michael A (Mike) — *Hockey Executive, Coach*
%Winnipeg Jets, Arena, 15-1430 Maroons Rd, Winnipeg MB R3G 0L5, Canada

Smith, Michael J — *Businessman*
%Lands' End Inc, 1 Lands' End Lane, Dodgeville, WI 53595, USA

Smith, Michael W — *Singer, Songwriter*
PO Box 25330, Nashville, TN 37202, USA

Smith, Moishe — *Artist*
PO Box 747, Hyde Park, UT 84318, USA

Smith, Neil — *Football Player*
%Kansas City Chiefs, 1 Arrowhead Dr, Kansas City, KS 64129, USA

Smith, Neil — *Hockey Executive*
%New York Rangers, Madison Square Garden, 4 Penn Plaza New York, NY 10001, USA

Smith, Norman R — *Educator*
%Wagner College, President's Office, Staten Island, NY 10301, USA

Smith, O C — *Singer*
%Headline Talent, 1650 Broadway, #508, New York, NY 10019, USA

Smith, Orin R — *Businessman*
%Englehard Corp, 101 Wood Ave S, Iselin, NJ 08830, USA

Smith, Osborne E (Ozzie) — *Baseball Player*
PO Box 8787, St Louis, MO 63101, USA

Smith, Pat — *Wrestler*
%Oklahoma State University, Athletic Dept, Stillwater, OK 47078, USA

Smith, Patti — *Singer*
%Beverly Smith, PO Box 188, Mantua, NJ 08051, USA

Smith, R Jackson — *Diver*
1 Deepwoods Lane, Old Greenwich, CT 06870, USA

Smith, Ralph — *Cartoonist*
%King Features Syndicate, 216 E 45th St, New York, NY 10017, USA

Smith, Rankin M, Sr — *Football Executive*
%Atlanta Falcons, 2745 Burnett Rd, Suwanee, GA 30174, USA

Smith, Ray E — *Religious Leader*
%Open Bible Standard Churches, 2020 Bell Ave, Des Moines, IA 50315, USA

Smith, Ray F — *Entomologist*
3092 Hedaro Court, Lafayette, CA 94549, USA

Smith, Raymond W — *Businessman*
%Bell Atlantic Corp, 1717 Arch St, Philadelphia, PA 19103, USA

Smith, Reggie (C Reginald) — *Baseball Player*
6168 Coral Pink Circle, Woodland Hills, CA 91367, USA

Smith, Rex — *Actor*
%Agency For Performing Arts, 9000 Sunset Blvd, #1200, Los Angeles, CA 90069, USA

Smith, Richard A — *Businessman*
%Harcourt General Inc, 27 Boylston St, Chestnut Hill, MA 02167, USA

Smith, Richard D — *Businessman*
%Smith's Food & Drug Centers, 1550 S Redwood Rd, Salt Lake City, UT 84104, USA

Smith, Richard E (Dick) — *Make-up Artist*
5313 Siesta Court, Sarasota, FL 34242, USA

Smith, Richard M — *Editor*
%Newsweek Magazine, Editorial Dept, 251 W 57th St, New York, NY 10019, USA

Smith, Riley — *Football Player*
2765 Government Blvd, Mobile, AL 36606, USA

Smith, Robert C *Editor*
%TV Guide Magazine, Editorial Dept, 100 Matsonford Rd, Radnor, PA 19087, USA

Smith, Robert Gray (Graysmith) *Editorial Cartoonist*
%San Francisco Chronicle, 901 Mission St, San Francisco, CA 94103, USA

Smith, Robyn *Thoroughbred Racing Jockey*
1155 San Ysidro Dr, Beverly Hills, CA 90210, USA

Smith, Roger *Actor*
2707 Benedict Canyon Dr, Beverly Hills, CA 90210, USA

Smith, Rolland *Commentator*
%CBS-TV, News Dept, 524 W 57th St, New York, NY 10019, USA

Smith, S Kinnie, Jr *Businessman*
%CMS Energy, Fairlane Plaza South, 350 Town Center Dr, Dearborn, MI 48128, USA

Smith, Samuel H *Educator*
%Washington State University, President's Office, Pullman, WA 99164, USA

Smith, Shawnee *Actress*
%Kincaid, 43 Navy St, #300, Venice, CA 90291, USA

Smith, Shelley *Model, Actress*
182 S Mansfield Ave, Los Angeles, CA 90036, USA

Smith, Sherwood H, Jr *Businessman*
%Carolina Power & Light Co, 411 Fayetteville St Mall, Raleigh, NC 27601, USA

Smith, Sinjin *Volleyball Player*
%Assn of Volleyball Pros, 15260 Ventura Blvd, #2250, Sherman Oaks, CA 91403, USA

Smith, Stanley R (Stan) *Tennis Player*
%ProServe, 1100 Woodrow Wilson Blvd, #1800, Arlington, VA 22209, USA

Smith, Steve(n D) *Basketball Player*
%Atlanta Hawks, 1 CNN Center, South Tower, Atlanta, GA 30303, USA

Smith, Steven L *Astronaut*
%NASA, Johnson Space Center, 2101 NASA Rd, Houston, TX 77058, USA

Smith, Taran Noah *Actor*
%Full Circle Mgmt, 6057 Rhodes Ave, North Hollywood, CA 91606, USA

Smith, Tom E *Businessman*
%Food Lion Inc, 2110 Executive Dr, Salisbury, NC 28147, USA

Smith, Tommie *Track Athlete*
%Santa Monica College, Athletic Dept, Santa Monica, CA 90405, USA

Smith, Tony *Football Player*
%Atlanta Falcons, 2745 Burnett Rd, Suwanee, GA 30174, USA

Smith, Tony *Artist*
%Pace Gallery, 32 E 57th St, New York, NY 10022, USA

Smith, Tubby *Basketball Coach*
%University of Georgia, Athletic Dept, Athens, GA 30613, USA

Smith, Vernon L *Economist*
2122 E Camino El Granado, Tucson, AZ 85718, USA

Smith, Vince *Singer, Songwriter*
%Process Talent Mgmt, 439 Wiley Ave, Franklin, PA 16323, USA

Smith, W Keith *Financier*
%Dreyfus Corp, 200 Park Ave, New York, NY 10166, USA

Smith, W Keith *Financier*
%Mellon Bank Corp, 1 Mellon Bank Center, 500 Grant St, Pittsburgh, PA 15219, USA

Smith, Wallace B *Religious Leader*
%Reorganized Church of Latter Day Saints, Box 1059, Independence, MO 64051, USA

Smith, Wayne T *Businessman*
%Humana Corp, 500 W Main St, Louisville, KY 40202, USA

Smith, Will *Actor*
330 Bob Hope Dr, Burbank, CA 91523, USA

Smith, William *Actor*
3250 W Olympic Blvd, #67, Santa Monica, CA 90404, USA

Smith, William Jay *Writer*
RR 1, Box 151, 62 Luther Shaw Rd, Cummington, MA 01026, USA

Smith, William R, Jr *Attorney*
1 Harbour Place, PO Box 3239, Tampa, FL 33601, USA

Smith, William Y *Army General*
%Institute for Defense Analyses, 1801 N Beauregard St, Alexandria, VA 22311, USA

Smith, Willie *Football Player*
%Cleveland Browns, 80 1st Ave, Berea, OH 44017, USA

Smithburg, William D *Businessman*
%Quaker Oaks Co, 321 N Clark St, Chicago, IL 60610, USA

Smithers, William *Actor*
11664 Laurelcrest Dr, Studio City, CA 91604, USA

Smithson, Peter D *Architect*
Cato Lodge, 24 Gilston Rd, London SW10 9SR, England

Smitrovich, Bill *Actor*
5075 Amestoy Ave, Encino, CA 91316, USA

Smits, Jimmy *Actor*
%El Sendero, PO Box 49922, Barrington Station, Los Angeles, CA 90049, USA

Smits, Rik *Basketball Player*
%Indiana Pacers, Market Square Arena, 300 E Market St, Indianapolis, IN 46204, USA

Smogolski, Henry R *Financier*
%Northwestern Savings & Loan, 2300 N Western Ave, Chicago, IL 60647, USA

Smolan, Rick *Photographer*
%Workman Publishers, 708 Broadway, New York, NY 10003, USA

Smoltz, John A *Baseball Player*
111 Royal Dornoch Dr, Duluth, GA 30155, USA

Smoot, George F, III *Astrophysicist*
%Lawrence Berkeley Laboratory, 1 Cyclotron Blvd, Berkeley, CA 94720, USA

Smothers, Dick *Comedian (Smothers Brothers)*
%SmoBro Productions, 8489 W 3rd St, #1078, Los Angeles, CA 90048, USA

Smothers, Tom *Comedian (Smothers Brothers)*
%SmoBro Productions, 8489 W 3rd St, #1078, Los Angeles, CA 90048, USA

Smucker, Paul H *Businessman*
%J M Smucker Co, 1 Strawberry Lane, Orrville, OH 44667, USA

Smucker, Richard K *Businessman*
%J M Smucker Co, 1 Strawberry Lane, Orrville, OH 44667, USA

Smucker, Timothy P *Businessman*
%J M Smucker Co, 1 Strawberry Lane, Orrville, OH 44667, USA

Smylie, Robert E *Governor, ID*
117 Locust St, Boise, ID 83712, USA

Smyth, Charles P *Physical Chemist*
245 Prospect Ave, Princeton, NJ 08540, USA

Smyth, Craig H *Art Historian*
PO Box 39, Cresskill, NJ 07626, USA

Smyth, Joe *Singer (Sawyer Brown)*
%TKO Artist Mgmt, 4219 Hillsboro Rd, #318, Nashville, TN 37215, USA

Smyth, Patty *Singer*
%Mark Spector Co, 850 7th Ave, #606, New York, NY 10019, USA

Smyth, Randy *Yachtsman*
%Sails by Smyth, 15640 Graham St, Huntington Beach, CA 92649, USA

Smythe, Danny *Musician (Box Tops)*
%Creative Entertainment Assoc, 2011 Ferry Ave, #U-19, Camden, NJ 08104, USA

Smythe, Quenton G M *WW II South Africa Army Hero (VC)*
54 Seadoone Rd, Amanzimtoti 4126, Natal, South Africa

Smythe, Reg *Cartoonist (Andy Capp)*
Whitegates, 96 Caledonian Rd, Hartlepool, Cleveland

Snead, Jesse Caryle (J C) *Golfer*
PO Box 782170, Wichita, KS 67278, USA

Snead, Norman B (Norm) *Football Player*
104 James Landing, Newport News, VA 23606, USA

Snead, Samuel J (Sam) *Golfer*
PO Box 544, Hot Springs, VA 24445, USA

Sneed, Joseph T *Judge*
%US Court of Appeals, Court Building, PO Box 193939, San Francisco, CA 94119, USA

Snegur, Mircea I *President, Moldova*
%President's Office, 23 Nicolae Iorge Str, 277033 Kishinev, Moldova

Sneider, Martin *Businessman*
%Edison Brothers Stores, 501 N Broadway, St Louis, MO 63102, USA

Sneider, Richard L *Diplomat*
211 Central Park West, New York, NY 10024, USA

Snell, Esmond E *Biochemist*
5001 Greystone Dr, Austin, TX 78731, USA

Snell, George D *Nobel Medicine Laureate*
21 Atlantic Ave, Bar Harbor, ME 04609, USA

Snell, Peter *Track Athlete*
6452 Dunston Lane, Dallas, TX 75214, USA

Snell, Richard *Businessman*
%Pinnacle West Capital Corp, 400 E Van Buren St, Phoenix, AZ 85004, USA

Snellings, Ronald L *Financier*
%Pentagon Federal Credit Union, PO Box 1432, Arlington, VA 22210, USA

Sneva, Tom *Auto Racing Driver*
3301 E Valley Vista Lane, Paradise Valley, AZ 85253, USA

Snider, Edward M *Hockey Executive*
1804 Rittenhouse Square, Philadelphia, PA 19103, USA

Snider, Edwin D (Duke) *Baseball Player*
3037 Lakemont Dr, Fallbrook, CA 92028, USA

Snider, Jeremy *Actor*
%"Bold & Beautiful", Bell-Phillip Prod, 7800 Beverly Blvd, Los Angeles, CA 90036, USA

Snider, R Michael *Medical Researcher*
%Pfizer Pharmaceuticals, Eastern Point Rd, Groton, CT 06340, USA

Snipes, Wesley *Actor*
%Creative Artists Agency, 9830 Wilshire Blvd, Beverly Hills, CA 90212, USA

Snipstead, Richard *Religious Leader*
%Free Lutheran Congregations Assn, 402 W 11th St, Canton, SD 57013, USA

Snodgrass, William D *Poet*
RD 1, Erieville, NY 13061, USA

Snodgress, Carrie *Actress*
3025 Surry St, Los Angeles, CA 90027, USA

Snoop Doggy Dogg (Calvin Broadus) *Rapper*
%Rush Artists Mgmt, 1600 Varick St, New York, NY 10013, USA

Snow, Hank *Singer*
PO Box 1084, Nashville, TN 37202, USA

Snow, Jack T *Football Player*
401 Purdue Circle, Seal Beach, CA 90740, USA

Snow, John W *Businessman*
%CSX Corp, James Center, 901 E Cary St, Richmond, VA 23219, USA

Snow, Percy *Football Player*
%Kansas City Chiefs, 1 Arrowhead Dr, Kansas City, KS 64129, USA

Snow, Phoebe *Singer, Songwriter*
%CHR Mgmt, 350 5th Ave, #5101, New York, NY 10118, USA

Snowdon (A C R Armstrong-Jones), Earl of *Photographer*
22 Launceston Place, London W8 5RL, England

Snyder, Bruce *Football Coach*
%Arizona State University, Athletic Dept, Tempe, AZ 85287, USA

Snyder, Gary S *Poet*
18442 Macnab Cypress Rd, Nevada City, CA 95959, USA

Snyder, Jimmy (The Greek) *Oddsmaker, Journalist*
%News America Syndicate, 1703 Kaiser Ave, Irvine, CA 92714, USA

Snyder, Laurence H *Educator*
2885 Oahu Ave, Honolulu, HI 96822, USA

Snyder, Richard E *Publisher*
Linden Farm, Boutonville Rd, PO Box 175, Cross River, NY 10518, USA

Snyder, Robert C *Businessman*
%Quanex Corp, 1900 West Loop S, Houston, TX 77027, USA

Snyder, Solomon H *Psychiatrist, Pharmacologist*
3801 Canterbury Rd, #1001, Baltimore, MD 21218, USA

Snyder, Tom *Commentator*
1225 Beverly Estates Dr, Beverly Hills, CA 90210, USA

Snyder, William D *Photographer*
%Dallas Morning News, Communications Center, Dallas, TX 75265, USA

Soames of Fletching, A Christopher J *Government Official, England*
%White's Club, St James's St, London SW1, England

Soares, Joao Clemente Baena *Government Official*
%Organization of American States, 17th & Constitution NW, Washington, DC 20006, USA

Soares, Mario A N L *President, Portugal*
Rua Dr Joao Soares #2-3, 1600 Lisbon, Portugal

Sobers, Garfield S (Garry) *Cricketer*
%Cricket Board, 9 Appleblossom, Petit Valley, Diego Martin, Trinidad

Soble, Ron *Actor*
%BDP Assoc, 10637 Burbank Blvd, North Hollywood, CA 91601, USA

Socol, Jerry M *Businessman*
%J Baker Inc, 555 Turnpike St, Canton, MA 02021, USA

Sodano, Angelo Cardinal *Religious Leader*
%Office of Secretary of State, 00120 Vatican City, Rome, Italy

Soderbergh, Steven A *Movie Director*
%Outlaw Productions, 12103 Maxwelton Rd, Studio City, CA 91604, USA

Soderquist, Donald G *Businessman*
%Wal-Mart Stores, 702 SW 8th St, Bentonville, AR 72716, USA

Soderstrom, Elisabeth — *Opera Singer*
19 Hersbyvagen, 181 42 Lidingo, Sweden

Soeda, Takao — *Financier*
%Tokai Bank of California, 534 W 6th St, Los Angeles, CA 90014, USA

Sofaer, Abraham D — *Attorney*
%Hughes Hubbard Reed, 1300 "I" St NW, Washington, DC 20005, USA

Sofia, Zuheir — *Financier*
%Huntington Bancshares, Huntington Center, Columbus, OH 43287, USA

Sofro, Barney — *Businessman*
%House of Fabrics, 13400 Riverside Dr, Sherman Oaks, CA 91423, USA

Soglo, Nicephore — *President, Benin*
%President's Office, Boite Postale 2028, Cotonou, Benin

Sohn Kee Chung — *Marathon Runner*
%Korean Olympic Committee, International PO Box 1106, Seoul, South Korea

Sokol, David L — *Businessman*
%California Energy Co, 10831 Old Mill Rd, Omaha, NE 68154, USA

Sokol, Marilyn — *Actress*
24 W 40th St, #1700, New York, NY 10018, USA

Sokoloff, Louis — *Physiologist, Neurochemist*
%National Mental Health Institute, 9000 Rockville Pike, Bethesda, MD 20892, USA

Sokolov, Grigory L — *Concert Pianist*
%Yolanta Skura, Opus 3, 420 W 24th St, New York, NY 10011, USA

Sokolove, James G — *Attorney*
1 Boston Place, Boston, MA 02108, USA

Sokomanu, George — *President, Vanuatu*
BP 105, D-5 Noumea Cedex, New Caledonia

Solari, Richard C — *Businessman*
%Granite Construction Inc, 585 W Beach St, Watsonville, CA 95076, USA

Soleri, Paolo — *Architect*
%Cosanti Foundation, 6433 Doubletree Rd, Scottsdale, AZ 85253, USA

Soles, P J — *Actress*
PO Box 2351, Carefree, AZ 85377, USA

Solh, Rashid — *Prime Minister, Lebanon*
%Chambre of Deputes, Place de l'Etoile, Beirut, Lebanon

Solomon, Arthur K — *Biophysicist*
27 Cragie St, Cambridge, MA 02138, USA

Solomon, David H — *Medical Scientist*
%University of California VA Wadsworth, Geriartics Dept, Los Angeles, CA 90024, USA

Solomon, Edward I — *Chemist*
%Stanford University, Chemistry Dept, Stanford, CA 94305, USA

Solomon, Ezra — *Educator*
775 Santa Ynez, Stanford, CA 94305, USA

Solomon, Harold — *Tennis Player*
1500 S Ocean Blvd, Pompano Beach, FL 33062, USA

Solomon, Richard L — *Psychologist*
72 Pollard St, Conway, NH 03818, USA

Solomon, Robert — *Economist*
8502 W Howell Rd, Bethesda, MD 20817, USA

Solomon, Yonty — *Concert Pianist*
43 Belsize Park Gardens, London NW3 4JJ, England

Solovyev, Anatoli Y — *Cosmonaut*
%Potchta Kosmonavtov, 141 160 Svyosdny Gorodok, Moskovskoi Oblasti, Russia

Solovyev, Vladimir A — *Cosmonaut*
Khovanskaya Ul D 3, Kv 28, 129 515 Moscow, Russia

Solow, Robert M — *Nobel Economics Laureate*
528 Lewis Wharf, Boston, MA 02110, USA

Solso, Theodore M — *Businessman*
%Cummins Engine Co, PO Box 3005, Columbus, IN 47202, USA

Solt, Ron — *Football Player*
%Indianapolis Colts, 7001 W 56th St, Indianapolis, IN 46254, USA

Soltan, Jerzy — *Architect*
6 Shady Hill Square, Cambridge, MA 02138, USA

Soltau, Gordy — *Football Player*
1111 Hamilton Ave, Palo Alto, CA 94301, USA

Solti, Georg — *Conductor*
Chalet Haut Pre, 1884 Villars Sur Ollons, Vaud, Switzerland

Solvay, Jacques — *Businessman*
%Solvay & Cie, Rue du Prince Albert 33, 1050 Brussels, Belgium

Solymosi, Zoltan *Ballet Dancer*
%Royal Ballet, Bow St, London WC2E 9DD, England

Solzhenitsyn, Aleksandr *Nobel Literature Laureate*
%Farrar Straus Giroux, 19 Union Square W, New York, NY 10003, USA

Somare, Michael T *Prime Minister, Papua New Guinea*
Karan, Murik Lakes, East Sepik, Papua New Guinea

Sombrotto, Vincent R *Labor Leader*
%National Letter Carriers Assn, 100 Indiana Ave NW, Washington, DC 20001, USA

Somers, Brett *Actress*
315 W 57th St, #4-H, New York, NY 10019, USA

Somers, Suzanne *Actress*
433 S Beverly Dr, Beverly Hills, CA 90212, USA

Somit, Albert *Educator*
830 E College, #21, Carbondale, IL 62901, USA

Sommars, Julie *Actress*
%Century Artists, 9744 Wilshire Blvd, #308, Beverly Hills, CA 90212, USA

Sommaruga, Cornelio *International Official, Switzerland*
%International Red Cross, 12 Grand-Mezel Place, 1204 Geneva, Switzerland

Sommer, Elke *Actress*
540 N Beverly Glen Blvd, Los Angeles, CA 90077, USA

Sommers, Gordon L *Religious Leader*
%Moravian Church, Northern Province, 1021 Center St, Bethlehem, PA 18018, USA

Sommers, Joanie *Singer*
%Lawrence International Corp, 10636 Santa Monica Blvd, #A, Los Angeles, CA 90025, USA

Sommerville, Jimmy *Singer*
%London Records, Chancellor House, Hammersmith, London W6 9QB, England

Somogi, Judith *Conductor*
%Herbert Barrett Mgmt, 1860 Broadway, New York, NY 10023, USA

Somogyi, Jozsef *Sculptor*
Marton Ut 3/5, 1038 Budapest, Hungary

Somorjai, Gabor A *Chemist*
%University of California, Chemistry Dept, Berkeley, CA 94720, USA

Sondheim, Stephen J *Composer, Lyricist*
300 Park Ave, #1700, New York, NY 10022, USA

Songaila, Antoinette *Astronomer*
%University of Hawaii, Astronomy Dept, Honolulu, HI 96822, USA

Sonja *Queen, Norway*
Det Kongelige Slott, Drammensveien 1, 0010 Oslo, Norway

Sonnenfeld, Barry *Movie Director*
%United Talent Agency, 9560 Wilshire Blvd, #500, Beverly Hills, CA 90212, USA

Sonnenschein, Hugo F *Educator*
%University of Chicago, President's Office, Chicago, IL 60637, USA

Sonsini, Larry W *Attorney*
%Wilson Sonsini Goodrich Rosati, 650 Page Mill Rd, Palo Alto, CA 94304, USA

Sonstelie, Richard R *Businessman*
%Puget Sound Power & Light, Puget Power Building, Bellevue, WA 98009, USA

Sontag, Susan *Writer*
470 W 24th St, New York, NY 10011, USA

Soose, Billy *Boxer*
PO Box 127, Tafton, PA 18464, USA

Sophia *Queen, Spain*
%Palacio de la Zarzuela, 28071 Madrid, Spain

Sorato, Bruno F *Financier*
%Union Bank of Switzerland, Bahnhofstr 45, 8000 Zurich, Switzerland

Sorel, Edward *Artist*
Rt 301, Carmel, NY 10512, USA

Sorel, Louise *Actress*
10808 Lindbrook Dr, Los Angeles, CA 90024, USA

Soren, Tabitha *Entertainer*
%MTV, News Dept, 10 Universal City Plaza, #3000, Universal City, CA 91608, USA

Sorensen, Jacki F *Physical Fitness Expert*
%Jacki's Inc, PO Box 289, DeLand, FL 32721, USA

Sorensen, Theodore C *Government Official*
345 Park Ave, New York, NY 10154, USA

Sorensen, Paul *Actor*
%Don Schwartz Assoc, 8749 Sunset Blvd, Los Angeles, CA 90069, USA

Sorenson, Richard K *WW II Marine Corps Hero (CMH)*
3393 Skyline Blvd, Reno, NV 89509, USA

Sorkin, Arleen — *Actress*
3226 N Knoll Dr, Los Angeles, CA 90068, USA

Sorlie, Donald M — *Test Pilot*
14612 44th Ave NW, Gig Harbor, WA 98332, USA

Soros, George — *Financier*
%Soros Fund Mgmt, 888 7th Ave, #3300, New York, NY 10106, USA

Sorsa, T Kalevi — *Prime Minister, Finland*
%Bank of Finland, PO Box 160, 00101 Helsinki, Finland

Sorvino, Mira — *Actress*
%Fox-Albert, 1697 Broadway, New York, NY 10019, USA

Sorvino, Paul — *Actor*
110 E 87th St, New York, NY 10128, USA

Sothern, Ann — *Actress*
PO Box 2285, Ketchum, ID 83340, USA

Sotin, Hans — *Singer*
Schulheide 10, 21227 Bendestorf, Germany

Sotirhos, Michael A — *Diplomat*
%American Embassy, A Leoforos Vassilissis Sofias 91, 106 60 Athens, Greece

Sotkilava, Zurab L — *Opera Singer*
%Bolshoi Theater, Teatralnaya Pl 1, 103009 Moscow, Russia

Soto, Jock — *Ballet Dancer*
%New York City Ballet, Lincoln Center Plaza, New York, NY 10023, USA

Soto, Mario M — *Baseball Player*
Joachs-Lachaustegui #42, Sur-Bani, Dominican Republic

Soto, Talisa — *Model, Actress*
%Flick East-West Talents, 9057 Nemo St, #A, West Hollywood, CA 90069, USA

Sotomayor, Antonio — *Artist*
3 Le Roy Place, San Francisco, CA 94109, USA

Sotomayor, Javier — *Track Athlete*
Miramar, Havana, Cuba

Sottile, Benjamin J — *Businessman*
%Gibson Greetings Inc, 2100 Section Rd, Cincinnati, OH 45237, USA

Sottsass, Ettore, Jr — *Industrial Designer*
Via Manzoni 14, 20121 Milan, Italy

Soul, David — *Actor*
RR 1, Box 288, Sandstone, MN 55072, USA

Soulages, Pierre — *Artist*
18 Rue des Trois-Portes, 75005 Paris, France

Soule, Charles E, Sr — *Businessman*
%Paul Revere Insurance Group, 18 Chestnut St, Worcester, MA 01608, USA

Sousa, Mauricio de — *Cartoonist (Monica)*
%Mauricio de Sousa Producoes, Rua do Curtume 745, Sao Paulo SP, Brazil

Soutar, Dave — *Bowler*
%Professional Bowlers Assn, 1720 Merriman Rd, Akron, OH 44313, USA

Soutar, Judy — *Bowler*
%Women's International Bowling Congress, 5301 S 76th St, Greendale, WI 53129, USA

Soutendijk, Renee — *Actress*
%Marion Rosenberg Office, 8428 Melrose Place, #C, Los Angeles, CA 90069, USA

Souter, David H — *Supreme Court Justice*
%US Supreme Court, 1 1st St NE, Washington, DC 20543, USA

Southard, Frank A, Jr — *Economist*
4620 North Park Ave, Chevy Chase, MD 20815, USA

Southern, Terry — *Writer*
RFD, East Canaan, CT 06024, USA

Southway, Peter — *Financier*
%Valley National Bancorp, 1445 Valley Rd, Wayne, NJ 07470, USA

Souza, Francis N — *Artist*
148 W 67th St, New York, NY 10023, USA

Souzay, Gerard — *Singer*
26 Rue Freycinet, 75116 Paris, France

Sovern, Michael I — *Educator*
%Columbia University, Law School, New York, NY 10027, USA

Sovey, William P — *Businessman*
%Newell Corp, Newell Center, 29 E Stephenson St, Freeport, IL 61032, USA

Sowell, Arnold — *Track Athlete*
1647 Waterstone Lane, #1, Charlotte, NC 28262, USA

Sowell, Thomas — *Economist*
%Stanford University, Hoover Institution, Stanford, CA 94305, USA

Soyer, David *Cellist (Guarneri String Quartet)*
6 W 77th St, New York, NY 10024, USA

Spacek, Sissy *Actress*
Beau Val Farm, Box 22, #640, Cobham, VA 22929, USA

Spacey, Kevin *Actor*
%Joanne Horowitz, 200 E 58th St, #7-H, New York, NY 10022, USA

Spader, James *Actor*
%International Creative Mgmt, 8942 Wilshire Blvd, Beverly Hills, CA 90211, USA

Spahn, Warren E *Baseball Player*
RR 2, Hartshorne, OK 74547, USA

Spain, James W *Writer*
42 Galle Face Court II, #42, Colombo 3, Sri Lanka

Spalti, Peter *Businessman*
%Sulzer Brothers Ltd, 8401 Winterhur, Switzerland

Spanarkel, Jim *Basketball Player*
1934 Harmon Cove Towers, Secaucus, NJ 07094, USA

Spander, Art *Sportswriter*
%San Francisco Examiner, Editorial Dept, 110 5th Ave, San Francisco, CA 94118, USA

Spane, Robert J *Navy Admiral*
Commander, Naval Air Force Pacific Fleet, NAS North Island, San Diego, CA 92135, USA

Spane, William T *Financier*
%BHC Securities, 2005 Market St, Philadelphia, PA 19103, USA

Spanier, Graham B *Educator*
%University of Nebraska, Chancellor's Office, Lincoln, NE 68588, USA

Spano, Joe *Actor*
%E C Assoc, 5140 Colfax Ave, #150, North Hollywood, CA 91601, USA

Spanos, Alexander G (Alex) *Football Executive*
%San Diego Chargers, Jack Murphy Stadium, San Diego, CA 92160, USA

Spark, Muriel S *Writer*
%David Higham, 5-8 Lower John St, Golden Square, London W1R 4H4, England

Sparks, Dana *Actress*
%Artists Agency, 10000 Santa Monica Blvd, #305, Los Angeles, CA 90067, USA

Sparks, David E *Financier*
%Meridian Bancorp, 35 N 6th St, Reading, PA 19601, USA

Sparlis, Al *Football Player*
13206 Mindanao Way, Marina del Rey, CA 90292, USA

Sparv, Camilla *Actress*
957 N Cole Ave, Los Angeles, CA 90038, USA

Speaks, Ruben L *Religious Leader*
%African Methodist Episcopal Zion Church, PO Box 32843, Charlotte, NC 28232, USA

Spear, Laurinda H *Architect*
426 Jefferson Ave, Miami Beach, FL 33139, USA

Spears, William D *Football Player*
63 Waterbridge Place, Ponte Vedra, FL 32082, USA

Spector, Elisabeth (Lisa) *Government Official*
%Resolution Trust Corp, 801 17th St NW, Washington, DC 20434, USA

Spector, Phil *Record Company Executive*
1210 S Arroyo Parkway, Pasadena, CA 91105, USA

Spector, Ronnie *Singer*
%Jonathan Greenfield, 39-B Mill Plain Rd, #233, Danbury, CT 06811, USA

Spedding, Frank H *Chemist, Physicist*
520 Oliver Circle, Ames, IA 50014, USA

Speier, Chris E *Baseball Player*
6114 E Montecito Ave, Scottsdale, AZ 85251, USA

Speight, Francis *Artist*
508 E 9th St, Greenville, NC 27858, USA

Speir, James D *Businessman*
%IMC Global, 2100 Sanders Rd, Northbrook, IL 60062, USA

Spelling, Aaron *Movie, Television Producer*
%Aaron Spelling Productions, 5700 Wilshire Blvd, #575, Los Angeles, CA 90036, USA

Spelling, Tori *Actress*
594 N Mapleton Dr, Los Angeles, CA 90024, USA

Spellman, John D *Governor, WA*
%Carney Stephenson Badley, Columbia Center, 701 5th Ave, Seattle, WA 98104, USA

Spence, Dave *Labor Leader*
%Horseshoers Union, Rt 2, Box 71-C, Englishtown, NJ 07726, USA

Spence, Gerry *Attorney*
%Spence Moriarity Schuster, 15 S Jackson St, Jackson, WY 83001, USA

Spence, Jonathan D *Historian*
691 Forest Rd, New Haven, CT 06515, USA

Spence, Roger F *Religious Leader*
%Reformed Episcopal Church, 2001 Frederick Rd, Baltimore, MD 21228, USA

Spence, Will B *Financier*
%Wachovia Bank of South Carolina, 1426 Main St, Columbia, SC 29201, USA

Spencer, Bud *Actor*
%Mistral Film Group, Via Archimede 24, 00187 Rome, Italy

Spencer, Donald C *Mathematician*
943 County Rd 204, Durango, CO 81301, USA

Spencer, Elizabeth *Writer*
402 Longleaf Dr, Chapel Hill, NC 27514, USA

Spencer, F Gilman *Editor*
%Denver Post, Editorial Dept, 1560 Broadway, Denver, CO 80202, USA

Spencer, Frank Cole *Surgeon, Educator*
560 1st Ave, New York, NY 10016, USA

Spencer, John *Actor*
%Barry Haft Brown, 165 W 46th St, #1108, New York, NY 10036, USA

Spencer, Melvin J *Religious Leader, Attorney*
5910 N Shawnee Ave, Oklahoma City, OK 73112, USA

Spencer, Susan *Commentator*
%CBS-TV, News Dept, 2020 "M" St NW, Washington, DC 20036, USA

Spencer, Timothy (Tim) *Football Player*
1435 Sherborne Lane, Powell, OH 43065, USA

Spencer-Devlin, Muffin *Golfer*
1561 S Congress Ave, #141, Delray Beach, FL 33445, USA

Spender, Percy C *Judge*
Headingley House, 11 Wellington St, Woolhara, Sydney NSW 2025, Australia

Sperber, Wendie Jo *Actress*
24121 Ventura Blvd, Calabasas, CA 91302, USA

Sperlich, Harold K *Businessman*
3333 W Shore Dr, Orchard Lake, MI 48324, USA

Sperlich, Peter W *Political Scientist*
39 Adeline Dr, Walnut Creek, CA 94596, USA

Spethmann, Dieter *Businessman*
Thyssen AG, Kaiser-Wilhelm-Str 100, 47166 Duisburg, Germany

Spicer, William E, III *Physicist*
785 Mayfield Rd, Palo Alto, CA 94305, USA

Spiegel, Henry W *Economist*
6848 Nashville Rd, Lanham, MD 20706, USA

Spiegelman, Art *Illustrator, Writer*
%Raw Books & Graphics, 27 Greene St, New York, NY 10013, USA

Spielberg, David *Actor*
11338 Cashmere St, Los Angeles, CA 90049, USA

Spielberg, Steven *Movie Director*
%DreamWorks SKG, 100 Universal City Plaza, Universal City, CA 91608, USA

Spielman, Chris *Football Player*
2110 Eastwood Ave NE, Massillon, OH 44646, USA

Spier, Peter E *Artist*
PO Box 566, Shoreham, NY 11786, USA

Spiers, Ronald I *Diplomat*
RR 1, Box 54-A, Middletown Rd, South Londonderry, VT 05155, USA

Spilhaus, Athelstan F *Meteorologist, Oceanographer*
PO Box 1063, Middlesburg, VA 22117, USA

Spillane, Mickey *Writer*
PO Box 265, Murrells Inlet, SC 29576, USA

Spilman, Robert H *Businessman*
%Bassett Furniture Industries, PO Box 626, Bassett, VA 24055, USA

Spina, David A *Financier*
%State Street Boston Corp, 225 Franklin St, Boston, MA 02110, USA

Spindler, Marc *Football Player*
%New York Jets, 1000 Fulton Ave, Hempstead, NY 11550, USA

Spindler, Michael H *Businessman*
%Apple Computer, 1 Infinite Loop, Cupertino, CA 95014, USA

Spinella, Stephen *Actor*
%William Morris Agency, 1325 Ave of Americas, New York, NY 10019, USA

Spiner, Brent *Actor*
6922 1/2 Paseo del Serra, Los Angeles, CA 90068, USA

Spinetti, Victor *Actor*
15 Devonshire Place, Brighton, Sussex, England

Spinks, Michael *Boxer*
%Centerville Rd, Wilmington, DE 19808, USA

Spinola, Antonio S R de *President, Portugal; Army Marshal*
%Ministerio de Defesa, 1300 Lisbon, Portugal

Spiro, Donald W *Financier*
%Oppenheimer Management Corp, 2 World Trade Center, New York, NY 10048, USA

Spitz, Mark *Swimmer*
383 Dalehurst Ave, Los Angeles, CA 90024, USA

Spitzer, Lyman, Jr *Astrophysicst*
659 Lake Dr, Princeton, NJ 08540, USA

Spivakovsky, Tossy *Concert Violinist*
29 Burnham Hill, Westport, CT 06880, USA

Splittorff, Paul W *Baseball Player*
4204 Hickory Lane, Blue Spring, MO 64015, USA

Spock, Benjamin M *Physician, Social Activist*
PO Box 1268, Camden, ME 04843, USA

Spohr, Arnold T *Ballet Director*
%Royal Winnipeg Ballet, 289 Portage Ave, Winnipeg MB R3B 2B4, Canada

Sponable, Jess M *Astronaut*
1 Chaco Court, Sandia Park, NM 87047, USA

Spong, John S *Religious Leader*
24 Rector St, Newark, NJ 07102, USA

Spoon, Alan G *Businessman*
%Washington Post Co, 1150 15th St NW, Washington, DC 20071, USA

Spooner, John *Writer, Financier*
%Houghton Mifflin Co, 215 Park Ave S, New York, NY 10003, USA

Sporck, Charles E *Businessman*
%National Semiconductor Corp, 2900 Semiconductor Dr, Santa Clara, CA 95051, USA

Spotswood, Denis *Royal Air Force Marshal, England*
Coombe Cottage, Hambleden, Oxon RG9 6SD, England

Sprague, George F *Geneticist, Agronomist*
494 W 10th Ave, #208, Eugene, OR 97401, USA

Sprague, Peter J *Businessman*
%National Semiconductor Corp, 2900 Semiconductor Dr, Santa Clara, CA 95051, USA

Sprague, William W, III *Businessman*
%Savannah Foods & Industries, PO Box 339, Savannah, GA 31402, USA

Sprayberry, James M *Vietnam War Army Hero*
745 Ledyard Place, Montgomery, AL 36109, USA

Sprewell, Latrell *Basketball Player*
%Golden State Warriors, Oakland Coliseum Arena, Oakland, CA 94621, USA

Spring, Sherwood C *Astronaut*
%Army Space Program Office, DAMO/FDX, 2810 Old Lee Highway, Fairfax, VA 22031, USA

Springer, Jeffrey R *Financier*
%Citizens Bancorp, 14401 Sweitzer Lane, Laurel, MD 20707, USA

Springer, Jerry *Entertainer*
PO Box 4115, Chicago, IL 60654, USA

Springer, Robert C *Astronaut*
PO Box 1751, Decatur, AL 35602, USA

Springfield, Dusty *Singer*
%Take Out Productions, 130 W 57th St, #13-A, New York, NY 10019, USA

Springfield, Rick *Singer, Actor*
15456 Cabrito Rd, Van Nuys, CA 91406, USA

Springs, Alice *Photographer*
7 Ave Saint-Ramon, #T-1008, Monte Carlo, Monaco

Springsteen, Bruce *Singer, Songwriter*
1224 Benedict Canyon Dr, Beverly Hills, CA 90210, USA

Sprinkel, Beryl W *Government Official*
20140 St Andrews Dr, Olympia Fields, IL 60461, USA

Sprinkle, Edward A (Ed) *Football Player*
%Motor Vacations Unlimited, Rt 20, Elgin, IL 60120, USA

Sprouse, James M *Judge*
%US Court of Appeals, PO Box 401, 122 N Court St, Lewisburg, WV 24901, USA

Spungin, Joel D *Businessman*
%United Stationers, 2200 E Golf Rd, Des Plaines, IL 60016, USA

Spurrier, Steve O *Football Player, Coach*
%University of Florida, Athletic Dept, PO Box 14485, Gainesville, FL 32604, USA

S

Spinetti - Spurrier

Spuzich, Sandra *Golfer*
%Ladies Professional Golf Assn, 2570 Volusia Ave, Daytona Beach, FL 32114, USA

Squier, Billy *Singer*
%Dera Assoc, 584 Broadway, #1201, New York, NY 10012, USA

Squire, Chris *Bassist (Yes)*
%Sun Artists, 9 Hillgate St, London W8 7SP, England

Squires, John *Computer Disc Drive Engineer*
%Conner Peripherals, 3081 Zanker Rd, San Jose, CA 95134, USA

Srb, Adrian M *Geneticist*
411 Cayuga Heights Rd, Ithaca, NY 14850, USA

St Clair, Robert B (Bob) *Football Player*
3312 Parker Hill Rd, Santa Rosa, CA 95404, USA

St Cyr, Lili *Exotic Dancer*
624 N Plymouth Blvd, #7, Los Angeles, CA 90004, USA

St George, William R *Navy Admiral*
862 San Antonio Place, San Diego, CA 92106, USA

St Jacques, Robert J *Businessman*
%Life Insurance Co of Georgia, 5780 Powers Ferry Rd NW, Atlanta, GA 30327, USA

St James, Lyn *Auto Racing Driver*
%MotorSports, 175 SW 20th Way, Dania, FL 33004, USA

St Jean, Garry *Basketball Coach*
%Sacramento Kings, 1 Sports Parkway, Sacramento, CA 95834, USA

St John of Fawsley, Norman A F *Government Official, England*
27 Charles St, London W1X 7HD, England

St John, Bill D *Businessman*
%Dresser Industries, PO Box 718, Dallas, TX 75221, USA

St John, H Bernard *Prime Minister, Barbados*
3 Enterprise, Christchurch, Barbados

St John, Jill *Actress*
%Borinstein Oreck Bogart Agency, 8271 Melrose Ave, #110, Los Angeles, CA 90046, USA

St John, Kristoff *Actor*
7101 Farralone Ave, #114, Canoga Park, CA 91303, USA

Staats, Elmer B *Government Official*
%Truman Scholarship Foundation, 712 Jackson Place NW, Washington, DC 20006, USA

Stabler, Ken M (Kenny) *Football Player*
%Stabler Co, 260 N Joachim St, Mobile, AL 36603, USA

Stack, Allen M *Swimmer*
PO Box 76, Honolulu, HI 96810, USA

Stack, Robert *Actor*
321 St Pierre Rd, Los Angeles, CA 90077, USA

Stackhouse, Jerry *Basketball Player*
%Philadelphia 76ers, Veterans Stadium, PO Box 25040, Philadelphia, PA 19147, USA

Stacy, Hollis *Golfer*
%Endicott, PO Box 10850, Palm Desert, CA 92255, USA

Stadler, Craig R *Golfer*
4601 S Columbine Court, Englewood, CO 80110, USA

Stadler, Sergei V *Concert Violinist*
Kaiserstr 43, 80801 Munich, Germany

Stadtman, Earl R *Biochemist*
16907 Redland Rd, Derwood, MD 20855, USA

Stafford, Harrison *Football Player*
Rt 1, Box 216-H, Edna, TX 77957, USA

Stafford, Jim *Singer, Songwriter*
PO Box 6366, Branson, MO 65615, USA

Stafford, Jo *Singer*
2339 Century Hill, Los Angeles, CA 90067, USA

Stafford, John R *Businessman*
%American Home Products Corp, 5 Giralda Farms, Madison, NJ 07940, USA

Stafford, Nancy *Actress*
13080 Mindanao Way, #69, Marina del Rey, CA 90292, USA

Stafford, Robert T *Governor/Senator, VT*
1 Sugarwood Hill Rd, RR 1, Box 3954, Rutland, VT 05701, USA

Stafford, Thomas P *Astronaut, Air Force General*
3212 E Interstate 240, Oklahoma City, OK 73135, USA

Stafford-Clark, Max *Theater Director*
7 Gloucester Crescent, London NW1, England

Stager, Gus *Swimming Coach*
%University of Michigan, Athletic Dept, Ann Arbor, MI 48104, USA

Staheli, Donald L — *Businessman*
%Continental Grain Co, 277 Park Ave, New York, NY 10172, USA

Stahl, Dale E — *Businessman*
%Gaylord Container Corp, 500 Lake Cook Rd, Deerfield, IL 60015, USA

Stahl, Lesley R — *Commentator*
%CBS-TV, News Dept, 51 W 52nd St, New York, NY 10019, USA

Stahle, Hans — *Businessman*
%Alfa-Laval, PO Box 12150, 102 24, Stockhom, Sweden

Stahr, Elvis J, Jr — *Conservationist*
16 Martin Dale N, Greenwich, CT 06830, USA

Stair, Charles W — *Businessman*
%ServiceMaster Co, 1 ServiceMaster Rd, Downers Grove, IL 60515, USA

Staley, Delbert C — *Businessman*
32 Polly Park Rd, Rye, NY 10580, USA

Staley, Robert W — *Businessman*
%Emerson Electric Co, 8000 W Florissant Ave, St Louis, MO 63136, USA

Staller Koons, Ilona (Cicciolina) — *Actress, Government Official*
%Diva Futura, Via Cassia 1818, 00123 Rome, Italy

Stallings, Gene C — *Football Coach*
%University of Alabama, Athletic Dept, PO Box 870323, Tuscaloosa, AL 35487, USA

Stallings, George — *Religious Leader*
%African American Catholic Congregation, 1015 "I" St NE, Washington, DC 20002, USA

Stallkamp, James H — *Financier*
%Bankers Trust Delaware, 1001 Jefferson St, Wilmington, DE 19801, USA

Stallone, Sylvester — *Actor*
30900 Broad Beach Rd, Malibu, CA 90265, USA

Stallones, Reuel — *Scientist*
12414 Modena Trail, Austin, TX 78729, USA

Stallworth, John — *Football Player*
%General Delivery, Brownsboro, AL 35741, USA

Stamos, John — *Actor*
2319 St George St, Los Angeles, CA 90027, USA

Stamos, Theodoros — *Artist*
%Louis Meisel Gallery, 141 Prince St, New York, NY 10012, USA

Stamp, Terence — *Actor*
%Markham & Froggatt, Julian House, 4 Windmill St, London W1P 1HF, England

Standish, J Spencer — *Businessman*
%Albany International Corp, PO Box 1907, Albany, NY 12201, USA

Stanfel, Dick — *Football Player, Coach*
1104 Juniper Parkway, Libertyville, IL 60048, USA

Stanfill, Dennis C — *Movie Executive*
908 Oak Grove Ave, San Marino, CA 91108, USA

Stanfill, William T (Bill) — *Football Player*
2307 Tara Dr, Albany, GA 31707, USA

Stang, Arnold — *Actor*
PO Box 786, New Canaan, CT 06840, USA

Stanier, John W — *Army Field Marshal, England*
%Coutts & Co, 440 The Strand, London SC2R 0QS, England

Stankard, Francis X — *Financier*
%Bank Leumi Trust, 579 5th Ave, New York, NY 10017, USA

Stankovic, Borislav — *Basketball Executive*
%FIBA, PO Box 70067, Kistlerhofstr 168, 81379 Munich, Germany

Stanky, Edward R (Eddie) — *Baseball Manager*
2100 Spring Hill Rd, Mobile, AL 36607, USA

Stanley, Allan H — *Hockey Player*
%Allan Stanley Hockey Camp, 15 Four Winds Dr, Toronto ON, Canada

Stanley, David — *Businessman*
%Payless Cashways, 2300 Main St, Kansas City, MO 64108, USA

Stanley, Florence — *Actress*
PO Box 48876, Los Angeles, CA 90048, USA

Stanley, Frank — *Cinematographer*
PO Box 2230, Los Angeles, CA 90078, USA

Stanley, Julian C, Jr — *Psychologist*
%Johns Hopkins University, Blumberg Center, Baltimore, MD 21218, USA

Stanley, Kim — *Actress*
1501 Montano St, #4, Santa Fe, NM 87501, USA

Stanley, Paul — *Singer, Guitarist (Kiss)*
%Kiss, 6363 Sunset Blvd, Los Angeles, CA 90028, USA

S

Staheli - Stanley

Stanley, Ralph — *Bluegrass Guitarist*
%Rebel Records, PO Box 3057, Roanoke, VA 24015, USA

Stanley, Richard H — *Businessman*
%HON Industries, 414 E 3rd St, Muscantine, IA 52761, USA

Stanley, Steven M — *Paleobiologist*
115 Overhill Rd, Baltimore, MD 21210, USA

Stanley, Walter — *Football Player*
4745 S Helena Way, Aurora, CO 80015, USA

Stans, Maurice H — *Secretary, Commerce*
211 S Orange Grove Ave, Pasadena, CA 91105, USA

Stansfield Smith, Colin — *Architect*
Three Ministers House, 76 High St, Winchester, Hants SO23 8UL, England

Stansfield, Lisa — *Singer*
PO Box 59, Ashwell, Herts SG7 5NG, England

Stantis, Scott — *Editorial Cartoonist (The Buckets)*
%Memphis Commerical-Appeal, Editorial Dept, 495 Union Ave, Memphis, TN 38103, USA

Stanton, Donald S — *Educator*
%Oglethorpe University, President's Office, Atlanta, GA 30319, USA

Stanton, Frank — *Broadcast Executive*
25 W 52nd St, New York, NY 10019, USA

Stanton, Harry Dean — *Actor*
14527 Mulholland Dr, Los Angeles, CA 90077, USA

Stanton, Jeff — *Motorcycle Racing Rider*
1137 Athens Rd, Sherwood, MI 49089, USA

Stanton, Susan — *Businesswoman*
%Payless Cashways Inc, 2301 Main St, Kansas City, MO 64108, USA

Staples, Mavis — *Singer*
2772 E 75th St, Chicago, IL 60649, USA

Stapleton, Jean — *Actress*
250 W Main St, #100, Charlottesvle, VA 22902, USA

Stapleton, Maureen — *Actress*
1-14 Morgan Manor, Lenox, MA 01240, USA

Stapleton, Walter K — *Judge*
%US Court of Appeals, 844 N King St, #33, Wilmington, DE 19801, USA

Stapp, John P — *Aerospace Scientist*
%New Mexico Research Institute, PO Box 553, Alamogordo, NM 88311, USA

Starfield, Barbara H — *Physician*
%Johns Hopkins University, Hygiene School, 624 N Broadway, Baltimore, MD 21205, USA

Stargell, Wilver D (Willie) — *Baseball Player*
1616 Shipyard Blvd, #278, Wilmington, NC 28412, USA

Stark, Freya M — *Explorer, Writer*
Via Canova, Asolo, Treviso, Italy

Stark, Jack L — *Educator*
%Claremont McKenna College, President's Office, Claremont, CA 91711, USA

Stark, Jurgen K — *Religious Leader*
%Church of Christ Scientist, 175 Huntington Ave, Boston, MA 02115, USA

Stark, Nathan J — *Lawyer*
4343 Westover Place NW, Washington, DC 20016, USA

Stark, Ray — *Movie Producer*
%MGM Studios, 10232 W Washington Blvd, Culver City, CA 90232, USA

Stark, Rohn T — *Football Player*
%Pittsburgh Steelers, 3 Rivers Stadium, 300 Stadium Circle, Pittsburgh, PA 15212, USA

Starker, Janos — *Concert Cellist*
1241 Winfield Rd, Bloomington, IN 47401, USA

Starks, John — *Basketball Player*
%New York Knicks, Madison Square Garden, 4 Penn Plaza, New York, NY 10001, USA

Starn, Douglas — *Photographer*
%Stux Gallery, 163 Mercer St, #1, New York, NY 10012, USA

Starn, Mike — *Photographer*
%Stux Gallery, 163 Mercer St, #1, New York, NY 10012, USA

Starnes, Vaughn A — *Surgeon*
%Stanford Univ Medical Center, Heart-Lung Transplant Program, Stanford, CA 94305, USA

Starr, Albert — *Cardiac Surgeon*
5050 SW Patton Rd, Portland, OR 97221, USA

Starr, B Bartlett (Bart) — *Football Player*
1400 Urban Center Dr, #400, Birmingham, AL 35242, USA

Starr, Blaze — *Exotic Dancer*
%Carrolltown Mall, Eldersburg, MD 21784, USA

Starr, Kay *Singer*
%General Artists Corp, 16810 Baijo Rd, Encino, CA 91436, USA

Starr, Kenneth W *Government Official, Judge*
%Pepperdine University, Law School, Malibu, CA 90265, USA

Starr, Leonard *Cartoonist (Annie, Kelly Green)*
46 Post Rd E, Westport, CT 06880, USA

Starr, Paul E *Sociologist*
%Princeton University, Sociology Dept, Green Hall, Princeton, NJ 08544, USA

Starr, Ringo *Singer (Beatles), Actor*
2029 Century Park Blvd, #1690, Los Angeles, CA 90067, USA

Starzl, Thomas E *Physician*
%University of Pittsburgh Medical School, Surgery Dept, Pittsburgh, PA 15261, USA

Stassen, Harold E *Governor, MN*
431 E Haskell St, #1, West St Paul, MN 55118, USA

Stastny, Anton *Hockey Player*
%Quebec Nordiques, 2205 Ave du Colisee, Quebec City PQ G1L 4W7, Canada

Stastny, Peter *Hockey Player*
%St Louis Blues, St Louis Arena, 5700 Oakland Ave, St Louis, MO 63110, USA

Stata, Ray *Businessman*
%Analog Devices Inc, 1 Technology Way, Norwood, MA 02062, USA

Station, Larry *Football Player*
%Pittsburgh Steelers, 3 Rivers Stadium, 300 Stadium Circle, Pittsburgh, PA 15212, USA

Staub, Daniel J (Rusty) *Baseball Player*
21509 17th Ave, Flushing, NY 11360, USA

Staubach, Roger T *Football Player*
%Staubach Co, 6750 LBJ Freeway, #1100, Dallas, TX 75240, USA

Stauffer, William A *Basketball Player*
4916 Harwood Dr, Des Moines, IA 50312, USA

Stauth, Robert E *Businessman*
%Fleming Companies, 6301 Waterford Blvd, Oklahoma City, OK 73118, USA

Staveley, William D M *Royal Navy Fleet Admiral, England*
%N Thames Health Authority, 40 Eastbourne Terrace, London W2 3QR, England

Stavro, Steve A *Hockey Executive*
%Toronto Maple Leafs, 60 Carlton St, Toronto ON M5B 1L1, Canada

Stavropoulos, William S *Businessman*
%Dow Chemical Co, 2020 Dow Center, Midland, MI 48674, USA

Stayskal, Wayne *Editorial Cartoonist*
PO Box 191, Tampa, FL 33601, USA

Stead, Eugene A, Jr *Physician*
5113 Townsville Rd, Bullock, NC 27507, USA

Steadman, J Richard *Orthopedic Surgeon*
1139 2nd, South Lake Tahoe, CA 95706, USA

Stearn, Carl W *Financier*
%Provident Bankshares Corp, 114 E Lexington St, Baltimore, MD 21202, USA

Stebbins, George L *Geneticist*
216 "F" St, #165, Davis, CA 95616, USA

Stecher, Theodore P *Astronomer*
%UIT Project, Goddard Space Flight Center, Greenbelt, MD 20771, USA

Steel, Amy *Actress*
331 N Martel Ave, Los Angeles, CA 90036, USA

Steel, Danielle F *Writer*
330 Bob Hope Dr, Burbank, CA 91523, USA

Steel, David M S *Government Official, England*
Aikwood Tower, Ettrick Bridge, Selkirkshire, Scotland

Steel, Dawn *Movie Executive*
%Atlas Entertainment, 345 N Maple Dr, #275, Beverly Hills, CA 90210, USA

Steele, Barbara *Actress*
442 S Bedford Dr, Beverly Hills, CA 90212, USA

Steele, Richard *Boxing Referee*
5009 Long View Dr, Las Vegas, NV 89120, USA

Steele, Shelby *Writer*
%San Jose State University, English Dept, San Jose, CA 95192, USA

Steele, Tommy *Singer, Actor*
%Mark Furness Ltd, 10/12 Garrick St, London WC2E 9BH, England

Steele, William W *Businessman*
%ABM Industries, 50 Fremont St, San Francisco, CA 94105, USA

Steele-Perkins, Christopher H *Photographer*
5 Homer House, Rushcroft Rd, London, England

Steen, Thomas *Hockey Player*
%Winnipeg Jets, Arena, 15-1430 Maroons Rd, Winnipeg MB R3G 0L5, Canada

Steenburgen, Mary *Actress*
3220 E Ojai Ave, Ojai, CA 93023, USA

Steere, William C, Jr *Businessman*
%Pfizer Inc, 235 E 42nd St, New York, NY 10017, USA

Stefanich, Jim *Bowler*
%Professional Bowlers Assn, 1720 Merriman Rd, Akron, OH 44313, USA

Stefanko, Robert A *Businessman*
%A Schulman Inc, 3550 W Market St, Akron, OH 44333, USA

Steffen, Christopher *Financier*
%Citibank, 399 Park Ave, New York, NY 10022, USA

Steffensen, Dwight A *Businessman*
%Bergen Brunswig Corp, 4000 Metropolitan Dr, Orange, CA 92668, USA

Steffes, Kent *Volleyball Player*
11106 Ave de Cortez, Pacific Palisades, CA 90272, USA

Steffy, Joe *Football Player*
%Broadway Buick, 259 Broadway, Newburgh, NY 12550, USA

Stegemeier, Richard J *Businessman*
%Unocal Corp, 1201 W 5th St, Los Angeles, CA 90017, USA

Steger, Joseph A *Educator*
%University of Cincinnati, President's Office, Cincinnati, OH 45221, USA

Steger, Will *Arctic Explorer*
%International Artic Project, 413 Wacouta St, #200, St Paul, MN 55101, USA

Stegmayer, Joseph H *Businessman*
%Clayton Homes, 623 Market St, Knoxville, TN 37902, USA

Steig, William *Writer, Artist*
301 Berkeley St, #4, Boston, MA 02116, USA

Steiger, Janet D *Government Official*
%Federal Trade Commission, Pennsylvania Ave & 6th St NW, Washington, DC 20580, USA

Steiger, Rod *Actor*
6324 Zumirez Dr, Malibu, CA 90265, USA

Stein, Bob *Basketball Executive*
%Minnesota Timberwolves, Target Center, 600 1st Ave N, Minneapolis, MN 55403, USA

Stein, Elias M *Mathematician*
132 Dodds Lane, Princeton, NJ 08540, USA

Stein, Gilbert (Gil) *Hockey Executive*
%National Hockey League, 650 5th Ave, #3300, New York, NY 10019, USA

Stein, Herbert *Government Official, Economist*
%American Enterprise Institute, 1150 17th St NW, Washington, DC 20036, USA

Stein, Horst *Conductor*
%Mariedi Anders Mgmt, 535 El Camino Del Mar, San Francisco, CA 94121, USA

Stein, Howard *Financier*
%Dreyfuss Corp, 200 Park Ave, New York, NY 10166, USA

Stein, J Dieter *Businessman*
%BASF Corp, 3000 Continental Dr N, Mt Olive, NJ 07828, USA

Stein, Joseph *Playwright*
1130 Park Ave, New York, NY 10128, USA

Stein, Robert *Editor*
%McCall's Magazine, Editorial Dept, 110 5th Ave, New York, NY 10011, USA

Stein, Robert B, Jr *Businessman*
%Dairy Mart Convenience Stores, 1 Vision Dr, Enfield, CT 06082, USA

Steinbach, Alice *Journalist*
%Baltimore Sun, Editorial Dept, 501 N Calvert St, Baltimore, MD 21202, USA

Steinbach, Terry L *Baseball Player*
750 Boone Ave N, Golden Valley, MN 55427, USA

Steinberg, David *Comedian*
4406 Haskell Ave, Encino, CA 91436, USA

Steinberg, Joseph S *Businessman*
%Leucadia National Corp, 315 Park Ave S, New York, NY 10010, USA

Steinberg, Leigh *Sports Attorney*
2727 Dunleer Place, Los Angeles, CA 90064, USA

Steinberg, Leo *Art Historian*
165 W 66th St, New York, NY 10023, USA

Steinberg, Robert M *Businessman*
%Reliance Group Holdings, 55 E 52nd St, New York, NY 10055, USA

Steinberg, Saul *Artist, Cartoonist*
%New Yorker Magazine, 20 W 43rd St, New York, NY 10036, USA

Steinberg, Saul P — *Businessman*
%Reliance Group Holdings, 55 E 52nd St, New York, NY 10055, USA

Steinberg, William R — *Labor Leader*
%American Radio Assn, 26 Journal Square, #1501, Jersey City, NJ 07306, USA

Steinberger, Jack — *Nobel Physics Laureate*
25 Chemin des Merles, 1213 Onex, Geneva, Switzerland

Steinbrenner, George M, III — *Baseball Executive*
512 Florida Ave, Tampa, FL 33602, USA

Steinem, Gloria — *Social Activist, Editor*
%Ms Magazine, Editorial Dept, 230 Park Ave, New York, NY 10169, USA

Steiner, George — *Writer*
32 Barrow Rd, Cambridge, England

Steiner, Jeffrey J — *Businessman*
%Fairchild Corp, 3800 W Service Rd, Chantilly, VA 22021, USA

Steinfeld, Jake — *Actor, Body Builder*
622 Toyopa Dr, Pacific Palisades, CA 90272, USA

Steinhardt, Richard — *Biologist*
%University of California, Biology Dept, Berkeley, CA 94720, USA

Steinhart, Ronald G — *Financier*
%Bank One Texas, 1717 Main St, Dallas, TX 75201, USA

Steinkraus, Bill — *Equestrian Rider*
PO Box 3038, Noroton, CT 06820, USA

Steinkuhler, Dean — *Football Player*
General Delivery, Palmyra, NE 68418, USA

Steinsaltz, Adin — *Religious Leader*
%Israel Talmudic Publications Institute, PO Box 1458, Jerusalem, Israel

Stella, Frank P — *Artist*
17 Jones St, New York, NY 10014, USA

Stelle, Kellogg S — *Physicist*
%Imperial College, Prince Consort Rd, London SW7 2BZ, England

Stelmach, Leigh S — *Businessman*
%Dollar General Corp, 104 Woodmont Blvd, Nashville, TN 37205, USA

Stemberg, Thomas G — *Businessman*
%Staples Inc, 100 Pennsylvania Ave, Framingham, MA 01701, USA

Stempel, Robert C — *Businessman*
%Energy Conversion Devices, 1647 W Maple Rd, Troy, MI 48084, USA

Stenerud, Jan — *Football Player*
10111 Wenonga Lane, Leawood, KS 66206, USA

Stenmark, Ingemar — *Skier*
Slalomvagen 9, 920 64 Tarnaby, Sweden

Stent, Gunther S — *Molecular Biologist*
145 Purdue Ave, Kensington, CA 94708, USA

Stepan, F Quinn — *Businessman*
%Stepan Co, 22 W Frontage Rd, Northfield, IL 60093, USA

Stepanian, Ira — *Financier*
%Bank of Boston Corp, 100 Federal St, Boston, MA 02110, USA

Stephanie — *Princess, Monaco*
%Palace Princier, Monaco-Ville, Monaco

Stephanopoulos, George R — *Journalist, Government Official*
%White House, 1600 Pennsylvania Ave NW, Washington, DC 20006, USA

Stephens, Jackson T — *Financier*
%Stephens Inc, 111 Center St, Little Rock, AR 72201, USA

Stephens, Olin James, II — *Naval Architect, Yacht Designer*
%Sparkman & Stephens, 79 Madison Ave, New York, NY 10016, USA

Stephens, Robert — *Actor*
%International Creative Mgmt, 76 Oxford St, London W1N 0AX, England

Stephens, Robert F — *Businessman*
%ATMOS Energy Corp, PO Box 650205, Dallas, TX 75265, USA

Stephens, Sanford (Sandy) — *Football Player*
1930 E 86th St, #111, Bloomington, MN 55425, USA

Stephens, W Thomas — *Businessman*
%Manville Corp, Ken-Caryl Ranch, PO Box 5108, Denver, CO 80217, USA

Stephens, Warren A — *Financier*
%Stephens Inc, 111 Center St, Little Rock, AR 72201, USA

Stephens, Woodford C (Woody) — *Thoroughbred Racing Trainer*
15534 Cairnyan Ct, Miami Lakes, FL 33014, USA

Stephenson, Dwight E — *Football Player*
6301 Hutchinson Rd, Miami Lakes, FL 33014, USA

S

Steinberg - Stephenson

Stephenson, Gordon — *Architect*
55/14 Albert St, Claremont WA 6010, Australia

Stephenson, Jan L — *Golfer*
7601 Della Dr, #276, Orlando, FL 32819, USA

Stephenson, Pamela — *Actress*
%John Reid Ent, Singes House, 32 Galena Rd, London W6 0LT, England

Stephenson, William V — *Businessman*
%First Brands Corp, 83 Wooster Heights Blvd, Danbury, CT 06810, USA

Stepnoski, Mark M — *Football Player*
%Houston Oilers, 6910 Fannin St, Houston, TX 77030, USA

Steppling, John — *Playwright*
%William Morris Agency, 151 S El Camino Dr, Beverly Hills, CA 90212, USA

Sterban, Richard A — *Singer (Oak Ridge Boys)*
329 Rockland Rd, Hendersonville, TN 37075, USA

Sterkel, Jill — *Swimmer*
%Indiana University, Athletic Dept, Bloomington, IN 47405, USA

Sterling, Jan — *Actress*
3959 Hamilton St, #11, San Diego, CA 92104, USA

Sterling, Philip — *Actor*
4114 Benedict Canyon Dr, Sherman Oaks, CA 91423, USA

Sterling, Robert — *Actor*
121 S Bentley Ave, Los Angeles, CA 90049, USA

Sterling, Tisha — *Actress*
PO Box 788, Ketchum, ID 83340, USA

Stern, Daniel — *Actor*
PO Box 6788, Malibu, CA 90264, USA

Stern, David J — *Basketball Executive*
%National Basketball Assn, Olympic Tower, 645 5th Ave, New York, NY 10022, USA

Stern, Fritz R — *Historian*
15 Claremont Ave, New York, NY 10027, USA

Stern, Gary H — *Financier*
%Federal Reserve Bank, 250 Marquette Ave, Minneapolis, MN 55401, USA

Stern, Howard A — *Entertainer*
%WXRK-FM Radio, 600 Madison Ave, New York, NY 10022, USA

Stern, Isaac — *Concert Violinist*
211 Central Park West, New York, NY 10024, USA

Stern, Leonard B — *Television, Movie Producer*
1709 Angelo Dr, Beverly Hills, CA 90210, USA

Stern, Richard G — *Writer*
%University of Chicago, English Dept, Chicago, IL 60637, USA

Stern, Robert A M — *Architect*
%Robert Stern Architects, 211 W 61st St, #500, New York, NY 10023, USA

Sternbach, Leo H — *Medical Chemist*
10 Woodmont Rd, Upper Montclair, NJ 07043, USA

Sternecky, Neal — *Cartoonist (Pogo)*
%Los Angeles Times Syndicate, Times Mirror Square, Los Angeles, CA 90053, USA

Sternfeld, Reuben — *Financier*
%Inter-American Development Bank, 1300 New York Ave NW, Washington, DC 20577, USA

Sternhagen, Frances — *Actress*
152 Sutton Manor Rd, New Rochelle, NY 10801, USA

Sterrett, Samuel B — *Judge*
%US Tax Court, 400 2nd St NW, Washington, DC 20217, USA

Sterzinsky, Georg Maximilian Cardinal — *Religious Leader*
%Archdiocese of Berlin, Wundstr 48/50, 14057 Berlin, Germany

Stetter, Karl — *Microbiologist*
%Universtat Regensburg, Universitatsstr 31, 93053 Regensburg, Germany

Steuber, Robert J (Bob) — *Football Player*
109 Forest Parkway, #1, Valley Park, MO 63088, USA

Stevens (Yusef Islam), Cat — *Singer, Songwriter*
Ariola Steinhauser Str 3, 81667 Munich, Germany

Stevens, Andrew — *Actor*
3965 Valley Meadow Rd, Encino, CA 91436, USA

Stevens, Brinke — *Actress*
8033 Sunset Blvd, #556, Los Angeles, CA 90046, USA

Stevens, Chuck — *Photographer*
1720 Mission St, #B, San Francisco, CA 94103, USA

Stevens, Connie — *Singer, Actress*
8721 Sunset Blvd, #PH-1, Los Angeles, CA 90069, USA

Stevens, Craig *Actor*
25 Central Park West, New York, NY 10023, USA

Stevens, Dorit *Actress, Model*
11524 Amanda Dr, Studio City, CA 91604, USA

Stevens, Fisher *Actor*
%William Morris Agency, 151 S El Camino Dr, Beverly Hills, CA 90212, USA

Stevens, Gary *Jockey*
%Thoroughbred Racing Assn, 3000 Marcus Ave, Lake Success, NY 11042, USA

Stevens, George, Jr *Movie Producer*
%New Liberty Productions, John F Kennedy Center, Washington, DC 20566, USA

Stevens, John Paul *Supreme Court Justice*
%US Supreme Court, 1 1st St NE, Washington, DC 20543, USA

Stevens, John R *Businessman*
%Eastern Utilities Assoc, 1 Liberty Square, Boston, MA 02109, USA

Stevens, Kevin M *Hockey Player*
%Boston Bruins, Boston Garden, 150 Causeway St, Boston, MA 02114, USA

Stevens, Ray *Singer, Songwriter*
%Ahab Music, 1708 Grand Ave, Nashville, TN 37212, USA

Stevens, Rise *Opera Singer*
930 5th Ave, New York, NY 10021, USA

Stevens, Robert B *Educator*
Masters Lodgings, Pembroke College, Oxford OX1 1DW, England

Stevens, Roger L *Theater Producer*
%President's Arts/Humanities Commission, Kennedy Center, Washington, DC 20566, USA

Stevens, Scott *Hockey Player*
%New Jersey Devils, Meadowlands Arena, PO Box 504, East Rutherford, NJ 07073, USA

Stevens, Shadoe *Actor, Radio Personality*
2570 Benedict Canyon Dr, Beverly Hills, CA 90210, USA

Stevens, Stella *Actress*
2180 Coldwater Canyon Dr, Beverly Hills, CA 90210, USA

Stevens, W D *Businessman*
%Mitchell Energy & Development, 2001 Timberloch Place, The Woodlands, TX 77380, USA

Stevenson, Adlai E, III *Senator, IL*
10 S LaSalle St, #3610, Chicago, IL 60603, USA

Stevenson, Juliet *Actress*
%Markham & Froggatt, Julian House, 4 Windmill St, London W1P 1HF, England

Stevenson, McLean *Actor*
PO Box 1668, Studio City, CA 91614, USA

Stevenson, Parker *Actor*
4875 Louise Ave, Encino, CA 91316, USA

Stevenson, Teofilo *Boxer*
%Comite Olimppicu, Hotel Havana, Libre, Havana, Cuba

Stever, H Guyford *Aeronautical, Space Engineer*
1528 33rd St NW, Washington, DC 20007, USA

Stevie B *Singer*
%Famous Artists Agency, 1700 Broadway, #500, New York, NY 10019, USA

Steward, H Leighton *Businessman*
%Louisiana Land & Exploration Co, 909 Poydras St, New Orleans, LA 70112, USA

Stewart of Fulham, R Michael M *Government Official, England*
Combe, Newbury, Berks, England

Stewart, Al *Singer, Songwriter*
%Chapman Co, PO Box 5549, Santa Monica, CA 90409, USA

Stewart, C Jim, II *Businessman*
%Stewart & Stevenson Services, 2707 North Loop W, Houston, TX 77008, USA

Stewart, Catherine Mary *Actress*
350 DuPont St, Toronto ON M5R 1Z9, Canada

Stewart, Dave *Keyboardist, Guitarist (Eurythmics)*
PO Box 245, London N89 QG, England

Stewart, David K (Dave) *Baseball Player*
1038 Canton Circle, Claremont, CA 91711, USA

Stewart, Donald W *Senator, AL*
9003 Teddy Rae Court, Springfield, VA 22152, USA

Stewart, Elaine *Actress*
1011 N Roxbury Dr, Beverly Hills, CA 90210, USA

Stewart, F Jay *Businessman*
%Morton International, 100 N Riverside Plaza, Chicago, IL 60606, USA

Stewart, Gary *Singer*
%Entertainment Artists, 819 18th Ave S, Nashville, TN 37203, USA

Stewart, Ian *Government Official, England*
%House of Commons, Westminster, London SW1A 0AA, England

Stewart, J W *Businessman*
%BJ Services, 5500 NW Central Dr, Houston, TX 77092, USA

Stewart, James *Football Player*
%Jacksonville Jaguars, 1 Stadium Place, Jacksonville, FL 32202, USA

Stewart, Jimmy *Actor*
918 N Roxbury Dr, Beverly Hills, CA 90210, USA

Stewart, John Y (Jackie) *Auto Racing Driver*
24 Rte de Divonne, 1260 Nyon, Switzerland

Stewart, Martha *Entertainer*
%Martha Stewart Entertaining, 10 Saugatuck Ave, Westport, CT 06880, USA

Stewart, Mary *Writer*
House of Letterawe, Lock Awe, Argyll PA33 1AH, Scotland

Stewart, Melvin, Jr *Swimmer*
1311 Lake Lauden, Knoxville, TN 37916, USA

Stewart, Norm *Basketball Coach*
%University of Missouri, Athletic Dept, Columbia, MO 65211, USA

Stewart, Patrick *Actor*
%Boyack, 9 Cork St, London W1, England

Stewart, Payne *Golfer*
%Leader Enterprises, 390 N Orange Ave, #2600, Orlando, FL 32801, USA

Stewart, Peggy *Actress*
11139 Hortense St, North Hollywood, CA 91602, USA

Stewart, Redd *Singer, Songwriter*
%Tessier-Marsh Talent, 505 Canton Pass, Madison, TN 37115, USA

Stewart, Robert H, III *Financier*
%Bank One Texas, 1717 Main St, Dallas, TX 75201, USA

Stewart, Robert L *Astronaut, Army General*
815 Sun Valley Dr, Woodland Park, CO 80863, USA

Stewart, Rod *Singer, Songwriter*
23 Beverly Park, Los Angeles, CA 90210, USA

Stewart, S Jay *Businessman*
%Morton International, 100 N Riverside Plaza, Chicago, IL 60606, USA

Stewart, Thomas *Opera Singer*
%Columbia Artists Mgmt Inc, 165 W 57th St, New York, NY 10019, USA

Stewart, Thomas D *Physical Anthropologist*
1191 Crest Lane, McLean, VA 22101, USA

Stich, Michael *Tennis Player*
Ernst-Barlach-Str 44, 25336 Elmshorn, Germany

Stickel, Fred A *Publisher*
%Portland Oregonian, 1320 SW Broadway, Portland, OR 97201, USA

Stickney, Dorothy *Actress*
13 E 94th St, New York, NY 10128, USA

Stieb, David A (Dave) *Baseball Player*
1960 Jeannie Lane, Gilroy, CA 95020, USA

Stieber, Tamar *Journalist*
%Albuquerque Journal, Editorial Dept, 7777 Jefferson NE, Albuquerque, NM 87109, USA

Stiefel, Ethan *Ballet Dancer*
%New York City Ballet, Lincoln Center Plaza, New York, NY 10023, USA

Stiers, David Ogden *Actor*
%GKAC, 12304 Santa Monica Blvd, #119, Los Angeles, CA 90025, USA

Stigers, Curtis *Singer*
%C Winston Simone Mgmt, 1790 Broadway, #1000, New York, NY 10019, USA

Stiglitz, Joseph E *Economist*
%Council of Economic Advisers, Old Executive Office Bldg, Washington, DC 20500, USA

Stigwood, Robert C *Movie, Theater, Music Producer*
%Barton Manor, Isle of Wight, Whippingham, East Cowes, PO32 6LB, England

Stiles, Alan *Publisher*
%Esquire Magazine, 2 Park Ave, New York, NY 10016, USA

Stilgoe, Richard *Lyricist*
%Noel Gray Artists, 24 Denmark St, London WC2H 8NJ, England

Still, Eric *Football Player*
%Houston Oilers, 6910 Fannin St, Houston, TX 77030, USA

Still, Ray *Concert Oboist*
%Chicago Symphony Orchestra, 220 S Michigan Ave, Chicago, IL 60604, USA

Still, Susan L *Astronaut*
%NASA, Johnson Space Center, 2101 NASA Rd, Houston, TX 77058, USA

Stiller, Jerry *Comedian*
118 Riverside Dr, #5-A, New York, NY 10024, USA

Stillings, Floyd *Rodeo Performer*
2118 S Baldwin Ave, Arcadia, CA 91007, USA

Stills, Stephen *Singer, Guitarist*
%Creative Artists Agency, 9830 Wilshire Blvd, Beverly Hills, CA 90212, USA

Stillwagon, Jim *Football Player*
890 Gatehouse Lane, Columbus, OH 43235, USA

Stillwell, Roger *Football Player*
25 Woodland Court, Novato, CA 94947, USA

Stilwell, Richard D *Opera Singer*
1969 Rockingham St, McLean, VA 22101, USA

Stine, Richard *Editorial Cartoonist*
8100 Hidden Cove Rd, Bainbridge Island, WA 98110, USA

Sting (Gordon Sumner) *Singer, Bassist, Actor*
%Outlandos, 2 The Grove, Highgate Village, London N16, England

Stingley, Darryl *Football Player, Executive*
%New England Patriots, Foxboro Stadium, Rt 1, Foxboro, MA 02035, USA

Stinnette, Joe L, Jr *Businessman*
%Fireman's Fund Insurance, 777 San Marin Dr, Novato, CA 94998, USA

Stinson, George A *Businessman*
Hunting Country Rd, Tryon, NC 28782, USA

Stipe, Michael *Singer (REM)*
%REM/Athens Ltd, 250 W Clayton St, Athens, GA 30601, USA

Stiritz, William P *Businessman*
%Ralston Purina Co, Checkerboard Square, St Louis, MO 63164, USA

Stirling, David *WW II Army Commando Hero*
22 S Audley St, London W1, England

Stirling, Linda *Actress*
4717 Laurel Canyon Blvd, #2068, North Hollywood, CA 91607, USA

Stiska, John C *Businessman*
%Triton Group, 550 W "C" St, San Diego, CA 92101, USA

Stitzlein, Lorraine *Bowling Executive*
%Professional Bowlers Assn, 1720 Merriman Rd, Akron, OH 44313, USA

Stock, Barbara *Actress*
13421 Cheltenham Dr, Sherman Oaks, CA 91423, USA

Stockdale, James B *Vietnam War Navy Hero (CMH), Admiral*
%Stanford University, Hoover Institution, Stanford, CA 94305, USA

Stockhausen, Karlheinz *Composer*
Stockhausen-Verlag, 51515 Kurten, Germany

Stockman, David A *Government Official, Financier*
%Blackstone Group, 345 Park Ave, New York, NY 10154, USA

Stockman, Shawn *Singer (Boyz II Men)*
%BIV Entertainment, 5 Bishop Rd, Vincentown, NJ 08088, USA

Stockton, Dave K *Golfer*
32373 Tres Lagos St, Mentone, CA 92359, USA

Stockton, Dick *Sportscaster*
715 Stadium Dr, San Antonio, TX 78212, USA

Stockton, John H *Basketball Player*
%Utah Jazz, 301 W South Temple, Salt Lake City, UT 84101, USA

Stockton, Richard L *Tennis Player*
%US Tennis Assn, 1212 Ave of Americas, New York, NY 10036, USA

Stockwell, Dean *Actor*
PO Box 6248, Malibu, CA 90264, USA

Stockwell, Guy *Actor*
6652 Coldwater Canyon Ave, North Hollywood, CA 91606, USA

Stoddard, Brandon *Television Executive*
240 N Glenroy Ave, Los Angeles, CA 90049, USA

Stodder, John W *Businessman*
%Jostens Inc, 5501 Norman Center Dr, Minneapolis, MN 55437, USA

Stoitchkov, Hristo *Soccer Player*
%FC Barcelona, Aristides Maillol S/N, 08 028 Barcelona, Spain

Stokes, Dewey R *Labor Leader*
%Fraternal Order of Police, 2100 Gardner Lane, Louisville, KY 40205, USA

Stokes, J J *Football Player*
%San Francisco 49ers, 4949 Centennial Blvd, Santa Clara, CA 95054, USA

Stokkan, Bill *Auto Racing Executive*
%Championship Auto Racing Teams, 755 W Big Beaver Rd, #800, Troy, MI 48084, USA

S

Stiller - Stokkan

Stoklos, Randy *Volleyball Player*
%Assn of Volleyball Pros, 15260 Ventura Blvd, #2250, Sherman Oaks, CA 91403, USA

Stolle, Frederick S *Tennis Player*
%Turnberry Isle Yacht & Racquet Club, 19735 Turnberry Way, North Miami, FL 33180, USA

Stolley, Paul D *Physician*
6424 Brass Knob, Columbia, MD 21044, USA

Stolley, Richard B *Editor*
%Time Inc, Time-Life Building, Rockefeller Center, New York, NY 10020, USA

Stolojan, Theodor *Prime Minister, Romania*
%Int'l Bank of Reconstruction-Development, 1818 "H" St NW, Washington, DC 20433, USA

Stoltenberg, Gerhard *Government Official, Germany*
Grauheindorferstr 108, 53111 Bonn, Germany

Stoltz, Eric *Actor*
401 S Burnside Ave, #2-F, Los Angeles, CA 90036, USA

Stoltzman, Richard L *Concert Clarinetist*
%Frank Saloman Assoc, 201 W 54th St, #4-C, New York, NY 10019, USA

Stone, Albert L *Thoroughbred Racing Executive*
700 Central Ave, PO Box 8427, Louisville, KY 40208, USA

Stone, Andrew L *Movie Director*
10478 Wyton Dr, Los Angeles, CA 90024, USA

Stone, Christopher *Actor*
23035 Cumorah Crest Dr, Woodland Hills, CA 91364, USA

Stone, Donald C *Government Official, Educator*
Robin Run Village, 5354 W 62nd St, #270, Indianapolis, IN 46268, USA

Stone, Doug *Singer, Songwriter*
PO Box 128, Orlinda, TN 37141, USA

Stone, Edward C, Jr *Space Physicist*
%Jet Propulsion Laboratory, 4800 Oak Grove Dr, #180-904, Pasadena, CA 91109, USA

Stone, Irving I *Businessman*
%American Greetings Corp, 1 American Rd, Cleveland, OH 44144, USA

Stone, Jack *Religious Leader*
%Church of Nazarene, 6401 The Paseo, Kansas City, MO 64131, USA

Stone, James L *Korean War Army Hero (CMH)*
1279 Cedarland Plaza Dr, Arlington, TX 76011, USA

Stone, Jesse, Jr *Educator*
%Southern University, President's Office, Baton Rouge, LA 70813, USA

Stone, Lawrence *Historian*
266 Moore St, Princeton, NJ 08540, USA

Stone, Leonard *Actor*
%Amaral Talent Agency, 10000 Riverside Dr, Toluca Lake, CA 91602, USA

Stone, Marvin L *Editor, Government Official*
6318 Crosswoods Circle, Lake Barcroft, Falls Church, VA 22044, USA

Stone, Oliver W *Movie Director, Screenwriter*
%Ixtlan Corp, 201 Santa Monica Blvd, #610, Santa Monica, CA 90401, USA

Stone, Peter H *Playwright, Scenarist*
160 E 71st St, New York, NY 10021, USA

Stone, Robert A *Writer*
%Donadio & Ashworth, 231 W 22nd St, New York, NY 10011, USA

Stone, Roger D *Political Consultant*
34 W 88th St, New York, NY 10024, USA

Stone, Roger W *Businessman*
%Stone Container Corp, 150 N Michigan Ave, Chicago, IL 60601, USA

Stone, Sharon *Actress*
%Tri-Star Pictures, 3400 Riverside Dr, Burbank, CA 91505, USA

Stone, Steven M (Steve) *Baseball Player, Sportscaster*
%WGN-TV, 435 N Michigan Blvd, Chicago, IL 60611, USA

Stone, W Clement *Businessman*
PO Box 649, Lake Forest, IL 60045, USA

Stonecipher, David A *Financier*
%Jefferson-Pilot Corp, 100 N Greene St, Greensboro, NC 27401, USA

Stonecipher, Harry C *Businessman*
%McDonnell Douglas Corp, PO Box 516, St Louis, MO 63166, USA

Stones, Dwight *Track Athlete*
12841 Newport Ave, Tustin, CA 92680, USA

Stookey, John H *Businessman*
%Quantum Chemical, 11500 Northlake Dr, Cincinnati, OH 45249, USA

Stookey, Paul *Singer (Peter, Paul & Mary), Songwriter*
%Newworld, Rt 175, South Blue Hill Falls, ME 04615, USA

Stoph, Willi *Head of State, East Germany*
Kohlsterstr 47, 12205 Berlin, Germany

Stoppard, Tom *Playwright*
%Peters Fraser Dunlop, Chelsea Harbour, Lots Rd, London SW10 0XF, England

Stoppelmoor, Wayne H *Businessman*
%Interstate Power Co, 1000 Main St, Dubuque, IA 52001, USA

Storaro, Vittorio *Cinematographer*
Via Divino Amore 2, 00040 Frattocchie Merino, Italy

Storch, David P *Businessman*
%AAR Corp, 1111 Nicholas Blvd, Elk Grove Village, IL 60007, USA

Storch, Larry *Actor*
336 West End St, #17-F, New York, NY 10023, USA

Storer, Peter *Broadcast Executive*
%Storer Broadcasting Co, 1177 Kane Concourse, Miami Beach, FL 33154, USA

Storey, David M *Playwright*
2 Lyndhurst Gdns, London NW3, England

Stork, Gilbert *Chemist*
459 Next Day Hill Dr, Englewood, NJ 07631, USA

Storm, Gale *Actress*
308 N Sycamore Ave, #104, Los Angeles, CA 90036, USA

Storm, Hannah *Sportscaster*
%NBC-TV, Sports Dept, 30 Rockefeller Plaza, New York, NY 10112, USA

Storr, Anthony *Psychiatrist, Therapist, Writer*
%Peters Fraser Dunlop, Chelsea Harbour, Lots Rd, London SW10 0XF, England

Story, Ralph *Commentator*
3425 Wonderview Dr, Los Angeles, CA 90068, USA

Stossel, John *Commentator*
%ABC-TV, News Dept, 153 Columbus Circle, New York, NY 10023, USA

Stott, Kathryn L *Concert Pianist*
Mire House, West Marton Near Skipton, Yorks BD23 3UQ, England

Stottlemyre, Melvin L (Mel) *Baseball Player*
9 S 3rd St, Yakima, WA 98901, USA

Stoudamire, Damon *Basketball Player*
%Toronto Raptors, 20 Bay St, #1702, Toronto ON M5J 2N8, Canada

Stover Irwin Russ, Juno *Diver*
601 Beachcomber Blvd, #370, Lake Havasu City, AZ 86403, USA

Stowe, David H, Jr *Businessman*
%Deere & Company, John Deere Rd, Moline, IL 61265, USA

Stowe, Madeleine *Actress*
%United Talent Agency, 9560 Wilshire Blvd, #500, Beverly Hills, CA 90212, USA

Stowers, James E, Jr *Financier*
%Twentieth Century Investors, 605 W 47th St, Kansas City, MO 64112, USA

Stoyanov, Krasimir M *Cosmonaut, Bulgaria*
%Potchta Kosmonavtov, 141 160 Svyosdny Gorodok, Moskovskoi Oblasti, Russia

Stoyanov, Michael *Actor*
%Borinstein Oreck Dogail Agency, 8271 Melrose Ave, #110, Los Angeles, CA 90046, USA

Stoyanovich, Pete *Football Player*
%Miami Dolphins, 7500 SW 30th St, Davie, FL 33329, USA

Strachan, Rod *Swimmer*
13812 Glenmere Dr, Santa Ana, CA 92705, USA

Stradlin, Izzy *Guitarist (Guns N' Roses)*
%Artists & Audience Entertainment, 83 Riverside Dr, New York, NY 10024, USA

Straight, Beatrice *Actress*
30 Norfolk Rd, Southfield, MA 01259, USA

Strait, George *Singer*
%Erv Woolsey Mgmt, 1000 18th Ave S, Nashville, TN 37212, USA

Stram, Henry L (Hank) *Football Coach, Sportscaster*
194 Belle Terre Blvd, Covington, LA 70433, USA

Strand, Mark *Poet*
%University of Utah, English Dept, Salt Lake City, UT 84112, USA

Strand, Robin *Actor*
%Gersh Agency, 232 N Canon Dr, Beverly Hills, CA 90210, USA

Strange, Curtis N *Golfer*
%Kingsmill Golf Club, 100 Golf Club Rd, Williamsburg, VA 23185, USA

Strangeland, Roger E *Businessman*
%Von's Companies, 618 Michillinda Ave, Arcadia, CA 91007, USA

Strasberg, Susan *Actress*
PO Box 847, Pacific Palisades, CA 90272, USA

S

Stoph - Strasberg

Strasser, Robin — *Actress*
152 E 82nd St, New York, NY 10028, USA

Strasser, Valentine E M — *President, Sierra Leone*
%President's Office, State House, Independence Ave, Freetown, Sierra Leone

Strassman, Marcia — *Actress*
520 18th St, Santa Monica, CA 90402, USA

Stratas, Teresa — *Opera Singer*
%Metropolitan Opera Assn, Lincoln Center Plaza, New York, NY 10023, USA

Stratton, Frederick P, Jr — *Businessman*
%Briggs & Stratton, PO Box 702, Milwaukee, WI 53201, USA

Stratton, Richard A — *Businessman*
%Nabors Industries, 515 W Greens Rd, Houston, TX 77067, USA

Stratton, William B — *Governor, IL*
%Chicago Bank of Commerce, 200 E Randolph Dr, Chicago, IL 60601, USA

Straub, Peter F — *Writer*
53 W 85th St, New York, NY 10024, USA

Straub, Robert W — *Governor, OR*
2087 Orchard Heights Rd NW, Salem, OR 97304, USA

Straus, Robert — *Behavioral Scientist*
%University of Kentucky, Behavioral Science Dept, Lexington, KY 40536, USA

Straus, Roger W, Jr — *Editor, Publisher*
%Farrar Straus Giroux, 19 Union Square W, New York, NY 10003, USA

Straus, William L, Jr — *Physical Anthropologist*
7111 Park Heights Ave, #506, Baltimore, MD 21215, USA

Strauss, Peter — *Actor*
%Movie Group, 1900 Ave of Stars, #1425, Los Angeles, CA 90067, USA

Strauss, Robert S — *Political Leader, Diplomat*
%Akin Gump Strauss Hauer Feld, 1700 Pacific Ave, #4100, Dallas, TX 75201, USA

Strausz-Hupe, Robert — *Diplomat*
White Horse Farm, 864 Grubbs Mill Rd, Newtown Square, PA 19073, USA

Straw, Edward M — *Navy Admiral*
Director, Defense Logistics Agency, Cameron Station, Alexandria, VA 22306, USA

Strawberry, Darryl E — *Baseball Player*
1419 Red Bluff Court, San Dimas, CA 91773, USA

Strawbridge, Francis R, III — *Businessman*
%Strawbridge & Clothier, 801 Market St, Philadelphia, PA 19107, USA

Strawbridge, Peter S — *Businessman*
%Strawbridge & Clothier, 801 Market St, Philadelphia, PA 19107, USA

Strawser, Neil — *Commentator*
130 "E" St SE, Washington, DC 20003, USA

Streep, Meryl — *Actress*
130 Paradise Cove Rd, Malibu, CA 90265, USA

Street, George L, III — *WW II Navy Hero (CMH)*
22 Linda Rd, Andover, MA 01810, USA

Street, Rebecca — *Actress*
711 9th St, #1, Santa Monica, CA 90402, USA

Street, William M — *Businessman*
%Brown-Forman Corp, 850 Dixie Highway, Louisville, KY 40210, USA

Streetman, Ben G — *Electrical Engineer*
3915 Glengarry Dr, Austin, TX 78731, USA

Strehler, Giorgio — *Theater Director*
%Piccolo Theatro di Milano, Via Ravello 2, 20121 Milan, Italy

Streisand, Barbra — *Singer, Actress, Director*
301 N Carolwood Dr, Los Angeles, CA 90077, USA

Streisinger, George — *Biologist*
%University of Oregon, Molecular Biology Institute, Eugene, OR 97403, USA

Streit, Clarence K — *Journalist*
2853 Ontario Rd NW, Washington, DC 20009, USA

Streitwieser, Andrew, Jr — *Chemist*
%University of California, Chemistry Dept, Berkeley, CA 94720, USA

Strekalov, Gennady M — *Cosmonaut*
%Potchta Kosmonavtov, 141 160 Svyosdny Gorodok, Moskovskoi Oblasti, Russia

Stretton, Ross — *Ballet Dancer*
%American Ballet Theatre, 890 Broadway, New York, NY 10003, USA

Strickland de la Hunty, Shirley — *Track Athlete*
22 Fraser Rd, Applecross WA 6153, Australia

Strickland, Amzie — *Actress*
1329 N Ogden Dr, Los Angeles, CA 90046, USA

Strasser - Strickland

Strickland, Gail *Actress*
340 E 72nd St, New York, NY 10021, USA

Strickland, Robert L *Businessman*
%Loew's Companies, State Highway 268 E, North Wilksboro, NC 28659, USA

Strickland, Rod *Basketball Player*
%Portland Trail Blazers, 700 NE Multnomah St, #600, Portland, OR 97232, USA

Strickler, Ivan K *Businessman*
PO Box 365, Iola, KS 66749, USA

Stricklyn, Ray *Actor*
852 N Genesee Ave, Los Angeles, CA 90046, USA

Strider, Marjorie V *Artist*
7 Worth St, New York, NY 10013, USA

Stringer, C Vivian *Basketball Coach*
%Rutgers University, Athletic Dept, New Brunswick, NJ 08903, USA

Stringer, Howard *Television Executive*
186 Riverside Dr, New York, NY 10024, USA

Stringfield, Sherry *Actress*
%Abrams-Rubaloff Lawrence, 8075 W 3rd St, #303, Los Angeles, CA 90048, USA

Stritch, Elaine *Singer, Actress*
%Michael Whitehall, 125 Gloucester Rd, London SW7 4TE, England

Stroessner, Alfredo *President, Paraguay*
Lago Sul, Brasilia, Brazil

Stroh, Peter W *Businessman*
%Stroh Brewery Co, 100 River Place Rd, Detroit, MI 48207, USA

Strolz, Hubert *Skier*
6767 Warth 19, Austria

Strom, Brock T *Football Player*
4301 W 110th St, Leawood, KS 66211, USA

Strom, Everald H *Religious Leader*
%Church of Lutheran Brethren, 1007 Westside Dr, Fergus Falls, MN 56537, USA

Strome, Stephen *Businessman*
%Handleman Co, 500 Kirts Blvd, Troy, MI 48084, USA

Strominger, Jack L *Biochemist*
%Harvard University, Biochemistry Dept, Cambridge, MA 02138, USA

Strong, Maurice F *Government Official, Canada*
%Ontario Hydro, 700 University Ave, Toronto ON M5G 1X6, Canada

Stroud, Don *Actor*
17020 W Sunset Blvd, #20, Pacific Palisades, CA 90272, USA

Stroud, Joe H *Editor*
%Detroit Free Press, Editorial Dept, 321 W Lafayette Blvd, Detroit, MI 48226, USA

Stroup, Theodore G, Jr *Army General*
Deputy Chief of Staff, Personnel, HdqsUSArmy, Pentagon, Washington, DC 20310, USA

Strouse, Charles *Composer*
171 W 57th St, New York, NY 10019, USA

Strube, Juergen F *Businessman*
%BASF Corp, Carl-Bosch Str 38, 67063 Ludwigshafen, Germany

Struchkova, Raisa S *Ballerina*
%Sovetskiy Ballet, Tverskaya 22-B, 103050 Moscow, Russia

Strudler, Robert J *Businessman*
%US Home Corp, 1800 West Loop S, Houston, TX 77027, USA

Struever, Stuart M *Anthropologist*
2000 Sheridan Rd, Evanston, IL 60201, USA

Strugnell, John *Theologian*
%Harvard University, Divinity School, 45 Francis Ave, Cambridge, MA 02138, USA

Strummer, Joe *Singer, Guitarist (Clash)*
%Clash, 268 Camden Rd, London NW1, England

Struthers, Sally *Actress*
%David Shapira Assoc, 15301 Ventura Blvd, #345, Sherman Oaks, CA 91403, USA

Strutz, Richard *Financier*
%National Bancorp of Alaska, 301 W Northern Lights Blvd, Anchorage, AK 99503, USA

Stuart, Barbara *Actress*
%Artists Group, 10100 Santa Monica Blvd, #2490, Los Angeles, CA 90067, USA

Stuart, Gloria *Actress*
884 S Bundy Dr, Los Angeles, CA 90049, USA

Stuart, John E *Businessman*
%Alco Standard Corp, PO Box 834, Valley Forge, PA 19482, USA

Stuart, Lyle *Publisher*
1530 Palisade Ave, #6-L, Fort Lee, NJ 07024, USA

Stuart, Marty	*Singer, Songwriter*
%Rothbaum & Garner, 119 17th Ave S, Nashville, TN 37203, USA	
Stuart, Mary	*Actress*
30 E 68th St, New York, NY 10021, USA	
Stuart, Maxine	*Actress*
%Century Artists, 9744 Wilshire Blvd, #308, Beverly Hills, CA 90212, USA	
Stuart, Roy	*Actor*
4948 Radford Ave, North Hollywood, CA 91607, USA	
Stubblefield, Dana	*Football Player*
%San Francisco 49ers, 4949 Centennial Blvd, Santa Clara, CA 95054, USA	
Stubbs, Imogen	*Actress*
%International Creative Mgmt, 76 Oxford St, London W1N 0AX, England	
Studeman, William O	*Navy Admiral*
Director, National Security Agency, Fort George Meade, MD 20755, USA	
Studenroth, Carl W	*Labor Leader*
%Molders & Allied Workers Union, 1225 E McMillan St, Cincinnati, OH 45206, USA	
Studer, Cheryl	*Opera Singer*
%International Performing Artists, 125 Crowfield Dr, Knoxville, TN 37922, USA	
Studstill, Patrick L (Pat)	*Football Player*
2235 Linda Flora Dr, Los Angeles, CA 90077, USA	
Stuiver, Minze	*Geological Scientist*
%University of Washington, Geological Sciences Dept, Seattle, WA 98195, USA	
Stukel, James J	*Educator*
%University of Illinois at Chicago, Chancellor's Office, Chicago, IL 60680, USA	
Stumpf, Kenneth E	*Vietnam War Army Hero (CMH)*
PO Box 94, Sparta, WI 54656, USA	
Stumpf, Paul K	*Biochemist*
764 Elmwood Dr, Davis, CA 95616, USA	
Stupski, Lawrence J	*Financier*
%Charles Schwab Corp, 101 Montgomery St, San Francisco, CA 94104, USA	
Sturckow, Frederick W (Rick)	*Astronaut*
%NASA, Johnson Space Center, 2101 NASA Rd, Houston, TX 77058, USA	
Sturdivant, John N	*Labor Leader*
%American Government Employees Federation, 80 "F" St NW, Washington, DC 20001, USA	
Sturdivant, Thomas V (Tom)	*Baseball Player*
825 SW 113th St, Oklahoma City, OK 73170, USA	
Sturgess, Thomas W	*Businessman*
%United Stationers, 2200 E Golf Rd, Des Plaines, IL 60016, USA	
Sturman, Eugene	*Sculptor*
1108 W Washington Blvd, Venice, CA 90291, USA	
Sturtevant, Julian M	*Chemist*
%Yale University, Chemistry Dept, PO Box 6066, New Haven, CT 06520, USA	
Stuzin, Charles B	*Financier*
%CSF Holdings, 1100 W McNab Rd, Fort Lauderdale, FL 33309, USA	
Styles, Margretta	*Educator*
2180 Mar East St, Bel Tiburon, CA 94920, USA	
Styron, William	*Writer*
12 Rucum Rd, Roxbury, CT 06783, USA	
Suad, Anthony	*Photographer*
%Denver Post, PO Box 1709, Denver, CO 80201, USA	
Suarez Gonzalez, Adolfo	*Prime Minister, Spain*
Sagasta, 33 Madrid 4, Spain	
Subotnick, Morton	*Composer*
121 Coronado Lane, Santa Fe, NM 87501, USA	
Subramanian, Shivan S	*Businessman*
%Allendale Mutual Insurance Co, Allendale Park, Johnston, RI 02919, USA	
Subroto	*Government Leader, Indonesia*
%OPEC, Obere Donaustr 93, 1020 Vienna, Austria	
Suchet, David	*Actor*
%Brunskill, 169 Queen's Gate, #8, London SW7 5EH, England	
Suchocka, Hanna	*Prime Minister, Poland*
%Prime Minister's Office, Ul Wiejska 48, 00-583 Warsaw, Poland	
Sudersham, Ennackel	*Theoretical Physicist*
%University of Texas, Physics Dept, Austin, TX 78713, USA	
Sudharmono	*Government Official, Indonesia; General*
%Vice President's Office, Jalan Merdeka Selatan 6, Jakarta, Indonesia	
Sudikoff, Jeffrey P	*Hockey Executive*
%Los Angeles Kings, Forum, PO Box 17013, Inglewood, CA 90308, USA	

Stuart - Sudikoff

Sudol, Edward L (Ed)	*Baseball Umpire*
415 Rivilo Blvd, Daytona Beach, FL 32118, USA	
Suenaga, Soichiro	*Businessman*
%Mitsubishi Heavy Industries, 5-1 Marubouchi, Chiyodaku, Tokyo, Japan	
Sues, Alan	*Actor*
9014 Dorrington Ave, Los Angeles, CA 90048, USA	
Suess, Hans E	*Geochemist*
%University of California, Chemistry Dept, La Jolla, CA 92093, USA	
Sugar, Bert Randolph	*Writer, Editor*
6 Southview Rd, Chappaqua, NY 10514, USA	
Sugar, Leo T	*Football Player*
816 Coutant, Flushing, MI 48433, USA	
Sugarman, Burt	*Movie Producer*
%Giant Group, 150 El Camino Dr, #303, Beverly Hills, CA 90212, USA	
Sugarmann, Josh	*Social Activist*
1650 Harvard St NW, Washington, DC 20009, USA	
Suggs, Louise	*Golfer*
%Ladies Professional Golf Assn, 2570 Volusia Ave, Daytona Beach, FL 32114, USA	
Sugiura, Hideo	*Businessman*
%Honda Motor Co, 27-8-6 Jingumae, Shibuyaku, Tokyo 150, Japan	
Suhara, Akira	*Businessman*
%Honshu Paper Co, 5-12-8 Ginza, Chuoku, Tokyo 104, Japan	
Suharto	*President, Indonesia; Army General*
%President's Office, 15 Jalan Merdeka Utara, Jakarta, Indonesia	
Suhl, Harry	*Physicist*
%University of California, Physicis Dept, San Diego, CA 92093, USA	
Suhor, Yvonne	*Actress*
%J Michael Bloom Ltd, 9255 Sunset Blvd, #710, Los Angeles, CA 90069, USA	
Suhr, August R (Gus)	*Baseball Player*
341 Hazel Ave, Millbrae, CA 94030, USA	
Suhrheinrich, Richard F	*Judge*
%US Court of Appeals, 315 W Allegan, Lansing, MI 48933, USA	
Sui, Anna	*Fashion Designer*
%Keeble Cavaco Duka, 853 7th Ave, #10-A, New York, NY 10019, USA	
Suitner, Otmar	*Conductor*
Platanestr 13, 13156 Berlin-Niederschonhausen, Germany	
Suk, Josef	*Concert Violinist*
Karlovo Namesti 5, 12000 Prague 2, Czech Republic	
Sukova, Helena	*Tennis Player*
1 Ave Grande Bretagne, Monte Carlo, Monaco	
Sulaiman, Jose	*Boxing Official*
%World Boxing Council, Genova 33, Colonia Juarez, Cuahtetemoc 0660, Mexico	
Suleymanoglu, Naim	*Weightlifter*
%Olympic Committee, Sisli, Buyukdere Cad 18 Tankaya, Istanbul, Turkey	
Culiotis, Elena	*Opera Singer*
Villa il Poderino, Via Incontri 38, Florence, Italy	
Sullins, William A, Jr	*Financier*
%Commerce Bancshares, 1000 Walnut St, Kansas City, MO 64106, USA	
Sullivan, Brendan V, Jr	*Attorney*
%Williams & Connolly, 725 12th St NW, Washington, DC 20005, USA	
Sullivan, Charles A	*Businessman*
%Interstate Bakeries Corp, 12 E Armour Blvd, Kansas City, MO 64111, USA	
Sullivan, Daniel J	*Businessman*
%Roadway Services Inc, 1077 Gorge Blvd, Akron, OH 44310, USA	
Sullivan, Danny	*Auto Racing Driver*
414 E Cooper St, #201, Aspen, CO 81611, USA	
Sullivan, Dennis P	*Mathematician*
%Queens College, Mathematics Dept, 33 W 42nd St, #706, New York, NY 10036, USA	
Sullivan, James N	*Businessman*
%Chevron Corp, 225 Bush St, San Francisco, CA 94104, USA	
Sullivan, Joseph P	*Businessman*
%American Health Properties, 6400 S Fiddler's Green Circle, Englewood, CO 80111, USA	
Sullivan, Joseph P	*Businessman*
%Vigoro Inc, 225 N Michigan Ave, Chicago, IL 60601, USA	
Sullivan, Kathleen	*Commentator*
5670 Wilshire Blvd, #213, Los Angeles, CA 90036, USA	
Sullivan, Kathryn D	*Astronaut*
2610 N Key Blvd, Arlington, VA 22201, USA	

S

Sudol - Sullivan

Sullivan, Leon H *Religious Leader*
%Zion Baptist Church, 3600 N Broad St, Philadelphia, PA 19140, USA

Sullivan, Louis W *Secretary, Health & Human Services*
%Morehouse School of Medicine, 720 Westview Dr SW, Atlanta, GA 30310, USA

Sullivan, Michael J (Mike) *Governor, WY*
1124 S Durbin St, Casper, WY 82601, USA

Sullivan, Pat *Football Player, Coach*
%Texas Christian University, Athletic Dept, Fort Worth, TX 76129, USA

Sullivan, Susan *Actress*
8642 Allenwood Rd, Los Angeles, CA 90046, USA

Sullivan, Timothy J *Educator*
%College of William & Mary, President's Office, Williamsburg, VA 23187, USA

Sullivan, Walter S *Journalist*
%New York Times, Editorial Dept, 229 W 43rd St, New York, NY 10036, USA

Sullivan, William J *Educator*
%Seattle University, President's Office, Seattle, WA 98122, USA

Sultan Salman Al-Saud *Astronaut, Saudi Arabia*
PO Box 18368, Riyadh 11415, Saudi Arabia

Sultan, Donald K *Artist*
54 N Moore St, New York, NY 10013, USA

Sulzberger, Arthur O, Jr *Publisher*
%New York Times, 229 W 43rd St, New York, NY 10036, USA

Summer, Donna *Singer*
18165 Eccles St, Northridge, CA 91325, USA

Summerall, George A (Pat) *Sportscaster*
10036 Sawgrass Dr, Ponte Vedra, FL 32082, USA

Summers, Carol *Artist*
2817 Smith Grade, Santa Cruz, CA 95060, USA

Summers, Dana *Cartoonist (Lug Nuts, Bound & Gagged)*
%Orlando Sentinel, 633 N Orange Ave, Orlando, FL 32801, USA

Summers, Lawrence H *Economist, Government Official*
%Treasury Department, 15th & Pennsylvania Ave NW, Washington, DC 20220, USA

Summers, William B, Jr *Financier*
%McDonald Co Investments, 800 Superior Ave, Cleveland, OH 44114, USA

Summitt, Pat Head *Basketball Coach*
%University of Tennessee, Athletic Dept, Knoxville, TN 37996, USA

Sumners, Rosalynn *Figure Skater*
%Barbara Kindness, 9912 225th Place SW, Edmonds, WA 98020, USA

Sun Yun-Suan *Prime Minister, Taiwan*
1 Chung Hsiao E Rd, Taipei 110, Taiwan

Sundance, Robert *Social Activist*
%California Indian Alcoholism Commission, 225 W 8th St, Los Angeles, CA 90014, USA

Sundlun, Bruce G *Governor, RI*
PO Box 15248, Riverside, RI 02915, USA

Sundquist, Donald K (Don) *Governor, Representative, TN*
%Governor's Office, State Capitol, Nashville, TN

Sundquist, Ulf *Businessman*
Ergo Consult Oy, Nordic Law, Mikonkatu 2, 00100 Helsinki, Finalnd

Sununu, John H *Governor, NH; Government Official*
24 Samoset Dr, Salem, NH 03079, USA

Suquia Goicoechea, Angel Cardinal *Religious Leader*
El Cardenal Arxobispo, San Justo 2, 28074 Madrid, Spain

Sura, Bob *Basketball Player*
%Cleveland Cavaliers, 2923 Statesboro Rd, Richfield, OH 44286, USA

Surtees, John *Auto Racing Driver*
%Team Surtees, Station Rd, Edenbridge, Kent TN8 6HL, England

Susa, Conrad *Composer*
433 Eureka St, San Francisco, CA 94114, USA

Suschitzky, Wolfgang *Photographer*
Douglas House, 6 Maida Ave, #11, London W2 1TG, England

Sushkevich, Stanislav S *Chairman of Soviet, Belarus*
%Chairman's Office, Soviet, Dom Pravitelstva, 220010 Minsk, Belarus

Susi, Carol Ann *Actress*
846 N Sweetzer Ave, Los Angeles, CA 90069, USA

Susman, Todd *Actor*
11462 Poema Place, #34-102, Chatsworth, CA 91311, USA

Sutcliffe, Richard L (Rick) *Baseball Player*
313 NW North Shore Dr, Parkville, MO 64151, USA

Suter, Albert E — *Businessman*
%Emerson Electric Co, 8000 W Florissant Ave, St Louis, MO 63136, USA

Suter, Gary — *Hockey Player*
%Calgary Flames, PO Box 1540, Station "M", Calgary AB T2P 389, Canada

Sutherland, Donald — *Actor*
%Creative Artists Agency, 9830 Wilshire Blvd, Beverly Hills, CA 90212, USA

Sutherland, Joan — *Opera Singer*
%Ingpen & Williams, 14 Kensington Court, London W8, England

Sutherland, Kiefer — *Actor*
9056 Santa Monica Blvd, #100, Los Angeles, CA 90069, USA

Sutherland, Peter D — *Government Official, Ireland*
68 Eglinton Rd, Dublin 4, Ireland

Sutter, Brent — *Hockey Player*
%Chicago Blackhawks, Chicago Stadium, 1800 W Madison St, Chicago, IL 60612, USA

Sutter, H Bruce — *Baseball Player*
1368 Hamilton Rd, Kennesaw, GA 30152, USA

Sutter, Ron — *Hockey Player*
%Quebec Nordiques, 2205 Ave du Colisee, Quebec City PQ G1L 4W7, Canada

Sutton, Donald H (Don) — *Baseball Player, Sportscaster*
2 Campanero W, Irvine, CA 92720, USA

Sutton, Eddie — *Basketball Coach*
%Oklahoma State University, Athletic Dept, Stillwater, OK 74078, USA

Sutton, George P — *Aeronautical Engineer*
725 Barrington Ave, #110, Los Angeles, CA 90049, USA

Sutton, Hal — *Golfer*
6917 Avondale Dr, Shreveport, LA 71107, USA

Sutton, Thomas C — *Businessman*
%Pacific Mutual Life Insurance, 700 Newport Center Dr, Newport Beach, CA 92660, USA

Suwa, Gen — *Anthropologist*
%University of California, Human Evolutionary Science Lab, Borkeley, CA 94720, USA

Suzman, Janet — *Actress*
%William Morris Agency, 31/32 Soho Square, London W1V 5DG, England

Suzuki, Eiji — *Businessman*
%Mitsubishi Chemical Industries, 2-5-2 Marunouchi, Tokyo 100, Japan

Suzuki, Osami — *Businessman*
%Suzuki Motor Corp, 300 Takatsuka, Kamimura, Hamanagun, Shizoka-ken, Japan

Suzuki, Robert — *Educator*
%California State University, President's Office, Bakersfield, CA 93311, USA

Suzuki, Seiji — *Businessman*
%Mitsubishi Chemical Industries, 2-5-2 Marunouchi, Tokyo 100, Japan

Suzuki, Toshifumi — *Businessman*
%Southland Corp, 2711 N Haskell Ave, Dallas, TX 75204, USA

Suzuki, Yuji — *Financier*
%Industrial Bank of Japan Trust, 245 Park Ave, New York, NY 10167, USA

Suzy (Aileen Mehle) — *Columnist*
18 E 68th St, #1-B, New York, NY 10021, USA

Svare, Harland — *Football Player, Coach*
3095 Caminito Sagunto, Del Mar, CA 92014, USA

Svedberg, Bjorn — *Businessman*
%L M Ericsson Telephone, Telefonaktiebiolaget, 126 11 Stockholm, Sweden

Svendsen, George — *Football Player*
2100 Mary Hills Dr, Golden Valley, MN 55422, USA

Svendsen, Louise A — *Museum Curator*
16 Park Ave, New York, NY 10016, USA

Svenson, Bo — *Actor*
1434 Princeton St, #D, Santa Monica, CA 90404, USA

Svetlanov, Yevgeni F — *Conductor*
Stanislavsky Str 14, #14, 103009 Moscow, Russia

Svoboda, Josef — *Architect*
%Laterna Magika, Lilova 9, 11000 Prague 1, Czech Republic

Swados, Elizabeth A — *Writer, Composer*
360 Central Park West, #16-G, New York, NY 10025, USA

Swaggart, Jimmy L — *Evangelist*
8919 World Ministry Ave, Baton Rouge, LA 70810, USA

Swaggert, H Patrick — *Educator*
%State University of New York, President's Office, Albany, NY 12222, USA

Swain, Donald C — *Educator*
%University of Louisville, President's Office, Louisville, KY 40292, USA

S

Suter - Swain

Swain, John C *Financier*
%Oppenheimer Mgmt, 2 World Trade Center, New York, NY 10048, USA

Swaminathan, Monkombu S *Geneticist*
%M S Swaminathan Foundation, 3 Cross St, Taramani, Madras 600113, India

Swan, Henry, II *Physician*
6700 W Lakeridge Rd, Lakewood, CO 80227, USA

Swan, John W *Premier, Bermuda*
%Cabinet Office, 105 Front St, Hamilton HM12, Bermuda

Swan, Richard G *Mathematician*
475 Oakdale Ave, Glencoe, IL 60022, USA

Swann, Lynn C *Football Player, Sportscaster*
%Swann Inc, 600 Grant St, #4800, Pittsburgh, PA 15219, USA

Swanson, August G *Physician*
3146 Portage Bay Place E, #H, Seattle, WA 98102, USA

Swanson, Dennis *Television Executive*
%ABC-Sports, 47 W 66th St, New York, NY 10023, USA

Swanson, Jackie *Actress*
847 Iliff St, Pacific Palisades, CA 90272, USA

Swanson, Judith *Actress*
%Persona Mgmt, 40 E 9th St, New York, NY 10003, USA

Swanson, Kristy *Actress*
145 S Fairfax Ave, #310, Los Angeles, CA 90036, USA

Swanson, Robert A *Businessman*
%Genentech Inc, 460 Point San Bruno Blvd, South San Francisco, CA 94080, USA

Swanson, Robert K *Businessman*
%Grossman's, 200 Union St, Braintree, MA 02184, USA

Swartz, Jacob T *Scientist*
New York University, 251 Mercer St, New York, NY 10012, USA

Swayze, Patrick *Actor*
%Wolf/Kasteller, 1033 Gayley Ave, #208, Los Angeles, CA 90024, USA

Swe, U Ba *Prime Minister, Myanmar*
84 Innes Rd, Yangon, Myanmar

Sweat, Keith *Songwriter, Singer*
PO Box 1002, Bronx, NY 10466, USA

Sweeney, D B *Actor*
%William Morris Agency, 151 S El Camino Dr, Beverly Hills, CA 90212, USA

Sweeney, Joan M *Financier*
%Allied Capital Advisers, 1666 "K" St NW, Washington, DC 20006, USA

Sweeney, John J *Labor Leader*
%Service Employees International Union, 1313 "L" St NW, Washington, DC 20005, USA

Sweeney, Walter F (Walt) *Football Player*
%Touchdown Ink, 1742 Garnet Ave, #130, San Diego, CA 92109, USA

Sweet, Sharon *Opera Singer*
%Metropolitan Opera Assn, Lincoln Center Plaza, New York, NY 10023, USA

Sweeting, Robert M *Financier*
%Banco Central Hispano, 221 Ponce de Leon Ave, Hato Rey, PR 00917, USA

Swenson, Inga *Actress*
3475 Cabrillo Blvd, Los Angeles, CA 90066, USA

Swenson, Rick *Dog Sled Racer*
%Trot-A-Long Kennel, Manley, AK 99756, USA

Swensson, Earl S *Architect*
%Earl Swensson Assoc, 2100 W End Ave, #1200, Nashville, TN 37203, USA

Swett, James E *WW II Marine Corps Hero (CMH)*
PO Box 327, Trinity Center, CA 96091, USA

Swift, Clive *Actor*
%Roxane Vacca Mgmt, 8 Silver Place, London W1R 3LJ, England

Swift, Hewson H *Biologist*
%University of Chicago, Molecular Genetics-Cell Biology Dept, Chicago, IL 60637, USA

Swift, Richard J *Businessman*
%Foster Wheeler Corp, Perryville Corporate Park, Clinton, NJ 08809, USA

Swift, Stephen J *Judge*
%US Tax Court, 400 2nd St NW, Washington, DC 20217, USA

Swift, William C (Bill) *Baseball Player*
16541 Redmond Way, #1006-C, Redmond, WA 98052, USA

Swilling, Pat *Football Player*
%Oakland Raiders, Oakland Coliseum, Oakland, CA 94621, USA

Swinburne, Nora *Actress*
52 Crammer Court, Whitehead's Grove, London SW3, England

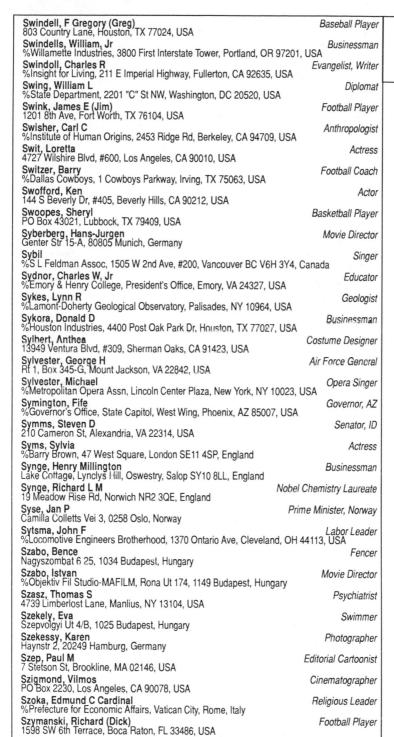

Swindell, F Gregory (Greg) — *Baseball Player*
803 Country Lane, Houston, TX 77024, USA

Swindells, William, Jr — *Businessman*
%Willamette Industries, 3800 First Interstate Tower, Portland, OR 97201, USA

Swindoll, Charles R — *Evangelist, Writer*
%Insight for Living, 211 E Imperial Highway, Fullerton, CA 92635, USA

Swing, William L — *Diplomat*
%State Department, 2201 "C" St NW, Washington, DC 20520, USA

Swink, James E (Jim) — *Football Player*
1201 8th Ave, Fort Worth, TX 76104, USA

Swisher, Carl C — *Anthropologist*
%Institute of Human Origins, 2453 Ridge Rd, Berkeley, CA 94709, USA

Swit, Loretta — *Actress*
4727 Wilshire Blvd, #600, Los Angeles, CA 90010, USA

Switzer, Barry — *Football Coach*
%Dallas Cowboys, 1 Cowboys Parkway, Irving, TX 75063, USA

Swofford, Ken — *Actor*
144 S Beverly Dr, #405, Beverly Hills, CA 90212, USA

Swoopes, Sheryl — *Basketball Player*
PO Box 43021, Lubbock, TX 79409, USA

Syberberg, Hans-Jurgen — *Movie Director*
Genter Str 15-A, 80805 Munich, Germany

Sybil — *Singer*
%S L Feldman Assoc, 1505 W 2nd Ave, #200, Vancouver BC V6H 3Y4, Canada

Sydnor, Charles W, Jr — *Educator*
%Emory & Henry College, President's Office, Emory, VA 24327, USA

Sykes, Lynn R — *Geologist*
%Lamont-Doherty Geological Observatory, Palisades, NY 10964, USA

Sykora, Donald D — *Businessman*
%Houston Industries, 4400 Post Oak Park Dr, Houston, TX 77027, USA

Sylbert, Anthea — *Costume Designer*
13949 Ventura Blvd, #309, Sherman Oaks, CA 91423, USA

Sylvester, George H — *Air Force General*
Rt 1, Box 345-G, Mount Jackson, VA 22842, USA

Sylvester, Michael — *Opera Singer*
%Metropolitan Opera Assn, Lincoln Center Plaza, New York, NY 10023, USA

Symington, Fife — *Governor, AZ*
%Governor's Office, State Capitol, West Wing, Phoenix, AZ 85007, USA

Symms, Steven D — *Senator, ID*
210 Cameron St, Alexandria, VA 22314, USA

Syms, Sylvia — *Actress*
%Barry Brown, 47 West Square, London SE11 4SP, England

Synge, Henry Millington — *Businessman*
Lake Cottage, Lynclys Hill, Oswestry, Salop SY10 8LL, England

Synge, Richard L M — *Nobel Chemistry Laureate*
19 Meadow Rise Rd, Norwich NR2 3QE, England

Syse, Jan P — *Prime Minister, Norway*
Camilla Colletts Vei 3, 0258 Oslo, Norway

Sytsma, John F — *Labor Leader*
%Locomotive Engineers Brotherhood, 1370 Ontario Ave, Cleveland, OH 44113, USA

Szabo, Bence — *Fencer*
Nagyszombat 6 25, 1034 Budapest, Hungary

Szabo, Istvan — *Movie Director*
%Objektiv Fil Studio-MAFILM, Rona Ut 174, 1149 Budapest, Hungary

Szasz, Thomas S — *Psychiatrist*
4739 Limberlost Lane, Manlius, NY 13104, USA

Szekely, Eva — *Swimmer*
Szepvolgyi Ut 4/B, 1025 Budapest, Hungary

Szekessy, Karen — *Photographer*
Haynstr 2, 20249 Hamburg, Germany

Szep, Paul M — *Editorial Cartoonist*
7 Stetson St, Brookline, MA 02146, USA

Szigmond, Vilmos — *Cinematographer*
PO Box 2230, Los Angeles, CA 90078, USA

Szoka, Edmund C Cardinal — *Religious Leader*
%Prefecture for Economic Affairs, Vatican City, Rome, Italy

Szymanski, Richard (Dick) — *Football Player*
1598 SW 6th Terrace, Boca Raton, FL 33486, USA

S

Swindell - Szymanski

T

T (Lawrence Tero), Mr — *Actor*
395 Green Bay Rd, Lake Forest, IL 60045, USA

Tabackin, Lew — *Jazz Flutist*
38 W 94th St, New York, NY 10025, USA

Tabai, Ieremia T — *President, Kiribati*
%South Pacific Forum Secretariat, Ratu Su Kuna Rd, GPO Box 856, Suva, Fiji

Taber, Carol A — *Publisher*
%Working Woman Magazine, 230 Park Ave, New York, NY 10169, USA

Tabitha 'Masentle — *Princess, Lesotho*
%Royal Palace, PO Box 524, Maseru, Lesotho

Tabone, Censu — *President, Malta*
%President's Office, The Palace, Valletta, Malta

Tabor, David — *Physicist*
8 Rutherford Rd, Cambridge CB2 2HH, England

Tabori, Kristoffer — *Actor*
172 E 95th St, New York, NY 10128, USA

Tabori, Laszlo — *Track Athlete*
2221 W Olive Ave, Burbank, CA 91506, USA

Tacha, Deanell R — *Judge*
%US Court of Appeals, 4830 W 15th St, Lawrence, KS 66049, USA

Tacke, David R — *Businessman*
%E-Systems Inc, 6250 LBJ Freeway, Dallas, TX 75266, USA

Taddei, Giuseppe — *Opera Singer*
%Metropolitan Opera Assn, Lincoln Center Plaza, New York, NY 10023, USA

Tagliabue, Paul J — *Football Executive*
%National Football League, 410 Park Ave, New York, NY 10022, USA

Tahara, Hishashi — *Businessman*
%Honshu Paper Co, 5-12-8 Ginza, Chuoku, Tokyo 104, Japan

Tait, John E — *Businessman*
%Penn Mutual Life Insurance, Independence Square, Philadelphia, PA 19172, USA

Taittinger, Jean — *Businessman*
%Cristallerie de Baccarat, 30 Bis Rue de Paradis, 75010 Paris, France

Taj Mahal — *Singer, Songwriter*
%Shankman DiBlasio Melina, 2434 Main St, Santa Monica, CA 90405, USA

Takacs-Nagy, Gabor — *Concert Violinist*
5265 Centennial Trail, Boulder, CO 80303, USA

Takahashi, Kokichi — *Businessman*
%Kobe Steel, 1-3-18 Wakinohamacho, Chuoko, Kobe 651, Japan

Takahashi, Michiaki — *Immunologist*
%Osaka University, Microbial Diseases Research Institute, Osaka, Japan

Takamatsu, Shin — *Architect*
%Shin Takamatsu Assoc, 36-4 Jobodaiincho Takeda, Fushimiku, Kyoto, Japan

Takano, Atsushi — *Financier*
%Fuji Bank & Trust, 2 World Trade Center, New York, NY 10048, USA

Takeda, Yutaka — *Businessman*
%Nippon Steel Corp, 2-6-3 Otemachi, Chiyodaku, Tokyo 100, Japan

Takei, George — *Actor*
3349 Cahuenga Blvd, #2, Los Angeles, CA 90068, USA

Takemitsu, Toru — *Composer*
3-15-56 Tamakomachi, #A-301, Higashi Murayama, Tokyo 189, Japan

Takeshita, Noboru — *Prime Minister, Japan*
3-5-9 Daisawa, Setagayaku, Tokyo, Japan

Tal, Josef — *Composer*
3 Dvira Haneviyah St, Jerusalem, Israel

Talbert, William F (Billy) — *Tennis Player*
%US Banknote Co, 345 Hudson St, New York, NY 10014, USA

Talbot, Don — *Swimming Coach*
%Canadian Sports Fed, 333 River Rd, Vanier, Ottawa ON K1L 8B9, Canada

Talbot, Nita — *Actress*
3420 Merrimac Rd, Los Angeles, CA 90049, USA

Talbott, John H — *Physician*
%Commodore Club, 177 Ocean Lane Dr, Key Biscayne, FL 33149, USA

Talbott, Michael — *Actor*
4250 Via Dolce, #118, Marina del Rey, CA 90292, USA

Talese, Gay — *Writer*
154 E Atlantic Blvd, Ocean City, NJ 08226, USA

Taliaferro, George — *Football Player*
%Innovative Health Systems, 3013 Stratfield Dr, Bloomington, IN 47401, USA

T (Lawrence Tero) - Taliaferro

Tallchief, Maria *Ballerina*
%Chicago City Ballet, 223 W Erie St, Chicago, IL 60610, USA

Talley, Darryl V *Football Player*
%Atlanta Falcons, 2745 Burnett Rd, Suwanee, GA 30174, USA

Talley, Gary *Musician (Box Tops)*
%Creative Entertainment Assoc, 2011 Ferry Ave, #U-19, Camden, NJ 08104, USA

Tallman, Patricia *Actress*
%Gold Marshak Assoc, 3500 W Olive Ave, #1400, Burbank, CA 91505, USA

Talmadge, Herman E *Governor/Senator, GA*
%Barnett & Alagia, 15 Circle Dr, Hampton, GA 30228, USA

Talu, Naim *Prime Minister, Turkey; Financier*
%Akbank TAS, Findukh, Istanbul, Turkey

Tamayo Mendez, Arnaldo *Cosmonaut, Cuba*
Calle 16, #504, c/5A y 7MA, Miramar, Ciudad Havana 11300, Cuba

Tamberlane, John *Financier*
%Republic Bank for Savings, 415 Madison Ave, New York, NY 10017, USA

Tamblyn, Russ *Actor*
2310 6th St, #2, Santa Monica, CA 90405, USA

Tambor, Jeffrey *Actor*
5526 Calhoun Ave, Van Nuys, CA 91401, USA

Tamm, Peter *Publisher*
%Axel Springer Verlag, Kochstr 50, 10969 Berlin, Germany

Tan, Amy R *Writer*
%G P Putnam's Sons, 200 Madison Ave, New York, NY 10016, USA

Tanana, Frank D *Baseball Player*
%New York Mets, Shea Stadium, Flushing, NY 11368, USA

Tananbaum, Andrew H *Financier*
%Century Business Corp, 119 W 40th St, New York, NY 10018, USA

Tananbaum, Stanley *Financier*
%Century Business Credit Corp, 119 W 40th St, New York, NY 10018, USA

Tandon, Sirjang Lal *Businessman*
%Tandon Corp, 301 Science Dr, #8025, Moorpark, CA 93021, USA

Tanen, Ned S *Entertainment Executive*
%Paramount Pictures Corp, 5555 Melrose Ave, Los Angeles, CA 90038, USA

Tanford, Charles *Physiologist*
Tarlswood, Back Lane, Easingwold, York YO6 3BG, England

Tange, Kenzo *Architect*
%Kenzo Tange Assoc, 7-2-21 Akasaka, Minato-ku, Tokyo, Japan

Taniguchi, Tadatsugu *Molecular Biologist*
%University of Osaka, Molecular & Cellular Biology Dept, Osaka, Japan

Tanksley, Steven D *Plant Geneticist*
%Cornell University, Plant Genetics Dept, Ithaca, NY 14853, USA

Tannen, Deborah F *Linguist*
%Georgetown University, Linguistics Dept, Washington, DC 20057, USA

Tannenwald, Theodore, Jr *Judge*
%US Tax Court, 400 2nd St NW, Washington, DC 20217, USA

Tanner Nahrgang, Elaine *Swimmer*
107-101 E 29th St, North Vancouver BC V7N 1C5, Canada

Tanner, Alain *Movie Director*
Rue du Point-du-Jour 12, 1202 Geneva, Switzerland

Tanner, Charles W (Chuck) *Baseball Manager*
34 Maitland Lane E, New Castle, PA 16105, USA

Tanner, Joseph R *Astronaut*
%NASA, Johnson Space Center, 2101 NASA Rd, Houston, TX 77058, USA

Tanner, Roscoe *Tennis Player*
1109 Gnome Trail, Lookout Mountain, TN 30750, USA

Tannous, Afif I *Government Official*
6912 Oak Court, Annandale, VA 22003, USA

Tanumafili, Malietoa, II *Head of State, Western Samoa*
%Government House, Valima, Apia, Western Samoa

Taofinu'u, Pio Cardinal *Religious Leader*
%Cardinal's Office, PO Box 532, Apia, Western Samoa

Tape, Gerald F *Physicist*
4970 Sentinel Dr, #502, Bethesda, MD 20816, USA

Tapie, Bernard R *Businessman, Sports Executive*
%Groupe Bernard Tapie, 24 Ave de Friedland, 75008 Paris, France

Tarantino, Quentin *Movie Director*
%A Band Apart Production, 10202 W Washington Blvd, Culver City, CA 90232, USA

T

Tallchief - Tarantino

Tarbell, Dean S *Chemist*
6033 Sherwood Dr, Nashville, TN 37215, USA

Tarkenton, Francis A (Fran) *Football Player, Businessman*
%Tarkenton & Co, 3340 Peachtree Rd NE, #444, Atlanta, GA 30326, USA

Tarnow, Robert L *Businessman*
%Goulds Pumps Inc, 300 WillowBrook Office Park, Fairport, NY 14450, USA

Tarpley, Roy *Basketball Player*
%Dallas Mavericks, Reunion Arena, 777 Sports St, Dallas, TX 75207, USA

Tarr, Curtis W *Government Official, Businessman*
%Intermet Corp, 2859 Paces Ferry Rd NW, #1600, Atlanta, GA 30339, USA

Tarr, Robert J, Jr *Businessman*
%Harcourt General, 27 Boylston St, Chestnut Hill, MA 02167, USA

Tarski, Alfred *Mathematician*
462 Michigan Ave, Berkeley, CA 94707, USA

Tartabull, Danilio (Dan) *Baseball Player*
16840 NW 79th Pl, Hialeah, FL 33016, USA

Tartikoff, Brandon *Television Executive*
1479 Lindacrest Dr, Beverly Hills, CA 90210, USA

Tarver, Jackson W *Publisher*
%Atlanta Journal-Constitution, 72 Marietta St, Atlanta, GA 30303, USA

Tasker, Steven J (Steve) *Football Player*
%Buffalo Bills, 1 Bills Dr, Orchard Park, NY 14127, USA

Tate, Albert, Jr *Judge*
%US Court of Appeals, 600 Camp St, New Orleans, LA 70130, USA

Tate, Jeffrey P *Conductor*
%Royal Opera House, Convent Garden, Bow St, London WC2E 7QA, England

Tatishvili, Tsisana R *Opera Singer*
%Tbilsi State Opera, Tbilisi, Georgia

Tatrai, Vilmos *Concert Violinist*
Zenemuveszeti Foiskola, Liszt Ference Ter 2, 1136 Budapest XIII, Hungary

Taub, Henry *Businessman*
%Automatic Data Processing, 1 ADP Blvd, Roseland, NJ 07068, USA

Taube, Henry *Nobel Chemistry Laureate*
441 Gerona Rd, Stanford, CA 94305, USA

Taubman, A Alfred *Businessman*
%Taubman Co, 200 E Long Lake Rd, Bloomfield Hills, MI 48304, USA

Taufa'ahau Tupou IV *King, Tonga*
%The Palace, PO Box 6, Nuku'alofa, Tonga

Taupin, Bernie *Lyricist*
1320 N Doheny Dr, Los Angeles, CA 90069, USA

Tauscher, Hansjorg *Skier*
Schwand 7, 87561 Oberstdorf, Germany

Tavener, John *Football Player*
197 N Main, Johnstown, OH 43031, USA

Tavener, John *Composer*
%Chester Music, 8-9 Firth St, London W1V 5TZ, England

Taverner, Sonia *Ballerina*
PO Box 129, Stony Plain AB, Canada

Tavernier, Bertrand R M *Movie Director*
%Little Bear Productions, 7-9 Rue Arthur Groussier, 75010 Paris, France

Taya, Maawiya Ould Sid'Ahmed *President, Mauritania; Army Officer*
%President's Office, Boite Postale 184, Nouakchott, Mauritania

Taylor, Aaron *Football Player*
%University of Notre Dame, Athletic Dept, Notre Dame, IN 46556, USA

Taylor, Arthur R *Educator, Businessman*
%Fordham University, Lincoln Center Campus, 113 W 60th St, New York, NY 10023, USA

Taylor, Billy *Jazz Pianist, Composer*
555 Kappock St, Bronx, NY 10463, USA

Taylor, Buck *Actor*
206 Via Colinas, Westlake Village, CA 91362, USA

Taylor, Carl E *Physician*
Bittersweet Acres, 1201 Hollins Lane, Baltimore, MD 21209, USA

Taylor, Cecil P *Jazz Pianist, Composer*
%PSI/Soul Note Records, 810 7th Ave, New York, NY 10019

Taylor, Charley *Football Player, Executive*
%Atlanta Falcons, 2745 Burnett Rd, Suwanee, GA 30174, USA

Taylor, Clarice *Actress*
380 Elkwood Terrace, Englewood, NJ 07631, USA

Taylor, Dave   *Hockey Player, Executive*
%Los Angeles Kings, Forum, PO Box 17013, Inglewood, CA 90308, USA

Taylor, Delores   *Actress*
20033 Big Rock Dr, Malibu, CA 90265, USA

Taylor, Don   *Movie Director*
1111 San Vicente Blvd, Santa Monica, CA 90402, USA

Taylor, Elizabeth   *Actress*
700 Nimes Rd, Los Angeles, CA 90077, USA

Taylor, Eric   *Artist*
13 Tredgold Ave, Branhope Near Leeds, W Yorkshire LS16 9BS, England

Taylor, Ernest-Frank   *Actor*
3857 Tracy St, Los Angeles, CA 90027, USA

Taylor, Fred R   *Basketball Coach*
%Golf Club, 4822 Miller Rd, New Albany, OH 43054, USA

Taylor, Frederick B   *Financier*
%United States Trust Co of New York, 114 W 57th St, New York, NY 10019, USA

Taylor, Gerard H   *Businessman*
%MCI Communications Corp, 1801 Pennsylvania Ave NW, Washington, DC 20006, USA

Taylor, Glen   *Basketball Executive*
%Minnesota Timberwolves, Target Center, 600 1st Ave N, Minneapolis, MN 55403, USA

Taylor, Gregory F   *Financier*
%Stifel Financial Group, 500 N Broadway, St Louis, MO 63102, USA

Taylor, Henry S   *Poet*
PO Box 23, Lincoln, VA 22078, USA

Taylor, J Herbert   *Botanist*
1414 Hilltop Dr, Tallahassee, FL 32303, USA

Taylor, James   *Singer, Songwriter*
%Peter Asher Mgmt, 644 N Doheny Dr, Los Angeles, CA 90069, USA

Taylor, James (Jim)   *Football Player*
8069 Summa Ave, #A, Baton Rouge, LA 70809, USA

Taylor, James A   *Vietnam War Army Hero (CMH)*
793 Hagemann Dr, Livermore, CA 94550, USA

Taylor, Joseph H, Jr   *Nobel Physics Laureate*
272 Hartley St, Princeton, NJ 08540, USA

Taylor, Kenneth N   *Publisher*
1515 E Forest Ave, Wheaton, IL 60187, USA

Taylor, Lance J   *Economist*
Old County Rd, PO Box 378, Washington, ME 04574, USA

Taylor, Lauriston S   *Physicist*
10450 Lottsford Rd, #3011, Mitchellville, MD 20721, USA

Taylor, Lawrence   *Football Player*
%"Stadium" Show, TNT-TV, Sports Dept, 1050 Techwood Dr, Atlanta, GA 30318, USA

Taylor, Lili   *Actress*
%William Morris Agency, 151 S El Camino Dr, Beverly Hills, CA 90212, USA

Taylor, Lionel   *Football Player, Coach*
%Texas Southern University, Athletic Dept, Houston, TX 77004, USA

Taylor, Mark L   *Actor*
7919 W Norton Ave, Los Angeles, CA 90046, USA

Taylor, Meshach   *Actor*
369 E Calaveras St, Altadena, CA 91001, USA

Taylor, Nicole R (Niki)   *Model*
728 Ocean Dr, Miami Beach, FL 33139, USA

Taylor, Paul B   *Dancer, Choreographer*
%Paul Taylor Dance Co, 552 Broadway, New York, NY 10012, USA

Taylor, Paul S   *Economist*
1163 Euclid Ave, Berkeley, CA 94708, USA

Taylor, Regina   *Actress*
%William Morris Agency, 151 S El Camino Dr, Beverly Hills, CA 90212, USA

Taylor, Renee   *Actress*
16830 Ventura Blvd, #326, Encino, CA 91436, USA

Taylor, Richard E   *Nobel Physics Laureate*
%Stanford University, Linear Accelerator Center, Box 4349, Stanford, CA 94309, USA

Taylor, Rip   *Comedian*
1133 N Clark Dr, Los Angeles, CA 90035, USA

Taylor, Rod   *Actor*
2375 Bowmont Dr, Beverly Hills, CA 90210, USA

Taylor, Roger   *Tennis Player*
39 Newstead Way, Wimbledon SW19, England

T

Taylor - Taylor

Taylor, Samuel A — Playwright
Meadow Rue, East Blue Hill, ME 04629, USA

Taylor, Telford — Attorney, Writer
54 Morningside Dr, New York, NY 10025, USA

Taylor, Thomas A — Businessman
%Amica Mutual Insurance, 10 Weybosset St, Providence, RI 02903, USA

Taylor, William O — Publisher
%Affiliated Publications, 135 Morrissey Blvd, Boston, MA 02128, USA

Taylor, Wilson H — Businessman
%Cigna Corp, 1 Liberty Place, Philadelphia, PA 19192, USA

Taylor-Young, Leigh — Actress
301 N Canon Dr, #215, Beverly Hills, CA 90210, USA

Tcherina, Ludmila — Ballerina
42 Cours Albert 1er, 75008 Paris, France

Tcherkassky, Marianna — Ballerina
%American Ballet Theatre, 890 Broadway, New York, NY 10003, USA

Te Kanawa, Kiri — Opera Singer
%Jules Haefliger Impressario, Postfach 4113, 6002 Lucerne, Switzerland

Teaff, Grant — Football Coach, Executive
8265 Forest Ridge Dr, Waco, TX 76712, USA

Teagle, Terry — Basketball Player
%Los Angeles Lakers, Forum, PO Box 10, Inglewood, CA 90306, USA

Teannaki, Teatao — President, Kiribati
%President's Office, PO Box 68, Bairiki, Tarawa Atoll, Kiribati

Tear, Robert — Opera Singer
11 Ravenscourt Court, London W6, England

Teasdale, Joseph P — Governor, MO
800 W 47th St, Kansas City, MO 64112, USA

Tebaldi, Renata — Opera Singer
Piazzetta della Guastella 1, 20122 Milan, Italy

Tebbetts, George R (Birdie) — Baseball Player, Manager
229 Oak Ave, Anna Maria, FL 33501, USA

Tebbit of Chingford, Norman B — Government Official, England
%House of Lords, Westminster, London SW1A 0PW, England

Tebbutt, Arthur R — Statistician
1511 Pelican Point Dr, Sarasota, FL 34231, USA

Teel, James E — Businessman
%Raley's, 500 W Capitol Ave, West Sacramento, CA 95605, USA

Teel, Joyce N — Businesswoman
%Raley's, 500 W Capitol Ave, West Sacramento, CA 95605, USA

Teerlink, Richard F — Businessman, Motorcycle Executive
%Harley-Davidson Inc, 3700 W Juneau Ave, Milwaukee, WI 53208, USA

Teets, John W — Businessman
%Dial Corp, 1850 N Central Ave, Phoenix, AZ 85004, USA

Teevens, Buddy — Football Coach
%Tulane University, Athletic Dept, New Orleans, LA 70118, USA

Teich, Malvin C — Electrical Engineer
%Columbia University, Electrical Engineering Dept, New York, NY 10027, USA

Teicher, Lou — Pianist (Ferrante & Teicher)
%Avant-Garde Records Corp, 12224 Avila Dr, Kansas City, MO 64145, USA

Teichner, Helmut — Skier
4250 Marine Dr, #2101, Chicago, IL 60613, USA

Teitelbaum, Philip — Psychologist
%University of Florida, Psychology Dept, Gainesville, FL 32611, USA

Teitell, Conrad L — Attorney
16 Marlow Court, Riverside, CT 06878, USA

Tekulve, Kenton C (Kent) — Baseball Player
1531 Sequoia, Pittsburgh, PA 15241, USA

Telegdi, Valentine L — Physicist
Eidgenossische Technische Hochschule, Houggerberg, Zurich, Switzerland

Tellep, Daniel M — Businessman
%Lockheed Corp, 4500 Park Granada Blvd, Calabasas, CA 91302, USA

Teller — Comedian, Illusionist (Penn & Teller)
%Earth's Center, PO Box 1196, New York, NY 10185, USA

Teller, Edward — Physicist
%University of California Livermore Laboratory, PO Box 808, Livermore, CA 94551, USA

Telnack, John J (Jack) — Automobile Designer
%Ford Motor Co, American Rd, Dearborn, MI 48121, USA

Teltscher, Eliot *Tennis Player, Coach*
%Pepperdine University, Athletic Dept, Malibu, CA 90265, USA

Temesvari, Andrea *Tennis Player*
%ProServe, 1100 Woodrow Wilson Blvd, #1800, Arlington, VA 22209, USA

Temirkanov, Yuri *Conductor*
%St Petersburg Philharmonic, Ul Brodskogo 2, St Petersburg, Russia

Temko, Allan B *Journalist*
%San Francisco Chronicle, Editorial Dept, 901 Misson, San Francisco, CA 94103, USA

Templeman of White Lackington, Sydney W *Judge*
Manor Heath, Knowl Hill, Woking, Surrey GU22 7HL, England

Templeton, Ben *Cartoonist (Motley's Crew)*
%Tribune Media Services, 435 N Michigan Ave, #1417, Chicago, IL 60611, USA

Templeton, Christopher *Actress, Singer*
11333 Moorpark St, North Hollywood, CA 91602, USA

Templeton, Garry L *Baseball Player*
13552 Del Pomonte Rd, Poway, CA 92064, USA

Templeton, John M *Financier*
%Lyford Cay Club, Box N-7776, Nassau, Bahamas

Tenace, F Gene *Baseball Player*
15368 Marker Rd, Poway, CA 92064, USA

Tenant, Anthony J *Businessman*
%Arthur Guinness & Sons, Royal Park Brewery, London NW10 7RR, England

Tengbom, Anders *Architect*
Kornhamnstorg 6, 111 27 Stockholm, Sweden

Tennant, Veronica *Ballerina*
%National Ballet of Canada, 157 King St E, Toronto ON M5C 1G9, Canada

Tennant, Victoria *Actress*
PO Box 929, Beverly Hills, CA 90213, USA

Tenney, Charles H, II *Businessman*
%Bay State Gas Co, 300 Friberg Parkway, Westborough, MA 01581, USA

Tenney, Jon *Actor*
%Agency For Performing Arts, 9000 Sunset Blvd, #1200, Los Angeles, CA 90069, USA

Tennllle, Toni *Singer (Captain & Tennille)*
7123 Franktown Rd, Carson City, NV 89704, USA

Tennstedt, Klaus *Conductor*
Rothenbaumchaussee 132-174, 20149 Hamburg, Germany

Tenorio, Pedro *Governor, CM*
%Governor's Office, Capitol Hill, Saipan, CM 96950, USA

Tenuta, Judy *Comedienne*
332 E Euclid Ave, Oak Park, IL 60302, USA

Tepper, Lou *Football Coach*
%University of Illinois, Assembly Hall, Champaign, IL 61820, USA

Ter Horst, Jerald F *Government Official, Journalist*
7815 Evening Lane, Alexandria, VA 22306, USA

Ter-Petrosyan, Levon *President, Armenia*
%President's Office, Parliament Building, Yerevan, Armenia

Teraoka, Masami *Artist*
41-048 Kaulu St, Waimanalo, HI 96795, USA

Teresa, Mother *Humanitarian, Nobel Peace Laureate*
Missionaries of Charity, 54-A Lower Circular Rd, Calcutta 700016, India

Tereschenko, Sergei A *Prime Minister, Kazakhstan*
%Prime Minister's Office, Dom Pravieelstra, 148008 Alma-Ata, Kazakhstan

Tereshkova, Valentina V *Cosmonaut*
%Soviet Woman's Committee, 6 Nemirovich-Danchenko, Moscow 103009, Russia

Terfel, Bryn *Opera Singer*
%Deutsche Grammaphon Records, 810 7th Ave, New York, NY 10019, USA

Terkel, Louis (Studs) *Writer*
850 W Castlewood Terrace, Chicago, IL 60640, USA

Terrile, Richard *Astronomer*
2121 E Woodlyn Rd, Pasadena, CA 91104, USA

Terry, Clark *Jazz Trumpeter*
218-14 36th Ave, Bayside, NY 11361, USA

Terry, Hilda *Cartoonist (Teena)*
8 Henderson Place, New York, NY 10028, USA

Terry, John Q *Architect*
Old Exchange, Dedham, Colchester, Essex, England

Terry, Megan *Playwright*
2309 Hanscom Blvd, Omaha, NE 68105, USA

Terry, Randall A *Anti-Abortion Activist*
%Operation Rescue National, PO Box 360221, Melbourne, FL 32936, USA

Terry, Richard E *Businessman*
%Peoples Energy Corp, 130 E Randolph Dr, Chicago, IL 60601, USA

Terry, Ronald A *Financier*
%First Tennessee National Corp, 165 Madison Ave, Memphis, TN 38103, USA

Terry, Tony *Singer*
%Artists Only Mgmt, 152-18 Union Turnpike, #12-S, Flushing, NY 11367, USA

Terry, Walter *Dance Critic*
%Saturday Review Magazine, 1290 Ave of Americas, New York, NY 10019, USA

Terzian, Jacques *Sculptor*
%Hunters Point Shipyard, Building 101, San Francisco, CA 94124, USA

Tesh, John *Entertainer*
%"Entertainment Tonight", Paramount, 5555 Melrose Ave, Los Angeles, CA 90038, USA

Teshoian, Nishan *Businessman*
%Keystone International, 9600 W Gulf Bank Dr, Houston, TX 75240, USA

Tesich, Steve *Writer*
%International Creative Mgmt, 40 W 57th St, New York, NY 10019, USA

Tessier-Lavigne, Marc *Neurobiologist*
1000 Chenery St, San Francisco, CA 94131, USA

Testaverde, Vinny *Football Player*
%Cleveland Browns, 80 1st Ave, Berea, OH 44017, USA

Testi, Fabio *Actor*
Via Siacci 38, 00197 Rome, Italy

Teter, Gordon E *Businessman*
%Wendy's International, 4288 W Dublin-Granville Rd, Dublin, OH 43017, USA

Tetley, Glen *Ballet Director, Choreographer*
15 W 9th St, New York, NY 10011, USA

Tetzlaff, Christian *Concert Violinist*
%Virgin Classics Records, 1790 Broadway, #2000, New York, NY 10019, USA

Tewes, Lauren *Actress*
1611 42nd Ave E, Seattle, WA 98112, USA

Tewkesbury, Joan F *Movie Director, Screenwriter*
%Creative Artists Agency, 9830 Wilshire Blvd, Beverly Hills, CA 90212, USA

Tews, Andreas *Boxer*
Hamburger Allee 1, 19063 Schwerin, Germany

Thacker, Brian M *Vietnam War Army Hero (CMH)*
11413 Monterey Dr, Wheaton, MD 20902, USA

Thagard, Norman E *Astronaut*
%NASA, Johnson Space Center, 2101 NASA Rd, Houston, TX 77058, USA

Thalheimer, Richard *Businessman*
%Sharper Image, 680 Davis St, San Francisco, CA 94111, USA

Than Shwe *Head of State, Myanmar; Army General*
%State Law Restoration Council, Signal Pagoda Rd, Yangon, Mynamar

Tharp, Twyla *Dancer, Choreographer*
%MPL Productions, 170 W 74th St, New York, NY 10023, USA

Thatcher of Lincolnshire, Margaret H *Prime Minister, England*
11 Dulwich Gate, Dulwich, London SE12, England

Thaves, Bob *Cartoonist (Frank & Earnest)*
PO Box 67, Manhattan Beach, CA 90267, USA

Thaw, John *Actor*
%John Redway Assoc, 5 Denmark St, London WC2H 8LP, England

Thaxter, Phyllis *Actress*
716 Riomar Dr, Vero Beach, FL 32963, USA

Thayer, Brynn *Actress*
956 Kaqawa St, Pacific Palisades, PA 90272, USA

Thayer, W Paul *Businessman, Government Official*
10200 Hollow Way, Dallas, TX 75229, USA

Theberge, James D *Diplomat*
4462 Cathedral Ave NW, Washington, DC 20016, USA

Theile, David *Swimmer*
84 Woodville St, Hendea, Brisbane 4011, Australia

Theismann, Joseph R (Joe) *Football Player, Sportscaster*
%JRT Assoc, 5912 Leesburg Pike, Falls Church, VA 22041, USA

Theodorakis, Mikis *Composer*
Epifanous 1, Akropolis, Athens, Greece

Theodosius (Lazor), Primate Metropolitan *Religious Leader*
%Orthodox Church in America, PO Box 675, Rt 25-A, Syosset, NY 11791, USA

Theroux, Paul E | Writer
35 Elsynge Rd, London SW18 2NR, England
Thesiger, Wilfred P | Explorer
15 Shelley Court, Tite St, London SW3 4JB, England
Theus, Reggie | Basketball Player
%New Jersey Nets, Byrne Meadowlands Arena, East Rutherford, NJ 07073, USA
Thewlis, David | Actor
%International Creative Mgmt, 76 Oxford St, London W1N 0AX, England
Thiandoum, Hyacinthe Cardinal | Religious Leader
Archeveche, BP 1908, Dakar, Senegal
Thibaudet, Jean-Yves | Concert Pianist
%IMG Artists, 22 E 71st St, New York, NY 10021, USA
Thibiant, Aida | Fashion Expert
%Institut de Beaute, 449 N Canon Dr, Beverly Hills, CA 90210, USA
Thicke, Alan | Actor
10505 Sarah St, Toluca Lake, CA 91602, USA
Thiebaud, Wayne | Artist
1617 17th Ave, Sacramento, CA 95814, USA
Thiele, Patrick A | Businessman
%St Paul Companies, 385 Washington St, St Paul, MN 55102, USA
Thiele, William E | Businessman
%North American Reinsurance, 237 Park Ave, New York, NY 10017, USA
Thiemann, Charles Lee | Financier
%Federal Home Loan Bank, PO Box 598, Cincinnati, OH 45201, USA
Thier, Samuel O | Educator, Physician
99-20 Florence St, #4-B, Chestnut Hill, MA 02167, USA
Thierry, John | Football Player
%Chicago Bears, Halas Hall, 250 N Washington Rd, Lake Forest, IL 60045, USA
Thiess, Ursula | Actress
1940 Bel Air Rd, Los Angeles, CA 90077, USA
Thiessem, Tiffani-Amber | Actress
%Gold Marshak Assoc, 3500 W Olive Ave, #1400, Burbank, CA 91505, USA
Thigpen, Lynne | Actress
35 W 20th St, New York, NY 10011, USA
Thimann, Kenneth V | Biologist
Quadrangle, 3300 Darby Rd, #3314, Haverford, PA 19041, USA
Thimmesch, Nicholas | Journalist
6301 Broad Branch Rd, Chevy Chase, MD 20815, USA
Thinnes, Roy | Actor
8016 Willow Glen Rd, Los Angeles, CA 90046, USA
Thirsk, Robert | Astronaut, Canada
%Astronaut Program, 6767 Rt de l'Aeroport, St-Hubert PQ J3Y 8Y9, Canada
Thode, Henry G | Chemist
%McMaster University, Nuclear Research Dept, Hamilton ON L8S 4M1, Canada
Thoma, Georg | Nordic Skier
Bisten 6, 79856 Hinterzarten, Germany
Thomas of Swynnerton, Hugh S | Historian
Well House, Sudbourne, Suffolk, England
Thomas, Aurelius | Football Player
PO Box 091157, Columbus, OH 43209, USA
Thomas, B Clendon | Football Player
7508 Runsey Rd, Oklahoma City, OK 73132, USA
Thomas, B J | Singer, Songwriter
%Grass-Goldstein Assoc, 13456 Cheltenham Dr, Sherman Oaks, CA 91423, USA
Thomas, Barbara S | Government Official
%News International, 1 Virginia St, London E1 9XY, England
Thomas, Betty | Actress, Director
PO Box 1892, Studio City, CA 91614, USA
Thomas, Billy M | Army General
8249 Clifton Farm Court, Community, VA 22306, USA
Thomas, Carmen | Actress
606 N Larchmont Blvd, #309, Los Angeles, CA 90004, USA
Thomas, Caroline Bedell | Physician
830 W 40th St, #259, Baltimore, MD 21211, USA
Thomas, Clarence | Supreme Court Justice
%US Supreme Court, 1 1st St NE, Washington, DC 20543, USA
Thomas, D M | Writer, Poet
Coach House, Rashleigh Vale, Tregolls Rd, Truro, Cornwall TR1 1TJ, England

Thomas, David — Concert Singer
74 Hyde Vale, Greenwich, London SE10 8HP, England

Thomas, Debra J (Debi) — Figure Skater
22 E 71st St, New York, NY 10021, USA

Thomas, Derrick — Football Player
%Kansas City Chiefs, 1 Arrowhead Dr, Kansas City, KS 64129, USA

Thomas, Dominic R — Religious Leader
%Church of Jesus Christ, 6th & Lincoln Sts, Monongahela, PA 15063, USA

Thomas, Donald A — Astronaut
%NASA, Johnson Space Center, 2101 NASA Rd, Houston, TX 77058, USA

Thomas, E Donnall — Nobel Medicine Laureate
%Hutchinson Cancer Research Center, 1124 Columbia St, Seattle, WA 98104, USA

Thomas, Elizabeth Marshall — Writer
80 E Mountain Rd, Peterborough, NH 03458, USA

Thomas, Emmitt — Football Player, Coach
%Washington Redskins, 21300 Redskin Park Dr, Ashburn, VA 22011, USA

Thomas, Frank E — Baseball Player
9060 Turnberry Dr, Burr Ridge, IL 60521, USA

Thomas, Frank J — Baseball Player
118 Doray Dr, Pittsburgh, PA 15237, USA

Thomas, Franklin A — Foundation Executive
%Ford Foundation, 320 E 43rd St, New York, NY 10017, USA

Thomas, Fred — Law Enforcement Official
%Metropolitan Police Dept, 300 Indiana Ave NW, Washington, DC 20001, USA

Thomas, Garet G — Financier
%Bankers Trust Delaware, 1001 Jefferson St, Wilmington, DE 19801, USA

Thomas, Gareth — Engineer
%University of California, Materials Science Dept, Berkeley, CA 94720, USA

Thomas, Harold E — Businessman
%TJ International, 200 E Mallard Dr, Boise, ID 83706, USA

Thomas, Heather — Actress
%Agency For Performing Arts, 9000 Sunset Blvd, #1200, Los Angeles, CA 90069, USA

Thomas, Helen A — Journalist
2501 Calvert St NW, Washington, DC 20008, USA

Thomas, Henry L, Jr — Football Player
%Detroit Lions, Silverdome, 1200 Featherstone Rd, Pontiac, MI 48342, USA

Thomas, J Gorman — Baseball Player
759 Tallwood Rd, Charleston, SC 29412, USA

Thomas, Jay — Actor
%KPWR-FM, 2600 W Olive Ave, Burbank, CA 91505, USA

Thomas, Jean — Ceramist
1427 Summit Rd, Berkeley, CA 94708, USA

Thomas, Jim — Basketball Executive
%Sacramento Kings, 1 Sports Parkway, Sacramento, CA 95834, USA

Thomas, Kurt — Gymnast
%George Wallach, 1400 Braeridge Dr, Beverly Hills, CA 90210, USA

Thomas, Kurt — Basketball Player
%Miami Heat, Miami Arena, Miami, FL 33136, USA

Thomas, Lawrason D — Businessman
%Amoco Corp, 200 E Randolph Dr, Chicago, IL 60601, USA

Thomas, Lee M — Government Official
%Enviromental Protection Agency, 401 "M" St SW, Washington, DC 20024, USA

Thomas, Llewellyn H — Theoretical Physicist
3012 Wycliff Rd, Raleigh, NC 27607, USA

Thomas, Marlo — Actress
420 E 54th St, #22-F, New York, NY 10022, USA

Thomas, Peter M — Financier
%Bank of America Nevada, 300 S 4th St, Las Vegas, NV 89101, USA

Thomas, Philip Michael — Actor
12156 W Dixie Highway, North Miami, FL 33161, USA

Thomas, R David (Dave) — Businessman
%Wendy's International, 4288 W Dublin-Granville Rd, Dublin, OH 43017, USA

Thomas, Richard — Actor
5261 Cleon Ave, North Hollywood, CA 91601, USA

Thomas, Richard L — Financier
%First Chicago Corp, 1 First National Plaza, Chicago, IL 60670, USA

Thomas, Robert D — Publisher
223 Mariomi Rd, New Canaan, CT 06840

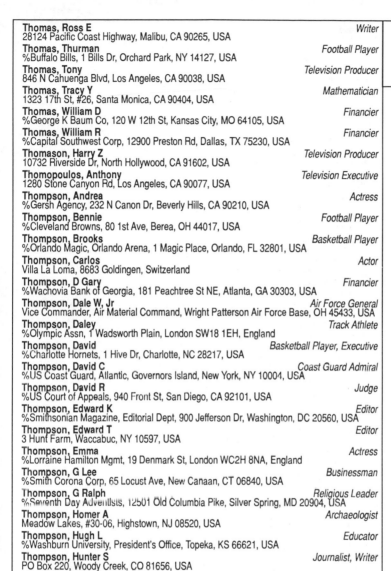

Thomas, Ross E *Writer*
28124 Pacific Coast Highway, Malibu, CA 90265, USA

Thomas, Thurman *Football Player*
%Buffalo Bills, 1 Bills Dr, Orchard Park, NY 14127, USA

Thomas, Tony *Television Producer*
846 N Cahuenga Blvd, Los Angeles, CA 90038, USA

Thomas, Tracy Y *Mathematician*
1323 17th St, #26, Santa Monica, CA 90404, USA

Thomas, William D *Financier*
%George K Baum Co, 120 W 12th St, Kansas City, MO 64105, USA

Thomas, William R *Financier*
%Capital Southwest Corp, 12900 Preston Rd, Dallas, TX 75230, USA

Thomason, Harry Z *Television Producer*
10732 Riverside Dr, North Hollywood, CA 91602, USA

Thomopoulos, Anthony *Television Executive*
1280 Stone Canyon Rd, Los Angeles, CA 90077, USA

Thompson, Andrea *Actress*
%Gersh Agency, 232 N Canon Dr, Beverly Hills, CA 90210, USA

Thompson, Bennie *Football Player*
%Cleveland Browns, 80 1st Ave, Berea, OH 44017, USA

Thompson, Brooks *Basketball Player*
%Orlando Magic, Orlando Arena, 1 Magic Place, Orlando, FL 32801, USA

Thompson, Carlos *Actor*
Villa La Loma, 8683 Goldingen, Switzerland

Thompson, D Gary *Financier*
%Wachovia Bank of Georgia, 181 Peachtree St NE, Atlanta, GA 30303, USA

Thompson, Dale W, Jr *Air Force General*
Vice Commander, Air Material Command, Wright Patterson Air Force Base, OH 45433, USA

Thompson, Daley *Track Athlete*
%Olympic Assn, 1 Wadsworth Plain, London SW18 1EH, England

Thompson, David *Basketball Player, Executive*
%Charlotte Hornets, 1 Hive Dr, Charlotte, NC 28217, USA

Thompson, David C *Coast Guard Admiral*
%US Coast Guard, Atlantic, Governors Island, New York, NY 10004, USA

Thompson, David R *Judge*
%US Court of Appeals, 940 Front St, San Diego, CA 92101, USA

Thompson, Edward K *Editor*
%Smithsonian Magazine, Editorial Dept, 900 Jefferson Dr, Washington, DC 20560, USA

Thompson, Edward T *Editor*
3 Hunt Farm, Waccabuc, NY 10597, USA

Thompson, Emma *Actress*
%Lorraine Hamilton Mgmt, 19 Denmark St, London WC2H 8NA, England

Thompson, G Lee *Businessman*
%Smith Corona Corp, 65 Locust Ave, New Canaan, CT 06840, USA

Thompson, G Ralph *Religious Leader*
%Seventh Day Adventists, 12501 Old Columbia Pike, Silver Spring, MD 20904, USA

Thompson, Homer A *Archaeologist*
Meadow Lakes, #30-06, Highstown, NJ 08520, USA

Thompson, Hugh L *Educator*
%Washburn University, President's Office, Topeka, KS 66621, USA

Thompson, Hunter S *Journalist, Writer*
PO Box 220, Woody Creek, CO 81656, USA

Thompson, J Lee *Movie Director*
9595 Lime Orchard Rd, Beverly Hills, CA 90210, USA

Thompson, Jack E *Businessman*
%Homestake Mining Co, 650 California St, San Francisco, CA 94108, USA

Thompson, James B, Jr *Geologist*
20 Richmond Rd, Belmont, MA 02178, USA

Thompson, James R *Governor, IL*
35 W Wacker Dr, Chicago, IL 60601, USA

Thompson, James R, Jr *Space Administrator*
%Orbital Sciences Corp, 620 Discovery Dr, #120, Huntsville, AL 35806, USA

Thompson, James W *Financier*
%NationsBank Corp, NationsBank Plaza, Charlotte, NC 28255, USA

Thompson, Jere W *Businessman*
%Southland Corp, 2711 N Haskell Ave, Dallas, TX 75204, USA

Thompson, John B *Basketball Coach*
%Georgetown University, Athletic Dept, Washington, DC 20057, USA

T

Thomas - Thompson

Thompson, John P — *Businessman*
%Southland Corp, 2828 N Haskell Ave, Dallas, TX 75204, USA

Thompson, Kay — *Singer, Actress*
300 E 57th St, New York, NY 10022, USA

Thompson, Kenneth L — *Computer Scientist*
366 Ridge Rd, Watchung, NJ 07060, USA

Thompson, Lea — *Actress*
7966 Woodrow Wilson Dr, Los Angeles, CA 90046, USA

Thompson, Linda — *Actress*
%Artists Group, 10100 Santa Monica Blvd, #2490, Los Angeles, CA 90067, USA

Thompson, Max — *WW II Army Hero (CMH)*
Rt 3, PO Box 56, Canton, NC 28716, USA

Thompson, Melvin E — *Governor, GA*
509 N Peterson St, Valdosta, GA 31601, USA

Thompson, N David — *Businessman*
%North American Reinsurance, 237 Park Ave, New York, NY 10017, USA

Thompson, Paul H — *Educator*
%Weber State University, President's Office, Ogden, UT 84408, USA

Thompson, Richard — *Singer, Guitarist*
PO Box 7095, New York, NY 10116, USA

Thompson, Richard C — *Publisher*
%US News & World Report Magazine, 2400 "N" St NW, Washington, DC 20037, USA

Thompson, Robert G K — *Army General, England*
Pitcott House, Winsford Minehead, Somerset, England

Thompson, Sada — *Actress*
PO Box 490, Southbury, CT 06488, USA

Thompson, Starley L — *Climatologist*
%National Atmospheric Research Center, PO Box 3000, Boulder, CO 80307, USA

Thompson, Tommy G — *Governor, WI*
%Governor's Office, State Capitol, PO Box 7863, Madison, WI 53707, USA

Thompson, William P — *Religious Leader*
%World Council of Churches, 475 Riverside Dr, New York, NY 10115, USA

Thomson of Fleet, Kenneth R — *Publisher*
%Thomson Newspapers, 65 Queen St W, Toronto ON M5H 2M8, Canada

Thomson, Gordon — *Actor*
%Noble Talent Mgmt, 2411 Yonge St, #202, Toronto ON M4P 2E7, Canada

Thomson, H C (Hank) — *Harness Racing Official*
PO Box 38, Mullett Lake, MI 49761, USA

Thomson, James A — *Research Company Executive*
%Rand Corp, 1700 Main St, Santa Monica, CA 90401, USA

Thomson, June — *Commentator*
%KNBC-TV, News Dept, 3000 W Alameda Ave, Burbank, CA 91523, USA

Thomson, Meldrim, Jr — *Governor, NH*
Mount Cube Farm, Orford, NH 03773, USA

Thomson, Peter W — *Golfer*
Carmel House, 44 Mathoura Rd, Toorak, VIC 3142, Australia

Thomson, Robert B (Bobby) — *Baseball Player*
122 Sunlit Dr, Watchung, NJ 07060, USA

Thomson, William R — *Financier*
%Asian Development Bank, Mandaluyong, Metro Manila, Philippines

Thon, William — *Artist*
%General Delivery, Port Clyde, ME 04855, USA

Thone, Charles — *Governor, NE*
%Erickson & Sederstrom, 301 S 13th St, #400, Lincoln, NE 68508, USA

Thoni, Gustav — *Skier, Coach*
39026 Prato Allo Stelvio-Prao BZ, Italy

Thora — *Actress*
1414 N Fairfax Ave, Los Angeles, CA 90046, USA

Thorburn, Clifford C D (Cliff) — *Snooker Player*
31 West Side Dr, Markham ON, Canada

Thorgren, Aya — *Model*
%Ford Model Mgmt, 344 E 22nd St, New York, NY 10010, USA

Thorn, George W — *Physician*
16 Gurney St, Cambridge, MA 02138, USA

Thorn, Rod — *Basketball Player*
%National Basketball Assn, Olympic Tower, 645 5th Ave, New York, NY 10022, USA

Thornburgh, Richard L — *Attorney General; Governor, PA*
%Kirkpatrick & Lockhart, 1800 "M" St NW, #900, Washington, DC 20036, USA

Thorne, Kip S *Physicist*
%California Institute of Technology, Physics Dept, Pasadena, CA 91125, USA

Thorne, Oakleigh B *Businessman*
%CCH Inc, 2700 Lake Cook Rd, Deerfield, IL 60015, USA

Thorne-Smith, Courtney *Actress*
11033 Massachusetts Ave, #19, Los Angeles, CA 90025, USA

Thornhill, Arthur H, Jr *Publisher*
50 S School St, Portsmouth, NH 03801, USA

Thornton, Andre *Baseball Player*
PO Box 395, Chagrin Falls, OH 44022, USA

Thornton, Kathryn C *Astronaut*
%NASA, Johnson Space Center, 2101 NASA Rd, Houston, TX 77058, USA

Thornton, Michael E *Vietnam War Navy Air Hero (CMH)*
118 Toler Place, Norfolk, VA 23503, USA

Thornton, Sigrid *Actress*
%William Morris Agency, 151 S El Camino Dr, Beverly Hills, CA 90212, USA

Thornton, William E *Astronaut*
%NASA, Johnson Space Center, 2101 NASA Rd, Houston, TX 77058, USA

Thornton, Winfred L *Businessman*
%St Joe Paper Co, 1650 Prudential Dr, Jacksonville, FL 32207, USA

Thornton-Sherwood, Madeleine *Actress*
32 Leroy St, New York, NY 10014, USA

Thorpe, J Jeremy *Government Official, England*
2 Orme Square, Bayswater, London W2, England

Thorpe, James *Library, Art Gallery Director*
%Huntington Library, 1650 Orlando Rd, San Marino, CA 91108, USA

Thorpe, Jim *Golfer*
%Professional Golfer's Assn, PO Box 109601, Palm Beach Gardens, FL 33410, USA

Thorpe, Otis H *Basketball Player*
%Detroit Pistons, Palace, 2 Championship Dr, Auburn Hills, MI 48057, USA

Thorsell, William *Editor*
%Toronto Globe & Mail, 444 Front St W, Toronto M5V 2S9, Canada

Thorsen, Howard B *Coast Guard Admiral*
Commander, Atlantic Area, US Coast Guard, Governors Island, New York, NY 10004, USA

Thorsness, Leo K *Vietnam Air Force Hero (CMH)*
PO Box 47, Indianola, WA 98342, USA

Threatt, Sedale *Basketball Player*
%Los Angeles Lakers, Forum, PO Box 10, Inglewood, CA 90306, USA

Threlkeld, Richard D *Commentator*
%CBS-TV, News Dept, 51 W 52nd St, New York, NY 10019, USA

Threshie, R David, Jr *Publisher*
%Orange County Register, 625 N Grand Ave, Santa Ana, CA 92701, USA

Throne, Malachi *Actor*
13067 Greenleaf St, Studio City, CA 91604, USA

Thulin, Ingrid *Actress*
Kevingestrand 7-B, 182 31 Danderyd, Sweden

Thunell, Lars H *Businessman*
%Home Insurance Co, 59 Maiden Lane, New York, NY 10038, USA

Thunman, Nils R *Navy Admiral*
1516 S Willemore Ave, Springfield, IL 62704, USA

Thuot, Pierre J *Astronaut*
%NASA, Johnson Space Center, 2101 NASA Rd, Houston, TX 77058, USA

Thurman, Maxwell R *Army General*
%Assn of US Army, 2425 Wilson Blvd, Arlington, VA 22201, USA

Thurman, Uma *Actress*
%Flick East-West Talents, 9057 Nemo St, #A, West Hollywood, CA 90069, USA

Thurmond, Nate *Basketball Player, Executive*
%Golden State Warriors, Oakland Coliseum Arena, Oakland, CA 94621, USA

Thurow, Lester C *Economist*
%Massachusetts Institute of Technology, Economics Dept, Cambridge, MA 02139, USA

Thurston, Frederick C (Fuzzy) *Football Player*
3510 E River Dr, Green Bay, WI 54301, USA

Thyssen, Greta *Actress*
444 E 82nd St, New York, NY 10028, USA

Thyssen-Bornemisza, Hans-Heinrich *Businessman, Art Collector*
Villa Favorita, 6796 Castagnola di Lugano, Switzerland

Tiainen, Juha *Track Athlete*
%Olympic Committee, Topeliuksenkatu 41 a A, Helsinki 25, Finland

T

Thorne - Tiainen

Tian Jiyun *Government Official, China*
%Vice Premier's Office, State Council, Beijing, China

Tiant, Luis C *Baseball Player*
1121 N Pine Island Rd, Ft Lauderdale, FL 33322, USA

Tibbets, Paul W *WW II Army Air Corps Hero*
5574 Knollwood Dr, Columbus, OH 43232, USA

Tice, George A *Photographer*
323 Gill Lane, #9-B, Iselin, NJ 08830, USA

Tichnor, Alan *Religious Leader*
%United Synagogue of America, 155 5th Ave, New York, NY 10010, USA

Tickner, Charlie *Figure Skater*
5410 Sunset Dr, Littleton, CO 80123, USA

Ticotin, Rachel *Actress*
%International Creative Mgmt, 8942 Wilshire Blvd, Beverly Hills, CA 90211, USA

Tidwell, Moody R, III *Judge*
%US Claims Court, 717 Madison Place NW, Washington, DC 20005, USA

Tiegs, Cheryl *Model*
%Barbara Shapiro, 2 Greenwich Plaza, #100, Greenwich, CT 06830, USA

Tiemann, Norbert T *Governor, NE*
7511 Pebblestone Dr, Dallas, TX 75230, USA

Tien, Chang-Lin *Educator*
%University of California, Chancellor's Office, Berkeley, CA 94720, USA

Tierney, Lawrence *Actor*
33 Brooks Ave, #3, Venice, CA 90291, USA

Tierney, Maura *Actor*
%"NewsRadio" Show, NBC-TV, 3000 W Alameda Ave, Burbank, CA 91523, USA

Tietjens, Norman O *Judge*
3509 Overlook Lane, Washington, DC 20016, USA

Tiffany (Renee Darwish) *Singer*
%Dick Scott Entertainment, 888 7th Ave, #2900, New York, NY 10106, USA

Tiffin, Pamela *Actress*
15 W 67th St, New York, NY 10023, USA

Tigar, Kenneth *Actor*
642 Etta St, Los Angeles, CA 90065, USA

Tiger, Lionel *Social Scientist, Anthropologist*
248 W 23rd St, #400, New York, NY 10011, USA

Tigerman, Stanley *Architect*
%Tigerman & McCurry, 444 N Wells St, #206, Chicago, IL 60610, USA

Tighe, Kevin *Actor*
PO Box 453, Sedro Wooley, WA 98284, USA

Tikkanen, Esa *Hockey Player*
%St Louis Blues, St Louis Arena, 5700 Oakland Ave, St Louis, MO 63110, USA

Tilberis, Elizabeth J *Editor*
%Harper's Bazaar Magazine, Editorial Dept, 1900 Broadway, New York, NY 10023, USA

Tilelli, John H, Jr *Army General*
Vice Chief of Staff, US Army, HqUSArmy, Pentagon, Washington, DC 20310, USA

Tilghman, Richard G *Financier*
%Crestar Financial Corp, 919 E Main St, Richmond, VA 23219, USA

Tiller, Nadja *Actress*
Via Tamporiva 26, 6976 Castagnola, Switzerland

Tilley, Patrick L (Pat) *Football Player, Coach*
5332 Goodgoin Rd, Ruston, LA 71270, USA

Tillinghast, Charles C, Jr *Businessman*
355 Blackstone Blvd, #530, Providence, RI 02906, USA

Tillis, Mel *Singer, Songwriter*
PO Box 1626, Branson, MO 65615, USA

Tillis, Pam *Singer, Songwriter*
PO Box 25304, Nashville, TN 37202, USA

Tillman, Robert L *Businessman*
%Lowe's Companies, State Highway 268 E, North Wilksboro, NC 28659, USA

Tilly, Jennifer *Actress*
%International Creative Mgmt, 8942 Wilshire Blvd, Beverly Hills, CA 90211, USA

Tilly, Meg *Actress*
%United Talent Agency, 9560 Wilshire Blvd, #500, Beverly Hills, CA 90212, USA

Tilson Thomas, Michael *Conductor, Concert Pianist*
%Harold Holt Ltd, 31 Sinclair Rd, London W14, England

Tilson, Joseph (Joe) *Artist*
Old Rectory, Christian Malford, Wilts SN15 4BW, England

Tilton, Charlene 22059 Galvez St, Woodland Hills, CA 91364, USA	*Actress*
Tilton, David L 800 Santa Barbara St, Santa Barbara, CA 93101, USA	*Businessman*
Tilton, Martha 760 Lausanne Rd, Los Angeles, CA 90077, USA	*Singer*
Tilton, Robert %Robert Tilton Ministries, PO Box 819000, Dallas, TX 75381, USA	*Evangelist*
Timakata, Fred %President's Office, Port Vila, Vanuatu	*President, Vanuatu*
Timbers, Stephen B %Kemper Corp, 1 Kemper Dr, Long Grove, IL 60047, USA	*Financier*
Timerman, Jacobo %Alfred A Knopf Inc, 201 E 50th St, New York, NY 10022, USA	*Publisher*
Timken, William R, Jr %Timken Co, 1835 Dueber Ave SW, Canton, OH 44706, USA	*Businessman*
Timme, Robert %Taft Architects, 807 Peden St, Houston, TX 77006, USA	*Architect*
Timmermann, Ulf Ahrenshooper Str 4, 13051 Berlin, Germany	*Track Athlete*
Timmins, Cali %The Agency, 1800 Ave of Stars, #400, Los Angeles, CA 90067, USA	*Actress*
Timmons, Richard F Commanding General, 8th US Army/UN Combined Forces Korea, APO, AE 96205, USA	*Army General*
Timofeyeva, Nina V %Bolshoi Theater, Teatralnaya Pl 1, 103009 Moscow, Russia	*Ballerina*
Timpe, Ronald E %Standard Insurance, 1100 SW 6th Ave, Portland, OR 97204, USA	*Businessman*
Tindemans, Leo Jan Verbertlei 24, 2520 Edegem, Belgium	*Prime Minister, Belgium*
Tindle, David 4 Rue Nande, 56260 Quemerie Sur Scorff Morbihan, France	*Artist*
Ting, Samuel C C 15 Moon Hill Rd, Lexington, MA 02173, USA	*Nobel Physics Laureate*
Ting, Walasse 100 W 25th St, New York, NY 10001, USA	*Artist*
Tinker, Grant A 531 Barnaby Rd, Los Angeles, CA 90077, USA	*Television Executive*
Tinkham, Michael 98 Rutledge Rd, Belmont, MA 02178, USA	*Physicist*
Tinsley, Bruce %USA Today, Editorial Dept, 1000 Wilson Blvd, Arlington, VA 22209, USA	*Editorial Cartoonist*
Tinsley, Gaynell C (Gus) 14343 Highland Rd, Rt 3, PO Box 485, Baton Rouge, LA 70821, USA	*Football Player*
Tinsley, Jackson B (Jack) %Fort Worth Star-Telegram, Editorial Dept, 400 W 7th St, Fort Worth, TX 76102, USA	*Editor*
Tiny Tim (Herbert Khaury) %Johnnie Martinelli Attractions, 888 8th Ave, New York, NY 10019, USA	*Singer, Songwriter*
Tippett, Andre %New England Patriots, Foxboro Stadium, Rt 1, Foxboro, MA 02035, USA	*Football Player*
Tippett, Michael K %Schott & Co, 48 Great Marlborough St, London W1V 2BN, England	*Composer, Conductor*
Tippie, Henry R %Rollins Truck Leasing Corp, 1 Rollins Plaza, Wilmington, DE 19803, USA	*Businessman*
Tippin, Aaron %Starstruck Publicity, PO Box 121996, Nashville, TN 37212, USA	*Singer, Songwriter*
Tipton, Daniel %Churches of Christ in Christian Union, Box 30, Circleville, OH 43113, USA	*Religious Leader*
Tipton, Eric G (Red) 125 Nina Lane, Williamsburg, VA 23188, USA	*Football Player*
Tiriac, Ion %Ion Tiriac/TV Enterprises, 251 E 49th St, New York, NY 10017, USA	*Tennis Player, Coach*
Tirimo, Martino 2 Combemartin Rd, London SW18 5PR, England	*Concert Pianist*
Tirole, Jean %Institut D'Economie Industrielle, Toulouse, France	*Economist*
Tisch, James S %Loews Corp, 667 Madison Ave, New York, NY 10021, USA	*Businessman*

Tisch, Laurence A *Businessman*
%CBS Inc, 51 W 52nd St, New York, NY 10019, USA

Tisch, Preston R *Government Official, Football Executive*
%Loews Corp, 667 Madison Ave, New York, NY 10021, USA

Tisch, Steve *Screenwriter*
14454 Sunset Blvd, Pacific Palisades, CA 90272, USA

Tisdale, Wayman *Basketball Player*
%Phoenix Suns, 201 E Jefferson St, Phoenix, AZ 85004, USA

Titov, Gherman S *Cosmonaut; Air Force General*
3 Hovanskaya Str, #8, 129515 Moscow, Russia

Titov, Vladimir G *Cosmonaut*
%Potchta Kosmonavtov, 141 160 Svyosdny Gorodok, Moskovskoi Oblasti, Russia

Tittle, Yelberton A (Y A) *Football Player*
611 Burleson St, Marshall, TX 75670, USA

Titus-Carmel, Gerard *Artist*
La Grand Maison, 02210 Oulchy Le Chateau, France

Tizard, Catherine A *Governor General, New Zealand*
Government House, Private Bag, Wellington, New Zealand

Tjeknavorian, Loris-Zare *Composer*
44 Coconut Row, #B-603, Palm Beach, FL 33480, USA

Tjoflat, Gerald B *Judge*
%US Court of Appeals, 311 Monroe St W, Jacksonville, FL 32202, USA

Tkachuk, Keith *Hockey Player*
%Winnipeg Jets, Arena, 15-1430 Maroons Rd, Winnipeg MB R3G 0L5, Canada

Tkaczuk, Ivan *Religious Leader*
%Ukrainian Orthodox Church, 90-34 139th St, Jamaica, NY 11435, USA

Toal, Lawrence J *Financier*
%Dime Bancorp, 589 5th Ave, New York, NY 10017, USA

Tober, Barbara D *Editor*
%Bride Magazine, Editorial Dept, 350 Madison Ave, New York, NY 10017, USA

Tobey, David *Basketball Referee*
740 Dearborn St, Teaneck, NJ 07666, USA

Tobey, Kenneth *Actor*
14155 Magnolia Blvd, #34, Sherman Oaks, CA 91423, USA

Tobias, Andrew *Writer*
%Micro Education Corp of America, 285 Riverside Ave, Westport, CT 06880, USA

Tobias, Randall L *Businessman*
%Eli Lilly Co, Lilly Corporate Center, Indianapolis, IN 46285, USA

Tobias, Robert M *Labor Leader*
%National Treasury Employees Union, 901 "E" St NW, Washington, DC 20004, USA

Tobiasse, Theo *Artist*
3 Quai Rauba Coupa, 06 Nice, France

Tobin, Don *Cartoonist (The Little Woman)*
24441 Calle Sonora, #324, Laguna Hills, CA 92653, USA

Tobin, James *Nobel Economics Laureate*
117 Alden Ave, New Haven, CT 06515, USA

Tobin, Robert G *Businessman*
%Stop & Shop Companies, PO Box 1942, Quincy, MA 02105, USA

Tocchet, Rick *Hockey Player*
%Los Angeles Kings, Forum, PO Box 17013, Inglewood, CA 90308, USA

Tocklin, Adrian M *Businessman*
%Continental Corp, 180 Maiden Lane, New York, NY 10038, USA

Toczyska, Stefania *Opera Singer*
%Metropolitan Opera Assn, Lincoln Center Plaza, New York, NY 10023, USA

Todd of Trumpington, Alexander R *Nobel Chemistry Laureate*
9 Parker St, Cambridge, England

Todd, Beverly *Actress*
488 Valley Ridge Ave, Los Angeles, CA 90043, USA

Todd, Hallie *Actress*
%Gersh Agency, 232 N Canon Dr, Beverly Hills, CA 90210, USA

Todd, James A, Jr *Businessman*
%Birmingham Steel Corp, 1000 Urban Center Dr, Birmingham, AL 35242, USA

Todd, Mark *Equestrian*
PO Box 507, Cambridge, New Zealand

Todd, Rachel *Actress*
8899 Beverly Blvd, #808, Los Angeles, CA 90048, USA

Todd, Richard *Actor*
Chinham Farm, Faringdon, Oxon SN7 8EZ, England

Todd, Virgil H *Religious Leader*
%Memphis Theological Seminary, 168 E Parkway S, Memphis, TN 38104, USA

Todea, Alexandru Cardinal *Religious Leader*
Archdiocese of Alba Julia, Str P P Aron 2, 3175 Blaj, Romania

Todorov, Stanko *Prime Minister, Bulgaria*
Narodno Sobranie, Sofia, Bulgaria

Toennies, Jan Peter *Physicist*
Ewaldstr 7, 37075 Gottingen, Germany

Tofani, Loretta A *Journalist*
%Philadelphia Inquirer, Editorial Dept, 400 N Broad St, Philadelphia, PA 19130, USA

Toffler, Alvin *Writer*
%Random House Inc, 201 E 50th St, New York, NY 10022, USA

Toft, Richard P *Financier*
%Chicago Title & Trust, 171 N Clark St, Chicago, IL 60601, USA

Tognini, Michel *Cosmonaut, France*
%CNES, 2 Place Maurice Quentin, 75039 Paris, France

Toia, Philip L *Financier*
%Dreyfus Corp, 200 Park Ave, New York, NY 10166, USA

Tokody, Ilona *Opera Singer*
%Hungarian State Opera, Andrassy Ut 22, 1062 Budapest, Hungary

Tolan, Robert (Bobby) *Baseball Player*
4145 Olympiad Dr, Los Angeles, CA 90043, USA

Toland, John W *Writer*
101 Long Ridge Rd, Danbury, CT 06810, USA

Tolbert, Berlinda *Actress*
1800 Ave of Stars, #400, Los Angeles, CA 90067, USA

Toles, Thomas G (Tom) *Editorial Cartoonist*
%Buffalo News, Editorial Dept, 1 News Plaza, Buffalo, NY 14203, USA

Tolkan, James *Actor*
%Paradigm Agency, 10100 Santa Monica Blvd, #2500, Los Angeles, CA 90067, USA

Toll, Bruce E *Businessman*
%Toll Brothers, 3103 Philmont Ave, Huntingdon Valley, PA 19006, USA

Toll, Robert I *Businessman*
%Toll Brothers, 3103 Philmont Ave, Huntingdon Valley, PA 19006, USA

Toller, William R *Businessman*
%Witco Inc, 1 American Lane, Greenwich, CT 06831, USA

Tolleson, John C *Financier*
%First USA, 2001 Bryan Tower, Dallas, TX 75201, USA

Tollett, Leland E *Businessman*
%Tyson Foods Inc, 2210 W Oaklawn Dr, Springdale, AR 72762, USA

Tolsky, Susan *Actress*
10815 Acama St, North Hollywood, CA 91602, USA

Tomasson, Helgi *Ballet Dancer, Director*
%San Francisco Ballet, 819 Lorraine Ave, Ardmore, PA 19003, USA

Tomaszewski, Henryk *Choreographer*
Al Debowa 16, 53-121 Wroclaw, Poland

Tomba, Alberto *Skier*
Castel dei Britti, 40100 Bologna, Italy

Tombaugh, Clyde W *Astronomer*
PO Box 306, Mesilla Park, NM 88047, USA

Tomei, Concetta *Actress*
630 Gayer Dr, Calabasas, CA 91302, USA

Tomei, Marisa *Actress*
%Altman Greenfield Selvaggi, 120 W 45th St, #3600, New York, NY 10036, USA

Tomey, Dick *Football Coach*
%University of Arizona, Athletic Dept, Tucson, AZ 85721, USA

Tominac, John J *WW II Army Hero (CMH)*
3234 Taylor Rd, Carmel, CA 93923, USA

Tomita, Stan *Photographer*
2439 St Louis Dr, Honolulu, HI 96816, USA

Tomjanovich, Rudolph (Rudy) *Basketball Player, Coach*
%Houston Rockets, Summit, Greenway Plaza, #10, Houston, TX 77277, USA

Tomko, Jozef Cardinal *Religious Leader*
Villa Betania, Via Urbano VIII-16, 00165 Rome, Italy

Tomlin, Lily *Comedienne, Actress*
%Omnipotent Theatricalz, PO Box 27700, Los Angeles, CA 90027, USA

Tomlinson, Charles *Writer*
%Bristol University, English Dept, Bristol BS8 1TH, England

Tomlinson, David *Actor*
Brook Cottage, Mursley, Bucks, England

Tomlinson, John *Opera Singer*
%Music International, 13 Ardilaun Rd, Highbury, London N5 2QR, England

Tomlinson, Kenneth Y *Editor*
%Reader's Digest Magazine, Reader's Digest Rd, Pleasantville, NY 10570, USA

Tomlinson, Mel A *Ballet Dancer*
1216 Bunche Dr, Raleigh, NC 27610, USA

Tomowa-Sintow, Anna *Opera Singer*
%Columbia Artists Mgmt Inc, 165 W 57th St, New York, NY 10019, USA

Tompkins, Angel *Actress*
9105 Morning Glory Way, Sun Valley, CA 91352, USA

Tone-Luc *Actor*
7932 Hillside Ave, Los Angeles, CA 90046, USA

Toneff, Robert (Bob) *Football Player*
18 Dutch Valley Lane, San Anselmo, CA 94960, USA

Tonegawa, Susumu *Nobel Medicine Laureate*
%Massachusetts Institute of Technology, Biology Dept, Cambridge, MA 02139, USA

Tonelli, John *Hockey Player*
%Los Angeles Kings, Forum, PO Box 17013, Inglewood, CA 90308, USA

Toner, Mike *Journalist*
%Atlanta Journal-Constitution, Editorial Dept, 72 Marietta, Atlanta, GA 30303, USA

Toney, Andrew *Basketball Player*
%Philadelphia 76ers, Veterans Stadium, PO Box 25040, Philadelphia, PA 19147, USA

Tonnemaker, F Clayton *Football Player*
212 S Cudd Ave, River Falls, WI 54022, USA

Tooker, Gary L *Businessman*
%Motorola Inc, 1303 E Algonquin Rd, Schaumburg, IL 60196, USA

Tooker, George *Artist*
PO Box 385, Hartland, VT 05048, USA

Toomey, Bill *Track Athlete*
%Olympic Training Foundation, 1904 Hotel Circle N, San Diego, CA 92108, USA

Toon, Al *Football Player*
%New York Jets, 1000 Fulton Ave, Hempstead, NY 11550, USA

Toon, Malcolm *Diplomat*
375 PeeDee Rd, Southern Pines, NC 28387, USA

Toot, Joseph F, Jr *Businessman*
%Timken Co, 1835 Dueber Ave SW, Canton, OH 44706, USA

Topfer, Morton L *Businessman*
%Dell Computer Corp, 9505 Arboretum Blvd, Austin, TX 78759, USA

Topol, Chaim *Actor*
%Brian Eagles, 236 Grays Inn Rd, London WC1X 8HB, England

Topping, Lynne *Actress*
%Sekura/A Talent Agency, PO Box 931779, Los Angeles, CA 90093, USA

Topping, Seymour *Editor*
5 Heathcote Rd, Scarsdale, NY 10583, USA

Torborg, Jeffrey A (Jeff) *Baseball Player, Manager*
5208 Ciesta Cove Dr, Sarasota, FL 34242, USA

Tork, Peter *Singer, Musician (Monkees)*
%16 Magazine, 233 Park Ave S, New York, NY 10003, USA

Torme, Mel *Singer*
%International Ventures, 1734 Coldwater Canyon Dr, Beverly Hills, CA 90210, USA

Torn, Rip *Actor*
%Hecht Co, 111 W 40th St, #2000, New York, NY 10018, USA

Torp, Niels A *Architect*
Industrigaten 59, PO Box 5387, 0304 Oslo, Norway

Torrance, Thomas F *Religious Leader, Educator*
37 Braid Farm Rd, Edinburgh EH10 6LE, Scotland

Torre, Joseph P (Joe) *Baseball Player, Manager*
6279 Sun Blvd, #507-H, St Petersburg, FL 33715, USA

Torrence, Dean *Singer (Jan & Dean), Songwriter*
18932 Gregory Lane, Huntington Beach, CA 92646, USA

Torrence, Gwen *Track Athlete*
PO Box 361965, Decatur, GA 30036, USA

Torres Gowen, Dara *Swimmer, Model*
%Trouble in New York Agency, 9 E 37th St, New York, NY 10016, USA

Torres, Jose *Boxer*
%NY State Athletic Commission, 270 Broadway, New York, NY 10007, USA

Torres, Liz *Singer, Actress*
%Atkins Assoc, 303 S Crescent Heights Blvd, Los Angeles, CA 90048, USA

Torres, Tico *Drummer (Bon Jovi)*
%Bon Jovi Mgmt, 250 W 57th St, #603, New York, NY 10107, USA

Torrey, Bill *Hockey Executive*
%Florida Panthers, 100 NE 3rd Ave, #1000, Fort Lauderdale, FL 33301, USA

Torrey, Rich *Cartoonist (Hartland)*
%King Features Syndicate, 216 E 45th St, New York, NY 10017, USA

Torrissen, Birger *Nordic Skier*
PO Box 216, Lakeville, CT 06039, USA

Torruella, Juan R *Judge*
%US Court of Appeals, PO Box 3671, San Juan, PR 00902, USA

Tortelier, Yan Pascal *Conductor*
%M A de Valmalete, Building Gaceau, 11 Ave Delcasse, 75635 Paris, France

Torvill, Jayne *Ice Dancer*
PO Box 16, Beeston, Nottingham NG9, England

Toski, Bob *Golfer*
160 Essex St, Newark, OH 43055, USA

Totenberg, Nina *Commentator*
%National Public Radio, News Dept, 615 Main Ave NW, Washington, DC 20024, USA

Totten, Robert *Movie Director*
13819 Riverside Dr, Sherman Oaks, CA 91423, USA

Totter, Audrey *Actress*
1945 Glendon Ave, #301, Los Angeles, CA 90025, USA

Toumanova, Tamara *Ballerina, Actress*
305 N Elm Dr, Beverly Hills, CA 90210, USA

Touraine, Jean-Louis *Immunologist*
%Edouard-Herriot Hospital, Place d'Arsonval, 69437 Lyons Cedex 03, France

Tournier, Michel *Writer*
Le Presbytere, Choisel, 78460 Chevreuse, France

Tousey, Richard *Physicist*
10450 Lottsford Rd, #231, Bowie, MD 20721, USA

Toussaint, Allen *Composer, Jazz Pianist*
%Sea Saint Recording Studio, 3809 Clematis Ave, New Orleans, LA 70122, USA

Tower, Horace L, III *Businessman*
%Stanhome Inc, 333 Western Ave, Westfield, MA 01085, USA

Tower, Joan P *Composer*
%Bard College, Music Dept, Annandale-on-Hudson, NY 12504, USA

Towers, Constance *Actress*
10253 Century Woods Dr, Los Angeles, CA 90067, USA

Towers, John *Businessman*
%AMAX Inc, 200 Park Ave, New York, NY 10166, USA

Towers, Kenneth *Editor*
%Chicago Sun-Times, Editorial Dept, 401 N Wabash, Chicago, IL 60611, USA

Towne, Robert *Movie Director, Screenwriter*
1417 San Remo Dr, Pacific Palisades, CA 90272, USA

Townes, Charles H *Nobel Physics Laureate*
%University of California, Physics Dept, Berkeley, CA 94720, USA

Townes, Harry *Actor*
251 N Burton Way, Palm Springs, CA 92262, USA

Townsend, Colleen *Actress*
%National Presbyterian Church, 4101 Nebraska Ave NW, Washington, DC 20016, USA

Townsend, Greg *Football Player*
%Philadelphia Eagles, 3501 S Broad St, Philadelphia, PA 19148, USA

Townsend, Ken W *Financier*
%Boatmen's First National Bank, PO Box 25189, Oklahoma City, OK 73125, USA

Townsend, Robert *Actor*
2934 1/2 N Beverly Glen Circle, #407, Los Angeles, CA 90077, USA

Townsend, Roscoe *Religious Leader*
%Evangelical Friends, 2018 Maple St, Wichita, KS 67213, USA

Townshend, Peter *Singer, Songwriter (Who)*
Boathouse, Ranelagh Dr, Twickenham, Middx TW1 1QZ, England

Toy, Sam *Businessman*
35 Stanhope Terrace, Lancaster Gate, London W2 2UA, England

Toyada, Eiji *Businessman*
%Toyota Motor Corp, 1 Toyotacho, Toyota City, Aichi Prefecture 471, Japan

Toye, Wendy *Choreographer, Ballerina*
%Jay Berning Co, Canberra House, 315 Regent St, London W1R 7YB, England

T

Torres - Toye

T

Toyoda, Shoichiro *Businessman*
%Toyota Motor Corp, 1 Toyotacho, Toyota City, Aichi Prefecture 471, Japan

Toyoda, Tatsuro *Businessman*
%Toyota Motor Corp, 1 Toyotacho, Toyota City, Aichi Prefecture 471, Japan

Tozzi, Giorgio *Opera Singer*
%RCA Records, 1540 Broadway, #900, New York, NY 10036, USA

Trabert, Tony *Tennis Player*
115 Knotty Pine Trail, Ponte Vedra, FL 32082, USA

Tracey, Margaret *Ballerina*
%New York City Ballet, Lincoln Center Plaza, New York, NY 10023, USA

Trachta, Jeff *Actor*
1040 N Maple St, Burbank, CA 91505, USA

Trachte, Don *Cartoonist (Henry)*
%King Features Syndicate, 216 E 45th St, New York, NY 10017, USA

Trachtenberg, Stephen J *Educator*
%George Washington University, President's Office, Washington, DC 20052, USA

Tracy, Arthur *Singer*
350 W 57th St, New York, NY 10019, USA

Tracy, Michael C *Artistic Director, Dancer*
%Pilobolus Dance Theater, PO Box 388, Washington Depot, CT 06794, USA

Tracy, Paul *Auto Racing Driver*
%Newman/Haas Racing, 500 Town Parkway, Lincolnshire, IL 60069, USA

Trafton, Stephen J *Financier*
%Glendale Federal Savings, 700 N Brand Blvd, Glendale, CA 91203, USA

Trager, Milton *Physical Therapist*
%Trager Institute, 33 Millwood St, Mill Valley, CA 94941, USA

Trager, William *Parasitologist*
%Rockefeller University, Parasitology Lab, 1230 York Ave, New York, NY 10021, USA

Train, Harry D, II *Navy Admiral*
1002 Magnolia Ave, Norfolk, VA 23508, USA

Train, Russell E *Government Official, Environmentalist*
%World Wildlife Fund, 1250 24th St NW, Washington, DC 20037, USA

Trainor, Bernard E *Marine Corps General*
80 Potter Pond, Lexington, MA 02173, USA

Trainor, Edward J *Businessman*
%Standex International, 6 Manor Parkway, Salem, NH 03079, USA

Tramiel, Jack *Businessman*
%Atari Corp, 1196 Borregas Ave, Sunnyvale, CA 94089, USA

Tramiel, Sam *Businessman*
%Atari Corp, 1196 Borregas Ave, Sunnyvale, CA 94089, USA

Trammell, Alan S *Baseball Player*
260 Guilford Rd, Bloomfield Hills, MI 48304, USA

Tranchell, Peter A *Composer*
%Caius College, Cambridge CB2 1TA, England

Trani, Eugene P *Educator*
%Virginia Commonwealth University, President's Office, Richmond, VA 23284, USA

Trask, Thomas E *Religious Leader*
%Assemblies of God, 1445 Boonville Ave, Springfield, MO 65802, USA

Traub, Charles *Photographer*
39 E 10th St, New York, NY 10003, USA

Trauscht, Donald C *Businessman*
%Borg-Warner Security, 200 S Michigan Ave, Chicago, IL 60604, USA

Trautwig, Al *Sportscaster*
%ABC-TV, Sports Dept, 77 W 66th St, New York, NY 10023, USA

Travaglianti, Edward *Financier*
%European American Bank, EAB Plaza, Uniondale, NY 11555, USA

Travalena, Fred *Singer*
4515 White Oak Place, Encino, CA 91316, USA

Travanti, Daniel J *Actor*
1077 Melody Rd, Lake Forest, IL 60045, USA

Travell, Janet G *Physician*
4525 Cathedral Ave NW, Washington, DC 20016, USA

Travers, Mary *Singer (Peter Paul & Mary)*
PO Box 135, Bearsville, NY 12409, USA

Travis, Cecil H *Baseball Player*
2260 Highway 138, Riverdale, GA 30296, USA

Travis, Nancy *Actress*
9869 Portola Dr, Beverly Hills, CA 90210, USA

Toyoda - Travis

Travis, Randy   *Singer, Songwriter*
%Lib Hatcher Mgmt, 1610 16th Ave S, Nashville, TN 37212, USA

Travolta, Ellen   *Actress*
5923 Wilbur Ave, Tarzana, CA 91356, USA

Travolta, John   *Actor*
1504 Live Oak Lane, Santa Barbara, CA 93105, USA

Treach   *Rapper (Naughty By Nature)*
%Flavor Unit Mgmt, 155 Morgan St, Jersey City, NJ 07302, USA

Treadway, Edward A   *Labor Leader*
%Elevator Constructors Union, 5565 Sterret Place, Columbia, MD 21044, USA

Treadway, James C, Jr   *Government Official*
Laurel Ledge Farm, Croton Lake Rd, RD 4, Mount Kisco, NY 10549, USA

Treadway, Kenneth   *Swimming Contributor*
%Phillips Petroleum Co, Adams Building, Bartlesville, OK 74003, USA

Treas, Terri   *Actress*
%Agency For Performing Arts, 9000 Sunset Blvd, #1200, Los Angeles, CA 90069, USA

Trebek, Alex   *Entertainer*
3405 Fryman Rd, Studio City, CA 91604, USA

Trebelhorn, Thomas L (Tom)   *Baseball Manager*
4344 SE 26th Ave, Portland, OR 97202, USA

Tree, Michael   *Violinist (Guarneri String Quartet)*
45 E 89th St, New York, NY 10128, USA

Treen, David C   *Governor, LA*
%Deutsch Kerrigan Stile, 755 Magazine St, New Orleans, LA 70130, USA

Treiman, Sam B   *Physicist*
60 McCosh Circle, Princeton, NJ 08540, USA

Trejos Fernandez, Jose J   *President, Costa Rica*
Apartado 10 096, 1000 San Jose, Costa Rica

Trelford, Donald G   *Editor*
20 Richmond Crescent, London N1 0LZ, England

Tremayne, Les   *Actor*
901 S Barrington Ave, Los Angeles, CA 90049, USA

Tremblay, Michael   *Writer*
294 Carre St Louis, #5-E, Montreal PQ H2X 1A4, Canada

Tremlett, David R   *Artist*
Broadlawns, Chipperfield Rd, Bovingdon, Herts, England

Tremont, Ray C   *Religious Leader*
%Volunteers of America, 3939 N Causeway Blvd, #400, Metairie, LA 70002, USA

Trenet, Charles   *Singer, Songwriter*
2 Rue Anatole-France, 11100 Narbonne, France

Trengganu   *Sultan of Trengganau State, Malaysia*
Istana Badariah, Kuala Trengganu, Trengganu, Malaysia

Trent, Gary   *Basketball Player*
%Portland Trail Blazers, 700 NE Multnomah St, #600, Portland, OR 97232, USA

Tretiak, Vladislav   *Hockey Player, Coach*
%Transglobal Sports, 94 Festival Dr, Toronto ON M2R 3V1, Canada

Tretyak, Ivan   *Army General, Russia*
%Ministry of Defense, 34 Nanerezhnaya M Thoreza, Moscow, Russia

Trevelyan, Edward N   *Yachtsman*
1515 Laguna St, #3, Santa Barbara, CA 93101, USA

Trever, John   *Editorial Cartoonist*
%Albuquerque Journal, 717 Silver Ave SW, Albuquerque, NM 87102, USA

Trevi, Gloria   *Singer*
%Leisil Ent, Ave del Parque 67 Col Napoles, Mexico City DF 03810, Mexico

Trevino, Lee B   *Golfer*
5757 Alpha Rd, #620, Dallas, TX 75240, USA

Trevino, Rick   *Singer*
%Vector Mgmt, PO Box 128037, Nashville, TN 37212, USA

Trevor, Claire   *Actress*
%Pierre Hotel, 2 E 61st St, New York, NY 10021, USA

Trevor, William   *Writer*
%Viking Press, 27 Wright's Lane, London W8, England

Treybig, James G   *Businessman*
%Tandem Computers, 19333 Vallco Parkway, Cupertino, CA 95014, USA

Tribbitt, Sherman W   *Governor, DE*
39 Hazel Rd, Dover, DE 19901, USA

Tribe, Laurence H   *Attorney, Educator*
%Harvard University, Law School, Griswold Hall, Cambridge, MA 02138, USA

T

Travis - Tribe

Trickle, Dick — Auto Racing Driver
%Stavola Racing, PO Box 339, Harrisburg, NC 28075, USA

Trigere, Pauline — Fashion Designer
498 Fashion Ave, #10-B-5, New York, NY 10018, USA

Trillin, Calvin M — Writer
%New Yorker Magazine, Editorial Dept, 20 W 43rd St, New York, NY 10036, USA

Trimble, Vance H — Editor
1013 Sunset Ave, Kenton Hills, KY 41011, USA

Trinh, Eugene — Astronaut
%Jet Propulsion Laboratory, 4800 Oak Grove Dr, Pasadena, CA 91109, USA

Trintignant, Jean-Louis — Actor
%Artmedia, 10 Ave George V, 75008 Paris, France

Trippi, Charles L (Charley) — Football Player
125 Riverhill Court, Athens, GA 30606, USA

Tritt, Travis — Singer, Songwriter
PO Box 440099, Kennesaw, GA 30144, USA

Troisgros, Pierre E R — Restauranteur
%Place Jean Troisgros, 42300 Roanne, France

Troitskaya, Natalia L — Opera Singer
Klostergasse 37, 1170 Vienna, Austria

Trost, Barry M — Chemist
24510 Amigos Court, Los Altos Hills, CA 94024, USA

Trost, Carlisle A H — Navy Admiral
10405 Windsor View Dr, Potomac, MD 20854, USA

Trotman, Alexander J — Businessman
%Ford Motor Co, American Rd, Dearborn, MI 48121, USA

Trott, Stephen S — Judge
%US Court of Appeals, US Courthouse, 550 W Fort St, Boise, ID 83724, USA

Trotter-Betts, Virginia — Labor Leader
%American Nurses Assn, 600 Maryland Ave SW, Washington, DC 20024, USA

Trottier, Bryan J — Hockey Player, Executive, Coach
%Pittsburgh Penguins, Civic Arena, Centre Ave, Pittsburgh, PA 15219, USA

Troup, Bobby — Musician, Actor
16074 Royal Oak St, Encino, CA 91436, USA

Troupe, Tom — Actor
8829 Ashcroft Ave, Los Angeles, CA 90048, USA

Troutt, William E — Educator
%Belmont College, President's Office, Nashville, TN 37212, USA

Trovoada, Miguel A C L — President, Sao Tome & Principe
%President's Office, Prago do Povo, Sao Tome, Sao Tome & Principe

Trowbridge, Alexander B, Jr — Secretary, Commerce
1823 23rd St NW, Washington, DC 20008, USA

Trower, Robin — Singer, Guitarist
%Stardust Entertainment, 2650 Glendower Ave, Los Angeles, CA 90027, USA

Troyat, Henri — Writer
%Academie Francaise, 23 Quai de Conti, 75006 Paris, France

Truax, Billy — Football Player
735 Ruth Ave, Gulfport, MS 39501, USA

Trubshaw, Brian — Test Pilot, Businessman
%British Aerospace, Filton, Bristol, England

Trucks, Virgil O (Fire) — Baseball Player
36 Santarem Circle, Punta Gorda, FL 33983, USA

Trudeau, Garry B — Cartoonist (Doonesbury)
271 Central Park W, #10-E, New York, NY 10024, USA

Trudeau, Jack — Football Player
%New York Jets, 1000 Fulton Ave, Hempstead, NY 11550, USA

Trudeau, Pierre E — Prime Minister, Canada
%Heenan Blaikie, 1250 Boul Rene-Levesque, Montreal PQ H3B 4Y1, Canada

Truitt, Anne D — Sculptor
3506 35th St NW, Washington, DC 20016, USA

Truly, Richard H — Astronaut, Space Administrator, Admiral
%Georgia Tech Research Institute, 400 10th St, Atlanta, GA 30332, USA

Truman, David B — Political Scientist
Tory Hill Rd, Box 308, Hillsdale, NY 12529, USA

Truman, James — Editor
%Conde Nast Publications, 350 Madison Ave, New York, NY 10017, USA

Trumka, Richard L — Labor Leader
%United Mine Workers, 900 15th St NW, Washington, DC 20005, USA

Trump, Donald J — *Businessman*
%Trump Organization, 725 5th Ave, New York, NY 10022, USA

Trump, Ivana — *Businesswoman*
725 5th Ave, New York, NY 10022, USA

Trumpy, Robert T (Bob), Jr — *Football Player, Sportscaster*
%NBC-TV, Sports Dept, 30 Rockefeller Plaza, New York, NY 10112, USA

Trundy, Natalie — *Actress*
6140 Lindenhurst Ave, Los Angeles, CA 90048, USA

Trusel, Lisa — *Actress*
2350 Allview Terrace, Los Angeles, CA 90068, USA

Tryggvason, Bjarni — *Astronaut, Canada*
%Astronaut Program, 6767 Rt de l'Aeroport, St-Hubert PQ J3Y 8Y9, Canada

Trzaskoma, Richard J — *Air Force General*
Commander, 22nd Air Force, Travis Air Force, CA 94535, USA

Tsai, Gerald, Jr — *Businessman*
%Delta Life Corp, 4370 Peacetree Rd NE, Atlanta, GA 30319, USA

Tsao, I Fu — *Chemical Engineer*
%University of Michigan, Chemical Engineering Dept, Ann Arbor, MI 48109, USA

Tschetter, Kris — *Golfer*
%Ladies Professional Golf Assn, 2570 Volusia Ave, Daytona Beach, FL 32114, USA

Tschudi, Hans-Peter — *President, Switzerland*
%Int'l Croix-Rouge Committee, Ave de la Paix 17, 1211 Geneva, Switzerland

Tse, Edmund S — *Businessman*
%American Life Insurance, 1 Alico Plaza, 600 King St, Wilmington, DE 19801, USA

Tsongas, Paul E — *Senator, MA*
%Foley Hoag Eliot, 1 Post Office Square, Boston, MA 02109, USA

Tsoucalas, Nicholas — *Judge*
%US Court of International Trade, 1 Federal Plaza, New York, NY 10278, USA

Tsui, John K — *Financier*
%First Hawaiian Bank, 1132 Bishop St, Honolulu, HI 96813, USA

Tsuji, Yoshifumi — *Businessman*
%Nissan Motor Co, 6-17-1 Ginza, Chuoku, Tokyo 104, Japan

Tsutsumi, Yoshiaki — *Businessman*
%Seibu Railway Co, 16-15-1 Minami Ikebukuro, Toshimaku, Tokyo 171, Japan

Tubbs, Billy — *Basketball Coach*
%Texas Christian University, Athletic Dept, Fort Worth, TX 76129, USA

Tucci, Stanley — *Actor*
%William Morris Agency, 151 S El Camino Dr, Beverly Hills, CA 90212, USA

Tuchman, Maurice — *Museum Curator*
%Los Angeles Museum of Art, 5905 Wilshire Blvd, Los Angeles, CA 90036, USA

Tuck, Jessica — *Actress*
%Brett Adams, 448 W 44th St, New York, NY 10036, USA

Tucker, J Walter, Jr — *Businessman*
%Keystone Consolidated Industries, 5430 LBJ Freeway, Dallas, TX 75240, USA

Tucker, Jim Guy — *Governor, AR*
%Governor's Office, 205 State Capitol Building, Little Rock, AR 72201, USA

Tucker, Keith A — *Businessman*
%Torchmark Corp, 2001 3rd Ave S, Birmingham, AL 35233, USA

Tucker, Marcia — *Museum Official*
%New Museum of Contemporary Art, 583 Broadway, New York, NY 10012, USA

Tucker, Tanya — *Singer*
PO Box 15245, Nashville, TN 37215, USA

Tucker, William E — *Educator*
%Texas Christian University, Chancellor's Office, Fort Worth, TX 76129, USA

Tuckwell, Barry E — *Concert French Hornist*
13140 Fountain Head Rd, Hagerstown, MD 21742, USA

Tudjman, Franjo — *President, Croatia*
%President's Office, Presidential Palace, Zagreb, Croatia

Tudor, John T — *Baseball Player*
14 Forest St, Peabody, MA 01960, USA

Tuerff, James R — *Businessman*
%American General Corp, 2929 Allen Parkway, Houston, TX 77019, USA

Tugwell, John — *Financier*
%National Westminster Bancorp, 10 Exchange Place, Jersey City, NJ 07302, USA

Tully, Daniel P — *Businessman*
%Merrill Lynch Co, World Financial Center North, 32 Vesey St, New York, NY 10007, USA

Tully, Darrow — *Publisher*
3001 Barret Ave, Plant City, FL 33567, USA

T

Trump - Tully

T

Tumanishvili, Mikhail I — *Theater Director*
Barnova Str 126-A, #8, 380079 Tbilsi, Georgia

Tumi, Christian W Cardinal — *Religious Leader*
Archveche, BP 272, Douala, Cameroon

Tune, Thomas J (Tommy) — *Dancer, Actor*
1501 Broadway, #1508, New York, NY 10036, USA

Tunney, Jim — *Football Referee*
%National Football League, Referees Office, 350 Park Ave, New York, NY 10022, USA

Tunney, John V — *Senator, CA*
106 Esparta Way, Santa Monica, CA 90402, USA

Tunnick, George — *Association Executive*
%National Assn of Female Executives, 127 W 24th St, New York, NY 10011, USA

Tupouto'a — *Crown Prince, Tonga*
%The Palace, PO Box 6, Nuku'alofa, Tonga

Tupper, C John — *Physician, Educator*
PO Box 2007, El Macera, CA 95618, USA

Turbyfill, John R — *Businessman*
%Norfolk Southern Corp, 3 Commercial Pl, Norfolk, VA 23510, USA

Turco, Richard P — *Atmospheric Scientist*
%R&D Assoc, 4640 Admiralty Way, Marina del Rey, CA 90292, USA

Turcotte, Ron — *Thoroughbred Racing Jockey*
PO Box 215, Van Buren, ME 04785, USA

Tureck, Rosalyn — *Concert Pianist*
%Tureck Bach Institute, 215 E 68th St, New York, NY 10021, USA

Turgeon, Pierre — *Hockey Player*
%Montreal Canadiens, 2313 St Catherine St W, Montreal PQ H3H 1N2, Canada

Turgeon, Sylvain — *Hockey Player*
%Montreal Canadiens, 2313 St Catherine St W, Montreal PQ H3H 1N2, Canada

Turkel, Ann — *Actress*
9877 Beverly Grove Dr, Beverly Hills, CA 90210, USA

Turkevich, Anthony L — *Chemist*
175 Briarwood Loop, Briarwood Lakes, Hinsdale, IL 60521, USA

Turley, Clarence M — *Financier*
%Roosevelt Bank, 900 Roosevelt Parkway, Chesterfield, MO 63017, USA

Turley, Joseph F — *Businessman*
%Gillette Co, Prudential Tower Building, Boston, MA 02199, USA

Turley, Robert L (Bob) — *Baseball Player*
1690 N Copeland Dr, Marco Island, FL 33937, USA

Turley, Stewart — *Businessman*
%Eckerd Corp, PO Box 4689, Clearwater, FL 34618, USA

Turlington, Christy — *Model*
%Ford Model Agency, 344 E 59th St, New York, NY 10022, USA

Turman, Glynn — *Actor*
%Agency For Performing Arts, 9000 Sunset Blvd, #1200, Los Angeles, CA 90069, USA

Turnbull, David — *Physicist*
77 Summer St, Weston, MA 02193, USA

Turnbull, William — *Artist*
%Waddington Galleries, 11 Cork St, London W1, England

Turnbull, William, Jr — *Architect*
%Turnbull Assoc, Pier 1 1/2, The Embarcadero, San Francisco, CA 94111, USA

Turner, Cal, Jr — *Businessman*
%Dollar General Corp, 104 Woodmont Blvd, Nashville, TN 37205, USA

Turner, Cathy — *Speed Skater*
PO Box 67747, Rochester, NY 14617, USA

Turner, Clyde (Bulldog) — *Football Player*
Rt 3, Box 62, Gatesville, TX 76528, USA

Turner, Clyde T — *Businessman*
%Circus Circus Enterprises, 2880 Las Vegas Blvd S, Las Vegas, NV 89109, USA

Turner, Edwin L — *Astrophysicist*
%Princeton University, Astrophysical Sciences Dept, Princeton, NJ 08544, USA

Turner, Eric — *Football Player*
%Cleveland Browns, 80 1st Ave, Berea, OH 44017, USA

Turner, Francis J — *Geologist*
2525 Hill Court, Berkeley, CA 94708, USA

Turner, Fred L — *Businessman*
%McDonald's Corp, McDonald's Plaza, 1 Kroc Dr, Oak Brook, IL 60521, USA

Turner, Ike — *Singer*
2360 Jupiter Dr, Los Angeles, CA 90046, USA

Tumanishvili - Turner

Turner, James C *Labor Leader*
%Operating Engineers Union, 1125 17th St NW, Washington, DC 20036, USA

Turner, James R *Baseball Player*
1004 Woodmont Blvd, Nashville, TN 37204, USA

Turner, James T *Judge*
%US Claims Court, 717 Madison Place NW, Washington, DC 20005, USA

Turner, Janine *Actress*
%Creative Artists Agency, 9830 Wilshire Blvd, Beverly Hills, CA 90212, USA

Turner, John G *Businessman*
%NWNL Companies, 20 Washington Ave S, Minneapolis, MN 55401, USA

Turner, John N *Prime Minister, Canada*
27 Dunloe Rd, Toronto ON M4V 2W4, Canada

Turner, Kathleen *Actress*
163 Amsterdam Ave, #210, New York, NY 10023, USA

Turner, Keena *Football Player, Coach*
1 Galvez, Stanford, CA 94305, USA

Turner, Morrie *Cartoonist (Wee Pals)*
%Creators Syndicate, 5777 W Century Blvd, #700, Los Angeles, CA 90045, USA

Turner, Norv *Football Coach*
%Washington Redskins, 21300 Redskin Park Dr, Ashburn, VA 22011, USA

Turner, R Gerald *Educator*
%University of Mississippi, Chancellor's Office, University, MS 38677, USA

Turner, Robert E (Ted), III *Communications, Sports Executive*
%Time Warner Inc, 75 Rockefeller Plaza, New York, NY 10019, USA

Turner, Ron *Football Coach*
%San Jose State University, Athletic Dept, San Jose, CA 95192, USA

Turner, Sherri *Golfer*
%Ladies Professional Golf Assn, 2570 Volusia Ave, Daytona Beach, FL 32114, USA

Turner, Stansfield *Navy Admiral, Law Enforcement Official*
1320 Skipwith Rd, McLean, VA 22101, USA

Turner, Steve *Guitarist (Mudhoney)*
%Reprise Records, 3300 Warner Blvd, Burbank, CA 91505, USA

Turner, Tina *Singer*
%Creative Artists Agency, 9830 Wilshire Blvd, Beverly Hills, CA 90212, USA

Turner, William B *Financier*
%Synovus Financial Corp, 901 Front St, Columbus, GA 31901, USA

Turner, William C *Diplomat*
4350 Camelback Rd, #240-B, Phoenix, AZ 85018, USA

Turner, William H *Financier*
%Chemical Bank New Jersey, 2 Tower Center, East Brunswick, NJ 08816, USA

Turnesa, Willie *Golfer*
28 Barksdale Rd, White Plains, NY 10607, USA

Turnley, David C *Photographer*
%Detroit Free Press, 321 W Lafayette Blvd, Detroit, MI 48226, USA

Turow, Scott F *Writer*
%Sonnenschein Carlin Nath Hosenthal, Sears Tower, #8000, Chicago, IL 60606, USA

Turrell, James *Artist*
%Skystone Foundation, PO Box 725, Flagstaff, AZ 86002, USA

Turrentine, Stanley W *Jazz Saxophonist*
%La Place Music, PO Box 396, Kensington, MD 20895, USA

Turro, Nicholas J *Chemist*
125 Downey Dr, Tenafly, NJ 07670, USA

Turturro, John *Actor*
16 N Oak St, Ventura, CA 93001, USA

Tusher, Thomas W *Businessman*
%Levi Strauss Assoc, 1155 Battery St, San Francisco, CA 94111, USA

Tushingham, Rita *Actress*
%International Creative Mgmt, 76 Oxford St, London W1N 0AX, England

Tusquets Blanca, Oscar *Architect*
%Tusquets Diaz Assoc, Cavallers 50, 08034 Barcelona, Spain

Tutin, Dorothy *Actress*
%Michael Whitehall, 125 Gloucester Rd, London SW7 4TE, England

Tutone, Tommy *Singer, Dancer*
%International Creative Mgmt, 40 W 57th St, New York, NY 10019, USA

Tuttle, Elbert P *Judge*
%US Court of Appeals, 56 Forsyth St NW, Atlanta, GA 30303, USA

Tuttle, O Frank *Geochemist*
PO Box 16, Greer, AZ 85927, USA

T

Turner - Tuttle

T

Tuttle, William G T, Jr *Army General*
%Logistics Management Institute, 6400 Godsboro Rd, Bethesda, MD 20817, USA

Tutu, Desmond M *Nobel Peace Laureate, Religious Leader*
Bishopscourt, Claremont Cape 7700, South Africa

Twardzik, Dave *Basketball Player, Executive*
%Golden State Warriors, Oakland Coliseum Arena, Oakland, CA 94621, USA

Tway, Bob *Golfer*
%Professional Golfer's Assn, PO Box 109601, Palm Beach Gardens, FL 33410, USA

Tweed, John N *Religious Leader*
%Reformed Presbyterian Church, 1117 E Devonshire Ave, Phoenix, AZ 85014, USA

Tweed, Shannon *Actress, Model*
2650 Benedict Canyon Dr, Beverly Hills, CA 90210, USA

Twibell, Roger *Sportscaster*
%ABC-TV, Sports Dept, 77 W 66th St, New York, NY 10023, USA

Twiggy (Leslie Lawson) *Model, Actress*
%N Shulman, 4 St George's House, 15 Hanover Square, London W1R 9AJ, England

Twilley, Howard *Football Player*
3109 S Columbia Circle, Tulsa, OK 74105, USA

Twogood, Jerry K *Businessman*
%Deluxe Corp, 1080 W County Rd "F", St Paul, MN 55126, USA

Twombly, Cy *Artist*
%Leo Castelli Gallery, 420 W Broadway, New York, NY 10012, USA

Twomey, David M *Marine Corps General*
%Marine Corps Headquarters, Washington, DC 20380, USA

Twomey, William P *Businessman*
%LTV Corp, 25 W Prospect Ave, Cleveland, OH 44115, USA

Twyman, John K (Jack) *Businessman, Basketball Player*
%Super Food Services Inc, 3233 Newmark Dr, Miamisburg, OH 45342, USA

Tydings, Joseph D *Senator, MD*
%Anderson Kill Olick, 2000 Pennsylvania NW, #7500, Washington, DC 20006, USA

Tyers, Kathy *Writer*
%Martha Millard Agency, 204 Park Ave, Madison, NJ 07940, USA

Tygart, W Barger *Businessman*
%J C Penney Co, PO Box 10001, Dallas, TX 75301, USA

Tyler, Anne *Writer*
222 Tunbridge Rd, Baltimore, MD 21212, USA

Tyler, Bonnie *Singer, Songwriter*
%Station Agency, 132 Liverpool Rd, London N1 1LA, England

Tyler, Harold R, Jr *Attorney*
%Patterson Belknap Webb Tyler, 30 Rockefeller Plaza, New York, NY 10112, USA

Tyler, Steven *Singer (Aerosmith), Songwriter*
%Collins Mgmt, 5 Bigelow St, Cambridge, MA 02139, USA

Tyner, Charles *Actor*
%Dade/Schultz Agency, 11846 Ventura Blvd, #100, Studio City, CA 91604, USA

Tyner, McCoy *Jazz Pianist, Composer*
%Abby Hoffer Ents, 223 1/2 E 48th St, New York, NY 10017, USA

Tyrell, Thomas N *Businessman*
%Birmingham Steel Corp, 1000 Urban Center Dr, Birmingham, AL 35242, USA

Tyrrell, Susan *Actress*
1489 Scott Ave, Los Angeles, CA 90026, USA

Tysoe, Ronald W *Businessman*
%Federated Department Stores, 7 W 7th St, Cincinnati, OH 45202, USA

Tyson, Cathy *Actress*
%Peters Fraser Dunlop, Chelsea Harbour, Lots Rd, London SW10 0XF, England

Tyson, Cicely *Actress*
315 W 70th St, New York, NY 10023, USA

Tyson, Donald J *Businessman*
%Tyson Foods Inc, 2210 W Oaklawn Dr, Springdale, AK 72762, USA

Tyson, Laura D *Economist*
%National Economic Council, 1600 Pennsylvania Ave NW, Washington, DC 20500, USA

Tyson, Mike G *Boxer*
6740 Tomiyasu Lane, Las Vegas, NV 89120, USA

Tyson, Richard *Actor*
%Parker Public Relations, 11500 W Olympic Blvd, #400, Los Angeles, CA 90064, USA

Tyus, Wyomia *Track Athlete*
1101 Kensington Ave, Los Angeles, CA 90019, USA

Tyzack, Margaret *Actress*
%Joyce Edwards, 275 Kennington Rd, London SE1 6BY, England

Tuttle - Tyzack

Ubriaco, Gene *Hockey Coach*
%Pittsburgh Penguins, Civic Arena, Centre Ave, Pittsburgh, PA 15219, USA

Uchida, Mitsuko *Concert Pianist*
26 Wadham Rd, London SW15 2LR, England

Udell, Rochelle *Editor*
%Conde Nast Publications Inc, 350 Madison Ave, New York, NY 10017, USA

Udenfriend, Sidney *Biologist*
%Roche Institute of Molecular Biology, 340 Kingsland St, Nutley, NJ 07110, USA

Udvar-Hazy, Steven F *Financier*
%International Lease Finance Corp, 1999 Ave of Stars, Los Angeles, CA 90067, USA

Udvari, Frank *Hockey Referee*
379-2 Gage Ave, Kitchener ON N2M 5E1, Canada

Ueberroth, Peter V *Baseball Executive, Olympics Official*
%Adia Services, 100 Redwood Shores Parkway, Redwood City, CA 94065, USA

Uehling, Barbara S *Educator*
%University of California, Chancellor's Office, Santa Barbara, CA 93106, USA

Uelses, John *Track Athlete*
3846 Exception Place, Escondido, CA 92025, USA

Ueltschi, Albert L *Businessman*
%FlightSafety Int'l, Marine Air Terminal, LaGuardia Airport, Flushing, NY 11371, USA

Uemura, Ko *Financier*
%Fuji Bank & Trust Co, 1 World Trade Center, New York, NY 10048, USA

Ufland, Len *Actor, Director*
4400 Hillcrest Dr, #901, Hollywood, FL 33021, USA

Uggams, Leslie *Singer, Actress*
%William Morris Agency, 1325 Ave of Americas, New York, NY 10019, USA

Ughi, Uto *Concert Violinist*
Cannareggio 4990/E, 30121 Venice, Italy

Uhl, Petr *Human Rights Activist*
Anglicka 8, 120 00 Prague 2, Czech Republic

Uhry, Alfred F *Playwright*
%Marshall Purdy, 226 W 47th St, #900, New York, NY 10036, USA

Ujiie, Junichi *Financier*
%Nomura Securities, 2 World Financial Center, 200 Liberty St, New York, NY 10281, USA

Ulanova, Galina S *Ballerina*
%Bolshoi Theater, Teatralnaya Pl 1, 103009 Moscow, Russia

Ulland, Olav *Skier*
2664 West Lake Sammamish Parkway SE, Bellevue, WA 98008, USA

Ullman, Norman *Hockey Player*
19 Averdon Crest, Don Mills ON M3A 1P4, Canada

Ullman, Tracey *Comedienne*
13555 D'Este Dr, Pacific Palisades, CA 90272, USA

Ullmann, Liv *Actress*
15 W 81st St, #13 D, New York, NY 10024, USA

Ullsten, Ola *Prime Minister, Sweden*
%Folkpartiet, PO Box 6508, 113 83 Stockholm, Sweden

Ulmanis, Guntis *President, Latvia*
%President's Office, Supreme Council, 11 Jeraba St, Riga 22681 PDP, Latvia

Ulrich, Laurel T *Historian*
%University of New Hampshire, History Dept, Durham, NH 03824, USA

Ulrich, Robert J *Businessman*
%Dayton Hudson Corp, 777 Nicollet Mall, Minneapolis, MN 55402, USA

Ultmann, John E *Physician*
5632 S Harper St, Chicago, IL 60637, USA

Ulusu, Bulent *Prime Minister, Turkey; Navy Admiral*
Ciftehavuzlar Yesllbahar 50-K 8/27, Kadikoy/Istanbul, Turkey

Ulvaeus, Bjorn *Singer (ABBA), Composer*
%Gorel Hanser, Sodra Brobanken 41A, Skeppsholmen, 111 49 Stockholm, Sweden

Ulvang, Vegard *Cross County Skier*
Fjellveien 53, 9900 Kirkenes, Norway

Umedo, Zenji *Businessman*
%Kawasaki Heavy Industries, 2-1-18 Nakamachidori, Chuoku, Kobe 650, Japan

Unanue, Emil R *Pathologist*
%Washington University Medical School, Pathology Dept, St Louis, MO 63110, USA

Underwood, Benton J *Psychologist*
1745 Stevens Dr, Glenview, IL 60025, USA

Underwood, Blair *Actor*
5682 Holly Oak Dr, Los Angeles, CA 90068, USA

U

Ubriaco - Underwood

Underwood, Cecil H — *Governor, WV*
609 13th Ave, Huntington, WV 25701, USA

Ungaro, Emanuel M — *Fashion Designer*
2 Ave du Montaigne, 75008 Paris, France

Ungaro, Susan Kelliher — *Editor*
%Family Circle Magazine, Editorial Dept, 110 5th Ave, New York, NY 10011, USA

Unger, Deborah — *Actress*
%International Creative Mgmt, 8942 Wilshire Blvd, Beverly Hills, CA 90211, USA

Unger, Jim — *Cartoonist (Herman)*
291 Britannia Rd, Ottawa ON K2B 5X5, Canada

Unger, Kay — *Fashion Designer*
%St Gillian Sportswear, 498 7th Ave, New York, NY 10018, USA

Unger, Leonard — *Diplomat*
31 Amherst Rd, Belmont, MA 02178, USA

Ungers, Oswald M — *Architect*
Belvederestr 60, 50933 Cologne, Germany

Unitas, John C (Johnny) — *Football Player*
5607 Patterson Rd, Baldwin, MD 21013, USA

Unkefer, Ronald A — *Businessman*
%Good Guys Inc, 7000 Marina Blvd, Brisbane, CA 94005, USA

Uno, Sosuke — *Prime Minister, Japan*
304 High Trio Akasaka Hatchome, 8-7-18 Akasaka, Minatoku, Tokyo 107, Japan

Unruh, James A — *Businessman*
%Unisys Corp, PO Box 500, Blue Bell, PA 19424, USA

Unruh, Jerry L — *Navy Admiral*
Commander, 3rd Fleet, FPO, AP 96601, USA

Unseld, Westley S (Wes) — *Basketball Player, Coach, Executive*
%Washington Bullets, Capital Centre, 1 Truman Dr, Landover, MD 20785, USA

Unser, Alfred (Al) — *Auto Racing Driver*
7625 Central NW, Albuquerque, NM 87121, USA

Unser, Alfred (Al), Jr — *Auto Racing Driver*
%Galles/Kraco Racing, PO Box 25047, Albuquerque, NM 87125, USA

Upbin, Hal J — *Businessman*
%Kellwood Co, 600 Kellwood Parkway, St Louis, MO 63017, USA

Updike, John H — *Writer*
675 Hale St, Beverly Farms, MA 01915, USA

Uphoff-Becker, Nicole — *Equestrian Rider*
Freiherr-von-Lanen-Str 15, 48231 Warendorf, Germany

Upshaw, Dawn — *Opera Singer*
%Columbia Artists Mgmt Inc, 165 W 57th St, New York, NY 10019, USA

Upshaw, Eugene (Gene) — *Football Player, Union Leader*
1102 Pepper Tree Dr, Great Falls, VA 22066, USA

Upton, Arthur C — *Physician*
1424 Seville Rd, Santa Fe, NM 87505, USA

Urban, Thomas N — *Businessman*
%Pioneer Hi-Bred Int'l, Capital Square, 400 Locust St, Des Moines, IA 50309, USA

Urbanchek, Jon — *Swimming Coach*
%University of Michigan, Athletic Dept, Ann Arbor, MI 48109, USA

Urben, Noel E — *Financier*
%BT Capital Corp, 280 Park Ave, New York, NY 10017, USA

Urich, Robert — *Actor*
15930 Woodvale Rd, Encino, CA 91436, USA

Uris, Leon M — *Writer*
PO Box 1559, Aspen, CO 81612, USA

Urist, Marshall R — *Orthopedic Surgeon*
%University of California Medical Center, Ortho/Bone Lab, Los Angeles, CA 90024, USA

Urmanov, Aleksei — *Figure Skater*
%Union of Skaters, Luzhnetskaya Nab 8, Moscow 119871, Russia

Urmson, Claire — *Model*
%Ford Model Agency, 344 E 59th St, New York, NY 10022, USA

Urquhart, Brian E — *Diplomat*
131 E 66th St, New York, NY 10021, USA

Urquhart, John A — *Businessman*
%Enron Corp, PO Box 1188, Houston, TX 77251, USA

Urquhart, Lawrence M — *Businessman*
%Burmah Oil, Burmah House, Pipers Way, Swindon, Wilts SN3 1RE, England

Urshan, Nathaniel A — *Religious Leader*
%United Pentecostal Church International, 8855 Dunn Rd, Hazelwood, MO 63042, USA

Ursi, Corrado Cardinal — *Religious Leader*
Via Capodimonte 13, 80136 Naples, Italy

Usery, William J, Jr — *Secretary, Labor*
2400 Virginia Ave, Washington, DC 20037, USA

Usher, Thomas J — *Businessman*
%USX Corp, 600 Grant St, Pittsburgh, PA 15219, USA

Ustinov, Peter — *Actor*
11 Rue de Silly, 92100 Boulogne, France

Ut, Nick — *Photographer*
%Associated Press, Photo Dept, 221 S Figueroa St, #300, Los Angeles, CA 90012, USA

Uteem, Cassam — *President, Mauritius*
%President's Office, Le Reduit, Port Louis, Mauritius

Utley, Garrick — *Commentator*
%ABC-TV, News Dept, 8 Carburton St, London W1P 7DT, England

Utzon, Jorn — *Architect*
%General Delivery, 3150 Hellebaek, Denmark

Uys, Jacobus J (Jamie) — *Movie Director*
PO Box 50019, Randburg, Transvaal 2125, South Africa

Uzawa, Hirofumi — *Economist*
Higashi 1-3-6, Hoya, Tokyo, Japan

Vacariou, Nicolae — *Prime Minister, Romania*
%Prime Minister's Office, Piata Victoriei 1, 71201 Bucharest, Romania

Vaccaro, Brenda — *Actress*
14423 Dickens St, #206, Sherman Oaks, CA 91423, USA

Vachon, Louis-Albert Cardinal — *Religious Leader*
%Seminaire de Quebec, 1 Rue des Remparts, Quebec QC G1R 5LY, Canada

Vachon, Rogatien R (Rogie) — *Hockey Player, Coach, Executive*
%Los Angeles Kings, Forum, PO Box 17013, Inglewood, CA 90308, USA

Vachss, Andrew H — *Writer*
299 Broadway, #1800, New York, NY 10007, USA

Vadim, Roger P — *Movie Director*
316 Alta Ave, Santa Monica, CA 90402, USA

Vaduva, Leontina — *Opera Singer*
%Royal Opera House, Covent Garden, Bow St, London WC2, England

Vaea of Houma, Baron — *Prime Minister, Tonga*
%Prime Minister's Office, Nuku'alofa, Tonga

Vagelos, P Roy — *Businessman*
1 Crossroads Dr, 500 Building "A", Bedminster, NJ 07921, USA

Vago, Pierre — *Architect*
Le Valparon, 77123 Nolsy-sur-Ecole, France

Vague, Richard W — *Financier*
%First USA, 2001 Bryan Tower, Dallas, TX 75201, USA

Vail, Thomas — *Editor*
%Cleveland Plain Dealer, Editorial Dept, 1801 Superior, Cleveland, OH 44114, USA

Vajiralongkorn — *Crown Prince, Thailand*
%Chitralada a Villa, Rangkok, Thailand

Valna, Andrew — *Movie Producer*
%Cinergi Productions, 2308 Broadway, Burbank, CA 90404, USA

Valar, Paul — *Skier*
PO Box 906, Franconia, NH 03580, USA

Valdez, Luis — *Playwright*
%El Teatro Capesino, 705 4th St, San Juan Bautista, CA 95045, USA

Vale, Jerry — *Singer*
1100 Alta Loma Rd, #1404, Los Angeles, CA 90069, USA

Valen, Nancy — *Actress*
15535 Riverside Dr, #4, Sherman Oaks, CA 91423, USA

Valente, Benita — *Opera Singer*
%Anthony Checchia, 135 S 18th St, Philadelphia, PA 19103, USA

Valente, Catarina — *Singer*
Via ai Ronci 12, 6816 Bissone, Switzerland

Valenti, Carl M — *Publisher*
%Information Services, Dow Jones Telerate, 200 Liberty St, New York, NY 10281, USA

Valenti, Jack J — *Movie Executive*
%Motion Picture Assn, 1600 "I" St NW, Washington, DC 20006, USA

Valentic, Nikica — *Prime Minister, Croatia*
%Prime Minister's Office, Radicev Tug 7, 41000 Zagreb, Croatia

Valentine, DeWain — *Artist*
59-230 Alapio Rd, Haleiwa, HI 96712, USA

Valentine, Donald T *Businessman*
%Cisco Systems, 170 W Tasman Dr, San Jose, CA 95134, USA

Valentine, Karen *Actress*
PO Box 1410, Washington Depot, CT 06793, USA

Valentine, Raymond C *Agronomist*
%University of California, Plant Growth Laboratory, Davis, CA 95616, USA

Valentine, Robert J (Bobby) *Baseball Player, Manager*
3504 Orchid Lane, Arlington, TX 76016, USA

Valentine, Scott *Actor*
662 N Van Ness Ave, #305, Los Angeles, CA 90004, USA

Valentine, William N *Physician*
PO Box 4698, Sun River, OR 97707, USA

Valentini Terrani, Lucia *Opera Singer*
Piazza Cavour 4, 35100 Padova, Italy

Valentino (Garavani) *Fashion Designer*
Palazzo Mignanelli, Piazza Mignanelli 22, 00187 Rome, Italy

Valenzuela, Fernando *Baseball Player*
3004 N Beachwood Dr, Los Angeles, CA 90068, USA

Valeriani, Richard G *Commentator*
23 Island View Dr, Sherman, CT 06784, USA

Vallee, Bert L *Biochemist, Physician*
56 Browne St, Brookline, MA 02146, USA

Vallee, Roy *Businessman*
%Avnet Inc, 80 Cutter Mill Rd, Great Neck, NY 11021, USA

Valletta, Amber *Model*
%Boss Models, 317 W 13th St, New York, NY 10014, USA

Valli, Alida *Actress*
Viale Liegi 42, 00100 Rome, Italy

Valli, Frankie *Singer*
5603 N Winton Court, Calabasas, CA 91302, USA

Vallone, Raf *Actor*
%Anne Alvares, Correa Panis, 18 Rue Troyon, 75017 Paris, France

Valo, Elmer W *Baseball Player*
571 Columbia Ave, Palmerton, PA 18071, USA

Valot, Daniel L *Businessman*
%Total Petroleum, 900 19th St, Denver, CO 80202, USA

Valtman, Edmund *Editorial Cartoonist*
41 Foothills Way, Bloomfield, CT 06002, USA

Van Allan, Richard *Opera Singer*
18 Octavia St, London SW11 3DN, England

Van Allen, James A *Physicist*
5 Woodland Mounds Rd, RFD 6, Iowa City, IA 52245, USA

Van Amerongen, Jerry *Cartoonist (The Neighborhood)*
2329 Newton Ave S, Minneapolis, MN 55405, USA

Van Andel, Jay *Businessman*
%Amway Corp, 7575 E Fulton St E, Ada, MI 49355, USA

Van Ark, Joan *Actress*
10950 Alta View Dr, Studio City, CA 91604, USA

Van Arsdale, Dick *Basketball Player, Executive*
3930 E Camelback Rd, Phoenix, AZ 85018, USA

Van Arsdale, Tom *Basketball Player*
3930 E Camelback Rd, Phoenix, AZ 85018, USA

Van Auken, John A *Tennis Contributor*
%Canadian Tennis Technology Ltd, PO Box 1538, Sydney NS B1P 6R7, Canada

Van Basten, Marco *Soccer Player*
%AC Milan, Via Turati 3, 20121 Milan, Italy

Van Breda Kolff, Bill (Butch) *Basketball Coach*
%Hofstra University, Athletic Dept, Hempstead, NY 11550, USA

Van Buren (Pauline Phillips), Abigail *Columnist (Dear Abby)*
%Phillips-Van Buren Inc, 9200 Sunset Blvd, #1003, Los Angeles, CA 90069, USA

Van Buren, Steve W *Football Player*
4212 Penn St, Philadelphia, PA 19124, USA

Van Citters, Robert L *Physiologist, Biophysicist*
%University of Washington Medical School, Physiology Dept, Seattle, WA 98815, USA

Van Dam, Jose *Opera Singer*
%Zurich Artists, Rutistr 52, 8044 Zurich-Gockhausen, Switzerland

Van Damme, Jean-Claude *Actor*
PO Box 4149, Chatsworth, CA 91313, USA

Van Dantzig, Rudi *Choreographer*
Emma-Straat 27, Amsterdam, Netherlands

Van de Ven, Monique *Actress*
%Marion Rosenberg Office, 8428 Melrose Place, #C, Los Angeles, CA 90069, USA

Van de Wetering, John E *Educator*
%State University of New York, President's Office, Brockport, NY 14420, USA

Van den Berg, Lodewijk *Astronaut*
%EG&G Corp, 130 Robin Hill Rd, Goleta, CA 93117, USA

Van den Haag, Ernest *Attorney, Writer*
118 W 79th St, New York, NY 10024, USA

Van der Klugt, Cor J *Businessman*
%Philips' Gloeilampenfabrieken, 5621 CT Eindhoven, Netherlands

Van der Meer, Simon *Nobel Physics Laureate*
4 Chemin des Corbillettes, 1218 GD-Saconnex, Switzerland

Van Deventer, Neill *Publisher*
%Cleveland Plain Dealer, 1801 Superior Ave, Cleveland, OH 44114, USA

Van Devere, Trish *Actress*
3211 Retreat Court, Malibu, CA 90265, USA

Van Doren, Mamie *Actress*
428 31st St, Newport Beach, CA 92663, USA

Van Dreelen, John *Actor*
%Paul Kohner Inc, 9300 Wilshire Blvd, #555, Beverly Hills, CA 90212, USA

Van Dusen, Granville *Actor*
2161 Ridgemont Dr, Los Angeles, CA 90046, USA

Van Dyke, Barry *Actor*
%William Morris Agency, 151 S El Camino Dr, Beverly Hills, CA 90212, USA

Van Dyke, Dick *Actor*
%William Morris Agency, 151 S El Camino Dr, Beverly Hills, CA 90212, USA

Van Dyke, Jerry *Actor*
%Kazarian/Spencer Assoc, 11365 Ventura Blvd, #100, Studio City, CA 91604, USA

Van Dyke, William G *Businessman*
%Donaldson Co, 1400 W 94th St, Minneapolis, MN 55431, USA

Van Eeghen, Mark *Football Player*
90 Woodstock Lane, Cranston, RI 02920, USA

Van Fleet, Jo *Actress*
54 Riverside Dr, New York, NY 10024, USA

Van Graafeiland, Ellsworth A *Judge*
%US Court of Appeals, Federal Building, 100 State St, Rochester, NY 14614, USA

Van Halen, Eddie *Guitarist (Van Halen)*
10100 Santa Monica Blvd, #2460, Los Angeles, CA 90067, USA

Van Hamel, Martine *Ballerina*
%Peter S Diggins Assoc, 133 W 71st St, New York, NY 10023, USA

Van Hellmond, Andy *Hockey Referee*
75 International Blvd, #300, Rexdale ON M9W 6L9, Canada

Van Hoften, James C D A *Astronaut*
%Bechtel Defense & Space Organization, 50 Beale St, San Francisco, CA 94105, USA

Van Horn, Richard L *Educator*
%University of Oklahoma, President's Office, Norman, OK 73019, USA

Van Horne, Keith *Football Player*
%Chicago Bears, Halas Hall, 250 N Washington Rd, Lake Forest, IL 60045, USA

Van Meter, Vicki *Pilot*
%James Van Meter, 902 Grove St, Meadville, PA 16335, USA

Van Otterloo, Eyk *Financier*
%Grantham Mayo Van Otterloo Co, 40 Rowes Wharf, Boston, MA 02110, USA

Van Pallandt, Nina *Actress, Singer*
845 E 6th St, Los Angeles, CA 90021, USA

Van Patten, Dick *Actor*
13920 Magnolia Blvd, Sherman Oaks, CA 91423, USA

Van Patten, Jimmy *Actor*
14111 Riverside Dr, #15, Sherman Oaks, CA 91423, USA

Van Patten, Joyce *Actress*
9220 Sunset Blvd, #206, Los Angeles, CA 90069, USA

Van Patten, Nels *Actor*
14435 Riverside Dr, #4, Sherman Oaks, CA 91423, USA

Van Patten, Timothy *Actor*
7461 Beverly Blvd, #400, Los Angeles, CA 90036, USA

Van Patten, Vincent *Actor*
13920 Magnolia Blvd, Sherman Oaks, CA 91423, USA

V

Van Dantzig - Van Patten

Van Peebles, Mario — *Actor*
11 Tuxedo, Glenridge, NJ 07028, USA

Van Riemsdijk, H A C — *Businessman*
%Phillip Gloeilampenfabrieken, 5621 CT Eindhoven, Netherlands

Van Runkle, Theodora — *Fashion Designer*
8805 Lookout Mountain Rd, Los Angeles, CA 90046, USA

Van Ryn, John — *Tennis Player*
350 Coconut Row, #28, Palm Beach, FL 33480, USA

Van Sant, Gus, Jr — *Movie Director*
%Addis-Wechsler, 955 S Carillo, Los Angeles, CA 90048, USA

Van Sant, R William — *Businessman*
%Lukens Inc, 50 S 1st Ave, Coatesville, PA 19320, USA

Van Staveren, Petra — *Swimmer*
%Olympic Committee, Surinamestraar 33, 2585 Le Harve, Netherlands

Van Stekelenburg, Mark — *Businessman*
%Rykoff-Sexton Inc, 761 Terminal St, Los Angeles, CA 90021, USA

Van Suan, Bruce — *Financier*
%Wasserstein Perella Group, 31 W 52nd St, New York, NY 10019, USA

Van Tamelen, Eugene E — *Chemist*
23570 Camino Hermoso Dr, Los Altos Hills, CA 94024, USA

Van Tuyl, Cecil — *Businessman*
%V T Inc, 8500 Shawnee Mission Parkway, Merriam, KS 66202, USA

Van Ummerson, Claire A — *Educator*
%Cleveland State University, President's Office, Cleveland, OH 44115, USA

Van Valkenburgh, Deborah — *Actress*
2025 Stanley Hills Dr, Los Angeles, CA 90046, USA

Van Wachem, Loedwijk C — *Businessman*
Royal Dutch/Shell, 30 Carel van Bylandtaan, 2596 HR The Hague, Netherlands

Van Zandt, Townes — *Singer, Songwriter*
4659 Popular Wood, Smyrna, TN 37167, USA

Van Zant, Steve — *Singer, Songwriter*
322 W 57th St, New York, NY 10019, USA

Vanbiesbrouck, John — *Hockey Player*
%Florida Panthers, Miami Arena, Miami, FL 33136, USA

Vance, Cyrus R — *Secretary, State*
%Simpson Thatcher Bartlett, 425 Lexington Ave, New York, NY 10017, USA

Vance, Robert S — *Judge*
%US Court of Appeals, 1800 5th Ave N, Birmingham, AL 35203, USA

Vandenburgh, Jane — *Writer*
%North Point Press, 1563 Solano Ave, #353, Berkeley, CA 94707, USA

Vanderberg Shaw, Helen — *Synchronized Swimming Coach*
%Heaven's Fitness, 301 14th St NW, Calgary AL T2N 2A1, Canada

Vanderbilt, Gloria — *Fashion Designer*
1349 Eagle Cove Rd, Jacksonville, FL 32218, USA

Vanderhoef, H Kent — *Businessman*
%Orange & Rockland Utilities, 1 Blue Hill Plaza, Pearl River, NY 10965, USA

Vanderhoef, Larry N — *Educator*
%University of California, President's Office, Davis, CA 95616, USA

Vanderhoof, John D — *Governor, CO*
%Club Twenty, 845 Grand, Grand Junction, CO 81501, USA

VanderMeer, John S (Johnny) — *Baseball Player*
4005 Leona Ave, Tampa, FL 33629, USA

Vandermeersch, Bernard — *Anthropologist*
%University of Bordeaux, Anthropology Dept, Bordeaux, France

Vanderstar, Cornelius C — *Businessman*
%International Aluminum Corp, 767 Monterey Pass Rd, Monterey Park, CA 91754, USA

Vanderveen, Loet — *Sculptor*
Lime Creek 5, Big Sur, CA 93920, USA

VanDerveer, Tara — *Basketball Coach*
%Stanford University, Athletic Dept, Stanford, CA 94305, USA

Vandewater, David T — *Businessman*
%Columbia/HCA Healthcare Corp, 201 W Main St, Louisville, KY 40202, USA

Vandeweghe, Ernie — *Basketball Player, Physician*
211 N Prairie Ave, Inglewood, CA 90301, USA

Vandeweghe, Kiki — *Basketball Player*
%Los Angeles Clippers, Sports Arena, 3939 S Figueroa St, Los Angeles, CA 90037, USA

Vandiver, S Ernest — *Governor, GA*
109 Hartwell Dr, Lavonia, GA 30553, USA

Vandross, Luther — *Singer*
%Alive Entertainment, 8912 Burton Way, Beverly Hills, CA 90211, USA

Vane, John R — *Nobel Medicine Laureate*
White Angles, 7 Beech Dell, Keston, Kent BR2 6EP, England

Vanek, John — *Basketball Referee*
9th St, RD 1, Nesquehoning, PA 18240, USA

Vaness, Carol — *Opera Singer*
%Metropolitan Opera Assn, Lincoln Center Plaza, New York, NY 10023, USA

Vangelis — *Composer*
%Apfel Co, 55 Welbeck St, London W1M 7RD, England

Vanilla Ice (Robby Van Winkle) — *Singer*
%QPM Inc, 2602 Mckinney Ave, #350, Dallas, TX 75204, USA

Vanity (Denise Matthews) — *Singer, Actress*
1871 Messino Dr, San Jose, CA 95132, USA

Vannelli, Gino — *Singer*
31270 La Baya Dr, #110, Westlake Village, CA 91362, USA

Vannoy, Walter M — *Businessman*
%Figgie International Inc, 4420 Sherwin Rd, Willoughby, OH 44094, USA

Varady, Julia — *Opera Singer*
%Colbert Artists Mgmt, 111 W 57th St, New York, NY 10019, USA

Varda, Agnes — *Movie Director*
%Cine-Tamaris, 86 Rue Daguerre, 75014 Paris, France

Varda, Chryssa — *Artist*
15 E 88th St, New York, NY 10128, USA

Varga, Imre — *Sculptor*
Bartha-Ut 1, Budapest XII, Hungary

Vargas Llosa, Mario — *Writer*
%PEN, 7 Duke St, London SW3, England

Vargas, Jay R — *Vietnam War Marine Corps Hero (CMH)*
7614 Rush River Dr, #139, Sacramento, CA 95831, USA

Varian, Hal R — *Economist*
2017 Vinewood Blvd, Ann Arbor, MI 48104, USA

Varley of Chesterfield, Eric G — *Government Official, England*
%Coalite Group, Buttermilk Lane, Bolsover, Derbyshire S44 6AB, England

Varmus, Harold E — *Nobel Medicine Laureate*
%National Institutes of Health, 9000 Rockville Pike, Bethesda, MD 20892, USA

Varnedoe, Heeth, III — *Businessman*
%Flowers Industries, 200 US Highway 19 S, Thomasville, GA 31792, USA

Varnedoe, J Kirk T — *Museum Director*
%Museum of Modern Art, 11 W 53rd St, New York, NY 10019, USA

Varrichone, Frank — *Football Player*
3 Shady Oak Lane, Natick, MA 01760, USA

Varton, Sylvie — *Singer*
%Scotti, 706 N Beverly Dr, Beverly Hills, CA 90210, USA

Varty, Keith — *Fashion Designer (Byblos)*
Bosco di San Francesco #6, Sirolo, Italy

Vasarely, Victor — *Artist*
83 Rue Aux Reliques, Annet-sur-Marne, 77410 Claye Souilly, France

Vasary, Tamas — *Concert Pianist*
9 Village Rd, London N3, England

Vasiliyev, Vladimir — *Ballet Dancer, Executive*
%Bolshoi Theater, Teatralnaya Pl 1, 103009 Moscow, Russia

Vasquez Rana, Mario — *Publisher*
%El Sol de Mexico, Guillermo Prieto 7, Mexico City DF, Mexico

Vass, Joan — *Fashion Designer*
%Joan Vass Inc, 117 E 29th St, New York, NY 10016, USA

Vassiliou, George V — *President, Cyprus*
PO Box 2098, Nicosia, Cyprus

Vassos, John — *Artist*
Comstock Hill Rd, Norfolk, CT 06850, USA

Vasyoutin, Vladimir V — *Cosmonaut*
%Potchta Kosmonavtov, 141 160 Svyosdny Gorodok, Moskovskoi Oblasti, Russia

Vasyuchenko, Yuri — *Ballet Dancer*
%Bolshoi Theater, Teatralnaya Pl 1, 103009 Moscow, Russia

Vatikiotis, Panayiotis J — *Educator*
55 Diamond Court, 153 Banbury Rd, Oxford OX2 7AA, England

Vaughan, Charles K — *Businessman*
%ATMOS Energy Corp, PO Box 650205, Dallas, TX 75265, USA

V

Vandross - Vaughan

V

Vaughn, Robert *Actor*
162 Old West Mountain Rd, Ridgefield, CT 06877, USA

Vaught, John H (Johnny) *Football Coach*
Highway North 6 W, Oxford, MS 38655, USA

Veasey, Craig *Football Player*
%Pittsburgh Steelers, 3 Rivers Stadium, 300 Stadium Circle, Pittsburgh, PA 15212, USA

Veasey, Josephine *Opera Singer*
Pound Cottage, St Mary Vourne, Andover, Hants, England

Vecsei, Eva H *Architect*
%Vecsei Architects, 1425 Rue du Fort, Montreal PQ H3H 2C2, Canada

Vecsey, George S *Columnist*
%New York Times, Editorial Dept, 229 W 43rd St, New York, NY 10036, USA

Vedder, Eddie *Singer (Pearl Jam)*
%Curtis Mgmt, 207 1/2 1st Ave S, #300, Seattle, WA 98104, USA

Vee, Bobby *Singer, Songwriter*
%Rockhouse Studio, PO Box 41, Sauk Rapids, MN 56379, USA

Vega, Suzanne *Singer, Songwriter*
%AGF Entertainment, 30 W 21st St, #700, New York, NY 10010, USA

Veiga, Carlos A Wahnon de C *Prime Minister, Cape Verde*
%Prime Minister's Office, Praca, 12 Septembre, Sao Tiago, Cape Verde

Veil, Simone *Government Official, France*
11 Place Vauban, 75007 Paris, France

Velaquez, Ramon Jose *President, Venezuela*
%Palacio de Miraflores, Avenida Urdanetal, Caracas 1010, Venezuela

Velasquez, Jorge L, Jr *Thoroughbred Racing Jockey*
770 Allerton Ave, Bronx, NY 10467, USA

Velasquez, Patricia *Model*
%Ford Model Mgmt, 344 E 59th St, New York, NY 10022, USA

Velazco, Sheila K *Labor Leader*
%National Federal Employees Federation, 1016 16th St NW, Washington, DC 20036, USA

Velgos, Alicia *Actress*
%William Morris Agency, 151 S El Camino Dr, Beverly Hills, CA 90212, USA

Velikhov, Yevgeni P *Physicist*
Moscow V-71, Leninski Prospekt 14, 117901 Moscow, USSR

Veljohnson, Reginald *Actor*
%Badgley McQueeney Connor, 9229 Sunset Blvd, #607, Los Angeles, CA 90069, USA

Vella, John *Football Player*
5350 Willow Glen Place, Castro Valley, CA 94546, USA

Vendela (Kirsebom) *Model*
%Ford Model Agency, 344 E 59th St, New York, NY 10022, USA

Vendler, Helen H *Educator*
54 Trowbridge St, #2, Cambridge, MA 02138, USA

Venet, Philippe *Fashion Designer*
62 Rue Francois 1er, 75008 Paris, France

Venetiaan, Ronald *President, Suriname*
%Presidential Palace, Onafhankelikheidsplein 1, Paramaribo, Suriname

Venkataraman, Ramaswamy *President, India*
Pothigai, Greenways Rd, Madras 600 028, India

Venter, J Craig *Molecular Biologist*
%Institute for Genomic Research, 932 Clopper Rd, Gaithersburg, MD 20878, USA

Venturi, Ken *Golfer*
%Eddie Elias Enterprises, 1720 Merriman Rd, #5118, Akron, OH 44313, USA

Venturi, Robert *Architect*
%Venturi Scott Brown Assoc, 4236 Main St, Philadelphia, PA 19127, USA

Venza, Jac *Broadcast Executive*
%WNET-TV, 356 W 58th St, New York, NY 10019, USA

Vera, Billy *Singer*
%Agency For Performing Arts, 9000 Sunset Blvd, #1200, Los Angeles, CA 90069, USA

Verba, Sidney *Political Scientist*
142 Summit Ave, Brookline, MA 02146, USA

Verdeur, Joe *Swimmer*
15 Bryn Mawr Ave, Bala-Cynwyd, PA 19004, USA

Verdi, Bob *Sportswriter*
%Chicago Tribune, 435 N Michigan Ave, Chicago, IL 60611, USA

Verdon, Gwen *Dancer, Actress*
26 Latimer Lane, Bronxville, NY 10708, USA

Verdugo, Elena *Actress*
PO Box 2048, Chula Vista, CA 91912, USA

Vaughn - Verdugo

Verdy, Violette *Ballerina*
44 W 62nd St, #44-C, New York, NY 10023, USA

Vereen, Ben *Actor, Dancer*
127 Broadway, #220, Santa Monica, CA 90401, USA

Verhoeven, Paul *Movie Director*
%Riverside Pictures, 1075 AA Amsterdam, Netherlands

Verhoogen, John *Geophysicist*
306 Santa Ana Ave, San Francisco, CA 94127, USA

Verity, C William, Jr *Secretary, Commerce*
120 Spanish Point Dr, Beaufort, SC 29902, USA

Verma, Inder M *Molecular Biologist*
%Salk Institute, 10010 N Torrey Pines Rd, La Jolla, CA 92037, USA

Vermeil, Dick *Football Coach, Sportscaster*
%CBS-TV, Sports Dept, 51 W 52nd St, New York, NY 10019, USA

Verna, Tony *Television Executive*
500 Ocampo Dr, Pacific Palisades, CA 90272, USA

Verne, Richard *Radio Executive*
%NBC Radio, 30 Rockefeller Plaza, New York, NY 10112, USA

Vernier-Palliez, Bernard M A *Diplomat, France*
25 Grande Rue, 78170 La Celle St Cloud, France

Vernon, Glen *Actor*
11123 Aqua Vista St, #103, North Hollywood, CA 91602, USA

Vernon, James B (Mickey) *Baseball Player*
100 E Rose Valley Rd, Wallingford, PA 19086, USA

Vernon, John *Actor*
15125 Mulholland Dr, Los Angeles, CA 90077, USA

Vernon, Kate *Actress*
%Innovative Artists, 1999 Ave of Stars, #2850, Los Angeles, CA 90067, USA

Vernon, Mike *Hockey Player*
%Detroit Red Wings, Joe Louis Arena, 600 Civic Center Dr, Detroit, MI 48226, USA

Vernon, Raymond *Economist*
1 Dunstable Rd, Cambridge, MA 02138, USA

Veronis, John J *Publisher*
%Veronis Suhler Assoc, 350 Park Ave, New York, NY 10022, USA

Verrell, Cec *Actress*
%Michael Slessinger Assoc, 8730 Sunset Blvd, #220-W, Los Angeles, CA 90069, USA

Verrett, Shirley *Opera Singer*
%International Management Group, 22 E 71st St, New York, NY 10021, USA

Versace, Dick *Basketball Coach*
%Turner Broadcast System, Sports Dept, 1050 Techwood Dr, Atlanta, GA 30318, USA

Versace, Gianni *Fashion Designer*
%Gianni Versace SpA, Via Gesu 12, 20121 Milan, Italy

Vessels, Billy W *Football Player*
4701 Santa Maria St, Coral Gables, FL 33146, USA

Vessey, John W, Jr *Army General*
Star Rt, Box 136-A, Garrison, MN 56450, USA

Vest, Charles M *Educator*
%Massachusetts Institute of Technology, President's Office, Cambridge, MA 02138, USA

Vest, George S *Diplomat*
5307 Iroquois Rd, Bethesda, MD 20816, USA

Vest, Jake *Cartoonist (That's Jake)*
1709 Carol Woods Dr, Apopka, FL 32703, USA

Vest, R Lamar *Religious Leader*
%Church of God, PO Box 2430, Cleveland, TN 37320, USA

Vetrov, Aleksandr *Ballet Dancer*
%Bolshoi Theater, Teatralnaya Pl 1, 103009 Moscow, Russia

Vettori, Ernst *Ski Jumper*
Fohrenweg 1, 6060 Absam-Eichat, Austria

Vettrus, Richard J *Religious Leader*
%Church of Lutheran Brethren, 707 Crestview Dr W, Union, IA 52175, USA

Viccellio, Henry (Butch), Jr *Air Force General*
Commander, Air Training Commmand, 1 "F" St, Randolph Air Force Base, TX 78150, USA

Vichich, William M *Financier*
%Citizens Federal Bank, 1 Citizens Centre, Dayton, OH 45402, USA

Vickers, Jon *Opera Singer*
%John Coast Agency, 1 Park Close, London SW1X 7PQ, England

Victoria *Crown Princess, Sweden*
%Royal Palace, Kung Slottet, Stottsbacken, 111 30 Stockholm, Sweden

V

Victorin (Ursache), Archbishop — *Religious Leader*
%Romanian Orthodox Church, 19959 Riopelle St, Detroit, MI 48203, USA

Vida, J D — *Test Pilot (SR-71)*
%OL Det 6, 2762LS/FT, Edwards Air Force Base, CA 93523, USA

Vidal, Gore — *Writer*
La Rondinaia Amalfi Ravello, Salerno, Italy

Vidal, Ricardo J Cardinal — *Religious Leader*
Chancery, PO Box 52, Cebu City 6401, Philippines

Videnov, Zhan — *Prime Minister, Bulgaria*
%Prime Minister's Office, 1 Dondukov Blvd, 1000 Sofia, Bulgaria

Vidmar, Peter — *Gymnast*
6 Flores, Foothill Ranch, CA 92610, USA

Vie, Richard C — *Businessman*
%Unitrin Co, 1 E Wacker Dr, Chicago, IL 60601, USA

Viehboeck, Franz — *Cosmonaut, Austria*
Brunnerbergstr 3021, 2380 Perchtoldsdorf, Austria

Vieillard, Roger — *Artist*
7 Rue de l'Estrapade, 75005 Paris, France

Vieira, Joao Bernardo — *Head of State, Guinea-Bissau; General*
Conselho de Estado, Bissau, Guinea-Bissau

Vieira, Meredith — *Commentator*
%"Day One" Show, ABC-TV, 77 W 66th St, New York, NY 10023, USA

Viereck, Peter — *Poet, Historian*
12 Silver St, South Hadley, MA 01075, USA

Viermetz, Kurt F — *Financier*
%J P Morgan Co, 60 Wall St, New York, NY 10005, USA

Viets, Robert O — *Businessman*
%CILCORP Inc, 300 Hamilton Blvd, Peoria, IL 61602, USA

Vigil, Selene — *Singer (7 Year Bitch)*
%Talent House, 1407 E Madison St, #41, Seattle, WA 98122, USA

Vigoda, Abe — *Actor*
8500 Melrose Ave, #208, West Hollywood, CA 90069, USA

Viguerie, Richard A — *Publisher*
%Viguerie Co, 7777 Leesburg Pike, Falls Church, VA 22043, USA

Viklund, William E — *Financier*
%Long Island Savings Bank, 201 Old Country Rd, Melville, NY 11747, USA

Viktorenko, Alexander S — *Cosmonaut*
%Potchta Kosmonavtov, 141 160 Svyosdny Gorodok, Moskovskoi Oblasti, Russia

Vila, Bob — *Home Repair Entertainer*
PO Box 749, Marstons Mills, MA 02648, USA

Vilas, Guillermo — *Tennis Player*
%Guy Cromwell Betz, Pembroke One Bldg, #525, Virginia Beach, VA 23462, USA

Vilenkin, Alex — *Physicist, Astronomer*
%Tufts University, Physics & Astronomy Dept, Medford, MA 02155, USA

Viljoen, Marais — *President, South Africa*
PO Box 5555, Pretoria 0001, South Africa

Villa, Carlos — *Artist*
1664 Grove St, San Francisco, CA 94117, USA

Villani, Edmond D — *Financier*
%Scudder Stevens Clark, 345 Park Ave, New York, NY 10154, USA

Villas Boas, Claudio — *Anthropologist, Explorer*
Parque Nacional do Xingu, Rua Capital Federal 309, 01259 Sao Paulo, Brazil

Villas Boas, Orlando — *Anthropologist, Explorer*
Parque Nacional do Xingu, Rua Capital Federal 309, 01259 Sao Paulo, Brazil

Villoria, Richard — *Educator*
%World Future Society, 4916 St Elmo Ave, Bethesda, MD 20814, USA

Vimond, Paul M — *Architect*
91 Ave Niel, 75017 Paris, France

Vincent, Jan-Michael — *Actor*
%David Krieff, 11693 San Vicente Blvd, #296, Los Angeles, CA 90049, USA

Vincent, Richard F — *Army Field Marshal, England*
%Midland Bank, Shaftesbury, Dorset SP7 8JX, England

Vincent, Vinnie — *Singer, Guitarist (Kiss)*
%International Talent Group, 729 7th Ave, #1600, New York, NY 10019, USA

Vines, C Jerry — *Religious Leader*
%First Baptist Church, 124 W Ashley St, Jacksonville, FL 32202, USA

Vines, William J — *Financier*
Cliffdale, Currabubula NSW 2342, Australia

Vinnie *Rapper (Naughty By Nature)*
%Flavor Unit Mgmt, 155 Morgan St, Jersey City, NJ 07302, USA

Vinson, James S *Educator*
%University of Evansville, President's Office, Evansville, IN 47722, USA

Vint, Jesse *Actor*
%BDP Assoc, 10637 Burbank Blvd, North Hollywood, CA 91601, USA

Vinton, Bobby *Singer*
%Rexford Productions, 9255 Sunset Blvd, #706, Los Angeles, CA 90069, USA

Vinton, Will *Animator*
%Will Vinton Productions, 2580 NW Upshur, Portland, OR 97210, USA

Viola, Bill *Sculptor*
282 Granada Ave, Long Beach, CA 90803, USA

Viola, Frank J, Jr *Baseball Player*
106 Coves Rub, Oyster Bay Cove, NY 11791, USA

Virata, Cesar E *Prime Minister, Philippines*
63 E Maya Dr, Quezon City, Philippines

Virdon, William C (Bill) *Baseball Manager*
1311 River Rd, Springfield, MO 65804, USA

Viren, Lasse *Track Athlete*
Suomen Urheilulitto Ry, Box 25202, 00250 Helsinki 25, Finland

Virolainen, Johannes *Prime Minister, Finland*
Kirkniemi, Lohja, Finland

Viry, Alain *Businessman*
%Willcox & Gibbs Inc, 150 Alhambra Circle, Coral Gables, FL 33134, USA

Viscardi Johnston, Catherine *Publisher*
%Mirabella Magazine, 200 Madison Ave, New York, NY 10016, USA

Viscuso, Sal *Actor*
6491 Ivarene Ave, Los Angeles, CA 90068, USA

Vise, David A *Journalist*
%Washington Post, Editorial Dept, 1150 15th St NW, Washington, DC 20071, USA

Vishnevskaya, Galina P *Opera Singer*
%Bolshoi Theater, Teatralnaya Pl 1, 103009 Moscow, Russia

Visitor, Nana *Actress*
914 N Kings Rd, #5, Los Angeles, CA 90069, USA

Viso, Michel *Spatinaut, France*
/ Domaine Chateau-Gaillard, 94700 Maisons-d'Alfort, France

Visscher, Maurice B *Physiologist*
120 Melbourne Ave SE, Minneapolis, MN 55414, USA

Visser, Lesley *Sportscaster*
%ABC-TV, Sports Dept, 77 W 66th St, New York, NY 10023, USA

Vitale, Alberto A *Publisher*
%Random House Inc, 201 E 50th St, New York, NY 10022, USA

Vitale, David J *Financier*
%First Chicago Corp, 1 First National Plaza, Chicago, IL 60670, USA

Vitale, Dick *Sportscaster*
%ESPN-TV, Sports Dept, ESPN Plaza, Bristol, CT 06010, USA

Vitito, Robert J *Financier*
%Citizens Banking Corp, 1 Citizens Banking Center, Flint, MI 48502, USA

Vittadini, Adrienne *Fashion Designer*
%Adrienne Vittadini Inc, 575 7th Ave, New York, NY 10018, USA

Vitti, Monica *Actress*
Via Vicenzo Tiberio 18, Rome, Italy

Vittorla, Joseph V *Businessman*
%Avis Inc, 900 Old Country Rd, Garden City, NY 11530, USA

Viviano, Joseph P *Businessman*
%Hershey Foods Corp, 100 Crystal A Dr, Hershey, PA 17033, USA

Vladeck, Judith P *Attorney*
%Vladeck Waldman Elias Engelhard, 1501 Broadway, New York, NY 10036, USA

Vlug, Dirk J *WW II Army Hero (CMH)*
1464 Seymour Ave NW, Grand Rapids, MI 49504, USA

Vo Nguyen Giap *Army General, Vietnam*
Dang Cong San Vietnam, 1-C Blvd Hoang Van Thu, Hanoi, Vietnam

Vo Van Kiet *Prime Minister, Vietnam*
%Prime Minister's Office, Hoang Hoa Thum, Hanoi, Vietnam

Vogel, Hans-Jochen *Government Official, West Germany*
Stresemanstr 6, 53123 Bonn-Bad Godesberg, Germany

Vogel, Matt *Swimmer*
246 Highland Ave, Oak Ridge, TN 37830, USA

V

Vinnie - Vogel

Vogelstein - Von Runkle

Vogelstein, Bert *Geneticist*
%Johns Hopkins University Medical School, Oncology Center, Baltimore, MD 21218, USA

Vogt, Carl W *Government Official*
%National Transportation Safety Board, 490 L'Enfant Plz SW, Washington, DC 20594, USA

Vogt, Peter K *Virologist*
%Univ of Southern California Med School, 2011 Zonal Ave, Los Angeles, CA 90033, USA

Vogt, Rochus E *Physicist, Astronomer*
%California Institute of Technology, Bridge Laboratory, Pasadena, CA 91125, USA

Voight, Jon *Actor*
13340 Galewood Dr, Sherman Oaks, CA 91423, USA

Voinovich, George V *Governor, OH*
%Governor's Office, State House, 77 S High St, Columbus, OH 43215, USA

Voiselle, William S (Bill) *Baseball Player*
RR 2, PO Box 318, Ninety Six, SC 29666, USA

Voisinet, James R *Businessman*
5909 Windmier Court, Dallas, TX 75252, USA

Vojta, George J *Financier*
%Bankers Trust New York Corp, 280 Park Ave, New York, NY 10017, USA

Volberding, Paul *Cancer Researcher*
%General Hospital AIDS Activities Dept, 995 Potrero Ave, San Francisco, CA 94110, USA

Volcker, Paul A *Government Official*
%James D Wolfensohn Inc, 599 Lexington Ave, New York, NY 10022, USA

Volk, Igor P *Cosmonaut*
%Potchta Kosmonavtov, 141 160 Svyosdny Gorodok, Moskovskoi Oblasti, Russia

Volk, Patricia *Writer*
%Raines & Raines, 71 Park Ave, New York, NY 10016, USA

Volk, Richard R (Rick) *Football Player*
12301 Woodcrest Lane, Glen Arm, MD 21057, USA

Volkema, Michael A *Businessman*
%Herman Miller Inc, 855 E Main St, Zeeland, MI 49464, USA

Volkmann, Elisabeth *Opera Singer*
%Agentur Doris Mattes, Merzstr 14, 81679 Munich, Germany

Volkov, Alexander A *Cosmonaut*
%Potchta Kosmonavtov, 141 160 Svyosdny Gorodok, Moskovskoi Oblasti, Russia

Vollbracht, Michaele *Fashion Designer, Artist*
%General Delivery, Safety Harbor, FL 34695, USA

Vollenweider, Andreas *Concert Harpist*
Sempacher Str 16, 8032 Zurich, Switzerland

Volynov, Boris V *Cosmonaut*
%Potchta Kosmonavtov, 141 160 Svyosdny Gorodok, Moskovskoi Oblasti, Russia

Volz, Nedra *Actress*
615 Tulare Way, Upland, CA 91786, USA

Von Aroldingen, Karin *Ballerina*
%New York City Ballet, Lincoln Center Plaza, New York, NY 10023, USA

Von Dohnanyi, Christoph *Conductor*
%Cleveland Orchestra, Severance Hall, Cleveland, OH 44106, USA

Von Einem, Gottfried *Composer*
Kapuzinergang 86, Hofberg, 1010 Vienna, Austria

Von Furstenberg, Betsy *Actress*
230 Central Park West, New York, NY 10024, USA

Von Furstenberg, Diane *Fashion Designer*
745 5th Ave, #2400, New York, NY 10151, USA

Von Furstenberg, Egon *Fashion Designer*
50 E 72nd St, New York, NY 10021, USA

Von Habsburg-Lothringem, Otto *Government Official, Germany*
Hindenburgstr 14, 82343 Pocking, Germany

Von Hartz, Maria del Carmen *Model*
%Ford Model Agency, 344 E 59th St, New York, NY 10022, USA

Von Klitzing, Klaus *Nobel Physics Laureate*
%Max Planck Institute, Heisenbergstr 1, 70569 Stuttgart, Germany

Von Kuenheim, Eberhard *Businessman*
%Bayerische Motorenwerke, Mauerkircherstr 105, 81925 Munich, Germany

Von Otter, Sophie *Opera Singer*
%Columbia Artists Mgmt Inc, 165 W 57th St, New York, NY 10019, USA

Von Oy, Jenna *Actress*
%J Michael Bloom Ltd, 9255 Sunset Blvd, #710, Los Angeles, CA 90069, USA

Von Runkle, Theodora *Costume Designer*
8805 Lookout Mountain Rd, Los Angeles, CA 90046, USA

Von Saltza Olmstead, Chris — *Swimmer*
7060 Fairway Place, Carmel, CA 93923, USA

Von Schack, Wesley W — *Businessman*
%DQE Inc, 1 Oxford Center, 301 Grant St, Pittsburgh, PA 15219, USA

Von Stade, Frederica — *Opera Singer*
1200 San Antonio Ave, Alameda, CA 94501, USA

Von Sydow, Max — *Actor*
Avd C-G Risberg, Strandvegen B, 114 56 Stockholm, Sweden

Von Thaden, Arthur G — *Businessman*
%BRE Properties, 1 Montgomery St, San Francisco, CA 94104, USA

Von Trotta, Margarethe — *Movie Director*
Turkenstr 91, 80799 Munich, Germany

Von Weizsacker, Carl-Friedrich — *Philosopher*
Aplenstr 14, 83139 Socking, Germany

Von Weizsacker, Richard — *President, Germany*
Meisenstr 6, 14195 Berlin, Germany

Vonk, Hans — *Conductor*
%St Louis Symphony, 1824 Garden St, Belleville, IL 62221, USA

Vonnegut, Kurt, Jr — *Writer*
PO Box 27, Sagaponack, NY 11962, USA

Voorhees, John J — *Dermatologist*
3965 Waldenwood Dr, Ann Arbor, MI 48105, USA

Vos Savant, Marilyn — *Writer*
%Parade Publications, 750 3rd Ave, New York, NY 10017, USA

Voss, James S — *Astronaut*
%NASA, Johnson Space Center, 2101 NASA Rd, Houston, TX 77058, USA

Voss, Janice E — *Astronaut*
%NASA, Johnson Space Center, 2101 NASA Rd, Houston, TX 77058, USA

Voulkos, Peter — *Artist*
951 62nd St, Oakland, CA 94608, USA

Voznesensky, Andrei A — *Poet*
Kotelnicheskaya Nab 1/15, Bl W, #62, 109240 Moscow, Russia

Vranitzky, Franz — *Chancellor, Austria*
%Chancellor's Office, Ballhausplatz 2, 1014 Vienna, Austria

Vreeland, Eleanor P — *Educator*
%Katherine Gibbs School, President's Office, New York, NY 10017, USA

Vu Van Mau — *Prime Minister, Vietnam*
132 Suon Nguyet Anh, Ho Chi Minh City, Vietnam

Vuarnet, Jean — *Skier*
Chalet Squaw Peak, 74110 Auoriaz, France

Vuitton, Henri-Louis — *Fashion Designer*
78 Bis Ave Marceau, 75000 Paris, France

Vuono, Carl E — *Army General*
5796 Westchester St, Alexandria, VA 22310, USA

Vyent, Louise — *Model*
%Pauline's Model Mgmt, 379 W Broadway, New York, NY 10012, USA

Von Saltza Olmstead - Vyent

Wachner, Linda J *Businesswoman*
%Warnaco Group, 90 Park Ave, New York, NY 10016, USA

Wachs, David V *Businessman*
%Charming Shoppes, 450 Winks Lane, Bensalem, PA 19020, USA

Wachs, Philip *Businessman*
%Charming Shoppes, 450 Winks Lane, Bensalem, PA 19020, USA

Wachtel, Christine *Track Athlete*
Helmut-Just-Str 5, 17036 Neubrandenburg, Germany

Wachter, Anita *Skier*
Gantschierstr 579, 6780 Schruns, Austria

Wackenhut, George R *Businessman*
%Wackenhut Corp, 1500 San Remo Ave, Coral Gables, FL 33146, USA

Wackenhut, Richard R *Businessman*
%Wackenhut Corp, 1500 San Remo Ave, Coral Gables, FL 33146, USA

Wacker, Jim *Football Coach*
%University of Minnesota, Athletic Dept, Minneapolis, MN 55455, USA

Waddell, John C *Businessman*
%Arrow Electronics Inc, 25 Hub Dr, Melville, NY 11747, USA

Waddell, John Henry *Artist*
Star Route 2273, Oak Creek Village Rd, Cornville, AZ 86325, USA

Waddington of Read, David *Governor General, Bermuda*
Government House, 11 Langton Hill, Pembroke HM13, Bermuda

Waddington, Leslie *Art Dealer*
%Waddington Galleries, 11 Cork St, London W1X 1PD, England

Wade, Edgar L *Religious Leader*
4466 Elvis Presley Blvd, #222, Memphis, TN 38116, USA

Wade, S Virginia *Tennis Player*
Sharstead Court, Sittingbourne, Kent, England

Wade, William J (Bill), Jr *Football Player*
PO Box 210124, Nashville, TN 37221, USA

Wadkins, Bobby *Golfer*
%Pros Inc, PO Box 673, Richmond, VA 23206, USA

Wadkins, Lanny *Golfer*
%Pros Inc, PO Box 673, Richmond, VA 23206, USA

Wadlow, Joan K *Educator*
%University of Alaska, Chancellor's Office, Fairbanks, AK 99775, USA

Wadsworth, Charles W *Chamber Pianist*
%Chamber Music Society, 225 E 79th St, New York, NY 10021, USA

Waelsch, Salome G *Geneticist*
90 Morningside Dr, New York, NY 10027, USA

Waetjen, Walter B *Educator*
4790 Sailors Retreat Rd, Oxford, MD 21654, USA

Wages, Robert E *Labor Leader*
%Oil Chemical Atomic Workers International Union, PO Box 2812, Denver, CO 80201, USA

Waggoner, J Virgil *Businessman*
%Sterling Chemicals, 1200 Smith St, Houston, TX 77002, USA

Waggoner, Lyle *Actor*
4450 Balboa Ave, Encino, CA 91316, USA

Waggoner, Paul E *Agronomist*
314 Vineyard Rd, Guilford, CT 06437, USA

Wagner, Chuck *Actor*
140 Claremont Ave, Verona, NJ 07044, USA

Wagner, David J *Financier*
%Old Ken Financial Corp, 1 Vandenberg Center, Grand Rapids, MI 49503, USA

Wagner, Gerrit A *Businessman*
%Royal Dutch/Shell Group, 30 Carel Van Bylandtlaan, The Hague, Netherlands

Wagner, Harold A *Businessman*
%Air Products & Chemicals Inc, 7201 Hamilton Blvd, Allentown, PA 18195, USA

Wagner, Jack *Actor*
1134 Alta Loma Rd, #115, West Hollywood, CA 90069, USA

Wagner, John *Cartoonist (Maxine)*
%Hallmark Cards, Shoebox Division, 101 McDonald Dr, Lawrence, KS 66044, USA

Wagner, Lindsay *Actress*
%International Creative Mgmt, 8942 Wilshire Blvd, Beverly Hills, CA 90211, USA

Wagner, Lisa *Bowler*
%Ladies Professional Bowlers Tour, 7171 Cherryvale Blvd, Rockford, IL 61112, USA

Wagner, Philip M *Columist*
Boordy Vineyard, PO Box 38, Riderwood, MD 21139, USA

Wachner - Wagner

Wagner, Robert *Actor*
1500 Old Oak Rd, Los Angeles, CA 90049, USA

Wagner, Robert T *Educator*
%South Dakota State University, President's Office, Brookings, SD 57007, USA

Wagner, Robin S A *Stage, Set Designer*
%Robin Wagner Studio, 890 Broadway, New York, NY 10003, USA

Wagner, Rodney B *Financier*
%J P Morgan Co, 60 Wall St, New York, NY 10005, USA

Wagner, Wolfgang M M *Opera Director*
Festspielhugel #3, 95445 Bayreuth, Germany

Wagoner, Dan *Dancer, Choreographer*
%Contemporary Dance Theater, 17 Duke's Rd, London WC1H 9AB, England

Wagoner, David R *Writer*
5416 154th Place SW, Edmonds, WA 98026, USA

Wagoner, Harold E *Architect*
331 Lindsey Dr, Berwyn, PA 19312, USA

Wagoner, Porter *Singer, Songwriter*
%Porter Wagoner Enterprises, PO Box 290785, Nashville, TN 37229, USA

Wahl, Ken *Actor*
480 Westlake Blvd, Malibu, CA 90265, USA

Wahlberg (Marky Mark), Mark *Singer, Actor*
63 Pilgrim Rd, Braintree, MA 02184, USA

Wahlen, George E *WW II Navy Hero (CMH)*
3437 W 5700 South, Roy, UT 84067, USA

Wahlgren, Olof G C *Editor*
Nicoloviusgatan 5-B, 217 57 Malmo, Sweden

Wahlstrom, Jarl H *Religious Leader*
Borgstrominkuja 1-A-10, 00840 Helsinki 84, Finland

Waigel, Theodor *Government Official, Germany*
%Finance Ministry, Graurheindorfer Str 108, 53117 Bonn, Germany

Waihee, John D, III *Governor, HI*
1164 Bishop St, #800, Honolulu, HI 96813, USA

Wain, Bea *Singer*
9955 Durant Dr, #305, Beverly Hills, CA 90212, USA

Wainer, Stanley A *Businessman*
1151 Hilary Lane, Beverly Hills, CA 90210, USA

Wainwright, James *Actor*
7060 Hollywood Blvd, #610, Los Angeles, CA 90028, USA

Wainwright, Loudon, III *Composer*
%Rosebud Agency, PO Box 174029, San Francisco, CA 94117, USA

Waite, Ralph *Actor*
93-317 Ironwood St, Palm Desert, CA 92260, USA

Waite, Ric *Cinematographer*
%Smith/Gosnell, 1515 Palisades Dr, #N, Pacific Palisades, CA 90272, USA

Waite, Terence H (Terry) *Religious Leader, Hostage*
%Travellers' Club, 106 Pall Mall, London SW1Y 5EP, England

Waits, Tom *Singer, Songwriter, Pianist*
421 S Serrano Ave, Los Angeles, CA 90020, USA

Waitz, Grete *Track Athlete*
Birgitte Hammers Vei 15-G, 1169 Oslo, Norway

Wajda, Andrzej *Movie Director*
Ul Jozefa Hauke Bosaka 14, 01-540 Warsaw, Poland

Wajnert, Thomas C *Financier*
%AT&T Capital Corp, 44 Whippany Rd, Morristown, NJ 07960, USA

Wakefield, Samuel N *Army General*
Commanding General, US Combined Arms Support Command, Fort Lee, VA 23801, USA

Wakefield, Timothy S (Tim) *Baseball Player*
2827 Choctaw Dr, Melbourne, FL 32935, USA

Wakeham of Maldon, John *Government Official, England*
%House of Lords, Westminster, London SW1A 0PW, England

Wakeman, Rick *Musician, Composer*
Bajonor House, 2 Bridge St, Peel, Isle of Man, United Kingdom

Walcott, Derek A *Nobel Literature Laureate*
%University of Boston, English Dept, Boston, MA 02215, USA

Walcott, Gregory *Actor*
22246 Saticoy St, Canoga Park, CA 91303, USA

Wald, George M *Nobel Medicine Laureate*
21 Lakeview Ave, Cambridge, MA 02138, USA

W

Wagner - Wald

Wald, Jeff — *Talent Agent*
1467 Chastain Parkway W, Pacific Palisades, CA 90272, USA

Wald, Patricia M — *Judge*
%US Court of Appeals, 3rd & Constitution Ave NW, Washington, DC 20001, USA

Wald, Richard C — *Television Executive*
35 Orchard Rd, Larchmont, NY 10538, USA

Waldegrave, William — *Government Official, England*
%House of Commons, Westminster, London SW1A 0AA, England

Walden, Robert — *Actor*
1450 Arroyo View Dr, Pasadena, CA 91103, USA

Walden, Robert E (Bob) — *Football Player*
909 E Alice St, Bainbridge, GA 31717, USA

Waldheim, Kurt — *President, Austria*
1 Lobkowitz Platz, 1010 Vienna, Austria

Waldner, Jan-Ove — *Table Tennis Player*
%Banda, Skjulstagatan 1O, 632 29 Eskilstuna, Sweden

Waldo, Carolyn — *Synchronized Swimmer*
%International Management Grp, 150 Bloor St W, Toronto ON M5S 2X9, Canada

Waldrop, Rob — *Football Player*
%University of Arizona, Athletic Dept, McKale Center, Tucson, AZ 85721, USA

Walenberg, Alan — *Publisher*
%Redbook Magazine, 224 W 57th St, New York, NY 10019, USA

Walesa, Lech — *Nobel Peace Laureate; President, Poland*
Ul Pilotow 17 D/3, Gdansk-Zaspa, Poland

Walgreen, Charles R, III — *Businessman*
%Walgreen Co, 200 Wilmot Rd, Deerfield, IL 60015, USA

Walken, Christopher — *Actor*
%International Creative Mgmt, 8942 Wilshire Blvd, Beverly Hills, CA 90211, USA

Walker, Alan — *Anthropologist*
%Johns Hopkins Medical School, Cell Biology/Anatomy Dept, Baltimore, MD 21205, USA

Walker, Alice M — *Social Activist, Writer*
720 Steiner St, San Francisco, CA 94117, USA

Walker, Ally — *Actress*
%Moore, 7920 Sunset Blvd, #400, Los Angeles, CA 90046, USA

Walker, B J — *Financier*
%First Union Corp, 301 S Tryon St, Charlotte, NC 28288, USA

Walker, Bree — *Commentator*
3347 Tareco Dr, Los Angeles, CA 90068, USA

Walker, Brian — *Cartoonist (Hi & Lois)*
%King Features Syndicate, 216 E 45th St, New York, NY 10017, USA

Walker, Catherine — *Fashion Designer*
65 Sydney St, Chelsea, London SW3 6PX, England

Walker, Charles B — *Businessman*
%Ethyl Corp, 330 S 4th St, Richmond, VA 23219, USA

Walker, Charles E — *Economist*
10120 Chapel Rd, Potomac, MD 20854, USA

Walker, Chris — *Actor*
%Rolf Kruger Mgmt, 121 Gloucester Place, London W1H 3PJ, England

Walker, Clay — *Singer*
%PLA Media, 1303 16th Ave S, Nashville, TN 37212, USA

Walker, Clint — *Actor*
Rodeo Flat Rd, Auburn, CA 95603, USA

Walker, Colleen — *Golfer*
%Ladies Professional Golf Assn, 2570 Volusia Ave, Daytona Beach, FL 32114, USA

Walker, David M — *Astronaut*
%NASA, Johnson Space Center, 2101 NASA Rd, Houston, TX 77058, USA

Walker, E Cardon — *Movie Executive*
%Walt Disney Productions, 500 S Buena Vista St, Burbank, CA 91521, USA

Walker, E Doak, Jr — *Football Player*
PO Box 773329, Steamboat Springs, CO 80477, USA

Walker, Greg — *Cartoonist (Hi & Lois)*
%King Features Syndicate, 216 E 45th St, New York, NY 10017, USA

Walker, Harry M — *Financier*
%Trustmark National Bank, 248 E Capital St, Jackson, MS 39201, USA

Walker, Herschel — *Football Player*
%New York Giants, Giants Stadium, East Rutherford, NJ 07073, USA

Walker, James E — *Educator*
%Middle Tennessee State University, President's Office, Murfreesboro, TN 37132, USA

Wald - Walker

Walker, James L (Jimmy) *Labor Leader*
%Fireman & Oilers Brotherhood, 1100 Circle 75 Parkway, Atlanta, GA 30339, USA

Walker, Jeffrey C *Financier*
%Chemical Venture Partners, 270 Park Ave, New York, NY 10017, USA

Walker, Jerry Jeff *Singer, Guitarist, Songwriter*
%Tried & True Music, PO Box 39, Austin, TX 78767, USA

Walker, Jimmie (J J) *Comedian*
8265 Sunset Blvd, #100, Los Angeles, CA 90046, USA

Walker, Joe Louis *Singer, Guitarist*
%American Famous Talent, 816 W Evergreen Ave, Chicago, IL 60622, USA

Walker, John *Track Athlete*
Jeffs Rd, RD Papatoetoe, New Zealand

Walker, John *Museum Curator*
%National Gallery of Art, 1729 "H" St NW, Washington, DC 20006, USA

Walker, John *Computer Engineer*
%Autodesk Inc, 2320 Marinship Way, Sausalito, CA 94965, USA

Walker, Joseph P *Businessman*
%CTS Corp, 905 West Blvd N, Elkhart, IN 46514, USA

Walker, Junior *Singer, Saxophonist*
PO Box 277, Battle Creek, MI 49016, USA

Walker, K Grahame *Businessman*
%Dexter Corp, 1 Elm St, Windsor Locks, CT 06096, USA

Walker, LeRoy T *Track Coach, Executive*
1208 Red Oak Ave, Durham, NC 27707, USA

Walker, Marcy *Actress*
%Leslie Bader, 10225 Donna Ave, Northridge, CA 91324, USA

Walker, Martin D *Businessman*
%M A Hanna Co, 200 Public Square, Cleveland, OH 44114, USA

Walker, Mort *Cartoonist (Beetle Bailey, Sarge)*
61 Studio Court, Stamford, CT 06903, USA

Walker, Peter E *Government Official, England*
Abbots Morton Manor, Grooms Hill, Abbots Morton, Worc WR7 4LT, England

Walker, Robert M *Financier*
%Union Bank, 350 California St, San Francisco, CA 94104, USA

Walker, Robert M *Physicist*
3 Romany Park Lane, St Louis, MO 63132, USA

Walker, Robert, Jr *Actor*
20828 Pacific Coast Highway, Malibu, CA 90265, USA

Walker, Ronald *Publisher*
%Smithsonian Magazine, 900 Jefferson Dr, Washington, DC 20560, USA

Walker, Ronald F *Financier*
%American Financial Corp, 1 E 4th St, Cincinnati, OH 45202, USA

Walker, Sandra *Opera Singer*
%Columbia Artists Mgmt Inc, 165 W 57th St, New York, NY 10019, USA

Walker, Sarah E B *Opera Singer*
152 Inchmery Rd, London SE6 1DF, England

Walker, Tonja *Actress*
4138 Augusta Dr, Crown Point, IN 46307, USA

Walker, Wesley D *Football Player*
10 Schoolhouse Way, Dix Hills, NY 11746, USA

Walker, William D *Businessman*
%Tektronix Inc, 26600 Southwest Parkway, Wilsonville, OR 97070, USA

Wall, Akure *Model*
%Elite Model Mgmt, 111 E 22nd St, #200, New York, NY 10010, USA

Wall, Art *Golfer*
PO Box 301, Sonoita, AZ 85637, USA

Wall, Brian A *Sculptor*
306 Lombard St, San Francisco, CA 94133, USA

Wall, David *Ballet Dancer*
%Royal Ballet, Bow St, London WC2E 9DD, England

Wall, Frederick T *Physical Chemist*
2468 Via Viesta, La Jolla, CA 92037, USA

Wall, John W *Financier*
%R I Hospital Trust National Bank, Hospital Trust Plaza, Providence, RI 02903, USA

Wall, Shannon J *Labor Leader*
%National Maritime Union, 346 W 17th St, New York, NY 10011, USA

Wallace Stone, Dee *Actress*
23035 Cumorah Crest Dr, Woodland Hills, CA 91364, USA

W

Walker - Wallace Stone

Wallace, Anthony F C *Anthropologist*
%University of Pennsylvania, Anthropology Dept, Philadelphia, PA 19014, USA

Wallace, Bruce *Geneticist*
940 McBryde Dr, Blacksburg, VA 24060, USA

Wallace, Craig K *Physician*
%National Institutes of Health, 9000 Rockville Pike, Bethesda, MD 20892, USA

Wallace, George C *Governor, AL; Educator*
3140 Fitzgerald Rd, Montgomery, AL 36106, USA

Wallace, Ian *Opera Singer*
%Peters Fraser Dunlop, Chelsea Harbour, Lots Rd, London SW10 0XF, England

Wallace, J Bransford *Businessman*
%Willis Corroon Corp, 26 Century Blvd, Nashville, TN 37214, USA

Wallace, Jane *Entertainer*
%"Under Scrutiny" Show, Fox-TV, PO Box 900, Beverly Hills, CA 90213, USA

Wallace, Marcia *Actress*
1312 S Genesee Ave, Los Angeles, CA 90019, USA

Wallace, Mike *Commentator*
%CBS-TV, News Dept, 524 W 57th St, New York, NY 10019, USA

Wallace, Rasheed *Basketball Player*
%Washington Bullets, Capital Centre, 1 Truman Dr, Landover, MD 20785, USA

Wallace, Rusty *Auto Racing Driver*
%Penske Racing, 6 Knob Hill Rd, Mooreville, NC 28115, USA

Wallace, W Ray *Businessman*
%Trinity Industries, 2525 Stemmons Freeway, Dallas, TX 75207, USA

Wallach, Eli *Actor*
90 Riverside Dr, New York, NY 10024, USA

Wallach, Timothy C (Tim) *Baseball Player*
10762 Holly Dr, Garden Grove, CA 92640, USA

Wallechinsky, David *Writer*
%William Morrow Co, 1350 Ave of Americas, New York, NY 10016, USA

Wallenberg, Peter *Businessman*
%Skandinaviska Enskilda Banken, 106 40 Stockholm, Sweden

Waller, Michael *Editor*
%Hartford Courant Co, 285 Broad St, Hartford, CT 06115, USA

Waller, Robert James *Writer*
%Aaron Priest Literary Agency, 708 3rd Ave, #2300, New York, NY 10017, USA

Waller, Ron *Football Player*
900 Concord Rd, Seaford, DE 19973, USA

Waller, William L *Governor, MS*
220 S President, Jackson, MS 39201, USA

Wallin, Winston R *Businessman*
%Medtronic Inc, 7000 Central Ave NE, Minneapolis, MN 55432, USA

Walling, Cheves T *Chemist*
PO Box 537, Jaffrey, NH 03452, USA

Wallis, Charles T *Financier*
%Back Bay Advisors, 399 Boylston St, Boston, MA 02116, USA

Wallis, Shani *Actress*
15460 Vista Haven, Sherman Oaks, CA 91403, USA

Walliser, Maria *Skier*
Selfwingert, 7208 Malans, Switzerland

Walmsley, Jon *Actor*
7101 Woodrow Wilson Dr, Los Angeles, CA 90068, USA

Walsh, Don *Underwater Explorer*
%International Maritime Inc, 839 S Beacon St, #217, San Pedro, CA 90731, USA

Walsh, Donnie *Basketball Coach, Executive*
%Indiana Pacers, Market Square Arena, 300 E Market St, Indianapolis, IN 46204, USA

Walsh, Joe *Singer, Guitarist (Eagles); Songwriter*
%David Spero Mgmt, 1670 S Belvoir Blvd, Cleveland, OH 44121, USA

Walsh, John *Television Host*
%"Most Wanted" Show, Fox-TV, 5151 Wisconsin Ave NW, Washington, DC 20016, USA

Walsh, John, Jr *Museum Curator*
%J Paul Getty Art Museum, 17985 Pacific Coast Highway, Malibu, CA 90265, USA

Walsh, Kenneth A *WW II Marine Air Corps Hero (CMH)*
1008 Riviera Dr, Santa Ana, CA 92706, USA

Walsh, Lawrence E *Government Official, Attorney*
1902 Bedford St, Oklahoma City, OK 73116, USA

Walsh, M Emmet *Actor*
%Gersh Agency, 232 N Canon Dr, Beverly Hills, CA 90210, USA

Wallace - Walsh

Walsh, Martin — *Association Executive*
%National Organization on Disability, 910 16th St NW, Washington, DC 20006, USA

Walsh, Patrick C — *Urologist*
%Johns Hopkins Hospital, Brady Urological Institute, Baltimore, MD 21205, USA

Walsh, Steve — *Football Player*
%New Orleans Saints, 1500 Poydras St, New Orleans, LA 70112, USA

Walsh, Steve — *Hockey Executive*
%New York Islanders, Veterans Memorial Coliseum, Uniondale, NY 11553, USA

Walsh, Sydney — *Actress*
%Innovative Artists, 1999 Ave of Stars, #2850, Los Angeles, CA 90067, USA

Walsh, William (Bill) — *Football Coach, Administrator*
%Stanford University, Athletic Dept, Stanford, CA 94305, USA

Walsh, William B — *Medical Administrator*
14473 N Spanish Garden Lane, Tucson, AZ 85737, USA

Walston, Ray — *Actor*
423 S Rexford Dr, #205, Beverly Hills, CA 90212, USA

Walter, James W — *Businessman*
%Walter Industries, 1500 N Dale Mabry Highway, Tampa, FL 33607, USA

Walter, Jessica — *Actress*
10530 Strathmore Dr, Los Angeles, CA 90024, USA

Walter, John R — *Businessman*
%R R Donnelley & Sons Co, 77 W Wacker Dr, Chicago, IL 60601, USA

Walter, Paul H L — *Labor Leader*
9 Walter Dr, Saratoga Springs, NY 12866, USA

Walter, Robert D — *Businessman*
%Cardinal Health Inc, 655 Metro Place S, Dublin, OH 43017, USA

Walter, Ulrich — *Astronaut, Germany*
%DLR, Astronautenburo, Linder Hohe, 51147 Cologne, Germany

Walters, Barbara — *Commentator*
33 W 60th St, New York, NY 10023, USA

Walters, Harry N — *Government Official*
%DHC Holdings Corp, 125 Thomas Dale, Williamsburg, VA 23185, USA

Walters, Julie — *Actress*
%International Creative Mgmt, 76 Oxford St, London W1N 0AX, England

Walters, Kirk W — *Financier*
%Northeast Savings, 50 State House Square, Hartford, CT 06103, USA

Walters, Peter I — *Businessman*
84 Eccleston Square, London SW1V 1PV, England

Walters, Susan — *Actress*
933 S Tremaine Ave, Los Angeles, CA 90019, USA

Walters, Vernon A — *Government Official, Army General*
2295 S Ocean Blvd, Palm Beach, FL 33480, USA

Walton, Jess — *Actress*
4702 Ethel Ave, Sherman Oaks, CA 91423, USA

Walton, Joseph (Joe) — *Football Coach*
%Robert Morris College, Athletic Dept, Corapolis, PA 15108, USA

Walton, S Robson — *Businessman*
%Wal-Mart Stores, 702 SW 8th St, Bentonville, AK 72712, USA

Walton, William T (Bill), III — *Basketball Player*
%NBC-TV, Sports Dept, 30 Rockefeller Plaza, New York, NY 10112, USA

Waltrip, Darrell L — *Auto Racing Driver*
PO Box 855, Franklin, TN 37065, USA

Waltrip, Robert L — *Businessman*
%Service Corp International, 1929 Allen Parkway, Houston, TX 77019, USA

Walworth, Arthur — *Writer*
North Hill, 865 Central Ave E, #206, Needham, MA 02192, USA

Walz, Carl E — *Astronaut*
%NASA, Johnson Space Center, 2101 NASA Rd, Houston, TX 77058, USA

Wambaugh, Joseph — *Writer*
3520 Kellogg Way, San Diego, CA 92106, USA

Wampler, Charles W, Jr — *Businessman*
%WLR Foods, PO Box 7000, Broadway, VA 22815, USA

Wan Li — *Government Official, China*
%State Council, National People's Congress, Tian An Men Sq, Beijing, China

Wang Tian-Ren — *Sculptor*
Shaanxi Sculpture Institute, Longshoucun, Xi'am, Shaanxi 710016, China

Wang, Charles B — *Businessman*
%Computer Associates Int'l, 1 Computer Associates Plaza, Islandia, NY 11788, USA

W

Walsh - Wang

W

Wang, Henry Y — *Chemical Engineer*
%University of Michigan, Chemical Engineering Dept, Ann Arbor, MI 48109, USA

Wang, Taylor G — *Astronaut, Physicist*
%Vanderbilt University, Microgravity Research Center, Nashville, TN 37235, USA

Wang, Vera — *Fashion Designer*
%Vera Wang Bridal House, 980 Madison Ave, New York, NY 10021, USA

Wang, Y C — *Businessman*
%Formosa Plastics Corp, 39 Chung Shang 3rd Rd, Kaohsiung, Taiwan

Wangchuk, Jigme Singye — *King, Bhutan*
%Royal Palace, Tashichhodzong, Thimphu, Bhutan

Wannstedt, David R (Dave) — *Football Coach*
%Chicago Bears, Halas Hall, 250 N Washington Rd, Lake Forest, IL 60045, USA

Wanzer, Bobby — *Basketball Player*
%St John Fisher College, Athletic Dept, Rochester, NY 14618, USA

Wapner, Joseph A — *Judge, Actor*
16616 Park Lane Place, Los Angeles, CA 90049, USA

Ward, Benjamin — *Law Enforcement Official*
%New York Police Commissioner's Office, 1 Police Plaza, New York, NY 10038, USA

Ward, Charlie — *Football, Basketball Player*
%New York Knicks, Madison Square Garden, 4 Penn Plaza, New York, NY 10001, USA

Ward, David — *Opera Singer*
1 Kennedy Cres, Lake Wanaka, New Zealand

Ward, David — *Educator*
%University of Wisconsin, President's Office, Madison, WI 53706, USA

Ward, Douglas Turner — *Actor, Playwright*
%Negro Ensemble Co, 1540 Broadway, New York, NY 10036, USA

Ward, Fred — *Actor*
1215 Cabrillo Ave, Venice, CA 90291, USA

Ward, Harvie — *Golfer*
%Grand Cyprus Golf Club, 1 N Jacaranda Dr, Orlando, FL 32836, USA

Ward, James (Skip) — *Actor*
PO Box 755, Beverly Hills, CA 90213, USA

Ward, James D — *Financier*
%Citizens Bancorp, 14401 Sweitzer Lane, Laurel, MD 20707, USA

Ward, John A, III — *Financier*
%Chase Manhattan Bank (USA), 1 Chase Manhattan Plaza, Wilmington, DE 19801, USA

Ward, Maitland — *Actress*
%"Bold & Beautiful" Show, CBS-TV, 7800 Beverly Blvd, Los Angeles, CA 90036, USA

Ward, Michael P — *Mountaineer, Surgeon*
%St Andrews's Hospital, Bow St, London E3 3NT, England

Ward, Milton H — *Businessman*
%Cyprus Minerals Co, 9100 E Mineral Circle, Englewood, CO 80112, USA

Ward, R Duane — *Baseball Player*
4505 Pacific St, Framington, MA 87402, USA

Ward, Rachel — *Actress*
%Judy Cann Mgmt, 110 Queen St, Woollahra NSW 2025, Australia

Ward, Robert — *Composer*
The Forest, 2701 Pickett Rd, #4029, Durham, NC 27705, USA

Ward, Robert R (Bob) — *Football Player*
8031 Telegraph Rd, Severn, MD 21144, USA

Ward, Sela — *Actress*
%International Creative Mgmt, 8942 Wilshire Blvd, Beverly Hills, CA 90211, USA

Ward, Simon — *Actor*
%International Creative Mgmt, 76 Oxford St, London W1N 0AX, England

Ward, Sterling — *Religious Leader*
%Brethren Church, 524 College Ave, Ashland, OH 44805, USA

Ward, Vincent — *Movie Director*
PO Box 423, Kings Cross, Sydney NSW 2011, Australia

Wardeborg, George E — *Businessman*
%WICOR Inc, 626 E Wisconsin Ave, Milwuakee, WI 53202, USA

Warden, Jack — *Actor*
23604 Malibu Colony Rd, Malibu, CA 90265, USA

Ware, Herta — *Actress*
PO Box 151, Topanga Canyon, CA 90290, USA

Wareham, James L — *Businessman*
%Wheeling-Pittsburgh Corp, 1134 Market St, Wheeling, WV 26003, USA

Warfield, Marsha — *Actress*
PO Box 691713, Los Angeles, CA 90064, USA

Wang - Warfield

Warfield, Paul D — *Football Player*
15476 NW 77th Court, #347, Hialeah, FL 33016, USA

Warfield, Ronald — *Businessman*
%Country Life Insurance, 1711 GE Rd, Bloomington, IL 61704, USA

Warfield, William C — *Opera Singer*
PO Box 1573, Champaign, IL 61824, USA

Wariner, Steve — *Singer, Songwriter*
%PBH Entertainment, 2910 Poston Ave, Nashville, TN 37203, USA

Waring, Todd — *Actor*
%Don Buchwald Assoc, 10 E 44th St, #500, New York, NY 10017, USA

Warioba, Joseph — *Prime Minister, Tanzania*
%Regional Administration Minister's Office, Dar es Salaam, Tanzania

Wark, Robert R — *Museum Curator*
%Huntington Library & Art Gallery, 1151 Oxford Rd, San Marino, CA 91108, USA

Warlock, Billy — *Actor*
6822 Lasaine Ave, Van Nuys, CA 91406, USA

Warmerdam, Cornelius (Dutch) — *Track Athlete*
3976 N 1st St, Fresno, CA 93726, USA

Warnecke, John Carl — *Architect*
300 Broadway, San Francisco, CA 94133, USA

Warner, David — *Actor*
%Julian Belfrage, 46 Albermarle St, London W1X 4PP, England

Warner, Douglas A, III — *Financier*
%J P Morgan & Co, 60 Wall St, New York, NY 10005, USA

Warner, John Christian — *Educator, Physical Chemist*
%St Barnabas Village, #411-A, 5850 Meridian Rd, Gibsonia, PA 15044, USA

Warner, Karl — *Track Athlete*
167 Heritage Rd, Rochester, NY 14617, USA

Warner, Malcolm-Jamal — *Actor*
PO Box 69646, Los Angeles, CA 90069, USA

Warner, Margaret — *Commentator*
%"MacNeil/Lehrer Newshour" Show, WNET-TV, 356 W 58th St, New York, NY 10019, USA

Warner, Philip G — *Editor*
%Houston Chronicle, Editorial Dept, 801 Texas Ave, Houston, TX 77002, USA

Warner, Todd — *Sculptor*
155 NW 11th St, Boca Raton, FL 33432, USA

Warner, Tom — *Television Producer*
%Carsey-Warner Productions, 4024 Radford Ave, Bldg 3, Studio City, CA 91604, USA

Warner, William W — *Writer*
2243 47th St NW, Washington, DC 20007, USA

Warnes, Jennifer — *Singer, Songwriter*
%Donald Miller, 12746 Kling St, Studio City, CA 91604, USA

Warnke, Paul C — *Government Official*
5037 Garfield St NW, Washington, DC 20016, USA

Warren, Frederick M — *Architect*
66 Cambridge Terrace, Christchurch 1, New Zealand

Warren, Jennifer — *Actress*
1675 Old Oak Rd, Los Angeles, CA 90049, USA

Warren, Kenneth S — *Physician*
%Picower Medical Research Institute, 350 Community Dr, Manhasset, NY 11030, USA

Warren, L D — *Editorial Cartoonist*
1815 William Howard Taft Rd, #203, Cincinnati, OH 45206, USA

Warren, Lesley Ann — *Actress*
%Passionflower, 2934 Beverly Glen Circle, #372, Los Angeles, CA 90077, USA

Warren, Michael — *Actor*
189 Greenfield Ave, Los Angeles, CA 90049, USA

Warren, Tom — *Triathlete*
2393 La Marque, Pacific Beach, CA 92109, USA

Warren, W Michael, Jr — *Businessman*
%Energen Corp, 2101 6th Ave N, Birmingham, AL 35203, USA

Warren, William D — *Businessman*
%National Re Corp, 777 Long Ridge Rd, Stamford, CT 06902, USA

Warrick, Ruth — *Actress*
903 Park Ave, New York, NY 10021, USA

Warshaw, Jerry — *Businessman*
%Presidential Life Insurance, 69 Lydecker St, Nyack, NY 10960, USA

Warshaw, Steven G — *Businessman*
%Chiquita Brands International, 250 E 5th St, Cincinnati, OH 45202, USA

W

Warfield - Warshaw

Warwick, Dionne — *Singer*
1583 Lindacrest Dr, Beverly Hills, CA 90210, USA

Washburn, Barbara — *Mapologist*
220 Somerset St, Belmont, MA 02178, USA

Washburn, Beverly — *Actress*
5201 Sale Ave, Woodland Hills, CA 91364, USA

Washburn, H Bradford, Jr — *Museum Official, Explorer*
220 Somerset St, Belmont, MA 02178, USA

Washburn, Sherwood L — *Anthropologist*
2797 Shasta Rd, Berkeley, CA 94708, USA

Washington, Claudell — *Baseball Player*
12 Charles Hill Rd, Orinda, CA 94563, USA

Washington, Denzel — *Actor*
4701 Sencola Ave, Toluca Lake, CA 91602, USA

Washington, Eugene (Gene) — *Football Player*
2725 Jewell Lane, Plymouth, MN 55447, USA

Washington, Gene A — *Football Player*
1177 California St, #1131, San Francisco, CA 94108, USA

Washington, Grover, Jr — *Jazz Saxophonist*
%Zane Mgmt, Bellevue, Broad & Walnut, #600, Philadelphia, PA 19102, USA

Washington, Joe — *Football Player*
Meadow Lark, 4 Treadwell Court, Lutherville, MD 21093, USA

Wasim Akram — *Cricketer*
%Lancashire Cricket Club, Old Trafford, Manchester M16 0PX, England

Wasmeier, Markus — *Skier*
83727 Schliersee, Germany

Wasmosy, Juan Carlos — *President, Paraguay*
%Palacio de Gobierno, Ave Mariscal Lopez, Asuncion, Paraguay

Wass, Ted — *Actor*
11733 Valleycrest Rd, Studio City, CA 91604, USA

Wasserburg, Gerald J — *Geophysicist*
1207 Arden Rd, Pasadena, CA 91106, USA

Wasserman, Dale — *Playwright*
Casa Blanca Estates, #37, Paradise Valley, AZ 95253, USA

Wasserman, Dan — *Editorial Cartoonist*
%Boston Globe, Editorial Dept, 135 Morrissey Blvd, Boston, MA 02128, USA

Wasserman, Lew R — *Entertainment Executive*
911 N Foothill Rd, Beverly Hills, CA 90210, USA

Wasserman, Rob — *Jazz Bassist*
%Steep Productions, 64 Molino Ave, Mill Valley, CA 94941, USA

Wasserman, Robert H — *Physiologist, Veterinarian*
%Cornell University, Veterinary Medicine College, Ithaca, NY 14853, USA

Wasserstein, Bruce — *Financier*
%Wasserstein Perella Group, 31 W 52nd St, #2700, New York, NY 10019, USA

Wasserstein, Wendy — *Playwright*
%Royce Carlton Inc, 866 United Nations Plaza, #4030, New York, NY 10017, USA

Watanabe, Milio — *Computer Scientist*
%Nippon Electric Co, Computer Labs, 5-33-1 Shiba, Tokyo, Japan

Watanabe, Moriyuki — *Businessman*
%Mazda Motor Corp, 3-1 Shinchi, Fuchucho, Akigun, Hiroshima 730-91, Japan

Watanabe, Sadao — *Jazz Saxophonist*
%Front Page News, 18509 Wellesley Ct, Sonoma, CA 95476, USA

Watanabe, Takeo — *Businessman*
%Mitsubishi Oil Co, 1-2-4 Toranomon, Minatoku, Tokyo 100, Japan

Watanabe, Youji — *Architect*
1-6-13 Hirakawacho, Chiyodaku, Tokyo, Japan

Waterman, Felicity — *Actress*
160 E Mountain Dr, Santa Barbara, CA 93108, USA

Waters, John — *Movie Director*
10 W Highfield Rd, Baltimore, MD 21218, USA

Waters, John B — *Government Official*
405 Burridge Waters Edge, Sevierville, TN 37862, USA

Waters, Kenneth R — *Businessman*
%MicroAge Inc, 2308 S 55th St, Tempe, AZ 85280, USA

Waters, Lou — *Commentator*
%Cable News Network, News Dept, 1050 Techwood Dr NW, Atlanta, GA 30318, USA

Waters, Richard — *Publisher*
20 Somerset Downs, St Louis, MO 63124, USA

Waters, Roger — *Singer, Bassist (Pink Floyd)*
%Ten Tenths Mgmt, 106 Gifford St, London N1 ODF, England

Waterston, Sam — *Actor*
RR Box 197, Easton St, West Cornwall, CT 06796, USA

Wathan, John D — *Baseball Manager*
1401 Deer Run Trail, Blue Springs, MO 64015, USA

Wathen, Thomas W — *Businessman*
%Pinkerton's Inc, 15910 Ventura Blvd, Encino, CA 91436, USA

Watkin, David — *Cinematographer*
6 Sussex Mews, Brighton BN2 1GZ, England

Watkins, Carlene — *Actress*
104 Fremont Place W, Los Angeles, CA 90005, USA

Watkins, Dean A — *Businessman*
%Watkins-Johnson Co, 3333 Hillview Ave, Palo Alto, CA 94304, USA

Watkins, John P — *Businessman*
%Food Lion Inc, 2110 Executive Dr, Salisbury, NC 28147, USA

Watkins, Lloyd I — *Economist*
RR 13, PO Box 111, Bloomington, IL 61704, USA

Watkins, Tasker — *WW II British Army Hero (VC), Judge*
5 Pump Court, Middle Temple, London EC4, England

Watkinson of Woking, Harold A — *Government Official, England*
Tyma House, Bosham Near Chichester, Sussex, England

Watley, Jody — *Singer*
%Levine/Schneider, 433 N Camden Dr, Beverly Hills, CA 90210, USA

Watrous, Bill — *Jazz Trombonist*
%Thomas Cassidy Inc, 0366 Horseshoe Dr, Basalt, CO 81621, USA

Watson Richardson, Pokey — *Swimmer*
4960 Maunalani Circle, Honolulu, HI 96816, USA

Watson, Albert M — *Photographer*
777 Washington St, New York, NY 10014, USA

Watson, Alberta — *Actress*
400 S Beverly Dr, #216, Beverly Hills, CA 90212, USA

Watson, Alexander F — *Diplomat*
%State Department, 2201 "C" St NW, Washington, DC 20520, USA

Watson, Arthel (Doc) — *Singer, Guitarist*
%Folklore Productions, 1671 Appian Way, Santa Monica, CA 90401, USA

Watson, Bobby — *Jazz Saxophonist*
%Abby Hoffer Ents, 233 1/2 E 48th St, New York, NY 10017, USA

Watson, Bobs — *Actor*
2700 Montrose Ave, Montrose, CA 91020, USA

Watson, Cecil J — *Physician*
%Abbott Northwestern Hospital, 2727 Chicago Ave, Minneapolis, MN 55407, USA

Watson, Elizabeth M — *Law Enforcement Official*
%Houston Police Department, Chief's Office, 61 Riesner St, Houston, TX 77002, USA

Watson, Harry — *Hockey Player*
20 Jonquil Crescent, Markham ON L3P 1T4, Canada

Watson, James D — *Nobel Medicine Laureate*
Bungtown Rd, Cold Spring Harbor, NY 11724, USA

Watson, James L — *Judge*
%US Court of International Trade, 1 Federal Plaza, New York, NY 10278, USA

Watson, Kenneth M — *Physicist, Oceanographer*
PO Box 9726, Rancho Santa Fe, CA 92067, USA

Watson, Martha — *Track Athlete*
5509 Royal Vista Lane, Las Vegas, NV 89129, USA

Watson, Mills — *Actor*
2824 Dell Ave, Venice, CA 90291, USA

Watson, Ned G — *Businessman*
%Jacobs Engineering Group, 251 S Lake Ave, Pasadena, CA 91101, USA

Watson, Paul — *Environmental Activist*
%Sea Shepherd Conservation Society, 1314 2nd St, Santa Monica, CA 90401, USA

Watson, Paul — *Photographer*
%Toronto Star, Editorial Dept, 1 Yonge St, Toronto ON M5E 1E6, Canada

Watson, Raymond L — *Entertainment Executive*
%Walt Disney Co, 500 S Buena Vista St, Burbank, CA 91521, USA

Watson, Stephen E — *Businessman*
%Dayton Hudson Corp, 777 Nicollet Mall, Minneapolis, MN 55402, USA

Watson, Thomas S (Tom) — *Golfer*
Commerce Tower, 911 Main St, #1313, Kansas City, MO 64105, USA

W

Waters - Watson

W

Watt, James G — *Secretary, Interior*
1800 N Spirit Dance Rd, Jackson Hole, WY 83001, USA

Watt, Tom — *Hockey Coach*
%Toronto Maple Leafs, 60 Carlton St, Toronto ON M5B 1L1, Canada

Wattenberg, Ben J — *Demographer*
%American Enterprise Institute, 1150 17th St NW, Washington, DC 20036, USA

Watters, Rickey — *Football Player*
%Philadelphia Eagles, 3501 S Broad St, Philadelphia, PA 19148, USA

Watterson, Bill — *Cartoonist (Calvin & Hobbes)*
%Universal Press Syndicate, 4900 Main St, #900, Kansas City, KS 64112, USA

Watterson, John B (Brett) — *Astronaut*
2508 Via Anacapa, Palos Verdes Estates, CA 90274, USA

Wattleton, A Faye — *Association Executive, Entertainer*
%Fischer-Ross Agency, 250 W 57th St, New York, NY 10107, USA

Watts, Andre — *Concert Pianist*
205 W 57th St, New York, NY 10019, USA

Watts, Charles R (Charlie) — *Drummer (Rolling Stones)*
%Rupert Lowenstein, 2 King St, London SW1Y 6QL, England

Watts, Claudius E, III — *Educator, Army General*
%The Citadel, President's Office, Charleston, SC 29409, USA

Watts, David H — *Businessman*
%Granite Construction Inc, 585 W Beach St, Watsonville, CA 95076, USA

Watts, Ernie — *Art Director, Stage Designer*
%International Creative Mgmt, 40 W 57th St, New York, NY 10019, USA

Watts, Ernie — *Jazz Tenor Saxophonist*
%Richard Barz Assoc, Rt 1, Box 91, Tannersville, PA 18372, USA

Watts, Glenn E — *Labor Leader*
%Communications Workers of America, 501 3rd St NW, Washington, DC 20001, USA

Watts, Heather — *Ballerina*
%New York City Ballet, Lincoln Center Plaza, New York, NY 10023, USA

Watts, Helen J — *Opera Singer*
Rock House, Wallis, Ambleston, Haverford-West, Dyfed SA62 5RA, Wales

Watts, Quincy — *Track Athlete*
%First Team Marketing, 10100 Santa Monica Blvd, #460, Los Angeles, CA 90067, USA

Watts, Stanley H — *Basketball Coach*
205 E 2950th St N, Provo, UT 84604, USA

Waugh, Auberon A — *Writer*
Combe Florey House, Combe Florey, Taunton, Somerset, England

Waugh, John S — *Chemist*
%Massachusetts Institute of Technology, Chemistry Dept, Cambridge, MA 02139, USA

Waxenberg, Alan M — *Publisher*
%Good Housekeeping Magazine, 959 8th Ave, New York, NY 10019, USA

Waxman, Al — *Actor*
87 Forest Hill Rd, Toronto ON M4V 2L6, Canada

Way, Alva O — *Businessman*
%IBJ Schroeder Bank & Trust Co, 1 State St, New York, NY 10004, USA

Wayans, Damon — *Actor*
12140 Summit Court, Beverly Hills, CA 90210, USA

Wayans, Keenen Ivory — *Movie Director, Actor*
16405 Mulholland Dr, Los Angeles, CA 90049, USA

Wayborn, Kristina — *Actress*
409 N Camden Dr, #105, Beverly Hills, CA 90210, USA

Wayland, Len — *Actor*
%Brooke Dunn Oliver, 9169 Sunset Blvd, #202, Los Angeles, CA 90069, USA

Wayne, June — *Artist*
1108 N Tamarind Ave, Los Angeles, CA 90038, USA

Wayne, Patrick — *Actor*
10502 Whipple St, North Hollywood, CA 91602, USA

Wazzan, Chafiq al- — *Prime Minister, Lebanon*
Rue Haroun El-Rashid, Immeuble Wazzan, Bierut, Lebanon

Weatherbie, Charlie — *Football Coach*
%Utah State University, Athletic Dept, Logan, UT 84322, USA

Weatherly, Shawn — *Actress*
12203 Octagon St, Los Angeles, CA 90049, USA

Weathers, Carl — *Actor*
10960 Wilshire Blvd, #826, Los Angeles, CA 90024, USA

Weatherspoon, Clarence — *Basketball Player*
%Philadelphia 76ers, Veterans Stadium, PO Box 25040, Philadelphia, PA 19147, USA

W

Weatherstone, Dennis — *Financier*
%J P Morgan Co, 60 Wall St, New York, NY 10005, USA

Weaver, Dennis — *Actor*
13867 County Road 1, Ridgway, CO 81432, USA

Weaver, Earl S — *Baseball Manager*
501 Cypress Pointe Dr W, Hollywood, FL 33027, USA

Weaver, Fritz — *Actor*
161 W 75th St, New York, NY 10023, USA

Weaver, James — *Cartoonist*
6251 Winthrop Ave, #12, Indianapolis, IN 46220, USA

Weaver, Robby — *Actor*
%Artists Group, 10100 Santa Monica Blvd, #2490, Los Angeles, CA 90067, USA

Weaver, Robert C — *Secretary, Housing & Urban Development*
215 E 68th St, New York, NY 10021, USA

Weaver, Sigourney — *Actress*
200 W 57th St, #1306, New York, NY 10019, USA

Weaver, Sylvester L (Pat), Jr — *Television Executive*
818 Deerpath Rd, Santa Barbara, CA 93108, USA

Weaver, Warren E — *Chemist*
7607 Horsepen Rd, Richmond, VA 23229, USA

Weaver, Warren W — *Financier*
%Commerce Bancshares, 1000 Walnut St, Kansas City, MO 64106, USA

Webb, Carl B — *Financier*
%First Nationwide Bank, 135 Main St, San Francisco, CA 94105, USA

Webb, Chloe — *Actress*
1244 Arden Rd, Pasadena, CA 91106, USA

Webb, Coyt — *Businessman*
%Southwestern Public Service, Tyler & 6th, Amarillo, TX 79170, USA

Webb, Jimmy — *Songwriter*
%Jimmy Webb Music Co, 1173-A 2nd Ave, #178, New York, NY 10021, USA

Webb, Lucy — *Comedienne*
1360 N Crescent Heights, #38, Los Angeles, CA 90046, USA

Webb, Richmond J — *Football Player*
%Miami Dolphins, 7500 SW 30th St, Davie, FL 33329, USA

Webb, Spud — *Basketball Player*
%Atlanta Hawks, 1 CNN Center, South Tower, Atlanta, GA 30303, USA

Webb, Tamilee — *Physical Fitness Instructor*
%ESPN-TV, ESPN Plaza, Bristol, CT 06010, USA

Webb, Veronica — *Model, Actress*
%Ford Model Agency, 344 E 59th St, New York, NY 10022, USA

Webber, Chris — *Basketball Player*
%Washington Bullets, Capital Centre, 1 Truman Dr, Landover, MD 20785, USA

Weber, Arnold R — *Educator*
%Northwestern University, President's Office, Evanston, IL 60208, USA

Weber, Bruce — *Photographer*
%Robert Miller Gallery, 41 E 57th St, New York, NY 10022, USA

Weber, Dick — *Bowler*
1305 Arlington Dr, Florissant, MO 63033, USA

Weber, Eugen — *Historian*
11579 Sunset Blvd, Los Angeles, CA 90049, USA

Weber, Pete — *Bowler*
1305 Arlington Dr, Florissant, MO 63033, USA

Weber, Robert M — *Cartoonist*
%New Yorker Magazine, 20 W 43rd St, New York, NY 10036, USA

Weber, Roy E — *Financier*
3340 Riverbend Dr, Ann Arbor, MI 48105, USA

Weber, Stephen L — *Educator*
%State University of New York, President's Office, Oswego, NY 13126, USA

Weber, Steven — *Actor*
2991 Hollyridge Dr, Los Angeles, CA 90068, USA

Weber, William P — *Businessman*
%Texas Instruments, 13500 North Central Expressway, Dallas, TX 75243, USA

Webster, Alexander (Alex) — *Football Player*
16 Shady Lane, Tequesta, FL 33469, USA

Webster, Mike — *Football Player, Coach*
%Pittsburgh Steelers, 3 Rivers Stadium, 300 Stadium Circle, Pittsburgh, PA 15212, USA

Webster, R Howard — *Publisher, Baseball Executive*
%Toronto Globe & Mail, 444 Front St W, Toronto ON M5V 2S9, Canada

Weatherstone - Webster

W

Webster, William H   *Law Enforcement Official*
4777 Dexter St NW, Washington, DC 20007, USA

Wechsler, Herbert   *Attorney, Educator*
179 E 70th St, New York, NY 10021, USA

Weddington, Sarah R   *Attorney*
709 W 14th St, Austin, TX 78701, USA

Wedemeyer, Herman C   *Football Player*
%Servco Pacific Inc, 900 Fort Street Mall, #500, Honolulu, HI 96813, USA

Wedgeworth, Ann   *Actress*
70 Riverside Dr, New York, NY 10024, USA

Wedgwood, C Veronica   *Historian*
Whitegate, Alciston Near Polegate, Sussex BN26 6UN, England

Weed, Maurice James   *Composer*
Givens Estates, Villa 21-F, Sweeten Creek Rd, Asheville, NC 28803, USA

Weege, Reinhold   *Television Producer*
199 E Lake Shore Dr #3-E, Chicago, IL 60611, USA

Weekly, John W   *Businessman*
%Mutual of Omaha Co, Mutual of Omaha Plaza, Omaha, NE 68175, USA

Weeks, Charles R   *Financier*
%Citizens Banking Corp, 1 Citizens Banking Center, Flint, MI 48502, USA

Weeks, John R   *Architect*
39 Jackson's Lane, Highgate, London N6 5SR, England

Weese, Harry M   *Architect*
118 N 1st St, Aspen, CO 81611, USA

Wefald, Jon   *Educator*
%Kansas State University, President's Office, Manhattan, KS 66506, USA

Wegman, William G   *Artist, Photographer*
431 E 6th St, New York, NY 10009, USA

Wegner, Hans   *Furniture Designer*
Tinglevej 17, 2820 Gentof'tte, Denmark

Wehmeier, Helge H   *Businessman*
%Bayer Corp, Mellon Center, 500 Grant St, Pittsburgh, PA 15219, USA

Wehrli, Roger R   *Football Player*
46 Fox Meadows Court, St Charles, MO 63303, USA

Weibel, Robert   *Pediatrician*
%University of Pennsylvania Med School, Pediatrics Dept, Philadelphia, PA 19104, USA

Weibring, D A   *Golfer*
1316 Garden Grove Court, Plano, TX 75075, USA

Weide, William W   *Businessman*
%Fleetwood Enterprises, 3125 Myers St, Riverside, CA 92503, USA

Weidemann, Jakob   *Artist*
Ringsveen, 2600 Lillehammer, Norway

Weidenbaum, Murray L   *Government Official, Economist*
6231 Rosebury Ave, St Louis, MO 63105, USA

Weidenfeld of Chelsea, Arthur G   *Publisher*
9 Chelsea Embankment, London SW3, England

Weider, Joe   *Publisher*
%Weider Health & Fitness, 21100 Erwin St, Woodland Hills, CA 91367, USA

Weidinger, Christine   *Opera Singer*
%Bielefelder Opernhaus, 33602 Bielefeld, Germany

Weidlinger, Paul   *Civil Engineer*
301 E 47th St, New York, NY 10017, USA

Weidman, Jerome   *Writer*
1230 Park Ave, New York, NY 10128, USA

Weidner, William P   *Businessman*
%Pratt Hotel Corp, 2 Galleria Tower, 13455 Noel Rd, Dallas, TX 75240, USA

Weikl, Bernd   *Opera Singer*
%Lies Askonas Ltd, 186 Drury Lane, London WC2B 5QD, England

Weiland (Scott)   *Singer (Stone Temple Pilots), Songwriter*
%Atlantic Records, 9229 Sunset Blvd, #900, Los Angeles, CA 90069, USA

Weilgos, Stanley C   *Financier*
%Northwestern Savings & Loan, 2300 N Western Ave, Chicago, IL 60647, USA

Weill, Claudia B   *Movie Director*
2800 Seattle Dr, Los Angeles, CA 90046, USA

Weill, Richard L   *Financier*
%MBIA Inc, 113 King St, Armonk, NY 10504, USA

Weill, Sanford I   *Businessman, Lawyer*
%Travelers Inc, 65 E 55th St, New York, NY 10022, USA

Wein, George — *Musical Producer*
%Festival Productions, 311 W 74th St, New York, NY 10023, USA

Weinbach, Arthur F — *Businessman*
%Automatic Data Processing, 1 ADP Blvd, Roseland, NJ 07068, USA

Weinberg, Alvin M — *Physicist*
111 Moylan Lane, Oak Ridge, TN 37830, USA

Weinberg, John L — *Financier*
%Goldman Sachs Co, 85 Broad St, New York, NY 10004, USA

Weinberg, Robert A — *Cancer Researcher, Biochemist*
%Whitehead Institute, 9 Cambridge Center, Cambridge, MA 02142, USA

Weinberg, Serg — *Businessman*
%Willcox & Gibbs Inc, 150 Alhambra Circle, Coral Gables, FL 33134, USA

Weinberg, Steven — *Nobel Physics Laureate*
%University of Texas, Physics Dept, Austin, TX 78712, USA

Weinberger, Caspar W — *Secretary, Defense & HEW; Publisher*
%Forbes Magazine, 60 5th Ave, New York, NY 10011, USA

Weinbrecht, Donna — *Skier*
%General Delivery, West Milford, NJ 07480, USA

Weiner, Art — *Football Player*
404 Kimberly Dr, Greensboro, NC 27408, USA

Weiner, Gerry — *Government Official, Canada*
%Cab du Ministre du Multiculturalisme, Ottawa ON K1A 0M5, Canada

Weiner, Timothy E — *Journalist*
%New York Times, Editorial Dept, 1627 "I" St NW, Washington, DC 20006, USA

Weiner, Walter H — *Financier*
%Republic New York Corp, 452 5th Ave, New York, NY 10018, USA

Weingarten, Reid — *Attorney*
%Steptoe & Johnson, 1330 Connecticut Ave NW, Washington, DC 20036, USA

Weinmeister, Arnie — *Football Player*
PO Box 70149, Seattle, WA 98107, USA

Weinstein, Arnold A — *Playwright, Lyricist*
%Columbia University, English Dept, New York, NY 10027, USA

Weinstein, Irwin M — *Internist, Hematologist*
9509 Heather Rd, Beverly Hills, CA 90210, USA

Weintraub, Jacob — *Art Gallery Owner*
%Weintraub Gallery, 988 Madison Ave, New York, NY 10021, USA

Weintraub, Jerry — *Movie Producer*
%Jerry Weintraub Productions, Lorimar Plaza, Burbank, CA 91505, USA

Weir, Bob — *Guitarist (Grateful Dead)*
%Grateful Dead, PO Box 1073, San Rafael, CA 94915, USA

Weir, Gillian C — *Concert Organist, Harpsichordist*
78 Robin Way, Tilehurst, Berks RG3 5SW, England

Weir, Judith — *Composer*
%Chester Music, 8/9 Frith St, London W1V 5TZ, England

Weir, Morton W — *Educator*
%Illinois University Foundation, Harker Hall, 1305 W Green St, Urbana, IL 61801, USA

Weir, Peter L — *Movie Director*
Post Office, Palm Beach NSW 2108, Australia

Weis, Robert E — *Businessman*
%Weis Markets, 1000 S 2nd St, Sunbury, PA 17801, USA

Weisberg, Ruth — *Artist*
2421 3rd St, Santa Monica, CA 90405, USA

Weisbrod, Burton A — *Economist*
%Northwestern University, Urban Affairs Center, Evanston, IL 60208, USA

Weisenburger, Randall J — *Businessman*
%Collins & Aikman Corp, 701 McCullough Dr, Charlotte, NC 28262, USA

Weiser, Irving — *Financier*
%Inter-Regional Financial Group, 60 S 6th St, Minneapolis, MN 55402, USA

Weisgall, Hugo D — *Composer, Conductor*
81 Maple Dr, Great Neck, NY 11021, USA

Weiskantz, Lawrence — *Psychologist*
%Oxford University, Experimental Psychology Dept, Oxford OX1 3UD, England

Weiskopf, Tom — *Golfer*
7580 E Gray Rd, Scottsdale, AZ 85260, USA

Weisman, Ben — *Composer*
4527 Alla Rd, #3, Marina del Rey, CA 90292, USA

Weisman, Neil J — *Financier*
%Chilmark Capital Corp, 139 W Saddle River Rd, Saddle River, NJ 07458, USA

W

Wein - Weisman

W

Weisman, Sam — *Actor*
10490 Selkirk Lane, Los Angeles, CA 90077, USA

Weisner, Maurice F — *Navy Admiral*
351 Woodbine Dr, Pensacola, FL 32503, USA

Weiss, Kenneth C — *Financier*
%Hyperian Capital Managment, 520 Madison Ave, New York, NY 10022, USA

Weiss, Melvyn I — *Attorney*
%Milberg Weiss Bershad, 1 Pennsylvania Plaza, New York, NY 10119, USA

Weiss, Michael — *Businessman*
%Limited Inc, 3 Limited Parkway, Columbus, OH 43230, USA

Weiss, Morry — *Businessman*
%American Greetings Corp, 1, American Rd, Cleveland, OH 44144, USA

Weiss, Paul — *Philosopher*
2000 "N" St NW, Washington, DC 20036, USA

Weiss, Theodore R — *Poet, Editor*
%Princeton University, QRL Poetry Series, 26 Haslet St, Princeton, NJ 08540, USA

Weissenberg, Alexis — *Concert Pianist*
%Columbia Artists Mgmt Inc, 165 W 57th St, New York, NY 10019, USA

Weisskopf, Victor F — *Physicist*
20 Bartlett Terrace, Newton, MA 02159, USA

Weissman, Robert E — *Businessman*
%Dun & Bradstreet Corp, 299 Park Ave, New York, NY 10171, USA

Weisz, William J — *Businessman*
%Motorola Inc, 1303 E Algonquin Rd, Schaumburg, IL 60196, USA

Weitz, Bruce — *Actor*
5030 Arundel Dr, Woodland Hills, CA 91364, USA

Weitz, John — *Fashion Designer*
%John Weitz Designs, 600 Madison Ave, New York, NY 10022, USA

Weitz, Paul J — *Astronaut*
3086 N Tam Oshanter Dr, Flagstaff, AZ 86004, USA

Weitzman, Howard L — *Attorney*
%Katten Muchin Zavis Weitzman, 1999 Ave of Stars, #1400, Los Angeles, CA 90067, USA

Weizman, Ezer — *President, Israel; Air Force General*
2 Haddekel St, Caesarea, Israel

Welbergen, Johannes C — *Businessman*
%Standard Elektrik Lorenz, Hellmuth-Hirth-Str 42, 70435 Stuttgart, Germany

Welch, Elisabeth — *Actress, Singer*
4-A Carpenters Close, London SW1, England

Welch, John F (Jack), Jr — *Businessman*
%General Electric Co, 3135 Easton Turnpike, Fairfield, CT 06431, USA

Welch, Kevin — *Singer, Songwriter*
%Dream Street Mgmt, 1460 4th St, #205, Santa Monica, CA 90401, USA

Welch, Raquel — *Actress*
540 Evelyn Place, Beverly Hills, CA 90210, USA

Welch, Robert L (Bob) — *Baseball Player*
1962 Jefferson St, San Francisco, CA 94123, USA

Welch, Tahnee — *Actress*
134 Duane St, #400, New York, NY 10013, USA

Weld, Tuesday — *Actress*
PO Box 367, Valley Stream, NY 11582, USA

Weld, William F — *Governor, MA*
%Governor's Office, State House, Boston, MA 02133, USA

Weldon, Fay — *Writer*
24 Ryland Rd, London NW5 3EA, England

Wellek, Rene — *Educator*
45 Fairgrounds Rd, Woodbridge, CT 06525, USA

Weller, Michael — *Playwright*
%Rosenstone/Wender, 3 E 48th St, New York, NY 10017, USA

Weller, Peter — *Actor*
%Bill Treusch Assoc, 853 7th Ave, #9-A, New York, NY 10019, USA

Weller, Ronny — *Weightlifter*
%VfL Duisburg-Sud, Am Forkelsgraben 55, 47259 Duisburg, Germany

Weller, Thomas H — *Nobel Medicine Laureate*
56 Winding River Rd, Needham, MA 02192, USA

Weller, Walter — *Conductor*
Doblinger Hauptstr 40, 1190 Vienna, Austria

Welling, Paul A — *Coast Guard Admiral*
Commander, Atlantic Area, Governor's Island, New York, NY 10004, USA

Weisman - Welling

Wellman, Mark — *Rock Climber*
%Visitor's Bureau, Yosemite National Park, CA 95389, USA

Wellman, William, Jr — *Actor*
410 N Barrington Ave, Los Angeles, CA 90049, USA

Wells, A Stanton — *Businessman*
%Barnes Group, 123 Main St, Bristol, CT 06010, USA

Wells, Carole — *Actress*
%Burton Moss Agency, 8827 Beverly Blvd, #L, Los Angeles, CA 90048, USA

Wells, Dawn — *Actress*
4616 Ledge Ave, North Hollywood, CA 91602, USA

Wells, Harry K — *Businessman*
%McCormick Co, 18 Loveton Circle, Sparks, MD 21152, USA

Wells, Herman B — *Educator*
1321 E 10th St, Bloomington, IN 47408, USA

Wells, Hoyt M — *Businessman*
%Goodyear Tire & Rubber Co, 1144 E Market St, Akron, OH 44316, USA

Wells, J Lyle — *Financier*
%UMB Financial Corp, 1010 Grand Ave, Kansas City, MO 64106, USA

Wells, James M, III — *Financier*
%Crestar Financial Corp, 919 E Main St, Richmond, VA 23219, USA

Wells, Kitty — *Singer*
264 Old Hickory Blvd, Madison, TN 35117, USA

Wells, Wayne — *Wrestler*
PO Box 3938, Edmond, OK 73083, USA

Welser-Most, Franz — *Conductor*
%Artists Management Co, Bildgass, 9494 Schaan, Liechtenstein

Welsh, George T — *Football Player, Coach*
%University of Virginia, Athletic Dept, Charlottesville, VA 22903, USA

Welsh, Moray M — *Concert Cellist*
28 Somerfield Ave, Queens Park, London NW6 6JY, England

Welsome, Eileen — *Journalist*
%Albuquerque Tribune, Editorial Dept, 7777 Jefferson NE, Albuquerque, NM 87109, USA

Welting, Ruth L — *Opera Singer*
%Bob Lombardo Assoc, 1 Harkness Plaza, 61 W 62nd St, New York, NY 10023, USA

Welty, John D — *Educator*
4411 N Van Ness Blvd, Fresno, CA 93704, USA

Wences, Senor — *Ventriloquist, Comedian*
204 W 55th St, #701-A, New York, NY 10019, USA

Wendelin, Rudolph A — *Cartoonist (Smokey the Bear)*
4516 7th St N, Arlington, VA 22203, USA

Wendelstedt, Harry H, Jr — *Baseball Umpire*
88 S St Andrews Dr, Ormond Beach, FL 32174, USA

Wenden, Michael — *Swimmer*
%Palm Beach Currumbin Center, Thrower Dr, Palm Beach Queens, Australia

Wenders, Wim — *Movie Director*
%Road Movies Filmproduktion, Potsdamerstr 199, 10785 Berlin, Germany

Wendt, Gary C — *Financier*
%General Electric Capital Corp, 260 Long Ridge Rd, Stamford, CT 06927, USA

Wendt, George — *Actor*
3856 Vantage Ave, Studio City, CA 91604, USA

Wenge, Ralph — *Commentator*
%Cable News Network, News Dept, 1050 Techwood Dr NW, Atlanta, GA 30318, USA

Wenner, Jann S — *Publisher*
%Straight Arrow Publications, 1290 Ave of Americas, New York, NY 10104, USA

Went, Frits W — *Botanist*
Lodestar Lane 3450, Reno, NV 89503, USA

Went, Joseph J — *Marine Corps General*
%Office of Assistant Commandant, Marine Corps Hdqs, Washington, DC 20380, USA

Wente, Jean R — *Businessman*
%California State Automobile Assn, PO Box 422940, San Francisco, CA 94142, USA

Wentz, Howard B, Jr — *Businessman*
%Tambrands Inc, 777 Westchester Ave, White Plains, NY 10604, USA

Wenzel, Andreas — *Skier*
Oberhul 151, Liechtenstein-Gamprin, Liechtenstein

Wenzel, Fred W — *Businessman*
13315 Fairfield Square Dr, Chesterfield, MO 63017, USA

Wenzel, Hanni — *Skier*
%General Delivery, Planken, Liechtenstein

Werber, William M (Bill) *Baseball Player*
11812 Quail Village Way, Naples, FL 33999, USA

Werner, Charles G *Editorial Cartoonist*
4445 Brown Rd, Indianapolis, IN 46226, USA

Werner, Ernest G G *Businessman*
%Shell Petroleum Co, 30 Carel Van Bylandtaan, The Hague, Netherlands

Werner, Helmut *Businessman*
%Daimler Benz AG, Mercedesstr 136, 70327 Stuttgart, Germany

Werner, Michael *Art Dealer*
%Michael Werner Ltd, 21 E 67th St, New York, NY 10021, USA

Werner, Pierre *Prime Minister, Luxembourg*
2 Rond-Point Robert Schuman, Luxembourg

Werner, Roger L, Jr *Television Executive*
%Prime Sports Ventures, 10000 Santa Monica Blvd, Los Angeles, CA 90067, USA

Werries, E Dean *Businessman*
%Fleming Companies, 6301 Waterford Blvd, Oklahoma City, OK 73118, USA

Wertheim, Jorge *Association Executive*
%UNESCO, Director's Office, UN Plaza, New York, NY 10017, USA

Wertheimer, Fredric M *Association Executive*
3502 Macomb St NW, Washington, DC 20016, USA

Wertheimer, Linda *Commentator*
%National Public Radio, News Dept, 2025 "M" St NW, Washington, DC 20036, USA

Wertheimer, Thomas *Entertainment Executive*
%MCA Inc, 100 Universal City Plaza, Universal City, CA 91608, USA

Werthen, Hans L O *Businessman*
%AB Electrolux, 105 45 Stockholm, Sweden

Wertmuller, Lina *Movie Director*
Piazza Clotilde, 00196 Rome, Italy

Wesker, Arnold *Writer*
37 Ashley Rd, London N19 3AG, England

Wesley, Kassie *Actress*
%"One Life to Live" Show, ABC-TV, 33 W 60th St, New York, NY 10023, USA

Wesselmann, Tom *Artist*
RD 1, Box 36, Long Eddy, NY 12760, USA

Wessels, Leon *Government Official, South Africa*
%Foreign Affairs Ministry, Private Bag X-152, Pretoria 001, South Africa

West, Adam *Actor*
PO Box 3477, Ketchum, ID 83340, USA

West, B Kenneth *Financier*
134 Green Bay Rd, #205, Winnetka, IL 60093, USA

West, Cornel *Theologian*
%Princeton University, Theology Dept, Princeton, NJ 08544, USA

West, Ernest E *Korean War Army Hero (CMH)*
912 Adams Ave, Wurtland, KY 41144, USA

West, Jake *Labor Leader*
%International Assn of Iron Workers, 1750 New York Ave NW, Washington, DC 20006, USA

West, Jerry A *Basketball Player, Executive*
%Los Angeles Lakers, Forum, PO Box 10, Inglewood, CA 90306, USA

West, John C *Governor, SC*
PO Drawer 13, Hilton Head Island, SC 29938, USA

West, Mark *Basketball Player*
%Detroit Pistons, Palace, 2 Championship Dr, Auburn Hills, MI 48057, USA

West, Morris L *Writer*
PO Box 102, Avalon NSW 2107, Australia

West, Robert H *Businessman*
%Butler Manufacturing Co, BMA Tower, Penn Valley Park, Kansas City, MO 64141, USA

West, Thomas L, Jr *Businessman*
%Variable Annuity Life Insurance, 2929 Allen Parkway, Houston, TX 77019, USA

West, Timothy *Actor*
%James Sharkey Assoc, 21 Golden Square, London W1R 3PA, England

West, William S *Businessman*
%West Co, 101 Gordon Dr, Lionville, PA 19341, USA

Westbrook, Michael *Football Player*
%Washington Redskins, 21300 Redskin Park Dr, Ashburn, VA 22011, USA

Westbrook, Peter *Fencer*
15 Washington Pl, #1-F, New York, NY 10003, USA

Westerberg, Verne E *Publisher*
%Vogue Magazine, 350 Madison Ave, New York, NY 10017, USA

W

Werber - Westerberg

Westerfield, Putney	Publisher
10 Greenview Lane, Hillsborough, CA 94010, USA	
Westheimer, David K	Writer
11722 Darlington Ave, #2, Los Angeles, CA 90049, USA	
Westheimer, Frank H	Chemist
3 Berkeley St, Cambridge, MA 02138, USA	
Westheimer, Ruth S	Sex Therapist, Psychologist
900 W 190th St, New York, NY 10040, USA	
Westin, Av	Television Executive, Journalist
%King World Productions, 1700 Broadway, New York, NY 10019, USA	
Westlake, Donald E	Writer
%Knox Burger Assoc, 39 1/2 Washington Square S, New York, NY 10012, USA	
Westling, Jon	Educator
7 Churchill Lane, Lexington, MA 02173, USA	
Westman, John W	Financier
%Banc One Arizona, 241 N Central Ave, Phoenix, AZ 85004, USA	
Westmoreland, James	Actor
8019 1/2 W Norton Ave, Los Angeles, CA 90046, USA	
Westmoreland, William C	Army General
107 1/2 Tradd St, Charleston, SC 29401, USA	
Weston, J Fred	Educator
258 Tavistock Ave, Los Angeles, CA 90049, USA	
Weston, Jack	Actor
420 Madison Ave, #1400, New York, NY 10017, USA	
Weston, Josh S	Businessman
%Automatic Data Processing, 1 ADP Blvd, Roseland, NJ 07068, USA	
Weston, Paul	Musician, Composer
%Hanover Music Corp, PO Box 6296, Beverly Hills, CA 90212, USA	
Weston, Randy	Jazz Pianist
PO Box 749, Maplewood, NJ 07040, USA	
Westphal, James A	Space Scientist
%California Institute of Technology, Planetary Sciences Dept, Pasadena, CA 91125, USA	
Westphal, Paul	Basketball Player, Coach
%Phoenix Suns, 201 E Jefferson St, Phoenix, AZ 85004, USA	
Westwood, Vivienne	Fashion Designer
The Lanterns, #3, Old School House, Bridge Lane, London SW11 3AD, England	
Wetherbee, James D	Astronaut
%NASA, Johnson Space Center, 2101 NASA Rd, Houston, TX 77058, USA	
Wetherill, George W	Geophysicist
%Carnegie Institution, Terrestrial Magnetism Dept, Washington, DC 20015, USA	
Wethington, Charles T, Jr	Educator
%University of Kentucky, President's Office, Lexington, KY 40506, USA	
Wetsel, Gary	Businessman
%Burland International, 100 Borland Way, Scotts Valley, CA 95066, USA	
Wetter, Friedrich Cardinal	Religious Leader
Kardinal-Faulhaber-Str 7, 80333 Munich, Germany	
Wetterau, Theodore C	Businessman
1401 S Brentwood Blvd, #760, St Louis, MO 63144, USA	
Wettig, Patricia	Actress
522 Arbamar Place, Pacific Palisades, CA 90272, USA	
Wetzel, Gary G	Vietnam War Army Hero (CMH)
PO Box 84, Oak Creek, WI 53154, USA	
Wetzel, John	Basketball Coach
%Portland Trail Blazers, 700 NE Multnomah St, #600, Portland, OR 97232, USA	
Wexler, Anne	Government Official
1317 "F" St NW, #600, Washington, DC 20004, USA	
Wexler, Haskell	Cinematographer
1341 Ocean Ave, #111, Santa Monica, CA 90401, USA	
Wexler, Jacqueline G	Educator
222 Park Ave S, New York, NY 10003, USA	
Wexler, Jerry	Record Producer
%Warner Bros Records, 75 Rockefeller Plaza, New York, NY 10019, USA	
Wexner, Leslie H	Businessman
%Limited Inc, 3 Limited Parkway, Columbus, OH 43230, USA	
Weyand, Frederick C	Army General
2121 Ala Wai Blvd, PH 1, Honolulu, HI 96815, USA	
Weyerhaeuser, George H	Businessman
%Weyerhaeuser Co, 33663 32nd Ave S, Tacoma, WA 98023, USA	

W

Westerfield - Weyerhaeuser

Weymouth, Tina *Bassist (Talking Heads)*
%Overland Productions, 1775 Broadway, #700, New York, NY 10019, USA

Whalley-Kilmer, Joanne *Actress*
PO Box 362, Tesuque, NM 87574, USA

Wharton, Clifton R, Jr *Educator, Government Official*
%State Department, 2201 "C" St NW, Washington, DC 20520, USA

Wharton, David *Swimmer*
%Ohio State University, Athletic Dept, Columbus, OH 43210, USA

Wheat, Francis M *Attorney*
%Gibson Dunn Crutcher, 333 S Grand Ave, Los Angeles, CA 90071, USA

Wheatley, E H *Publisher*
%Vancouver Sun, 2250 Granville St, Vancouver BC V6H 3G2, Canada

Wheatley, Tyrone *Football Player*
%New York Giants, Giants Stadium, East Rutherford, NJ 07073, USA

Wheaton, David *Tennis Player*
4430 Manitou Rd, Tonka Bay, MN 55331, USA

Wheaton, Wil *Actor*
2603 Seapine Lane, La Crescenta, CA 91214, USA

Wheeler, C E *Labor Leader*
%Railway Carmen Brotherhood, 4929 Main St, Kansas City, MO 64112, USA

Wheeler, Daniel S *Editor*
%American Legion Magazine, 700 N Pennsylvania St, Indianapolis, IN 46204, USA

Wheeler, H Anthony *Architect*
Hawthornbank House, Dean Village, Edinburgh EH4 3BH, Scotland

Wheeler, Harold A *Radio Engineer*
4900 Telegraph Rd, #523, Ventura, CA 93003, USA

Wheeler, John A *Physicist*
1904 Meadow Lane, Highstown, NJ 08520, USA

Wheeler, Thomas B *Businessman*
%Massachusetts Mutual Life Insurance, 1295 State St, Springfield, MA 01111, USA

Wheeler-Bennett, R C *Businessman*
%Thomas Borthwick & Sons, St John's Lane, London EC1M 4BX, England

Whelan, Wendy *Ballerina*
%New York City Ballet, Lincoln Center Plaza, New York, NY 10023, USA

Whelchel, Lisa *Actress*
17647 Orna Dr, Granada Hills, CA 91344, USA

Whinnery, Barbara *Actress*
%Gold Marshak Assoc, 3500 W Olive Ave, #1400, Burbank, CA 91505, USA

Whinnery, John R *Electrical Engineer*
1 Daphne Court, Orinda, CA 94563, USA

Whipple, Fred L *Astronomer*
35 Elizabeth Rd, Belmont, MA 02178, USA

Whipple, Thomas A *Businessman*
%Kash n' Karry Food Stores, 6422 Harney Rd, Tampa, FL 33610, USA

Whishaw, Anthony *Artist*
7-A Albert Place, Victoria Rd, London W8 5PD, England

Whitacre, Edward E, Jr *Businessman*
%Southwestern Bell Corp, 175 E Houston, San Antonio, TX 78205, USA

Whitacre, John *Businessman*
%Nordstrom Inc, 1501 5th Ave, Seattle, WA 98101, USA

Whitaker, Forest *Actor*
10345 W Olympic Blvd, #200, Los Angeles, CA 90064, USA

Whitaker, Jack *Sportscaster*
PO Box 342, Bridgehampton, NY 11932, USA

Whitaker, Louis R (Lou) *Baseball Player*
803 Pipe, Martinsville, VA 24112, USA

Whitbread, Fatima *Track Athlete*
5 Hemley Rd, Orsett, Essex, England

Whitcomb, Edgar D *Governor, IN*
PO Box 23, Hayden, IN 47245, USA

White of Rhymney, Eirene L *Government Official, England*
64 Vandon Court, Petty France, London SW1H 9HF, England

White, Alan R *Philosopher*
%The University, Hull HU6 7RX, England

White, Alvin S (Al) *Test Pilot*
201 Pecan Lane, Georgetown, TX 78628, USA

White, Barry *Singer, Songwriter*
14248 Valley Vista, Sherman Oaks, CA 91423, USA

White, Betty *Actress, Comedienne*
PO Box 3713, Granada Hills, CA 91394, USA

White, Byron R *Supreme Court Justice, Football Player*
%US Supreme Court, 1 1st St NE, Washington, DC 20543, USA

White, Charles *Football Player, Administrator*
%University of Southern California, Heritage Hall, Los Angeles, CA 90089, USA

White, Danny *Football Player*
%White Companies, 12655 N Central Expressway, #115, Dallas, TX 75243, USA

White, Dwight *Football Player, Financier*
%Daniels & Bell Inc, 9 Wall St, New York, NY 10005, USA

White, Edmund V *Writer*
%Maxine Groffsky, 2 5th Ave, New York, NY 10011, USA

White, Edward A (Ed) *Football Player*
%General Delivery, Julian, CA 92036, USA

White, Frank *Baseball Player*
5335 W 96th St, Shawnee Mission, KS 66207, USA

White, Frank *Governor, AR*
1 Andover Dr, #7, Little Rock, AR 72227, USA

White, Gilbert F *Geographer*
624 Pearl St, #302, Boulder, CO 80302, USA

White, Jesse *Actor*
1944 Glendon Ave, #304, Los Angeles, CA 90025, USA

White, John H *Photographer*
%Chicago Sun-Times, 401 N Wabash Ave, Chicago, IL 60611, USA

White, Joy *Singer*
%Rothbaum & Garner, 1101 17th Ave S, Nashville, TN 37212, USA

White, Judith M *Biologist*
%University of San Francisco, Biology Dept, San Francisco, CA 94117, USA

White, Karyn *Singer*
%Warner Bros Records, 3300 Warner Blvd, Burbank, CA 91505, USA

White, Kate *Editor*
%Redbook Magazine, Editorial Dept, 224 W 57th St, New York, NY 10019, USA

White, Lari *Singer, Songwriter*
%William Carter Career Mgmt, 1114 17th Ave S, #204, Nashville, TN 37212, USA

White, Lorenzo *Football Player*
%Cleveland Browns, 80 1st Ave, Berea, OH 44017, USA

White, Marco P *Chef*
The Restaurant, Knightsbridge, London SW1, England

White, Martha G *Publisher*
%London Free Press, 369 York St, London ON N6A 4G1, Canada

White, Michael S *Movie, Theater Producer*
13 Duke St, St James's, London SW1 6DB, England

White, Mike *Football Coach*
%Oakland Raiders, Oakland Coliseum, Oakland, CA 94621, USA

White, Nera *Basketball Player*
Rt 3, Box 165, Lafayette, TN 37083, USA

White, Raymond P, Jr *Oral Surgeon*
1506 Velma Rd, Chapel Hill, NC 27514, USA

White, Reginald H (Reggie) *Football Player*
%Green Bay Packers, 1265 Lombardi Ave, Green Bay, WI 54304, USA

White, Robert L *Labor Leader*
%National Postal Employees Alliance, 1644 11th St NW, Washington, DC 20001, USA

White, Robert M *Test Pilot, Air Force General*
PO Box 2488, APO, AE, NY 09063, USA

White, Robert M *Meteorologist*
Somerset House II, 5610 Wisconsin Ave, #1506, Bethesda, MD 20815, USA

White, Robert M, II *Journalist*
1824 Phelps Place NW, #1813, Washington, DC 20008, USA

White, Roy H *Baseball Player*
297-101 Kinderkamack, Oradell, NJ 07649, USA

White, Sammy *Football Player*
%Minnesota Vikings, 9520 Viking Dr, Eden Prairie, MN 55344, USA

White, Sherman E *Football Player*
PO Box 1856, Pebble Beach, CA 93953, USA

White, Slappy *Comedian*
933 N La Brea Ave, Los Angeles, CA 90038, USA

White, Steven A *Navy Admiral, Businessman*
%Stone & Webster Engineering Corp, 245 Summer St, Boston, MA 02210, USA

W

White - White

W

White, Tim D — *Anthropologist*
%University of California, Human Evolutionary Studies Lab, Berkeley, CA 94720, USA

White, Vanna — *Entertainer, Model*
2600 Larmar Rd, Los Angeles, CA 90068, USA

White, Willard W — *Opera Singer*
10 Montague Ave, London SE4 1YP, England

Whitehead, Alfred K — *Labor Leader*
%International Assn of Fire Fighters, 1750 New York Ave NW, Washington, DC 20006, USA

Whitehead, George W — *Mathematician*
25 Bellevue Rd, Arlington, MA 02174, USA

Whitehead, John C — *Financier, Government Official*
%AEA Investors, 65 E 55th St, New York, NY 10022, USA

Whitehead, John C — *Research Executive*
%Brookings Institute, 1775 Massachusetts Ave NW, Washington, DC 20036, USA

Whitehead, Richard F — *Navy Admiral*
%American Cage & Machine Co, 135 S LaSalle St, Chicago, IL 60603, USA

Whitelaw of Penrith, William S A — *Government Official, England*
%House of Lords, Westminster, London SW1A 0PW, England

Whitelaw, Billie — *Actress*
Rose Cottage, Plum St, Glensford , Suffolk C010 7PX, England

Whiteley, Benjamin R — *Businessman*
%Standard Insurance, 1100 SW 6th Ave, Portland, OR 97204, USA

Whitemore, Willet F, Jr — *Cancer Researcher*
2 Hawthorne Lane, Plandome, NY 11030, USA

Whitfield, Lynn — *Actress*
6950 Oporto Dr, Los Angeles, CA 90068, USA

Whitfield, Mal — *Track Athlete*
1322 28th St SE, Washington, DC 20020, USA

Whitford, Brad — *Guitarist (Aerosmith)*
%Collins Mgmt, 5 Bigelow St, Cambridge, MA 02139, USA

Whiting, Margaret — *Singer*
41 W 58th St, #5-A, New York, NY 10019, USA

Whitlam, E Gough — *Prime Minister, Australia*
Westfield Towers, 100 William St, Sydney NSW 2011, Australia

Whitley, Chris — *Singer*
%Assis/Wechsley Assoc, 955 S Carillo Dr, #300, Los Angeles, CA 90048, USA

Whitley, Michael R — *Businessman*
%KU Energy Corp, 1 Quality St, Lexington, KY 40507, USA

Whitman, Christine Todd — *Governor, NJ*
%Governor's Office, State House, 125 W State St, Trenton, NJ 08608, USA

Whitman, Marina Von Neumann — *Economist*
%University of Michigan, Business Administration Dept, Ann Arbor, MI 48109, USA

Whitman, Slim — *Singer*
1300 Division St, #103, Nashville, TN 37203, USA

Whitman, Stuart — *Actor*
749 San Ysidro Rd, Santa Barbara, CA 93108, USA

Whitmire, Donald B (Don) — *Football Player*
3817 Winterset Dr, Annandale, VA 22003, USA

Whitmire, Melburn G — *Businessman*
%Cardinal Health Inc, 655 Metro Place S, Dublin, OH 43017, USA

Whitmore, James — *Actor*
4990 Puesta del Sol, Malibu, CA 90265, USA

Whitmore, James, Jr — *Actor*
1284 La Brea St, Thousand Oaks, CA 91362, USA

Whitmore, John R — *Financier*
%Bessemer Group, 100 Woodbridge Center Dr, Woodbridge, NJ 07095, USA

Whitney, CeCe — *Actress*
840 N Ogden Dr, Los Angeles, CA 90046, USA

Whitney, Grace Lee — *Actress*
PO Box 69, Coarsegold, CA 93614, USA

Whitney, Hassler — *Educator*
%Institute for Advanced Study, Olden Lane, Princeton, NJ 08540, USA

Whitney, Jane — *Entertainer*
5 TV Place, Needham, MA 02194, USA

Whitney, Ruth R — *Editor*
%Glamour Magazine, Editorial Dept, 350 Madison Ave, New York, NY 10017, USA

Whitsell, Dave — *Football Player*
2441 W 79th St, Long Grove, IL 60047, USA

White - Whitsell

Whitsitt, Robert J — *Basketball Executive*
%Seattle Supersonics, 190 Queen Ave N, PO Box C-900911, Seattle, WA 98109, USA

Whittaker, Roger — *Singer, Songwriter*
%Tembo Music Canada, 284 Church St, Oakville ON L6J 7N2, Canada

Whittingham, Charles A — *Publisher*
11 Woodmill Rd, Chappaqua, NY 10514, USA

Whittingham, Charles E — *Thoroughbred Racing Trainer*
88 Lowell Ave, Sierra Madre, CA 91024, USA

Whittle, Christopher — *Publisher*
%Whittle Communications, 333 W Main Ave, Knoxville, TN 37902, USA

Whitton, Margaret — *Actress*
%William Morris Agency, 151 S El Camino Dr, Beverly Hills, CA 90212, USA

Whitwam, David R — *Businessman*
%Whirlpool Corp, 2000 N State St, Rt 63, Benton Harbor, MI 49022, USA

Whitworth, Kathrynne A (Kathy) — *Golfer*
%General Delivery, Roanoke, TX 76262, USA

Whitworth, William — *Editor*
%Atlantic Monthly Magazine, Editorial Dept, 745 Boylston St, Boston, MA 02116, USA

Whyte, William H — *Writer*
175 E 94th St, New York, NY 10128, USA

Wiatt, James A — *Entertainment Executive*
%International Creative Mgmt, 8942 Wilshire Blvd, Beverly Hills, CA 90211, USA

Wiberg, Kenneth B — *Chemist*
160 Carmalt Rd, Hamden, CT 06517, USA

Wiberg, Pernilla — *Skier*
Katterunsvagen 32, 60 210 Norrkopping, Sweden

Wiborg, James H — *Businessman*
%Univar Corp, 6100 Carillon Point, Kirkland, WA 98033, USA

Wichmann, Herbert — *Government Official, Germany*
Ohnhorstr 29, 22609 Hamburg, Germany

Wichterle, Otto — *Chemist, Inventor (Soft Contact Lens)*
U Andelky 27, 162 00 Prague 6, Czech Republic

Wick, Charles Z — *Government Official*
%US Information Agency, 400 "C" St SW, Washington, DC 20002, USA

Wickenheiser, Robert J — *Educator*
%St Bonaventure University, President's Office, St Bonaventure, NY 14778, USA

Wicker, Thomas G — *Writer, Journalist*
169 E 80th St, New York, NY 10021, USA

Wickes, Mary — *Actress*
2160 Century Park East, #503, Los Angeles, CA 90067, USA

Wickham, John A, Jr — *Army General*
13590 N Fawnbrooke Dr, Tucson, AZ 85737, USA

Wickremesinghe, Ranil — *Prime Minister, Sri Lanka*
%Prime Minister's Office, 150 R A De Mel Mawatha, Colombo 3, Sri Lanka

Wicks, Ben — *Editorial Cartoonist*
38 Yorkville Ave, Toronto ON M4W 1L5, Canada

Widdoes, Kathleen — *Actress*
%Don Buchwald Assoc, 10 E 44th St, #500, New York, NY 10017, USA

Wideman, John Edgar — *Writer*
%University of Massachusetts, English Dept, Amherst, MA 01003, USA

Widerberg, Bo — *Movie Director*
%Svenska Filminstitutet, Kungsgatan 48, Stockholm C, Sweden

Widmark, Richard — *Actor*
%International Creative Mgmt, 8942 Wilshire Blvd, Beverly Hills, CA 90211, USA

Widom, Benjamin — *Chemist*
%Cornell University, Chemistry Dept, Ithaca, NY 14853, USA

Widseth, Edwin C — *Football Player*
1666 Coffman St, #117, St Paul, MN 55108, USA

Wiedemann, Josef — *Architect*
Im Eichgeholz 11, 80997 Munich, Germany

Wiederkehr, Joseph A — *Labor Leader*
%Roofers Waterproofers & Allied Workers, 1125 17th NW, Washington, DC 20036, USA

Wiedorfer, Paul J — *WW II Army Hero (CMH)*
2506 Moore Ave, Baltimore, MD 21234, USA

Wieschaus, Eric F — *Nobel Medicine Laureate*
%Princeton University, Genetics Dept, Princeton, NJ 08544, USA

Wiesel, Elie — *Writer, Nobel Peace Laureate*
200 E 64th St, New York, NY 10021, USA

W

Whitsitt - Wiesel

Wiesel, Torsten N *Nobel Medicine Laureate*
%Rockefeller University, Neurobiolgy Lab, York & 66th, New York, NY 10013, USA

Wiesen, Richard A *Educator*
%D'Youville College, Administrative Offices, 320 Porter Ave, Buffalo, NY 14201, USA

Wiesenthal, Simon *War Crimes Activist*
%Jewish Documentation Center, Salztorgasse 6, 1010 Vienna, Austria

Wiest, Dianne *Actress*
127 W 79th St, New York, NY 10024, USA

Wigdale, James B *Businessman*
%M&I Marshall & Isley Corp, 770 N Water St, Milwaukee, WI 53202, USA

Wiggin, Paul *Football Player, Coach*
5220 Malibu Dr, Edina, MN 55436, USA

Wiggins, James Russell *Editor, Diplomat*
Carlton Cove, HC 63, Box 436, Brooklin, ME 04616, USA

Wigglesworth, Marian McKean *Skier*
%General Delivery, Wilson, WY 83014, USA

Wightman, Arthur S *Mathematician, Physicist*
16 Balsam Lane, Princeton, NJ 08540, USA

Wigle, Ernest D *Cardiologist*
101 College St, Toronto ON M56 1L7, Canada

Wijetunga, Hondoval D B *President, Sri Lanka*
%President's Office, Republic Square, Colombo 1, Sri Lanka

Wilander, Mats *Tennis Player*
%Einar Wilander, Vickersvagen 2, Vaxjo, Sweden

Wilberforce, Richard O *Judge*
8 Cambridge Place, London W8, England

Wilbraham, John H G *Concert Cornetist, Trumpeter*
9 D Cuthbert St, Wells, Somerset BA5 2AW, England

Wilbur, Doreen *Archery Athlete*
1401 W Lincoln Way, Jefferson, IA 50129, USA

Wilbur, Richard P *Poet*
87 Dodswells Rd, Cummington, MA 01026, USA

Wilbur, Richard S *Physician, Association Executive*
PO Box 70, Lake Forest, IL 60045, USA

Wilby, James *Actor*
%International Creative Mgmt, 76 Oxford St, London W1N 0AX, England

Wilcox, David *Singer, Songwriter*
%The Agency, 41 Britain St, #200, Toronto ON M5A 1R7, Canada

Wilcox, Larry *Actor*
10 Appaloosa Lane, Bell Canyon, Canoga Park, CA 91307, USA

Wilcutt, Terence W *Astronaut*
%NASA, Johnson Space Center, 2101 NASA Rd, Houston, TX 77058, USA

Wild, Earl *Concert Pianist*
2233 Fernleaf Lane, Worthington, OH 43235, USA

Wild, Jack *Actor*
%London Mgmt, 2-4 Noel St, London W1V 3RB, England

Wilde, Kim *Singer, Songwriter*
Big M House, 1 Stevenage Rd, Nebworth, Herts SG3 6AN, England

Wilde, Patricia *Ballerina, Artistic Director*
%Pittsburgh Ballet Theater, 2900 Liberty Ave, Pittsburgh, PA 15201, USA

Wildenstein, Daniel L *Art Historian, Dealer*
%Wildenstein Co, 57 Rue la Boetie, 75008 Paris, France

Wilder, Alan *Synthesizer Musician (Depeche Mode)*
PO Box 326, London SW6 6RL, England

Wilder, Billy *Movie Director*
10375 Wilshire Blvd, Los Angeles, CA 90024, USA

Wilder, Don *Cartoonist (Crock)*
%North America Syndicate, 235 E 45th St, New York, NY 10017, USA

Wilder, Gene *Actor, Movie Director*
%Pal-Mel Productions, 1511 Sawtelle Blvd, #155, Los Angeles, CA 90025, USA

Wilder, James *Football Player*
%Washington Redskins, 21300 Redskin Park Dr, Ashburn, VA 22011, USA

Wilder, James *Actor*
%United Talent Agency, 9560 Wilshire Blvd, #500, Beverly Hills, CA 90212, USA

Wilder, L Douglas *Governor, VA*
2509 E Broad St, Richmond, VA 23223, USA

Wildmon, Donald *Social Activist*
%National Federation of Decency, PO Box 1398, Tupelo, MS 38802, USA

Wiles, Andrew — *Mathematician*
%Princeton University, Mathematics Dept, Princeton, NJ 08544, USA

Wiley, Don C — *Biochemist*
%Children's Hospital, Molecular Medicine Lab, 320 Longwood Ave, Boston, MA 02115, USA

Wiley, Lee — *Singer*
%Country Crossroads, 7787 Monterey St, Gilroy, CA 95020, USA

Wiley, Richard E — *Government Official*
3818 Woodrow St, Arlington, VA 22207, USA

Wiley, William T — *Artist*
PO Box 654, Woodacre, CA 94973, USA

Wilford, John Noble, Jr — *Journalist*
232 W 10th St, New York, NY 10014, USA

Wilhelm, J Hoyt — *Baseball Player*
3102 N Himes Ave, Tampa, FL 33607, USA

Wilkening, Laurel L — *Educator*
%University of California, Chancellor's Office, Irvine, CA 92717, USA

Wilkens, Leonard R (Lenny), Jr — *Basketball Player, Coach*
%Atlanta Hawks, 1 CNN Center, South Tower, Atlanta, GA 30303, USA

Wilkerson, Isabel — *Journalist*
%New York Times, Editorial Dept, 229 W 43rd St, New York, NY 10036, USA

Wilkes, Glen — *Basketball Coach*
%Stetson University, Athletic Dept, Campus Box 8359, DeLand, FL 32720, USA

Wilkes, Jamaal — *Basketball Player*
7846 W 81st St, Playa del Rey, CA 90293, USA

Wilkes, Maurice V — *Computer Engineer*
%Olivetti Research Ltd, 24-A Trumpington St, Cambridge CB2 1QA, England

Wilkie, David — *Swimmer*
Oaklands, Queens Hill, Ascot, Berkshire, England

Wilkin, Richard E — *Religious Leader*
%Winebrenner Theological Seminary, 701 E Melrose Ave, Findlay, OH 45840, USA

Wilkins, Gerald — *Basketball Player*
%Vancouver Grizzlies, 788 Beatty St, #300, Vancouver BC V6B 2M1, Canada

Wilkins, Maurice H F — *Nobel Medicine Laureate*
30 St John's Park, London SE3, England

Wilkins, Roger — *Journalist*
%George Mason University, 207 East Building, Fairfax, VA 22030, USA

Wilkinson, Dan — *Football Player*
%Cincinnati Bengals, 200 Riverfront Stadium, Cincinnati, OH 45202, USA

Wilkinson, Geoffrey — *Nobel Chemistry Laureate*
%Imperial College, Chemistry Dept, London SW7 2AY, England

Wilkinson, Harry J — *Businessman*
%SPS Technologies, 101 Greenwood Ave, Jenkintown, PA 19046, USA

Wilkinson, John — *Businessman*
%Connecticut General Life Insurance, 900 Cottage Grove Rd, Bloomfield, CT 06002, USA

Wilkinson, June — *Actress*
3653 Fairesta St, La Crescenta, CA 91214, USA

Wilkinson, Signe — *Editorial Cartoonist*
%Philadelphia Daily News, Editorial Dept, 400 N Broad, Philadelphia, PA 19130, USA

Will, George F — *Columnist*
1208 30th St NW, Washington, DC 20007, USA

Will, Maggie — *Golfer*
217 Maple St, Whiteville, NC 28472, USA

Willard, Fred C — *Actor, Comedian*
%William Morris Agency, 151 S El Camino Dr, Beverly Hills, CA 90212, USA

Willard, Kenneth H (Ken) — *Football Player*
%Ken Willard Assoc, 3071 Viewpoint Rd, Midlothian, VA 23113, USA

Willcocks, David V — *Concert Organist*
13 Grange Rd, Cambridge CB3 9AS, England

Willebrands, Johannes Cardinal — *Religious Leader*
%Council for Promoting Christian Unity, Via dell'Erba I, 00120 Rome, Italy

Willem-Alexander — *Crown Prince, Netherlands*
%Huis ten Bosch, The Hague, Netherlands

Willes, Mark H — *Publisher, Businessman*
%Times Mirror Co, Times Mirror Square, Los Angeles, CA 90053, USA

Willet, E Crosby — *Stained Glass Artist*
%Willet Stained Glass Studios, 10 E Moreland Ave, Philadelphia, PA 19118, USA

Willey, Gordon R — *Archaeologist*
25 Gray Gardens E, Cambridge, MA 02138, USA

W

Wiles - Willey

Willhite, Gerald *Football Player*
5700 Logan St, Denver, CO 80216, USA

William *Prince, England*
%Kensington Palace, London W8, England

William, David *Actor, Theater Director*
194 Langarth St E, London ON N6C 1Z5, Canada

William, Edward *Religious Leader*
%Bible Way Church, 5118 Clarendon Rd, Brooklyn, NY 11203, USA

Williams of Crosby, Shirley *Government Official, England*
%Social & Liberal Democrats, 4 Cowley St, London SW1P 3NB, England

Williams of Elvel, Charles C P *Government Official, England*
48 Thurloe Square, London SW7 2SX, England

Williams, A C *Medical Researcher*
%University of Birmingham, School of Medicine, Birmingham, England

Williams, Andy *Singer*
161 Berms Circle, #3, Branson, MO 65616, USA

Williams, Anson *Actor*
24615 Skyline View Dr, Malibu, CA 90265, USA

Williams, Arthur E *Army General*
Chief of Engineers/CG, USAEC, 20 Massachusetts Ave NW, Washington, DC 20314, USA

Williams, Barry *Actor, Singer*
3646 Reina Court, Calabasas, CA 91302, USA

Williams, Ben *Football Player*
5961 Huntview Dr, Jackson, MS 39206, USA

Williams, Betty *Nobel Peace Laureate*
PO Box 725, Valparaiso, FL 32580, USA

Williams, Billy *Cinematographer*
%Coach House, Hawkshill Place, Esher, Surrey KT10 9HY, England

Williams, Billy Dee *Actor*
2114 Beech Knoll Rd, Los Angeles, CA 90046, USA

Williams, Billy L *Baseball Player*
586 Prince Edward Rd, Glen Ellyn, IL 60137, USA

Williams, Bob *Football Player*
602 Stone Barn Rd, Towson, MD 21286, USA

Williams, Brian *Basketball Player*
%Los Angeles Clippers, Sports Arena, 3939 S Figueroa St, Los Angeles, CA 90037, USA

Williams, C Wayne *Educator*
%University of NY State, Regents College, President's Office, Albany, NY 12203, USA

Williams, Cara *Actress*
146 S Peck Dr, Beverly Hills, CA 90212, USA

Williams, Charles L (Buck) *Basketball Player*
%Portland Trail Blazers, 700 NE Multnomah St, #600, Portland, OR 97232, USA

Williams, Cindy *Actress*
6712 Portshead Rd, Malibu, CA 90265, USA

Williams, Clarence, III *Actor*
%Flick East-West Talents, 9057 Nemo St, #A, West Hollywood, CA 90069, USA

Williams, Clarke M *Businessman*
%Century Telephone Enterprises, 100 Century Park Dr, Monroe, LA 71203, USA

Williams, Clyde *Religious Leader*
%Christian Methodist Episcopal Church, 4466 E Presley Blvd, Memphis, TN 38116, USA

Williams, Colleen *Commentator*
%KNBC-TV, News Dept, 3000 W Alameda Ave, Burbank, CA 91523, USA

Williams, Darnell *Actor*
%Artists Group, 10100 Santa Monica Blvd, #2490, Los Angeles, CA 90067, USA

Williams, Dave H *Businessman*
%Alliance Capital Managment, 1345 Ave of Americas, New York, NY 10105, USA

Williams, Deniece *Singer*
1414 Seabright Dr, Beverly Hills, CA 90210, USA

Williams, Derek T D *Businessman*
%Pall Corp, 2200 Northern Blvd, East Hills, NY 11548, USA

Williams, Dick Anthony *Actor*
%International Creative Mgmt, 8942 Wilshire Blvd, Beverly Hills, CA 90211, USA

Williams, Don *Singer, Songwriter*
%Moress Nanas Shea, 1209 16th Ave S, Nashville, TN 37212, USA

Williams, Donald E *Astronaut*
%Science Applications Int'l, 17049 El Camino Real, #202, Houston, TX 77058, USA

Williams, Doug *Football Player, Coach*
%US Naval Academy, Athletic Dept, Annapolis, MD 21402, USA

Williams, Dudley *Ballet Dancer*
%Alvin Ailey Dance Theatre, 1519 Broadway, New York, NY 10036, USA

Williams, E Virginia *Artistic Director, Choreographer*
%Boston Ballet, 19 Clarendon St, Boston, MA 02116, USA

Williams, Easy *Actor*
%Don Schwartz Assoc, 8749 Sunset Blvd, Los Angeles, CA 90069, USA

Williams, Edy *Model*
1638 Blue Jay Way, Los Angeles, CA 90069, USA

Williams, Elmo *Movie Director, Producer*
1249 Iris St, Brookins, OR 97415, USA

Williams, Eric *Basketball Player*
%Boston Celtics, 151 Merrimac St, #500, Boston, MA 02114, USA

Williams, Erik *Football Player*
%Dallas Cowboys, 1 Cowboys Parkway, Irving, TX 75063, USA

Williams, Esther *Swimmer, Actress*
9377 Readcrest Dr, Beverly Hills, CA 90210, USA

Williams, Gary *Basketball Coach*
%University of Maryland, Athletic Dept, College Park, MD 20742, USA

Williams, George C *Financier*
%Allied Capital Advisers, 1666 "K" St NW, Washington, DC 20006, USA

Williams, Hal *Actor*
8730 Sunset Blvd, #220-W, Los Angeles, CA 90069, USA

Williams, Hank, Jr *Singer, Songwriter*
%Hank Williams Jr Ents, PO Box 850, Paris, TN 38242, USA

Williams, Harold M *Museum Executive*
%J Paul Getty Museum, 17985 Pacific Coast Highway, Malibu, CA 90265, USA

Williams, Harrison A, Jr *Senator, NJ*
PO Box 2, Holland Rd, Bedminster, NJ 07921, USA

Williams, Harvey *Football Player*
%Kansas City Chiefs, 1 Arrowhead Dr, Kansas City, KS 64129, USA

Williams, Hershel W *WW II Marine Corps Hero (CMH)*
3491 Wire Branch Rd, Ona, WV 25545, USA

Williams, Hosea *Religious Leader, Civil Rights Activist*
PO Box 170188, Atlanta, GA 30317, USA

Williams, J Kelley *Businessman*
%First Mississippi Corp, 700 North St, Jackson, MS 39202, USA

Williams, J McDonald *Businessman*
%Trammell Crow Co, Trammell Crow Center, 2001 Ross Ave, Dallas, TX 75201, USA

Williams, Jack K *Medical Administrator*
%Texas Medical Center, 1133 M D Anderson Blvd, Houston, TX 77030, USA

Williams, James (Froggy) *Football Player*
296 Sugarberry Circle, Houston, TX 77024, USA

Williams, James A *Army General*
8928 Maurice Lane, Annandale, VA 22003, USA

Williams, James B *Financier*
%SunTrust Banks, 25 Park Place NE, Atlanta, GA 30303, USA

Williams, James Elliott *Vietnam War Navy Hero (CMH)*
139 Preston Dr, Pawleys Island, SC 29585, USA

Williams, JoBeth *Actress*
%Pasquin, 3529 Beverly Glen Blvd, Sherman Oaks, CA 91423, USA

Williams, Joe *Singer*
3337 Knollwood Court, Las Vegas, NV 89121, USA

Williams, John *Concert Guitarist*
%Harold Holt Ltd, 31 Sinclair Rd, London W14 0NS, England

Williams, John (Hot Rod) *Basketball Player*
%Phoenix Suns, 201 E Jefferson St, Phoenix, AZ 85004, USA

Williams, John A *Writer*
693 Forest Ave, Teaneck, NJ 07666, USA

Williams, John G, Jr *Navy Admiral*
2300 "E" St NW, Washington, DC 20037, USA

Williams, John L *Football Player*
%Pittsburgh Steelers, 3 Rivers Stadium, 300 Stadium Circle, Pittsburgh, PA 15212, USA

Williams, John T *Conductor, Composer*
%Boston Pops Orchestra, Symphony Hall, 301 Massachusetts Ave, Boston, MA 02115, USA

Williams, Joseph D *Businessman*
%Warner-Lambert Co, 201 Tabor Rd, Morris Plains, NJ 07950, USA

Williams, Joseph H *Businessman*
%Williams Companies, 1 Williams Center, Tulsa, OK 74172, USA

Williams, Joseph R *Publisher*
%Memphis Commerical Appeal, 495 Union Ave, Memphis, TN 38103, USA

Williams, L Stanton *Businessman*
%PPG Industries, 5 The Trillium, Pittsburgh, PA 15238, USA

Williams, Lucinda *Singer*
%Metropolitan Entertainment, 7 N Mountain Ave, Montclair, NJ 07042, USA

Williams, Mark *Bowler*
%Professional Bowlers Assn, 1720 Merriman Rd, Akron, OH 44313, USA

Williams, Mary Alice *Commentator*
%NYNEX Corp, Public Relations Dept, 1113 Westchester Ave, White Plains, NY 10604, USA

Williams, Mason *Singer, Pianist*
PO Box 25, Oakbridge, OR 97463, USA

Williams, Matt *Screenwriter*
%Zeiderman, 211 E 48th St, New York, NY 10017, USA

Williams, Matthew D (Matt) *Baseball Player*
10661 Fanfol Lane, Scottsdale, AZ 85258, USA

Williams, Maurice J *Association Executive*
%Overseas Development Council, 1875 Connecticut Ave NW, Washington, DC 20009, USA

Williams, Michael *Actor*
%Julian Belfrage, 46 Albermarle St, London W1X 4PP, England

Williams, Micheal *Basketball Player*
%Minnesota Timberwolves, Target Center, 600 1st Ave N, Minneapolis, MN 55403, USA

Williams, Montel *Entertainer*
%Montel Williams Show, 1481 Broadway, New York, NY 10036, USA

Williams, O L *Religious Leader*
%United Free Will Baptist Church, 1101 University St, Kinston, NC 28501, USA

Williams, Otis *Singer (Temptations)*
%Star Directions, 9255 Sunset Blvd, #610, Los Angeles, CA 90069, USA

Williams, Patrick M *Composer*
3156 Mandeville Canyon Rd, Los Angeles, CA 90049, USA

Williams, Paul *Songwriter, Actor*
8545 Franklin Ave, Los Angeles, CA 90069, USA

Williams, Phillip L *Publisher*
%Times Mirror Co, Times Mirror Square, Los Angeles, CA 90053, USA

Williams, Prince Charles *Boxer*
%Champs Gym, 1243 N 26th St, Philadelphia, PA 19121, USA

Williams, R Neil *Financier*
%Premier BanCorp, 451 Florida St, Baton Rouge, LA 70801, USA

Williams, Redford B, Jr *Internist*
%Duke University Medical School, Box 3708, Durham, NC 27706, USA

Williams, Reggie *Basketball Player*
%Denver Nuggets, McNichols Arena, 1635 Clay St, Denver, CO 80204, USA

Williams, Reginald (Reggie) *Football Player*
540 Madison Ave, #3200, New York, NY 10022, USA

Williams, Richard E *Cartoonist (Pink Panther)*
3193 Cahuenga Blvd W, Los Angeles, CA 90068, USA

Williams, Richard H (Dick) *Baseball Manager*
1608 Starside Dr, Las Vegas, NV 89117, USA

Williams, Robert C *Businessman*
%James River Corp of Virginia, 120 Tredegar St, Richmond, VA 23219, USA

Williams, Robin *Comedian*
1100 Wall Rd, Napa, CA 94558, USA

Williams, Robin M, Jr *Social Scientist*
414 Oak Ave, Ithaca, NY 14850, USA

Williams, Roger *Pianist*
16150 Clear Valley Place, Encino, CA 91436, USA

Williams, Ron *Bowler*
5700 Westchase Dr, North Richland Heights, TX 76180, USA

Williams, Roy *Basketball Coach*
%University of Kansas, Athletic Dept, Allen Field House, Lawrence, KS 66045, USA

Williams, Simon *Actor*
%Jonathan Altaras Assoc, 2 Goodwins Court, London WC2N 4LL, England

Williams, Stacey *Model*
%Next Model Mgmt, 115 E 57th St, #1540, New York, NY 10022, USA

Williams, Stephanie *Actress*
1269 S Orange Dr, #1, Los Angeles, CA 90019, USA

Williams, Stephen *Anthropologist*
1017 Foothills Trail, Santa Fe, NM 87505, USA

Williams, Sterling L *Businessman*
%Sterling Software, 8050 North Central Expressway, Dallas, TX 75206, USA
Williams, Steven *Actor*
%Geddes Agency, 1201 Greenacre Blvd, West Hollywood, CA 90046, USA
Williams, T Franklin *Physician*
%Monroe Community Hospital, Director's Office, Rochester, NY 14620, USA
Williams, Theodore *Businessman*
%Bell Industries, 11812 San Vicente Blvd, Los Angeles, CA 90049, USA
Williams, Theodore S (Ted) *Baseball Player, Manager*
PO Box 1629, Hernando, FL 34442, USA
Williams, Thomas S Cardinal *Religious Leader*
Viard, 21 Eccleston Hill, PO Box 198, Wellington 1, New Zealand
Williams, Tonya Lee *Actress*
%Artists Agency, 10000 Santa Monica Blvd, #305, Los Angeles, CA 90067, USA
Williams, Treat *Actor*
215 W 78th St, #10-A, New York, NY 10024, USA
Williams, Ulis *Track Athlete*
%Compton Community College, Dean of Students Office, Compton, CA 90221, USA
Williams, Van *Actor*
PO Box 4758, Ketchum, ID 83340, USA
Williams, Vanessa *Model, Singer, Actress*
50 Old Farm Rd, Chappaqua, NY 10514, USA
Williams, W Clyde *Religious Leader*
%Christian Methodist Episcopal Church, 2805 Shoreland Dr, Atlanta, GA 30331, USA
Williams, Walt *Basketball Player*
%Sacramento Kings, 1 Sports Parkway, Sacramento, CA 95834, USA
Williams, Walter Ray, Jr *Bowler*
%Professional Bowlers Assn, 1720 Merriman Rd, Akron, OH 44313, USA
Williams, Wendy Lian *Diver*
%Advantage International, 1025 Thomas Jefferson St NW, #450, Washington 20007, USA
Williams, Wendy O *Singer*
PO Box 2039, New York, NY 10013, USA
Williams, William A *Astronaut*
%Environmental Protection Agency, 200 SW 35th St, Corvallis, OR 97333, USA
Williams, William J *Businessman*
7640 Waterfall Trail, Chagrin Falls, OH 44022, USA
Williams, Willie L *Law Enforcement Official*
%Los Angeles Police Dept, 150 S Los Angeles St, Los Angeles, CA 90012, USA
Willams-Dourdan, Roshumba *Model*
%Bethann Model Mgmt, 36 N Moore St, #36-N, New York, NY 10013, USA
Williamson, Ernest L *Businessman*
%Louisiana Land & Exploration Co, 909 Poydras St, New Orleans, LA 70112, USA
Williamson, Fred *Actor, Football Player*
3920 N Lake Shore Dr, Chicago, IL 60613, USA
Williamson, Henry G, Jr *Financier*
%BB&T Financial Corp, 233 W Nash St, Wilson, NC 27893, USA
Williamson, Keith *Air Force Marshal, England*
%National Westminster Bank, Fakenham, Norfolk, England
Williamson, Marianne *Psychotherapist*
%Los Angeles Center for Living, 650 N Robertson Blvd, Los Angeles, CA 90069, USA
Williamson, Nicol *Actor*
%International Creative Mgmt, 76 Oxford St, London W1N 0AX, England
Williamson, Ron W *Financier*
%Citibank (South Dakota), 701 E 60th St N, Sioux Falls, SD 57104, USA
Williamson, Samuel R, Jr *Educator*
%University of the South, President's Office, Sewanee, TN 37375, USA
Willingham, Tyrone *Football Coach*
%Stanford University, Athletic Dept, Stanford, CA 94395, USA
Willis, Austin *Actor*
%BDP Assoc, 10637 Burbank Blvd, North Hollywood, CA 91601, USA
Willis, Bruce *Actor*
1453 3rd St, #420, Santa Monica, CA 90401, USA
Willis, Gordon *Cinematographer*
11849 W Olympic Blvd, #100, Los Angeles, CA 90064, USA
Willis, Kelly *Singer*
%ATS Mgmt, 8306 Appalachian Dr, Austin, TX 78759, USA
Willis, Kevin A *Basketball Player*
%Miami Heat, Miami Arena, Miami, FL 33136, USA

W

Williams - Willis

W

Willis, William K (Bill)　　　　　　　　　　　　　　　*Football Player*
1158 S Waverly, Columbus, OH 43227, USA

Willison, Bruce G　　　　　　　　　　　　　　　　　*Financier*
%First Interstate Bancorp, 633 W 5th St, Los Angeles, CA 90071, USA

Willoch, Kare I　　　　　　　　　　　　　　*Prime Minister, Norway*
Blokkaveien 6-B, 0282 Oslo, Norway

Willoughby, H William　　　　　　　　　　　　　　　*Financier*
%CRI Inc, 11200 Rockville Pike, Rockville, MD 20852, USA

Wills Moody Roark, Helen　　　　　　　　　　　　*Tennis Player*
PO Box 22095, Carmel, CA 93922, USA

Wills, Garry　　　　　　　　　　　　　　　　　　　*Writer*
%Northwestern University, History Dept, Evanston, IL 60201, USA

Wills, Maurice M (Maury)　　　　　　　　　　　*Baseball Player*
30100 Town Center Dr, #0209, Laguna Niguel, CA 92677, USA

Wilmer, Harry A　　　　　　　　　　　　　　　　*Psychiatrist*
%Texas Health Science Center, Psychiatric Dept, San Antonio, TX 78284, USA

Wilmers, Robert G　　　　　　　　　　　　　　　　*Financier*
%Manufacturers & Traders Trust, 1 M&T Plaza, Buffalo, NY 14203, USA

Wilmore, Melvin A　　　　　　　　　　　　　　*Businessman*
%Ross Stores, 8333 Central Ave, Newark, CA 94560, USA

Wilmouth, Robert K　　　　　　　　　　　　　　　*Financier*
%LaSalle National Corp, 135 S LaSalle St, Chicago, IL 60603, USA

Wilson, A N　　　　　　　　　　　　　　　　　　　*Writer*
21 Arlington Rd, London NW1 7ER, England

Wilson, Alexander G (Sandy)　　　　　　　　　　　*Composer*
2 Southwell Gardens, #4, London SW7 4SB, England

Wilson, Allan B　　　　　　　　　　　*Molecular Biologist*
%University of California, Molecular Biology Dept, Berkeley, CA 94724, USA

Wilson, Ann　　　　　　　　　　　　　　　*Singer (Heart)*
%Levine/Schneider, 433 N Camden Dr, Beverly Hills, CA 90210, USA

Wilson, August　　　　　　　　　　　　　　　　　*Writer*
PO Box 21368, Seattle, WA 98111, USA

Wilson, Blenda J　　　　　　　　　　　　　　　　*Educator*
%California State University, President's Office, Northridge, CA 91330, USA

Wilson, Brian D　　　　　　　　*Singer (Beach Boys), Songwriter*
2049 Century Park East, #2450, Los Angeles, CA 90067, USA

Wilson, C Kemmons　　　　　　　　　　　　　*Businessman*
3615 S Galloway Dr, Memphis, TN 38111, USA

Wilson, Carl　　　　　　　　　　*Singer (Beach Boys), Songwriter*
8860 Evan View Dr, Los Angeles, CA 90069, USA

Wilson, Cassandra　　　　　　　　　　　　　　　　*Singer*
%Bennett Morgan Assoc, 1282 Rt 376, Wappingers Falls, NY 12590, USA

Wilson, Colin A St John　　　　　　　　　　　　　*Architect*
Highbury Crescent Rooms, 70 Ronalds Rd, London N5 1XW, England

Wilson, Colin H　　　　　　　　　　　　　　　　　*Writer*
Tetherdown, Trewallock Lane, Gorran Haven, Cornwall, England

Wilson, David　　　　　　　　　　　　　　　　　　*Actor*
%Susan Smith Assoc, 121 N San Vicente Blvd, Beverly Hills, CA 90211, USA

Wilson, David Mackenzie　　　　　　　　　　*Museum Director*
%The Lifeboat House, Castletown, Isle of Man

Wilson, Demond　　　　　　　　　　　　　　　　　*Actor*
%Church of God in Christ, Fort Washington, MD 20022, USA

Wilson, Donald M　　　　　　　　　　　　　　　*Publisher*
4574 Province Line Rd, Princeton, NJ 08540, USA

Wilson, Doug　　　　　　　　　　　　　　　*Hockey Player*
%Chicago Blackhawks, Chicago Stadium, 1800 W Madison St, Chicago, IL 60612, USA

Wilson, Earl L　　　　　　　　　　　　　　*Baseball Player*
PO Box 662, Ponchatoula, LA 70454, USA

Wilson, Earle L　　　　　　　　　　　　　　*Religious Leader*
%Wesleyan Church, PO Box 50434, Indianapolis, IN 46250, USA

Wilson, Edward O　　　　　　　　　　　　*Zoologist, Writer*
9 Foster Rd, Lexington, MA 02173, USA

Wilson, Eric C T　　　　　　　　　*WW II British Army Hero (VC)*
Woodside Cottage, Stowell, Sherborne, Dorset, England

Wilson, Eugene　　　　　　　　　　　　　　　　　*Skier*
PO Box 912, Coleraine, NH 55722, USA

Wilson, F Paul　　　　　　　　　　　　　　　　　*Writer*
%Albert Zuckerman, Writers House, 21 W 26th St, New York, NY 10010, USA

Wilson, F Perry — *Chemical Engineer*
11656 Lake House Court, North Palm Beach, FL 33408, USA
Wilson, Flip — *Comedian*
21970 Pacific Coast Highway, Malibu, CA 90265, USA
Wilson, Gahan — *Cartoonist, Writer*
%Michelle Urry, 747 3rd Ave, New York, NY 10017, USA
Wilson, Gary L — *Businessman*
%Northwest Airlines Corp, 5101 Northwest Dr, St Paul, MN 55111, USA
Wilson, Geoffrey H — *Businessman*
%Southern Electric PLC, Littlewick Green, Maidenhead, Berkshire, England
Wilson, George B (Mike), Jr — *Football Player, Army General*
1062 Lancaster Ave, Rosemont, PA 19010, USA
Wilson, Gerald — *Jazz Trumpeter, Composer*
4625 Brynhurst Ave, Los Angeles, CA 90043, USA
Wilson, Harold E — *Korean War Marine Corps Hero (CMH)*
125 Shadydale Dr, Lexington, SC 29073, USA
Wilson, Harry C — *Religious Leader*
%Wesleyan Church Int'l Center, 6060 Castleway West Dr, Indianapolis, IN 46250, USA
Wilson, J Lawrence — *Businessman*
%Rohm & Haas Co, 100 Independence Mall W, Philadelphia, PA 19106, USA
Wilson, J Tylee — *Businessman*
PO Box 2057, Ponte Vedra, FL 32004, USA
Wilson, James M — *Geneticist*
%Univ of Pennsylvania Medical Center, Genetics Dept, Philadelphia, PA 19104, USA
Wilson, James Q — *Educator*
%University of California, Graduate Management School, Los Angeles, CA 90024, USA
Wilson, James R — *Businessman*
%Thiokol Corp, 2475 Washington Blvd, Ogden, UT 84401, USA
Wilson, Jean D — *Physician*
%Southwestern Internal Medical Center, 5323 Harry Hines Blvd, Dallas, TX 75235, USA
Wilson, Jeannie — *Actress*
General Delivery, Hailey, ID 83333, USA
Wilson, John D — *Educator*
%Washington & Lee University, President's Office, Lexington, VA 24450, USA
Wilson, Johnnie E — *Army General*
Deputy Chief of Staff Logistics, HdqsUSArmy, Pentagon, Washington, DC 20310, USA
Wilson, Kenneth G — *Nobel Physics Laureate*
%Ohio State University, Physics Dept, Columbus, OH 43210, USA
Wilson, Lanford — *Playwright*
%International Creative Mgmt, 40 W 57th St, New York, NY 10019, USA
Wilson, Lawrence F (Larry) — *Football Player, Executive*
%Arizona Cardinals, 8701 S Hardy Dr, Tempe, AZ 85284, USA
Wilson, Linda S — *Educator*
%Radcliffe College, President's Office, Cambridge, MA 02138, USA
Wilson, Louis H, Jr — *WW II Marine Corps Hero (CMH); General*
1030 Wembly Rd, San Marino, CA 91108, USA
Wilson, Malcolm — *Governor, NY*
50 Main St, #7, White Plains, NY 10606, USA
Wilson, Marc D — *Football Player*
10820 157th Ave NE, Woodinville, WA 98072, USA
Wilson, Mary — *Singer (Supremes)*
1601 E Flamingo Rd, Las Vegas, NV 89110, USA
Wilson, Mary — *Singer (Heart)*
%Levine/Schneider, 433 N Camden Dr, Beverly Hills, CA 90210, USA
Wilson, Melanie — *Actress*
12946 Dickens St, Studio City, CA 91604, USA
Wilson, Michael H — *Government Official, Canada*
%Industry & Science Dept, 235 Queen's St, Ottawa ON K1A OH5, Canada
Wilson, Nancy — *Singer*
%Bowen Agency, 504 W 168th St, New York, NY 10032, USA
Wilson, Neal C — *Religious Leader*
%Seventh-Day Adventists, 12501 Old Columbus Pike, Silver Spring, MD 20904, USA
Wilson, Olin C — *Astronomer*
616 Terry Lane, West Lafayette, IN 47906, USA
Wilson, Pete — *Governor, Senator, CA*
%Governor's Office, State Capitol Building, #100, Sacramento, CA 95814, USA
Wilson, Ralph, Jr — *Football Executive*
%Buffalo Bills, 1 Bills Dr, Orchard Park, NY 14127, USA

W

Wilson - Wilson

W

Wilson, Robert E (Bobby)	Football Player
811 W Lubbock St, Brenham, TX 77833, USA	
Wilson, Robert M	Actor
%Byrd Hoffman Foundation, 131 Varick St, #908, New York, NY 10013, USA	
Wilson, Robert N	Businessman
%Johnson & Johnson, 1 Johnson & Johnson Plaza, New Brunswick, NJ 08904, USA	
Wilson, Robert R	Physicist
916 Stewart Ave, Ithaca, NY 14850, USA	
Wilson, Robert W	Nobel Physics Laureate
9 Valley Point Dr, Holmdel, NJ 07733, USA	
Wilson, Sarah	Religious Leader
%Friends United Meeting, 101 Quaker Hill Dr, Richmond, IN 47374, USA	
Wilson, Sheree J	Actress
7218 S Jan Mar Court, Dallas, TX 75230, USA	
Wilson, Sloan	Writer
PO Box 510, Colonial Beach, VA 22443, USA	
Wilson, William J	Sociologist
PO Box 197, Lincoln, NM 88338, USA	
Wilson, Willie J	Baseball Player
3905 W 110th St, Leawood, KS 66211, USA	
Wilson, Woody	Cartoonist (Rex Morgan, MD)
%North America Syndicate, 235 E 45th St, New York, NY 10017, USA	
Wilson-Johnson, David R	Opera Singer
28 Englefield Rd, London N1 4ET, England	
Wiltshire, Richard W	Businessman
%Home Beneficial Life Insurance, 3901 W Broad St, Richmond, VA 23230, USA	
Wiltshire, Richard W, Jr	Businessman
%Home Beneficial Life Insurance, 3901 W Broad St, Richmond, VA 23230, USA	
Wilzig, Siggi B	Financier
%Trust Co of New Jersey, 35 Journal Square, Jersey City, NJ 07306, USA	
Wimmer, Brian	Actor
3434 Bengal Blvd, Salt Lake Cty, UT 84121, USA	
Wimmer, Maria	Actress
Osserstr 16, 81679 Munich, Germany	
Winans, BeBe	Singer
%DAS Communications, 83 Riverside Dr, New York, NY 10024, USA	
Winans, CeCe	Singer
%DAS Communications, 83 Riverside Dr, New York, NY 10024, USA	
Winbergh, Gosta	Opera Singer
%Columbia Artists Mgmt Inc, 165 W 57th St, New York, NY 10019, USA	
Winbush, Angela	Singer, Songwriter
%Bowen Agency, 504 W 168th St, New York, NY 10032, USA	
Wincer, Simon G	Movie Director
PO Box 241, Toorak, VIC 3142, Australia	
Winder, Sammy	Football Player
%Winder Construction Co, 4823 Green Crossing Rd, Jackson, MS 39213, USA	
Winders, Wim	Movie Director
%Paul Kohner Inc, 9300 Wilshire Blvd, #555, Beverly Hills, CA 90212, USA	
Windle, William F	Anatomist
229 Cherry St, Granville, OH 43023, USA	
Windlesham (D J G Hennessy), Baron	Government Official, England
Brasenose College, Oxford OX1 4AJ, England	
Windom, William	Actor
5455 Sylmar Ave, #1601, Van Nuys, CA 91401, USA	
Windsor, Marie	Actress
9501 Cherokee Lane, Beverly Hills, CA 90210, USA	
Windust, Penelope	Actress
%Writers & Artists Agency, 924 Westwood Blvd, #900, Los Angeles, CA 90024, USA	
Winfield, David M (Dave)	Baseball Player
14970 Hickory Greens Court, Fort Myers, FL 33912, USA	
Winfield, Paul	Actor
5693 Holly Oak Dr, Los Angeles, CA 90068, USA	
Winfield, Rodney M	Artist
444 Laclede Place, St Louis, MO 63108, USA	
Winfrey, Oprah	Entertainer
%Harpo Productions, 110 N Carpenter St, Chicago, IL 60607, USA	
Wing, Toby	Actress
PO Box 1197, Lake Elsinore, CA 92531, USA	

Wilson - Wing

Wingate, David A — *Businessman*
33 Applegreen Dr, Old Westbury, NY 11568, USA

Winger, Debra — *Actress*
20220 Inland Ave, Malibu, CA 90265, USA

Winkler, Hans-Gunter — *Equestrian Rider*
Dr Rau Allee 48, 48231 Warendorf, Germany

Winkler, Henry — *Actor, Television Director*
PO Box 49914, Los Angeles, CA 90049, USA

Winkler, Irwin — *Movie Producer*
%Irwin Winkler Productions, 211 S Beverly Dr, #220, Beverly Hills, CA 90212, USA

Winn, George M — *Businessman*
%Fluke Corp, 6920 Seaway Blvd, Everett, WA 98203, USA

Winn, Kitty — *Actress*
%Artists Agency, 10000 Santa Monica Blvd, #305, Los Angeles, CA 90067, USA

Winner, Michael R — *Movie Director, Producer*
31 Melbury Rd, London W14 8AB, England

Winningham, Mare — *Actress*
PO Box 19, Beckwourth, CA 96129, USA

Winograd, Shmuel — *Mathematician, Computer Scientist*
235 Glendale Rd, Scarsdale, NY 10583, USA

Winokur, Herbert S, Jr — *Businessman*
%Dyncorp, 2000 Edmund Halley Dr, Reston, VA 22091, USA

Winpisinger, William W — *Labor Leader*
%Machinists & Aerospace Union, 9000 Machinists Place, Upper Marlboro, MD 20772, USA

Winship, Thomas — *Editor*
Old Concord Rd, South Lincoln, MA 01773, USA

Winslow, Barry N — *Financier*
%Great Lakes Bancorp, 401 E Liberty St, Ann Arbor, MI 48104, USA

Winslow, Michael — *Comedian*
18653 Ventura Blvd, #635, Tarzana, CA 91356, USA

Winsor, Jackie — *Artist*
%Paula Cooper Gallery, 155 Wooster St, New York, NY 10012, USA

Winsor, Kathleen — *Writer*
115 E 67th St, New York, NY 10021, USA

Winston, George — *Pianist, Composer*
%Dancing Cat Productions, PO Box 639, Santa Cruz, CA 95061, USA

Winston, Hattie — *Actress*
13025 Jarvis Ave, Los Angeles, CA 90061, USA

Winston, Patrick H — *Computer Scientist*
%Massachusetts Institute of Technology, Technology Square, Cambridge, MA 02139, USA

Winston, Roland — *Physicist (Nonimaging Optics)*
5217 S University Ave, #C, Chicago, IL 60615, USA

Winter, Edgar — *Singer, Guitarist*
1325 El Hito Circle, Pacific Plsds, CA 90272, USA

Winter, Edward D — *Actor*
181 N Saltair Ave, Los Angeles, CA 90049, USA

Winter, Fred (Tex) — *Basketball Coach*
%Chicago Bulls, 1901 W Madison St, Chicago, IL 60612, USA

Winter, Frederick T — *Thoroughbred Racing Jockey, Trainer*
Montague House, Eastbury, Newbury, Berks RG16 7JL, England

Winter, J Burgess — *Businessman*
%Magma Copper Co, 7400 N Oracle Rd, Tucson, AZ 85704, USA

Winter, Johnny — *Singer, Guitarist*
%Slatus Mgmt, 208 E 51st St, #151, New York, NY 10022, USA

Winter, Max — *Football Executive*
%Minnesota Vikings, 9520 Viking Dr, Eden Prairie, MN 55344, USA

Winter, Raymond F — *Businessman*
%BIC Corp, 1 Bic Dr, Milford, CT 06460, USA

Winter, William F — *Governor, MS*
633 N State St, Jackson, MS 39202, USA

Winters, Jonathan — *Comedian*
945 Lilac Dr, Santa Barbara, CA 93108, USA

Winters, Shelley — *Actress*
457 N Oakhurst Dr, Beverly Hills, CA 90210, USA

Wintour, Anna — *Editor*
%Vogue Magazine, Editorial Dept, 350 Madison Ave, New York, NY 10017, USA

Wintour, Charles V — *Editor*
60 East Hatch, Tisbury, Wilts SP3 6PH, England

Winwood, Steve *Singer, Songwriter*
%William Morris Agency, 1325 Ave of Americas, New York, NY 10019, USA

Winzenried, Jesse D *Financier*
%Securities Investor Protection Corp, 805 15th St NW, Washington, DC 20005, USA

Wirahadikusuman, Umar *Government Official, Indonesia; General*
Jalan Teuku Umar 61, Jarkata 10310, Indonesia

Wire, William S, II *Businessman*
6119 Stonehaven Dr, Nashville, TN 37215, USA

Wirkin, Gary M *Businessman*
%Service Merchandise Co, PO Box 24600, Nashville, TN 37202, USA

Wirth, Billy *Actor*
%Michael Slessinger Assoc, 8730 Sunset Blvd, #220-W, Los Angeles, CA 90069, USA

Wirtz, Arthur M, Jr *Hockey Executive*
%Chicago Blackhawks, Chicago Stadium, 1800 W Madison St, Chicago, IL 60612, USA

Wirtz, W Willard *Secretary, Labor*
1211 Connecticut Ave NW, Washington, DC 20036, USA

Wirtz, William W *Hockey Executive*
DeWindt Rd, Winnetka, IL 60093, USA

Wisdom, Norman *Comedian*
%Johnny Mans, The Maltings, Brewery Rd, Hoddesdon, Herts EN11 8HF, England

Wise, George S *Educator*
5500 Collins Ave, Miami Beach, FL 33140, USA

Wise, Robert E *Movie Director, Producer*
2222 Ave of Stars, #2303, Los Angeles, CA 90067, USA

Wiseman, Joseph *Actor*
382 Central Park West, New York, NY 10025, USA

Wishart, Leonard P, III *Army General*
%Non-Legislative/Financial Services, US House of Representatives, Washingt 20515, USA

Wishnick, William *Businessman*
%Witcon Corp, 1 American Lane, Greenich, CT 06831, USA

Wisniewski, Stephen A (Steve) *Football Player*
%Oakland Raiders, Oakland Coliseum, Oakland, CA 94621, USA

Wisoff, Peter J K *Astronaut*
%NASA, Johnson Space Center, 2101 NASA Rd, Houston, TX 77058, USA

Wistert, Albert A (Ox) *Football Player*
256 Gunnell Rd, Grants Pass, OR 97526, USA

Wistert, Alvin *Football Player*
10250 W Seven Mile Rd, Northville, MI 48167, USA

Withers, Jane *Actress*
4249 Stern Ave, Sherman Oaks, CA 91423, USA

Withers, Pick *Drummer (Dire Straits)*
%Damage Mgmt, 10 Southwick Mews, London W2, England

Witherspoon, Jimmy *Singer*
4200 Don Tapia Place, Los Angeles, CA 90008, USA

Witherspoon, Tim *Boxer*
%Carl King, 32 E 69th St, New York, NY 10021, USA

Witkin, Joel-Peter *Photographer*
1707 Five Points Rd SW, Albuquerque, NM 87105, USA

Witkop, Bernhard *Chemist*
3807 Montrose Driveway, Chevy Chase, MD 20815, USA

Witt, Katarina *Figure Skater*
%Arts & Promotions, Bergerstr 295, 60385 Frankfurt/Main, Germany

Witt, Paul J *Screenwriter*
16032 Valley Vista Blvd, Encino, CA 91436, USA

Witten, Edward *Theoretical Physicist*
%Institute for Advanced Study, Olden Lane, Princeton, NJ 08540, USA

Wittman, Randy *Basketball Player, Coach*
%Dallas Mavericks, Reunion Arena, 777 Sports St, Dallas, TX 75207, USA

Wobst, Frank *Financier*
%Huntington Bancshares, Huntington Center, Columbus, OH 43287, USA

Woessner, Mark M *Businessman, Publisher*
%Bertelsmann AG, Carl-Bertelsmann-Str 270, 39264 Gutersloh, Germany

Woetzel, Damian *Ballet Dancer, Choreographer*
%New York City Ballet, Lincoln Center Plaza, New York, NY 10023, USA

Wogan, Gerald N *Toxicologist*
%Massachusetts Institute of Technology, Toxicology Div, Cambridge, MA 02139, USA

Wogsland, James W *Businessman*
%Caterpillar Inc, 100 NE Adams St, Peoria, IL 61629, USA

Wohl, Dave *Basketball Coach, Executive*
%Miami Heat, Miami Arena, Miami, FL 33136, USA

Wohlhuter, Rick *Track Athlete*
1558 Brittany Court, Wheaton, IL 60187, USA

Woit, Dick *Physical Fitness Expert*
%Lehman Sports Center, 2700 N Lehmann Court, Chicago, IL 60614, USA

Woiwode, Larry *Writer, Poet*
%State University of New York, English Dept, Binghamton, NY 13901, USA

Wojtowicz, R P *Labor Leader*
%Railway Carmen Union, 3 Research Place, Rockville, MD 20850, USA

Wolaner, Robin P *Publisher*
%Sunset Publishing Corp, 80 Willow Rd, Menlo Park, CA 94025, USA

Wolf, Dale E *Governor, DE*
Lieutenant Governor's Office, Legislative Hall, Legislative Ave, Dover, DE 19901, USA

Wolf, David A *Astronaut*
%Kennedy Space Center, Code TP-TMS-A, NASA, Kennedy Space Center, FL 32899, USA

Wolf, Frank *Publisher*
%Seventeen Magazine, 850 3rd Ave, New York, NY 10022, USA

Wolf, Sigrid *Skier*
6652 Elbigenalp 45-A, Austria

Wolf, Stephen M *Businessman*
%United Airlines Corp, 1200 E Algonguin Rd, Elk Grove Village, IL 60005, USA

Wolfbein, Seymour L *Government Official, Economist*
East 706 Parktown, 2200 Benjamin Franklin Parkway, Philadelphia, PA 19130, USA

Wolfe, George C *Theater Director*
%Shakespeare Festival, 425 Lafayette St, New York, NY 10003, USA

Wolfe, John F *Publisher*
%Columbus Dispatch, 34 S 3rd St, Columbus, OH 43215, USA

Wolfe, Kenneth L *Businessman*
%Hershey Foods Corp, 100 Crystal A Dr, Hershey, PA 17033, USA

Wolfe, Naomi *Poet*
%Royce Carlton Inc, 866 United Nations Plaza, New York, NY 10017, USA

Wolfe, Thomas K (Tom), Jr *Writer*
21 E 79th St, New York, NY 10021, USA

Wolfenden of Westcott, John F *Educator*
White House, Guildford Rd, Westcott Near Dorking, Surrey, England

Wolfensohn, James D *Financier*
%World Bank Group, 1818 "H" St NW, Washington, DC 20433, USA

Wolfenstein, Lincoln *Physicist*
%Carnegie-Mellon University, Physics Dept, Pittsburgh, PA 15213, USA

Wolfermann, Klaus *Track Athlete*
%Puma Sportschu, Postfach 1420, 91074 Herzogenraurach, Germany

Wolff, Hugh *Conductor*
%Affiliate Artists, 37 W 65th St, #601, New York, NY 10023, USA

Wolff, Jon A *Geneticist*
1122 University Bay Dr, Madison, WI 53705, USA

Wolff, Sanford I *Labor Leader*
8141 Broadway, New York, NY 10023, USA

Wolff, Tobias *Writer*
%Syracuse University, English Dept, Syracuse, NY 13244, USA

Wolff, Torben *Biologist, Zoologist*
2900 Hellerup, Denmark

Wolford, Will *Football Player*
%Indianapolis Colts, 7001 W 56th St, Indianapolis, IN 46254, USA

Wolfson, Louis E *Businessman, Thoroughbred Racing Owner*
10205 Collins Ave, Bal Harbour, FL 33154, USA

Wollenberg, Richard P *Businessman*
%Longview Fibre Co, PO Box 639, Longview, WA 98632, USA

Wollman, Harvey *Governor, SD*
RR 1, Box 43, Hitchcock, SD 57348, USA

Wolper, David L *Movie Producer*
1833 Rising Glen Rd, Los Angeles, CA 90069, USA

Wolpert, Julian *Geographer*
4588 Provinceline Rd, Princeton, NJ 08540, USA

Wolszczan, Alexander *Astronomer*
%Pennsylvania State University, Astronomy Dept, University Park, PA 16802, USA

Woltz, H O, III *Businessman*
%Insteel Industries, 1373 Boggs Dr, Mount Airy, NC 27030, USA

W

Woltz, Howard O, Jr *Businessman*
%Insteel Industries, 1373 Boggs Dr, Mount Airy, NC 27030, USA

Womack, Bobby *Singer*
4735 Sepulveda Blvd, #430, Sherman Oaks, CA 91403, USA

Womack, Robert R *Businessman*
%Zurn Industries, 1 Zurn Place, Erie, PA 16505, USA

Wonder, Stevie *Singer, Songwriter*
%Steveland Morris Music, 4616 W Magnolia Blvd, Burbank, CA 91505, USA

Wong, Albert *Computer Engineer*
26796 Vista Terrace, Lake Forest, CA 92630, USA

Wong, B D *Actor*
%Agency For Performing Arts, 888 7th Ave, New York, NY 10106, USA

Wonham, Frederick S *Financier*
%United States Trust Co of New York, 114 W 47th St, New York, NY 10036, USA

Woo, John *Movie Director*
%Garth Productions, 20th Century Fox, 10201 W Pico Blvd, Los Angeles, CA 90064, USA

Woo, Peter K C *Businessman*
%Hongkong & Kowloon Wharf & Godown Co, 7 Canton Rd, Kowloon, Hong Kong

Wood, C Norman *Air Force General*
5440 Mount Corcoran Place, Burke, VA 22015, USA

Wood, David C *Financier*
%Norwest Financial, 206 8th St, Des Moines, IA 50309, USA

Wood, Elijah *Actor*
760 N La Cienega Blvd, #200, Los Angeles, CA 90069, USA

Wood, Godfrey *Hockey Executive*
%Boston Bruins, Boston Garden, 150 Causeway St, Boston, MA 02114, USA

Wood, James *Businessman*
%Great Atlantic & Pacific Tea Co, 2 Paragon Dr, Montvale, NJ 07645, USA

Wood, James N *Museum Director*
%Art Institute of Chicago, 111 S Michigan Ave, Chicago, IL 60603, USA

Wood, Lana *Actress*
4129 Woodman Ave, Sherman Oaks, CA 91423, USA

Wood, Maurice *Physician*
RR 2, Box 543-B, Hot Springs, VA 24445, USA

Wood, Nigel *Astronaut, England*
Church Crookham, Aldershot, England

Wood, Richard *Football Player, Coach*
%New England Patriots, Foxboro Stadium, Rt 1, Foxboro, MA 02035, USA

Wood, Richard D *Businessman*
%Eli Lilly Co, Lilly Corporate Center, Indianapolis, IN 46285, USA

Wood, Robert E *Publisher*
%Peninsula Times Tribune, 435 N Michigan Ave, #1609, Chicago, IL 60611, USA

Wood, Robert J *Astronaut*
%McDonnell Douglas Corp, PO Box 516, St Louis, MO 63166, USA

Wood, Ron *Guitarist (Rolling Stones)*
2077 Mandeville Canyon, Los Angeles, CA 90049, USA

Wood, Sharon *Mountaineer*
PO Box 1482, Canmore AB T0L 0M0, Canada

Wood, Sidney B B *Tennis Player*
300 Murray Place, Southhampton, NY 11968, USA

Wood, Thomas H *Publisher*
%Atlanta Constitution, 72 Marietta St NW, Atlanta, GA 30303, USA

Wood, Wilbur F *Baseball Player*
3 Elmsbrook Rd, Bedford, MA 01730, USA

Wood, William B, III *Biologist*
%University of Colorado, Molecular Biology Dept, Boulder, CO 80309, USA

Wood, William V (Willie) *Football Player*
7941 16th St NW, Washington, DC 20012, USA

Wood, Willis B, Jr *Businessman*
%Pacific Enterprises, 633 W 5th St, Los Angeles, CA 90071, USA

Woodard, Alfre *Actress*
602 Bay St, Santa Monica, CA 90405, USA

Woodard, Lynette *Basketball Player*
%Kansas City School District, 1211 McGee St, Kansas City, MO 64106, USA

Woodcock, Leonard *Labor Leader, Diplomat*
2404 Vinewood Blvd, Ann Arbor, MI 48104, USA

Wooden, John R *Basketball Player, Coach*
17711 Margate St, #102, Encino, CA 91316, USA

Woodhead, Cynthia   *Swimmer*
PO Box 1193, Riverside, CA 92502, USA

Woodhouse, John F   *Businessman*
%Sysco Corp, 1390 Enclave Parkway, Houston, TX 77077, USA

Woodhull, John R   *Businessman*
%Logicon Inc, 3710 Skypark Dr, Torrance, CA 90505, USA

Woodiwiss, Kathleen E   *Writer*
%Avon Books, 959 8th Ave, New York, NY 10019, USA

Woodley, David   *Football Player*
%Pittsburgh Steelers, 3 Rivers Stadium, 300 Stadium Circle, Pittsburgh, PA 15212, USA

Woodling, Eugene R (Gene)   *Baseball Player*
926 Remsen Rd, Medina, OH 44256, USA

Woodring, Wendell P   *Geologist, Paleontologist*
6647 El Colegio Rd, Goleta, CA 93117, USA

Woodruff, Judy C   *Commentator*
%Cable News Network, News Dept, 820 1st St NE, Washington, DC 20002, USA

Woods, Barbara Alyn   *Actress*
%Geddes Agency, 1201 Greenacre Blvd, West Hollywood, CA 90046, USA

Woods, Donald   *Social Activist*
%Atheneum Publishers, 866 3rd Ave, New York, NY 10022, USA

Woods, G David   *Financier*
%ABN AMRO Securities USA, 335 Madison Ave, #1400, New York, NY 10017, USA

Woods, J Mark   *Businessman*
%Anacomp Inc, 11550 N Meridian St, Indianapolis, IN 46240, USA

Woods, James   *Actor*
760 N La Cienega Blvd, Los Angeles, CA 90069, USA

Woods, James D   *Businessman*
%Baker Hughes Inc, 3900 Essex Lane, Houston, TX 77027, USA

Woods, John W   *Financier*
%AmSouth Bancorp, 1900 5th Ave N, Birmingham, AL 35203, USA

Woods, Michael   *Actor*
%Metropolitan Talent Agency, 4526 Wilshire Blvd, Los Angeles, CA 90010, USA

Woods, Nan   *Actress*
%Geddes Agency, 1201 Greenacre Blvd, West Hollywood, CA 90046, USA

Woods, Philip W (Phil)   *Jazz Clarinetist, Saxophonist*
PO Box 278, Delaware Water Gap, PA 18327, USA

Woods, Rose Mary   *Presidential Secretary*
1194 W Cambridge St, Alliance, OH 44601, USA

Woodson, Abraham B (Abe)   *Football Player*
PO Box 4749, Carson, CA 90749, USA

Woodson, Robert R   *Businessman*
%John H Harland Co, 2939 Miller Rd, Decatur, GA 30035, USA

Woodson, Roderick K (Rod)   *Football Player*
%Pittsburgh Steelers, 3 Rivers Stadium, 300 Stadium Circle, Pittsburgh PA 15212, USA

Woodson, Warren B   *Football Coach*
6010 Angleblum Circle, Dallas, TX 75248, USA

Woodward, C Vann   *Historian*
83 Rogers Rd, Hamden, CT 06517, USA

Woodward, Edward   *Actor, Singer*
Ravens Court, Calstock, Cornwall PL18 9ST, England

Woodward, James H, Jr   *Educator*
%University of North Carolina, Chancellor's Office, Charlotte, NC 28223, USA

Woodward, Joanne   *Actress*
1120 5th Ave, #1-C, New York, NY 10128, USA

Woodward, John F   *Navy Admiral, England*
%Navy Secretary, Defense Ministry, Whitehall, London SW1A 2BE, England

Woodward, Kirsten   *Fashion Designer*
%Kirsten Woodward Hats, 26 Portobello Green Arcade, London W10, England

Woodward, Robert U (Bob)   *Journalist*
%Washington Post, Editorial Dept, 1150 15th St NW, Washington, DC 20071, USA

Woodward, Roger   *Concert Pianist*
%LH Productions, 2/37 Hendy Ave, Coogee NSW 2034, Australia

Woofter, R D   *Businessman*
%TNP Enterprises, PO Box 2943, Fort Worth, TX 76113, USA

Woolard, Edgar S, Jr   *Businessman*
%E I Du Pont de Nemours Co, 1007 N Market St, Wilmington, DE 19898, USA

Wooldridge, Dean E   *Businessman*
4545 Via Esperanza, Santa Barbara, CA 93110, USA

W

Woodhead - Wooldridge

Woolery, Chuck *Entertainer*
620 N Linden Dr, Beverly Hills, CA 90210, USA

Wooley, Sheb *Singer, Songwriter*
Rt 3, Box 231, Sunset Island Trail, Gallatin, TN 37066, USA

Woolford, Donnell *Football Player*
%Chicago Bears, Halas Hall, 250 N Washington Rd, Lake Forest, IL 60045, USA

Woolley, Catherine *Writer*
PO Box 71, Higgins Hollow Rd, Truro, MA 02666, USA

Woolley, Kenneth F *Architect*
26 Lang Rd, Centennial Park NSW 2021, Australia

Woolridge, Orlando *Basketball Player*
%Philadelphia 76ers, Veterans Stadium, PO Box 25040, Philadelphia, PA 19147, USA

Woolsey, Clinton N *Neurophysiologist*
106 Virginia Terrace, Madison, WI 53705, USA

Woolsey, Elizabeth D *Skier*
Trail Creek Ranch, Wilson, WY 83014, USA

Woolsey, R James *Law Enforcement Official*
%Shea & Gardner, 1800 Massachusetts Ave NW, Washington, DC 20036, USA

Woosnam, Ian H *Golfer*
Dyffryn, Morda Rd, Oswestry, Shropshire SY11 2AY, Wales

Wooten, Jim *Commentator*
%ABC-TV, News Dept, 1717 De Sales St NW, Washington, DC 20036, USA

Wootten, Morgan *Basketball Coach*
%De Matha High School, Athletic Dept, Hyattsville, MD 20781, USA

Wootton, Charles G *Diplomat*
%Chevron Corp, 555 Market St, San Francisco, CA 94105, USA

Wopat, Tom *Actor*
2614 Woodlawn Dr, Nashville, TN 37212, USA

Word, Weldon R *Engineer (Paveway Smart Bomb)*
Brookhaven, Northshore Dr, Rt 2, Box 293-BB, Hawkins, TX 75765, USA

Worden, Alfred M *Astronaut*
%B F Goodrich Research Center, 9921 Brecksville Rd, Brecksville, OH 44141, USA

Worgull, David *Religious Leader*
%Wisconsin Evangelical Lutheran Synod, 1270 N Dobson Rd, Chandler, AZ 85224, USA

Worley, Joanne *Actress*
4714 Arcola Ave, North Hollywood, CA 91602, USA

Worndl, Frank *Skier*
Burgsiedlung 19-C, 87527 Sonthofen, Germany

Worsley, Lorne (Gump) *Hockey Player*
%Minnesota North Stars, Sports Center, 7901 Cedar Ave S, Bloomington, MN 55425, USA

Worth, Irene *Actress*
333 W 56th St, New York, NY 10019, USA

Worthen, John E *Educator*
%Ball State University, President's Office, Muncie, IN 47306, USA

Worthington, Melvin L *Religious Leader*
%Free Will Baptists National Assn, 5233 Mt View Rd, Antioch, TN 37013, USA

Wortman, J John *Businessman*
%Amerisure Insurance Co, 28 W Adams Ave, Detroit, MI 48226, USA

Wossner, Mark M *Businessman*
%Bertelsmann AG, Carl-Bertelsmann Str 25, 33311 Gutersloh, Germany

Wottle, Dave *Track Athlete*
9245 Forest Hill Lane, Germantown, TN 38139, USA

Wouk, Herman *Writer*
%BSW Literary Agency, 3255 "N" St NW, Washington, DC 20007, USA

Woytowicz-Rudnicka, Stefania *Concert Singer*
Al Przyjaciol 3 M 13, 00-565 Warsaw, Poland

Wray, Donald E *Businessman*
%Tyson Foods Inc, 2210 W Oaklawn Dr, Springdale, AR 72762, USA

Wray, Fay *Actress*
2160 Century Park East, #1901, Los Angeles, CA 90067, USA

Wright, Charles Alan *Attorney*
5304 Western Hills Dr, Austin, TX 78731, USA

Wright, Clyde *Baseball Player*
528 Jeanine Ave, Anaheim, CA 92806, USA

Wright, Cobina, Jr *Actress*
1326 Dove Meadow Rd, Solvang, CA 93463, USA

Wright, Donald C (Don) *Editorial Cartoonist*
%Palm Beach Post, Editorial Dept, 2751 S Dixie Highway, West Palm Beach, F 33405, USA

Wright, Donald F — *Publisher*
%Los Angeles Times, Times Mirror Square, Los Angeles, CA 90053, USA

Wright, Ernie H — *Football Player*
4858 Renovo Way, San Diego, CA 92124, USA

Wright, Felix E — *Businessman*
%Leggett & Platt Inc, 1 Leggett Rd, Carthage, MO 64836, USA

Wright, Gerald — *Theater Director*
%Guthrie Theatre, 725 Vineland Place, Minneapolis, MN 55403, USA

Wright, Irving S — *Physician*
25 East End Ave, New York, NY 10028, USA

Wright, J Oliver — *Diplomat, England*
Burstow Hall, Horley, Surrey H6 9SR, England

Wright, James C, Jr — *Representative, TX; Speaker*
Lanham Federal Office Building, 819 Taylor St, Fort Worth, TX 76102, USA

Wright, Jay — *Poet*
%General Delivery, Piermont, NH 03779, USA

Wright, Louis B — *Historian*
3702 Leland St, Chevy Chase, MD 20815, USA

Wright, Louis D — *Football Player*
3826 S Dawson St, Aurora, CO 80014, USA

Wright, Max — *Actor*
%Bresler Kelly Kipperman, 15760 Ventura Blvd, #1730, Encino, CA 91436, USA

Wright, Michael W — *Businessman*
%SuperValu Inc, 11840 Valley View Rd, Eden Prairie, MN 55344, USA

Wright, Michelle — *Singer*
%PLA Media, 1303 16th Ave S, Nashville, TN 37212, USA

Wright, Mickey — *Golfer*
%Ladies Professional Golf Assn, 2570 Volusia Ave, Daytona Beach, FL 32114, USA

Wright, Rayfield — *Football Player*
PO Box 30513, Phoenix, AZ 85046, USA

Wright, Raymond R — *Vietnam War Army Hero (CMH)*
490 Joyce St, Mineville, NY 12956, USA

Wright, Rick — *Keyboardist (Pink Floyd)*
%Ten Tenths Mgmt, 106 Gifford St, London N1 ODF, England

Wright, Robert C — *Television Executive*
%National Broadcasting Co, 30 Rockefeller Plaza, New York, NY 10112, USA

Wright, Robert F — *Businessman*
%Ameralda Hess Corp, 1185 Ave of Americas, New York, NY 10036, USA

Wright, Robin — *Actress, Model*
%Creative Artists Agency, 9830 Wilshire Blvd, Beverly Hills, CA 90212, USA

Wright, Stan — *Track Coach*
7955 La Riveria Dr, Sacramento, CA 95826, USA

Wright, Teresa — *Actress*
948 Rowayton Wood Dr, Norwalk, CT 06854, USA

Wright, Timothy W — *Navy Admiral*
Commander, 7th Fleet, FPO, AP 96601, USA

Wrighton, Mark S — *Chemist*
%Massachusetts Institute of Technology, Chemistry Dept, Cambridge, MA 02139, USA

Wrightson, Bernie — *Diver*
924 Birch Ave, Escondido, CA 92027, USA

Wrigley, William — *Businessman*
%William Wrigley Jr Co, 410 N Michigan Ave, Chicago, IL 60611, USA

Wroughton, Philip L — *Financier*
%Marsh & McLennan Companies, 1166 Ave of Americas, New York, NY 10036, USA

Wszola, Jacek — *Track Athlete*
Ul Chrzanowskiego 7 m 70, 04-381, Warsaw, Poland

Wu Cheng-Chung, John B Cardinal — *Religious Leader*
%Catholic Diocese Center, 16 Caine Rd, Hong Kong

Wu Xiuquan — *Government Official, China; Army Officer*
%Beijing Institute for International Strategic Studies, Beijing, China

Wu, Chien-Shiung — *Physicist*
15 Claremont Ave, New York, NY 10027, USA

WuDunn, Sheryl — *Journalist*
%New York Times, Editorial Dept, 229 W 43rd St, New York, NY 10036, USA

Wulff, Kai — *Actor*
%Barr Agency, PO Box 69590, Los Angeles, CA 90069, USA

Wulsin, Henry H — *Businessman*
%Colonial Penn Group, PO Box 1990, Valley Forge, PA 19482, USA

W

Wright - Wulsin

W

Wunderlich, Hermann — *Businessman*
%Bayer Corp, Mellon Center, 500 Grant St, Pittsburgh, PA 15219, USA

Wunderlich, Paul — *Artist*
Haynstr 2, 20949 Hamburg, Germany

Wunsch, Carl I — *Oceanographer*
78 Washington Ave, Cambridge, MA 02140, USA

Wuorinen, Charles P — *Composer*
%Howard Stokar Mgmt, 870 West End Ave, New York, NY 10025, USA

Wurster, Donald F — *Businessman*
%National Indemnity Co, 3024 Harney St, Omaha, NE 68131, USA

Wurtell, C Angus — *Businessman*
%Valspar Corp, 1101 3rd St S, Minneapolis, MN 55415, USA

Wurtzel, Alan L — *Businessman*
%Circuit City Stores, 9950 Maryland Dr, Richmond, VA 23233, USA

Wyatt, J Whitlow (Whit) — *Baseball Player*
Box 56, Buchanan, GA 30113, USA

Wyatt, Jane — *Actress*
651 Siena Way, Los Angeles, CA 90077, USA

Wyatt, Joe B — *Educator*
%Vanderbilt University, Chancellor's Office, Nashville, TN 37240, USA

Wyatt, Oscar S, Jr — *Businessman*
%Coastal Corp, 9 Greenway Plaza, Houston, TX 77046, USA

Wyatt, Shannon — *Actress*
8949 Falling Creek Court, Annandale, VA 22003, USA

Wyatt, Sharon — *Actress*
24549 Park Grande, Calabasas, CA 91302, USA

Wyche, Samuel D (Sam) — *Football Coach*
%Tampa Bay Buccaneers, 1 Buccaneer Place, Tampa, FL 33607, USA

Wyeth, Andrew — *Artist*
%General Delivery, Chadds Ford, PA 19317, USA

Wyeth, James Browning — *Artist*
%General Delivery, Chadds Ford, PA 19317, USA

Wykle, Kenneth R — *Army General*
DCinC, US Transportation Command, Scott Air Force Base, IL 62225, USA

Wyle, Noah — *Actor*
%IFA Talent, 8730 Sunset Blvd, #490, Los Angeles, CA 90069, USA

Wyler, Gretchen — *Actress*
15115 Weddington St, Van Nuys, CA 91411, USA

Wylie, Paul — *Figure Skater*
%International Management Group, 1 Erieview Plaza, #1300, Cleveland, OH 44114, USA

Wyly, Sam — *Businessman*
%Sterling Software, 8080 North Central Expressway, Dallas, TX 75206, USA

Wyman, Jane — *Actress*
PO Box 1317, Elfers, FL 34680, USA

Wyman, Louis C — *Senator, NH; Judge*
121 Shaw St, Manchester, NH 03104, USA

Wyman, Thomas H — *Financier*
%S G Warburg Co, Equitable Center, 787 7th Ave, New York, NY 10019, USA

Wyman, William G (Bill) — *Bassist (Rolling Stones)*
%Ripple Records, 2705 Glendower Ave, Los Angeles, CA 90027, USA

Wymore, Patrice — *Actress*
Port Antonio, Jamaica, British West Indies

Wynder, Ernst L — *Internist*
%American Health Foundation, 320 E 43rd St, New York, NY 10017, USA

Wyner, George — *Actor*
3450 Laurie Place, Studio City, CA 91604, USA

Wynette, Tammy — *Singer*
%George Richey, 1222 16th Ave S, #22, Nashville, TN 37212, USA

Wynn, Early — *Baseball Player*
567 Fallbrook Dr, Venice, FL 34292, USA

Wynn, Stephen A — *Businessman*
%Mirage Resorts, 3400 Las Vegas Ave S, Las Vegas, NV 89109, USA

Wynter, Dana — *Actress*
Glenmacnass, Glendalough, County Wicklow, Ireland

Wyse, Henry W (Hank) — *Baseball Player*
1133 SE 14th St, Pryor, OK 74361, USA

Wysocki, Charles — *Artist*
PO Box 441, Cedar Glen, CA 92321, USA

Wunderlich - Wysocki

Xenakis, Iannis *Composer, Architect, Engineer*
9 Rue Chaptal, 75009 Paris, France

Xie Bingxin *Writer*
%Central Nationalities Institute, Residental Quarters, Beijing 100081, China

Xie Jin *Movie Director*
%Shanghai Film Studio, 595 Caoxi Beilu, Shagnhai, China

Xu Shuyang *Sculptor*
%Zhejiang Academy of Fine Arts, PO Box 169, Hangzhou, China

Xuxa (Maria da Graca Meneghel) *Entertainer*
%"El Show de Xuxa", KMEX-TV, 6255 Sunset Blvd, #1600, Los Angeles, CA 90028, USA

Yablans, Frank *Movie Producer*
100 Bull Path, East Hampton, NY 11937, USA

Yackira, Michael W *Businessman*
%FPL Group, 700 Universe Blvd, Juno Beach, FL 33408, USA

Yaeger, Andrea *Tennis Player*
PO Box 10970, Aspen, CO 81612, USA

Yager, Faye *Social Activist*
%Children of the Underground, 902 Curlew Court NW, Atlanta, GA 30327, USA

Yagi, Yasuhiro *Businessman*
%Kawasaki Steel Corp, 2-2-3 Uchisaiwaicho, Chiyodaku, Tokyo 100, Japan

Yago, Bernard Cardinal *Religious Leader*
Arceveche, Ave Jean-Paul II, 01 BP 1287, Abidjan 01, Cote d'Ivoire

Yakovlev, Aleksandr N *Government Official, Russia*
%Prisoner Rehabilitation Commission, Ul Iljinka 8/4, 103132 Moscow, Russia

Yalow, Rosalyn S *Nobel Medicine Laureate*
%Veterans Administration Medical Center, 130 W Kingsbridge Rd, Bronx, NY 10468, USA

Yamada, Eiichi *Businessman*
%Citizen Watch Co, 2-1-1 Nishi, Shinjulu, Tokyo 160, Japan

Yamada, Hajime *Financier*
%Mitsubishi Bank, 2-7-1 Marunouchi, Chiyodaku, Tokyo 100, Japan

Yamada, Osamu (Sam) *Financier*
%Bank of California, 400 California St, San Francisco, CA 94104, USA

Yamaguchi, Kristi T *Figure Skater*
4841 Norris Rd, Fremont, CA 94536, USA

Yamaguchi, Tamotsu *Financier*
%Union Bank, 350 California St, San Francisco, CA 94104, USA

Yamaguchi, Yoshio *Financier*
%Yasuda Trust & Banking Co, 1-2-1 Tarsu, Chuoku, Tokyo 103, Japan

Yamaji, Hiroyuki *Financier*
%Daiwa Bank Trust, 75 Rockefeller Plaza, New York, NY 10019, USA

Yamamoto, Kenichi *Businessman*
%Mazda Motor Corp, 4-6-19 Funairi-Minami, Minamiku, Hiroshima, Japan

Yamamoto, Masashi *Financier*
%Fuji Bank & Trust, 2 World Trade Center, New York, NY 10048, USA

Yamamoto, Takuma *Businessman*
%Fujitsu Ltd, 1-6-1 Marunouchi, Chiyodaku, Tokyo 100, Japan

Yamanaka, Seiichiro *Financier*
%Mitsui Trust & Banking Ltd, 2-1-1 Nihonbashi, Muromachi, Tokyo 103, Japan

Yamanaka, Tsuyoshi *Swimmer*
6-10-33-212 Akasaka, Minatoku, Tokyo, Japan

Yamani, Sheikh Ahmed Zaki *Government Official, Saudi Arabia*
Chermignon Near Crans-Montana, Valais, Switzerland

Yamaoka, Seigen H *Religious Leader*
%Buddhist Churches of America, 1710 Octavia St, San Francisco, CA 94109, USA

Yamasaki, Yoshiki *Businessman*
%Mazda Motor Corp, 3-1 Fuchacho-Shinchi, Akigun, Hiroshima, Japan

Yamashita, Hideaki *Businessman*
%Ashai Glass Co, 2-1-2 Marunouchi, Chiyodaku, Tokyo 100, Japan

Yamashita, Isamu *Businessman*
%Mitsui Engineering & Shipbuilding, 5-6-4 Tsukiji, Tokyo 104, Japan

Yamashita, Toshihiko *Businessman*
%Matsushita Electric Industrial, 1006 Kadoma City, Osaka 571, Japan

Yamashita, Yasuhiro *Judo Athlete, Coach*
640 Sanada, Hiratsuka, Kanagawa 259-12, Japan

Yancey, James D *Financier*
%Synovus Financial Corp, 901 Front St, Columbus, GA 31901, USA

Yancy, Emily *Actress*
%Henderson/Hogan Agency, 247 S Beverly Dr, #102, Beverly Hills, CA 90212, USA

X-Y

Xenakis - Yancy

Y

Yang Shangkun *President, China; Army General*
%Overseas Chinese Affairs Committee, Beijing, China

Yang, Chen Ning *Nobel Physics Laureate*
3 Victoria Court, St James, NY 11780, USA

Yankelovich, Daniel *Social Scientist*
%Public Agenda Foundation, 6 E 39th St, #900, New York, NY 10016, USA

Yankovic, (Weird) Al *Comedian*
8842 Hollywood Blvd, Los Angeles, CA 90069, USA

Yankovic, Frankie *Accordionist*
4853 Bostonian Loop, Heritage Lake, New Port Richey, FL 34655, USA

Yannas, I V *Mechanical Engineer, Medical Researcher*
%Massachusetts Institute of Technology, Engineering School, Cambridge, MA 02139, USA

Yanni (Chryssomallis) *Keyboardist, Songwriter*
6714 Villa Madera Dr SW, Tacoma, WA 98499, USA

Yanofsky, Charles *Biologist*
725 Mayfield Ave, Stanford, CA 94305, USA

Yarborough, Cale *Auto Racing Driver*
%Yarborough Racing, 2723 W Palmetto St, Florence, SC 29501, USA

Yarborough, William P *Army General*
160 Hillside Rd, Southern Pines, NC 28387, USA

Yarbrough, Curtis *Religious Leader*
%General Baptists Assn, 100 Stinson, Popular Bluff, MO 63901, USA

Yarbrough, Glenn *Singer (Limelighters)*
2835 Woodstock Ave, Los Angeles, CA 90046, USA

Yard, Mollie *Women's Activist*
1000 16th St NW, Washington, DC 20036, USA

Yardley, George *Basketball Player*
%George Yardley Co, 17260 Newhope, Fountain Valley, CA 92708, USA

Yarmolinsky, Adam *Government Official, Attorney*
3700 33rd Place NW, Washington, DC 20008, USA

Yarnell, Lorene *Mime (Shields & Yarnell)*
7615 W Norton Ave, #1, Los Angeles, CA 90046, USA

Yarrow, Peter *Singer (Peter Paul & Mary), Songwriter*
27 W 67th St, #5-E, New York, NY 10023, USA

Yary, A Ronald (Ron) *Football Player*
18 Kenilworth Dr, Cresskill, NJ 07626, USA

Yasbeck, Amy *Actress*
2170 Century Park East, #1111, Los Angeles, CA 90067, USA

Yasinsky, John B *Businessman*
%GenCorp, 175 Ghent Rd, Fairlawn, OH 44333, USA

Yastrzemski, Carl M *Baseball Player*
4621 S Ocean Blvd, Highland Beach, FL 33487, USA

Yasufuka, Terayoshi *Financier*
%Sanwa Bank California, 444 Market St, San Francisco, CA 94111, USA

Yasui, Tadashi *Financier*
%Mitsubishi Trust & Banking, 4-5 Marunouchi, Tokyo 100, Japan

Yasuma, Susumu *Financier*
%Industrial Bank of Japan Trust, 245 Park Ave, New York, NY 10167, USA

Yates, Albert C *Educator*
%Colorado State University, President's Office, Fort Collins, CO 80523, USA

Yates, Brock W *Sportswriter*
%Car & Driver Magazine, Editorial Dept, 2002 Hogback Rd, Ann Arbor, MI 48105, USA

Yates, Cassie *Actress*
520 Washington Blvd, #175, Marina del Rey, CA 90292, USA

Yates, Edward D *Businessman*
%DENTSPLY International, 570 W Colleg Ave, York, PA 17404, USA

Yates, Peter J *Movie Director*
334 Caroline Ave, Culver City, CA 90232, USA

Yates, Ronald W (Ron) *Air Force General*
Commander, AF Materiel Command, Wright Patterson Air Force Base, OH 45433, USA

Yates, Sandra *Publisher*
%Ms Magazine, 119 W 40th St, New York, NY 10018, USA

Yauch, Adam (MCA) *Rapper (Beastie Boys)*
%Gold Mountain Ent, 3575 Cahuenga Blvd W, #450, Los Angeles, CA 90068, USA

Yeager, Charles E (Chuck) *Test Pilot, Air Force General*
PO Box 128, Cedar Ridge, CA 95924, USA

Yeager, Cheryl L *Ballerina*
%American Ballet Theatre, 890 Broadway, New York, NY 10003, USA

Yang Shangkun - Yeager

Yeager, Jeana *Experimental Airplane Pilot*
PO Box 352, Campbell, TX 75422, USA

Yeager, Waldo E *Businessman*
%Seaway Food Town, 1020 Ford St, Maumee, OH 43537, USA

Yearley, Douglas C *Businessman*
%Phelps Dodge Corp, 2600 N Central Ave, Phoenix, AZ 85004, USA

Yearwood, Trisha *Singer*
PO Box 150245, Nashville, TN 37215, USA

Yeliseyev, Alexei S *Cosmonaut*
%Bauman Higher Technical School, Baumanskaya Ul 5, 107 005 Moscow, Russia

Yellen, Janet L *Financier, Government Official*
%Federal Reserve Board, 20th St & Constitution Ave NW, Washington, DC 20551, USA

Yellen, Linda B *Television Producer, Director*
3 Sheridan Square, New York, NY 10014, USA

Yeltsin, Boris N *President, Russian Federation*
%Russian Central Committee, 4 Staraya Ploshchad, 103073 Moscow, Russia

Yendo, Masayoshi *Architect*
%Nakajima Building, 5-6-8 Ginza, Chuoku, Tokyo 104, Japan

Yeohlee (Teng) *Fashion Designer*
%Yeohlee, 530 7th Ave, New York, NY 10018, USA

Yeoman, William F (Bill) *Football Coach*
%University of Houston, Athletic Dept, Houston, TX 77204, USA

Yeosock, John J *Army General*
411 Taberon Rd, Peachtree City, GA 30269, USA

Yepes, Narciso *Concert Guitarist*
%Deutsche Grammaphon Records, 810 7th Ave, New York, NY 10019, USA

Yepremian, Garabed S (Garo) *Football Player*
1 East Mount Vernon St, Oxford, PA 19363, USA

Yerkovich, Anthony *Television Producer*
1802 Ashland Ave, Santa Monica, CA 90405, USA

Yeston, Maury *Composer*
%Flora Roberts, 157 W 57th St, New York, NY 10019, USA

Yeutter, Clayton K *Secretary, Agriculture*
%Republican National Committee, 3110 1st St SE, Washington, DC 20003, USA

Yevtushenko, Yevgeniy A *Poet*
Kutuzovski Prospekt 2/1, #101, 121248 Moscow, Russia

Yhouse, Paul A *Businessman*
%Holnam Inc, 6211 Ann Arbor Rd, Dundee, MI 48131, USA

Yilmaz, A Mesut *Prime Minister, Turkey*
%Motherland Party, Balgat, Ankara, Turkey

Yma Sumac *Singer*
%Alan Eichler Assoc, 1524 LaBaig Ave, Los Angeles, CA 90028, USA

Yoakam, Dwight *Singer*
%Dwight Yoakam Tours, 6363 Sunset Blvd, #712, Los Angeles, CA 00020, UOA

York, Robert J *Judge*
%US Claims Court, 717 Madison Place NW, Washington, DC 20005, USA

Yoder, Hatten S, Jr *Petrologist*
%Geophysical Laboratory, 5251 Broad Branch Rd NW, Washington, DC 20015, USA

Yodh, Arjun *Physicist*
%University of Pennsylvania, Physics Dept, Philadelphia, PA 19104, USA

Yodoyman, Joseph *Prime Minister, Chad*
%Prime Minister's Office, N'Djamena, Chad

Yoken, Mel B *Writer*
261 Carroll St, New Bedford, MA 02740, USA

Yokich, Stephen P *Labor Leader*
%United Auto Workers Union, 800 E Jefferson Ave, Detroit, MI 48214, USA

Yokoyama, Soichi *Financier*
%Bank of Tokyo, 6-3 Nihombashi, Hongokucho, Chuoku, Tokyo 103, Japan

Yontz, Kenneth F *Businessman*
%Sybron Corp, 411 E Wisconsin Ave, Milwaukee, WI 53202, USA

York, Francine *Actress*
12725 Ventura Blvd, #F, Studio City, CA 91604, USA

York, Herbert F *Physicist*
6110 Camino de la Costa, La Jolla, CA 92037, USA

York, John J *Actor*
4804 Laurel Canyon Blvd, #212, Valley Village, CA 91607, USA

York, Michael *Actor*
9100 Cordell Dr, Los Angeles, CA 90069, USA

Y

York, Michael M *Journalist*
%Lexington Herald-Leader, Editorial Dept, Main & Midland, Lexington, KY 40507, USA

York, Susannah *Actress*
%Jonathan Altarass Assoc, 2 Goodwins Court, London WC2N 4LL, England

Yorkin, Alan (Bud) *Movie Producer, Director*
%Bud Yorkin Productions, 345 N Maple Dr, #206, Beverly Hills, CA 90210, USA

Yorkin, Peg *Feminist Activist*
%Fund for Feminist Majority, 1600 Wilson Blvd, #704, Arlington, VA 22209, USA

Yorks, Richard A *Businessman*
%Prudential Insurance, Prudential Plaza, 751 Broad St, Newark, NJ 07102, USA

Yorzyk, William *Swimmer*
417 Forest Hills Rd, Springfield, MA 01128, USA

Yoshida, Kanetake *Financier*
%Union Bank, 350 California St, San Francisco, CA 94104, USA

Yoshikuni, Jiro *Financier*
%Bank of Yokohama, 5-47 Honcho, Nakaku, Yokohoma 231, Japan

Yoshimura, Junzo *Architect*
8-6-3 Mejiro, Toshimaku, Tokyo, Japan

Yoshiyama, Hirokichi *Businessman*
%Hitachi Ltd, 1-5-1 Marunouchi, Chiyodaku, Tokyo 100, Japan

Yost, Edward F J (Eddie) *Baseball Player*
48 Oak Ridge Rd, Wellesley, MA 02181, USA

Yost, Paul A, Jr *Coast Guard Admiral*
%James Madison Memorial Foundation, 200 "K" St NW, Washington, DC 20001, USA

Yothers, Tina *Actress*
15521 Kennard St, Hacienda Heights, CA 91745, USA

Youdelman, Robert A *Businessman*
%Allen Group, 25101 Chagrin Blvd, Beachwood, OH 44122, USA

Youman, Roger J *Editor*
%TV Guide Magazine, Editorial Dept, 100 Matsonford Rd, Radnor, PA 19087, USA

Younce, Leonard A (Len) *Football Player*
300 S River St, Enterprise, OR 97828, USA

Young of Farnworth, Janet M *Government Official, England*
%House of Lords, Westminster, London SW1A 0PW, England

Young, A Thomas *Businessman*
%Martin Marietta Corp, 6801 Rockledge Dr, Bethesda, MD 20817, USA

Young, Alan *Actor*
%Artists Group, 10100 Santa Monica Blvd, #2490, Los Angeles, CA 90067, USA

Young, Andrew *Ambassador; Mayor, Atlanta*
%Law International Inc, 1000 Abernathy Rd NE, Atlanta, GA 30328, USA

Young, Burt *Actor*
%Irv Schechter Co, 9300 Wilshire Blvd, #410, Beverly Hills, CA 90212, USA

Young, Charles E *Educator*
%University of California, Chancellor's Office, Los Angeles, CA 90024, USA

Young, Connie *Cyclist*
%US Cycling Federation, 1750 E Boulder St, Colorado Springs, CO 80909, USA

Young, Dean *Cartoonist (Blondie)*
%King Features Syndicate, 216 E 45th St, New York, NY 10017, USA

Young, Donna Caponi *Golfer*
%Ladies Professional Golf Assn, 2570 Volusia Ave, Daytona Beach, FL 32114, USA

Young, Faron *Singer, Songwriter*
%Tessier-Marsh Talent, 505 Canton Pass, Madison, TN 37115, USA

Young, Frank E *Research Scientist, Government Official*
%Health & Human Services Dept, 200 Independence Ave SW, Washington, DC 20201, USA

Young, George *Track Athlete*
Rt 1, Box 479, Casa Grande, AZ 85222, USA

Young, Gerald O *Vietnam War Air Force Hero (CMH)*
317 Eden Rd, Anacortes, WA 98221, USA

Young, H Edwin *Religious Leader*
%Southern Baptist Convention, 901 Commerce St, Nashville, TN 37203, USA

Young, J Warren *Publisher*
%Boys Life Magazine, 1325 Walnut Hill Rd, Irving, TX 75038, USA

Young, Jerry *Religious Leader*
%Grace Brethren Church Fellowship, 855 Turnbull St, Delona, FL 32725, USA

Young, Jesse Colin *Singer, Songwriter*
%Ridgetop Music, PO Box 130, Point Reyes, CA 94956, USA

Young, Jim *Football Coach*
%US Military Academy, Athletic Dept, West Point, NY 10966, USA

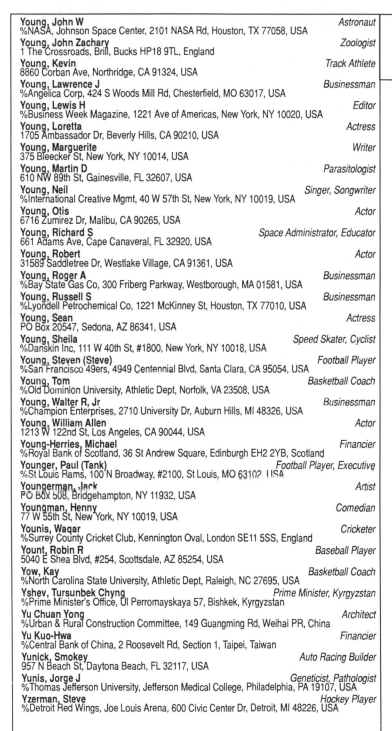

Young, John W — *Astronaut*
%NASA, Johnson Space Center, 2101 NASA Rd, Houston, TX 77058, USA

Young, John Zachary — *Zoologist*
1 The Crossroads, Brill, Bucks HP18 9TL, England

Young, Kevin — *Track Athlete*
8860 Corban Ave, Northridge, CA 91324, USA

Young, Lawrence J — *Businessman*
%Angelica Corp, 424 S Woods Mill Rd, Chesterfield, MO 63017, USA

Young, Lewis H — *Editor*
%Business Week Magazine, 1221 Ave of Americas, New York, NY 10020, USA

Young, Loretta — *Actress*
1705 Ambassador Dr, Beverly Hills, CA 90210, USA

Young, Marguerite — *Writer*
375 Bleecker St, New York, NY 10014, USA

Young, Martin D — *Parasitologist*
610 NW 89th St, Gainesville, FL 32607, USA

Young, Neil — *Singer, Songwriter*
%International Creative Mgmt, 40 W 57th St, New York, NY 10019, USA

Young, Otis — *Actor*
6716 Zumirez Dr, Malibu, CA 90265, USA

Young, Richard S — *Space Administrator, Educator*
661 Adams Ave, Cape Canaveral, FL 32920, USA

Young, Robert — *Actor*
31589 Saddletree Dr, Westlake Village, CA 91361, USA

Young, Roger A — *Businessman*
%Bay State Gas Co, 300 Friberg Parkway, Westborough, MA 01581, USA

Young, Russell S — *Businessman*
%Lyondell Petrochemical Co, 1221 McKinney St, Houston, TX 77010, USA

Young, Sean — *Actress*
PO Box 20547, Sedona, AZ 86341, USA

Young, Sheila — *Speed Skater, Cyclist*
%Danskin Inc, 111 W 40th St, #1800, New York, NY 10018, USA

Young, Steven (Steve) — *Football Player*
%San Francisco 49ers, 4949 Centennial Blvd, Santa Clara, CA 95054, USA

Young, Tom — *Basketball Coach*
%Old Dominion University, Athletic Dept, Norfolk, VA 23508, USA

Young, Walter R, Jr — *Businessman*
%Champion Enterprises, 2710 University Dr, Auburn Hills, MI 48326, USA

Young, William Allen — *Actor*
1213 W 122nd St, Los Angeles, CA 90044, USA

Young-Herries, Michael — *Financier*
%Royal Bank of Scotland, 36 St Andrew Square, Edinburgh EH2 2YB, Scotland

Younger, Paul (Tank) — *Football Player, Executive*
%St Louis Rams, 100 N Broadway, #2100, St Louis, MO 63102, USA

Youngerman, Jack — *Artist*
PO Box 508, Bridgehampton, NY 11932, USA

Youngman, Henny — *Comedian*
77 W 55th St, New York, NY 10019, USA

Younis, Waqar — *Cricketer*
%Surrey County Cricket Club, Kennington Oval, London SE11 5SS, England

Yount, Robin R — *Baseball Player*
5040 E Shea Blvd, #254, Scottsdale, AZ 85254, USA

Yow, Kay — *Basketball Coach*
%North Carolina State University, Athletic Dept, Raleigh, NC 27695, USA

Yshev, Tursunbek Chyng — *Prime Minister, Kyrgyzstan*
%Prime Minister's Office, Ul Perromayskaya 57, Bishkek, Kyrgyzstan

Yu Chuan Yong — *Architect*
%Urban & Rural Construction Committee, 149 Guangming Rd, Weihai PR, China

Yu Kuo-Hwa — *Financier*
%Central Bank of China, 2 Roosevelt Rd, Section 1, Taipei, Taiwan

Yunick, Smokey — *Auto Racing Builder*
957 N Beach St, Daytona Beach, FL 32117, USA

Yunis, Jorge J — *Geneticist, Pathologist*
%Thomas Jefferson University, Jefferson Medical College, Philadelphia, PA 19107, USA

Yzerman, Steve — *Hockey Player*
%Detroit Red Wings, Joe Louis Arena, 600 Civic Center Dr, Detroit, MI 48226, USA

Y

Young - Yzerman

Zabaleta, Nicanor — *Concert Harpist*
Villa Izar, Aldapeta, 20009 San Sebasatian, Spain

Zaban, Erwin — *Businessman*
%National Service Industries, 1420 Peachtree St NE, Atlanta, GA 30309, USA

Zabel, Steven G (Steve) — *Football Player*
2413 Brookdale Ave, Edmond, OK 73034, USA

Zable, Walter C — *Businessman*
%Cubic Corp, 9333 Balboa Ave, San Diego, CA 92123, USA

Zable, Walter J — *Businessman*
%Cubic Corp, 9333 Balboa Ave, San Diego, CA 92123, USA

Zaborowski, Robert R J M — *Religious Leader*
%Mariavite Old Catholic Church, 2803 10th St, Wynadotte, MI 48192, USA

Zabriskie, John L — *Businessman*
%Upjohn Co, 7000 Portage Rd, Kalamazoo, MI 49001, USA

Zacharias, Donald W — *Educator*
%Mississippi State University, President's Office, Mississippi State, MS 39762, USA

Zacharius, Walter — *Publisher*
475 Park Ave S, New York, NY 10016, USA

Zachary, Frank — *Editor*
%Town & Country Magazine, Editorial Dept, 1700 Broadway, New York, NY 10019, USA

Zadeh, Lotfi A — *Computer Scientist (Fuzzy Logic)*
904 Mendocino Ave, Berkeley, CA 94707, USA

Zadora, Pia — *Actress, Singer*
%Par-Par Productions, 9560 Wilshire Blvd, Beverly Hills, CA 90212, USA

Zadrick, Shana — *Model*
%Men/Women Model Mgmt, 20 W 20th St, New York, NY 10011, USA

Zaentz, Saul — *Movie Producer*
%Saul Zaentz Co, 2600 10th St, Berkeley, CA 94710, USA

Zaffaroni, Alejandro C — *Biochemist*
%Alza Corp, 950 Page Mill Rd, Palo Alto, CA 94304, USA

Zafy, Albert — *President, Madagascar*
%President's Office, Iavoloha, Antananarivo, Madagascar

Zahn, Geoffrey C (Geof) — *Baseball Player*
30470 Sloan Canyon, Saugus, CA 91384, USA

Zahn, Paula — *Commentator*
%CBS-TV, News Dept, 51 W 52nd St, New York, NY 10019, USA

Zahn, Wayne — *Bowler*
%Professional Bowlers Assn, 1720 Merriman Rd, Akron, OH 44313, USA

Zaitsev, V M (Slava) — *Fashion Designer*
%Moscow Fashion House, Prospekt Mira 21, Moscow, Russia

Zaklinsky, Konstantin — *Ballet Dancer*
%Kirov Ballet Theatre, 1 Ploshchad Iskusstv, St Petersburg, Russia

Zaks, Jerry — *Theater Director*
%Helen Merrill, 337 W 22nd St, New York, NY 10011, USA

Zal, Roxana — *Actress*
1450 Belfast Dr, Los Angeles, CA 90069, USA

Zalapski, Zarley — *Hockey Player*
%Hartford Whalers, Coliseum, 242 Trumbell St, #800, Hartford, CT 06103, USA

Zale, Tony — *Boxer*
17643 Lilac Ln, Tinley Park, IL 60477, USA

Zaleznik, Abraham — *Businessman*
%Ogden Corp, 2 Penn Plaza, New York, NY 10121, USA

Zamba, Frieda — *Surfer*
2706 S Central Ave, Flagler Beach, FL 32136, USA

Zamecnik, Paul C — *Physician*
%Worcester Experimental Biology Foundation, 222 Maple St, Shrewsbury, MA 01545, USA

Zamfir, Gheorghe — *Conductor*
Dr Teohari Str 10, Bucharest, Romania

Zamora Rivas, Ruben I — *Government Official, El Salvador*
%National Constituent Assembly, San Salvador, El Salvador

Zampetis, Theodore K — *Businessman*
%Standard Products Co, 2130 W 110th St, Cleveland, OH 44102, USA

Zandano, Gianni — *Financier*
%First Los Angeles Bank, 2049 Century Park East, Los Angeles, CA 90067, USA

Zander, Robin — *Singer, Guitarist (Cheap Trick)*
1818 Parmenter St, #202, Middleton, WI 53562, USA

Zane, Billy — *Actor*
843 N Las Palmas Ave, Los Angeles, CA 90038, USA

Zane, Lisa *Actress*
209 S Orange Dr, Los Angeles, CA 90036, USA

Zankel, Arthur S *Financier*
%First Manhattan Co, 437 Madison Ave, New York, NY 10022, USA

Zanuck, Lili Fini *Movie Producer, Director*
%Zanuck Co, 202 N Canon Dr, Beverly Hills, CA 90210, USA

Zanuck, Richard D *Movie Producer*
%Zanuck Co, 202 N Canon Dr, Beverly Hills, CA 90210, USA

Zanuso, Marco *Architect*
Piazza Castello 20, Milan, Italy

Zanussi, Krzysztof *Movie Director*
Kaniowska 114, 01-529, Warsaw, Poland

Zapata, Carmen *Actress*
6107 Ethel Ave, Van Nuys, CA 91401, USA

Zapf, Hermann *Book, Type Designer*
2 Hammarskjold Plaza, New York, NY 10017, USA

Zappa, Dweezil *Actor*
PO Box 5265, North Hollywood, CA 91616, USA

Zappa, Moon *Actress*
335 N Maple Dr, #361, Beverly Hills, CA 90210, USA

Zarb, Frank G *Government Official, Financier*
%Alexander & Alexander Services, 1211 Ave of Americas, New York, NY 10036, USA

Zariski, Oscar *Mathematician*
122 Sewall Ave, Brookline, MA 02146, USA

Zarkhi, Aleksandr G *Movie Director*
Cherniachovskogo Str 4, #105, 125319 Moscow, Russia

Zarkin, Herbert J *Businessman*
%Waban Inc, 1 Mercer Rd, Natick, MA 01760, USA

Zarnas, August (Gust) *Football Player*
850 Jennings St, Bethlehem, PA 18017, USA

Zasloff, Michael *Geneticist*
%National Child Health Institute, 9000 Rockville Pike, Bethesda, MD 20205, USA

Zaslow, Jeffrey L (Jeff) *Columnist*
%Chicago Sun-Times, Editorial Dept, 401 N Wabash, Chicago, IL 60611, USA

Zatopek, Emil *Track Athlete*
Nad Kazankov 3, 171 00 Prague 7, Czech Republic

Zatopkova, Dana *Track Athlete*
Troja, 171 00 Prague 7, Czech Republic

Zawinul, Josef (Joe) *Jazz Synthesizer, Composer*
%International Music Network, 112 Washington St, Marblehead, MA 01945, USA

Zawoluk, Robert *Basketball Player*
%General Delivery, Mineola, NY 11501, USA

Zax, Stanley R *Businessman*
%Zenith National Insurance, 21255 Califa St, Woodland Hills, CA 91367, USA

Zeamer, Jay *WW II Army Air Corps Hero (CMH)*
123 Commercial St, PO Box 602, Boothbay Harbor, ME 04538, USA

Zech, Lando *Government Official*
%Nuclear Regulatory Commission, 1717 "H" St NW, Washington, DC 20555, USA

Zech, Ronald H *Businessman*
%GATX Corp, 500 W Monroe, Chicago, IL 60661, USA

Zeffirelli, G Franco *Movie Director*
448 Via Appia Pignatelli, 00178 Rome, Italy

Zeh, Geoffrey N *Labor Leader*
%Maintenance of Way Employees Brotherhood, 12050 Woodward, Detroit, MI 48203, USA

Zeien, Alfred M *Businessman*
%Gillette Co, Prudential Tower Building, Boston, MA 02199, USA

Zeigler, Heidi *Actress*
%Mary Grady Agency, 4444 Lankershim Blvd, #207, North Hollywood, CA 91602, USA

Zeikel, Arthur *Financier*
%Merrill Lynch Asset Mgmt, 800 Scudders Mill Rd, Plainsboro, NJ 08536, USA

Zeitlin, Zvi *Concert Pianist*
204 Warren Ave, Rochester, NY 14618, USA

Zell, Samuel *Businessman*
%Itel Corp, 2 N Riverside Plaza, Chicago, IL 60606, USA

Zeman, Jacklyn *Actress*
6930 Dume Dr, Malibu, CA 90265, USA

Zemeckis, Robert L *Movie Director*
PO Box 5218, Santa Barbara, CA 93150, USA

Zemke, E Joseph *Businessman*
%Amdahl Corp, 1250 E Arques Ave, Sunnyvale, CA 94086, USA

Zenawi, Hailu *President, Ethiopia*
%President's Office, PO Box 5707, Addis Ababa, Ethiopia

Zendejas, Tony *Football Player*
%St Louis Rams, 100 N Broadway, #2100, St Louis, MO 63102, USA

Zender, Hans *Conductor, Composer*
Am Risebheck, 65812 Bad Soden, Germany

Zerbe, Anthony *Actor*
245 Chateaux Elise, Santa Barbara, CA 93109, USA

Zernial, Gus E *Baseball Player*
5902 E Belmont Ave, Fresno, CA 93727, USA

Zeroul, Lamine *President, Algeria; Army General*
%President's Office, Al-Mouradia, Algiers, Algeria

Zevi, Bruno *Architect*
Via Nomentana 150, 00162 Rome, Italy

Zevon, Warren *Singer, Songwriter*
%Peter Asher Mgmt, 644 N Doheny Dr, Los Angeles, CA 90069, USA

Zhamnov, Adam *Hockey Player*
%Winnipeg Jets, Arena, 15-1430 Maroons Rd, Winnipeg MB R3G 0L5, Canada

Zhang Aiping *Government Official, China; Army General*
%Ministry of Defense, State Council, Beijing, China

Zhang Xian *Writer*
%Jiangsu Branch, Chinese Writers' Assn, Nanjing, China

Zhang Xianliang *Writer*
%Ningxia Writers' Assn, Yinchuan City, China

Zhang Yimou *Movie Director*
%Xi'an Film Studio, Xi'an City, Shanxi Province, China

Zhao Yanxia *Opera Singer*
%Beijing Opera Theatre, Beijing, China

Zhao Ziyang *Prime Minister, China*
1 Zhong Nan Hai, Beijing, China

Zhelev, Zhelyu *President, Bulgaria*
%President's Office, 2 Dondukov Blvd, 1123 Sofia, Bulgaria

Zheng, Wei *Astronomer*
%Johns Hopkins Universities, Astronomy Dept, Baltimore, MD 21218, USA

Zhirinovsky, Vladimir V *Government Leader, Russia*
%Liberal Democratic Party, Rybnikov Per 1, 103045 Moscow, Russia

Zhitnik, Alexel *Hockey Player*
%Buffalo Sabres, Memorial Stadium, 140 Main St, Buffalo, NY 14202, USA

Zholobov, Vitali M *Cosmonaut*
Ul Yanvarskovo Vostaniya D 12, 252 010 Kiev, Ukraine

Zhu Rongji *Government Official, China*
%Vice Premier's Office, State Council, Xi Changan Jie, Beijing, China

Zia, B Khaleda *Prime Minister, Bangladesh*
%Prime Minister's Office, Sher-e-Banglangar, Dhaka, Bangladesh

Zidek, George *Basketball Player*
%Charlotte Hornets, 1 Hive Dr, Charlotte, NC 28217, USA

Ziegler, Dolores *Opera Singer*
%Lynda Kay, 2702 Crestworth Ln, Buford, GA 30519, USA

Ziegler, Henri A L *Aviation Engineer, Businessman*
55 Blvd Lannes, 75116 Paris, France

Ziegler, Jack *Cartoonist*
%New Yorker Magazine, Editorial Dept, 20 W 43rd St, New York, NY 10036, USA

Ziegler, John A, Jr *Hockey Executive*
1 Detroit Center, 500 Woodward Ave, #4000, Detroit, MI 48226, USA

Ziegler, Larry *Golfer*
6209 Dartmoor Ct, Orlando, FL 32819, USA

Ziegler, Peter D *Financier*
%Ziegler Companies, 215 N Main St, West Bend, WI 53095, USA

Ziegler, R Douglas *Financier*
%Ziegler Companies, 215 N Main St, West Bend, IN 53095, USA

Ziegler, Ronald L *Government Official, Journalist*
%National Assn of Chain Drug Stores, 413 N Lee St, Alexandria, VA 22314, USA

Ziegler, William, III *Businessman*
%American Maize-Products Co, 250 Harbor Dr, Stamford, CT 06902, USA

Ziemann, Sonja *Actress*
Via del Alp Dorf, 7500 St Moritz, Switzerland

Ziering, Ian *Actor*
%Guttman & Pam, 118 S Beverly Dr, #201, Beverly Hills, CA 90212, USA

Ziff, William B, Jr *Publisher*
%Ziff-Davis Publishing Co, 1 Park Ave, New York, NY 10016, USA

Ziffren, Kenneth *Attorney*
%Ziffren Brittenham Branca, 2121 Ave of Stars, #3200, Los Angeles, CA 90067, USA

Zigler, Edward F *Educator*
%Yale University, Bush Child Development Center, New Haven, CT 06520, USA

Zikes, Les *Bowler*
%Beverly Lanes, 8 S Beverly Ln, Arlington Heights, IL 60004, USA

Zimbalist, Efrem, Jr *Actor*
1448 Holsted Dr, Solvang, CA 93463, USA

Zimbalist, Stephanie *Actress*
%William Morris Agency, 151 S El Camino Dr, Beverly Hills, CA 90212, USA

Zimerman, Krystian *Concert Pianist*
%Deutsche Grammaphon Records, 810 7th Ave, New York, NY 10019, USA

Zimm, Bruno H *Chemist*
2522 Horizon Way, La Jolla, CA 92037, USA

Zimmer, David R *Businessman*
%CORE Industries, 500 N Woodward Ave, Bloomfield Hills, MI 48304, USA

Zimmer, Donald W (Don) *Baseball Manager*
10124 Yacht Club Dr, St Petersburg, FL 33706, USA

Zimmer, Hans *Composer*
1547 14th St, Santa Monica, CA 90404, USA

Zimmer, Kim *Actress*
25561 Almendra Dr, Santa Clarita, CA 91355, USA

Zimmer, William H *Financier*
%Cincinnati Financial Corp, PO Box 145496, Cincinnati, OH 45250, USA

Zimmerman, Gary *Football Player*
%Denver Broncos, 13655 E Dove Valley Pkwy, Englewood, CO 80112, USA

Zimmerman, James M *Businessman*
%Federated Department Stores, 7 W 7th St, Cincinnati, OH 45202, USA

Zimmerman, John T *Neuroscientist*
%University of Colorado Medical School, Neurology Dept, Denver, CO 80202, USA

Zimmerman, Mary Beth *Golfer*
%Ladies Professional Golf Assn, 2570 Volusia Ave, Daytona Beach, FL 32114, USA

Zimmerman, Raymond *Businessman*
%Service Merchandise Co, PO Box 24600, Nashville, TN 37202, USA

Zimmermann, Egon *Skier*
%Hotel Kristberg, 67644Am Arlberg, Austria

Zindel, Paul *Playwright*
%Harper & Row Publishers, 10 E 53rd St, New York, NY 10022, USA

Zinder, Norton D *Geneticist*
450 E 63rd St, New York, NY 10021, USA

Zindler, Marvin *Commentator*
%KTRK-TV, News Dept, 3310 Bissonnet, Houston, TX 77005, USA

Zinke, Olaf *Speedskater*
J Bobrowski Str 22, 12626 Berlin, Germany

Zinman, David J *Conductor*
%Baltimore Symphony, 1212 Cathedral St, Baltimore, MD 21201, USA

Zinnemann, Fred *Movie Director*
37 Bloomfield Rd, London W9, England

Zlatoper, Ronald J *Navy Admiral*
37 Makalapa Dr, Honolulu, HI 96818, USA

Zmed, Adrian *Actor*
22103 Avenida Morelos, Woodland Hills, CA 91364, USA

Zmeskal, Kim *Gymnast*
%Karolyi's World Gym, 17203 Bamwood Dr, Houston, TX 77090, USA

Zmievskaya, Galina *Figure Skating Coach*
%International Skating Rink, 1375 Hopmeadow St, Simsbury, CT 06070, USA

Zoeller, Frank (Fuzzy) *Golfer*
3802 Cormorant Point Dr, Sebring, FL 33872, USA

Zoffinger, George R *Financier*
%CoreStates New Jersey National Bank, 370 Scotch Rd, Pennington, NJ 08534, USA

Zook, John E *Football Player*
145 Farm Track, Roswell, GA 30075, USA

Zoran *Fashion Designer*
157 Chambers St, #1200 , New York, NY 10007, USA

Zorich, Chris *Football Player*
%Chicago Bears, Halas Hall, 250 N Washington Rd, Lake Forest, IL 60045, USA

Zorich, Louis *Actor*
%Susan Smith Assoc, 121 N San Vicente Blvd, Beverly Hills, CA 90211, USA

Zorina, Vera *Actress, Ballet Dancer*
247 E 61st St, New York, NY 10021, USA

Zorn, Jim *Football Player, Coach*
%Utah State University, Athletic Dept, Logan, UT 84322, USA

Zou Jiahua *Government Official, China*
%Communist Central Committee, Zhonganahai, Beijing, China

Zouikin, Tania *Financier*
%Batterymarch Financial Management, 200 Clarendon St, Boston, MA 02116, USA

Zoungrana, Paul Cardinal *Religious Leader*
Archeveche, BP 1472, Ouagadougou 01, Burkina Faso

Zsigmond, Vilmos *Cinematographer*
%Feinstein & Shorr, 16133 Ventura Blvd, #800, Encino, CA 91436, USA

Zubi, Mahmud al- *Prime Minister, Syria*
%Prime Minister's Office, Shahbandar St, Damascus, Syria

Zubrod, C Gordon *Physician*
177 Ocean Lane Dr, Key Biscayne, FL 33149, USA

Zucaro, A C *Businessman*
%Old Republic International, 307 N Michigan Ave, Chicago, IL 60601, USA

Zucchini, Michael R *Financier*
%Fleet Financial Group, 50 Kennedy Plaza, Providence, RI 02903, USA

Zucker, David *Movie Producer, Director*
%Zucker Productions, Sony, 10202 W Washington Blvd, Culver City, CA 90232, USA

Zucker, Jerry *Movie Director*
481 Denslow Ave, Los Angeles, CA 90049, USA

Zuckerman, Mortimer B *Publisher*
%Boston Properties, 599 Lexington Ave, New York, NY 10022, USA

Zuckert, Bill *Actor*
%Allen Goldstein Assoc, 5015 Lemona Ave, Sherman Oaks, CA 91403, USA

Zudov, Vyachselav D *Cosmonaut*
%Potchta Kosmonavtov, 141 160 Svyosdny Gorodok, Moskovskoi Oblasti, Russia

Zuendt, William F *Financier*
%Wells Fargo Co, 420 Montgomery St, San Francisco, CA 94104, USA

Zukerman, Eugenia *Concert Flutist*
%Brooklyn College of Music, Bedford & "H" Aves, Brooklyn, NY 11210, USA

Zukerman, Pinchas *Concert Violinist*
%Shirley Kirshbaum Assoc, 711 West End Ave, #5-KN, New York, NY 10025, USA

Zukofsky, Paul *Concert Violinist*
%University of Southern California, Schoenberg Institute, Los Angeles, CA 90089, USA

Zulu, Alphaeus H *Religious Leader*
PO Box 177, Edendale, Natal 4505, South Africa

Zumwalt, Elmo R, Jr *Navy Admiral*
%Admiral Zumwalt Consultants, 1500 Wilson Blvd, Arlington, VA 22209, USA

Zuniga, Daphne *Actress*
%Constellation, PO Box 1249, White River Junction, VT 05001, USA

Zurbriggen, Pirmin *Skier*
%Hotel Larchenhof, 3905 Saas-Almagell, Switzerland

Zwanzig, Robert W *Chemical Physicist*
5314 Sangamore Rd, Bethesda, MD 20816, USA

Zweig, George *Theoretical Physicist*
%Los Alamos National Laboratory, MS B276, PO Box 1663, Los Alamos, NM 87544, USA

Zweig, Martin E *Financier*
%Zweig Companies, 900 3rd Ave, New York, NY 10022 USA

Zwick, Edward M *Movie Director, Producer*
%Skywalker Sound, 1861 S Bundy, #314, Los Angeles, CA 90025, USA

Zwilich, Ellen Taaffe *Composer*
%Music Assoc of America, 224 King St, Englewood, NJ 07631, USA

Zych, Leonard A *Financier*
%Chemical Financial Services, 250 W Huron, Cleveland, OH 44113, USA

Zydeco (Stanley Dural Jr), Buckwheat *Singer, Accordionist*
%Ted Fox Productions, PO Box 561, Rhinebeck, NY 12572, USA

Zykina, Lyudmila G *SInger*
Kotelnicheskaya Nab Y-15 Korp B, #64, Moscow, Russia

Zylis-Gara, Teresa *Opera Singer*
16-A Blvd de Belgique, Monaco-Ville, Monaco

NECROLOGY

Abbott, George	*Theater Producer*
Abs, Hermann J	*Financier*
Adams, Stanley	*Lyricist*
Adrian, Iris	*Actress*
Aguirre, Hank	*Baseball Player*
Akins, Claude	*Actor*
Albritton, Dave	*Track Athlete*
Aldrich, Hulbert S	*Financier*
Aldridge, Kay	*Actress*
Aleksandrov, Anatoly P	*Physicist*
Alfven, Hannes O G	*Nobel Laureate*
Allers, Franz	*Conductor*
Almeida, Laurindo	*Jazz Guitarist*
Ambers, Lou	*Boxer*
Anderson, Glenn M	*Representative, CA*
Anderson, Lindsay	*Movie Director*
Anderson, Paul	*Weightlifter*
Anfinsen, Christian B	*Nobel Laureate*
Anselmo, Rene	*Businessman*
Arcel, Ray	*Boxing Trainer*
Arnold, Danny	*Movie Producer, Director*
Arnon, Daniel I	*Biochemist*
Aspin, Les	*Secretary, Defense*
Atwood, Donald J, Jr	*Businessman*
Aubrey, James T, Jr	*Movie Producer*
Aylestone, Bowden	*Government Official*
Bagnell, Francis (Reds)	*Football Player*
Baker, George P	*Educator*
Ball, George W	*Government Official*
Ball, Joseph H	*Senator, MN*
Bar-Lev, Haim	*General*
Barber, Jerry	*Golfer*
Barrault, Jean-Louis	*Actor, Producer*
Bartell, Dick	*Baseball Player*
Basquette, Lina	*Actress*
Batten, James K	*Publisher*
Baudouin I	*King, Belgium*
Bazargan, Mehdi	*Premier, Iran*
Beck, Jeffrey P	*Financier*
Beery, Noah, Jr	*Actor*
Begelman, David	*Movie Producer*
Bell, David R (Gus)	*Baseball Player*
Belluschi, Pietro	*Architect*
Bender, Stanley	*WW II Hero (CMH)*
Bennett, John Coleman	*Theologian*
Bennett, Wallace F	*Senator, UT*
Bennett, William T, Jr	*Diplomat*
Benson, Erza Taft	*Sec Agriculturer*
Beregovoi, Georgi T	*Cosmonaut*
Bergsma, William L	*Composer*
Bernays, Edward L	*Businessman*
Bestor, Arthur E	*Historian*
Biggs, Vernon	*Football Player*
Bill, Max	*Architect, Artist*
Black, Fischer	*Economist*
Blair, Frank	*Commentator*
Blake, Hector (Toe)	*Hockey Coach*
Blaustein, Albert P	*Attorney, Educator*
Bloch, Robert	*Writer*
Bolt, Robert 0	*Plauwright*
Bondarchuk, Sergei F	*Movie Director*
Bonica, John J	*Anesthesiologist*
Bonnett, Neil	*Auto Racing Driver*
Booke, Sorrell	*Actor*
Boone, Walter F	*Navy Admiral*
Borch, Fred J	*Businessman*
Boros, Julius	*Golfer*
Borotra, Jean	*Tennis Player*
Bosley, Bruce	*Football Player*
Botvinnik, Mikhail M	*Chess Player*
Boulle, Pierre	*Writer*
Boutin, Francois	*Thoroughbred rainer*
Bray, Ray	*Football Player*
Brazzi, Rossano	*Actor*
Brennan, Joseph R	*Basketball Player*
Brett, Jeremy	*Actor*
Brewer, Edward E	*Businessman*
Briles, Herschel F	*WW II Hero (CMH)*
Brody, S Steven	*Businessman*
Brooks, Cleanth	*Writer, Educator*
Brooks, Phyllis	*Actress*
Brophy, Brigid	*Writer*
Brown, Raymond (Tay)	*Football Player*

Bryant, Douglas W	*Librarian*
Buckner, Teddy	*Jazz Musician*
Bukowski, Charles	*Writer*
Burger, Warren	*Chief Justice*
Burkhardt, Hans	*Artist*
Burri, Alberto	*Artist*
Burroughs, Robert P	*Pension Expert*
Busby, Matthew	*Soccer Executive*
Butenandt, Adolf	*Nobel Laureate*
Buttram, Pat	*Actor*
Cabot, Paul C	*Financier*
Cain, Stanley A	*Ecologist, Botanist*
Calloway, Cab	*Jazz Band Leaderr*
Camras, Marvin	*Inventor*
Candy, John	*Comedian*
Canetti, Elias	*Nobel Laureate*
Carey, MacDonald	*Actor*
Carlough, Edward J	*Labor Leader*
Caron, Bob	*WW II Photographer*
Carpino, Francesco	*Religious Leader*
Carter, Janis	*Actress*
Carter, Kevin	*Photographer*
Cater, Douglass	*Educator*
Chadwick, Florence	*Channel Swimmer*
Chadwick, Gloria C	*Skiing Administrator*
Chenery, Hollis B	*Economist*
Chung Il Kwon	*Prime Minister, S Korea*
Church, Alonzo	*Philosophe*
Chute, Marchette	*Writer*
Cisler, Walker Lee	*Engineer*
Clampitt, Amy K	*Poet*
Clavell, James	*Writer*
Clayton, Jack	*Movie Director*
Claytor, W Graham	*Government Official*
Cobain, Kurt	*Singer, Songwriter*
Colbert, Lester L	*Businessman*
Coleman, James S	*Sociologist*
Collado, Emilio G	*Government Official*
Collins, Dorothy	*Singer*
Colosio, Luis D	*Government Official*
Conn, Jerome W	*Medical Researcher*
Connor, James P	*WW II Hero (CMH)*
Conrad, William	*Actor*
Cook (Derek Raymond), Robin	*Writer*
Cook, Elisha, Jr	*Actor*
Cook, Peter E	*Comedian*
Cordeiro, Joseph	*Religious Leader*
Cornfeld, Bernard	*Businessman*
Cosell, Howard	*Sportscaster*
Cotten, Joseph	*Actor*
Craigie, Laurent	*Test Pilot*
Crawford, Frederick C	*Businessman*
Creach, Pappa John	*Singer, Violinist*
Critchfield, Richard P	*Writer, Journalist*
Crosby, Gary	*Actor*
Cuccinello, Tony	*Baseball Player*
Culverhouse, Hugh F	*Football Executive*
Curless, Dick	*Singer, Songwriter*
Curry, John	*Figure Skater, Choreographer*
Cushing, Peter	*Actor*
Cziffra, Georges	*Concert Pianist*
Dandridge, Ray	*Baseball Player*
Dano, Royal	*Actor*
Darden, Severn	*Actor*
Darmojuwono, Just	*Religious Leader*
David, Mack	*Songwriter*
Davis, Bernard D	*Microbiologist*
Day, Leon	*Baseball Player*
De Grey, Roger	*Artist*
Decourtray, Albert	*Religious Leader*
Del Portillo, Alvaro	*Religious Leader*
Delfont of, Bernard	*Movie Executive*
Delvaux, Paul	*Artist*
Demske, James M	*Educator*
Desai, Morarji R	*Prime Minister, India*
Devitt, James E	*Businessman*
Di Tolla, Alfred W	*Labor Leader*
Dials, Lou	*Baseball Player*
Dicker, Richard	*Businessman*
Djilas, Milovan	*Government Official*
Dodson, Jack	*Actor*
Donnelly, Charles	*Air Force General*
Doucette, John	*Actor*

Name	Title	Name	Title
Downes, Ralph W	Concert Organist	Greenewalt, Crawford	Businessman
Downs, Johnny	Actor, Dancer	Grey, Aida	Fashion Expert
Du Bridge, Lee	Physicist, Educator	Griffiths, Frank	Hockey Executive
Duke, Angier Biddle	Diploma	Grimsby, Roger	Commentator
Duncan, George H	Radio Executive	Griswold, Erwin N	Government Official
Dunlap, Robert G	Businessman	Groza, Alex	Basketball Player
Durrell, Gerald M	Naturalist, Writer	Guinan, Matthew	Labor Leader
Eagles, Tommy Joe	Basketball Coach	Haas, Walter A, Jr	Businessman
Eazy-E (Eric Wright)	Rapper	Haasen, Peter	Physicist
Eckert, J Presper, Jr	Inventor	Haberler, Gottfried	Economist
Eckman, John W	Businessman	Habyarimana, Juv	President, Rwanda
Edwards, George C, Jr	Judge	Haddix, Harvey	Baseball Player
Eisenstaedt, Alfred	Photographer	Hamilton, Tom	Football Player
Elgart, Les	Orchestra Leader	Hanke, Lewis U	Historian
Elkin, Stanley L	Writer	Hanks, Sam	Racing Driver
Ellison, James	Actor	Hansen, Kenneth N	Businessman
Ellison, Ralph W	Writer	Hardy, Maurice G	Businessman
Emeleus, Harry J	Chemist	Harrington, Fred H	Historian
Emhardt, Robert	Actor	Harris, Claude	Representative, AL
Ende, Michael	Writer	Harris, Harry	Geneticist
Engman, Lewis	Government Official	Harris, Phil	Comedian
Ennals, David H	Government Official	Harrison, Albertis S, Jr	Governor, VA
Enrique y Tarancon, V	Religious Leader	Harvey, Alfred	Cartoonist
Erdelyi, Miklos	Conductor	Hatoyama, Iichiro	Government Official
Erikson, Erik H	Psychoanalyst	Hauser, Philip M	Sociologist
Ewell, Tom	Actor	Hawkins, Erick	Choreographer
Falicov, Leopoldo M	Physicist	Henry, David D	Educator
Fangio, Juan Manuel	Racing Driver	Henry, William A, III	Journalist
Faubus, Orval E	Governor, AR	Herriot, James	Veterinarian, Writer
Feather, Leonard	Jazz Critic	Highsmith, Patricia	Writer
Feeney, Charles	Baseball Executive	Hill, John A	Businessman
Felt, Irving M	Businessman	Hitch, Charles J	Educator
Ferrell, Riick	Baseball Player	Hoad, Lew	Tennis Player
Filer, John H	Businessman	Hobby, Oveta Culp	Secretary, HEW
Finks, Jim	Football Executive	Hodgkin, Dorothy C	Nobel Laureate
Finley, Murray H	Labor Leader	Holman, Nat	Basketball Coach
Firestone, Raymond C	Businessman	Holst, J Jorgen	Government Official
Firkusny, Rudolf	Concert Pianist	Home (Alec Douglas-Home), Lord	M, England
Fischer, Annie	Concert Pianist	Honecker, Erich	Head of State, E Germany
Fistoulari, Anatole	Conductor	Honochick, Jim	Baseball Umpire
Flaherty, Ray	Football Coach	Hordern, Michael	Actor
Flanders, Ed	Actor	Horgan, Paul	Writer
Flood, Daniel J	Representative, PA	Horsfall, James G	Plant Pathologist
Fonseca, Bruno	Artist	Horton, Mildred McAfee	Navy Admiral
Foote, H Robert)	WW II Hero (VC)	Houser, Allan	Artist
Ford, Louis Henry	Religious Leader	Houser, Clarence (Bud)	Track Athlete
Fortmann, Daniel J	Football Player	Howard, James H	WW II Hero (CMH)
Fowler, William A	Nobel Laureate	Howard, Jimmie	Vietnam War Hero (CMH)
Francis, Sam	Artist	Huff, Paul B	Korean War Hero (CMH)
Franklin, Melvin	Singer (Temptations)	Hunt, Hugh S	Theater Director
Franklin, William H	Businessman	Hunter, Howard W	Religious Leader
Fraser, Gretchen	Skier	Hyman, Phyllis	Singer
Freed, Bert	Actor	Hyuga, Hosai	Businessman
Frehm, Walter	Cartoonist	Ingram, E Bronson	Businessman
Freleng, Friz	Animator	Ionesco, Eugene	Writer
Frondizi, Arturo	President, Argentina	Isoda, Ichiro	Financier
Fuchs, Fritz F	Obstetrician	Ives, Burl	Actor, Singer
Fukuda, Takeo	M, Japan	Jackson, Norman C	WW I Hero (VC)
Fulbright, J William	Senator, AR	Jerne, Niels K	Nobel Laureate
Furcolo, Foster	Governor, MA; Judge	Jobim, Antonio Carlos	Jazz Guitarist
Furness, Betty	Consumer Advocate	John, Fritz	Mathematician
Furrer, Reinhard	Astronaut, Germany	Johnson, William S	Chemist
Gabor, Eva	Actress	Jones, Roger W	Government Official
Gaither, Alonzo (Jake)	Football Coach	Jones, Tristan	Explorer, Writer
Galan, Augie	Baseball Player	Jones, Warren L	Judge
Gallo, Dean A	Representative, NJ	Joseph, Keith S	Government Official
Gamsakhurdia, Zviad	PM, Georgia	Judd, Donald C	Sculptor
Ganilau, Penaia K	President, Fiji	Judd, Walter H	Representative, MN
Garcia, Jerry	Guitarist, Composer	Julia, Raul	Actor
Garrone, Gabriel	Religious Leader	Kabibble (, Ish	Comedian
Gary, Raymond	Governor, IN	Kaminsky, Max	Jazz Trumpeter
Gatton, Danny	Guitarist	Kane, Art	Photographer
Gee, Thomas G	Judge	Kappel, Frederick R	Businessman
Gerstacker, Carl A	Businessman	Katcavage, Jim	Football Player
Gerulaitis, Vitas	Tennis Player	Katz, Milton	Attorney, Educator
Gibson, Alexander D	Conductor	Kay, Connie	Jazz Drummer
Gifford, Frances	Actress	Kearney, Richard D	Government Official
Giuggio, John P	Businessman	Keene, Christopher	Conductor
Glennan, T Keith	Space Administrator	Kelly, John	Labor Leader
Godjnov, Alexander	Ballet Dancer, Actor	Kelly, Nancy	Actress
Goebel, Walther F	Biochemist	Kennedy, L Vern	Baseball Player
Goldberg, Irvin L	Judge	Kennedy, Rose	Mother of President
Gonzalez, Pedro J	Singer, Composer	Kerr, James R	Businessman
Gonzalez, Pancho	Tennis Player	Kessel, Dimitri	Photographer
Gordon, Gale	Actor	Ketcham, Hank	Cartoonist
Goria, Giovanni	Prime Minister, Italy	Kienholz, Edward	Artist
Grace, J Peter	Businessman	Kim Il Sung	President, North Korea
Grant, James P	Government Official	Kingsley, Sidney	Writer

NECROLOGY

Kirby, George	Comedian
Kirby, Jack (King)	Cartoonist
Kirk, Russell A	Columnist
Kleene, Stephen C	Mathematician
Knoll, Erwin	Legal Activist, Writer
Knox, Alexander	Actor
Koch, Howard	Screenwriter
Kohler, Georges J F	Nobel Laureate
Koontz, Raymond	Businessman
Koscina, Sylvia	Actress
Kostal, Irwin J	Conductor
Kouma, Ernest	Korean War Hero (CMH)
Kramer, Paul J	Plant Physiologist
Krim, Arthur B	Movie Executive
Krumm, Daniel J	Businessman
Kuchel, Thomas H	Senator, CA
Kuhn, Maggie	Social Activist
Kukrit Pramoj	P M, Thailand
Kunstler, William	Human Rights Activist
Kunz, Erich	Opera Singer
Kurtz, Efrem	Conductor
Lamborghini, Ferruccio	Businessman
Lancaster, Burt	Actor
Lane, Priscilla	Actress
Lansing, Robert	Actor
Lantz, Walter	Animator
Lapsley, William W	Businessman
Lasch, Christopher	Historian
Lash, Don	Track Athlete
Lasker, Mary	Civic Worker
Lassen, Clyde E	Vietnam War Hero (CMH)
Layton, Joe	Dancer, Choreographer
Lazar, Irving (Swifty)	Literary Agent
Lazarev, Vassily G	Cosmonaut
Lebow, Fred	Marathon Executive
Lee, Robert Edwin	Playwright
Lejeune, Jerome J L M	Geneticist
Leontovich, Eugenie	Actress
Lesch, George H	Businessman
Levin, Harry T	Educator, Writer
Levinson, Daniel	Educator, Psychologist
Ley, Margaretha	Fashion Designer
Lipsig, Harry H	Attorney
Lleras o, Carlos	President, Colombia
Loeb, William	Editor
Long, Clarence	Representative, MD
Lopat, Eddie	Baseball Player
Louis Ferdinand H	Prince, Prussia
Lubin, Arthur	Movie Director
Luciano, Ron	Baseball Umpire
Lupino, Ida	Actress, Director
Lutoslawski, Witold	Composer
Luyten, Willem J	Astronomer
Lwoff, Andre	Nobel Laureate
MacKinnon, George E	Judge
Madigan, Edward	Secretary, Agriculture
Maier, Henry W	Mayor, Milwaukee
Maier, Ulrike	Skier
Mancini, Henry	Composer, Pianist
Mantle, Mickey C	Baseball Player
Marshall, Catherine	Writer
Martin, Charles E	Cartoonist
Martin, Ernest	Theater, Movie Producer
Marty, Francois	Religious Leader
Masina, Giulietta	Actress
Masserman, Jules H	Psychoanalyst
Mata, Eduardo	Conductor
Mattus, Reuben	Businessman
Maung Maung Kha, U	President, Myanmar
Maxwell, Vera H	Fashion Designer
May, John L	Religious Leader
May, Rollo	Psychiatrist
McCabe, Charles	Columnist
McCann, Owen	Religious Leader
McClure, Doug	Actor
McCoy, Charles B	Businessman
McCracken, G Herbert	Football Coach
McGuire, Frank J	Basketball Coach
McNally, Stephen	Actor
McRae, Carmen	Singer
Meister, Alton	Biochemist
Mellanby, Kenneth	Entomolgist, gist
Merbah, Kasdi	Prime Minister, Algeria
Mercouri, Melina	Actress
Merrill, James	Writer
Meyer, Louis	Auto Racing Driver
Michael, Edward S	WW II Hero (CMH)
Michelangeli, Arturo B	Concert Pianist
Millar, Margaret	Writer
Mitchell, Cameron	Actor
Moertel, Charles G	Physician
Moffett, William A	Museum Official
Montgomery, Elizabeth	Actress
Monzon, Carlos	Boxer
Moore, Charles W	Architect
Moore, Richard A	Diplomat
Moore, Terry B	Baseball Player
Morgan, Dennis	Actor, Singer
Morgan, Henry	Actor
Morgan, William W	Astronomer
Morrill, Priscilla	Actress
Morris, John M	Editorial Cartoonist
Moschino, Franco	Fashion Designer
Moses, Gilbert	Movie, Theater Director
Mosienko, William	Hockey Player
Moya, J Hidalgo	Architect
Muir, Jean E	Fashion Designer
Munger, George (Red)	Football Coach
Munro, Hamish N	Biochemist
Murphy, Franklin D	Educator, Publisher
Murphy, William B	Businessman
Natcher, William H	Representative, KY
Natwick, Mildred	Actress
Naumann, William L	Businessman
Nauta, Walle J H	Anatomist
Needham, Joseph	Biochemist
Nelson, Harriet	Actress, Singer
Nelson, Lindsey	Sportscaster
Neumann, Vaclav	Conductor
Nichols, CheChet	Baseball Player
Nickerson, Albert L	Businessman
Nier, Alfred O C	Physicist
Niles, Wendell	Entertainer
Nilsson, Harry	Singer, Songwriter
Nixon, Richard M	President, USA
Nizer, Louis	Attorney, Writer
Novotna, Jarmila	Opera Singer
Ntaryamira, Cyprien	President, Burundi
Nu, U	Prime Minister, Burma
O'Kane, Richard	WW II Hero (CMH)
O'Neal, Patrick	Actor
O'Neill, Thomas P (Tip)	House Speaker
O'Toole, John E	Businessman
Odinga, A Oginga	Government Official
Ogarkov, Nikolay I	Army Marshal
Olson, Everett C	Paleobiologist
Onassis, Jacqueline	President 's Wife
Ongania, Juan Carlos	President, Argentina
Onoe, Baiko, II	Kabuki Dancer
Osborn, Robert C	Cartoonist
Osborne, Gregory	Ballet Dancer
Osborne, John	Playwright
Overcash, Reece A, Jr	Businessman
Oxenhorn, Harvey	Writer
Pappenheimer, Alwin M, Jr	Biologist
Parsons, Geoffrey	Concert Pianist
Pass, Joe	Jazz Guitarist
Patinkin, Don	Economist
Patten, Edward J	Representative, NJ
Pauling, Linus C	Nobel Laureate
Paupini, Giuseppe	Religious Leader
Pavan, Pietro Cardinal	Religious Leader
Penry, Richard	Vietnam War Hero (CMH)
Peierls, Rudolph	Physicist
Peppard, George	Actor
Perpich, Rudy	Governor, MN
Perry, Frank	Movie Director
Perry, Fred	Tennis Player
Petrie, Milton J	Businessman
Pfaffmann, Carl	Physiological
Phoumi Vongvichit	President, Laos
Pilkington, L Alastir B	Engineer, Inventor
Pilous, Rudy	Hockey Coach, Executive
Place, B C Godfrey	WW II Hero (VC)
Pleasence, Donald	Actor
Plunkett, Roy J	Inventor
Polyansky, Anatoliy T	Architect
Ponnamperuma, Cyril A	Chemist
Pope-Hennessy, John	Museum Director
Popper, Karl	Philosopher
Porter, Eric	Actor
Potter, Dennis	Writer
Preston, Lewis T	Financier
Preus, Jacob A O	Religious Leader
Price, George	Cartoonist
Primus, Pearl	Dancer, Choreographer

Prothro, Tommy	Football Coach
Pye, A Kenneth	Educator
Quennell, Peter	Writer
Ralston, Esther	Actress
Rambo, Dack	Actor
Ratner, Max	Businessman
Ray, Dixy Lee	Governor, WA
Raye, Martha	Comedienne
Redenbacher, Orville	Businessman
Reese, Jimmie	Baseball Coach
Renaud, Madeleine	Actress
Rey, Fernando	Actor
Reynolds, Allie P	Baseball Player
Reynolds, Robert O	Football Player
Rhodes, Hari	Actor
Rich, Charles A (Charlie)	Singer
Richter, Hans W	Writer
Rie, Lucie	Ceramist
Riesel, Victor	Columnist
Roberts, Dennis J	Governor, RI
Robertson, James D	Anatomist
Robinson, Cleveland L	Labor Leader
Roche, John P	Political Scientist
Rodger, George W A	Photographer
Roebling, Mary G	Financier
Rogers, Ginger	Actress
Rogers, Henry	Public Relations Expert
Roland, Gilbert	Actor
Rollins, Orville W	Businessman
Romero, Cesar	Actor
Romney, George W	Secretary, HUD
Roosa, Stuart A	Astronaut
Rossi, Agnelo Cardinal	Religious Leader
Rozsa, Miklos	Composer
Rubin, Jerry	Political Activist
Rudolf, Max	Conductor
Rudolph, Wilma	Track Athlete
Rush, Kenneth	Government Official
Rusk, Dean	Secretary, State
Rutledge, W A	Businessman
Ryan, John T, Jr	Businessman
Sagendorf, Forrest (Bud)	Cartoonist
Salk, Jonas E	Physician, Scientist
Salomon, Richard	Businessman
Saltzman, Charles E	Financier
Saltzman, Harry	Movie, Theater Producer
Samuel, Primate	Religious Leader
San Romani, Archie J	Track Athlete
Sargent, Dick	Actor
Sarton, May	Author, Poet
Sauer, George	Football Player, Coach
Savalas, Telly	Actor
Scali, John A	Commentator
Scharrer, Berta V	Anatomist
Schiller, Karl	Government Official
Schmidt, Ernest J	Basketball Player
Schmitt, Francis O	Neurobiologist
Schneerson, Menachem	Religious Leader
Schwartzberg, Howard	Judge
Schwarz, Rudolf	Conductor
Schweitzer, Pierre-Paul	Financier
Schwinger, Julian S	Nobel Laureate
Scott, Fred	Actor
Scott, Hugh D, Jr	Senator, PA
Seldes, George	Writer
Seligman, Henry	Nuclear Scientist
Sellin, Thorsten	Sociologist
Senna, Ayrton	Auto Racing Driver
Shackleton, Edward	Government Official
Shad, John S R	Government Official
Shannon, James A	Medical Administrator
Shapp, Milton J	Governor, PA
Sharkey, Jack	Boxer
Sharp, Eric	Businessman
Shaw, Harry A, III	Businessman
Shea, Charles W	WW II Hero (CMH)
Sherrod, Robert L	Writer
Shilts, Randy	Writer
Shore, Dinah	Singer
Shulman, Irving	Writer
Shutt, Edwin H, Jr	Businessman
Siad Barre, Muhammed	Leader, Somalia
Sigler, Franklin E	WW II Hero (CMH)
Sikes, Robert L F	Representative, FL
Silk, Leonard S	Economist, Columnist
Simms, Ginny	Singer
Simpson, Adele	Fashion Designer
Singh, G Zail	President, India
Singh, Swaran	Government Official, India
Skala, Lilia	Actress
Smith, Hal	Actor
Smith, John	Government Official
Smith, Margaret Chase	Senator, ME
Smith, Oliver	Theatrical Designer
Smith, Page	Educator
Smith, Willie Mae Ford	Singer
Smithson, Alison M	Architect
Smoktunovsky, Innokenty M	Actor
Solandt, Ormond M	Physiologist
Somes, Michael	Ballet Dancer
Souphanouvong	President, Laos
Spadolini, Giovanni	Prime Minister, Italy
Spender, Stephen	Writer, Poet, Critic
Sperry, Roger W	Nobel Laureate
Spivak, Lawrence	Commentator
Spoehr, Alexander	Anthropologist
Sprague, E Russell	Businessman
Squire, Katherine	Actress
Stacy, Jess	Jazz Pianist
Stander, Lionel	Actor
Steegmuller, Francis	Writer
Steinberg, Dick	Football Executive
Steinke, Gil	Football Coach
Stennis, John C	Senator, MS
Stephens, Helen	Track Athlete
Stibitz, George R	Inventor
Stone, Ezra	Actor
Stone, Michael P W	Government Official
Stowe, Leland	Journalist
Stratton, Julius A	Physicist
Strode, Woody	Actor
Strom, Earl	Basketball Referee
Styne, Jule	Composer, Producer
Suchon, Eugen	Composer
Sulkin, Sidney	Editor
Sullivan, Barry	Actor
Sutton, Grady	Actor
Swainson, John B	Governor, MI
Swann, Donald I	Comedian, Composer
Swayze, John Cameron	Commentator
Swenson, Swen	Actor, Dancer
Tagliavini, Ferruccio	Opera Singer
Tandy, Jessica	Actress
Tang, Thomas	Judge
Taper, S Mark	Financier
Tarancon, Enrique	Religious Leader
Tax, Sol	Anthropologist
Taylor, Chuck	Football Player, Coach
Taylor, Dub	Actor
Taylor, George	Botanist
Taylor, Peter M H	Writer
Tedrow, Irene	Actress
Temin, Howard M	Nobel Laureate
Tenney, Mesh	Thoroughbred Trainer
Thorneycroft, G E P	Government Official
Throneberry, Marv	Baseball Player
Timbers, William H	Judge
Timken, William R	Businessman
Timmerman, George B, Jr	Governor, SC
Tinbergen, Jan	Nobel Laureate
Tippit, Jack	Cartoonist
Tobias, Harry	Composer
Tobin, Genevieve	Actress
Townsend, Dallas S, Jr	Commentator
Travers, Bill	Actor
Turner, Lana	Actress
Upham, Charles H	WW II Hero (VC & Bar)
Urban, Matt L	WW II Hero (CMH)
Uwilingiyimana, Agathe	PM Rwanda
Van de Kamp, Peter	Astronomer
Venuta, Benay	Singer, Actress, Dancer
Versalles, Zoilo	Baseball Player
Victor, Paul-Emile	Explorer, Civil Engineer
Vines, H Ellsworth	Tennis Player
Volpe, John A	Secretary, Transportation
Wade, L Margaret	Basketball Coach
Wain, John B	Writer
Walcott, Jersey Joe	Boxer
Walker, John C	Plant Pathologist
Walker, Sydney	Actor
Walker, Wilbert A	Businessman
Walsh, Michael H	Businessman
Walton, Ernest T S	Nobel Laureate
Wang, Hao	Philosopher
Warner, Jack M	Movie Producer
Watanabe, Michio	Government Official

NECROLOGY

Waters, Frank	Writer
Watson, Wilson D	WW II Hero (CMH)
Watts, James	Surgeon
Wayne, David	Actor
Weaver, Monte M	Baseball Player
Wells, Frank	Entertainment Executive
Wells, John W	Geologist
Welsh, Matthew	Governor, IN
Wessner, Kenneth T	Businessman
Wetherby, Lawrence W	Governor, KY
White, William S	Journalist
Whitten, Jamie L	Representative, MS
Wiesner, Jerome B	Engineer
Wigglesworth, Vincent B	Entomologist
Wigner, Eugene P	Nobel Laureate
Wilkinson, Charles (Bud)	Football Coach
Williams, Ike	Boxer
Williams, Robley C	Biophysicist
Wilson n, Harold	Prime Minister, England
Wilt, Fred	Track Athlete, Coach
Winfrey, Bill	Thoroughbred Racing Trainer
Wohlstetter, Charles	Businessman
Wolff, Roger F	Baseball Player
Wolfman Jack	Disc Jockey
Worner, Manfred	Government Official
Wright, Jerauld	Navy Admiral, Diplomat
Wyatt, Katy Rodolph	Skier
Wyckoff, Ralph W G	Physicist
Wylie, Laurence W	Educator
Yancey, Bert	Golfer
Yang Dezhi	Army General, China
Yariv, Aharon	Army General, Israel
Yegorov, Boris B	Cosmonaut
Yen, Chia-Kan	President, Taiwan
Young, Terence	Movie Director
Zetterling, Mai E	Movie Director, Actress
Zimmerman, Charles J	Businessman

U.S. SENATE MEMBERSHIP & ADDRESSES

The men and women below are current members of the U.S. Senate. They can all be reached by writing in care of U.S. Senate.
Letters should be addressed:

The Honorable Jane/John Doe
U.S. Senator from ---
% U.S. Senate
Washington, D.C 20510 USA

Dear Mr./ Ms. Senator ---:

Abraham, Spencer	Michigan	Dorgan, Byron L	North Dakota
Akaka, Daniel K	Hawaii	Exon, J James	Nebraska
Ashcroft, John	Missouri	Faircloth, Duncan M (Lauch)	North Carolina
Baucus, Max S	Montana	Feingold, Russell D	Wisconsin
Bennett, Robert F (Rob)	Utah	Feinstein, Dianne	California
Biden, Joseph R, Jr	Delaware	Ford, Wendell H	Kentucky
Bingaman, Jeff	New Mexico	Frist, Bill	Tennessee
Bond, Christopher (Kit)	Missouri	Glenn, John H, Jr	Ohio
Boxer, Barbara	California	Gorton, Slade	Washington
Bradley, William W (Bill)	New Jersey	Graham, D Robert (Bob)	Florida
Breaux, John B	Louisiana	Gramm, W. Phillip (Phil)	Texas
Brown, Hank	Colorado	Grams, Rodney D (Rod)	Minnesota
Bryan, Richard H	Nevada	Grassley, Charles E	Iowa
Bumpers, Dale	Arkansas	Gregg, Judd A	New Hampshire
Burns, Conrad	Montana	Harkin, Thomas R	Iowa
Byrd, Robert C.	West Virginia	Hatch, Orrin G	Utah
Campbell, Ben Nighthorse	Colorado	Hatfield, Mark O	Oregon
Chafee, John H	Rhode Island	Heflin, Howell T	Alabama
Coats, Daniel R	Indiana	Helms, Jesse	North Carolina
Cochran, Thad	Mississippi	Hollings, Ernest F (Fritz)	South Carolina
Cohen, William S	Maine	Hutchison, Kay Bailey	Texas
Conrad, Kent	North Dakota	Inhofe, James M	Oklahoma
Coverdell, Paul D	Georgia	Inouye, Daniel K	Hawaii
Craig, Larry E	Idaho	Jeffords, James M (Jim)	Vermont
D'Amato, Alfonse M	New York	Johnston, J. Bennett, Jr	Louisiana
Daschle, Thomas A	South Dakota	Kassebaum, Nancy Landon	Kansas
DeWine, Michael	Ohio	Kempthorne, Dirk A	Idaho
Dodd, Christopher J	Connecticut	Kennedy, Edward M (Ted)	Massachusetts
Dole, Robert J	Kansas	Kerry, J Robert (Bob)	Nebraska
Domenici, Pete V	New Mexico	Kerry, John F	Massachusetts

Kohl, Herbert H	Wisconsin	Pryor, David H	Arkansas
Kyl, Jon L	Arizona	Reid, Harry M	Nevada
Lautenberg, Frank R	New Jersey	Robb, Charles S	Virginia
Leahy, Patrick J	Vermont	Rockefeller, John D, IV	West Virginia
Levin, Carl	Michigan	Roth, William V, Jr.	Delaware
Lieberman, Joseph I	Connecticut	Santorum, Richard J (Rick)	Pennsylvania
Lott, Trent	Mississippi	Sarbanes, Paul S	Maryland
Lugar, Richard G	Indiana	Shelby, Richard C	Alabama
Mack, Corneilus M (Connie), III	Florida	Simon, Paul	Illinois
McCain, John S, III	Arizona	Simpson, Alan K	Wyoming
McConnell, Mitch	Kentucky	Smith, Robert C	New Hampshire
Mikulski, Barbara A	Maryland	Snowe, Olympia J	Maine
Moseley-Braun, Carol	Illinois	Specter, Arlen	Pennsylvania
Moynihan, Daniel Patrick	New York	Stevens, Theodore F	Alaska
Murkowski, Frank H	Alaska	Thomas, Craig	Wyoming
Murray, Patty	Washington	Thompson, Fred Dalton	Tennessee
Nickles, Donald L	Oklahoma	Thurmond, J Strom	South Carolina
Nunn, Samuel (Sam)	Georgia	Warner, John W	Virginia
Pell, Clairborne De B	Rhode Island	Wellstone, Paul D	Minnesota
Pressler, Larry	South Dakota		

U.S. HOUSE OF REPRESENTATIVES MEMBERSHIP & ADDRESSES

The men and women below are current members of the U.S. House of Representatives. They can all be reached by writing in care of U.S. Senate. Letters should be addressed:

> The Honorable Jane/John Doe
> U.S. Representative from ---
> % U.S. House of Representatives
> Washington, D.C 205102USA

> Dear Mr./ Ms. Representative ---:

Abercrombie, Neil	Hawaii	Blute, Peter I	Massachusetts
Ackerman, Gary L	New York	Boehlert, Sherwood L	New York
Allard, Wayne	Colorado	Boehner, John A	Ohio
Andrews, Robert E	New Jersey	Bonilla, Henry	Texas
Archer, William R (Bill), Jr	Texas	Bonior, David E	Michigan
Armey, Richard K	Texas	Bono, Sonny	California
Bachus, Spencer T, III	Alabama	Borski, Robert A, Jr	Pennsylvania
Baesler, Scotty	Kentucky	Boucher, Frederick C (Rick)	Virginia
Baker, Richard H	Louisiana	Brewster, Bill K	Oklahoma
Baker, William P (Bill)	California	Brooks, Susan	California
Baldacci, John	Maine	Browder, J Glen	Alabama
Ballenger, T Cass	North Carolina	Brown, Corrine	Florida
Barcia, James A	Michigan	Brown, George E, Jr	California
Barr, Bob	Georgia	Brown, Sherrod	Ohio
Barrett, Thomas M	Wisconsin	Brownback, Sam	Kansas
Barrett, William E (Bill)	Nebraska	Bryant, Ed	Tennessee
Bartlett, Roscoe G	Maryland	Bryant, John W	Texas
Barton, Joe L	Texas	Bryce, Deborah	Ohio
Bass, Charles	New Hampshire	Bunning, James P D (Jim)	Kentucky
Bateman, Herbert H (Herb)	Virginia	Burr, Richard	North Carolina
Becerra, Xavier	California	Burton, Dan L	Indiana
Beilenson, Anthony C	California	Buyer, Stephen E	Indiana
Bensten, Ken	Texas	Callahan, H L (Sonny)	Alabama
Bereuter, Douglas K	Nebraska	Calvert, Ken	California
Berman, Howard L	California	Camp, Dave	Michigan
Bevill, Tom	Alabama	Canady, Charles T	Florida
Bilbray, Brian P	California	Cardin, Benjamin L	Maryland
Bilirakis, Michael	Florida	Castle, Michael N	Delaware
Bishop, Sanford D, Jr	Georgia	Chabot, Steve	Ohio
Bliley, Thomas J (Tom), Jr	Virginia	Chambliss, Saxby	Georgia

V.I.P. Address Book

U.S. HOUSE OF REPRESENTATIVES

Chapman, James L (Jim)	Texas	Farr, Sam	California
Chenoweth, Helen	Idaho	Fattah, Chaka	Pennsylvania
Christensen, Jon	Nebraska	Fawell, Harris W	Illinois
Chrysler, Dick	Michigan	Fazio, Vic	California
Clay, William (Bill), Sr	Missouri	Fields, Cleo	Louisiana
Clayton, Eva M	North Carolina	Fields, Jack M	Texas
Clement, Bob	Tennessee	Filner, Robert (Bob)	California
Clinger, William F (Bill), Jr	Pennsylvania	Flake, Floyd H	New York
Clyburn, James E	South Carolina	Flanagan, Michael Patrick	Illinois
Coble, Howard	North Carolina	Foglietta, Thomas M	Pennsylvania
Coburn, Tom	Oklahoma	Foley, Mark	Florida
Coleman, Ronald D	Texas	Forbes, Michael P	New York
Collins, Barbara-Rose	Michigan	Ford, Harold E	Tennessee
Collins, Cardiss R	Illinois	Fowler, Tillie K	Florida
Collins, Michael A (Mac)	Georgia	Fox, Jon D	Pennsylvania
Combest, Larry	Texas	Frank, Barney	Massachusetts
Condit, Gary A	California	Franks, Gary A	Connecticut
Conyers, John, Jr	Michigan	Franks, Robert D (Bob)	New Jersey
Cooley, Wes	Oregon	Frelinghuysen, Rodney	New Jersey
Costello, Jerry F	Illinois	Frisa, Daniel	New York
Cox, C Christopher	California	Frost, J Martin	Texas
Coyne, William J	Pennsylvania	Funderburk, David	North Carolina
Cramer, Robert E (Bud), Jr	Alabama	Furse, Elizabeth	Oregon
Crane, Philip M	Illinois	Gallegly, Elton W	California
Crapo, Michael D	Idaho	Ganske, Greg	Iowa
Cremeans, Frank A	Ohio	Gejdenson, Samuel	Connecticut
Cubin, Barbara	Wyoming	Gekas, George W	Pennsylvania
Cunningham, Randall (Duke)	California	Gephardt, Richard A	Missouri
Danner, Patsy Ann (Pat)	Missouri	Geren, Preston (Pete)	Texas
Davis, Thomas M, III	Virginia	Gibbons, Samuel M (Sam)	Florida
De la Garza, Eligio (Kika)	Texas	Gilchrest, Wayne T	Maryland
Deal, Nathan	Georgia	Gillmor, Paul E	Ohio
DeFazio, Peter A	Oregon	Gilman, Benjamin A	New York
DeLauro, Rosa L	Connecticut	Gingrich, Newton L (Newt)	Georgia
DeLay, Thomas D (Tom)	Texas	Gonzalez, Henry B	Texas
Dellums, Ronald V	California	Goodlatte, Robert W (Bob)	Virginia
Deutsch, Peter	Florida	Goodling, William F	Pennsylvania
Diaz-Balart, Lincoln	Florida	Gordon, Bart	Tennessee
Dickey, Jay W, Jr	Arkansas	Goss, Porter J	Florida
Dicks, Norman D	Washington	Graham, Lindsey	South Carolina
Dingell, John D, Jr	Michigan	Green, Gene	Texas
Dixon, Julian C	California	Greenwood, James C	Pennsylvania
Doggett, Lloyd	Texas	Gunderson, Steve C	Wisconsin
Dooley, Calvin M, Jr	California	Gutierrez, Luis V	Illinois
Doolittle, John T	California	Gutknecht, Gil	Minnesota
Dornan, Robert K (Bob)	California	Hall, Ralph M	Texas
Doyle, Mike	Pennsylvania	Hall, Tony P	Ohio
Dreier, David T	California	Hamilton, Lee H	Indiana
Duncan, John J, Jr	Tennessee	Hancock, Melton D (Mel)	Missouri
Dunn, Jennifer B	Washington	Hansen, James V	Utah
Durbin, Richard J	Illinois	Hastert, J Dennis	Illinois
Edwards, Chet	Texas	Hastings, Alcee L	Florida
Ehlers, Vernon J	Michigan	Hastings, Doc	Washington
Ehrlich, Robert L, Jr	Maryland	Hayes, James A (Jimmy)	Louisiana
Emerson, William	Missouri	Hayworth, J D	Arizona
Engel, Eliot L	New York	Hefley, Joel M	Colorado
English, Phil	Pennsylvania	Hefner, W G (Bill)	North Carolina
Ensign, John	Nevada	Heineman, Frederick Kenneth	North Carolina
Eshoo, Anna G	California	Herger, Wally W, Jr	California
Evans, Lane	Illinois	Hilleary, Van	Tennessee
Everett, Terry	Alabama	Hilliard, Earl F	Alabama
Ewing, Thomas W	Illinois	Hinchey, Maurice D, Jr	New York

U.S. HOUSE OF REPRESENTATIVES

Hobson, David L	Ohio
Hoekstra, Peter	Michigan
Hoke, Martin R	Ohio
Holdon, Tim	Pennsylvania
Horn, J Stephen	California
Hostettler, John	Indiana
Houghton, Amory, Jr	New York
Hoyer, Steny H	Maryland
Hunter, Duncan L	California
Hutchinson, Y Tim	Arkansas
Hyde, Henry J	Illinois
Inglis, Robert D (Bob)	South Carolina
Istook, Ernest J (Jim), Jr	Oklahoma
Jacobs, Andrew, Jr	Indiana
Jefferson, William J (Jeff)	Louisiana
Johnson, Eddie Bernice	Texas
Johnson, Nancy L	Connecticut
Johnson, Samuel (Sam)	Texas
Johnson, Timothy P	South Dakota
Johnston, Harry A, II	Florida
Jones, Walter B, Jr	North Carolina
Kanjorski, Paul E	Pennsylvania
Kaptur, Marcy	Ohio
Kasich, John R	Ohio
Kelly, Sue W	New York
Kennedy, Joseph P, II	Massachusetts
Kennedy, Patrick J	Rhode Island
Kennelly, Barbara Bailey	Connecticut
Kildee, Dale E	Michigan
Kim, Jay	California
King, Peter T	New York
Kingston, Jack	Georgia
Kleczka, Gerald D	Wisconsin
Klink, Ron	Pennsylvania
Klug, Scott L	Wisconsin
Knollenberg, Joseph (Ken)	Michigan
Kolbe, James T (Jim)	Arizona
LaFalce, John J	New York
LaHood, Ray	Illinois
Lambert, Blance M	Arkansas
Lantos, Thomas P	California
Largent, Steve	Oklahoma
Latham, Tom	Iowa
LaTourette, Steven C	Ohio
Laughlin, Gregory H	Texas
Lazio, Rick A	New York
Leach, James A S (Jim)	Iowa
Lee, Sheila Jackson	Texas
Levin, Sander M	Michigan
Lewis, Jerry	California
Lewis, John R	Georgia
Lewis, Ron	Kentucky
Lightfoot, Jim Ross	Iowa
Linder, John E	Georgia
Lipinski, William O	Illinois
Livingston, Robert L (Bob), Jr	Louisiana
LoBiondo, Frank A	New Jersey
Lofgren, Zoe	California
Longley, James B, Jr	Maine
Lowey, Nita M	New York
Lucas, Frank D	Oklahoma
Luther, William P (Bill)	Minnesota
Maloney, Carolyn B	New York
Manton, Thomas J	New York
Manzullo, Donald A	Illinois
Markey, Edward J	Massachusetts
Martinez, Matthew G, Jr	California
Martini, Bill	New Jersey
Mascara, Frank R	Pennsylvania
Matsui, Robert T	California
McCarthy, Karen	Missouri
McCollum, I William (Bill), Jr	Florida
McCrery, Jim	Louisiana
McDade, Joseph M	Pennsylvania
McDermott, James A (Jim)	Washington
McHale, Paul	Pennsylvania
McHugh, John M	New York
McInnis, Scott S	Colorado
McIntosh David M	Indiana
McKeon, Howard P (Buck)	California
McKinney, Cynthia A	Georgia
McNulty, Michael R	New York
Meehan, Martin T	Massachusetts
Meek, Carrie P	Florida
Menendez, Robert	New Jersey
Metcalf, Jack	Washington
Meyers, Jan	Kansas
Mfume, Kweisi	Maryland
Mica, John L	Florida
Miller, Dan	Florida
Miller, George	California
Minge, David	Minnesota
Mink, Patsy Takemoto	Hawaii
Moakley, John Joseph	Massachusetts
Molinari, Susan K	New York
Mollohan, Alan B	West Virginia
Montgomery, Gillespie V (Sonny)	Mississippi
Moorhead, Carlos J	California
Moran, James P, Jr	Virginia
Morella, Constance A	Maryland
Murtha, John P	Pennsylvania
Myers, John T	Indiana
Myrick, Sue	North Carolina
Nadler, Jerrold L (Jerry)	New York
Neal, Richard E	Massachusetts
Nethercutt, George	Washington
Neumann, Mark W	Wisconsin
Ney, Bob	Ohio
Norwood, Charlie	Georgia
Nussle, James A (Jim)	Iowa
Oberstar, James L	Minnesota
Obey, David R	Wisconsin
Olver, John W	Massachusetts
Ortiz, Solomon P	Texas
Orton, William H (Bill)	Utah
Owens, Major R O	New York
Oxley, Michael G	Ohio
Packard, Ronald	California
Pallone, Frank, Jr	New Jersey
Parker, Michael (Mike)	Mississippi
Pastor, Ed	Arizona
Paxon, L William (Bill)	New York
Payne, Donald M	New Jersey
Payne, Lewis F, Jr	Virginia
Pelosi, Nancy	California
Peterson, Collin C	Minnesota

746

U.S. HOUSE OF REPRESENTATIVES

Peterson, Douglas (Pete)	Florida
Petri, Thomas E	Wisconsin
Pickett, Owen B	Virginia
Pombo, Richard W	California
Pomeroy, Earl R	North Dakota
Porter, John E	Illinois
Portman, Rob	Ohio
Poshard, Glenn W	Illinois
Quillen, James H (Jimmy)	Tennessee
Quinn, Jack	New York
Radanovich, George P	California
Rahall, Nick Joe, II	West Virginia
Ramstad, Jim	Minnesota
Rangel, Charles B	New York
Reed, John F (Jack)	Rhode Island
Regula, Ralph	Ohio
Richardson, William B (Bill)	New Mexico
Riggs, Frank	California
Rivers, Lynn Nancy	Michigan
Roberts, Charles P (Pat)	Kansas
Roemer, Timothy J	Indiana
Rogers, Harold (Hal)	Kentucky
Rohrabacher, Dana	California
Ros-Lehtinen, Ileana	Florida
Rose, Charles G, III	North Carolina
Roth, Toby	Wisconsin
Roukema, Margeret S	New Jersey
Roybal-Allard, Lucille	California
Royce, Edward R (Ed)	California
Rush, Bobby L	Illinois
Sabo, Martin O	Minnesota
Salmon, Matt	Arizona
Sanders, Bernard (Bernie)	Vermont
Sanford, Mark	South Carolina
Sawyer, Thomas C	Ohio
Saxton, H James	New Jersey
Scarborough, Joe	Florida
Schaefer, Daniel L (Dan)	Colorado
Schiff, Steven H	New Mexico
Schroeder, Patricia S	Colorado
Schumer, Charles E	New York
Scott, Robert C (Bobby)	Virginia
Seastrand, Andrea	California
Sensenbrenner, F James, Jr	Wisconsin
Serrano, José E	New York
Shadegg, John	Arizona
Shaw, E Clay, Jr	Florida
Shays, Christopher	Connecticut
Shuster, E G (Bud)	Pennsylvania
Sisisky, Norman	Virginia
Skaggs, David E	Colorado
Skeen, Joseph R	New Mexico
Skelton, Isaac Newton (Ike), IV	Missouri
Slaughter, Louise M	New York
Smith, Christopher H	New Jersey
Smith, Lamar S	Texas
Smith, Linda	Washington
Smith, Nick	Michigan
Solomon, Gerald B H	New York
Souder, Mark Edward	Indiana
Spence, Floyd D	South Carolina
Spratt, John M, Jr	South Carolina
Stark, Fortney N (Pete)	California
Stearns, Clifford B (Cliff)	Florida
Stenholm, Charles W	Texas
Stockman, Steve	Texas
Stokes, Louis	Ohio
Studds, Gerry E	Massachusetts
Stump, Bob	Arizona
Stupak, Bart T	Michigan
Talent, James M	Missouri
Tanner, John S	Tennessee
Tate, Randy	Washington
Tauzin, Wilbert J (Billy)	Louisiana
Taylor, Charles H	North Carolina
Taylor, Gene	Mississippi
Tejeda, Frank	Texas
Thomas, William M	California
Thompson, Bennie G	Mississippi
Thornberry, William M (Mac)	Texas
Thornton, Ray	Arkansas
Thurman, Karen L	Florida
Tiahrt, Todd	Kansas
Torkildsen, Peter G	Massachusetts
Torres, Esteban E	California
Torricelli, Robert G	New Jersey
Towns, Edolphus	New York
Traficant, James A, Jr	Ohio
Tucker, Walter R, III	California
Upton, Frederick S	Michigan
Velazquez, Nydia M	New York
Vento, Bruce F	Minnesota
Visclosky, Peter J	Indiana
Volkmer, Harold L	Missouri
Vucanovich, Barbara F	Nevada
Waldholtz, Enid Greene	Utah
Walker, Robert S	Pennsylvania
Walsh, James T	New York
Wamp, Zach	Tennessee
Ward, Mike	Kentucky
Waters, Maxine	California
Watt, Melvin L	North Carolina
Watts, J C	Oklahoma
Waxman, Henry A	California
Webber, Catherine	Oregon
Weldon, Dave	Florida
Weldon, W Curtis	Pennsylvania
Weller, Gerald C (Jerry)	Illinois
White, Rick	Washington
Whitfield, Edward	Kentucky
Wicker, Roger	Mississippi
Williams, Pat	Montana
Wilson, Charles (Charlie)	Texas
Wise, Robert E, Jr	West Virginia
Wolf, Frank R	Virginia
Woolsey, Lynn C	California
Wyden, Ronald L	Oregon
Wynn Albert R	Maryland
Yates, Sidney R	Illinois
Young, Donald E	Alaska
Young, C W (Bill)	Florida
Zeliff, Willaim H, Jr	New Hampshire
Zimmer, Richard A (Dick)	New Jersey

Abrams-Rubaloff Lawrence	8075 W 3rd St, #303	Los Angeles, CA 90048, USA
Abrams Artists	420 Madison Ave, #1400	New York, NY 10017, USA
ACC	102 Ryders Lane	East Brunswick, NJ 08816, USA
Aces Agency	6820 Katherine Ave	Van Nuys, CA 91405, USA
Advantage International	1025 Thomas Jefferson NW	Washington 20007, USA
Agency, The	1800 Ave of Stars, #400	Los Angeles, CA 90067, USA
Agents Artistiques Beaume	4 Rue De Ponthieu	75008 Paris, France
Ambrosio/Mortimer	9150 Wilshire Blvd, #175	Beverly Hills, CA 90212, USA
Ambrosio/Mortimer	165 W 46th St, #1109	New York, NY 10036, USA
Amsel Eisenstadt Frazie	6310 San Vicente Blvd, #401	Los Angeles, CA 90048, USA
Agency For Performing Arts	9000 Sunset Blvd, #1200	Los Angeles, CA 90069, USA
Agency For Performing Arts	888 7th Ave	New York, NY 10106, USA
Agentur Killer	54 Harthauser Str	81545 Munich, Germany
Arthur, (Irvin) Assoc	9363 Wilshire Blvd, #212	Beverly Hills, CA 90210, USA
Artists Agency	10000 Santa Monica Blvd, #305	Los Angeles, CA 90067, USA
Artists Group	10100 Santa Monica Blvd, #2490	Los Angeles, CA 90067, USA
Artmedia	10 Ave George V	75008 Paris, France
Associated Talent Int'l	1320 Armacost Ave, #2	Los Angeles, CA 90025, USA
Atkins Assoc	303 S Crescent Heights Blvd	Los Angeles, CA 90048, USA
Associated Booking Agency	1995 Broadway, #501	New York, NY 10023, USA
Badgley Connor	9229 Sunset Blvd, #311	Los Angeles, CA 90069, USA
Barr, (Rickey) Agency	PO Box 69590	Los Angeles, CA 90069, USA
Barz, (Richard A) Assoc	Rt 1, Box 91	Tannersville, PA 18372, USA
Bauman Hiller Assoc	5757 Wilshire Blvd, #PH 5	Los Angeles, CA 90036, USA
Bauman Hiller Assoc	250 W 57th St, #803	New York, NY 10107, USA
BDP Assoc	10637 Burbank Blvd	North Hollywood, CA 91601, USA
Beall, (Harry) Mgmt	PO Box 4	Shutesbury, MA 01702, USA
Belfrage, Julian	46 Albermarle St	London W1X 4PP, England
Belson & Klass Assoc	144 S Beverly Blvd, #405	Beverly Hills, CA 90212, USA
Berkeley Agency	2608 9th St	Berkeley, CA 94710, USA
Bethann Model Mgmt	36 N Moore St, #36-N,	New York, NY 10013, USA
Big J Productions	PO Box 24455	New Orleans, LA 70184, USA
Bikoff, (Yvette) Agency	8721 Santa Monica Blvd, #21	West Hollywood, CA 90069, USA
Blake Agency	415 N Camden Dr, #121	Beverly Hills, CA 90210
Blanchard, (Nina) Enterprises	957 N Cole Ave	Los Angeles, CA 90038, USA
Bloom, (J Michael) Ltd	9255 Sunset Blvd, #710	Los Angeles, CA 90069, USA
Bloom, (J Michael) Ltd	233 Park Ave S, #1000,	New York, NY 10017, USA
Bloom, Lloyd	1440 S Sepulveda Blvd, #110,	Los Angeles, CA 90025, USA
Bennett Morgan Assoc,	1282 Rt 376	Wappingers Falls, NY 12590, USA
Borinstein Oreck Bogart	8271 Melrose Ave, #110	Los Angeles, CA 90046, USA
Borman Sternberg	9220 Sunset Blvd, #320	Los Angeles, CA 90069, USA
Bresler Kelly Kipperman	15760 Ventura Blvd, #1730	Encino, CA 91436
Breslin, (Herbert) Inc	119 W 57th St	New York, NY 10019, USA
Brewis, (Alexis) Agency	12429 Laurel Terrace Dr	Studio City, CA 91604, USA
Brillstein Productions	9150 Wilshire Blvd, #350	Beverly Hills, CA 90212, USA
Brooke Dunn Oliver	9169 Sunset Blvd, #202	Los Angeles, CA 90069, USA
Brothers Mgmt,	141 Dunbar Ave	Fords, NJ 08863, USA
Buchwald, (Don) Assoc	9229 Sunset Blvd, #710	Los Angeles, 90069, USA
Buchwald, (Don) Assoc	10 E 44th St, #500	New York, NY 10017, USA
Burton, (Iris) Agency	1450 Belfast Dr	Los Angeles, CA 90069, USA
Calder Agency	19919 Redwing St	Woodland Hills, CA 91364, USA
Camden ITG Talent Agency	822 S Robertson Blvd, #200	Los Angeles, CA 90035, USA
Cassidy, (Thomas) Inc	0366 Horseshoe Dr	Basalt, CO 81621, USA
Columbia Artists Mgmt Inc	165 W 57th St	New York, NY 10019, USA
Carlyle, (Phyllis) Mgmt	5300 Melrose Ave, #305-E	Los Angeles, CA 90038, USA
Carroll, (William) Agency	139 N San Fernado Rd, #A	Burbank, CA 91502, USA
Cunningham-Escott-Dipene	10635 Santa Monica Blvd	Los Angeles, CA 90025, USA
Cunningham-Escott-Dipene	118 E 25th St, #600	New York, NY 10010, USA
Century Artists	9744 Wilshire Blvd, #308	Beverly Hills, CA 90212, USA
Charter Mgmt	8200 Wilshire Blvd, #218	Beverly Hills, CA 90211, USA
Chasin Agency	8899 Beverly Blvd, #716	Los Angeles, CA 902048 USA
Chatto & Linnit	Prince of Wales, Coventry St	London W1V 7FE, England

Circle Talent Assoc	433 N Camden Dr, #400	Beverly Hills, CA 90210, USA
Clark, (Dick) Agency	3003 W Olive Ave	Burbank, CA 91505, USA
Click Model Mgmt	881 7th Ave	New York, NY 10019, USA
Coast To Coast Talent Group	4942 Vineland Ave, #200	North Hollywood, CA 91601, USA
Colbert Artists Mgmt	111 W 57th St	New York, NY 10019, USA
Commercials Unlimited	9601 Wilshirre Blvd, #620	Beverly Hills, CA 90210, USA
Conner, (Hall) Agency	9169 Sunset Blvd	Los Angeles, CA 90069, USA
Contemporary Artists	1427 3rd St Promenade, #205	Santa Monica, CA 90401, USA
Conway Van Gelder Robinson	18-21 Jermyn St	London SW1Y 6HB, England
Cosden, (Robert) Enterprises	3518 Cahuenga Blvd W, #216	Los Angeles 90068, USA
Craig Agency	8485 Melrose Place, #E	Los Angeles, CA 90069, USA
Creative Artists Agency	9830 Wilshire Blvd	Beverly Hills, CA 90212, USA
Creative Entertainment Assoc	2011 Ferry Ave, #U-19	Camden, NJ 08104, USA
Cumber, (Lil) Agency	6363 Sunset Blvd, #701	Los Angeles, CA 90028, USA
Curtis Brown	162-168 Regent St	London W1R 5TB, England
Dade/Schultz Agency	11846 Ventura Blvd, #100,	Studio City, CA 91604, USA
Daish, (Judy) Assoc	83 Eastbourne Mews	London W2 6LQ, England
DeLeon Artists	4031 Panama Court	Piedmont, CA 94611, USA
DGRW	1650 Broadway	New York, NY 10019, USA
Diamond Artists	215 N Barrington Ave	Los Angeles, CA 90049, USA
Diamond Artists	170 West End Ave, #3-K	New York, NY 10023, USA
Doty, (Patricia) Assoc	13455 Ventura Blvd, #210	Sherman Oaks, CA 91423, USA
Duncan Heath Assoc	Paramount House, 162 Wardour	London W1V 3AT, England
Elite Model Mgmt	111 E 22nd St, #200	New York, NY 10010, USA
Entertainment Talent Agency	PO Box 1821	Ojai, CA 93024, USA
Epstein-Wyckoff-Lamanna	280 S Beverly Dr, #400	Beverly Hills, CA 90212, USA
Famous Artists Agency	1700 Broadway, #500	New York, NY 10019, USA
Farrell, (Eileen) Agency	PO Box 15189	North Hollywood, CA 91615, USA
Felber, (William) Agency	2126 Cahuenga Blvd	Los Angeles, CA 90068, USA
Film Artists Assoc	7080 Hollywood Blvd, #1118	Los Angeles, CA 90028, USA
First Artists Assoc	10000 Riverside Dr, #10	Toluca Lake, CA 91602, USA
Flick East-West Talents	9057 Nemo St, #A	West Hollywood, CA 90069, USA
Flick East-West Talents	881 7th Ave	New York, NY 10019, USA
Ford Model Agency	344 E 59th St	New York, NY 10022, USA
Freed, (Barry) Co	2029 Century Park East, #600	Los Angeles, CA 90067, USA
Front Line Mgmt	8900 Wilshire Blvd, #300	Beverly Hills, CA 90211, USA
Gage Group	9255 Sunset Blvd, #515	Los Angeles, CA 90069, USA
Gage Group	315 W 57th St, #4-H	New York, NY 10019, USA
Dale Garrick Int''l	8831 Sunset Blvd, #402	Los Angeles, CA 90069, USA
Dale Garrick Int''l	117 W 48th St	New York, NY 10020, USA
Geddes Agency	1201 Greenacre Blvd	West Hollywood, CA 90046, USA
Geller, (Susan) Assoc	335 N Maple Dr, #254	Beverly Hills, CA 90210, USA
Gersh Agency	232 N Canon Dr	Beverly Hills, CA 90210, USA
Gerler/Stevens Assoc	3349 Cahuenga Blvd, #2	Los Angeles, CA 90068, USA
Gersh Agency	130 W 42nd St, #1804	New York, NY 10036, USA
Gewald, (Robert) Mgmt	58 W 58th St	New York, NY 10019, USA
Gibson, (J Carter) Agency	9000 Sunset Blvd, #801	Los Angeles, CA 90069, USA
Gold Marshak Assoc	3500 W Olive Ave, #1400	Burbank, CA 91505, USA
Gores/Fields Agency	10100 Santa Monica Blvd, #2500	Los Angeles, CA 90067, USA
Gorfaine/Schwarz/Roberts	3301 Barham Blvd, #201	Los Angeles, CA 90068, USA
Gordon Co	12700 Ventura Blvd, #340	Studio City, CA 91604, USA
Gray/Goodman	211 S Beverly Dr, #100	Beverly Hills, CA 90212, USA
Greenevine Agency	110 E 9th St, #C-1005	Los Angeles, CA 90079, USA
Hallmark Entertainment	8033 Sunset Blvd, #1000	Los Angeles, CA 90046, USA
Halsey, (Jim) Co	PO Box 40703	Nashville, TN 37204, USA
Halsey, (Jim) Co	3225 S Norwood Ave	Tulsa, OK 74135
Hatcher, (Lib) Mgmt	1610 16th Ave S	Nashville, TN 37212, USA
Henderson/Hogan Agency	247 S Beverly Dr, #102	Beverly Hills, CA 90212, USA
Henderson/Hogan Agency	850 7th Ave, #1003	New York, NY 10019, USA
Hill, (Terry M) Assoc	6430 Variel Ave, #101	Woodland Hills, CA 91367, USA
Hoffer, (Abby) Enterprises	223 1/2 E 48th St	New York, NY 10017, USA
HTM/Headliner Talent Mgmt	7200 France Ave S, #330	Edina, MN 55435, USA
Hutton Mgmt	200 Fulham Rd	London SW10 9PN, England
Innovative Artists	1999 Ave of Stars, #2850	Los Angeles, CA 90067, USA

Int'l Creative Mgmt	8941 Wilshire Blvd	Beverly Hills, CA 90212, USA
Int'l Creative Mgmt	76 Oxford St	London SW10 9PN, England
Int'l Creative Mgmt	40 W 57th St	New York, NY 10019, USA
Int'l Creative Mgmt	38 Via Siacci	00917 Rome, Italy
Int'l Creative Mgmt	33 Rue Marbeuf	75008 Paris, France
Int'l Management Group	1 Erieview Plaza, #1300	Cleveland, OH 44114, USA
Int'l Management Group	Pier House, Chiswick	London W4M 3NN, England
Jennings, (Thomas) Assoc	28036 Dorothy Dr, #210-A	Agoura, CA 91301, USA
Jovanovic, Management	24 Kathi-Kobus-Str	80797 Munich, Germany
Joyce Agency	370 Harrison Ave	Harrison, NY 10528, USA
Karg/Weissenbach Assoc	329 N Wetherly Dr, #101	Beverly Hills, CA 90211, USA
Katz, (Raymond) Enterprises	345 N Maple Dr, #205	Beverly Hills, CA 90210, USA
Kazarian/Spencer Assoc	11365 Ventura Blvd, #100	Studio City, CA 91604, USA
Killer, Agentur	54 Harthauser Str	81545 Munich, Germany
Kjar, (Tyler) Agency	10643 Riverside Dr	Toluca Lake, CA 91602, USA
Kohner, (Paul) Inc	9300 Wilshire Blvd, #555	Beverly Hills, CA 90212, USA
Kosden, (Robert) Agency	7135 Hollywood Blvd, #PH-2	Los Angeles, CA 90046, USA
Kurland, (Ted) Assoc	173 Brighton Ave	Boston, MA 02134, USA
Lantz Office	888 7th Ave	New York, NY 10106, USA
LA Talent	8335 Sunset Blvd	Los Angeles, CA 90069, USA
Lee, (Buddy) Attractions	38 Music Square E, #300	Nashville, TN 37203, USA
Lemond/Zetter Inc	8370 Wilshire Blvd, #310	Beverly Hills, CA 90211, USA
Levine/Schneider	433 N Camden Dr	Beverly Hills, CA 90210, USA
Lichtman, (Terry) Agency	4439 Worster Ave	Studio City, CA 91604, USA
London Mgmt	2-4 Noel St	London W1V 3RB, England
Lookout Mgmt	506 Santa Monica Blvd	Santa Monica, CA 90401, USA
Lovell Assoc	1350 N Highland Ave, #24	Los Angeles, CA 90028, USA
Lustig Talent Enterprises	235 Sunrise Ave	Palm Beach, FL 33480, USA
Majestic Tours	29701 Kinderkarmack Rd	Oradell, NJ 07649, USA
Markham & Froggatt	Julian House, 4 Windmill St	London W1P 1HF, England
Mars Talent	168 Orchid Dr	Pearl River, NY 10965, USA
Marshak Wyckoff Assoc	280 S Beverly Dr, #400	Beverly Hills, CA 90212, USA
Mattes, Agentur	14 Merzstr	81679 Munich, Germany
MCA Concerts	100 Universal City Plaza	Universal City, CA 91608, USA
MEW Inc	8489 W 3rd St, #1100	Los Angeles, CA 90048, USA
MGA/Mary Grady Agency	4444 Lankershim Blvd, #207	North Hollywood, CA 91602, USA
Mishkin Agency	2355 Benedict Canyon Dr	Beverly Hills, CA 90210, USA
Monarch Productions	8803 Mayne St	Bellflower, CA 90706, USA
Monterey Peninsula Artists	PO Box 7308	Carmel, CA 93921, USA
Morris, (William) Agency	151 S El Camino Dr	Beverly Hills, CA 90212, USA
Morris, (William) Agency	1325 Ave of Americas	New York, NY 10019, USA
Morris, (William) Agency	2325 Crestmoor Rd	Nashville, TN 37215, USA
Morris, (William) Agency	31/32 Soho Square	London W1V 5DG, England
Morris, (William) Agency	Lamontstr 98	81679 Munich, Germany
Morris, (William) Agency	Via Giosue Carducci	00187 Rome, Italy
Moss, (Burton) Agency	8827 Beverly Blvd, #L	Los Angeles, CA 90048, USA
Moss, (H David) Assoc	733 N Seward St, #PH	Los Angeles, CA 90038, USA
Metropolitan Talent Agency	4526 Wilshire Blvd	Los Angeles, CA 90010, USA
Nathe, (Susan) Assoc	8281 Melrose Ave, #200	Los Angeles, CA 90046, USA
Nationwide Entertainment Services	770 Regents Rd, #113-90	San Diego, CA 92122, USA
Next Model Mgmt	115 E 57th St, #1540	New York, NY 10022, USA
Paradigm Agency	200 W 57th St, #900	New York, NY 10019, USA
Pauline's Model Mgmt	379 W Broadway,	New York, NY 10012, USA
Pecoraro, (George)	3680 Madrid St	Las Vegas, NV 89121, USA
Peters, A D	10 Buckingham St	London WC2H 6BO, England
Peters Fraser Dunlop	Chelsea Harbour, Lots Rd	London SW10 0XF, England
PMK Public Relations	955 S Carillo Dr, #200	Los Angeles, CA 90048, USA
PMK Public Relations	1776 Broadway, #800	New York, NY 10019, USA
Premier Talent Agency	3 E 54th St, #1400	New York, NY 10022, USA
Progressive Artists Agency	400 S Beverly Dr, #216	Beverly Hills, CA 90212, USA
ProServe	1100 Woodrow Wilson Blvd	Arlington, VA 22209, USA
Producers Inc	11806 N 56th St	Tampa, FL 33617, USA
Ramsay, Margaret	14-A Goodwins Court, St Martin's	London WC2N 4LL, England
Rapp Enterprises	9200 Sunset Blvd, #620	Los Angeles, CA 90069, USA

Rascoff/Zysblat Organization	110 W 57th St, #PH	New York, NY 10019, USA
Redway, (John) Assoc	5 Denmark St	London WC2H 8LP, England
Reid, (John) Ent	Singes House, 32 Galena Rd	London W6 0LT, England
Rich, (Elaine) Mgmt	2400 Whitman Place	Los Angeles, CA 90068, USA
Robinson, (Dolores) Mgmt	10683 Santa Monica Blvd	Los Angeles, CA 90025, USA
Rogers & Cowan Agency	1888 Century Park East, #500	Los Angeles, CA 90067, USA
Rollins Joffe Morra Brezne	10201 Pico Blvd, #5	Los Angeles, CA 90064, USA
Rose, (Jack) Agency	9255 Sunset Blvd, #603	Los Angeles, CA 90069, USA
Rosenberg, (Marion) Offic	8428 Melrose Place, #C	Los Angeles, CA 90069, USA
Rossen, (Natalie) Agency	11712 Moorpark St, #204	Studio City, CA 91604
Rothberg, Arlyne	850 S Devon Ave	Los Angeles, CA 90024, USA
Rothschild, (Charles) Productions	330 E 48th St	New York, NY 10017, USA
Ruffalo, (Joseph) Mgmt	9655 Wilshire Blvd, #850	Beverly Hills, CA 90212, USA
Rush Artists Mgmt	1600 Varick St	New York, NY 10013, USA
Russo, Lynn	3624 Mound View Ave	Studio City, CA 91604, USA
Sanders Agency	8831 Sunset Blvd, #304	Los Angeles, CA 90069, USA
Sanders Agency	1204 Broadway, #304	New York, NY 10001, USA
Sanford-Beckett-Skouras	1015 Gayley Ave, #300	Los Angeles, CA 90024, USA
Savage Agency	6212 Banner Ave	Los Angeles, CA 90038, USA
Schechter, (Irv) Co	9300 Wilshire Blvd, #41	Beverly Hills, CA 90212, USA
Schiffman Ekman Morrison	156 5th Ave	New York, NY 10010, USA
Schiowitz/Clay/Rose	1680 N Vine St, #614	Los Angeles, CA 90028, USA
Schoen, (Judy) Assoc	606 N Larchmont Blvd, #309	Los Angeles, CA 90004, USA
Schut, (Booh) Agency	11350 Ventura Blvd, #206	Studio City, CA 91604, USA
Schwartz, (Don) Assoc	8749 Sunset Blvd	Los Angeles, CA 90069, USA
Scotti Bros	2114 Pico Blvd	Santa Monica, CA 90405, USA
Sekura/A Talent Agency	PO Box 931779	Los Angeles, CA 90093, USA
Selected Artists Agency	3575 Cahuenga Blvd W, #201	Los Angeles, CA 90068, USA
Smith/Gosnell	1515 Palisades Dr, #N	Pacific Palisades, CA 90272, USA
Shapira, (David) Assoc	15301 Ventura Blvd, #345	Sherman Oaks, CA 91403, USA
Shiparo-Lichtman Talent Agency	8827 Beverly Blvd	Los Angeles, CA 90048, USA
Sharkey, (James) Assoc	21 Golden Square	London W1R 3PA, England
Shaw Concerts	1900 Broadway, #200	New York, NY 10023, USA
Shepherd Agency	9034 Sunset Blvd, #100	Los Angeles, CA 90069, USA
Sherrell, (Lew) Agency	1354 Los Robles	Palm Springs, CA 92262, USA
Shlessinger, (Michael) Assoc	8730 Sunset Blvd, #220	Los Angeles, CA 90069, USA
Shapiro-Lichtman Agency	8827 Beverly Blvd	Los Angeles, CA 90048, USA
Shriver, Evelyn	1313 16th Ave S	Nashville, TN 37212, USA
Silver Massetti Agency	8730 Sunset Blvd, #480	Los Angeles, CA 90069, USA
Silver Massetti Agency	145 W 45th St, #1204	New York, NY 10036, USA
Smith, (Susan) Assoc	121 N San Vicente Blvd	Beverly Hills, CA 90211, USA
Smith, (Susan) Assoc	192 Lexington Ave	New York, NY 10016, USA
Special Artists Agency	335 N Maple Dr, #36	Beverly Hills, CA 90210, USA
Stein & Stein	9200 Sunset Blvd, #707	Los Angeles, CA 90069, USA
St James's Mgmt	22 Groom Place	London SW1, England
Stone Manners Agency	8091 Selma Ave	Los Angeles, CA 90046, USA
Subrena Artists	330 W 56th St, #18-M	New York, NY 10019, USA
Sutton Barth Vennari	145 S Fairfax Ave, #310	Los Angeles, CA 90036, USA
Talent Group Inc	9250 Wilshire Blvd, #208	Beverly Hills, CA 90212, USA
Tannen, (Herb) Assoc	1800 N Vine St, #120	Los Angeles, CA 90028, USA
Thomas (Robert) Agency	28051 Dequindre Rd	Madison Heights, MI 48071, USA
Tisherman Agency	6767 Forest Lawn Dr, #115	Los Angeles, CA 90068, USA
Tobias, (Herb) Agency	8571 Holloway Dr, #1	Los Angeles, CA 90069, USA
Twentieth Century Artists	15315 Magnolia Blvd, #429	Sherman Oaks, CA 91403, USA
United Talent Agency	9560 Wilshire Blvd, #50	Beverly Hills, CA 90212, USA
Variety Artists International	15490 Ventura Blvd	Sherman Oaks, CA 91403, USA
Wain, (Erika) Agency	1418 N Highland Ave, #102	Los Angeles, CA 90028, USA
Webb, (Ruth) Enterprises	7500 Devista Dr	Los Angeles, CA 90046, USA
Wilhelmina Artists	8383 Wilshire Blvd, #65	Beverly Hills, CA 90211, USA
Wilder Agency	3151 Cahuenga Blvd W, #310	Los Angeles, CA 90068, USA
Wilhelmina Artists	300 Park Ave	New York, NY 10010, USA
Wolf/Kasteller	1033 Gayley Ave, #208	Los Angeles, CA 90024, USA
Wolfman Jack Entertainment	Rt 1, Box 56	Belvidere, NC 27919, USA
Writers & Artists Agency	924 Westwood Blvd, #900	Los Angeles, CA 90024, USA

Writers & Artists Agency	19 W 44th St, #1000	New York, NY 10036, USA
Yusem, (Gene) Assoc	PO Box 67-B-69	Los Angeles, CA 90067, USA
ZBF Agentur	Ordensmeisterstr 15-16	12099 Berlin, Germany

SYNDICATE ADDRESSES

Creators Syndicate	5777 W Century Blvd, #700	Los Angeles, CA 90045, USA
King Features Syndicate	216 E 45th St	New York, NY 10017, USA
North America Syndicate	235 E 45th St	New York, NY 10017, USA
Times-Mirror Syndicate	Times-Mirror Square	Los Angeles, CA 90053, USA
Tribune Media Services	64 E Concord St	Orlando, FL 32801, USA
United Feature Syndicate	200 Park Ave	New York, NY 10166, USA
United Media Syndicate	200 Park Ave	New York, NY 10166, USA
United Press International	5 Pennsylvania Plaza	New York, NY 10001, USA
Universal Press Syndicate	4900 Main St, #900	Kansas City, KS 64112, USA
Universal Press Syndicate	4400 Fairway Dr	Fairway, KS 66205, USA
Universal Press Syndicate	Time-Life Building	New York, NY 10020, USA
Universal Press Syndicate	1301 Spring Oaks Circle	Houston, TX 77055, USA

MAJOR TELEVISION STATION ADDRESSES

American Broadcasting System

WSB-TV	1801 W Peachtree St NE	Atlanta, GA 30309, USA
WCVB-TV (Boston)	5 TV Place	Needham, MA 02194, USA
WLS-TV	190 N State St	Chicago, IL 60601, USA
WFAA-TV	606 Young St	Dallas, TX 75202, USA
WXYZ-TV (Detroit)	20777 W Ten Mile Rd	Southfield, MI 48037, USA
KTRK-TV	3310 Bissonnet Dr	Houston, TX 77005, USA
KABC-TV	4151 Prospect Ave	Los Angeles, CA 90027, USA
WPLG-TV	3900 Biscayne Blvd	Miami, FL 33137, USA
WVUE-TV	1025 S Jefferson Davis Pkwy	New Orleans, LA 70125, USA
WABC-TV	7 Lincoln Square	New York, NY 10023, USA
WPIV-TV	4100 City Line Ave	Philadelphia, PA 19131, USA
KGO-TV	900 Front St	San Francisco, CA 94111, USA
WJLA-TV	3007 Tilden St NW	Washington, DC 20008, USA

Columbia Broadcasting System

WBZ-TV	1170 Soldiers Field Rd	Boston, MA 02134, USA
WBBM-TV	630 N McClurg Court	Chicago, IL 60611, USA
KHOU-TV	1945 Allen Parkway	Houston, TX 77019, USA
KCBS-TV	6121 Sunset Blvd	Los Angeles, CA 90028, USA
WCIX-TV	8900 NW 18th Terrace	Miami, FL 33172, USA
WWL-TV	1024 N Rampart St	New Orleans, LA 70116, USA
WCBS-TV	524 W 57th St	New York, NY 10019, USA
KYW-TV	101 S Independence Mall E	Philadelphia, PA 19106, USA
KPIX-TV	855 Battery St	San Francisco, CA 94111, USA
WUSA-TV	4100 Wisconsin Ave NW	Washington, DC 20016, USA

Fox Television

WAGA-TV	1551 Briarcliff Rd NE	Atlanta, GA 30306, USA
WFXT-TV (Boston)	1000 Providence Highway	Dedham, MA 02026, USA
WFLD-TV	205 N Michigan Ave	Chicago, IL 60601, USA
KDFW-TV	400 N Griffin St	Dallas, TX 75202, USA
WJBK-TV (Detroit)	16550 W Nine Mile Rd	Southfield, MI 48075, USA
KRIV-TV	3935 Westheimer Rd	Houston, TX 77027, USA
KTTV-TV	5746 W Sunset Blvd	Los Angeles, CA 90028, USA
WSVN-TV	1401 79th St Causeway	Miami, FL 33141, USA
WNOL-TV	1661 Canal St	New Orleans, LA 70112, USA
WNYW-TV	205 E 67th St	New York, NY 10021, USA
WTXF-TV	330 Market St	Philadelphia, PA 19106, USA
KTVU-TV (San Francisco)	PO Box 22222	Oakland, CA 94623, USA
WTTG-TV	5151 Wisconsin Ave NW	Washington, DC 20016, USA

National Broadcasting Company

| WXIA-TV | 1611 W Peachtree St NE | Atlanta, GA 30309, USA |

V.I.P. Address Book

WMAG-TV	454 N Columbus Dr	Chicago, IL 60611, USA
KXAS-TV	3900 Barnett St	Fort Worth, TX 76103, USA
WDIV-TV	550 W Lafayette Blvd	Detroit, MI 48231, USA
KPRC-TV	8181 Southwest Freeway	Houston, TX 77074, USA
KNBC-TV (Los Angeles)	3000 W Alameda Ave	Burbank, CA 91523, USA
WTVJ-TV	316 N Miami Ave	Miami, FL 33128, USA
WDSU-TV	520 Royal St	New Orleans, LA 70130, USA
WNBC-TV	30 Rockefeller Plaza	New York, NY 10112, USA
WMGM-TV (Philadelphia)	1601 New Rd	Linwood, NJ 08221, USA
KRON-TV	1001 Van Ness Ave	San Francisco, CA 94109, USA
WRC-TV	4001 Nebraska Ave NW	Washington, DC 20016, USA

CABLE TELEVISION CHANNEL ADDRESSES

American Christian Television	6350 West Freeway	Fort Worth, TX 76150, USA
Arts & Entertainment	235 E 45th St	New York, NY 10017, USA
Black Entertainment Network	1232 31st St NW	Washington, DC 20007, USA
British Broadcasting Company	Wood Lane	London W12 8QT, England
C-SPAN	400 N Capitol St NW	Washington, DC 20001, USA
Cable News Network	100 International Blvd NW	Atlanta, GA 30303, USA
Canadian Broadcasting Company	1500 Bronson Ave	Ottawa ON K1G 3J5, Canada
Canadian Television Network	42 Charles St E	Toronto ON M4Y 1T5, Canada
Capital Cities/ABC	77 W 66th St	New York, NY 10023, USA
Cartoon Network	1050 Techwood Dr NW	Atlanta, GA 30318, USA
Christian Broadcasting Network	1000 Centerville Turnpike	Virginia Beach, VA 23463, USA
Cinemax	1100 6th Ave	New York, NY 10036, USA
Columbia Broadcasting System	51 W 52nd St	New York, NY 10019, USA
Comedy Central	1775 Broadway	New York, NY 10019, USA
Consumer News & Business	2200 Fletcher Ave	Fort Lee, NJ 07024, USA
Country Music Television	2806 Opryland Dr	Nashville, TN 37214, USA
Discovery Channel	7700 Wisconsin Ave	Bethesda, MD 20814, USA
Disney Channel	3800 W Alameda Ave	Burbank, CA 91505, USA
E! (Entertainment Television)	5670 Wilshire Blvd	Los Angeles, CA 90036, USA
ESPN (Entertainment & Sports)	ESPN Plaza, 935 Middle St	Bristol, CT 06010, USA
Family Channel	PO Box 64549	Virginia Beach, VA 23467, USA
Fox Broadcasting Co	10201 W Pico Blvd	Los Angeles, CA 90035, USA
FX (Fox Net)	PO Box 900	Beverly Hills, CA 90213, USA
Granada Television	36 Golden Square	London W1R 2AX, England
Home Box Office (HBO)	1100 6th Ave	New York, NY 10036, USA
Home Shopping Network	PO Box 9090	Clearwater, FL 34618, USA
Learning Channel	7700 Wisconsin Ave	Bethesda, MD 20814, USA
Lifetime	309 W 49th St	New York, NY 10019, USA
Madison Square Garden Network	2 Pennsylvania Plaza	New York, NY 10001, USA
Movie Channel (TMC)	1633 Broadway	New York, NY 10019, USA
MTV (Music Television)	1515 Boadway	New York, NY 10036, USA
Nashville Network (TNN)	2806 Opryland Dr	Nashville, TN 37214, USA
National Broadcasting Company	30 Rockefeller Plaza	New York, NY 10112, USA
Nickelodeon	1515 Broadway	New York, NY 10036, USA
PBS (Public Broadcasting System)	1320 Braddock Place	Alexandria, VA 22314, USA
Playboy Channel	9242 Beverly Blvd	Beverly Hills, CA 90210, USA
Prime Ticket Network	10000 Santa Monica Blvd	Los Angeles, CA 90067, USA
QVC Inc	1365 Enterprise Dr	West Chester, PA 19380, USA
Sci-Fi Channel	1230 Ave of Americas	New York, NY 10020, USA
Showtime Network	1633 Broadway	New York, NY 10019, USA
TBN (Trinity Broadcast Network)	PO Box "A"	Tustin, CA 92711, USA
TBS (Turner Broadcasting System)	100 International Blvd NW	Atlanta, GA 30303, USA
Telemundo Group	1740 Broadway	New York, NY 10019, USA
TNT (Turner Network Television)	1050 Techwood Dr NW	Atlanta, GA 30318, USA
TVA	1600 De Maisonneuve Blvd E	Montreal PQ H2L 4P2, Canada
Univision Network	605 3rd Ave	New York, NY 10158, USA
USA Cable Network	1230 Ave of Americas	New York, NY 10020, USA
VH-1 (Video Hits One)	1515 Broadway	New York, NY 10036, USA
Viewer's Choice	909 3rd Ave	New York, NY 10022, USA
Weather Channel	2600 Cumberland Parkway NW	Atlanta, GA 30339, USA

RECORD COMPANY ADDRESSES

A&M Records	1416 N La Brea Ave	Los Angeles, CA 90028, USA
Angel Records	1750 N Vine St	Los Angeles, CA 90028, USA
Angel Records	810 7th Ave	New York, NY 10019, USA
Arista Records	8370 Wilshire Blvd, #300	Beverly Hills, CA 90211, USA
Arista Records	6 W 57th St	New York, NY 10019, USA
Asylum Records	9229 Sunset Blvd, #718	Los Angeles, CA 90069, USA
Asylum Records	75 Rockefeller Plaza	New York, NY 10019, USA
Atlantic Records	9229 Sunset Blvd, #900	Los Angeles, CA 90069, USA
Atlantic Records	75 Rockefeller Plaza	New York, NY 10019, USA
Blue Note Records	6920 Sunset Blvd	Los Angeles, CA 90028, USA
Capitol Records	1750 N Vine St	Los Angeles, CA 90028, USA
Capitol Records	810 7th Ave	New York, NY 10019, USA
Chrysalis Records	8730 Sunset Blvd	Los Angeles, CA 90069, USA
Chrysalis Records	810 7th Ave, #4	New York, NY 10019, USA
Deutsche Grammaphon	810 7th Ave	New York, NY 10019, USA
Elektra Records	75 Rockefeller Plaza	New York, NY 10019, USA
EMI America Records	6920 Sunset Blvd	Los Angeles, CA 90028, USA
EMI America Records	810 7th Ave	New York, NY 10019, USA
Epic Records	21211 S Highland Ave	Los Angeles, CA 90019, USA
Epic Records	550 Madison Ave	New York, NY 10022, USA
Geffen Records	9100 Sunset Blvd	Los Angeles, CA 90069, USA
Geffen Records	1755 Broadway	New York, NY 10019, USA
Island Records	8920 Sunset Blvd, #200	Los Angeles, CA 90069, USA
Island Records	400 Lafayette St, #500	New York, NY 10003, USA
London Records	810 7th Ave	New York, NY 10019, USA
MCA Records	70 Universal City Plaza	Universal City, CA 91608, USA
MCA Records	1755 Broadway	New York, NY 10019, USA
Mercury Records	810 7th Ave	New York, NY 10019, USA
Motown Records	6255 Sunset Blvd	Los Angeles, CA 90028, USA
Nonesuch Records	75 Rockefeller Plaza	New York, NY 10019, USA
Phillips Records	810 7th Ave	New York, NY 10019, USA
Polygram Records	3800 W Alameda Ave, #1500	Burbank, CA 91505, USA
Polygram Records	Worldwide Plaza, 825 8th Ave	New York, NY 10019, USA
Polydor Records	3800 W Alameda Ave	Burbank, CA 91505, USA
Polydor Records	810 7th Ave	New York, NY 10019, USA
RCA Records	6363 Sunset Blvd, #429	Los Angeles, CA 90028, USA
RCA Records	1540 Broadway, #900	New York, NY 10036, USA
Reprise Records	3300 Warner Blvd	Burbank, CA 91505, USA
Reprise Records	75 Rockefeller Plaza	New York, NY 10019, USA
Rhino Records	10635 Santa Monica Blvd	Los Angeles, CA 90025, USA
Sire Records	3300 Warner Blvd	Burbank, CA 91505, USA
Sire Records	75 Rockefeller Plaza	New York, NY 10019, USA
Sony/Columbia Records	2100 Colorado Ave	Santa Monica, CA 90404, USA
Sony/Columbia Records	51 W 52nd St	New York, NY 10019, USA
Verve Records	Worldwide Plaza, 825 8th Ave	New York, NY 10019, USA
Virgin Records	338 N Foothill Rd	Beverly Hills, CA 90210, USA
Virgin Records	1790 Broadway, #2000	New York, NY 10019, USA
Warner Bros Record	3300 Warner Blvd	Burbank, CA 91505, USA
Warner Bros Records	75 Rockefeller Plaza	New York, NY 10019, USA
Windham Hill Records	1416 N La Brea Ave	Los Angeles, CA 90028, USA

PUBLISHER ADDRESSES

Atheneum Publishers	866 3rd Ave	New York, NY 10022, USA
Ballatine Books	201 E 50th St	New York, NY 10022, USA
Bantam Books	1540 Broadway	New York, NY 10036, USA
Crown Publishers	225 Park Ave S	New York, NY 10003, USA
Delacorte Press	1540 Broadway	New York, NY 10036, USA
Dodd Mead Co	6 Ram Ridge Rd	Spring Valley, NY 10977, USA
Doubleday Co 1	540 Broadway	New York, NY 10036, USA
Dutton, (E P) Co	2 Park Ave	New York, NY 10016, USA
Farrar Straus Giroux	19 Union Square W	New York, NY 10003, USA
Grove Press	841 Broadway	New York, NY 10003, USA

Harcourt Brace Jovanovich	111 5th Ave	New York, NY 10003, USA
Harper & Row Publishers	10 E 53rd St	New York, NY 10022, USA
Holt, (Henry) Inc	115 W 18th St	New York, NY 10011, USA
Houghton Mifflin Co	215 Park Ave S	New York, NY 10003, USA
Knopf, (Alfred A) Inc	201 E 50th St	New York, NY 10022, USA
Little Brown Co	34 Beacon St	Boston, MA 02108, USA
McGraw Hill Book Co	1221 Ave of Americas	New York, NY 10011, USA
MacMillan Inc	866 3rd Ave	New York, NY 10022, USA
Morrow, (William) Co	1350 Ave of Americas	New York, NY 10016, USA
New American Library	1633 Broadway	New York, NY 10019, USA
Norton, (W W) Co	500 5th Ave	New York, NY 10110, USA
Pocket Books	1230 Ave of Americas	New York, NY 10020, USA
Prentice-Hall Inc	Rt 9-W	Englewood Cliffs, NJ 07632, USA
Putnam's Sons, G P	200 Madison Ave	New York, NY 10016, USA
Random House Inc	201 E 50th St	New York, NY 10022, USA
Scribner's Sons, Charles	866 3rd Ave	New York, NY 10022, USA
Simon & Schuster Inc	1230 Ave of Americas	New York, NY 10020, USA
St Martin's Press	175 5th Ave	New York, NY 10010, USA
Viking Press	375 Hudson St	New York, NY 10014, USA

PROFESSIONAL SPORTS TEAM ADDRESSES

Baseball

Atlanta Braves	County Stadium, PO Box 4064	Atlanta, GA 30302, USA
Baltimore Orioles	333 W Camden Ave	Baltimore, MD 21201, USA
Boston Red Sox	Fenway Park, 4 Yawkey Way	Boston, MA 02215, USA
California Angels	Anaheim Stadium, PO Box 2000	Anaheim, CA 92803, USA
Chicago Cubs	1060 W Addison St	Chicago, IL 60613, USA
Chicago White Sox	333 W 35th St	Chicago, IL 60616, USA
Cincinnati Reds	100 Riverfront Stadium	Cincinnati, OH 45202, USA
Cleveland Indians	Cleveland Stadium	Cleveland, OH 44114, USA
Colorado Rockies	2001 Blake St	Denver, CO 80205, USA
Detroit Tigers	Tiger Stadium, 2121 Trumbell	Detroit, MI 48216, USA
Florida Marlins	100 NE 3rd Ave	Fort Lauderdale, FL 33301, USA
Houston Astros	Astrodome, PO Box 288	Houston, TX 77001, USA
Kansas City Royals	PO Box 419969	Kansas City, MO 64141, USA
Los Angeles Dodgers	1000 Elysian Park Ave	Los Angeles, CA 90012, USA
Milwaukee Brewers	County Stadium, 201 S 46th St	Milwaukee, WI 53214, USA
Minnesota Twins	501 Chicago Ave S	Minneapolis, MN 55415, USA
Montreal Expos	PO Box 500, Station "M"	Montreal PQ H1V 3P2, Canada
New York Mets	Shea Stadium	Flushing, NY 11368, USA
New York Yankees	Yankee Stadium, 161st & River	Bronx, NY 10451, USA
Oakland Athletics	Oakland Coliseum	Oakland, CA 94621, USA
Philadelphia Phillies	Veterans Stadium, PO Box 7575	Philadelphia, PA 19101, USA
Pittsburgh Pirates	Three Rivers Stadium	Pittsburgh, PA 15212, USA
San Diego Padres	PO Box 2000	San Diego, CA 92112, USA
Seattle Mariners	Kingdome, PO Box 4100	Seattle, WA 98104, USA
San Francisco Giants	Candlestick Park	San Francisco, CA 94124, USA
St Louis Cardinals	250 Stadium Plaza	St Louis, MO 63102, USA
Texas Rangers	PO Box 901111	Arlington, TX 76004, USA
Toronto Blue Jays	300 Bremner Blvd	Toronto ON M5V 3B3, Canada

Football

Arizona Cardinals	8701 S Hardy D	Tempe, AZ 85284, USA
Atlanta Falcons	2745 Burnett Rd	Suwanee, GA 30174, USA
Buffalo Bills	1 Bills Dr	Orchard Park, NY 14127, USA
Carolina Panthers	227 W Trade St, #1600	Charlotte, NC 28202, USA
Chicago Bears	Halas Hall, 250 N Washington Rd	Lake Forest, IL 60045, USA
Cincinnati Bengals	200 Riverfront Stadium	Cincinnati, OH 45202, USA
Cleveland Browns	80 1st Ave	Berea, OH 44017, USA
Dallas Cowboys	1 Cowboys Parkway	Irving, TX 75063, USA
Denver Broncos	13655 E Dove Valley Parkway	Englewood, CO 80112, USA
Detroit Lions	Silverdome, 1200 Featherstone	Pontiac, MI 48342, USA
Green Bay Packers	1265 Lombardi Ave	Green Bay, WI 54304, USA

Houston Oilers	6910 Fannin St	Houston, TX 77030, USA
Indianapolis Colts	7001 W 56th St	Indianapolis, IN 46254, USA
Jacksonville Jaguars	1 Stadium Place	Jacksonville, FL 32202, USA
Kansas City Chiefs	1 Arrowhead Dr	Kansas City, KS 64129, USA
Miami Dolphins	7500 SW 30th St	Davie, FL 33329, USA
Minnesota Vikings	9520 Viking Dr	Eden Prairie, MN 55344, USA
New England Patriots	Foxboro Stadium, Rt 1	Foxboro, MA 02035, USA
New Orleans Saints	1500 Poydras St	New Orleans, LA 70112, USA
New York Giants	Giants Stadium	East Rutherford, NJ 07073, USA
New York Jets	1000 Fulton Ave	Hempstead, NY 11550, USA
Oakland Raiders	Oakland Coliseum	Oakland, CA 94621, USA
Philadelphia Eagles	3501 S Broad St	Philadelphia, PA 19148, USA
Pittsburgh Steelers	3 Rivers Stadium, Stadium Circle	Pittsburgh, PA 15212, USA
San Diego Chargers	Jack Murphy Stadium	San Diego, CA 92160, USA
Seattle Seahawks	11220 NE 53rd St	Kirkland, WA 98033, USA
San Francisco 49ers	4949 Centennial Blvd	Santa Clara, CA 95054, USA
St Louis Rams	100 N Broadway, #2100	St Louis, MO 63102, USA
Tampa Bay Buccaneers	1 Buccaneer Place	Tampa, FL 33607, USA
Washington Redskins	21300 Redskin Park Dr	Ashburn, VA 22011, USA

Basketball

Atlanta Hawks	1 CNN Center, South Tower	Atlanta, GA 30303, USA
Boston Celtics	151 Merrimac St, #500	Boston, MA 02114, USA
Charlotte Hornets	1 Hive Dr	Charlotte, NC 28217, USA
Chicago Bulls	1901 W Madison St	Chicago, IL 60612, USA
Cleveland Cavaliers	2923 Statesboro Rd	Richfield, OH 44286, USA
Dallas Maverick	Reunion Arena, 777 Sports St	Dallas, TX 75207, USA
%Denver Nuggets	McNichols Arena, 1635 Clay St	Denver, CO 80204, USA
Detroit Pistons	Palace, 2 Championship Dr	Auburn Hills, MI 48057, USA
Golden State Warriors	Oakland Coliseum Arena	Oakland, CA 94621, USA
Houston Rockets	Summit, Greenway Plaza, #10	Houston, TX 77277, USA
Indiana Pacers	Market Sq Arena, 300 E Market	Indianapolis, IN 46204, USA
Los Angeles Clippers	Sports Arena, 3939 S Figueroa	Los Angeles, CA 90037, USA
Los Angeles Lakers	Forum, PO Box 10	Inglewood, CA 90306, USA
Miami Heat	Miami Arena	Miami, FL 33136, USA
Milwaukee Bucks	Bradley Center, 1001 N 4th St	Milwaukee, WI 53203, USA
Minnesota Timberwolves	Target Center, 600 1st Ave N	Minneapolis, MN 55403, USA
New Jersey Nets	Byrne Meadowlands Arena	East Rutherford, NJ 07073, USA
New York Knicks	Madison Square Garden	New York, NY 10001, USA
Orlando Magic	Orlando Arena, 1 Magic Place	Orlando, FL 32801, USA
Philadelphia 76ers	Veterans Stadium, Box 25040	Philadelphia, PA 19147, USA
Phoenix Suns	201 E Jefferson St	Phoenix, AZ 85004, USA
Portland Trail Blazers	700 NE Multnomah St, #600	Portland, OR 97232, USA
Sacramento Kings	1 Sports Parkway	Sacramento, CA 95834, USA
San Antonio Spurs	600 E Market St, #102	San Antonio, TX 78205, USA
Seattle Supersonics	190 Queen Ave N	Seattle, WA 98109, USA
Toronto Raptors	20 Bay St, #1702	Toronto ON M5J 2N8, Canada
Utah Jazz	301 W South Temple	Salt Lake City, UT 84101, USA
Vancouver Grizzlies	788 Beatty St, #300	Vancouver BC V6B 2M1, Canada
Washington Bullets	Capital Centre, 1 Truman Dr	Landover, MD 20785, USA

Hockey

Anaheim Mighty Ducks	1313 S Harbor Blvd	Anaheim, CA 92803, USA
Boston Bruins	Boston Garden, 150 Causeway	Boston, MA 02114, USA
Buffalo Sabres	Memorial Stadium, 140 Main	Buffalo, NY 14202, USA
Calgary Flames	PO Box 1540, Station "M"	Calgary AB T2P 389, Canada
Chicago Blackhawks	Chicago Stadium, 1800 Madison	Chicago, IL 60612, USA
Colorado Avalanch	McNichols Arena, 1635 Clay St	Denver, CO 80204, USA
Dallas Stars	211 Cowboys Parkway	Irving, TX 75063, USA
Detroit Red Wings	Louis Arena, 600 Civic Center Dr	Detroit, MI 48226, USA
Edmonton Oilers	Northlands Coliseum	Edmonton AB T5B 4M9, Canada
Florida Panthers	100 NE 3rd Ave, #1000	Fort Lauderdale, FL 33301, USA
Hartford Whalers	Coliseum, 242 Trumbell St	Hartford, CT 06103, USA
Los Angeles Kings	Forum, PO Box 17013	Inglewood, CA 90308, USA
Minnesota North Stars	Sports Center, 7901 Cedar S	Bloomington, MN 55425, USA

      V.I.P. Address Book

Montreal Canadiens	2313 St Catherine St W	Montreal PQ H3H 1N2, Canada
New Jersey Devils	Meadowlands Arena, Box 504	East Rutherford, NJ 07073, USA
New York Islanders	Veterans Memorial Coliseum	Uniondale, NY 11553, USA
New York Rangers	Madison Square Garden	New York, NY 10001, USA
Ottawa Senators	301 Moodie Dr, #200	Nepean ON K2H 9C4, Canada
Philadelphia Flyers	Spectrum, Pattison Place	Philadelphia, PA 19148, USA
Pittsburgh Penguins	Civic Arena, Centre Ave	Pittsburgh, PA 15219, USA
Quebec Nordiques	2205 Ave du Colisee	Quebec City PQ G1L 4W7, Canada
San Jose Sharks	525 W Santa Clara St	San Jose, CA 95113, USA
St Louis Blues	St Louis Arena, 5700 Oakland	St Louis, MO 63110, USA
Tampa Bay Lightning	Mack Center, 501 E Kennedy	Tampa, FL 33602, USA
Toronto Maple Leafs	60 Carlton St	Toronto ON M5B 1L1, Canada
Vancouver Canucks	100 N Renfrew St	Vancouver BC V5K 3N7, Canada
Washington Capitals	USAir Arena	Landover, MD 20785, USA
Winnipeg Jets	Arena, 15-1430 Maroons Rd	Winnipeg MB R3G 0L5, Canada

OTHER SPORTS ORGANIZATION ADDRESSES

Amateur Athletic Union	3600 W 86th St	Indianapolis, IN 46268, USA
Amateur Softball Assn	2801 NE 50th St	Oklahoma City, OK 73111, USA
American Bicycle Assn	PO Box 718	Chandler, AZ 85226, USA
American Bowling Congress	5301 S 76th St	Greendale, WI 53129, USA
American Horse Show Assn	220 E 42nd St	New York, NY 10017, USA
American Hot Rod Assn	111 N. Hayford Rd	Spokane, WA 99204, USA
American Kennel Club	51 Madison Ave	New York, NY 10010, USA
American League (Baseball)	350 Park Ave	New York, NY 10022, USA
American Motorcycle Assn	PO Box 6114	Westerville, OH 43081, USA
American Power Boat Assn	17640 E Nine Mile Rd	East Detroit, MI 48021, USA
American Pro Soccer League	122 "C" St, NW	Washington, DC 20001, USA
American Water Ski Assn	799 Overlook Dr, SE	Winter Haven, FL 33882, USA
Assn of Int'l Amateur Boxing	Postamt Volkradstr, Postlagernd	10319 Berlin, Germany
Assn of Int'l Marathon & Road Races	20 Trongate	Glasgow G1 5ES, England
Assn of Ski Racing Professionals	148 Porters Point Rd	Colchester, VT 05446, USA
Assn of Surfing Professionals	16691 Gothard St	Huntington Beach, CA 92648, USA
Assn of Tennis Professionals	200 Tournament Players Rd	Ponte Vedra, FL 32082, USA
Assn of Volleyball Professionals	15260 Ventura Blvd	Sherman Oaks, CA 91403, USA
Canadian Football League	110 Eglinton Ave	Toronto, ON M4R 1A3, Canada
Canadian National Sports Center	1600 James Naismith Dr	Gloucestor ON KJB 5N4, Canada
Championship Auto Racing Teams	755 W Big Beaver Rd, #800	Troy, MI 48084, USA
Fed de Int'l Hockey	Avenue des Arts 1	1040 Brussels, Belgium
Fed de Int'l Ski	Worbstr 210	3073 Gumligen B, Bern, Switzerland
Fed Int'l de Canoe	G Massaia 59	50134 Florence, Italy
Fed Int'l de Football Assn	PO Box 85, Hitzigweg 1	8030 Zurich, Switzerland
Fed Int'l de Tir a l'Arc (Archery)	Via Cerva 30	20122 Milan, Italy
Fed of Int'l Volleyball	Ave de la Gare 12	1001 Lausanne, Switzerland
Fed of Int'l Amateur Cycling	Via Cassia N 490	00198 Rome, Italy
Fed of Int'l Basketball	Kistlerhofstr 168	81379 Munich, Germany
Fed of Int'l Bobsleigh/Tobogganing	Via Piranesi 44/b	20137 Milan, Italy
Fed of Int'l du Sport Automobiles	8 Place de la Concorde	75008 Paris, France
Fed of Int'l Equestrian	Bolligenstrasse 54	Berne 32, Switzerland
Fed Int'l de Gymnastics	Juraweg 12	3250 Lyss, Switzerland
FIFA Women's Football Assn	37 Sussex Rd, Ickenham	Middx UB10 8PN, England
Formula One Driver's Assn	2 Rue Jean Jaures	1836 Luxembourg
Indy Car Racing	390 Enterprise Court	Bloomfield Hills, MI 48302, USA
Int'l Badminton Federation	24 Winchcombe House	Cheltenham, Glos GL52 2NA, England
Int'l Baseball Association	201 S Capitol Ave, #490	Indianapolis, IN 46225, USA
Int'l Boxing Federation	134 Evergreen Place	East Orange, NJ 07018, USA
Int'l Cricket Council	Lord's Cricket Ground	London NW8 8QN, England
Int'l Curling Federation	2 Coates Crescent	Edinburgh EH3 7AN, England
Int'l Game Fish Assn	1301 E Atlantic Blvd	Pompano Beach, FL 33060, USA
Int'l Hot Rod Assn	PO Box 3029	Bristol, TN 37625, USA
Int'l Ice Hockey Federation	Bellevuestr 8	1190 Vienna, Austria
Int'l Jai Alai Assn	5 Calle Aldamar	San Sebastian 3, Spain
Int'l Judo Federation	Ave del Trabajo 2666, CP 1406	Buenos Aires, Argentina

Int'l Luge Federation	Olympiadestr 168	8786 Rottenmann, Austria
Int'l Motorsports Assn	PO Box 10709	Tampa, FL 33679, USA
Int'l Olympic Committee	Chateau de Vidy	1007 Lausanne, Switzerland
Int'l Roller Skating Federation	1500 S 70th St	Lincoln, NE 68506, USA
Int'l Rugby Football Board	PO Box 902	Auckland, New Zealand
Int'l Skating Union	Promenade 73	7270 Davos-Platz, Switzerland
Int'l Sled Dog Racing Assn	PO Box 446	Nordman, ID 83848, USA
Int'l Softball Federation	2801 NE 59th St	Oklahoma City, OK 73111, USA
Int'l Surfing Assn	Winston Ave	Branksome People,Dorset, England
Int'l Table Tennis Federation	53 London, St Leonards-Sea	East Sussex TN37 6AY, England
Int'l Tennis Federation	Palliser Rd, Barons Court	London W14 9EN, England
Int'l Volleyball Federation	Avenue de la Gare 12	1003 Lausanne, Switzerland
Int'l Weightlifting Federation	Rosemberg Hp U1	1374 Budapest PF 614, Hungary
Int'l Yacht Racing Union	60 Knightsbridge, Westminster	London SWEX 7JX, England
Ladies Professional Bowlers Tour	7171 Cherryvale Blvd	Rockford, IL 61112, USA
Virginia Slims Women's Tennis	3135 Texas Commerce Tower	Houston, TX 77002, USA
Ladies Professional Golf Assn	2570 Volusia Ave	Daytona Beach, FL 32114, USA
Little League Baseball	PO Box 3485	Williamsport, PA 17701, USA
Major Indoor Lacrosse League	2310 W 75th St	Prairie Village, KS 66208, USA
Major League Baseball	350 Park Ave	New York, NY 10022, USA
Nat Archery Assn	1 Olympic Plaza	Colorado Springs, CO 80909, USA
Nat Assn of Intercollegiate Athletics	1221 Baltimore Ave	Kansas City, MO 64105, USA
Nat Assn of Stock Car Racing	1801 Speedway Blvd	Daytona Beach, FL 32015, USA
Nat Basketball Assn	645 5th Ave	New York, NY 10022, USA
Nat Collegiate Athletic Assn	6201 College Ave	Overland Park, KS 66211, USA
Nat Football League	410 Park Ave	New York, NY 10022, USA
Nat Hockey League	650 5th Ave	New York, NY 10019, USA
Nat Hot Rod Assn	2035 Financial Way	Glendora, CA 91740, USA
Nat League (Baseball)	350 Park Ave	New York, NY 10022, USA
Nat Professional Soccer League	229 3rd St NW	Canton, OH 44702, USA
Nat Rifle Assn	11250 Waples Mill Rd	Fairfax, VA 22030, USA
Nat Tractor Pullers Assn	6969 Worthington-Galena Rd	Worthington, OH 43085, USA
Professional Bowlers Assn	1720 Merriman Rd	Akron, OH 44313, USA
Professional Golf Assn	100 Ave of Champions	Palm Beach Gardens, FL 33418, USA
Professional Golf Assn Seniors Tour	112 T P C Blvd	Ponte Vedra Beach, FL 32082, USA
Professional Rodeo Cowboys Assn	101 Pro Rodeo Dr	Colorado Springs, CA 80919, USA
Special Olympics	1350 New York Ave NW	Washington, DC 20005, USA
Thoroughbred Racing Assn	420 Fair Hill Dr	Elkton, MD 21921, USA
Union Int''l de Tir (Rifle)	Bavariaring 21	80336 Munich, Germany
US Auto Club	4910 W 16th St	Speedway, IN 46224, USA
US Bobsled & Skeleton Assn	PO Box 828	Lake Placid, NY 12946, USA
US Cycling Federation	1750 E Boulder St	Colorado Springs, CO 80909, USA
US Figure Skating Assn	20 1st St	Colorado Springs, CO 80906, USA
US Luge Assn	PO Box 651	Lake Placid, NY 12946, USA
US Olympic Committee	1 Olympic Plaza	Colorado Springs, CO 80909, USA
US Polo Assn	120 Mill St	Lexington, KY 40507, USA
US Skiing Assn	PO Box 100	Park City, UT 84060, USA
US Tennis Assn	Flushing Meadow	Flushing, NY 11368, USA
US Trotting Assn	750 Michigan Ave	Columbus, OH 43215, USA
US Youth Soccer Assn	PO Box 18404	Memphis, TN 38181, USA
USA Rugby	830 N Tejon	Colorado Springs, CO 80903, USA
USA Track & Field	1 Hoosier Dome	Indianapolis, IN 46225, USA
Women's Basketball Assn	4011 N. Bennington	Kansas City, MO 64117, USA
Women's Int'l Bowling Congress	5301 S 76th St	Greendale, WI 53129, USA
Women's Int'l Surfing Assn	PO Box 512	San Juan Capistrano, CA 92675, USA
Women's Pro Volleyball Assn	1730 Oak St	Santa Monica, CA 90405, USA
Women's Tennis Assn	133 1st St NE	St Petersburg, FL 33701, USA
World Boardsailing Assn	Feldafinger Platz 2	81477 Munich, Germany
World Boxing Assn	Rodrigo Sazagy, Apartado	4070 Panama City, Panama
World Boxing Council	Genova 33, Colonia Juarez	Cuahtemoc 0660, Mexico
World Taekwondo Federation	San 76 Yuksam-Dong	Kangnam-Ku, Seoul, Korea
World Team Tennis	445 N Wells St	Chicago, IL 60610, USA
World Union of Karate Organizations	1-15-16 Toranomon, Minatoku	Tokyo 105, Japan
World Wrestling Federation	1055 Summer St	Stamford, CT 06905, USA

SPORTS HALLS OF FAME ADDRESSES

Academy of Sports	4 Rue de Teheran	75008 Paris, France
Amateur Athletic Foundation	2141 W Adams Blvd	Los Angeles, CA 90018, USA
American Water Ski Hall of Fame	799 Overlook Dr SE	Winter Park, FL 33884, USA
Auto Racing Hall of Fame	4790 W 16th St	Speedway, IN 46224, USA
College Football Hall of Fame	5540 Kings Island Dr	Kings Island, OH 45034, USA
Hockey Hall of Fame	Exhibition Place	Toronto, ON M6K 3C3, Canada
Int'l Boxing Hall of Fame	PO Box 425	Canastoga, NY 13032, USA
Int'l Gymnastics Hall of Fame	227 Brooks St	Oceanside, CA 92054, USA
Int'l Motor Sports Hall of Fame	PO Box 1018	Talladega, AL 35160, USA
Int'l Surfing Hall of Fame	5580 La Jolla Blvd	La Jolla, CA 92037, USA
Int'l Swimming Hall of Fame	1 Hall of Fame Dr	Fort Lauderdale, FL 33316, USA
Int'l Tennis Hall of Fame	194 Bellevue Ave	Newport, RI 62840, USA
Int'l Women's Sports Hall of Fame	342 Madison Ave	New York, NY 10173, USA
Lacrosse Hall of Fame Foundation	White Athletic Center	Baltimore, MD 21218, USA
Ladies Pro Golf Assn Hall of Fame	2570 Volusia Ave	Daytona Beach, FL 32114, USA
Lawn Tennis Museum	All England Lawn Tennis Club	Wimbledon, England
Naismith Basketball Hall of Fame	1150 W Columbus Ave	Springfield, MA 01101, USA
Nat Baseball Hall of Fame	PO Box 590	Cooperstown, NY 13326, USA
Nat Bowling Museum/Hall of Fame	111 Stadium Plaza	St. Louis, MO 63102, USA
Nat Cowboy Hall of Fame	1700 NE 63rd St	Oklahoma City, OK 73111, USA
Nat Football Foundation Hall of Fame	1865 Palmer Ave	Larchmont, NY 10538, USA
Nat Museum of Racing	Union Ave	Saratoga Springs, NY 12866, USA
Nat Ski Hall of Fame	Poplar & Mather	Ishpeming, MI 49849, USA
Nat Softball Hall of Fame	2801 NE 50th St	Oklahoma City, OK 73111, USA
Nat Sprint Car Hall of Fame	1402 N Lincoln Ave	Knoxville, IA 50138, USA
Nat Track & Field Hall of Fame	PO Box 120	Indianapolis, IN 46206, USA
Nat Wrestling Hall of Fame	405 W Hall of Fame Ave	Stillwater, OK 74074, USA
Pro Bowlers Assn Hall of Fame	1720 Merriman Rd	Akron, OH 44313, USA
Pro Football Hall of Fame	2121 George Halas Dr NW	Canton, OH 44708, USA
Pro Golf Assn Hall of Fame	100 Ave of Champions	Palm Beach Gardens, FL 33418, USA
Pro Golf Assn Tour Hall of Fame	112 TPC Blvd	Ponte Vedra, FL 32082, USA
Pro Golf Assn World Golf Hall of Fame	PGA Blvd, PO Box 1908	Pinehurst, NC 28374, USA
Pro Rodeo Hall of Champions	101 Pro Rodeo Dr	Colorado Springs, CO 80919, USA
Sportcasters/Sportswriters HofF	322 E Innes St	Salisbury, NC 28144, USA
Trapshooting Hall of Fame	601 W Vandalia Rd	Vandalia, OH 45377, USA
Trotter Horse Museum/Hall of Fame	PO Box 590	Goshen, NY 10924, USA
US Bicycling Hall of Fame	1 W Main St	Somerville, NJ 08876, USA
US Figure Skating Assn Hall of Fame	20 1st St	Colorado Springs, CO 80906, USA
US Golf Association Golf Museum	Golf House	Far Hills, NJ 07931, USA
US Hockey Hall of Fame	Hat Trick Ave	Eveleth, MN 55734, USA
US Olympic Committee Hall of Fame	1750 E Boulder St	Colorado Springs, CO 80909, USA
Volleyball Hall of Fame	444 Dwight St	Holyoke, MA 01040, USA
Women's Bowling Hall of Fame	5301 S 76th St	Greendale, WI 53129, USA
Yachting Hall of Fame	PO Box 129	Newport, RI 02840, USA

BIBLIOGRAPHY

OTHER SOURCES FOR CELEBRITIES, DIGNITARIES & ORGANIZATIONS

Academy Players Directory, Academy of Motion Picture Arts & Sciences, 8949 Wilshire Blvd, Beverly Hills, CA 90211, USA
African Who's Who, African Journal Ltd, 54-A Tottenham Court Rd, London W1P 08T, England
Biographical Dictionary of Governors of the US, Meckler Publishing, Ferry Lane W, Westport, CT 06880, USA
Biographical Dictionary of US Executive Branch, Greenwood Press, 51 Riverside Ave, Westport, CT 06880, USA
Celebrity Access, Celebrity Access Publications, 20 Sunnyside Ave, Mill Valley, CA 94941, USA
Congressional Directory, Superintendent of Documents, US Government Printing Office, Washington, DC 20402, USA
Contemporary Architects, St Martin's Press, 175 5th Ave, New York, NY 10010, USA
Contemporary Designers, Gale Research Co, Book Tower, Detroit, MI 48226, USA
Contemporary Theatre, Film & Television, Gale Research Co, Book Tower, Detroit, MI 48226, USA
Corporate Yellow Book, Leadership Directories, 104 5th Ave, #200, New York, NY 10011, USA
Editor & Publisher International Yearbook, 575 Lexington Ave, New York, NY 10022, USA
International Artists Community, Postfach 11 05, 35112 Fronhausen, Germany
International Directory of Films & Filmmakers, St James Press, 175 5th Ave, New York, NY 10010, USA
International Talent & Touring Directory, 1515 Broadway, New York, NY 10036, USA
International Who's Who, Europa Publications Ltd, 18 Bedford Square, London WC1B 3JN, England
International Who's Who in Music, Biddles Ltd, Walnut Tree House, Guildford, Surrey GU1 1DA, England
Kraks BlaBog, Nytorv 17, 1450 Copenhagen K, Denmark
Major Companies of the Far East, Graham & Trotman Ltd, 66 Wilton Rd, London SW1V 1DE, England
Major Companies of Europe, Graham & Trotman Ltd, 66 Wilton Rd, London SW1V 1DE, England
Martindale-Hubbell Law Directory, Reed Publishing, Summit, NJ 07902, USA
Moody's International Manual, Moody's Investors Service, 99 Church St, New York, NY 10007, USA
National Directory of Addresses & Telephone Numbers, Omnigraphics Inc, Penobscot Building, Detroit, MI 48226, USA
New Address Book, Perigee Books, Putnam Publishing Grp, 200 Madison Ave, New York, NY 10016, USA
Notable Australians, Paul Hamlyn Pty Ltd, 31 176 S Creek Rd, Dee Why, WA 2099, Australia
Notable New Zealanders, Paul Hamlyn Pty Ltd, 31 Airedale St, Auckland, New Zealand
Prominent Personalities in USSR, Scarecrow Press, Metuchen, NJ 08840, USA
Sports Address Bible, Global Sports Productions, 1223 Broadway, #102, Santa Monica, CA 90404, USA
US Court Directory, Government Printing Office, Washington, DC 20401, USA
US Government Manual, National Archives & Records Service, General Services Administration, Washington, DC 20408, USA
Who's Who, A & C Black Ltd, St Martin's Press, 175 5th Ave, New York, NY 10010, USA
Who's Who in America, Marquis Who's Who, 200 E Ohio St, Chicago, IL 60611, USA
Who's Who in American Art, R R Bowker Co, 1180 Ave of Americas, New York, NY 10036, USA
Who's Who in American Politics, R R Bowker Co, 1180 Ave of Americas, New York, NY 10036, USA
Who's Who in Canada, Global Press, 164 Commanden Blvd, Agincourt ON M1S 3C7, Canada
Who's Who in France, Editions Jacques Lafitte SA, 75008 Paris, France
Who's Who in Germany, Verlag AG Zurich, Germany
Who's Who in Israel, Bronfman Publishers Ltd, 82 Levinsky St, Tel Aviv 61010, Israel
Who's Who in Poland, Graphica Comense Srl, 22038 Taverreiro, Italy
Who's Who in Scandinavia, A Sutter Druckerei GmbH, 4300 Essen, Germany
Who's Who in Switzerland, Nagel Publishers, 5-5 bis de l'Orangeris, Geneva, Switzerland
Who's Who in the Theatre, Pitman Press, 39 Parker St, London WC2B 5PB, England
Who's Who in Washington, Tiber Reference Press, 4340 East-West Hwy, Bethesda, MD 20814, USA
Writer's Directory, St James Press, 213 W Institute Place, Chicago, IL 60610, USA
World Almanac, Funk & Wagnalls, 1 International Blvd, #444, Mahway, NJ 07495, USA

V.I.P. ADDRESS BOOK UPDATES

KEEP YOUR V.I.P. ADDRESS BOOK CURRENT ! ! !

The U.S. Bureau of Statistics says almost 20 percent of people move yearly. Not only do people change places of residence, many change business affiliations.

- athletes get traded
- entertainers change agents
- businesspeople change jobs
- politicians leave or change office

How do you stay abreast of changes? . . . Through the **V.I.P. ADDRESS BOOK UPDATES**! These updates will keep you on top of:

- changed addresses
- invalid addresses
- new V.I.P.s
- deaths

The **V.I.P. ADDRESS BOOK UPDATES** is the same size and format as the **V.I.P. ADDRESS BOOK**. The UPDATES are published annually in mid-year. Cost of the updates is $24.95 postpaid (California residents add $2.12 for sales tax). Fill out and mail the coupon below. Foreign orders add $4.00 for overseas shipping. Include check or money order. MasterCard, Visa and American Express orders accepted. Credit card orders call 1-(800) 258-0615. No C.O.D. orders.

Please send _____ copies to **V.I.P. ADDRESS BOOK UPDATES** at $24.95 per year (California residents add $2.12 sales tax).

NAME_____

ADDRESS _____

CITY _____ STATE _____ ZIP _____

Mail this coupon with check, money order or credit card number to:

V.I.P. ADDRESS BOOK UPDATES
%Associated Media Companies Ltd.
1212 Porta Ballena
Alameda, CA 94501

Phone Number (510) 814-8255   **Fax Number (510) 814-8355**

V.I.P. ADDRESS CORRECTIONS

Bad addresses are a fact of life for all directories.

Even though all names and addresses have been checked prior to publication of this edition with the United States Postal Service through its National Change of Address program, addresses continually change as people move residences or go to new jobs.

If your letters are returned due to an expired or incorrect address listed in the V.I.P. ADDRESS BOOK, we will try to help you obtain updated addresses.

We will check our files to see if a later or alternate address is available if you do the following:

- Send the front of returned envelope and any postal service markings on the envelope.

- Each inquiry must be limited to one address.

- List additional names in case there are no later or alternate addresses in our files.

- If more than one name is included, only the first name will be researched for an updated or alternate address.

- If you are a purchaser of this book and registered with us for that purchase, the fee is $1.00 for each address request. The request must include a self-addressed, stamped envelope.

- If you are not a purchaser of this book and not registered with us, the fee is $2.00 for each address request. The request must include a self-addressed, stamped envelope.

- Do not send requests for address corrections for people not listed in this book.

Your address correction requests should be mailed to:

V.I.P. ADDRESS BOOK CORRECTIONS

Associated Media Companies Ltd.

1212 Porta Ballena

Alameda, CA 94501

Phone Number — (510) 814-8255   Fax Number — (510) 814-8355

> Requests without the handling fee or the self-addressed, stamped envelope will not receive replies.

V.I.P. ADDRESS BOOK MAILING LISTS

The address list of the V.I.P. ADDRESS BOOK contains approximately 25,000 addresses. These addresses may be rented for one-time use only on 3-up pressure sensitive labels.

Prices include a set-up cost and a price per category depending upon the number of names ordered. There is a minimum shipping and handling charge.

Address labels may be rented as a complete list or in the following categories:

- Actors
- Architects
- Artists
- Astronauts/Cosmonauts
- Athletes/Coaches
- Business Leaders
- Cabinet Members
- Cartoonists
- Comedians
- Composers
- Concert Performers/Conductors
- Dancers/Choreographers
- Editors/Publishers/Journalists
- Educators
- Fashion Designers/Models
- Government Leaders

- Heroes/Explorers
- Labor Leaders
- Medical Researchers
- Military Leaders
- Musicians
- Nobel Price Winners
- Opera Performers
- Producers/Directors
- Psychologists/Psychiatrists
- Photographers
- Religious Leaders
- Research Scientists
- Royalty
- Social Activists
- Singers
- Writers

All orders must be in writing and include a sample mailing piece. Associated Media Companies reserves the right to refuse orders for its labels.

For information or a brochure on costs, please write or call:

V.I.P. ADDRESS BOOK MAILING LISTS
Associated Media Companies Ltd.
1212 Porta Ballena
Alameda, CA 94501
Phone Number — (510) 814-8255   Fax Number — (510) 814-8355

CD-ROM

V.I.P. ADDRESS BOOK FILE

Available March, 1996

Now available for the first time, a CD-ROM version of the V.I.P. ADDRESS BOOK. The CD-ROM version is called the V.I.P. ADDRESS BOOK FILE. The latest and most complete listing of V.I.P.'s in all fields will be available for the first time in March of 1996 from Associated Media Companies Ltd.

The CD-ROM version will be compatible with both PCs and MacIntosh computers.

Cost of the CD-ROM will be $94.95. California residents should add $8.07 sales tax. Foreign orders should add $9.50 for overseas shipping and handling.

To reserve your copy, fill out and mail the coupon below today. Be sure to include your check or money order. MasterCard, Visa and American Express orders are accepted. For credit card orders, call 1-800-258-0615. No C.O.D. orders will be accepted.

Please send me _____ copies of the V.I.P. ADDRESS FILE CD-ROM AT $94.95. (California residents add $8.07 sales tax; Foreign orders add $9.50 per copy for shipping and handling.)

Name _____

Address _____

City _____ State _____ Zip _____

Country _____

American Express ☐   MasterCard ☐   Visa ☐

Credit Card Number _____

Expiration Date _____

Signature _____

Mail this coupon with your check, money order or credit card number to:

THE V.I.P. ADDRESS FILE (CD-ROM)

Associated Media Companies Ltd.

1212 Porta Ballena

Alameda, CA 94501

Phone Number — (510) 814-8255   Fax Number — (510) 814-8355

V.I.P. ADDRESS BOOK MULTIPLE ORDER CARD

THE V.I.P. ADDRESS BOOK

Associated Media Companies Ltd.

1212 Porta Ballena

Alameda, CA 94501

Phone Number — (510) 814-8255   Fax Number — (510) 814-8355

Please send _____ copies of the 1996-97 V.I.P. ADDRESS BOOK at
$_____ each. Quantity orders are priced as follows:

1 copy	$94.95 each
2-4 copies	$85.46 each
5-12 copies	$80.71 each
13-49 copies	$75.96 each
50-99 copies	$71.21 each
100-199 copies	$66.47 each
200 or more copies	$56.97 each

California residents add 8.5% for sales tax. Foreign orders write for information on overseas shipping costs.

Check or money order for $_____ is enclosed.

PURCHASE ORDER NUMBER _____

NAME_____

TITLE _____

ORGANIZATION _____

ADDRESS _____

CITY _____ STATE _____ ZIP _____

COUNTRY _____

SIGNATURE _____

Book design by Lee Ann Nelson. Cover logo is Corvinus Skyline. Body type is Swiss Narrow. Production by Nelson Design, 1 Annabelle Lane, San Ramon, California 94583, USA.

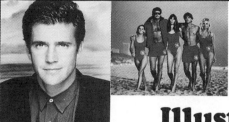

Illustrated
Photo-Autograph Catalog

Hummerdude's is a complete one-stop source for ALL your photo and autograph needs. We have <u>THOUSANDS</u> of unsigned photos, you can send to celebrities to receive Free autographs. Every photo is illustrated, so you can **Look BEFORE You Buy**! We sell signed cards, photos and collectibles too! Order our catalog today!

<u>1,000</u>'s of Photos!   <u>100</u>'s of Stars!

o **Movie/TV Stars**   o **Music Artists**

o **Models**   o **Star Trek**   o **MORE**

Member U.A.C.C. (Universal Autograph Collectors Club)

<u>4x6 - 8x10 size photos</u>   <u>Topless poses</u>!

Write to Stars for <u>FREE</u> autographs!

<u>Highest Quality GUARANTEED</u>!   <u>Low Prices</u>!

Easy Order [MasterCard] [VISA] Phone - Fax - Mail

<u>To Order</u>: To receive our BIG Catalog and Supplements, send $5 cash, check or money order to the address below.

Hummerdude's * P.O. Box 4348-VP * Dunellen, NJ * 08812
Phone: (908) 424-9367 Monday - Friday 10AM - 4PM E.S.T.

An Invitation To Join The

The Universal Autograph Collector's Club is the largest organization of its kind in the world with members in over thirty countries. Our journal, *The Pen and Quill*, is published six times a year and features articles in all fields of autograph collecting as well as information useful to today's collector. Members are also given opportunities to purchase through the club autographic material at far below Dealer prices. The UACC also sponsors shows around the world and publishes low cost reference works to aid the collector in their autograph quests. Best of all, the UACC is an organization of collectors and run by collectors.

For membership information, please write:

UACC Dept. V.
P.O. Box 6181
Washington, DC 20044-6181